Pan Am's USA Guide

Everything You Need to Know
About 50 Great States—and
U.S. Territories

McGraw-Hill Company
New York   St. Louis   San Francisco
Hamburg   Mexico   Toronto   Sydney

Library of Congress Cataloging in Publication Data

Main entry under title:

Pan Am's USA guide.

  Includes index.
  1. United States—Description and travel—
1960-   —Guide-books. I. Pan American World
Airways, Inc. II. Title: USA guide.
E158.P27 1982   917.3′04927   81-15628
ISBN 0-07-048434-1   AACR2

1 2 3 4 5 6 7 8 9 0 D O D O 8 7 6 5 4 3 2

Contents

Acknowledgments

We wish to acknowledge the supervision and project coordination by The DR Group, Inc., and the work of McGraw-Hill World News bureaus and correspondents throughout the United States in updating and assembling the information for this Guide. We also wish to acknowledge the assistance of state offices and agencies who cooperated in providing accurate, up-to-date facts and figures.

Editorial supervision for Pan Am: Maureen A. Hickey.

Photo Credits: United States Travel Service; Arizona Office of Tourism; Chicago Convention & Tourism Bureau, Inc.; Goodman Travel; The Goodyear Corporation; Greater Reno Chamber of Commerce; Guenther-Lawrence Public Relations; Hawaii Visitors Bureau; Massachusetts Department of Commerce & Development, Division of Tourism; Michigan Travel Commission; Milwaukee Convention & Visitors Bureau; New York Convention & Visitors Bureau; Pennsylvania Bureau of Travel Development; Portland Chamber of Commerce; Puerto Rico Tourism Development, Inc.; South Dakota Tourism; Vermont Travel Division; Walt Disney Productions; Washington Convention & Visitors Association.

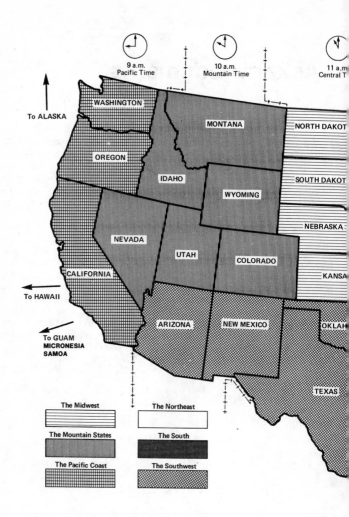

9 a.m.
Pacific Time

10 a.m.
Mountain Time

11 a.m.
Central T

To ALASKA

WASHINGTON

MONTANA

NORTH DAKOT

OREGON

SOUTH DAKOT

IDAHO

WYOMING

NEBRASKA

To HAWAII

NEVADA

UTAH

COLORADO

KANSA

CALIFORNIA

To GUAM
MICRONESIA
SAMOA

ARIZONA

NEW MEXICO

OKLAH

TEXAS

The Midwest

The Northeast

The Mountain States

The South

The Pacific Coast

The Southwest

12 noon
Eastern Time

NESOTA

WISCONSIN

MICHIGAN

IOWA

ILLINOIS   INDIANA   OHIO

MISSOURI

KENTUCKY

ARKANSAS

TENNESSEE

MISSISSIPPI

ALABAMA   GEORGIA

LOUISIANA

FLORIDA

MAINE

VERMONT

NEW HAMPSHIRE

NEW YORK

MASSACHUSETTS

RHODE ISLAND
CONNECTICUT

PENNSYLVANIA

NEW JERSEY

DELAWARE
MARYLAND

WEST
VIRGINIA

VIRGINIA

NORTH CAROLINA

SOUTH
CAROLINA

PUERTO RICO
AND
THE VIRGIN ISLANDS

Introduction

The United States of America, as a nation, was founded on the premise that all men are "endowed with certain inalienable rights . . . (to) life, liberty and the pursuit of happiness." It has made that premise a reality by welcoming and assimilating immigrants from everywhere, until, today, over 200 million Americans share a cumulative heritage embracing every part of the world.

The United States is a big country, straddling the North American continent and wide expanses of ocean as well. It means things small and homemade as well as gigantic and automated. And the easy blend of those extremes is a characteristically American achievement. Despite the almost incredible growth of its industries, the US still harbors vast acreages of virgin forest, and its efficiently cultivated farmlands regularly produce more of the world's foodstuffs than do those of any other nation. It is the homeland of such varied international figures as Abe Lincoln, Buffalo Bill, Lindbergh, Henry Ford, Mickey Mouse, Al Capone, Elizabeth Taylor, Li'l Abner, Eleanor Roosevelt, Rockefeller and Snoopy.

Few countries can match the varied scenery and climate of the United States . . . from the icy remoteness of northern Alaska in winter to the dormant volcanoes and lush vegetation of Hawaii year 'round. America is a major part of Pan Am's world of travel. Apart from Hawaii and Alaska, America forms one contiguous country 3000 miles wide and 1500 miles from North to South. Within that single land mass, you'll find California's Mojave Desert, New Mexico's Petrified Forest, the plantations, bayous and beaches of the South, the seemingly endless grainfields of the Midwest, the soaring majesty of the Rocky Mountains, the color and splendor of Niagara Falls and the Grand Canyon of the Colorado. Away from the major cities, the United States landscape is still largely unspoiled. For the visitor there's the wildest possible choice of sights, activities and climate. In a three-week vacation, for example, you could comfortably visit three locations so diverse in their ambience and physical characteristics that you'd feel you've enjoyed a series of different vacations.

Impressive architecture is another of America's "most varied" features. From the downtown "Twin Towers," you'll get a close-up view of one of the world's most spectacular skylines . . . the skyscrapers of Manhattan against the East, West, North and/or South horizon. But dramatic buildings are not confined to New York.

Actually, some of the most notable architecture—including the world's tallest building—is in Chicago. Atlanta's "downtown of tomorrow," Houston's Astrodome, San Francisco's hill-climbing cable cars, Boston's historic Faneuil Hall . . . whichever cities you visit, you'll find more than enough of interest to fill the time you have available. And the towns and villages also contain a wealth of interesting "local" architecture, from the Spanish adobes of the Southwest to the classic simplicity of New England's colonial settlements, with their village greens, white clapboard buildings and weatherbeaten "saltboxes."

TIPS FOR VISITORS

In the main, you'll find the United States an exceptionally hospitable country. Its varied immigrant heritage has nurtured an authentic respect and empathy for strangers . . . to the point that it's hard to remain a stranger for long. Informality is the most immediately notable hallmark of American society . . . so don't be hesitant about asking questions of practically anyone. Most Americans will be genuinely glad to give you their views on any and every aspect of American life and culture . . . from local events to national history and accomplishments.

Your local Pan Am office and your travel agent will gladly help you find out whatever you need to know. You'll also find innumerable helpful sources of information wherever you go. For example, many cities have their own Visitors' Bureaus to provide information on local attractions and to act as a referral service for almost any type of travel inquiry you might have.

In addition, the International Visitors' Information Service in Washington, DC (202-872-8747) operates a Language Bank to help foreign visitors with any language problems they might encounter. Staffers speak a total of nearly 40 languages and can help with most translation problems. The Language Bank is part of the National Council for International Visitors (202-332-1028) which, as part of its duties to promote international understanding through travel, oversees the American tours of sponsored visitors and can provide referrals to some 90 NCIV affiliate offices around the country.

In the event of travel difficulty, Travelers' Aid has offices all over the country and specializes in helping travelers who need assistance as a result of illness, accident, loss, robbery or any other crisis situation. Just dial "O" and the telephone operator will help you find the nearest Travelers' Aid office. Dialing "O" is a quick method of finding help in any emergency, and your hotel operator will call a doctor for you if needed.

The fear is sometimes expressed that travel in the United States will be too expensive. But, although living luxuriously in a major US city is as expensive as it would be elsewhere, traveling in America can be surprisingly reasonable. Hotel and motel rooms, almost always with private bath, may cost as little as $12 a day. There's the widest choice of restaurants—to suit any tastes or budget, and many low-priced surprises (such as excellent quality American wines).

REQUIREMENTS FOR VISITORS TO THE USA

If you're coming to the United States from abroad for a vacation or on business and you are not a US citizen, you'll need a passport and visa. (Citizens of Canada, Mexico, and British subjects residing in Canada, Bermuda, the Bahamas and Cayman Island are exempt from these requirements.) For your visitor's visa, apply either in person or by mail to your nearest US Embassy or Consulate. The following documents are required: your passport (valid for at least six months longer than your intended visit), one passport-size photograph, and evidence (such as a round-trip ticket) of your intention to return home after your visit, as opposed to remaining to seek employment. Usually, a visa is valid for a visit as long as six months for each entry. There is no US entry tax levied on passengers coming into the country.

The United States allows nonresidents to bring the following items into the country free of duty and internal revenue tax as a personal exemption: one quart of alcoholic beverages (by persons at least 21 years old), 200 cigarettes, or 50 cigars, or 3 pounds of smoking tobacco (or proportionate amounts of each); items necessary for personal comfort or special purpose of visit (cameras, sporting equipment, baby carriage, typewriter, etc.); and personal effects such as jewelry and clothing. These possessions need not accompany you to the US to be entitled to free entry. Nonresidents are also allowed $100 duty allowance and tax-free exemption for gifts accompanying them provided they intend to remain in the US for more than 72 hours, and provided such "gift exemption" or part thereof has not been claimed within the preceding 6 months. 100 cigars may be included in this gift exemption, and is in addition to quantities allowed under the personal exemption. Regarding money, only amounts of $5,000 or more require the filing of a report of transaction with US Customs. Pets are subject to health, agriculture and customs requirements. And, without special permission, narcotic drugs, meats, fruits, vegetables, plants and plant products, or furs or skins of endangered species such as leopard and crocodile may not be brought into the country.

Sometimes at US gateways, Customs will refuse to clear some personal effects or other items. After they're turned over to the airline's freight department and post entered onto the freight manifest for the flight, the passenger, or a Customs broker retained by him, must then make a Customs entry for the importation or transit of the goods. Because of the expense for the handling and paperwork, Pan Am now assesses the passenger $25 for this service.

Facts About the USA

Population: 226,505,825 (February 1981)

Size: 3,536,855 square miles, including Alaska and Hawaii. The fourth largest country in the world, the USA follows the USSR, Canada and China.

Capital: Washington, District of Columbia

Public Holidays

New Year's Day, 1 January
Washington's Birthday, 3rd Monday in February
Memorial Day, last Monday in May
Independence Day, 4 July
Labor Day, 1st Monday in September
Columbus Day, 2nd Monday in October
Veteran's Day, 4th Monday in October
Thanksgiving Day, 4th Thursday in November
Christmas Day, 25 December

Climate: Climatic conditions in America are as diverse as the ethnic backgrounds of Americans, from the Arctic regions of Northern Alaska to the year-round summer of Hawaii. On the mainland, blustery winters "up north" and steamy summers "down south," with some of the world's most equitable weather in the state of California.

Clothing: From a practical point of view, your wardrobe should be as varied as the US climate areas you plan to visit. Because of this diversity—at the same time of year, you could go skiing in one part of the US, and swimming in another—you'd be wise to bring at least one outfit to reflect either end of the temperature scale. (And wise too, to check the weather charts throughout this book, broken down by state and month of the year.) From the fashion consideration, styles are as free and casual and individual as the American people. From blue jeans to ballgowns, Americans dress for the occasion. During the day, women should be comfortable in a sweater or blouse and skirt or slacks; men in trousers and shirt or sweater, with or without a sports jacket. At night, women might change to a dress, or a dressier material; men might add a tie or change to a suit. Because the most important consideration is your comfort and convenience, start with a basic, flexible wardrobe of easy-care, drip-dry fabrics, and add the special outfits that reflect your special vacation interests.

Traveling with Children: People and places in the US try to make traveling with small children convenient and pleasant. Most restaurants are equipped with high chairs and will gladly warm special foods and formulas. Many, especially nationwide chain restaurants, offer children's menus—smaller portions at reduced prices. Supermarkets sell a wide variety of fine prepared foods in jars for infants and toddlers; also disposable diapers and other infant needs. You may even purchase prepared, sterile formula in disposable bottles or cans that do not require refrigeration. Reliable babysitting services are no problem either; inquire at the reception desk at your hotel or motel.

Currency: American money is based on the decimal system: one dollar ($1) = 100 cents (¢). The most commonly used bills (paper money) are $1, $5, $10 and $20; coins consist of the penny (1¢), nickel (5¢), dime (10¢), quarter (25¢), half-dollar (50¢) and the new dollar ($1).

Government: The United States is a federation of the 50 states in its Union. As regulated by the Constitution, power is divided among three branches, executive, legislative and judicial. On the federal level, these areas of responsibility are represented by: executive—a President and his administration; legislative—Congress, consisting of the Senate and House of Representatives (representing every state in the Union), judicial—a nine-member Supreme Court. All powers not constitutionally assigned to the federal government are relegated to the individual states, each of which has its own semi-autonomous government, usually structured similarly to the federal government. Because of this, local laws vary from state to state, and visitors are likely to encounter inconsistencies in liquor licensing, driving laws and state taxes.

Language: The English you'll hear on the American side of the Atlantic is quite different from the language spoken in Great Britain. It's "American English," an entity of its own. Variations in word usage, sentence structure, idiom and inflection are very distinct. And, within the language you'll hear further, regional differences: sonorous southern "drawls," assimilated "old world" accents, the clipped "twang" of Midwesterners and the "broad 'a' and ignored 'r' sounds" of New Englanders. "American English" is an adventure in language, one you're sure to enjoy. Non-English-speaking visitors will find Americans patient and eager to understand . . . and enclaves throughout the US where their own and many other languages are spoken.

Religion: As America is the "melting pot" of the people of the world, it is the same for the religions of the world. Although predominantly Christian (both Roman Catholic and various Protestant denominations), there is hardly any religion on earth not practiced in America. And, in most major cities, places of worship conduct services in one or more foreign languages.

Electricity: The standard national electricity supply is 110 volts, 60 cycles AC. All power points take a standard two-blade ungrounded plug.

Time Zones: The continental United States has four main time zones: Eastern, Central, Mountain and Pacific. This means that when it is 12 noon in the Eastern Time Zone (for instance, New York), it's 11am in the Central Zone (e.g. Chicago), 10am in the Mountain Zone (e.g. Denver), and 9am in the Pacific Zone (e.g. Los Angeles). Hawaii is two hours beyond that, at 7am, . . . and Alaska is so big, parts of it lie within four different time zones. Unless Congress changes the current law, the continental US adopts "daylight savings time" on the fourth Sunday in April and returns to "standard time" on the fourth Sunday in October.

Banks: Banks are plentiful throughout the USA. Although banking hours vary—by region or day, staying open later on traditional "paydays" or for a half-day Saturday—most are open Monday-Friday, from 9am to 3pm. Except within major seaboard cities, there are few banks that can exchange foreign currency. Should you need to make an exchange in the US, look for facilities at the airports. Try also to obtain an international credit card such as American Express, MasterCard or VISA (BankAmericard), as these cards are widely accepted throughout the US for a variety of purposes.

Laundry: Whether it's washing or dry-cleaning, services are excellent and abundant in America. From quick ("same day") services provided by major hotels to economical "do-it-yourself" facilities in coin-operated establishments, keeping your clothes in shape is no problem in American cities or towns.

Tipping: America is a very service-oriented society, and tipping is a way of life. 15% is the normal rate for hotel or restaurant checks. 25¢ to hat-check clerks and 25-35¢ per bag to porters is customary. Tip taxi drivers 20% of fare or thereabouts. Tips in barbershops and beauty parlors are between 15-20% to everyone who attends you in proportion to the cost of their service. You need not tip hotel chambermaids in establishments where you have not stayed for several days. Tour guides usually depend on a tip, especially if you are part of a particular group excursion.

Mail and Telephones: Postage stamps may be purchased at post offices or from vending machines in stores, hotels, transportation terminals and the like. Post Offices are generally open 8am to 6pm, Monday through Friday, and until 12 noon on Saturdays. First-class mail automatically is routed by air if appropriate and costs 18¢ for the first ounce within the US and to Canada and Mexico. To countries other than Canada and Mexico, the first-class surface rate is 30¢ for the first ounce and airmail is 40¢ per half ounce up to and including 2 ounces, except to Central America, Colombia, Venezuela, the Caribbean Islands, Bahama, Bermuda and St Pierre & Miquelon (35¢ per half ounce up to and including 2 ounces). When writing to an address within the US you should try to use the "Zip Code," a 5-digit number which designates a geographical area, and is designed to speed delivery. US post offices do not provide telegraph services, but you may send international messages via the Western Union Telegraph Company, with offices throughout the US.

Public coin-operated telephones can be found virtually everywhere in America: on street corners, in restaurants, public buildings, stores and gasoline stations, and along the highways. To get the "dial tone" that will allow you to place a call, you must deposit a dime (10¢) (some states 20¢) before dialing any number. Local calls cost a dime for the first three minutes, and involve dialing a 7-digit number. Long-distance calls are more expensive and require the dialing of a 3-digit prefix or "area code" preceding the local number. Rates are less expensive for calls you dial yourself (as opposed to having the operator place it), and least expensive for calls made in the evening or on weekends. To find a phone number in any city, simply dial the area code, followed by 555-1212 and you'll get the Directory Assistance Operator. For calls from the US to countries abroad, dial "O" and ask for the Overseas Operator.

There are two kinds of telephone directories: the general directory (or "white pages"), with alphabetical listing by last name; and the classified directory (or "Yellow Pages"), with listings of practically all businesses and services available in the area, categorized alphabetically according to their business or nature of service. A cross-referenced index at the beginning of the directory will help you locate the category you seek. Many Yellow Pages also include local guide maps and almost all directories provide a general listing of emergency telephone numbers.

Newspapers: US newspapers are local rather than national. The major exceptions are the *New York Times* and *Wall Street Journal* which are available the same day in major cities across the nation. Airmail editions of newspapers from other countries are available at airports and international newsstands in most metropolitan areas.

TV and Radio: For the most part, television is commercially supported in America. While a certain amount of this programming is local, many of the programs are provided by the major national networks (ABC, CBS and NBC). In large cities such as New York or Los Angeles, there may be a choice of seven or more standard viewing channels, and programming almost 24 hours a day. There is also a public network (PBS), subsidized by the government and private grants, that broadcasts educational, cultural, news and special entertainment programs, without advertisements. And wherever you go in the States, you'll never be far from a local radio station—"AM" stations with more "popular" music and commercial messages; "FM," as a rule, having fewer commercial messages.

Accommodations: Accommodations in America are usually modern, clean and efficiently operated. They basically fit into three categories: hotels, motels (also "motor inns" or lodges) and "tourist" or "guest houses," and range from luxurious and expensive to plain and inexpensive. All the better hotels and motels tend to be air-conditioned in summer and centrally-heated in winter and include a private bath, telephone and television/radio in every room. Larger hotels will typically feature lobbies with shops and services of all kinds: newsstands, beauty parlors, jewelers, travel agents and car rental and airline offices. Hotels outside of central city areas (particularly "resort" hotels) also offer a variety of sport facilities—tennis courts, golf courses, perhaps equestrian or water sports activities—as do many of the larger resort motels.

At one time, motels were simple, inexpensive roadside cabins for motorists; now many offer accommodations comparable in luxury to hotels. The principal difference between a hotel and motel is that motels offer free parking near your room (although you usually have to carry your own baggage), and many times you have direct access from your car to your room and needn't enter a central lobby. Many motels are part of nationwide chains that offer "800" telephone numbers and inter-motel reservations. A few of the major chains are: *Holiday Inn*, 800-238-5510; *Howard Johnson*, 800-654-2000; *Ramada Inn*, 800-228-2828; *Sheraton Motor Inn*, 800-325-3535 and *TraveLodge*, 800-255-3050.

Hotels and motel rates are usually lower in small towns than in large cities, and generally stable year-round. In resort areas, rates vary with the season, so the applicable prices quoted throughout this guide are the lowest available in that area's busiest or "high" season. You can generally book accommodations in hotels (and major chain metropolitan motels) on American Plan (AP) or European Plan (EP). AP usually includes all three meals with the cost of your room, although some food items may be considered extra and charged for as such. EP means no meals are included. Another option, the Modified American Plan (MAP) includes breakfast and dinner, but no lunch. And a Continental Plan (CP) means that a continental breakfast—coffee and rolls—is included.

In this guide, we use the following format for specifying information about accommodations—Hotel Name, telephone number and price range for a particular size room. "S" denoting a single room, "D," a double, and location relative to city center. Further, unless otherwise noted by symbols AP, MAP or CP, the rates quoted herein are based exclusively on the European Plan—no meals.

Occasionally, if a rate is followed by "PP," it means that it is the price per person. A modest hotel tax is levied on most accommodations in America.

Tourist or Guest Houses—generally similar to the European "bed-and-breakfast" arrangement—are advantageous alternatives for the economy-minded traveler. Ranging from convenient, "no reservation necessary" Rooming Houses in a large city to quaint New England inns complete with fireplaces and antique furniture, such establishments offer rooms in private houses that are clean and comfortable (but often without private bath facilities). Tourist-home facilities in most localities are inspected by local tourist authorities to ensure that they are of a consistently high standard. Individual state tourist boards can supply lists of acceptable local establishments. In the cities, the YMCA and YWCA (Young Men's or Women's Christian Association) hotels offer excellent accommodations for those on a strict budget.

Camping is yet another alternative, greatly enjoyed by many thousands of Americans. The vast choice of campsites provides a great way to see the USA and really get to know the people. Operated by state and national park and forest authorities (sometimes, Indian Reservations too), most sites provide drinking water, washrooms and outdoor fireplaces; others also include individual electrical, gas and septic hook-ups. (Check with the American Forestry Association, Wilderness Society and Sierra Club for information about organized wilderness camping and hiking tours.) Other possible kinds of accommodations are youth hostels and trailer (caravan) parks—government or commercially operated—scattered throughout the country.

Transportation: Although the airplane and the automobile are the two dominant modes of transportation in America, travel by train and by bus is popular. Particularly for the pleasure traveler, trains and buses afford an economical, leisurely way to see more of this vast country in a limited amount of time.

Buses provide a great way to experience the diversity of the United States, from the big cities to delightful off-the-beaten-path towns and villages. Buses can be rather luxurious in America, complete with restrooms, hostesses, meals served on board and even observation decks. Again, unlimited mileage *See the USA* Passes are available from Greyhound and Eagle Passes from Continental Trailways. Prices are: $240.30 for 15 days, $347.10 for one month.

Travel by air is a way of life in America. Americans think nothing of "hopping a plane" for business or pleasure. Pan Am has expanded its service within the US making available many key US cities to visitors from abroad and America alike. Service is excellent and so frequent that, between certain major destinations—San Francisco and Los Angeles, and New York and Boston for example—you can simply go to the airport, board a "shuttle" without a reservation, and pay for your fare enroute. Jumbo jets to single engine—there is some kind of airplane to take you practically anywhere you want to go in the US.

The automobile is responsible for giving Americans the flexibility and mobility that makes a 50-mile drive to an irresistible restaurant a matter of course. America's highway system is the most extensive in the world, and cars are everywhere. Travel by car is a very personal way to see the country, and car rentals are easy to arrange and relatively inexpensive. Choose from special rate packages ranging from three-day "weekenders" to longer unlimited mileage plans. You can consult the Yellow Pages of the local telephone directory or call the following companies, toll-free, to reserve a car: Avis, 800-331-1212; Budget, 800-228-9650;

Hertz, 800-654-3131; National, 800-328-4567. Most car rental firms also have offices at airports and in many major hotels.

Because America's network of roads and highways is so modern, driving can be a most enjoyable experience. The travel conveniences you need can be found along most major thoroughfares—rest areas where you can park, obtain food and refreshments, find lodging and have your car serviced, often 24 hours a day. Some highways in the US are toll roads requiring payment in porportion to the miles driven. Roads are generally well marked, as are variable speed limits. The maximum speed limit is 55 miles per hour. Road system maps are available, for a small charge, at most gas stations. In this guide, four main types of roads are identified as they appear on maps and road signs, and each type is further defined by a number following the appropriate symbol. Interstate highways—represented by an "I"—are four-lane high-speed roads with no cross traffic. US highways ("US"), are generally highways with limited cross traffic. State highways—denoted according to the official abbreviations of each state—may have cross traffic, lower speed limits, and are usually two-lanes. Secondary state roads (called "routes") are also usually two lanes.

Regarding local public transportation, most city bus fares are flat rates regardless of distance traveled (usually 50¢), and many require that you have exact change for the fare. New York, Boston, Philadelphia, and Washington, D.C. have underground subway systems; Chicago has underground and elevated subway trains, and San Francisco has both subways and its famous cable cars. Subway tokens can be purchased at stations. Taxis are available at airports, other transportation terminals and hotels. Also found roaming the streets of any large city, taxis with their "availability light" on may be hailed with a wave or a whistle and a little bit of luck. In smaller locations taxi services may be telephoned for.

Food and Drink: Every type of food in the world is available somewhere in the USA. There is, however, a truly American cuisine—good plain preparation of fresh basic ingredients, served in hearty portions, and generally reasonably priced. A typical American breakfast includes fruit juice, eggs ("any style"), bacon or sausages, toast and coffee. Or try pancakes or waffles with rich maple syrup. Lunch is a very flexible meal for Americans that can range from a quick sandwich at a "fast food shop" to a leisurely meal at a sophisticated restaurant. Dinner also varies dramatically place to place, person to person. Just as you can be sure of being able to get a hamburger or hot dog anywhere in America for lunch, you can get a steak for dinner. A very standard American "steak house" dinner would include a salad (perhaps from a tempting choice at a laden salad bar), a baked Idaho or Maine potato (split, buttered and dressed with sour cream, chopped bacon or chives), and apple pie a la mode (with ice cream) for dessert. Try regional specialties, seafood, such as a "clam and lobster bake" in New England, Pennsylvania Dutch country foods; Southern fried chicken with "greens, peas and rice and red-eye gravy"; spicy Louisiana Creole dishes; beef and dairy foods in the Midwest; Mexican-American foods in the Southwest. Because much of American eating is convenience-oriented, you'll usually be able to find any of several franchised chain restaurants, "take-out" foods such as Chinese or pizza, and even "drive-ins," where you can pull into a parking lot and be served in your car. For major cities in this guide, you'll find a selection of recommended restaurants.

Liquor Laws—serving age, hours, etc.—differ from state to state, and sometimes, county to county. But basically, they are more lenient than, for example, those of Great Britain, so it's usually easy to get a drink at any reasonable hour. "Cocktail hour" in America runs anywhere from about 4:30 to dinnertime, around 8pm or so. Try some of these favorite cocktails and exotic-sounding libations: Manhattan, Rusty Nail, Harvey Wallbanger, Bloody Mary, Mint Julep, Grasshopper, Tequila Sunrise, and Singapore Sling, to name just a few. While whiskey nearly always means Scotch in other countries, in America it can indicate Scotch, Bourbon, or Rye blended. American beers are lighter than European beers, similar to lager, and always served chilled. Choose from a wide variety of beers and ales. US wines have made quite a name for themselves—particularly those from California and New York State. They compare very favorably with good European wines, and are usually lower in price and consistent in quality. You may buy wine, liquor and beer by the bottle at retail liquor or "package" stores, or, in states where not available at retail stores, in "state" liquor stores. In many states, you must be able to prove that you are over 21 years of age to purchase liquor.

Entertainment and the Arts: What constitutes "a night out" in America is too varied for generalization. However, you'll never lack for something interesting to do, wherever you are. From discotheque dancing in New York to barn dancing in Iowa, simmering jazz in small, smokey New Orleans clubs to the "big acts" in Las Vegas casino/nightclubs. Theater, Motion Pictures, Concerts, Flea Markets and Fairs, Lectures. And shows for everything: autos, boats, flowers, etc. For opera lovers the United States is an undiscovered land of opportunity. In 1979-1980 over 10 million people saw 9,391 operatic performances, 3,361 of which were American works. At the present time there are 986 organizations producing operas—some are professional companies, others are workshops at academic institutions. Chances are you won't have to look very far to find a top quality opera performance wherever you are.

And the same is true for concerts by symphony orchestras. With 1,570 symphony orchestras across the country, from small local orchestras to the large, national, big-budget operations, almost any city of any size will have a symphony orchestra near it. In fact, there were 22,250 performances in 1979-1980 enjoyed by over 23 million people. Many of the concerts were given during summer months at festivals, some of which are quite well-known especially those at Tanglewood (MA), Saratoga (NY), Wolftrap Farm Park, (VA), Blossom Center (OH), and the Hollywood Bowl in Los Angeles. For more information on these concerts as well as those with other types of music, just pick up the local newspaper— you can hear the sounds of good music in all 50 states.

Shopping: Anything you could possibly want to buy, you should be able to find in America. Shopping for it should be fun, too whether you're looking for a big bargain or an ordinary item in a chain department store, or poking around for a unique gift in a specialty shop. And bargains there are—for example, wash n'wear cotton clothing in a tremendous range of styles, sizes and prices, and household gadgets, unmatched for variety and low cost anywhere in the world. Watch for discount stores across the country; by cutting down on overhead, they can sell top line brands at virtually wholesale prices.

Store hours are generally 9-5:30 or 10-6 with at least one late shopping night in large cities, with stores open until 9 or 9:30pm. US stores and shops do not usually close for lunch. The amount, if any, of state sales tax is provided in the general statistics at the beginning of each chapter; there may also be a city sales tax levied on certain items.

Sports: America is a very sportsminded country with all kinds of athletic activity, individual and team. In person or on television, you can almost always see some professional game being played—baseball in spring and summer, football in the autumn, basketball and ice hockey in the winter. And tennis, golf, car racing, swimming, squash, fishing, soccer, jogging, even kiteflying are all a part of the American sports scene. Americans are avid sports spectators and participants, whose enthusiasm is very infectious. Why not join in? This guide will tell you what's going on where and when.

Let's Hear From You: To supplement the constant check and revision work being done on this guide by hundreds of people all over the United States, Pan Am would welcome your personal comments—areas you've found helpful; points that may be incorrect; areas where you'd like additional information. Please address your input to: Att: Sales Promotion Department, Pan American World Airways, Inc., Pan Am Building, New York, New York 10166.

The information in this guide is as accurate and up to date as we could make it, as of the date of issue. However, because of changing conditions and the possibility of typographic and other human error, the publisher disclaims responsibility for absolute accuracy.

Comparative Table of Clothing Sizes

All over the world there are different ways of sizing things up. If in doubt, it is always best to try on a garment before purchase.

MEN'S CLOTHING

Suits

UK	34	35	36	37	38	39	40	41	42
USA	34	35	36	37	38	39	40	41	42
European	44	46	48	49½	51	52½	54	55½	57

Shirts

UK		14½	15	15½	16	16½	17	17½	18
USA		14½	15	15½	16	16½	17	17½	18
European		37	38	39	41	42	43	44	45

Shoes

UK			6	7	8	9	10	11	12
USA			7	8	9	10	11	12	13
European			39½	41	42	43	44½	46	47

WOMEN'S CLOTHING

Dresses

UK		10	12	14	16	18	20
USA		8	10	12	14	16	18
European		38	40	42	44	46	48

Cardigans, Sweaters, Blouses

UK		32	34	36	38	40	42
USA		8	10	12	14	16	18
European		38	40	42	44	46	48

Shoes

UK	3	3½	4	4½	5	5½	6	6½	7
USA	4½	5	5½	6	6½	7	7½	8	8½
European	35½	36	36½	37	37½	38	38½	39	39½

CHILDREN'S CLOTHING CHART

Dresses and Coats (knitwear one size larger)

UK		18	20	22	24	26
USA		3	4	5	6	6X
European		98	104	110	116	122

For older children, sizes generally correspond with their age.

Shoes

UK	7	8	9	10	11	12	13	1	2	3	4	5½
USA	8	9	10	11	12	13	1	2	3	4½	5½	6½
European	24	25	27	28	29	30	32	33	34	36	37	38½

Weights, Measures, Temperatures

WEIGHT
(1 pound = 0.454 kilogram)

Kilograms	1	2	3	4	5	6	7	8
Pounds	2.2046	4.4	6.6	8.8	11.0	13.2	15.43	17.64

LIQUID MEASURES
(1 Imperial gallon = 1.2 US gallons or 4.5 liters.)

Liters	1	2	3	4	5	6
US Gal	0.264	0.53	0.79	1.06	1.32	1.58

Liters	7	8	9	10	50	100
US Gal	1.85	2.11	2.38	2.64	13.20	26.40

LENGTHS AND DISTANCES
(1 foot = 0.3048 meter; 1 meter = 39 inches)
(1 mile = 1.609 kilometers. Roughly speaking 1 kilometer = ⅗ mile)

Meters	1	2	3	4	5	6
Feet	3.3	6.6	9.8	13.1	16.4	19.7

Meters	7	8	9	10	50	
Feet	23.0	26.2	29.5	32.8	164.0	

Kilometers	1	2	3	4	5	6
Miles	0.62	1.24	1.86	2.48	3.11	3.73

Kilometers	7	8	9	10	20	
Miles	4.35	4.97	5.58	6.20	12.40	

TEMPERATURE

Centigrade	40	39	38	37	36	35
Fahrenheit	104.0	102.2	100.4	98.6	96.8	95

Centigrade	34	33	32	31	30	29
Fahrenheit	93.2	91.4	89.6	87.8	86.0	84.2

Centigrade	28	27	26	25	24	23
Fahrenheit	82.4	80.6	78.8	77.0	75.2	73.4

Centigrade	22	21	20	19	18	17
Fahrenheit	71.6	69.8	68.0	66.2	64.4	62.6

Centigrade	16	15	14	13	12	11
Fahrenheit	60.8	59.0	57.2	55.4	53.6	51.8

Centigrade	10	9	8	7	6	5
Fahrenheit	50.0	48.2	46.4	44.6	42.8	41.0

Centigrade	4	3	2	1	0	−1
Fahrenheit	39.2	37.4	35.6	33.8	32.0	30.2

Centigrade	−2	−3	−4	−5	−6	−7
Fahrenheit	28.4	26.6	24.8	23.0	21.2	19.4

Major Airport Information

ALABAMA
Birmingham (BHM) Municipal, 5 miles NE of city. Tel: (205)595-0533. Ground transportation includes rental cars, courtesy cars, limousines and taxis. Accommodation at field at **Best Western Airport Hotel** (592-0061, S$32up/D$38up).

Mobile (MOB) Bates Field, 11 miles W of city. Tel: (205)342-0510. Ground transportation includes rented cars, courtesy cars, limousines and taxis. Accommodations 8 minutes from field at **Ramada Airport Inn** (344-8030, S$40/D$48).

Montgomery (MGM) Dannelly Field, 7 miles SW of city. Tel: (205)281-5040. Ground transportation includes rental cars, limousines and taxis. Accommodations 2 miles from the field include the **Holiday Inn Southwest** (281-1660, S$26up/D$31up).

ALASKA
Anchorage (ANC) International, 4.3 miles SW of city. Tel: (907)266-1400. Ground transportation includes rental cars, limousine service and taxis. Accommodations include **Best Western Barratt Inn** (277-1525, S$45up/D$51up) 1 mile from field. **Anchorage International Inn** (274-5564, S$38up/D$46up) on International Airport Road not quite 3 miles from the field.

Fairbanks (FAI) International, 3.5 miles SW of city. Tel: (907)452-2151. Ground transportation includes rental cars, courtesy cars, limousine service and taxis. Accommodations at **Klondike Inn** (479-6241, S$37up/D$42up).

Juneau (JNU) International, 6 miles NW of city. Tel: (907)789-0600. Ground transportation includes rental cars and taxis. No accommodations at field.

ARIZONA
Phoenix (PHX) Sky Harbor International, 4 miles E of city. Tel: (602)273-3300. Ground transportation includes rental cars, courtesy cars, limousine service, buses and taxis. Accommodations include **Sheraton Airport Inn** (275-3634, S$40up/D$42up) on airport grounds; **Rodeway Inn-Airport** (273-1211, S$22-24/D$26-28) ½ mile from field, with courtesy car service to and from airport; **Holiday Inn-Airport** ½ mile from field (267-0611,

S$30up/D$40up); **Best Western Country Village Motor Hotel** (273-7251, S$30up/D$37up) 3 minutes from field; **Flamingo Airport Inn** (275-6211, S/D$8.95-15) ½ mile from field; and **Kon Tiki Hotel** (244-9361, S$17-30/D$18-35) 1 mile from field.

ARKANSAS

Hot Springs (HOT) Memorial Field, 3 miles SW of city. Tel: (501)624-3306. Ground transportation includes rental cars, limousines and taxis. Accommodations include **Ramada Inn** (624-4441, S$28.50up/D$33.50up) 7 blocks from field, and **Holiday Inn Lake Hamilton** (525-1391, S$28up/D$37up) 6 miles from field.

Little Rock (LIT) Adams Field, 3 miles E of city. Tel: (501)372-3439. Ground transportation includes rental cars, limousines, buses and taxis. Accommodations a few minutes from field at **Americana Inn** (372-4392, S$31-42/D$36-47), **Sheraton Little Rock Inn** (374-3331, S$42up/D$50up) 5 minutes from field, **Holiday Inn Convention Center** (376-2071, S$31up/D$39up) 2 miles from field, and **Quality Inn** (376-8301, S$20-22/D$24-26) 4 miles from field.

CALIFORNIA

Los Angeles (LAX) International, 17 miles SW of city. Tel: (213)646-4265. Ground transportation includes rental cars, courtesy cars, limousines, buses and taxis. Accommodations include **Airport Marina Hotel** (670-8111, S$34up/D$40up) 2 miles from field, **Marriott Inn** (641-5700, S$48-58/D$58-68) 1 mile from field, and **Hyatt House Hotel** (670-9000, S$42-52/D$47-57) ¼ mile from field.

Sacramento (SMF) Metropolitan, 11 miles NW of city. Tel: (916)929-5411. Ground transportation includes rental cars, courtesy cars, limousines and taxis. Accommodations at the field at **Host International Hotel** (922-8071, S$35/D$40).

San Diego (SAN) International-Lindbergh Field, 3 miles NW of city. Tel: (714)291-3900. Ground transportation includes rental cars, courtesy cars, buses and taxis. Accommodations include **Royal Quality Inn** (224-3621, S$28-35/D$31-41) 3 minutes from field, **Sheraton Harbor Island Hotel** (291-2900, S$50up/D$62up/Suites $160up) ½ mile from field, and **Sheraton Inn Airport** (291-6400, S$45up/D$55up/Suites $125up) 1½ miles from field.

San Francisco (SFO) International, 15 miles SE of city. Tel: (415)761-0800 or 876-2131. Ground transportation includes rental cars, courtesy cars, limousines, buses and taxis. Accommodations include **San Francisco Airport Hilton** (589-0770) at airport entrance, **Holiday Inn** (589-7200, S$44up/D$51up) 3 miles from field, and **Travelodge International Inn** (583-9600) 3 miles from field.

COLORADO
Denver (DEN) Stapleton International, 5 miles E of city. Tel: (303)398-3844. Ground transportation includes rental cars, courtesy cars, limousines, buses and taxis. Accommodations 1 mile from field at **Holiday Inn** (321-6666, S$39up/D$44up), **Ramada Inn** (388-6161, S$44up/D$50up), and **Sheraton Inn** (333-7711, S$41up/D$49up/Suites $86up).

CONNECTICUT
Hartford-Brainard (HFD), 2 miles SE of city. Tel: (203)566-7037. Ground transportation includes rental cars and taxis. Accommodations include **Koala Inn** (249-5811) and **Chalet Inn** (529-9306), both 1 mile from field.

New Haven (HVN) Tweed Municipal, 4 miles SE of city. Tel: (203)787-8283. Ground transportation includes rental cars and taxis. Accommodations include **Holiday Inn Downtown** (777-6221, S$35up/D$44up) 4 miles from field, and **Howard Johnson's Long Wharf** (562-1111, S$37.50-42.50/D$44.50-52.50) 3 miles from field.

New London/Groton Trumbull Airport (GON), 3 miles SE of Groton, 6 miles SE of New London. Tel: (203)445-8549. Ground transportation includes rental cars and taxis. Accommodations include **Holiday Inn** in Groton (445-8141, S$35.50up/D$42.50up) 2 miles from field.

DELAWARE
Wilmington (ILG) Greater Wilmington Airport, 5 miles S of city. Tel: (302)328-5656. Ground transportation includes rental cars, courtesy cars, limousines, buses and taxis. Accommodations include **Quality Inn-Skyways Motel** (328-6666, S$15-20/D$18-22) adjacent to field, **Gateway Motor Lodge** (328-1383, S$14-17/D$17-22) 1 mile from field, and **Ramada Inn** (658-8511, S$34up/D$39up) 2 miles from field.

DISTRICT OF COLUMBIA
Washington National (DCA), 3 miles S of city. Tel: (703)557-2045. Ground transportation includes rental cars, courtesy cars, limousines, buses and taxis. Accommodations 1 mile from field at **Hospitality House Motor Inn** (920-8600, S$21-25/D$25-30) and **Holiday Inn** (521-1600, S$47up/D$54up) and 10 minutes from field at **Howard Johnson's** (684-7200, S$54-58/D$62-66).

Dulles International (IAD), 26 miles W of city. Tel: (703)471-7596. Ground transportation includes rental cars, courtesy cars, limousines and taxis. Accommodations include **Dulles Marriott Hotel** (471-9500) at field, and **Dulles Holiday Inn** (471-7411, S$42up/D$50up) 3½ miles from field.

FLORIDA
Fort Lauderdale-Hollywood (FLL) International, 4 miles SW of city. Tel: (305)765-5910. Ground transportation includes limousines, taxis and rental cars. Accommodations include **Howard Johnson's Airport Lodge**

(921-5325, S$29-45/D$33-45) at field, and **Holiday Inn Airport** (584-4000, S$45up/D$50up) 5 minutes from field with free transportation to and from field.

Jacksonville (JAX) International, 15 miles N of city. Tel: (904)757-2261. Ground transportation includes rental cars, courtesy cars, limousines and taxis. Accommodations include **Holiday Inn** (757-3110, S$30/D$34) 2 miles from field, and **Rodeway Inn** (757-0990) 5 minutes from field with free airport pickup.

Key West (EYW) International, 2 miles E of city. Tel: (305)296-5439. Ground transportation includes rental cars, limousines and taxis. Accommodations at the **Holiday Inn** (294-2571, S$40up/D$46up) 2 miles from field.

Miami (MIA) International, 9 miles NW of city. Tel: (305)526-2000. Ground transportation includes rental cars, courtesy cars, limousines, buses and taxis. Accommodations at field include **Miami International Airport Hotel** (526-5900) and **Holiday Inn-Miami International Airport** (885-1941, S$48up/D$53up) ¾ miles from field.

Tampa (TPA) International, 6 miles W of city. Tel: (813)883-3400. Ground transportation includes rental cars, courtesy cars, limousines and taxis. Accommodations include **Tampa Airport Resort** (877-6131) 5 minutes from field, **Host International Airport Hotel** (879-5151) at field, and **Admiral Benbow Inn** (879-1750) 1 mile from field.

St. Petersburg–Clearwater International (PIE), 9 miles N of city. Tel: (813)531-1451. Ground transportation includes rental cars, limousines and taxis. Accommodations include **St. Petersburg Hilton Inn** (360-1811). On the Gulf.

West Palm Beach–Palm Beach International (PBI), 3 miles W of city. Tel: (305)683-5722. Ground transportation includes rental cars, courtesy cars, limousines and taxis. Accommodations include **Howard Johnson's** (582-2581, S$31-50/D$33-62) 1 mile from field, **Ramada Inn** (683-8810, S$34up/D$40up) 1½ miles from field, and **Breakers Hotel** (665-6611) 3 miles from field.

GEORGIA
Savannah (SAV) Municipal, 8 miles NW of city. Tel: (912)964-0514. Ground transportation includes rental cars, limousines and taxis. Accommodations include **Quality Inn Airport** (964-1421, S$20/D$25) at airport.

HAWAII
Honolulu (HNL) International, 4 miles NW of city. Tel: (808)836-6411. Ground transportation includes rental cars, courtesy cars, buses and taxis.

Accommodations include **Holiday Inn Airport** (836-0661, S$37up/ D$42up) ½ mile from field, **Pacific Marina Airport Inn** (836-1131) 1 mile from field, and **Ramada Inn Airport** (836-3636, S$38up/D$40up) 4 miles from field.

IDAHO
Boise (BOI) Air Terminal–Gowen Field, 4 miles S of city. Tel: (208)383-3111. Ground transportation includes rental cars, limousines, buses and taxis. Accommodations include **Holiday Inn** (344-8365 S$34up/D$40up) ½ mile from field.

ILLINOIS
Chicago (ORD) O'Hare International, 16 miles NW of city. Tel: (312)686-2200. Ground transportation includes rental cars, limousines, taxis and buses. Accommodations include **Air Host** (678-4470) at airport, **Howard Johnson's O'Hare** (671-6000, S$38-62/D$38-62) 3 minutes from field, and **Ramada O'Hare Resort Hotel** (827-5131, S$53up/D$63up) 5 minutes from field.

Peoria (PIA) Greater Peoria Airport, 6 miles SW of city. Tel: (309)697-8272. Ground transportation includes taxis, car rentals and limousine service. Accommodations at **Jumers Castle Lodge** (673-8040) about 3 miles from airfield.

Springfield (SPI) Capital Airport, 3 miles NW of city. Tel: (217)528-7551. Ground transportation includes taxis, car rentals, limousine and courtesy cars. Accommodations at field at **Capital Sky Lodge Motel** (544-3431) while **Holiday Inn** provides free courtesy transportation (529-7171, S$32.75up/D$37.75up) and is close to Abraham Lincoln's home, tomb and monument and Governor's Mansion.

INDIANA
Indianapolis (IND) Weir-Cook International, 7 miles SW of city. Tel: (317)247-6271. Ground transportation includes rental cars, courtesy cars, limousines, buses and taxis. Accommodations adjacent to field include **Hilton Inn Airport** (244-3361) **Holiday Inn Airport** (244-6861, S$40up/ D$45up), and **Ramada Inn** (247-5171, S$38up/D$43up).

IOWA
Des Moines (DSM) Municipal, 3 miles SW of city. Tel: (515)283-4255. Ground transportation includes rental cars, courtesy cars, limousines and taxis. Accommodations include **Best Western Airport Inn** (287-6464, S$32up/D$38up), 2 blocks from field, and **Hyatt House** (285-4310, S$33/ D$42) 1 mile from field.

KANSAS
Dodge City (DDC) Municipal, 5 miles NE of city. Tel: (316)227-3351. Ground transportation includes rental cars and taxis. Accommodations

include **Best Western Silver Spur Lodge** (227-2125, S$22up/D$26up) 4 miles from field.

KANSAS CITY—see MISSOURI

Topeka (TOP) Philip Billard Municipal, 2 miles NE of city. Tel: (913)234-2602. Ground transportation includes rental cars and taxis. Accommodations include **Holiday Inn Downtown** (232-7721, S$24-29/D$29-34) 3 miles from field, **Ramada Inn** (233-8981, S$25up/D$30up) 3 miles from field.

Wichita (ICT) Municipal, 6 miles SW of city. Tel: (316)942-8101. Ground transportation includes rental cars, courtesy cars and taxis. Accommodations include **Best Western Canterbury Inn** (942-7911, S$38up/D$44up) 2 miles from field, **Sheraton Motor Inn** (943-2181, S$31up/D$36up/Suites $57up) 1 mile from field, and **Hiway Inn Motel** (943-1244) 2 miles from field.

KENTUCKY

Louisville (SDF) Standiford Field, 5 miles N of city. Tel: (502)368-6524. Ground transportation includes rental cars, courtesy cars, limousines, buses and taxis. Accommodations include **Holiday Inn South** (964-3311, S$35up/D$43up) 3 miles from field, and **Executive Inn** (367-6161), ½ mile from field.

LOUISIANA

Baton Rouge (BTR) Ryan Airport, 5 miles N of city. Tel: (504)356-1401. Ground transportation includes rental cars, courtesy cars, limousines and taxis. Accommodations include **Best Western Inn** (356-2531, S$25up/ D$31up) 4 miles from field, **Baton Rouge Hilton** (923-2323) 8 miles from field, and **Sheraton Inn** (923-2244, S$25up/D$33up) 8 miles from field.

New Orleans (MSY) Moisant International, 12 miles W of city. Tel: (504)729-2591. Ground transportation includes rental cars, courtesy cars, limousines, buses and taxis. Accommodations include **Hilton Inn** (721-3471) adjacent to field, **Rodeway Inn** (721-8571) adjacent to field, and **Ramada Inn** (721-6211, S$43up/D$53up) ½ mile from field.

MAINE

Bangor (BGR) International, 3 miles W of city. Tel: (207)947-0384. Ground transportation includes rental cars, courtesy cars and taxis. Accommodations include **Holiday Inn** (947-0101, S$26up/D$30up) 1 mile from field, and **Howard Johnson's** (942-5251, S$28-36/D$30-44) 1 mile from field.

Portland (PWM) Municipal, 2 miles SW of city. Tel: (207)774-7301 or 775-5451. Ground transportation includes rental cars, limousines, buses and taxis. Accommodations include **Sheraton Inn** (775-6161, S$30up/

D$38up) ½ mile from field, and **Ramada Inn** (774-5611, S$32up/D$42up) 1 mile from field.

MARYLAND
Baltimore (BAL) Washington International, 9 miles S of city. Tel: (301)787-7079 ext. 283. Ground transportation includes rental cars, courtesy cars, buses and taxis. Accommodations include **International Hotel** (761-7700) at field, and **Holiday Inn** (796-8400, S$55up/D$65up) 1 mile from field.

MASSACHUSETTS
Boston (BOS) Logan International, 4 miles N of city. Tel: (617)567-5400. Ground transportation includes rental cars, courtesy cars, limousines, buses and taxis. Accommodations include **Logan Airport Hilton Inn** (569-9300) at field, and **Ramada Inn-Airport** (569-5250, S$54up/D$61up) 3 miles from field.

Hyannis (HYA) Barnstable Municipal, 1 mile N of city. Tel: (617)775-2020. Ground transportation includes rental cars, taxis and limousines (on request). Accommodations include **Holiday Inn** (775-6600, S/D$39up) ¼ mile from field, and **Sheraton Regal Inn** (771-3000, S$30up low season, $60 high/D$30up low season, $60 high/Suites $60-$250) ¾ miles from field.

MICHIGAN
Detroit (DTW) Metropolitan Wayne County, 17 miles S of city. Tel: (313)274-8100. Ground transportation includes rental cars, courtesy cars, limousine, public transport, taxis. Accommodations include **Holiday Inn** (728-2800, S$45up/D$50up), **Ramada Inn** (729-6300, S$52up/D$62up).

MINNESOTA
Minneapolis-St. Paul (MSP) International, 8 miles S of city. Tel: (612)726-1717. Ground transportation includes rental cars, courtesy cars, limousines and taxis. Accommodations include **Holiday Inn Airport** (854-4000, S$46/D$54) 3 miles from field, **Sheraton Airport Inn** (854-1771, S$49up/D$54up) 1 mile from field, and **Marriott Inn** (854-7441) 3 miles from field.

MISSISSIPPI
Jackson (JAN) Municipal, 7 miles E of city. Tel: (601)939-5631. Ground transportation includes rental cars, courtesy cars, limousines and taxis. Accommodations include **TraveLodge Airport** (939-4011, S$32-38/D$38-42) at field, and **Airways Inn** (939-3515, S$15/D$22) about 10 minutes from downtown and 5 miles from airport.

Natchez–Adams (HEZ) Municipal, 6 miles NE of city. Tel: (601)442-5171. Ground transportation includes rental cars, taxis. Accommodations are **Holiday Inn** (442-3686, S$29up/D$34up) 7 miles from airport.

MISSOURI

Kansas City (MCI) International, 18 miles N of city. Tel: (816)243-5200. Ground transportation includes rental cars, courtesy cars, limousine service, buses and taxis. Accommodations at airfield include **Marriott's Hotel** (464-2200, S$48-60/D$58-70) and 1 mile from airport is **Holiday Inn International Airport** (464-2345, S$25up/D$35up).

St. Louis (STL) Lambert International, 11 miles NW of city. Tel: (314)426-7777. Ground transportation includes rental cars, courtesy cars, limousine service, buses and taxis. Accommodations include **Best Western Executive International** (731-3800, S$30up/D$37up) and **Hilton Inn** (426-5500, S$29-36/D$36-43) both adjacent to airport and **Ramada Inn Airport** (426-4700, S$42up/D$50up) just 1 mile from field.

MONTANA

Billings (BIL) Logan International, 2 miles NW of city. Tel: (406)245-8989. Ground transportation includes rental cars, courtesy cars, buses and taxis. Accommodations include **Rimrock Lodge** (252-7107, S$20/D$22) and **Holiday Inn East** (245-6611, S$29up/D$34up), slightly more distant, about 6 minutes from field.

Great Falls (GTF) International, 4 miles SW of city. Tel: (406)727-3404. Ground transportation includes rental cars, courtesy cars, limousine service and taxis. Accommodations include **Best Western Heritage Inn** (761-1900, S$34up/D$41up) 2 miles from airport, **Best Western Ponderosa Inn** (761-3410, S$25up/D$33up) about 6 minutes from field, and **Holiday Inn** (761-4600, S$27up/D$33up) about 3 miles from field and about 7 minutes from downtown.

NEBRASKA

Lincoln (LNK) Municipal, 4 miles NW of city. Tel: (402)435-2925. Ground transportation includes rental cars, courtesy cars, limousines, buses and taxis. Accommodations ½ mile from airfield at **Holiday Inn Airport** (475-4971, S$32up/D$37up) and **Best Western Airport Inn** (475-9541, S$23up/D$28up) and 1½ miles from the field at **Ramada Inn Airport** (475-5911, S$28up/D$34up).

Omaha (OMA) Eppley Air Field, 3 miles NE of city. Tel: (402)422-6800. Ground transportation includes rental cars, courtesy cars, limousines and taxis. Accommodations at **Best Western Airport Inn** (348-0222, S$26/D$33) 1 block from airport terminal, and **Ramada Airport Inn** (342-5100, S$37up/D$43up) approximately 1 mile from field.

NEVADA

Las Vegas (LAS) McCarran International, 3 miles S of city. Tel: (702)739-5211. Ground transportation includes rental cars, courtesy cars, limousines, buses and taxis. Accommodations 1 mile from airport at **Tropicana**

Hotel (739-2222,S/D$45-65) and **Las Vegas Marina Hotel/Casino** (739-1500, S/D$42-56) both on the strip.

Reno (RNO) International, 2 miles SE of city. Tel: (702)785-2575. Ground transportation includes rental cars, courtesy cars and taxis. Accommodations 2 miles from airport at **Holiday Inn–Reno South** (825-2940 S$29up/D$36up), and at numerous nearby hotels, including **McCarlie's High Sierra Hotel & Casino** (358-6900, S/D$45-55) 5 minutes from field.

NEW HAMPSHIRE
Manchester (MHT) Municipal–Grenier Field, 4 miles S of city. Tel: (603)622-1951. Ground transportation includes rental cars, limousines and taxis. Accommodations include **Sheraton Wayfarer Inn** (622-3766, S$39up/D$47up) 4 miles from field; **Holiday Inn** (669-2660, S$35up/D$43up) 7 miles from airfield; and **Howard Johnson's Motor Lodge** (668-2600, S$36.90-44.90/D$42.90-50.90) 5 miles from the field.

Concord (CON) Municipal, 1½ miles E of city. Tel: (603)224-4033. Ground transportation includes rental cars and taxis. Accommodations include **Ramada Inn** (224-9534, S$41/D$51) 1 mile from airport, and **New Hampshire Highway Hotel** (225-6687, S$18-28/D$30-36) ¾ mile from the field.

NEW JERSEY
Atlantic City (AIY) Bader Field, 1 mile W of city. Tel: (609)347-5894. Ground transportation: taxis. Accommodations adjacent to airport at **Oasis Motel** (344-9085).

Newark (EWR) International, 3 miles S of city. Tel: (201)961-2000. Ground transportation includes rental cars, courtesy cars, limousines, buses and taxis. Accommodations adjacent to airport at **Howard Johnson's Newark Airport** (824-4000, S$48-55/D$53-60), **Sheraton Inn Newark Airport** (527-1600, S$59up/D$65up), and **Holiday Inn North** (589-1000, S$48up/D$53up).

Trenton (TTN) Mercer County, 7 miles NW of city. Tel: (609)882-1600. Ground transportation includes rental cars, courtesy cars, limousines, buses and taxis. Accommodations 6 miles from airport at **Trenton Inn** (989-7100, S$26/D$35).

Teterboro (TEB) Airport, 1 mile SW of city. Tel: (201)288-1775. Ground transportation includes rental cars, courtesy cars, limousines, buses and taxis. Accommodations 1 mile from the airport at **The Sheraton Heights** (288-6100, S$61up/D$64up).

NEW MEXICO
Albuquerque (ABQ) International, 4 miles S of city. Tel: (505)766-7894. Ground transportation includes rental cars, courtesy cars, limousines, buses and taxis. Accommodations include **Albuquerque Hilton Inn** (243-

8661, S$43-53/D$53-63), 10 minutes from field with free airport transportation.

Santa Fe (SAF) Municipal, 9 miles S of city. Tel: (505)471-0828. Ground transportation includes rental cars and taxis. Accommodations include **Sheraton Santa Fe Inn** (982-5591, S$40up/D$50up) 7 miles from airport; **Santa Fe Hilton** (988-2811, S$32-45/D$42-55) 8 miles from airport.

Taos (SKX) Municipal, 8 miles N of city. Tel: (505)758-4995. Ground transportation includes rental cars and taxis. Accommodations 8 miles from airport at **Holiday Inn** (758-8611, S$45up/D$50up) and 8½ miles from airport at **Best Western Kachina Lodge** (758-2275, S$34up/D$56), **Taos Inn** (758-2233, S$18-20/D$20-21).

NEW YORK
Albany (ALB) County Airport, 8 miles NW of city. Tel: (518)869-5312. Ground transportation includes rental cars, courtesy cars, limousines, buses and taxis. Accommodations include **Americana Inn** (869-9271, S$44-50/D$52-57) ½ mile from field; and **Sheraton Airport Inn** (458-1000, S$42up/D$48up) 1 mile from airport.

Buffalo (BUF) Greater Buffalo International, 9 miles E of city. Tel: (716)632-3115. Ground transportation includes rental cars, courtesy cars, limousines, buses and taxis. Accommodations at Buffalo airport include **Executive Motor Hotel** (634-2300 S$28-35/D$36-42) and 1 mile from the airport at **Holiday Inn International Airport** (634-6969, S$36up/D$43up).

Lake Placid (LKP) Airport, 1 mile SE of city. Tel: (518)523-2473. Ground transportation includes rental cars, limousines and taxis. Accommodations include **Thunderbird Motor Inn** (523-2439, S/D$28-36) 2 miles from airport, and **Ramada Inn** (523-2587, S$30up/D$38up) 2½ miles from airport.

New York City (JFK) John F. Kennedy International, 15 miles SE of city. Tel: (212)656-4444. Ground transportation includes rental cars, courtesy cars, limousines, buses and taxis. Accommodations at JFK Airport include **Holiday Inn** (995-5000, S$59up/D$66up), and **Airport Hilton Inn** (322-8700, S$51-97/D$73-119).

New York City (LGA) La Guardia Airport, 8 miles NE of city. Tel: (212)476-5072. Ground transportation includes rental cars, courtesy cars, limousines, buses and taxis. Accommodations at the airport include **Holiday Inn** (898-1225, S$75up/D$87up), **Sheraton Inn** (446-4800, S$62up/D$72up), and **Travelers Hotel** (335-1200, S$42/D$48).

Poughkeepsie (POU) Dutchess County, 5 miles S of city. Tel: (914)462-2600. Ground transportation includes rental cars and taxis. Accommodations include **Holiday Inn** (473-1151, S$37up/D$47up) 9 miles from the airport, **Dorchester Motor Lodge** (297-3757, S$25/D$30) 2 miles from airport, and the **Airport Motel** (462-2200) located at the airport.

Rochester (ROC) Monroe County, 4 miles SW of city. Tel: (716)436-5624. Ground transportation includes rental cars, courtesy cars, buses and taxis. Accommodations within ½ mile of airport include **Sheraton Inn Airport** (235-6030, S$43up/D$53up), **TraveLodge Airport** (436-4400, S$31/D$35) and **Holiday Inn** (328-6000, S$43up/D$48up).

Syracuse (SYR) Hancock International, 7 miles N of city. Tel: (315)454-3263. Ground transportation includes rental cars and taxis. Accommodations include **Syracuse Airport Inn** (454-9362, S$28-32/D$31-38) located at airport, **Howard Johnson's Motor Lodge North** (454-3266, S$28.50-32.50/D$35.00-37.00) 3 miles from airport, and **Ramada Inn** (457-8670, S$37/D$40up) 2 miles from field.

White Plains (HPN) Westchester County, 4 miles NE of city. Tel: (914)946-9000. Ground transportation includes rental cars, limousines and taxis. Accommodations include **White Plains Hotel** (761-8100, S$54-64/D$64-74) 7 miles from airport; and **Holiday Inn** (592-5680, S$50up/D$54up) and **Rye Hilton Inn** (639-6300, S$63-87/D$81-105), both 8 miles from airport.

NORTH CAROLINA
Charlotte (CTL) Douglas Municipal, 2 miles W of city. Tel: (704)374-2822. Ground transportation includes rental cars, courtesy cars, limousines, buses and taxis. Accommodations include **Best Western Charlotte Airport Motel** (392-5311, S$29/D$35) at the airport, and **Holiday Inn Airport** (394-4301, S$35up/D$41up) 1½ miles from airport.

Raleigh/Durham (RDU) Airport, 12 miles NW of Raleigh, 12 miles SW of Durham. Tel: (919)781-0200 or 596-2321. Ground transportation includes rental cars, courtesy cars, limousines and taxis. Accommodations include **Triangle Motel** (787-8121, S$18/D$22) located at airport; **Sheraton Crabtree Motor Inn** (787-7111, S$34up/D$38up) 8 miles from airport, and **Howard Johnson's Motor Lodge** (782-8718, S$33-48/D$39-54) approximately 10 minutes from airport.

NORTH DAKOTA
Bismarck (BIS) Municipal, 3 miles SE of city. Tel: (701)222-6502. Ground transportation includes rental cars and taxis. Accommodations include **Best Western Town House Motor Inn** (223-8001, S$30up/D$36up) 5 miles from airport; **Best Western Kirkwood Motor Inn** (258-7700, S$30up/D$36up) 2 miles from airport; and **Holiday Inn** (233-9600, S$31up/D$41up) 5 miles from airport.

Fargo (FAR) Hector Field, 3 miles NW of city. Tel: (701)237-0727. Ground transportation includes rental cars and taxis. Accommodations 3 miles from the field include **Biltmore Motor Lodge** (282-2121, S$17/D$22-25) and **Town House Inn** (232-8851, S$21.50/D$29); and 4 miles from the field at **Holiday Inn** (282-2700, S$33/D$43).

Grand Forks (GFK) International, 6 miles NW of city. Tel: (701)775-6293. Ground transportation includes rental cars, limousines and taxis. Accommodations 2 miles from airport at **Holiday Inn** (772-7131, S$29up/D$37up) and **Best Western Westward Ho Motel** (775-5341, S$19up/D$25up), and 5 miles from the airport at **Ramada Inn** (775-3951, S$31.50up/D$39.50up).

OHIO

Cincinnati (CVG) Greater Cincinnati Airport, 4 miles E of Covington, Ky. Tel: (606)283-3151. Ground transportation includes car rentals, courtesy cars, limousines, taxis. Accommodations at airport in **Americana Inn** (283-3285) and **Ramada Inn** (371-4700, S$28up/D$34).

Cincinnati (LUK) Municipal Airport, Tel: (513)321-4132. Ground transportation includes taxis, courtesy cars, car rentals. Accommodations 2 miles away at **El Rancho Rankin** (231-4000) and **Mariemont Inn** (271-2100).

Cleveland (CLE) Hopkins International, 12 miles SW of city. Tel: (216)265-6000. Ground transportation includes rental cars, courtesy cars, limousines, public and taxis. Accommodations on airport grounds at **Hotel Sheraton Hopkins** (267-1500, S$49up/D$59up), 5 minutes away **Holiday Inn** (267-1700, S$35up/D$41up); 8 minutes from downtown, **Sheraton Airport Inn** (267-9800, S$34up/D$39up); and 15 minutes from downtown at **Howard Johnson** (267-2350, S$30-35/D$32-37).

Cleveland (BKL) Burke-Lakefront, Tel: (216)781-6411. Ground transportation includes taxis, public, car rentals, courtesy cars. Accommodations minutes from the heart of Cleveland are **Holiday Inn** (524-8050, S$35up/D$40up); **Sheraton Inn and Hotel** (731-5800, S$31-33/D$34-36).

Columbus (CMH) Port Columbus International, 8 miles E of city. Tel: (614)239-4000. Ground transportation includes taxis, car rentals, limousines. Accommodations at field at **Sheraton Inn** (237-2515, S$39up/D$44up) and **Holiday Inn** 3 miles from airport (861-0321, S$33.50up/D$41.50up). Also **Holiday Inn** at airport (237-6360, S$39up/D$46up).

Dayton (DAY) James M. Cox Municipal, 13 miles N of city. Tel: (513)898-4631. Ground transportation includes car rentals, taxis, limousines, courtesy cars. Accommodations on airport property at **Dayton Airport Hotel** (898-1000, S$49-56/D$56-65).

Toledo (TOL) Toledo Express, 17 miles SW of city. Tel: (419)865-2351. Ground transportation includes taxis, limousines, car rentals, courtesy cars. Accommodation 7 miles from the airport is **Ramada Inn Southwyck** (865-1361, S$40/D$49).

OKLAHOMA
Oklahoma City (OKC) Will Rogers World Airport, 7 miles SW of city. Tel: (405)681-5311. Ground transportation includes car rentals, courtesy cars, limousines, public and taxis. Accommodations 2 miles from airport at **Holiday Inn West** (942-8511, S$34/D$40). At the airport and 2 miles from business district is **Sheraton Inn** (681-7511, S$38up/D$44up) and at the airport is the **Hilton Inn West** (947-7681, S$28-37/D$30-47).

Tulsa (TUL) International, 6 miles N of city. Tel: (918)835-8412. Ground transportation includes taxis, car rentals and limousines. Accommodations within 6 miles at **Camelot Inn** (747-8811).

OREGON
Eugene (EUG) Airport, Mahlon Sweet Field, 8 miles NW of city. Tel: (503)687-5430. Ground transportation includes car rentals, limousines and taxis. Accommodations 5 miles from airport at **TraveLodge** (342-1109) or a half mile from downtown at the **Holiday Inn** (342-5181, S$29up/D$35up).

Portland (PDX) International, 5 miles NE of city. Tel: (503)231-5000. Ground transportation includes car rentals, courtesy cars, limousines, public, taxis. Accommodations on airport grounds at **Sheraton Inn** (288-7171, S$46up/D$52up); 1½ miles from airport at the **Cosmopolitan Airtel** (255-6511); and 3 miles S of airport is the **Chumaree Rodeway Inn** (256-4111).

Salem (SLE) McNary Field, 2 miles SE of city. Tel: (503)588-6314. Ground transportation includes car rentals, limousines, public and taxis. 3 miles from the airport are accommodations at the **International Marion Dunes** (363-4123).

PENNSYLVANIA
Allentown (ABE)-Bethlehem-Easton Airport, 3 miles N of city. Tel: (215)264-2381. Ground transportation includes public, car rentals and taxis. Accommodations 3 miles from airport at **Sheraton Inn Allentown** (437-9876, S$32.50up/D$41up). Opening summer '81 **Sheraton Airport** (212)581-8100 (temporary).

Altoona (AOO) Blair County Airport, 12 miles S of city. Tel: (814)793-3872. Ground transportation by taxi. Accommodations at the **Minuet Manor Motel** (742-8441).

ERIE (ERI) International Airport, 4 miles SW of city. Tel: (814)833-4258. Ground transportation of taxi, car rental and public. Downtown accommodations 6 blocks away at **Holiday Inn Downtown** (456-2961, S$36up/

D$43up); and 3 miles from downtown are the **Quality Inn Scott's** (838-1961) and the **Quality Inn Downtowner** (456-6251).

Harrisburg (MDT) International Airport, 8 miles SE of city. Tel: (717)774-3022. Ground transportation includes taxis, public and car rentals. Accommodations 10 minutes from airport at the **Sheraton Harrisburg Inn** (774-2721, S$44up/D$56up), and 5 minutes from downtown at the **Host Inn Harrisburg** (939-7841) and the **Penn Harris Motor Inn** (763-7117).

Lancaster (LNS) Municipal Airport, 5 miles N of city. Tel: (717)569-1221. Ground transportation includes taxis, car rentals, limousines and courtesy cars. Accommodations 4 miles from airport at **Holiday Inn** (393-0771, S$24up/D$34up) or in the heart of town at **Brunswick Motor Inn** (397-4801, S$26/D$32-38.50).

Philadelphia (PHL) International Airport, 10 miles S of city. Tel: (215)492-3000. Ground transportation includes taxis and car rentals, courtesy cars and limousines. Accommodations on airport grounds at **Sheraton Airport Inn** (365-4150, S$56up/D$62up) and just 3 miles from the airport is the **Ramada Inn** (521-9600, S$39up/D$45 up).

Pittsburgh (PIT) Greater International Airport, 12 miles W of city. Tel: (412)771-2500. Ground transportation includes taxis, car rentals and limousines. Accommodations on terminal grounds include **Sheraton Motor Inn** (262-2400, S$47up/D$53up), **Holiday Inn** (262-3600, S$53/D$59), and **Howard Johnson's** (771-5200, S$38-48/D$44-54).

Scranton (AVP) Wilkes-Barre-Scranton Airport, 5 miles SW of city. Tel: (717)457-7371. Ground transportation includes taxis, car rentals, limousines and courtesy cars. Accommodations within 9 miles at **Holiday Inn** (343-4771, S$33up/D$40up), and 2 miles away at **Howard Johnson's** (654-3301, S$30-34/D$34-40).

RHODE ISLAND
Providence (PVD) T.F. Green State Airport, 9 miles S of city. Tel: (401)737-4000. Ground transportation includes taxis, car rentals, limousines, and courtesy cars. Adjacent to airport are accommodations at **Sheraton Motor Inn** (738-4000, S$48up/D$53up) and **Quality Inn Airport** (739-0600).

Newport (NPT) State Airport, NE of city. Tel: (401)846-2200. Ground transportation includes taxis, car rentals and courtesy cars. Accommodations ½ mile from airport at **Newport Motor Inn** (846-7600, S$34-75/D$40-75).

SOUTH CAROLINA
Charleston (CHS) Municipal Airport, 6 miles NW of city. Tel: (803)744-4155. Ground transportation includes taxis, limousines, car rentals,

courtesy cars. Accommodations adjacent to airport at **Holiday Inn** (744-1621, S$35up/D$45up); downtown at **Mills House Hotel** (577-2400, S/D$80).

Columbia (CAE) Metropolitan Airport, 7 miles SW of city. Tel: (803)794-3419. Ground transportation includes taxis, public and car rentals. Accommodations 5 minutes from airport at **Best Western Host of America Motel** (782-6525, S$28up/D$34up) or 2 blocks from state capitol, **Carolina Inn** (799-8200, S$21.50-23/D$28-30).

SOUTH DAKOTA
Rapid City (RAP) Municipal Airport, 9 miles SE of city. Tel: (605)394-4195. Ground transportation includes taxis, car rentals and limousines. Accommodations include 36 motels and hotels, among them **Holiday Inn** (348-1230, S$30up/D$38up) and **Alex Johnson Hotel** (342-1210).

Sioux Falls (FSD) Joe Foss Field Airport, 3 miles N of city. Tel: (605)336-0762. Ground transportation includes taxis, limousines, public, car rentals and courtesy cars. Accommodations adjacent to airport at **Holiday Inn** (336-1020, S$30up/D$36up) and 2 miles south at **Ramada Inn** (336-0650, S$30up/D$36up).

TENNESSEE
Chattanooga (CHA) Lovell Field Airport, 4 miles E of city. Tel: (615)892-1666. Ground transportation includes car rentals and limousines. Accommodations include **Sheraton Inn South** (894-6820, S$30up/D$36up); **Quality Inn Cascades** (698-1571); and **Days Lodge** (894-7480).

Knoxville (TYS) McGee-Tyson Airport, 13 miles S of city. Tel: (615)970-2773. Ground transportation includes car rentals, limousine and public. Accommodations directly across from airport at **Quality Inn Airport** (577-2528); **Holiday Inn Airport** (577-1674, S$26up/D$34up).

Memphis (MEM) International Airport, 10 miles SE of city. Tel: (901)345-7777. Ground transportation includes taxis, car rentals, limousine and courtesy cars. Accommodations on airport grounds at **Sheraton Inn** (332-2370, S$34up/D$44up), **Rodeway Inn–Airport** (345-1250, S$32-38/D$38-44) and **Quality Inn–Airport** (332-8980).

Nashville (BNA) Metropolitan Airport, 5 miles S of city. Tel: (615)367-3000. Ground transportation includes taxis, car rentals and public. Accommodations adjacent to airport at **Hilton Inn** (244-5472) and **Rodeway Inn** (255-4611, S$26/D$36).

TEXAS
Amarillo (AMA) Air Terminal, 10 miles E of city. Tel: (806)335-1671. Ground transportation includes car rentals and limousines. Accommodations at airport in **Hilton Inn** (373-3071, S$32-47/D$43-58); 10 minutes

from airport at **Inn of Amarillo** (376-4211, S$18-22/D$25-30); and 4 miles from airport the **Quality Inn** (372-8101, S$28/D$37).

Austin (AUS) Robert Mueller Municipal Airport, 4 miles NE of city. Tel: (512)472-5439. Ground transportation includes taxis, car rentals and courtesy cars. Accommodations near airport include **Ramada Inn** (452-2581, S$34up/D$38up) and the **Marriott Hotel** (458-6161, S$52-60/D$62-76); **Austin Hilton Inn** (451-5757, S$46-63/D$58-75).

Dallas–Fort Worth (DFW) Regional Airport, 17 miles W of city. Tel: (214)574-3112. Ground transportation includes taxis, public, car rentals and courtesy cars. Accommodations at airport in **Marina Hotel** (453-8400, S$42/D$48); 5 minutes to **Holiday Inn** (255-7147, S$49up/D$55up), and **Ramada Inn** (579-8911, S$47up/D$55up).

Dallas (DAL) Love Field, 7 miles NW of city. Tel: (214)352-2663. Ground transportation includes car rentals, courtesy cars, public and taxis. Accommodations at airport in **Ramada Inn** (265-7711, S$39/D$45) and the **Rodeway Inn** (357-1701).

El Paso (ELP) International Airport, 8 miles NE of city. Tel: (915)772-4271. Ground transportation includes taxis, car rentals and courtesy cars. Accommodations at airport in **Hilton Inn** (778-4241) and **Ramada Inn** (778-3341, S$26up/D$32up).

Houston (IAH) Intercontinental Airport, 20 miles N of city. Tel: (713)443-4731. Ground transportation includes taxis, limousines, car rentals, public, courtesy cars. Accommodations at airport include **Quality Inn Intercontinental Airport** (446-9131, S$49-56/D$56-62), and the **Host International** (443-2310, S$58-62/D$66-70).

San Antonio (SAT) International Airport, 8 miles N of city. Tel: (512)824-5335. Ground transportation includes courtesy cars, limousines, public, taxis, car rentals. Accommodations at airport include **Best Western Motor Inn** (344-8331, S$32up/D$39up); **La Quinta Motor Inn** (828-0781); **Ramada Inn** (344-4581, S$36up/D$42up).

UTAH
Salt Lake City (SLC) International Airport, 3 miles NW of city. Tel: (801)539-2400. Ground transportation includes car rentals, courtesy cars, limousines, public, taxis. Accommodations near airport at **Holiday Inn** (533-9000, S$35up/D$42up); and 3 miles away are **Hotel Utah Motor Inn** (328-8901) and the **Temple Square Hotel** (355-2961).

VERMONT
Burlington (BTV) International Airport, 3 miles E of city. Tel: (802)863-2874. Ground transportation includes taxis and car rentals. 2 miles from airport is **Best Western Redwood** (862-6421, S$22up/D$28up), 3 miles,

Colonial Motor Inn (862-5754, S$16-24/D$18-26) and **Sheraton Burling-ton Inn** (862-6576, S$25up/D$30up).

VIRGINIA
Norfolk (ORF) Regional Airport, 8 miles E of city. Tel: (804)857-3351. Ground transportation includes car rentals and taxis. Airport accommoda-tions at **Quality Inn** (855-3355, S$18-24/D$20-24).

Richmond (RIC) Richard E. Byrd International Airport, 8 miles SE of city. Tel: (804)222-7361. Ground transportation includes car rentals, cour-tesy cars, limousines, public, taxis. Accommodations at airport, **Holiday Inn** (222-6450, S$35up/D$39up) and **Ramada Inn** (222-2780, S$34up/D$42up).

Williamsburg (PHF, Newport News) Patrick Henry International Airport, 18 miles SE of city. Tel: (804)229-9256. Ground transportation includes taxis and car rentals. Accommodations at **Best Western Patrick Henry Inn** (229-9540, S$20up/D$30up).

WASHINGTON
Seattle (SEA)-Tacoma International Airport, 14 miles S of city. Tel: (206)433-5385. Ground transportation includes car rentals, courtesy cars, limousines, taxis. Accommodations near airport premise include **Best Western Airport Inn** (878-1814, S$30up/D$33up), and **Seattle Airport Hilton** (244-4800).

Spokane (GEG) International Airport, 7 miles SW of city. Tel: (509)624-3218. Ground transportation includes courtesy cars, limousines, taxis, and car rentals. Accommodations at airport in **Ramada Inn** (838-5211, S$30up/D$34up); 2 miles from airport is **Holiday Inn** (747-2021, S$31up/D$38up).

WEST VIRGINIA
Charleston (CRW) Kanawha County, 4 miles NE of city. Tel: (304)342-8818. Ground transportation includes car rentals, courtesy cars, limou-sines, taxis. 4 miles from airport is **Holiday Inn** (343-4521, S$36.50up/D$42.50up).

Huntington (HTS) Tri-State Airport, 9 miles W of city. Tel: (304)453-6165. Ground transportation includes taxis, limousines and car rentals. Accommodations 3 miles to downtown at **Holiday Inn East** (529-1331, S$30up/D$33up).

WISCONSIN
Madison (MSN) Municipal Airport, 5 miles NE of city. Tel: (608)266-6540. Ground transportation includes taxis, limousines, courtesy cars, car

rentals. Accommodations at **Holiday Inn** (244-4703, S$33up/D$40up) 3 miles from airport, and **Ramada Inn** (244-2481, S$30up/D$34up).

Milwaukee (MKE) General Mitchell, 6 miles S of city. Tel: (414)747-5300. Ground transportation includes car rentals, courtesy cars, limousines, public, taxis. Accommodations at airport include **Best Western Midway Motor Lodge** (769-2100, S$43up/D$53up) and **Ramada Inn Airport** (764-5300, S$36up/D$40up).

WYOMING
Cheyenne (CYS) Municipal Airport, 1 mile N of city. Tel: (307)637-6400. Ground transportation includes taxis and car rentals. Accommodations within 1 mile of airport include **Best Western Hitching Post Inn** (638-3301, S$31up/D$37up), **Downtowner Motor Inn** (634-1331).

Useful Telephone Numbers

The following is a list of NATIONAL COUNCIL FOR INTERNATIONAL VISITORS offices around the USA who provide information to visitors. Telephone Monday-Friday 9-5 (except as otherwise noted in individual listings).

ALABAMA
HUNTSVILLE—Huntsville-Madison County Council for International Visitors: (205)536-5911 ext. 260

ARIZONA
PHOENIX—World Affairs Council of Phoenix: (602)254-3345 or 258-3411
TUCSON—Hospitality International Tucson: (602)327-7341 ext. 355

ARKANSAS
LITTLE ROCK—Little Rock Council for International Visitors: (501)225-0216

CALIFORNIA
RIVERSIDE—International Relations Council of Riverside: (714)787-4113
SACRAMENTO—People-to-People Council of Greater Sacramento: (916)441-1424
SAN FRANCISCO—International Hospitality Center: (415)986-1388
STANFORD—Bechtel International Center, Office for Foreign Visitors, Stanford University: (415)497-1984

COLORADO
DENVER—Institute of International Education, Rocky Mountain Office: (303)837-0788
DENVER—International Hospitality Center: (303)832-4234

CONNECTICUT
HARTFORD—World Affairs Center: (203)236-5277 or 236-4331 or 633-2835 (weekend)
WESTPORT—International Hospitality Committee of Fairfield County: (203)966-0464 or 762-7232

DELAWARE
WILMINGTON—Delaware Council for International Visitors: Tuesdays & Fridays 9:30am-1pm (302)655-3341 ext. 31; all other times (302)239-4412 or 239-4258

DISTRICT OF COLUMBIA (WASHINGTON, DC)
WASHINGTON—Foreign Student Service Council: (202)232-4979
WASHINGTON—International Visitors Information Service: (202)872-8747

FLORIDA
GAINESVILLE—Gainesville Council for International Friendship: (904)392-1860
MIAMI—Council for International Visitors of Greater Miami: (305)379-4610
WINTER PARK/ORLANDO AREA—Mid-Florida Council for International Visitors: (305)859-9570

ILLINOIS
CHICAGO—International Visitors Center of Chicago: (312)332-5875
FREEPORT—International Fellowship Committee: (815)232-3340
SPRINGFIELD—Springfield Commission on International Visitors: (217)546-0775
STERLING—Sterling–Rock Falls International Fellowship Committee: (815)625-5896

INDIANA
INDIANAPOLIS—International Visitors Service: (317)251-2414

IOWA
SIOUX CITY—Mayor's Committee for International Visitors: (712)255-1080

KENTUCKY
LOUISVILLE—University of Louisville, International Center: (502)588-6602

MARYLAND
BALTIMORE—Baltimore Council for International Visitors: (301)837-7150

MASSACHUSETTS
BOSTON—Center for International Visitors for Greater Boston: (617)742-0460
CAMBRIDGE—Harvard University Marshal's Office: (617)495-5724
CAMBRIDGE—Massachusetts Institute of Technology: (617)253-2851
SPRINGFIELD—World Affairs Council of the Connecticut Valley: (413)782-2054
WORCESTER—International Center of Worcester: (617)752-8414

MICHIGAN
ANN ARBOR—University of Michigan, International Center: (313)764-9310

DETROIT—International Visitors Council of Metropolitan Detroit: (313)259-2680

EAST LANSING—Community Volunteers for International Programs: (517)353-1735

FLINT—Flint Committee to Welcome International Visitors: (313)238-6722 or 655-4076

MINNESOTA

MINNEAPOLIS/ST PAUL—Minnesota International Center: (612)373-3200

WORTHINGTON—Worthington-Crailsheim International: (507)376-6121 from 8am until 4pm; at other times 376-4011

MISSOURI

KANSAS CITY—Chamber of Commerce of Greater Kansas City: (816)221-2424

ST LOUIS—St Louis Council on World Affairs: (314)361-7333 (from 9 to 4)

MONTANA

BOZEMAN—Bozeman Council of International Visitors: (406)587-0859 or 586-5372

NEBRASKA

GRAND ISLAND—Grand Island Council for International Visitors: (303)382-3190

LINCOLN—Mayor's Committee for International Friendship: (402)489-3339

OMAHA—Kiwanis Club of Omaha: (402)345-9999

NEW HAMPSHIRE

DURHAM—New Hampshire Council on World Affairs: (603)862-1683

NEW MEXICO

ALBUQUERQUE—Committee for International Visitors: (505)299-6754

SANTA FE—Council on International Relations: (505)982-4931 (mornings only)

NEW YORK

ALBANY—International Center: (518)436-9741

BUFFALO—Buffalo World Hospitality Association: (716)882-6900

NEW YORK CITY—International Center of New York: (212)245-8278

ROCHESTER—Rochester International Friendship Council: (716)461-2794

ROCHESTER—International Visitors Program Service, Rochester Association for the United Nations: (716)232-1080

SYRACUSE—International Center of Syracuse: (315)471-0252 or 471-1222

OHIO
AKRON—Hosting International Travellers: (216)928-5555
CINCINNATI—Cincinnati International Visitors Center: (513)241-7384 (9 to 4)
COLUMBUS—Central Ohio Council for International Visitors: (614)451-6459
DAYTON—Dayton Council on World Affairs: (513)223-6203
TOLEDO—International Institute of Greater Toledo: (419)241-9178

OKLAHOMA
OKLAHOMA CITY—International Visitors Council, Chamber of Commerce: (405)232-6381
TULSA—Council for International Visitors: (918)585-1201

OREGON
PORTLAND—World Affairs Council of Oregon: (503)229-3049

PENNSYLVANIA
PHILADELPHIA—Philadelphia Council for International Visitors: (215)823-7261
PITTSBURGH—Pittsburgh Council for International Visitors: (412)682-6151

RHODE ISLAND
NEWPORT—Newport Council for International Visitors: (401)846-0222
PROVIDENCE—World Affairs Council: (401)751-1272

SOUTH CAROLINA
COLUMBIA—Columbia Council for Internationals: (803)782-1865

TENNESSEE
KNOXVILLE—Knoxville Area International Council: (615)974-3177
MEMPHIS—Memphis Council for International Friendship: (901)526-6201 or 274-3506 or 754-8730
NASHVILLE—Vanderbilt University Office of International Services: (615)322-2753

TEXAS
AUSTIN—International Hospitality Committee of Austin: (512)471-1211
DALLAS—Dallas Committee for Foreign Visitors: (214)528-4889 [after hours call (214)321-1163]
EL PASO—El Paso Council for International Visitors: (915)544-7880
HOUSTON—Houston International Service Committee, Institute of International Education, Southern Office: (713)223-5454

UTAH
SALT LAKE CITY—International Visitors—Utah Council: (801)532-4747

VERMONT
BURLINGTON—Vermont Council on World Affairs: (802)863-3539

VIRGINIA
NORFOLK—Norfolk–Virginia Beach Committee for International Visitors: (804)481-0814

WASHINGTON
EPHRATA—Ephrata's International Friends: (509)754-4611 ext. 258
SEATTLE—World Affairs Council of Seattle: (206)682-6986
SPOKANE—Spokane International Exchange Council: (509)747-6963
YAKIMA—Yakima Valley Council for International Visitors: (509)877-2079 [after hours (509)457-5113]

WISCONSIN
MILWAUKEE—Hospitality International: (414)933-0521

Alabama

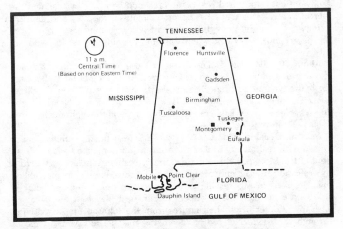

Area	50,708 square miles	Population	3,742,000
Capital	Montgomery	Sales Tax	4%

Weather	Jan	Feb	Mar	Apr	May	Jun	Jul	Aug	Sep	Oct	Nov	Dec
Av Temp (°C)	12	13	16	20	24	28	28	28	26	21	15	12
Days of Rain	10	10	11	7	8	12	17	14	10	6	7	11

Alabama, like its sister southern states, is developing at a rapid rate and the visitor may suddenly be transported from the sleepy countryside to one of the modern industrial cities. But rapid change is something Alabamans have learned to live with since large areas of land in the north of the state were, seemingly overnight, made into large areas of water by the Tennessee Valley Authority (TVA). And a rural area where sharecroppers once scratched out a sparce living is now producing rockets and other space-related vehicles such as the Space Shuttle.

In the northern half of the state the **Cumberland Mountains,** in concert with the **Tennessee River,** make for a variety of scenic beauty, with peaks, sometimes snowy, long ridges, wind-sculptured crags, and deep gorges and canyons. These are particularly beautiful in the fall. The Muscle Shoals project, built by the TVA in the northwest corner of Alabama, centers on the cities of **Muscle Shoals, Florence, Sheffield,** and **Tuscumbia,** and has created marvelous lakes for fishing, water skiing, and sailing.

Florence stands beside **Wilson Dam,** the world's highest lift lock at 100 ft, and the largest ceremonial Indian mound in the Tennessee Valley is also located here. Among the old houses still standing in the town is the log cabin where W. C. Handy, composer of *St Louis Blues* and *Memphis Blues*, was born in 1873. Tuscumbia's most famous citizen was Helen Keller, the remarkable woman who battled valiantly to overcome the handicap of an early childhood without sight, speech, or hearing. At her birthplace the pump still stands where her lifelong companion, Anne Sullivan, first established real communication with her by teaching the word "water." This scene has become famous in the play and film *The Miracle Worker*. Summer theater productions of the play are presented on the grounds every Friday and Saturday evening during July and August.

About 50 miles east of Tuscumbia is **Decatur** where you can spend the day at the unique wave-making pool at **Point Mallard**. (It's used for hydrodynamic testing). Be sure also to visit the Civil War **Old State Bank Building** and the **Burleson-Hinds-McEntire Home**. Nearby is the **Joe Wheeler State Park** where the family can spend the night in attractive cabins or camping out.

Leaving Decatur, take Alt. 72 East to **Mooresville**, a genuine pioneer village with real history in its past. Andrew Johnson, who became President of the U.S. upon the assassination of Abraham Lincoln, was a tailor by profession and the only president without the benefit of formal schooling. He lived in Mooresville as an apprentice tailor, and his home is still lived in here. While not open to tourists, it may be viewed—along with many other original structures from the Johnson era—by driving through the town. Not too far down the road is **Bell Mina**, home of two of the state's early governors.

Further east is **Huntsville**, population 142,238, and the first English-speaking community in what today is Alabama. Other firsts include the first public library, first Alabama bank, first railroad, and first capital of the state. Today it regards itself as *Rocket City, Space Age Capital to the World*. This is also where former German rocketeer Werner von Braun and his team researched moon-flight and missiles. The **Alabama Space and Rocket Center** houses the largest aerospace exhibit in the US and is to be found on Alt. 72 East. Open 9-5 daily. Admission: $4 adults, $2.25 senior citizens, military personnel, and children 6-12. Tour buses from the Center take visitors to the **Marshall Space Flight Center**. Adults $2.75, senior citizens, military personnel, and children $1.50. In addition, **Huntsville** has an **Observatory & Planetarium** plus the Urritt Museum at Monte Sano Mountain, all well worth the visit. The $15-million **Von Braun Civic Center** complex is the location of numerous cultural events. Some 27 Huntsville groups provide performing and participating programs in music, theater, song, dance, literature, film, painting, sculpture, photography, handicrafts, and other arts. The **Huntsville Museum of Art** is to be found here. Some 10 miles west of the city is **Jetplex**, one of the most modern airport facilities in the US. **The Skycenter Hotel** (772-9661, S$30-34/D$36-60) has accommodations and restaurant facilities. **Huntsville Hilton** (533-1400, S$27-31/D$33-37) is across from

Civic Center. **Carriage Inn** (837-5555, S$23-28/D$27-32), 2 miles west of Center; **Sheraton** (837-3250, S$32/D$40), 10 miles to airport.

Eastward on the Tennessee River is **Scottsboro,** where backwoodsmen have for generations held a "barter day" market on the first Monday of each month. Along I-50 near Fort Payne are the beautiful **De Soto Falls** and the **Little River Canyon,** one of the deepest canyons east of the Rockies. **Weiss Lake** and **Sequoyah Cave** are nearby. The Cherokee Indians went underground at Sequoyah to avoid zealous government agents who were trying to force them from their land. See **Manitou Cave** with its fascinating rock formations. And just south and west of Ft Payne is **Guntersville,** on the lake of the same name, the home of the hydroplaning fraternity and with its own exceptionally popular **Boat Racing Festival.**

Turning southwest you come to **Noccalula Falls,** which dive off a 100-foot ledge near Gadsden, and the **Ave Maria Grotto** on the campus of **St Bernard College** in Cullman. Here a Benedictine monk devoted a lifetime to creating precise miniatures of 150 famous churches and shrines around the world. Southwest of Gadsden, near Oneonta, is the **Horton Mill Covered Bridge,** 220 feet long and higher above the water than any other covered bridge in America. It is one of 14 preserved in the state. Open daily. Admission: free.

BIRMINGHAM, Alabama's largest city, population 282,068, is to the south of Cullman on US 31/I-65. Jefferson, St Clair, Shelby, Walker, and Birmingham counties have a total population of 820,200. The first settlers arrived in Jones Valley (Birmingham) in 1813, though it was not until 1871 that Birmingham was incorporated. On **Red Mountain,** Vulcan Park, US31S, stands an unusual 55-ft statue of **Vulcan,** mythical Roman God of the forge. It is elevated on a 124-ft pedestal and is the largest iron figure ever cast. What makes this edifice so unusual is that the statue holds a light. If it shines green, it informs viewers that no traffic deaths have occurred on the streets of Birmingham within the past 24 hours. The color red signifies a fatal accident. The statue has an interesting past. In 1905 it was part of the Birmingham District Exhibit at the Louisiana Purchase Exposition in St Louis. Today, a high-speed elevator takes you to the top which is a climate-controlled, glass-enclosed observation deck where a panoramic view of the Birmingham area may be enjoyed. (Call 254-2628 for further information). Places of interest in Birmingham include: **Arlington Home and Gardens (1822),** open daily 9-4:30, Sunday 1-4:30, closed Monday. (780-5656) National Register of Historic Places. Birmingham's only antebellum mansion. Once the headquarters for Union General James H. Wilson. **Birmingham Botanical Gardens,** Open dawn to dusk. Stroll through the authentic Japanese Gardens, complete with Tea House given as a gift from Japan to Birmingham. Free. **Bessemer Southern Railway Terminal,** Bessemer. Example of small turn-of-the-century depot. National Register of Historic Places. **Highland Avenue-Rhodes Park Historic District,** dates back to 1880s. The district consists of a three-block section and park. A number of original homes have

3

been preserved and are in use as private residences. National Register of Historic Places. The **Birmingham-Jefferson Civic Center**, a sports, entertainment, and convention complex, is located in the heart of downtown. **Birmingham Museum of Art**, also in the downtown area, has fine silver and Wedgwood collections. Open daily 10-5, Sunday 2-6, closed Monday. Accommodations in the downtown area include **Cabana Motel**, (252-7141, S$16.95/D$27.50); **Hyatt Birmingham** (251-2221, S$42-50/D$56-74), **Holiday Inn-Civic Center** (328-6320, S$28/D$34-38); **Trave-Lodge-Civic Center** (324-6605, S$25-31/D$29-43); **Sheraton** (328-8560, S$32-39/D$42-49). Also located in the downtown area and adjacent to the Medical Center are: **Ramada Inn-Medical Center** (933-7700, S$32-36/D$32-40); **Passport Inn** (933-1900, S$17.90/D$20.90); **Holiday Inn-20th Place** (323-7211, S$35-40/D$42-45); **Birmingham Hilton** (933-9000, S$38-56/D$48-64). South of the city are the **Sheraton Mountain Brook Inn** (870-3100, S$32-37/D$39-42); **Ramada Inn-South** (822-6030, S$25-29/D$29-33); **Quality Inn South** (942-2041, S$32-36/D$39-42); **Rodeway Inn** (942-0010, S$27-30/D$32-35); **Red Carpet Inn of America Crest** (942-2031, S$22-28/D$28-42). Restaurants include **Rossi's** for Italian cuisine, **Jimez's Restaurant** for creole food, **Steve Leontis Smokehouse** for Southern Barbeque. Seafood is available at **John's** and **Bright Star Restaurant**. **Sumo Japanese Steak House** and **Trader Ku's** provide oriental fare.

Forty miles east of Birmingham in Talladega, is the **Alabama International Speedway**, located on I-20. Two stock car international races are held annually, **the Winston 500** in early May and **The Talledega 500** in early August. Tours available upon request.

Fifty-six miles southwest of Birmingham is **Tuscaloosa**, home of the **University of Alabama**, and once the state capital. There are several antebellum buildings on this fine 425-acre campus. In Tuscaloosa, sample the food at **The Landing** (steaks/seafood), or stop for breakfast or dinner at the **Waysider Restaurant**, 15th Street and Greensboro Avenue.

Montgomery, 100 miles south of Birmingham and 180 miles north of Mobile, was incorporated in 1819 and in 1846 was chosen as the site of the State Capital. It was in Montgomery that the world's first electric street car began operation on April 7, 1885. In the early 1900s, the Wright Brothers established a flight school on the site of the present-day Maxwell Air Force Base. Places of interest in Montgomery include **First White House of the Confederacy**, Washington and Union Streets, which is filled with personal memorabilia of Jefferson Davis, President of the Confederate States; the **State Capitol**, Dexter Avenue, which is open daily 8-4:30 pm, free; the **W. A. Gayle Planetarium**, 1010 Forest Avenue (265-6225). Adults $1.50, students-through grade 12-75¢. Open Tuesday & Thursday 3:45 pm, Saturday & Sunday 3:30 pm; **Jasmine Hill Sculpture Gardens**, US Highway 231 North. Featuring reproductions of famous works of art in a natural setting. Classical sculpture and fountains brought from Greece and Italy. Open March-November, Tuesday-Sunday 9-5. Adults $1.50, children 6-12, 50¢, under 6 free.

For rates and information on city tours, call 265-1731 or 265-7886. Accommodations in the downtown area include: **Holiday Inn-State Capi-**

tol, (265-0741, S$33/D$39); **Town Plaza Motor Inn,** (269-1561, S$18/ D$22); **Whitley Hotel,** (262-6461, S$24/D$32); and **Downtowner Motor Inn,** (264-2231, S$29.50/D$36). To the south is **Governors House Motor Inn,** (288-2800, S$36/D$41-50). Good places to eat include **Elite Café** (seafood); **Morrison's Cafeteria, Twickenham Station, Sahara, Riviera Restaurant** (beef & seafood); **Mr. G's** (beef); **Varon's** (Italian) and **Beverly Restaurant** (Mexican).

East of Montgomery is **Tuskegee,** where Booker T. Washington founded the **Tuskegee Institute** for blacks in 1881. On the campus is **The Oaks,** Dr Washington's home, where his study has been preserved; an extensive library contains practically every book ever published about the black man in the South. Also preserved is the laboratory where the brilliant black scientist George Washington Carver proved that there was more to the peanut than anyone suspected, and thereby almost single-handedly revolutionized the agricultural economy of the South. The charming city of **Eufaula,** on the Georgia border southeast of Montgomery, has a number of fine antebellum mansions, some open year round and others during the annual **Pilgrimage** in April; there is also an annual antique show. This is a Mecca for fishermen and the **Alabama Fresh-Water Fishing Rodeo** is held in May on Lake Eufaula, a 500-mile shoreline teaming with bass, crappie and bream. Near the Florida border is Dothan, which holds the **National Peanut Festival** every October, a few miles west is **Enterprise.** The world's only monument to the boll weevil was erected here in gratitude to the pest for initiating the diversification of the economy. This insatiable little insect decimated the entire cotton production of the South and forced the region to start growing other crops in the 1920s.

City to Visit

MOBILE

Mobile is situated at the head of Mobile Bay, about 35 miles north of the Gulf of Mexico. The Spaniards explored the area from about 1519 to 1559, but it was left to the French to establish the first permanent settlement in 1711. Originally known as Fort St Louis, it was the capital of French Louisiana for several years. America didn't get a firm grip on it until the War of 1812. When the Civil War came, the city's splendid harbor was a convenient route by which the Confederacy received supplies from Europe and the West Indies, despite an attempted federal blockade from 1861. However, in 1864, Admiral David Farragut arrived with his ironclad boats and effectively obstructed the passage of supplies. On April 12, 1865, General E. R. S. Canby and company arrived and the city fell to Northern forces.

The years that followed were difficult for Mobile, but the opening of the Panama Canal in 1914 brought foreign trade and a healthy economic outlook for the future. Now Mobile is the hub of the thriving **Gulf Intra-**

coastal Waterway, and four navigable rivers, running deep inland, carry freight to and from the city. Freighters from all over the world arrive at the Alabama State Docks. Manufacturing also contributes heavily to the local economy.

Many of the city's old homes and tree-lined streets have retained much of the charm and influence of the French and Spanish periods. Azaleas, brought from France in 1754, bloom extravagantly in late winter and early spring along a 35-mile route known as the **Azalea Trail.** Mobile has thoughtfully maintained an attractive blend of hectic waterfront activity and casual southern gentility.

WHAT TO SEE

Fort Conde-Charlotte House, 18th century, has rooms decorated in the style of each period of its history; open 10-4 Tue-Sat. Adults $1.50, children 50¢. **Oakleigh House** (1833-38) is shaded by magnificent oaks; its pre-Civil War period furniture is worth inspecting along with Mardi Gras relics. The **Phoenix Museum** has antique fire-fighting equipment dating back to 1819. Visit the submarine *USS Drum* and the battleship *USS Alabama,* permanently docked in honor of Alabamans who served in World War II and Korea.

ACCOMMODATIONS

Located in mid-town are **Mobile TraveLodge** (433-3921, S$29-39/D$30-39); **Best Western Admiral Semmes Motor Hotel** (433-2771, S$22-29/D$30-34); **Sheraton** (438-3431, S$33/D$40); **Holiday Inn-Downtown** (433-6923, S$24-28/D$27-31). The **Quality Inn** (344-3410, S$33.50-36.50/D$40.50-43.50) is midway between the airport and downtown. **Howard Johnson Motor Lodge** (471-2402, S$31/D$40-43) is near Bellingrath Gardens, a little farther out. Other good spots west of town are **Rodeway Inn-Government Street** (471-5371, S$29/D$34): **Holiday Inn-West** (661-5431, S$25-29/D$28-32), and **Town House Motor Hotel** (438-4653, S$12-15/D$16-18). Tax 7%.

RESTAURANTS

Burke's Seafood for steaks, seafood; **Wintzell's Oyster House; Constantine's; Bayley's;** and **Rousso's** are good places to eat in Mobile.

ARTS AND MUSIC

The large **Municipal Theater** and adjacent **Municipal Auditorium** handle lavish stage and operatic productions. Paintings, drawings, prints, lectures, films and fine art symposiums can be found at the **Mobile Municipal Art Gallery and Museum;** open 10-4:45 Tue-Sat, 12-4:45 Sun. Interesting murals decorate the **Commercial Guaranty Bank Building,** formerly the **Waterman Building,** and **E.A. Roberts Building.** The **Opera Guild** sponsors productions with famous guest artists.

SHOPPING

Most downtown stores are open weekdays 9-6; evenings until 9 at Bel Air Mall and Spring Dale Plaza.

SPORTS

Golf and tennis are played throughout the year. You can sail or water-ski in the bay or swim from miles of sandy beaches, go deep-sea fishing for tarpon, marlin and other big fish, or angle for speckled trout. At certain times the bay "boils over" with fish and shellfish which get stranded in the shallows. When this happens, you will be able to catch as much fish as you can carry. Another colorful event is **The Blessing of the Shrimp Fleet** at **Bayou LaBatre** on the last Sunday in July.

CALENDAR OF EVENTS

Senior Football Bowl Game and **Camellia Club Flower Show,** January; **Mobile Azalea Trail** along 35 miles, February-March: **Mardi Gras** parties and balls, culminating in exuberant parades, carnivals and costume balls; the **Krewe de Bienville Ball,** open to visitors 10 days before Ash Wednesday; **Mobile Jazz Festival,** May; **Dauphin Island Regatta,** April; **Alabama Deep-Sea Fishing Rodeo,** off Dauphin Island, third weekend in July; **Greater Gulf State Fair,** October; **Cascading Chrysanthemums,** November; **Candlelight Christmas** at Oakleigh, December.

WHERE TO GO NEARBY

Bellingrath, south of town near Theodore, has magnificently landscaped gardens that are in bloom the year-round. Special seasons are late September to April for hundreds of varieties of camellias, February to April for azaleas, May for hydrangeas and gardenias, November for chrysanthemums, and December for poinsettias. The **Bellingrath Mansion** has priceless furnishings and works of art; separate admission charges to house and gardens, both open daily. South of the city on the west side of Mobile Bay is **Dauphin Island,** reached by a toll-free bridge.

Here **Fort Gaines** and old weapons recall the Battle of Mobile Bay. **Fort Morgan,** the last Confederate bastion to fall in the Civil War, stands on a matching strip of land extending from the southern tip of the eastern shore. Admiral Farragut's famous ironclad *USS Tecumseh*, victim of a Confederate torpedo, lies deep in the three-mile gap of water that was the only entry to Mobile Bay. Fort Morgan is about 100 miles by car via upper Mobile Bay; take the tunnel and continue down the eastern shore.

On the way are some charming villages where many city people have fishing camps and summer homes; see the beautiful **Greek Orthodox Church** at Malbis. Down at **Point Clear,** 23 miles southeast of Mobile, the **Grand Hotel** (928-9201, S$45/D$75 MAP) maintains the luxurious traditions established when its predecessor, built in 1847, was the first resort hotel in the South. Here there is sailing, water-skiing, freshwater and deep-sea fishing, golf at the **Lakewood Club,** tennis, horseback riding, pool and beach, shooting in season, and dancing.

Gulf State Park—located at Gulf Shores, southeast of Mobile, the 6,000-acre park has 2.5 miles of beachfront, a lodge, restaurant and convention facilities, as well as a beach pavilion and an 825-foot fishing pier on the Gulf. Slightly off the beach are an 18-hole golf course, large modern campground, lakeside vacation cottages, picnic area, tennis courts, and freshwater fishing. (Lodge-convention complex operated by **Araserv Inc.,** Drawer K, Gulf Shores, **Gulf State Park Resort** (968-7531, S$21.50-43/ D$24-46).

FURTHER STATE INFORMATION

Birmingham Avenue Chamber of Commerce, 2027 First Avenue North, Birmingham, AL (tel: 323-5461). **Greater Birmingham Convention and Visitors Bureau,** 2027 First Avenue North, Birmingham, AL 35203 (tel: 252-9825). Convention and Visitors Division, **Montgomery Chamber of Commerce,** P.O. Box 79, Montgomery, AL 36101. **Alabama Bureau of Publicity and Information,** 532 South Perry St, Montgomery, AL 36130. Out of State 800-633-5763. **Alabama Chamber of Commerce,** 468 South Perry, AL 36101 (tel: 834-6000). Hunting and fishing: **Division of Fish and Game,** Department of Conservation, Montgomery, AL 36130. **Mobile Chamber of Commerce,** PO Box 2187, Mobile, AL 36601.

 Consulates in Mobile: Belgium, Bolivia, Costa Rica, Denmark, Dominican Republic, El Salvador, Finland, France, Germany, Guatemala, Haiti, Honduras, Italy, Japan, Korea, Mexico, Nicaragua, Norway, Panama, South Africa, Spain, Sweden, Thailand, Venezuela.

USEFUL TELEPHONE NUMBERS
Mobile

Police	438-7211
Fire	438-7311
Mobile Infirmary	431-2400
University of South Alabama Medical Center	471-7000
Chamber of Commerce	433-6951
Pan Am Reservations	(800)231-0260

Birmingham

Crisis Center	323-7777
Police	328-9311
Fire	251-1291
Brookwood Medical Center Emergency	877-1930
Chamber of Commerce	323-5461
Pan Am Reservations	(800)231-1841

Montgomery

Emergency Number	911
Police	832-4720
Fire	263-1003
St Margaret's Hospital	265-5661
Baptist Medical Center	288-2100
Chamber of Commerce	834-5200
Pan Am Reservations	(800)535-6764

Alaska

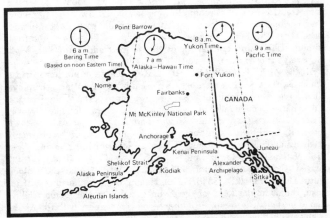

Area	589,757	Population	406,000
Capital	Juneau	Sales Tax	none

Weather

	Jan	Feb	Mar	Apr	May	Jun	Jul	Aug	Sep	Oct	Nov	Dec
Av Temp (°C)	−4	−3	−1	3	8	11	13	12	9	5	1	−2
Days Rain/Snow	18	18	18	17	17	15	17	18	20	23	20	21

Time Zone the state has four time zones. Juneau and the southeast is on Pacific Time; Yukon Time is one hour behind Juneau; Fairbanks and Anchorage are two hours behind Juneau on Alaska Time; Nome is three hours behind Juneau on Bering Sea Time.

In 1959 Alaska joined the Union as the 49th and largest state; it is more than twice the size of Texas. Alaska first caught the attention of Europe when Vitus Bering, a Dane, sailed through the straits now bearing his name. The area was also visited by Captain James Cook in 1778. From about 1799 the Russians took an abiding interest in Alaska and its wealth of furs, but eventually they sold it to the United States in 1867. A few years later, the Gold Rush of 1886 brought a flood of prospectors, some of whom settled down to become the core of the new American population. But today oil is the most valuable natural asset.

The early settlers found themselves in a huge and beautiful, if sometimes dangerous, country, from the steep-walled fjords of the southwest to the wide stretches of the Bering coast and the icy expanse of the Beaufort Sea. The name "Alaska" comes from an Aleut word meaning "great land," which was no understatement. Its vastness is an appropriate setting for North America's highest mountain, **Mt McKinley** (20,320 feet) and the continent's longest river, the **Yukon** (2,300 miles). The population of more than 406,000 includes military personnel, Eskimos, Indians and Aleuts.

Alaska's game make it a sportsmen's paradise, and a profitable industry has developed from it. May-September are the best months to fish for huge trout, pike and salmon. Hunting safaris bag Dall sheep, moose, deer, caribou, walrus, grizzly and black bears from early August to mid-December. The game provides good eating, too. In summer the fresh salmon, halibut and crab are a particular treat and many hotels will prepare your own catch for you.

On the **ALEXANDER ARCHIPELAGO,** along the northern British Columbia coast, Alaska's territory is a gloriously scenic scattering of mountainous islands and peninsulas. **Skagway,** terminus of the White Pass and Yukon narrow-gauge railroad, the terminus of the new Klondike Highway 2 from Dawson City, is also a major port for cruise ships. The town retains its Gold Rush atmosphere with a good museum of the era, many original buildings, a "gambling" saloon, an office of the **Klondike Gold Rush National Historic Park,** and costumed **Days of '98 Festival.** Centrally located: the **Klondike Hotel** (983-2273, S$55/D$65) and the **Golden North Hotel** (983-2214, S$45/D$59). **Haines,** 80 miles northwest of Juneau, stands at the head of the **Lynn Canal** with the scenic **Chilkat Range** in the background. From here, you can connect with the Alaska Highway heading north; only ferries go south from Haines. This is the home of the Chilkat Indian Dancers, who have toured widely in the US and abroad; here they perform in an authentic Indian tribal house. Stay at the **Thunderbird Motel** (766-2131, S$35/D$42), **Hotel Halsingland** (766-2353, S$37/D$42), noted for its Swedish cuisine, or the **Town House Motel** (766-3301, S$35/D$42), all centrally located.

JUNEAU, Alaska's capital, on the mainland side of Gastineau Channel nestled between towering mountains, is 2½ hours by air from Fairbanks and 1½ hours from Anchorage. Places to visit include the **Alaska State Museum, Governor's Mansion,** the **State Capitol,** and **Mendenhall Glacier.** In July the **Golden North Salmon Derby,** a three-day contest offering prizes for big fish, attracts sportsmen from all over the United States. Hotels include the **Baranof** (800-426-0600, S$60/D$70), downtown and an established favorite; **Breakwater Inn** (586-6303, S$42/D$47), at the north entrance to town; **Prospector** (586-3737, S$50/D$56), and the **Cape Fox Sheffield House** (586-6900, S$60-63/D$73-79), waterfront, downtown.

Glacier Bay National Park and Preserve, between Haines and Sitka, has only recently become accessible to the average traveler. Here mountainsides are streaked with hundreds of glaciers, and the area is noted for its big game, seals, whale and salmon. Accommodations are available at the **Glacier Bay Lodge** (697-3221, S$44/D$56). The charm of the old Russian days is still alive at **Sitka,** on an island to the south of Glacier

Bay. Here is **St. Michael's Cathedral,** with a treasury of icons and ecclesiastical art. A large collection of restored totems is at the **Sitka National Historical Park,** and Russian and Indian relics are displayed in the **Centennial Building.** The little city, surrounded by water of an intense blue, looks up to **Mt Edgecumbe.** Many of the inhabitants, descendants of the Tlingit Indians, are skilled craftsmen. Modern hotels include the **Potlatch House Hotel** (747-8611, S$25-30/D$29-48), seven blocks from the airport, **Shee Atika Lodge** (800-426-0670, S$48/D$54), and **Sheffield House Sitka** (800-544-0970, S$52-56/D$62-66). **Ketchikan** on the southeast tail of the archipelago, is the "Gateway Port of Alaska" because it is the nearest major port to the 48 contiguous United States. Visit the **Saxman Indian village** totem park two miles south of town and **Totem Bight Park** north of town. The **Ketchikan Salmon Derby** is held in June. Hundreds of fishing boats make this their home port. Hotels available are the **Hilltop Motel** (225-5166, S$49/D$54), the **Ingersoll** (225-2124, S$30-40/D$40-50), centrally located; the **Gilmore** (225-2174, S$35-45/D$40-50), and the **Marine View Plaza** (225-6601, S$48/D$52).

Inland, **Denali National Park and Preserve** (3,030 square miles) lies midway between Fairbanks and Anchorage. Motorcoach excursion tours operate from both cities. **Fort Yukon,** just above the Arctic Circle, can be reached by air from Fairbanks. It is a large Athabascan Indian fishing village and trading post on the Yukon River.

The **KENAI PENINSULA,** 80 miles south of Anchorage, offers superb scenery, great hunting and fishing. The spectacular **Portage Glacier** and **Visitor Center** are accessible by highway and motorcoach excursion. En route, you can visit **Alyeska,** the state's most popular ski resort; open the year round.

Volcanoes dot the terrain at **Katmai National Park and Preserve,** on the far-flung **ALASKA PENINSULA.** This monument offers more than 4,200 square miles of ocean bays, fjords and lagoons. The interior is comprised of wilderness forests and numerous chains of lakes. The park offers outstanding opportunities to the adventurous sightseer, canoeist, backpacker and sport fisherman. A valid Alaska fishing license is required to fish for rainbow trout, salmon and grayling in the park. The National Monument is accessible only by air or charter boat. Package tours are available. The Alaska Peninsula is part of the Aleutian Range which includes the broad-sweeping Aleutian Islands. The islands reach 2,000 miles southwest to a point only an hour by airplane from Siberia.

Kodiak, on an island across the Shelikof Strait from Katmai, is known as "King Crab Capital of the World." Fishing is the mainstay of Kodiak's economy, the home port of one of the largest fishing fleets in the Pacific. The town also has 19 canneries and processors. It is the headquarters for the big game hunter in search of Kodiak brown bear, the world's largest carnivorous animal. Flightseeing tours are available. Nearby is the largest **US Coast Guard Station** in the United States, **Sheffield House of Kodiak** (800-7544-0970, S$57-62/D$67-72), overlooking harbor, and **Shelikof Lodge** (486-4141, S$50/D$54), downtown.

Nome is 510 miles northwest of Anchorage, facing the Bering Sea and the Seward Peninsula. It still has Gold Rush atmosphere. Accommodations are at the **Nome Nugget Inn** (433-2205, S$66/D$78). Watch King Island Eskimos make beautiful ivory carvings. Flying north from Nome, you will be within 150 miles of Siberia, just across the **Bering Strait**, before putting down at **Kotzebue**, one of the oldest and largest of Alaska's Eskimo communities. Visit the **Museum of the Arctic** to better understand the Eskimo culture. Hotels here include **Wien Arctic Hotel** (243-4100, S$65/D$75), and **Nul-Luk-Vik Hotel** (442-3331, S$67/D$77-88), downtown.

Barrow, the largest Eskimo community is the northernmost point in the United States. It is located on the shores of the Arctic Ocean, 330 miles above the Arctic Circle. Daily flights are available from Fairbanks and Anchorage. No roads go into Barrow, but you may see a traffic jam of snowmobiles. Barrow is the headquarters of the North Slope Borough, the largest political subdivision in the US. The hotel is the **Top of the World** (852-3900, S$112/D$123). Night life can be found at the **Polar Bear Theater,** which converts into a dance hall, **Alice's Café** and **The Hut** recreation center. Even though most homes have freezers, nature still provides the deep freeze where whale meat, walrus, seal, caribou and fish are stored year round in natural ice cellars. The Midnight Sun shines around the clock up here from 10 May to 2 August. Tour months in the Arctic are usually June, July and August.

Cities To Visit

ANCHORAGE

Anchorage, in south central Alaska overlooking Cook Inlet, is the state's largest and fastest-growing city. The population is 204,328 including 18,011 at two military bases, **Fort Richardson** and **Elmendorf Air Force Base.** It is Alaska's social, financial, trade and distribution center. Oil tankers call year round at the city-operated **Port of Anchorage.** Anchorage also serves as a stopover for Orient- and Europe-bound foreign air carriers operating over the Polar route.

WHAT TO SEE

Conducted tours of the town include **Earthquake Park** with reminders of the catastrophic Good Friday earthquake in 1964; **Lake Hood-Lake Spenard** complex with the world's largest concentration of floatplanes; **Pacific University** and the **University of Alaska. Anchorage Historical and Fine Arts Museum** has a permanent exhibit outlining the history of Alaska, summer hours 9-6 daily, 1-5 Sun. Also visit the **Wildlife Museum. Heritage Library** contains out-of-print books, old maps and original Gold Rush newspapers, open Monday through Friday, 1-4. A statue of Captain James Cook stands in the **New Resolution Park** overlooking Cook Inlet at the end of Third Avenue. Be sure to visit the Alaska Zoo.

The Sun and Raven Totem near Ketchikan, Alaska, tells the story of a great flood and how Raven helped man to survive.

ACCOMMODATIONS

In downtown Anchorage there are the **Anchorage TraveLodge** (272-7561, S$48/D$58), the **Anchorage Westward Hilton Hotel** (272-7411, S$40-60/D$56-66); **Holiday Inn of Anchorage** (279-8671, S$47/D$59); **Captain Cook Hotel** (276-6000, S$72-80/D$84-90, Suites $92-230); **Sheffield House of Anchorage** (276-7676, S$60/D$70); the **Traveler's Inn** (277-1511, S$42/D$49); the **Sheraton Anchorage Hotel** (800-325-3535, S$63-68/D$68-78, Suites $135 and up). Closer to the airport are the **Golden Lion Motel** (278-4561, S$49/D$57 and up), and the **Northern Lights Inn** (276-4500, S$39.63/D$46.11, Suites $55). Hotel Tax: 5%

RESTAURANTS

Most dining spots in Anchorage are located in hotels: the **Whale's Tail** and **Crow's Nest** in the Hotel Captain Cook; the **Top of the World** at the Anchorage Westward Hotel; **Kobuk Kettle** in the Traveler's Inn and the **King's Dining Room** in the Holiday Inn, and the **Golden Lion**, to name a few. Other excellent new restaurants are the **Cattle Company, Elevation 92, Simon & Seafort, Clinkerdagger Bickerstaff, Petts,** and **Oriental Gardens.** Italian, oriental, Mexican, and Indian cuisines may be sampled in Anchorage.

CALENDAR OF EVENTS

Annual Midnight Sun 600 Snowmobile Race. Anchorage to Fairbanks and return, January; **Anchorage Fur Rendezvous** featuring the **World Championship Sled Dog Race**, February; **Alaska Festival of Music**, mid-June.

WHERE TO GO NEARBY

Bordering Anchorage on the east, **Chugach State Park** is open to hikers and mountain climbers. A climb to the top of **Flattop Mountain** affords a panoramic view of **Cook Inlet** and the **Susitna Valley,** including the towering **Mount McKinley.** Twenty-six miles north of Anchorage are the interesting **Eklutna Indian Burial Grounds.** Forty miles south of Anchorage, **Mount Alyeska** is open with its year-round lift service for skiers.

FAIRBANKS

Fairbanks, with a population of 60,227, plus 16,000 military personnel, is Alaska's second largest city. It is the terminus of the Alaska Railroad and the Alaska, Steese and Richardson Highways. As the "Gateway to the Arctic" it is a popular departure point for excursions to the far north. It was the bustling construction headquarters for the Trans-Alaska pipeline project, the 800-mile pipeline from Alaska's North Slope to Valdez.

WHAT TO SEE

Alaskaland, a frontier-style park, is on the Chena River. Visit the former Yukon sternwheeler *Nenana,* which now has a restaurant on board. **Gold Rush Town** has an authentic collection of pioneer buildings. Try to see the **Pioneer Museum** and **Mining Valley,** with original gold-mining equipment, and the **Eskimo and Indian Villages.** Children will enjoy the "Gay 90s" train ride and wildlife park. The **University of Alaska** campus has a museum and experimental farm. River cruises on the two *Discovery* sternwheelers stop at an Indian fishing village, June to September; adults $18, children $9.

From about mid-May to mid-September, one of the city's most popular jaunts is out to Ester City for an evening at the **Malamute Saloon,** with Robert Service poetry as part of the entertainment.

ACCOMMODATIONS
Leading hotels in the downtown area include the **Fairbanks Inn** (456-6602, S$55/D$65) **Traveler's Inn** (456-7722, S$64/D$74); **Golden North Hotel** (479-6201, S$29-39/D$32-50); **Klondike Inn** (479-6241, S$32/D$35-40). Hotel Tax: 5%

RESTAURANTS
Among the more interesting places to eat are the **Steak Pit, Club 11, Switzerland** and the **Bear'N Seal Restaurant** in the Traveler's Inn of Fairbanks. Other restaurants include the **Black Angus, Hungry Dog Café, Pumphouse Restaurant and Saloon,** the **Ranch Dinner House.**

SHOPPING
Fairbanks is one of the better centers for those in search of Eskimo artifacts of all kinds. **Alaska House and Art Gallery, Arctic Travelers' Gift Shop** and the **Gold Pan Trading Post** all offer a wide selection of Eskimo handicrafts. The **Mukluk Shop** specializes in interesting fur designs unique to Alaska. If you get a chance, tour the workshops and observe the furriers and craftsmen at work.

CALENDAR OF EVENTS
North American Sled Dog Championship Race attracts *mushers* (sled drivers) from all over the state and some from the eastern US, March; **Midnight Sun Festival,** 21 June, when the **Goldpanners** play baseball at midnight and one can take photographs as if it were noon; 800-mile **Yukon Marathon** two-day riverboat race, late June; annual celebration of gold's discovery in Fairbanks, with pioneer activities, parades and contests, late July; **Tanana Valley Fair,** garden produce displays, August.

WHERE TO GO NEARBY
Six and a half miles out of Fairbanks on Richardson Highway is the **Eskimo Museum and Trophy Room** which features life-size exhibits of Alaskan wildlife, Eskimo artifacts; there are Eskimo arts and crafts for sale in the **Gift Shop.** Tour the **Silver Fox Gold Mine** north of Fairbanks, an operating mine producing gold, silver, lead and zinc; rates are $3 adults, $1.50 students under 12. Forty-five miles southwest of Fairbanks is **Nenana** on the banks of the Tanana River. It is the distribution center for traffic along the Interior River system. Two-day bus tours are offered

to **Mt McKinley** as well as a 2½-hour aerial tour leaving from Merrill Field for $155 per person.

DENALI NATIONAL PARK AND PRESERVE

Best time to go is late May to mid-September. Be prepared for daytime temperatures ranging from −1°C when the weather is cool, wet and windy, to 27°C on dazzlingly sunny days. Wildflowers carpet the mountain slopes from mid-June through August, when the sun shines 18 hours a day, with only semi-darkness the remaining six hours. Summer is also the mosquito season; take insect repellent. In late August and early September, the foliage is rich in color, and moose and caribou are readily seen.

If you go by train, which will also transport your car, the park is eight hours north of Anchorage and four hours south of Fairbanks. A landing strip for small planes is near the park entrance. The Denali (Indian name for McKinley) Highway from **Paxson,** 160 miles east, is usually passable from about 1 June to mid-September. The Fairbanks-Anchorage Highway is paved and open all year.

Mount McKinley Park Hotel (683-2215, S$51/D$59) is open 25 May-30 September. The hotel serves breakfast for guests departing on the 6am sightseeing bus tour. Also available are **Alaska Railroad** car accommodations, $25 (without bath). The **McKinley Chalets** (S$69/D$75) and **Camp Denali,** north of Wonder Lake, have housekeeping tent-cabins and rustic chalets with a communal dining room. There are also seven campgrounds within the park on a first-come, first-served basis. Carry your own fuel because firewood is scarce. For reservations, write McKinley Park Station Hotel, Denali NP, McKinley, AK 99755.

With approximately 3,030 square miles it is the second largest park in the US national park system, exceeded only by Yellowstone National Park. A highland region flanks the northern Alaska Range and contains **Mount McKinley,** North America's highest mountain.

Some prefer early in the morning for sightseeing. Mt. McKinley, highest point in the continent, rises 20,320 feet above sea level at the South Peak and 19,470 feet at the North Peak. The two peaks are known collectively as the "Churchill Peaks." Other mountains in the perpetually snow-capped range are from 12,000 to 17,000 feet high but the park road climbs only to 3,980 feet. The scenery is overwhelming. Many mountain glaciers, as many as 30 or 40 miles long, are still active. Broad glacial streams flow down five valleys crossed by the **Park Road,** from where the immensity of Mt McKinley seems very near. Wildlife in the park is protected; over 130 varieties of birds, some migrating from Japan and Hawaii every spring, and 37 kinds of mammals inhabit the park. **Igloo Canyon** is a good place to get photos of moose and white Dall sheep. Grizzly bears are frequently seen around **Sable Pass** and the **Tŏklat River. Wonder Lake** is near the end of Park Road.

The swampy forest throughout the Park below the timberline is composed of dark green conifers and deciduous trees. Most of the park is above the timberline, with diverse grasses, bushes, moss and lichen in the wet tundra, and flowering plants in the higher dry areas. The perpetual snow line begins about two miles below the mountain peaks. Several nature trails leave from the Mount McKinley Park Hotel for short distances. Get detailed information at ranger stations on local conditions before starting any cross-country hikes. A daily bus wildlife tour leaves from the park hotel.

The National Park Service shows movies at **McKinley Hotel.** Evening programs are presented by ranger naturalists at several campgrounds. Sled dog demonstrations are conducted daily.

FURTHER STATE INFORMATION
State Division of Tourism, Pouch E, Juneau, AK 99811. Hunting and Fishing: **Department of Fish and Game,** Subport Building, Juneau, AK 99811. National Parks: National Park Service, 540 W. 5th, Anchorage, AK 99501; National Forest of Alaska, PO Box 1628, Juneau, AK 99801.

Consulates in Anchorage: Denmark, Finland, France, Germany, Italy, Japan, Korea, Norway, Sweden.

In Juneau: France, Norway.

USEFUL TELEPHONE NUMBERS IN ANCHORAGE
Emergency (Ambulance, Fire, Police)	911
Poison Control Center	274-6535
Providence Hospital	276-4511
Alaska Hospital & Medical Center	276-1131

Arizona

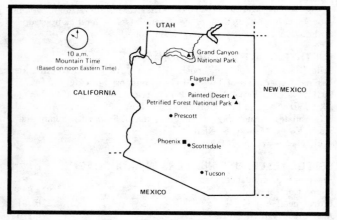

Area	113,909 square miles	Population	2,717,866
Capital	Phoenix	Sales Tax	5%

Weather

	Jan	Feb	Mar	Apr	May	Jun	Jul	Aug	Sep	Oct	Nov	Dec
Av Temp (°C)	10	12	15	20	24	29	32	31	28	22	15	11
Days no rain	4	4	3	2	1	1	4	5	3	3	2	4

No daylight saving time.

Like much of the Southwest, Arizona was first inhabited by cliff-dwelling Indians who abandoned their drought-striken villages before 1300 AD. Later, numerous Indian tribes populated this area, some of whom developed relatively sophisticated social and agricultural systems. One of these tribes, the Hohokam, settled in the Phoenix area and devised an irrigation system of canals to cultivate large areas of the desert which later were incorporated into the present irrigation system of the Valley. In 1540 Coronado crossed the area with his *conquistadores* in his fruitless search for gold, and in 1692 the Jesuit padre, Eusebio Francisco Kino, established a toehold for the church. Settlers and miners later trickled in, but Indian uprisings in 1802 and 1827, combined with an assortment of Mexican revolutions, made many miners, settlers and ranchers reconsider their choice of neighborhood. Eventually, Mexico replaced Spain as owner and in 1848 ceded the Territory of New Mexico to the United States. The American government combined part of this with the Gadsden Purchase of 1853, and in 1863 Arizona became a US territory. In 1912 it became the 48th state in the Union.

The state, which has more than a million acres of desert under irrigation, is divided topographically into the plains of the southwest and the mountains and plateau regions of the northeast. The **Colorado River** takes credit for the shape of much of the landscape including the Grand Canyon, Lake Powell and Lake Mead.

Entering the northeast section of Arizona from New Mexico via I-40 from Gallup one meets the **Petrified Forest National Park** where trees have turned to rock. The park, 148 square miles, is open during daylight hours every day. There are good motels in **Holbrook,** 19 and 24 miles from the two park entrances, but there are no overnight facilities of any kind inside the park. Meals, souvenirs and gasoline are provided, year round, at the **Painted Desert Oasis** (north) and **Rainbow Forest Lodge** (south), which are connected by the 28-mile park road. If approaching the park from I-40, stop for information at the **Painted Desert Visitor Center.** If coming from US 180, stop at the **Rainbow Forest Museum.** Between 180 and 200 million years ago, this region, which is now 5,300 to 6,200 feet above sea level, was part of a low, swampy area inhabited by dinosaur-like reptiles and primitive aquatic life. Tall conifers grew on higher, drained sites. When the trees fell, many were buried in streams loaded with silica which, over millions of years, petrified them into multicolored stone. Near the south entrance are the **Long Logs,** piled like jackstraws. **Jasper Forest,** viewed from a scenic overlook, is a valley scattered with petrified logs in greenish colors typical of jasper quartz. **Agate Bridge** is one petrified log, 111 feet of it exposed to form a natural bridge over a 40-foot ravine. **Blue Mesa,** on a spur road, is a beautiful area showing the way erosion continually re-shapes the landscape. **Newspaper Rock,** on another spur, is covered with petroglyphs (picture writing) drawn by prehistoric Indians. **Puerco Ruin** contains the remains of an Indian village abandoned about 600 years ago. The **Painted Desert,** an awesome, barren region formed by the erosion of soft clay, can be viewed from various lookout points at the north end of the park. Its countless shades are most vivid early in the morning and at sunset. Jeep tours can be arranged through the Park Service via the north entrance.

North of the park stretches the giant **Navajo Indian Reservation** and inside it the smaller **Hopi Indian Reservation. Canyon de Chelly National Monument** covers four periods of Indian history from the year 348 to 1300. The canyons here are the summer homes of over 300 Navajo, who grow peaches, farm and graze their animals on the canyon floor. Automobile traffic is restricted, but **Justin's Thunderbird Lodge** (674-5443, S$28-35/D$35-45) conducts tours by jeep from mid-May until mid-October. To get into the canyons hire a Navajo guide for a horseback tour. The **Navajo National Monument** is the largest and most complex of Arizona's cliff dwellings. The area lies west of Kayenta, on US 160, and is best explored on foot or horseback with a Navajo guide. In Kayenta, there are **Goulding's Monument Valley Lodge** (727-3231, S$30/D$35), open March to November; **Holiday Inn** (697-3221, S$28-34/D$38), and the **Wetherill Inn** (697-3231, S$20-28/D$26-34); all three of which can arrange jeep tours.

Wupatki National Monument, about 45 miles north of Flagstaff, was a prosperous city back in the 12th century. Among its apartment-like houses is one containing more than 100 rooms. **Sunset Crater National Monument** (nearer Flagstaff) is the cone of an extinct volcano. It is surrounded by fields of cinder dunes, lava, spatter cones and inactive hot springs. A footpath leads to the summit, 1,000 feet.

FLAGSTAFF is situated at an elevation of 6,980 feet. **Northern Arizona University** is here. Also early in July are the **Hopi Craftsman Show** and the **Navajo Craftsman Show,** both at the **Museum of Northern Arizona.** Among numerous motels east of town on US 66 are **Little America** (779-2741, S$42-48/D$46-52), **Chalet** (774-2779, S$16/D$16-20), **King's House Lodge** (744-7186, S$20-25/D$52), **Pony Soldier** (526-2388, S$18-21/D$21-24), and **Ramada Inn-East** (526-1399, S$20-40/D$24-40). West of Flagstaff are **Holiday Inn, Imperial 400, Ramada Inn** and **TraveLodge.** South of the city are **Rodeway Inn, Time Motel** and others. High season rates (May to October) are S$25-36/D$40-52. **Arizona Snow Bowl,** a ski resort, is in the nearby San Francisco Peaks. Facilities include a day lodge, ski shop and ski rentals. The chair lift climbs to 11,800 feet. **Lowell Observatory** is one of the country's most important astronomical observatories. The planet Pluto was discovered from here in 1930; guided tours Monday to Friday. **Sedona,** at Oak Creek, offers art colonies and good restaurants.

Try not to miss the **Tuzigoot National Monument,** southwest of Flagstaff, with a pueblo dwelling which probably housed 400 persons around 1300 AD. The adjoining museum contains material from the site; open daily. **Payson** is surrounded by the **Tonto National Forest;** excellent for hunting and fishing. An annual rodeo is held in mid-August. **Zane Grey's Cabin** is 17 miles northeast of Payson; open March to November, closed Tuesday; free.

Prescott is 5,346 feet up in the mountains. The **Frontier Days Celebration and Rodeo** on 4 July dates from 1888, and is one of the biggest in the west. Over on the Nevada border is **Lake Havasu City. London Bridge,** which once spanned the River Thames, is here. It leads to a man-made island complete with airport, marina, golf course, campsite and motels. **Havasu National Wildlife Refuge** offers a home to all the migrating birds which pass on their way to Mexico and the Northwest.

In the **SOUTHWEST** region of Arizona, the infamous **Yuma Territorial Prison** (1876-1909) is open daily. The **Fort Yuma Indian Reservation** is the site of the **Catholic Indian Mission.** The sand dunes west of town are the scene of many desert motion pictures. Major events in **Yuma** include the **Silver Spur Rodeo** in February; **Yuma County Fair** in late March; and the **Father Garces Celebration of the Arts,** including films, from the last week in April to the first week in May. The **Stardust** (783-8861, S$21-34/D$28-40) is an outstanding resort hotel. Alternative hotels are the **Ramada Inn, Romney, Royal Inn, Yuma Cabana, Holiday Inn,**

Rodeway and TraveLodge; rates are S$28-40/D$32-44. **Painted Rock State Historic Park** lies in the Gila Bend Valley between Yuma and Casa Grande.

The construction of **Roosevelt Dam,** east of Phoenix on the Salt River, in 1911 provided water for irrigation, power for industry and helped to create **Big Surf,** an "ocean" in the desert at **Tempe.** The **Apache Trail,** built to get supplies from Phoenix and Globe to the Roosevelt Dam site, closely follows the ancient route which the Apaches found to be the best trail through this complicated canyon country.

The most accessible of the cliff dwellings in **SOUTH CENTRAL** Arizona are preserved at the **Tonto National Monument** on the edge of the **San Carlos Indian Reservation. Globe,** center of a silver boom and now a copper-mining town, is west of the reservation. Be in Globe for the **Gila County Gem and Mineral Show,** 1 February. The **Copper Manor, Ember, El Rancho** and **El Rey** motels are about S$28/D$36, while **Copper Hills Motel** at Miami is S$33/D$35. The **Southwestern Archaeological Center** of the Department of Interior is at the Gila Pueblo near Globe; open daily, free.

From **Safford,** the **Swift Trail** winds its way 36 miles to the top of **Mount Graham,** 10,720 feet high, called "the mountain of flowers." Try the trout fishing in **Riggs Flat Lake.** Excellent camping grounds are maintained by the Forest Service. **Tombstone,** made famous in American movies as a Wild West town, is located near the southeast corner of Arizona, south of Tucson. The **Bird Cage Theater** still has the original furnishings and fancy interior which dates from 1881. **Boothill Graveyard** is full of bad guys, most of them unmourned. **O.K. Corral** is where Wyatt Earp and his brothers dismantled the Clanton family in 1881. **Tombstone Courthouse State Historical Monument and Museum** is devoted to relics and mementos of the early days. The old courtroom was the scene of many famous trials, and the reconstructed gallows are in a rear courtyard. **Wyatt Earp Museum** and the **Wells Fargo Museum** contain wax figures, photographs and documents. Underground mine tours of an old silver shaft are offered daily.

Tumacacori National Monument preserves the abandoned Mission San Jose, begun by the Franciscans in 1800 but never completed. **Saguaro National Monument** just east of Tucson, contains one of the densest stands of cactus in America.

Cities to Visit

PHOENIX

Phoenix, population 781,000, is in the south-central part of the state, 189 miles north of the Mexican border. Hundreds of years ago the Hohokam Indians lived in the Phoenix region but disappeared before the first white settlers arrived in 1864. Lord Duppa, a member of the party, named the new community after the mythical bird that rose from its ashes after being destroyed by fire. Phoenix is in the middle of an agricultural area but has grown steadily as a resort because of its excellent climate. Phoenix is a fairly cosmopolitan city and one of the fastest-growing resort centers of the southwest. Homes are generally ranch-style and much emphasis is placed on outdoor living.

WHAT TO SEE

You'll want to see the **State Capitol Building; Pueblo Grande,** an excavated Indian ruin; the **Arizona Museum** with relics of pioneer days (open afternoons November through May); **Heard Indian Museum** features anthropological displays of the Southwest tribes. **Phoenix Art Museum** is outstanding.

Parks and zoos include **Papago Park,** about eight miles east of the city center, with the **Phoenix Zoo,** one of the West's largest zoos which has a rare herd of Arabian oryx, and the **Desert Botanical Gardens,** with a unique desert plant collection. **Encanto Park** in central Phoenix has exotic plants and trees. **South Mountain Park,** eight miles south, contains more than 14,000 acres of canyons, peaks, rock formations and shrubs.

ACCOMMODATIONS

All accommodations in Phoenix are air conditioned. Hotel rates change according to the season, with the highest charges made during winter months; summer rates are considerably lower. The rates which follow are for the winter season. Downtown location (all with swimming pools): **Caravan Inn** (244-8244, S$38/D$44), **Chalet Inn** (252-3477, S$20/D$22), **Del Webb's Towne House** (279-9811, S$60/D$60), **Doubletree Inn of Phoenix** (248-0222, S$45/D$70), **Granada Royale Hometel** (957-1910, S$69/D$79), **Adams-Hilton Hotel** (257-1525, S$60-84/D$75-90), **Hyatt Regency** (257-1525, S$60-70/D$70-80), **Los Olivos Lodge Hotel** (258-6911, S$37/D$41), **Park Central Motor Hotel** (277-2621, S$44/D$50): **Ramada Inn Downtown** (258-3411, S$28-44/D$38-52). Ten miles north of city center is **The Pointe** (997-2626, S$104/D$114). Adjacent to the airport: **Sheraton Airport Inn** (993-0800, S$40/D$47). Scottsdale area, 10 miles from Sky Harbor International Airport: **Del Webb's La Posada Resort Hotel** (952-0420, S$100/D$100), **Doubletree Inn-Scottsdale Mall** (994-9203, S$75-90/D$90-100), **Scottsdale Hilton** (948-7750, S$85-105/D$100-115), **Doubletree Inn-Fashion Square** (947-5411, S$64-80/D$74-90). There are scores of attractive, modern resort-type motels in and around Phoenix, including **Holiday Inn** and **TraveLodge,** in the city and at the airport. Typical European Plan rates are from S$25-30/D$28-35. Free campsites are available in **Tonto** and **Prescott** national forests, and in the **Oak Creek Canyon.** Hotel Tax: 5%

RESTAURANTS

In Phoenix: **John's Green Gables,** unusual, well-prepared dishes; **Navarre's** specializes in prime ribs and steak; **Hungry Tiger** features seafood, lobster tank and decorative aquarium; **Nantucket Lobster Trap** for flown-in seafood; fairly expensive. More moderate are **Woody's El Nido, GuadalaHar-**

"Running" the Grand Canyon is not all hectic adventure, with many placid stretches allowing proper attention to the spectacular scenery.

23

ry's and **Macayo,** Mexican and American food; **Beef Eaters, Durant's, Victoria Station, North Bank, Stockyards,** for beef and steaks are all popular locally. In Scottsdale, **Chez Louis, Etienne** and **La Chaumiere** specialize in French cuisine; **Dale Anderson's, Pink Pony, Glass Door, Quilted Bar,** and **The Other Place** have fine American food; fairly expensive. **La Posada** (Mexican). **Ianuzzi's** (Italian) is expensive. **Pacific Seafood Co.** and **Trader Vic's** specialize in food from Chinese ovens, international menu. **El Chorro Lodge** 12 miles northeast in Mesa, exceptional food; **Pinnacle Peak Patio,** 14 miles northeast of Scottsdale, specializes in steaks, old West atmosphere.

ENTERTAINMENT

Dining and dancing during the winter season in the **Gold Room** of the Arizona Biltmore and at **Carefree Inn, Mountain Shadows, Safari Hotel, Sunburst, Registry.** Music and entertainment at the **Green Gables, Lulu Belle's, Playboy Club,** and **French Quarter.** For the younger set, **Mr. Lucky's. The Village Inn** is a pizza parlor featuring folk music. **The Organ Stop** has pizza and organ concerts.

ARTS AND MUSIC

Art Museum, general exhibit of paintings and sculpture; closed Mondays, holidays. **Heard Museum,** Indian arts and crafts, including Senator Barry Goldwater's collection of Kachina dolls; closed August. The **Phoenix Symphony Association,** the **Phoenix Musical Theater, Phoenix Little Theater,** and **Windmill Dinner Theater** give a series of performances. Symphonies, jazz and rock concerts are staged at the **Grady Grammage Auditorium** in the **Veteran's Memorial Coliseum,** and also in the new **Civic Plaza Concert Hall.**

SHOPPING

Stores remain open Monday and Thursday evening until 9. Various shopping centers in the Phoenix-Scottsdale area: **Fifth Avenue Merchants' Association,** Indian jewelry, arts and crafts as well as fashion boutiques; **Biltmore Fashion Park** and **Town and Country Shopping Center, Chris-Town** and **Park Central** in Phoenix and **Metro Center** north on Black Canyon Highway.

SPORTS

There is big-league baseball to watch during March, when the **San Francisco Giants, Chicago Cubs, Milwaukee Brewers, Seattle Mariners,** and Oakland "A's" are in the area for preseason training. Professional basketball is played by the **Phoenix Suns,** professional Major Indoor League Soccer by the **Phoenix Inferno.** There are also intercollegiate athletic events at **Arizona State University** at Tempe. Horse and dog racing with pari-mutuel betting from September through May; and many rodeos. Golf may be played at four city courses and some 30 semipublic and resort golf courses. Horseback riding, tennis, and fishing are popular. Snow skiing within easy driving distance of the Valley of the Sun, accommodations available November-March.

CALENDAR OF EVENTS

Arizona Livestock Show, early January; **Superstition Mountain Lost Gold Trek,** early March; **Yaqui Ceremonials,** held at Guadalupe, Easter; **Arizona State Fair,** November: **World's Championship Rodeo,** March; **Phoenix Open Golf Tournament,** January; **Cactus Show,** Desert Botanical Garden, late February. In Scottsdale: **All-Arabian Horse Show,** February; **National Indian Art Show,** March.

WHERE TO GO NEARBY

Hieroglyphic Canyon and its picture writing, seven miles south in South Mountain Park; **Scottsdale,** 12 miles east, an interesting community with shops specializing in Arizona arts and crafts. Important resort hotels in Scottsdale open all year include **Arizona Biltmore, The Inn at McCormick Ranch, Hermosa Inn** and **Mountain Shadows,** and the **Inn at Carefree,** 20 miles north. Rates with all meals average S$75/D$180. **Guadalupe Village,** 12 miles southeast, a Yaqui Indian community. Drive to the east and see **Camelback Mountain** and to the west to see the citrus groves and lettuce fields. **Apache Trail,** beginning 35 miles east of Phoenix, winds through mountain scenery to Globe. **Grand Canyon National Park, Petrified Forest National Park; Casa Grande,** at Coolidge, 57 miles southeast, old Indian ruins. Rafting trips on the **Colorado River** rapids through the Grand Canyon. Twenty miles northwest of Phoenix, visit **Taliesin West,** the architectural school and former winter home of Frank Lloyd Wright.

TUCSON

Tucson (pronounced *too-sahn*), population 400,506, is in south-central Arizona, on the Santa Cruz River, about 125 miles south of Phoenix and 67 miles north of the Mexican border. The region was first explored in the mid-16th century by the Spaniards Fray Marcos de Niza, Coronado and others. In 1699 it was the site of an Indian settlement named Stjukshon. From 1720 to 1767 a Spanish Jesuit mission, San Xavier del Bac, was established nine miles south, but residents were finally driven out by the Indians. It is still in use as a church. In 1776, the Spanish established a Franciscan mission on the site of present-day Tucson, supported by the military. It remained a walled town until 1864, when under the terms of the Gadsden Purchase the area became US territory and was included as a State three years later. From 1867 to 1877 Tucson was the capital of the Arizona Territory. The Southern Pacific Railroad in 1880 gave impetus to development, and in 1883 it was chartered as a city. One of the oldest communities in the southwest, Tucson is virtually surrounded by mountains.

WHAT TO SEE

Arizona State Museum, on the **University of Arizona** campus, Indian archaeological exhibits. **Arizona Historical Society,** near the entrance to the university campus, historical exhibits. **Old Tucson**, 12 miles west of Tucson Mountain Park Road, has 130-building replicas of Tucson in 1860; it is used for movies and TV shows. **Tucson Mountain Park** is 14 miles west, where the **Arizona-Sonora Desert Museum** has exhibits of live animals and plants native to Arizona and Sonora, Mexico. The museum is open year round from 8:30 till sundown. Admission for adults is $4; ages 13-17, $2.25; ages 12-6, .75¢, children under 6 are free. **Saguaro National Monument** is known for its cactus; **Colossal Cave**, 20 miles southeast, an interesting interior with many unusual formations. See **Kitt Peak National Science Observatory**, 50 miles west of Tucson. **Armory and Randolph Parks** in the city.

ACCOMMODATIONS

Hotel rates change several times during the year; rates given here are for the winter. **Marriott Hotel** (624-8711, S$57-71/D$62-80), moderate deluxe convention and resort hotel adjacent to the Community Convention Hall. Also centrally located are the **Plaza International Hotel** (327-7341, S$41/D$45) and the **Royal Inn of Tucson** (622-8871, S$46/D$46). Among many fine air-conditioned motels within two miles of downtown Tucson are the **Executive Inn, Flamingo Motor Hotel** and **Sahara Motor Inn**, all north; the **Desert Inn, Ramada Inn** and **Sheraton Pueblo**, all west; and the **Holiday Inn-South**. Approximately three miles from the center are **Aztec Inn** (S$40.50/D$48) and **Doubletree Inn** (881-4200, S$74/D$84), near Randolph Park and municipal golf courses; **Ghost Ranch Lodge, Hilton Inn** and **Wayward Winds Lodge** on Miracle Mile northwest of center city; and the **Spanish Trail Motel** near Downtown Tucson Airport. Rates range from S$30-40/D$35-50. Resorts and guest ranches in the area: **Arizona Inn,** near the University of Arizona; **Saddle and Surrey Ranch Resort** at the Tucson Mountain Wildlife Area; **Tanque Verde Ranch**, 20 miles east of the downtown area (rocky mountain trails); **Westward Look Resort Hotel**, 10 miles north; **White Stallion Ranch**, 17 miles northwest; and **Wild Horse Ranch Club**, 14 miles from the center. Winter rates, including all meals, average S$70-215/D$116-250. Camping facilities at **Palo Verde Picnic Grounds**, about 14 miles west of Tucson; and at **Mt Lemmon**, 30 miles northwest of the city.

RESTAURANTS

Most restaurants in the area are moderately-priced. **La Fuente, Old Adobe Patio, Casa Molina,** and **Pancho's**, Mexican food; **El Corral, Cork 'N Cleaver, The Vineyard** for steaks; **Coat of Arms** and **Rancho Del Rio's Tack Room** for continental cuisine; and **Palamino Continental**, one of the nicer restaurants around town. **Paulo's, Plank House,** and **Ye Olde Lantern** for beef; **Marco's, La Cucina, Vito's** and **Scordato's**, Italian dishes; **Kon Tiki** and **Ports O' Call** for Polynesian food. For seafood: **Nantucket Lobster Trap** and **Solarium**.

ENTERTAINMENT
Spanish Trail, Hilton Inn, the End Zone, Barons, Doubletree Inn, Sheraton Pueblo Inn, Pirate's Den and the Smuggler's Inn are all small bars—with live music.

ARTS AND MUSIC
Tucson Museum of Art has exhibitions of works by local artists and permanent collections of pre-Columbian and Spanish art; open Tuesday through Saturday 10-5, Sunday 1-5, closed August. The University of Arizona Museum of Art has permanent displays of Renaissance and international contemporary paintings, open daily 10-5, Sunday 2-5. The Tucson Symphony Orchestra performs during the winter. There are band concerts at Armory Park and Randolph Park on Sunday evenings, October through March. The Sunday Evening Forum presents lecture circuit entertainers at the University of Arizona Auditorium every Sunday at 8pm; free. October through April the university offers plays at its Fine Arts Center. The Arizona Civic Theater and the Comedy Dinner Theater are professional resident companies. Concerts and ballet are held throughout the year at the Community Center.

SHOPPING
Along Speedway Road there are many shopping malls and stores of all types. Most downtown stores remain open every night except Tuesday and Saturday until 9; Sunday 12-5 at shopping centers.

SPORTS
Horse racing at Rillito Race Track on Saturday and Sunday during the winter; greyhound racing for about 45 evenings (season varies). The University of Arizona is a PAC-10 Conference Member during the fall. Rodeo competitions are popular here, with several held each year. Major-league spring baseball training during March at Hi Corbett Field. Tucson Toros of the Pacific Coast League play baseball during the summer at Hi Corbett Field. There are 22 golf courses both private and public in and around Tucson; Randolph Golf Course and El Rio are open to the public. Swimming is available in public pools from June to September.

CALENDAR OF EVENTS
The Tucson Open Golf Tournament is held in January; Tucson Rodeo (La Fiesta des los Vaqueros), February; Livestock Show, at the Tucson Rodeo Grounds, in the spring; Yaqui Indian Holy Week Ceremonials, Easter week; San Xavier Fiesta, Friday after Easter; Fiesta de la Placita, Mexican fiesta event, April; Tucson's Birthday, August; Pima Country Fair at Pima County Fairgrounds, largely agricultural, during the fall.

WHERE TO GO NEARBY
Saguaro National Monument, 18 miles east, remarkable display of cactus. Casa Grande Ruins about 55 miles northeast. Tumacacori National Monu-

ment, 55 miles south; **Chiricahua National Monument**, 80 miles east. **Organ Pipe Cactus National Monument**, 60 miles west of town, near Ajo. **Tucson Mountain State Park**, eight miles west. **Nogales** and **Sonora**, Mexico, are 60 miles south.

GRAND CANYON NATIONAL PARK

Grand Canyon National Park, in northwest Arizona, is 277 miles long, a mile deep and as much as 18 miles wide. It is one of the most spectacular natural phenomena of the world, the product of 10 million years of erosion by the Colorado River and elements of nature—rain, wind, and snow. Bizarre formations, precipices, amphitheaters, and buttes of limestone and sandstone glow in warm tones of gold, orange, rust, and mauve, giving the impression at certain times of movement. Even though the **North** and **South Rims** are only 10 miles apart, there is a difference in elevation of 1,364 feet, making them quite different in climate, vegetation, and wildlife.

The South Rim is open year round. Elevation here ranges from 5,750 to 7,400 feet, so if summer days are warm, nights are always cool. Summertime temperature at the 2,300-foot level may reach 51°C and the Canyon floor is often "June-warm" when there is snow on the rims in the winter. Summertime reservations should be made well in advance at Grand Canyon Village for rooms in the hotel and lodge on the South Rim: **Bright Angel Lodge and Cabins** (638-2401, S$30/D$40); **El Tovar Hotel** (638-2631, S$37/D$42); and **Grand Canyon Motor Lodge** (638-2401, S$24-26/D$24-30). There is a large trailer court there, too; stay limited to 15 days, 1 May to 31 October. **Mather Campground** is open all year.

A well-paved road skirts the South Rim for nearly 35 miles of awesome vistas. At the **Hopi Indian Reservation** ancient crafts still thrive. Landmarks include **Hermit's Rest; Hopi Point; Hopi House; Yavapai Museum**, containing model of Grand Canyon's geologic formations and specimens of local plant and animal life; **Tusayan Ruin and Museum**, prehistoric pueblo and museum of earliest inhabitants; **Lipan Point**, regarded by many as the most thrilling view. Make advance reservations if you plan to take the two-day muleback trip down **Bright Angel Trail** to Phantom Ranch. Mule tours are restricted to people over 12 years old and weighing under 200 pounds; you also need to be able to withstand height.

The less-visited North Rim is open from mid-May to mid-October and is at its best in September. North Rim elevations are about 8,000 to 9,000 feet, so even summer days are cool here. **North Rim Campground** and **Grand Canyon Lodge** (638-2611, S$25-35/D$30-40) are open midMay to mid-October. From Grand Canyon Lodge there is a short ridge path to **Bright Angel Point**, reaching out into **Bright Angel Valley**. The **Kaibab Trail** starts at the North Rim Ranger Station and runs down Bright Angel Valley, passing **Ribbon Falls** to reach the bottom of the canyon at **Phantom Ranch. Cape Royal** is 22 miles by paved road from Grand Canyon Lodge; there one has an impressive view of the **Painted Desert,**

One of the most awesome sights in the world, the Grand Canyon in Arizona attracts visitors from all over the world.

and further along at **Point Imperial** and **Angel's Window** there are other vantage points of the canyon.

FURTHER STATE INFORMATION
Arizona Office of Tourism, 1645 West Jefferson, Room 417, Phoenix, AZ 85007. Hunting and Fishing: **Game and Fish Commission,** 222 West Greenway Road, Phoenix, AZ 85023. **Phoenix Chamber of Commerce,** 34 W. Monroe, Phoenix, AZ 85004. **Phoenix and Valley of the Sun Convention Bureau,** 2701 E. Camelback Rd., Phoenix, AZ 85016. **Tucson Chamber of Commerce,** 420 W Congress Street, Tucson, AZ 85701. **Tucson Convention Bureau,** PO Box 5547, Tucson, AZ 85701. National Parks: **Grand Canyon National Park** (Superintendent), Holbrook, AZ 86025. **Pan Am** office, Financial Center, 3443 North Central Avenue, Phoenix, AZ 85012; tel: 252-6747.

Consulates in Phoenix: Belgium, Denmark, El Salvador, Finland, France, Germany, Italy, Mexico, Nicaragua, Norway, Panama, Senegal, Sweden.

In Tucson: Mexico.

USEFUL TELEPHONE NUMBERS
Phoenix
St Joseph's Hospital	241-3000
Mesa Lutheran Hospital	834-1211
Legal Aid Society	258-3434
Chamber of Commerce	254-5521
A.A.A.	252-7751
Pan Am Reservations	252-6747

Tucson
St Joseph's Hospital	296-3211
Tucson General Hospital	327-5431
Legal Aid Society	623-9461
Chamber of Commerce	792-1212
A.A.A.	623-5871
Rotary	623-2281
Kiwanis Club	623-5791
Pan Am Reservations	(800) 421-2707

Arkansas

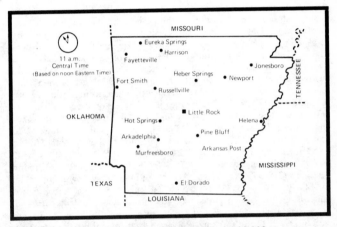

Area	53,225 square miles				**Population**		2,280,000					
Capital	Little Rock				**Sales Tax**		3%					

Weather	Jan	Feb	Mar	Apr	May	Jun	Jul	Aug	Sep	Oct	Nov	Dec
Av Temp (°C)	0	4	9	16	21	26	31	30	25	17	11	6
Days of Rain	13	7	12	9	10	4	3	1	11	4	8	3

Arkansas is a blend of the graciousness of the Old South and the rugged pioneer spirit of the frontier. Even the terrain seems to reflect the dichotomy with broad, flat expanses of delta lowlands and rugged elevations of the Ozark and Ouachita Mountains.

The area came into American hands in the bargain called the Louisiana Purchase and was considered a part of Missouri until 1819, when it became a territory in its own right. The cotton gin did for Arkansas what mineral finds were to do for the western states. Its development brought farmers into an area which had formerly been the province of the frontiersman. These new settlers founded their society on King Cotton and the slave system, which later caused Arkansas to join with the Confederacy during the Civil War. The state was the site of numerous skirmishes, and endured one decisive conflict, the Battle of Pea Ridge, which saved Missouri for the Union.

Arkansas is still essentially an agrarian state, but its biggest cash yield is from timber products. In addition, it has a considerable income from tourism and an annual production of minerals valued at over $667 million,

31

including 96% of the nation's domestic bauxite. The Ozark Mountains slant across northwestern Arkansas, and the Ouachitas, although only 1,000 to 2,800 feet high, form a picturesque wilderness in the southwestern section. About 55% of the state is forested, and there are 453,868 acres of lakes, 9,740 miles of streams, and many bayous, springs and caves.

In the center of the state is the capital city of **LITTLE ROCK**, a good point from which to start a tour. Often called the "City of Roses", Little Rock is ringed by areas of great scenic beauty. Situated on the south bank of the Arkansas River, it received its name from Benard de la Harpe, who in 1722 sighted an outcropping of rock and named it *La Petite Roche* or Little Rock. It was a hunting and trapping outpost for many years, gaining in importance because of its strategic location. Little Rock is the home of the *Arkansas Gazette,* whose former editor, Harry Ashmore, won the Pulitzer Prize for his editorials on the school integration controversy in 1957. Downtown hotels and motels include **Coachman's Inn** (372-6271, S$24-28/D$30-34), heated pool; **Sam Peck Motor Inn** (376-1304), S$27-30/ D$32.55-34.65), popular dining room; **Holiday Inn Downtown** (376-2071; S$30/D$37), **Camelot Hotel** (372-4371, S$42-50/D$48-56); **Americana Inn** (372-4392, S$36/D$42), with 267 rooms; **Sheraton** (372-3331, S$42/D$50), pool, and near downtown; **Hilton Inn** (644-5020, S$46-54/D$56-64) which is popular for its busy disco. Downtown is anchored by a landscaped pedestrian mall—Metrocentre Mall. Excellent cuisine and assorted atmospheres are to be found at **Jacques and Suzanne, Cajun's Wharf, Polyasian,** and several other restaurants. Because the area is dry on Sundays, (alcoholic beverages are not sold) it may be worth noting the private clubs: **American Legion Club** (372-8762), the **Checkmate Club** (376-2777) in downtown North Little Rock, the **Wine Cellar Lounge** (666-9985) west of downtown Little Rock. You may join as a temporary member for a nominal fee which entitles you to consume alcoholic beverages on Sunday. **Pinnacle Mountain State Park** at Little Rock's western edge emphasizes environmental education. Adams Field Airport is four miles southeast of the city. The northern and southern roads to town also have many modern motels. The **Quapaw Quarter** is the historic section of Little Rock, representing exactly one quarter of the township. Here are the **Arkansas Art Center,** which has changing exhibits in sculpture, ceramics, photography, and painting, and the **Museum of Science and Natural History,** housed in the **Old Arsenal,** near where General Douglas MacArthur was born in 1880 when his father commanded the fort. The two state capitol buildings represent different periods in the state's history. The current **State Capitol** is patterned on the one in Washington; the **Old State House** (1836-1911) is a beautifully styled Greek revival building, now a museum which includes the inaugural gowns of governors' wives. The **Arkansas Territorial Restoration** recalls the pioneer era of the early 1800s. There are five main buildings and seven companion outbuildings set among beautiful flower and herb gardens. Built in 1820 and beautifully restored 120 years later, this tranquil scene provides a fascinating glimpse into the past. The charm of the Victorian age is recorded at **Villa Marre,** an Italianate mansion built in 1881 and one of the many restored homes in this historic district. The **University of Arkansas Medical Science Campus** and **Little Rock Air Force Base** attract many visitors. The **Arkansas State Fair and Livestock Exposition** is held here in late September and early October. The performing arts are well represented in Little Rock through the **Arkansas Repertory Theatre,** the **Arkansas Opera Theatre, Ballet Arkansas,** and the **Arkansas Symphony Orchestra. Murry's Dinner Playhouse** (562-3131) combines good food and theater. Although there are several discothéques, a good start is at **Track's Inn,** located in a large restored railroad terminal, **The Train Station,** featuring good restaurants, bars, and other entertainment. At **North Little Rock** is **The Old Mill,** which with its water wheel that turns, was visible in the opening sequence of the movie "Gone with the Wind." The city is the location of **McCain Mall,** the state's largest indoor shopping center, and has the berth for **The Arkansas Explorer,** an overnight excursion boat.

Once a land of swamps and impenetrable forests, **NORTHEASTERN ARKANSAS** today has vast stretches of rice paddies, extensive soybean fields and cotton crops. **Heber Springs,** about 40 miles north of Little Rock, used to be a sleepy little village, but it sprang to life after a dam created **Greers Ferry Lake** in 1963. The town now provides water-skiing, boating, scuba diving and all the other appurtenances of a thriving resort. The **Red Apple Inn** (362-3111), S$49-59/D$52-75) is a popular resort on the lake. The seven mineral springs in the town still attract local people who credit them with having cured everything from warts to mange. A "piece up the road" is **Mountain View,** which has been isolated for so long that old-time Ozark music has been handed down unchanged for generations. In May 1973 the **Ozark Folk Center** (269-3851) opened as a major preservation and interpretive effort of the State Parks and Tourism Department. Here hill country musicians perform the Anglo-Saxon ballads of their forefathers with guitar, banjo, fiddle, "pickin' bow," and the mountain dulcimer, and also demonstrate local crafts. Open May through October (closed Mon and Tue through May and September; Mon through October) admission is $2.50 adults, $1.50 children. **The Arkansas Folk Festival and Handicraft Fair** is held in Mountain View the second, third and fourth weekends in April. Also near Mountain View are the **Blanchard Springs Caverns.** The **Dripstone Trail** tour features a cavern large enough to hold three football fields and is open year around. The new, more difficult *Discovery Trail,* which is open Memorial Day Weekend through Labor Day, has 600 steps, takes nearly two hours to cover and boasts of magnificent calcite formations. The **Buffalo National River,** north of town, is a classic canoe stream. Accommodations and campsites are available at the **National River Park's Buffalo Point.** Northeast of Little Rock is the Jackson County seat of **Newport.** Three miles away on AR 69 is the **Jacksonport Courthouse Museum,** a restored 1869 brick building reflecting various periods in delta life. It is located in the **Jacksonport Historic State Park,** which provides facilities for picnicking and fishing.

In the northeast corner of the state, **Jonesboro** is the home of **Arkansas State University**, the second-largest college in the state. The library houses the **University Museum**, which records archaeological, geological, pioneering, and Civil War events. **Craighead Forest Lake** is nearby. Enhanced by the flowering dogwood in the spring, **Crowley's Ridge State Park** encircles rolling hills and lakes and a ridge of windblown silt and dust (loess), a geologic oddity which extends from Missouri through the delta to **Helena Village Creek State Park.** Crowley's Ridge offers camping, fishing, swimming, and hiking. Some 12 miles north of Interstate 40 at **Forrest City. Blytheville,** on I-55, is the center of the delta's cotton region. You can fish year round and hunt duck in season at **Big Lake National Wildlife Refuge.** South of Blytheville is **Wilson,** built to resemble an English Tudor village, an oddity of charm in these flat delta farmlands. This Mississippi Delta country highlights the Great River Road of Arkansas, a section of historic route between the Gulf of Mexico and Canada in the far north. **West Memphis** is popular for **Southland Greyhound Park,** a busy dog-racing track, open spring through fall.

Follow the Mississippi River, which is the eastern boundary line of the state separating it from the states of Tennessee and Mississippi, south to **Helena,** an important riverport. Here you can recapture a feeling of the Old South through its lovely homes built before the Civil War. At the **Phillips County Museum,** adjacent to the library, a panorama of Arkansas history unfolds through various exhibits. The largest rice mill in the world serves as a landmark for Stuttgart, West of Helena. Around the town are rice paddies, just like those in Asia, except that these are flooded every third year and stocked with fish. On the first Saturday of the winter duck season in late November or early December, **Stuttgart** is host to the **World Championship Duck Calling Contest and Waterfowl Festival.** In the **White River National Wildlife Refuge** you can bag deer, turkey, squirrel, and raccoon. Elsewhere, duck hunting is unusually good because the ducks are attracted to the rice fields in the fall. Nearby is the site of one of the oldest settlements west of the Mississippi, the **Arkansas Post National Memorial.** The area included the first capital of the Arkansas Territory and was the home of the *Arkansas Gazette,* which began publication November 20, 1819 and is the oldest newspaper west of the Mississippi. A wildlife sanctuary, fishing, boating, a dogtrot logcabin (a reconstruction of an early 1800s homestead), and picnicking facilities are located here. On the Arkansas River between Arkansas Post and Little Rock is **Pine Bluff,** the second oldest city in the state. The **Southeastern Arkansas Arts and Science Center** is in the Civic Center, which was designed by Edward Durrell Stone. The city's new convention center features many top-name recording artists and entertainers. Many fine old houses maintain the charm and dignity of the antebellum period. **Du Bocage,** built in 1866, is a restored Greek revival mansion furnished with antiques.

There are several towns of interest to the southwest of Little Rock, beginning with **Arkadelphia** on I-30 and the Ouachita River; it is the home of **Henderson State College** and **Ouachita Baptist University.** Fishing is said to be excellent at the nearby **DeGray Reservoir,** where the state's resort park offers a lodge, 18-hole golf course, tennis courts, a marina and campgrounds. The city of **Camden** is as far north as riverboats can go on the Ouachita River. The **Chidester House** (1848) used to be a stagecoach stop and was the first house in town to have wallpaper and a sewing machine; usually open Tuesday through Sunday. Other fine old houses are open during special tour weeks in May and October. Three hundred unknown graves are in the **Confederate Cemetery. Poison Springs Battleground State Historical Monument,** where the South stopped the North from invading Texas, is 11 miles west. **White Oak State Lake Park** is noted for its bass, bream and crappie. Oil well derricks are visible in **Magnolia,** southwest of Camden. Oil was discovered here in 1937 and there are more than 800 wells in the vicinity. **El Dorado** has been happily oil-rich since 1921; the **Oil Belt Golf Tournament** draws big crowds on Labor Day weekend. The only diamond mine on the North American Continent is in **Crater of Diamonds State Park** at Murfreesboro. You can dig for your own gems for $2. Two miles northwest are the **Caddo Burial Mounds,** site of a prehistoric Indian Village. **Old Washington State Historic Park,** south of Murfreesboro, was the capital of Arkansas during the Confederacy and is full of historical memories. The **Block-Catts House** (1828), **Royston House** (1830) and **Garland House** (1836) are open daily. In the old restored Tavern, Stephen Austin and Davy Crockett met to recruit an army which later perished at The Alamo. And in the **Blacksmith Shop,** James Black reportedly made James Bowie the first of his famous knives. **Texarkana,** at the southwest corner of the state, lies equally in Texas and Arkansas.

An excursion into the mountainous northwest can lead you into some of the most tranquil valleys in Arkansas. The **OZARKS,** with 1,055,000 acres, are curiously isolated; a maze of steep valleys plunging through wooded hills seemed to discourage all but the most determined settlers. A whole folklore has evolved here, handed down in flinty phraseology. Northwest of Little Rock is **Petit Jean State Park,** encompassing rugged mountainous areas, Cedar Falls, Cedar Creek Canyon, Indian Cave with pictures by the aborigines, Bear Cave Rocks and miles of developed trails. Adjoining the park are **Winrock Farms,** the demonstration farms owned by the late Governor Winthrop Rockefeller's son, Winthrop Paul Rockefeller. Headquarters of the **Ozark National Forest,** Russellville can be reached from AR 7, one of the most beautiful drives in the state. Nuclear 1, the state's first nuclear power plant, is nearby. From a crest of 1800 feet in **Mount Nebo State Park,** you can appreciate the majesty of Arkansas River Valley. Further west, the state's most popular wine country, complete with tasting and eating facilities, was established at **Altus** by Swiss-German settlers. **Holla Bend National Wildlife Refuge** close by harbors many endangered species, including gold and bald eagles, egrets and herons.

In the **NORTHWEST,** on the Oklahoma border, is the bustling manufacturing town of **Fort Smith.** The fort was originally built in 1817 as defense against the Indians. As the center of a lawless territory after the gold strike in California, it was assigned its own federal court. Here at **Fort Smith National Historic Site**, "Hanging Judge" Issac Charles Parker sentenced 151 men to die. In 1895 Judge Parker summed up his philosophy of law by saying, "It is not the severity of punishment but the certainty of it that checks crime nowadays." His courtroom and the foundations of the first fort have been preserved. The **Old Fort Museum** is in the former commissary. The **Fort Smith Art Center** occupies a home that was built in 1865. The 22-square-block **Belle Grove Historic District** has several restored frontier homes open for tours. The **Crawford County Court House**, built in 1841, is across the Arkansas River east of **Fort Smith**, and adjoins a similarly restored district where the old **Butterfield State Coach** stopped on its route between St Louis and San Francisco. The Frisco Railroad depot and many old downtown stores reflect accurate, restored glimpses of the past. The **University of Arkansas,** home of the football and basketball **Razorbacks,** is in Fayetteville, north of Fort Smith. On the campus are science, natural history and ethnological exhibits at **University Museum** in Old Main, and a **Fine Arts Center,** where traveling exhibits of paintings are displayed. **Mount Gaylor,** highest point in the Arkansas Ozarks, rises into a haze of cloud 25 miles south of Fayetteville. Between Fayetteville and Fort Smith are large sandstone outcroppings in the **Devil's Den State Park.** Relax here and explore the adjacent hillsides honeycombed by deep cracks and fissures.

Deep in the Ozarks is the little resort town of **Harrison.** This is a good base for exploring the area. **Holiday Inn** (741-2191, S$21/D$28). **Siesta Motel** (743-1000, S$18D$22), **Ramada Inn** (741-7611, S$23-29/D$28-45), and the **Oasis** (732-1200, S$15-18/D$18-28), are open all year. Out on the pretty AR 7 are the **Bryant Art Museum** (741-5367), open spring through fall. Farther out, Al Capp's **Dogpatch USA** comes alive in an amusement park that includes stagecoach and train rides, and a tour of **Dogpatch Cavern**; open daily from Memorial Day to Labor Day. Next door is **Marble Falls Resort** which offers manmade snow for skiers from 15 December-15 March, year-round ice skating, and an antique car collection. **Diamond Cave** and **Hurricane River Cave** are also worth exploring in the Harrison vicinity, and so is the frontier recreation in the **Rally Hill Museum and Heritage Center.** The backwoods creeks and rivers provide excellent fishing. Northwest of Harrison is **Berryville,** where side arms that belonged to Jesse James, Pancho Villa and Wild Bill Hickok are among a remarkable collection of guns, antiques and handicrafts at the **Saunders Museum.** For an unusual thrill, picnic underground at **Mystery Cave** which contains a lake stocked with trout. In the southwest, **HOT SPRINGS,** the "Spa City of the United States," sits in a valley rimmed by five mountains of the Quachita Range. And it is probably the only American city that almost entirely surrounds a national park.

Most downtown motels and hotels have higher rates during the spring racing season at Oaklawn Park. **Arlington Hotel** (623-7771, S$36-46/D$46-56), famous for thermal baths; **Avanelle** (624-2521; S$26-29/D$32-35), heated pool, near race track; **Downtowner** (624-5521, S$22-50/D$33-

60), thermal baths, in Hot Springs National Park; **Holiday Inn** (624-3321, S$28/D$32), heated pool; **Best Western Hot Springs Inn** (624-4436, S$21-25/D$26-33.55); **Majestic Hotel** (623-5511, S$21-39/D$25-43), thermal baths; **Ramada Inn** (624-4441, S$30.50/D$33.50-36.50), heated pool; **Royal Vista Inn** (624-5551, S$26/D$30), heated pool, near race track; **Travelier** (624-4681, S$21/D$28), heated pool. South of town is **Buena Vista Lake Resort** (525-1321, S$22/D$24), with a variety of facilities, such as fishing, skiing, boats, children's playground, and a heated pool. **The Vapors** night club attracts nationally known entertainers. Favorite family places to dine are **Mollie's** and the **Mayflower**, which features a kosher-style and American menu. Before leaving Hot Springs, visit the indoor mechanical village, **Tiny Town,** where you can see animated figures less than three inches tall, and the **I.Q. Zoo** where "psychologically trained" animals perform. In the fine arts field you can tour **Dryden Potteries** or view an exhibit by local or regional artists at the **Southern Association Fine Arts Center.** Monkeys and alligators are displayed at the **Alligator Farm.** Other attractions are **Animal Wonderland,** horse-drawn carriage rides and a new historical drama. **"The Adventures of Hernando DeSoto, Conquistador,"** re-enacts DeSoto's discovery in 1541 of this land of thermal springs. The city's **Magic Springs Family Fun Park,** which features amusement rides, craft shops, live shows and other activities, spread across some 75 acres on US 70 east of town. West of the city is the 470-acre **Mid-America Park,** a development with industrial, educational, and entertainment facilities and **Mid-America Center,** an unusual museum with aesthetic experiences of energy, life, and matter, fulfilling a reputation of "a museum to amuse."

The charm of Victorian days still lingers at **Wildwood,** a restored mansion enhanced by a handsome handcarved stairway of wild cherry wood. You can dig your own quartz crystals at **Coleman's Crystal Mine,** north of town on AR 7. The sport of kings flourishes at the **Oaklawn Race Track** from early February to early April. June brings the **Arkansas Fun Festival,** with folklore, art and industrial exhibits; and the **Arts and Crafts Fair** occurs in early October.

West of Hot Springs is the large, primitive **Ouachita National Forest** with 1,572,879 acres. In the forest is **Lake Ouachita State Park,** with campsites, cabins, boat dock and café located on a cove of Lake Ouachita. **Rich Mountain,** the highest point between the Rockies and the Appalachians, is one of the attractions of **Queen Wilhelmina State Park,** near Mena. Accommodations are at the **Queen Wilhelmina Inn.** On the mountain are more than 100 species of moss, ferns and flowers. To view the whole panorama, take the 2-mile railroad trip in the summer. Nearby is **Talimena Scenic Drive** to Oklahoma.

EUREKA SPRINGS is the spa city of the Ozark Mountains. Its 63 cold natural springs flow in grottos sprinkled throughout the town. The entire central business district is listed on the National Record of Historic Places. Gingerbread architecture of a bygone era attests that the town is the oldest resort in the Ozark region. Many of the colorful homes are shown on the listing of Historic Places. This "Little Switzerland of

America" town is famous for its seven-story hotel with each floor having a ground-floor entrance, and a church entered through its bell tower. The **Folk Festival** is a gala pageant of folklore and folk songs highlighted by a Barefoot Ball here in October. A unique attraction is *Christ of the Ozarks*, a seven-story concrete figure which stands with outstretched arms at the summit of Magnetic Mountain. Near the base is the amphitheater where *The Great Passion Play*, depicting Christ's last week on earth, is performed from May through October every year. Adjacent is the **Christ Only Art Gallery** with 400 studies of Jesus Christ in different media. **Eureka Springs Historical Museum**, with 19th-century artifacts, and **Hatchet Hall**, the boarding house where Carrie Nation lived and made her last temperance address, are in midtown. The 1886 **Crescent Hotel** (253-9766, S$28-38/D$30-65) has been restored to its former opulence and is the town's most enduring symbol. The stroller will enjoy a path that connects the Crescent with downtown. To add to your visit, try such attractions as **Onyx Cave**; **Miles Mountain Musical Museum** displaying hundreds of music boxes and instruments; **Dinosaur Park**, where prehistoric monsters are recreated; and **Blue Spring**, one of the largest springs in the Ozarks, which gushes out 38 million gallons in 24 hours. In **Pea Ridge National Military Park**, north of **Rogers** (mentioned earlier), Union forces scattered Confederate regiments after a bloody 2-day engagement in March 1862 and helped save Missouri for the Union. Exhibits and a slide presentation are furnished at the Visitors Center, and a 7-mile scenic drive leads to points of battle.

HOT SPRINGS NATIONAL PARK

Tiny by national standards, the park occupies only one and two-thirds square miles and is almost completely surrounded by the city of Hot Springs. The 47 hot springs, bubbling out of the five low mountains in the park, were neutral territory before the white man came. Here Indian braves of all tribes could soak away their ailments in peace. **The Visitor Center,** on the corner of Reserve and Central Avenues, displays the human, geological and natural history of the park. **Bathhouse Row** has seven bathing establishments, operated under federal inspection, where you can enjoy whirlpool baths, showers, massages, and alcohol rubs. **The Libbey Memorial Physical Medicine Center** accepts hydrotherapy patients who have been recommended by local federally registered physicians; a list of physicians is available at park headquarters. Two display springs have been left in their natural state; the other 45 are now sealed so their 67°C waters can be scientifically cooled and piped to bathhouses and drinking fountains. Unlike most spa waters, Hot Springs water tastes good.

About 18 miles of hiking and horseback riding trails wind through the surrounding tree-shaded hills where redbud and dogwood bloom in spring, magnolias are creamy-white in summer, and the foliage flames into vibrant colors in autumn. Summer campfire programs and nature hikes are conducted by park naturalists. Activity schedules can be obtained at the Visitor Center. Sports in the area include golf, fishing, and boating.

The park is recommended year round. Most hotels have higher rates from early February to early April during the racing season at **Oaklawn Park.** There is a wide choice of hotels and motels in town and resort hotels on nearby **Lakes Ouachita** and **Hamilton.** Some of the city hotels are supplied with thermal waters from the hot springs. **Gulpha Gorge Campground** is a lovely rustic area in the northeast section of the park; 14-day stay limit from 1 April to 31 October, 30 days the rest of the year.

FURTHER STATE INFORMATION

Department of Parks and Tourism, 149 State Capitol, Little Rock, AR 72201. Hunting and fishing: **Game and Fish Commission,** State Capitol Grounds, Little Rock, AR 72201. **Greater Little Rock Chamber of Commerce,** 1 Spring Street, Little Rock, AR 72201. National Parks: **Hot Springs National Park** (Superintendent), Box 1219, Hot Springs, AR 71901.

USEFUL TELEPHONE NUMBERS IN LITTLE ROCK

St Vincent Infirmary	661-3866
Baptist Medical Center	227-2300
General Medical	664-3402
Legal Services	376-3423
Events & Tourist Info (Telefun)	372-3399
Information and Referral Service	374-4411
Pan Am Reservations	(800) 231-0256

California

Area	158,693 square miles				**Population**	23,618,562						
Capital	Sacramento				**Sales Tax**	6%						

Weather	Jan	Feb	Mar	Apr	May	Jun	Jul	Aug	Sep	Oct	Nov	Dec
Av Temp (°C)	12	13	14	15	17	18	21	21	20	18	16	14
Days of Rain	6	6	5	4	1	1	1	5	1	2	4	6

In any other country California would not be a state but a nation in its own right. It is large enough, rich enough, thickly populated enough, and certainly varied enough to make many a good-sized country look small. The Spanish, in the 18th century, were the first settlers in California, and established a chain of missions all along the coast and inland. Nearby, *presidios* with small military staffs were established to protect the missions from hostile natives and possible invaders. By 1823 Franciscan fathers had founded 21 missions along *El Camino Real* (the Royal Road), extending from San Diego near the Mexican border nearly 600 miles to Sonoma north of San Francisco. US 101 runs nearly parallel to this historic route, and the old missions are among the most beautiful buildings in the United States.

By 1821 California had become a province of Mexico. Twenty years later, when the first wagon train of pioneers began arriving, there were fewer than 400 of these eastern settlers already living there. By 1845, however, 4,000 had arrived and were busily establishing farms, vineyards, and businesses. During the war between Mexico and the United States

(1846-1848), the settlers declared California's independence and, with relatively little bloodshed, in 1848 Mexico formally ceded California. Nine days before the signing of the Treaty of Guadalupe-Hidalgo, which ended the war, gold had been discovered at Sutter's Mill near Sacramento. The Gold Rush of 1849, the most bizarre and frenzied migration in history, started California on a course of prosperity that continues to this day.

Californians have a magnificent setting in which to enjoy their prosperity. There are only four large shipping harbors on its coast, leaving vast stretches of shoreline free for recreational use. There are 24 national forests, totalling 20 million acres and 20 wilderness areas where fishing and hunting are plentiful and 17 national park service areas, including seashores, recreation areas, monuments, etc. It was 1928 when efforts of the Save-the-Redwoods League and others led to the founding of the California State Park System, which boasts now of more than 200 units. One of the state's proudest possessions is the magnificent coast redwoods which provided the inspiration for creation of the state park system. These great trees once stretched in a nearly continuous strip from the Oregon border to below Monterey on the west side of the Coast Range. Some of the finest remaining primeval redwoods in California state parks owe their existence to the Save-the-Redwoods League, which has raised $23 million to purchase redwood lands, to become one of the wonders of the world. The mighty **Sierra Nevada** range stretches down the eastern side of the state in an awesome panorama of peaks; about 40 are 5,000 to 8,000 feet high and 11 are more than 14,000 feet.

When packing for a trip to California, take warm clothes if you plan to be high in the mountains; otherwise, keep your wardrobe flexible so you can add or peel off layers as required. California has some of the country's most spectacular scenery, with mostly dormant and extinct volcanoes, canyons, immense expanses of barren rock, plunging waterfalls, alpine meadows, and beautiful lakes of which Tahoe is the most famous. **Death Valley**, enclosed by mountain ranges, is about 50 miles long and 20 to 25 miles wide. Although a few places in the Colorado Desert are sometimes hotter, Death Valley beats anywhere else in the world for combined heat and aridity. Each region of the state has its own eccentricities of climate. US 395 Highway, stretching from the California-Oregon border near Goose Lake on the north, through eastern California and western Nevada, passes west of Death Valley before joining Highway 15 in the Mojave Desert, offering unsurpassed scenery. US 395 connects with Calif. 178 and 190 to the Death Valley Monuments and Park. US 95 passes east of the park and connects with Nev. 72, 58, and 29 to the park. Interstate 15 passes southeast of the park and connects with Calif. 127 to the park. Limited bus and air service are available from Las Vegas, Nev., to Death Valley. Always one of the state's major tourist attractions, Death Valley has four widely separated campgrounds, Furnace Creek, Grapevine, Stovepipe Wells, and Wildrose Canyon. Resorts provide lodging and other commercial services at two locations within the national monument and information can be obtained by writing to Fred Harvey, Inc., P.O. Box 187, Death Valley, CA 92328. The National Park Service provides gasoline, curios, and snack bar services at Scotty's Castle, which is one of the highly popular Death Valley attractions.

If you are driving to California, the following are suggested routings. If you enter California on I-8 from Yuma, Arizona, you will skirt the Mexican border all the way west to San Diego. **Imperial Valley** was an arid desert but irrigation has made it possible to grow lettuce, melons, and other produce. **El Centro,** 52 feet below sea level, is the major town here. To the north is the **Salton Sea,** to the west are **Vallecito Mountains, Anza-Borrego Desert State Park,** and a great many Indian reservations.

If you enter the state on I-10 from Phoenix, Arizona, the first town you reach is **Blythe,** in the **Palo Verde Valley** where there is great fishing and boating on the **Colorado River.** Most of the US's palm dates come from **Indio,** 63 miles west of Blythe, where there is a real Arabian atmosphere complete with camel races at the **Riverside County Date Festival** in mid-February. North of Indio is **Joshua Tree National Monument** which has dramatic desert scenery, particularly when the rare *Yucca Brevifolia* bloom from March through May. **Palm Springs** is at the foot of San Jacinto Peak.

I-40 cuts across Arizona from Flagstaff and crosses over the Colorado River entering California at **Needles,** named for its weird stone peaks, a popular stop for fishermen and devotees of abandoned mining towns. From here it's mountains and desert all the way to **Barstow,** one-time wagon train station and outfitter for miners and "desert rats." I-15, an excellent highway into California from Las Vegas, crosses the **Mojave Desert** to Barstow and then angles down to **Los Angeles.** Beyond the **Tehachapi Mountains** to the west of Barstow lies **Bakersfield** on the edge of the **San Joaquin Valley.** Already doing well with prosperous farms, Bakersfield had a gold rush in 1885 and a more lasting windfall when oil was discovered in 1899; while there visit the **Kern County Museum and Pioneer Village.** Accommodations at Bakersfield include **Casa Royale Best Western** (327-3333, S$26-36/D$30-40); **Hilton Inn,** 200 rooms, (327-0681, S$29-41/D$37-49), and **Ramada Inn,** 200 rooms (327-9651, S$35-43/D$39-47).

Route 99 goes from Bakersfield north to **Fresno,** passing through some of the richest agricultural land in the world. The city of Fresno's attractions include the **Kearney Mansion,** home of one of the area's pioneers in agriculture. It is open Wednesdays through Sundays and holidays from 2pm to 4:30pm, starting the first weekend in March and continuing to 30 December, closed Thanksgiving and Christmas Days. Admission is $1 for adults and 25¢ for children ages 6-17. Fresno boasts of one of the better zoos in California at **Roeding Park,** where there also are many recreational facilities. The zoo is open daily from 10-5, adults $1 and children under 15 are 25¢. **Fort Miller Blockhouse Museum** is open Saturday, Sunday and holidays from 1pm to 5pm and Storyland is open 10-5 from 1 May to mid-September daily and weekends, also holidays and vacation periods the rest of the year, except between 1 December and 31 January when it is closed. Adults $1, children under 3 free. Fresno is host to the **West Coast Relays,** a track and field meet, on the second Saturday in May. The city, population 215,396, is only 54 miles from Yosemite National Forest and is near Sierra National Forest.

The **Fresno Hilton Hotel** (485-9000, S$29-41/D$37-49), with 205 units, is located on the downtown Mall, one of the first Malls in California. The **Holiday Inn-Airport** (252-3611, S$36-43/D$39-50, subject to change) has 207 units. **Smuggler's Inn** (226-2200, toll free (800) 742-1911, CA., S$36-43/D$39-50), with 210 units. Other accommodations include: **Hill House** (268-6211, S$24-27/D$28-31); **Quality Inn** (233-5781, S$23-33/D$30-33); **Ramada Inn** (244-4040, S$30-35/D$35-40); **Travelodge Fresno North** (486-3220, S$24/D$28-32); **Travelodge Roeding Park** (233-5886, S$24/D$27-32); **Village Inn** (226-2100, S$27-29/D$31-34); **Water Tree Inn** (222-4445, S$30-34/D$36-42). Most of those listed have restaurants and some have cocktails and entertainment. Fresno has many top eating establishments and it is claimed that you can get some of the best Armenian food served anywhere. At the **Big Yellow House,** a family restaurant, table d'hote dinners served family style with two entrees at a modest price. Other popular restaurants include the Armenian-style **Stanley's, Nicola's,** featuring Italian food; **Papagallo's Mexican** eatery; **Pardini's** at Piccadilly Square, serving continental foods, **Velvet Turtle,** noted for its rack of lamb, prime ribs, and beef Wellington, and **Hungry Tiger,** celebrated for Irish dinners.

Following the **PACIFIC COAST** north from Los Angeles, US 101 goes to **San Luis Obispo** where Father Junipero Serra founded the mission in 1772. From here you can continue north on US 101 inland to **King City,** the best place to make a detour to see the rock formation at **Pinnacles National Monument.** Or you can follow the twisting route US 1 along the coast and see some of the most beautiful and awe-inspiring coastline scenery in the world. William Randolph Hearst's magnificently-decorated estate is at **San Simeon,** high on **La Cuesta Encantada** (The Enchanted Hill) overlooking the Pacific. The estate, now a state historic monument, is open daily except Thanksgiving, Christmas and 1 January. There is a choice of 3 tours and all tickets are usually sold out by mid-morning. A good deal of walking and stair climbing is involved in each tour. Advance reservations are usually necessary in summer. For prices, information and reservations, write to Hearst Reservation Office, Department of Parks and Recreation, Box 2390, Sacramento 95811. Further up the coast is **Big Sur,** a retreat high above the ocean that has become the home of many artists and writers. About 30 miles north of here is the lovely **Monterey Peninsula** which includes the communities of Monterey, Pacific Grove, Pebble Beach, and Carmel.

If you enter California from **Reno** on Interstate 80 or **Carson City,** Nevada, on Highway 50, by all means see **Lake Tahoe,** one of the most attractive resort areas in the United States. Divided by the California-Nevada border in the northern Sierra Nevada, Tahoe is the highest freshwater lake in the world and has been a mecca for travelers for years because of its unsurpassed natural beauty, all-year recreation and a fine selection of restaurants, accommodations and entertainment. The 75-mile drive circling Lake Tahoe is said to contain more recreational, historic, and scenic points of interest than any other comparable area in the United States. The lake is only 28 miles from Nevada's Capital, Carson City, 58 miles from Reno, Nev., and 198 miles from San Francisco. Lodging/motel reservations can be made from California by calling the toll free number 800-822-5974 (South Tahoe Tours). From other western states the toll free number is 800-648-5450. On the Nevada side, where gambling is legal, there are seven casinos on the south end of the lake and four on the north shore, all operating 24 hours a day. Throughout the year, the world's greatest performers in show business are featured. Lake Tahoe visitors like to compare their feelings with that of Mark Twain, who wrote: "The air up there in the clouds is pure and fine, bracing and delicious. And why shouldn't it be? It is the same the angels breathe." Hotels and motels on both the California and Nevada sides of the lake change rates between the winter and summer. Tahoe is near famous **Squaw Valley**, one of the great winter sports areas and site of the 1960 Winter Olympics. At Squaw, as it is popularly known, are enough slopes, accommodations and restaurants to please any sports-person or visitor seeking to absorb the beauty of the valley and its surrounding mountains. Squaw Valley reservations and package plans can be made by calling, toll free, 800-824-7954, excluding California, Alaska, and Hawaii. In California a collect call can be made through 916-583-5585. Also near Lake Tahoe is **Donner Memorial State Park** (adjacent to Interstate 80), where a museum recounts the tragic tale of the Donner Party, trapped there in the savage winter of 1846-47.

One hundred miles west of Lake Tahoe, **SACRAMENTO** as capital of the nation's most populated state, offers many attractions of historical significance as well as reflecting the vitality of a prosperous, growing city. **Sutter's Fort,** has been restored to recreate the features of the establishment as they were in founder John Sutter's time. An Indian museum filled with artifacts adjoins Sutter's Fort, open daily 10-5. Admission 50¢ for adults, children 25¢. **State Indian Museum,** open daily 10-5. Admission free. A short distance away on the banks of the **Sacramento River** is one of the west's greatest historic areas—Old Sacramento. In a 28-acre area, California's early years have been given new life. The "city that brought you the Gold Rush" has restored with authenticity its great heritage. In Old Sacramento the **B. F. Hastings Building** has become a state museum to commemorate the site of the western terminus of the Pony Express. It was here also that the California Supreme Court conducted its deliberations in the early years of California. At the site is a statue of the first Pony Express rider who set off from Sacramento on April 4, 1860 on the first leg of the journey to St Joseph, Missouri, with the mail pouches. Nearby is the restored **Eagle Theater,** the first theater in California, and the **Central Pacific Passenger Station.** A gigantic state railroad museum opened in Old Sacramento in 1981. The 3-floor, 100,000 square-foot-structure, said to be unequaled anywhere in the world, is a showcase for over 40 interpretive exhibits and 21 pieces of historic railroad stock. Admission, adults $2. Children free. From 1849-1870, Sacramento possibly was America's best known city—an exciting hub of commerce and vital life-blood to the Gold Country. James Marshall, an employee of John Sutter, found flecks of gold in the tailrace water at a sawmill at Colusa, a short distance northeast of Sacramento, triggering the Gold Rush of 1849. Sacramento's central location provides an excellent base for visits to the historic mining towns lining the Sierra Nevada foothills. In putting Sacramento's best foot forward, the state legislature has appropriated nearly $70 million to remodel the State Capitol, rising majestically with its gold-plated dome in a park filled with hundreds of varieties of trees and plants. The home of 13 governors prior to 1967, the old Governor's Mansion a few blocks away from the Capital has become a major tourist attraction. The Victorian-Gothic 3-floor mansion was built in 1887 by a hardware merchant. Lincoln Steffens, the author, lived there as a child and it was bought by the state for $32,500 in 1903 as the home for California governors. The last to live in it was Ronald Reagan. Many other Victorian homes are being restored to their former beauty. One of the city's proudest possessions is the **E. B. Crocker Art Gallery,** the oldest art museum in the West.

Midtown Sacramento accommodations are offered by a large number of hotels and motels. Among them are the **Capitol Plaza Holiday Inn** (445-0100, S$44-48/D$50-54), adjacent to the Old Sacramento historic area. Other midtown hotel/motel accommodations include: **Mansion Inn** (444-8000, S$34/D$41-46); **Vagabond Motor Hotel** (446-1481, S$36/ D$44-47); **Best Westen Ponderosa** (441-1314, S$27/D$32-34); **Americana** (444-3980, S$20/D$24-28); **Mansion View Lodge** (443-6631, S$18/D$22-24); **Discovery Motor Inn** (442-6971, S$23-/D$27-31). Some of the larger hotels and motels a short distance from downtown Sacramento include the new **Ramada/El Rancho** (371-6731, S$32/D$38-42); **Red Lion Motor Inn** (929-8855, S$45-51/D$53-59); **Sacramento Motor Inn** (922-8041, S$39-45/D$47-53); **Woodlake Inn** (922-6251, S$28/D$34-40); **Rodeway Inn** (488-4100, S$24/D$30-35); **Holiday Inn North** (927-3492, S$26.50/ D$29.50-31.50); **Holiday Inn South** (422-3760, S$27/D$29.50-34.50); **Host International Hotel** (922-8071, S$48/D$43), and **Rancho Murieta Country Club** (985-7200, S/D$45-110).

Old Sacramento alone has 27 eating and drinking establishments, including the first restaurant and tavern in the area, the **Firehouse,** a structure which housed in early days a horsedrawn fire engine. The Firehouse flambé entrees and desserts have become famous. Reservations are required, 422-4772. Another popular restaurant in Old Sacramento is **D. O. Mills & Co.,** where dining is in a Victorian bankinghouse atmosphere. There are two **Stuart Anderson's Black Angus** restaurants in the Sacramento area. Many Chinese restaurants are popular, including **Frank Fat's,** located downtown and patronized by the governors and other politicians. **The Fox and Goose Pub,** also in downtown Sacramento, serves traditional English food and drinks. Supper clubs include the **Galactica 2000** in downtown Sacramento, one of California's largest discos, designed around a space age theme. Reservations are required, 443-2000.

Nearly 100 restaurants and taverns feature dancing, ranging from disco to country, and jazz. Many have live music. **Vangari's** (448-1723), a new lunch and dinner house with jazz music at night, opened early in 1981 and is a popular dining and entertainment center in downtown Sacramento. It offers valet parking. Traditionally, there is a global parade to Old Sacramento the Memorial Day weekend when the annual Sacramento Dixieland Jubilee is held. Some jazz enthusiasts compare it to the New Orleans Festival in popularity and the growing number of crowds each year back up that assessment. Another event of nationwide interest in the California gold country is the Calaveras County Jumping Frog Jubilee at Angels Camp (near Sacramento and 2½ hours drive from San Francisco), a sport popularized during Mark Twain's days in the gold mining camps, and held in May of each year. Less than 50 miles from Sacramento is highway 49 which reaches such historic gold mining communities as **Grass Valley, Nevada City, Placerville,** and **Jackson. Coloma,** where gold was discovered in California, is a short distance off Highway 49 on Route 193.

Amtrak, America's inter-city rail passenger service, has a toll-free number for information and reservations—800-648-3850. Seven airlines provide service to and from the Sacramento Metropolitan Airport for connections, if desired, to PAN AM flights out of San Francisco or Los Angeles. Regional Transit runs frequent buses downtown and out to the suburbs and nearby communities; $1 buys an all-day pass. Information on how to get there on Regional Transit, call 444-BUSS. Greyhound Bus Lines run from Sacramento to destinations all over the country. Call 444-6800 (24 hours) for schedules and rates. Trailways runs north on Interstate 5 to Seattle and south on Highway 99 to Los Angeles with stops in between. Call 443-2044 for schedules, rates and other destinations.

The first major stop on I-5 north of Sacramento is Red Bluff, shipping point for the livestock and produce of the upper Sacramento Valley and a popular headquarters for hunters and anglers. The important Red Bluff Bull Sale is held in late January and there's a good rodeo in this picturesque "cow" town in April. About 50 miles east of Red Bluff is Lassen Volcanic National Park, a fine winter sports area.

Redding, about 25 miles north of Red Bluff on Interstate 5, has many attractions for visitors and is within easy distance of some of the more spectacular scenic areas of California. There is a comparatively close view of the snow-covered cone of **Mount Shasta,** which towers 11,000 feet and nearby, where the Cascade Mountains join the Sierra Nevada, there is Lassen Peak in **Lassen Volcanic National Park.** After a period of inactivity for several thousand years, Lassen Peak gave forth with several small volcanic eruptions in 1914 and 1915 and small amounts of steam have been visible periodically since from the plug dome volcano. There are free guided tours at **Shasta Dam** (8 miles north of Redding) one of the world's largest dams which harnesses the Sacramento River to provide water for irrigation throughout the Sacramento and San Joaquin Valleys, and via a 444-mile canal that serves domestic, industrial, and irrigation water as far south as Los Angeles. The guided tours of the dam and hydroelectric powerplant are daily 9-5 1 May-30 September and at 10, noon and 2pm the rest of the year. The spectacularly beautiful **Lake Shasta Caverns** is a must-see for visitors. Two-hour tours by bus and boat provide access to the well-lighted caves. Trips are daily, every hour 9-5 from 1 May-30 September, and 3 times daily the rest of the year, weather permitting. Closed Thanksgiving, Christmas and New Year's Day. Cost, adults $6, ages 5-15, $3.50. In Redding's **Caldwell Park** there is a museum of art, historical and Indian exhibits, open Tuesday through Sunday 10-5 from 1 June through 31 August and from noon until 5:00pm the rest of the year. Closed holidays. Free admission. The restored gold rush town in **Shasta State Historical Park** is 6 miles from Redding. The old courthouse, converted to a museum, is open daily, adults 50¢, those under 18 25¢, closed Thanksgiving and Christmas. Redding is the access point for the surrounding **Whiskeytown-Shasta Trinity National Recreation** area and Shasta-Trinity National Forest, areas of good hunting, fishing, water sports and camping. House boating is very good with rentals by the week as low as $100 per person (minimum of 6 people); contact for information Shasta-Cascade Wonderland Assn; (916) 243-2643. **The Coleman National Fish Hatchery,** where salmon are hatched for later releases into the Sacramento River to begin the cycle that takes them to the Pacific Ocean to grow before returning to their river home to breed.

There are many motels and hotels in Redding, the latest being 194-unit **Red Lion Motor Inn** (241-8700, S$33-34/D$34-45); **Holiday Inn** (246-1500, S$31.50/D$35-38), with 163 units; **Shasta Inn** (241-8200, S$38-45/D$44-51), 147 units; **Americana Lodge** (241-7020, S$22/D$26); **Best Western Inn** (246-1000, S$28-32/D$33-37); **Bridge Bay Resort** (275-3021, S$27-38/D$27-55); **Ponderosa Inn-Best Western** (241-6300, S$23-27/D$27-34), and **Vagabond Motor Hotel** (243-1555, S$28-31/D$31-38). **Hospitality House** has a 24-hour restaurant and free boat and trailer parking. The **Shasta Inn** boasts of "gourmet cuisine" and live entertainment at its new **Wintoon Dining Room and Bar.**

Cities To Visit

LOS ANGELES

Los Angeles is in southwestern California, 400 miles south of San Francisco and 125 miles north of San Diego. The first explorers arrived in the region in 1769 and the actual settlement was begun in 1781. The original name was El Pueblo de Nuestra Senora la Reina de los Angeles de Porciuncula (the village of Our Lady the Queen of the Angels of Porciuncula); this was conveniently shortened to Los Angeles or, irreverently, L.A. Los Angeles was incorporated as a city in 1850 after Mexico ceded California.

Los Angeles consists of many elements and a mixed population. Resi-

CALIFORNIA

dents are from all over the United States and native-born Californians are in the minority. One of the country's most diverse cities, it is within a few hours of beaches, desert, and mountain ski resorts. The population is 2,952,511, metropolitan area 7,455,721.

WHAT TO SEE

To see the old Spanish landmarks, visit **Olvera Street,** with its shops, restaurants, curiosities; most interesting in the evening. **Avila Adobe** is a reconstructed Spanish ranch house on Olvera Street. The **Old Mission Church,** on North Main Street at Sunset Boulevard, is the oldest in the city.

In central Los Angeles, visit **Chinatown** shops and bazaars and dine in a Chinese restaurant. See **Little Tokyo,** restored as an authentic Japanese community of shops, gardens, restaurants, and nightclubs. A few blocks north of this region is **El Pueblo de Los Angeles State Historical Park,** covering 11 blocks and depicting California life as it was in the days of the Indians, Mexicans, and pioneer Americans. **Arco Plaza** is downtown's "City Beneath The City"—with 10 restaurants and 50 shops. The **Civic Center's** boundaries are the Hollywood Freeway, Grand Avenue, First and San Pedro streets. The art galleries on **La Cienega Boulevard** are especially interesting on open-house Monday nights when the latest paintings and sculptures are on view.

Los Angeles radio and television studios are all interesting; visit the **Universal Studios, CBS** and **NBC Studios,** all of which have tours. There are also tours past the homes of Hollywood stars. The colorful **Farmer's Market** is best visited in the middle of the day; enjoy an outdoor lunch there. Visit **Mann's Chinese Theater** (formerly Grauman's) in Hollywood to examine the footprints, handprints, and hoofprints of the stars. If time permits, see the port of Los Angeles and drive through Los Angeles' superbly-kept suburban residential areas.

Parks and zoos in Los Angeles include **Forest Lawn Memorial Park** in Hollywood Hills, with statues and historical memorials; **Marineland,** 25 miles south at Palos Verdes, ocean fish and whales in a modern open aquarium; **Griffith Park,** on Mt Hollywood, with the **Los Angeles Zoo,** an observatory and planetarium, satellite exhibit, and travel museum. Los Angeles is also a good spot for fall and spring whale-watching trips and party boat fishing year-round. **Fern Dell,** adjoining Griffith Park, has beautiful rare ferns. The **Rose Garden** in **Exposition Park** has 17,000 rosebushes, 120 varieties. Exposition Park also is the home of the 92,000-seat **Los Angeles Memorial Coliseum** and 16,000-seat indoor **Sports Arena,** centers for some of the West's most spectacular sports and entertainment. There are also the fine **Botanical Gardens at UCLA: Descanso Gardens** in suburban La Canada, featuring camellias, orchids, rose and Japanese gardens, rare western flowers and plants, and the **Los Angeles State and County Arboretum** with interesting plants from all over the world and numerous parks.

Principal schools: **California Institute of Technology; Occidental College; Southwestern University,** business courses; **University of California**

Los Angeles, CA has the most extensive, the most complex and the most
highly developed freeway system in the world.

at Los Angeles; University of Southern California, technical and professional subjects.

ACCOMMODATIONS

In the central business district: **Biltmore** (624-1011, S$62-92/D$78-108, toll free (800) 421-0156 US, (800) 252-0175 CA, 1,022 rooms, a convention headquarters; **Los Angeles Hilton** (629-4321, S$60-80/D$75-95); **Mayflower Hotel** (624-1331, toll free (800) 421-8851, S$44-60/D$51-68); **Hyatt Regency Los Angeles** (683-1234, toll free (800) 228-9000 US, (800) 268-7530 Canada, S$75-90/D$90-105); **New Otani Hotel and Garden** (629-1200, toll free (800) 421-8795 US, (800) 252-0197 CA, S$75-84/D$90-99); **Los Angeles Bonaventure** (624-1000, toll free (800) 288-3000, 1,500 rooms, S$75-95/D$90-110).

Near the International Airport: **Airport Century Inn** (649-4000, toll free (800) 421-2048, S$30-32/D$34-36); **Hyatt Hotel-LAX** (670-9000, toll free (800) 228-9000, S$57-67/D$63-72/Suites $150-325); **Los Angeles Marriott** (641-5700, S$50-58/D$58-66/Suites $125 up); **Manchester House Motel** (649-0800, S$26-30/D$32-50); **Marina Del Rey Marriott Inn** (822-8555, toll free (800) 228-9290, S$62-80/D$74-92); **Sheraton Plaza La Reine** (624-1111, toll free (800) 334-8484, S$54-72/D$64-82), 810 rooms; **Travelodge International Hotel** (645-4600, toll free (800) 255-3050, S$58/D$66).

West of the business district: **Hotel Bel Air** (472-1211, S$85-125/D$90-150); **Beverly Hills Hotel** (276-2251, toll free (800) 223-6625, S$72-150/D$81-165), famous, luxurious attractive setting; **Beverly Hillcrest Hotel** (277-2800, toll free (800) 421-3212 US, 252-0174 CA S$64-74/D$74-86); **Beverly Wilshire Hotel** (275-4282, toll free (800) 421-4354 US, 282-4804 CA, S$115-130/D$135-150); **Century Plaza** (277-2000, toll free (800) 228-3000, S$72-94/D$87-109/Suites $170-520).

In the Wilshire district: **Ambassador** (387-7011, toll free (800) 421-0182 US, (800) 252-0385 CA, S$51-88/D$63-100), large, 23 garden acres, 17 shops; **Hotel Chancellor** (383-1183, toll free (800) 421-8260, S$25.50/D$42.50); **Hyatt Wilshire Hotel and Conference Center** (381-7411, toll free (800) 228-9000, S$51-77/D$66-97).

In Hollywood: **Hyatt on Sunset** (656-4101, S$49-60/D$64-75); **Hollywood Roosevelt** (469-2442, S$36-48/D$41-53), 381 rooms with pool, shops.

In North Hollywood: **Sheraton Universal Hotel** (980-1212, S$56-65/D$66-77/Suites $110-170); **Beverly Garland's Howard Johnson Resort Lodge** (980-2000, toll free (800) 654-2000, S$52-64/D$58-79). Hotel Tax 6%.

RESTAURANTS

A fantastic variety of food and cuisines; the local favorites are grilled meats, salads, fruits, and fresh vegetables. You'll enjoy a Caesar salad, often served as an appetizer. Deli and soup restaurants are very popular. For outstanding French food, **Bernard's** in the Biltmore Hotel, and **Fran-**

cois at 555 South Flower St are rated high, $18 to $24 at Bernard's, and $24 and up at Francois. Also in the downtown area, **Angel's Flight** in the Hyatt Regency, $6-12 offers American dinners in its revolving rooftop restaurant. **A Thousand Cranes** in the New Otani Hotel specializes in Japanese food, $12-18, and **El Paseo Inn** on Olvera Street, $6-12, features Mexican/American/Spanish dishes. **Curtain Call**, $6-12, American/Continental, and **Pacific Dining Car**, $12-18, offers steaks, veal, seafoods, served in a dining car setting—both are located downtown. In the west Los Angeles-Beverly Hills area there are the **Brown Derby-Beverly Hills**, $12-18, American/Continental; **Senor Pico & Mama Gruber Restaurant**, $18-24, for Mexican foods served in the grand manner; **Lawry's The Prime Rib**, $12-18, presented in an English decor. In the Wilshire area, dinner can be enjoyed in the popular **Perino's Restaurant** with an elegant 18th-century motif, featuring veal, fish, pasta, and steaks—over $24. There is a **Brown Derby** in Hollywood at the famous Hollywood and Vine, a meeting place of the entertainers, with such specialties as Cobb salad and grapefruit cake, dinners $12-18. Little kitchens and restaurants dot the **Farmer's Market** at Third and Fairfax Avenue, serving food from around the world, $6 and under.

ENTERTAINMENT

Live entertainment abounds in the Los Angeles area; many of the larger hotels and nightclubs offer a wide diversity and atmosphere. Nightlife centers in the Hollywood-West Hollywood-Beverly Hills area, with countless nightclubs, stage shows, and discos appealing to all interest and age groups. Many performers eventually make it to the "big time" in the entertainment field. Downtown spots offering entertainment include: **Beaudry's** in the Bonaventure Hotel, the **Down Under Restaurant** in the Gala Inn Towne Hotel, and **Tokyo Kaikan**. Disco and jazz are featured at the **Hollywood Roosevelt Garden Room Lounge**, and at **La Bella Fontana** Beverly Wilshire Hotel.

ARTS AND MUSIC

Los Angeles is a major cultural center, and offers a variety of excellent art, music and theatrical events. The **Los Angeles County Museum of Art,** on Wilshire Boulevard, consists of three pavilions containing many art treasures. Outdoor decor is embellished with fine sculptures and mobiles. **Hunting Art Gallery** has paintings and sculpture; **California Museum of Science and Industry** includes a space display and the Shirley Temple Doll Collection. The **County Museum of Natural History** and the **Southwest Museum** display Indian handicrafts and relics, closed mid-August to mid-September. The J. Paul Getty Museum at Malibu has an outstanding art collection, and equally interesting is the collection at the Norton Simon Museum of Art in nearby Pasadena.

Broadway presentations can be seen at the **Dorothy Chandler Pavilion, Mark Taper Forum** and the **Ahmanson Theater** in the Music Center or **Huntington Hartford Theater** in Hollywood. Century City's new **Shubert**

Theatre offers many fine pre- and post-Broadway productions. Principal musical groups are the **Los Angeles Philharmonic Orchestra, Light Opera Association** and **Hollywood Bowl Association,** which sponsors the famous **Symphony Under the Stars** in July and August. Dorothy Chandler Pavilion, Mark Taper Forum and Howard Ahmanson Theater form the **Music Center of Los Angeles County,** in the vicinity of the Civic Center. It has been hailed by both musicians and architects as a perfect complex of buildings for musical and theatrical productions; conducted tours are available. There are over 75 legitimate theaters in greater Los Angeles, plus three auditoriums at UCLA in Westwood. All offer programs in drama, music, and dance.

SHOPPING

Stores are open daily, some open evenings. For department stores downtown, try **Bullock's, JW Robinson,** or the **Broadway Plaza.** In San Pedro you can find **Ports O'Call,** an array of craft and gift shops. For books, try the **Pickwick Bookstore** on Hollywood Boulevard. Numerous shopping plazas are located throughout the Los Angeles metropolitan area. From smart shopping with valet parking on Beverly Hills' fashionable Rodeo Drive, to uniquely hand-crafted discoveries in Los Angeles' Mexican Olvera street, Little Tokyo, and Chinatown, the shopper is sure to find surprises.

Southern California sets the pace in sports and beach wear for both men and women; many local shops have good buys. You can ship California citrus fruits, avocados and nuts to friends and relatives at home.

SPORTS

Horse racing at **Santa Anita** and **Hollywood Parks** and at **Del Mar** track, just north of San Diego, pari-mutuel betting. Also on Sundays in Mexico at **Agua Caliente.** Many college football games in the area are scheduled by USC and UCLA, plus a varied program of other college sports. Los Angeles has two major league baseball teams, the **Los Angeles Dodgers** and the **California Angels;** the **Rams** are a professional football team, now located in Anaheim. The **Los Angeles Lakers** play pro basketball and the **Los Angeles Kings** pro hockey. Los Angeles also has a professional soccer team. The **Los Angeles Coliseum** holds many sporting events; visit the **Sports Arena** and the **Forum** for indoor events.

Golf can be played all year round at a large number of public and private courses, and there are many tennis courts. Fishing in chartered boats from fishing piers is often good; freshwater fishing in the lakes is variable. For swimming and surfing, the surrounding region offers many public beaches such as **Playa Del Rey, Will Rogers, Malibu, Laguna** and **Cabrillo Beaches.** Los Angeles has many swimming pools, public and private; the bathing season is from May through September. Winter sports are good in the **Big Bear** and **Lake Arrowhead** regions. Check at your hotel or motel for specific times and locations for local sports activities.

CALENDAR OF EVENTS

Tournament of Roses and **Rose Bowl Football Game**, 1 January; **Easter Sunrise Services**, at the Hollywood Bowl; **Los Angeles County Fair**, at Pomona about 25 miles east of downtown, September. The **Glen Campbell Los Angeles Open** golf tournament is held in February. In May the big event is the **Cinco de Maya** Mexican celebration on Olvera Street.

WHERE TO GO NEARBY

If you enjoy the beach, **Santa Monica**, 15 miles west of downtown Los Angeles and Malibu Beach, about 25 miles west, are ideal. **Long Beach,** with 8 miles of wide, sandy beaches, now has the **Queen Mary** as a maritime museum and a convention center. It's possible to stay on the Queen Mary as a hotel (435-3511, toll free (800) 421-3732 S$45-65/D$48-78), Queen Mary Hotel, 384 rooms.

Disneyland, southeast of Los Angeles in nearby Anaheim, is accessible by car or bus from Los Angeles or by Grayline Tours. Open throughout the summer months from 8am to 1am daily. The rest of the year, it is open Wednesday through Friday from 10am to 6pm, Saturday and Sunday from 9am to 7pm. There is something for everyone in this land of adventure. Stroll along Main Street USA for a sample of Americana, *circa* 1890. New Orleans Square recreates the ambience and setting of that city's fabulous French Quarter. The many "lands" include Adventureland; Bear Country, the newest, featuring the "Country Bear Jamboree"; Frontierland; Fantasyland; the World of Children; and Tomorrowland. Over 20 restaurants and refreshment centers offer a wide selection of menus. Disneyland features more than 30 colorful boutiques and specialty shops. Special services available are banking facilities, pet care, storage lockers, and a baby station. Accommodations are available at the **Disneyland Hotel** (778-6600, toll free (800) 854-6165 US, (800) 422-7325 CA, S$65-70/C$70-84), 1,100 rooms, adjacent to the park and linked to it by the Disneyland-Alweg Monorail System. Additional hotels and motels are located in the immediate area.

See also **Knotts Berry Farm,** Buena Park, 2 miles south of the Santa Ana freeway. This is a recreated gold-rush town with train and stagecoach rides, gold mine tour, and restaurant. **Santa Barbara,** 92 miles northwest, is a famous resort with good selection of accommodations. **Lake Arrowhead,** 83 miles east, is another good spot for a vacation. **Palm Springs,** about 125 miles southeast, is the famous winter resort in the desert, but extremely hot during the summer months. To the south of Los Angeles are such small communities as **Newport Beach, Balboa,** and **Laguna Beach. La Jolla,** near San Diego, is one of the most beautiful small towns on the coast. The **Salton Sea,** 160 miles southeast, 241 feet below sea level, is interesting. Flights to **Catalina Island,** 25 miles offshore from Los Angeles, are available, and the round trip can be made in a day. **Channel Islands National Monument** (Santa Barbara and Anacapa Islands) 65 miles north of Los Angeles is a large rookery of sea lions, nesting sea birds, unique plants and animals. Arrangements to visit the islands by private boat can be made at Oxnard or Ventura. **Huntington, Doheny,** and **San Clemente Beaches** are all state park areas offering swimming and picknicking. **Palomar Mountain State Park,** about 100 miles southeast, has mountain scenery and camping; the **Palomar Observatory** is nearby. **Mt San Jacinto State Park,** 120 miles southeast, is a forest wilderness. **Joshua Tree National Monument,** approximately 160 miles east, has large numbers of Joshua trees, interesting roads and wild animals. You can also drive through **Lion Country Safari,** a 500-acre preserve 60 miles south of Los Angeles, where over 800 imported animals roam free. The **Renaissance Pleasure Fair at Paramount Ranch** in Agoura, just off US 101, includes foods, crafts, plays, and music of the medieval and Renaissance periods, weekends in May.

MONTEREY PENINSULA

A hundred miles south of San Francisco lies the Monterey Peninsula surrounded by Monterey Bay, the Pacific Ocean, and Carmel Bay. The peninsula was first seen by Europeans in 1542 when Juan Rodriguez Cabrillo, a Portuguese adventurer in the service of Spain, sighted Point Pinos. In 1602 Sebastian Vizcaino, sailing from Acapulco on the Mexican coast, landed on the peninsula, named his harbor El Puerto de Monterey and took possession of the country in the name of Spain. The spot was rediscovered in 1770 by Father Crespi and Father Junipero Serra. Father Serra founded the Mission San Carlos Borromeo on the site of the present **Royal Presidio Chapel.** The following year the mission was moved 5 miles south of Monterey where the **Carmel Valley** slopes gently to the sea. The King of Spain recognized Monterey as the capital of California in 1775, but in 1822 it became part of the Mexican Republic and alternated with Los Angeles as a provincial capital. Yankee fishermen and traders who began to visit Monterey planted the seeds of discontent with Mexican rule, and in 1846 Commodore John Drake Sloat raised the American flag over the city. In September 1849 the first constitutional convention in California met in Monterey's **Colton Hall.**

Monterey has a Spanish-Mexican-American tradition of grace, color and warmth. The peninsula's year-round equable climate, a notable absence of heavy industry and a lively program of sports and cultural activities had made the region one of California's most fascinating resort areas.

WHAT TO SEE

The "17-Mile Drive" ($4 per car) around the shoreline of the peninsula from Pacific Grove, continuing to the **Carmel Mission** and climbing back over the hill to Monterey, is a delight. The **Camera Obscura,** along the 17-mile drive, offers a panoramic view of wildlife and trees in the area. Sightseeing tours of the peninsula are available, including the spectacular 17-Mile Drive Tour by Monterey Peninsula Tours, Inc., daily except Sunday—$11.50 per person from Carmel, and $13 from Monterey (375-1550). In Monterey the **Path of History,** marked by an orange-red line painted down the center of the streets throughout the town, leads to every old house of distinction, each of which is marked with a plaque explaining its history. The stops include the **Old Pacific Building,** now a historical museum, built in 1835 as a seaman's hotel; **Old Custom House; Vizcaino-Serra** landing place; **Historical Wax Museum,** privately owned; the **First Theater; Casas Soberanes, Gutierrez, Soto, Alvarado** and **Vasquez,** picturesque adobes; **Colton Hall; Larkin House,** (closed Mondays and Tuesdays) 1835 home furnished with period pieces; and **Stevenson House,** whose most famous guest was Robert Louis Stevenson. Other spots are **Cannery Row** with its former sardine processing facilities made famous by John Steinbeck's book, *Cannery Row,* buildings are now used as shops, studios and restaurants.

In **Pacific Grove,** nearby, are **Ocean View Boulevard; Point Pinos; the Pacific Grove Lighthouse,** open weekends and holidays; and **Pacific Grove Museum of Natural History.** In **Carmel,** further south on the peninsula, see the **Mission** and its museum, and the distinctive architecture of its homes.

Parks and zoos in the area include the **Butterfly Trees Park** in Pacific Grove October to March, "home" of Monarch butterflies; Monterey cypress trees at **Cypress Point. Seal** and **Bird Rocks,** home of innumerable cormorants, gulls and seals; **Fanshell Beach,** covered with brightly colored shells and sea-polished stones at certain times of year; **Crocker Grove,** containing the largest and oldest Monterey cypress. "Dennis the Menace Playground" is the popular name of **Monterey Playground,** created by Hank Ketchum, the cartoonist.

ACCOMMODATIONS

In Monterey: **Casa Munras Garden Inn** (375-2411, S$48/D$66), a 10-minute walk to historic Fisherman's Wharf; **Cypress Gardens Motel** (373-2761, S$36/D$50), pets allowed; **Reef Motel** (373-3203, S$30/D$34), South Sea island decor; **Hyatt Del Monte** (372-7171, S$70/D$90) adjacent to Del Monte Golf Course, dancing, nightly entertainment; **Doubletree Inn** (649-4511, S$68/D$95), at Fisherman's Wharf; **Hotel San Carlos** (375-2662, S$23/D$50), ocean view, within walking distance of historical landmarks. At Pebble Beach: The deluxe **Lodge at Pebble Beach** (624-3811, European plan, modified American plan available, $110-120), on 17-Mile Drive off Highway 1.

In Pacific Grove: **Borg's Ocean Front Motel** (375-2406, $36-55); **Asilomar Conferences Center** (372-8016, European and American Plan, 289 rooms, $15-42); **Lighthouse Lodge** (375-6288, $24-58), **Sunset Motel** (375-3936, $28-38).

In Carmel: **Best Western Carmel Resort Inn** (624-3113, $38-80); **Highlands Inn** (624-3801, $96-130), golf and tennis arrangements; **Carmel Holiday Inn** (624-3864, $66-75); **Wayside Inn** (624-5336, $32-80); **Village Inn** (624-3864, $34-50). Hotel Tax: 6%

RESTAURANTS

Fish is the star of the Monterey cuisine; sole, sea bass, filet of fresh tuna, red snapper, swordfish steak and salmon. Don't fail to sample the shellfish, abalone steaks and fresh crab. Along Fisherman's Wharf are **Mike's, Ange-**

lo's, Cerrito's, Neptune Table, Lou's Fish Grotto, Rappa's, specializing in freshly caught fish. Cannery Row's restaurants include **The Outrigger, Whaling Station Inn, Sardine Factory, Neil de Vaughn's, York of Cannery Row,** and **Captain's Cove,** providing a wide variety of cuisine. Other dinner houses abound in the Monterey area and among the popular are **The Rogue, Old Bath House, Peter B's. Consuelo's** and **Zapeda's** specialize in authentic Mexican food. **Clock Garden Restaurant, The Ginza Restaurant, The Brasserie,** and **Whaler** are others of note.

Pacific Grove restaurants include **Asilomar, Bertolucci's, Korean Sunset, Old Bath House, Old Europe, Tinnery at the Beach.** Carmel also has outstanding eating places, such as **Adobe Inn, Pine Inn, Clam Box, La Playa Hotel, French Poodle, Scandia, Shabu Shabu** (for Japanese dishes), **La Marmite, L'Escargot,** and **Le Coq d'Or.** At Pebble Beach there are **Club XIX, Cypress Room,** and **Taproom,** and at Big Sur the restaurants include **River Inn, Nepenthe, Ventana,** and **Rocky Point.** The Monterey Peninsula, especially the Carmel area, long has been a mecca for artists and art lovers. The latest count shows Carmel with 75 art galleries; Monterey with 17; Pacific Grove, 8; 2 in Carmel Valley, and 1 each in Seaside and Fort Ord. The area also has 14 museums, offering a wide variety of cultural, historical, and natural history information, ranging from early Pacific Coast Indian and Mission artifacts to historic material from the first days of California. All museums are free and many are in historic sites of interest. The museums include the **Monterey Peninsula Museum of Art,** open 10-5 Tue through Fri, 1-4 Sat and Sun. Annual events include the **Bach Festival** in July and the world famous **Monterey Jazz Festival** in September. Monterey has California's **First Theater,** featuring 19th-century melodramas throughout the year. There are 14 other theater groups in the Monterey Peninsula, and the Carmel Music Society, now in its 54th season, is active in bringing prominent groups to the area for concerts. Carmel's **Golden Bough Circle Theatre** gives contemporary and classic plays in-the-round on Friday, Saturday and Sunday nights; the **White Oaks Theater** in Carmel has a talented stock company performing Thursday through Sunday evenings; and the **Studio Restaurant & Theater** in Carmel offers light comedy and musicals at 8:30 every evening, and dinner is served at 6:30 and 7:30.

SHOPPING

Shopping is a favorite pasttime, particularly in Carmel; the village has more than 150 shops offering everything from Australian boomerangs to New Zealand tikis. **Ocean Avenue** houses one international specialty shop-after another.

SPORTS

Golf tournaments, horse racing, sports car racing at **Laguna Seca Raceway.** The peninsula, famous for golfing facilities, has 13 golf courses. In Monterey is the public **Laguna Seca Golf Ranch.** A famous private course is **Pebble Beach Golf Links;** also in Pebble Beach is the public **Peter**

Hay Par-Three Golf Course. There are more than 20 tennis courts. The salmon fishing season begins in mid-February and the **Monterey Salmon Derby** is from May-September. Sport-fishing boats head out early every morning from **Fisherman's Wharf** in Monterey; arrangements should be made the night before. There are also horses to ride on the over 100 miles of bridle trails through the **Del Monte Forest** accessible from Pebble Beach stables. There are other riding stables in Monterey and Carmel Valley. Bicycles and boats also can be rented.

CALENDAR OF EVENTS
Bing Crosby Pro-Am Tournament, January and February; **National Rugby Tournament** in March; **Pebble Beach-Los Altos Hunt and Steeplechase** in April; **Pebble Beach Hunter Trails, Del Monte Kennel Club Dog Show, Monterey County Pops Concert** in May; **California State Amateur Golf Tournament, NCGA Senior Golf Tournament, Sprints, Laguna Seca Raceway** in June; **Bach Festival, Obon Festival, National Horse Show, Matthew Jenkins Sailboat Regatta, Scottish Highland Games, NCGA Public Links Golf Tournament** in July; **National Horse Show, Monterey County Fair, Historic Automobile Races, International Motorcycle Races Laguna Seca** in August; **Monterey Jazz Festival, Gem and Mineral Show, Carmel Mission Festival Arabian Horse Show** in September; **Trans-Am Championship, Laguna Seca, Butterfly Parade, Wine Stomp** in October; **Golden Domino Tournament** in November; **Women's State Golf Championship Tournament,** and **California Wine Festival** in December.

WHERE TO GO NEARBY
Three 1-day trips from the Monterey Peninsula area: Highway 1 to the **Hearst Castle** atop its "Enchanted Hill" at San Simeon; **Pinnacles National Monument,** spiral rock formations 500-1,200 feet high and a variety of volcanic features, and the **Salinas Valley;** and **San Juan Bautista** and **Fremont Peak.** Three old Spanish missions, **Soledad, San Antonio,** and **San Miguel** are in South Monterey County. Each is a pleasant day's trip from the Peninsula, or all three may be included in a weekend loop drive. Information on side trips can be obtained from the Monterey Peninsula Chamber of Commerce and Visitors and Convention Bureau (649-3200).

Neaby state or national parks include **Asilomar Beach State Park** in Pacific Grove, with white sand dunes, green pines, fuschia-colored ice plants, and great green rollers; **Point Lobos State Reserve,** rugged 1,250 acre peninsula forming southern headland of Carmel Bay; **Pfeiffer-Big Sur State Park,** 820 beautiful acres with stands of sycamore and redwood, where there is swimming in river-fed pools, trout and steelhead fishing, 13 miles of well-marked hiking trails, more than 200 individual campsites, a lodge, cabins, picnic facilities, dining room and grocery store. Big Sur also has access to some 500 miles of trail leading into the far reaches of **Los Padres National Forest.**

PALM SPRINGS

Palm Springs is in southern California at the foot of the San Jacinto Mountains; Los Angeles is 104 miles northwest. In 1774 this desert oasis was known to the Spanish settlers of California as Agua Caliente because of its hot springs. In 1853 a US government survey party rediscovered it and by 1872 it was a regular stop on the stagecoach run between Prescott, Arizona and Los Angeles. In 1876 the Southern Pacific Railroad tracks were laid near the town but it remained quietly unknown to the outside world until 1913, when its healthy climate and pleasant surroundings began to attract visitors. In 1915 its first schoolhouse was built, and in 1938 it was large enough to receive its charter as a city. During World War II the adjacent region was used as a desert combat training center. Today its fame rests largely on its popularity as a resort. Visualize a beautiful mountain background, undulating desert covered with modern homes, palm trees, 7,000 swimming pools, luxurious clubs and hotels, add to that a touch of Hollywood glamour, and you'll have a general idea of Palm Springs. Permanent population about 36,000. However, winter population of the surrounding Coachella Valley is approximately 150,000. Principal streets are Palm Canyon Drive and Indian Avenue.

WHAT TO SEE

The desert fauna and flora in the area interest many visitors. The **Palm Springs Desert Museum** has exhibits of the plants and animals of the Southwest. Unusual birds include the nighthawk, rock wren, road runner, and poorwill; there are bighorn sheep in the mountains and coyotes on the plains. Common flora are bushes, cholla cactus, and sage; the largest concentration of smoke trees in the US is about 4 miles away. The Washingtonia palms in the nearby canyons are of great interest. Parks and zoos include the **Ruth Hardy Park** and **Moorton's Desertland Botanical Gardens** on South Palm Canyon Drive.

The **Palm Springs Aerial Tramway**, 6 miles from the center of town, carries 80 passengers at a time from 2,643-foot level of **Mt San Jacinto** to the 8,516-foot level and offers truly spectacular views. Beautiful stations at both terminals have shops, restaurants and observation terraces. **Palm Canyon,** 6 miles south, has a forest of Washingtonia palms estimated to be over 1,000 years old. **Andreas Canyon** is 5 miles south, where sparkling water courses over great boulders. **Tahquitz Falls,** just south of Palm Springs is where melting snow forms a great veil of water during the winter and spring. This water occasionally contains high bacteria counts and may not be drunk. The date groves at **Indio** are 26 miles southeast.

ACCOMMODATIONS

Palm Springs has become increasingly popular during the summer months when hotel rates are substantially lower, but the major tourist activity is from September through June, with the height of the season from December through mid-April. There are more than 200 hotels in the city, with winter season rates among the larger, more expensive and luxurious ones ranging from $28-375 per person. In this category are the **Canyon Hotel** with 18-hole championship golf course, **Gene Autry's, Palm Springs Spa, Hilton Riviera Hotel,** the **Sheraton-Oasis, Sheraton Plaza.** Small but luxurious are **La Siesta Villas, La Marcha,** and **Orchid Tree Hotel.** Large and less expensive are the **Dunes, Hyatt Lodge, Marriott's Rancho Las Palmas Resort, Ramada Inn, Royal Inn** and **Sands,** all S$50/D$80 up. Hotel Tax: 6%. The Chamber of Commerce provides assistance to tourists. (714) 325-1577, especially important in making hotel reservations. Summer rates in Palm Springs often drop to half their winter cost.

RESTAURANTS

Good restaurants and a variety of cuisines are available, though some close during the summer. Mexican food: **Casa Camargo, El Torrido** and the **Sombrero Room.** French and German: **La Petite Marmite, Garden Room** in the Palm Springs Biltmore, **Mr. A's.** Cantonese: **Lamb's Gardens, Don the Beachcomber's.** Steak, chops: **Dominick's, Kobe Steak House.** Italian: **Casa Roma, Banducci's Bit of Italy** and **Georgio's.** There are good hotel dining rooms and many snack bars throughout the city.

ENTERTAINMENT

Dancing or entertainment at **Palm Springs Spa, Biltmore, Laff Stop, Ocotillo Lodge, Sheraton-Oasis, Riviera** and **Canyon Hotel,** all moderate to expensive.

ARTS AND MUSIC

The **Desert Museum** has desert exhibits, field trips; numerous galleries feature paintings by local artists. Open 10-5 Tue through Sat. Admission $1.50, children free.

SHOPPING

The principal stores are **I Magnin, J Magnin, Silverwoods, Bullock's Wilshire, Saks Fifth Avenue, Robinson's, W and J Sloan, J. C. Penney,** and **Desmond's,** all branches of Los Angeles stores. There are also many fine specialty shops including **Neal's Apparel** for women's clothing, the **Oasis,** fine men's wear, and **Walker Scott.** Best buys are western and resort clothes and Indian jewelry.

SPORTS

There are rodeos, horse shows, polo matches, golf and tennis tournaments. Palm Springs has 40 public and private golf courses and numerous tennis courts. Swimming is a favorite sport. The fishing season is from 1 May to 31 October. There is some hunting for duck, doves, quail, deer and rabbits. For additional information, contact the Palm Springs Convention & Visitors Bureau, 714-327-8411.

CALENDAR OF EVENTS

Palm Springs Mounted Police Rodeo, January; **Riverside County Fair and Date Festival,** in Indio, 26 miles southeast, and the annual **Bob Hope**

Golf Classic, a 5-day, 90-hole tournament played over 4 courses, January; **Desert Circus Week,** fanfare, parades, March; and **Colgate Dinah Shore Golf Tournament,** April.

WHERE TO GO NEARBY

Joshua Tree National Monument, 60 miles east, is open all year round; the park has beautiful rock formations and is home of the Joshua trees which bear waxy white blooms each spring. **Mt San Jacinto State Park,** 55 miles away, has lovely woodlands, mountains, hiking and camping grounds.

SAN DIEGO

San Diego is in southern California on the Mexican border, facing San Diego Bay and the Pacific Ocean. It was here the first European set foot in California—Juan Cabrillo, a Portuguese explorer in the service of Spain, in 1542. In 1769 the Spanish priest Father Junipero Serra established the first of his California missions here, calling it San Diego de Alcala. In 1825 it became the Mexican capital of California; in 1846, after the outbreak of the Mexican War, United States forces defeated the Mexicans at the Battle of San Pasqual and General Frémont took the city, raising the flag for the first time in California. San Diego was incorporated as a city in 1850 but lost its charter 2 years later when the community began to dwindle. With the building of the Sante Fe Railroad, however, the community revived and in 1872 was again chartered as a city. Today it is a major seaport and the headquarters of the Eleventh Naval District.

San Diego retains much of its old Spanish-Mexican atmosphere. Famous for its almost perfect climate, it has attracted tourists and permanent residents from all over the country. It is California's second largest city, population 874,826, with a total census figure of 1,859,623 for San Diego County.

WHAT TO SEE

Visit the adobe buildings in **Old Town San Diego State Historic Park,** the original site of the city. Here you'll find **Casa de Estudillo; Old Whaley House,** now a museum; and **Casa de Lopez,** historic landmark now a museum and candle shop. Particularly interesting is the **Mission San Diego de Alcala,** 7 miles from town. On **Point Loma,** near the spot where Cabrillo first set eyes on California, are the old **Lighthouse, Cabrillo National Monument** and cliffs. The *Star of India* at the San Diego waterfront is a nautical museum. Take the San Diego-Coronado Bay Bridge to Coronado to see **Hotel del Coronado,** built in the 1880s, and one of the showplaces of the resort area. Parks include beautiful **Balboa Park,** with the **Natural History Museum, Museum of Man, Aerospace Museum** and the **Reuben H. Fleet Space Theater** in the northeast part of town. The **San Diego Zoological Gardens** in the park is one of the world's best zoos, and has moving sidewalks and a "Skyfari" aerial tramway. Balboa Park has plants from all over the world; its **Rosecroft Begonia**

Gardens has rare tropical plants and driftwood displays. There is an aquarium at the **Scripps Institution of Oceanography** in La Jolla and **Sea World** in **Mission Bay Park.**

A typical 3-hour conducted tour of the San Diego district costs $8. There are also daily 2-hour cruises of San Diego Bay. Gray Line (231-9922) has guided tours of San Diego and vicinty, including the zoo, Sea World, Point Loma, and San Diego and Tijuana, Mexico. Cush Tours (293-7870) has a "Two Nation Vacation" package of 5 days and 4 nights in San Diego and Ensenada, Baja California, including car, lodging and attractions but not food at $124 per person. Scenic plane and helicopter flights, winery tours, and walking tours of the Old Town San Diego State Historic Park are available.

Principal school: **San Diego State University, University of California at San Diego, United States International University, University of San Diego** and 6 2-year junior colleges.

ACCOMMODATIONS

In the central area are **El Cortez** (232-0161, S$30/D$40), a leading hotel; **US Grant** (232-3120, S$32-43/D$36-43), older, convenient. On Shelter Island in San Diego Bay are **Kona Inn** (222-0421, S$34/D$44-52); **Half Moon Inn** (224-3411, S$49-55/D$59-65); **Shelter Island Inn** (222-0551, S$40-44/D$46-50). At Mission Bay are **Bahai Motor Hotel** (488-0551, S$44-50/D$44-52); **Hilton Hotel** at the Embaracadero, (276-4010, S$44-60/D$55-72); **Hyatt Islandia** (224-3541, S$43-67/D$58-82); **Vacation Village Hotel** (274-4630, S$52-68/D$60-78). At La Jolla, **The Inn at La Jolla** (454-6121, S$30-36/D$35-40); **La Jolla Travelodge** (454-0791, S$35-45/D$39-45); **La Jolla Village Inn** (453-5500, S$40-48/D$48-54), where one green fee gives you a choice of half a dozen courses to play golf, including world famous Torrey Pines; **La Valencia Hotel** (454-0771, S$55-67/D$63-75); **Royal Inn** (459-4461, S$43-55/D$48-60), and **Torrey Pines Inn** (453-4420, S$30-45/D$35-50). There are also many apartment hotels and motels within the city, in beach resort areas, and along the highways. The famous **Hotel del Coronado** (435-6611, S/D$49-125/DD$59-125) is reached from midtown San Diego by the San Diego-Coronado Bay Bridge. Conveniently located near the airport, are the **Sheraton Inn-Airport,** (291-6400, S$40-60/D$50-70); **Town and Country Hotel-Convention Center** (291-7131, S$45-60/D$50-65), and **Travelodge Tower** at Harbor Island, 3 minutes from airport (291-6700, S$49-69/D$70-90/DD$80-120). San Diego winter rates from October to May are lower than the summer rates quoted here. Hotel Tax: 6%.

RESTAURANTS

San Diego specializes in a variety of fresh seafood; Mexican dishes are also popular. Downtown there are the **Grill Room,** US Grant Hotel, very good, fairly expensive; **Fontaine Bleau Dining Room** at the Little America Westgate Hotel, superb food in superlative surroundings, expensive; **Lubach's,** on the waterfront; **Nino's** or **John Tarantino's,** Italian fare and seafood beside the bay; **Anthony's Star of the Sea Room,** very good, fairly expensive. In Coronado are the famous **Prince of Wales Grille** and **Coronado Chart House** at Hotel del Coronado; **Su Casa** and **La Casa Blanca Dining Room,** genuine Mexican food, attractive atmosphere, also the **Aztec Dining Rooms 1 & 2.** At La Jolla is **L'Escargot Restaurant,** French, **Anthony's Fish Grotto,** seafood, and **Top O'The Cove,** famous for seafood, and film and TV stars. At Mission Valley, **Benihana of Tokyo,** oriental food, moderate in price.

ENTERTAINMENT

Downtown: **El Cortez Hotel,** dancing nightly except Sunday in the **Sky Room; Mickie Finn's; America's No. 1 Speakeasy,** closed Sunday and Monday; **Backstage at the Off Broadway Theater,** after show entertainment. Shelter Island: **Bali Hai,** dancing, Polynesian floor show, nightly except Monday; **Shelter Island Inn,** dancing and entertainment nightly except Sunday; **Voyager Room,** Kona Inn, dancing nightly except Monday. Mission Bay: dancing or entertainment at **Hilton Inn, Islandia, Catamaran** and **Vacation Village.** Mission Valley: Master Host Inn has dancing nightly in the **Coral Room** and **Palais 500** has dancing and entertainment Tuesday through Saturday. Coronado: **Ocean Terrace Room** at Hotel del Coronado, dancing and entertainment Tuesday through Sunday.

ARTS AND MUSIC

The Old Globe Theater in Balboa Park, a replica of the one in London, offers the **National Shakespeare Festival** with professional actors in repertory during the summer. In Balboa Park are the **Fine Arts Gallery; House of Pacific Relations,** displays of national costumes, music and dances of various international groups; and the **Spanish Village,** arts and crafts. **Spreckels Outdoor Organ** gives free concerts during July and August; check with hotel or in newspapers for days and times of concerts. There are summer concerts in the **San Diego Bowl** and **San Diego State University. San Diego Civic Theater,** downtown community concourse, gives plays, musicals and concerts throughout the year. Cabaret-style **Coronado Playhouse** presents performances throughout the year. **Mission Playhouse,** in Old San Diego, presents theater-in-the-round all year. The **La Jolla Museum of Contemporary Art** features an extensive permanent collection and rotating exhibitions. Closed Mondays. Admission, $1.

SHOPPING

Downtown department stores include **Bullock's Wilshire, Robinson's** and **I Magnin,** open Monday through Saturday 9:30-5:30. Most shopping centers open 9:30-9 daily.

SPORTS

The **San Diego Padres** play professional baseball during the spring, summer and fall at the **San Diego Stadium.** College football games are played by the four local colleges. **San Diego Chargers,** professional National Football League team, also play at San Diego Stadium. **The San Diego Gulls** are the professional ice hockey team and the **San Diego Sockers** are the professional soccer team. Horse racing has a 42-day season from late July to mid-September at **Del Mar**; pari-mutuel betting. Jai alai games are played at the **Fronton Palacio** in Tijuana, Mexico. There is greyhound racing most nights of the year and thoroughbred horse racing on week-ends at **Caliente Race Course** in Tijuana and bullfights during the season from May through September. San Diego has 65 golf courses, both public and private. For swimming and skin diving, there are over 70 miles of fine ocean beaches. Water-skiing, sailing and boating are popular at **San Diego** and **Mission Bays**. San Diego is a good starting point for deep-sea fishing by chartered or party boats. Freshwater fishing is also available, and there are many opportunities for hunting in the mountains to the east.

CALENDAR OF EVENTS

Moby Dick Parade, annual migration of California grey whales, mid-December through April; **Annual Fishing Derbies,** deep-sea, late March through September; **San Diego National Shakespeare Festival,** 8 June through 9 September; **Southern California Exposition,** at Del Mar, 21 June through 4 July. There is also the **Corpus Christi Fiesta,** held annually in June, at Pala Mission, with open masses, processions, games and dances; Indian tribal dances annually in July at Mission San Luis Rey; **Trek to the Cross,** historic pageant, 10-11 July; **Old Mission Fiesta** at San Diego de Alcala, mid-July; **America's "finest city"** celebration is held in San Diego in August. **La Jolla Rough Water Swim and Aqua Fiesta,** early September; **Cabrillo Festival,** late September; **Annual Mother Goose Parade,** Sunday prior to Thanksgiving; **San Diego Bay Christmas Light Boat Parade,** 20 December. **Old Town Fiesta de la Primavera** in May; and **Fiesta de la Quadrilla** in December.

WHERE TO GO NEARBY

To the north are such delightful communities as **La Jolla, Carlsbad, Oceanside, Laguna Beach** and **Balboa;** all have hotels, motels or cottages offering good accommodations. Drive to **Mt Palomar,** 55 miles distant, site of the world's largest telescope. **Palomar Mountain State Park,** 63 miles north, near the Palomar Observatory, has beautiful mountains and trails; camping and picknicking. Across the bay from San Diego is **Coronado,** ideal for a vacation with its miles of beaches stretching south almost to the Mexican border. **Borrego Springs Desert Resort** is about 90 miles northeast. Pleasant trips may be made by automobile into Mexico, by way of **Tijuana,** about 15 miles south. People driving their own cars must get insurance coverage before going in, many losses are not covered. A good toll road runs from Tijuana south 60 miles to **Ensenada** with lovely oceanside scenery; bullfights, horse and dog races, jai alai games, Mexican souvenirs, and Mexican food abound in Tijuana. It is best to eat cooked food and drink bottled water.

State parks in the vicinity are **Cuyamaca Rancho State Park, Laguna Mountain Recreation Area** and **Cleveland National Forest,** approximately 45 miles northeast, all large forest areas with picnicking and camping facilities. **Anza-Borrego Desert State Park,** about 90 miles northeast; history, desert scenery and **Borrego Springs** resort area.

SAN FRANCISCO

San Francisco is on the central coast of California, on a peninsula bounded by the Pacific Ocean on the west, Golden Gate Bridge on the north, and San Francisco Bay on the east. Juan Cabrillo, a Portuguese explorer, may have sighted the bay in the early 16th century, and it is known that Sir Francis Drake sailed right by it in 1579; generally, credit for the discovery of the bay is given to Don Gaspar de Portola, who arrived in 1769.

In 1776 the Spanish established the mission and presidio of Santa Dolores and in 1777 the priest Father Junipero Serra set up the Mission of San Francisco, though the community was then called Yerba Buena. In 1806 the Russians sought to establish an outpost in the area from which they could supply their Alaskan possessions, but they settled for a spot 100 miles north which they eventually abandoned in 1841. In 1821 the region came under Mexican rule, but in 1846, after the outbreak of the Mexican War, the town was seized and occupied by US naval forces. In 1847 its name was changed to San Francisco.

With the discovery of gold in California in 1848 the town began to boom as a port of entry for thousands of prospectors, and chartered as a city in 1850. It gained further importance when it became the terminus of the Pony Express in 1860 and of the trans-continental railroad in 1869. The great earthquake and fire of 1906 destroyed much of the city but it rallied quickly and today is the banking and shipping capital of the West. In 1945 San Francisco gained the distinction of being the scene of the first organizational meeting of the United Nations Organization and of the signing of its charter.

Built on 40 hills between the mountains and the sea, San Francisco is a beautiful and sophisticated town. It is also a financial and business area of prime importance. In 1966 a Gallup poll in the US named San Francisco the city that most people would like to live in, and the city with the most beautiful setting. Many of its streets have steep grades and the weather is often on the damp side, but the loyalty of San Franciscans remains steadfast—and most visitors understand why. Population is 674,063.

WHAT TO SEE

Wandering about San Francisco can be fascinating. A 50¢ fare takes visitors anywhere on bus, cable car or trolley, and transferring from one to another is possible. The famous cable cars are undergoing restoration due to be completed 1984, however there are cable cars running at various times. Call Muni Railway, 673-6864, for directions and schedules. There are many conducted tours of the city. Gray Line (771-4000) has three morning or afternoon tours of the main points of interest for $9 adults; $4.50 children. Because the city is compact, it is easy to walk between major points of interest. **Chinatown,** the largest Chinese community outside Asia, is next to the shopping district around **Union Square;** the financial district and **Nob Hill** are near both. Gray Line has evening tours of Chinatown, with dinner $18.75 adults; $15.65 children, or without $10.50 adults; $7.40 children. **North Beach** section is the haunt of the "beat generation" of poets and writers. Near here and all within walking distance of each other are **Ghirardelli Square** with many little shops and restaurants; **The Cannery** with its maze of craft shops; and **Fisherman's Wharf,** famous for its atmosphere and seafood restaurants. Tours of the harbor by boat or helicopter available at the Wharf; do not miss the trip over to **Alcatraz,** the famous prison closed since 1963. Book in advance. Other points of interest include: **Civic Center,** with municipal, state and federal buildings and public library; the new **Davies Symphony Hall; Opera House;** the **San Francisco Museum of Modern Art,** in the Veterans Memorial Building; the **Ferry Building,** which houses the **World Trade Center; Japan Center; Telegraph Hill** with **Coit Tower; Cable Car Barn; Gold Gate Bridge,** connecting San Francisco with Marin County and the Redwood Highway; **San Francisco-Oakland Bay Bridge; Mission Dolores; Presidio,** a US military reservation; **Sigmund Stern Memorial Grove; Cliff House** and **Seal Rocks;** the Exploratorium at the **Palace of Fine Arts,** and the **Bay Area Rapid Transit System,** with sleek, silent, computer-run trains and stations decorated with mosaic murals.

Parks and zoos include the **Golden Gate Park** with over 1,000 acres of recreational facilities, a conservatory, planetarium, The Steinhart Aquarium, De Young Museum, Japanese Tea Garden and Stow Lake. **Lincoln Park** has fine views of San Francisco Bay ocean, also a golf course. **Aquatic Park** and **San Francisco Zoo.**

ACCOMMODATIONS

Leading hotels are the **Hyatt Regency** (788-1234, S$85-110/D$145-170), financial, Chinatown; **Miyako** (922-3200, S$62-82/D$82-102), Japantown, 1 mile west of Union Square; **San Francisco Hilton and Tower** (771-1400, S$61-81/D$113-133), centrally located; **Sheraton Palace** (392-8600, S$58-69/D$86-98), centrally located and famous for Garden Court. By Union Square, the **St Francis** (397-7000, S$60-75/D$120-145); the **Sir Francis Drake** (392-7755, S$59-69/D$89-99); **Hyatt** on Union Square (398-1234, S$85-105/D$120-140). In the downtown area are less expensive hotels: **Bellevue Hotel** (474-3600, S$54-60/D$68-74); **Californian** (885-2500, S$44-54/D$48-58); **Chancellor Hotel** (362-2004, S$34-38/D$38-42); **Commodore International** (855-2464, S$35-40/D$45-50); **El Cortez Hotel** (775-5000, S$34-40/D$38-44); **Manx** (421-7070, S$39-43/D$45-48); Perched on top of Nob Hill are the elegant **Fairmont Hotel** (772-5000, S$82-102/D$125-145), panoramic view of the city; **INTER·CONTINENTAL Mark Hopkins Hotel** (392-3434, S$85-100/D$115-130), with the famous "Top of the Mark" bar; **Stanford Court** (989-3500, S$88-108/D$118-138). One block from the Golden Gate Bridge is **Best Western Civic Center Motor Inn** (621-2826, S$40-45/D$50-55). Nearly a dozen state parks near the city have camping facilities. Hotel Tax: 6%.

RESTAURANTS

A gourmet's paradise of seafood restaurants is located on the docks of **Fisherman's Wharf**, port of San Francisco's fishing fleet. **Ghirardelli Square**, nearby, is a pleasant plaza of restaurants and shops built within the framework of a 19th-century chocolate factory overlooking the bay. Try the local shrimp, Dungeness crabs, California rex sole, abalone, sand dabs and clams; *cioppino*, a great local favorite, is a cross between a soup and a stew, made with several kinds of seafood. Of the hundreds of restaurants in the city, these are some of the better known: **Amelio's**, attractive, Italian food, fairly expensive; **Alfred's**, good for crab, steaks and Italian specialties, expensive; **Modesto Lanzone's**, Italian; **Doros**, Montgomery Street on Jackson Square, **Grison's Steak House**, on Van Ness Avenue, good, moderate to expensive; **House of Prime Rib**, on Van Ness Avenue, and **Ben Jonson**, in the Cannery, English fare. For French cuisine: **Alexis, Le Club**, classical French cuisine, Nob Hill, outstanding; **Fleur de Lys, La Bourgogne, Le Trianon, La Mirabelle** and **L'Orangerie, Le Central**, French Alsacienne, **Jacks**, in the financial district, popular for over a century, **La Cabana**, off in residential area but one of the finest. French-American cuisine: **Ernie's**, North Beach, beautifully decorated, serving French and Continental food; both in the rather expensive category, reservations advisable. Other distinctive restaurants include: **Trader Vic's** (and the original of the numerous Trader Vic's around the world), Cosmo Place, downtown; and **Imperial Palace**, strictly Chinese and located in Chinatown; **Blue Fox**, Merchant Street, downtown, Continental, expensive; **Rocca's**, Civic Center near Opera House, Italian-Continental cuisine; also for Italian cuisine, **Vanessi's**, one of the oldest and best, and **Original Joe's Restaurant**, Chestnut Street in the Marina area. For early American specialties try **North Beach Restaurant**. Reservations for most restaurants are essential.

For other foreign cuisine restaurants try these representative selections: **Omar Khayyam**, downtown, well-known for international specialties, **Cathay House, Kan's, Empress of China, Golden Pavilion, Tao Tao**, all in Chinatown, for gourmet Chinese cuisine. Also note the **Mandarin** and **Far East Café**. **India House**, Jackson Street, in Jackson Square area, and **Taj of India**, Pacific Avenue, North Beach, East Indian food. For Japanese cuisine: **Yamato Sukiyaki House**, California Street in Chinatown; **Nikko Sukiyaki**, Van Ness Avenue; **Bush Garden**, Bush Street, downtown; **Mingei Ya**, Union Street, with Japanese garden entrance; **Tokyo Sukiyaki**, Fishmerman's Wharf. **Schroeder's**, Front Street, in the financial district, established 1893, for German food; **Little Sweden**, O'Farrell Street, downtown for smorgasbord only. Other suggested dining places are **Rolf's**, Beach Street, opposite Aquatic Park, Continental cuisine in attractive dining room; on Telegraph Hill, the **Shadows**, with German-American food, and **Julius' Castle**, with a Continental menu, both have good views; **Ondine**, in Sausalito across the Bay, on the water's edge with a bay view. If you are downtown, **Tad's Steak House**, Powell Street, is a quick place for steaks. Seafood: **Alioto's**, since 1925, **Castagnola, Fisherman's Grotto, Franciscan, Tarantino's**, all on Fisherman's Wharf; **Bernstein's, Fish**

San Francisco's exquisite Golden Gate Bridge . . . one of the truly beautiful structures of the century.

Grotto, Powell Street, downtown; **Sam's Grill** and **Tadich Grill**, in the financial district. You can also find Greek, Mexican and Spanish restaurants, as well as other French, German, Italian, Swedish and Swiss restaurants in San Francisco. For inexpensive eating, try **El Sombrero**, great Mexican food; **Pam Pam East**, 24-hour coffee shop with savory food; **Lefty O'Doul's**, Hofbrau style meals; **The Hippo**, with an incredible variety of deluxe hamburgers; and the excellent **Connie's**, for a West Indian theme.

ENTERTAINMENT

Dancing at the Fairmont Hotel on Nob Hill, the St Francis and the Sir Francis Drake, downtown. Popular night spots include **McGoon's**, for dixieland and jazz; the **Boarding House** and **Great American Music Hall** both feature name bands and performers.

ARTS AND MUSIC

San Francisco Museum of Art, on the two top floors of the Veterans Memorial Building in Civic Center, specializes in modern and contemporary art; closed Monday. The **M. H. De Young Memorial Museum** in Golden Gate Park has an extensive collection of American and European art. In the west wing is the **Asian Art Museum** where the marvelous **Avery Brundage Collection** is housed. The **California Palace of the Legion of Honor** in a beautiful setting high on a bluff has a large collection of French art.

The **Maritime Museum,** at the foot of Polk Street, and the **National Maritime Museum,** at the foot of Hyde Street, have seafaring exhibits, the latter a floating museum of old-time shops. **Chinatown Wax Museum** depicts tales of old Chinatown.

The city has a rich musical life. The **San Francisco Symphony Orchestra** gives concerts from early December to late May. The **San Francisco Opera Company's** fall season lasts 11 weeks beginning in mid-September, with the spring season starting in February. The **San Francisco Ballet** performs in December and in the spring. Pop concerts are held at the Civic Auditorium during July and August. San Francisco is an active theatrical city, with regular professional productions given at the **Curran, Marines' Memorial, On Broadway Theater, Golden Gate, Alcazar, Phoenix, Little Fox** and the **Geary Theater,** home of the American Conservatory Theater. The universities in the area have frequent productions.

SHOPPING

Most stores are open until 9 on Monday evenings. Sutter St is the principal area for shopping around Union Square, as well as Market St. **Gump's,** a famed city landmark, has unusual antiques and art objects and specializes in Oriental goods. Among other stores are **I Magnin, Macy's, Emporium, Joseph Magnin, Liberty House** and branches of New York stores such as **Brooks Brothers, Dunhill's, Saks Fifth Avenue,** and **Tiffany's.** Shop in Chinatown; at the **Japan Center;** on **Ghirardelli Square,** former chocolate factory, now with shops and restaurants. **The Cannery,** formerly a fruit-packing plant, now housing specialty shops and restaurants; and at **Cost Plus Imports,** on Taylor Street, near Fisherman's Wharf, which carries exotic and inexpensive imports. **Upper Grant Avenue** in North Beach has specialty shops for leather and other handcrafted gift items and apparel. Good regional buys are needlework, leathercrafts, objets d'art, and oriental goods.

SPORTS

Professional baseball is played by the **San Francisco Giants** at **Candlestick Park** and by the **Oakland Athletics** at **Oakland Coliseum;** professional football games at Candlestick Park by **San Francisco "49ers"** during the fall season and **Oakland Raiders** at Oakland Coliseum. The **Warriors** are the pro basketball team, playing at the Oakland Coliseum. San Francisco is represented in women's professional basketball by the **Pioneers.** The city also has a men's professional soccer team, the **Fox.** College athletic events, including football, are scheduled at the **University of California at Berkeley** and at **Stanford University** in Palo Alto. There is horse racing at **Golden Gate Fields** in Albany and at **Bay Meadows** in San Mateo and pari-mutuel betting. Boxing and wrestling matches, rodeos and other sporting events take place at the **Cow Palace.**

Other sports include archery, bowling, golf, horseback riding, ice skating, roller skating, swimming, tennis. Deep-sea fishing in nearby waters is often very good; freshwater fishing is variable. Check your hotel or motel and local papers to find out what's "running."

CALENDAR OF EVENTS

San Francisco National Sports and Boat Show, Cow Palace, January; **Chinese New Year Festival,** January or February, depending on year; **California Home Furnishings and Decorating Show,** Brooks Hall, March to April; **St Patrick's Day Parade,** March; **Easter Sunrise Service,** Mt Davidson; **Cherry Trees in Bloom,** Japanese Tea Garden, Golden Gate Park, first week in April; **Nihonmachi Cherry Blossom Festival,** Japan Center mid-April. **Latin American Fiesta and Parade,** early May; **Fourth of July** celebration and fireworks display, Crisp Field, Presidio. **Municipal Outdoor Art Festival,** September; **Columbus Day Celebration,** a 4-day fiesta centered on Columbus Day weekend. **San Francisco International Film Festival,** Palace of Fine Arts Theater, mid-October; **Imported Automobile show,** Brooks Hall, late November.

WHERE TO GO NEARBY

A day at Sausalito is worthwhile. Ferries operate throughout the day. Shop and leisurely explore this seaside resort. The **Golden Gate National Recreation Area** is an area of 34,000 acres of land and water encompassing greater San Francisco and Oakland. It offers many recreational facilities as well as historical points of interest, and the Golden Gate Bridge. Suggestions for 1 day trips in the general area include **Mt Tamalpais** and **Point Reyes National Seashore,** located 25 miles north of the city, for those who enjoy outdoor life. Slightly to the northeast of Mt Tamalpais are **Sonoma** and **Napa** valleys, with vineyards and beautiful scenery; be sure to visit one of the wineries. (A guide for the wineries, both north and south, is available at the Convention and Visitors' Bureau.) **Muir Woods National Monument,** just 17 miles north, with giant redwood trees may be seen with a half-day tour by Grayline or Muir Woods. Much farther north is the redwood region with the popular **Russian River** and **Clear Lake** resort areas; northeast of this district is **Mt Shasta** and its surrounding lakes and streams.

California has many national parks including **Redwood, Sequoia,** and **Kings Canyon,** with giant trees, and **Lassen Volcanic National Park,** which until the eruption of **Mt St Helens** in Washington State, had been the only active (currently dormant) volcano in the mainland US. These should not be missed by any visitor, although they are some distance from San Francisco. San Francisco is a good starting point for an extended trip to beautiful **Yosemite National Park** to the east. There are also 10 state parks within a radius of 150 miles of San Francisco, all with camping facilities. Several are situated along the coast, some in the famous redwood groves.

LASSEN VOLCANIC NATIONAL PARK

The park is at the junction of the Sierra Nevada and Cascade mountains, about 100 miles due north of Sacramento. It's best in summer, but there is a lively winter-sports center for skiers of every proficiency near the Sulphur Works entrance.

Lassen Peak volcanos, now dormant, erupted in 1914 and continued to belch steam and lava for 7 years. The park is exciting with hot springs, bubbling mudpots, seam-spouting fumaroles, lava flows, boiling lakes and volcanic cones. It is important to stay on the marked trails. **Lassen Park Road,** open June to October, winds up and down mountains for nearly 30 miles, connecting the southern and northern entrance stations on the west side of the park. In the **Sulphur Works** thermal area, **Bumpass Hell,** largest hot springs in the park, is reached in a 2½ hour round-trip hike from the road along a trail fringed with alpine flowers; **Lassen Peak Trail** can be conquered in a 3-5 hour round-trip to the 10,457-foot summit. **Summit Lake** is a popular campground with nightly nature programs, fishing; **Devastated Area** is where a forestry program is trying to soften the bleakness of an area totally stripped of life by 1915 lava flows; **Chaos Crags, Jumbles,** and **Dwarf Forest,** are in a turbulent-looking region formed by lava plugs pushing up through vents in the earth and subsequent volcanic explosions and avalanches; there are valiant little conifers struggling up among the rocks. Other points of interest are **Lily Pond Nature Trail** and **Reflection Lake.** The eastern part of the park is traversed on foot or horseback, although there are adequate roads to **Butte Lake,** which is near the barren **Cinder Cone** in a region of lava beds and colorful volanic ash dunes; also to **Horseshoe** and **Juniper** lakes; and to **Drakesbad** near **Boiling Springs Lake.** A fishing license is required and California laws must be observed if you want to catch trout in the many lakes and streams. Rowboats, canoes and other non-motorized boats may be used on most lakes. **Drakesbad Guest Ranch** (tel: (916) 595-3306 or (916) Drakesbad 2 via Susanville operator, S$37/D$68; bungalows S$42.50/D$79.50) is situated in an isolated valley within the park, while **Mineral Lodge** (916-595-4422, a private operation with accommodation fees subject to change)

REDWOOD NATIONAL PARK

May to October is the best time for a visit to avoid coastal fog. The world's tallest trees are the mighty redwoods *(Sequoia sempervirens)*, which grow 300 or more feet tall; some are 2,000 years old. The highway through the park is shadowed by their towering immensity. The tallest trees measured by the National Geographic Society in 1963, are found along **Emerald Mile**, where in summer you can hike off **Bald Hills Road**, half a mile from the US 101 turnoff, to **Redwood Creek**, southeast of the Prairie Creek section. About 2 miles up Bald Hills Road is the trail head for a very pleasant short hike through **Lady Bird Johnson Grove** to **Dedication Site**. One of the finest trees is in the northern **Jedediah Smith Redwoods State Park** area; it stands 320 feet high and is 21 feet in diameter. **Gold Bluff Beach**, which has campsites and naturalist programs in summer, is a refuge for Roosevelt elk, and the Pacific coast sand here is flecked with genuine gold flakes. There is great fishing for salmon, trout and steelhead in park streams. When this park was created on 2 October 1968, it was the culmination of a 90-year fight to acquire and protect the gigantic redwoods, and the acquisition of private lands cost more than all the other national parks combined. The headquarters for **Redwood National Park** is located in Crescent City. Information, exhibits, interpretive publications, and programs are available there. For 24-hour information about the park, telephone (707) 464-6101.

There is a wide choice of established campgrounds in the state parks of **Del Norte Coast, Jedediah Smith Redwoods** and **Prairie Creek** which, with the addition of 30,512 acres of privately owned lands, make up the country's newest national park. **Crescent City**, near the north end, is a popular resort with good motels.

SEQUOIA AND KINGS CANYON NATIONAL PARKS

Generals Highway, a magnificently scenic 47-mile route, begins at Ash Mountain entrance to this magnificent park. Shooting up on your right is **Moro Rock**, an unusual monolith 6,700 feet high with a stairway to the top. Stop at the **Lodgepole Visitor Center** for information on the park's geological features. The **Giant Forest** contains some of the most immense sequoias; most massive living thing is **General Sherman Tree**, 272 feet tall, 101.6 feet in diameter, and estimated to be 3,500 years old. Beyond is **Wolverton**, where there are slopes in winter for skiers of all standards. Among wilderness hikes in this area is the ranger-conducted tour in summer through lovely **Crystal Cave**. The **General Grant** and **Redwood Mountain Groves** area contains the mighty **General Grant Tree, General Lee** and **Hart Tree**, among other titans, which, despite their great ages, continue to produce fertile seeds that sprout into young Christmas tree-shaped sequoias. Here too is the **Centennial Stump** of the tree felled for the 1875 Philadelphia World's Fair, and nearby is **Big Stump Basin** with the remains of early logging depredation before John Muir and other naturalists saved the trees. Beyond the highway, partially closed in winter, is the steep-walled valley of **Kings Canyon** leading to **Cedar Grove**, information center and take-off point for mountain trails. The high country can be explored only on foot or with the help of pack and saddle horses which can be hired at many places in the park. The superb mountain scenery culminates in **Mt Whitney**, 14,495 feet, the highest point in North America outside of Alaska. Mt Whitney can be climbed by anyone in good physical condition. There is a trail all the way to the top. The two parks, blending into an area about 65 miles long, have a primitive grandeur in which wildlife lives as freely as it has for thousands of years.

Tourist facilities, including accommodations, here from late May, when high mountain passes become traversable, to mid-September, but Generals Highway, leading to the biggest sequoia trees, is kept clear year round, except for short periods during heavy snowstorms. Advance reservations should be made for housekeeping cabins or rooms in the lodges; most are open from late May to mid-September, some all year. There are 12 major campgrounds, 5 easily accessible to trailers; 14-day stay limit. Most campgrounds are open from 1 June until September snows, but **Potwisha Camp** is open all year. Reservations for facilities, ranging from cabins to superior motels and cabins, can be made by calling Sequoia National Park (209-565-3373, and Grant Grove (King's Canyon National Park) (209-335-2314). Rates are reasonable but subject to change without notice, (S/D$14-32) at Sequoia and at Kings Canyon. Other accommodations in the area include: **Best Western Holiday Lodge** (561-4119, S$19-27/D$22-32); **Giant Forest Lodge** (565-3373, S/D$24); **Grant Grove Lodge** (335-2314, S/D$21.50); **M Bar J Ranch** (337-2513, S$38/D$70), **Stony Creek Village** (565-3373, S$25) and situated between two of the largest trees in the world. Rates at private lodges usually change from year to year, depending on the season.

YOSEMITE NATIONAL PARK

The park is in the Sierra Nevada, about a 5-hour drive due east of San Francisco. In May and June, melting snows become thundering cascades so tremendous that Yosemite Valley throbs with their pounding, while dogwood, azalea, fern and jupines spring to life and bears emerge from hibernation. From mid-June to early September all park facilities are in full swing. July and August are glorious in the high Sierra, but be prepared for cold nights. In September and October the park seems washed in gold and the air fairly sparkles. Under a mantle of snow and low clouds the mountains and high meadows are silent and incredibly beautiful. Each season in Yosemite has its own loveliness. All backpacking requires permit, some areas close during high fire-danger time.

Upper Yosemite Falls continues with a constant cascade of clear waters in one of the world's most scenic parks.

Yosemite Valley, 7 miles long and about a mile wide, is enclosed by cliffs rising 2,000 to 4,000 feet high. Here, early in the season, you'll see—and hear—the **Upper** and **Lower Yosemite Falls** plunging a total of 2,425 feet. Less high but remarkably graceful are the famous **Bridalveil, Vernal, Illilouette, Nevada** and **Ribbon** falls. Massive rock formations rise in bold granite precipices to dominate the skyline—**El Capitan, North Dome, Half Dome, Three Brothers, Cathedral Spires,** and others. The **Yosemite Museum** is most informative about the park's geologic formations, the 220 species of birds, 75 species of mammals, its huge trees and lovely flowers. Schedules are posted here for campfire programs throughout the park and for ranger-naturalist conducted hikes. For a tremendous panoramic view of Yosemite Valley, look down upon it 3,254 feet below from **Glacier Point,** open May to October. **Mariposa Grove,** at the south entrance, is full of immense sequoias. The northbound highways joins Glacier Point Road to **Badger Pass,** a major winter sports resort from mid-December to mid-April. **Tioga Road,** open summer until October snows, is 8,000 to 10,000 feet high, with plants, wildlife and temperatures similar to those in Canada's Hudson Bay region. Follow the 5½-mile trail down from the road to **Waterwheel Falls,** fed from the Tuolumne River. Saddle horses can be hired at many points in the park. There are bus tours into the park the year round from Merced and Fresno. From San Francisco by car take Interstate 580, then Interstate 5 to the Gustine off-ramp and State Highway 140 to Yosemite Valley. From Los Angeles, take Highway 99 to Fresno, then Highway 41 from Fresno. Yosemite Transportation System provides connecting bus service on to Yosemite from Merced and Fresno for those wishing to ride Amtrak from San Francisco or Los Angeles to either of those two cities. And Greyhound or Continental service is available to Merced or Fresno. Also scheduled flights are available to these cities. Between 1 May and 30 Sept., the Yosemite Transportation System links Yosemite with Merced, Fresno and Lee Vining on a daily basis. Reservations for transportation should be made at least 24 hours in advance by calling (209) 373-4171.

Yosemite Lodge and **Curry Village** are open year round, and the luxurious **Ahwahnee Hotel** closes for only a week or two after Thanksgiving, reopening before Christmas. Other hotels and lodges are open from mid-May or mid-June until just after Labor Day; advance reservations imperative in the summer and highly advisable at other times. Excellent camps in the high mountains greet hikers and horseback explorers with hot showers and well-prepared meals. There are also 2,400 campsites in the park; 7-day stay limit in Yosemite Valley, 14 days elsewhere from 1 June to 15 September, 30 days the rest of the season. Special trailer park at **Wawona.** Family tent, cabin accommodations at Curry Village and at **Housekeeping Camp** on the Merced River. In Yosemite National Park accommodations are available at **The Ahwanee** (393-4171, S$62/D$70); **Curry Village** (373-4171, Rooms $33/Cabins $17-26/Tents $12.50), and **Yosemite Lodge** (373-4171, S/D$32-42, Cabins $17-26).

FURTHER STATE INFORMATION

State Office of Visitor Service, P.O. Box 1499, Sacramento, CA 95805. **Department of Commerce,** Division of Tourism, 1400 Tenth Street, Sacramento, CA 95814. Hunting and Fishing: **Department of Fish and Game,** 1416 Ninth Street, Sacramento, CA 95814. **Sacramento Convention & Visitors' Bureau,** 1100 14th Street, Sacramento, CA 95814. **Southern California Visitors' Council,** 705 West Seventh Street, Los Angeles, CA 90017. **Beverly Hills Visitors and Convention Bureau,** 239 S. Beverly Drive, Beverly Hills CA 90212 (213) 271-8174; **Carmel Business Association,** PO Box 444, Carmel, CA. **Monterey Peninsula Chamber of Commerce,** PO Box 1770, Monterey, CA 93940. **Palm Springs Convention and Visitors' Center,** Municipal Airport Terminal, Palm Springs, CA 92262. **San Diego Convention and Visitors Bureau,** 1200 Third Avenue, Security Pacific Plaza, San Diego, CA 92101. **San Francisco Convention and Visitors' Bureau,** Fox Plaza, 1390 Market Street, San Francisco, CA 94102. National Parks: **National Park Service,** 450 Golden Gate Avenue, Box 36063, San Francisco, CA 94102. State Parks: *California State Park System* published by **State Department of Parks and Recreation,** PO Box 2390, Sacramento, CA 95811. **Lassen Volcanic National Park,** Superintendent, Mineral, CA 96063. **Redwood National Park,** Superintendent, Drawer N, 501 "H" Street, Crescent City, CA 95531; other information stations at Orick and Klamath. **Sequoia and Kings Canyon Parks,** Superintendent, Three Rivers, CA 93271. For overnight reservations, **Government Services, Inc.,** Sequoia National Park, CA 93262 or Kings Canyon National Park, CA 93633; call (209) 565-3373. **Yosemite National Park,** Superintendent, CA 95389. **Pan Am** offices: 222 Stockton Street, San Francisco, CA 94108 and One California Street, San Francisco, CA 94111 (tel: 626-6600) and at San Francisco International Airport (tel: 397-5200); 601 South Grand Avenue, Los Angeles, CA 90017 (tel: 381-5771); 222 Broadway, San Diego, CA 92101 (tel: 234-7321).

Consulates in Los Angeles: Argentina, Australia, Austria, Belgium, Bolivia, Brazil, Canada, Chile, Colombia, Costa Rica, Denmark, Dominican Republic, Ecuador, El Salvador, Estonia, Finland, France, Germany, Great Britain, Guatamala, Guyana, Honduras, Iceland, Israel, Italy, Jamaica, Japan, Korea, Latvia, Lebanon, Liberia, Lithuania, Malta, Mexico, Netherlands, Nicaragua, Norway, Panama, Peru, Philippines, Portugal, Republic of China, Spain, Sri Lanka, Sweden, Switzerland, Thailand, Turkey, Venezuela, and Western Samoa.

In San Francisco: Argentina, Australia, Austria, Belgium, Boliva, Brazil, Canada, Chile, Colombia, Costa Rica, Cyprus, Denmark, Dominican Republic, Ecuador, Egypt, El Salvador, Fiji, Finland, France, Germany, Great Britain, Greece, Guatamala, Haiti, Honduras, Iceland, India, Indonesia, Ireland, Italy, Japan, Republic of Korea, Lesotho, Liberia, Republic of Malawi, Malaysia, Malta, Mexico, Monaco, Republic of Nauru, Nepal, Netherlands, New Zealand, Nigeria, Norway, Panama, Paraguay, People's Republic of China, Peru, Philippines, Portugal, Senegal, South Africa, Spain, Sweden, Switzerland, Tunisia, Turkey, Union of Soviet Socialist Republics, Uruguay, Venezuela, Yugoslavia.

In San Diego: Belgium, Chile, Colombia, Costa Rica, Denmark, El Salvador, Finland, France, Germany, Guatemala, Honduras, Italy, Japan, Mexico, Netherlands, Norway, Panama, Sweden.

USEFUL TELEPHONE NUMBERS
Los Angeles

Police	625-3311
Fire	384-3131
Ambulance	483-6721
Beverly Hospital	723-0951
Bella Vista Hospital	723-7241
Chamber of Commerce	629-0711
Legal Aid	487-3320
Los Angeles Tours	346-0673
Pan Am Reservations	381-5771

San Diego

Police	236-5911
Fire	238-1212
Ambulance	236-5911
Community Hospital	234-4341
Mercy Hospital	294-8111
Legal Aid Society	232-2214
Chamber of Commerce	232-0124
Tourist Information	435-3356
Pan Am Reservations	234-7321

San Francisco

Police	553-0123
Fire	861-8020
Ambulance	431-2800
St Luke's Hospital	647-8600
Mount Zion Hospital	567-6600
Legal Aid	495-7374
Chamber of Commerce	392-4511
Tourist Information	433-4109
Pan Am Reservations	626-6600

Palm Springs

Police & Fire	327-1441
Ambulance	327-1313
Palm Springs Medical Center	323-4211
Desert Hospital	323-6251
Dental Emergency	325-5928
Legal Clinic	568-1162
Chamber of Commerce	325-1577
Visitors Information	329-6403
Pan Am Reservations	(800) 262-1801

Colorado

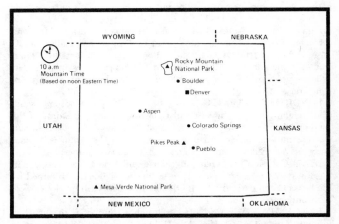

Area	104,247 square miles	**Population**	2,772,000
Capital	Denver	**Sales Tax**	3%

Weather	Jan	Feb	Mar	Apr	May	Jun	Jul	Aug	Sep	Oct	Nov	Dec
Av Temp (°C)	−2	0	2	8	13	19	23	22	17	11	3	−2
Days Rain/Snow	6	6	8	9	10	9	9	8	6	5	5	5

Gold and silver were lures to early visitors, but today the mountains and scenery of Colorado are the chief attractions. There are more than 1,140 peaks above 10,000 feet, and mountain resorts have open-slope skiing of the highest international standards.

In 1806 Captain Zebulon Pike, a US Army officer, made an unsuccessful assault on one of the state's highest mountains, failed and said that it could never be climbed. The summit was reached a few years later but not by Pike, although it was named after him. **Pike's Peak,** one of the most conspicuous in the Rocky Mountains, is now a national attraction. It inspired Katherine Lee Bates to write the song *America the Beautiful*. By the spring of 1859, when it seemed that most of the country was making for Colorado in the quest for gold, many traveled with the slogan "Pike's Peak or Bust". Mining towns sprang up everywhere but, by the time the boom had passed, the state had been more or less permanently settled.

The **NORTHEASTERN** part of the state is dominated by Colorado's share of the Great American Plains, an impressive expanse of waving buffalo grass, dotted with prairie dog villages, and still roamed by herds of antelope. Entering the state on I-70 north of Burlington is the **Bonny Reservoir,** surrounded by an expanse of wildflowers and grasses, where there is year-round water skiing, fishing, boating, and hunting in season. **Fort Morgan,** on I-76, is the site of the **Jackson State Recreation Area,** which offers camping, fishing, and swimming. **Sterling,** in the northeast corner, was a stop for westward-bound settlers, and you can trace their route at the **Overland Trail Museum.** Further west on CO 14 outside Sterling is **Pawnee National Grasslands,** teeming with prairie birds and other mountain and plain wildlife. **Fort Collins,** at the junction of CO 14 and I-25, spans the **Cache la Poudre River,** known as Colorado's "**Trout Route.**" **Colorado State University** and the **Pioneer Museum,** with its collection of Indian artifacts, are also here. The **University of Northern Colorado** is at **Greeley.**

In **NORTH CENTRAL** Colorado, **Boulder** has the handsome, sandstone buildings of the **University of Colorado,** with the backdrop of the **Flatiron Mountain Range** rising behind it. The university boasts an outstanding museum on early man and geological samples. Skiing is 16 miles away at **Lake Eldora** from November to April. Two of the most scenic drives in Colorado, the **Trail Ridge Road** and **Bear Lake Road,** are in the **Rocky Mountain National Park** northwest of Boulder. Rimmed by the peaks of the park, the town of **Estes Park** offers a tramway view of the **Continental Divide.**

In **NORTHWESTERN** Colorado, **Steamboat Springs** is the gateway to **Routt National Forest. Howelsen Hill** here offers fine skiing for novice and expert. The **Winter Carnival** in Steamboat Springs is held the second week in February. **Craig,** the center of Colorado's northwest, is known for its **Ride 'n Tide Days Rodeo,** the third weekend in July, and for the deep canyons of the **Green** and **Yampa** rivers.

Continuing south on CO 13, then west on I-70, you will find **Grand Junction,** the hub of Colorado's Western Slope. **Grand Mesa** is the world's largest flat-top mountain, less than an hour's drive away. **Colorado National Monument,** an area of eroded and brilliantly colored rock formations, is 10 miles west off I-70. Heading east on I-70, you'll come into the **White River National Forest** at **Glenwood Springs,** where you can join jeep tours or hunt, fish, and camp. **Sunlight Ski Area** is open from late November to early April; see the **Vapor Cave Baths** and **Glenwood Hot Springs Pools.**

Aspen, to the southeast, is popular for hiking, climbing, horseback riding, swimming, fishing, and pack trips as well as snow skiing. It is well-known as a cultural center: **Ballet West, Aspen Theatre Institute,** and the **Center of the Eye Photography School** are located here. The charm of old days is still evident in Victorian landmarks such as **Hotel Jerome,** the **Red Onion,** and **Wheeler Opera House.** The **Aspen Music Festival and School** are held from late June through August. In midtown, try **Aspen Square** (925-1000, S$44-80/D$44-72 summer; S$70-120/D$70-120 winter), year round condominium; **Boomerang Lodge** (925-3416, S$30-38/D$36-42 summer; S$70-74/D$70-82 winter), small, modern, open

The slopes at Aspen offer exciting challenge to skiers of every level of ability, from the beginner to the skilled world-class skier.

year round as is the **Continental Inn** (925-1150, S$42-48/D$42-48 summer; S$68-up/D$68-up winter); **Fifth Avenue Condominiums** (925-2260, S$60/D$60 summer; S$90/D$130 winter) 3-day minimum, has a variety of accommodations. One and a half miles northwest on CO 82 is **Pomegranate Inn** (925-2700, S$40-70/D$40-70 summer; S$70-100/D$70-100 winter), with rooms decorated in the style of the late 1800s, riding stables, and other sports facilities. Among many good restaurants in Aspen, try the **Copper Kettle, Arthur's Chinese, Guido's Swiss Inn** and **Jerome Hotel** for an international gourmet menu, and **Skiers' Chalet Steak House,** a favorite family dining spot.

Vail, part Tyrolean and part Old West, is another top skiing and year-round resort community in the **White River National Forest;** hunting in season, as well as golf, tennis, riding, swimming, jeep trips in summer, sleigh rides in winter, and alpine wildflower safaris. From mid-November to mid-April, rates at Vail's elegant hotels are at a peak. **Christiania-at-Vail, Kiandra/Talisman Lodge,** the **Lodge at Vail, Mountain Haus, Ram's Horn Lodge,** and **Talisman Lodge** are about S$40-48/D$50-62 summer; S$70-90/D$90-140 winter. **Beaver Creek,** a SuperSki Resort developed by Vail Associates east of Vail, with accommodations and amenities surpassing its parent resort. **Leadville,** south of Vail on US 24, is the highest incorporated city in the US, standing at an elevation of 10,200 feet; it earns the nickname of *"Cloud City".* See **Matchless Mine, Tabor House, Baby Doe Cabin, Tabor Opera House, Vendome Hotel, House with the Eye, Healy House,** and the **Dexter Cabin,** all maintained by the State Historical Society.

High in the Rockies, near the Continental Divide, is **Breckenridge,** where you can ski six months in the year or hunt and fish in season. The **Little Britches Rodeo** is the first week of August; the **Ullr Dag Winter Festival** the first week of February. Moving farther north, you can relax in the silence of the peaks rimming **Dillon Reservoir** or ski in alpine country at **Arapahoe Basin Ski Area,** 12 miles east on US 6, November to May. North of I-70 is **Central City,** a historic mining town. Don't miss the famous **"Face on the Bar Room Floor"** in the Teller House Hotel and relive mining days at the **Central Gold Mine and Museum.** There are outstanding productions at the **Central City Opera and Drama Festival,** where stars from the Metropolitan Opera and films appear during the summer. **Golden,** on US 6, once the capital of Colorado Territory, is now the home of the well-known **Colorado School of Mines.** An outstanding **Geological Museum** is on the campus. The **Lariat Trail,** a winding, precipitous route leading to the top of **Lookout Mountain** and **Buffalo Bill Cody's Museum** and grave begins here.

In **CENTRAL** Colorado, **Colorado Springs** claims to be one of the five most beautiful cities in the US. Named for the numerous mineral springs in the area, the town is an important cultural, tourist, and military center. The **North American Air Defense Command** has its headquarters here, along with the **United States Air Force Academy;** open to visitors. Downtown hotels include **Antler's Plaza** (473-5600, S$38-46/D$46-54, **Four Seasons Motor Inn** (576-5900, S$40/D$48 summer; S$47/D$57 winter); and the **Hilton Inn** (598-7656, S$40/D$48 summer, S$32/D$40 winter). Five miles southwest of downtown on CO 122, one of the world's finest resorts, **The Broadmoor** (634-7711, S$75-110/D$75-110 summer; S$47-70/D$49-70 winter), has 36 holes of golf, tennis, year round ice skating, snow skiing, sightseeing and the nearby **Cheyenne Mountain Zoo.** The **Colorado Springs Fine Arts Center** has a fine southwestern religious, folk and Indian art collection. The **Opera Association, Choral Society, Symphony Orchestra, Civic Players, Broadmoor International Theater** and **Town Hall** sponsor outstanding presentations.

South on I-25 is the industrial city of **Pueblo,** to which the **Colorado State Fair** in late August draws thousands of visitors. There's also a good rodeo in summer. Nearby is **San Isabel National Forest,** one of the West's most extensive mountain playgrounds. **Canon City,** on US 50, is the center of a recreation area focusing on **Royal Gorge** of the Arkansas, reached by tram from its rim and spanned by a breath-taking suspension bridge.

Following I-25 south to **Trinidad,** you can take in **Bloom House** of Victorian vintage and tour the **Baca House Pioneer Museum,** which recalls the years when Bat Masterson was marshal here.

Another of Colorado's major skiing centers, in the **SOUTHWEST** section of the state, is **Crested Butte,** 28 miles north of Gunnison. Fourteen miles from Montrose is the rugged **Black Canyon of the Gunnison National Monument,** aptly described by the Indians as "the place of high rocks and much water" and the canyon is a naturalist's delight. Near the borders of Colorado, New Mexico, Utah and Arizona, is **Cortez,** a home base for tours of the **Mesa Verde National Park.** The **Stoner Ski Area** is 28 miles north of Mesa Verde. Set on the old Navajo Trail, **Durango** is ringed by the **San Juan National Forest,** 27 miles west of Mesa Verde, which makes an ideal camping site. Billy the Kid was a noted visitor to Durango. You can take to the slopes from Thanksgiving to mid-April at **Purgatory Ski Area;** the **Silverton** is a narrow gauge passenger train which passes through spectacular canyon scenery not far from the Continental Divide. **The Navajo State Recreation Area** provides camping, water, and fishing and has an airstrip. Farther north is one of the state's best-known rodeos, the **Ski-Hi Stampede** at Monte Vista.

City to Visit

DENVER

Denver, the capital of Colorado and a major business center for the Rocky Mountain region, was established as a permanent settlement when gold was discovered at Cherry Creek in 1858. It was incorporated as a city in 1861 and made state capital in 1876 when Colorado was admitted to the Union. Known as the "Mile High City," Denver is at a higher altitude (5,280 ft.) than any other capital city in the U.S. Denver grew from a settlement of 60 cabins and a saloon into the present modern, skyscraping metropolis with a metropolitan population of 1,690,000.

WHAT TO SEE

In downtown Denver, see the new **Denver Art Museum,** featuring one of the best collections of American Indian art in the US. Adjacent to it, is the **Civic Center,** with its **Voorhees Memorial, Greek Theater,** and **Public Library.** Nearby is the gold-domed **State Capitol Building.** Step back into history at the new **State Historical Society Museum** and see its exhibits of pioneer, mining, and Indian days. Visit the restored 19th-century residence of Molly Brown of "Unsinkable Molly Brown" fame, about whom a popular play and motion picture were based. **Larimer Square** and **Ninth Street Park,** the historic gaslight district. Also the **United States Mint,** 300 block, West Colfax Avenue, can be visited Monday through Friday, except holidays; closed for inventory several weeks in June. From visitors' gallery you can watch metal being manufactured into coin "blanks" and then by giant presses into US currency. For an impressive view of the surrounding **Rocky Mountains,** visit the 31st floor observation area of the **Security Life Building.** Denver has 100 beautiful parks. **Cheesman Park,** southeast of business district, has a beautiful view of the Rockies, a marble pavilion and a mountain-peak finder. **City Park,** east of the business district, maintains a zoo, golf course, and the **Museum of Natural History,** with a collection of native animals and birds. Also in the museum is a new planetarium designed for comfortable star-gazing. **Washington Park,** in south Denver, has flower gardens and picnic areas. Other important parks are **Berkeley, Mountain View, Sloan's Lake** and **Observatory.** Gray Line and several other sightseeing companies have conducted city tours for about $8.

ACCOMMODATIONS

In Central Denver: **Brown Palace Hotel** (825-3111, S$65-80/D$75-90), world famous with exceptional service; **Plaza Cosmopolitan** (861-9000, S$36-50/D$40-62, popular and convenient; **Denver Hilton Hotel** (292-3600, S$39-61/D$51-73), elegant; **Executive Tower Inn** (571-0300, S$48-52/D$56-60), new, spectacular mountain views; **Hampshire House** (837-1200), S$31-51/D$38-58), swimming pool, sundeck; **Radisson Denver** (861-2000, S$36-42/D$48-54), roof top pool; **Regency Inn** (433-6131, S$48/D$56-62), **Fairmont Hotel** (571-1200, S$58-80/D$70-95). There are many excellent motor hotels near Denver. At Stapleton International Airport: **Hilton Inn-Airport** at I-70 and Peoria, in the industrial and residential section; **Holiday Inn-Airport,** one half mile from Stapleton International; **Malibu Airport Inn,** 15 minutes from downtown; **Ramada Inn-Airport Quebec Street,** one mile northwest of Stapleton and **Ramada Inn-Airport Smith Road,** three minutes away; **Sheraton Inn,** opposite the airport; **Skyway Airport Inn,** three blocks from I-70 between Mile Hi and Montbello Industrial parks; **Stouffer's Denver Inn,** at airport entrance. Other accommodations include the **Capri Motor Inn,** 10 miles from downtown Denver; **Cherry Creek Inn,** four miles from the airport; **Continental Denver,** on the edge of downtown; **Holiday Inn,** at seven locations in addition to the airport; **Howard Johnson's North,** I-70 at US 287 and **Howard Johnson's South,** I-25 at Colorado 70; **Marriott,** southeast of the city on I-25 and Hampden Avenue, 15 minutes from the airport; **Riviera Motel,** on US Highways 36, 40 and 287; **TraveLodge,** three minutes from downtown and **TraveLodge At Denver North,** intersection I-25 and I-70; **Writer's Manor,** south of the city, 20 minutes from airport. Rates average S\$42-50/D\$50-60; many have discounts for overseas visitors. Hotel Tax: 3-7½%

RESTAURANTS
Colorado beef and Rocky Mountain trout are local specialties. The **Normandy,** the **Broker, Top of the Rockies,** and the **Quorum** are outstanding. The **North Woods Inn** and the **Hungry Farmer** offer American dishes served while one views breathtaking scenes of the Rockies. Foreign restaurants include **Chateau Pyrenees,** French, **Mario's,** Italian; the **Lotus Room,** Chinese; and the **Alpine Village Inn,** Bavarian. For steaks try the **Golden Ox, The Fort, El Rancho, Henrici's, Alexander Graham's,** and the **Colorado Mine Company.** At Brown Palace Hotel, famous for prime ribs of beef, are two fine restaurants: the **Palace Arms** and the **San Marco Room. Sperte's Laffite** has great oysters.

ENTERTAINMENT
San Marco Room at the Brown Palace Hotel has pleasant dining, dancing, entertainment; and the **Outrigger Room** at the Cosmopolitan Hotel features Polynesian atmosphere. **The Lady and The Dove** is one of the best dining and dancing spots. **Country Dinner Playhouse** offers dining with revues of Broadway shows. **Emerson Street East** is a supper club known for its good food and excellent entertainment. **Turn of the Century, Yesterday's, Café Nepenthes, Zeno's, Stapleton Plaza** feature top-name entertainment.

ARTS AND MUSIC
The **Denver Symphony Orchestra** performs regularly from October to May at the **Denver Center for the Performing Arts.** The **Red Rocks Theater,** near Denver at the foot of the mountains, is a spectacular outdoor theater for concerts. Among dramatic attractions are presentations at the Denver Auditorium Theater throughout the year, and summer stock at the **Elitch Theater** nightly, June through August. Band concerts are held at the **Electric Fountain,** City Park, nightly, July-August.

SHOPPING
Stores are open Monday and Thursday evenings until 9. Shopping downtown is along 16th Street, from **Cleveland Place** to **Arapahoe Street,** and the side streets nearby. Boutiques and gift shops are found in **Larimer Square** and the district around 3rd Avenue in Cherry Creek.

SPORTS
Professional baseball is played by the **Denver Bears** in the American Association. The **Denver Broncos** play pro football in the National League. The **Denver Nuggets** play pro basketball, and the **Colorado Rockies** play

NHL hockey. The **University of Denver** and **University of Colorado** play basketball; and the **University of Colorado** and **Colorado School of Mines** play college football. There is horse racing for 60 days beginning mid-April and dog racing in the evenings for about four months starting in March; pari-mutuel betting.

Denver has seven municipal 18-hole golf courses, many tennis courts and several swimming pools open during the summer. Fishing is particularly good in Colorado, with the season running year round; non-resident 2-day fishing license $5, renewable; non-resident annual $25. The big-game hunting season is mid-October to early November, deer license $90, elk license $135, antelope $100, bear $50, mountain lion $150, turkey $20, small game $25. Skiing is superb in Colorado. The slopes at **Aspen** and **Vail** impress even European experts. **Winter Park,** 62 miles west of Denver in the Arapahoe National Forest, is known for its ideal powder snow, ski school, and accommodations. There are over 36 areas in the state offering the best of skiing, and railroads and buses run "snow specials" to the resorts. There's a winter carnival each February at **Steamboat Springs.** Ski season is mid-November to mid-May.

CALENDAR OF EVENTS

National Western Stock Show and Rodeo, January; **Easter Sunrise Service; Pike's Peak Auto Hill Climb,** 4 July; **Colorado State Fair,** at Pueblo, late August. Important events are held at **Currigan Convention Hall,** seating about 14,000, and at **McNichols Sports Arena.**

WHERE TO GO NEARBY

Just an hour away are beautiful mountains and parks. Visit the **Red Rocks Park,** with its unusual rock formations; **Lookout Mountain,** a mile west of Denver, features Buffalo Bill's grave and museum. **Pike's Peak** is about 75 miles south. **The Air Force Academy,** 60 miles south, is just north of Colorado Springs. The springs are the site of the famous **Broadmoor Hotel,** a resort complex with a ski area, an Olympic skating arena, and two noted golf courses. Many guest ranches offer jeep expeditions and cook-outs as part of their entertainment schedule. The mining towns of **Central City, Georgetown,** and **Leadville** should be visited. Seventy-one miles northwest of Denver is **Estes Park,** an important resort hotel center.

MESA VERDE NATIONAL PARK

The park, in the southwestern corner of the state, is open year round, but facilities are somewhat curtailed between mid-October and mid-May. The park is 6,900 to 8,572 feet above sea level, so while summer days may be warm, nights are always chilly and winter frosts start early in the autumn.

On the 21-mile mountain road from the park entrance to park headquarters, stop at **Park Point Lookout,** from which you can see 60 miles to **Four Corners,** where Colorado, New Mexico, Arizona, and Utah meet. Then stop at the **Navajo Hill Visitor Center** or **Chapin Mesa Museum.**

More than 40 pithouses and pueblos can be seen from the two six-mile loops of **Ruins Road.** Cliff dwellings can be entered only on ranger-conducted tours. **Spruce Tree House,** near the museum, contains 114 living rooms, many with original roofs intact, and eight *kivas* (ceremonial chambers). **Cliff Place,** discovered in 1888, contains more than 200 rooms and 23 kivas under its vaulted cave roof. **Balcony House,** high on the west wall of Soda Canyon, is a classic example of Pueblo architecture and a shrewd choice of an impregnable site. **Square Tower House,** no admittance but easily seen from the road, is unique for its four-story tower against the cliff. **Sun Temple,** overlooking Fewkes and Cliff canyons, was an ideal spot for ceremonial rites, but the structure was abandoned before completion. Nightly campfire programs, from early June to September, deal with the area's natural and human history and are often enlivened by Navajo Indian tribal dances. As you leave the park, stop at **Far View House** and **Pipe Shrine House,** mesa-top pueblos built between 1000 and 1200 AD. Excavations nearby teem with archaeologists in summer. Hiking in the park is restricted because the smallest shard underfoot might be a clue to the people who once lived in these cliffs.

A deluxe motel, **Far View Motor Lodge,** is open from mid-May to mid-October at the summit of Chapin Mesa (advance reservations advisable from 1 June through Labor Day). **Morfield Campground** for tents and trailers is open from about 1 May to 15 October, 14-day-stay limit, 1 June to 7 September. In winter, camping is permitted in the picnic area near park headquarters. In and near **Durango,** 38 miles east of the park, you will find a good choice of motels and summer-season dude ranches.

ROCKY MOUNTAIN NATIONAL PARK

The park is 65 miles north of Denver. The best time for a visit is June to September but be prepared for cold days and nights.

Valleys in the park are about 8,000 feet above sea level, and 62 mountain peaks rise to 12,000 feet or more. **Trail Ridge Road** is one of the world's most spectacular highways. For 11 of its 44 miles it is above the timberline and at one point reaches 12,183 feet—high enough to be abreast of the surrounding mountaintops. Stop at the **Alpine Visitor Center** at Fall River Pass for exhibits and information. The road crosses the Continental Divide at **Milner Pass** and then proceeds south beside the plunging Colorado River to beautiful **Grand Lake.** The short drive from the **Moraine Park Visitor Center** (information, exhibits, park literature) takes you through Glacier Creek Valley to **Bear Lake,** where the rocky east face of the **Front Range** shoots abruptly skyward. Most park trails can be explored on horseback, a good way to travel if you're not used to hiking in thin mountain air. You must register at the nearest ranger station before climbing tricky **Long's Peak,** 14,256 feet. Pick up a Colorado license and check fishing regulations before you angle for trout in the icy-cold lakes and streams. Most waters can be fished year round. **Hidden Valley,** seven miles from the Fall River Entrance, is the center for ice skating, skiing, and other snow sports from December to mid-April. The park is a refuge for bighorn sheep, elk, deer, black bear, and mountain lion.

Most of the numerous lodges, inns and motels around Estes Park, outside the main entrance, however, have lower rates after Labor Day and until mid-June. There are seven major campgrounds in the park, most of them accessible to trailers; seven-day-stay limit. There are also many back-country campsites along the 300 miles of trails.

FURTHER STATE INFORMATION

Visitors Information Center, 225 West Colfax Avenue, Denver CO 80202. Hunting and Fishing: **Division of Wildlife,** 6060 Broadway, Denver, CO 80216. Skiing: **Colorado Ski Country USA,** 1410 Grant, Denver, CO 80203; **Colorado Dude and Guest Ranch Association,** 34557 Upper Bear Creek Road, Evergreen, CO 80439. National Parks: **Mesa Verde National Park** (Superintendent), CO 81330. **Rocky Mountain National Park** (Superintendent), Estes Park, CO 80517. **Pan Am** office, 818 17th Street, Denver, CO 80202; tel: 629-0251.

Consulates in Denver: Belgium, Costa Rica, Denmark, Dominican Republic, El Salvador, Finland, France, Germany, Guatemala, Italy, Korea, Mexico, Nicaragua, Norway, Paraguay, Peru, Senegal, Sweden, Switzerland.

USEFUL TELEPHONE NUMBERS

All Emergencies	911
Rocky Mountain Poison Center	629-1123
Metro Denver Dental Society (referral service)	789-0573
Denver Medical Society	861-1221
Legal Aid Society	837-1313
Chamber of Commerce (Denver)	534-3211
Weather Reports & Travel conditions	639-1212
Pan Am Reservations (Denver)	629-0251

Connecticut

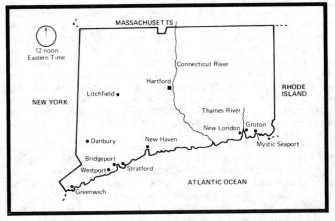

Area	5,009 square miles		**Population**	3,107,576							
Capital	Hartford		**Sales Tax**	7.5%							

Weather	Jan	Feb	Mar	Apr	May	Jun	Jul	Aug	Sep	Oct	Nov	Dec
Av Temp (°C)	−3	−3	2	9	16	20	23	22	17	12	5	−2
Days Rain/Snow	10	11	11	11	11	11	10	10	9	8	12	12

Connecticut, one of the original 13 American colonies, is a blend of good rolling farmland, pretty colonial villages, old seaports and handsome residential suburbs. Because of its size—only Delaware and Rhode Island are smaller—the traveler can see much of this state in a relatively short time. Covered bridges, gracious old houses, white churches, and rambling stone walls dot the hilly countryside. From Mystic Seaport, once the homebase for the clipper ship traders, to New London's Old Town Mill, a sense of America's beginnings pervades Connecticut.

First known as "The Nutmeg State," the legislature renamed it "The Constitution State" in 1959, because its Fundamental Orders, adopted in 1639, are considered to be the first written constitution in America. This model document established a continuing government with the full consent of the people and later served as a model for the United States Constitution. *Yankee* ingenuity has developed a proud tradition of historical "firsts." In 1740 Edward and William Pattison made the first tinware in America and founded the tradition of the famous "Yankee peddlers" by peddling their wares from house to house.

The many local summer stock theater companies, because of their fine reputation and close proximity to Broadway, attract the nation's leading actors. Future Broadway shows often "try out" on Connecticut's summer circuit.

Collectors of antiques will take special delight in local flea markets, auctions and country fairs. Along Connecticut's southern coast on Long Island Sound, there are numerous public beaches. The state has also set aside an unusually large proportion of its inland area for public parks and forests. Some 85 state parks total about 30,300 acres, while 29 state forests cover some 132,800 acres. These areas are open for hiking, hunting, camping and other outdoor recreation.

New England winters seem to bring to life Currier and Ives paintings and Christmas card scenes of midnight sleigh rides across the countryside, ice skating on glassy, smooth ponds and of snow-bound farmhouses. Come spring, mountain laurel, the official state flower, grows in abundance on the rocky hillsides. White dogwood and pink azaleas are also common and the Dogwood Festival in **Greenfield Hill** is an annual tourist attraction.

Because the state's western boundary meets New York State, many cities serve as communities for the thousands of people who daily commute to work in Manhattan. **Greenwich** on the New York state line is just 28 miles from Times Square. **Stamford, Darien, Norwalk,** and **Westport** are other fashionable residential communities for city executives. When you visit the area, you'll understand why they choose to return to the luscious greenery and the fresh country air after a hard day's work in the city.

The *Hartford Courant* is said to be the oldest continuously published newspaper in the United States. It was founded in 1764 and became a daily in 1837; George Washington was among its early subscribers. The colony's first paper mill was opened in **Norwich** in 1766. The first pocket knives made in the US came from **Lakeville. Meriden** is the home of the International Silver Company, the largest manufacturer of sterling and plated silverware in the world. They have been producing silver plate since the Rogers Brothers introduced the electrolytic process in 1847. Until The American Thread Company was opened in **Willimantic** in 1854, most thread had to be imported. Agriculture is still of considerable importance throughout Connecticut; poultry, dairy products and tobacco grown in the Connecticut River Valley provide the largest source of agricultural income.

The ivy-covered campus of **Yale University,** chartered in 1701, has dominated **New Haven** since 1716. New Haven has many excellent restaurants including **Basil's,** Greek fare (live Greek music); **Blessing's,** Chinese; **India Inn** for curries; **Leon's,** Italian; **Old Heidelberg** for varsity flavor, steaks and beer; **Louis' Lunch,** originator of the hamburger in the US; **Poor Lad's,** French; and for authentic homemade country style food, try **Annie's Firehouse Soup Kitchen.** The first law school in the country was established in **Litchfield** in 1784. The state-supported University of Connecticut is based at **Storrs,** with five branches throughout the state. Connecticut is a leading state in urban renewal projects. Hartford's **Constitution Plaza,** a building complex in the downtown business area, and New Haven's **Church Street Center,** a redevelopment, restoration and rebuilding of community and housing facilities, are considered among the most successful urban renewal projects in the country.

Essex, a small township in Middlesex and on the Connecticut River, is redolent of the history of former times with numerous Colonial era homes. You may take boat tours on the river and on Long Island Sound, and a ride on a privately operated, restored railroad. **The Griswold Inn** (767-0991, S/D$30-36) has been offering fine food and accommodations to travelers since the 18th century. Reservations essential.

Greenwich's **Audubon Center** is a kind of summer camp for adults, with a self-guided nature trail and a 475-acre nature preserve; open Tuesday to Saturday 9-5, 50¢. **Putnam Cottage** in Greenwich, built in 1690, is the house from which General Israel Putnam escaped the Redcoats in 1779; open Monday, Thursday to Saturday, 10-5, 50¢. The **Bruce Museum,** also located in Greenwich, has over 20,000 exhibits, including wildlife dioramas and a zoo; open Monday-Friday 10-5, Sunday 2-5, free. In Cos Cob the **Bush-Holley House,** a restored "saltbox" house built in 1685, includes **John Rogers Museum** and **Crafts Shop.**

About 15 miles north of Norwalk, **Ridgefield** boasts a 99-foot-wide, tree-shaded street surrounded by 18th-century houses. The **Aldrich Museum of Contemporary Art,** 258 Main Street, has changing exhibits, a sculpture garden and gallery tours on Saturday at 2:30 and 3:30; open March through December, Saturday and Sunday 2-5. **Stonehenge,** on Danbury Road, Rte 7, north of Wilton, is considered by many gourmets to be the best restaurant in Connecticut. Chef-owned, the house specialties include their own trout, rack of lamb, pheasant, and Swiss pastries.

The great **Danbury State Fair,** at **Danbury,** 20 miles north of Norwalk, has been held annually since 1869. It runs for 10 days in early October. **Candlewood Lake,** Connecticut's largest, is more than 14 miles long with 60 miles of coastline. There are swimming, fishing, picnicking facilities and summer cottages available. The **Candlewood Theater** in New Fairfield presents Broadway comedies and musicals from late June through early September; a children's show is held on Tuesdays at 11am in July. For information call (203) 746-2451.

The **Westport Country Playhouse** in **Westport** is one of the state's best-known summer theaters and many future Broadway shows are tried out there. The season is mid-June through early September, Monday to Friday at 8:30pm; Wednesday matinee at 2:30; Saturday at 6 and 9; children's shows on Fridays; box office number is (203) 227-4177. The **Player's Tavern,** in an attached building, is open for dinner, 6-10, and after the theater for supper and entertainment, 10-2. The **Mid-Fairfield County Youth Museum,** 10 Woodside Lane, has a five-mile nature trail and a 54-acre wildlife sanctuary; free. The **Westport New Englander** on E. State Street, Westport (259-5236, S$47-53/D$65) offers pool, cabanas, and sundeck during the summer season. There are many exceptionally good restaurants in the Westport area. Among these are the **Arrow,**

with Italian and American dishes, including sandwiches, recommended
for families; **The Moorings,** on the Saugatuck River near Long Island
Sound, has continental and American cuisine. **Chez Pierre** offers an intimate café atmosphere with terrace and fireplace; the **Clam Box** is a
big favorite with seafood specialties and special children's plates; and
the **Red Barn** offers a special early-bird dinner on Sunday, noon to 3.
The Three Bears was originally a colonial tavern and **Werners** has a continental menu, plus Belgian specialties.

  Bridgeport's most famous citizen and onetime mayor was none other
than the great showman P. T. Barnum. The annual **Barnum Festival,**
held from late June to 4th of July, is a spectacular show with circus
and side-show, local Tom Thumb, Lavinia Warren and Jenny Lind contests, and a big parade on the 4th of July. **The Barnum Museum,** 804
Main Street, has many circus props, including General Tom Thumb's
wardrobe tailored for his 28-inch height; open Monday-Friday 2-5, September through June, Monday-Friday 2-4, July and August. **Seaside Park**
on Long Island Sound, at the foot of Park Avenue, has 210 acres including
a two-and-a-half-mile seawall. The beach is open to the public daily,
Memorial Day through Labor Day. The **Museum of Art, Science and
Industry,** 4450 Park Avenue, offers planetarium shows and exhibits. **Holiday Inn** (366-5421, S$42/D$48) provides reliable accommodations. Outside of town and close to Fairfield are the **Bridgeport Motor Inn** (367-
4404, S$31.10/D$36.55), at Exit 24 of the Connecticut Turnpike, and
the **Merritt Parkway Motel** (259-5264, S/D$32-$36) at exits 44 and 45
of the Merritt Parkway.

  The **American Shakespeare Theater at Stratford** is modeled after the
original Globe theater in London and the program is fashioned after
the original Stratford-on-Avon festival in Britain bringing the state international prominence. Leading Shakespearean performers appear here,
July through early September. Performances are scheduled so visitors
can see three plays, two Shakespearean, during a short visit. The 12-
acre site adjacent to the **Housatonic River** provides a lovely riverside
setting and picnic area. Strolling troubadors serenade you before the
show and during intermission. There are also free tours of the theater
complex, Sundays 2-4, November through January. For information call
(203) 378-7321; or in New York City (212)WO-6-3900. **Howard Johnson's
Motor Inn** (375-5666, S$37.50/D$47.50) and the **Stratford Motor Inn**
(378-7351, S$37/D$44), both have pools, and the **Mermaid Tavern,** at
the Stratford Motor Inn, offers an English and American menu, dancing
and entertainment.

Cities to Visit

HARTFORD

Hartford, the capital of Connecticut, is in the north central part of the
state, on the **Connecticut River,** which originates in northern New Hamp-

shire and empties into Long Island Sound. New York City is 115 miles southwest. The site was first used in 1623 as a Dutch trading post called the "House of Hope." It was colonized in 1635 by Reverend Thomas Hooker and his followers from Newtowne, now Cambridge, Massachusetts. The city was named after Hertford, England, two years later and was incorporated in 1784.

Hartford is an industrial area devoted to manufacturing, particularly aircraft engines, and is the insurance capital of the country with several dozen major companies maintaining their home offices here. Population 158,017.

WHAT TO SEE

The **Mark Twain Memorial,** the house in which Twain wrote *Tom Sawyer, Huckleberry Finn, The Prince and the Pauper* and many other classics; the **Harriet Beecher Stowe House,** the home of the author of *Uncle Tom's Cabin,* who taught school in Hartford; and the **Old State House,** 1796 architectural masterpiece by Charles Bulfinch, now a museum, are of great interest. **Constitution Plaza,** one of the nation's most impressive urban renewal projects; **State Capitol;** the various buildings of the large insurance companies; and **Traveler's Tower,** the tallest building in the state, offering a view of Greater Hartford and Connecticut River Valley, should also be seen. **Elizabeth Park,** rose gardens; **Bushnell Park,** in center of town; **Goodwin and Keney Parks,** golf courses; **Colt and Pope Parks,** swimming. **Environmental Centers, Inc.,** formerly the Children's Museum of Hartford, has exhibits of colonial life, primitive peoples, fossils and a **Planetarium.** Open Monday-Saturday 9-5, Sunday 1-5. Among the colleges and schools are **Trinity College,** the **University of Connecticut Law School** and the **University of Hartford.**

ACCOMMODATIONS

Downtown hotels include **Sonesta** (278-2000, S$60-90/D$70-100), **Sheraton Hartford** (728-5151, S$57-72/D$67-82), **Holiday Inn** (549-2400, S$38/D$46), **Governor's House Motel,** at 440 Asylum Street (246-6591, S$32-36/D$43-47). There are also many motels on major highways leading into Hartford: **Carville's Motor Lodge,** two miles north of downtown; **Howard Johnson's Motor Lodge,** Flanders Rd, (739-6921, S$28/D$32), **Howard Johnson's** and **Travelers** motor lodges at Rocky Hill, south of Hartford on I-91; and the **Farmington Motor Inn** at Farmington, southwest of Hartford, Junction Route 4 and Route 10. Rates average S$24/D$30. **Lighthouse Inn & Motor Lodge** (S$30/D$40).

RESTAURANTS

Hotels serve good food; **Frank's Italian Restaurant,** Italian-American cooking; **Adajians,** shish kebab; **Honiss' Seafood Restaurant,** famous for seafood, specialty scrod. **The South Seas,** Polynesian-Chinese food; **Hearthstone,** charcoal-broiled steaks; **Last National Bank,** a reconverted bank vault, and **Valle's Steak House,** steak and lobster, are moderate to expensive in price. **The Signature,** in the city's new Civic Center, is one of the most popular—and expensive—in town. **The Marble Pillar,** German, wiener schnitzel a specialty, reservations evenings only.

ENTERTAINMENT

There is dancing usually at the **Sheraton, Sonesta,** and **Materese's.** Bars and restaurants serve liquor from 9am to 1am daily, to 2am on Friday and Saturday evenings, noon to 11pm on Sunday.

ARTS AND MUSIC

Wadsworth Atheneum, outstanding art museum, embracing the Colt, Morgan, and Avery memorial collections; paintings, sculpture, porcelains, bronzes, furniture, tapestry; open Tuesday through Saturday 11-4, Sunday 1-5. **Horace Bushnell Memorial Hall,** programs of concerts, opera and other artistic performances. The **Hartford Symphony** performs about 10 times during the year. Summer theaters in the Hartford area include **Nutmeg Summer Playhouse, Oakdale Musical Theater,** and **Ivoryton.** During the winter, the **Hartford Stage Company** and the **Hartford Ballet** are active and touring companies appear in Hartford's Bushnell Memorial Hall.

SHOPPING

The central shopping area is located on **Main Street,** home of **G. Fox & Co.,** one of New England's largest department stores. West Hartford has many specialty shops, including branches of New York City stores such as **Lord & Taylor,** and a huge shopping complex **West Farms Mall,** opened Mon thru Sat 10-9:30 and Sun 12-5. The **Hartford Civic Center** has a variety of stores and crafts displays which are opened Mon thru Fri 10-9, Sat 10-6 and Sun 12-5.

SPORTS

Golf, tennis, horseback riding, and swimming are available in the city's many excellent parks. There is good fishing in nearby lakes and streams and on the **Connecticut** and **Farmington Rivers,** white water canoeing on the **Farmington River,** and salt-water fishing along the coastline. There are college football games during the fall and professional hockey and basketball during the winter. The **New England Whalers** hockey team plays its home games at the Hartford Civic Center and the **Boston Celtics** basketball team visits there. The **Aetna World Cup Tennis Tournament** is held in March.

CALENDAR OF EVENTS

Travel Show, late winter; **Boat Show,** early spring; **Sportsmen's Show,** spring; **New England Fiddle Contest,** May; **Rose Festival,** June; **New Haven Antiques Show,** June; **Home Show,** late winter; **House and Garden Tour,** May; **Hartford Civic Arts Festival,** June; **Plaza Garden Fair,** September in the Civic Center Coliseum. The **Sammy Davis, Jr. Greater Hartford Open Golf Tournament** is the biggest sporting event of the year.

WHERE TO GO NEARBY

The **American Clock** and **Watch Museum** in **Bristol** has over 600 clocks, dating from 1790, on display in a house built in 1801; open April through October, daily except Monday 1-5. Also in Bristol, the annual **Chrysanthemum Festival** of music, art, theater, and dance is held for two weeks in early October. In East Haddam, the famous **Goodspeed Opera House,** originally built in 1876, has been restored and musicals are presented mid-June through Labor Day. At **Gillette Castle State Park,** the 24-room medieval castle built for and designed by actor William Gillette, is open Memorial Day through Columbus Day, daily 11-5. The former estate has been converted into a state park encompassing 171 acres overlooking the Connecticut River. Picnic area available. **Dinosaur State Park** in Rocky Hill has more than 1,000 dinosaur prints and tracks under a plastic dome, open all year 10-5. The **University of Connecticut** in Storrs, established in 1881, has an impressive campus for 20,000 students in nearby Storrs. The **Nutmeg Summer Playhouse,** on the campus, is open late June through mid-August.

NEW LONDON AND GROTON

New London and Groton are in southeastern Connecticut on Long Island Sound and the Thames River, midway between the great metropolitan centers of New York and Boston.

Originally called Nameaug (fishing place) by the Pequot and Mohegan Indian tribes that inhabited the area, the New London settlement began when the Massachusetts General Court granted John Winthrop, Jr., the right to make a claim at Pequot in 1645, extending east to the Mystic River. In 1658 the site was named New London in honor of London, England. Groton's first settlers came in 1650. It was not until 1705, however, that is was set off from New London as a separate town. Groton took its name from Governor Winthrop's home town in England. New London was a meeting place for privateers during the Revolution and an important whaling port during the 19th century. Groton was a famous shipbuilding center as early as 1724 and in 1955 produced the world's first atomic-powered submarine.

Shipbuilding has been the outstanding industry in both New London and Groton throughout the years. This is as true now in the age of atomic-powered submarines, modern yachts, cutters, and cruisers as it was in the days of clipper ships and whaling vessels. Many old vessels are preserved in the village of **Mystic** nearby. New London has one of the finest deepwater ports on the Atlantic coast. Four major military installations are located in the region: the US Submarine Base, the US Coast Guard Academy, the Underwater Sound Laboratory, and the US Coast Guard Training Station. Population of New London is 30,720, Groton 38,230.

WHAT TO SEE

In New London: see the first lighthouse on Connecticut coast, activated in 1760; **Shaw Mansion,** built in 1755 and the Naval Office of the State during the Revolution; **Hempsted House,** built in 1678, with a fine selection of early American furniture; **Old Town Mill,** a reconstruction of the oldest power plant in the United States; **Whale Oil Row,** a row of four Greek revival houses, built in 1830. One building houses a new **Whaling Museum.**

In Groton: **Daboll Homestead** where the first school of navigation was conducted from 1805-73 and the **US Naval Submarine Base.** Boats leave in summer from the boat dock in Groton on several daily one-hour, seven-mile trips on the Thames, passing the US Naval Submarine Base, US Coast Guard Academy, and other points of interest. A **Submarine Library and Museum** at the US Naval Submarine Base has very interesting submarine models, flags, memorabilia, and a research center tracing the history of submarines with books, photos, and data. Open Monday to Friday 9-4, Saturday and holidays 10-4, Sunday 1-4; admission by appointment only; apply to Submarine Base Visitor Control Officer; free. For information on tours call the Public Information Office. Groton is also the home of the world's largest private builder of submarines. **The Electric Boat Division of General Dynamics Corporation** built the first diesel-powered submarine in 1912 and the first nuclear-powered submarine, the *Nautilus,* in 1955.

Principal parks: **Ocean Beach Park** in New London offers swimming, picnic area, amusements, and playground area; **Bates Woods Park** and **Nature Center** has a picnic area, playground, and zoo area; **Thames Science Center** in New London has class and field activities for children all year; and **Mitchell Woods Park** in New London has tennis courts.

Colleges and schools in the area include **Connecticut College, Mitchell College,** a two-year branch of the **University of Connecticut,** and the **US Coast Guard Academy.**

ACCOMMODATIONS

In Groton try the **Holiday Inn** (445-8141, S$38.50/D$42.50), one block south of I-95. Across the Thames in New London are the **Holiday Inn** (442-0631, S/D$52.50) and **Lamplighter Motel** (442-7227, S$14-26/D$16-24), both along I-95. Other good motels nearby include **Niantic Motor Lodge, Starlight Motor Inn,** and **TraveLodge-New London South,** all at Exit 74 of the Connecticut Turnpike near Niantic; and the **Mystic Motor Inn** (536-9604, S/D$30-$70), and **Seaport Motor Inn** (536-2621, S$55/D$60), at the Mystic Seaport exit of I-95; Hotel Tax 7½%.

RESTAURANTS

In New London try the **Lighthouse Inn,** overlooking Long Island Sound, **Ye Olde Tavern,** open-hearth cooking with a tavern motif, **Chuck's Steak House, The Ships Wheel,** and **Anthony's Steam Carriage.** In nearby Mystic, **The Seafarer** and the **Seamen's Inne** have lots of atmosphere. All are moderate to expensive. In Groton try the **Yankee Fisherman, Seahorse Restaurant,** seafood; **Ming Garden, Chinese Kitchen,** Chinese; **The Ground Round.**

Majestic sailing ships, such as the Charles W. Morgan *and the* Joseph Conrad *(above), now peacefully berthed for boarding and exploration, are a part of the authentic display at Mystic Seaport, CT.*

ENTERTAINMENT

There is dancing on Friday and Saturday nights at the **Holiday Inn,**
New London, at **Groton's Holiday Inn,** and at the **Groton Motor Inn**
on Saturday evening.

ARTS AND MUSIC

Lyman Allyn Museum, Mohegan Avenue in New London, shows fine
examples of colonial artifacts, 18th- and 19th-century furniture, an extensive collection of doll furniture, and early American and modern French
paintings; open Tuesday-Saturday 1-5, Sunday 2-5. **Connecticut College
School of Dance** presents a summertime **American Dance Festival.** Performances sponsored by the **Connecticut College Concert Series** often
feature nationally known musical soloists and symphony orchestras. The
Eastern Connecticut Symphony Orchestra appears at the **Palmer Auditorium** as does the US Coast Guard Band.

SHOPPING

In addition to the antique shops and sophisticated shopping malls, New
London has all kinds of nautical supply stores where you can find everything imaginable for the family boat. Unique is the **Olde Mistick Village**
shopping mall.

SPORTS

Coast Guard Academy athletic events are good spectator sports. There
is good fishing in nearby lakes and streams, and salt-water fishing along
the coastline. Golf, tennis, and swimming are available in the many parks.

WHERE TO GO NEARBY

Harkness Memorial State Park in Waterford has formal gardens, a museum of bird paintings, and an Italian mansion, once the home of tycoon
Edward S. Harkness. One section of the park is set aside for the enjoyment
of the handicapped; fishing and picnicking permitted. **Fort Griswold State
Park** south of Groton has a 135-foot monument to the 84 Revolutionary
War soldiers killed there, and a Daughters of the American Revolution
museum. **Rocky Neck State Park** at East Lyme has swimming and picnic
facilities. Similar facilities and hiking trails at **Fort Shantok Park,** Mont-
ville. **Bluff Point Park,** in Groton, and **Sheldon Neck State Park** have
been left natural and undeveloped. There are also two state forests
nearby: **Nehantic,** in East Lyme, with picnic area, fishing, shooting, and
hiking; and **Pachaug** at Voluntown, with swimming, picnicking, fishing,
shooting, and hiking.

    Mystic Seaport and Museum, route 27 on the Mystic River, has a unique
replica of a 19th-century marine village, berth of whaleship *Charles Morgan* and square-rigged *Joseph Conrad* and many other old vessels; outstanding collection of marine objects; museum and a planetarium. Also
in Mystic, **Museum of Transportation** and a row of old sea captains' homes
in an excellent state of preservation. The **Mystic Marinelife Aquarium**
is open daily.

FURTHER STATE INFORMATION

Connecticut Department of Commerce, 210 Washington Street, Hartford, CT 06106. Hunting and fishing: **State Department of Environmental Protection,** State Office Building, Hartford, CT 06115. **Chamber of Commerce of Southeastern Connecticut,** 105 Huntington Street, New London, CT 06320. **Greater Hartford Convention and Visitors Bureau,** One Civic Center Plaza, Hartford, CT 06103. **Department of Public Affairs,** Mystic Seaport, Mystic, CT 06355. **New England Vacation Center,** 1268 Avenue of the Americas, New York, NY 10019.

Consulates in Hartford: Bolivia, France, Italy, Peru.

USEFUL TELEPHONE NUMBERS
Hartford
Medical Service	522-1234
Mount Sinai Hospital	242-4431
Hartford Hospital	524-3011
Fire	522-1234
Police	522-0111
State Police	566-5930
Legal Aid Society	566-6360
Tourist Information	521-7150
Pan Am Reservations	249-9651

New London
Emergency Medical Service	443-4381
Lawrence & Memorial Hospital	442-0711
Fire	443-4381
Police	443-4315
State Police	848-1201
Legal Aid	442-3934
Chamber of Commerce	443-8332
Pan Am Reservations	(800) 223-9762

Delaware

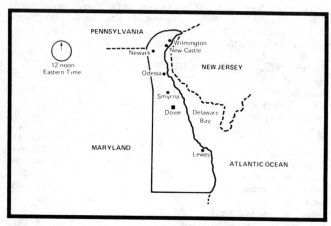

Area	2,057 square miles					**Population**		595,225					
Capital	Dover					**Sales Tax**		None					
Weather		Jan	Feb	Mar	Apr	May	Jun	Jul	Aug	Sep	Oct	Nov	Dec
Av Temp (°C)		1	1	5	11	17	22	24	24	20	14	7	2
Days Rain/Snow		1	9	9	11	11	9	9	9	7	7	9	10

For a state only 96 miles long and 35 miles across at its widest, Delaware has many nicknames. It is called the "Blue Hen State" for the fiery game-cocks that accompanied a crack Delaware regiment in the Revolutionary War. It is the "First State" because it was the first to ratify the United States Constitution. It is the "Corporations' State" because its legal structure is advantageous for companies wishing to become incorporated, and it is the home of some chartered firms. And Delaware is the "Diamond State" because of its great value in contrast to its small size.

Named for Lord De La Warr, Governor of Virginia, the state's early history is a record of a continual scramble for control among the Dutch, Swedish, Finnish, and English colonists. After all this quieted down, Delaware sailed virtually unscathed through history. During the Revolution only one minor battle occurred in the state, at Cooch's Bridge; only the town of Lewes had any trouble from the British during the War of 1812 and no Civil War battles at all were fought in Delaware. In 1802 Eleuthere Irenee du Pont, a French immigrant, built a gunpowder plant beside the Brandywine Creek that grew into a corporation respected the world over. Today nearly everyone in the world has used products that originated in the Du Pont Laboratories in Wilmington as the du Ponts aimed their chemists' talents in a positive direction.

The state is hilly in the north, tapering off to sea level in the south. "Downstate" is anywhere south of the Chesapeake and Delaware Canal that connects the **Delaware River** with **Chesapeake Bay.** It's a region of centuries-old houses in charming little towns, prosperous farms and lots of wonderful places to go fishing in both fresh and salt water. Delaware's principal farm product is broiler chickens, but probably its most memorable meals consist of freshly-caught fish and shellfish. Whether you enter Delaware from Pennsylvania or from New Jersey via the twin **Delaware Memorial Bridges,** you immediately arrive in Wilmington. Only 3 miles south of the bridges, but well off the main highway, little **New Castle** lies beside the river. Here the **Green** was laid out by Dutchman Peter Stuyvesant in 1655 and **The Strand,** still cobble-stoned, is lined with brick houses over 200 years old. Many historic homes are open to the public on New Castle Day, the third Saturday in May. Other buildings open most of the time are the **Amstel House** (*circa* 1780) and **Old Dutch House** (*circa* 1690), both with genuine colonial furnishings; **Immanuel Church** (1703) and **Old Presbyterian Church** (1701); **Old Court House,** the colonial capitol, and three miles out, **Buena Vista** (1846) with Empire furnishings. Fifteen miles west of Wilmington is the college town of **Newark,** with the University of Delaware, home of the "Fighting Blue Hens" football team. Stop and see the **Iron Hill Natural Museum,** and a 90-foot observation tower overlooking the Revolutionary War **Cooch's Bridge** battleground, built on the site of General Washington's Lookout.

Once a prosperous grain-shipping center named after the Russian port on the Black Sea, **Odessa,** further south, was an important station on the Underground Railroad, a railroad system to help fugitive slaves escape to Canada or other places of safety, during the Civil War. Stop there to see the **Corbit-Sharp House** and **Wilson-Warner House,** two very handsome Georgian mansions built side by side in the 18th century and filled with antiques. **Smyrna** has the **Allee House** (1753) and **The Lindens** (pre-1725), open to the public. East of town is the large **Bombay Hook National Wildlife Refuge.**

Just north of **Frederica** on US 113 is **Barratt's Chapel,** regarded as the cradle of Methodism in America. **Lewes** (pronounced *Lewis*) is a salty old town on Delaware Bay proud of having been bombed (just a little bit) in the War of 1812. Here the first European settlement was established by the Dutch in 1631. The **Zwaanendael** (Valley of the Swans) **Museum** commemorates this settlement, which was destroyed by Indians in less than a year. Old houses are open and there's an antiques market on **Lewes Day,** an annual celebration, commemorating the founding, the first Saturday in August. A series of special events are planned, beginning in May and lasting through September. Car ferries connect Lewes with **Cape May** in the neighboring state of New Jersey. Stretching southward from Cape Henlopen are **Rehoboth Beach, Bethany Beach, Fenwick Island,** and **Delaware Seashore State Parks,** popular summer resorts with the Atlantic pounding on their eastern beaches, and the sheltered waters of the **Indian River** and **Little Assawoman Bay** on their western shores. Delaware may be tiny, but it has a lot to offer if you get off the main highways and look around.

DOVER has been the state capital since 1777. In response to orders issued by William Penn, the town was originally laid out around The Green in 1717, and 18th- and 19th-century houses still surround it. The **Old State House** (1787-92) is in elegant Georgian colonial style. The **Delaware State Museum** has exhibits illustrating many phases of Delaware life, from a genuine log cabin built by Swedish settlers to Apollo space suits. Southeast of town is the **John Dickinson Mansion** (1740), home of the "Penman of the Revolution." Try to be in town for **Old Dover Days**, held annually the first weekend in May. Motels, ranging from about S\$20-30/D\$25-35 are the **Quality Inn South, Sheraton Inn-Dover, Ramada Inn, Quality Inn Towne Point, Holiday Inn,** and **Capital City Motor Lodge.** There is outstanding sea food at the **Blue Coat Inn.**

Year-round racing activities can be seen at **Dover Downs,** just north of the city. This race track offers stock car and other auto racing, thoroughbred trotters, and a variety of entertainment shows. Be sure to see the **Mason-Dixon 500** in May and the CRC Chemicals 500 in September.

City to Visit

WILMINGTON

Seven years after the Indian massacre of the Dutch colony at Lewes, Swedish colonists, led by Peter Minuit, founded the first permanent European settlement at Fort Christiana in 1638. In 1655 Dutch forces led by the formidable pegleged Governor of New Netherland, Peter Stuyvesant, took the fort and renamed it Altena. The English, under the Duke of York, came along in 1664 and captured all the Dutch territory in America. Thus while the Swedish had ruled for over 15 years and the Dutch for 9, the English retained power for 112 years. Industrious Quakers, a religious sect who moved in from Pennsylvania in the 1730s, renamed the town for the Earl of Wilmington. Mills and manufacturing industries begun in the early 1700s, thrived on the abundant water power and transportation facilities. Now large chemical research and manufacturing facilities have made modern Wilmington the "Chemical Capital of the World."

WHAT TO SEE
Market St. Mall; the **Marine Terminal;** Old Swedes Church (1698); the site of **Fort Christiana;** exhibits of Continental Army uniforms and equipment in the Delaware Historical Society's chambers in the **Old Town Hall** (1798). **Brandywine Park** has an enchanting zoo, with a special section for children. The zoo has recently been renovated and features new exhibits. Admission: adults, \$1, children 50¢.

The Henry Francis du Pont Winterthur Museum, 6 miles northwest of the city, has unquestionably the nation's greatest collection of Early American furnishings. From massive Dutch wardrobes to gracefully swooping staircases, every piece is authentic and was once part of an American home from 1640 to 1840. There are more than 100 rooms, each perfectly furnished in its own period. Fourteen rooms in the South Wing are open from 10:00-4:00; the gardens are open from mid-April through October. Tours of the entire house, in groups of 4, take a full day and are by advance reservation only. Write to the Reservations Office, Winterthur Museum, Winterthur, Delaware 19735. The newly opened Delaware Museum of Natural History (route 52, in Greenville) has over 100 exhibits including rare shells, extinct and vanishing species of birds and a lifelike panorama of African animals. Also in Greenville is the Hagley Museum on the property where the Du Pont mills prospered for more than a century. The premises are devoted to industrial development in America and depict its evolution from the colonial mills of Brandywine Valley to 20th-century corporate business. Eleutherian Mills, also on the property, was built by the first du Pont in 1803, enlarged in 1805 and 1853 and was the family home until 1958; open to the public in spring and fall.

ACCOMMODATIONS

In downtown Wilmington, Hotel Du Pont (656-8121, S$63-68.50/D$78.50-98); Radisson Wilmington Hotel (800-228-9822, S$50-60/D$60-72). In Wilmington's northern suburbs, 1 to 5 miles from center city: El Capitan Motor Hotel (695-9436, S$31/D$36); Sheraton-Brandywine Inn (800-325-3535, S$55-60/D$61-70); Brandywine Hilton Inn (792-2701, S$36-56/D$46-66); Tally Ho Motor Lodge (478-0300, S$25.44/D$30.74, tax included); Holiday Inn North (478-2222, S$31-35/D$36-40). South of Wilmington, 1 to 5 miles from center city. Kent Manor Motel (659-9431, S$18-27/D$25-27); Ramada Inn (800-228-2828, S$34-37/D$39-42); Howard Johnson's Motor Lodge, New Castle (800-654-2000, S$31-35/D$36). Southwest of Wilmington, 12 miles from center city: Holiday Inn South (737-2700, S$31/D$37); Howard Johnson's Motor Lodge, Newark (800-654-2000, S$36/D$42); Sheraton Inn-Newark (800-325-3535, S$38-44/D$42-48). Hotel tax 6%.

RESTAURANTS

Especially recommended are the Hotel Du Pont Green Room and Brandywine/Christina Rooms, Columbus Inn, Town Wharf, Town House, Sal's Place, The Crab Shack, The Magic Wok, the Executive Inn, Constantinou's House of Beef, Winkler's, Remedio's and Leounes' Town Talk.

ENTERTAINMENT

In Wilmington and the nearby suburbs, there is dancing nightly at The Alley, the Sheraton-Brandywine Inn, Brandywine Hilton Inn, Ramada Inn, Kent Manor Inn, Tally Ho Motor Lodge and Sheraton Inn-Newark.

ARTS AND MUSIC
The **Delaware Art Museum** features the Phelps Collection of Andrew Wyeth, works by Winslow Homer and a collection of Pre-Raphaelite art. Art shows include the **Brandywine Arts Festival** in Brandywine Park, second Saturday in September, and the **Clothesline Fair** at the City Hall, first Tuesday-Thursday in May. The **Delaware Symphony** presents concerts featuring outstanding artists. The **Delaware Theatre Company**, 303 N. French Street, Wilmington, has regularly-scheduled performances by a company of resident professionals. **The Playhouse** is a theater in the Du Pont Building where shows are often tried out before going on to Broadway. The **Grand Opera House**, Delaware's center for the performing arts, offers an outstanding selection of cultural events. **Candlelight Dinner Theater** is at Arden, six miles north of town. The **Stone Balloon** in nearby Newark offers dancing to the music of rock, jazz, and country-western bands. Live jazz is presented nightly at the **Flight Deck** in downtown Wilmington. On most weekends there are live jazz performances in Wilmington at **Oscar's**, **The Crepe Chalet**, and **Zink's**.

SPORTS
Tracks near Wilmington, with pari-mutuel betting, feature flat racing from late May to early August; harness racing from May through September. There are public and private golf courses, numerous tennis courts and fresh- and salt-water fishing the whole length of the state.

CALENDAR OF EVENTS
Swedish Colonial Days, Fort Christiana, late March; **Wilmington Garden Day**, May; **Day In Old New Castle**, third Saturday in May; **Scottish Games**, Fair Hill, 3 miles west of Newark, 1st Saturday in June; **Separation Days**, New Castle, June; **Brandywine Arts Festival**, early September.

WHERE TO GO NEARBY
Fort Delaware State Park is situated on **Pea Patch Island**, reached by boat from Delaware City; there are the **Civil War Museum** and recreational facilities. **Brandywine Creek** and **Lum's Pond** are state parks in the area. **Longwood Gardens**, once an estate of the Du Pont family, is in nearby Kennet Square, Pa. The public is invited to tour the formal gardens and see the fountain displays. Concerts and plays are scheduled throughout the summer. Delaware is part of the **Delmarva** peninsula, which it shares with Maryland and Virginia, and so is close to these states as well as to eastern Pennsylvania and western New Jersey.

FURTHER STATE INFORMATION
Southern Delaware Tourist Information, Milford, DE 19963 (tel: 422-3300); **Delaware State Chamber** of Commerce, 1102 West St., Wilmington, 19801 (tel: 655-7221); **Delaware State Travel Service**, 630 State College Road, PO Box 1404, Dover, 19901 (tel: in state—800-282-8667, out of state—800-441-8846); **Greater Wilmington Convention and Visitors Bureau**, PO Box 111, Wilmington, 19899 (tel: 4088 or 4064); **State Game**

and Fishing Commission, William Penn Street, Dover, DE 19901. Recreation Promotion Service (tel: 656-8364). **Consulates in Wilmington: Peru**

USEFUL TELEPHONE NUMBERS
Southern Delaware—Sussex County
Beebe Hospital, Lewes	645-3000
Legal Aid, Georgetown	856-0038
Legal Aid, Dover	645-3000

Wilmington/North Delaware
Wilmington Medical Center	428-1212
Legal Referral	658-5278
Pan Am Reservations	(800) 223-9762

Florida

Area	58,560 square miles					Population		9,567,112			
Capital	Tallahassee					**Sales Tax**		4%			

Weather	Jan	Feb	Mar	Apr	May	Jun	Jul	Aug	Sep	Oct	Nov	Dec
Av Temp (°C)	19	20	21	23	25	27	28	28	27	25	22	20
Days Rain		8	8	8	6	8	12	15	15	14	9	6	8

While searching for the Fountain of Youth, the Spanish explorer Juan Ponce de Leon landed on the east coast of Florida in 1513. Although he didn't find it, nearly 34 million visitors each year continue the quest amid sun and sea. Many are so captivated that they settle permanently. No place in the state is more than 70 miles from either the Atlantic Ocean or the Gulf of Mexico; Florida's coastline of bays and beaches stretches for 8,426 miles. **Lake Okeechobee,** covering 700 square miles, is one of more than 30,000 lakes. Occupying the most southern latitude in continental USA, Florida has a world-famous wintertime climate, although there are occasional cold spells, even as far south as Miami. Summertime, from May through October, is decidedly hot and humid but made bearable by ocean breezes and air conditioning. The rainy months, and official hurricane season, are June through October, but storms of disastrous proportions are rare.

Visitors have an enormous choice of places to stay, from inexpensive rooming houses to hotels and motels in all price ranges and all stages of luxury, and from campsites to sleek waterfront condominiums. Resort hotels may move up and down through 10 price changes in 12 months. Late April through May and September through October are the least expensive months; February and March are the most costly.

From Thanksgiving through April there are parades, fairs and festivals, horse, dog and car races, golf, tennis and fishing tournaments, arts and crafts shows, concerts, and plays. From about mid-February into April, major league baseball teams come from all over the country for spring training in the Florida sunshine.

The state has five distinct areas. **NORTH FLORIDA** extends from **Pensacola** (pop 66,500) in the "panhandle" east to **Jacksonville** (pop 584,700). Winters are cooler here than on the peninsula, and the area has an Old South flavor similar to neighboring Georgia. Pensacola, which changed hands 17 times among five different nations from 1596 to 1865, is the home of the US Naval Air Station where pilots have trained since 1914. **Tallahassee** (pop 90,600) is the state capital, and Jacksonville is a commercial city and major Atlantic port and resort. Although Jacksonville is not the typical Florida resort, it does provide an excellent stepping-off point for the countryside around. And Jacksonville Beach has numerous guest accommodations for those who want business and leisure. (The city is headquarters for the region of many nationally known companies, particularly in the insurance field.) Accommodations in Jacksonville include **Holiday Inns South** and **West** (398-3331, S$28/D$29-34; 387-4661, S$27/D$32); **Jacksonville Hilton** (398-8800, S$44-66/D$57-79); **Ramada Inn East** (725-5093, S$28/D$38), and **Rodeway Inn** (757-0990, S$27-40/D$32-40) close to the airport, among others. At Jacksonville Beach, in addition to **Holiday Inns, Ramada Inn,** averaging S$23-26/D$26-29, there are beachfront villas at **Sawgrass Resort** (285-2661, 2br-4br $120-160), **Sea Turtle Inn** (249-7402, S$36/D$45), oceanfront, and **Sheraton Beach Resort Inn** (249-7231, S$36-40/D$42-46), all rooms oceanfront.

Perhaps the most rewarding of local excursions is a visit to nearby **St Augustine** (pop 12,800), dating from 1585, some forty minutes drive south on the **East Coast,** and generally reckoned to be the nation's oldest city. And it's an incredible place, with a continuous record of the time visually seen in the changing forms of the architecture—the range runs from narrow, almost medieval streets to stone fortifications and elaborate ecclesiastical architecture. Then there is the scrupulous restoration of buildings from times gone by. Perhaps the scope of the record of the ages may be shown in the changing uses of a building known today as St Francis Inn, and formerly as Dummitt House. Back in 1576, it was a chapel for the first order of Franciscan monks to settle here. Later it became regimental headquarters to a group of Redcoats stationed in the vicinity. At another time it was used as the local gaol (jail), and at still another—during the Civil War—as a clearinghouse for spies. St Augustine and its history are too detailed for more comment here, but the best book on the subject—*St Augustine's Historical Heritage*—is available from the information booth on San Marco Avenue, close to this ancient city's gates. Founded in 1565, the city has a plenitude of Spanish colonial homes, churches, and museums. Accommodations in St Augustine include **Mon-**

son **Motor Lodge** (829-2277, S\$16/D\$24) near the center of the historical and restoration area at Downtown Bayfront, and **Ponce de Leon Lodge** (824-2821, S\$24/D\$29), a golf and tennis resort, among many others. Continuing south is **Marineland of Florida**, with six whale and porpoise performances daily and close-up views of bizarre sea creatures in the Wonder of the Sea display. Just south is the first of a series of tourist resorts that continue down the coast to Miami. **Ormond Beach** (pop 19,100) and **Daytona Beach** (pop 49,300), which today is a haven for college students during the spring vacation period, were early favorites with the motoring set, and such non pareil as Louis Chevrolet, Henry Ford, Barney Oldfield, R. E. Olds all spent time here with their creations. Racers Bluebird and Sir Malcom Campbell came to set world records, on the 23-mile-long, hard-packed sand beach at Daytona. These days, motor enthusiasts swarm to the Daytona International Speedway, the world's fastest track, a giant oval some 2.5 miles long. Late February is when the Daytona 500 is held, while July 4 sees the big stock car meet, and sports cars race over Labor Day weekend. Farther south is **Cape Canaveral** and the **John F. Kennedy Space Center.** Inland is Florida's lake country, with moss-covered trees, ranches incongruously secured with barbed wire fencing, and the sweet scented moist air from the land. At **Melbourne** (pop 42,600)—a favored hopping-off point for private pilots Bahamas-bound or venturing further down to the Caribbean—begins another 100 mile plus strip of beach with resorts large and small, some fishing villages where fishing and not tourism is still life's mainstay, and the so-called millionaires fashionable resort of **Palm Beach** (an island, actually) and neighboring **West Palm Beach** (combined population 70,200) with its rococo mansions.

The story of Palm Beach and its neighbor is not without irony. Henry Flagler, an associate of the original Rockefeller, and a railroad baron in his own right, got interested in the area in 1893. He went to work quickly and created the Royal Poinciana Hotel, and by judicious word of mouth was able to persuade such illustrious citizens as the Wanamakers, Wideners, and Stotesburys to venture south. As a winter version of fashionable Newport RI, Palm Beach was almost an instant success with most of America's rich and socially conscious gentry. The consequence of all this was the construction of West Palm Beach as quarters for the servants of the rich.

Today both Palm Beach and West Palm Beach have become two of the more exclusive of the Florida resorts, while offering extraordinarily good value to all during the summer months. A good way to see just how glamorous a spot the Palm Beach area has become and to see how a town perched on a barrier beach between the Atlantic Ocean and Lake Worth has been developed is to take the drive on A1A for the views of the fine estates, luxurious hotels, and shining condominiums. Strolling on Worth Avenue, to windowshop (or shop) or merely to be seen, is fun. The **Flagler Museum** in Palm Beach is the old Henry Flagler Mansion, restored in all its period luxury. The **Norton Gallery of Fine Art** and **Dreher Park Zoo** and the **Science Museum** are in West Palm

Beach (or West Palm, as the locals say it). **Morikani Park,** 6 miles west of Delray, is a Japanese Museum and garden. **Lion Country Safari,** about 17 miles inland of West Palm, is an excellent preserve of African animals; visitors must keep car windows closed, so an air-conditioned car is advisable (or you can rent a car at the entrance for the excursion). In addition, there are many beautiful beaches, sports fishing, plus greyhound racing at **Palm Beach Kennel Club,** harness racing at **Pompano Park,** tennis, skin/scuba-diving, and air boat rides at **Loxahatchee Wildlife Preserve.** For food, there's a wide range of choices from quaint places where you can eat freshly caught seafood under a thatched roof to elegant gourmet restaurants with continental atmosphere. A resident and tourist favorite in Palm Beach is **Testa's,** with sidewalk tables in a tropical setting. Another with an enduring reputation for good food is **Petite Marmite,** a bit more expensive but not prohibitive. Serious gastronomes make the pilgrimage to nearby Boca Raton—just south of Boynton Beach—for the elegance and quality of **La Vieille Maison,** one of the best restaurants in Florida and offering an expensive *prix fixe* dinner with an emphasis on the dishes of Provence and the French and Italian Rivieras. Architecturally interesting, this restaurant is in a historic Mizner era house that has been transformed into a Mediterannean-styled haven for those interested in good fare and comfortable surroundings, including courtyards and fountains and an interesting collection of Old World antiques. For a different change of pace there's **The Downunder,** just a few steps away in Fort Lauderdale. Descriptions vary from rustic Creole waterfront tavern (with a touch of the California about it), to reminiscences of New Orleans or New York with its collection of *art nouveau* and Victorian memorabilia. The cuisine is basic French, with borrowings from others which include Polynesian. Two other notable French restaurants are **Le Dome of the Four Seasons** and **Le Cordon Bleu.** But if you are in a South Seas mood, you can go to **Mai-Kai** for Polynesian and Oriental cuisine. Also in Fort Lauderdale is the **Plum Room** and **Il Giardino,** and for discoing **Club 51** and **Yesterdays.** For brunch on Sundays, the perennially fashionable **The Breakers** (655-6611, S$150/D$120 up) is a ritual and a new **INTER · CONTINENTAL HOTEL** is due to open Feb 1982. The building itself is an ornate, almost fantasylike grand hotel, with two golf courses on the property, a beach club, plus tennis, swimming, fine dining, nightly music and entertainment; and it's one of the truly five-star hotels around town. Then there's **The Colony,** a favorite of the late Duke of Windsor (655-5430, S/D$36-75 per room) and located in the resort area itself. Numerous other excellent accommodations abound, all offering incredible value for money in this area. **Nando's** and **Bernard's** offer splendid fare, but please don't overlook the many family-style and fast-food type restaurants in the area. They're good because they have to be to meet the competition, and they often provide attractive, appetizing, and reasonable dining for the tourist in a hurry. **Marakesh, Abbey Road,** and **Tiffany's** are among the more popular discothèques.

Local events in the Palm Beach area include the **South Florida Fair** at the end of January, while the **West Palm Beach Auditorium** (toll-free number: 800-223-1814) features sports, concerts, circus, and ballet. The **Atlanta Braves** train at West Palm through April.

Boca Raton has moderately priced motels, but one of the top places to stay is the **Boca Raton Hotel & Club,** a pink-and-white complex set amid magnificently landscaped gardens; winter rates run from $120 double per day to as high as $1,200 for the presidential suite. **Fort Lauderdale** is a charming oceanfront resort city renowned for its yachting. Just south is **Port Everglades,** where luxury ships depart for Caribbean and round-the-world cruises. Miami and Miami Beach are connected by causeways. **Everglades National Park** occupies much of the southwestern corner of the state. Rangers conduct guided tours through this unique subtropical area. There are a variety of facilities available including boat rentals, restaurants, and motels. The **FLORIDA KEYS** are a crescent of nearly 1,000 islets curving around the southern tip of Florida, some 150 miles out into the Gulf of Mexico. The toll-free Overseas Highway, with more than 40 bridges, reaches out over the waters bringing the visitor over more than 100 miles to its termination at **Key West,** just 90 miles from Cuba.

The concept of linking these islets with the mainland was that of the same Henry Flagler who dreamed so successfully the resorts of Palm and West Palm Beaches. His idea was an extension of his eastern seaboard railroad—to Cuba. The last stage of the journey would have been provided by a ferry. But the depression of the late 20s and a vicious hurricane in 1935 put paid to those plans. And it was not until the federal government stepped in that the Overseas Highway was successfully created.

There are a number of fairly large islands on the way to Key West, each with its own local characteristics, including **Key Largo,** an important scuba center in the US with the John Pennekamp Coral Reef State Park, a protected marine park of more than 150 square miles. You can rent all and any equipment here. **Islamorada, Upper Matecumbe Key, Long Key,** and **Marathon** are all popular with fishing folk (both above and below the water) while **Big Pine Key** is home to the indigenous Key deer.

And then there's Key West. Some 120 miles from Florida, this tiny island (just 2 by 4 miles) was originally settled in the early 1820s by pirates, wreckers, sailors, and fishermen, all who depended upon the sea for their livelihood. Many came from the Bahamas, and their descendants proudly call themselves "conchs" (pronounced konks, after the edible spiral-shaped sea mollusk to be found in these waters). Many of these early settlers' simple wooden houses have been restored—and sell for astonishing prices—and the *Old Town* is now a spruced-up historic section with numerous quaint shops and beautiful renovations. *New Town* has concrete block houses and shopping centers.

Despite the changes, Key West maintains its low-keyed pace and there is still a real sense of "manana" in the daily tempo of life. Dress is informal, and Key West formal wear means a colorful sports shirt and slacks for men, and a Key West handprint dress for women.

Part of today's culture has to do with the immigration of many Cubans during the late 1800s who started the local cigar industry. Today, the only cigar maker left works in the cigar shop on Pirate's Alley, but the former cigar makers' cottages, and even a couple of their factories, still stand. Interestingly, descendants of these early workers are now among the islet's most respected families, and Spanish—especially Spanish mixed with English—is frequently heard. Cuban dishes such as picadillo, black beans, and rice are so common as to be a staple in hospitals and school cafeterias.

But the magic of Key West is perhaps most visible at sunset. From all over the island, by bike, on foot, by car, people head for Mallory Square as the sun begins to go down. On a broad concrete dock two blocks long the show begins. Acrobats, a guitarist, the Solares Hill String Band, a juggling act—whoever is in town and feels like it—starts performing. The "banana bread man" comes along, plying his wares from his bicycle. The Iguana Man with his pets draped over his shoulder stoops to let a youngster pet. The crowd, local and newcomer alike, eddies from act to act, to the beat of a bongo drum at the far end. A pause, and the sun drops—to applause and the clicking of cameras. The sunset is glorious and the feeling is: free.

The season runs from mid-December through mid-April, with reductions during the non-peak season. A favorite with movie stars and literati is **Pier House Motel** (294-9541, S/D$80-125), with an excellent restaurant and several bars. **Marriott's Casa Marina Resort** (296-3535, S/D$60-75) is the beautifully restored grand hotel of Mr. Flagler's empire and originally completed in 1931. The original building features a magnificent stone arched veranda, and the best tropical island view in Key West. It's one of the few hotels with tennis courts. For more isolated living there's **Key Ambassador Hotel** (296-3500, S/D$66-78) and **Key Wester Motel** (296-5671, S/D$68), both near the airport. **The Santa Maria Motel, Holiday Inn,** and **Blue Lagoon Hotels** average S$46/D$78, while at **Eden House** (296-6868, S$35-38/D$40-44) you can enjoy one of the older Key West hotels, renovated a few years ago. Ceiling fans and straw rugs provide atmosphere. Two blocks from harbor. Bike rentals at entrance.

For an initial get-acquainted tour of the island, the **Conch Tour Train** (294-5161) offers a 1½-hour narrated tour of the entire island: Old Town, New Town, beaches, harbor area, and the old Naval Station (off-limits for the casual visitor, requiring a pass to enter). The trains, pulled by jeeps disguised as locomotives, leave three depots every hour from 9am to 4pm. Depots are on Roosevelt Boulevard near the intersection of US 1, at the corner of Angela and Duval Streets, and at Front and Duval Streets. Fare is $5.00 adult and $2.50 child.

Old Town Trolley Tours features a narrated tour aboard a vehicle outfitted like an old-fashioned trolley car. The Trolley's small size permits travel through narrow, winding streets. Fare for adult, $5.00. Children ride free with adult. For getting around on your own, the directions given in *Key West, the Last Resort,* a popular local paperback, are thorough and informative.

The **Key West Sightseeing Boat** offers a 1¾-hour narrated cruise of the island's waterfront four times a day, plus a sunset cruise at 5:30pm. Fare: Adult $5.00, students $2.50, children under 12, free.

Glass Bottom Sightseeing Boat Fireball (296-6293) offers four tours daily of the reef located 7 miles out in the Atlantic. Fare: $7.50 adult, $3.50 child.

Reservations are definitely needed for eating out during the season, and restaurants include **Chez Emile,** authentic French cuisine, ambiance old country inn; **Bagatelle,** located in a restored "conch" house; **Port of Call** and **Pier House Restaurant,** both excellent and include such local items as shrimp salad, Key Lime Pie, all expensive; as is **Henry's,** at Marriott's Casa Marina, **Antonia's,** cuisine of northern Italy, homemade pasta, very elegant. Others include **Hukilau,** Polynesian fare, **Rooftop Cafe, The Deck, Captain Bob's Shrimp Dock Restaurant** for the best fried shrimp on the island, shrimp jambalaya and honey rolls a specialty, **El Cacique,** Cuban-American, and **Half Shell Raw Bar,** for conch chowder.

Live theater is available at **Waterfront Playhouse, Tennessee Williams Fine Arts Center,** and **Red Barn Theatre,** plus four first-run movie houses in the shopping center. **Captain Tony's** is the oldest bar in Key West (formerly known as Sloppy Joe's where Ernest Hemingway sipped his grog). **Surfside Six** is a good spot to relax and watch the sun go down. Try **Top of La Concha** and **Copa Cabana Disco,** located in the Key West Inn's former convention center. Other popular discos are **The Monster** and **Fitzgerald's.**

Florida's **WEST COAST** is comfortable and less expensive than the east coast and has an air of settled stability. Due west of Miami on the Gulf of Mexico is **Naples** (pop 15,800), an upper-income community that carefully guards the environment. Naples boasts a beautiful Gulf beach and a midtown 1,000-foot fishing pier. First erected in the late 1800s, it was swept away by Hurricane Donna in 1960 and then rebuilt. There are many fine restaurants and beachfront accommodations including the **Beach Club Hotel** (261-2222, S/D$45-95, more expensive in season), **Sheraton Edgewater Inn** (642-6511, S/D$30-50), both at the beach, the **Naples Bath & Tennis Club** (261-5777, S/D$90-95), just 5 minutes from the shore, and **Cove Inn Marina Resort** (642-7161, S$27 up/D$32 up) located at Crayton Cove. Nearby Marco Island offers similarly excellent accommodations and recreation at **Marriott's Marco Island Beach Hotel and Villas** (394-2511, S/D$65 up). Working north from Naples, you reach fast-growing **Fort Myers** (pop 37,500). Called the "City of Palms," Fort Myers was the winter home of Thomas A. Edison. Henry Ford, his friend and admirer, lived next door. Edison's home and laboratory on the 14-acre estate are now a municipally operated attraction, open daily and with guided tours. Accommodations include **Cape Coral Country Club Inn** (542-3191, S$21-23/D$25-43); **Holiday Inn Fort Myers Beach** (463-5711, S$25-43/D$56-61); **Lahaina Inn** (463-5751, S/D$27-29) at beach; and **Pink Shell Cottage Resort** (463-6181, S/D$35-92) also at beach, among many others. Offshore is **Sanibel Island,** renowned for rare seashells washed up on 14 miles of sandy beaches. The huge **J. N. "Ding"**

Darling National Wildlife Refuge is a good place to see nature birds. **Sarasota** (pop 50,136) is the cultural hub of Florida. Accommodations in Sarasota include **Best Western Aku Tiki Inn** (388-2840, S/D$38-65) with its own private beach; **Colony Beach & Tennis Resort** (388-3681, D$36-150) with apartments on the Gulf; **Four Winds Beach Resort** (383-2411, D$36 to $160 deluxe penthouse suite) also private beach; and **Sheraton Sandcastle** (325-3535, S/D$55-95).

Tampa (pop 279,000), freighter port and industrial city, is Florida's third-largest city. The old **Tampa Bay Hotel,** now the University of Tampa, was modeled on the Alhambra in Spain and is complete with minarets. It was in the backyard of this hotel that Teddy Roosevelt trained his "Rough Riders" for the Spanish-American War. Within Tampa is **Ybor City,** named for a cigar manufacturer who established the dominant industry; it retains its original Latin atmosphere with fine Spanish cafés and restaurants. Visit **Busch Gardens** with its free-roaming African veldt animals and exotic performing birds. **Tampa International Airport** is a bustling traffic center and so modern that it is an attraction itself. Among the many fine restaurants in the Tampa area, including those with Spanish flavor, is world-famous **Bern's Steak House,** where the wine list is an encyclopedic collector's item, the vegetables organically grown by the restaurant, and the meal memorable. There are numerous excellent hotels in Tampa, including **Bay Harbor Inn** (835-2541, S$45-46/D$46-56) with its own private beach, **Causeway Inn Beach Resort** (884-7561, S$25-48/D$29-53), plus **Best Western, Holiday Inn, Howard Johnson's, Quality Inn, Ramada, Sheraton, TraveLodge,** and others providing a complete range of prices. **St Petersburg** (pop 222,500), known as a retreat for the retired, is actually a lively town with activities for people of all ages. The *St Petersburg Independent* gives free newspapers if the sun doesn't shine! Accommodations in the St Petersburg area include the **Bayfront Concourse, The Breckenridge, Belleview Gulf, Don Cesar Beach Resort,** averaging S$24-55/D$35-65; **Happy Dolphin Inn** (360-7011, S$20-46/D$35-55), and **St Petersburg Beach Hilton** (360-1811, S$28-45/D$35-40) among many others. Close by is a string of resort villages such as **Tarpon Springs,** known for its sponge diving and good Greek restaurants. Inland, farther north, is **Weeki Wachee,** home of remarkable underwater mermaid shows, which audiences watch through windows 16 feet below the water's surface.

Low, rolling hills and lakes make **CENTRAL FLORIDA** a different kind of resort area. It has enormous citrus groves and fruit, vegetable, and cattle farms. **Gainesville** is the site of the **University of Florida** and the **Florida State Museum. Ocala** (pop 39,800), deep in thoroughbred horse country, is near the crystal-clear **Silver Springs** which may be toured in glass-bottom boats. **Orlando** (pop 115,100) is an attractive resort city. Precisely in the middle of the state, Orlando was a quiet agricultural town that attracted only a modest number of retirees and tourists but became a "boom" city with the advent of **Walt Disney World,** 20 miles to the south, and **Kennedy Space Center,** 60 miles to the east. Accommodations in the Orlando area include: **Holiday Inn** (351-3500, S$32-46/

D$46-52), **Days Inn** (841-3731, S$32.88/D$27.88), near Disney World; and **Gateway Inn** (351-2000, S/D$32-45). West of Orlando is the **Florida Citrus Tower,** in **Clermont;** the view encompasses 2,000 square miles of citrus groves and lakes. **Cypress Gardens,** 5 miles southwest of Winter Haven, has been superbly landscaped with tropical plants, but is more famous for the breathtaking water-ski shows performed here four times daily, year round. **Lake Wales,** site of winter performances of the **Black Hill Passion Play,** is near the **Bok Singing Tower.** Here on top of Iron Mountain (only 325 feet) carillon recitals take place daily at 3pm. **Sebring,** surrounded by citrus groves, holds the **International Grand Prix Sports Car Race** in mid-March.

Cities To Visit

MIAMI AND MIAMI BEACH

When Henry Flagler extended his Florida East Coast Railroad south to Miami in 1896, the area was occupied by only a few farming homesteaders and some rather questionable people who salvaged cargos from ships wrecked on the offshore reefs. Flagler had no sooner built the Royal Palm Hotel when the Spanish-American War broke out; profiteers speedily filled the hotel, and a somewhat confused government dispatched 7,500 soldiers to protect 1,500 Miamians from invasion. Word spread around the country after that about Miami's wintertime climate, subtropical vegetation, and ideal location on Biscayne Bay.

When the Florida land boom flared up in the early 1920s, it seemed that everyone in America wanted to own property in Miami. After the real estate bubble burst in 1926, Miami simmered along with slow but steady growth that erupted into an incredible hotel-building spree from the 1950s onwards.

Miami Beach is on a slim thread of land, 3½ miles east of Miami, between Biscayne Bay and the Atlantic Ocean. **Collins Avenue,** named after the man who first saw development possibilities in this former mangrove swamp, extends the full length of the beach for a distance of about 8 miles. From 71st Street southward, Collins Avenue has a succession of huge oceanfront condominium apartment houses and hotels, each trying to be more opulent and stunning than the next. Miami Beach exists to give vacationers and conventioneers the time of their lives. Miami, despite its many diversions, seems very sensible and businesslike in comparison. Population 351,427 in Miami proper; 91,200 in Miami Beach. The Greater Miami area is composed of 27 municipalities with a total population of more than 2,000,000.

WHAT TO SEE

Remember to look around while driving to see the soothing views of **Biscayne Bay** from the causeways across to Miami Beach. For a glimpse of true luxury, visit the marinas, especially the huge **Miamarina,** in downtown Miami with an attractive dockside restaurant, to admire the splendid yachts or stroll through the village atmosphere of **Coconut Grove** a few miles south of downtown Miami, the **Venetian Pool,** and "**Miracle Mile**" of shops in Coral Gables. The **Museum of Science** has exhibits spanning Florida history from the peninsula's formation to space exploration far in the future. There is an entrance fee for the **Planetarium** shows, given at 1, 2:30, and 8pm weekdays, and at 5:30 and 10pm Saturdays. There is a show in Spanish at 9:30pm Sunday. The **Wax Museum** presents historic Florida events with life-sized figures in over 40 dioramas; open 9:30 to 9:30 daily and from 10:30 to 9:30 Sunday. The **Seaquarium** on Rickenbacker Causeway has performing killer whales and sharks, lion fish, porpoises, and seals, and is open 9-5:30. Almost directly across the highway is the fairly new **Planet Ocean** with sophisticated, educational, and entertaining exhibits of earth's "inner space," its exploration and utilization. **Spanish Monastery Cloisters,** North Miami Beach, an 800-year-old building transported from Spain and set in lovely formal gardens; sculptures and fine architecture; open weekdays and Sunday afternoons. **Vizcaya,** the ornately beautiful Italian Renaissance *palazzo* built for industrialist James Deering; superb antique furnishings and gardens; open daily 10-5, Wednesdays 10-10. Outstanding rare plants can be seen in the **Fairchild Tropical Gardens** in **Coral Gables** and at the **Miami Beach Garden Center** near Convention Hall. In South Miami, the **Serpentarium** is a spectacular attraction where venoms are extracted from king cobras and other poisonous snakes for use in antivenins and for medical research. Open daily. Gray Line has a 4-hour, 70-mile tour by bus for $10 covering the Greater Miami Area—Miami and Miami Beach. Conducted visits to nightclubs are handled by Leblang's Tours. The Island Queen offers a 2-hour trip from Miami Marina, $3-$5. Boat trips around Miami give a new perspective on the city and are a good way to see stunning waterfront homes. Tours above the city in a blimp are sometimes available, and a number of companies offer helicopter excursions ($15-25 and up) including visits to The Everglades.

ACCOMMODATIONS

Rates in Miami hotels do not fluctuate with the seasons quite as drastically as those in Miami Beach hotels. Rates given here apply from early December to April or early May, depending upon each hotel's policy; rooms can average as much as 50% less in summer. Miami International Airport is located 5 miles northwest of Miami and accommodations include the **Best Western Miami Airport Inn** (871-2345, S$40-58/D$46-64); **Holiday Inn International Airport** (885-1941, S$48-56/D$53-61); **Miami Skyways Motel** (871-3230, S$25-29/D$29-33); and the **Quality Inn Airport** (871-4350, S$36/D$56). Midtown Miami: **Coconut Grove Hotel** (858-2500, S/D$65 up), overlooking the bay and across the street from the Coconut Grove Marina; **Columbus Hotel** (373-4411, S$51-61/D$56-66, with complimentary breakfast); **Dupont Plaza** (358-2541, S$52-55/D$62-65) directly on Biscayne Bay waterfront, luxury apartment suites available, pool, spa; **Holiday Inn** (854-2070, S$20-24/D$30-40), near entrance to

Rickenbacker Causeway; **Everglades Hotel** (379-5461, S$63-71/D$71-81), Biscayne Boulevard; and **Four Ambassadors** (377-1966, S$90-105/D$98-115), on the bay, palatial with executive suites, fresh and saltwater pools. Also located on the mainland is the **Doral Hotel** and **Country Club** (532-3600, S/D$111-124), famous luxury resort on a 2,400-acre estate with 5 golf courses, 19 tennis courts, all water sports, and nightly entertainment. The **Miami Lakes Inn & Country Club** (821-1150, S$65/D$75) is near airport. Hotel tax is 6% in Greater Miami.

Miami Beach oceanfront: Among the most impressive hotels are the **Americana, Beau Rivage,** north of 71st Street; south of it are the **Carillon, Deauville, Doral-on-the-Ocean, Eden Roc Hotel, Fountainebleau Hilton; Montmartre** and **Konover Hotel.** Winter rates, S/D$95-150. Rates at most hotels drop astonishingly in the summer with two or three meals, cut-rate excursions to Walt Disney World, and even cruises to the Bahamas included. Big-name performers who appear in the hotels' nightclubs in winter are scarce in summer, but there is still excellent summer entertainment for adults, and all kinds of supervised fun for children. Some other outstanding Beach hotels, all south of 71st Street and averaging D$24-68 in winter, are the **Algiers, Barcelona, Cadillac, di Lido, Holiday Inn-22nd Street, Lucerne, Sans Souci, Seville,** and **Versailles.**

Greater Miami area: There are more than 850 hotels and motels with 65,000 units in all price ranges. The chambers of commerce of Miami-Dade County, Miami Beach, Coral Gables, and other municipalities will furnish complete lists and give further information.

Key Biscayne: The most luxurious resorts are the **Key Biscayne Hotel & Villas, Royal Biscayne Hotel,** and **Sonesta Beach Hotel,** all located on the ocean. Less expensive is the **Silver Sands Oceanfront Motel.**

RESTAURANTS

Among hundreds of eating places in Greater Miami are: **Casa Santino, Flamenco Supper Club, The Hasta, Jamaica Inn, Piccadilly Hearth, Prince Hamlet, Food among the Flowers, Arthur's Eating House, Pietro's, Tony Roma's,** and **Horatio's,** moderate to expensive; **Don Julio's** and **Centro Vasco,** Mexican, Spanish, and American, moderate; **The Rusty Pelican** and **Miamarina,** for interesting waterfront views. In downtown Miami, the restaurants in the Omni and Four Ambassadors hotels are varied and better than average. **Raimondo's,** on 79th Street, is notable for northern Italian cuisine. Prices are high but seem fitting. Some of the better restaurants in Greater Miami close between mid-May and mid-October. On Miami Beach are **Joe's Stone Crab, Mike Gordon's** and **Tony's Fish Market** for seafood; **Nick and Arthur's, The Embers, The Forge,** for steaks; **Gaucho Steak House** for steaks; **Gatti's,** Italian; **Mai-Kai,** Polynesian. **Wolfies** and the **Rascal House** are excellent Jewish deli-type restaurants where you can also get full meals. For the white table-cloth, seltzer-bottle treatment, the **Famous** lives up to its name. The better eating places in Miami Beach tend to be expensive, and it is wise to reserve ahead, unless you dine very early or after 8:30pm. **Cafe Chauveron** in Bay Harbor Island and **Chez Vendome** in the David William

Hotel in Coral Gables are all elegantly continental and among the more expensive restaurants. Since some of Havana's best chefs are now in the Miami area, there are hundreds of good Cuban restaurants, especially along SW 8th Street in Miami. **Les Violins,** in downtown Miami, is a Cuban nightclub and restaurant patterned after those in pre-Castro Cuba. There is a 6% Miami Beach restaurant tax.

ENTERTAINMENT

The most famous entertainers and dance orchestras in the country appear at Miami Beach in winter at the big hotel nightclubs; check local papers to see which stars are appearing and where. Many hotels have less expensive entertainment in their cocktail lounges or other rooms, often with dancing, and there are many other nightclubs all over the city. On the disco scene, **Cricket Club** and **Ménage** are popular.

ARTS AND MUSIC

Bass Museum of Art, Miami Beach, European paintings and tapestries; Tuesday-Saturday 10-5. **Lowe Art Gallery,** on University of Miami campus in Coral Gables, sculpture and painting, special exhibits and annual shows; open Tuesday-Saturday 10-5, Sunday 2-5, Wednesday evenings 8-10 from October-May, closed in August. Ballet, symphony, and opera performances are held in the **Dade County Auditorium** in Miami and the **Miami Beach Auditorium.** Theaters include the **Player's State Theater,** housed in the Museum of Science, and the **Coconut Grove Playhouse,** both in Miami. **The Ring Theater** is at the University of Miami in Coral Gables. The **Miami Beach Theater of the Performing Arts** offers a full winter season of Broadway shows with New York casts.

SHOPPING

Good buys are locally made women's clothing and swimsuits. Popular take-home souvenirs are coconut candies, citrus fruits, tropical jellies, and seashell ornaments. Stores are open from 9:30 to 5:30, and to 9 on Monday evenings. **Burdine's** and **Jordan Marsh** are excellent department stores in Miami. The **Omni Mall** adjoining Jordan Marsh in downtown Miami contains dozens of shops ranging from $1 novelties to expensive European imports. The Miami central business district is a beehive of small shops catering to Latin visitors with the emphasis on electronics and small appliances. If you have the time to shop, investigate Miami's important wholesale garment district close to downtown where outlet shops offer substantial savings. **Flagler Street** is a street of small international shops.

   Lincoln Road Mall on Miami Beach has nice shops, but the most elegant shopping area on the Beach is in **Bal Harbour** across from the Americana Hotel. **Mike's Cigars** of Miami Beach is stacked floor to ceiling with fine cigars from all over the world.

SPORTS

The world champion **Miami Dolphins** play professional football in the **Orange Bowl Stadium** in the fall. See professional big-league baseball during the March training season; boxing and wrestling events are scheduled year round. **Calder Race Course,** open May through January; horse racing too at **Hialeah** from mid-January to early March; and at **Gulfstream Park** during the winter season. There is jai alai at the **Miami Fronton** and **Dania Jai Alai Palace** from December to mid-April. Greyhound racing is held throughout the year at the **Miami Beach Kennel Club, Biscayne Kennel Club, Flagler Dog Track,** and **Hollywood Dog Track.** There are 39 golf courses in the area, of which 18 are open to the public, and 7 are semiprivate; hotels offer guest privileges.

At least 30 species of well-known game fish are among the 600 known species of salt- and freshwater fish around Miami and Miami Beach. Fishing is free from seawalls, beaches, and the MacArthur and Rickenbacker causeways. You can go deep-sea fishing with a crowd on a big boat, or charter your own craft and guide for real deep-sea fishing from a number of sources. Miles upon miles of beaches are open to the public; there is water-skiing and some surfing. Tennis is very popular, and other diversions run the gamut from archery to bicycling and volleyball.

CALENDAR OF EVENTS

Orange Bowl Festival, parade on New Year's Eve and football game on New Year's Night; **International Boat Show,** mid-February; **Flower Show,** March; **The New York Yankees** train through April in Fort Lauderdale; **Pan American Week,** April; **International Folk Festival,** May; **Poinciana Festival,** early June; **Bowling Tournament of the Americas,** July; **Metropolitan Fishing Tournament,** mid-December to mid-April; **Polo at the Royal Palm Polo Club in Boca Raton,** Dec-April. Boat races and regattas are held year round.

WHERE TO GO NEARBY

Hialeah Park, famous for winter horse racing in an exotic setting, also has a flamingo colony and an exhibit of carriages and stagecoaches. It is open year round. **Parrot Jungle,** 11 miles south off US 1, is served by Gray Line tour buses. **Coral Castle** is 25 miles south. **Everglades National Park,** entrance about 40 miles southwest, can also be toured independently or by bus. This giant park, covering almost the entire southern tip of the state, is a cornucopia of wildlife—a mixture of plants and animals of the subtropics with northern drifters and visitors. The kingpin of the Everglades ecological balance is the alligator. Here, too, are the only crocodiles on the North American continent. For a special treat, fly over to Nassau or some other Bahamian island for the day, or longer. Gambling casinos operate year round in Nassau and Grand Bahama.

SARASOTA

Sarasota stands on the west coast of Florida facing Sarasota Bay. Causeways stretch out to four resort islands fronting the **Gulf of Mexico.** Known to early Spanish explorers, Sarasota was little more than a fishing village until 60 families migrated there from Scotland in 1885 and promptly laid out one of the nation's first golf courses. In 1927 John Ringling chose

Sarasota as the winter headquarters for the Ringling Brothers and Barnum and Bailey Circus. Sarasota Bay's protected waters are ideal for water-skiing, boating, and fishing.

WHAT TO SEE

The great **Ringling Estate** is on US 41, near the airport north of town. Here you will find the superb **Ringling Museum of Art** with its remarkable collection of paintings by Rubens, Rembrandt, Gainsborough, El Greco, and many other masters. Beside the museum is the charming **Asolo Theater,** reconstructed from an 18th-century theater formerly in a castle near Venice, Italy. **Ca'd'Zan,** built in 1925 at a cost of $1,500,000, is the Venetian palace which John and Mabel Ringling furnished, set in magnificent gardens overlooking the water. The **Circus Hall of Fame** is world-famous for its collections of circus trappings and mementos of great performers, puppet shows daily for children, and live circus acts during the winter and summer seasons. Automobiles in the **Bellm's Cars and Music of Yesterday,** off US 41, have been beautifully preserved; exhibits date from 1897. You will also find one of the world's largest collections of music boxes here; open daily. At **Lionel Train Museum,** you can operate trains yourself; open daily. See rare birds at the **Sarasota Jungle Gardens.** Watch glass ornaments made at the **Glass Blowers;** open daily except Sunday, 9-5, free. Two-hour sightseeing boat trips leave at 1pm from the **Marina Jack** at Bayfront Park. *The Dixie* is a replica of a Mississippi paddle wheeler; daily excursions at 11am and 3pm, with moonlight cruises starting at 8pm on Wednesdays. Special cruises to tropical bird sanctuaries at **Robert's Bay** and **Siesta Key.**

ACCOMMODATIONS

There is a wide variety of arrangements throughout the area ranging from campsites for a tent or a trailer, efficiency apartments to hotel suites, daily or weekly rates, high or low season. The prices quoted here are high-season rates for January through April. They can be as much as 50% less in mid-summer. In mainland Sarasota are **Hyatt Sarasota** (366-9000, S$63-71/D$75-83); **Hilton Inn Longboat Key** (388-2451, S$52-73/D$62-92); **Holiday Inn Lido Beach** (388-3941, S$40-77/D$58-91); **Golden Host Best Western** (355-5141, S$30/D$60) two miles north on US 41; **Rodeway Inn** (365-1900, S/D$28-56), US 41 and Gulfstream Avenue; **Quality Inn South** (955-9841, S$24-32/D$28-43), 1 mile south on US 41; **St Armand** (388-2161, S/D$25-40), located on Gulf. **Lido Key** is directly out from Sarasota's main street and is well known for its luxury shops. All of the following resort motels are in Lido Beach, right on the Gulf of Mexico: **Azure Tides** (388-2101, S/D$25-37); **Gulf Beach** (388-2127, D$26 up); **Sheraton Sandcastle** (388-2181, S/D$59-95); **Limetree Rodeway Inn** (388-2111, S$50-70/D$55-75), on Lido Beach. On Longboat Key, farther north, accommodations stretch along Gulf of Mexico Drive. Some, more remote, are more exclusive and more expensive than others: **Colony Beach & Tennis Resort** (388-3681, S/D$85-145); **Diplomat** (383-3791, S$47-55/D$60-85); **Far Horizons** (383-2441, S/D$90-195); **Four Winds**

Beach Resort (383-2411, D$36up); **Sea Horse Beach Resort** (383-2417, S/D$28-75); **Tropics** (383-2431, S/D$15-35). Hotel tax: 4%

RESTAURANTS

In downtown Sarasota are **The Ranch House,** great homemade pastries, **Foley's,** and the **Brewmaster.** East of downtown are **House of Chong,** outstanding Cantonese cuisine, closed Monday; **Martine's,** huge salad bar and steaks; **Davey's Locker,** seafood and steaks. Another favorite for seafood and steaks is **Zinn's.** On St Armands Key are the **Columbia,** a branch of Tampa's famous Spanish restaurant; the **Grenadier,** steaks and roasts; **Tail o' the Pup,** charcoal-broiled steaks, chicken, and seafood. On Longboat Key there are glamorous surroundings and entertainment nightly at the **Colony Beach & Tennis Resort** and the excellent **Buccaneer Inn.** The **Raft and Reef** is moderately priced and the food good, with such locally caught fish as pompano a specialty. The **King's Court** at the Sheraton Sandcastle and **The Pub** at Lido Beach Inn are outstanding. For the dancing crowd, **The Place, Gregg's Greenhouse,** and **Far Horizons** are disco spots.

ART AND MUSIC

The Ringling Museum of Art houses a distinguished collection of baroque art; open Monday to Friday 9am-10pm, Saturday 9-5, Sunday 1-5, children under 12 free. The galleries of the **Sarasota Art Association,** in the Civic Center, are open Monday to Friday 10-5, Saturday and Sunday 1-4, October-May, free. Other exhibits at the **Longboat Key Art Center,** at the north end of the island; and at **Oehlschlaegar Galleries, Beaux Art Gallery,** and **C. J. Bronson Gallery** on St Armands Key. The **Florida West Coast Symphony Orchestra** presents regular subscription concerts, gala pop concerts, and children's concerts. The **Performing Arts Hall** in the Civic Center is designed for all kinds of musical and dramatic entertainment. The **Asolo Theater** presents operas, concerts, art films, and plays.

SHOPPING

The **Circle** on St Armands Key is a succession of delightful shops selling smart resort-type clothing for men and women, and decorative treasures from all over the world. **Sarasota Square** and **Town and Country** are popular shopping areas. **Siesta Key** also has a shopping center.

SPORTS

The **Woodcrest Golf Club** has nine holes lighted for play at night. The **De Sota Lakes Golf Club** is rated with the top 40 in the nation. **Longboat Key Golf and Tennis Club** has 17 water hazards. Boating, fishing, and water sports at the **Marina Jack** at Sarasota's Bayfront Park, where there is also a fine marina for private yachts. Power and sail boats and fishing and water-skiing equipment are available at many other spots also. Fishing from the causeways and bridges may produce catches of tasty trout, snapper, and pompano; try also for the big game fish out in the gulf. Shuffleboard, lawn bowling, tennis, and other typical resort sports thrive here. And during spring training in mid-February to early April, you can see exhibition baseball; the Chicago White Sox train in Sarasota, and the Pittsburgh Pirates work out in Bradenton. There is greyhound racing May-September.

CALENDAR OF EVENTS

King Neptune Pageant Week, activities including coronation ball early April; water-ski shows at Marina Jack, January to March, Sundays at 2; **International Tarpon Tournament,** April to July; **Sailor's Circus,** April; **Festival of Lights,** December.

WHERE TO GO NEARBY

Although many circus people live—and informally rehearse their acts—in Sarasota's **La Tosca** trailer park, the official winter headquarters is in **Venice,** 18 miles south, where you might see a preview of next summer's show in the rehearsal hall and arena. Just east of Venice is **Warm Mineral Springs,** claimed to be helpful in easing the pains of arthritis and rheumatism. Also in the area are large cattle ranges where cowboys work with big herds of Black Angus, Whiteface Herefords, and warm-climate Brahmans and Santa Gertrudis; visit the **Sarasota Cattle Auction,** held in Arcadia every Wednesday. **Myakka River State Park,** 17 miles east of Sarasota, has wildlife sanctuaries, fishing, boating, bicycling, and horseback riding. **Sunshine Skyway** takes motorists high above the junction of lower Tampa Bay and the Gulf of Mexico to St Petersburg, Clearwater, Tarpon Springs, and other Gulf towns.

DISNEY WORLD

Grown-ups who reluctantly agree to take their children or grandchildren to Walt Disney World could be in for a surprise; they'll very likely enjoy every minute of it. This make-believe world of fantasy is constructed as solidly as any city. And the construction continues. When completed, Walt Disney World will include two complete towns, two railways, five lakes, three golf courses, a fleet of 200 ships, and a 7,500-acre wildlife preserve. Here you can experience the past and the future in a delightful atmosphere.

Occupying a 2,500-acre site 20 miles southwest of Orlando. All indoor attractions are air conditioned, and the whole place is kept spotlessly clean. But even with all the transportation available, a lot of walking is involved. Comfortable shoes are necessary, and a hat or parasol is advisable during the summer months.

WHAT TO SEE

The Magic Kingdom is similar to Disneyland in California, but favorite old shows have been improved and new ones added. You can travel "20,000 Leagues Under the Sea" in a submarine and see different marine scenes ranging from sunken Caribbean pirate ships to what it's like under the polar ice cap. The **Haunted Mansion,** with its ghostly waltzers opening coffins, disembodied talking heads, and amiable skeletons, is a triumph of Disney technicians; you'll want to see it twice. **Fantasyland,** behind golden-spired Cinderella's Castle, is where the "Small World" dolls perform. Throughout the Magic Kingdom adorable Disney characters come to life and send little children into ecstasies when they meet Mickey Mouse, Snow White, and other characters. The tableau in the **Hall of Presidents** is so ingenious that all 39 figures, from Washington to Reagan, seem to live and breathe. Outside in **Liberty Square,** a fife and drum corps performs 11 times a day. **Adventureland** includes a jungle cruise in an African launch and a cruise past pirate dungeons and fuming towns in "Pirates of the Caribbean." **Frontierland** recreates the Old West; don't miss the hilarious Country Bear Jamboree and the newest ride on Thunder Mountain. The old-time **Main Street** has a penny arcade, silent film cinema, ice cream parlor, and some good shops. Scientifically authentic **Tomorrowland** includes RCA's popular **Space Mountain,** a simulated rocket ride. The average visitor puts in a 9-hour day trying to see as much as he can, and there's still a lot left for the next visit.

General admission is: $8 for adults, $7 for juniors aged 12-13, and $5 for children aged 3-11. These tickets include one day's unlimited use of the transportation system, admission to the Magic Kingdom, and admission to all free exhibits and entertainment. There are a number of admission options, including Guided Tour (5 Adventures plus complete tour of facility, $13.50 adults and juniors, $10 children) and 10 Adventures arrangement, $11.50 adults, $10.50 juniors—12 to 17, $9.50 children. Disney World is open daily from 9-7 in winter with extended evening hours during summer, holidays, and selected Saturday nights.

ACCOMMODATIONS

The incredible success of the Orlando Walt Disney World "vacation kingdom" has led to an immense boom in hotels and hostelries, and in numerous new amenities nearby, such as the **Mead Botanical Gardens, Loch Haven Park and Art Center, John Young Museum and Planetarium** to name but a few. But while there are many hotels, there are also many visitors and it is wisest to ensure your accommodations by advance reservation. The **Lake Buena Vista** offers town houses and vacation villas. **Fort Wilderness** is for campers and has lots of outdoor activities; campsites are $22 per night. There are also a great many hotels and motels adjacent to the Disney property and in nearby Orlando. Just 10 minutes from Disneyland is **Marriott's Orlando Inn** (351-2420, S/D$55-75) with two pools, six tennis courts, and much more, **Orlando Hyatt House** (846-4100, S/D$60-80), **Sheraton Parkway Inn** (851-8730, S$18/D$22) near Disney World, **Olympic Villas** (351-2420, S$35-45/D$40-50) also but minutes from Disney World.

RESTAURANTS

Gracious evening dining at the **Papeete Bay Verandah** in the Polynesian Village Hotel, and in the **Gulf Coast Room,** an elegant continental restaurant in the Contemporary Resort Hotel, reservations required in both. Casual attire is accepted in the other hotel dining rooms and in the numerous restaurants in the Magic Kingdom. Prices for snacks, soft

Mickey Mouse and his companions, Pluto and Goofy, keeping in step with the marching band in Disney World's Magic Kingdom near Orlando, Florida.

© *Walt Disney Productions*

drinks, and meals are surprisingly reasonable, the highest being under $10 for a complete dinner with prime ribs of beef in the **King Stefan's Banquet Hall. The Empress Lilly** at the Walt Disney World Village dock (an 1800s-style Mississippi stern-wheeler) serves seafood and French gourmet delicacies. Carried-in picnic lunches are not permitted in the Magic Kingdom. However, there are picnic areas just outside the main entrance to Disney World.

ENTERTAINMENT

On warm summer nights there are brilliant fireworks displays, concerts, dancing under the stars, dazzling water pageants, and guest appearances by famous entertainers in the **Top of the World** at the Contemporary Hotel, which also has an excellent restaurant. Paddlewheel steamers make sunset and moonlight cruises, and there are also family dinner shows in the **Old West** and **South Sea Islands.** Out in Fort Wilderness campers are treated to canoe and wilderness tours, nature films, campfire sing-alongs, country-western entertainment, and unique "old west" dining at **Pioneer Hall.**

SPORTS

On the Disney complex grounds there are three 18-hole championship golf courses; greens fee is $16, including golf cart. You can go boating on the **Seven Seas Lagoon** and **Bay Lake** in just about anything from a pedal boat to a speedboat or an eight-passenger outrigger canoe; rates vary according to the craft. Water-skiing, tennis, bicycling, archery, and fishing are available, and there are shuffleboard and volleyball courts.

WHERE TO GO NEARBY

Thirty minutes west of Walt Disney World is **Ringlings Bros. Barnum & Bailey's Circus,** in Barnum City. Ten minutes north off Interstate 4 is **Wet'n Wild,** a water park. Also in the area is **Sea World.** The **John F. Kennedy Space Center,** operated by NASA, the National Aeronautics and Space Administration, is on **Merritt Island,** about 210 miles north of Miami and 60 miles east of Walt Disney World. On 20 July 1969, Neil Armstrong and Edwin Aldrin became the first men to step onto the surface of the moon. You can relive the excitement of this and of all the other US space flights in exhibits and movies at **The Kennedy Space Center Visitor Information Center,** 6 miles south of **Titusville.** Scale models and real spacecraft are displayed. The center is open every day of the year except Christmas Day. Two-hour air-conditioned bus tours of the area include the building where astronauts train for flights, the **Air Force Space Museum, Mission Control Center, Apollo Launch Pads,** and the **Vehicle Assembly Building,** where the towering spacecraft are put together. **Holiday Inn** (269-2121, S$16-19/D$19-25) is 5 miles south of downtown Titusville and **Quality Inn Apollo** (267-9111, S$16-18/D$18-20) is 2 miles south of downtown, both on US 1.

The public is permitted to tour the Space Center unescorted in private cars only on Sundays from 9-3, Space Center operations permitting. Mis-

America's massive rocket ready for take off at the launching pad, Cape Kennedy, Florida.

sile launchings still draw crowds, though they are not as overwhelming as they once were; Florida visitors may call (800-432-2153) toll-free for launch information.

There are several places of interest nearby. **Cocoa,** population 16,700, is on the Indian River, facing Merritt Island and long known as a shipping port for citrus fruits and as a winter vacation town. **Howard Johnson's Motor Lodge** (632-4210, S$24-30/D$29-39), 1 mile north on US 1, and **Quality Inn** (632-4561, S$16-30/D$18-36), 4 miles north on US 1, are good. **Cocoa Beach** is right on the Atlantic Ocean. The resort is reached by a causeway from Cocoa that crosses the Indian River, Merritt Island, and the broad Banana River. Lively and sophisticated, the town is about midway between Patrick Air Force Base and the town of **Cape Canaveral,** where the **Museum of Sunken Treasure** displays gold and silver salvaged from the Spanish plate fleet that sank offshore in a 1715 hurricane. Try deep-sea and river fishing and some of the nightclubs with entertainment. **Atlantis Beach Lodge** (783-9430, S$16-20/D$22-26); **Holiday Inn** (783-2271, S$36-46/D$46-56); **Howard Johnson's Motor Lodge** (783-9481, S$30-35/D$35-49) are excellent, and are all located on FLA A1A, within 1½ miles south of FLA 520.

Titusville, population 31,494, is on the mainland north of Cocoa, facing the **Merritt Island National Wildlife Refuge,** a sanctuary for migratory waterfowl.

FURTHER STATE INFORMATION

Division of Tourism, Florida Department of Commerce, Collins Building, Tallahassee, FL 32304. **Miami-Metro Department of Publicity and Tourism,** 499 Biscayne Boulevard, Miami, FL 33132. **Sarasota County Chamber of Commerce,** PO Box 308, Sarasota, FL 33578. **Walt Disney World,** PO Box 40, Lake Buena Vista, FL 32830, tel: (305) 824-4321 (information); PO Box 78, tel: (305) 824-8000 (reservations). **Pan Am offices,** 110 S.E. 3rd Ave., Miami, FL 33131 and 147 Alhambra Circle, Coral Gables, FL 33134.

Consulates in Miami: Argentina, Austria, Belgium, Bolivia, Brazil, Chile, Colombia, Costa Rica, Denmark, Dominican Republic, Ecuador, El Salvador, France, Germany, Great Britain, Guatemala, Haiti, Honduras, Italy, Jamaica, Lesotho, Mexico, Netherlands, Nicaragua, Norway, Paraguay, Peru, Spain, Sweden, Venezuela.

USEFUL TELEPHONE NUMBERS IN MIAMI

Police	579-6111
Fire & Emergency Medical	374-3131
Poison Info Center	325-6799
Mount Sinai Medical Center	674-2121
Hialeah Hospital	693-6100
Legal Services	638-6666
Tourist Info	887-7852
Chamber of Commerce	374-1800
Pan Am Reservations	874-5100

Georgia

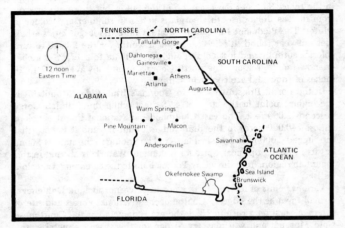

Area	58,876 square miles				**Population**		5,400,851					
Capital	Atlanta				**Sales Tax**		3%					

Weather	Jan	Feb	Mar	Apr	May	Jun	Jul	Aug	Sep	Oct	Nov	Dec
Av Temp (°C)	9	10	12	17	21	26	27	27	22	17	11	9
Days of Rain	12	10	12	9	9	10	12	9	7	6	8	11

Georgia has been featured in enough films to be at least visually familiar to millions who have never visited it. *Tobacco Road* showed the plight of the southern Georgia small farmer; *Gone with the Wind* depicted and romanticized central Georgia plantation life and the Reconstruction era following the Civil War; *Deliverance* showed the world the breathtaking beauty of the mountains and rivers in northern Georgia; and half a dozen films have revealed the eerie charm and hidden dangers of the Okefenokee Swamp.

On February 12, 1733 the last of the 13 colonies was founded by General James Oglethorpe. George II of England released debtors from the prisons to go with Oglethorpe but only 12 came. The purpose of the granting of 50 acres in the new world to settlers was to act as a buffer to the Spanish area to the south and for economic reasons. Georgia flourished and became one of the great states of the South. Many years later, however, her fortunes were reversed when, as a member of the Confederacy, she seceded from the Union in 1861 and suffered greatly both during the war and the subsequent Reconstruction period.

Once extending to the Mississippi, Georgia still is the largest state east of the mighty river. Spreading wide from the Atlantic to the Chatta-hoochee River and stretching tall from Florida to Tennessee and the Carolinas, the state also justly claims a stimulating diversity of climate and topography. Georgia's coast, about 100 miles, has a balmy winter climate; even in January and February the daytime temperatures are in the teens. Summer days may be in the 30C's, but there are breezes from the sea. Inland, south Georgia is hotter in summer and colder in winter. The **Piedmont Plateau,** midstate, where the larger cities are, is pleasant year round. It's brisk enough in winter for the foliage to turn color beautifully and just cold enough for Atlanta to average 3 inches of snow for the season. The north Georgia mountains average 7 to 10 inches of snow and are cooler in summer.

In the north, **Brasstown Bald** in Georgia's **Blue Ridge Mountains** is the highest point in the state at 4,784 feet while the **Tallulah Gorge** descends 2,000 feet. The vast **Chattahoochee National Forest** envelops almost 740,000 acres in the Blue Ridge Mountains and it is here that the rugged 2,000-mile **Appalachian Trail** beginning in the state of Maine has its southern tip, near Springer Mountain. Waterfalls abound in this mountain region, from the wispy **Toccoa Falls** to the cascading **Amicalola Falls.**

Various points of interest in this northeast corner include **Dahlonega,** a small town at the edge of Chattahoochee National Forest and site of America's first gold rush in 1828; the era is depicted at the **Courthouse Gold Museum** and you may try to pan for this precious metal at the **Gold Hills of Dahlonega** or **Crisson Mines.** Continuing south is **Gaines-ville,** situated on the shore of the huge man-made **Lake Sidney Lanier;** the lake provides fishing and a variety of water sports. This is the site of Lake Lanier Islands, a state-owned family resort area complete with a **Stouffer's Pine Isle Resort Hotel,** camping, rental cottages, rental house-boats, 18-hole golf course, tennis, and horseback riding.

In the northwest corner of the state is the **Chickamauga and Chatta-nooga National Military Park.** The Visitor Center on US 27 will provide complete information for your tour of this Civil War battlefield. About 100 miles south is the **Kennesaw Mountain National Battlefield Park,** near Marietta. Here the Union led by Sherman and the Confederate by Johnston fought one of the strategic battles of Sherman's Atlanta cam-paign during the Civil War. A few months later, in the fall of 1864, the formidable Sherman carved a path of destruction from Atlanta to Savannah with such relentless force that it became known as Sherman's "March to the Sea."

About 80 miles east of Marietta is the pleasant town of **Athens** with the **University of Georgia** (the oldest chartered state university in the US) and lovely old mansions. To the southeast of Athens is **Augusta,** founded by Oglethorpe in 1735, just 2 years after he established Savan-nah; both towns are among the oldest in the country. The **Gertrude Herbert Institute of Art** is housed in the magnificent **Ware Mansion** which cost $40,000 to build in 1818. The **Harris-Pearson-Walker House** (c 1797), formerly the MacKay House, was built by tobacco merchant Ezekiel Harris. Visible from the house are the Augusta Canal, constructed in the 1840s, the chimney of the Confederate Powderworks, and two 19th-century cotton mills, all testimony to Augusta's commercial and industrial heritage. Augusta is known to the world as the home of the exclusive **Augusta National Golf Club** which is host every April to the famous **Masters Golf Tournament.**

Traveling southwest from Augusta through the central section of the state, you'll pass through **Milledgeville.** This town escaped destruction during Sherman's infamous march, leaving future generations with an architectural history of the rare and gracious homes of the 1830s and 1840s. **Macon** is a modern industrial city with some fine pre-Civil War homes, the **Hay House** in particular. **Wesleyan College** (1836) was the first to grant degrees to women. Two miles east of Macon on US 80 is the **Ocmulgee National Monument,** an archaeological find of temple mounds, an earth-covered lodge, and other remains of Indian tribes of long ago. South of the town on GA 49 is the **Andersonville National Historical Site and Cemetery.** Here is the location of the notorious Confederate prison where some 13,000 Union soldiers died, mainly of neglect. Andersonville is a tragic monument to the inhumanity that accompanied the Civil War throughout the nation. At the far side of Sumter County lies the village of **Plains** (663 pop), home of Jimmy Carter, the first southern President of the nation since the Civil War. South of Macon on I-75 is **Tifton** which features the **Georgia Agirama** development, a 70-acre farm and village depicting life in the late 1800s.

West of Macon is a delightful area that focuses on **PINE MOUNTAIN. Warm Springs,** a tiny place known to Georgians for decades as a health spa, was discovered by Franklin D. Roosevelt in 1924 three years after he became a victim of polio. Under his patronage the town became the world's foremost center for the treatment of this disease. The **Little White House** became the President's Georgia home, where he died on 12 April 1945. This rambling cottage remains in precisely the same state it was in on the day of his death. Even the famous unfinished portrait by Elizabeth Shoumatoff for which Roosevelt was sitting at the time remains in its place. Also on the grounds are a museum and carriage house with Roosevelt's special hand-operated car.

Then, about 5 miles east in the pretty little town of **Manchester,** is probably Georgia's most peculiar tourist attraction. It is called *Magic Hill,* and what you do is this: stop your car facing up the hill, turn off the engine and release the brakes. Astonishingly, the car will roll up the hill of its own accord. While there are many local and scientific theories, nobody really understands why. The local traffic policeman will direct you to Magic Hill.

Up Pine Mountain and along its ridge is the **Franklin Delano Roosevelt State Park,** located on land once a part of the President's farm. There is a handsome bell-shaped swimming pool built from local flagstone and, at the summit of the mountain, an English-style coaching tavern with a restaurant and a view. A mile farther along you come to the extraordinary **Callaway Gardens.** Here is a 2,500-acre recreation and educational complex situated around 13 lakes and offering four golf courses, tennis, fishing, swimming, and sunbathing on a mile-long sand beach; water-skiing, horseback riding, quail hunting (October to March), and to complete the list of attractions, the **Florida State "Flying High" University Circus,** which performs near the swimming beach from mid-June through August. Accommodations include 175 one- and two-bedroom A-frame family cottages in addition to the **Callaway Gardens Inn** (663-2281, S/D$50); the picturesque Garden Clubhouse and the Plantation Room at the Inn serve fine Southern food. The **Callaway Gardens Lodge** is often used as an executive retreat or by hunting parties; a convenient small airport is located nearby.

In the easternmost part of the state is **SAVANNAH** (see Cities To Visit section). Farther south, near the Florida border, Waycross is one of the entrances to the **Okefenokee Swamp,** a national wildlife refuge, which is roughly 20 miles wide and 40 miles long. The swamp got its name, which is Seminole Indian for "land of the trembling earth," because in places you can stamp your foot and the earth (which may be only peat at that point) will tremble. The Okefenokee has its own fascinating, primitive beauty with moss-draped cypresses and myriad wildlife. Experienced guides conduct a variety of interpretive tours through this shadowy wilderness, enabling you to enjoy your visit to the fullest.

Driving north along the coast, you come to **Brunswick,** "The Shrimp Capital of the World," where Sidney Lanier wrote his enchanting poems under his favorite oak overlooking the **Marshes of Glynn.** A toll causeway will take you across the wide, grassy marshes to **St Simon's Island,** the largest of the three famous "Golden Isles." St Simon's is a bustling beach resort with a good choice of accommodations and restaurants. Wander through the beautiful grounds of **Ft Frederica,** the largest and most expensive fortification built by the British in America. It is an excavation and includes some standing buildings; open daily from 8am to 5pm (except Christmas and Thanksgiving) and admission is free. The **Museum of Coastal History** is in the lighthouse keeper's house at the base of the lighthouse; free admission, open Tues-Sat, 10-4, and Sun, 1:30-4.

Another bridge takes you to the second isle, **Sea Island,** where you can drive among beautiful homes that have housed wealthy families for decades. The **Cloisters** (638-3611, 1 Dec-14 Feb, S$59-104/D$88-132; 15 Feb-14 Mar, S$62-144/D$90-172; 15 Mar-31 May, S$82-178/D$114-210; 1 June-30 Nov, S$68-160/D$100-192) is a beautiful Mediterranean-style resort hotel that is a home-away-from home for genteel, monied families. It rarely has a vacancy near Christmas, so try for another time of year.

The third isle is **Jekyll Island,** from 1888-1942 the private playground of a handful of famous multimillionaire American families such as J. P. Morgan, the Rockefellers, Goulds, and Vanderbilts. It is a beautiful place, reached by causeway from Brunswick, and has many modern motel rooms in the range D$25-40.

Although famous as "The Peach State," Georgia leads the nation in peanut production and is a major producer of pecans, fowl, and pork. Pimintos, imported from Spain years ago, now flourish in fields once devoted almost exclusively to cotton. Turnip greens, collards, and hominy grits are foods the visitor might find unfamiliar. Barbecue is one Georgia specialty the world knows little about. It may sound familiar, but it's not just steak broiled over charcoal. It's a whole side of meat, typically pork, but frequently beef, roasted very slowly over hickory fires and constantly basted with a spicy sauce until every bite of the meat tastes of smoke and seasoning. It is served as a main dish or in sandwiches, often with Brunswick stew, a soup of chicken, pork, beef, and vegetables so thick it can be eaten with a fork. Even the smallest Georgia town will have at least one restaurant specializing in barbecue meals.

Cities To Visit

ATLANTA

Many would say Atlanta is the capital of the southeastern United States as well as of Georgia. Certainly, it is the transportation, business, sports, shopping, and cultural hub of the region, even though it is a comparatively new city. Anyone who has seen *Gone With the Wind* will know that the original little town practically ceased to exist following the siege by Sherman's army in 1864. Modern Atlanta dates from that time and has grown into a metropolis of proud, ambitious, and courteous people. By any standard it is one of America's finest cities. But in spite of its rapid growth it has managed to retain, in both its appearance and its people, an extraordinary quality of grace. In the spring, blooming dogwood trees turn the city into a garden, and the visitor will find himself treated more like a friend than a stranger. Population metropolitan area, 2,100,000.

WHAT TO SEE

Peachtree Center provides a glimpse into the 21st century with its futuristic style and architecture. Its skyscrapers have glass-enclosed aerial walkways high above the streets, opening up vistas of mile after mile of treetops that give Atlanta her park-like ambience. A short distance away, this time beneath the streets, is historic **Underground Atlanta** where Atlanta was born in 1837 as the southeastern terminus of the Western & Atlantic Railroad (the name Atlanta probably derives from the feminine form of Atlantic). **Five Points,** the intersection of five major downtown thoroughfares, once was the site of a drugstore whose pharmacist first concocted and sold a now-famous beverage, Coca-Cola. Not far from the company's new world headquarters building is **The Varsity,** the world's largest outdoor drive-in restaurant. **The Georgia State Capitol Building,** its dome covered in gold leaf mined in Dahlonega in North

Georgia, houses the **Georgia State Museum of Science and Industry. Omni International** is a megastructure that contains under one roof two 14-story office towers, luxury hotel of the same name, restaurants, lounges, three-level shopping bazaar and designer boutiques, six movie theaters, and an Olympic-sized skating rink. Adjacent are the striking **Omni Coliseum** and the mammoth **Georgia World Congress Center.**

Just east of the city center is the **Martin Luther King Jr. Historic District,** 2 blocks that contain the Nobel Peace Prize winner's birth house, the Ebenezer Baptist Church where he preached, and his simple tomb guarded by an eternal flame. Several miles to the southwest is the **Wren's Nest,** the gabled Victorian cottage where Joel Chandler Harris wrote his enchanting stories of Uncle Remus, Br'er Rabbit, Br'er Fox, Tar Baby, and other critters. **Grant Park,** to the east, is home of **Atlanta Zoo** and the **Cyclorama,** a 50-foot-high, 400-foot-circumference painting with three-dimensional figures and narration that depicts the 1864 Civil War Battle of Atlanta. (The Cyclorama is closed while undergoing restoration.) **Georgia Institute of Technology** (Georgia Tech), one of the finest engineering schools in the nation, is located in the downtown area, as is **Georgia State University.** These are but two of the city's six institutions of higher learning, which also include **Emory University** and **Atlanta University,** the latter an affiliation of six colleges that constitute the largest center of Black private higher education in the world.

Northeast of the city, towards Decatur, is **Fernbank Science Center,** which tries to bridge the gap between scientific knowledge and the citizen's awareness of his rapidly changing society. It boasts one of the largest planetariums in the nation, a hall with natural science and other exhibits, the original Apollo 6 capsule, and a 65-acre forest with 2 miles of walking trails.

The northwest section of the city contains what has been described as "the most beautiful residential suburbs in the world." Here, among trees and private mansions, is located the **Governor's Mansion,** built in 1968 in Greek Revival style, and the Atlanta Historical Society's **Swan House,** a 1928 mansion that formerly was a private home, and **Tullie Smith House,** a restored 1840s Georgia farmhouse.

Gray Line, MARTA, and Arnel Tours have sightseeing tours of the city that include these and other areas. A typical tour takes 4 hours and costs $7-$10 adults, $3.50-$7 children 6-11. Gray Line has two tours worth noting: The **Black Heritage Tour,** which includes the Martin Luther King, Jr., Historic District and Black residential areas (Fri-Sun, 1 Apr-Labor Day); and the **Gone with the Wind Tour,** which includes the Gone with the Wind Museum, Big Shanty Museum, Kennesaw Battleground, and concludes with lunch at the Smith House (Sun, Mon, Wed, and Fri). MARTA operates a 3- and a 5-hour tour, sites including Martin Luther King, Jr. Memorial, Georgia Tech, Emory University, Governor's Mansion, and Stone Mountain.

Other sights worth knowing about are the **Atlanta State Farmers Market, Atlanta Botanical Gardens, Oakland Cemetery,** and **Rhodes Memorial Hall.**

The Peachtree Center, a glistening, modern commercial area in Atlanta, boasts the Hyatt Regency Atlanta with its architecturally notable glass-bubble elevators and the bustling 70-story Peachtree Plaza Hotel.

ACCOMMODATIONS

Within an easy, 8-block walking radius (4 blocks each way from main thoroughfare Peachtree Street) downtown hotels include the **Atlanta American-Quality Inn Motor Hotel** (688-8600, S$35-48/D$45-48); **Atlanta Hilton** (659-2000, S$57-88/D$75-106); **Atlanta Marriott** (659-6500, S$52-69/D$66-83); **Holiday Inn-Downtown** (659-2727, S$40-44/D$44-46); **Hyatt Regency Atlanta** (577-1234, S$59-82/D$79-102), a tourist attraction in itself, for this is where the soaring atrium lobby—this one's 22 stories—futuristic "bubble" elevators, and revolving rooftop lounge had their origins; **Omni International Hotel** (659-0000, S$79-94/D$97-112); **Peachtree Center Plaza Hotel** (659-1400, S$67-87/D$85-105), at 723 cylindrical feet and 70 stories the world's tallest hotel. In the convenient downtown-to-midtown area (within 2 miles) there are **Habersham Hotel** (577-1980, S$45-65/D$55-75); **Atlanta Biltmore Hotel** (881-9500, S$38-42/D$46-50); **Colony Square Hotel** (892-6000, S$52-72/D$62-82); **Ladha Continental Hotel** (892-6800, S$35-40/D$40-50); **Sheraton Atlanta Hotel** (881-6000, S$50-61/D$62-73). Two hotels north of downtown, within walking distance of Lenox Square, are **Tower Place Hotel** (231-1234, S$52/D$62) and **Terrace Garden Inn** (261-9250, S$48-54/D$58-64). Excellent motels are on all approaches to the city and near the airport, including a **Hilton Inn** (767-0281, S$39-54/D$51-66), **Holiday Inn** (762-8411, S$36/D$44), **Sheraton** (768-6660, S$40-48/D$45-56), and a **Marriott** (659-6500, S$54-71/D$68-85). Most motor hotels, as well as most downtown high-rise hotels, have pools. Hotel tax: 3%.

TRANSPORTATION

All the national car rental companies have counters at the airport and downtown, and at many of the larger hotels. The sleek, futuristic MARTA bus fleet covers the entire Metro area. Fare is 50¢ (exact change required) and transfers are free. Bus schedules and transportation maps are available without cost at several downtown supervising points. MARTA operates the nearly completed 53-mile rail system. Fare is 50¢ and transfers to interconnecting bus service are free. Stations of interest are **5 Points** (largest), the **Omni**, and **Georgia State University**.

RESTAURANTS

Atlanta has five award-winning restaurants: **The Abbey** (French), **Brennan's of Buckhead** (continental; cousin of the New Orleans clan), **The Midnight Sun** (Scandinavian), **The French Restaurant** (in the Omni International Hotel), and **Nikolai's Roof** (in the Atlanta Hilton, where there's normally a 6-week waiting list for the two-sittings-per-night Russian/continental prix fixe meal). There's excellent dining at other hotels as well, including Colony Square's **Toulouse** and Peachtree Plaza's **Sun Dial**, where the novelty is revolving atop the world's tallest hotel. For down-home cooking there's downtown's **Aunt Pittypat's Porch** and suburban **Aunt Fanny's Cabin**, for years a pillar of the best in Southern cooking. For atmosphere, **The Mansion** is located in a former Victorian home, and **Anthony's** is housed in an authentic, relocated antebellum home. Among other good places to eat are **Pleasant Peasant, The Country Place, Coach and Six, McKinnon's Louisiane, Pano's and Paul's, La Grotta, Joe Dale's Cajun House,** and **The Fish Market** (in Lenox Square).

ENTERTAINMENT

Pick up a copy of *Key, Where, Travelhost, Around Atlanta,* or, best of all, the Saturday weekend magazine section of the *Atlanta Journal-Constitution* for an introduction to entertainment spots and current weekly and monthly happenings. The **Hyatt Regency Atlanta** and **Peachtree Plaza** hotels have elegant rooms for drinking, dancing, and floorshows while **Aunt Pittypat's Porch** features continuous old-time silent movies in its Rocking Chair Lounge. In **Underground Atlanta's** gaslit atmosphere you can listen to jazz, folk guitar, Dixieland band, or bouzouki. Jazz and country music can be found at a number of spots around the city. The **Alliance Theatre** at the Atlanta Memorial Arts Center presents popular productions from Shakespeare to current Broadway shows during its October-May series. Other regularly performing professional theater groups are **Academy Theatre** (October-May) and **Theatre of the Stars,** which stages Broadway productions anchored by big-name performers at the Atlanta Civic Center (also site of the spring performance of the Metropolitan Opera and touring dance companies).

The **Omni Coliseum** features a packed schedule of big-name rock and pop concerts, as well as circuses, ice skating extravaganzas, horse shows, and rodeos. **The Fox Theatre** stages performances by top performers, plus touring theater and dance companies. The yearly (June) **Jazz Festival** in **Atlanta-Fulton County Stadium** is a big draw.

ARTS AND MUSIC

The **Atlanta Memorial Arts Center,** a multipurpose arts complex, was built in 1968 entirely with privately donated funds. Here, the internationally acclaimed **Atlanta Symphony Orchestra** performs from December through April in 1,800-seat Symphony Hall under the direction of Robert Shaw, in addition to an outdoor summer season that includes free Sunday evening performances in Piedmont Park. **The High Museum of Art** exhibits permanent collections of European and American paintings, sculpture, and decorative arts; 13th-through-18th-century Italian paintings and northern Italian sculpture from the Samuel H. Kress Collection; and 19th- and 20th-century prints and photographs. The Center also houses The Alliance Theatre (see Entertainment), **The Atlanta Children's Theatre,** and **The Atlanta College of Art.**

SHOPPING

Downtown stores generally are open from 10am to 6pm. In addition to venerable **Rich's,** the largest and oldest department store in the southeast, and **Davison's,** an affiliate of New York's Macy's, there is the five-level **Peachtree Center Shopping Gallery** and the more than 35 shops in Omni's **International Bazaar,** plus designer boutiques. **Lord & Taylor,**

Saks Fifth Avenue, and Tiffany have branches in **Phipps Plaza** on the north end of town, and **Neiman-Marcus, Rich's, Davison's, Rive Gauche, Courrèges,** and **Charles Jourdan** are but a few of the fine shops in the impressive **Lenox Square** center across Peachtree Road from Phipps (open 10am-9:30pm daily except Sunday, when stores are open noon-5pm). Lenox Square has recently opened a new three-level **Market Place** adjacent to the mall. It consists of 45 new stores, five restaurants, and many fast-food and specialty shops.

SPORTS

The huge (58,000 seats) **Atlanta-Fulton County Stadium** is home ground for three professional sports teams—**Atlanta Braves** baseball, **Atlanta Falcons** football, and **Atlanta Chiefs** soccer. The **Atlanta Hawks** play pro basketball in the 17,000-seat **Omni Coliseum. Georgia Tech** and other colleges field first-rate teams in a number of intercollegiate sports. There are 75 golf and country clubs in Atlanta and outlying areas, more than 40 of them within easy range and at least 15 of which are open to the public. Spring brings the annual **Atlanta Golf Tournament** and **Lady Michelob Golf Classic. Atlanta International Raceway** is 25 miles south of the city and **Road Atlanta,** site of the American Road Race of Champions, is 60 miles northeast. There's even snow skiing, and you have to travel only 15 minutes to find it at **Vining Ski Ridge,** where there's a single slope 580 feet long with a vertical drop of 125 feet. Only catch: the snow is artificial; Atlanta's weather seldom brings the real thing.

CALENDAR OF EVENTS

The Steeplechase, mid to late March; **Dogwood Festival,** with sports events, concerts, art exhibits, and tours of homes in posh and/or historic neighborhoods, and the **Atlanta 500** race in April; the **Atlanta Arts Festival,** in Piedmont Park, a big affair embracing all forms of the arts, mid-May; the **Dixie 500** and **Grand National Circuit Stock Car Races,** June; **Peachtree Road Race,** second-largest foot race in the country, and **Salute to America Parade,** July 4.

WHERE TO GO NEARBY

Six Flags Over Georgia (10 miles west of town on I-20) is a 276-acre park that has enough going on to occupy the whole family. Open 10am to midnight Fri-Sat; 10am to 10pm Sun-Thurs. More than 100 rides, shows, and attractions run the gamut from the Mindbender, the world's only triple-loop roller coaster, to the 70 hand-carved horses of the Riverview Carousel. One-day admission for an unlimited number of attractions is $10.95 for both adults and children; 2-day admission is $15.95; children under 3 admitted free. **Stone Mountain Park,** 16 miles east of Atlanta, is 3,200 acres surrounding the world's largest exposed mass of granite, on which is carved the world's largest relief sculpture, the equestrian figures of Confederacy President Jefferson Davis and Confederate Generals Robert E. Lee and Thomas "Stonewall" Jackson. For a close-up look at the impressive monument, take the cable car to the top (for the hardier, there's a hiking trail). Also within the park are an **Antebellum Plantation** with 19 authentic old buildings and houses brought in from around the state, a delightful **Antique Auto and Music Museum,** scenic railroad ride with Indian "attack" around the mountain's base, paddlewheeler rides on the lake, and facilities for camping, fishing, golf, tennis, picnicking, and swimming. **Stone Mountain Inn,** for a prolonged vacation, has 90 rooms (469-3311, S$30-34/D$34-41.50). Admission to the park is $2.50 per car and a booklet valid for eight attractions is $8.95 adults, $5.50 children; choice of four attractions is $5.50 adults, $3.25 children. **Historic Roswell,** 25 miles north of Atlanta, is a small community that was spared destruction during the 1864 Battle of Atlanta and so retains many fine pre-Civil War homes, a few of which can be toured. Columned **Bulloch Hall,** childhood home of President Theodore Roosevelt's mother, is open during special events. **Lake Lanier Islands,** four connecting state-owned islands just 45 minutes from downtown, offers 1,200 recreational acres with facilities for camping, swimming, tennis, picnicking, sailing, and horseback riding. Accommodations vary from houseboats to cottages (945-8331, two bedrooms $45-75) to **Stouffer's Pine Isle Resort Hotel** with tennis courts and 18-hole golf course (945-8921, S$46-54/D$62-70).

SAVANNAH

When General James Oglethorpe arrived in the colonies in 1733 he chose the spot on which Savannah now stands for his first settlement. It was about 17 miles up the **Savannah River** from the ocean, offering both a deep-water harbor and a high bluff on which to perch the town. He chose well. The design of America's "First Planned City" was selected by Oglethorpe and based on 5 squares which still exist today. Savannah thus became Georgia's oldest city and, indeed, one of the oldest in the country. By amazing fortune beautiful parts of the city have survived.

Fires in 1796 and 1820 opened large parts of the city for accommodating the Georgian colonial and Greek revival mansions that were then coming into vogue. When the Civil War broke out, the city became an important Confederate stronghold and one of the crucial links with England, which was aiding the South by buyings its cotton. Then General Sherman arrived at the end of his famous march from Atlanta, and the city surrendered before any damage occurred. Urban blight became the next enemy, and by the mid-20th century Savannah was showing her age. In 1955 the restoration era began with the Historic Savannah Foundation encouraging the restoration of 1,100 historically significant buildings and the beautification of parks and squares. The 2½-square-mile restored downtown area is a model for city revitalization. As a result Savannah is probably more attractive today than at any time in its history. Savannah's shirt-sleeve climate makes outdoor recreation a pleasure virtually year round. The area has a temperate climate with a seasonal mean temperature of 51°F in spring, 80°F in summer, and 66° in autumn. Population, 141,634.

WHAT TO SEE

It is suggested that any visitor to Savannah stop at the **Visitors Center** (open 8:30-5 daily, 9-5 weekends) to plan his itinerary. The center is housed in the station of the former Central of Georgia, the state and the US's first railroad.

Much has been made of the city's historic waterfront—those industrial warehouses that remain to salute the days of cotton's importance. Today, rejuvenated as the **Riverfront Plaza Park**, the 9-block concourse is for strolling, ship-watching, and shopping. Its boundaries—those self-same warehouses—are now some of the better places to get acquainted with boutiques, antique stores, restaurants and pubs, galleries and craft shops, and museums. While in the area see **Factors Walk**, passageways into the past, connecting the cotton warehouses to the upper levels of the City. Walls of oyster shells, ballast, and brick abound the entire area. Also the **Waving Girl Statue** depicts the legend of Florence Martus who was know in every port for her vigilance to her fiance who sailed away in the late 1800s and never returned. Florence waved a white scarf by day and a lantern by night to every ship that passed her lighthouse home for 44 years . . . but in vain.

Ships of the Sea Museum, open daily 10-5, located on bluff street above the Riverfront Plaza area, contains an outstanding and comprehensive collection of models, scrimshaw, figureheads, and numerous other seafaring artifacts of *tradition America*. Children under 7 free, 7-12 75¢, adults $2.

For a sea-going voyage, from the harbor, try the *Harbor Queen* or *Waving Girl* that make regular daily excursions up and down the river, plus scheduled roundtrips to **Hilton Head** and the **Dafuskie Islands** plus the twilight cocktail cruises, many of which require reservation. The **Historic Savannah Foundation** conducts tours of the restored area. The **Negro Heritage Trail** has three walking or driving tours highlighting historic sites significant in Black history (tel: 233-2027 for reservations). **Carriage Tours of Savannah** (tel: 236-6756) show the city's charms at a leisurely pace. There are also **Walking and Biking Tape Tours** for rent at the Visitors Center. For current data, call the **Historic Savannah Foundation** (tel: 233-3597) or **Savannah Scenic** (tel: 355-4296). A number of industrial, conventional, and other commercial tours are available by arrangement with local businesses involved. Among the many historic points of interest are: **Juliette Gordon Low Birthplace**—Oglethorpe at Bull Street. Our first registered National Historic Landmark. Built 1818-1821. Home of Gordon Family. Juliette Gordon Low founded the Girl Scouts in 1912 in Savannah. **Telfair Academy Of Arts And Sciences**—Barnard and State Streets. Former home of the Telfair Family. One of Southeast's oldest museums. Contains important paintings, statuary and antique furniture. Admission charged. **Davenport House**—Habersham and State Streets. (1820) Built by Isaiah Davenport. Now a museum. This home is a fine example of Georgian architecture. A public garden of 18th-century design is now open. Admission charged. **Owens-Thomas**

House—Abercorn and State Streets. (1816) Designed by William Jay. Contains many architectural innovations as well as original and fine period furnishings. **The Green-Meldrim House**—Bull and Harris Streets, on Madison Square, where Sherman lived for several months after arriving in Savannah. Exquisite Gothic architecture, and serves today as the parish house of St John's Episcopal Church. **Fort Pulaski** (1829-1849), Robert E. Lee's first engineering assignment after graduation from West Point. Most of the above are open daily except national holidays.

ACCOMMODATIONS

Visitors to Savannah have a wide variety of lodging choices among the city's hotels, motels, and inns. The newest hotel, the **Hyatt Regency Savannah** (238-1234, S$47-60/D$69-72), is built on a 30-foot bluff facing Bay Street. Its location is said to be at the very spot where Oglethorpe stepped off his ship to found the colony of Georgia. The **De Soto Hilton** (232-0171, S$43-54/D$57-68), in the heart of the historic district, is one of Savannah's most famous hotels. For relaxation and sports, try the **Sheraton Savannah Inn & Country Club** (897-1612, S$50-55/D$60-65), on Wilmington Island Rd, 15 minutes from city center. Downtown motels include the **Ramada Inn** (232-1262, S/D$33-38), **Downtowner Motor Inn** (233-3531, S$28-34/D$34-38), and **Quality Inn** (236-6321, S$21-25/D$25-29).

There is a growing interest in small inns that offer an alternative to hotels and motels. These include **Bed and Breakfast** (233-9481, S$20/D$24 CP), in a renovated Federalist townhouse in the heart of the historic district; **Four Seventeen Inn** (233-6380, suite S/D$55, family of four, $75), built in 1872; and **Liberty Inn** (233-1007, S/D$65-90), built in 1834.

RESTAURANTS

Savannah is known for its delicious seafood. **Old Pink House,** 23 Abercorn St (282-4286) superb continental and regional dishes served in intimate small rooms of an 18th-century house; **17 Hundred 90 Restaurant,** 307 E President (235-7122) 19th-century atmosphere; **Chart House,** 202 W Bay St (234-6686) features steaks and prime ribs. The award-winning **Pirate's House** is located in Savannah's historic Trustees' Garden, serves buffet and lunch as well as regular menu fare at lunch and dinner, plus 35 fabulous desserts; **Watson's Crab House Restaurant** serves fresh local seafood in an informal atmosphere. Overlooking a picturesque waterway at Thunbolt (outside of town) is **Tassy's Pier, Inc.** specializing in seafood prepared with imagination; for reasonable and casual homestyle eating try **Morrison's Cafeteria,** 15 Bell St.

CALENDAR OF EVENTS

Georgia Week, February; **St Patrick's Day, Annual Tour of Homes & Gardens,** March; **Night in Old Savannah,** April; **Savannah Days,** last week in April, first in May, takes place in Johnson Square. Ethnic food and entertainment with everything priced under $1. All monies donated to the Girl Scouts; **Savannah Scottish Games,** May; **Blessing of the Fleet,** June; **Oktoberfest,** October; **Holiday Delights,** December.

FURTHER STATE INFORMATION

Pan Am, 3445 Peachtree Rd., N.E., Atlanta, GA 30305; **Tourist Division,** Georgia Department of Industry and Trade, 1400 North Omni International, Atlanta, Georgia 30303. Tel. 404-656-3590. In Atlanta: **Atlanta Convention and Visitors Bureau,** 233 Peachtree Street, N.E., Suite 200, Atlanta, Georgia 30303. Tel. 404-659-4270; in Savannah: **Savannah Visitors Center,** 301 West Broad Street, Savannah, Georgia 31499. Tel: 233-3067.

Consulates in Atlanta: Austria, Barbados, Belgium, Bolivia, Brazil, Canada, Colombia, Costa Rica, Denmark, Dominican Republic, El Salvador, Finland, France, Germany, Grenada, Guatemala, Honduras, Iceland, Israel, Italy, Japan, Korea, Luxembourg, Mexico, Nicaragua, The Netherlands, Panama, Senegal, Sweden, Switzerland, Turkey, United Kingdom.

USEFUL TELEPHONE NUMBERS IN ATLANTA

Ambulance	294-2222
Police	658-6666
Fire	659-2121
Poison Control Center	588-4400
Grady Memorial Hospital	588-4307
Doctors Hospital	938-2811
Legal Counseling & Preventive Law Clinic	586-0696
Chamber of Commerce	524-8481
Tourist Information	393-4761
Pan Am Reservations	688-9830

Savannah

Ambulance	352-8122
Police	233-9321
Fire	232-5552
Tourist Information	233-3067
Pan Am Reservations	232-0256

Hawaii

Area	6,425 square miles					Population	965,000					
Capital	Honolulu					Sales Tax	4%					

Weather	Jan	Feb	Mar	Apr	May	Jun	Jul	Aug	Sep	Oct	Nov	Dec
Av Temp (°C)	23	22	23	23	24	26	26	26	26	26	24	23
Days of Rain	10	10	9	9	7	6	8	7	7	10	10	11

If you have never been to Hawaii, you may think of it in terms of surf-boards and pineapple punch or a kind of tropical suburb of Los Angeles. But Hawaii is much more than this. Just over 2,000 miles west of San Francisco and at about the same latitude as Cuba, Hawaii is the genuine Pacific Paradise of the United States. Clear water and superb beaches offer the best in every kind of water sport—swimming, skin- and scuba diving, small and big game fishing, sailing and, of course, surfing on the giant waves that roll in from the Pacific.

The state is actually a group of islands with **Hawaii** the biggest, about the size of Connecticut and Rhode Island together. But **Oahu,** 44 miles long and 30 miles wide, is the commercial and vacation center and con-tains the capital, **Honolulu.** There are some 965,000 Polynesian, Oriental, and Caucasian inhabitants on the seven main islands with 762,020 of the total population living in the City and County of Honolulu, which is all the island of Oahu. The superb climate, lush tropical vegetation, magnificent vistas, exciting food, hula dancers, and Hawaii's beautiful resorts make this vacation spot different from any other in the US. A long way from home, perhaps, but that's a small consideration for what could be the vacation of a lifetime. All of the islands described below can be reached by air.

The island of **HAWAII,** known as the "Big Island," is dominated by the spirit of *Pele,* the fire goddess who, it is said, causes the volcanoes **Mauna Loa** and **Kilauea** to erupt. You will want to go to Kilauea and to **Halemaumau,** the fire pit thought to be Pele's home.

Make your headquarters in the city of **Hilo,** the orchid capital and second largest city in the islands; the **Naniloa Surf Hotel** (935-0831, S$56-65/D$49-68) is excellent, and worth noting are the **Sheraton Waiakea** (961-3041, S$45 up/D$48 up); the **Hilo Lagoon** (935-9311, S$29-42/D$32-45); **Hilo Hawaiian** (935-9361, S$37-52/D$40-56); **Hilo Bay** (935-0861, S$24-41/D$27-44). Or base yourself in the **Kailua-Kona** resort area, or in the National Park section, about 25 miles from Hilo; stay at the **Volcano House** (967-7321, S$28-38/D$31-41) situated on the edge of Kilauea's crater.

Among other places to visit on Hawaii are **Akaka Falls** at the end of magnificent tropical gardens and **Kalapana Beach,** which has black sand churned from the lava of the volcano. Paradoxically, there is skiing in winter on the volcano slopes, also hunting for wild goat. Visit **Parker Ranch** nearby. On the **Kona** coast of the island there is marvelous fishing; stay at the **Hotel King Kamehameha** (329-2911, S$44-64/D$48-68), **Kona Hilton** (329-3111, S$46-72/D$52-82). Just north of the Kailua-Kona area at the ancient site of Kaupulehu lies **Kona Village** (325-5555, S$125-210/D$165-250), a remote Polynesian hideaway resort. And at Kawaihae, the magnificent, luxurious **Mauna Kea Beach Hotel** (882-7222, S$170-210/D$185-230) rises above the shoreline.

KAUAI, where Captain Cook landed, is known as the "Garden Island" because of its magnificent foliage. The **Coco Palms Hotel** (822-4921, S$52-65/D$54-67) near the mouth of the Wailua River; the **Sheraton Kauai** (742-1661, S$64-69/D$67-82) at **Poipu** and **Kauai Surf Hotel** (245-3631, S$52-86/D$55-89) at **Lihue** are modern and excellent, and have everything from swimming pools to Saturday-night hula shows. Less expensive are the **Poipu Beach** (742-1681, S$44-54/D$46-56), **Hanalei Bay Resort** (826-6522, S$45-53/D$45-53), **Kauai Resort** (245-3931, S$35-67/D$38-70), **Poipu Village-Cottages** (742-1619, $28-74), **Islander Inn-Kauai** (822-4931, S$39-42/D$43-46). Kauai is an island where a rented car is useful, for exploring the hills and the area's beautiful beaches, including Hanalei, one of the finest of any of the islands, where the luxurious **Club Mediteranee** overlooks the location where *South Pacific* was filmed. There are also, on the lee side, the **Barking Sands,** with five-foot coral and lava dunes, where the sand, when rubbed, is said to sound like a dog barking. There is a "sliding bathtub" here, where falls spray down a natural chute into a fresh-water swimming pool. Also worth seeing is the **Wailua River,** where you can take a boat trip through the hyacinth-filled water to the lovely **Fern Grotto.**

The villages on the island of **MAUI** are set on hills that rise from sea level to **Haleakala,** the world's largest dormant volcano, whose cinder cones stand among the unique Hawaiian silversword flowers with brilliant yellow and magenta blooms. You can descend to the floor of the crater on horseback. Between **Haleakala National Park** and the sea is a vast natural jungle, much of it still unexplored. See the **Seven Pools,** focal point of the **Kipahulu Valley** with its plunging waterfalls and rare wild birds. Among the island's luxury hotels are the **Hana Maui** (248-8211, S\$106 up/D\$139 up), **Royal Lahaina Hotel** (661-2611, S\$56-73/D\$58-75) and the **Sheraton-Maui** (661-0031, D\$62-75/D\$65-78). Also worth noting at **Lahaina** is **TraveLodge** (661-3661, S\$46-48/D\$46-48). In addition, the **Inter-Continental Maui** (879-1922, S\$73-98/D\$75-100), on the western slope of the inactive **Haleakala Volcano.** More moderately priced are the **Maui Beach** (877-0061, S\$27-36/D\$30-38) and the **Maui Palms Hotel** (877-0071, S\$27-36/D\$30-38) in Kahului. For a trip into the past, visit the **Pioneer Inn** (661-3636, S\$25-31/D\$28-33) on the Lahaina waterfront. Among the newer hotels are the **Hyatt Regency Maui** (667-7474, S\$85-135/D\$85-135) and the **Kaanapali Beach Hotel** (661-0011, S\$51-65/D\$53-67) at Kaanapali Beach. The road from **Wailuku** to **Hana** is noted for its spectacular scenery. The oldest US school west of the Rockies (1831) should be seen in Lahaina and the biggest banyan tree in the islands. **Kaanapali** has an outstanding golf course. While on Maui try to see a hukilau (community fishing party) at **Hana.** The quaint six-mile excursion "sugar cane train" of the Lahaina, Kaanapali, and Pacific Railroad is another attraction.

MOLOKAI island is almost completely in its natural state, and has pretty ranches and pineapple plantations. Wild deer roam all over the island. Hunting is permitted and the game fishing is great. Stay at the Pau Hana Inn (536-7545, S\$12-35/D\$15-40), at the Sheraton Molokai (552-2555, S\$52-62/D\$55-65), or the Molokai Shores Condo Apts (S\$38-58/D\$38-58).

Lanai Island offers a perfect, nearly idyllically quiet vacation. Wholly owned by Dole Pineapple, the place to stay is the Lanai Lodge in Lanai City (pop. 2,125). Reservations for the 11 rooms are essential (S\$32-37/D\$35-50). There's an attractive 9-hole golf-course, no fees. Good swimming is to be found at **Manele Beach Bay** and **Shipwreck Beach,** accessible by 4-wheel drive vehicles. And there's hunting, fishing, and hiking. There's positively no commercial entertainment, and movies are shown when enough people want to attend!

City To Visit

HONOLULU, OAHU

WHAT TO SEE
The Hawaii Visitors' Bureau in Waikiki, 2270 Kalakaua Ave., Suite 801 (tel: 923-1811), a section of Honolulu, can supply you with all kinds of information, maps, guides, and a calendar of events. Free entertainment

includes the **Kodak Hula Show** on Tuesday, Wednesday, and Thursday mornings all year, adjacent to the **Waikiki Shell**, and tours of Hawaiian wood carving and perfume factories daily. For a panoramic view of Honolulu harbor, the city and its hills, visit the **Aloha Tower**. The **Hawaiian Wax Museum** presents a historical panorama of Hawaii's royal monarchy. Visit **Paradise Park**, an area featuring shows of exotic and beautiful birds. Guided tours through pineapple canneries and sugar mills are available during most of the year. Worthwhile is a walk through **Chinatown**, to see the exotic jumble of apothecary, jade and food shops. Try to visit the **Punchbowl**, the National Memorial Cemetery of the Pacific. From the rim of this extinct volcano you can enjoy a sweeping view of Honolulu, from **Diamond Head Crater**, the city's greatest landmark, to the International Airport. **Foster Gardens** has a profusion of tropical flowers, trees and shrubs indigenous to this part of the Pacific. The **Arizona Battleship Memorial** is accessible by Navy shuttle boat free of charge at Halawa Gate Pearl Harbor on Kamehameha (route 90) highway.

GETTING AROUND

The Bus goes almost everywhere on Oahu, at very reasonable cost (50¢ for adults, including free transfers from one bus to another, and free to senior citizens, including tourists). Guided bus tours and City Tours around Oahu cost about $9.50 to $11.20 and are very comfortable, or you can do it on your own aboard TheBus from **Waikiki**: Take Bus #5 or Bus #8 to Ala Moana Shopping Center; transfer to a Kaneohe/Wahiawa Bus for a 4-hour circle trip via **Pali, Kailua Kaneohe,** the **Polynesian Cultural Center, North Shore, Haleiwa, Wahiawa.** Buses leave every half hour from 5a.m. to 6p.m. Round trip is just 50¢. The weekly visitors' guide, *"Where,"* (free at most hotel desks) details all the possible mini-cost excursions. Taxis are best called by phone; they are metered at $2 up for the first mile and $1 for each additional mile. Limousines with chauffeur-guides cost around $18 up per hour per vehicle. For those who'd like to drive themselves, driving conditions in Honolulu are similar to those in any other US city.

Inter-Island Tours: Hawaiian and **Aloha Airlines** run dozens of inexpensive flights between island airports, and there are also several air-taxi charter and helicopter services.

HOW TO GET THERE

Flying time to Honolulu International Airport from New York is 11½ hours; from San Francisco, 5¼ hours; from Guatemala City, 9½ hours; from Tokyo, 6½ hours. The Gray Lines Airporter Service costs to Honolulu $3.50 per person, $6.00 round trip.

ACCOMMODATIONS

The **Cinerama Reef** (923-3111, S$26-56/D$28-58) on Waikiki Beach. The Halekulani Hotel (923-2311, S$45-75/D$45-75), also on the beach, is quiet and pleasant and features garden cottages. Other good hotels on the beach include the huge **Hilton Hawaiian Village** (949-4321, S$46-76/

The silhouette of Diamond Head overlooks the year-round resort for surf, sand and sail on world renowned Waikiki Beach.

143

D$52-82 up); the **Kahala Hilton** (734-2211, S$93-183 up/D$96-185 up), overlooking the Waialae Golf Course; the **Moano** (922-3111, S$38-69/ D$41-72), the **Princess Kaiulani** (922-5811, S$31-49/D$34-52); the **Royal Hawaiian** (923-7311, S$62-90 up/C$65-93 up), the best known hotel in the island; the **Sheraton-Waikiki** (922-4422, S$57-87/D$60-90). Near the beach is the towering **Ilikai Hotel** (949-3811, S$60 up/D$60-90 up), with a view of the Ala Wai Yacht harbor. Also note the **Hale Pua Hotel**—all studios (923-9693, S/D$29-33) and **Hyatt Regency Hotel** (922-9292, S/ D$65-95 up) and both just one block from the beach. There are also many small hotels and apartment hotels which are available by the day, week or month. Make reservations in advance. General Excise tax: 4%.

RESTAURANTS

There are many restaurants and hotels serving international food in Honolulu and, of course, excellent Chinese and Japanese restaurants. The *luau*, which is a Hawaiian feast, features the Hawaiian dish *poi*, a paste made of the root of the taro plant, and Hawaiian roast suckling pig, cooked by hot rocks in an *imu* (underground oven). Be sure to sample the local fruits and juices, such as pineapple, guava nectar, passion-fruit and papaya. Outstanding restaurants in Waikiki for continental cuisine are the **Captain's Galley** in the Moana-Surfrider Hotel and **Michel's** in the Colony Surf Hotel. The revolving **La Ronde,** high above Waikiki, and the **Top of the I** in the Ilikai Hotel are both restaurants with panoramic views of the city. For steaks, try the **Whaler's Broiler** in the Ala Moana Hotel or **Canlis Broiler. The Pagoda Floating Restaurant,** featuring its owner's collection of Japanese carp, is very popular. Visit the **Willows** and try their popular coconut cream pie. **Fisherman's Wharf** is ideal for lunch or dinner and features *mahi-mahi,* the delicately flavored island fish, plus an excellent selection of other seafood. Best known among the many fine Chinese restaurants are **Wo Fat's** in downtown Honolulu, the **China House Restaurant** in the Ala Moano Center. There are a number of picturesque Japanese teahouses in Honolulu.

Some of the places featuring *luau* food and traditional Polynesian entertainment are the **Hilton Hawaiian Village, Kahala Hilton** and the **Royal Hawaiian;** by reservation only. Less formal is the **Wailana Coffee House** (open 24 hrs), near Hawaiian Village Hotel. Among the best spots for cocktails in the Waikiki area are the Royal Hawaiian Hotel, the **Captain Cook Bar** in the Surfrider, **Michel's** at the Colony Surf, the **Kamaaina Bar** at the Moana, the **House Without a Key** at the Halekulani, and **Top of the I** at the Ilikai Hotel.

ENTERTAINMENT

There is a tremendous variety of night life in Hawaii: the **Blue Dolphin Room** has turn-of-the-century Hawaiian atmosphere in the Outrigger Hotel, dining and old style Hawaiian entertainment; **Catamaran** Restaurant in the **Holiday Inn-Waikiki,** nightly entertainment; **Duke Kahanamoku's** features a Polynesian "spectacular"; the Halekulani Hotel's **Coral Lanai** and the Kahala Hilton's **Hala Terrace,** Hawaiian entertainment.

At most night clubs you can see a good hula, and a few places offer Polynesian, Tahitian and Samoan entertainment.

ART AND MUSIC

The **Honolulu Academy of Arts** contains interesting collections of Oriental and Western art and special exhibitions of Pacificana and modern art. **Bishop Museum** houses some of the finest collections of Pacificana, including the famous featherwork of the Hawaiians and relics and crafts from the entire Pacific. **Queen Emma Museum** is the beautiful summer palace of this former Queen at the time Hawaii had rulers. It contains many collections of personal and household relics of the Victorian era in which she lived. **The Archives,** next to **Iolani Palace,** contain important and valuable Hawaiian documents, relics, and old photographs of early island history. The Palace, which has undergone extensive restoration, has the only throne room on US soil. Tours are available by reservation only. Theaters include the **Honolulu Community Theater,** the dramatic center of the **University of Hawaii,** and the **Hawaiian Performing Arts** at the **Manoa Valley Theater** near the University of Hawaii.

The **Honolulu Symphony** is the leading musical organization of the islands. Visitors can enjoy good music presented by the finest guest artists in the **Neal S. Blaisdell Center** and "under the stars" in the **Waikiki Shell.** Outstanding is the **Royal Hawaiian Band,** which presents numerous free concerts of Hawaiian music. Polynesian water ballet is performed at the Sheraton-Waikiki.

SHOPPING

The interesting purchases are Chinese and Japanese objets d'art and other Asian goods. The many fine stores in downtown Honolulu and in Waikiki have wide selections of hand-blocked linens, silks, carved Hawaiian woods, and imported teak items. Waikiki's **International Market Place** is where you should look for perfumes, native jams and jellies, textiles, shell, and black and pink coral jewelry, open evenings. Another worthwhile place to visit is the huge **Ala Moana Shopping Center** near Waikiki, easily accessible by bus or car.

SPORTS

Polo, wrestling, boxing, baseball, soccer, and football events are scheduled year-round. Expert instructors and all the necessary equipment can be rented for scuba and skin diving, water-skiing and, of course, surfing. Equally exciting, but less strenuous, are outrigger canoe rides and catamaran cruises. Fishing is sensational, whether you spear reef fish, learn native net casting, or go out for marlin in a fully equipped charter boat. Of the many yacht clubs, several sponsor weekly sailing competitions. There are public tennis courts at **Ala Moana** and **Kapiolani Parks,** where equipment can be rented.

There are fine hiking trails on all the islands, with numerous campsites on mountain slopes and at beach parks. Superb bird and game hunting in the mountainous regions of Oahu and all the islands; guides available.

For those who perfer archery, some areas permit game hunting with bow and arrow, and targets are always available in **Kapiolani Park** in Honolulu. The city has bowling alleys, too. The **Ala Wai** in Waikiki, and **Pearl** golf course just 20 minutes from Waikiki, the **Hawaii Kai** and **Pali** are fine public golf courses.

CALENDAR OF EVENTS

All mainland holidays are observed plus **Chinese New Year, Lei Day** (May Day); **Kamehameha Day,** 11 June; **Prince Kuhio Day** (Hawaii's first delegate to Congress), 26 March. **Aloha Week,** held the third full week of October, is similar to Mardi Gras.

WHERE TO GO NEARBY

Other Oahu Island attractions are: **Sea Life Park** at **Makapuu Point,** with underwater walking tours around the huge glass reef tanks; the **Porpoise Theater** where scientific training is being conducted in conjunction with military and governmental research programs. Forty miles north of Waikiki is the **Polynesian Cultural Center** at Laie, where six authentic native villages are reproduced from Samoa, New Zealand, Fiji, Tahiti, Tonga, and rural Hawaii; there are also shops, entertainment, interesting food. Open daily except Sunday; there are 8-hour bus-trips to the Center from Waikiki for $40.20, adult; child's fare, $20.10, which includes admission fee, a *luau* and a spectacular Polynesian show. The trip should be arranged through a tour company.

HALEAKALA NATIONAL PARK

The park is located on the island of **Maui,** 26 miles southeast of Kahului Airport. It is a spectacular place, in scenery, luxuriant vegetation, and peace and quiet. The season is year round, but be prepared for showers and a 19°C nighttime temperature drop on the mountain, even in summer. Winters are apt to be windy, rainy and cold at high elevations; even snow is possible. The crater is usually cloud-free until midmorning and again late in the afternoon and evenings.

"**The House of the Sun**" is a gigantic, color-splashed volcanic crater, its rim rising to 10,023 feet above sea level. **Puu Ulaula Observatory,** on the highest point, affords a vast view 3,000 feet down into the lunar landscape dotted with weird cinder cones. They seem small from such a height but one is 1,000 feet tall. On a clear day you can see practically all of the Hawaiian Islands. **Kalahaku Overlook,** 9,324 feet, is another good vantage point from which you'll also see a patch of silversword, the dramatically splashy plants that burst into hundreds of yellow- and magenta-hued flowers in midsummer. Within the crater, the floor of which covers 19 miles, are 30 miles of well-marked trails through a region reminiscent of the moon's surface; a permit is required for all trips into the crater. With advance reservations you can take a conducted horseback tour of from one to four days, for which you need carry only food, water canteen and personal gear. See the flamboyant flowers on **Silver-**

sword Loop Trail; the brilliantly colored *iwi, apapane,* and *amakihi* and the rare *nene,* the Hawaiian goose and other native birds.

The choice of accommodations on Maui ranges from luxury hotels to rustic campsites. Facilities within the park, however, consist solely of three cabins, accessible only on foot or horseback, with bunks for 12 in each. Cabin-space reservations must be made in advance. Go prepared, for the nearest eating place is 12 miles from the park, the nearest gas station 18 miles away, the nearest shops even further.

HAWAII VOLCANOES NATIONAL PARK

Covering an area of 344 square miles the park is located about 30 miles southwest of **Hilo** on Hawaii and 96 miles from Kona-Kailua. Rental cars are available at both places.

For your introduction to the area, visit the **Park Museum.** Then continue clockwise along the 11-mile **Crater Rim Drive,** passing through tropical jungles, areas all but destroyed by volcanic activity, piles of pumice and comparatively young lava flows. Beyond **Byron Ledge Lookout,** you can walk nearly 500 feet into the weird **Thurston Lava Tube** on the edge of the shadowy **Tree Fern Forest.** Past **Kilauea Iki Lookout** is the spooky **Devastation Trail,** a wooden walkway across the lava-strewn and bleached-bare trees felled by the 1959 eruption. Then on to the **Kilauea Overlook, Hawaiian Volcano Observatory,** and the malodorous **Sulfur Bank.** The **Chain of Craters Road,** extending from Kilauea Crater to the seacoast at Kalapana, passes five pit craters, some spatter cones, and **Wahaula Heiau,** an ancient temple. The road has been recently restored (the lava flows removed) and is now open all the way. The new **Wahaula Visitor Center** has an interesting museum of man's history in the region. West of Kilauea is magnificent **Mauna Loa,** world's largest mountain, which rises 13,677 feet above the sea and extends 18,000 feet below the surface. Off the **Mauna Loa Strip Road** is a self-guiding nature trail through **Kipuka Puaulu,** a forest of rare native trees inhabited by equally rare birds. The road terminates 6,662 feet up the mountain, where there is a glorious view. From here it is a tough, 18-mile hike up the trail to the summit. Allow three days and be sure to check with park headquarters before attempting this or any other backpacking hikes.

Since May, 1969, **Mauna Ula,** a new satellite volcano along **Kilauea's** east rift, has been active, burying 10,000 acres of the parklands. The **Halemaumau** crater was active between November, 1967 and July, 1968.

The famous **Volcano House Hotel** is 4,000 feet up Kilauea; there are three campgrounds and two rest-houses on Mauna Loa. You could also stay nearby in some of the Kona coast resorts, or in Hilo.

FURTHER STATE INFORMATION

Hawaii Visitors' Bureau, 2270 Kalakaua Avenue, Waikiki, HI 96815, tel: 923-1811; Room 1407, 441 Lexington Avenue, New York, NY 10017; 3440 Wilshire Boulevard, Los Angeles, CA 90010; and at Suite 1530, Marshall Field Annex, 25 East Washington Street, Chicago, IL 60602;

Park information: the Superintendent, **Haleakala National Park,** 537 Makawao; Maui, HI 96768; Superintendent, **Hawaii Volcanoes National Park,** Hawaii, HI 96718. **Pan Am** offices, 2340 Kalakaua Avenue, Honolulu, HI 96815, tel: 955-9111; 1021 Bishop Street, Honolulu, HI 96815, tel: 955-9111.

Consulates in Honolulu: Australia, Belgium, Denmark, Dominican Republic, Finland, France, Germany, Guatemala, Indonesia, Italy, Japan, Korea, Mexico, Monaco, Nauru, Netherlands, Norway, Peru, Philippines, Portugal, Sweden, Switzerland, Thailand.

USEFUL TELEPHONE NUMBERS IN HONOLULU

Emergency (Ambulance, Fire & Police)	911
Castle Memorial Hospital	261-0841
Queen's Medical Center	538-9011
Poison Information Center	941-4411
Legal Aid Society of Hawaii	536-4302
Chamber of Commerce of Hawaii	531-4111
Tourist Information	923-1811
Dentist Information	536-2135
Pan Am Reservations	955-9111

Idaho

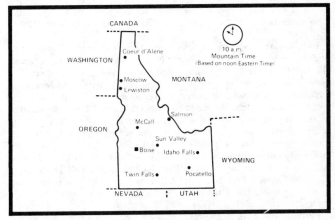

| Area | 82,557 square miles | **Population** | 943,600 |
| **Capital** | Boise | **Sales Tax** | 3% |

Weather	Jan	Feb	Mar	Apr	May	Jun	Jul	Aug	Sep	Oct	Nov	Dec
Av Temp (°C)	−2	1	5	10	15	19	24	22	17	11	4	0
Days Rain/Snow	13	10	9	8	8	7	2	2	4	7	10	12

Idaho has vast areas still uninhabited and a population density averaging only 9.5 people per square mile. You are seldom out of sight of mountains in Idaho, and there are massive peaks and great rivers frothing and plunging through precipitous canyons.

Idaho is the "Gem State"; 72 different kinds of precious and semi-precious stones are found here. Hunters know there is more wildlife in the Idaho mountains than in any other state. Apart perhaps from the cougar, Idaho's varied wildlife is every bit as enjoyable if you're armed with nothing more lethal than a camera. The fishing in the rivers, lakes, ponds, reservoirs, and streams is world famous for record breaking catches. There are lakes and reservoirs for swimming, water-skiing, and boating of all kinds throughout the state, and winter sports abound.

Entering **CENTRAL** Idaho on US 93 near the Montana border, you come to the small town of **Salmon**, a popular place to pick up a guide and supplies for the **Salmon National Forest** and the vast **Idaho Primitive Area. Lemhi Pass**, 7,373 feet high, is where Lewis and Clark crossed the Continental Divide. There's a monument on ID 28 to Sacajawea, their Indian girl guide; and nearby is the ghost town of **Lemhi,** where the Mormons tried to found a settlement in 1855. The **Salmon River** is the famous "River of No Return" that plunges over nearly 250 major rapids before it empties into the Snake River on the western Idaho border. Reservations for float trips down the river must be made well in advance. Continuing south on US 93, you pass through **Sawtooth National Recreational Area** and Ketchum, a year-round resort town and also the home of the late Ernest Hemingway. Northeast of Sun Valley, in the **Lost River Range,** is the highest point in Idaho, **Mount Borah,** 12,662 feet high.

In **SOUTHERN** Idaho a line of towns follows the **Snake River** on its undulating course westward. North is an immense lava field, of which the **Craters of the Moon National Monument** is only a small part. The eerie cones, craters, and crags were created by massive underground explosions that spewed lava everywhere. Most of the caves you can explore are so cold that the ice in them never melts. The modern campground here is designed so that each camper has his own "crater." The nearest town is **Arco,** the first in the country to get all its power from atomic energy. About 30 miles west of Idaho Falls is the Energy Research & Development Administration's **Idaho National Engineering Laboratory.** Big crowds arrive in **Idaho Falls** for the Sportsmen's Jamboree in May, the **Pioneer Days Rodeo** in late July and the **War Bonnet Roundup** in early August. The **Driftwood, Westbank, Littletree,** and **Bonneville** motels are about S$14-26/D$15-29.

Farther downriver is **Pocatello,** industrial city and key transportation point. Near here are the restored **Fort Hall** trading post (1834-60), **Fort Hall Indian Reservation** and the vast **American Falls Reservoir.** To the south and east is a region bubbling with hot springs. Accommodations in Pocatello: The **Bannock Motor Inn** (233-1260, S$13-16/D$15-20) and **TraveLodge** (232-8140, S$22-28/D$28-34), both located in the city center; and **Holiday Inn** (237-1400, S$27/D$32), **Hilton Inn** (223-2200, S$24-32/D$29-37), **Cottontree** (237-7650, S/D$24-60), and **Rodeway** (237-0020, S$24-27/D$28-31), between the city center and airport. Best restaurants are **Elmer's Pancake & Steak House** and **Sambo's.** At **Twin Falls** is the **Perrine Memorial Bridge,** a dizzying 476 feet above the Snake River. **Shoshone Falls** here are 52 feet higher than Niagara. Accommodations in Twin Falls: **Littletree Inn** and **Holiday Inn,** both 1 mile from center, average rates about S$24-33/D$31-38. The world famous **Balanced Rock** is near Buhl. Caused by wind erosion, it is a top-heavy, 40-foot high stone poised on a base that measures only 18 inches by 36 inches. The **Snake River Trout Ranch** is probably the world's largest. Try to see **Thousand Springs,** cascading into the Snake River and **Banbury Hot Springs** (32°C). South of Mountain Home on the **Bruneau River,** a tributary of the Snake River, is **Bruneau Canyon,** a narrow, 67-mile-long chasm rimmed by cliffs 2,000 feet high.

SOUTHWESTERN Idaho is sheep country, and the nation's largest concentration of Basques from the European Pyrenees work as shepherds in the area. The Basque shepherds have influenced the local cuisine so you'll find some surprises on the menus; Basque dancing has also caught on here. The **Basque Festival,** an annual celebration, is held mid-summer.

Boise (boy-zee), the capital, is the largest city in the state with a population of 154,000. See the display of minerals and valuable stones in the **Capitol Building.** The **Julia Davis Park** has the **State Historical Museum, Boise Gallery of Art,** and a log cabin village reminiscent of pioneer days. Lovely formal gardens and a fountain are in **Ann Morrison Memorial Park.** In the mountains near Boise are **Idaho City** and **Silver City,** two genuine ghost towns that blossomed during the gold boom in the 1860s. Accommodations in the center of Boise: **TraveLodge, Safari, Owyhee Plaza, Red Lion Inn Downtowner,** and **Sheraton Downtowner,** averaging S$24-38/D$26-42. Nearby are the **International Dunes** and **Boisean Lodge,** averaging S$18-25/D$22-28, and the **Rodeway Inn** and **Holiday Inn,** averaging S$29-36/D$35-42. Best restaurants are **Chart House, Black Angus, Elmer's Pancake and Steak House, Ray's Seafood Restaurant, The Royal, Gamekeeper, The Sandpiper, Jake's, Peter Schott's, Pengilly's 12th Floor Gin Mill, Sand Bar, Stagecoach,** and **Kitty Hawk** (airport).

In the mountains 16 miles north of Boise (45 minutes on good road) is **Bogus Basin** ski area with 31 major runs served by 5 double chairlifts. The longest runs are 1.5 miles with 1,500 feet of vertical rise. Lifts operate daily with three continuing until 10pm each night. **The Red Lion Downtowner** offers ski packages including lodging, day/night lift tickets, area tour, round trip bus ticket and local taxes (double, 3-day, $54/5-day $90); lodging, day/night lift tickets, lunch, dinner, area tour, round trip bus tickets, after-ski cocktail and local taxes (double, 3-day, $78/5-day, $130). Skiers are transported back and forth to Bogus Basin each day.

North of Boise is **McCall,** on Payette Lake, where the **Brundage Mountain Ski Area** booms from November through April. Arrangements here can be made for pack trips into the Idaho Primitive Area. The major resort is **Shore Lodge** (634-2244, S$23-26/D$29-32). **Weiser** (wee-zer) lies at the point where the Weiser River joins the Snake on the Oregon line. You might come here for the rodeo in the first week in June, or for the **National Oldtime Fiddlers' Contest and Festival** in June; the **National Fiddlers' Hall of Fame** is in Weiser. But the big attraction is **Hells Canyon,** which has recently become accessible from Weiser. This is the deepest gorge on the continent, hemmed in by solid rock walls that average 5,500 feet. Towering along the Idaho side are the **Seven Devils Mountains,** their snowy 9,000-foot granite peaks reflected in lakes as clear as glass. Campsites and recreation areas have been created by Idaho Power Company at reservoirs formed by **Brownlee Dam, Oxbow Dam,** and **Hells Canyon Dam.** This is a great area for fishing and hunting in season. The best views of the canyon are from **Cuprum** (kew-prum), but driving on the mountain roads can be hair-raising.

Lewiston is at the base of **NORTHERN** Idaho. **Royal Motor Inn** and **Sacajawea Lodge** average S$16-20/D$19-23, while the **Tapadera Motor Inn** is slightly more expensive at S/D$27-47. There are boat trips from Lewiston up the **Grand Canyon of the Snake River** lasting the day; or others that go farther and take 2 days or 3 days on large boats with your cabin and meals included in the fare. **Luna House** (1910) is now a museum of pioneer relics and Indian artifacts; open Tuesday to Saturday and Sunday afternoons, free. There are tours of **Potlatch Forests, Inc,** the world's largest white pine sawmill (no children under 10). Lewiston has a **Fine Arts Festival** in June, a rousing rodeo on the weekend after Labor Day, and the **Nez Percé County Fair,** held here in mid-September. The **Nez Percé Historical Park,** east of Lewiston, is made up of 22 separate sites scattered over 12,000 square miles. There are numerous campsites in the forests, and the park sections are devoted to the culture of the early pioneers and the Nez Percé tribe. The **Lewis and Clark Trail** runs alongside US 12, which passes through the park heading eastward over **Lolo Pass** (elevation 5,233 feet) and then up to Missoula, Montana. North of Lewiston is **Moscow,** home of the **University of Idaho,** which has an unusually beautiful campus. The city also claims to be the "Dried Pea and Lentil Capital of the World." Moscow is surrounded by rich, rolling farmland, a sort of breathing space before you plunge into the slender panhandle of cold blue lakes, mountains, forested hills, and fish-filled streams and rivers. **Coeur d'Alene** is on the northern end of the beautiful lake of the same name and has such a pleasant climate that it is becoming a popular place for retired people. Special events here are a midlake fireworks display on 4 July; the **Scottish Tattoo,** last weekend in July; **Kootenai County Rodeo** in late July; and the **Kootenai County Fair** in early September. The scenery all around here is breathtaking. The forest-lined **St Joe River,** supposedly the world's highest navigable river, offers good fishing. East of Coeur d'Alene is **Kellogg,** site of the country's largest silver mine and the great **Bunker Hill** lead mine and smelter; tours Monday to Friday, June through August. South of Kellogg is **Jackass Ski Bowl,** where the snow lingers from December to mid-May.

In the **NORTHWEST** corner of the state is **Sandpoint,** near the famous Schweitzer Ski Basin, season late November to mid-April, overlooking **Lake Pend Oreille.** The lake, hemmed in by mountains, is well stocked with game fish, of which the huge Kamloops rainbow trout is the most highly prized. **Farragut State Park,** popular for scout gatherings, is where America's First Boy Scout World Jamboree was held in 1967.

SUN VALLEY

Sun Valley, in south central Idaho, is at the foot of the spectacular **Sawtooth Mountain Range,** and is the most complete winter sports area in North America. Sun Valley is a year-round resort; the sunshine seems more golden and the air crisper here than anywhere on earth. Summer and winter sports are superb, and there is hunting in season.

WHAT TO SEE

Skate year round on the outstanding Olympic-size artificial ice rink; swim in the three pools, two of which are outdoor, warm-water, and glass-enclosed. During the summer, tennis and riding schools are in session; pack trips and hayrides can be arranged. Art instruction is given at the

Hells Canyon, on Idaho's Snake River, is the continent's deepest gorge, accessible by jetboat from Lewiston or downstream from below Hells Canyon Dam. The more adventurous can actually enter the turbulent raceway, skimming the rapids as far as Willow Creek

creative arts center. Winter sports are unexcelled: 15 ski lifts to slopes for every type of skier on **Dollar Mountain** and **Baldy Mountain**. The well-known **Sun Valley Ski School** has more than 200 instructors. Sleigh rides and snowmobiling are also available during the winter season. This valley was a favorite retreat for Ernest Hemingway; monuments to the writer's memory and work can be seen here.

ACCOMMODATIONS

Sun Valley Resort (tel: 622-4111) is the original complex in the area. Besides the Inn (S$39-69/D$45-150), the resort also offers luxurious accommodations at its lodge and in its condominiums. **Elkhorn** (tel: 622-4541) at Sun Valley is a new and developing sister resort with its own runs and lifts for winter sports, golf courts and tennis courts for summer. The **Elkhorn Village Inn** has rooms (S/D$60) while the **Condos** have studios (S/D$65) and one- to four-bedroom apartments ranging from $80-160 up. Off-season rates lower. Motels in **Ketchum**, a half-mile from Sun Valley resort, include **Tamarack Lodge,** (726-3344, S/D$43-59), **Heidelberg Friendship Inn** (726-5361, S/D$29-49), and **Christiania Lodge** (726-3351, $28-55/D$28-65). Hotel tax: 3%

RESTAURANTS

Trail Creek Cabin is well-known for barbecues. **Duchin Dining Room** is also recommended. **The Ram** and the **Ore House** are at Sun Valley and the **Chart House** at Elkhorn. In nearby Ketchum, **Warm Springs Ranch Inn** features steak and trout.

ENTERTAINMENT

Movies, concerts, summer theater, dancing indoors or under the stars. The **Palace** is a night club for teenagers.

SHOPPING

Shopping malls at both Sun Valley and Elkhorn for clothes, gifts and sports equipment. Shopping hours 9-5, some stores open until 9 on Friday nights.

FURTHER STATE INFORMATION

Division of Economic and Community Affairs, State Capitol Building, Room 108, Boise, ID 83707. Hunting and Fishing: **Information and Education Division, Idaho Fish and Game Department,** PO Box 25, Boise, ID 83707.

USEFUL TELEPHONE NUMBERS

Boise

Information referral number	378-0111
Boise Chamber of Commerce	344-5515
St Alphonsus Hospital	378-2121
St Luke's Hospital	386-2222
Red Cross	344-2593
Idaho Legal Aid Services	345-0106

Illinois

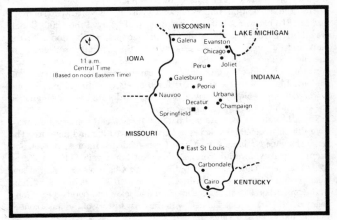

Area	56,400 square miles	**Population**	11,418,461
Capital	Springfield	**Sales Tax**	5%

Weather	Jan	Feb	Mar	Apr	May	Jun	Jul	Aug	Sep	Oct	Nov	Dec
Av Temp (°C)	−3	−2	2	9	16	21	24	23	19	13	4	−1
Days Rain/Snow	10	10	12	13	12	11	9	8	9	8	10	11

Illinois, the Prairie State, could be thought of as the pantry of America. It is a key food-producing region and its highly progressive farmers play no small part in keeping the nation well fed. Its importance can be judged by the active commodity market in Chicago, which you should try to visit. This is a clearing house for much of the nation's farm produce and on a minute-by-minute basis determines the price Americans will pay for their groceries. Eighty-five percent of Illinois land is cultivated, and the yield from 40 different crops alone is second only to California.

Illinois is also the land of Lincoln; students of US history will find it a treasure house of information, reminders, and documents of the famous president, who grew up in the state.

The state is bordered on the west by the Mississippi, on the east by the Ohio and Wabash Rivers, and on the north by Lake Michigan. The first white men arrived in 1673 when the French priest Jacques Marquette and explorer Louis Jolliet came down the Mississippi, turned east, and headed up the Illinois River to beach their canoes on land now occupied by the skyscrapers of Chicago. Five years later, La Salle estab-

155

lished Fort Creve Coeur near Peoria. In 1682 a fort was erected in what is now **Starved Rock State Park,** and the first permanent settlement was established by the French in 1700 as a fur-trading center. The French ruled until the English gained the title in 1763, and the British expanded their domain and captured Fort de Chartres in 1765, but the British stay was brief. The American colonies were expanding, and for a time the state was claimed as a county by Virginia.

After the Revolution, Illinois became a part of the Northwest Territory and in 1818 became a state. Through the early part of the 1800s Illinois was the last frontier, where settlers and pioneer folk battled with the Sauk and Fox Indians. Settlers surged into the land after settlement of the Black Hawk Wars in 1832. Later, the young "backwoods" attorney Abraham Lincoln entered politics; his career marked the beginning of modern Illinois. Lincoln's support for projects of railroads, canals, and waterway routes along the river highways bordering the state signalled the beginning of its rapid development.

The 100 state parks, state and national forests, and conservation areas give Illinois over 400,000 acres of land for recreation and pleasure. The huge **Shawnee National Forest** near Carbondale has impressive rock out-croppings, lakes, a wildlife refuge, hiking, and horse trails. Skiing is offered at **Antioch** and **Galena,** deer hunting in the **Chain o'Lakes** region and near **Havana.** Camping is permitted in more than 50 parks and the fishing in the more than 220 streams and 453 public lakes and ponds is excellent. Many of the parks are associated with the early history of Indians, pioneer homes, old forts, and Lincoln.

Springfield, almost in the center of the state and easily reached from Chicago or St Louis on I-55, is located on the Sangamon River. Settled in 1818 by hunters from South Carolina, it was selected as the state capital through the efforts of Abraham Lincoln and eight other members of the Illinois legislature, known as the "Long Nine." Springfield has not been the only capital of Illinois; there were two others—Vandalia and Kaskaskia. Springfield, the heart of *Lincolnland,* was Lincoln's home for 25 years and is where he is buried. At the corner of Eighth and Jackson is the first and only house Lincoln ever owned; open daily, free. In the **State Historical Library** in the **Old State Capitol** is the desk at which he wrote his first inaugural address. The **Lincoln Tomb** in **Oak Ridge Cemetery** has a 117-foot spire and a 10-foot statue. Bronze plaques are engraved with the *Gettysburg Address,* his farewell speech to Spring-field and his second inaugural address; open daily, free. The former capi-tol, now called the **Old State Capitol,** where Lincoln made his famous "House Divided" speech, is restored and furnished with originals and reproductions of the times; open daily, free. The **Lincoln Herndon Law Office,** across from the Old State Capitol Building, is where Lincoln prac-ticed law. Open 7 days a week, all year round; for American visitors, there is a small fee; international visitors, free.

Follow the Post Road to various Lincoln-related attractions in the area. Important Lincoln documents and memorabilia are in the State Historical Library. The **Lincoln Marriage Home** and **Lincoln Life Museum** show the restored wedding parlor and dioramas depicting Lincoln's life, open April-October. **Lincoln Depot Museum,** open April-October, is on the site of his farewell address when he left Illinois to become president; life-sized mannequins of Lincoln and his wife are shown. **Illinois State Museum** is one of the best in the country, featuring exhibits of the fine, applied and natural arts with audiophones to explain the exhibits. **Thomas Reese Memorial Carillon** in Washington Park has 66 bells in a 132-foot tower and three observation decks. The **Vachel Lindsay Home** presents original manuscripts and drawings of the poet; open June-August. The **International Carillon Festival** is held in the last week of June, and the **Illinois State Fair** lasts for 10 days in mid-August. Boat regattas are conducted on 4 July and Labor Day. **Holiday Inn East** (529-7171, S$31.75-37.75/D$37.54-42.75), **Howard Johnson's Downtown** (544-3466, S$22-25/D$24-30), **Inn of the Lamplighter** (529-5454, S/D$28-38), and **State House Inn** (253-5661, S/D$32-55) provide good accommodations. Restaurants: the **Georgian** for seafood; **Balestri's** for chicken; **John's Supper Club,** featuring dinner and entertainment; and the **Glade** for Cantonese dishes, all at moderate prices.

Carbondale, home of **Southern Illinois University,** is south of Springfield and situated in lovely countryside. **Crab Orchard National Wildlife Refuge** and its 17,000-acre man-made lake provide hunting, fishing, camping, and swimming opportunities. **Giant City State Park,** with picturesque rock formations and an ancient "Stone Fort" of prehistoric origin, is 10 miles south of the city in **Shawnee National Forest. Giant City Lodge** (618-457-4921, S$20/D$25), open March to mid-November, has excellent country food, as does **Ma Hale's** restaurant in nearby Grand Tower.

Petersburg, north of Springfield on IL 97, is close to **New Salem State Park,** a complete reconstruction of **New Salem Village** as it was when Lincoln was there in the 1830s. It includes homes, stores, and the only original building, the **Onstott Cooper Shop.** The sternwheeler *Talisman* offers hourly riverboat trips in the summer. The park is open year round. The **New Salem Carriage Museum** has over 100 horse-drawn vehicles, a covered bridge and zoo; open daily May-November. In Petersburg itself is the **Edgar Lee Masters Memorial Home,** boyhood home of the author of *Spoon River Anthology;* open Memorial Day-Labor Day, free. Also in Petersburg is the **Illinois Country Opry,** and nearby is the **Clayville Stagecoach Stop,** including a historic tavern, crafts and a country kitchen.

Northeast of Springfield the vast campus of the **University of Illinois** spreads across the twin cities of **Champaign** and **Urbana.** There are interesting tours of the university buildings, including the **Krannert Art Museum and Center for the Performing Arts.** The striking **Assembly Hall** has one of the world's largest edge-supported domes. Advance hotel reservations are advisable during home football weekends in the fall, when hotel rates usually go up a little. In Champaign, try the **Ramada Inn** (217-352-7891, S$29-52/D$35-52), excellent dining room; **Holiday Inn, Howard Johnson's** and **Paradise Inn** are about S$22-28/D$28-36. In Urbana, **Holiday Inn** and **Howard Johnson's Motor Lodge** are about S$25-

35/D$29-40. **Decatur,** a soybean-processing center, has a replica of the first courthouse in Macon County, where Lincoln practiced law. **Sheraton Motor Inn** (217-877-7255, S$27/D$30-35) offers good accommodation. **Du Quoin,** halfway between Dowell and Elville, is famous for the $100,000 **Hambletonian Stake,** the world's leading harness race, held during the Du Quoin State Fair, the 10 days before Labor Day. Southwest is **Carmi,** where the 460-mile **Lincoln Trail** enters the state. **Ratcliff Inn,** where Lincoln stayed in 1840 while attending a political rally, is restored as a museum; open Monday-Saturday, free.

Peoria, on the banks of the Illinois River, is in the heart of the rich farming basin and is believed to be the oldest settlement in the state. **Bradley University** is here. **Glen Oak Park Zoo** has displays of birds and fish, and a pet compound which allows children to handle small animals. **Lakeview Center for the Arts and Sciences** is a recreation, education, arts, and science center, including the **Peoria Art Museum** and **Lakeview Planetarium;** open Tuesday to Sunday. Free tours are available of **Fort Creve Coeur State Park,** the settlement founded by La Salle in 1680. **Jumer's Castle Lodge** (309-673-8040, S$39/D$43), with Bavarian dining room, and **Ramada Inn** (673-6461, S$31-39/D$36-43), serving French cuisine, are outstanding. **Clayton House, Holiday Inn,** and **Howard Johnson's** are also excellent at about S$30-38/D$32-40.

Southwest of Peoria near Lewiston is an unusual new museum; **Dickson Mounds State Museum of Illinois Indians** is built over more than 200 Indian graves, with skeletons intact, that were excavated in the late 1920s; open daily, free. The **Carl Sandburg Birthplace** in downtown **Galesburg,** 49 miles northwest of Peoria, is a restored 3-room cottage containing antique furnishings, a Lincoln room, and Sandburg memorabilia; open Tuesday-Sunday, free. **Knox College** is also here, site of one of the Lincoln-Douglas debates. **Bishop Hill,** north of Galesburg, was settled in 1846 by Swedish immigrants seeking religious freedom in a communal-utopian colony. The "Jansonists" were superb craftsmen, as you can see from the details of the 14 original buildings now restored. One, the **Colony Church,** contains a sanctuary large enough to seat 1,000 worshippers and a collection of early American paintings that show how the colonists lived; open daily, free. The **Valkomen Inn** in Bishop Hill is noted for its food.

Monmouth has a Prime Beef Festival each September. It is the birthplace of the lawman Wyatt Earp, and **Pioneer Cemetery** is the burial place of many of his relatives. **Moline,** farm implement capital of the world, is worth a stop to see the **Deere & Company** building designed by Eero Saarinen; open daily, free. **Rock Island** began with **Fort Armstrong,** on the large island in the middle of the Mississippi, where the blockhouse has been reconstructed. It was here that Black Hawk, the brilliant Sauk Chieftain, was defeated in 1832. The first railroad bridge over the Mississippi was built across Rock Island in 1854. As a hub of transportation, the island became a major government arsenal in 1862; modern arms are now developed here. The **John M. Browning Museum** has an important collection of all kinds of firearms, from the oldest to the newest. Rock Island was the site of a prison for Confederate soldiers during the Civil War; nearly 5,000 are buried in the **National Cemetery** at the east end of the island. East of Rock Island and near the twin cities of **Peru** and **La Salle** is **Matthiessen State Park Nature Area,** with a deer reservation, canyon paths, and caves; open daily. **Starved Rock State Park** occupies 6,000 acres on the Illinois River. The name comes from a legend that a band of Indians, isolated by their enemies on the peak, starved to death. Excursion boats operate on the river from May to October. **Joliet,** further east, is one of the state's leading industrial centers. It also has the biggest stockyards, the **Chicago/Joliet Livestock Marketing Center:** (815) 423-5005. Best time for tours, Monday to Friday; free. The **Brandon Road Locks** on the **Lake-to-Gulf Waterway** south of the city are among the largest in the world. In Joliet there are two Holiday Inns: **Holiday Inn West** (815/725-2180, S$31/D$36); **Holiday Inn South** (815/729-2000, S$31/D$36); and a **Sheraton Motor Inn** (815/727-6544, S$23/D$29.50).

The **Mississippi River,** forming Illinois' western boundary, rolls inexorably along, and seems quite indifferent to all the history that has occurred near its banks. **Cairo,** pronounced *kay-row,* is the most southern town in Illinois. The Ohio River joins the Mississippi here, and the town is well protected with levees. In Cairo **Magnolia Manor** (1869) was the scene of an elegant reception for President and Mrs. Ulysses S. Grant. **Fort Kaskaskia State Park** is upriver and the site of famous **Fort Kaskaskia,** built by the French in 1736 but later destroyed to prevent British occupation. Nearby is the **Garrison Hill Cemetery,** where 3,800 settlers are buried. **Belleville** is the location of the 200-acre **National Shrine of Our Lady of the Snows.** An outdoor altar combines with a large amphitheater as the center of activities. There is a replica of the grotto at Lourdes, France; open daily; pilgrimage season is 1 May through 2 November. **Hyatt Lodge** (618/234-9400, S$19-24/D$28-36) offers good rooms. **East St Louis,** across the Mississippi from its namesake, is the stopping place for the 650-acre **Cahokia Mounds State Park.** The park preserves the remains of the only prehistoric Indian village north of Mexico, and has 40 Indian mounds, a museum, and camping and picnicking areas; open daily. Also in the area is the summer-long **Mississippi River Festival of Music** at Edwardsville.

It is worthwhile following the Mississippi as close as you can on secondary roads. Between the bridges that cross over to Keokuk hilltop, and Fort Madison, Iowa, the little town of **Nauvoo** clings to an Illinois hilltop on a bend in the river. In 1839 Joseph Smith, founder of the Church of Jesus Christ of Latter-Day Saints (Mormons), settled here with his followers, hoping to escape the persecution which had hounded them out of New York, Ohio, and Missouri. Far larger and more prosperous than Chicago was in those days, the Mormon city had a population of 14,000 industrious citizens before trouble found them here, too. Joseph Smith and his brother were murdered in nearby **Carthage** in 1844. Brigham Young, the new leader, decided to abandon the town and go west. Today, Utah Mormons have restored a number of the homes as they used to be. The first and last houses Joseph Smith lived in have been restored, and Brigham Young's home and many other authentic buildings are open daily. Two other religious groups were attracted to Nauvoo: the Icarians, a French sect, and a group of German Roman Catholics, who started a little wine industry. Blue cheese ripened beautifully in the old wine cellars, and there is now a great **Wine and Cheese Festival** every year on the Saturday and Sunday before Labor Day. Very good regional food, including Mississippi catfish, is served in the attractive **Hotel Nauvoo** (217-453-2211, S$18.50-32.50/D$21.50-39.50).

If you continue north along the Mississippi you will come to the little town of **Galena,** one of the architectural gems of the midwest. Its beauty is accentuated by steep residential streets rising on each side of the elongated Main Street. Ulysses S. Grant came to Galena in 1860, when his heavy drinking outweighed his valor in the Mexican War. At the outbreak of the Civil War, he organized the Galena militia and, eventually, made generals out of nine of his Galena friends. The handsomely preserved **U.S. Grant Home** was presented to him as a gift in 1865 and still contains many original furnishings; open daily. The **Dowling House** (1826) was originally a trading post for lead miners; open May to October. The large brick **Orrin Smith House** (1852) belonged to a riverboat captain at a time when Galena's river often flooded, making the town the only US post office with a rowboat as standard equipment. There are exceptionally good Civil War paintings and relics in the **Galena Historical Society Museum.** The **Market House** (1845) was an elegant Greek revival shelter for outdoor fruit and vegetable dealers. The **Stockade and Underground Refuge** were where townsfolk hid during the Black Hawk Wars; open May to October. **Grace Episcopal Church** (1848) is an exquisite little English Gothic church; its organ, made in 1838, traveled from Philadelphia to New Orleans and then up to Galena by steamboat. There are open-house tours on many pre-Civil War mansions during the second weekend in June and last weekend in September. The **De Soto House Hotel** (815-777-9208, S$12-21/D$16-28.50) is a restored historic hotel. The **Victorian Mansion** (815-777-0675, S$20.50-24/D$23-26.50) also offers good accommodation. The nearby **Chestnut Mountain Ski Resort** has the famous **Chestnut Mountain Lodge** (815-777-1320, S$26.50-32/D$34-42, rates higher during ski season), a very attractive summer and winter resort, rates slightly lower in summer. There are daily tours, mid-April to September, of historic **Vinegar Hill Lead Mine and Museum,** 6 miles north of town. The discovery of lead deposits helped put Galena on the map as early as the 18th century. The most direct way to go to Chicago from Galena is through Freeport, Rockford, and on to the Northwest Tollway.

On the outskirts of Chicago, the small town of **Lisle** is the home of the **Morton Arboretum.** Here you will find specimens of more than 4,800 varieties of plants. Crabapples blossom in early May, the lilac season is in late May, and the shrubs and trees are spectacular in October; open daily. The **Cantigny War Memorial Museum** in nearby **Wheaton** recreates through dioramas the valiant history of the First Infantry Division in

World Wars I and II; open Tuesday to Sunday, free. The **Robert R. McCormick Museum** is the former home of the founding editor and publisher of the *Chicago Tribune*. The grounds are an exercise in experimental gardening, and wooded paths are mixed with tanks and weapons; open Wednesday to Sunday; free. **Evanston**, site of **Northwestern University**, is a beautiful suburb along Lake Michigan north of Chicago. The **Deering Library** at the university has a rare book display; campus tours are offered Monday to Saturday. The **Evanston Historical Society Museum**, home of Charles G. Dawes, vice-president under Calvin Coolidge, and the **Frances E. Willard House**, home of the national temperance movement leader, are open for inspection. **The Café Provencal** offers gourmet French dining, and **Fanny's** restaurant has delighted generations with its good food.

City To Visit

CHICAGO

A frontier outpost of less than a dozen cabins in 1803, Chicago was incorporated as a town in 1833, and 4 years later as a city. By 1890 it had become the second largest city in the nation; by 1930 the fourth largest in the world. The **Chicago River** runs through the heart of the city; its flow was reversed in 1871 to save beautiful **Lake Michigan** from pollution, and it now drains into the Mississippi River by way of the Illinois River. Completion of the St Lawrence Seaway gave Chicago direct access to international trade.

Chicago is a gigantic industrial and economic center. Fond of large-scale fairs and shows, proud of its tall buildings, it also has an extensive system of attractive city parks. The population is 2,969,570; metropolitan area, 7,032,000. The central business and shopping area is called **"The Loop,"** for there the city-bound elevated trains make a complete circle before heading back to where they came from. This district contains many of the department stores and office buildings, although the "Magnificent Mile" of Michigan Avenue, north of the Loop, has become the city's most elegant shopping area. Chicago's public transit system is excellent. Call 836-7000 for route instructions to any destination.

WHAT TO SEE

Archicenter, exhibits, slide shows, and special events exploring Chicago's architectural heritage; **Adler Planetarium; Art Institute of Chicago,** with an extensive collection of French Impressionist paintings; **Chicago Academy of Sciences**, natural history of the Chicago region; **Chicago Historical Society**, especially noted for its Lincoln collection; the renovated **Chicago Public Library Cultural Center,** with beautiful mosaic tile interior and stained-glass ceiling, featuring exhibits and lectures; **Field Museum of Natural History**, extensive exhibits on anthropology, botany, geology, and zoology; **Museum of Contemporary Art,** changing exhibits, films, and lectures; **Museum of Science and Industry,** fascinating exhibits relating to scientific, engineering, industrial, and medical progress; **Oriental Institute,** cultural objects from the Near East; **Shedd Aquarium,** featuring a coral reef tank; the **Art Institute of Chicago,** with extensive Far Eastern and French Impressionist collections, hosting major exhibits.

Chicago has several notable sculptures. Pablo Picasso's 50-foot high unnamed statue stands in front of the **Civic Center** on Randolph and Clark, and nearby, the **First National Plaza** boasts Marc Chagall's vivid "Four Seasons" mosaic. Alexander Calder's "Flamingo" is in the **Federal Plaza** at the corner of Dearborn and Jackson. The **Sears Tower** on Adams and Wacker houses another Calder, this one a mobile. Harry Bertoia's copper and brass "sounding sculpture" makes music above the reflecting pool at the **Standard Oil (Indiana) Plaza** on Randolph, east of Michigan Avenue. At the **University of Chicago,** "Nuclear Energy," a huge bronze piece by Henry Moore, stands near the spot where Enrico Fermi and his associates first split the atom.

Many conducted tours of the city are available, including several by boat. Among the most interesting sights are **Buckingham Fountain** in Grant Park, **Chinatown, Lake Point Tower Apartments, Marina City's** riverside circular apartments, the huge **Merchandise Mart, Navy Pier,** the **Tribune Tower,** and the **Wrigley Building.** The world's largest commodity market is on the fourth floor of the **Board of Trade** building.

Chicago is justly proud of its 548 public parks. Outstanding are: **Grant Park,** built along the downtown lakefront on land reclaimed from Lake Michigan; **Jackson Park,** stretching along the lake shore on the South Side; and **Lincoln Park** on the lake to the north. The **Lincoln Park Zoo** houses a well rounded collection and a special children's zoo. West of downtown Chicago is **Brookfield Zoo,** where animals are exhibited in natural settings. The **Lincoln Park** and **Garfield Park Conservatories** house permanent collections of tropical and exotic plants and feature special seasonal flower shows. **The Cook County Forest Preserve** District maintains five nature centers in the Chicago area, each with a different terrain.

Chicago has about 50 colleges and universities and over 200 technical and vocational schools. Some of the more famous ones: **Northwestern University,** courses in law, medicine, and business; **University of Chicago,** a progressive institution famous for physics, chemistry, and nuclear science, also for medicine, law, and business; **University of Illinois,** branch schools of medicine, engineering, and business; **Loyola University,** which specializes in medicine, law, art, and business administration. Other Chicago area schools include **Barat College, DePaul University, Illinois Institute of Technology, Lake Forest College, Mundelein College,** and **Roosevelt University.** Chicago also has an extensive city college system, consisting of nine community colleges.

There is a church here for almost every established religious group; many have foreign-language services. Detailed information may be had from the Chicago Church Foundation. Of special interest is the **Chicago**

Temple, which is the tallest church in the world—568 feet at the tip of its spire. The unique **Baha'i Temple** is in **Wilmette,** a northern lakefront suburb.

BUILDINGS

Chicago is a city of architectural distinction. The city fostered the genius of Louis Sullivan, whose **Auditorium Theatre** on Michigan Avenue and **Carson, Pirie, Scott** department store on State Street should be seen. Chicago was once the center of the Prairie School of Architecture, and the home of Frank Lloyd Wright. The city boasts 60 of Wright's buildings, many of which are located in the western suburb of Oak Park, where the architect resided. The Chicago School of Architecture Foundation and the Oak Park Tour Center offer walking tours of his buildings. William Le Baron Jenny conceived and executed the design for the Home Life Insurance Company Building, which was torn down in the 1930s. But the building was the forerunner for the breathtaking towers that now pierce the Chicago skyline. The Archicenter, operated by the Chicago Architecture Foundation, sponsors walking, biking, and bus tours of architectural points of interest. Phone 312/782-1776.

The **John Hancock Center,** designed by the city's largest architectural firm, Skidmore, Owings & Merrill, rises to 1,127 ft, the Standard Oil building is slightly higher, and the Sears Tower is the world's tallest, at 1,454 ft. It is second in floor space only to the Pentagon. These are three of the world's tallest buildings. The **Water Tower Place,** a 76-story, 859 ft concrete-framed building, also houses a 7-story marble-exterior shopping complex. Glass elevators give an interesting ride. For a fee, the public can view the Chicago panorama from several of its skyscrapers, the John Hancock Center, the **Prudential Building,** and the Sears Tower.

ACCOMMODATIONS

Downtown near business, shopping: **Blackstone** (427-4300, S\$49-59/ D\$58-68), on South Michigan Avenue overlooking Grant Park; **Conrad Hilton** ((922-4400, S\$55-73/D\$70-88), one of the country's largest; **Palmer House** (726-7500, S\$70-90/D\$85-105), a luxurious Loop landmark; **Americana Congress** (427-3800, S\$62-70/D\$82-90), near Grant Park.

North, near nightclubs, beaches, the smartest shops: **Allerton** (440-1500, S\$45/D\$50-55), quiet, convenient; **Ambassador East** (787-7200, S\$85-105/D\$100-120), regal elegance just off North Michigan Avenue; **Ambassador West** (787-7900, S\$60-90/D\$75-90), convenient and comfortable; **Continental Plaza** (943-7200, S\$68-118/D\$89-138), a luxury hotel, facing John Hancock Center, all rooms with color TV; **Drake** (787-2200, S\$51-98/D\$28-118); **Executive House** (346-7100, S\$66-84/D\$76-94), comfortable and convenient; **Hyatt Regency Chicago** (565-1000, S\$84-104/D\$99-119); **Marriott Hotel** (836-0100, S\$76-99/D\$91-114); **Raphael Hotel** (943-5000, S\$55-70/D\$65-80); **Ritz Carlton** (266-1000, S\$99-119/D\$109-139), luxurious; **Sheraton Plaza** (787-2900, S\$65-105/D\$80-120); **Knickerbocker**

Hotel (751-8100, S\$76-100/D\$88-120); **Park Hyatt** (280-2222, S\$110-130/ D\$130-150); **Whitehall** (944-6300, S\$105-125/D\$125-145), elegant.

Motels: In the Loop and Lake Shore Drive area, **Ascot House, Avenue Hotel, Best Western, Essex Inn, Holiday Inn—Lakeshore, La Salle Motor Lodge, Ramada Inn,** and the **McCormick Inn.** Rates have an extremely wide range, S\$23-96/D\$26-108. There are over a dozen motels near O'Hare Airport. Hotel Tax: 5-7%.

RESTAURANTS

American food: There are excellent dining rooms in major hotels, including the remodeled and elegant **Empire Room** in the Palmer House, restored to its 1920s splendor. In addition there are **Vittles, Gene & Georgetti, Lawry's, Sage's East, The Waterfront, Arnie's** (Near North Side), **Kinzie Steak House,** and **That Steak Joynt** on North Wells. Others on the Near North Side include the award-winning **Biggs Restaurant, The Embers** (3), **The Bakery, Nantucket Cove,** and the **Wrigley Building Restaurant. Binyon's** and **Don Roth's Blackhawk** are outstanding in the Loop. Moderately priced in the downtown area are the **Epicurean** and **Stouffer's Top of the Rock.**

Foreign food: Café de Paris, Chez Paul, Frere Jacques, Le Bastille, Le Mignon, Jacques, La Cheminée, Le Bordeaux, L'Epuisette, Jovan, Le Perroquet, L'Escargot, and **Maxim's de Paris;** all French on the Near North Side and all moderate to expensive. Good Italian restaurants, more moderately priced: **Riccardo's, The Italian Village, Gino's East,** and **Pizzeria Uno** and **Due** or **Giordano's** for great pizza. German and moderate: **Math Igler's, Black Forest, Zum Deutschen Eck,** and **The Berghoff.** Mexican: **La Hacienda del Sol, La Margarita, Su Casa,** and **Meson del Lago.** Greek: **Diana's, Greek Islands,** and **Parthenon** in Greek Town. Chinese: **Don the Beachcomber** (moderately expensive), **Chiam, Dr. Shen's, Abacus, Mandarin House, Jimmy Wong's, Wing Yee's,** and **Lee's Chinese Restaurant.** Japanese: **Azuma House, Benihana of Tokyo,** moderately expensive, **Ron of Japan** and **Kamehachi of Tokyo. The Magic Pan,** creperie, **Les Oeufs, Omelettes** and **Jasands,** hamburgers, all moderate. Famous hotel dining rooms, all expensive: **Cape Cod Room** in the Drake Hotel, **Trader Vic's** at the Palmer House, **Kon-Tiki Ports** at the Sheraton Chicago, and the **Consort Room** at the Continental Plaza.

ENTERTAINMENT

Empire Room at the Palmer House; **Arnie's; The Pump Room** at the Ambassador East Hotel; **Avenue One** and **Terrace Lounge** at the Drake; **Blue Max,** at the Hyatt Regency O'Hare and **Mill Run** in suburban Niles, name entertainers. Rush Street is one of the city's night life centers. Numerous dinner theaters include **Drury Lane, Arlington Park, Forum,** and **Candlelight Dinner Playhouse. Second City,** in Old Town, has topical reviews. There are many community theaters on Lincoln Avenue and in Old Town. See *Chicago* magazine or local newspaper entertainment sections for schedules.

Chicago's behemoth in the sky—the Sears Tower—looms above the midwestern metropolis' horizon to a height of 1,454 ft, making it the tallest building in the world.

ARTS AND MUSIC

The **Chicago Symphony** performs at **Orchestra Hall** on Thursday evenings, Friday afternoons, and Saturday evenings in season. The **Lyric Opera** season opens in the fall. Enjoy ballet and other musical events in **Sullivan's Auditorium Theater, Civic Opera House,** and **Arie Crown Theater.** Outstanding stage productions are presented in various theaters in the city and suburbs. In summer, stock companies perform in **Theater-on-the-Lake** at the **Fullerton Pavilion.** There are also outdoor concerts at the **Grant Park** bandshell and at **Ravinia Park** (in north suburban Highland Park), both places famous for their varied programs. **Facets Multimedia** and the **Midwest Film Center** show current and old films, as well as foreign and experimental movies.

SHOPPING

There are many fine shops along North Michigan Avenue, Chicago's "Magnificent Mile," including the new Water Tower Place, featuring both **Lord & Taylor** and **Marshall Field** department stores. Field's also has an outstanding store in the Loop, which gives conducted tours to groups on weekdays by appointment. Most stores are open Monday and Thursday evenings until 9, other days until 5:45pm. **Northbrook Court,** about 20 minutes from Chicago (exit Lake-Cook Road off Edens Expressway in Northbrook) is an elegant shopping center with stores such as Lord & Taylor, **I Magnin, Brooks Brothers,** and **Neiman-Marcus.**

SPORTS

Horse racing is in season from April through late fall; pari-mutuel betting. The **Chicago White Sox** play professional baseball in the American League and the **Chicago Cubs** in the National League. The **Bears** are the city's pro football team. The **Blackhawks** play professional ice hockey and the **Chicago Sting** play pro soccer. The **Bulls** play pro basketball. **The Chicago Hustle** is the city's professional woman's basketball team. In addition, there is a good selection of college athletic events.

There are scores of fine golf courses, public and private, in the Chicago vicinity. Tennis is also available at public parks and at country clubs. Lake Michigan offers boating, swimming and fishing; no license is required for fishing in the lake and many people angle from the piers.

WHERE TO GO NEARBY

If you can get away from the excitement and fascination of Chicago, **Illinois Beach State Park,** about 50 miles north, offers swimming and picnic facilities. The **Chain o'Lakes** region includes the antique centers of **Richmond, Long Grove,** and **Frankfort.** The lovely old communities of **Geneva, Batavia,** and **St Charles** along the Fox River are also noted for antique shops and good dining facilities, in particular the **Mill Race Inn,** a converted grist mill on the river in Geneva. **McHenry County,** west of Chicago, is known for its hundreds of preserved acres as a conservation district, and for the town of **Woodstock,** with its restored buildings and antique shops.

FURTHER STATE INFORMATION

Illinois Office of Tourism, Department of Business and Economic Development, 205 West Wacker Drive, Chicago, IL 60606. Hunting and Fishing: **Department of Conservation,** State Office Building, Springfield, IL 62706. **Chicago Convention and Tourism Bureau,** 332 South Michigan Avenue, Chicago, IL 60604; tel: 922-3530. **Chicago Association of Commerce and Industry,** 130 S. Michigan Avenue, Chicago, IL 60603; tel: 786-0111. **Pan Am,** 18 South Michigan Avenue, Chicago, IL 60603; tel: 332-4900.

Consulates in Chicago: Argentina, Australia, Austria, Barbados, Belgium, Bolivia, Brazil, Burundi, Canada, Chile, Republic of China, Colombia, Costa Rica, Denmark, Ecuador, El Salvador, Finland, France, Germany, Great Britain, Greece, Guatemala, Haiti, Honduras, Iceland, India, Iran, Ireland, Israel, Italy, Jamaica, Japan, Korea, Lebanon, Liberia, Lithuania, Luxembourg, Mexico, Monaco, Netherlands, Nicaragua, Norway, Panama, Paraguay, Peru, Philippines, Poland, Senegal, Spain, Sri Lanka, Sweden, Switzerland, Thailand, Turkey, Uruguay, Venezuela, Yugoslavia.

USEFUL TELEPHONE NUMBERS IN CHICAGO

General Emergency	911
Metrohelp (medical)	929-5150
Dental Clinic Northwest University	649-8350
Traffic Info	731-8383
Road Conditions	283-6204
Travel Info (Public Transport)	836-7000
Legal Assistance Foundation	341-1070
Legal Aid Bureau	922-5625
Weather	936-1212
Kiwanis	943-2300
Pan Am Reservations	332-4900

Indiana

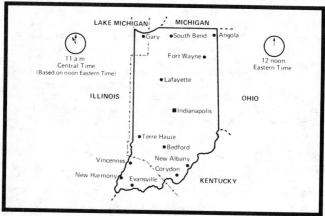

Area	36,291 square miles					**Population**		5,374,000				
Capital	Indianapolis					**Sales Tax**		4%				

Weather	Jan	Feb	Mar	Apr	May	Jun	Jul	Aug	Sep	Oct	Nov	Dec
Av Temp (°C)	−2	−1	−4	10	16	22	24	23	19	13	5	−1
Days Rain/Snow	11	10	12	12	12	10	9	8	8	7	10	11

Indiana, sitting astride the industrial and agricultural region of mid-America, sees itself as the crossroads of the nation. For while the smallest of states west of the Allegheny Mountains, it rates amongst national leaders in terms of population, industrial manufacturing, and agriculture. **Lake Michigan** touches on the north, the **Ohio River** runs along the entire southern boundary, and the **Wabash River** makes its way along the southwest border with Illinois. Peculiar to the northern section of the state are the sand dunes and beaches of Lake Michigan and the famous lake districts, a remnant of the Ice Age. A 45-mile segment which touches on the Lake is host to huge steel mills and oil refineries, making this one of the world's greater industrial centers.

The central section, consisting of a level plain seemingly as smooth as the hardwood floors in many of the state's historic homes, is broken only by river valleys and occasional low ridges and is one of the richest farming regions in the United States. Southern Indiana, which contains the most striking scenery in the state, is a region of deep valleys, sharp ridges, and the foothills of the **Cumberland Mountains**, called the

"Knobs". The great limestone belt, from **Bloomington** to the Ohio River, is pocked by caves, sinkholes, mineral springs, and disappearing streams. The lovely **Ohio Valley**, forming a narrow, hilly, and in some places rugged border with Kentucky, begins to widen and becomes level in the southwestern part of the state, ending at **Evansville.**

Much of the heritage of Indiana involves the Indians who lived here, and who left their traces in curious groups of still existing earthworks. In 1670 two Frenchmen, Father Marquette and Louis Joliet, wandered across northern Indiana preaching to the Indians. After the French and Indian War, most of the territory came under British control for a time, but American control was clearly established after 1811 and the Battle of Tippecanoe.

More than 1,000 lakes and streams, many restocked annually with game fish, provide excellent sport, and the 32 state parks, forests, and recreation areas offer many outdoor activities. Fishing is especially good near **La Porte, Rome City,** and **Warsaw Lake** where raft trips are popular for stream fishing. Quail, deer, and pheasant hunting are excellent in **Enos, Knox,** and **North Judson.**

The good state roads allow easy traveling from such places as the **Dunes State Park** on Lake Michigan to Lincoln's boyhood home in **Spencer County** and the grave of his mother, Nancy Hanks Lincoln, at the **Lincoln Boyhood National Memorial,** 30 miles northwest of Evansville. Also visit the prehistoric Indian mounds at **Mounds State Park** outside Anderson and **Wyandotte Cave,** third largest in the US. Then continue to the restored pioneer settlement with gristmill, general store, distillery, and sawmill at **Spring Mill,** east of Mitchell; or to that famous post office, **Santa Claus, Indiana.**

Travelers entering from Ohio on I-90, or from Michigan on I-69, find themselves in the lake country around **Angola,** where more than 100 spring-fed lakes are stocked with blue gill and bass. **Redwood Best Western Motor Inn** (665-9451, S$23/D$28) offers very good accommodations, while **Holiday Inn** (665-9471, S$30/D$38-40) at Lake Charles and **Potawatomi Inn** (833-1077, S$25/D$30-37) on Lake James at Park provide lodging nearby. **Pokagon State Park** on **Lake James** near Angola is a year-round recreational center with swimming, boating, fishing, horseback riding, and nature hikes in the summer, and ice-skating, ice-boating, and a 1700-foot toboggan slide in winter. Just south of Angola is **Auburn,** former center for production of the classic Auburns, Cords, and Duesenbergs. These antique autos are featured in a museum and annual **Labor Day Rally** in Auburn.

Further south on I-69 is **FORT WAYNE,** home of the **Lincoln Museum,** open Monday to Friday, free; and the **Cathedral of the Immaculate Conception,** with its Bavarian stained-glass windows. Architectural attractions include the new **Performing Arts Center** designed by Louis Kahn and **Concordia College** designed by Eero Saarinen. Besides being the burial place for John Crawford, better known as "Johnny Appleseed", there is **Franke Park,** featuring a large bird sanctuary and children's zoo. **Marriott Inn** (484-0411, S$32-46/D$50-54) which boasts its popular Scotland

Yard Disco and the **Ramada Inn** (432-0511, S\$37/D\$43) are both within 5 miles of the town's center. Also 8 miles from the center of Fort Wayne at Baer Field is the **Hilton Inn** (747-9171, S\$32-49/D\$45-62). Taxi into town from the Hilton, which is at the airport, is \$7.50. Try the **Café Johnell** for excellent French cuisine. Moving 40 miles south, **Amishville USA,** outside Berne, is an authentic Amish farm where visitors may jaunt around the area in a horse-drawn buggy or sleigh in winter; open daily. **Richmond** was one of the first communities founded by the Society of Friends. The **Wayne County Historical Museum,** built in 1865, occupies the former meeting house and contains a pioneer kitchen, open mid-February to mid-December. Traveling due west from Richmond to **Indianapolis,** visitors pass through the stagecoach towns along the **Old National Road** (US 40). Attractive restorations and good antique hunting characterize this drive.

Continue westward towards Chicago from Angola, and you pass through **Elkhart,** famous for making musical instruments since 1875. It may be worth noting that Indiana has given the nation such musicians as Hoagy Carmichael, Paul Dresser, Cole Porter, Tom Westerdorf, and famed Albert von Tilzer. Just beyond is **SOUTH BEND** home of the **University of Notre Dame.** Tours of the Notre Dame campus are given daily in the summer, by appointment the rest of the year. **University Galleries** in O'Shaughnessy Hall contain many famous paintings and a collection of furniture and art objects owned by the Borgia and Medici families; open daily. **Sacred Heart Church** is one of the finest Gothic structures in the US with its famous altar and Gregori murals. **The Log Chapel** is a replica of the chapel built in 1830 by the first priest ordained in the US. **The Grotto of Lourdes** is a beautiful reproduction of the original grotto in the French Pyrenees. **Storyland Zoo** off route 20, is set in a heavily wooded area with miniature train and picnicking. The influence of the early French missionaries and fur traders can be seen in the restored **Pierre Navarre Cabin** and the **Council Oak Tree,** a 400-year-old tree under which La Salle held council with chiefs of the Miami and Illinois Confederations in 1681. Numerous good motels in South Bend, including the **Americana Inn** (232-3941, S\$44-60/D\$50-66) in the center of town, The **Morris Inn** (234-0141, S\$31/D\$37) on the Notre Dame Campus, **Randalls Inn** (272-7900, S\$22/D\$26) 1½ miles from business district, and **Ramada Inn** (272-5220, S\$30-33/D\$34-37). In nearby Mishawaka the former Kamms Beer Brewery has been converted into a unique shopping mall, the **100 Center.**

GARY is the largest US city founded in the 20th century. The city was chosen in 1906 as the site of the main plant of the US Steel Corporation. A river was moved, sand dunes pulled down, and vast sections drained to make way for the influx of factories and for the building of workers' homes. The sight of the red-glowing cupolas turning out more than 8 million tons of steel annually is stirring by daylight and awesome against the night sky. If you head for Indianapolis from Gary via I-65, you'll pass through **Lafayette.** Lafayette and its neighbor, West Lafayette, home of **Purdue University,** is named after the Marquis de Lafayette, in honor of his service to the United States during the Revolutionary War. **Tippecanoe Battlefield State Memorial** is 7 miles north, off IN 43, marking the site of the battle in 1811 where General William Henry Harrison defeated the Indians led by Tecumseh and his brother, The Prophet. The Indian tribes were outraged about losing 3 million acres of their lands, now Southern Indiana, and had gone on the warpath against settlers. **Tippecanoe County Historical Association Museum** contains local historical relics. On special occasions there are performances here by an 18th-century style fife and drum corps at the reconstructed blockhouse in **Fort Quiatenon. Columbia Park** has one of the largest zoos in the state and recreational facilities. Hotels include **Holiday Inn** (567-2131, S$33/D$40), **Sheraton Inn** (463-5511, S$32/D$40), and **TraveLodge** (743-9661, S$31/D$37-45). Northwest Indiana is also the location of the state's four ski resorts.

Southwest of Indianapolis is **TERRE HAUTE**, one of the major cities on the banks of the Wabash River and the location of the **Indiana State University.** This was the birthplace of composer Paul Dresser, novelist Theodore Dreiser, and Eugene V. Debs, the early socialist labor leader. The homes of Debs and Dresser have been restored and reopened for free tours. Interestingly, in addition to its musicians, Indiana numbers amongst its authors: James Whitcomb Riley, Gene Stratton Porter, Pulitzer Prize winner Booth Tarkington, and Lew Wallace. Less remembered is that the celebrated sociological studies by Dr Alfred C. Kinsey of Indiana University, **Sexual Behaviour of the Human Male and Female. Early Wheels Museum** has antique vehicles; open Monday to Friday, free. **Swope Art Gallery** contains an outstanding collection of 19th- and 20th-century American paintings; open Tuesday through Sunday, closed in August. **Imperial House Terre Haute** (234-4816, S$18/D$27) and **Holiday Inn** (232-6081, S$35/D$42) provide good accommodations. **Best Western of Terre Haute** (234-7781, S$32/D$39) is also good. Also southwest of Indianapolis and home of **Indiana University,** is **BLOOMINGTON.** While visiting this university town catch a performance of the school's opera company. Among the many motels in Bloomington are the **Holiday Inn** (332-9453, S$32-40/D$37-45) and the **Best Western Fireside Inn** (332-2141, S$32/D$39). Fifteen minutes south in the Hoosier National Forest, **The Inn of the Four Winds** (824-9904, S/D$58-68), on Lake Monroe; offers a resort atmosphere.

VINCENNES, Indiana's oldest city, is on the banks of the Wabash River, halfway between Evansville and Terre Haute. It stands amid peach and apple orchards, truck farms and livestock pastures. Fur trading brought about the establishment in 1732, of Fort Vincennes, which fell to the British in 1763, then was captured by George Rogers Clark in 1779. At the first division of the Northwest Territory in 1800, it became the capital of the Indiana Territory. **George Rogers Clark National Historic Park,** commemorates the winning of the Northwest. **Harrison Mansion,** built in 1804 by William Henry Harrison, later ninth president of the United States, is open daily. The **Old Cathedral** was built in 1826 on the site of the first log church, and in the spire is the same bell, since recast, which hung in the tower of the original building; open daily. Behind the church is **Simon Brute Library,** oldest in the state, containing 5,000 volumes, some dating from the 14th century; open daily. The **Elihu Stout Print Shop** is the home of one of the earliest newspapers in the old Northwest. Stay at **Executive Inn** (886-5000, S$19-27/D$23-31) or **Holiday Inn** (886-9900, S$28-40/D$34-46).

EVANSVILLE, the state's second-largest city, is the home of two universities, parks, horse racing and the unusual **Angel Mounds State Memorial,** a 421-acre archaeological site full of Indian relics; open daily, free. The **Executive Inn** (424-8000, S$30-42/D$35-49) and the **Jackson House** (423-7816, S$22/D$24) provide good lodging. Have dinner at **F's Steak House** or **Joe Larvo's Three Coins Restaurant. New Harmony,** 20 miles northwest of Evansville, was the location of two of early America's attempts at communal living. Many traces of the older settlement, first organized in 1814, are found at the **New Harmony State Memorial,** which includes two buildings and a garden labyrinth; open May through October, Tuesday-Sunday, free. **Roofless Church** features a dome by architect Philip Johnson and a bronze sculpture by Jacques Lipchitz.

Travelers heading south move into the **Lake Monroe** region and its nearby town of **Bedford,** which has many limestone quarries. The **Mark III Motel** (275-5935, S$20/D$23) in this small town makes a good headquarters while exploring the many attractions in the area. **Pioneer Mothers' Memorial Forest,** 1 mile south of Paoli, is used for ecological studies. **Avoca State Fish Hatchery,** free admission, breeds sunfish, bass, and bluegill to stock the state's lakes. **Spring Mill State Park** is one of the most successful historical restorations in the country. **Spring Mill Village,** a frontier trading post founded about 1815, is set in a secluded hollow entirely enclosed by towering hills. The park includes many of the original buildings and is surrounded by 100 acres of virgin woodland. Underground boat trips are available in **Twain** and **Donaldson Caves;** open daily. The mineral springs at **French Lick** are famous as a health and vacation resort situated on 1,600 acres of woodland. The **French Lick Sheraton Hotel** (935-9381, S$70-100/D$90-120, all meals included) offers excellent accommodations with a number of special packages available for tennis, golf including clinics, horseback riding, trap/skeet shooting, and spa.

Just off busy I-64 some of the best touring and sightseeing in the state is found in the Ohio Valley. The city of **Columbus** includes some outstanding examples of modern architecture. In **New Albany,** shipbuilders of the last century produced two record-setting steamboats, the *Robert E. Lee* and the *Eclipse.* Steamboat races, shows, and parades are scheduled for 3 days in early May. The **Culbertson Mansion,** a 26-room Victorian home completed in 1868, is open Tuesday to Sunday, April-November. For a real treat take a boat ride through the restored canal town of **Metamora,** or take the scenic **Whitewater Valley Railroad,** the world's longest standard gauge railroad.

A short distance to the west is **Corydon,** briefly the state capital in the early 1800s, the site of the only Indiana battle of the Civil War not marked by a memorial. The **Corydon Capitol State Museum,** open daily in summer and closed Sunday and Wednesday in winter, offers a historical museum and a classic collection of furniture reproductions. **Wyandotte Cave,** known for its huge underground mountain, and **Squire Boone Caverns,** a large travertine dam formation, are open daily. West along I-64 at the US 231 exit is the entrance to the **Lincoln Boyhood National Memorial,** just south of Lincoln City. Included here are **Abraham Lincoln Hall,** built to resemble a chapel, and the **Nancy Hanks Lincoln Hall,** a museum and auditorium. Along the wall of the semicircular walk connecting the two halls are five sculptured panels depicting important periods in Lincoln's life; open daily, free.

City to Visit

INDIANAPOLIS

Central location and better than average ground and air transportation facilities have contributed to making Indianapolis the nation's second largest city among those not located on navigable waterways. The city is especially favoured as being the crossroads of no less than 5 interstate highways. The first settlers arrived at what is now Indianapolis in 1820. A year later the Indiana Assembly's special commission selected the site as the state capital. The plan of the city was designed by Ralston, assistant to Major L'Enfant, who laid out Washington, DC. It is a combination of the "spider web" of Versailles, France, and the regular squares of Washington, DC. The city was incorporated in 1874.

"Hoosiers", as the people of Indiana are called, are notably friendly and hospitable to tourists and newcomers. One item a prospective visitor to the Hoosier State should know, is where the term "Hoosier" comes from. The answer is that it all depends on who's telling the story, for replies can range from an early canal contractor, by name Sam Housier, who preferred to hire men from Indiana, or to the early pioneer greeting of "Who's hyer?" In English, a hoo is still used to mean a small hill, while in earlier times a "hoozer" meant a hill dweller. Their capital is typically Midwestern. Business activities flourish and there is a good diversification of trade and agriculture. Population is 704,045. The central part of the town has "Mile Square", where the main shopping centers, hotels, public buildings, and some industries are situated. There are several multi-million-dollar shopping centers, but a great deal of the business activity remains in the "Mile Square" area.

WHAT TO SEE

State Capitol, erected in 1878, with its gold dome, and built of the finest local limestone, is open Monday to Friday 8:15-4:45. **Clowes Memorial Hall** is an architecturally impressive center for concerts, plays, opera. **Soldiers' and Sailors' Monument,** rising 285 feet, is one of the tallest columns in the US; it has a museum in the basement and an observation platform reached by an elevator; open daily 9-4; 25¢ admission. **Indiana State Museum**, admission free; **Scottish Rite Cathedral**, old-world architecture, is noted for its carillon, conducted tours, no charge; **Children's Museum** (free); **Indianapolis Motor Speedway**, just outside the city limits, a 2½ mile paved oval, with a golf course near the entrance, and a racing museum at main entrance; open daily 9-5. **Indianapolis Museum of Art**, remarkable collection, with beautiful grounds; also see the **Federal Building**; **World War Memorial**; national headquarters of the American Legion; **Indiana University Medical Center, James Whitcombe Riley's Home; Benjamin Harrison Memorial Home;** and **Butler University Planetarium**, open Saturday and Sunday 3-5 and 7-9. **Conner Prairie Pioneer Settlement and Museum**, restored pioneer settlement with tours April-October, is also interesting, as is **Union Station**, on the site of the first union railroad station in the country. **The State Library and Historical Building** houses an extensive collection of material on state history and development.

Riverside Park offers playing fields, golf, canoeing, boating; other parks in the city also have a variety of recreational facilities. **Riverside Fish Hatchery**, just north of Riverside Park, is interesting; open daily. **Garfield Park** has an enclosed greenhouse, sunken gardens, picnic areas and an outdoor theater. **Indianapolis Zoo** is open daily; admission charge. **Eagle Creek Park**, the largest city park in the nation, is located on West 71st Street off I-65. Its facilities include canoe, rowboat, and sailboat rentals, and a swimming beach. Admission is $2.25 per car.

ACCOMMODATIONS

Hotels in Indianapolis include: **Atkinson Hotel** (639-5611, S$35-45/D$40-50), downtown; **Hilton Inn** (244-3361, S$48-58/D$64-72), at airport; **Indianapolis Hilton Hotel** (635-2000, S$54-62/D$64-72), in the heart of town; **Essex Hotel** (639-4501, S$31/D$42-45) excellent and downtown; **Stouffers Indianapolis** (924-1241, S$31/D$40); **Hyatt Regency Indianapolis** (632-1234, S$55-80/D$67-95); **Marriott Inn** (352-1231, S$46-52/D$53-59) northeast center of town; **Sheraton East** (897-4000, S$44/D$49); **Sheraton West** (248-2481, S$54-57/D$57-67), at the airport. Fine motels include **Holiday Inn** (7 locations throughout town), **Howard Johnson's** (downtown and at the raceway), **Indianapolis Motor Speedway, Quality Inn** (downtown and near the fairgrounds), **Ramada Inn** (4 throughout town), and **Rodeway Inn** (near the airport and in the eastern section), and **Stouffers** (downtown). Rates range from S$25-30/D$36-40. Hotel Tax: 9%.

RESTAURANTS

Chanteclair Sur le Toit, King Cole and **La Tour,** (on the 37th floor of Indiana National Bank Tower, with spectacular view) superb food; quite expensive. **Italian Village, La Scala** for Italian food; **Mon Reve** and **Chez Jean,** authentic French cuisine; **St Elmo's Steak House,** excellent steaks; **Key West Shrimp House** and **Captain Alexander's Wharf,** very good seafood and steaks served in an attractive setting; **Mickler's Sirloin Inn,** east of city on US 40, good for steak; **Good Earth Cafeteria,** vegetarian;

Indianapolis . . . "500". Over 300,000 people gather annually to watch the world's fastest automobiles compete in the "greatest spectacle in racing."

Hawthorn Restaurant; Hollyhock Hill; Iron Skillet; Kendall Inn; René's, French; Sirloin Inn and **TGI Friday, Laughner's Cafeterias** in 4 locations, **Ralf's Delicatessen,** and **Shapiro's Kosher Cafeteria;** all moderate. **Jong Mea, Lantern Room, L. S. Ayres Tea Room, Wm. H. Block & Co Tea Room;** very reasonable.

ENTERTAINMENT
Dinner dancing at several of the hotels, including the Atkinson Hotel, the **Indianapolis Hilton, Hyatt Regency, Marriott Inn** and **Stouffer's Indianapolis;** all fairly expensive. Away from the hotels is **Lucifers** at the Keystone-at-the-Crossing; and the **Hummingbird,** 71st and Keystone.

ARTS AND MUSIC
John Herron Art Institute, art objects and paintings from all over the world. **The Morris Butler Museum** has mid-Victorian decorative arts; **Museum of Indian Heritage,** exhibits depicting Indian culture. Regular concerts are given by the **Indianapolis Symphony Orchestra** at **Clowes Memorial Hall** on the campus of Butler University, as is opera by the recently formed Indianapolis Opera Company, and by the **Jordan Conservatory of Music.** The Butler Ballet also performs here from late fall through spring. Free band concerts and variety shows in summer.

SHOPPING
Keystone at the Crossing is a new multi-level shopping center which has found numerous patrons, as have the boutiques to be found on North Side. Bargains abound at **Broad Ripple** and **Zionsville,** both slightly off the beaten track.

SPORTS
The **Indianapolis 500** race, inaugurated in 1911, is the largest single-day sporting event in the world; related events of 500 Festival occur throughout May. With many colleges in the vicinity, there is a good variety of sporting events including football, basketball, baseball, ice hockey, and track. Spectators enjoy the **Indiana Pacers,** professional basketball team, the **Indianapolis Indians,** professional baseball club, and the **Racers,** who play ice hockey. State basketball finals engender "Hoosier Hysteria", a wild excitement for local teams. There are extensive facilities for golf, tennis, and swimming in public parks and private clubs. Hunting and fishing are available. The **US Open Clay Court Championships,** a weeklong tournament attracting national and world celebrity players, is conducted in August at the **Indianapolis Sports Center.**

CALENDAR OF EVENTS
Sportsmen's Show, early spring; **Home Show,** about April; **Sport Car Show** and **Indianapolis 500** automobile race, late May; **Indiana State Fair,** late August; **Fall Foliage Festival,** October; **Pioneer Christmas Festival** at Conner Prairie, each of the three weekends before Christmas.

WHERE TO GO NEARBY

Brown County State Park in Nashville has accommodations at **Brown Country Inn** (988-2291, S$27-30/D$35-38) and **Ramada Inn** (988-2284, S/D$35-53). Nashville is also noted for its quaint shops and restaurants and also boosts itself as an artists' colony. **Turkey Run State Park** in Marshall has **Turkey Run Inn;** open all year. **Clifty Falls State Park** at Madison has **Clifty Falls Inn;** open all year. **Pokagon Park** has **Potowatomi Inn** at Angola; open all year. **Dunes State Park at Chesterton** has two hotels, **Duneside** and **Dunes,** open April to October. Other nearby attractions include **Indiana Beach** in Monticello and **Billie Creek Village,** a recreated turn-of-the-century town.

FURTHER STATE INFORMATION

Department of Commerce, Room 336, State House, Indianapolis, IN 46204. Hunting and Fishing: **Indiana Department of Natural Resources,** 612 State Office Building, Indianapolis, IN 46204. **Indianapolis Chamber of Commerce,** 320 North Meridian Street, Indianapolis, IN 46204. **Convention and Visitors' Bureau,** 100 South Capitol Avenue, Indianapolis, IN 46225.

   Consulates in Indianapolis: France, West Germany.

USEFUL TELEPHONE NUMBERS FOR INDIANAPOLIS

Police, Fire, Ambulance	911
Poison Control	927-3033
Community Hospital	353-1411
Wishard Memorial Hospital	639-6671
Legal Aid Society	635-9538
Chamber of Commerce	635-4747
Pan Am Reservations	800-621-2909

Iowa

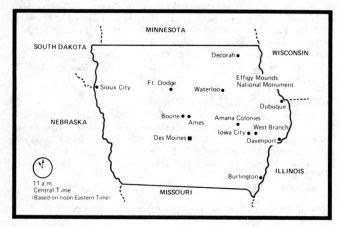

Area	56,290 square miles	Population	2,913,400								
Capital	Des Moines	**Sales Tax**	3%								

Weather	Jan	Feb	Mar	Apr	May	Jun	Jul	Aug	Sep	Oct	Nov	Dec
Av Temp (°C)	−7	−5	1	9	16	22	25	23	19	12	3	−4
Days Rain/Snow	7	7	10	10	11	11	9	9	9	7	6	7

Iowa, named after the Sioux Indian word for "beautiful land," is a state of cornfields and prairies. It is also very rich in American history. A favorite Indian hunting ground and scene of bitter warfare, Iowa was part of the Louisiana Purchase and was first explored by the Frenchmen Marquette and Joliet in 1673. Lewis and Clark, the US military explorers, also crossed the vast tract of land in 1804 on their arduous journey to the northwest coast. The Lewis and Clark Trail runs for 193 miles along the Missouri River from Council Bluffs, named after a meeting between the explorers and the Oto and Missouri Indians, to Sioux City. Much of their trail can now be followed on I-29.

Although the state's economy benefits from some 4,000 manufacturing firms, the emphasis is on farming: 95% of Iowa's total land area is farmland and the state grows 20% of the nation's corn. Iowa's recreation chiefly centers on its 50,000 acres of lakes and 15,000 miles of streams. There are many state parks and preserves and six state forests. The lake regions of southcentral, north and northwest Iowa, easily accessible from Des Moines on I-35, are the state's most popular water playground areas.

Lake Okoboji, in the northwest, is one of only three natural blue water lakes in the world. Iowans and visitors flock here for swimming and golf in the summer, then return in winter for skiing, snowmobiling and ice fishing. The **Best Western Brooks Lodge & Golf Club** (332-2161, S$16.50-40.50/D$22.50-44.50) is one of several places to stay.

To the west, the **Ochevaedan Burial Mound** rises 170 feet above the countryside.

SIOUX CITY, site of one of the nation's largest stockyards, holds its annual **River-Cade Celebration** in late July. **Sioux City Public Museum** has exhibits illustrating life in pioneer and Indian days; open Tuesday to Sunday, free. **Rodeway Inn** (277-1550, S$29-34/D$35-40) offers good accommodations; the **Holiday Inn, Imperial 400, Palmer House,** and **Howard Johnson's** are about S$26-30/D$31-35. The **Normandy,** three miles north of town, serves unlimited portions of good food.

The city of **Davenport** lies in the eastern part of the state on I-80. The **Davenport Municipal Art Gallery** houses an impressive collection of paintings and sculpture. Driving south, through the romantic river region, you come to **Burlington,** where **Steamboat Days** and **Dixieland Jazz Festival** are in full swing here in June. **West Branch** was the birth place of the late President Herbert Hoover; the **Herbert Hoover National Historic Site** includes his restored home. **Iowa City,** on the Iowa River, is the home of the **University of Iowa.** Nearby **Coralville Lake** provides year-round recreational facilities including fishing and camping. The **Amana Colonies,** northwest of Iowa City, are a group of seven closely united villages which form a communal center. They were settled in the 1850s by the Amana Society, a sect whose members came from Germany seeking religious freedom. The villages are organized on the basis of a joint stock corporation which absorbs its profits from and has as its stockholders the people of the Amana settlement. The annual **Oktoberfest** is held here in early October. The **Holiday Inn** (668-1175, S$25-28/D$31-34) offers good accommodation. The **Ox Yoke Inn, Ronneburg** and other restaurants are noted for their hearty German food and family-style service.

North of Des Moines lies **Ames,** home of **Iowa State University,** and **Boone,** birthplace of Mamie Eisenhower. The **Kate Shelly High Bridge,** near Boone, is the longest double track railroad bridge in America. **Ledges State Park** is of geological significance, with its unusual sandstone ledges. **Fort Dodge** has an exact replica of the original 1850 fort, open mid-May to mid-September. The **Starlight Village Motel** (573-7177, S$26-31/D$34-40) offers a quiet room and a sauna in Fort Dodge.

Visitors entering Iowa from southwestern Wisconsin cross the Mississippi at **Dubuque,** the state's oldest city, where it is hilly enough for an inclined railway cable car. **New Melleray Abbey** (founded 1849) is a Trappist Monastery known for delicious homemade breads and honey. North of Dubuque is picturesque **McGregor** in a land of caves and Indian burial grounds. **Effigy Mounds National Monument,** outside Marquette, contains the remains of a prehistoric Indian society; open daily. Continuing north you come to **Wonder Cave** and its 75-foot stalactites, near

Decorah; open late May-September. Norwegian visitors will be especially interested in Decorah's **Norwegian-American Museum;** open May-October. About 12 miles southwest of Decorah, in Spillville, is **Bily Clocks,** an exhibit of elaborately hand-carved musical clocks made by the Bily Brothers. Still farther south, at Festina, is the **St. Anthony of Padua Chapel,** built by a soldier who served under Napoleon. In Nashua, **"The Little Brown Church in the Vale"** is a sentimental landmark for thousands of visitors every year. The city of **Waterloo** looms large on the agricultural scene. The **National Dairy Cattle Congress** attracts huge crowds in September. **Holiday Inn, Howard Johnson's, Quality Inn-Midtown** and **Ramada Inn** average S$29/D$33-38. Try to be in Tama for the **Mesquakie Annual Pow Wow,** held four days during early August, with authentic dancing and tours of the Indian settlement.

City to Visit

DES MOINES

Des Moines had its beginning in 1834 when a fort was built at the fork of the Raccoon and Des Moines Rivers after treaties with the Sauk and Fox Indian tribes. According to old Indian stories, the river on whose banks this fort was built was known as the "Moingonia." Later it was shortened to "Moin" by French explorers, who called the stream *"la rivière des moines."* The city gets its name from the river. When the fort was ready, the land surrounding was thrown open for settlement. By 1853 there were about 500 inhabitants in the settlement and the city of Des Moines was incorporated. It became the capital of the state in 1857. One of the first places in the United States to adopt a city planning system, Des Moines started to undergo remodeling in 1924 and grew into a spacious, beautiful city noted for its many flowers and trees. The city has a population of 190,910, metropolitan area 330,000.

WHAT TO SEE

Drake University, with eight buildings designed by Eero Saarinen, is interesting. **Des Moines Center of Science and Industry** in Greenwood Park has natural and physical science exhibits and planetarium shows. The gold-domed **State Capitol,** guided tours during the summer; **Living History Farms,** with many interesting displays which recreates early Iowa life on three fully operative farms: a pioneer farm of 1840, a horse farm of 1900 and a Farm of the Future. **Salisbury House** is a 42-room mansion housing valuable art objects and paintings as well as a library of letters and first editions, guided tour by appointment only. **Des Moines Botanical Center** (283-4148) houses over 1,000 plant varieties, from cacti to orchids. Admission: adults 50¢, children 25¢.

ACCOMMODATIONS

Three centrally located hotels are the **Fort Des Moines** (243-1161, S$30-40/D$35-45), the **Savery** (244-2151, S$28-40/D$35-48), and the new **Mar-**

riott Hotel (245-5500, S$45-60/D$55-70). **Holiday Inn** (283-0151, S$33/ D$38) and **Ramada Inn** (288-5251, S$34-40/D$40-50) are downtown. **Hyatt House** (285-4310, S$35-45/D$45-55) is near the airport, and is excellent. Numerous good motels around the city include **Clayton House,** 6 miles northwest; **Des Moines Hilton Inn,** near the airport; **Holiday Inn,** at three locations in addition to the downtown inn; **Howard Johnson's Motor Lodge,** at two locations. Rates range from S/D$29-39. West on I-80, **Breckenridge West Mark Inn** (223-8500, S$36/D$49). Hotel tax: 5%.

RESTAURANTS

Johnny & Kay's in the Hyatt House for seafood and steak, moderate to expensive; **Wimpy's Steak House,** Italian-American cooking, moderate; **Babe's,** interesting antiques and works of art; **Cloud Room** in the airport terminal; **Noah's Ark,** international cuisine; **Bishop Buffet,** good food cafeteria-style; **Guidos** in the Savery; **The Pier,** nautical decor and menu.

ENTERTAINMENT

The Raintree for dinner and entertainment, reservations a must; **Ingersoll's Dinner Theater;** plus two discos—**The Denver** and **Sight & Sound Inc; Charlie's Showplace.**

ARTS AND MUSIC

Des Moines Art Center, exhibitions, **Junior Art Museum,** art reference library, concert hall; open daily except Monday, free. The **State Capitol** has valuable paintings, mosaics, and statues. Concerts are put on by the **Civic Music Association, Friends of Music,** and the **Des Moines Symphony Orchestra. Community Playhouse, Drama Workshop,** and **Des Moines Civic Ballet** stage theatrical and dance events.

SHOPPING

Most stores are open from 10-5:30. The leading store is **Younker's** located in downtown Des Moines.

SPORTS

Veterans Memorial Auditorium, seating 15,000 people, is the headquarters for state basketball tournaments, major ice shows, and similar events. **Drake University** has its relays and other collegiate sports. There is also football and **Triple-A** baseball. Swimming at six public pools. Des Moines has two municipal and three privately owned golf courses.

CALENDAR OF EVENTS

Drake Relays, outstanding collegiate track meet, late April; **National Hot Air Balloon Races,** held 12 miles from Des Moines in Indianola, early August; **State Fair,** one of the nation's greatest fairs; late August.

WHERE TO GO NEARBY

The many state parks and nature preserves offer fishing and boating; camping sites in about 40 parks. Visit the **Doll Museum** in Le Grand;

hundreds of rose bushes in **State Center,** the rose center of Iowa; Indian craft for sale in **Mesquaki Indian Settlement; Adventureland** is a large family amusement park some seven miles northeast of Des Moines, and near Altoona. Here is a re-creation of turn-of-the-century Iowa, with vintage trolley cars, just one of a series of spectacular rides. Dolphin and sea lion shows daily. Admission, which includes all rides and entertainment, $9.95, children aged 4 thru 11, $8.95, and **Pella,** a town of Dutch influence which has a **Tulip Festival** in May.

FURTHER STATE INFORMATION

Iowa Development Commission, Travel Development Division, 250 Jewett Building, Des Moines, IA 50309. Hunting and Fishing: **State Conservation Commission,** 300 Fourth Street, Des Moines, IA 50319. **Greater Des Moines Chamber of Commerce,** 8th and High Streets, Des Moines, IA 50307.

   Consulate in Des Moines: Danish.

USEFUL TELEPHONE NUMBERS IN DES MOINES

Broadlawn Polk County Hospital	282-2253
Des Moines General Hospital	265-9540
Iowa Lutheran	283-5120
Iowa Methodist Medical Center	283-6423
Danish Consulate	244-4201
Des Moines Chamber of Commerce	283-2161
Rotary Club of Des Moines (Hotel Fort Des Moines)	244-6028
Kiwanis Club	279-8821
Pan Am Reservations	(800) 621-2909

Kansas

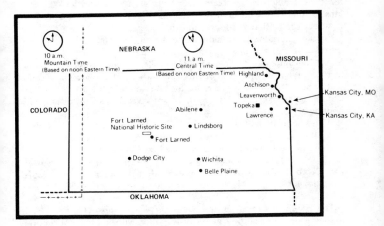

Area	82,264 square miles	Population	2,369,000
Capital	Topeka	Sales Tax	3%

Weather	Jan	Feb	Mar	Apr	May	Jun	Jul	Aug	Sep	Oct	Nov	Dec
Av Temp (°C)	0	2	7	14	19	25	27	27	22	16	7	2
Days Rain/Snow	5	5	7	7	10	10	9	7	8	6	4	6

The geographical center of the continental US, Kansas is a state both of prairies and high plains. The Spaniard Francisco de Coronado, searching for gold in the land of "Quivira" believed to be a wealthy region northeast of the Great Bend in the Arkansas River, first explored the region in 1541 when it was home to the Kansa, Osage, Pawnee, and Wichita Plains Indians. France and Spain claimed the land in the 1600s and 1700s, and it finally came into United States hands as part of the Louisiana Purchase. It became a territory in 1854 and statehood arrived just in time for the Civil War; Kansas was torn between free-state and proslavery forces.

Much of present-day Kansas has its roots in the pioneer and trade routes which passed through the state. The forts which protected the frontier during the white man's push westward gave their names to towns such as **Fort Leavenworth, Fort Riley, Fort Larned, Fort Hays,** and **Fort Scott.**

The rolling plains of Kansas stretch east and west across the state, gradually reaching into the **Smoky Hills** in the north and the sandy **Red Hills** of the south, sometimes rising to elevations of 3,000 feet. The **Great Plains** in the west have short grass, cactus, irrigated farming, and, where buffalo once grazed, endless "waves of grain." Eastern Kansas is green, fertile, and hilly, with wooded river valleys, streams, and lovely lakes. Most of the land is devoted to agriculture, with the state ranking first in wheat production and fourth in cattle.

Kansans consider their state to be among the country's most progressive. It was the first to grant women municipal suffrage and the first to permit them to hold municipal office. When Kansas became a territory, it had a population of only 700. Although it has grown substantially, there is still plenty of room for recreation in the 23 state parks and 26 major lakes. In addition, there are several excellent fishing and hunting areas.

With a population of 164,250, Kansas City KS is the sister city to Kansas City MO, a fact that often confuses first-time visitors. Kansas City, Kansas is home to the **University of Kansas Medical Center.**

Accommodations in Kansas City, KS include **Best Western's Colonial Inn** (236-6880, S$28-34/D$33), **Best Western's Flamingo Motel** (287-5511, S$24/D$28), and **Holiday Inn Downtown Towers** (342-6919, S$28/D$33).

The 233-mile Kansas Turnpike and I-70 leave Kansas City and lead to **Lawrence,** home of the **University of Kansas,** with an excellent **Natural History Museum.** Because of its tie with the New England states and an anti-slavery bias, Lawrence and its neighboring communities were frequent targets of attacks and burnings in 1860 by Southern sympathizers who would ride across from Missouri on pillaging expeditions. Exhibits here include a panorama of North American animals and "Comanche," the horse that survived Custer's Last Stand; open daily, free. In addition, the University of Kansas includes the **William Allen White School of Journalism,** and the **Helen Foresman Spencer Art Museum.** The Museum was started in 1878 and it has the oldest University art collection west of the Mississippi River. The **Virginia Inn Motel** (843-6611, S$19/D$22-25) and **Ramada Inn** (842-7030, S$25-37/D$33-45) are located just west of the turnpike interchange.

Leavenworth is north of Lawrence on the Missouri River and is the oldest city in the state. The **Fort Leavenworth Museum** displays examples of military dress and transport wagons of the pioneer days, all keyed to the influence of nearby **Fort Leavenworth,** a 7,000-acre military post established in 1827. Its **Command and General Staff College** is the largest tactical school in the world for advanced military training. In Leavenworth also is the federal penitentiary. Further north, **Atchison** is symbolic of the western expansion of the railroad. A railroad from St Joseph, Missouri, first financed by an Atchison city bond issue in 1859, was the first direct rail connection eastward from a point so far west. **Benedictine College** has a good view of the **Missouri River.** Visit the **Abbey Church,** copied from Benedictine monasteries of the Middle Ages, and the St

Scholastica Chapel, noted for its distinctive architecture. North near the Nebraska border is **Highland,** a small town and the home of the **Iowa, Sac, and Fox Indian Museum,** containing pioneer relics and Indian artifacts.

TOPEKA, (population 122,100) the state capital, grew up as a railroad town. Northwest lies the original capital of the state, **Manhattan,** now home to **Kansas State University.** The **Kansas State Historical Society and Museum,** across from the State House grounds, is one of the nation's largest historical societies. The museum displays relics of Indian artifacts, Coronado, John Brown, the cattle trade, and has some pioneer exhibits; open daily, free. **The Topeka Art Guild** features a fairly comprehensive collection of mid-Western painters. **Gage Park,** a 146-acre exposition near the downtown area, contains recreational facilities, beautiful gardens and a zoo which includes a Children's Zoo; park and zoo open daily. The world-famous **Menninger Foundation** mental health complex is at the western edge of the city. In midtown, **Holiday Inn** (232-7721, S$32-38/D$39-44) and **Ramada Inn** (233-8981, S$25-44/D$30-48) offer good accommodation. **Howard Johnson's** (266-4700, S$26-29/D$30-35) is 3 miles south of downtown at the Kansas Turnpike exit 8. **Le Flambeau Club** in Topeka is noted for its French cuisine and comfortable surroundings. More informal is **Robbie's,** also good. West along I-70 is **Fort Riley,** established in 1853 to protect Santa Fe Trail traffic. Visit the **US Cavalry Museum,** open daily, free, and the Memorial to the US Cavalry, where "Chief," the last cavalry horse, died in 1968 and is buried. Topeka is the site of the **Mid-America Fair,** held annually each September.

In **ABILENE,** (population, 6,430) further west, famed in earlier days as the northern terminus of the **Chisholm Trail** and governed at various times by Tom Smith and "Wild Bill" Hickok, you can see the **Eisenhower Center.** It covers 13 acres of landscaped grounds and encompasses the Eisenhower family home, presidential library, a museum and the **Meditation Chapel,** where the president was buried in 1969; open daily. Other attractions include the new **Miro Zoo;** open daily, and the **Greyhound Hall of Fame,** of particular interest because the sport began near Abilene. Accommodations in Abilene include: **Best Western's Priem's Pride Motel** (263-2800, S$18-22/D$21-25) and **Trails End Motel** (263-2050, S$12-15/D$15-19). Also of note is "Old Abilene Town," a period reconstruction of a wild west habitation. Nearby the **Old Abilene Opera House** stages plays dealing with America's past. **Salina** is a turning point for southern Kansas exploration. Here is the **Indian Burial Pit,** enclosed grave with artifacts and the skeletal remains of 140 Indians; open daily. Other relics and artifacts are to be found at the **Smokey Hill Historical Museum** at Oakdale Park. The **Airliner Motel, Holiday Inn** and **Trade Winds** are within 1 and 1½ miles of downtown and are moderately priced. On your way south to **Wichita** and **Belle Plaine** on I-35, you may want to stop in **Lindsborg,** a small town that is a center of a Swedish culture and home of **Bethany College.**

Cities to Visit

DODGE CITY

Now a progressive wheat and livestock center with a population of 15,626, Dodge City is a magnet for visitors who come to pick up the flavor of the frontier days. As everyone knows, Dodge City was a rugged frontier town which became a major terminus for the cattle drives north from Texas.

WHAT TO SEE

Visit the replica of the notorious **Front Street** where Wyatt Earp, Doc Holiday, and Bat Masterson controlled the lawless buffalo hunters, cowboys, soldiers, and settlers. "Miss Kitty" and her girls put on an oldtime show every night in the summer at the **Long Branch Saloon.**

The famous **Beeson Museum** is packed with items actually used by Dodge City's 19th-century gunmen. **Boot Hill,** where slow-drawing gunmen were buried with their boots on, is noted for the wry humor on its tombstones and the original **Hangman's Tree.** Behind the cemetery is **Boot Hill Museum,** open daily, with a collection of six-shooters and the eerie **Open Grave.** Nearby is the genuine **Fort Dodge Jail,** moved here from its original site. Also interesting in and near town are the **H. B. Bell Memorial Fountain** and the **Yoked Oxen Memorial;** the **100th-Meridian Twin Sun Dials;** the **Home of Stone,** built in 1881 of native stone and shown with many of its original Victorian furnishings; and vestiges of the **Sante Fe Trail** on US 50, 9 miles west.

Of contemporary interest are the **Municipal Auditorium,** a handsome center for cultural and sports events, and the modern **Sale Barn** of the **McKinley Winter Livestock Commission Company,** where over 250,000 head of cattle are auctioned annually. The **Dodge City Feed Yards,** where cattle are fattened before being shipped to market, have a capacity of 90,000 head. **Dodge City Days,** with parades, carnival, and rodeo, is held the third weekend in July.

ACCOMMODATIONS

Dodge City TraveLodge (225-4196, S$24-26/D$26-28), 1 mile west of city center and Boot Hill, **Best Western Silver Spur Lodge** (227-2125, S$22-26/D$24-30), 7 blocks west of Boot Hill, and **Holiday Inn** (227-8146, S$29-36/D$34-41) offer good accommodations. **The Astro Friendship Inn** (227-8146, S$18-22/D$26), is a few blocks west of Boot Hill on business route US 50. Campsites are at **Ford County State Lake** and **Miller Campground.** Hotel Tax: 3%

ENTERTAINMENT

Try the **Lamplighter Club, Cowtown Club,** and Silver Spur Lodge for good entertainment. And don't forget to check out the Long Branch

Saloon where nightly from 1 June through Labor Day Miss Kitty and the girls will entertain you to turn-of-the-century can-can while sarsaparilla and "red-eye whiskey" are served at the bar. For authentic southern-fried chicken, try the **Cottage Inn,** where the home baked pastries are also good.

SPORTS
Two golf courses are in town; swimming and archery in **Wright Park;** fishing and boating at **Ford County Lake** nearby.

WHERE TO GO NEARBY
Cedar Bluff Reservoir and State Park is 85 miles northeast in Trego Co.

WICHITA

A modern, cosmopolitan and friendly city, Wichita, population 267,748, ranks second among major cities in having the cleanest air. Wichita is home to a significant portion of the nation's aerospace industry and Boeing Aircraft production and is headquarters of the Beech and Cessna Aircraft companies, both formed by pioneers of flight in the early years of the century. Today, Cessna has become the largest manufacturer of general aviation aircraft in the world. Learjet also produces planes in Wichita.

WHAT TO SEE
Cow Town is a restored village showing the city's early history; open April to October, Tuesday-Sunday. **Sedgwick County Zoo** is one of the most outstanding in the country; open daily. Tours of local aircraft manufacturing plants arranged by the Chamber of Commerce.

ACCOMMODATIONS
Among the best hotels are the **Holiday Inn Plaza** (264-1181, S$32/D$35-38), **the Broadview Hotel** (264-0171, S$25/D$30-33), **Ramada Inn Central** (267-9281, S$31/D$36-38), and **The Wichita Royale** (263-2101, S$32-36/D$44-46), all downtown. The **Wichita Hilton Inn** (686-7131, S$34-52/D$48-66) is in midtown. Near the airport are **Canterbury Inn** (942-7911, S$34-52/D$37-49) and **Town & Country Lodge** (942-2273, S$15-18/D$20-22), and others. Hotel Tax: 3%

RESTAURANTS
The **Hickory House** specializes in seafood and steaks. **Steak and Ale** has delicious food at modest prices served in Tudor-style dining rooms with open fires, while **Brown's Grill East** has a pleasant family atmosphere. There's a beautiful view of the city from Holiday Inn Plaza's 25th-floor restaurant.

ENTERTAINMENT
Plenty of nightclub activity. Try **Lancers Downtown** and **Le Bistro Club,** good floor shows; **Ship's Tavern,** fitted out like the interior of an early

sailing ship; and the **Penthouse,** overlooking the city from the Holiday Inn Plaza.

ARTS AND MUSIC

Watch for performances by the excellent **Wichita Symphony Orchestra.** The **Wichita Art Museum** includes a large collection of American paintings and the Naftzger European print collection; open Tuesday through Sunday. The **Wichita Art Association** building, set in grounds of 15 acres, has displays changing monthly, an art school and children's theater; open September through June, Tuesday to Sunday, free.

SHOPPING

Stop at **Shepler's,** the world's largest Western store. Good shopping also at the **Mall, Twin Lakes Shopping Center** and **Towne East Shopping Center.**

SPORTS

Swimming and golf at several of the public parks; boating and fishing at **Sante Fe Lake,** 7 miles east, or **Lake Afton,** 5 miles west. **The National Semi-pro Baseball Tournament** is held in mid-August.

WHERE TO GO NEARBY

The **Barlett Arboretum** in Belle Plaine, 20 miles south of Wichita, makes a pleasant morning or afternoon excursion from the city. Open daily, the 20-acre display includes hundreds of varieties of trees, rare vines, shrubs, and formal gardens.

FURTHER STATE INFORMATION

Department of Economic Development, (Tourist Bureau), 503 Kansas Avenue, Topeka, KS 66603. Hunting and Fishing: **Forestry, Fish and Game Commission,** PO Box 1028, Pratt, KS 67124. **State Park and Resources Authority,** 503 Kansas Avenue, Topeka, KS 66603. **Wichita Convention and Visitors' Bureau,** 350 West Douglas, Wichita, KS 67202.

Consulates in Kansas City: Colombia, Germany, Italy, Sweden. For other consulates in Greater Kansas area, see Missouri.

Consulate in Wichita: Costa Rica.

USEFUL TELEPHONE NUMBERS IN DODGE CITY

Emergency (Ambulance, Fire & Police)	911
Dodge City Regional Hospital	225-9050
Meade District Hospital	873-2141
Chamber of Commerce	227-3119
Pan Am Reservations	(800) 621-7107

Kentucky

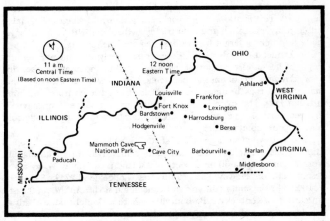

Area	40,395 square miles					**Population**		3,498,000				
Capital	Frankfort					**Sales Tax**		5%				
Weather	Jan	Feb	Mar	Apr	May	Jun	Jul	Aug	Sep	Oct	Nov	Dec
Av Temp (°C)	2	2	6	13	18	23	25	25	21	14	7	2
Days of Rain	12	11	13	12	11	10	11	8	7	7	10	11

Explorers who followed the Ohio and Mississippi rivers heard there was good land in the interior. Settlers in Virginia knew that the Shawnees and Cherokees had an immense hunting preserve teeming with buffalo, deer, and small game. The problem was how to reach it with so many mountains blocking the way. The Indians already knew about a path that ran from Portsmouth, Ohio, through the Cumberland Gap to Tennessee and in 1750 and 1751 white men scouted the area. Later, James Harrod, a Pennsylvania trader, went down the Ohio and inland in 1774 to found Harrodsburg, the first white settlement in Kentucky. But it was the persistent Daniel Boone who came back again and again until he could confidently lead a band of settlers through the gap to the Kentucky River where Boonesborough was founded in 1775. Once the mountain barrier was conquered, pioneers swarmed into the region.

Among the earliest were Scottish-Irish immigrants from Pennsylvania who knew how to distill whiskey from rye. One year the rye crop failed but corn grew tall in the fields of Bourbon County. By substituting corn for rye, they invented the famous bourbon, and Kentucky has been the national headquarters for bourbon ever since. Clear, cold water rising from springs in layers of limestone rock is one of the secrets of good bourbon. Those pure springs and the mineral-rich forage of the bluegrass country were also a unique asset for the propagation of a superior breed of horse. Today, beautiful horses and fine whiskey are synonymous with Kentucky. This is also a major coal-mining and tobacco-growing state, but crop diversification and industrial growth, along with tourism, have made Kentucky a target for businessmen and vacationers.

The **Daniel Boone National Forest** runs nearly the full north-south length of the eastern portion of the state. A wildly mountainous, heavily wooded region, it contains the spectacular **Red River Gorge** with towering cliffs, natural rock bridges, and waterfalls; guided tours from mid-June to Labor Day. The sparsely settled mountains east of the forest haven't changed much since Boone's day, and neither have the rugged, religious, self-sufficient mountaineers.

The only town of any size in **EASTERN KENTUCKY** is Ashland, population 27,064, an industrial city across the Ohio River from Huntington, West Virginia. About 50 miles south of Ashland is the **Jenny Wiley State Resort Park** on Dewey Lake, with **May Lodge** (886-2711, S$13-19/D$19.28-28), day and night golf and a mountain skylift. In the southeastern corner of Kentucky is **Barbourville**, where a **Daniel Boone Festival** is held the second weekend in October and the **Dr Thomas Walker State Shrine** commemorates the first white man to discover the Cumberland Gap in 1750. **Harlan**, the state's coal mining center, is at the start of the **Little Shepherd Trail**, known through scenes described in *The Little Shepherd of Kingdom Come* by John Fox. It crosses **Kingdom Come State Park** with its dramatic rock formations; nearby is **Big Black Mountain**, 4,145 feet, the highest point in Kentucky. The Visitors Center for the **Cumberland Gap National Historical Park** is at Middlesboro; settlers traveled through this pass along Boone's "Wilderness Road", to extend the boundaries of the frontier.

Just west of the elongated Daniel Boone National Forest is **Berea**, home of the famous **Berea College.** Here there is no tuition, and mountain youths put themselves through school with their high quality ceramics, weaving, furniture, homemade candy and other items. The students also run **Boone Tavern** (986-9341, S$11-23/D$17-24), where they produce excellent meals from typical southern ingredients; highly recommended. The **Kentucky Guild of Artists and Craftsmen's Fair,** with lots of folk singing too, is held here in May. **Churchill Weavers,** the country's largest hand-weaving firm, is on the north end of town; self-guided tours Monday-Friday 8-4. About midway between Berea and Lexington is **Fort Boonesborough State Park** and a complete reconstruction of the fort built by Daniel Boone and his settlers.

CENTRAL KENTUCKY is bluegrass country, dominated by **Louisville** (pop. 317,503) and **Lexington.** Lexington is surrounded with those famous white-fenced farms where thoroughbred race horses are raised and trained. The Chamber of Commerce, at 421 North Broadway (254-4447), will give you maps and information about horse farms open to visitors. Don't miss the splendid statue atop the grave of **Man o'War,** the beloved racehorse that died in 1947, located in the $39 million **Kentucky Horse Park.** Also visit the **Headley-Whitney Museum of Jewels** and ornate doll-houses; **Waveland State Shrine, Ashland,** where Henry Clay lived from 1811 until his death in 1852; **Hopemont** (1814), home of the dashing Confederate leader of Morgan's Raiders; the **University of Kentucky; Transylvania College,** chartered in 1780; the graves of famous men in the **Lexington Cemetery;** and **Keeneland Race Course,** where promising thoroughbreds are trained year round, raced in April and October, and sold at important sales in July, September, and November. There are race meets at **Red Mile Trotting Track** from late April to mid-June, and late September through the first week in October. Lexington also has the world's largest loose-leaf tobacco market, with auctions in December through February. Between Lexington and **Harrodsburg,** where there is a replica of the state's first pioneer fort and some beautiful old homes, is Pleasant Hill, better known as **Shakertown.** Here the celibate members of the United Society of Believers in Christ's Second Appearance main-tained a community between 1809 and 1910. Perfectionist craftsmen, the Shakers built and furnished their stone and brick buildings so meticu-lously that "restoration" of the community required little more than a good spring cleaning. The old Shaker recipes were just as skillful, and reservations are advised if you hope to dine in **The Trustees House** (734-5411). The Inn at Shakertown (734-5411, S$15-25/D$25-37) also serves delicious meals and has rooms furnished just as they were in the Shakers' era.

The major city in **WESTERN KENTUCKY** is **Paducah,** laid out in 1827 by explorer William Clark, who named it for a friendly Chickasaw Indian chief. The **Alben W. Barkley Monument** displays Indian and pio-neer artifacts, and mementos of Vice-President Alben W. Barkley and Irvin S. Cobb, the city's most famous native sons. Only 20 miles east of Paducah the **Land Between the Lakes** begins, one of the country's largest back-to-nature recreation areas, with lots of free camp sites, family cot-tages and luxurious lodges along the lovely western shore of **Lake Barkley** and two of the largest man-made lakes in the world. There are three major state resort parks on the lakes, **Kentucky Dam Village, S.R.P., Kenlake S.R.P.** and **Lake Barkley S.R.P.** At the **Environmental Education Center Station** in **Land Between The Lakes** there are films and displays of plant and animal life.

Kentucky is more of a border state than most border states. Its people have the charm and courtly manners of Southern USA, but can quickly display the crackling energy of Northerners. Both Abraham Lincoln and Jefferson Davis, the opposing presidents during the Civil War, were born in Kentucky. Split by its two allegiances, the state sent 73,000 men into the Union Army and 35,000 to fight for the Confederacy. Although sev-eral battles and skirmishes took place in Kentucky, the state remained theoretically neutral.

City to Visit

LOUISVILLE

Early explorers using the Ohio River were confronted by churning rapids that descended about 30 feet over a distance of a mile. Canoes had to be hauled ashore and carried to an area of calm water, which seemed a natural place for a settlement. George Rogers Clark founded Louisville in 1778 and named it after King Louis XVI of France. (The local pronunciation is *Loo-uh-vull.*) A canal was built in 1830 so that flatboats could bypass the falls. Although it is a leading industrial city, it manages to retain its gracious beauty. Louisville is situated in about the middle of Kentucky's northern boundary, and is within easy reach of the state's other interesting cities and famous landmarks. Population 317,503; metropolitan area 950,000.

WHAT TO SEE

Churchill Downs, where the Kentucky Derby has been run annually since 1875, has a **Derby Museum** at the grounds entrance; open daily 9:30-4:30, except 9-11 on race days, free. The **Kentucky Railway Museum** thrills train lovers; open noon to 5 Saturdays, Sundays and holidays from Memorial Day to October. The *Belle of Louisville,* a genuine 19th-century sternwheeler, has been refurbished in all its splendor and is anchored at the **Riverfront Plaza,** downtown; river cruises, from Memorial Day through Labor Day about 2pm on Tuesday-Sunday, moonlight cruises Tuesday and Saturday evenings at 8:30pm (582-2547). **Cave Hill Cemetery** is outstanding for its beautiful landscaping. Also drive through Louisville's lovely, rolling parks, the largest of which is **Cherokee Park.** The **Museum of Science and History,** open Monday to Saturday 9-5, Sunday 1-5. Adults $1, students 75¢, children under 12, 50¢. Fine old homes can be seen on a walking tour of **St James** and **Belgravia Courts,** south of Central Park between Fourth and Sixth Streets. Another historic section of early 1800s homes and quaint shops is **Butchertown,** an area founded by German butchers, just east of downtown. **Farmington,** on Bardstown Road was designed by Thomas Jefferson, built in 1810 and furnished entirely with antiques made before 1820; open Tuesday to Saturday 10-4:30, Sunday 1:30-4:30. **Locust Grove,** out on Blankenbaker Lane, was the last home of explorer George Rogers Clark, who lived here from 1809 until his death in 1818; hours are the same as for Farmington. Louisville's downtown riverfront, a major new development, is a delightful place to fritter away some time enjoying a drink and a snack and watching the boats go by. Just across the river, in **Jeffersonville,** Indiana, is the fascinating **Howard Steamboat Museum,** open April to November, weekdays, 10-4, Sundays 1-4. There are 14 colleges and universities in the city; the **University of Louisville,** founded in 1798, is the nation's oldest municipal university. Guided tours of the city and listings of other museums and events are available at Founders Square.

A variety of industrial tours are also offered, including a pottery workshop, distillery, cigarette factories, and a public livestock market.

ACCOMMODATIONS
Right in midtown are the huge, smart new **Hyatt Regency** (587-3434, S$47-75/D$59-90); **Galt House**, 598-5200, S$38-48/D$46-55); the very fine **Louisville Inn** (582-2241, S$28-34/D$36-44). Other midtown accommodations include **Holiday Inn-Midtown, Howard Johnson's Downtown, Louisville TraveLodge,** and **Rodeway Inn,** rates about S$31-42/D$36-42. At the airport, the **Executive Inn Motel** (367-6161, S$35-38/D$41-44) and the **Executive West** (367-2251, S$35-37/D$41-45). During Kentucky Derby weekend, the first Saturday in May, nearly all hotels and motels raise their rates and may have a minimum-stay requirement of three days. This applies not only to establishments in town but to those on highways leading into town both in Kentucky and in Indiana, across the river. You should make your reservations far in advance if you intend to be there at Derby time.

RESTAURANTS
In midtown there are **Casa Grisanti,** fine Italian-American; **Lamb's** at the Hyatt Regency; huge seafood buffet and live lobster at **The New Orleans House; Charley's,** steaks, seafood, crepes; **The Spire** is the Hyatt's Regency's revolving restaurant with a view. Roast prime rib a specialty; and the elegant new **Savoy Restaurant and Bar. Galt House,** overlooking the river; Stouffer's **Top of the Tower,** with a great view; **Kunz's the Dutchman,** very popular but closed Sundays and major holidays. Farther out are the well-known **Bauer's Since 1870; Bill Boland's Dining Room; Hasenour's; Captain's Quarters,** overlooking the river, dinner dancing on weekends; **Embassy Supper Club;** and **Hoe Kow,** Cantonese. About 20 miles east of the city at Simpsonville, try the historic **Old Stone Inn** and **Claudia Sanders',** the restaurant run by the widow of the famous Colonel Sanders; in a building near his white frame house. While in Louisville, try a refreshing (and potent) mint julep, properly served in a chilled silver cup.

ENTERTAINMENT
The **Empire Room** at the Executive Inn and the **Embassy Supper Club,** both rather expensive, are outstanding among many night spots with dancing, dining and floor shows. Consult local newspapers. Beer is the only alcoholic beverage served in Louisville on Sunday, while virtually the rest of the state is dry.

ARTS AND MUSIC
The numerous contributions made by citizens to the **Louisville Fund** gives the city an unusually active cultural life. **The Kentucky Opera Association, Louisville Orchestra, Louisville Civic Ballet** and touring Broadway play companies put on a full schedule of performances at the **Macauley Theater,** from early autumn until summer. The **Actors Theater**

of Louisville, widely acclaimed as the nation's leading regional theatre, has productions by a local theatrical company. Shakespeare is performed during the summer in **Central Park**. The **J. B. Speed Art Museum**, on the University of Louisville campus, is especially rich in decorative arts of all eras; open Tuesday to Saturday 10-4, Sunday 2-6. The **Filson Club**, a distinguished historical society, displays rare Indian and pioneer relics; open Monday to Friday 9-5, free. Other art works at the **Frame House Gallery** in midtown and the **Little Gallery** of the Hadley Pottery in Butchertown.

SHOPPING

Downtown stores are open until 9 on Monday evenings; most surburban shopping centers are open until 9 or 10 every night. The new pedestrian mall on lower Fourth Street makes midtown shopping a pleasure. Very smart little shops are out in **Butchertown's Bakery Square**, where 18th- and 19th-century houses have been restored.

SPORTS

Oxmoor Steeplechase is in mid-April. Spring race meet is held at **Churchill Downs**, late April to early June; more thoroughbred racing during the fall meet in November. New riders and horses work out in summer at **Commonwealth Race Course;** harness racing in spring and summer at **Louisville Downs**. The Louisville metropolitan area has 12 public golf courses. Fishing is permitted year-round in all public waters. Water sports can be enjoyed on the Ohio River and in nearby lakes. Major sports events take place at the midtown **Convention Center** and at the **Kentucky Fair and Exposition Center** near Standiford Field; stock car races are held at the **Fairgrounds Motor Speedway** on Fridays and Saturdays, April to September. There are professional and collegiate baseball and football in season.

CALENDAR OF EVENTS

Kentucky Derby Festival with 10 days of balls and parties, **Pegasus Parade**, river boat race between the *Belle of Louisville* and the *Delta Queen*, culminating in "The Run for the Roses," late April-early May; **Open House Tours of Homes**, mid-May; **Bluegrass Music Festival of the USA**, mid-September; May-early June; **Kentucky State Fair**, mid-August; **Salute to Arts**, mid-September.

WHERE TO GO NEARBY

A good guide for one-day trips from Louisville is distributed free by the Brown and Williamson Tobacco Corporation, 1600 West Hill Street. Try to devote one day to the cave region, about 100 miles south. The **Mammoth Onyx Cave** is at **Horse Cave**. The **Diamond Caverns, Jesse James**, and **Hundred Domes Caves** are near **Park City**. Mammoth Cave National Park is 10 miles west of **Cave City** on KY 70.

On another day, follow the 120-mile loop formed by US Highways 31-W and 31-E, south of Louisville. **Bardstown** has beautiful old **Federal Hill** mansion that inspired Stephen Foster to write *My Old Kentucky Home*, and **Wickland**, the beautifully furnished Georgian residence (1813) where three state governors have lived. The valuable art works in **St Joseph's Cathedral** (1819) were the gift of exiled Louis Philippe, who lived in **Talbot Tavern** before returning to the French throne in 1830. The **Barton Museum** depicts the whole history of bourbon whiskey with exhibits, bottles, posters and other memorabilia from pre-Colonial days through Prohibition. South of **Hodgenville** is the log cabin in which Abraham Lincoln was born, now cherished within a magnificent building at the **Abraham Lincoln Birthplace National Historic Site.** Visitors, understandably, cannot go inside the Gold Bullion Depository at **Fort Knox,** but the **Patton Museum of Cavalry and Armor** can be seen here.

East of Louisville is the renowned bluegrass country of great horse farms. **Frankfort** is the state capital, and Daniel Boone and his wife were buried here in 1845. Visit the **Capitol, Governor's Mansion, Liberty Hall,** the **Orlando Brown House,** the newly renovated **Old State Capital** and adjoining **Kentucky History Museum,** and the **Kentucky Military History Museum** overlooking the Kentucky River, for a glimpse of early Kentucky.

MAMMOTH CAVE NATIONAL PARK

The park has about 80 square miles above ground, and the cave itself occupies an area about 10 miles in diameter. The cave system consists of the world's largest network of caverns and corridors, 170 miles in length. It is located about 23 miles northeast of Bowling Green and is open year round. The cave temperature is also 12°C so you'll need a coat or sweater. Wear comfortable, sturdy shoes for lots of walking and some climbing.

The **Mammoth Cave Hotel** (758-2225, S$19-25/D$32-38) has a kennel available for pets. There is also a large campsite with a 14-day stay limit. Motels in small towns surrounding the park: **Brownsville, Cave City, Horse Cave** and **Park City.**

All cave trips start at the Visitor Center, where audio-visual programs and exhibits are a valuable introduction to the formations underground. Choose from various conducted tours of 1½ to 7 hours' duration. Some tours descend through pits and domes and along rocky corridors to see stalactites, lovely travertine formations and the blind fish from **Crystal Lake.** Other trips pass through the area mined for nitrate used in gunpowder during the War of 1812, to the narrow corridor of Fat Man's Misery, the Bottomless Pit, Mammoth Dome with its superb fluted columns, and perhaps Echo River, the deepest point open to visitors. Visitors on some tours also can stop for lunch in the Snowball Room 267 feet underground. Back on the surface, you'll enjoy following the **Cave Island Nature Trail** on the island in Green River and taking a scenic cruise up **Green River,** May to October.

FURTHER STATE INFORMATION

Kentucky Department of Tourism, Capitol Plaza Tower, Frankfort, KY 40601. Hunting and Fishing: **Department of Fish and Wildlife Resources,** Capital Plaza Tower, Frankfort, KY 40601. **Louisville Chamber of Commerce,** 300 West Liberty Street, Louisville, KY 40202. **Louisville Visitors Bureau,** Founders Square, 501 W. Muhammad Ali Blvd. Louisville, KY 40202. National Parks: **Mammoth Cave National Park** (Superintendent), KY 42259.

Consulates in Louisville: Belgium, El Salvador.

USEFUL TELEPHONE NUMBERS IN LOUISVILLE

Emergency Medical Services	587-3911
Southwest Jefferson Community Hospital	933-2110
State Police	765-6118
Crisis and Information Center	589-4313
Poison Control Center	589-8222
Tourist Information	582-3732
Chamber of Commerce	582-2421
Legal Aid	584-1254
Pan Am Reservations	800-621-2909

Louisiana

Area	48,253 square miles	Population	4,203,972
Capital	Baton Rouge	Sales Tax	6%

Weather	Jan	Feb	Mar	Apr	May	Jun	Jul	Aug	Sep	Oct	Nov	Dec
Av Temp (°C)	13	14	16	20	24	27	28	28	26	21	16	13
Days of Rain	9	9	9	7	8	10	15	13	10	6	6	10

Louisiana, part of the southland that gave birth to the blues, earned almost $2.5 billion from the 15,000,000 out-of-state visitors. Perhaps no other state has a magnetism quite like Louisiana's and no city is quite like the legendary New Orleans with its nostalgic jazz festivals, galas, parades, and magnificent French Creole cuisine. The state's architecture is particularly fine. Generally, you will see two types of well-preserved houses—those dating from the French and Spanish periods and those adapted from the Greek revival style, which flourished prior to the Civil War.

Spaniards were the first to discover the region in 1541 when Hernando de Soto was exploring the Mississippi River. But it was the French under La Salle who gave a name to the area, as a mark of respect for Louis XIV. The Creoles are descendants from the French and Spanish days. Fearing he would lose Louisiana to Britain and in need of cash for his military expeditions, Napoleon sold the territory to the United States in 1803. The settlers did not at first welcome the idea of being tied to the US but, when faced with the possibility of English rule, they rallied behind Andrew Jackson to defeat the British in the celebrated battle of New Orleans in 1815.

Forests of emerald green, rivers, and prominent hills dominate the northern part of the state, while in the southern section many people have settled near the bayous where they fish, trap, crab, and do a little farming. However, fresh discoveries of oil and natural gas, notably the finds of the "Tuscaloosa Trend," an energy-rich belt of deposits centering around Baton Rouge, are bringing changes. Much of the southern third of the state is Acadian by ancestry. "Cajuns" are descended from the French Canadians who were driven in a forced exile called Le Grand Derangement from Nova Scotia (Acadia) by the British in 1755.

SHREVEPORT, in the northwest corner of the state on I-20, is a good place to begin a tour of Louisiana. Here, on the **Red River,** the pace is brisk, the accent southwestern, the vision wide, and the history Deep South. **The Louisiana State Fair,** one of the top 10 in the nation, is held here for two weeks in October every year. One of the gala's main attractions is the **Louisiana State Exhibit Museum,** with dioramas of Louisiana's resources, antiques, and contemporary items; open year round. The **Spar Planetarium** offers a changing series of programs, as does the **Barnwell Art and Garden Center.** Don't miss the **Norton Art Gallery,** which features American and European paintings, sculpture, glass, a Wedgwood collection, and manuscripts from the 15th to 20th centuries. The highlight of the museum, however, is the collection of Western art by Frederic Remington and Charles M. Russell. Before you leave, visit old **Shreve Square** for dining and entertainment in an authentic 1890s setting. In April the city stages **Holiday in Dixie,** a 10-day festival commemorating the Louisiana Purchase; also from April to December the roses are in bloom on the 118 acres of the **American Rose Center** gardens. From late spring through early fall, enjoy thoroughbred racing at **Louisiana Downs.** Visit the relocated, restored historic buildings at the **Pioneer Heritage Center.** Open to school groups by appointment weekdays, to the general public, Sunday afternoons. Admission for adults, $2.

You can capture the spirit of the Confederacy at **Mansfield,** south of Shreveport on LA 171. Two miles southeast is **Mansfield Battlepark and Museum,** commemorating the decisive battle of 8 April 1864 which ended the Red River Campaign. The Yankees were heavily defeated here, ending the attempt of the Union to capture river ports. Before departing, drive through Mansfield's tree-lined streets for a view of its antebellum mansions.

North of Shreveport off US 71 are the oil towns of **Rodessa** and **Plain Dealing,** the latter bordered on the north by **Dogwood Drive,** a beautiful floral trail which winds among some of Louisiana's highest hills. **Minden** is westward on I-20, and 6 miles away are the remains of **Germantown,** a communal village founded in the early 19th century. **Lake Bistineau State Park** is close by, with a variety of outdoor activities.

Beginning in the northeast section of the state and preserving the charm and tradition of yesteryear is the **DELTA COUNTRY,** along the Mississippi River. Near **Epps** is the **Poverty Point State Commemorative**

Area with some of America's most remarkable prehistoric Indian mounds, whose fascinating history is interpreted by graphic exhibits and artifacts. Open daily and Sunday afternoons. Toward **Milliken's Bend** on LA 65 is the site of **Grant's March Route.** The only antebellum plantation home spared by the federal forces in this area was **Winter Quarters,** and it is open to the public, near Newellton. **Lake Bruin State Park,** with numerous blue herons and white egrets, is nearby.

Monroe, in the northeast corner of the state, is notable for its splendid 100-acre **Louisiana Purchase Gardens and Zoo.** At **Karoli Park** in West Monroe is the *Louisiana Legend,* an outdoor historical drama, presented every Friday during July and early August.

St Joseph, on the Mississippi along US 65, is a restored old river town which resembles a turn-of-the-century steamboat center. Here, dating back to antebellum days, are **Christ Church Rectory** and **Bondurant House,** both open the last two weeks in March and first two weeks in April; the **Davidson House** of 19th-century vintage, originally built around a log cabin; **Tensas Parish Courthouse,** in the Greek revival style; the **Tensas Parish Public Library** and **Plantation Museum,** displaying items of early plantation life. South is the old river center of **Waterproof.**

The hub of central Louisiana is **ALEXANDRIA,** home of **Louisiana State University** (the main campus of Louisiana State University (LSU) is in Baton Rouge) and the restored colonial-era **Kent Plantation House.** In nearby **Pineville** are the **National Cemetery and Louisiana College. Hot Wells,** with its soothing mineral springs, is 20 miles northwest, and **Cotile Recreation Center** is 18 miles west. Encircling this vicinity is **Kisatchie National Forest** with bayous, lakes, and facilities for outdoor camping and recreation; good deer and quail hunting. Here, too, is a 30-mile floral haven, the beautiful **Wild Azalea Trail.**

Southeast on LA 1 is **Marksville** and the **State Prehistoric Indian Park,** site of six ancient Indian mounds, a village site dating between 300 and 600AD and a museum established by the Smithsonian Institution with artifacts and special Indian exhibits. This vicinity is populated by the Tunica-Biloxi Indians, who live on land presented to their ancestors by the Spanish.

To trace the history of the **CANE RIVER COUNTRY,** journey to **Cloutierville,** northeast of Alexandria off LA 1. Here is the **Bayou Folk Museum,** a raised house in a pleasant garden typifying the early Louisiana architecture of the Creoles. Spanning the Cane River is the oldest settlement in the Louisiana Purchase Territory, **Natchitoches.** See "pure" French colonial architecture at the **Roque House Museum,** built of cypress beams with mud and moss fillings, and dating from 1790. It is open from March to August and from 1-23 December. Try to see the fascinating spiral ironwork stairway of the **Hughes Building** and the restored **Old Lemee House** (1830). You can see fine examples of religious architecture of the mid-19th century at the **Catholic Church of the Immaculate Conception and Trinity Episcopal Church.** The **American Cemetery** is on the site of the original Fort St Jean Baptiste, erected in 1735. Just west of Natchitoches, near Robeline, is **Los Adaes Historical Park,** site of a historic Spanish mission and fort, and locale of the first capital of Spanish Texas. Situated between Cloutierville and Natchitoches is **Melrose,** a plantation established by an African-born, freed slave in the 1700s; it encompasses many architectural treasures. The showplace is open year round, by appointment, or during the tour season, the second weekend in October, at which time a Cane River tour of other plantations is also offered.

Northwest of Alexandria is **Many** on LA 171. Nearby, wild and cultivated flowers range over 4,700 acres in picturesque parkland at **Hodges Gardens;** visit the wildlife refuge and an outdoor theater. Father south, along Hwy 6, is **Fort Jesup State Commemorative Area,** a restored frontier post established in 1822 by Zachary Taylor. An 1830s army kitchen and reconstructed officers' quarters can be viewed. West of Many and along the Texas border lies the **Toledo Bend Reservoir,** a mammoth man-made lake and recreational site. South of Many, on US 171, is **Fisher,** a vintage turn-of-the-century sawmill village with a restored town center. Heading south toward **Leesville** on LA 171, you can see the **Fort Polk Military Reservation.**

In the southwest section of the state on I-10 is **LAKE CHARLES,** the nation's leading rice port and an industrial center for oil, rubber, chemicals, and cattle. You can stroll across **McNeese State University** campus or tour the **Imperial Calcasieu Museum** with items of local historical interest. In late spring, **Contraband Days,** a water pageant with a pirate theme, is held here. **North Beach,** along I-10, has white sand, good swimming, water-skiing, sailing, and sun bathing by the city's lakefront. Starting at nearby **Sulphur,** and following a southerly course, is the scenic **Creole Nature Trail,** leading through marsh and swamp lands, and along the Gulf Coast, through **Sabine Wildlife Refuge,** and the unique **Rockefeller Wildlife Refuge.** To the east is **Lacassine National Wildlife Refuge,** a 31,000-acre preserve for hunting, fishing, and wildlife. At Jennings is the **Zigler Museum,** containing dioramas of Louisiana wildlife, exhibits, and antiques. Nearby, off I-10, is the **Louisiana Oil and Gas Park,** a recreational site with vintage building replicas and exhibits reflecting early oil industry days in Southwest Louisiana. A few miles to the north at **Elton** you can buy crafts at the **Coushatta Indian Cultural Center and Trading Post,** specializing in unique baskets woven from swamp cane, pine needles, and other wild natural fibers. Continuing east on I-10 a unique collection of rice-farming memorabilia, exhibited in a typical old Acadian building, can be viewed at **Blue Rose Museum** in Crowley. Founded by French Acadians from Nova Scotia in 1823, **Lafayette,** a city which considers itself the "capital of French Louisiana" or the "capital of Acadiana," is called the Hub City and is the dominant center of the oil and gas industry in the area (Acadiana). Also to be seen in Lafayette is the **Acadian Village,** a restored site with relocated pioneer and period buildings from early Acadiana days, surrounded by about 10 acres of tropical gardens. Off La. Highway 93 at La. Highway 342. Open daily except major holidays. Admission $2 adults, $1 children and senior citizens. See St John Cathedral and the St John Oak on St

John Street near downtown Lafayette. Lafayette faces the **Vermilion River** and is a highpoint of the 21-mile Azalea Trail which is in bloom from late February to late March. Here you can see **University of Southwestern Louisiana,** with its incredibly beautiful and scenic Cypress Lake, the fine **Art Center for Southwestern Louisiana,** and **Evangeline Downs,** a race track. **Lafayette Museum** was the home of the first Democratic governor of the state, Alexander Mouton. Carnival costumes and an outstanding collection of Acadiana are displayed.

Festivals seem to be going on at all times of the year in Acadiana (French Louisiana), especially at Mardi Gras when small French communities celebrate with rustic, traditional Mardi Gras festivals, not as elaborate or as crowded as New Orleans', but scenic nonetheless, and very enjoyable. The unique local music includes Cajun bands and zydeco bands (black adaptation of French and blues music) featuring fiddles, accordion, guitar, drums, washboard, etc. Lafayette's popular **Festivals Acadiens** has the watchword, *"laissez les bon temps rouler,"* ("let the good times roll"). The festival takes place on the third weekend of September and features Cajun food, dance, music, arts and crafts.

Opelousas, a major oil, gas, and agrarian hub and gateway to the Acadiana Trail, is north on US 90. Visit the **Jim Bowie Museum** which commemorates Bowie's adventures, and try to attend the **Louisiana Yambilee,** given in honor of the yam (sweet potato) in October. A few miles north is **Washington,** an old steamboat town which maintains the dignity and charm of antebellum days. The classically styled **Arlington House** (1829) and **Magnolia Ridge** are both open daily. LA 10 leads you northwest to **Ville Platte,** or "flat town," rich in Acadian lore. The *Tournoi,* an ancient knightly joust which once delighted spectators in medieval France, is a highlight of the **Louisiana Cotton Festival** staged in October.

Turning southeast, head toward the **BAYOU TECHE** region below Lafayette. The **Bayou Teche,** the most romantic of all bayous, is characterized by giant banks and cypress trees laced with moss. The highways are bordered by impressive sugar cane fields and oil refineries. Fanning out from the river banks are acres of black fertile loam deposited by floods. Dotted along the river are colorful French towns. **St Martinville,** on LA 31, is probably the most fabled old town in this vicinity. The town figures prominently in Longfellow's epic poem *Evangeline.* See something of the early days of the Cajuns in the volumes of historical records at the **Courthouse,** and **Evangeline Oak,** where Evangeline and her Gabriel are said to have been reunited. In the 157-acre **Longfellow-Evangeline State Commemorative Area** are the **Acadian House Museum,** said to have been occupied by Louis Arceneaux, Longfellow's Gabriel. Also see the **Acadian Craft Shop.** The grave of Emmeline Labiche, the original Evangeline, is in the cemetery of **St Martin of Tours Catholic Church.** Nearby **Loreauville** is the site of the **Acadian Heritage Museum** with 30 walk-in village buildings and farm shops. The chief city of the Bayou Teche, on US 90, is **New Iberia.** Reflecting the influence of the French and Spanish, the town was founded in the late 1700s. Set amid mossy oaks and a profusion of tropical plants is **Shadows on the Teche,** a 16-room townhouse erected in the 1830s. Be sure to view the marble statue of the Roman Emperor Hadrian, carved around 130AD; it stands adjacent to the Iberia Savings Bank in New Iberia. Three miles away on LA 86 is **Justine,** known for its charming 1822 antebellum mansion with additions built in 1848 and 1894.

Avery Island, lush in foliage, is 10 miles southwest of New Iberia. Actually a mountain of rock salt, the island contains a 200-acre **Jungle Garden** with many thousands of camellias, azaleas, iris, tropical plants, ferns, and bamboo. A fine statue of Buddha, dating from 1000AD, stands in the **Chinese Garden.** Successful efforts to save the egret, or snowy heron, were made here, and the flocks have been joined by crane, heron, and many varieties of wild duck and geese. The island is now the site of the largest egret colony in the United States; summer and spring are the best times to see them. Heading south to **Franklin,** visit the recently restored antebellum mansion, **Oaklawn Manor.** Its six large Doric columns, wrought iron chandeliers, and marble flooring are from the old St Louis Hotel in New Orleans. Another columned house is **Albania Plantation** at Jeanerette on LA 20. Its unsupported spiral staircase and renowned collection of antique dolls from all over the world should not be missed. Visitors may stay in a cottage on the grounds; reservation advised.

In the southwest corner of the state, south of New Orleans, is **Lafitte,** a former haunt of Pirate Jean Lafitte. In this quaint fishing village north of **Barataria Bay** he and his men used to transport booty in cypress *pirogues* or Indian boats. On the Sunday after Mother's Day, the **World Championship Pirogue Races** are staged here. For some of the choicest saltwater fishing in the nation, don't miss **Grand Isle** at the south end of LA 1. It also has a fine beach and a state park with camping facilities.

In southeastern Louisiana, upriver on the Mississippi, is **BATON ROUGE,** the state capital. Named "Red Stick" by the French, for the red pole used by the Houma and Bayougoula Indian tribes to mark the boundaries of their respective lands, the city is a hub of industrial activity with a port which ranks fourth in the nation. Baton Rouge boasts the nation's tallest **Capitol Building,** with a lavish **Memorial Hall** and an observation tower which offers a panoramic view of the city. On the capitol grounds is the **Old Arsenal,** constructed in 1835. It is now a historical museum housing relics that represent and explain state history. Across **Capitol Lake** is the modified Greek revival-style **Governor's Mansion,** a 40-room mansion furnished in 18th-century decor and built in 1963; open to the public by appointment. In contrast to the contemporary architecture of the new capitol is the turreted Gothic design of the **Old State Capitol** (1847). Its winding staircase, stained-glass dome, and art gallery are features you shouldn't miss. The **New State Capitol** is a magnificent structure completed in 14 months by the famous ex-governor Huey Long. With one of the finest planetariums in the South, the **Louisiana Arts and Science Center** is located in downtown. South of the central business district is **Magnolia Mound,** oldest wooden structure in Louisiana and one of the oldest plantation homes, dating to the colonial era. Now a community museum, the house contains period furniture and artifacts. Surrounding gardens are faithful to colonial period. Three miles south is **Louisiana State University,** one of the largest centers for higher education in the South. **Mount Hope Plantation,** a recently restored early 19th-century house on Highland Road, is located inside city limits.

Drive north from Baton Rouge on US 61 for a view of opulent plantation homes built in the Feliciana country by the landed gentry who drew on cotton and sugar for their income. **Oakley Plantation,** in the **Audubon Memorial State Commemorative Area at St Francisville,** is the first stop. Here John James Audubon, the ornithologist, tutored the plantation owner's daughter and drew 32 of his *Birds of America* series. St Francisville, "two miles long and two yards wide," is a charming old town spread over a narrow ridge. While you're here, enter **Grace Episcopal Church,** founded in 1826 and shelled during the Civil War. **Rosedown,** just east of town, is a lavishly reconstructed antebellum mansion dating from 1835; its formal gardens are fashioned in the 17th-century style. Six miles north is **The Cottage,** a plantation which mirrors life in the Spanish period. The farm's school, offices, and slaves quarters are also part of the tract. In the **New Roads** vicinity is **Parlange Plantation,** an outstanding example of *bousillage,* mud wall architecture; the house dates from 1750.

Some of the lovely homes south of Baton Rouge are **Oak Alley** (1830), with a magnificent avenue of oak trees leading to the river. Near Burnside on LA 942 is **Houmas House.** Formerly a large sugar plantation, the restored building was the setting for the film, *Hush, Hush, Sweet Charlotte.* Other mansions open for tour along the Old River Road between Baton Rouge and New Orleans include **Nottoway Plantation,** recently restored. With its unique design and 54 rooms, it ranks as the largest plantation house in the South. **San Francisco Plantation** is a restored mansion in the "steamboat Gothic" style. **Destrehan Manor Plantation** is of Creole West-Indian design and is the oldest extant plantation house on the Mississippi River.

City to Visit

NEW ORLEANS

New Orleans is in southeastern Louisiana, on the Mississippi River. To the north of the city is **Lake Pontchartrain,** to the east **Lake Borgne,** and 60 miles to the south is the Gulf of Mexico. The original settlement was founded by the Frenchman Jean LeMoyne, Sieur de Bienville, in 1778 and named after the Duke of Orleans. In 1762, against the wishes of its French inhabitants, New Orleans was ceded to Spain. In 1803 it was returned to France and only 20 days later ceded to the United States under the terms of the Louisiana Purchase. The city's strategic position has twice subjected it to military assault. In 1815 General Andrew Jackson successfully defended it against a British attack at the Battle of New Orleans—the final engagement of the War of 1812. In 1862 the city, then a Confederate stronghold, was captured and occupied by Union forces. But its strategic position has also brought New Orleans prosperity and today it is the second largest port in the country and a leading center of the petrochemical industry.

New Orleans prides itself on being the "Most Interesting City in the United States." Famous for its Creole cuisine and fine restaurants, its old French Quarter, its nightclubs and Dixieland jazz, and the **Louisiana Superdome,** the city has a character that is easy to sense but difficult to describe—a mixture of sophistication, honky-tonk, and Southern hospitality all blended to make New Orleans unique. Population 557,761, metropolitan area 1,183,606.

WHAT TO SEE

Undoubtedly the greatest attraction for tourists is the **French Quarter,** which still retains some of its appearance of 150 years ago. The 50-square block *Vieux Carre* (Old Square) formed the original city. Streets are narrow, buildings have exquisite wrought-iron balconies and railings, there are patios and courtyards and many historic spots. Wandering about on your own in the French Quarter can be delightful. **Pirate's Alley** is a narrow, picturesque passageway located off **Jackson Square** alongside of **St Louis Cathedral,** America's oldest; **Bourbon Street** is best at night; **Royal Street** has some delightful shops and opens onto lovely courtyards. The **Louisiana Wildlife Museum,** on Royal, houses an unusual collection of birds. See the **Cabildo,** erected in 1795, scene of the signing of the Louisiana Purchase; **St Louis Cathedral,** erected in 1794; **Pontalba Apartments,** erected in 1849 by the Baroness Pontalba, daughter of the colony's richest man during the Spanish era and reputedly the first apartment houses in the United States; the **1850 House,** which depicts a time when New Orleans was supreme and the style of life very fashionable; **Absinthe House,** built in 1806, now a public bar and restaurant; and the restored **French Market.** The Cabildo has some artifacts from the former Mardi Gras Museum. See the history of the city and state at the **Musee Conti Wax Museum.**

The **Piazza D'Italia** is a new attraction to New Orleans' highlights. Located on Poydras Street only a few blocks from the Mississippi River, it is the monument to the city's Italian population. Tour the garden district and **St Charles Avenue** where visitors can get an idea of what lavish Southern living is all about. Or enjoy a breezy ride on the St Charles Avenue street-car, the only such line left in the city and one of the last remaining vintage street-car routes in America. Enjoy one of New Orleans' best tourist bargains—a 1½-hour street-car ride from Canal Street up St Charles Avenue, to Carrolton and back: 40¢ one way. People who come to New Orleans generally already know about Royal Street and its prized antiques shops, but they should know that **Magazine Street** is also lined with shops offering some of the best buys in the country. And Magazine Street cuts through **Audubon Park,** with its newly refurbished **Audubon Zoological Garden,** featuring more than a thousand animals in fascinating, naturalistic settings.

The French Quarter of New Orleans still manages to exclude an Old-World charm and the flavor of its origins more than one hundred and fifty years ago.

See the unusual old cemeteries in **Cities of the Dead,** where some of the tombs containing the remains of original settlers and old celebrities have stained-glass windows and are adorned with statues. Other interesting spots in town are **International House; International Trade Mart,** topped with a revolving cocktail lounge and observation deck with a panoramic view of the city; French cemeteries, in various places in the city, with ornate, above-ground tombs and vaults; the old **US Mint Building,** which is being restored and scheduled to reopen in September 1981 as a community museum, featuring jazz and Mardi Gras memorabilia; and the **Ursuline Convent; US Customs House;** and the 14-acre **Civic Center** near the central business district. There are many conducted tours of New Orleans; a typical 3-hour tour costs $9-12 per person; a 4-hour nightlife tour costs between $25-30, including cover charge, one drink, and gratuities at each club. There are also horse-drawn carriages for hire (about $6-10 per person) and boat trips on the Mississippi—a 2½-hour trip costs about $10-15. For the more adventurous there are **Bayou Cruises** for $15-25 per person.

Principal parks: **City Park,** in the northern part of the city, a huge area with three public golf courses, many amusements and recreational facilities, including a children's "storyland." The famous **Dueling Oaks,** where affairs of honor were once settled, are also in City Park. **Audubon Park** has a zoo, aquarium, attractive grounds with an excellent view of the Mississippi, open daily, free. And in the French Quarter is **Jackson Square.**

Take the Algiers Ferry from Canal Street to the West Bank and walk down Delaronde Street for atmosphere of iron fence work and turn of the century homes.

Principal schools: **Tulane University,** founded in 1834, coeducational; **Southern University** and **H. Sophie Newcomb College,** for women, affiliated with Tulane. **Louisiana State University Medical School** and the **University of New Orleans** are branches of the main establishment in Baton Rouge.

ACCOMMODATIONS

Instead of the big hotels, some tourists may prefer guest houses that offer the cozy charm of French Quarter Life. There are a number of these with overnight accommodations in historic settings and some that include breakfast in the arrangements. With varying amenities, rates range from $35 to $250 per night. The **Hyatt Regency** is a striking hotel and is accented by a breathtaking atrium and glass elevator, (561-1234, S$60-88/D$88-108.) The Hyatt is right at the Superdome. In the French Quarter: **Bienville House** (529-2345, S$45-60/D$70-90), charmingly furnished; **Bourbon Orleans Ramada** (523-5251, S$48-65/D$50-85); **Chateau Motor Hotel** (524-9636, S$34-40/D$40-46, Suites $58-80), near **St Louis Cathedral; Corn Stalk Hotel** (525-1515, S$50 up/D$70 up), **Maison de Ville** (561-5858, S$50-65/D$60-75), **Marie Antoinette** (522-0801, S$62-95/D$67-95 up), on Rue Toulouse; **Marriott Hotel** (581-1000, S$62-95/D$67-95 up); **Montelleone** (523-3341, S$62-95/D$67-95), convenient, rooftop pool; **Place d'Armes Motor Hotel** (523-4531, S$40 up/D$50 up), on Jackson Square; **Provincial Hotel** (581-4995, S$45-55/D$50-55), near the French Market; **Royal Orleans Hotel** (529-5333, S$75-109/D$85-118), with rooftop pool; **Royal Sonesta** (586-0300, S$75-128/D$85-128, Suites $225 up); **Saint Ann** (581-1881, S$65-110/D$75-125), **Vieux Carre Motor Lodge** (524-0461, S$45-85/D$55-110), luxurious atmosphere. Near the French Quarter in the business district: **Fairmont Hotel** (529-7111, S$60-100/D$80-120), a leading convention center; **Le Pavillon** (581-3111, S$85/D$95). **The Pontchartrain** (524-0581, S$55-95/D$65-115, Suites $135-250), 1½ miles from midtown on St Charles Avenue, specializes in personalized service and fine Creole food. **New Orleans Hilton & Tower** (561-0500, S$75 up/D$85 up, Suites $225 up); **Sheraton Chateau Le Moyne Hotel** (581-1303, S$65 up/D$75 up). At the airport, 11 miles from town: **Candelight Hilton, Holiday Inns,** and **Town House Motor Hotel.** All hotels are air conditioned; most have French- and Spanish-speaking personnel. Hotel Tax: 9%.

RESTAURANTS

New Orleans is one of the most famous cities in the country for food and restaurants. Dress in most restaurants is casual but some require men to wear jackets and most do not accept reservations. Its seafood, particularly the shrimp, oysters, and crab, is renowned; local fish such as pompano, trout, and redfish are exceptional. Famous dishes include oysters Rockefeller (baked with a spinach-herb mixture), gumbos (soups thickened with okra), and café brulot (black coffee with spices and liquor). One of the city's newest restaurants, but one that has been widely acclaimed since its opening, is **Crozier's** in eastern New Orleans, a small, romantic spot that offers some of the best French cuisine available. The menu is small but everything is worthwhile. Then there's **La Provence**, which will require a ride on the Causeway over Lake Pontchartrain, since it is located in Mandeville, but a trip there won't be forgotten. It, too, offers French cuisine in a cozy, dim atmosphere, and you can dress exactly the way you feel, barring shorts and tee-shirts, of course. French Quarter restaurants include **Antoines,** one of the most famous, exceptional food, expensive; **Arnaud's,** outstanding, many fine specialties, moderate to expensive; **Brennans,** atmosphere, patio, famous for breakfasts, local specialties, expensive; **Galatoire's,** famous for crabmeat preparations, moderate to expensive. The **Rib Room** in the Royal Orleans Hotel specializes in superb ribs, excellent service. **Kolb's,** just out of the French Quarter, has German specialties, moderate. For an inexpensive dinner of spaghetti try the **Spaghetti Factory.** In the Garden District, there are **Commander's Palace,** good food, noted for seafood, moderate; **Dunbar's,** luxurious home atmosphere, advanced reservations essential, expensive; **Caribbean Room** in the Pontchartrain Hotel, quiet and refined, excellent French, Creole, and Cajun cuisine. Out (and just off) Canal Street is **Christian's,** a superb continental restaurant housed in a former church, expensive. For true continental coffeehouse atmosphere and devastating pastries in this area go to **Les Patisseries aux Quatre**

Saisons. And for great baked goods and pastries try **La Marquis.** On the west bank of the Mississippi River is **LeRuth's,** an exceptionally fine restaurant that has been highly praised by area gourmets. **Bruning's Restaurant** overlooking Lake Pontchartrain is noted for its wide variety of good seafood, moderate. Near the lake there is **Masson's Beach House,** featuring Creole and seafood specialties. **Tchoupitoulas Plantation Restaurant,** outside the city, is excellent, and reservations are necessary. **Bart's, Elmwood Plantation,** and the **Pontchartrain Hotel's** Caribbean Room are some of the better places to eat around town.

ENTERTAINMENT

There are dining, dancing, and floor shows in principal hotels. The French Quarter offers extremely informal entertainment, much of it rough and ready and not suited to all tastes; they come to life about 5 pm. Best known are: **Al Hirt's Club, The Famous Door, Pat O'Brien's, Old Absinthe Bar, Maison Bourbon, Pete Fountain's, French Quarter Inn. The Paddock Lounge, Chris Owens;** all feature authentic Dixieland jazz. Walk down Bourbon Street; it's famous for its honky-tonks, but you'll have to use your own judgement. Some are interesting, others merely "joints." Some of America's most authentic Dixieland, played by oldtime jazzmen, is available at **Preservation Hall,** in the heart of the French Quarter. Pick up a copy of *What To Do Or See In New Orleans* for other suggestions. Fast becoming another focal point for nightlife in the New Orleans area is **Fat City,** the suburban answer to the French Quarter's gaiety. Located a few blocks off the interstate from the French Quarter to the airport— about 20 minutes drive from downtown.

ARTS AND MUSIC

New Orleans Museum of Art, paintings and art exhibits, provides a tour through the history of art; open Tuesday to Saturday 10-5, Sunday 1-6; $1 for adults, 50¢ for children 12-18 (except for special international exhibits). **Institute of Middle American Research,** at Tulane University, has outstanding Mayan collections; open Monday to Friday 9-5; free. **Louisiana State Museum,** in the Cabildo, has exhibits of French and Spanish colonial Louisiana, open Tuesday to Sunday 10-4:30, admission 50¢.

Musical activities include concerts by the **New Orleans Philharmonic Symphony Orchestra** and performances by the **New Orleans Opera House Association.** Other musical events are the **Summer Pops** concert series, the **New Orleans Jazz Club** concerts, and musicals and operas put on by the **New Orleans Recreation Department. New Orleans Music and Drama Foundation** stages local productions of Broadway musicals, as does the newly reopened and refurbished **Saenger Theatre,** downtown.

SHOPPING

New Orleans has four major shopping centers outside of the French Quarter, two located in suburban Jefferson Parish, one in eastern New Orleans, and there's **Uptown Square,** located not far from Audubon Park near the river. **Lakeside** and **Clearview** are two popular shopping centers—malls—which can be reached by I-10 West. **The Plaza** in Lake Forest can be reached by taking the I-10 East. Stores are open Monday through Saturday 10-5:30, Thursday 10-8:30, and some on Sunday. **Oakwood Shopping Mall,** on the west bank of the Mississippi River in Gretna, is a small but smart shopping area that can be reached via the Mississippi River Bridge. The major department stores are found on **Canal Street** adjacent to the **Vieux Carre.** For smaller, intriguing shops try the French Quarter, or browse on **Magazine Street** or **Brulatour Courtyard** at 520 Royal Street.

SPORTS

Horse racing at the **Fair Grounds** from Thanksgiving through March, daily except Sunday. Night racing at **Jefferson Downs,** mid-October through mid-April. There's also college and professional football, played in one of New Orleans' most famous landmarks, the **Louisiana Superdome,** located downtown and just off I-10. Guided tours of this remarkable facility are offered daily. There are seven private and five public golf courses and tennis courts in parks and at private clubs. Salt-water fishing in the gulf and fresh-water fishing in **Lake Pontchartrain** are year-round sports. There's never a problem finding something to do—and enjoy doing in New Orleans or nearby. Fishing on the lakefront is just the beginning. For adventurous souls, a trip down Chef Menteur Highway into some of the out-lying marsh areas for fishing is a treat, but try also fishing off of **Grand Isle** (depending on traffic, it takes about one hour twenty to two and a half hours), where many of the deep-sea fishermen go for a ride into the Gulf of Mexico. Then there's ice skating in the big rink at the **Plaza Shopping Center** in **Lake Forest,** as well as many other regular roller skating rinks throughout the city. The hunting season runs from October through February.

CALENDAR OF EVENTS

Mardi Gras, nationally famous festival of elaborate galas, parades, and masquerades, 10-day period before Lent, approximately mid or late February or early March; **Spring Fiesta,** tours of local homes and gardens with outdoor art show in Pirate's Alley, beginning the Friday after Easter; **New Orleans Jazz and Heritage Festival,** local artists and musicians of international repute in concerts, seminars, and parades, five days in May. Louisiana's fabled cuisine is showcased each summer at the **New Orleans Food Festival,** staged on the closest weekend to July 4.

WHERE TO GO NEARBY

Fort Pike (in Fort Pike State Commemorative Area), 30 miles east of town, and **Fort Macomb,** 20 miles east, are old forts that have been restored. **Fountainebleau State Park,** on Lake Pontchartrain, 25 miles north, has water-sport facilities. **Chalmette National Historical Park,** about 6 miles south of the city, was where General Andrew Jackson defeated the British in the last major battle of the War of 1812. There is a museum on the second floor of the restored **Rene Beauregard House**

overlooking the battlefield. The modern steamboat replica of the *Mississippi Queen* and the vintage *Delta Queen* have seasonal excursions from New Orleans up the Mississippi and back, stopping at key historic cities along the river.

If you want to see the bayou country where Jean Lafitte used to roam, 5-hour bayou cruises on the *Becky Thatcher* are available, but do include much of the industrial area. Delightful **Longue Vue House and Gardens** are just a few minutes' drive from the central business district. From 60 to 90 miles east of New Orleans are the Mississippi resort towns on the Gulf of Mexico, including **Waveland, Biloxi, Pass Christian, Gulfport,** and **Long Beach.** Swimming is best in hotel and motor pools.

FURTHER STATE INFORMATION

Louisiana State Office of Tourism, Box 44291, Baton Rouge, LA 70804. Hunting and Fishing: **Louisiana Wildlife and Fisheries Commission,** 400 Royal Street, New Orleans, LA 70130. **New Orleans Chamber of Commerce,** PO Box 39240, New Orleans, LA 70130; and **International House,** 607 Gravier Street, New Orleans, LA 70130. **Greater New Orleans Tourist and Convention Commission,** 334 Royal Street, New Orleans, LA 70130. **Baton Rouge Area Convention & Visitors Bureau,** Old State Capitol, Baton Rouge, LA 70821. **Lafayette Parish Convention & Visitors Commission,** PO Drawer 52066, Lafayette, LA 70505. **Shreveport-Bossier Convention and Tourist Commission,** 408 Market Street, PO Box 1761, Shreveport, LA 71166.

Consulates in New Orleans: Argentina, Austria, Belgium, Bolivia, Brazil, Canada, Chile, Colombia, Costa Rica, Denmark, Dominican Republic, Ecuador, El Salvador, Finland, France, Germany, Great Britain, Greece, Guatemala, Haiti, Honduras, India, Italy, Japan, Korea, Liberia, Mexico, Monaco, Netherlands, Nicaragua, Norway, Panama, Paraguay, Peru, Philippine Republic, Portugal, Senegal, South Africa, Spain, Sri Lanka, Sweden, Switzerland, Thailand, Turkey, Upper Volta, Uruguay, Venezuela.

USEFUL TELEPHONE NUMBERS IN NEW ORLEANS

Mercy Hospital	486-7361
Jo Ellen Smith Memorial Hospital	361-7131
Ochsner Foundation Hospital	838-3000
Fire	581-3473
Police	822-4161
State Police	568-5751
Legal Aid Bureau	523-2597
Chamber of Commerce	527-6900
Tourist Information	566-5011
Pan Am Reservations	529-5192

Maine

Area	33,215 square miles				**Population**	1,123,560						
Capital	Augusta				**Sales Tax**	5%						

Weather

	Jan	Feb	Mar	Apr	May	Jun	Jul	Aug	Sep	Oct	Nov	Dec
Av Temp (°C)	−6	−5	0	6	12	17	20	19	15	9	3	−3
Days Rain/Snow	11	10	11	12	13	11	9	10	8	9	12	11

Maine boasts some beautiful unspoiled wilderness areas. The state is a great favorite for a vacation with year-round hunting, fishing, camping, swimming, sailing, skiing, and snowmobiling for the sportsman, and art galleries, auctions, country fairs, historic sites, horse races, and cruises for those who prefer something less strenuous. Known as the Pine Tree State, Maine is the top producer of the nation's low-bush blueberries, and the third largest producer of potatoes. The state is also known for its lobsters, and the manufacture of toothpicks. Mainstay of its economy, however, is the wood processing industry, with paper the most important single product. It is the country's easternmost state and the only one bordering on just one other state—New Hampshire.

Maine is practically as big as the other five New England states combined—320 miles long and 210 miles wide. Of this, over four fifths, or 17,000,000 acres, are forest preserve. **Acadia National Park** is the only national park in New England and the oldest east of the Mississippi. **Mt Cadillac,** 1,532 feet, is located within the park.

Inhabitants of Maine's coastal region are referred to as "Down-Easters," a term which dates back to the time when the local sailors referred to the return trip from Boston, with the wind at their backs, as a "down-hill run" or "going down east." **Kittery,** on the **SOUTHERN COAST,** is an old sea town incorporated in 1647 and once an important shipbuilding, shipping and lumbering center. Submarines are built and repaired at the **Portsmouth** (N.H.) **Navy Yard,** located on a small island in the Piscataqua River just off Kittery. **Lady Pepperrell House** in Kittery is an elaborate two-story Georgian house built in 1760. **Valle's Steak House** and **Warren's Lobster House** are fine restaurants in Kittery. Up the coast from Kittery to **Portland** is an area full of sunny, sandy beaches which provide excellent fishing, swimming, and cruising.

Along the coast line, **York's** beaches and pine groves have been a favorite summer playground since the early 17th century. A walking tour of historic **York Village** includes the **Old Gaol Museum,** built in 1653 and used as a jail until 1860; **Emerson-Wilcox House,** originally built as a private home in 1740 and later used as a tavern and post office; the **Elizabeth Perkins House** (1686); **Jefferd's Tavern,** mid-18th century; a 1745 school house; and the parish **Congregational Church** on the village green, built in 1747. Fishing, sailing, and boating at **York Harbor** and **Cape Neddick,** swimming and picnicking at the harbor, the cape, and local beaches. An annual craft fair is held here in late August. York's local motels include **Anchorage Motor Inn** (363-5112, S$26.50-46.50), ocean view; **Dockside Guest Quarters** (363-2868, S$20-30/D$24.50-32), rooms and units, adjacent to the Marina, free breakfast.

Stage Neck Inn (363-3850, S$35-60/D$45-75) is a popular resort on a private peninsula in York Harbor; each room has a view of the river, harbor, or ocean, heated salt-water pool, café. **Hickory Stick Farm's Dockside Restaurant** offers a fine view of York Harbor. **Cape Neddick Lobster Pound,** on the harbor, has a lobster tank and open kitchen. Another popular restaurant in York is the **Nubble Light. Boon Island,** the locale of a Kenneth Roberts novel, can be seen from the shore. The 18th-century **Hamilton House,** in South Berwick, was the scene of Sarah Orne Jewett's *The Tory Lover;* the **Vaughan Woods State Memorial,** off ME 236 on the east bank of Salmon Falls River, has 250 wooded acres with foot trails.

Back on the coast, **Ogunquit, Wells,** and **Kennebunkport,** the famous trio of artists' and actors' colonies, provide summer theatrical entertainment and a number of noteworthy art galleries. The white sand beach at Ogunquit runs for three miles and has some of the best swimming on the Atlantic. Walkers will enjoy **Marginal Way** along the cliffs overlooking the ocean. There are several local art galleries; the seascapes and little harbor at **Perkins Cove** in Ogunquit have attracted a growing art colony. Hotels in the Ogunquit area include: **The Cliff House & Motels** (646-5124, S/D$59-65), on the ocean; **Colonial Village Motel** (646-2794, D$50-75, weekly $250-280), heated Olympic size pool, cottages; **Dolphin Post Motor Inn** (646-7586, D$50-75), on the ocean; **Dunelawn** (646-2403, D$35-55), a converted Georgian mansion set in a seven-acre estate facing river, dunes, and ocean; and **Sea Chambers Motor Lodge** (646-9311, D$42-45), ocean view.

Ogunquit has some of New England's finest restaurants; **Old Village Inn, Chef Wilhelm's** for fine German food. **Barnacle Billy's** at Perkins Cove features an open kitchen; choose your own lobster and then dine on the dock over the water. **Le Chateaubriand** has a continental menu and view of the ocean. You can select your own lobster at **Ogunquit Lobster Pond,** where they also have outdoor cooking and dining in the pine grove. **Poor Richard's Pub,** in a historic 1780 tavern, is noted for the lobster ramekin. **Whistling Oyster** has a continental menu, serves Sunday brunch, and has a view of the harbor. Other popular dining and lodging spots in Ogunquit include **Lookout East Motor Inn** (646-5501, D$18-46), and **Sparhawk** (646-5562, S/D$44-48). One of Maine's most popular summer theaters, the **Ogunquit Playhouse,** is also located here.

North along the coast, **Wells** used to be a coastal farming center with some commercial fishing, until it was discovered by vacationers; there is fishing, swimming at the beaches. **Atlantic Motor Inn** (646-7061, S/D$20-55) is on the ocean; **Sea Gull Motor Inn** (646-7082, S/D$20-40) has a heated pool, good for families. Author Kenneth Roberts used the **Kennebunkport** area at the mouth of the **Kennebunk River** as the scene for *Arundel.* A famous shipbuilding town, Kennebunkport now has a permanent art and literary colony and is a popular summer resort. The **Seashore Trolley Museum** has more than 90 antique streetcars from the US and abroad; trolley rides, picnicking. Swimming at **Cleaves Cove** and **Goose Rocks Beach;** fishing from local bridges and wharfs. Hotels in the area: **The Colony** (967-3331, S$67/D$87), spacious grounds opposite the ocean, heated salt-water pool, dancing; the **Nonantum** (967-3338, S$40-60/D$62-86), pleasant, on the river, heated salt-water pool; **Seacrest Inn on the Sea** (967-2125, S/D$30-34), overlooks the coast offering both inn and motel accommodation; **Shawmut Motor Inn** (967-3931, S/D$44-68), on a secluded bluff, overlooks the ocean, has heated salt-water pool, café featuring New England fare; **The Captain Lord Mansion** (967-3141, S$35/D$55); **Village Cove Inn** (967-3393, S/D$45) and **Narragansett-By-The-Sea-Hotel** (967-4741, S$24-33/D$38-44). The **Olde Grist Mill Restaurant,** overlooking the river, has been owned and operated by the same family since 1749; country store, lobster and shore dinners, home baking, porch dining. **Spicer's Gallery** on Cape Porpoise stands on a century old pier.

Kennebunk, on the Mousam and Kennebunk Rivers, is another 18th-century shipbuilding town. The **First Parish Church,** built in 1774, has a bell cast by Paul Revere. **Old Orchard Beach,** 12 miles from Portland, has a crescent beach seven miles long and about 700 feet wide, with surf casting at the southern end of the beach off **Ocean Park.** Hotels, cottages, boardwalk, pier and amusements attract thousands of tourists in season. Motels include the **Diplomat** (934-4621, S/D$48-51), on the ocean, pool; **Executive** (934-4637, S/D$48), near the beach, pool; the **Gull Motel** (934-4321, D$30-38) on the beach; **New Normandie Motor**

Inn (934-2533, S$18-35/D$20-50) oceanfront; **Sandpiper Motel** (934-2733, S/D$48-50). Also **Americana Motel** (934-2292, S/D$35); and **Royal Anchor Motor Lodge** (934-4521, S$24/D$34), one mile north of city center.

Scarborough Downs, formerly Maine's only flat racing track, offers harness racing during the summer months.

Brunswick, to the east, used to be a great lumbering center, but today the town is mostly concerned with trade and education. **Bowdoin College,** founded in 1794, has 1,000 students. Nathaniel Hawthorne, Longfellow, Rear Admiral Robert E. Peary and President Franklin Pierce studied here. **Brunswick Music Theater,** on the campus, features professional players in Broadway musicals, late June through early September. The **Brunswick Naval Air Station** is based here. **Harriet Beecher Stowe House,** built in 1806, where she wrote *Uncle Toms Cabin,* is now a restaurant. Duck hunting at **Merrymeeting Bay,** tuna fishing on **Bailey Island,** 17 miles south on the northern shore of Casco Bay. Swimming and picnicking at **Thomas Point Beach** and **Coffin's Pond;** the latter also has winter skiing, ice skating, and tobogganing. The **Bowdoin Steak House** in Brunswick offers fine fare and an extensive range of music to eat by.

Bath, on the west bank of the **Kennebec River,** has been a shipbuilding center for almost four centuries, and today it is the leading center for building guided missile frigates. **Bath Marine Museum** traces the maritime history of Maine since 1607, emphasizing 19th-century wooden shipbuilding. **Ocean View Park,** picnicking, swimming; **Reid State Park,** swimming, fishing, picnicking; **Sheraton Motor Inn at Bath** (443-9741, S$24/D$34).

In the **WESTERN LAKES REGION, Sebago Lake** is about 16 miles long and 10 miles wide. Many resort communities are tucked in along the shore and behind the wooden hills. **Sebago** is the home of the landlocked salmon. About 250,000 salmon are hatched and released annually at the state fish hatchery in **Casco;** open daily. **Sebago Lake State Park,** south of **Naples,** has a 1,300-acre recreational area with sand beaches, fishing, picnicking, camping, boating and snowmobiling. Located at Naples is the **Chute Homestead** (693-6425, D$29-34). **Pleasant Mountain Ski Area,** at Bridgton, has a year-round chair lift. Water from the famous mineral springs at **Poland Spring** has been bottled and shipped around the world since the 1840s. Accommodations are available at the **Inn at Poland Spring** (998-4351, S$25-60). The **Shaker Museum** at Sabbathday Lake on ME 26 is part of the cooperative community founded there in 1783. The 14-building **Shaker Village** complex and museum exhibits Shaker furniture, woodenware, and handicrafts; open Memorial Day through September.

AUGUSTA has been the state capital since 1832. Charles Bulfinch drew the original design for the **State House** building in 1829. **Blaine House,** the 28-room executive mansion, adjoins the State House. **Fort Western Museum,** opposite City Hall, has a pre-Revolutionary, restored 20-room barracks, plus reproductions of a stockade and blockhouses. Huge granite quarries are found from **Hallowell** up to **North Jay.** An annual pageant the third week in July is held at Hallowell, famed for its old homes, antique and craft shows.

Franklin County Fair, at **Farmington** in late May, attracts visitors from all over. The **University of Maine** at Farmington, founded in 1864, has over 1,300 students. **Nordica Homestead Museum,** birthplace of the famous American singer, Lillian Nordica, exhibits mementos of her opera career, along with original 19th-century furnishings. **Skowhegan,** on the Kennebec River, is still used for log driving. The annual **State Fair** is held here in mid-August. **Lakewood Theater** in Madison is a famous summer playhouse founded in 1900; it features current Broadway shows.

Waterville forms the center of the **Belgrade** and **China Lakes** resort area, and **Colby College,** chartered in 1813, is here. The college has its own ski area, north on Upper Main Street. Motels located in central Waterville are: **Howard Johnson Motor Lodge** (873-3335, S\$31.50-39.50/ D\$41.50-51.50) and **Holiday Inn** (873-0111, S\$24-35/D\$28-48). Recommended restaurants are the **Silent Woman,** with an old English atmosphere, the **Silver Street Tavern** and **The Manor.** The Silver Street Tavern offers jazz and folk music.

The charming seaside towns and villages along the Maine midcoast are noted for their quaint shops, colonial architecture, historic harbors and modern marinas, art galleries and museums. **BOOTHBAY HARBOR** is a delightful old seaport on the peninsula between the Sheepscot and Damariscotta rivers. From June through mid-October, river and ocean cruises leave the harbor for hourly and day-long trips to **Monhegan Island,** with the highest cliffs on the New England coast, and **Squirrel Island.** Supper cruises, clambakes and fishing trips are also available. On **Cabbage Island** in Linekin Bay traditional clambakes are held twice daily. For boat schedule call 633-4333. Windjammer schooners cruise the Maine coast and sail into the harbor en masse for **Windjammer Days** in mid-July, fishing, salt- and fresh-water swimming, picnicking at **Crab and Lobster Wharf.** Local motels include **Brown's Wharf Motel** (633-5440, S/D\$39-69), facing the harbor, restaurant in 18th-century saltshed overlooking the water; **Fisherman's Wharf** (633-5090, S/D\$35-45), harbor view; **Lake View Motel** (633-5381, S/D\$18-46), overlooking fresh-water lake, private sand beach; **Ocean Gate Motor Inn** (633-3321, S/D\$22-69), on 80 acres with harbor view units, heated pool; **Ocean Point Inn** (633-4200, S/D\$24.50-36.50), on a peninsula at Linekin Bay entrance, lodge and cottage accommodations. The 15 acre **Linekin Bay Resort** (633-2494, S\$21-30, weekly \$147-210), heated salt-water pool, lobster cookouts; **Newagen Inn** (633-4152, S\$18-25/D\$22-32), 400 acres, all sports; and **Spruce Point Inn** (633-4152, S\$45-60.50/D\$84-95), on a 100-acre wooded peninsula with a beautiful ocean view, heated and salt-water pools and beach, are three lovely places to stay. Reservations are recommended at local restaurants since this is such a popular resort. The **Tugboat Inn** and the **Thistle Inn** are recommended. **The Blue Ship** is a good restaurant for families.

Thomaston, a trading post during its first hundred years, remains a shipbuilding center and has gained a reputation as a yachting and resort community. **Montpelier,** a reproduction of the late 18th-century home owned by General Henry Knox, hero of the Revolutionary War and first US Secretary of War, has original furnishings. **Rockland** is the chief town of **PENOBSCOT BAY,** with commercial fishing and light industry, in addition to resort facilities. Popular dining and lodging places at Rockland include **Samoset Resort** (594-2511, S$28-56/D$38-62); **Trade Winds Motel** (594-2131, D$34-40); **Navigator Motor Inn** (596-6661, D$29-40), and the **Red Jacket Restaurant.** The **Farnsworth Library and Art Museum** in Rockland has several works by Andrew and James Wyeth. The **Farnsworth Homestead,** a Greek revival mansion, is open early June through late September. The **Maine Seafoods Festival,** a four-day food fair held the first weekend in August, features local dishes in a giant tent, plus a parade and entertainment. **Vinalhaven,** a fashionable resort island, has fishing, swimming, and boating; ferry service from Vinalhaven to Rockland.

North of Rockland is **Camden,** the summer home of many artists, writers and musicians; excellent boating on Penobscot Bay and weekly cruises along the coast on old-time schooners, mid-June through mid-September. Sightseeing cruises on the bay, daily June through September. **Camden Hills State Park** has picnicking, camping and snowmobiling; skiing at **Camden Snow Bowl.** The **Old Conway House and Barn,** an authentically restored 18th-century farmhouse, has carriages and sleighs on exhibit in the barn and a blacksmith shop. **Garden Club Open House Day,** a tour of homes and gardens, is held the third Thursday in July. Local motels are **Snow Hill** (236-3452, S$18.40/D$20.50), 4 miles from central Camden; and **Whitehall Inn** (263-3391, S$26-40/D$56), ¾ mile from central Camden. As the name suggests, diners can choose lobster from the pool at the **Lobster Pound,** overlooking Penobscot Bay. **Warren Island State Park,** at Islesboro, offers camping, fishing, picnicking and a three-mile ferry ride from **Lincolnville. Searsmont,** to the west, was the locale for many of Ben Ames Williams' country stories.

Belfast is an old seaport town on the west shore of Penobscot Bay. **Lake St George State Park,** in Liberty, has 360 acres; fishing, boating, swimming, picnicking, camping, and snowmobiling. The important poultry industry in this area sponsors an annual six-day **Maine Broiler Festival,** held at the city park in mid-July. **Belfast Motor Inn** (388-2740, S/D$18-26), overlooking the bay and **Colonial Gables Motel** (338-4000, D$24-26), private sand beach on the bay, provide accommodation.

Moose Point State Park offers a splendid view of Penobscot Bay and picnicking in the pine groves. The **Penobscot Marine Museum** includes an 1845 Town Hall and 19th-century homes which have been restored and furnished with period pieces and marine memorabilia. The town maintains a wharf and boat landing. **The Yardarm Motel** (548-2404, S$22/D$25), overlooking the bay, family rates, is located in Searsport. **Kob's Lobster Pound Restaurant** has a large picnic area and a bay view. **Fort Knox** at Prospect, is one of the largest Civil War forts.

The **Blue Hill** area of Penobscot and Acadia counties is the setting of many Mary Ellen Chase novels. The region is also famous for its late-summer county fair with livestock shows, cooking and needlework contests, handcrafted Rowantrees pottery, and fine trout and pan fishing. The principal commercial city in northern Maine and the state's third largest city is **BANGOR**. It was the world's foremost lumber market at the end of the last century and today pulp paper and wood products are still its leading industries. The **Bangor International Airport** is located four miles west of the center of the city. **The Hilton Inn** (947-6721, S$19-31/D$25-37) is adjacent to the airport. The **Paul Bunyan Statue**, on Main Street, is 31 feet high. The annual **Paul Bunyan Snowmobile Derby** is held the last weekend in January and the **Bangor Fair**, one of the nation's oldest, is held in midsummer. Accommodations in Bangor include: **Best Western White House** (862-3737, S$14-24/D$18-28); **Holiday Inn** (947-8651, S$26-35/D$28-44); **Howard Johnson's Motor Lodge** (942-5251, S$26-36/D$28-44) and about 10 minutes from the airport; **Queen City Charter House** (942-4611, S/D$18.50); **Ramada Inn** (947-6961, S$32/D$39) and **Stable Inn** (989-3200, S$20-25/D$24-26). Popular restaurants include **Pilot's Grill, The Red Lion,** the **White Elephant,** the **Chateau Restaurant** in the Hilton Inn at the Airport, **Murray's Steak House** in nearby Brewer and **Benjamin's Tavern.** The **Bangor Mall** is a $25 million, 74-store complex, totaling 500,000 square feet. North of Bangor, **Orono,** in the Penobscot Valley, is the home of the **University of Maine,** founded in 1865. **The Penobscot Indian Reservation,** on a small island north of Old Town, still has several hundred Indians. Annual attractions are the **Indian Pageant** in July and the **Hunter's Breakfast,** which is served in the city park on the first day of the fall hunting season. **Ellsworth,** 25 miles southeast of Bangor, was the second-biggest lumber shipping port in the world in the early 19th century. **The Black Mansion,** off US 1, is an 1802 Georgian house with original furnishings and old carriages and sleighs in the carriage house. **Le Domaine,** French food and homemade pastries, and the **Hilltop House** are recommended.

BAR HARBOR lies at the entrance to Acadia National Park. It is the largest town on **Mt Desert Island,** which has been called one of the most beautiful islands on the Atlantic Coast. The area is dotted with resorts, motels, guest houses, cabins and summer homes. **Seal Cove Automobile Museum** has more than 100 antique and classic autos and motorcycles. Freshwater swimming in **Echo Lake.** Salt-water swimming four miles south at **Sand Beach;** fishing, hiking, horseback riding. Ferry service to Swans Island from Bass Harbor. The new **Atlantic Oakes By-The-Sea** (288-5218, S/D$27-51), heated pool, free breakfast; **Bar Harbor Motel Inn** (228-5159, S/D$28-58), motel on the shore front, hotel overlooking the water, heated pool; **Frenchman's Bay Motel** (288-3321, D$32-34) opposite the ferry terminal, overlooking the bay; **Wonder View Motor Lodge** (288-3358, D$42) heated pool, near Nova Scotia ferry; are all good. Local restaurants specializing in shore dinners include **Harbor View, High Seas, Testa's, Tripp's** and **Young's Lobster Pot.** Daily ferry service to **Cranberry Isles,** off Mt Desert Island, in summer. There's also daily ferry service to Yarmouth, Nova Scotia, on the 600-passenger ship MS Bluenose (tel: 207-288-3395). Reservations must be made far in advance.

In **Northeast Harbor**, Asticou Inn (276-3344, S$56-64/D$78-90); **Harbourside Inn** (276-3272, S/D$27-48); near the docks; **Kimball Terrace Inn** (276-3383, S/D$27-48), overlooking the harbor, heated pool; **The Claremont Hotel** and cottages (244-5036, S$39-49/D$66-81) on Somes Sound; all are good. The **Jordan Pond House Restaurant** in Seal Harbor overlooks **Jordan Pond** and the mountains in Acadia National Park. Take tea on the lawn and try some of their homemade ice cream. **Yarmouth**, 10 miles out of Portland, is one of the oldest **Casco Bay** summer resorts. The annual **Clam Festival** is held here the third weekend in July, followed by the **Vacationland Agricultural Fair**, early August. In Yarmouth there are the **Down-East Village Motel** (846-5161, D$22-30) and **Homewood Inn** (846-3351, S/D$26-44), pool, sports, and restaurant featuring New England menu and homemade baked goods, buffet style.

Washington County, on the easternmost border, is one of America's finest fishing areas and "the sardine capital of the world." The region also produces almost all of the nation's processed blueberries. **Machias** *(muhchy-as)*, founded in 1763, is particularly recommended for hunting bear and deer and fishing for salmon and striped bass. The **Burnham Tavern**, built in 1770, is now a museum. **Quoddy Head State Park**, 481 acres south of Lubec, is the easternmost point in the US. Smoked herring and packed sardines are the local industries. **Roosevelt Campobello International Park** on **Campobello Island,** is jointly operated by Canada and the US. This is where the young Franklin D. Roosevelt maintained his summer home and was stricken with polio. The 3,000-acre park and his home are open daily, mid-May to October. At the southern end of Passamaquoddy Bay, **Eastport**, on Moose Island, is the easternmost city in the US. Several hundred Indians remain on the **Passamaquoddy Reservation** to the north at Pleasant Point. A free ferry connects **Deer Island** to the Canadian mainland.

Maine's **NORTHERN LAKES DISTRICT** is one of the nation's last frontiers, famous for its lakes, mountains, forests, and huge watersheds. **Mt Blue State Park** at Weld offers swimming, camping, and a view from the summit, 3,000 feet above sea level. **Small's Falls**, in Madrid, is another scenic picnic spot.

The entire region around **Rangeley Lake State Park** is noted for its landlocked salmon. **Saddleback** and **Sugarloaf/USA** are famous winter ski resorts, and lifts also operate for summer sightseers. The century-old slate quarries at Monson are still productive.

Lily Bay State Park, eight miles north of Greenville, is a 924-acre park on **Moosehead Lake,** with excellent fishing, swimming, boating, and picnicking, and snowmobiling. **Squaw Mountain** at Moosehead is nearby and the chair lift takes sightseers to the summit daily, June through September. **Squaw Mountain Lodge** (695-2272, D$32-44) at Moosehead, has an indoor heated pool, sauna, playground, tennis, entertainment, restaurant and cafeteria during the ski season. **The Cottages** on Moosehead Lake (695-2422, D$28-30/$125-195 weekly) is a secluded colony on the lake with private beach, fishing, boating. Moosehead Lake is the largest in Maine, 40 miles long and 20 miles wide. It is the state's wilderness sports center, with hunting and fishing, camping, hiking and canoeing, surrounded by pine, spruce and fir. On the west shore of the lake, the **Moosehead Motel** (534-7787, S/D$22-32) in Rockwood has a heated pool, all sports. Its restaurant overlooks the lake and will cook your catch, though steak is the specialty. **Jackman** is another hunting and fishing center; there are many lodges and campsites for visitors. The rustic 35,000-acre **Attean Lake Resort** (668-3792, S$45/D$75) is an island family camp with cabins. **Sky Lodge & Motel** (668-2171, S$20-24/D$26-29) has a panoramic view of the mountain from its restaurant. Percival P. Baxter, two-term governor (from 1921-1925), sought to create a wilderness park around **Mount Katahdin,** the state's highest peak, 5,268 feet, but met with no success. Finally he bought the land himself and gave the 2,000,000-acre park to the state, on condition that it was left in its natural state. **Baxter State Park,** 26 miles northwest of Millinocket, can be approached from Greenville, Patten, or Millinocket. There are eight campgrounds and 140 miles of trails. Reservations may be made through the Reservations Clerk, Millinocket, Maine 04462, Tel (207) 723-5140. The **Allagash Wilderness Waterway,** a 95-mile passage through the Northern Maine Woods, is for experienced canoeists only.

Aroostook County is larger than Connecticut and Rhode Island combined. During the third week in July when the nation's potato capital is in full bloom, **Fort Fairfield** hosts the **Potato Blossom Festival. Presque Isle** is also famous for its potatoes, fishing, hunting, and swimming. The **Northern Maine Fair** is held here the first week in August. **Aroostook State Fair** is held here the first week in July. **Aroostook State Park** has 577 acres with swimming, fishing, boating, picnicking, camping, and snowmobiling. **Mars Hill** is 14 miles southeast. The **Aroostook Experimental Farm** is operated by the University of Maine to improve potato and sugar production. Local harness racing is at **Bangor Raceways,** late June through August. **Caribou** is a potato-shipping center. The **Nylander Museum** has geological exhibits. Fishing, hunting, swimming, and boating on local lakes.

At the northern end of US 1 is **Fort Kent.** A bridge connects the town with Clair, New Brunswick, across the St John River in Canada. **Fort Kent Ski Areas** is nearby on US 1.

City To Visit

PORTLAND

Portland, the birthplace of Henry Wadsworth Longfellow, is in southwestern Maine, on Casco Bay, and borders on Fore River and Back Cove. The city was the state capital from 1820 to 1831 and an important seaport since colonial days. The largest city in Maine, Portland has salty breezes and delightful architecture. Population 61,530; metropolitan area 232,500. There's daily ferry service to Yarmouth, Nova Scotia on the MS Carlisle.

WHAT TO SEE

Wadsworth-Longfellow Home, built 1785; open during summer 9:30-4:30, adult admission $2.50, children under 12, 75¢. Follow "History Trail" from the old **Chamber of Commerce** building (1830) to such historic landmarks as the **Portland Observatory** (1807), where wives watched for their husbands' ships; **Tate House** (1755); **Portland Head Light** (1791), in nearby Cape Elizabeth; **Victoria Mansion** (1863); **Fort Gorges** (1858); **Eastern Cemetery** (established 1688); and many other charming old places. The **Eastern** and **Western Promenades** offer fine views of the surrounding area. Take a three-hour boat trip across Casco Bay. **Deering Oaks** is the outstanding park here, with beautiful gardens, tennis and other recreational facilities. Other popular tourist attractions are the **Maine Historical Society,** which has an extensive historical and genealogical library; the **Portland Museum of Art,** open 10am Tuesday through Saturday; the **Sweat Museum** attached to the Museum of Art; and the **Payson Gallery of Art** located on the campus of **Westbrook College** in the city. Ferry service between Portland and Yarmouth, Nova Scotia, is available in the summer.

ACCOMMODATIONS

Located in downtown Portland are the **Eastland Motor Hotel** (775-5411, S$26.25/D$33.60) and the **Holiday Inn Downtown** (775-2311, S$34/D$43). Also centrally located in Portland are the **Ramada Inn** (744-5611, S$32/D$42); **Executive Inn** (773-8181, S$34/D$44). Located near Portland are the **Holiday Inn West** (774-5601, S$32/D$36); the **Sheraton Inn South Portland** (775-6161, S$54/D$62); **Howard Johnson's Motor Lodge** (774-5861, S$30-46/D$38-52). Nearest camping site is at **Sebago Lake State Park,** some 35 miles from town. Hotel tax: 5%.

RESTAURANTS

Lobster, steamed or fried clams and fresh seafood are Maine specialties; try to attend a Maine clambake, and don't miss homemade blueberry pie. The following are all first class restaurants—**Old Port Tavern, F. Parker Reidy's, Seaman's Club, Hollow Reed, DiMillo's Lobster House, Amigo's** (Mexican) and **34 Exchange Street** for French fare, located in the Old Port Exchange. **Boone's** for seafood; **Roma Café** for continental cuisine; both moderate. Reasonably priced meals at **Valle's Steak House.** Other good restaurants include the **Art Gallery, Merry Manor** and **The Galley.** For Italian food, the **Village Café.** Many hotels have excellent dining rooms. Jazz spots include the **Horsefeathers** on Middle Street, **Bridgeway** in South Portland, and **Squire Morgan's** on Market Street. Top 40 music is offered at **Holiday Inn Downtown, Holiday Inn West,** and **Ramada Inn,** all in Portland, and the **Merry Manor** in South Portland. **The Landing** on Commercial Street and the **Executive Inn** on Congress

Street feature disco. The **Great New England Music Hall** offers rock and **Dock Fore** on Fore Street is a piano bar.

ARTS AND MUSIC

The **Portland Museum of Art** is open daily 10-5, Sunday 2-5, free. **Maine Historical Society** has objects of local historical interest; open all year, Monday to Friday 10-5; October through May. Saturday 10 to noon, free. Concerts are given by the **Portland Symphony Orchestra;** organ recitals on the Kotzschmar Organ in **City Hall Auditorium.** Nearby summer theaters at **Ogunquit, Brunswick, Monmouth,** and **Thomas Playhouse** in South Casco. **Portland Players, Portland Lyric Theater,** and **Children's Theater** give amateur productions the year round. The newest major attraction in Portland is the $8.5 million, 7,000 seat **Cumberland County Civic Center** (775-3458), located in the city's downtown section, which has featured major country-western and rock concerts, ice-shows, big-time boxing matches, hockey, and the **Boston Pops** orchestra. The center is also home to the **Maine Mariners**—a Philadelphia Flyers farm club—which captured the American Hockey League Championships in 1977-78 and 1978-79. For ticket information, call 775-3458. A similar, but smaller facility is the **Augusta Civic Center,** in Augusta. The **Profile Theater,** professional group, presents regular dramatic productions throughout the year in Portland.

SHOPPING

Stores remain open until 5:30 Tuesday, Wednesday, Friday and Saturday; open Monday and Thursday until 9. **Maine Mall** in South Portland is open every day and evening except Sundays. One of Portland's most attractive sight-seeing and shopping areas is the **Old Port Exchange,** near the waterfront, which is now a bustling center of shops, studios, and restaurants. The new $8 million, 350,000 square-foot **Lewiston Mall** has some 50 specialty shops. Lewiston is 34 miles north of Portland, and is Maine's second largest city.

SPORTS

Harness racing at **Scarborough Downs** from late May to September. Parimutuel betting at all races. Stockcar races at **Beech Ridge Speedway,** weekends only. Portland has a municipal golf course and there are many other public and private courses in the vicinity. Tennis courts at **Deering Oaks Park.** Public deep-sea fishing boats leave Portland for daily runs; boats are available on charter. **Sebago Lake,** 21 miles northwest, is known for landlocked salmon and trout. Good hunting is found in southern Maine for small game. Ocean swimming is available at many beaches to the north and south of the city. Maine ranks among the top four ski areas in the United States.

CALENDAR OF EVENTS

Yacht Races, July and August; **Maine Open Golf Championship,** August. Schoolboy sports are held at the **Portland Exposition Building,** which was the city's main sports center until the **Cumberland County Civic Center** was built in 1977.

WHERE TO GO NEARBY

Bradbury Mountain State Park, 22 miles northeast, beautiful views, hiking, trails, winter sports facilities. **Two Lights State Park** at Cape Elizabeth, picnic grounds with dramatic coastal scenery. **Crescent Beach State Park** at Cape Elizabeth, picnicking and bathing. **Sebago Lake State Park,** 30 miles northeast, known for lake bathing, boating, fishing, other sports. **Reid State Park,** 46 miles northeast, ocean bathing, trails, picnic areas, surf fishing. **Wolf Neck State Park** is just off Route 1 south of **Freeport,** 21 miles northeast of Portland. The park features shoreline hiking trails, salt marshes, and a bird sanctuary. Freeport is the home of L. L. Bean, world famous sporting goods mail order firm.

ACADIA NATIONAL PARK

The park, located 156 miles northeast of Portland and 47 miles southeast of Bangor, encompasses **Mount Desert Island, Schoodic Peninsula,** facing the island across **Frenchman Bay;** and on **Isle au Haut,** reached by mail boat from Stonington, Connecticut. It offers a unique combination of natural resources with **Cadillac Mountain,** largest in the area, rising 1,532 feet above the sea, sandy beaches, woodlands, 5 large lakes, and numerous ponds and streams as well as the open ocean. It covers more than 65 square miles and is the home of land and water birds, deer, fox, and beaver. The park is open year round. Glorious foliage can be seen in September.

Try not to miss the view of the Atlantic and little boat-dotted bays, distant islands, and surf crashing below the pine hills from **Cadillac Mountain. Ocean Drive** is one of the world's most scenic highways. **Great Head** is a rocky headland with a spectacular plunge to the shore; **Thunder Hole** has incoming waves which sound like the slamming of a gigantic door; and **Spouting Horn** is a rock formation that often shoots surf skyward like a geyser. Also see **Jordan Pond House,** traditional restaurant for lobster and teatime popovers. **Abbe Museum of Archaeology,** local Indian relics; open 30 May to mid-September, free. **Nature Center,** natural history exhibits; open 10 May to 20 October, free. Sea cruises are accompanied by park naturalists who will explain the area's granite formation, its wildflowers, birds, animals and fish. Cruises include a stop at **Islesford Museum** on Little Cranberry Island. Hiking trails wander for nearly 150 miles across the park; conducted nature walks from 1 July to Labor Day. **Schoodic Point** is the only section of the park on the mainland, encircled by a cliff highway from which you get beautiful views anytime but especially dramatic ones after a storm. Isle au Haut, a completely untouched wilderness, offers boating and fishing in park lakes, license required, and from shorelike rocks and deep-sea fishing boats; inland swimming at **Echo Lake Beach** and **Sand Beach** below Great Head is fine for tanning, but the Atlantic is very cold here even in August.

Two campsites, two-week-stay-limit, are open 30 May to 1 October;

Situated off Maine's barren, rocky coastline, Portland Head Lighthouse continues to beam in sailors and fisherman.

for reservations, call 238-5000, toll free. There are several year-round motels in Bar Harbor and rambling Down East-style summer hotels in the little towns of **Northeast Harbor, Southwest Harbor** and **Sea Harbor,** where rates usually include all meals. Advance reservations imperative in July and August.

FURTHER STATE INFORMATION

Maine State Chamber of Commerce, 477 Congress Street, Portland, ME 04111; **Maine Publicity Bureau,** 142 Free St., Portland, ME 04102; Camping Information: **Maine Co-operative Campground Owners Association,** Stewart Street, Lewiston, ME 04240. **Greater Portland Chamber of Commerce,** 142 Free Street, Portland, ME 04101. National Parks: **Acadia National Park** (Superintendent), Hulls Cove, ME 04644.

Consulates in Portland: France, Italy, Norway, Panama, Sweden.

USEFUL TELEPHONE NUMBERS IN PORTLAND

Fire	911
Police	911
Ambulance	911
Pine Tree Legal Assistance	774-8211
Portland Chamber of Commerce	772-2811
Portland Public Library	773-4761
Pan Am Reservations	800-223-6260

Maryland

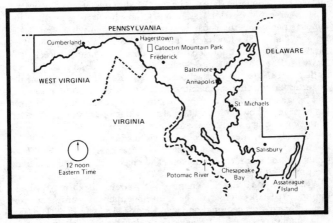

Area	10,577 square miles	Population	4,216,446
Capital	Annapolis	Sales Tax	4%

Weather	Jan	Feb	Mar	Apr	May	Jun	Jul	Aug	Sep	Oct	Nov	Dec
Av Temp (°C)	2	2	6	12	18	23	25	24	20	14	8	2
Days Rain/Snow	10	9	11	11	11	9	8	10	7	7	9	9

Maryland had things in its favor from the beginning. As Captain John Smith recorded after his exploration of Harford County in 1608: "Heaven and earth never agreed better to frame a place for man's habitation. Here are mountains, hills, plains, valleys, rivers and brooks all running most pleasantly into a Faire Bay compassed but for the mouth with fruitful and delightsome land." But though heaven and earth were agreed on how to frame the state, Maryland and its neighbors were not. The early history was fraught with all kinds of litigations that kept batteries of lawyers busy for decades. Possibly one reason people could devote so much time to legal matters was because everything else was going so smoothly. There were no serious troubles with the local Indians; the mild climate and rich soil speedily produced good crops, and the settlers, aware of what had caused trouble in other colonies in the New World, wisely followed different tactics.

Charles I granted the original charter for Maryland, a colony for persecuted Roman Catholics, to occupy all the territory between the Potomac River and the 40th parallel, the line upon which Philadelphia now stands. With admirable navigation the *Ark* and the *Dove* moved smartly up the **Potomac River** and 200 colonists stepped ashore on St Clement's

Island (now **Blakistone Island**) on 25 March 1634. The first permanent settlement was established at St Mary's, which served as the capital until 1694, when **Annapolis** was given the honor. By then, boundary disputes were arising with Virginia to the south and Pennsylvania to the north, and for generations the state was involved in disputes over its dimensions. Finally surveyors Charles Mason and Jeremiah Dixon established the famous straight lines that separate Maryland from Pennsylvania and Delaware (1763-67). The flow of the Potomac River, which begins in West Virginia, makes Maryland less than 2 miles wide near Hancock. The fuss with Virginia about the dividing line across Chesapeake Bay was settled in 1877 to the satisfaction of mapmakers, if not to that of the oyster fishermen from both states. In 1791 Maryland donated some of its acreage for the formation of the District of Columbia. This largesse has been repaid by the installation of many huge government agencies, which now bring added income to the state's coffers.

Although sometimes overlooked by visitors heading toward Washington, DC, Maryland has a lot to offer the vacationer and tourist. There is much to see that is old and famous, and much that is new and shaping the world of tomorrow.

WESTERN MARYLAND, composed of **Garrett, Allegheny, Washington,** and **Frederick** counties, is a beautiful, mountainous year-round resort area with activities centered on **Deep Creek Lake State Park.** The lake, with 65 miles of shoreline, provides swimming, boating, fishing, hunting, and camping. The highest point in Maryland is **Backbone Mountain** nearby, rising to 3,360 feet. On **Marsh Mountain,** 3,080 feet, is the famous **Wisp Ski Area,** where you can expect ideal snow conditions, artificial if necessary, from mid-December until well into March. The biggest concentration of motels is around the lake and at **Oakland.**

Cumberland, focal point of Allegheny County, is squeezed between the Potomac River and the Pennsylvania line, with mountains rising on three sides. Accommodations in Cumberland at **Algonquin Motor Inn, Best Western Braddock Motor Inn, Continental Motel,** averaging S$13-24/D$17-27, and the **Holiday Inn** at slightly higher prices. **Wills Creek** bisects the city; it was here that Fort Cumberland was built in 1754 as a British defense against the French and their Indian allies. George Washington's first military headquarters were in **Riverside Park.** Just west of town is the **Narrows,** a deep gorge through the **Allegheny Mountains,** a natural gateway to the Ohio Valley. The first major road westward was laid here in 1806; an original tollhouse still stands; today the route is a section of US 40, which extends from New Jersey to California. The nation's first railroad (Baltimore and Ohio) came to Cumberland in 1842. In 1850, the Chesapeake and Ohio Canal established its western terminus at Cumberland, and sections are still visible. Cumberland is characteristic of the nation's growth as it pivoted its focus from defending the East (as a colonial outpost) to exploring the West (as supply depot for overland commerce). East on route 40 in a state park is **Fort Frederick** (1756), where costumed militiamen recreate the drills of the Maryland Line soldiers of the Revolution on the last weekends of June, July and August.

Hagerstown, near the Pennsylvania border, where the *Hagers-Town Town and Country Almanack* has been published since 1797, is a modern industrial city with some handsome old buildings. Holiday Inn, Quality Inn, Sheraton Motor Inn, Ramada Inn, and Best Western Venice Motel are about S\$22-32/D\$26-40. The Jonathan Hager House (1739-40) was built directly above two springs as a combination home, fortress and fur trading post; a pioneer museum adjacent is open Tuesday to Sunday from 1 May to 1 October. The elegant Miller House has a 3-story spiral staircase; open daily except Monday. Valley Store in "Mansion House" has a unique collection of 19th-century country store stock and furnishings. The Antietam National Battlefield Site is at Sharpsburg, south of Hagerstown on MD 65. The battleground is virtually unchanged since 17 September 1862, when six generals were killed and 23,110 Union and Confederate soldiers were killed or wounded on the bloodiest day of the Civil War. Here Clara Barton (later founder of the American Red Cross) attended the wounded while Commissary Sgt. Wm. McKinley (later US President) served food and coffee to his men from Ohio. East of here are Crystal Grotto, a limestone cavern, and the crude stone tower that was the first Washington Monument, built on a mountain near Boonsboro in 1827. Nearby is Gathland State Park, with a monument erected in 1896 by George Alfred Townsend, youngest correspondent of the Civil War, as a memorial to his fellow newsmen.

Continuing south you will come to Frederick, which may be completely modern agriculturally and industrially, but it is still the pretty little churchspired city "Greenwalled by the hills of Maryland" that was described by John Greenleaf Whittier. His poem, *Barbara Frietchie* (sic), describes the legend that while leading his troops towards their destiny at Antietam, General "Stonewall" Jackson saw a Union flag waving from the dormered house at 156 West Patrick Street. When he ordered the flag shot down, the aged Barbara Fritchie shamed him by shouting out, "Shoot if you must, this old gray head, but spare your country's flag." The Barbara Fritchie Home and Museum is interesting; two famous visitors paused on a journey from Washington during World War II. While Roosevelt waited in the car, Churchill saluted the flag and recited all 60 lines of John Greenleaf Whittier's poem *Barbara Frietchie*. The home of Roger Brooke Taney (1799) contains furnishings and memorabilia of the Supreme Court justice who swore in seven Presidents including Lincoln. There is also a collection of the mementos of Francis Scott Key, author of the *Star-Spangled Banner*, the US national anthem; open daily in summer. Accommodations in Frederick at the Holiday Inn (622-5141, S\$32-34/D\$37-43) and Red Horse Motor Inn (622-0281, S\$21/D\$30). Three miles south of town is Monocacy Battlefield, where the Confederates lost their chance to capture Washington, DC.

Catoctin Mountain Park, a beautiful forested wilderness adjoining Camp David, the retreat of US presidents, is north of Frederick at Thurmont. At Emmitsburg, near the Pennsylvania line, you will find the Grotto of Lourdes, the first National Catholic Shrine in America and a replica of the French shrine and the Mother Seton Shrine. New Market, east of town on US 40, is a nationally famous antique center.

CENTRAL MARYLAND stands on the pleasantly rolling uplands of the **Piedmont Plateau**. All the highways seem to coverge on **Baltimore** but there are many attractions along the way. In the **NORTHWESTERN SECTION** is the **Shriver Homestead and Mill** at Union Mills on US 140. This rambling, 24-room house has been continuously occupied since 1797 by members of the family of Sargeant Shriver (Peace Corps director during the Kennedy administration); open daily May to November. **Westminster** is where rural free mail delivery began in 1899. The **Carroll County Farm Museum** recalls the hardworking days of 1850 when farms were entirely self-supporting. To the southwest of Baltimore is the International Gift Shop of the Church World Service Mission at **New Windsor**, where you can buy unusual items from all over the world. Northeast of Baltimore is **Aberdeen**, home of the vast Aberdeen Proving Ground, where the **Army Ordnance Museum** contains the world's largest collection of mobile and armored war weapons. Another 28 miles north on Route 213 is **Chesapeake City**, the western terminus of the deepwater Chesapeake and Delaware Canal. **Schaefer's Restaurant** at the water's edge of the canal, is a popular place to watch the year-round parade of ocean-going ships and pleasure craft.

The area between Washington, DC and Baltimore is an extension of both cities. Just 5 miles northwest of Washington is the **Clara Barton House** in Glen Echo, with the original furnishings and gardens that were designed by the founder of the American Red Cross; open daily except Mondays and holidays. The **Potomac River's Great Falls**, another 10 miles up the Potomac River, are a spectacular sight. The old **Chesapeake and Ohio Canal**, begun in 1828, bypasses the falls; the lovely canalside park all the way from Georgetown to the falls and the museum in the **Great Falls Tavern** (1828-30) are worth seeing. Farther north, just off Route 1270, is **Gaithersburg**, with the impressive buildings of the **National Bureau of Standards**, where both measurements and quality standards are established, and the National Geographical Society's handsome **Membership Center**. In the same suburban Maryland area is **Rockville**, the home of the famous **Olney** and **Shady Grove Theaters**. The **Beall-Dawson Mansion** (1815) gives a peek into how Maryland's upper crust lived in the 19th and early 20th centuries; open Tuesday to Saturday, afternoons.

SOUTHERN MARYLAND is where the earliest traditions of the state were founded, where the aristocratic passion for fast horses, pleasure boating and similar delights were financed by the big tobacco plantations. On the fringes of Washington, DC are **College Park**, home of the University of Maryland and the nearby **Agricultural Research Center** of the US Department of Agriculture. **Laurel** is world-famous for its great international horse race. In Laurel, stay at **Best Western Laurel East Motel** or **Howard Johnson's Motor Lodge**, averaging S$22-26/D$26-30, or at **Holiday Inn** at slightly higher rates. **Bowie** also has a great race track, and it is where American thoroughbred racing began. In Bowie, stay at **Holiday Inn** (464-2200, S$28-32/D$30-34). **Columbia**, a new city begun in the 1960s, is a fine experiment in town planning; the **Merriweather-Post Pavilion** hosts various cultural events, including the **Baltimore Symphony Orchestra** in the summer. **The Cross Key Inn** (730-3900, S$35-

48/D$42-56) just 9 miles east of Baltimore/Washington International Airport is a convenient place to stay.

Annapolis, founded in 1649 and named in honor of Princess Anne of England, is the state capital and a true treasure of early American life. The downtown area (1 square mile) is a national historic district with 300 years of architecture gracefully converted to modern uses. Historic Annapolis Inc, in the old Treasury building, has sightseeing information and guides on hand to conduct "walk in" tours daily, year round. Many of the 18th-century houses that line the quaint, narrow streets are open to the public during **Heritage Weekend,** the third weekend in October.

The **United States Naval Academy,** founded in 1845, is open to visitors daily March through November; tours leave from the Visitors' Center at Gate 1. You'll want to see **Bancroft Hall,** the world's largest dormitory, with the *Tecumseh* figurehead that midshipmen smear with warpaint before every Army-Navy football game. At noon everyday while school is in session more than 4,200 midshipmen march in formation into the mess hall. The **Chapel** contains the tomb of John Paul Jones, a naval hero of the Revolution. The **Naval Academy Museum** has a collection of ship models and items pertaining to the history of the US Navy. **June Week,** in late May to early June, is packed with activities to help celebrate graduation ceremonies.

Annapolis' elegant **State House** is the nation's oldest state capitol building (1772-79). It was also the first peacetime capital of the United States from 26 November 1783 to 13 August 1784. George Washington resigned his commission on 23 December 1783 in the lovely **Old Senate Chamber** where, a few weeks later, the Treaty of Paris brought the Revolution to an official end. Antique furnishings and portraits decorate the chambers and the **Flag Room** contains the only known remaining banner carried in a Revolutionary battle. **St John's College,** founded in 1696, has some fine old buildings and a tulip poplar, the 600-year-old Liberty Tree under which early colonists signed a peace treaty with the Susquehannock tribe in 1652. Other notable landmarks in Annapolis are the **Old Treasury Building** (1735); **Hammond-Harwood House Museum** (1774); **Chase-Lloyd House** (1774); **Paca House** (1768); **St Ann's Church,** established in 1692; **Reynolds Tavern** (1735), now the public library; and the **London Town Publick House** (1750), 5 miles south of town.

The **Hilton Inn** (268-7555, S$46-65/D$56-65) overlooks the harbor; **The Maryland Inn** (263-2641, S$18-27/D$23-30) is at Church Circle and Main Street; **Holiday Inn** (268-5031, S$30-32/D$34-36), **Howard Johnson Motor Lodge** (757-1600, S$24-27/D$28-34), and **Thr-rift Inn** (224-2800, S$30-34/D$37) are 3 miles southwest on US 301 and US 50.

North of Annapolis is the 7.7 mile **Chesapeake Bay Bridge,** which heads you towards the eastern shore beaches. **Solomon's Island,** where the Patuxent River joins the bay, is a fishing and boating center and site of the **Chesapeake Biological Laboratory.** In St Mary's County, between the Patuxent and the Potomac, is **St Mary's City,** where the first permanent settlement in Maryland was established. Monuments, excavations, and markers show what happened here in 1634, but if you're there on a Wednesday or Saturday you'll be delighted with the Amish Market at **Charlotte Hall,** where you can buy everything from antiques to home-made bread. Jousting matches are a big feature of the **County Fair** throughout the summer into late September. Near Piney Point on the Potomac is the **Harry Lundeberg School,** where "classrooms" are an exciting assortment of all kinds of watercraft; the school is sponsored by the Seafarer's International Union. From April to July there are rousing tobacco auctions, Monday to Friday, at **Upper Marlboro, Wayson's Corner, Waldorf, La Plata** and **Hughesville.** This whole section of Maryland is dotted with fine old homes of tobacco planters. **Sotterley,** on the Patuxent, southeast of Oakville, has been a working plantation since 1730; open daily June to October.

The **DELMARVA PENINSULA,** which Maryland shares with Delaware and Virginia, is Maryland's eastern shore; it is easily accessible but not yet flooded with sightseers. The wealthier inhabitants maintain smart estates and live a pleasant routine of riding, shooting, boating, and house parties. Crusty "watermen" who live in ancient villages along the indented bay go out in a great variety of craft in search of oysters, crabs, and all the other seafood. The bay is ideal for boating from early May through October.

Most visitors head south after crossing the **Bay Bridge,** more correctly known as the William Preston Lane, Jr, Memorial Bridge. Just off US 50 is **Wye Oak,** Maryland's official tree, the largest in the US and well over 400 years old. Close by is **Wye Mills,** a picturesque village representing authentic colonial America. The Mill produces the same kind of flour that was ground for Washington's troops at Valley Forge; it may be purchased in small quantities on a limited basis and the Mill is open for tours. **Easton** is picturesque and full of antique shops. The **Holiday Inn** and **Tidewater Hotel** are about S\$20-30/D\$26-34, while the **Easton Manor Inn** is slightly less expensive. The **Old Friends Third Haven Meetinghouse** (1682) is where William Penn often attended services; open daily by request, contact resident of the grounds, tel: 822-4606. Little roads lead eastward to wispy peninsulas deeply indented with bays and inlets. **St Michaels** is delightful; they still ring the Ship Carpenter's Bell three times a day in St Mary's Square, and the city's twisty streets are lined with weathered 17th- and 18th-century houses with gingerbread-trimmed galleries. The **Chesapeake Maritime Museum** preserves historic ships and relics of the old days on the bay. St Michaels' **Crab Claw** restaurant overlooks the harbor. **Oxford** is now a yachting center but it was an international shipping port in the 17th and 18th centuries; dine at the **Robert Morris Inn,** former home of the financier of the American Revolution. The **Choptank River** in Talbot County is a favorite spot for duck hunters. Across the mouth of the Choptank is **Cambridge,** a deep-water port which holds a **Sailing Regatta** in July, **Power Boat Regatta** in late July or early August, and boating just for the fun of it all summer long. Among many wildlife sanctuaries in the sea is the **Blackwater National Wildlife Refuge.** Probably one of the oldest churches in the US still in use is **Old Trinity Church** (1675, restored), 8 miles southeast of Cambridge.

Salisbury, largest city on the eastern shore, is a commercial center and host of the **National Indoor Tennis Championship Tournament** in February. Northwest of town is one of the boundary stones of the **Mason-Dixon Line** bearing the coat of arms of Lord Baltimore and Wm Penn. These stones established the traditional line between North and South during the Civil War. In Salisbury, accommodations at **Best Western Statesman Hotel, Holiday Inn, Howard Johnson's Motor Lodge,** and **Quality Inn** average S$20-30/D$24-36. South of Salisbury is the village of **Princess Anne,** with many beautiful old buildings; the **Olde Princess Anne Days** festival draws large crowds in October. **Crisfield,** Maryland's largest seafood processing center, is also a yachting town. If the feeling of salt air and an atmosphere detached from the 20th century appeals to you, take the excursion offered by the passenger ferry from Crisfield to the 300-year-old fishing villages on Smith Island. In spring, summer and early fall the boat sets sail daily at 12:30 pm arriving at the island at about 1:40 pm. An island tour including a family-style dinner at one of the islander's homes is part of the excursion, and the boat returns to the mainland at 4:05 pm. arriving at Crisfield at 5:15 pm. **Tangier Island,** in Virginia's share of the bay, is also reached by ferry from Crisfield. Northeast of the town on MD 667 is the **Rehobeth Presbyterian Church** (1705), the first of its denomination in America. Farther north is **Pocomoke City** on the river with a strangely tropical air. **Twin Towers Motel** (957-2111, S$13-19/D$19-25), **Holiday Inn** (957-3000, S$25-27/D$32-35), and **Quality Inn** (957-1300, S$21-28/D$24-34) provide accommodations. The **Annual National Bass Round-Up** is held from 1 May through October, and the **Annual Pocomoke River Crappie Contest** is waged from 1 April to 15 May. **Snow Hill,** where the Pocomoke River is non-tidal, is a great center for fresh-water fishing; see the strange historic relics in the **Julia Purnell Museum** and visit the impressive ruins of the **Nassawango Iron Furnace** erected in the 1820s. Now you are almost at **Ocean City,** which has a year-round population of less than 1,500, yet can accommodate 200,000 visitors in summer. The sand beach is 10 miles long, there's a 3-mile boardwalk lined with all kinds of amusements, and there is an endless parade of resort hotels where high season rates operate from about mid-June through Labor Day, reduced rates in spring and autumn; nearly all hotels are closed from November through March. Ocean City is famous for its deep-sea fishing, which is good nearly all the year. South of Ocean City is the **Assateague Island National Seashore** with conducted walks and demonstrations in summer; wild ponies roam the dunes.

City To Visit

BALTIMORE

The earliest settlers arrived here in 1634; in 1649 the Religious Toleration Act was passed, making Baltimore and Maryland unique as places with freedom of worship. Incorporated as a city in 1797, Baltimore did not begin to grow until 1827 when the Baltimore and Ohio Railroad was chartered. It was one of the few cities in the country where the allegiance of the people was divided between the North and South during the Civil War. The city has the salty flavor of a seaport, the bustle of an industrial area, and the dignity of a financial center. The deep-water port—on Chesapeake Bay—is the principal East Coast shipping point for coal, grain, and spice, and an important center in the nation's maritime trade. The Bay itself is almost 200 miles in length and its shorelines encompass a variety of settlements from small fishing villages to near deserted creeks where herons home, small harbors, and large, elegant stately homes of mansions and palaces set amid lushly landscaped grounds and of course, Annapolis, home of the US Naval Academy and much much more. The waters of the Bay are a home away from home for a vast confraternity of sailing folk, have generated a number of locally designed sailboats including the Chesapeake Sharpie, and numerous ships' architects and boat builders are to be found ashore. It is a city of established wealth and of world-famous educational and cultural institutions. Population: 800,000; metropolitan population 2,164,000.

WHAT TO SEE

Follow the **Star-Spangled Banner Trail** to major historic sites: **Fort McHenry**, where Francis Scott Key wrote words of *The Star Spangled Banner*, inspired by the flag flying over the fort during the 25-hour bombardment by the British; **Flag House**, a museum; **Shot Tower**, built in 1829; **George Washington Monument**; the home of **Edgar Allan Poe**, in which the author lived during the 1830s. Interestingly, he revisited the city in 1849, staying just long enough to die and be buried at the nearby **Westminster Presbyterian Church Cemetery**. His home is open Saturday, 1-4; **Baltimore Ohio Transportation Museum** with a unique collection of railroad locomotives and memorabilia dating from 1829; the Baltimore Inner Harbor, where you see the *USS Constellation*, launched in 1797 as the first ship in the US Navy; **Johns Hopkins Hospital**; and **Baltimore Civic Center.** Two harbor tours are offered, one 30-minute excursion up river to Fort McKinley on the *Defender* at $4 adults, $2 children, and a 90-minute river excursion on the *Patriot*, at $4 adults, $2 children. Outstanding among the educational institutions are the **University of Maryland**, which includes the oldest dental college in the United States and the **Johns Hopkins University** and its world renowned medical school. Other establishments include **Loyola College, Notre Dame of Maryland, St Mary's Seminary, Goucher College** for women, **Morgan State College,** and **St John's College** in nearby Annapolis. **The Peabody Institute and Conservatory of Music** has a magnificently designed library, and offers free noon concerts on Wednesdays during semesters (call 837-0600 for information). The **Maryland Historical Society** has some excellent examples of 18th- and 19th-century clothing, furniture, and silver, while at **Lexington Market**—an historic and colorful indoor market since the 1780s—you can experience the continuing bustle and hustle of individual entrepreneurs and merchants, with more than 100 kiosks, stores, boutiques, and shops. Take a break at **John W. Faidley Seafood** to sample the largest oysters to be had in the world; market closed Sundays. The **Washington Monument,** the original and completed in 1829, provides a superb bird's eye view of the city and harbor that is worth the effort of climbing the more than 200 steps to the top—no elevator, but good exercise. Baltimore also has some fine recreational areas. **Druid Park Zoo** is an outstanding collection of 1,000 specimens from all the world; open daily 10-4:30. **Sherwood Gardens** is open to the public during the spring. Other parks are **Gwynns Falls, Patterson, Carroll,** and **Clifton.**

City Hall, a charming yet impressive example of Renaissance architecture, was completed in the 1870s and underwent extensive renovation for its 100th birthday in 1975. The result has been the preservation of the best of what was old so that inside it's a pleasing blend of ancient and modern, while the exterior was left alone-that is, excepting the gold leaf which now adorns the cupola. If City Hall represents some of Baltimore's best from the past, the splendid modernity of **Charles Center** with its skyscrapers and plazas—and the downtown business area—the **Peabody Library** and the internationally acclaimed **Johns Hopkins University** and medical complex plus the national heritage of **Fort McHenry,** provide some of the best examples of American architecture in combining form with function over the years. Charles Center is an essentially integrated 22-acre development that combines business accommodations and luxury apartments with piazzas, fountain displays, and overhead walkways. **One Charles Center** is one of the better known (and more photographed) of the buildings in this area, being a soaring 24-story tower of bronze-tinted glass designed by the renowned L. Mies van der Rohe. Also of interest is the futuristic **Morris Mechanic Theater,** designed by John M. Johansen, while **Hopkins Plaza** features concerts by the Baltimore Symphony Orchestra (resident conductor Sergiu Comissiona) and the **Civic Center** hosts everything from trade shows to hard rock.

ACCOMMODATIONS

Baltimore Hilton Inn (653-1100, S$36-46/D$46-54) in Charles Center, pool; **Lord Baltimore Hotel** (539-8400, S$39-48/D$49-58), 1 block from Civic Center, true Maryland cuisine: **Holiday Inn-Downtown** (685-3500, S$48 up/D$57 up), across from Civic Center; and **Sheraton Inn-Johns Hopkins** (k675-6800, S$32-45/D$38-55), 15 minutes from shopping and financial districts, across from Johns Hopkins Hospital. Numerous motels on highways into the city, including the **Cross Keys Inn** (532-6900, S$42-50/D$52-60) off I-83 at Village of Cross Keys; Holiday Inn at 12 locations including one at the airport; **Howard Johnson's,** one at I-695 (Beltway) exit 15 and one at airport; **Marriots Hunt Valley Inn,** (666-7000, S$64-76/D$76-88) at I-83 and Shawan Road; **Meushaw's Motor Inn,** at I-695 exit 17; **Quality Inn West,** at I-695 exit 15; and **Warren House,** 1 mile south of I-695 exit 20. **International Hotel** (761-7700, S$60-85/D$72-97) is only 3 minutes from the airport with free bus service. Also at **Colony 7 Motor Inn, Holiday Inn,** and **Howard Johnson's Motor Lodge,** which average S$29-51/D$34-57. Nearest camping site is in **Patapsco State Park,** which also has various recreational facilities. Hotel Tax: 4-9%.

RESTAURANTS

Maryland fried chicken, terrapin soup or stew and steamed hard-shell crabs are "musts" for the gourmet. **Brass Elephant,** northern Italian cuisine in a 19th-century robber baron's princely town house; **Peerce's,** elegant and good; **Danny's,** *Holiday* award winner, great for roast beef and steaks; **Marconi,** where the specialty of this Franco-Italian house is filet of sole prepared in delightfully tasteful and inventive ways; **Tio Pepe Restaurant,** excellent Spanish cuisine; and **Haussner's,** for draft Bavarian beer and authentic *Kloesse* (German potato dumplings), a big place with a menu to match its size, features hearty German dishes and seafood; **Ikaros,** Greek. Other very good places to dine include **Eager House; Chiapparelli's, Valeggias,** and **Sabatinos** for Italian dishes; **Circle One,** French-American cuisine specializing in *flambé* dishes, steak, and prime ribs; the **Pimlico Hotel** restaurant, near the track, is a long-time favorite for seafood and steak lovers. Some restaurants close Sundays or Mondays.

ENTERTAINMENT

Try the **Grog Shop** at Lord Baltimore Hotel or **Circle One** in the Holiday Inn-Downtown. East Baltimore Street is famous for its "Block"—a street of bars which tends to be a little rough at night.

ARTS AND MUSIC

Baltimore Museum of Art, outstanding Oriental and French modern art, open Tuesday to Friday 11-5, Saturday 10-5, Sunday 1-5; free. **Peale Museum,** historical collection; open Tuesday to Friday 10:30-4:30, Saturday and Sunday 1-5; free. **Maryland Historical Society,** collection of antique furniture and library of Americana; open Tuesday to Saturday 11-4; Sundays 1-4 (closed Sundays, July and August), free. **Walters Art Gallery,** one of the country's greatest collections of art of all periods; open Monday 1-5, Tuesday to Saturday 11-5, Sunday 2-5; free. **Lyric Theater,** weekly musical programs. Baltimore was the first US city to sponsor a municipal orchestra with a full season of programs. The city also has a **Civic Opera Company. Morris Mechanic Theater,** with distinctive modern architecture, offers Broadway productions; **Center Stage** is Baltimore's professional repertory theater. **Painters Mill Music Fair** and other dinner-theater complexes present concert artists and Broadway musical shows.

SHOPPING

Most stores are open from 10 to 5:30; Thursday evenings until 8. Major department stores downtown include Hecht Company, Stewart's, Hamberger's, and Hutler's.

SPORTS

Ice hockey and World Team tennis are held at the **Baltimore Civic Center.** Professional major league baseball is played by the **Baltimore Orioles,** pro football by the **Colts,** pro soccer by the **Comets** at **Memorial Stadium;** college football by the Navy and University of Maryland. There are four race tracks—**Bowie** meets from 1 January through mid-March, **Pimlico** mid-March through the third week in July (the Preakness is run on the third Saturday in May), **Timonlum** from the third week in July through the first week in September, **Bowie** from the second week in September through the third week in October, **Laurel** from the last week in October to the end of December. There is harness racing at **Ocean Downs** during the summer season. Saltwater fishing in **Chesapeake Bay** and at **Ocean City**; freshwater fishing at **Bush** and **Miles Rivers.** Wildlife is plentiful in Maryland, with hunting for wild turkeys, squirrels, deer, rabbit, and ducks. Swimming at Chesapeake Bay beaches. Golf at numerous public and private courses; there are many tennis courts in the vicinity.

CALENDAR OF EVENTS
Maryland House and Garden Pilgrimage, April to May; **Preakness Festival Week,** May; **June Week** at Annapolis, Navy graduation; **Baltimore City Fair,** September; *Oktoberfest,* October. Special local holidays are Maryland Day, 25 March, and Defender's Day, 12 September.

WHERE TO GO NEARBY
Gambrill State Park, 54 miles away; beautiful scenery and trails. **Elk Neck,** 53 miles away; fishing, water sports. **Patapsco State Park,** 10 miles away; waterfalls, picnic facilities. **Fort Frederick State Park,** 92 miles away; museum, recreational facilities. Other parks include **Gathland, Wye Oak, Fort Tonolway, Sandy Point,** and **Dans Mountain. Ocean City,** about 130 miles southeast, offers beach cottages, swimming, deep-sea fishing. **Deep Creek Lake,** 185 miles west, has tennis, swimming, boating, hunting, fishing, golf, camping.

FURTHER STATE INFORMATION
Pan Am office, 6755 Elkridge Road, Baltimore, MD 21240; **Division of Tourist Development,** 2525 Riva Road, Annapolis, MD 21401; **Fish and Wildlife Administration,** PO Box 231, Annapolis, MD 21404; **Baltimore Promotion and Tourism Office,** 110 West Baltimore Street, Baltimore, MD 21201.

Consulates in Baltimore: Argentina, Belgium, Bolivia, Colombia, Costa Rica, Denmark, Dominican Republic, Ecuador, El Salvador, Finland, France, Great Britain, Guatemala, Honduras, Italy, Netherlands, Nicaragua, Norway, Panama, Senegal, Sweden, Tunisia, Uruguay, Venezuela.

USEFUL TELEPHONE NUMBERS IN BALTIMORE
Ambulance	396-1111
Police	222-3333
Fire	685-1313
Poison Control	528-7701
Providence Hospital Inc.	225-2000
St Agnes Hospital	368-6550
Legal Aid Bureau	539-5340
Chamber of Commerce	539-7600
Tourist Information	752-8632
Pan Am Reservations	685-2115

Massachusetts

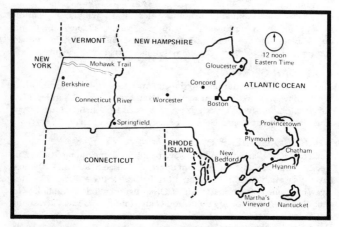

Area	8,257 square miles	**Population**	5,728,288
Capital	Boston	**Sales Tax**	5%

Weather

	Jan	Feb	Mar	Apr	May	Jun	Jul	Aug	Sep	Oct	Nov	Dec
Av Temp (°C)	−1	−1	3	9	15	20	23	22	19	13	7	1
Days Rain/Snow	12	11	12	12	11	10	9	10	9	9	12	11

In the late autumn of 1620 a tiny shipload of English settlers was making for a point south of the Hudson River. It is interesting to speculate what might have happened had the ship not been diverted by a storm, for it was the *Mayflower*, which stopped briefly at the tip of Cape Cod, then continued to Plymouth where the Pilgrims founded the first permanent English colony north of Virginia, the Massachusetts Bay Colony. Their provisional instrument of government, the "Mayflower Compact," formed the basis of American Democracy, and from that time no other colony was to play a more important role in the formation of the United States of America.

The Boston Massacre in 1730 and the Boston Tea Party in 1773 were landmarks on the way to the American Revolution, which began in 1775 in Concord and Lexington. In the same year General George Washington took command of the Continental Army in Cambridge, and a year later he captured Boston in the first major American victory of the war.

After the Revolution Massachusetts became and remains a key industrial state, as well as the home of the authors of a great deal of classic

American literature. This includes Thoreau's *Walden*, Melville's *Moby Dick*, Louisa May Alcott's *Little Women*, Longfellow's *Wayside Inn*, Hawthorne's *House of Seven Gables*, Whittier's *Snow Bound*, Emerson's *Essays*, William Cullen Bryant's *Thanatopsis* and Mary Baker Eddy's *Science and Health*. The state's poets include Emily Dickinson, Amy Lowell, James Russell Lowell, Robert Lowell, Edna St. Vincent Millay, Edward Arlington Robinson and e.e. cummings. With its literary traditions and such august institutions as the Massachusetts Historical Society and the lavishly sponsored Boston Symphony Orchestra, the state is at the cultural heart of America.

Massachusetts has also contributed, in numbers far out of proportion to its size, some of America's most distinguished historians, educators, statesmen, lawyers, social reformers and scientists. And, with its extraordinarily varied topography, the state offers the visitor a large choice of vacation activities.

The small New England town of **PLYMOUTH** (population 18,606) along the South Shore still reflects much of the quiet colonial charm and quaintness of the early America that followed the landing of the Pilgrims. Exhibits are open April through November and tickets may be purchased at the Ticket to History booth, on State Pier, open daily 9-5. They sell a combination ticket only for the *Mayflower* ship and the Plantation, ages 3-13, $3, over 13, $5.75. **Plymouth Rock,** beside the harbor on Water Street. **Plimoth Plantation,** 3 miles south, contains **Pilgrim Village,** a replica of a 1627 community, complete with 12 houses, a fort, and meetinghouse. Costumed guides re-enact the pilgrim's daily life. The **Indian Campsite,** within the Plantation, is open only mid-June through Labor Day. *Mayflower II,* at the State Pier on Water Street, is a replica of the original ship which brought the Pilgrims to America. Just north of Plymouth Rock on Sandwich Street, the **Howland House** and **Harlow Old Fort House** are open. The **Jenney Mill** on Spring Lane is a replica of Plymouth's first gristmill and grinds corn by water power; a candle-making shop is also on the premises (open daily May-Dec, admission free). Be sure to see also the **Cranberry World Museum** (free). The *Cape Cod Princess* leaves **State Pier,** crossing **Cape Cod Bay** with a 3-hour stopover in **Provincetown,** daily, weather permitting, May through October; if you prefer, stay on board at Provincetown and continue for 3 hours of whale-watching. **Miles Standish State Forest** has 13,000 acres with swimming, boating, fishing, camping and snowmobiling. Motels in Plymouth include: **Governor Bradford Motor Inn** (746-6200, S$28-38/ D$32-58) and **Governor Carver** (746-7100, S$32-46/D$36-56). Popular area restaurants are: **Bert's** and **McGrath's,** overlooking the bay; **Currier's, Ernie's,** and **Mayflower Seafoods,** on the dock. Eat at the **Sandwich and Deli Shop** at the corner of North and Main Streets, or take out cold cuts.

Miles Standish and John Alden were among the party who came to the **Duxbury** area in search of more farmland. **Alden House** was built in 1653 by Jonathan Alden, son of John and Priscilla (open daily 9:30-5 June-Sept, admission charged). The 130-foot-high **Standish Monument,** with an observation tower, stands in **Standish Reservation,** a recreational area south of the city; picnicking May through mid-October. Duxbury had America's first annual county fair in 1638. The **King Caesar House** is an elegant example of Federal period architecture (open end of June-Sept Tues-Sun, admission charged). **Fiddler's Green Restaurant** is known for its Sunday buffet and home baking. Farther north along the coast, **Scituate** is a historic town and established coastal resort. **Cohasset** is probably best known for the **South Shore Music Circus,** featuring professional players in Broadway musicals and comedies; late June through early September. **Hugo's Lighthouse,** overlooking the harbor, is an award-winning restaurant. The **Red Lion Inn** offers dining in a 1704 house. **Quincy,** at the northern end of the shore, near Boston, was the home of the Adams family, which included two presidents and John Hancock, first signer of the *Declaration of Independence.* The **Adams National Historical Site** includes a 1731 house with original furnishings mid-April to mid-November, 9-5, cost 50¢, under 16 free; the **John Adams and John Quincy Adams Birthplaces,** where the second and sixth presidents of the US were born, open mid-April to mid-October, 9-5.

Continuing south inland, **South Carver** is the largest cranberry-producing town in the world. The miniature **Edaville Railroad,** the only 2-foot gauge railroad in the country, with antique locomotives, coaches, parlor car, and open sightseeing cars, takes visitors on a 5½-mile trip through the cranberry bogs. A museum contains an antique toy train collection and a 19th-century store. The train ride alone costs $2 for ages 3-12, $4 above 12; a combo ticket that includes the museum is $2.50/$5.

New Bedford, in the southeast corner of **BRISTOL COUNTY,** is the city that whaling built and was once the greatest whaling port in the world. The **Old Dartmouth Historical Society and Whaling Museum** has an accurate half-scale replica of a square-rigged whaler and visitors are welcome aboard (open 9-5 Mon-Sat, 1-5 Sun, adults $1.50/children 75¢). You can follow the **Moby Dick** trail on a marked tour. Annual **Whaling City Days** feature a 3-day celebration in late June with a blessing of the fleet, a parade, and a flea market. **Buttonwood Park** has a botanical garden and zoo. There is swimming at the foot of **Hazelwood Park** and **East Beach.** Saltwater fishing in **Buzzards Bay** and freshwater fishing in local ponds. **Fall River,** the other major city in the area, is probably best known as the scene of the Lizzie Borden axe murder trial in the 1890s. The battleship *Massachusetts* has been permanently enshrined here in Battleship Cove as the state war memorial; also visit the **Marine Museum** (combination ticket, 13 and older, $4, 12 and under $2; open Mon-Fri 9-4:30, Sat-Sun 10-5). Eat in the Wardroom of the *Massachusetts* or dine at the **Gangplank Restaurant** overlooking Battleship Cove. Heading north, **Taunton** has a popular dog racing track.

Continuing north, bypassing Boston on MA 128, you come upon **Lexington** in **MIDDLESEX COUNTY.** The **Old Buckman Tavern,** on the Lexington village green, vintage 1700, was the rendezvous of the Minutemen. **Munroe Tavern,** built in 1695, served as the British headquarters during the Revolutionary War. A statue of the Minutemen's commander, Captain Parker, stands on Lexington common where the first line of resistance was formed against the British. At the **Hancock-Clarke House** (1698) John Hancock and Samuel Adams were awakened by Paul Revere with the news of the British advance. The three houses are open 19 April through October, 10-5 daily, 1-5 Sundays; cost, adults $1 for each house or $2.25 for a combo ticket, children 16 and under 25¢. For further information as well as guides, visit the **Lexington Visitors' Center** (July-Nov, 9-5; rest of year 10-4). Just west of Lexington, in **Concord,** is the famous **Old North Bridge** where, on that historic day in April 1775, "the embattled farmers stood and fired the shot heard round the world." Here too is peaceful **Walden Pond,** immortalized by Henry David Thoreau. **The Old Manse** was home to Ralph Waldo Emerson and Nathaniel Hawthorne (open daily June through October, except Tuesday, 10-4:30, Sun 1-4:30; admission adults $2, ages 11-16 $1, 10 and under 75¢.) Louisa May Alcott lived for many years at **Orchard House,** where she wrote *Little Women* (open daily early Apr-early Oct 10-4:30, Sun 1-4:30, adults $2, ages 6-12 $1). At **Sleepy Hollow Cemetery,** you can visit the graves of Emerson, Thoreau, the Alcotts, Hawthorne, and other prominent Concordians. **Grand Meadows National Wildlife Refuge,** 1 mile north on the banks of the Concord River, has excellent nature trails along the refuge dikes. **Walden Pond State Reservation,** 1½ miles south, consists of about 150 acres surrounding the famous 64-acre pond; picnicking, boating, and fishing. Also visit the **Antiquarium House Museum** which has 15 rooms, including a replica of Emerson's study and equipment Thoreau used at Walden Pond (open daily 10-4:30, Sun 2-4:30, adults $2, children $1).

Longfellow's *Tales of Wayside Inn* were written about a 17th-century tavern in **Sudbury.** This historic and literary shrine has been restored and its rooms have been furnished with beautiful period pieces. Now called **Longfellow's Wayside Inn** (443-8846, S$20/D$25), it was originally opened around 1686 and is the oldest operating inn in the US. The charming restaurant features New England specialties. The grounds also include a gristmill with an operating water wheel and the school immortalized in the children's rhyme *Mary Had a Little Lamb.* On 19 April, each year, more than 200 local men in costume re-enact the 1775 march of the Sudbury Minutemen from the common to the Old North Bridge in Concord.

Still within Middlesex County, **Lowell** (30 miles north of Boston) was the birthplace of James McNeill Whistler. His portrait of his mother is the only American painting in the Louvre. The family home, built in 1823, is open September through June (2-4, adults $1, children 50¢). The **Speare House Restaurant** specializes in steak and Greek *souvlaki;* guests enter its medieval castle atmosphere across a moat. Lowell is the site of the **Lowell National Historical Park,** where old textile mills and some of the boarding houses of the "mill girls," showing the birth of the American Industrial Revolution, may be seen. A **Lowell Museum** with textile machinery and other mementoes of the period from the 1830s has been established. Within the city may also be seen the remnants of the old Lowell to Boston **Middlesex Canal,** at which horses along the banks pulled passengers and freight before the railroad era. **Groton** (pronounced *graht'n*), about 35 miles west of Lowell and a lovely colonial town, is the home of the **Groton School** and **Lawrence Academy,** two prominent boys' preparatory schools.

If you enter **ESSEX COUNTY** from the North Shore, the 85-foot tower in **High Rock Park,** in the center of **Lynn,** will afford you a marvelous view. Northwest of the city, **Lynn Woods,** on MA 129, is one of the largest city parks in the nation. **Swampscott** has been a popular summer resort outside Boston since the late 19th century. The **Mary Baker Eddy House,** where the Christian Science movement was founded in the late 1860s, is open mid-May through mid-October. Farther north along the shore, **Marblehead** stands on a hill overlooking the harbor. It was originally a fishing community and the narrow, crooked streets remain. **Fort Sewall,** at the harbor entrance, was built in 1742 and used through the Spanish-American War. The **Jeremiah Lee Mansion,** built in 1768, is a good example of Georgian architecture (open May 15-Oct 12, 9:30-4 Mon-Sat). The home of the local historical society, it contains the original furnishings. **King Hooper Mansion,** built in 1728, has been restored (open Tues-Sun, 1-4). Sailing races are held on weekends in the summer, capped by Marblehead's annual **Race Week,** the end of July. The **Atlantic** and the **Barnacle** are popular restaurants serving New England fare.

Salem is the home of Nathaniel Hawthorne, *The House of Seven Gables,* and the witchcraft persecutions of 1692. The town streets, squares, homes, museums, and waterfront still reflect its glorious past when it was a foremost US port. **Chestnut Street** is one of the world's most beautiful streets, lined with the former homes of wealthy Salem clipper captains and owners. Among the many historic houses are those built by Samuel McIntire. The **House of Seven Gables,** built in 1668, which inspired Hawthorne's novel, is open daily till 4:30, July to Labor Day. **Pioneers' Village** (open daily June-Nov, by appointment starting end of Oct), in Forest River Park, contains 12 buildings in a reproduced 1630 settlement including the **Governor's House** and blacksmith's forge. **Salem Maritime National Historic Site** (open daily till 7, July-Sept, till 5, rest of year) contains the old **Custom House** (admission free), built in 1819, where Hawthorne worked for three years as port surveyor. **Derby House,** built in 1761, is the oldest brick house in Salem and is furnished as one of the prosperous sea merchants' homes. The **Salem Witch Museum** dramatizes the witch hunts of the 1690s with a sight and sound presentation (open summer daily till 7:30, winter times vary). The **Essex Institute** offers one of the finest collections of local historical objects in the US (open Tues-Sat 9-4:30, Sun 2-5). For further information regarding Salem's sights contact Salem Chamber of Commerce, 18 Hawthorne Blvd., telephone 744-0004. Also the residents are proud of their historic past and celebrate **Heritage Days** for one week in mid-August. Accommodations in Salem at **The Coach House Inn** (744-4092, S$28-40/D$32-60) and **The Hawthorne Inn** (744-4080, S$20-32/D$32-38).

Farther north along the coast is **Beverly,** a popular summer resort

This half-scale reproduction of a whaler fascinates visitors at the Whaling Museum in New Bedford, MA, which was not so long ago the whaling capitol of the world.

where the **North Shore Music Theater** (tel: 922-8500) sponsors a 5-week **Shakespeare Festival** in April and May. Broadway musicals and comedies are performed in-the-round, late June through early September. Beverly's **Yankee Homecoming Week,** in early August, attracts visitors to its historic house tours, harbor cruises, sailboat races, and lobster festival. These homes include **Balch House,** one of the oldest wooden frame houses in the US, built in 1636, and **John Hale House,** erected in 1694 by Nathan Hale's great-grandfather, the town's first minister. **Cabot House,** 1781, now houses the Beverly Historical Society. All three houses are open mid-June to mid-Oct, Wed-Sat 10-4, Sun 1-4, admission adults $1, children 50¢. A combination ticket to see the houses is $3. Swimming at local parks and beaches; fishing, boating, and scuba-diving near **Glover's Wharf. Commodore Restaurant** offers colonial atmosphere, complete with an old mill wheel and lighthouse. The **Sword & Shield** has an open hearth and an Old English motif.

Gloucester, on **CAPE ANN,** was settled in 1623 and has been a famous fishing port since that time. A bronze statue of the *Gloucester Fisherman,* on the harbor, was erected as a memorial to the local fishermen lost at sea, said to total as many as 10,000 over the last three centuries. An annual memorial service is held at the statue the last Monday in May. A 4-day **St Peter's Fiesta,** sponsored by Italian-American fishermen, is held the weekend nearest to 29 June. Fireworks, a parade, the blessing of the fleet, and sports events highlight the well-attended festivities. **Hammond Castle,** built like a typical medieval structure, has pipe organ concerts during spring and summer (open daily except Jan 10-4, adults $3, children $1). Recommended motels are: **Captain's Lodge Motel** (281-2420, S$22-38/D$27-38) and **Twin Light Manor** (283-7500, S$28-46/D$32-48), both open year round; **Bass Rocks Motor Inn** (283-7600, S/D$34-56), overlooking the ocean, and **Rockaway House** 283-2592, S/D$22-50) are open May-Nov. **Captain Courageous** restaurant, on a cove with an excellent view of the harbor, is very popular locally. **Easterly Inn, Gloucester House** on the wharf, the **New Tavern,** and **The Surf** feature New England seafood menus. **The Rudder** is a converted fish-packing store with a dining porch overlooking the harbor. Try the **Raven** for an out-of-the-ordinary continental cuisine with a Middle Eastern touch.

The Gloucester summer resort region includes **Rockport,** the famous artists' colony near the tip of Cape Ann. The **Main Street, Dock Square,** and **Bearskin Neck** offer a wide choice of shopping and dining possibilities. It is also a quaint fishing village, and a weather-worn lobster house on a wharf has been named "Motif No. 1," designating it as the single most-popular subject of paintings in the US. Art galleries and studios dot the coast from **Eastern Point** southeast of Gloucester to **Annisquam.** The Rockport Art Association (open Mon-Sat 9:30-4:30), housed in the **Old Tavern** built in 1770, sponsors a tour of artists' studios and homes in July and the annual **Artist Costume Ball** in August. Also visit the **Paper House** at nearby Pigeon's Cove; built entirely from newspaper, with walls 215 thicknesses deep, its furnishings are also constructed of newspaper. Stay at **Peg Leg Inn** (546-2352, S/D$22-40), opposite the beach, restaurant has greenhouse dining and an ocean view; open year round. **Yankee Clipper Inn** (546-3407, S/D$60-65), terraced grounds overlooking the ocean, heated salt-water pool; **Ralph Waldo Emerson Inn** (546-6321, S$20-31/D$28-48); and **Seaward Inn** (546-6792, S$32/D$56-72) are open May-Oct. **Blacksmith Shop Restaurant**, overlooking the harbor, features Greek specialties. **Oleana-by-the-Sea** overlooks the ocean and features a Scandinavian-American menu.

To the west, **Ipswich** is naturally the home of the celebrated Ipswich clam and may possibly have more 17th-century houses than any other US town, claiming over 50 built before 1725. The **John Whipple House**, built in 1640, contains period furniture (open mid-April to November). The garden has a representative collection of medicinal herbs and plants. Nearby, the **John Heard House**, built in 1795, is furnished with Oriental pieces from the China sea trade (open May to mid-October). Hours for both houses are 10-5 Tues-Sat; 1-5 Sun; admission adults $2 for each house and $3 for a combination ticket. **Crane's Beach**, on the bay, is among the best on the Atlantic coast. **Jack Hackett's Lakeside Restaurant**, overlooking a lake, has a New England tavern atmosphere.

In northeast Massachusetts, **Newburyport**, at the mouth of the Merrimack River, gained its early prosperity from the shipping and shipbuilding industries. The great Federalist houses along High Street belonged to the successful shipowners and captains. **Tristram Coffin House** was built in the 1650s (open June-mid-Sept Tues, Thurs, weekends 1-5). The Historical Society is located in the 17-room **Cushing House**, built in 1808 (open May-Nov, Tues-Sat 10-4, Sun 2-5, adults $1.50, children 50¢). Plum Island, 6 miles southeast, is the site of the **Parker River National Wildlife Refuge**, which is open for year-round nature study, swimming, picnicking, and fishing. Beach plum and cranberry picking, late August through mid-October. Newburyport stages a **Yankee Homecoming** celebration during 9 days in late July-early August.

Salisbury State Beach Reservation includes an amusement center, fishing, boating, swimming, picnicking, and camping. The **John Greenleaf Whittier Home** (open March through December, Tues-Sat 10-4, admission adults $1, children 50¢), in Amesbury, contains the Garden Room where he wrote *Snow-Bound, The Barefoot Boy,* and other works. The poet lived here from 1836 until his death in 1892. The Whittier birthplace, described in *Snow-Bound,* is nearby in **Haverhill.**

The **Merrimack Valley Textile Museum**, in North Andover, traces textile manufacturing of 1750-1890, and has spinning demonstrations (open 9-5 except Mondays, adults $2, children $1). Local manufacturers in **Andover** tried to bypass the Japanese by growing their own mulberry trees to feed silkworms, but it didn't work and they had to settle for making woolens and rubber goods. Andover is best known for **Phillips Academy** for boys, the oldest incorporated school in the US, founded in 1778. **Abbot Academy,** the oldest incorporated school for girls in New England, was founded in 1829. **Boston Hill Ski Area** is four miles southeast of North Andover. **Andover Inn** (475-5903, S$30/D$37) is on the academy campus. **Beef 'N Bottle** and **Ivanhoe Room** both feature Old English tavern decor.

Continuing southeast, **Peabody** is the world's leading leather city. The American steel industry was founded in **Saugus** when the first ironworks were built here in 1646. The **Ironworks** contains the reconstructed blast furnace, forge, and mills (open daily 9-5, free). The **Ironmaster's House,** home of the first proprietor, stands just as it did in 1648. The national historic site is open April through October.

Entering central Massachusetts, **Leominster,** in northern **WORCES-TER COUNTY,** is the birthplace of "Johnny Appleseed," who traveled across the country planting apple orchards. **Johnny Appleseed Civic Day** is celebrated on the first Saturday in June. **Benjamin Hill Ski Area** is 7 miles to the east and **Pheasant Run Ski Area** is 2 miles west. To the east, **Harvard** was the locale of two idealistic communities. A Shaker Society was founded here in the late 18th century, and Bronson Alcott attempted to establish a New Eden at **Fruitlands** farmhouse (open June-Oct, Tues-Sun 1-5, admission adults $2, children 7-17 50¢, under 7 free). The restored colonial kitchen and items belonging to the Alcott family are on view. The **Old Shaker House** displays handicrafts and products. Princeton has an exceptional **Antique Auto Museum.**

Worcester, the principal city in central Massachusetts, is a cultural and educational center. The **Higgins Armory Museum** has the best collection of medieval armor in the US (open daily except Mon, free). The **Worcester Art Museum** includes a complete room from a 12th-century Benedictine priory brought over from France, as well as Greek and Roman pottery and sculpture (open Tues-Sat, Sun 2-6, free). There's also a **Science Center,** with a planetarium and oceanarium (open Mon-Fri 10-5, Sat-Sun 12-5, admission adults $2.50, children and senior citizens $1.50). Worcester is the home of **Clark University** and **College of the Holy Cross. Elm Park** was the first land set aside for a public park in the US. The city's annual **Music Festival** is the country's oldest, founded in 1859, and features world-renowned symphony orchestras and guest soloists in five concerts in late August. There's **Holiday Inn** (791-2291, S$36-50/D$41-50) and **Howard Johnson's** (791-5501, S$31-36/D$40-43). **Putnam and Thurston** has been a Worcester dining landmark since 1858; **Franklin Manor** is also popular. **Spencer State Forest,** south on MA 31, contains the **Howe Homestead** and **Cobblestone Monument.** Elias Howe developed the first practical sewing machine in 1845, and his uncles invented the truss bridge and spring bed.

Farther southwest toward **Sturbridge, Old Sturbridge Village** (open daily 9:30-5:30, admission adults $7, children $3) takes visitors back to a complete New England country town in the early 19th century. Surrounding the peaceful village green, more than 38 buildings include typical homes of the time, a gristmill and herb farm, blacksmith shop, and printing office. The village store is filled with genuine 19th-century goods and all the buildings house the tools, furniture, and homespun textiles that were once used or made there. Craftsmen and guides, in period costume, show how people lived, worked, and traded. The craftsmen demonstrate weaving, printing, spinning, and making pottery, pewter, tin, and cabinets, as well as the family arts of cooking over a fireplace, herb gardening, and candle-dipping. Farm animals work in the village just as they did in the old days; horses draw carts for visitors to ride. The village includes dining and picnic areas. Suggested motels include: **Best Western American Motor Lodge** (347-9121, S$22-30/D$30-40); **Carriage House** (347-9000, S$33/D$43), on a lake, heated pool; **Publick House Inn** (347-3313, S$20/D$30-40), colonial atmosphere, New England menu; **Sturbridge Orchard Inn** (347-9555, S$26/D$33), heated pool; **Treadway Motor Inn** (347-3391, S$26-34/D$30-38); **Quality Colonial Motel** (347-3306, S$20-28/D$24-32); and **Sheraton Sturbridge Inn** (347-7393, S$25-35/D$33-48). **North Oxford** is the birthplace of Clara Barton, founder of the American Red Cross. **Webster** is a water-ski center with the biggest natural lake in Massachusetts. It has an Indian name—Lake Chargoggagogmanchaugagogchaubunagungamaung. Translated, that means, "You fish on your side, I fish on my side, nobody fish in the middle."

HAMPSHIRE and **HAMPDEN COUNTIES** in the western part of the state, comprise Massachusetts' "Pioneer Valley." The **Connecticut River** is the longest river in New England and has inspired numerous artists and writers. Mark Twain wrote *Tom Sawyer* and *Huckleberry Finn* on its river banks. Fossilized footprints of dinosaurs have been discovered here. The counties contain lively cities and quiet woods where wild deer still roam. **Springfield**, on the Connecticut River, was settled in 1636 and became an active trading post. Today the town boasts over 200 industrial plants and a fine cultural center. The **Library and Museums Center** (open Tues-Sat 1-5, Sun 2-5, free), occupying a quadrangle at State and Chestnut Streets, includes the **Museum of Fine Arts,** with one of the country's leading Oriental art collections, and a **Science Museum,** with an aquarium and planetarium. **Storrowton** contains a group of reconstructed New England buildings—a country store, schoolhouse, meetinghouse, and tavern. The **National Basketball Hall of Fame** (open daily 10-5, admission adults $2.50, children 6-15 $1) is on the Springfield College campus. Basketball was invented here; it got its name from the peach basket and ball used in the original game. The facilities at **Forest Park** include tennis, a zoo, picnicking; also **Brimfield State Forest** and **Granville State Forest** for swimming, fishing, and hunting. The **Eastern States Exposition** is the biggest industrial-agricultural fair in the east, held 10 days in mid-September. The **Storrowton Theater,** on the exposition grounds, offers musical shows in-the-round mid-June through mid-September; **Stage West,** on the same grounds, offers repertory theater, mid-November through late-April. There are many hotels and motels in the Springfield area. Among the motels are **Marriott at Baystate West** (781-7111, S$44-52/D$56-64), in downtown, sauna; **Seven Gables** (783-2111, S$18-22/D$22-26), on lake with private sand beach, pool. The **Student Prince and Fort** is a popular downtown restaurant, with German-American menu. **Vincent's Steak House** has an oyster bar and open-hearth cooking.

Laurel Week in **Westfield,** a town noted for its flora, takes place around the third week in June when selected trails for walking and looking are posted. **Grandmother's Garden** includes a century-old well; **Stanley Park** and **Carillon** contain vast floral displays. A covered bridge, reconstructed mill with grinding stone, and a blacksmith shop are in the pond area. The **Rose Garden** grows over 50 varieties. There are carillon and organ concerts throughout the summer.

North of Westfield is **Holyoke,** the first planned industrial city in the US. Volleyball was invented here in the late 19th century by a physical education teacher at the local YMCA. **Mt Tom State Reservation** and **Mt Tom Ski Area,** north of the city, provide year-round sports. The **Log Cabin Restaurant** offers a fine view of the valley.

South Hadley is probably best known as the home of **Mount Holyoke College,** founded in 1837. The summit of **Mt. Holyoke,** 954 feet high, in Skinner State Park, gives a panoramic view of the Connecticut Valley. **Hadley Farm Museum** (open May-15 Oct, Tues-Sun till 4:30, free), by the Hadley village green, is a restored 1782 barn with original household and farm items, plus an old stagecoach, oxcart, complete smithy, and the first broom-making machinery. **Smith College,** founded in 1871, is in nearby **Northampton. Acadia Wildlife Sanctuary** has self-guiding nature trails and guided tours. The annual **Three County Fair,** with farm shows and pari-mutuel horse racing, is held in Northampton, Labor Day week. Places to stay: **Northampton Colonial Hilton Inn** (586-1211, S$27-33/D$37-43); **Hotel Northampton** (584-3100, S$22-26/D$28-32), includes old Country Store and rustic **Wiggins Tavern,** featuring home baking and a New England menu. On Main Street there is **Fitzwilly's** for a relaxing lunch or supper served in cozy surroundings, or **Paul and Elizabeths,** where health food is served with imagination and a gourmet touch.

Amherst is a quiet college town centered around **Amherst College,** founded in 1821. The **University of Massachusetts,** with over 20,000 students, is to the north, and **Hampshire College,** established through the joint initiative of Smith, Amherst, Mount Holyoke, and the University of Massachusetts, is south of the city. **Lord Jeffrey Inn** (253-2576, S$18/D$28-30), on the Amherst green, has colonial furnishings and a notable restaurant.

The **Mohawk Trail** stretches 63 miles, west to east, from the Massachusetts-New York line in the northwest corner of the state to Millers Falls on the Connecticut River. Log cabins may be rented through the Mohawk State Forest Supervisor by the week. **Greenfield** is the eastern terminus of the trail. Forty miles west along MA2, high in the Berkshire Hills, is **Williamstown,** which centers around **Williams College,** 1 block east of the village green. Founded in 1793, over 1,400 students attend classes on the campus. The **Sterling and Francine Clark Art Institute** has superb painting, silver, and sculpture collections (open daily 10-5, free). **Williamstown Summer Theater** offers dramas and musicals in July and August. Local motels include: **Berkshire Hills** (458-3950, S$28-33/D$32-35), pool; and **The Williams Inn** (458-9371, S$36-46/D$42-56). Favorite restaurants are **Elwal Pines,** with dining on the terrace, while **Le Country** offers a continental and American menu. South of Williamstown, on Route 7 in nearby **New Ashford,** is the outstanding **Mill on the Floss,** in a lovely 200-year-old house with an inviting open kitchen.

New England's only natural bridge, a rock formation immortalized by Hawthorne in his *American Notebook,* is just north of **North Adams.** Two connected recreation areas, **Mohawk Trail** and **Savoy Mountain State Forest,** offer swimming, fishing, hunting, camping and snowmobiling. **Graylock State Reservation** contains **Mt Graylock,** the highest point in the state, 3,491 feet; skiing and snowmobiling, fishing, hunting and camping facilities. **Valley Park Campground,** southeast of town, also has boating, fishing and swimming. North Adams' **Fall Foliage Festival,** in late September or early October, includes a parade and entertainment. The **Berkshire East Ski Area** is nearby in Charlemont. Stay at the **North Adams Sheraton** (664-4561, S$24-31/D$27-37).

The **Bridge of Flowers,** at Shelburne Falls, is the only one of its kind in the world. Colorful shrubs and flowers, planted by the community, cover the 400-foot, five-arch concrete span. It's a spectacular sight any season and floodlighted nightly in summer. The **Bridge of Flowers Art Festival** is held here in late August. **Sweetheart-Scenic Dining Restaurant** offers a New England menu, waterfall, and splendid view of the valley.

South of the Mohawk Trail, **Deerfield** is noted for its beautiful historic homes and for **Deerfield Academy.** Mile-long **Old Deerfield Street,** dotted with 17th-, 18th-, and 19th-century homes, is one of the most charming streets in the country. **Frary House,** built before 1700, was an 18th-century inn and stagecoach stop. **Wilson Printing House** displays an early 19th-century printing operation. Combination tickets to the homes and guide service are available at Hall Tavern, early May through early November. (All historic Deerfield homes open year round 9:30-4:30 Mon-Sat, 11-4:30 Sun.) Deerfield Academy, founded in 1797, is an exclusive boys' preparatory school. Its first building, **Memorial Hall Museum,** was built in 1797 (open May to Nov, 10-4:30 Mon-Fri, 2:30-4:30 Sat-Sun, admission adults $2, students $1.50, children 6-12 75¢). **Deerfield Inn** (774-5587, S/D$60-65), adjacent to the Academy, was founded in 1884; its restaurant is furnished with antiques. **Mt Sugarloaf State Reservation,** in South Deerfield, has a hiking trail and paved road to the summit; excellent view of the Connecticut River Valley. **Turners Falls, Millers Falls, Montague City,** and **Erving** are worth visiting for their historical sites and Indian battlements. **Orange,** to the east, is the leading sport parachuting center.

Theaters and concerts, multiple sports, and recreational areas, plus natural scenic glories contribute to the year-round vacation attractions of the **BERKSHIRE HILLS.** Over 80,000 acres of forest in 17 state parks offer camping, hunting, fishing, and swimming, while skiing is the most exciting winter sport, with more than 20 areas in the region. In the southwest corner, **Sheffield,** the first town in Berkshire County, was settled in 1725, thus starting the movement along the **Housatonic River.** Two covered bridges spanning the river still remain. **Great Barrington** is the shopping and resort center for the southern Berkshires. Skiing at **Butternut Basin, Otis Ridge,** and **Catamount.** Boating, fishing, hunting, swimming, camping, picnicking, and snowmobiling in **Beartown State Forest. Monument Mountain** is just north of town. **Mt Everett State Reservation** has a 2,624-foot summit. Pari-mutuel racing at the **Barrington Fair** in early September. **Berkshire Motor Inn** (528-3150, S$25-44/D$28-50) is a good place to stay.

Continuing north, **Stockbridge** was established as an Indian mission in 1734 and was the home of Norman Rockwell, the famous painter and illustrator. The **Field Chime Tower** on the mission site plays concerts every summer evening and **Berkshire Garden Center** has a herb trail and rock gardens. **Chesterwood** was the studio of sculptor Daniel Chester French, who modeled the statue of Lincoln at the Lincoln Memorial in Washington, DC, and of the Minutemen in Concord. Plaster casts of most of his works are on display daily, mid-June through mid-September. The **Old Corner House** (open Mon-Sun 10-5, admission adults $2, children under 12 50¢), a restored 18th-century Georgian house on Main Street, has several original Normal Rockwell paintings, including his self-portrait. The **Berkshire Theater Festival** in the **Berkshire Playhouse** is open July through September. **Red Lion Inn** (298-5545, S$22-40/D$32-52), open since 1773, has a heated pool and an excellent restaurant.

The world-renowned **Jacob's Pillow Dance Festival,** in the Ted Shawn Theater, east of Lee, features outstanding performances by international dance companies, late June through late August. **Morgan House Restaurant,** established in 1850, offers home cooking in a charming colonial tavern atmosphere.

Tanglewood, in **Lenox,** is the home of the Boston Symphony Orchestra's summer **Berkshire Festival,** founded in 1939. Tanglewood is the 200-acre estate where Hawthorne lived and wrote. Guided tours of the estate and formal gardens are available during the festival. The **Music Shed** has seating for 6,000. Chamber music programs are held in the theater, which seats over 1,000. **Pleasant Valley Wildlife Sanctuary** and **Stockbridge Bowl,** a pretty lake, are nearby. **October Mountain State Forest** includes 17,000 acres for boating, camping, and hunting. Recommended accommodations in Lenox: **Eastover Resort** (637-0625, rates on request), an extensive resort designed especially for young adults, offering a wide range of sports and entertainment; **Wheatleigh Inn** (637-0610, S$45-55/D$70-100 BB); **Holiday Inn** (637-1100, S$20-62/D$27-66), heated pool; and **Yankee Motor Lodge** (499-3700, S$27-45/D$24-49), pool. **Lenox House** and **William Henry Inn** are popular local restaurants. If you are in the mood for a French extravaganza, try the **Gateways Inn** for a memorable dinner.

Pittsfield, in the central Berkshires, claims two Shaker villages. **Hancock Shaker Village,** 5 miles west, is a restoration of the original complex, which was founded in 1790 and vacated in 1960 (open daily June-Nov 9:30-5, admission adults $4.50, students $3.50, children 3-12 $1). It includes an 1826 round stone barn and 17 other buildings reflecting community life. **Mt Lebanon Shaker Village,** on the site of a colony founded in 1774, also contains original and restored buildings; open daily, early June through late July. **Berkshire Athenaeum** has a Herman Melville collection. Skiing at **Bousquet, Jiminy Peak,** and **Brodie Mountain. South Mountain Concerts** feature chamber music, opera, and recitals by renowned artists, weekends June through October; **Young Audience Concerts** in July and August. The **Berkshire County Fair,** held in September, has pari-mutuel horse racing. Pittsfield hotels: **Berkshire Hilton Inn** (S$24-46/D$30-52), indoor heated pool; **Liberty Court** (443-9431, $20-30), heated pool; **Pittsfield TraveLodge** (443-5661, S$32-47/D$39-47); and **Springs Motor Inn** (458-5945, S/D$39-54), heated pool, 9 miles north of Pittsfield in New Ashford on Route 7. **Yellow Aster Restaurant,** in a 200-year-old house, offers pleasant fireside dining. **The Springs** has a continental and American menu, and the **Busy Bee's** reasonably priced lunch is recommended for families.

City To Visit

BOSTON

> "Here's to good old Boston
> Land of the bean and the Cod.
> Where the Lowells talk only to Cabots
> And the Cabots talk only to God."

The above was originally recited by someone now forgotten at a Harvard University function in 1905. It is known to the Cabots of Boston as "The Poem."

Boston, the capital of Massachusetts, is in the eastern end of the state on the Mystic and Charles rivers and the Atlantic Ocean. Boston Harbor is at the head of Massachusetts Bay and Fort Point Channel is to the south. The first settlement was established by English Puritans in 1630 under Governor John Winthrop, the new community being named after a town in Lincolnshire, England. Two years later it became the capital of the Massachusetts Bay Colony. Boston grew in importance as a shipping center during the following century, steadily opposing British trade policies in the colonies. The "Boston Tea Party," in which tea from docked ships was thrown into Boston Harbor, helped solidify public opinion and hastened the American Revolution. Boston was incorporated as a city in 1822.

The older portion of the city has an old-world atmosphere and crooked, narrow streets. Its historic sights make Boston a must for any student of America's past. Many European visitors prefer it to any other United States city. Population 562,118, metropolitan area 3,918,000.

WHAT TO SEE

Boston is filled with historic places. A good way for the visitor to get oriented is to view the city from the 50th-floor Observatory at the **John**

Hancock Tower, where there's a model of the city as it was in 1775, together with telescopes for distant viewing—you can see the New Hampshire hills on a clear day—commentaries, plus a 7-minute film of a helicopter ride over town. A second starting point is the Prudential Skywalk's similar 50th-story viewing area. On the ground floor of the building is a multi-media 50-minute show which plays throughout the day, while on the 52nd floor is Top of the Hub, a restaurant from which you can view arriving and departing aircraft from Logan International Airport. Most visitors enjoy wandering along Freedom Trail, a marked walking tour about 1¼ miles through old Boston. Start at the Information Center on Boston Common; then continue on to Park St Church completed in 1809 and according to Henry James the "most interesting mass of bricks and mortar in America"; and King's Chapel, Granary Burying Ground, City Hall, Old South Meeting House, Old State House (where the *Declaration of Independence* was originally read in Boston on 18 July 1776), overlooking the site of the Boston Massacre, Faneuil Hall, often called the "Cradle of Liberty," the 200-year-old Haymarket Square Market; Paul Revere House, probably the oldest wood structure in Boston, was built in the early 1670s and was almost 100 years old when Revere moved in in 1770 (the house is still furnished as he left it in the style of the 1770s); Old North Church and Copp's Burying Ground. Three large old former market buildings in the Faneuil Hall area have undergone extensive renovation, and now house many small specialty shops, restaurants, and fast-food places. There are strolling musicians and other entertainment in the area. Also worthwhile are the quietly aristocratic Federalist mansions on Beacon Hill, now mostly private clubs and the exquisite Louisburg Square; the Boston Athenaeum; Bunker Hill Monument; Boston Navy Yard; "Old Ironsides," the *US Constitution*, on view daily 10-4. The Christian Science Mother Church is very impressive; across the street in the Christian Science Publishing Society building is the famous Mapparium, huge hollow replica of the world. Visit the fabulous New England Aquarium, which has over 2,000 fish and the largest ocean tank (200,000 gallons) in the world (Mon-Thurs 9-5, Fri till 9, weekends 9-6, admission adults $4, children $2.50). The Kennedy Library (open 9-5 daily) is in South Boston and in nearby Milton see the Museum of the American China Trade (Tues-Sun 1-4, admission adults $3, students $1.50, children under 12 free).

Also visit Boston Tea Party Ship and Museum, full-scale brig, *Beaver II;* visitors may throw tea chests overboard (daily, 9 to dusk, admission adults $1.75, ages 5-14 $1); Prudential Skywalk, exhibits and view of city (9am-11pm Mon-Thurs, until midnight Fri-Sat, 10am-11pm Sun, admission adults $1.75, ages 5-15 85¢); Museum of Transportation, autos, carriages, antique bicycles (daily 10-5, Fri till 9, admission adults $3.50, ages 3-15 $2.50); Whites of Their Eyes, new pavilion depicts the battle of Bunker Hill (daily June to Sept 9:30-6:30, the rest of the year until 4:30, admission adults $1.50, children 75¢); Museum of Afro-American History, in oldest Black church building in US, will arrange Black Heritage Trail Tour (daily 1-4, adults $1/children 50¢). Recently eight new walking trails were established in Boston. **Gray Line** provides Freedom Trail and museum tours, adults $8.50, children $4.25. Most museums and exhibits are free to children under 6, reduced rates for senior citizens. Many of Boston's attractions have reduced rates on Friday evenings.

Beacon Hill is a tradition in the life of Boston and its citizens. For the visitor, can walk through these quiet tree-lined streets—still lighted by gas lamps at night—and where shuttered brick townhouses provide an anonymous facade behind which the wealthy and socially prominent of Boston's families (The Boston Brahmins, as they have sometimes called themselves) lived—as some still do to this day. The hill takes its name from a system of leading lights—beacons—that were hoisted on yards to provide navigational information to mariners who were making night landfalls in the 1630s. Today, any echo of its marine past is muted, and the eye catches the fashionable bow fronts of the dwellings and the tint of purple glass. Originally thought to have been caused by the action of the sun on defective plate glass, it quickly became sought after as an outward sign of material success. But the nouveau riche who attempted to duplicate the glass of the earlier establishments were unable to achieve the same softness of tint. It now appears probable that the original glass was prepared according to the methods of the medieval guilds, who before the advent of mineral dyes, used vegetable dyes that were activated by sunlight. This same tint may still be seen in a number of European cathedrals where the stained glass dates back to the 11th and 12th centuries.

Harvard University, founded 1636 in the suburb of Cambridge, is an outstanding university offering courses in a wide variety of subjects; **Radcliffe College** is affiliated with it. Walking tours of the campus leave every day Mondays through Fridays at 11:15, 1:15 and 2:15pm from Byerly Hall, the undergraduate admissions' office at 8 Garden St., Cambridge. The tour lasts about an hour. Other important schools in the area are **Boston College, Boston University, Massachusetts Institute of Technology, New England Conservatory of Music, Northeastern University, St John's Seminary, Simmons College, Tufts University,** and **Wellesley College** for women.

Franklin Park has rose gardens, golf course, woodland walks. The great "Boston Kite Festival" is held annually at Franklin Park, when upwards of 30,000 people camp out for the day to watch thousands of kites go skyward. Appropriately, the park is named after America's most famous kite flyer, Benjamin Franklin. The event is usually held on the second Saturday in May. **Boston Common,** in the heart of the city, is particularly pleasant during the summer. **Boston Public Garden** has a pond with swanboats (in use Apr-Sept, adults 75¢, children 30¢) and pretty floral displays. **Arnold Arboretum** is known for its fine collection of plants and trees. **Isabella Stewart Gardner Museum** has a Venetian garden with changing floral displays.

There is a wide choice of conducted sightseeing tours; a typical city tour takes 3 hours and costs from about $8.50.

ACCOMMODATIONS

Boston hotels. Downtown Boston: **Avery** (482-8000, S$25-38/D$30-46), good commercial hotel; **57 Park Plaza Hotel** (432-5700, S$59/D$69), cocktail lounge, two movie theaters, roof-garden dining, pool, sauna; **Parker House** (227-8600, S$70-106/D$80-116), traditional landmark, restaurant, cocktail lounge; **Ritz Carlton** (536-5700, S$80-90/D$90-100), distinguished elegance, adjacent to Public Gardens; **Copley Plaza** (267-5300, S$70-90/D$82-104), old updated hotel near Trinity Church, French restaurant; **Copley Square** (536-9000, S$38-46/D$49-50), restaurant lounge; **Lenox** (536-5300, S$55-66/D$67-68), opposite Library, good commercial hotel; **Midtown Motor Inn** (262-1000, S$43-53/D$48-58), near Prudential Building; **Sheraton-Boston** (236-2000, S$73-80/D$86-93), basement garage, health club, 5 restaurants, covered access to John B. Hynes Veteran's Auditorium in Prudential Center; **Hyatt Regency** (492-1234, S$67-93/D$82-108), in Cambridge, across the Charles River from Boston, new, ultra-modern high-rise hotel, with all refinements; **Boston Park Plaza Hotel** (426-2000, S$55-84/D$67-96), near Boston Common and Garden, restaurant, cocktail lounge; **Colonnade** (261-2800, S$78-84/D$89-100), in Prudential Center. At Logan International Airport: **Hilton** (569-9300, S$43-67/D$53-87); **Ramada Inn** (569-5250) 2 miles from Logan Airport at North Station. Two miles from downtown in Fenway area: **Children's Inn** (731-4700, S$31/D$33), near Museum of Fine Arts, Isabella Stewart Gardner Museum, universities. Numerous motels in and around the city provide overnight lodgings in a wide variety of costs. Hotel tax: 5.7%

TRANSPORTATION

Public transportation is available to those visitors averse to driving through the congested city traffic. The Massachusetts Bay Transportation Authority (MBTA) provides a complete system of subways, trolleys, and buses servicing the suburbs as well as the city proper. MBTA runs from 5:20am to 1am. Subways 50¢, surface lines 25¢; exact change required on surface lines. The MBTA's routes now cover over 188 miles, with stops at 14 major beaches from Nantasket on the South Shore to Marblehead on the North Shore. Points of interest near MBTA stations include the Museum of Science, the *USS Constitution*, Bunker Hill Monument, Symphony Hall—and more than 100 places people like to visit. Commuter rail cars to outlying communities run from both the North and South Stations.

RESTAURANTS

Boston restaurants serve usually until 10-11 Friday and Saturday nights. **Charley's Eating and Drinking Place** on Newbury Street and **Ken's** in Copley Square serve until 1am and 3am respectively.

Local specialties include seafood and brown bread, codfish balls, lobster and clam dishes, Indian pudding and New England Boiled Dinner. **Locke-Ober,** classic food, expensive; **Joseph's,** French food, very good, expensive. **Anthony's Pier 4** and **Jimmy's Harborside,** seafood, expensive; **Kev-**

in's Wharf, seafood, moderate and **The Chart House**, popular, on the waterfront, steak and seafood, no reservation accepted. More moderate-priced restaurants include **Jake Wirth's**, German dishes; **Lechner's Gourmet Restaurant**, specializing in German food, moderately expensive. **Felicia's, Cafe Marliave**, and **Stella's**, Italian food; **Athens Olympia**, Greek specialties. Good New England-style food at **Patten's** and **The Warren Tavern**. Fine seafood at the **Union Oyster House. Nine Knox St**, elegant, expensive, reservation only. **The Voyagers**, one of Boston's newest and well spoken for. **Zachary's** (at the Colonnade), **57 Restaurant, Maitre Jacques** and the **Ritz Carlton** all have excellent French and continental cuisine; expensive. American food at: **Durgin Park**, fine ambiance, moderate prices. **Delmonico's** in the Hotel Lenox, turn-of-the century restaurant with piano entertainment; moderately expensive. **Cybele's** is at the Market Place in Faneuil Hall, one of the liveliest spots in town. **Bay Tower Room** features a continental cuisine, expensive; **Gallagher**, moderate to expensive, offers American and European fare. **Maison Robert**, new excellent restaurant, expensive; **Top of the Hub** at the Prudential Tower, panoramic view of city, moderately expensive. **Cafe Budapest**, an elegant excellent Hungarian restaurant. **Daudin-Bouffant**, intimate French restaurant, expensive. **Casa Romeo**, moderately priced gourmet Mexican food. **Polcari's** and **Joe Tecce's** both have moderately priced Italian food. The best moderately priced seafood restaurant in Boston is **Dini's**. For moderately expensive Japanese try **Benihana of Tokyo**. Boston is known for its many Chinese restaurants in the Hudson and Tyler streets district. In Cambridge, try **Legal Seafoods**, communal tables, excellent fish.

ENTERTAINMENT

Dancing and entertainment at the **Sheraton Boston, Hilton Inn, Holiday Inn, The Last Hurrah** at the Parker House, and at numerous small lounges. Dynamic sound and light are offered at **Kimmies Disco**, 230 Mass. Ave, Cambridge. **Boston-Boston the Discotheque**, across from Fenway Park, claims to be New England's largest new disco, complete with fog-covered dance floor. The **Kenmore Square** area offers the following jazz, rock and discothèques: **Lucifer's, Celebration, King's Row, Copperfields, Future** and **Pooh's**. Downtown try **Burke's Place** and **Scotch 'n Sirloin Lounge**. North of Boston in Beverly is **Sandy's Jazz Revival**, featuring top Dixieland performers.

ARTS AND MUSIC

Boston's **Museum of Fine Arts** houses Roman, Greek, Oriental, Near East, and early American art objects; Wed-Sun 10-5, Tues till 9pm. **Isabella Stewart Gardner Museum** is an Italian villa complete with classic art, furniture (open Tues. 1-9:30pm except in July & August when it is open from 1-5:30pm). Concerts are held all year except July and August; for information call 734-1359. In the **Children's Museum**, all exhibits are participative (Tues-Sun 10-5, admission adults $3.50, ages 3-15 $2.50). **Museum of Science** has scientific exhibits, planetarium (Mon-Thurs 9-4,

Fri till 10pm, Sat 9-5, Sun 10-5, admission adults $4, children $2.50). **Fogg Art Museum** at Harvard is considered by many to be the best university museum in the country (Mon-Sat 9-5, Sun 2-5, free). **Institute of Contemporary Art** has modern art (open Tues-Sat 10-5, Wed until 9pm, Sun 12-5, admission adults $1.25, children 50¢).

The excellent **Boston Symphony Orchestra** (226-1492) performs during the winter season at **Symphony Hall**, when there is also a wide choice of other concerts, opera and ballet. The **Boston Pops** (tel: 266-1492) plays during May and June. There are Esplanade Concerts held in the open air at **Hatch Memorial Shell** during July.

Boston is considered a good theater town, and many Broadway productions are presented at the **Shubert, Wilbur,** and **Colonial** theaters. There are also two "off-Broadway" theaters, and summer playhouses within reach of Boston at Beverly, Cohasset, Holyoke, Martha's Vineyard, Marblehead, Plymouth, Hyannis and Dennis. Repertory companies such as the **Theater Company of Boston,** the **Loeb Drama Center,** and the **New Theater** in Cambridge offer experimental theater. Other theaters are: **Boston Center for the Arts** (426-5000), sponsors variety of cultural events including OM Theatre, Boston Ballet, Boston Philharmonic; **National Center for Afro-American Artists** in Roxbury (442-8820), theater, dance.

SHOPPING

Stores open daily 9:30-6, Monday and Wednesday until 8 during the summer, 9 the rest of the year. Boston's major department stores, **Jordan Marsh** and **Filene's** are located on **Washington Street** directly across from each other. **Newbury Street** is lined with art galleries and boutiques. **Boylston Street** is known for its specialty shops, including **Shreve, Crump & Low Company,** a fine jewelry and silver store established after the Revolutionary War. One hundred and fifty new retail stores and 17 restaurants in the restored Faneuil Hall Marketplace near Boston's waterfront draw a million visitors a month. Three market buildings, the Quincy, North and South, have been renovated.

SPORTS

There is horse racing at **Suffolk Downs** from 1 Jan. to 4 July; 17 Sept-31 Dec (1:30pm post time, closed Tues) and dog racing at **Wonderland Dog Track** in Revere, (closed Sun), from March to December. Professional baseball is played by the **Red Sox,** basketball by the **Celtics,** ice hockey by the **Bruins,** football by the **Patriots,** tennis by the **Lobsters** May through August. There is also a choice of collegiate athletic events scheduled by **Harvard University** and other institutions in the vicinity.

There are good facilities for golf and tennis at many public parks and private clubs. Swimming is available at various pools and ocean bathing at nearby **Nantasket, Revere, Carson, City Point, Malibu,** and **Orient Heights** beaches. The **Charles River** is used for regattas and boating on its upper portion near Cambridge. Numerous party boats leave for deep-sea fishing excursions.

CALENDAR OF EVENTS

Opera Company of Boston season, starts mid-January; **New England Home Show,** March; **Boston Marathon,** 3rd Monday in April; **John Williams' Boston Pops Concerts** begin late April: **Summerthing** sponsors festivals, workshops, ethnic-month events and performances; **National Tennis Championships,** mid-August, at Longwood Cricket Club, Brookline; **Boston Symphony** season, begins late September; **Christmas Festival,** December, Boston Common decorated in lights. Boston recognizes a different ethnic group each month with a variety of special exhibits, performances, lectures, and festivals.

WHERE TO GO NEARBY

Cape Cod, Martha's Vineyard, and **Nantucket** are excellent vacation areas. **Plymouth Rock** is only 37 miles south of Boston just off MA3; nearby is **Plimoth Plantation,** a 17th-century restoration. Nine miles north of Boston is the **Saugus Ironworks,** where Joseph Jenks founded America's iron and steel industry in 1646. **Cape Ann** is a delightful resort area, rich in New England atmosphere, only about 30 miles northeast of Boston. If you take the shore route, you'll pass through **Salem.** See the **House of Seven Gables, Peabody Museum, Essex Institute Museum,** and the captivating fishing town of **Gloucester** which, like **Rockport** on Cape Ann, is a popular artists' colony. At **Old Sturbridge,** an hour's drive southwest of Boston, is a fascinating reconstructed early American village, in some ways similar to Williamsburg. In western Massachusetts are the rolling hills of the **Berkshires,** offering music and the arts in a perfect setting, particularly the **Tanglewood** music festival in Lenox and the **Jacob's Pillow** dance recitals near Lee; there are also many summer theaters in the area. The best ski areas in the northeast—in Maine, New Hampshire, Massachusetts, and Vermont—are only 2 to 4 hours from Boston.

Nearby parks include: **Blue Hills Reservations** and **Houghton's Pond,** 12 miles southwest, picnic areas, boating, bathing, sport facilities; **Salisbury Beach State Reservation,** 40 miles northeast, ocean bathing, sand dunes, fishing; **Douglas State Park,** 40 miles southwest, good sandy beach at **Wallum Lake,** bathhouse, picnic areas; **Willard Brook State Forest,** 50 miles west, fishing, hiking, hunting, swimming; **Harold Parker State Forest,** 18 miles north, ponds, fishing, bridle trails; **Walden Pond State Reservation,** 21 miles northwest, good swimming, fishing, boating; **Miles Standish State Forest,** 40 miles south; **Crane's Beach** for swimming, 25 miles northeast.

CAPE COD

Cape Cod is a peninsula at the southeastern end of Massachusetts, extending eastward from the Cape Cod Canal, and north to Provincetown, a total distance of about 70 miles. Cape Cod Bay is to the north, the Atlantic Ocean to the east, **Nantucket Sound** to the south, and **Buzzards Bay** and **Cape Cod Canal** to the west. The Cape is dotted with some 365 lakes and ponds.

About 1602 the region was visited by the English explorer Bartholomew Gosnold. Because many codfish were caught, the region was named Cape Cod. The Pilgrims arrived in 1620, landing at Provincetown before proceeding to Plymouth. The Cape was sparsely settled for a long time, fishing and agriculture being the principal occupations. It has since become a delightful summer resort with an early American atmosphere.

Cape Codders, according to many people, are the saltiest of all American types. They are said to represent one of the last strongholds of "rugged individualism," many of them being artisans or fishermen. Most year-round residents live simply and conservatively. Population is about 100,000, swollen by many thousands during the summer.

WHAT TO SEE

At Barnstable, see the **Coach House and Crocker Tavern;** at Bourne, the **Aptucxet Trading Post.** Chatham has **Chatham Light, Monomoy Point** and **Atwood House. Dennis** is an art center and there is usually an exhibit scheduled. At Eastham, there are the famous old **Nauset Beach Light** and **Old Windmill.** The beach at **Nauset Light** and the neighboring **Coast Guard Beach** comprise some of the East Coast's finest shoreline. Falmouth has its famous **Congregational Church,** and there are interesting exhibits at **Falmouth Historical Society.** Harwich has **Brooks Park** and **Brooks Library.** Hyannis is the best place for shopping and has boat service to Nantucket and Martha's Vineyard in summer months. **Sandwich** is where the famous glass was made; there is a good collection at the **Sandwich Glass Museum** (daily Apr-Nov, 9:30-4:30, adults $1.50, under 12 25¢). Visit **Heritage Plantation** of Sandwich (daily May-mid-Oct, 10-5, adults $3, children 6-11 $1) with its antique cars, arts and crafts museum, military museum, and gardens. Near Sandwich is **Shawme State Forest,** with picnic areas and beautiful woodlands.

Provincetown is the tourist's favorite, an artists' colony at the very end of the Cape; the **Provincetown Playhouse,** granddaddy of American summer stock theaters, was founded in 1915, produces seven plays from July through Labor Day. Symphony Orchestra gives summer concerts here. See the **Heritage Museum,** the **Pilgrim Memorial Monument** (open daily 9-5 summer, 9:30-4:30 rest of year, adults $2.25, children $1), the popular beaches. Take a ride in a "beach buggy" over the sands or go for a sail. **Truro,** where the Pilgrims first found drinking water, is a tiny town that has retained much of its colonial atmosphere. Check locally for dune tours. The **Museum of Truro** features a collection of historical artifacts. **Wellfleet** is pleasant to visit; be sure to see **Sunset Hill.** South Wellfleet is headquarters of the **Cape Cod National Seashore,** 29,000 acres of unsurpassed scenery. Visitors Centers at Eastham and Provincetown supply information and maps. In Brewster the **Drummer Boy Museum** (daily mid-May-Oct, 9:30-5, adults $2.50, 12-16 $1.50, 6-11 75¢) and the **New England Fire and History Museum,** both on route 6A, are good historians' haunts. **West Brewster** is a tiny village; here visitors may watch the **Stony Brook Mill** in operation; open Wednesday and Saturday afternoons.

Woods Hole, at the base of the Cape, is a busy town with steamers leaving for Martha's Vineyard and Nantucket; visit the **Aquarium of the Bureau of Commercial Fisheries** (daily mid-June-mid-Sept, 10-5, free). **Yarmouth** is an attractive town; see the **Thacher House** and its antiques. There are numerous conducted sightseeing tours. In West Yarmouth's **Aquarium of Cape Cod's Aqua Circus,** see performing dolphins, sea lions and alligators.

ACCOMMODATIONS

Many large, old-style hotels are well maintained in a dignified fashion and generally offer rooms and meals starting at $35 per person daily. New construction is largely confined to cottage colonies and motels, some simple, others extremely luxurious. Cottages range in price from $150 up per week. A charming compromise is the small inn, many of which have as few as four or five rooms and offer friendly hospitality; rates start at about $25 per day. Some recommended accommodations: **Chatham Bars Inn** (945-0096, D$100-120); **Coonamesset** (548-2300, D$30-43), in Falmouth, traditional Cape Cod buildings, pool, popular restaurant specializing in seafood; **Nauset Knoll Lodge** (255-2364, D$24), upcape in Orleans, overlooking Nauset Beach.

RESTAURANTS

There are dozens of good restaurants scattered all over the Cape, principally near the larger communities. Many provide dance music and entertainment. Local specialties are cranberries, clam chowder, fried clams, and lobsters—baked, stuffed, boiled, steamed, broiled, or stewed—all ocean fresh.

ARTS AND MUSIC

Provincetown Heritage Museum, colonial kitchen, glassware, special exhibits. Chatham's Atwood House, beautiful antiques. Bourne's Aptucxet Trading Post, relics of Pilgrim days. Most of these open during the summer only; all charge admission fees.

Principal summer theaters are the **Cape Playhouse** (Dennis); **Falmouth Playhouse** (Coonamesset), **Cape Cod Melody Tent** (Hyannis), **Orleans Arena Theater** (Orleans), **The College Light Opera Company, Highfield Theater** (Falmouth), **Monomoy Theater** (Chatham), **Harwich Junior Theater** (Harwich), **Provincetown Playhouse** (Provincetown), and **Yarmouth Playhouse** (South Yarmouth).

SHOPPING

Furniture shops specialize in early New England reproductions. In addition, there are hundreds of antique shops, and also stalls where small handicraft items are offered along the road. Homemade jams and jellies, particularly the unusual wild beach-plum jelly, and hand-made candles are worth buying.

SPORTS

The region abounds with facilities for golf, tennis, horseback riding, fishing, sailing, and swimming. Ocean bathing is particularly good at any of the numerous beaches; saltwater fishing from chartered boats and piers and surf casting; also freshwater trout, bass. A series of service roads along scenic routes provide bicycle and walking trails.

CALENDAR OF EVENTS

Blessing of the Fleet, Provincetown, June; **Cape Cod Art Association** Show and annual **Antiques Fair,** Hyannis, July; **Beachcombers Costume Ball,** Provincetown, and **Barnstable County Fair,** Mashpee, July; **Antiques Fair,** Chatham, and **Indian Summer Princess Pageant,** Hyannis, August; **Cape Cod Tuna Tournament,** August; **Cape Cod Indian Summer Golf Tournament,** October.

WHERE TO GO NEARBY

Roland Nickerson State Park, 3 miles east of Brewster, has campsites and bathing areas. There is a National Seashore, about 29,000 acres of beach and sand dunes on the Atlantic side of the peninsula. Martha's Vineyard and Nantucket may be reached by car ferry from Hyannis and Woods Hole.

MARTHA'S VINEYARD

Martha's Vineyard, New England's largest island, lies 6 miles south of Cape Cod. It can be reached from Woods Hole by regular steamer service and car ferry. There is also airplane service direct from New York and Boston. Roughly triangular in shape, with 105 square miles of area, the island is about 16 miles long and varies from 1 to 10 miles in width. Its colored cliffs and terrain in many ways resemble England's Isle of Wight, complete with English-style fogs.

Settled early in the 17th century, Martha's Vineyard became an important whaling port, later fell into decline, but for more than 50 years has been a popular resort in summer, when the permanent population of about 6,500 swells to about 40,000. The beautiful homes of daring sea captains, the local legends and relics of the Indians, and historic lore of early seafaring explorers are all part of the island's unique charm.

While day excursions to the island are popular with sightseeing tourists, the Vineyard has its greatest appeal for people who come for several weeks of sports and relaxation or for the entire summer, returning faithfully year after year. The island offers a healthful mild climate, clear air, varied picturesque surroundings of sweeping moors, colorful cliffs, pounding surf, and sheltered beaches, charming little fishing villages, and facilities for casual sports, providing an atmosphere of uncrowded, unhurried living, private or social as you choose.

Principal towns are **Vineyard Haven,** a port for the island steamers; **Gay Head,** with its rugged cliffs, lighthouse, and American Indian settlement with interesting burial grounds; **Menemsha,** an excellent harbor, usually crowded with fishing boats, a popular subject for artists; **Oak Bluffs,** with amusing Victorian architecture and excellent beaches, also a port for the island ferries; and **Edgartown,** the county seat, its fine old homes built with whaling fortunes and historical exhibits of interest.

ACCOMMODATIONS

Accommodations in Edgartown include the **Harborside Inn** (627-4321, S/D$61-80), **Colonial Inn** (627-4711, S$24-34/D$30-43), **Harbor View Hotel** (627-4333, S/D$65-75), **Dagget House** (627-4600, S/D$30-50), and **Edgartown Inn** (627-4794, S$26-36/D$28-40). Other hotels on the island are **Wesley House,** at Oak Bluffs, **Mansion House** and **Vineyard Harbor Motel,** at Vineyard Haven, and **Menemsha Inn,** in the Chilmark area. Among the restaurants, aside from the hotels, are the **Seafood Shanty** in **Edgartown,** the **Home Port** in Menemsha and **Boston House** in Oak Bluffs. Prices at most hotels and cabins are moderate. Popular activities available here are deep-sea and surf fishing, sailing, golf, swimming, and horseback riding, and boats are available for rent.

NANTUCKET

Nantucket is the county seat of **Nantucket Island,** which lies in the Atlantic Ocean some 30 miles south of Cape Cod. Boat connections to the island cross the **Nantucket Sound.** To the west is **Muskeget Channel;** south and east is the Atlantic Ocean.

The island was first settled in 1658 by Thomas Macy, who purchased it from the Indians. Two years later the Coffins, Folgers, Gardners, Swains, Mayhews, Barnards, and others arrived from England. Descendants of these first families still live on the island. Nantucket became famous for its ships, captains, and seafaring men who sailed all over the world; later it became a whaling port, although subsequently New Bedford became the more important whaling center. Before the turn of the century, the island became a summer resort, but it is as lovely in autumn and an unexpected delight in winter.

Nantucket still retains its salty flavor and is rich in the tradition of the men who sailed the seven seas. The well-preserved homes ranging from handsome mansions to charming lean-to houses, quaint cobblestone streets, and the relaxed and calm atmosphere all take you back to colonial days. Still called the "Little Gray Lady of the Sea," it is an unspoiled resort. Population is about 3,500, increasing to about 25,000 during summer months. The island is about 14 miles long and 3 to 6 miles wide.

WHAT TO SEE

Nantucket is more a mood, a sense of living in the past, than a place with particular sights. Tour the island with an automobile or cycle and see the little communities of **Siasconset, Quidnet,** and **Wauwinet** with their weathered grey shingle houses. In June rambler roses cover the small cottages. In early fall, the rolling moors become very colorful, changing in hue from week to week. Tracks across the moors are wonderful for hiking (and getting lost) but never too far from civilization. The peace and beauty of the clean white beaches is relaxing and there is an eerie quality to the island's fogs. A 200-year-old windmill, which still operates, is interesting to explore. Walk down the cobblestones of Nantucket's principal street; see the perfectly preserved mansions topped by "widows' walks" where sailing-ship captains' wives watched for their husbands' return. The **Jethro Coffin House** is attractively furnished, open daily 10-5. The **Nantucket Whaling Museum** has a good collection (daily May 23-Oct 13 10-5, rest of year 1:30-4:30, Adults $1/Children 50¢/Children under 5 free). See the **Maria Mitchell Observatory**, open to the public Monday evenings. Sightseeing buses offer a 40-mile tour of the island.

ACCOMMODATIONS
Nantucket hotels: **Beachside Motel** (228-2241, S$38/D$48); **Harbor House** (228-1500, S$35-70/D$40-75); **Jared Coffin House** (228-2400, S$20-25/D$40-55); **White Elephant Inn** (228-2500, S/D$55-85). Off season rates are $8-10 lower. The **Gordon Folger Hotel & Cottages** (228-0313, S$20-30/D$30-42) are open May-Oct only. Rooms are also available at attractive guest houses in cottages and apartments in town.

RESTAURANTS
Among the restaurants in the town of Nantucket, all moderately expensive, are **The Club Car** and **The Tavern**—both have good food; **Harbor House**, entertainment; **Cap'n Tobey's Chowder House**, entertainment; the popular **Mad Hatter; The Relaxed Lobster. The Company of the Cauldron** (tel: 228-4016) and **India House** (tel: 228-9043) both require reservations. Popular, smaller places include the **Opera House**, a discothèque. The **White Elephant Inn** and **Jared Coffin House** feature nightly entertainment and particularly fine meals. Many restaurants and hotels have pleasant cocktail lounges with entertainment. There are also several interesting places in the other communities nearby, particularly **The Chanticleer** in 'Sconset, with outdoor dining in a lovely rose garden.

ARTS AND MUSIC
There are many amateur and professional art shows and much activity here; this is an artists' colony. There is a sidewalk exhibit during August, plus many other small shows. The **Kenneth Taylor Galleries** show works by Nantucket artists free. A theatrical group gives stock-company performances during July and August, with a new play each week. The **Nantucket Musical Arts Society** presents recitals, mostly of classical works, in the Unitarian Church in July and August.

SHOPPING
Curio shops and antique stores, as well as stores selling necessities and old-fashioned penny candies, can be found throughout the town.

SPORTS

There are two public golf courses, and tennis courts are also available. Bicycling is popular all over the island. Deep-sea fishing is good and requires a license. The favorite sport is ocean bathing on one of the island's fine beaches, but water-skiing and sailing are also popular. The **Nantucket Yacht Club** holds annual races.

FURTHER STATE INFORMATION

Division of Tourism, Massachusetts Department of Commerce and Development, 100 Cambridge Street, Boston, MA 02202. Hunting and Fishing: **Division of Fisheries and Game,** Department of Natural Resources, State Office Building, 100 Cambridge Street, Boston, MA 02202. **Convention and Visitors Bureau,** Great Boston Chamber of Commerce, 125 High Street, Boston, MA 02110. **Cape Cod Chamber of Commerce,** Hyannis, MA 02601 (362-3225). **Martha's Vineyard Chamber of Commerce,** Vineyard Haven, MA 02568 (228-1750). **Massachusetts Hotel/Motel Association,** 73 Tremont Street, Boston, MA 02108 (227-1616); **Central Massachusetts Tourist Council,** Suite 350 Mechanics Tower, Worcester, MA 01608 (753-2924); **Pan Am,** 150 Federal Street, Boston, MA 02110; tel: 1-800-223-9762.

Consulates in Boston: Argentina, Austria, Barbados, Belgium, Bolivia, Canada, China, Colombia, Costa Rica, Denmark, Dominican Republic, Ecuador, El Salvador, Finland, France, Germany, Great Britain, Greece, Guatemala, Haiti, Honduras, Iceland, Ireland, Israel, Italy, Japan, Korea, Lebanon, Mexico, Monaco, Netherlands, Norway, Panama, Paraguay, Peru, Portugal, Senegal, Spain, Sweden, Switzerland, Turkey, Venezuela.

USEFUL TELEPHONE NUMBERS

Referrals for professional medical and legal services in an emergency are made for tourists by the following:

Massachusetts Medical Society	536-8812
Massachusetts Dental Society	237-6511
Legal Aid Society	376-2880
Pan Am Reservations	800-223-9762

Michigan

Area	58,216 square miles					Population		9,189,000				
Capital	Lansing					Sales Tax		4%				

Weather

	Jan	Feb	Mar	Apr	May	Jun	Jul	Aug	Sep	Oct	Nov	Dec
Av Temp (°C)	−3	−3	2	9	15	21	24	23	18	12	5	−1
Days Rain/Snow	13	12	12	12	12	11	9	9	9	9	11	13

It might seem strange that a state which places a heavy emphasis on manufacturing should also have so much to offer tourists. While Michigan does produce more motor vehicles, more auto parts, boats, engines, refrigerators, and office equipment than any other part of the United States, the tourist here is offered some of the finest opportunities for outdoor adventure. There are more than 32,000 miles of Great Lakes' shoreline, 11,000 inland lakes, 36,000 miles of streams, and more ski resorts than could be sampled in 20 visits to the state. The natives call it the Great Lake State.

French explorers were the first to penetrate the Lower Peninsula region, quickly followed by trappers eager to barter with Indians, and then soldiers to guard the strategic points of trade. The French and Indians teamed up to fight and lose to the British, who were later forced to retreat into Canada after the American colonies successfully revolted.

In the 1840s, the great forests gave birth to a booming but brief lumber industry. Copper and iron mining were also started at this time primarily in the Upper Peninsula. Finally, at the turn of the century, the automobile industry arrived. Today, the **St Lawrence Seaway** makes international ports of such places as Bay City, through Saginaw Bay. The Coho, Chinook, and Atlantic salmon make great sport for fishermen throughout the summer and during early fall. Winter ice fishing excursions to the thousands of frozen lakes are often accompanied by the town festivals, most famous of which is the "Tip-Up-Town" weekend at **Houghton Lake.** Deer hunters with guns or bows take to the forest in November.

The college community of **Ann Arbor** in the **SOUTH CENTRAL** region is the home of the **University of Michigan,** and a good place to begin the trip north. Located off US 23, the university was founded in 1817 in Detroit and moved to Ann Arbor in 1837. **Burton Memorial Tower** houses the Baird Carillon; the **Matthaei Botanical Gardens,** where exotic plants bloom year round, is open daily, free; the **William L. Clements Library** houses noted collections of Americana, original manuscripts and rare books. **Weber's Inn** (769-2500, S$35/D$43) is excellent, just outside town. West of Ann Arbor, off I-94 is the town of Marshall, where you will find **The American Museum of Magic** as well as one of the best dinners in Michigan at **Win Schuler's.** Fresh fish and prime ribs are the specialties, and there are delicious baked goods fresh from the oven. **Battle Creek** is the central headquarters for the famous **Kellogg Company;** free tours are available Monday-Friday. Further east on I-94 is **Kalamazoo,** a pleasant city made famous in several songs. It is the home of **Kalamazoo College,** one of the oldest in the state.

Traveling northeast, you come to **Lansing,** the capital city of Michigan; visit the state building complex and the **State Capitol** building. **Carl G. Fenner Arboretum** provides many live animal and Indian exhibits, including American prairie vegetation. The park is opened 8-5 (weather permitting) and is free. The neighboring community of **East Lansing** is the home of **Michigan State University.**

The industrial city of **Flint,** in **EASTERN** Michigan, has guided tours of the **Buick Motor Co,** Monday to Friday at 9:30 and 1:30. **Chevrolet Flint Truck Assembly Plant** is open for conducted tours at 9:30 and 1:00 weekdays. There are no tours of automobile plants during new model changeover in August. **Howard Johnson's** in Flint averages S$34-36/D$40-48. **Port Huron** to the east is on two great waterways, **Lake Huron** and the St Clair River, which provide the backdrop for the **Blue Water Festival** and famous **Port Huron to Mackinac** sailboat race in mid-July. The **Museum of Arts and History** is open Wednesday to Sunday. **Howard Johnson's** (984-1522, S$29/D$38) provides good accommodations.

Heading west toward I-75, try to stop in **Frankenmuth.** The **Glockenspiel Tower** at the **Frankenmuth Bavarian Inn** contains a 35-bell carillon which plays at 11, noon, 3, 6, 9 and 10 daily. Superb chicken dinners are served family-style at **Zehnder's,** just down the street from **Bronner's,** a series of shops which display Christmas decorations all the year. A **Bavarian Festival** is held the second full week in June. **Saginaw** is at the head of the valley which is one of the most fertile agricultural districts in the state. Two of the area's leading crops are beans and sugar beets. A museum displays the glories of the great lumber industry which died by 1890 when the local timber supply was exhausted. **Bay City** is the home of the **Museum of the Great Lakes,** open Monday-Friday, free, and offers facilities for sailing and fishing in Saginaw Bay.

Albert E. Sleeper State Park is near Caseville at the tip of the thumb jutting into Lake Huron. Across the bay is **Tawas City,** a sleepy summer resort with excellent sailing; boat rentals available. The beautiful **Rifle** and **Au Sable** rivers have many places to rent canoes along their shores. **Rifle River State Park** near Rose City has trout fishing in its fast-running streams as well as peaceful sandy beaches. Paddlewheel river boat trips on the Au Sable travel more than 19 miles and last two hours. Boats depart from **Foot Dam,** on River Road six miles from **Oscoda,** and from **Five Channels Dam,** 19 miles west at the junction of MI 65 and West River Road.

Houghton Lake is the center of a beautiful region surrounding **NORTHERN** Michigan's largest inland lake. The area's vast forests provide excellent bird and game hunting. The **Tip-Up-Town Festival** is held on the ice the third weekend in January. **Val Halla Motel** (422-5137, S/D$28), with spacious, shaded grounds, offers good accommodations. The **King's Table Restaurant,** at Bill Oliver's Lakefront Lodge, serves dinner in a rustic setting. **Hartwick Pines State Park,** seven miles northeast of Grayling on MI 93, is a lovely wooded area which includes some 250-year-old virgin pines. **Fred Bear Museum,** open daily, has an extensive collection of trophy game taken by bow and arrow. **Call of the Wild Museum** at Gaylord displays 150 wild animals and game birds in their natural setting, with sound effects. **Indian River Shrine** at the base of beautiful Burt Lake is the world's largest crucifix, supporting a seven-ton statue of Christ mounted on a 55-foot redwood cross. **Burt Lake State Park** nearby has fine camping facilities (call 517-275-5151 for information on all State Park vacancies).

The **Old Lighthouse,** built in 1840 at **Presque Isle Harbor,** 25 miles north of Alpena off US 23, has been restored. **Grand Lake** and the harbor are among the most spectacular sights in the state. Northeast on US 23 is **Cheboygan,** a center for summer and winter sports. The city has a large ice-skating rink; fishing for bass, pike and bluegill in the nearby lakes is excellent.

The Dutch settlement town of **Holland** is a good place to begin a tour of the Lake Michigan Coast. The **Dutch Village** here has flowering gardens, imported Dutch goods and picturesque buildings; open year-round. Tours are available of the village and the **Wooden Shoe Factory. Windmill Island** is an unusual municipal park open mid-May through 31 October. The annual **Holland Tulip Time Festival** in mid-May has been held since 1929. **Point West Motel** (335-5894, S$55/D$65, lower in winter), at the west end of **Lake Macatawa,** has recreational facilities along with tastefully appointed rooms.

The city of **GRAND RAPIDS,** northeast on MI 21, received its name from the rapids of the Grand River. Once the site of an Ottawa Indian village, it later became a trading post of the American Fur Company. It is the home of former President Gerald R. Ford. The **Roger B. Chaffee**

Planetarium presents lecture-demonstration programs year-round. The city museum's **Gaslight Village** re-creates the period from 1870 to 1900; free, open daily. **John Ball Park Zoological Gardens** is open daily. **Circle in the Park Theater** at the John Ball Pavilion stages musicals from mid-June to September. **Cannonsburg Ski Area,** 10 miles northeast via US 131, has full skiing facilities. Choose from many comfortable motels at Grand Rapids, including **Cascade Motor Inn, Pick Motor Inn, Midway Motor Lodge, Ramada Inn, TraveLodge,** several **Holiday Inns,** and **Howard Johnson's** with rates averaging S$18-43/D$23-50.

Traveling northwest but along the Lake Michigan Coast, you come to **Muskegon** and **Ludington** on the coast. In the center of blueberry country, Ludington has day and night ferry service year round to Milwaukee and Manitowoc, Wisconsin; $14 for cars, $8 for adult passengers, one way. Concerts, plays and ballets are performed in **Cartier Park** and also at **Lincoln Lake.** Continuing north, **Traverse City** is the center of Michigan's cherry-growing belt; the **National Cherry Festival** is celebrated here in July. **Cherry County Playhouse** offers summer stock theater with nationally known stars from early July to early September. **Sugar Loaf Village, Traverse City Holiday, Schuss Mountain, Crystal Mountain, Shanty Creek, Timber Lee,** and **Hickory Hills** have many ski tows and runs. **Colonial Inn, Park Place Motor Inn,** and **Fox Haus Motor Lodge** provide rooms averaging S$36-44/D$40-52. **Beef Tree Inn** and **Shield's** serve good dinners. The towns of **Bellaire** and **Old Mission** offer good exploring among antique and junk emporiums.

Petoskey, a resort and health center, is on **Little Traverse Bay.** The famous fossilized pieces of coral called Petoskey stones can still be found along waterways. Within a 30-minute drive are five major ski resorts, including **Walloon Hills, Boyne Falls,** and **Thunder Mountain.** Shop for antiques here. The **Coach House, Best Western Inn, Hayner Motel,** and **The Inn on the Hill** offer comfortable attractive accommodations at average rates of S$34/D$36-40. **This Ole House** specializes in casserole dishes; **Holiday House** serves "live" lobster, prime ribs and its own baked goods. The **Lodge of Charlevoix** (547-6565, S$44/D$48) has rooms with balconies. Boats and planes leave regularly in the summer for **Beaver Island** which was once the only monarchy in the continental United States. It was ruled by Mormon King James Jessie Strang in the early 1840s. **St James** is a good hunting, fishing, and boating center.

Harbor Springs is an exclusive resort area near the ski resorts of **Nub's Nob** and **Boyne Highlands. Birchwood Inn** (626-2151, S/D$39-52) has good rooms. The Boyne Highlands complex, one of the best ski areas in the state, is five miles east off US 131; there is a ski package plan in winter, golf plan in summer. From **Mackinaw City** the **Mackinac Bridge** takes you to Michigan's Upper Peninsula in 10 minutes. At 8,614 feet it is the world's longest suspension bridge, although its center span is shorter than those of the Golden Gate Bridge in San Francisco and the Verrazano-Narrows Bridge in New York.

Michigan's Upper Peninsula is a haven for sportsmen and naturalists. It covers a small area north of the Straits of Mackinac. There are white-sand shorelines on Lakes Superior, Michigan, and Huron, and inland areas with evergreen mountains, birch forests, swiftly running streams and many beautiful waterfalls; invigorating swimming; adventuresome boating; fishing for bass, perch, pike, trout, and many other fish; hunting for deer, bear, rabbit, fox and beaver; shooting for pheasant, partridge, grouse and duck. Accommodations can vary from a cabin in the woods to a resort hotel, depending on your inclination. Many Michigan hosts will, if notified in advance, meet buses, trains and airplanes. There are often special rates during the off season. Restaurant specialties include lake trout and seafood; prices are moderate.

MACKINAC ISLAND is reached by ferry from St Ignace and Mackinaw City and by air from Pellston, Detroit and St Ignace. Once a strategic military stronghold fought over by England and France for supremacy of the rich fur trading area of the northwest, the island is now a quiet summer resort with many scenic features. On it stands **Old Fort Mackinac.** Built in 1780, it commands the Straits; open daily 22 May-1 September. The famous, resplendently Victorian **Grand Hotel** (847-3331, S$100/D$140-180 AP), with an incredibly long veranda, is open from mid-May to early October. It was recently completely renovated. The quaint old **Chippewa Hotel** (847-3341, S$38/D$48) faces the Straits. Automobiles are banned and transportation is by carriage, horse or bicycle. **John Jacob Astor House,** original headquarters of the American Fur Company, is open daily, mid-June to September. There is a carriage tour of scenic and historic points of interest daily in summer.

The Mackinac Bridge joins the Upper Peninsula at **St Ignace.** Leading resort hotels in the area include **Dettman's** (643-9882, S/D$36-38) and the **Georgian House** (643-8411, S/D$38-48), both open year round. Heading north on I-75 you come to **Sault Ste Marie** where you can see the famous **Soo Locks,** the world's busiest. From two observation towers, ships can be watched as they transfer past the unnavigable rapids of the St Mary's River between Lake Superior and the lower elevation of Lake Huron. Famous **Welch Lock Tours** through American and Canadian locks (two hours) leave several times daily from late May to mid-October; $8.25 adults, $4 children, under six free. There are also conducted tours through the *SS Valley Camp,* a typical Great Lakes ore carrier moored at a wharf in the Soo. Visit the **Tower of History** and the **Shrine of Missionaries,** dedicated to early Jesuit missionaries. In midtown Sault Ste Marie are the **Mid City Motel** (632-6822, S/D$22-26) and the **La France Terrace Motel** (632-7823, S/D$26-34). South of town near I-75 are the **Colonial Inn** (632-2170, S/D$35-36) and the **Skyline Motel** (632-3393, D$32-35). Some rates are lower after Labor Day.

The **Tahquamenon River,** which flows into Lake Superior at **Whitefish Bay,** was made famous in Henry Wadsworth Longfellow's *Hiawatha.* The 200-foot-wide **Upper Falls** thunders down a 40-foot cliff. The **Lower Falls,** a few miles downstream, is a succession of stepped cascades. The river and forest are accessible by car or boat in spring, summer or fall. Camping facilities are available near the rapids and bay shore. **Tahquamenon Falls State Park,** 16 miles north of **Hulbert** in the heart of the lumber country, is visited by more than 100,000 people a year. From **Slater's Landing,** 10 miles north of Hulbert, you can board a river boat for a 4½-hour round trip down the Tahquamenon River; daily 1st July-Labor Day; Sat-Sun 15-30 June, Labor Day-10 October; adults $8, children 5-11 $4. At **Soo Junction,** 17 miles east of **Newberry,** you can ride the **Toonerville Trolley,** a narrow gauge railroad running six miles through thick forest.

The **Upper Peninsula State Fair** is held every third week of August at **Escanaba,** to the south on Lake Michigan. Near Escanaba is **Fayette Ghost Town,** a state park that was once a thriving iron center and port. **Iron Mountain,** further west, is a lovely resort center with the world's highest artificial ski slide. On a wooded peninsula at Marquette is **Presque Isle Park,** with trails and varied recreational facilities. There are interesting mining, lumbering and geological displays at the **Marquette County Historical Society Museum.** Seven miles north are exceptional views from Sugar Loaf Mountain, with a trail to the summit. At **Ishpeming** is the **National Hall of Fame and Ski Museum.** Operated by the US Ski Association, it houses national trophies and old ski equipment. An **International Ski Tournament** is held in Ishpeming each February.

Hancock and **Houghton,** facing each other across the man-made **Portage Canal,** lie in the area of America's original mining capital. The area was the scene of the first great mineral strike in the western hemisphere. The copper-bearing geological formations are believed to be the oldest rock strata in the world. Hancock, mostly populated by people of Finnish descent, is known for its **Suomi College** and fine Finnish choirs. East of town is the **Arcadian Copper Mine,** which has conducted tours. In Houghton, where boats and seaplanes leave for Isle Royale National Park in Lake Superior, is the **Michigan Technological University** with its radiation facilities and nuclear reaction equipment. The **A.E. Seaman Mineralogical Museum,** houses one of the nation's best mineral collections. Beautiful **Copper Harbor** is the northernmost point in Michigan on the top of the **Keweenaw Peninsula.** There are many resort facilities here as well as **Fort Wilkins State Park** with its restored fort buildings and stockade. The park's historical museum houses pioneer relics and early mining equipment; open 15 May to 15 October.

City To Visit

DETROIT

Detroit, with a population of more than 1,257,879, with a blend of different races, nationalities and cultures. It has few traditions and considerably more interest in the future than in the past. In 1701 the French established a trading post calling it "Fort Pontchartrain du Detroit"—Fort Pontchartrain of the Strait. The British captured it in 1760 during the Seven Years' War and even after defeat in the Revolution they did not give up control until 1796. During the War of 1812 the city was surrendered to the British attacks under unexplained circumstances, without the defending American army firing a single shot; it was retaken by the US the next year. Detroit was incorporated in 1815 as a village and as a city nine years later. Its growth may be attributed directly to the automobile; many of Michigan's workers are directly involved in the industry.

WHAT TO SEE

A symbol of Detroit's new image, the **Renaissance Center**, is five glass towers on the waterfront that contain offices, hotel facilities, many specialty shops, restaurants, and a theater. The **Detroit Civic Center** covers 75 acres of the downtown riverfront and includes **Cobo Hall**—one of the largest and finest exhibition buildings in the nation, **Hart Plaza** with the **Dodge Riverfront Fountain, Ford Auditorium,** and the **Joe Louis Sports Arena.** Other highlights of a visit include the **Fort Wayne Military Museum,** well-preserved pre-Civil War fort with original barracks and powder magazine, Indian, and military exhibits. Northwest of Detroit is **Cranbrook,** a distinguished private school: building by Eero Saarinen, fountains and sculptures by Carl Milles, including the **Cranbrook Academy of Art Museum** and the **Cranbrook Institute of Science** (645-3142). If possible visit the **Henry Ford Museum** and **Greenfield Village,** about 12 miles west, with historic houses, buildings, and interesting displays of American culture; open daily 9-5; adults $8, children 6-12 $4 (under 6 free). Also visit the **Detroit Historical Museum** and the **Detroit Science Center,** which has many participatory exhibits and a space theater with a tilted dome that features 3-dimensional films; admission $2.50, ages 2-5, 75¢ (833-1892). **Belle Isle** is an island park connected to Detroit by a free bridge. The island has an aquarium, the **Belle Isle Nature Center, Belle Isle Zoo** with an elevated walkway through trees for views of animals roaming uncaged, and the **Doussin Great Lakes Museum.** There are picnic grounds and facilities for swimming, canoeing, horseback riding, tennis, and golf. The **Detroit Zoological Park** is north of Detroit and is one of the largest and most modern zoos in the US. Surroundings designed to simulate the natural habitat of the animals are laid out over 122 acres (398-0900). Cruises on the **Bob-Lo** boats to a Canadian Island amusement park are offered Memorial Day to Labor Day.

ACCOMMODATIONS

Hotels in Detroit: **Detroit Plaza** in the Renaissance Center (568-8200, S$85-100/D$100-120); **Pontchartrain** (965-0200, S$59-79/D$74-94), elegance in French tradition; **St Regis Hotel** (873-3000, S$65/D$77), very good accommodations; **Book Cadillac** (256-8000, S$40/D$50), extremely large, well-run hotel; **Hilton Inn** (292-3400, S$43/D$47), near airport; **Dearborn Inn** (271-2700, S$50/D$58); and **Hyatt Regency Dearborn** (593-1234, S$60-90/D$95-105) next to Ford Motor Co World Headquarters. A wide selection of motel and motor hotel accommodations includes the **Coach and Lantern, Cranbrook House, Holiday Inns, Howard John-**

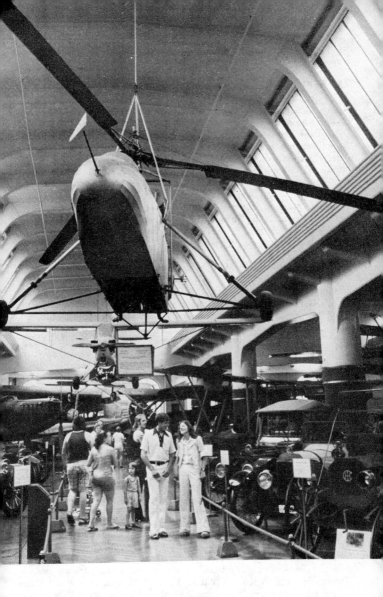

The Henry Ford Museum in Dearborn, MI has more than just motorcars on its 14 acres of exhibits—all under one roof.

son's, **Stouffer's Northland Inn**, **TraveLodges** and the **Troy Hilton**. Rates average S$35-46/D$39-58. Hotel Tax: 4%.

RESTAURANTS

The city's cosmopolitan character has produced some fine foreign restaurants. Oriental: **Yamato's**, authentic Japanese dishes; **Mikado** or **Victor Lim's**, Oriental decor, exotic drinks. French: **Pontchartrain Wine Cellars**, Parisian bistro-type atmosphere and a gourmet menu, **La Fontaine** (in the Plaza Hotel). German: **The Little Cafe**, German beer, quaint Bavarian decor; **Schweizer's**, open since 1862. Greek: **Grecian Gardens, New Hellas Cafe**, and a wide range of others in Greek Town. Italian: **La Lanterna**, informal, open till 3am, **Mario's**, a long list of genuine Italian dishes; **Roma Cafe**, city's oldest Italian restaurant. Mexican: **Mexican Village**, old-style Mexican dinners; **Acapulco Restaurant**, authentic atmosphere. Middle Eastern: **The Sheik Cafe**, shish kebab and shish kafta, Arabic decor and background music. Polish: **The Ivanhoe Cafe; Under the Eagle**, with all Polish dishes. Polynesian: **Chin Tiki**, exotic drinks and decor, sarong-clad waitresses; **Golden Buddha**, on far east side. **Benno's Restaurant**, exquisite cuisine. Most foreign-food restaurants listed also serve American food. American: **The Summit**, a revolving restaurant atop the Plaza Hotel, with spectacular views of Motor City and nearby Canada. **Jim's Garage**, "early garage" decor includes antique hood ornaments and license plates; **Soup Kitchen** and **Woodbridge Tavern**, casual, inexpensive in the warehouse district close to downtown. **Ttopinka's on the Boulevard**, Old English setting; **Berman's Chop House, London Chop House, Little Harry's**, great beef, expensive; **Sinbad's**, casual, popular on the Detroit River. **Traffic Jam**, 20th-century Detroit decor, smorgasbord; **Ye Old Steak House** in Windsor (Ontario), delicious Canadian and American beef. Seafood: **Joe Muer's**, claims best seafood in the Midwest; **Mario's of Windsor** (Ontario), fresh Canadian and imported fish. For popular seafood try **Charley's Rawbar & Seafood** (Pontchartrain Hotel). Try **Nemo's** for hamburgers and beer and **Russell's**, good steaks and chili.

ENTERTAINMENT

Detroit is a lively city. From May through September each weekend brings a different Ethnic Festival in the waterfront civic center with special foods, drinks and entertainment. A trolley ride down Washington Blvd takes you through the city (25¢). After dark all the establishments listed feature some form of live entertainment, and most serve food. **db's Club** (in the Hyatt Regency Dearborn) offers a weekly schedule of top names in entertainment; **Top of the Ponch**, in Hotel Pontchartrain, rooftop supper club, dancing; **The Cedars Lounge**, Middle Eastern decor and menu; **Top Hat**, Canadian nightclub, dancing; **Grecian Gardens**, authentic Greek dining; **London Chop House**, one of America's top restaurants, dancing, expensive; **Bakers Keyboard Lounge**, excellent jazz; **Celabration Lounge** (Plaza Hotel); **Rembrandt's**, bluegrass; **Raven Gallery**, folk music, no liquor; **Salamandre Bar**, reminiscent of Paris bistros;

Dakota Inn, German Songfest; **Dewey's in Michigan Inn,** Piper Alley (east side) and **Fanny's** in the Troy Hilton, all popular singles' spots. For discos, **Oscar's, My Fair Lady, L'Esprit.**

ARTS AND MUSIC

Detroit Institute of Arts is a series of art galleries; open daily except Monday, 9:30-5:30. **Cranbrook Academy Art Galleries** in suburban Bloomfield Hills presents works of contemporary artists, shows changing selections from an outstanding permanent collection. **Children's Museum,** art exhibits for children; weekdays 1-4, Saturdays in October-May 9-4; free. The **International Institute** has arts and crafts exhibits of 43 countries. The luxurious **Fisher Theater** in midtown offers pre-Broadway productions and top road company hits. The **Hilberry, Bonstelle** and **Meadowbrook Theaters** give good performances, as well as do **Mercy College** and the **Music Hall Center for the Performing Arts.**

The University of Detroit's **Performing Arts Center** offers theatrical productions October-April. The **Detroit Symphony Orchestra** gives a series of concerts during the winter, and the "Symphony Under the Stars" series in June. **Pine Knob** (40 miles north on I-75), outdoor concerts during summer with top name entertainment. The **Meadowbrook Festival** offers concerts in the summer and there are band concerts in **Belle Isle Park. P'Jazz** at Hotel Pontchartrain and **Renaissance Live** offer summer weekday concerts.

SHOPPING

Stores remain open Thursday evenings until 9. **Downtown Detroit,** general retail; **Renaissance Center,** specialty stores; **Dumouchelle Art Galleries Co,** art and antiques. Detroit and its suburbs have a number of enormous and excellent shopping centers.

SPORTS

The **Detroit Tigers** play professional baseball; the **Lions,** professional football, at the **Silverdome** (suburban Pontiac); the **Red Wings,** ice hockey; **Detroit Pistons,** professional basketball, also at Silverdome. There is speedboat racing during summer months; horse racing at **Detroit Race Course** and **Hazel Park** from March to early December. **University of Michigan** college football and **University of Detroit** college basketball in the 101,000-seat stadium in Ann Arbor, 38 miles west. Harness or thoroughbred racing year round at **Windsor Raceway** and **Detroit Race Course.** Numerous public and private facilities for golf, tennis and all water sports. Skiing, cross-country and downhill, and other winter sports are available nearby.

CALENDAR OF EVENTS

Auto Show, November; **Society of Automotive Engineers Meeting,** February; **International Freedom Festival** (Detroit and Windsor, Ontario), June to early July; **State Fair,** August.

WHERE TO GO NEARBY

North of Detroit is the **St Clair River** section, particularly good for a fishing vacation. There are many waterfront resorts near **Port Huron**, known for its beaches and sailboat races. **Port Austin,** about 115 miles north, offers many vacation opportunities. Ann Arbor is a distinctive, cultural college town, 38 miles west.

In an area from 30 to 60 miles northwest of Detroit are a series of recreational parks. The most important are the several **Dodge Brothers State Parks, Kensington Park, Island Lakeport** and **Proud Lake** recreational areas; these have fishing, camping and sports facilities. Canada is a five-minute drive via the auto tunnel or Ambassador Bridge to Ontario.

ISLE ROYALE NATIONAL PARK

Isle Royale has changed very little since the French temporarily annexed it to Canada in 1669. Nearly 50 different species of fish are found in 30 lakes and nearly 25 miles of trout streams; no license required except for Lake Superior waters. Primitive but well-marked trails wander through the forests for 115 miles, offering good back-packing opportunities and guiding hikers to geological landmarks, inland lakes, secluded campsites, lookout towers and ancient mine ruins. Indians worked the rocky shores for copper at least 3,900 years ago, and there was another rush of copper mining in the 19th century. **Greenstone Ridge,** reaching a height of 1,377 feet at **Ishpeming Point,** is the 40-mile trail connecting Rock Harbor with Windigo on **Washington Harbor.** The island's only transportation is by foot, on 120 miles of trails, or by boat. With advance notice you can arrange to be left or picked up at your campsite. The calm inland waters are ideal for exploring in your own small boat but are not recommended for swimming. Illustrated nature programs are presented on the island and there are conducted half-day nature walks. Moose are common on the island, and 200 species of birds have been recorded.

About 45 miles long and nine miles wide, the park is accessible by boat from Houghton and Copper Harbor, Michigan, and from Grand Portage, Minnesota; also by seaplane from Houghton. There are free parking areas at mainland take-off points because there are no roads for cars on the island. Vessels will carry canoes and other boats under 20 feet long. The park is open for hardy campers, bearing all their own supplies, from early May through mid-October. The **Lodge and Inn** are open from 15 June-5 September, and minimum supplies are available at the Lodge store. Take warm clothes. **Rock Harbor Lodge** (482-2890, S$49/D$77), at the northeast end, has both hotel-type and housekeeping rooms (2-day minimum $41/day), store and gift shop. There is another small store on the southwestern end. Room reservations should be made at least three weeks in advance. The 31 campsites on the shores and inland lakes have a 14-day-stay limit; one-night limit on **Rock Harbor**

Campground. Only three sites have treated water; boil drinking water at the others.

FURTHER STATE INFORMATION

Michigan Tourist Council, 300 South Capital Avenue, Lansing, MI 48926. Hunting and Fishing: **Department of Natural Resources,** Mason Building, Lansing, MI 48926. **Southeastern Michigan Travel and Tourist Association,** 350 American Ctr. Bldg., Southfield, MI 48034 (booklet describing vacation regions). **Upper Peninsula Travel and Recreation Association,** PO Box 400 PA, Iron Mountain, MI 49801. **Greater Detroit Chamber of Commerce,** 150 Michigan Avenue, Detroit, MI 48226 (business and industrial information). **Metropolitan Detroit Convention and Visitors' Bureau,** 100 Renaissance Center, Suite #1950, Detroit, MI 48243. **City of Detroit, Department of Public Information,** City-County Building, Detroit, MI 48226 (tours, tel: 224-5585). National Parks: **Isle Royale National Park** (Superintendent), Houghton, MI 49931. **Pan Am** office, 1231 Washington Boulevard, Detroit, MI 48226 (tel: 354-0500) and Metropolitan Airport, Detroit, MI 48242 (tel: 274-8850).

Consulates in Detroit: Australia, Austria, Belgium, Canada, Denmark, Dominican Republic, France, Germany, Great Britain, Israel, Italy, Japan, Lebanon, Malta, Mexico, Netherlands, Norway, Sweden.

USEFUL TELEPHONE NUMBERS IN DETROIT

General Emergency (Fire, Police, Medical)	911
Legal Aid	961-3545
Dental Referral	341-4600
Medical Referral	963-1640
Travelers Aid	962-6740
Pan Am Reservations	354-0500

Minnesota

Area	84,068 square miles	**Population**	4,077,148
Capital	St Paul	**Sales Tax**	4%

Weather	Jan	Feb	Mar	Apr	May	Jun	Jul	Aug	Sep	Oct	Nov	Dec
Av Temp (°C)	−13	−12	6	3	10	15	19	18	12	7	−3	−10
Days Rain/Snow	9	7	10	10	12	12	10	9	9	8	8	9

Minnesota calls itself the "Land of 10,000 Lakes," but there are actually 12,034 freshwater lakes, some extending to over 10 acres, and scores of smaller ones. Minnesota also has 25,000 miles of rivers and streams. When the first French explorers entered the territory in the mid-16th century, they found the Ojibwa and Sioux Indians casually traveling great distances in their birch-bark canoes. Minnesota's lakes and rivers formed an ideal transportation system then and still do today, both for freight barges on the Mississippi and for canoes in the lakes. The Mississippi, which begins in Lake Itasca, gathers tributaries all the way down to the Gulf of Mexico. The Red River, forming most of the state's western boundary, flows north 545 miles from its source into Hudson Bay. A host of streams arising from lakes in the northeast carry a bit of Minnesota through the Great Lakes to the Atlantic Ocean.

Although the first explorers and fur traders were French and the first settlers British, Minnesota could be considered a North American offshoot of Scandinavia. During the 1880s, Scandinavians arrived in large numbers to find Germans already solidly settled and prospering on the rich farmlands. There was plenty of room for everyone, however. The Swedes tended to settle on farms in the east central region, the Norwegians headed north to the forests, and the Danes scattered around the central and southern sections where they boosted Minnesota into the forefront of the dairy industry. The other large national groups are from Finland, Poland, and Czechoslovakia. Thousands of Indians live on Minnesota's large reservations and go out in canoes, as their ancestors did, to gather the valuable and delicious wild rice.

Minnesota has all the familiar motels for tourists who are just passing through, but where it really excels is in summer resort lodges. They are invariably on lakes or rivers and have every facility for fishing and water sports; there's usually a golf course nearby. Larger resorts have dancing and entertainment, both indoor and outdoor game programs, heated swimming pools, and special activities for children; rates usually include two or three meals a day and are moderately priced. Wherever there are resort hotels there are usually economical cottages for rent on a weekly basis, often with a boat included. These can be great for a family vacation. Many cottages offer a wide choice of sports facilities similar to those of more expensive hotels. If you want to get around without leaving the water, houseboat vacations are becoming very popular, especially for families. Rentals are low, and even novices can safely handle this kind of craft.

Camping is down to a fine art here. Not only are sites admirably equipped, but many stores cater especially to the needs of people who live outdoors. Fishing probably keeps more people outdoors than any other single activity. There's no closed season on such panfish as perch, sunfish, crappies, and rock bass. The lake trout season is generally mid-January to mid-March and mid-May through September, but can vary from area to area so that it is advisable to check with the Department of Natural Resources; stream trout season is March through September in North Shore streams and elsewhere; bass is generally June to mid-February; northern pike, muskie, and walleye are in season from mid-May through January. The 60 state parks are game refuges, but there is state forest hunting in season for deer, moose, bear, elk, and game birds. The beaver, almost completely destroyed by two centuries of rapacious trappers, is again building his excellent little dams in the security of the state's protection, which also extends to many other valuable fur-bearing animals.

"Hiawathaland" is in the **SOUTHEASTERN** toe bounded by the Mississippi. Heading north along the river valley you come to **Winona**, a tidy, New Englandish river port for both pleasure boats and freight barges. **Sugar Loaf** is a distinctive limestone formation of a 500-foot bluff where the Sioux used to hold ceremonies. The *Julius C. Wilkie* is a retired paddle-wheeler, now a museum of old-time riverboat lore; open May through September. The **Bunnell House**, south of town, and **Pickwick Mill** are intriguing relics of a bygone era. Continuing up the river, you pass through **Frontenac**, which had some of the first private summer cottages and perhaps the first tourist hotel in Minnesota. Affluent Southerners came by riverboat from as far as New Orleans to revel in Minnesota's wonderful summer air. Just beyond is **Red Wing**, famous for pottery and dinnerware. You can pick up some bargains here. Nearby are **Welch Village** and **Mt Frontenac** ski areas.

ROCHESTER is the focal point of southeastern Minnesota. Dr William Mayo, who had emigrated from England in 1845, set up his medical practice in Rochester in 1863. He was joined by his sons, William James and Charles Horace, who became surgical geniuses. Other young doctors came to learn their techniques and the great **Mayo Clinic** evolved. People come here from all over the world to consult the Mayo specialists; it is estimated that there are some 8,000 patients and other transients in town every day the year round. A system of heated subways speeds ambulatory and wheelchair patients to the clinic, the Rochester Diet Kitchen, and the new Methodist Hospital.

The subway is directly accessible from several hotels. These include the **Arthur Hotel** (282-3881, S$13-18/D$20-24), the **Kahler Hotel** (282-2581, S$30-74/D$41-80), and the **Kahler Hotel Zumbro** (282-2721, S$11.25-33.25/D$19.50-44.50). Courtesy cars to the clinic are provided by the **Galaxy Hotel, Holiday Inn-Downtown,** and **Holiday Inn-South,** averaging S$27.50-38/D$36.50-46. The **Fiksdal** (288-2671, S$24.75/ D$34.75) is opposite St. Mary's Hospital; **Gas Light Inn** (289-1824, S$16-20/D$23.50-26.50) is adjacent to it. There are many other motels, and most of Rochester's accommodations have special facilities for wheelchairs. All hotels and motels are 9 to 12 miles from Rochester airport. Popular restaurants include **Michael's, The Bank,** the **Penthouse** and the **Elizabethan Room** in the Kahler Hotel, and **Depot House.** The **Chanticleer Room** at the airport is also popular. Though local cuisine is apt to be sophisticated, there is an unusually large choice of cafeterias in Rochester to help the medical visitor cope with the limitations imposed by special diets.

There are free conducted tours of the complex of clinic buildings. The **Mayo Medical Museum,** open daily, has life-size anatomical exhibits, illustrations of typical operations, educational films, and demonstrations of how various organs work. **Mayowood,** built by Dr Charles Horace Mayo in 1910-11 and later the home of his son Dr Charles William Mayo, is a 38-room mansion which the family donated to the county in 1965; interesting family furnishings and fine antiques. Conducted Mayowood tour buses leave from the **Olmsted County Historical Center and Museum** on Salem Road SW; daily afternoon tours except Monday from June to August, reduced schedule in April-May, September-November. Professional stage productions are held in the **Civic Theater,** and the **Rochester Symphony Orchestra** performs in the **Mayo Civic Auditorium.** A new $1.25 million **Rochester Community College Theater** opened in November 1975. **International Business Machines** occupies a handsome building designed by Eero Saarinen.

Rochester is a good base for touring "Hiawathaland," where the fishing is superb. **Owatonna** was named for a beautiful Indian princess who was restored to health by drinking the mineral spring water here. **Northfield** is the home of the excellent **Carleton College** and **St Olaf College,** known for its widely traveled choir. Every September there is a re-enactment of that hectic day in 1876 when Frank and Jesse James and the Younger gang tried to hold up Northfield's First National Bank. The important **Freeborn County Fair** is held early in August in Albert Lea. Austin is host to the **Mower County Fair** the second week in August.

"Pioneerland" is the name for **SOUTHWESTERN** Minnesota, though pioneer legends are kept alive throughout the state. **Mankato,** population about 27,200, is the largest town in the area and makes a good headquarters for exploration. **Holiday Inn,** 1 mile north, and the **Mankato Inn Towne Motel** are about S$27-29/D$36-38. **Hubbard House** (1871), a typical Victorian mansion, is part of the **Blue Earth County Historical Society Museum.** Unusual furnishings include three fireplaces looted from Southern plantations during the Civil War and the house's original bathroom fixtures. There's also an authentic log cabin dating from 1873 preserved in the basement; open afternoons Tuesday to Sunday. A few miles west is **New Ulm,** where the rich valley of the Minnesota River reminded early German settlers of river valleys in their homeland. They founded the city in 1854 naming it after Ulm on the Daube. The **Defenders' Monument** on Center Street honors the staunch citizens, who stayed and fought the Sioux, enabling noncombatants to escape to Mankato. The ruins of **Waraju Distillery** give some indication of the damage wrought by the Indians who were finally defeated when they attacked **Fort Ridgely,** northwest of town. **Hermann's Monument,** towering above the distillery ruins, recalls a German hero who defeated the Romans 1,853 years before his countrymen's troubles with the Sioux. There are more memories of the 1862 uprising in **St Peter,** north of Mankato. **Traverse des Sioux State Park,** just northwest of town, is where the Sioux sold the US government 19 million acres of southwestern Minnesota territory for 4.5¢ an acre. That was in 1851, and realization that they'd been cheated led to the Indian troubles of 1862. **Gustavus Adolphus College** is unusual for its ultramodern **Christ Chapel** and **Alfred Nobel Gallery** in the Nobel Hall of Science.

Pipestone National Monument is near the South Dakota border. This is one of the most sacred spots in the country for Indians of all tribes. They came here to quarry the unusual red stone and make it into *calumets,* their ceremonial peace pipes. Actually a very hard red clay, the material is called "catlinite" after George Catlin, the artist-explorer who first described it after a visit in 1833. Longfellow also made the quarry notable in his *Song of Hiawatha,* published in 1855. To this day, only Indians may take stone from the quarry and they still make it into ceremonial pipes used by Indians all over the country and also into a variety of souvenir items. This is the only pipestone quarry in the country. *Song of Hiawatha* pageants are presented in an outdoor theater in late July and early August.

"The Heartland," stretching up through **CENTRAL** and **NORTHERN**

Minnesota, has at least 2,500 lakes teeming with walleye and muskie. Here you will find an abundance of resorts, campsites, and trailer parks. This beautiful region begins at **St Cloud**, 65 miles northwest of Minneapolis. With a population of 41,400, it is highly industrialized while still looking comfortably homey. All around are granite quarries which have supplied stone for stately buildings throughout the country. Attractively situated on the Mississippi, St Cloud has some unusually nice parks, and the presence of three colleges keeps the town lively. Marcel Breuer designed the strikingly modern buildings of **St John's University. Sauk Center**, on I-94, is about 40 miles west of St Cloud. In this town is the plain little frame house where novelist Sinclair Lewis lived until he was 18; open year round. Many of the author's original manuscripts and letters are exhibited in the **Sinclair Lewis Interpretive Center** just off Interstate Highway 94 on SR (State Road) 27. **Little Falls,** about midway between St Cloud and Brainerd, was the home of "Lucky Lindy" and his father, Charles A. Lindbergh, Sr. Their restored home (1907) and the interpretive center contain memorabilia of the congressman and his son, who made the first solo flight across the Atlantic in 1927.

Within a radius of only 25 miles from **Brainerd** are 464 lakes in deep forests. There are golf courses too, and a host of resort hotels with many facilities for daytime sports and evening entertainment. The **Paul Bunyan Center** just west of town is a delightful amusement park presided over by a huge animated figure of the legendary lumberman; open late May-Labor Day. **Lumbertown, USA,** is on the shore of **Gull Lake**, northwest of Brainerd. This is a good replica of a Minnesota lumber town of the 1870s, with re-creations of typical homes and business buildings. There are also cruises on the *Blue Berry Belle* riverboat, and rides on a replica of the first Northern Pacific train. The financing arrangements of this line, which was finally completed in 1883, caused such a panic on Wall Street that the New York Stock Exchange was closed for 10 days in 1873. Lumbertown is open from late May until mid-September. The **Deer Forest and Storybook Land,** just south of Nisswa and just north of Gull Lake, delights children with its tame deer and other animals; there are turtle races on Wednesday afternoons in Nisswa. Sports car races are featured in the **Brainerd International Speedway** from June to August. Fine fishing is found all around Brainerd, but **Mille Lacs Lake** claims to be the best anywhere for walleye. On the western shore is the excellent **Mille Lacs Indian Museum.** Northeast of Brainerd are the open-pit mines of the **Cuyuna Iron Range,** and in **Aitkin** farther east on US 210, are the **Ak Sar Ben Gardens.** Here, amid rock gardens and waterfalls, is a lake full of tame fish that visitors can feed.

Park Rapids, northwest of Brainerd, is another very popular resort town ringed with lakes, streams, forests, fine resort hotels, and cottage colonies. **Aqua Park Aquarium** features more than 100 local fish in a huge tank, and **Deer Town,** open from Memorial Day to Labor Day, is a replica of an old frontier town with tame deer that can be fed by hand. Only 21 miles north of here is **Lake Itasca,** the source of the Mississippi. The surrounding state park has very good camping facilities and modern housekeeping log cabins with big stone fireplaces. Lake Itasca is full of muskie and other prize fish, and is ideal for boating and canoeing. State-operated **Douglas Lodge** (266-3656) overlooks the lake and surrounding forest; cabins also available. Guided tours usually leave from the lodge, and a museum and gift shop are nearby. East of the park, on the highway between Brainerd and Bemidji, is the town of **Walker.** It claims to be America's finest spot for muskie and there are some spectacular catches made during the **Muskie Derby,** July-August. Resorts, motels, and cottages can be found all around **Leech Lake,** which is also popular with people who like to spend their vacations in houseboats. Information on houseboat rentals, fishing, and resorts can be obtained at the Leech Lake Chamber of Commerce in Walker. The same building houses the local **Museum of Natural History and Indian Arts and Crafts** with its collection of Indian arts and crafts. The **Chippewa National Forest** is spread around the lakes in this area. A few sections of it are wildlife refuges, but elsewhere there is very good hunting in the autumn. In winter, the area is alive with snowmobilers and skiers.

Bemidji stands on Lake Bemidji and the Mississippi River. Enormous statues of Paul Bunyan and Babe, his blue ox, are on the lakeshore. You can learn all about this powerful pair in the **(Bunyan House) Information Center,** where you will also find a fireplace built with stones from every US state and Canadian province. There are very fine collections of Indian artifacts in the **Historical and Wildlife Museum,** which also features stuffed wildlife of the area and an aquarium of local fish. Hunting, fishing, and winter sports make Bemidji far more than just a summer resort. The **Paul Bunyan Playhouse** offers professional productions from late June-late August. The **Paul Bunyan Water Carnival** is held on the 4th of July weekend and the **Birchmont Golf Tournament** is held in July. From Bemidji the highway goes up through **Blackduck,** where autumn fishing and duck shooting are said to be excellent. **Kelliher** is near the vast **Red Lake Indian Reservation.**

Waskish, where the walleye fishing season opens every spring, is the last town before the wilderness begins. Then you come to **Baudette,** a border post into Canada and gateway to the wild **Lake of the Woods** area, with its 14,000 little islands. At the very top of Minnesota is the **Northwest Angle,** which juts into the big lake from Canada and is accessible only by boats or small planes.

"Viking Land" is what Minnesotans call the **WESTERN** strip of their state that runs along the North Dakota border. In the southern part of the region is the town of **Alexandria,** which claims to be the "Birthplace of America." Scholars still argue about whether Vikings ever came this far inland, and there's still doubt about the runic inscription, supposedly carved in 1362, that is on the boulder discovered here in 1898. A huge Viking statue identifies the **Runestone Museum.** More than 200 lakes are in the vicinity along with good resort hotels. The **Resorters Golf Tournament** is held every August in Alexandria. Northwest of here is

Fergus Falls, a major dairy produce center built on the hills surrounding Lake Alice. **Pebble Lake Recreation Center** is just south of town. **Detroit Lakes** is one of the state's most elaborate resort towns. Along the new "Mile of Beach" are parks and illuminated fountains, while out on the water are speedboats, canoes, sailboats, and water skiers. There are many lakes in the area and accommodations ranging from campsites to luxury resorts. The **Northwest Water Carnival** is held in Detroit Lakes in mid-July, the **Pine to Palm Golf Tournament** is in mid-August, and the **Becker County Fair** is the second week in August. Northeast of town are the **Tamarac National Wildlife Refuge** and the large **White Earth Indian Reservation. Moorhead,** on the border, is Minnesota's industrial and shopping center for the Red River Valley. **Concordia College** and **Moorhead State College** are here. The latter sponsors a **Straw Hat Summer Theater** from mid-June to mid-August. The flat, rich land stretches northward here in vast acreages of sugar beets, wheat, potatoes, and other crops. There is a canoe trail in **Red Lake River,** near the town of Thief River Falls. The **Agassiz National Wildlife Refuge** is northeast of town.

The "Arrowhead" is the wild triangle of towering forests in **NORTHEASTERN** Minnesota, with myriad lakes and streams, and huge open pit iron mines. This exciting region begins at **Duluth** named for the Sieur du Luht who claimed the territory for Louis XIV of France in 1679. But even before that, canoe loads of furs often started from this ideal harbor on their long trip to France. Today as the western terminus of the Great Lakes-St Lawrence Seaway, Duluth has 49 miles of docks. The combined harbors of Duluth and neighboring Superior, Wisconsin, handle the second-largest amount of tonnage in the US. This is an especially remarkable achievement in view of the fact that the seaway is closed by ice for 115-125 days from early December to early April. The harbor is protected by a range of cliffs rising 600 to 800 feet. From the **Enger Tower** on Skyline Parkway you get a superb view of the busy waterway.

A slim strip of land, **Minnesota Point,** extends 7 miles from Duluth-Superior, enclosing the harbor from Lake Superior. Here you can see the unique **Aerial Lift Bridge** which goes up to let ships come into the harbor. The visitor can see the gigantic grain elevators, ore docks, freighters, and **Inter-State Bridge** from the sightseeing boat that makes 2-hour harbor cruises; daily from 1 June to 15 October, weather permitting. Relics from this old city's early days are displayed in the **St Louis County Historical Society Museum.** The **A.M. Chisholm Museum** contains antique toys and Indian pioneer weapons, plus interesting models of lumber camps and fur trading posts. Both museums are housed in the new **St Louis County Heritage and Arts Center.** Pottery and oil lamps dating from the first century are displayed in the **Bible House,** as well as very old bibles and religious scrolls. The **Tweed Museum of Art,** on the campus of the **University of Minnesota-Duluth,** has a good collection of 16th-20th-century art. Other places to see are the **Duluth Zoo,** open daily; **Lake Superior Marine Museum,** containing ship models and memorabilia of the area's early shipping years; and **Spirit Mountain**, a year-round recreation complex and major skiing area.

Midtown accommodations include the **Holiday Inn** (727-8821, S$30/D$36) and the **Radisson Duluth Hotel** (727-8981, S$39-44/D$49-54). Others in the area are the **Voyager Motel**, the **Downtown**, and the **Duluth Hotel**. The **Buena Vista** is about a mile northwest of center. Rates for these hotels and motels average S$17-22/D$20-27. On US 61, heading northeast from town, are the **Best Western Edgewater East** and **Edgewater West** and **Lake Aire Motel**, all about 2 miles from downtown with rates averaging S$19-30/D$22-31.

The Arrowhead country north of Duluth provides seclusion almost beyond belief. If you tour it with a backpack and canoe, you can spend days or weeks in a wilderness unchanged since the explorers went through three hundred years ago. Some roads are planned for development areas but transportation is mostly by boat. This is a dramatically scenic area of large glaciated lakes, great exposed rocks of the Canadian Shield, deep forests, and protected wildlife.

Extending farther east along the Canadian line is the **Boundary Waters Canoe Area** in the immense **Superior National Forest**. Travel through here is by canoe, just as the French fur traders did. But if you prefer a more comfortable journey, one of the most beautiful drives in the US is along US 61, which follows the shore of Lake Superior for 152 miles from Duluth to Grand Portage. **Two Harbors**, 25 miles from Duluth, is a pretty little port town where the **Lake County Historical Society** displays the first steam locomotive that hauled iron ore in Minnesota. The museum also exhibits the modern *Mallet*, the world's most powerful steam-powered locomotive; open late May through September. **Grand Marais** lies at the foot of the **Gunflint Trail**, which rambles through forests for 58 miles to the Canadian border. A string of attractive lodges lies on the trail, beginning 10 miles inland from Grand Marais. They're equipped with guides, boats, and canoes in summer, and some have snowmobiles as well as facilities for ice fishing in winter. **Lutsen**, a major ski resort, lies just south of Grand Marais. **Grand Portage** at the eastern tip of the "Arrowhead," was the first white settlement in the state, although most of the local populace are now Indians. Forest rangers are on hand in summer to answer questions about the reconstructed stockade and other typical buildings. There are two excursion boats from Grand Portage to Michigan's beautiful **Isle Royale National Park**, 20 miles out in Lake Superior.

Returning on US 61, turn inland on MN 1, which goes up to **Ely**. This is a major resort town and the jumping-off place for the **Boundary Waters Canoe Area**. Local outfitters can provide everything you'll need. Ely has a golf course and is near the **Hidden Valley Winter Sports Area** and each January is host to the **American Championship Sled Dog Races**. The **Voyageur Visitor Center**, which maintains a museum of exhibits pertaining to this historic region, is open from mid-May to Labor Day. A great vein of iron ore runs from just west of Ely all the way over to

Grand Rapids. The **Vermilion Iron Range,** which shipped its first ore in 1884, extends from Lake Vermilion to Babbitt, southwest of Ely. Also near Lake Vermilion is **Tower Soudan State Park,** a large recreational area which offers tours of the underground mine.

The **Mesabi Range,** one of the world's richest mineral deposits, runs from near Hibbing to Virginia. This area was the province of lumberjacks until the Merritt brothers discovered the Range in 1887. John D. Rockefeller bought them out in 1893 for only $420,000. At **Virginia,** you can visit the **Rouchleau Mine,** June to Labor Day. From an observation platform, the visitor can see the workings of the vast open-pit mine, 600 feet below. **Chisholm** has the **Iron Range Interpretive Center,** situated on the edge of the inactive Glen Open pit mine. Open year round, the Center offers film presentations together with geological and natural history exhibits. From observation points on both sides of the road you can see open-pit mining all along the highway from Chisholm to **Hibbing.** On the north side of Hibbing is the awesome **Hull-Rust Mahoning Mine,** nearly 5 miles across, up to a mile wide, and as much as 535 feet deep; a viewing platform is open from 1 June through Labor Day. As the mine grew, it took over the town site, so Hibbing was relocated 2 miles south, whereupon two bright young men started driving commuters between the two points. That was the beginning of the Greyhound Bus Lines. Big events in Hibbing are the **Winter Carnival** in mid-February; the international **Last Chance Curling Bonspiel** in early April; and the St Louis County Fair the last week in July. The **Best Western Kahler Motel** (262-3481, S$34/D$39-41) has a heated indoor pool and entertainment.

Grand Rapids is on the western end of the Mesabi Range, and is also where the Mississippi River starts to become navigable. With hundreds of lakes and other rivers in all directions, you could get in a canoe and paddle for miles. The *Mississippi Melodie Showboat* stages musicals and revues on weekend evenings in July. **Sugar Hills** is a year-round resort area 14 miles southwest of town. It includes a golf course, entertainment center, and a ski area that booms from Thanksgiving to Easter. The **Quadna Mountain Ski Area,** 6 miles farther south, is another thriving resort, open all year. The University of Minnesota sponsors the **Summer Arts Study Center** here from mid-June to mid-August. Both areas have excellent lodges. **International Falls** is 116 miles north of Grand Rapids. You may think you've reached the end of civilization up here, but the town is an important border post into Canada and a supply point for the area. A 26-foot-tall statue of Smokey the Bear is a reminder to be careful of fires in the huge forests. The town stands on **Rainy Lake** which opens into lakes and streams that are ideal for exploring in a canoe or rented houseboat. The **Holiday Inn** (283-4451, S$29-36/D$39-44) and **Thunderbird Lodge** (286-3151, S$18-24/D$22-32) are among many motels and lodges in town and in the surrounding woods. **Crane Lake,** farther east on the Canadian line, has campsites, lodges, and houseboats to help you rough it in style. The landscape is dotted with forest-covered islands. During July there is a colorful festival to commemorate the French *voyageurs.*

Cities To Visit

MINNEAPOLIS AND ST PAUL

Minneapolis and St Paul lie in the east central part of Minnesota on the Mississippi River. St Paul, the capital of the state, is 10 miles east of its "twin city," Minneapolis. **Lake Minnetonka,** 15 miles west of Minneapolis, is a large, beautiful lake with fishing, boating, and swimming. Other large lakes in Minneapolis are **Calhoun, Harriet, Cedar, Nokomis,** and **Lake of the Isles. Lake Phalen** and **Lake Como** lie within St. Paul. **White Bear Lake,** 8 miles north of the capital, has bathing beaches and fishing. **St Croix River,** 12 miles east of St Paul, is particularly scenic. It is thought that the first white man to visit the area was Father Louis Hennepin, a French Franciscan priest who arrived in 1683. The entire territory was at first French. In 1763 the English acquired the region east of the Mississippi which became part of the United States at the end of the American Revolution. The area west of the river was ceded by France to the United States through the Louisiana Purchase of 1803. In 1819, **Fort Snelling** was established to protect the fur traders from the warring Chippewa and Sioux Indians. Today, Fort Snelling is open to the public and offers a "living museum" with a fort population living as people did in the 1820s. St Paul was originally the site of a fur-trading post near the fort and was known as Pig's Eye Landing or Pig's Eye, thought to be named after the leader of a squatter's camp at the river landing near the fort. Then, in 1841, when Father Gaultier built a log chapel there, it became known as St Paul's Landing. In 1849 it was named the capital city of the Territory of Minnesota. Minneapolis was incorporated as a town in 1856 and 12 years later became a city. In 1858, when Minnesota was admitted to the Union, St Paul became the state capital. Minneapolis and St Paul have been engaged in a longstanding but friendly rivalry. Minneapolis is an attractive large city, filled with parks and lakes. It has grown to greatness in a comparatively brief period of time. St Paul is beautifully situated on the Mississippi River, which winds through the town. Many streets are picturesque, narrow, and hilly; others are completely modern. Together, Minneapolis and St Paul form a major cultural and educational center. The population of Minneapolis is 363,940; St Paul 262,980.

WHAT TO SEE

In Minneapolis, see the 57-story **IDS Tower** with its observation deck; open daily, adults $2.00, children and senior citizens $1.50. Then see **University of Minnesota** campus; **Minneapolis Institute of Arts; Fort Snelling; Minneapolis Grain Exchange.** The **Science Museum and Planetarium,** with its time and space gallery, natural history, geology, and Egyptian mummy collections, is located at the Minneapolis Public Library. The sophisticated **Dayton's** department store is worth a visit. Tours are available through **General Mills** and other large companies if you call in advance. A worthwhile automobile trip is a ride around Lakes Calhoun, Harriet, Cedar, Nokomis, and Lake of the Isles. Also see the **Mississippi River Lock and Dam No. 1.** A 2½-hour conducted sightseeing tour of the city costs $8.75, Memorial Day-Labor Day. The Minneapolis Park Board has set up a self-guided scenic drive. There are boat trips on many of the lakes and on the Mississippi River in summer.

In St Paul, see *God of Peace*, the huge revolving Indian statue at City Hall; **Ramsey House,** home of the state's first territorial governor; **Summit Avenue** with its mansions and churches; the **Minnesota State Historical Society,** early state historical objects, open Monday through Saturday 8:30-5, Sunday 1-4, free; the **Old Federal Courts Building;** the **State Capitol,** tours Monday-Friday 9-4, Saturdays 10-4, and Sundays 1-3; reservations advised; **Indian Mounds Park,** pre-historic Indian ruins and a recreational area; and the **Science Museum,** with its 180° Omnitheater, which shows science films daily. Greyline offers a number of tours running from 2½ to 7 hours. A 6-hour conducted tour of St Paul costs about $6, Memorial Day-Labor Day; a combined 6½ hour tour of Minneapolis and St Paul costs $13, and is available through the Metropolitan Transit Commission.

Minneapolis is known for its 153 parks and 22 lakes. **Minnehaha Park** is renowned for **Minnehaha Falls,** mentioned in Longfellow's *Song of Hiawatha.* Interesting displays at **Kenwood Parkway Demonstration Gardens; Eloise Butler Wild Flower Garden,** open daily, April-November; and **Lyndale Park,** beautiful rose gardens.

In St Paul are **Como Park,** with zoo, amusement center, conservatory, floral displays, lake; **Phalen Park,** swimming, beach, boating; **Highland Park,** golf course, swimming pool, amusement section. There is a state fish hatchery on Point Douglas Road, open Monday through Friday 8-4:30.

The Minnesota Zoological Garden in Apple Valley has a variety of exotic animals from all parts of the world, as well as creatures native to the state. All are displayed in their natural habitat. Daily 9-5 1 May-30 September; remainder of year 9-4; adults $3, senior citizens and ages 12-16, $1.50, ages 6-11, $1. The Metropolitan Transit Commission provides bus service May-September from both Minneapolis and St Paul.

Principal schools in Minneapolis: **University of Minnesota,** founded in 1851; over 54,000 students now enrolled; coeducational; outstanding for medicine, dentistry, graduate work, agriculture and education. **Augsburg College,** founded 1869, coeducational; **Minneapolis College of Art and Design;** and **Metropolitan College of Law.**

Principal schools in St Paul: **Hamline University,** coeducational, arts and science courses; **Macalester College,** coeducational, arts and science courses; **College of St Thomas; College of St Catherine,** for women. Also **Luther Seminary, St Paul Seminary, Bethel College, Concordia College** and **William Mitchell College of Law.** The **Institute of Agriculture,** part of the University of Minnesota, is noted for its research work. The small but famous **St Olaf** and **Carleton** colleges are in Northfield, about 35 miles south of St Paul.

ACCOMMODATIONS

In Minneapolis: **Curtis Hotel and Motor Lodge** (340-5300, S\$30-40/D\$35-44); **Holiday Inn-Downtown** (332-0371, S\$49/D\$55); **Leamington Hotel** (370-1100, S\$40/D\$48); **Leamington Motor Inn** (355-9551, S\$19-27/D\$32-40); **Marquette Inn** (332-2351, S\$64-79/D\$74-89), in the IDS Center, and the **Northstar Inn** (338-2288, S\$52-60/D\$65-75), in the Northstar Center, both connected by skyway system to the business hub of the city; **Radisson Hotel Downtown** (333-2181, S\$42-48/D\$52-58); and the **Sheraton Ritz** (336-5711, S\$57-65/D\$67-75), on Nicollet Mall; all downtown. Other hotels and motels in or near the city include **Concord Motel, Fair Oaks Motel,** and **Normandy Motor Inn,** with rates averaging S\$29-36/D\$31-51; **Hopkins House,** 9 miles west, and **Holiday Airport South, Howard Johnson's, Marriott Inn, Radisson South,** and **Thunderbird,** 8 to 12 miles south of the center of Bloomington. Rates average S\$37-60/D\$42-67. **L'Hotel de France** (835-1900, S\$58-90/D\$70-102) is 15 miles southwest. Hotel Tax: 4-7%.

In St Paul: **Capp Towers Motor Hotel** (227-7331, S\$36/D\$42); **Holiday Inn-St Paul State Capitol** (227-8711, S\$40/D\$47); **Radisson St. Paul** (292-1900, S\$46-52/D\$58-64), all downtown. **Paul's Place Inn** (633-6333, S\$33/D\$42) is 8 miles northwest. Many motels are situated on the outskirts of town on US 12 and MN 55. Hotel Tax: 4-7%.

RESTAURANTS

No one should fail to try the locally caught trout, walleyed pike, and whitefish. In Minneapolis: **Charlie's Cafe Exceptionale** and **Murray's** are the business men's favorites for steaks, expensive; **Wine Cellar, New French Cafe,** and **Les Quatres Amis,** excellent, continental cuisine, expensive; **Flame Room** at the Hotel Radisson, good food specialties, entertainment nightly, expensive; **Rosewood Room** at the Northstar and **Orion Room** atop the IDS both very elegant and very expensive; **Black Angus, The Butcherblock** for steaks, moderately expensive; **Waikiki Room** at the Hotel Leamington, Hawaiian and Polynesian food specialties and atmosphere, expensive; **Guadalaharry's, Anthony's Wharf, Taiga,** and **Pracna** on Main are on part of the reconstructed waterfront, moderate. **Normandy Kitchen,** in the business area, moderate. Within a half-hour ride from town are **Michael's, The Chalet, White House,** and **Jax, Howard Wong's, The Szechuan Star, The Criterion,** and **Eddie Webster's;** all have good food and are moderately expensive. **Camelot** is excellent and expensive. L'Hotel de France, **Henrici's,** and **Franco's** are within 10 minutes of the airport, 20 minutes from downtown Minneapolis; moderately expensive, good food.

In St Paul: Dining rooms of the **St Paul** and **Radisson St Paul** hotels, good meals, moderate; **Manor** and **Gannon's** for steaks and chicken, both moderate; **Blue Horse** and **Smuggler's Inn,** more expensive; **Saji-Ya,** Japanese specialties; **Sweden House,** smorgasbord; **Don the Beachcomber's,** Polynesian food, moderately expensive; **Lee's Highland Village Inn,** steaks, moderate; **Lexington,** steaks and seafood, moderate. Other good, moderate-priced restaurants include **The Coachman, Golden Steer,** and

Fran O'Connell's. **The Venetian Inn** in north St Paul, 10 minutes from downtown St Paul, has good Italian style cooking; moderately expensive.

ARTS AND MUSIC

In Minneapolis: **Walker Art Center,** exhibits and excellent permanent collection of contemporary art; open Tuesday-Saturday 10-8, Sunday 12-6, 1 June-28 February; Tuesdays-Sundays 10-5, also Wednesday 5-8, remainder of year; free. **Minneapolis Institute of Arts,** fine, large art collection; open Tuesday-Saturday 10-5, Sunday 1-5, also Thursday 5-9; free. **University of Minnesota Art Gallery,** contemporary art; open daily, free. **Bell Museum of Natural History,** general exhibits; open daily, free. **American Swedish Institute,** Swedish arts and crafts; open Tuesday through Saturday 1-4, Sundays 1-5; $1 adults, students 6-21, 50¢. Guided tours by appointment only. The **Minnesota Theater Company** performs in repertory at the internationally known **Guthrie Theater** from June through late January or early February. **Old Log Theater,** professional performances; **The Cricket Theater; Chanhassen Dinner Theater; Children's Theater Company** of the Minneapolis Institute of Arts; and the amateur **Theater-in-the-Round.**

The **Minnesota Orchestra** performs regularly at **Orchestra Hall.** During July and August there are free band concerts by various artists every evening at the **Lake Harriet** pavilion. The New York Metropolitan Opera gives performances in Minneapolis in late spring every year. Consult the newspapers for other musical events. The Minnesota Orchestra performs on the University of Minnesota campus, late May to August and October to early May.

In St Paul: **St Paul Arts and Science Center,** art center gallery and workshop, science museum, general scientific exhibits, semi-professional theater, and concert chambers, and the unique **Omnitheater,** a domed planetarium which shows 3-D films on various scientific phenomena (call for show times); most functions free. There are grand and light opera performances given by the **St Paul Civic Opera Association. St Paul Civic Center** presents Broadway roadshows; **Chimera** is also active during most of the season.

SHOPPING

The pedestrian **Nicollet Mall** in downtown Minneapolis is the city's main shopping thoroughfare, with many specialty shops and large department stores. The skyway system, a large network of enclosed above-the-street pedestrian bridges, connects the buildings in the downtown area. Stores are open 9:30-6, Monday and Thursday evenings until 9. **Gokey,** nationally known for outdoor wear and sports equipment, is on West Fifth Street in the heart of St. Paul's business district. **Southdale,** a large three-tiered shopping mall, is near the airport.

SPORTS

Professional major-league baseball is played by the **Minnesota Twins;** professional football by the **Vikings;** pro ice hockey by the **North Stars;**

and professional soccer by the **Minnesota Kicks.** Big Ten football, baseball, and basketball are played by the University of Minnesota's **Golden Gophers.** Several smaller colleges also have active sports programs. Automobile racing at the **Minnesota State Fair** for 10 days ending Labor Day. With much freezing weather during the winter, ice skating and other winter sports are very popular; there are 27 winter ski resorts in the metropolitan region. Ice fishing is particularly good in the area. Summertime brings water sports, golf, tennis, hunting, and fishing; non-resident fishing license is $10 for the season, $5.00 for three days.

CALENDAR OF EVENTS

In Minneapolis: **Ice Follies,** April; **Svenskarnas Dag,** June; **Minneapolis Aquatennial,** 10 days of water shows, parades, and entertainment, July; **Minnesota Renaissance Festival,** September.

In St Paul: **Winter Carnival Week,** late January to early February; **Minnesota Golf Classic,** mid-June; **Minnesota State Fair,** 10 days preceding Labor Day.

WHERE TO GO NEARBY

Six parks in the **Hennepin County Park Reserve** district in and around Minneapolis; **Minneapolis Valley Restoration Project** at Shakopee, 25 miles southwest of Minneapolis, re-creating life on the river in the 1850s; the new **Valley Fair Amusement Park** near Shakopee, a multimillion dollar family entertainment theme park with rides, campgrounds, vaudeville; **University of Minnesota Arboretum,** 30 miles west of Minneapolis; **St Croix Islands State Park,** 36 miles northeast, a scenic area; **William O'Brien State Park,** 41 miles northeast, picnic facilities. **St Croix State Park,** about 100 miles north, beautiful forest region, with fishing, camping sites, cabins. **Nerstrand Woods State Park,** 71 miles southeast, rugged wooded areas, and **Itasca State Park,** where the Mississippi River begins.

Farther away: **Brainerd Lake Region,** about 130 miles northwest, is the leading resort area in the state, with a wide variety of accommodations, many fine lakes, and delightful wooded areas. Other resort spots are Aitkin, Alexandria, **Annandale,** Bemidji, **Crosby, Deer River, Deerwood,** Detroit Lakes, Ely, **Glenwood, Hackensack, Orr,** Park Rapids, **Perham,** Walker, **White Bear Lake** and **Willmar.** Northeastern Minnesota is famous for its "Canoe Country," recommended to those who enjoy outdoor camping trips. At **Fort Snelling State Park,** on the Minnesota and Mississippi Rivers, is historic Fort Snelling, old fort and frontier outpost; open May through October.

FURTHER STATE INFORMATION

Department of Economic Development, 480 Cedar Street, St Paul, MN 55101. Hunting, Fishing and Parks: **Department of Natural Resources,** Centennial Building, St Paul, MN 55101. **Minneapolis Convention and Tourism Commission,** 15 S. Fifth Street, Minneapolis, MN 55402. **St Paul Area Chamber of Commerce,** Suite 300, Osborn Building, St Paul, MN 55102.

Consulates in Minneapolis: Belgium, Canada, Chile, Colombia, Costa Rica, Denmark, El Salvador, Finland, France, Federal Republic of Germany, Great Britain, Iceland, Japan, Korea, Malta, Mexico, Netherlands, Norway, Peru, Sweden, Switzerland.

USEFUL TELEPHONE NUMBERS
Minneapolis
Police	348-2345
Fire	348-2345
Ambulance	347-3151
Medical Society	375-0000
Poison	347-3141
Dental Emergency	333-5052
Road Info	296-3076
Pan Am Reservations	800-621-2909

St. Paul
Police	291-1234
Fire	224-7371
Medical Society	224-1857
Poison	221-2113
Pan Am Reservations	800-621-2909

Mississippi

Area	47,716 square miles					**Population**		2,520,638			
Capital	Jackson					**Sales Tax**		5%			

Weather	Jan	Feb	Mar	Apr	May	Jun	Jul	Aug	Sep	Oct	Nov	Dec
Av Temp (°C)	9	10	14	18	23	27	28	28	25	19	13	10
Days of Rain	11	9	10	9	9	7	10	11	8	6	7	11

Between the arrival of Hernando de Soto in 1540 and the granting of statehood in 1817, Mississippi lived under the flags of Spain, France, and Britain. Although the state flew the US flag as early as 1798, the Yazoo Land Fraud—in which the state of Georgia, claiming the region, sold lots to speculators—was not settled until the federal government intervened in 1802; the Louisiana Purchase of 1803 solved the problem of access via the river the state is named for. Mississippi was admitted to the Union in 1817. The Choctaw, Chickasaw, and Natchez Indian tribes did not settle their land claims until 1832. A slave-owning state, Mississippi nevertheless bore the epithet "The Magnolia State" and until the Civil War, its concepts of peace and prosperity made it one of the richest in the nation with property assessments alone totaling $510 million in 1860.

The era coincided with the fashion of Greek revival architecture, and wealthy plantation owners built some of America's most gracious pillared mansions, often with Spanish galleries, French wrought-iron grillwork, and touches of the Gothic revival. Beautiful furnishings were imported from Europe to enrich the interiors. The whole effect was invariably charming, and it is easy to visualize the carefree house parties and balls that were the pattern for life among Mississippi's aristocracy until it all came to a crashing end with the outbreak of the Civil War in 1861.

It took Mississippi a long time to recover from those tragic years. Indeed, it was not until the 1920s that property assessments reached pre-Civil War levels, though in devalued dollars. Too many battles had been fought across its rich plantations, and landowners, who had been dependent upon slaves to plant and harvest their cotton, run their homes, and raise their children, now had no one but themselves to perform these tasks. Then a plague of boll weevils nearly finished the cotton fields, and railway trains put the exciting Mississippi steamboats out of business. But slowly, gallantly, the state has recovered, though without renouncing its history, through a long period of transition. Nevertheless, it was only in 1965 that industrial employment moved ahead of agriculture in terms of work provided.

Cotton is still very important but no longer king of the economy. Large forests of hardwood trees put Mississippi among the nation's leading lumber producers. More people are engaged in industry than work in the fields, and oil and gas wells gush out a steady profit. Indeed, the state is a leading producer of natural gas and oil. Tourism is another major industry. People come from all over to see the restored mansions which recall that storybook antebellum era, to visit the great battlefields, and to enjoy Gulf Coast winter resorts along the Old Spanish Trail.

Inland, rolling hills cover most of the state. Summers are hot and humid. Winters are brief, but you can expect some cold weather from December through February, a situation alien to this Deep South atmosphere.

If you have come this far without trying "soul food," Mississippi is a good place to experience the unique tastes of turnip greens, crisp fried okra, stuffed baked ham, hush puppies, catfish, and barbecue sauces blazing with chili peppers. From early-day Indian stews to modern cocktail appetizers, the pecan has found its way into all aspects of the Mississippi cuisine, and Gulf shrimp and oysters are other delicious local dishes.

Mississippi's **Gulf Coast,** rich in historic sites, is both a great summer and winter resort area. A 28-mile-long sand beach extends east from **Pass Christian** (pronounced *chris-tee-an*) through **Gulfport** to **Biloxi** (pronounced *bu-lux-i*). At Gulfport (population 39,450), accommodations at **Sheraton-Gulfport Inn** (864-0050, S$29/D$35); **Ramada** and **Holiday Inns** averaging S$28-30/D$34-37; and at **Best Western** (864-4650, S$26/D$37). In Biloxi (population 49,134), try **Broadwater Beach Hotel** (388-2211, S$50/D$55); **Royal D'Iberville** (388-4141, S$40-48/D$48-56), with its challenging PGA courses at Marsh Island, St. Andrews Sunkist, Bayon View, Hickory Hills, and Pass Christian Isles; or **Sea Gulf Motel** or **White House Hotel/Motel** averaging S$22-23/D$23-35. Branches of most other motels here at the usual price. Just west of Biloxi is **Beauvoir,** the last home of Jefferson Davis, president of the Confederacy; it is interestingly furnished with his own possessions. Beyond is **Gautier** where the antebellum **Old Home Place** plantation, home of the Gautier family, is open for tours and cruises on the **Pascagoula River** in the sternwheeler, *Magnolia Blossom,* daily, year round. See the **Old Spanish Fort** and the museum outside **Pascagoula,** another resort town and ship building center, near the Alabama border. In the northern part of the state, just 30 miles above Oxford, is little **Holly Springs,** a perfect gem of stately antebellum homes and churches that are featured during the town's annual "pilgrimage" (tour of old mansions), the last weekend in April.

In recent years Mississippi has given the US more creative writers, *per capita,* than any other state. Richard Wright *(Native Son, Black Boy),* the first modern spokesman for his race, was born in Natchez. Eudora Welty *(The Optimist's Daughter* and many distinguished short stories) lives in **Jackson,** the state capital, where the **Governor's Mansion,** the oldest executive mansion in the nation designated as a National Landmark, and **The Oaks** are outstanding antebellum homes. Jackson, population 200,338, has been a center for all-American conspiracies since pre-Civil War days. It was an apparent haven for Aaron Burr and for numerous plottings since. It was sacked by the Federal Army in 1863, but has not lost its penchant for individuality. The Old Capitol, which now houses the state's **Historical Museum** is a fine example of Greek Renaissance architecture. It has been recently renovated. Accommodations include: **Passport Inn** (982-1011, S$23/D$27), **Stonewall Jackson** (354-1653, S$18/D$22), and **Airways Inn Motel** (939-3513, S$20/D$25), plus **Admiral Benbow** (948-4161, S$28/D$35), four **Holiday Inns** averaging S$31-35/D$37-40, and **Howard Johnson, Jackson Hotel,** and **Sheraton** running rather more. **Motel 6** chain breaks price barrier here at North Frontage Road (948-3682, S$12/D$15) with simple and clean, basic accommodation. Tennessee Williams *(The Glass Menagerie, A Streetcar Named Desire)* was born in **Columbus,** a small city with over 100 houses built before the Civil War. Some homes in Columbus are open to the public during the **Columbus Pilgrimage** in early April as well as all year for touring. Check with the Columbus Chamber of Commerce. William Faulkner, Nobel Prize-winning giant of American literature, wrote about the fictional "Yoknapatawpha County" and "Jefferson," which were really Lafayette County and Oxford. His home is preserved next to the University of Mississippi campus ("Ole Miss") in **Oxford.**

Mississippi has about 30 parks with well-developed facilities for sports and camping. The **Natchez Trace Parkway,** still under development, follows the old Indian trail that became the 500-mile post road in the early 1800s which connected Natchez with Nashville, Tennessee. Except for road-surfacing, the scene along the Trace is much as it was when all traffic was on foot or on horseback; a free film, *Path of Empire,* tells the exciting story of the Trace's history at parkway headquarters in **Tupelo.** Historic sites en route from north to south include **Brices Cross Roads National Battlefield Site,** near Baldwyn, the **Tupelo National Battlefield** and the **Chickasaw Indian Village,** near Tupelo, and the Emerald Mound, near Natchez. About 70 miles north of Natchez is **Vicksburg National Military Park,** considered one of the country's most interesting battlefields. Cannons stand in their battery positions; breastworks, rifle pits, and the ruins of forts remain as they were over 100 years ago. There are nearly 1,600 memorials, statues, monuments, and markers honoring both Union and Confederate soldiers who took part in the 47-day siege that ended in the fall of **Vicksburg** on 4 July 1863. Exhibits in the Visitors Center clarify the plan and action of this crucial campaign, which dealt a mortal blow to the South. In the town itself are **Candon Hearth, Cedar Grove,** and **McRaven,** three homes which provide both an architectural and military history of the town. There is an exceptional museum of Civil War relics in the **Old Courthouse,** where Grant ran up the Union flag after his victory. Popular restaurants include **Tumminellos,** featuring an Italian-American cuisine; the **Old Southern Tea Room,** Southern specialties; and **The Glass Kitchen,** home-style food with a cafeteria for those who choose not to order from the menu.

City To Visit

NATCHEZ

Natchez (population 21,732) is in southwestern Mississippi, beautifully situated on high bluffs overlooking the Mississippi River. When the French explorers La Salle and Tonti arrived in 1682, they found the site occupied by friendly Natchez Indians; the tribe subsequently became less hospitable when Le Moyne de Bienville came in 1716 to establish Fort Rosalie. Thirteen years later, the Indians captured and destroyed the fort, but it was a brief victory. In 1763 Natchez became a British possession, only to fall to Spain in 1779. Spaniards laid out the town site, erected a number of fine buildings, encouraged tobacco growing, and departed peaceably in 1798 when the Mississippi Territory was annexed to the United States. After the Louisiana Purchase in 1803 opened the Mississippi River to American control, Natchez became first a major river port and then one of the world's leading cotton centers.

The great wealth generated during the early 1800s was partially invested in fine residences, and Natchez has at least 35 antebellum homes that are outstanding for their architecture and furnishings. Fortunes were lost during the Civil War, but many of the lovely homes are still occupied by descendants of the original owners. The courtly traditions of the Old South have been preserved, and Natchez has a distinct aura of aristocracy.

WHAT TO SEE

If it hadn't been for the determined members of the Pilgrimage Garden Club and Natchez Garden Club, Natchez could have moldered in oblivion. The great mansions, which have been restored at the coaxing of the garden clubs, are scattered all over town and are often in considerable contrast to their surrounding neighborhoods. There are more than 35 antebellum homes, of outstanding architecture and interior furnishing, and in spring and fall these are open to visitors, although still occupied in many instances by the descendants of their former owners. Among

Longwood, the famous octagonal Moorish structure built around a glass-enclosed rotunda, is but one of a number of unusual mansions to be seen in Natchez, MS.

the lovely old homes open to the public during the **Natchez Pilgrimage** in March is **Stanton Hall,** sumptuous with Carrara marble mantels, bronze chandeliers, and huge French mirrors, all brought by chartered sailing ship from Europe; it has lovely gardens and a restaurant in a restored carriage house; open year round.

Connelly's Tavern, overlooking the Mississippi, was built before 1795, and flew the US flag in 1797 despite the Spanish rulers. This was the gathering place for adventurers who plied the river or set off for the Natchez Trace. The Tavern's guest list ranged from outlaws to a prince who became King Louis Philippe of France; fine period furnishings in Spanish provincial architecture. **Rosalie,** occupied since 1820, was head-quarters of the Union Army in 1863. **The Elms,** shaded by huge oaks, is designed and furnished to the taste of the Spanish governor for whom it was built in 1782. **Melrose** (1845), a classic example of the stately ante-bellum home, is exquisitely furnished with the original carved rosewood furniture, French brocade draperies, Egyptian marble fireplaces, and an Audubon landscape of Natchez. All four buildings are open daily except for Thanksgiving, Christmas Eve, and Christmas Day.

Green Leaves (pre-1812) contains a rare collection of hand-painted Audubon china, and the immense live oak in the backyard is believed to have sheltered Natchez Indian councils. **Longwood,** the famous octago-nal Moorish extravaganza built around a glass-enclosed rotunda, was only partly completed when the Yankee workmen heard of the outbreak of the Civil War; tools and paint buckets remain just as they left them. Set amid oaks draped with Spanish moss, the house has an eerie atmo-sphere. Open year round, 7 days a week, the home offers expansive grounds that invite picnickers. **Dunleith** (1847), said to be haunted by a harp-playing spinster, is completely surrounded by huge columned galleries; **D'Evereux** (1840), a perfect example of Greek revival architec-ture, often entertained statesman Henry Clay; both are open year round.

Gloucester (pre-1803) was built in the Georgian style before Greek revival became fashionable. **Arlington** (1816), another Georgian mansion, has original furnishings which recall dazzling social whirls. **The Briars** (1812) is the stately home in which Jefferson Davis married Varina Howell in 1845; open year round. There are many more great Natchez houses, each with a romantic history. During the *Pilgrimage* there is a variety of tours for a ticketbook price of $12.50 adults, $6.25 children. The price includes the viewing of five homes and tickets can be used on any one of the Pilgrimage days. To see five homes usually takes 4 hours. Twenty of the Pilgrimage homes are open year round. A delightful *Confederate Pageant* depicting the Old South is presented four evenings a week for the entire month during the Pilgrimage, and the satiric *Southern Expo-sure* is staged on alternate evenings. The *"Mississippi Medicine Show,"* a showboat type entertainment, can be enjoyed by groups all year except at Pilgrimage time. At **Natchez-under-the-Hill** the *Delta and Mississippi Queens* dock each week, and it is then that the sounds of Southern jazz are to be heard around town. Natchez is also the end of the Natchez Trace Parkway, an historic and scenic route which runs the upstream way back to Nashville TN. In the early days, pioneers would sell their goods at the dock and then return upriver by horse or on foot along this trail. This pleasant town has managed to preserve its diverse history—as a number of movie makers have discovered—the courtly traditions of the Old South still remain and Natchez has a subtle but distinct aura of its former aristocracy.

ACCOMMODATIONS

On US 61 South: **Days Inn Motel** (445-8291, S$20/D$24), **Prentiss Motel,** 10 minutes from the center of Natchez (442-1691, S$28/D$33). On US 61 North, 1½ miles from Natchez center: **Holiday Inn** (442-3686, S$30/D$35). On Highway 98/84 overlooking the Mississippi River: **Ramada Hilltop Inn** (446-6311, S$30/D$40). Hotel Tax: 5%. All rates go up slightly during the Pilgrimage in March, at which time it is also possible to get rooms in some of the houses on display and in other private homes.

RESTAURANTS

Many of the restaurants in the city feature the southern specialties of fried chicken and catfish. Two restaurants with fine food and atmosphere are the **Carriage House,** well spoken for in neighboring areas and noted for its fresh mint juleps, and the **Side Track. The Post House,** a recent restoration of the oldest building on the Natchez Trace, now serves typical Dixie fare as does the **Rendezvous,** specializing in steak and seafood. Note also **Cock-of-the-Walk,** for catfish specialties at Natchez-under-the-Hill.

ENTERTAINMENT

Several of the motels feature nightly combos for dancing and listening.

SHOPPING

The recently opened **Natchez Mall** is home to a number of stores and boutiques, including both **McRaes** and **Coles** department stores. Fashionable women's wear is to be found at **Ullman's,** while **Benoist's** is fine for men's wear. A number of boutiques have sprung up over the past few years, and the Tracetown shopping center can occasionally surprise with bargains.

Antique dealers and others who collect antiques make regular pilgrimages to Natchez for the fine *objects* to be found here. And on Sundays there's a Thieves Market that brings a crowd of regulars to buy and barter.

SPORTS

Natchez has a public golf course, private golf club, baseball fields, and tennis courts. Fishing and hunting are good in the vicinity.

CALENDAR OF EVENTS

Natchez Pilgrimage, March; **Confederate Memorial Day,** 26 April; **Craft Fair,** handmade goods for sale, first week in October; **Territorial Fair**

and **Horse Show,** October. Tours of antebellum mansions are available year round.

WHERE TO GO NEARBY

Rosemont, the boyhood home of Jefferson Davis, is at **Woodville,** 33 miles south of Natchez. About a 2-hour drive due east of Natchez is **Laurel,** home of Masonite products and site of the excellent **Lauren Rogers Library and Museum of Art,** which also contains the world's largest collection of baskets. There are camping, picnicking, swimming, hunting, and fishing in **Homochitto National Forest,** which covers much of the land south toward the Louisiana border. Just off Natchez Trace Parkway, 12 miles northeast of Natchez, is **Emerald Mound,** the nation's third-largest Indian mound, with a dozen mounds within 25 miles of it. Vicksburg is only about 70 miles north of Natchez.

FURTHER STATE INFORMATION

Division of Tourism, Mississippi Department of Economic Development; PO Box 849, Jackson, MS 39205. Hunting and Fishing: **Wildlife and Conservation Commission,** Box 451, Jackson, MS 39205. **Natchez-Adams County Chamber of Commerce,** PO Box 725, Natchez, MS 39120. **Natchez Pilgrimage Headquarters,** PO Box 347, Natchez, MS 39120.

USEFUL TELEPHONE NUMBERS
Natchez

Emergency (Fire, Police & Ambulance)	911
Jefferson Davis Memorial Hospital	442-2871
Natchez Community Hospital	446-7711
Chamber of Commerce	445-4611
Tourist Information	442-5849
Pan Am Reservations	800-535-6764

Jackson

Emergency (Fire, Police & Ambulance)	911
Hinds General Hospital	376-1000
Mississippi Baptist Medical Center	968-1000
Mississippi Highway Police	982-1212
Legal Services	948-6752
Chamber of Commerce	948-7575
Pan Am Reservations	800-535-6764

Missouri

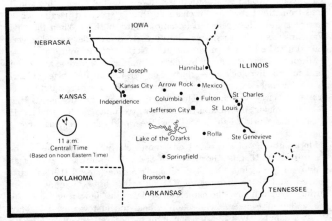

Area	69,686 square miles				**Population**	4,867,000						
Capital	Jefferson City				**Sales Tax**	4%						
Weather		Jan	Feb	Mar	Apr	May	Jun	Jul	Aug	Sep	Oct	Nov	Dec
Av Temp (°C)		0	2	6	13	19	24	28	27	22	16	7	2
Days Rain/Snow		7	7	9	10	11	11	8	8	8	7	6	7

It might be said that Missouri was the first of the post-Revolution states to benefit in any lasting way from the tourist trade. Since it formed the western bank of the Mississippi for quite a distance, it had seen travelers in some numbers by the time it came into the possession of the United States in 1803 as part of the Louisiana Purchase. The next year Lewis and Clark, the US military explorers, chose St Louis as the starting point for their trip up the Missouri River to the Oregon Territory and the Pacific Ocean. After that, people poured in and out of the state. Missouri became the jumping-off place for both the Santa Fe Trail to the Southwest and the Oregon Trail to the great Northwest. And for a while it must have seemed that everybody was passing through and not much interested in Missouri itself. However, a sufficient number of tourists found the state attractive, for it quickly became the last outpost of civilization instead of the new frontier.

When time came to apply for statehood, Missouri suddenly found itself in the middle of a national controversy. At the time, states were either "free states" or "slave states," and the free states wanted Missouri admitted as one of their number. But the cotton gin had been invented, and Southern farmers, many of whom had been in favor of the abolition of slavery, began to readjust their principles. It had become clear that cotton would grow nicely in Missouri, and slaves were needed to reap cotton.

A great deal of hard bargaining was done on both sides, and the result became known as the "Missouri Compromise." The arrangement was that Missouri would be admitted as a slave state, but any further admissions from the Louisiana Purchase north of a specified parallel would be free states. Thus, Missouri became a state in 1821. When the Civil War broke out 40 years later, the unresolved attitude toward slavery caused it to be badly torn between the North and the South.

Missouri has grown since those days in wealth and stature as an agricultural, mining, livestock, and industrial center. It is the birthplace of Mark Twain (Samuel G. Clemens), one of America's finest writers, and former president Harry S. Truman. The state has also produced Thomas Hart Benton, a major American artist, and also the infamous Jesse James. In 1904 at the World's Fair in St. Louis, the world's first ice cream cones were sold.

Florissant, one of the oldest and most colorful communities in the state, is about 15 miles northwest of St Louis. Entered by way of an avenue of giant elms, **Old St Ferdinand's Shrine** (*circa* 1819) adjoins a convent and historical museum. The old white brick building is open during daylight hours. The name Florissant means "flowering," and here the **Valley of Flowers Celebration** is held the first weekend in May. Westward on I-70 is **St Charles,** one of the earliest settlements in Missouri and site of the first state capital. The town provides a walking tour for visitors. View the first **Missouri State Capitol** with period furnishings, *circa* 1820; the **County Historical Society Museum,** which safeguards the personal effects of Daniel Boone and the other pioneers; **Bushnell Pioneer Museum** with replicas of old village shops, open May to November only; and the Tudor-Gothic buildings of the **Lindenwood Colleges.** Thirteen miles west on I-70 is **Fort Zumwalt State Park,** which encloses the remains of the oldest hewn-timber cabin north of the Missouri River. Camping and picnic facilities are available.

South of I-70 on US 54 is **Fulton,** where Winston Churchill delivered his "Iron Curtain" address in March 1946 at **Westminster College.** The **Winston Churchill Memorial and Library** has been established at the college in a church which stood in London for 800 years until moved to Fulton in 1966. Churchill memorabilia includes a bust by Jacob Epstein, leaded glass windows, the document John F. Kennedy signed, while President, to make Sir Winston an honorary US citizen, the original text of the "Iron Curtain" speech, and a memorial statue of Winston Churchill.

Some of the finest saddle horses in the world are bred in **Mexico,** a town north of I-70 on US 54. Home of the **Missouri Military Academy,** Mexico also has the **Audrain County Historical Society Museum.** This restored 1857 mansion has fine Currier and Ives and antique doll collections. Overlooking the bluffs of the Salt River is the **Mark Twain State Park** at Florida, north on MO 107. The 1,192 acres of rugged terrain are a backdrop for the **Mark Twain Shrine,** which houses the cabin in which the author Samuel Clemens was born. The facility contains many of his personal belongings and the original manuscript of *Tom Sawyer.*

HANNIBAL still retains the flavor of the Mississippi River's steamboat days. This was the boyhood town of Samuel Clemens. You can see his personal effects in his father's law office, now the **Mark Twain Museum** and **Boyhood Home.** Adjoining the building is a replica of the fence which Tom's Aunt Polly wanted whitewashed. Nearby is the **Becky Thatcher House.** Clemens made his last visit to Hannibal in 1892 when he addressed a group at the **Rockcliffe Mansion,** now restored in art nouveau décor. The **Pilaster House,** where the author's father died, features a vintage drugstore, kitchen, and doctor's office. North is **Cardiff Hill,** with an expansive view of the Mississippi and life-size bronze statues of Tom Sawyer and Huck Finn. South of town is **Mark Twain Cave,** where Injun Joe supposedly died. A statue of the author overlooks the Mississippi bluffs at **Riverview Park.** Also of interest is the **Molly Brown House,** where the "Unsinkable" Molly Brown (about whom a popular play and motion picture were based) was born. You can ride the Twainland Express train, May-August, and sign up for a river excursion leaving from Steamboat Landing, 15 May to Labor Day. **Tom Sawyer Days,** a national fencepainting contest, is held in early July. Accommodations in Hannibal include **Best Western Hannibal House** (221-7950, S$18-24/ D$22-28), **Best Western Holiday Inn** (221-6610, S$25-27/D$30-40), **Best Western Mark Twain Motor Inn** (221-1490, S$18-25/D$22-28).

A center for higher education, **COLUMBIA** is westward on I-70. The oldest university west of the Mississippi, the **University of Missouri,** or "Mizzou," was founded in 1839. Its **Ellis Library** contains 1½ million volumes and in its rare book room has a page from the Gutenberg Bible. Greek and Roman art, the Kress Study Collection of Italian paintings, and a Far and Near East collection are also in the library. Adjacent to the library is the **Missouri Historical Society** with paintings by George Caleb Bingham, who was professor of art here, and a collection of works by and about Mark Twain. The **Journalism Historical Museum** is located at the university's **School of Journalism,** the world's oldest college for journalists. An outstanding horse show is a highlight of the **Boone County Fair** held in Columbia in early August. Accommodations in Columbia include: **Hilton Inn** (445-8531, S$23-30/D$28-37); **Holiday Inn-East** (449-2491, S$34-39/D$42-48); **Ramada Inn** (449-0051, S$32 up/D$40 up).

South of Columbia, spanning the steep bluffs of limestone near the Missouri River, is the capital of the state, **JEFFERSON CITY.** Noted for its fine art collection, the **State Capitol** is built in Italian Renaissance style from Carthage gray marble. Works by Alexander S. Calder and N. C. Wyeth are hung inside. The chief attractions are the Thomas Hart Benton murals. A Missouri genre painter, Benton uses legendary and historical themes in his work, including Huck Finn and his friend Jim, the James Boys, a political rally, and even a country kitchen. Before leaving the capitol, explore the **Missouri State Museum** which includes an Indian burial restoration and collections of Civil War relics, firearms, gems, and even zithers. Memorabilia of five wars, antiques, and the inaugural ball gowns of many first ladies of the state are on display in the **Cole County Historical Society Museum.** Overlooking the city is **Lincoln University,** founded by Union soldiers in 1866 for the education of blacks. Midtown motels include the **Holiday Inn-Downtown, Ramada Inn** and **Rodeway Inn;** about S\$29/D\$36. At Lake of the Ozarks, some 40 miles southwest of the city, are a number of resorts, including **Marriott's Tan-Tar-A-Resort** (348-3131, S/D\$70-90), **Lodge of the 4 Seasons** (365-3001, S/D\$70-100). There are also tent and camping facilities on this popular lake with 1,375 miles of shoreline. North on US 54, near Eldon, are the **Fantasy World Caverns,** which include an Indian burial ground with skeletons and artifacts. At **Camdenton** are **Kelsey's Antique Cars** and the **Camden County Historical Museum,** stocked with antique tools and arrowheads.

Of historic interest on I-70 is the little town of **Arrow Rock,** part of the old Santa Fe Trail. The restored **Old Tavern** still welcomes visitors. **George Caleb Bingham's House** can be viewed from June to August. Sign up for the walking tour of the town, which includes the **Log Courthouse, Gun Shop** and **Chapel;** April through October. In the **Arrow Rock State Historic Site** you'll find historical markers which designated the **Old Santa Fe Trail;** camping and picnicking facilities here. Continuing north to **Laclede,** one arrives at the childhood home of General "Black Jack" John Pershing. Preserved as a memorial, the house displays Victorian furnishings and personal memorabilia. Nearby is an 1836 covered bridge.

Independence, in western Missouri, was the start of the Santa Fe Trail in 1831 and the Old Oregon Trail in 1843. It was also the home of Harry S. Truman; the **Harry S. Truman Library and Museum** is on a knoll overlooking Slover Park. The dungeon-like cells of the **Jackson County Jail and Marshal's Home** once held Frank James, notorious outlaw in the late 1800s. A replica of the first **Jackson County Courthouse,** built of logs in 1827, is on display. Independence is also the headquarters for the **Reorganized Church of the Latter-Day Saints. Fort Osage,** the first US outpost in the Louisiana Territory, was constructed by William Clark in 1808.

Lexington was the site of a Confederate victory and one of the largest battles in the Western Campaign. **Lafayette County Courthouse,** one of the oldest still in use, has a cannonball that was fired into its east column. At **Lexington State Park** is **Anderson House,** an 1853 brick dwelling used by both forces as a field hospital in the attack. Ten miles southeast is the beautiful **Confederate Memorial State Park.** The **Museum of Yesteryears** exhibits authentic relics of a bygone era.

The historic **Liberty Jail** is housed in a museum in the center of **Liberty.** Mormon prophet Joseph Smith is said to have received several revelations concerning doctrines of the Mormon Church while confined here. **William Jewel College** has rare collections of Elizabethan and Puritan literature in its library. Nearby **Excelsior Springs** is widely known as a health spa. North is **Watkins Mill State Park** with the **Watkins Woolen Factory,** *circa* 1861. To see how early woolens were woven by the machinery of this period, take one of the guided tours. **The Jesse James Farm,** where the famous outlaw was born, is at **Kearney.**

North on I-29, **ST JOSEPH** was the eastern terminus of the Pony Express. The **Pony Express Stables,** now a museum, directed the operation from St Joseph to Sacramento, California. St Joseph was also the terminus of the first railroad to cross the state. The 110-room **Patee House,** once one of the finest hotels west of the Mississippi, now contains the reconstructed Pony Express and railroad offices, as well as other historical items and documents. Visit the **Jesse James Home** where the outlaw was killed, and the **Doll Museum. Missouri Western State College,** the **Albrecht Gallery,** with outstanding 19th- and 20th-century art, and the **St Joseph Museum,** with rare Chinese and Eskimo items, are also of interest. Nearby is **Lewis and Clark State Park** where the fishing is good.

In southwest Missouri, two miles west of **Diamond,** stands the **George Washington Carver National Monument.** Born a slave on this farm, he became an outstanding teacher, humanitarian, botanist, agronomist, and leader. The Visitor Center contains mementos of his life, and a self-guiding trail leads you through the farm. The **Harry S. Truman Birthplace Memorial Shrine,** a restored frame house with period furnishings, is at **Lamar,** north on US 71. Early in September, the four-day **Farm and Industrial Exposition** is staged here. Southeast is **Springfield,** home of **Central Bible College, Drury College, Evangel College,** and **Southwest Missouri State University.** The **Springfield Art Museum** has changing exhibits. Ten miles southwest of town are the rolling hills of **Wilson's Creek National Battlefield,** site of a Civil War battle for control of Missouri. Wild Bill Hickok served as a Union scout and spy in Springfield during this period.

The resort area of **Branson** was immortalized by Harold Bell Wright's best-selling novel *Shepherd of the Hills.* For old-time hillbilly comedy and music, visit the **Mountain Music Theater,** four miles west of town, open April to October; and the **Baldknobbers Hillbilly Jamboree,** three miles west, open last Saturday in April to the last Saturday in October. Motels in the area include **Branson Inn, Holiday Inn, Lampliter** and the **Roark;** about S$15-30/D$18-40. Wood carving, basket weaving, glass blowing and many other crafts from years past are kept alive at **Silver Dollar City,** where the **National Crafts Festival** is held in October. Explore some of **Marvel Cave's** 32 miles of passageways or stop at one of the recreational spots along the 800-mile shoreline of **Table Rock Reservoir.**

East on I-44 is **Rolla,** where the University of Missouri has an outstanding **Minerals Museum** with more than 3,500 specimens from all over the world. The **Autos of Yesteryear Museum** is well worth a visit. In mid-August, attend the **Central Missouri Regional Fair. Meramec State Park,** with camping and fishing facilities, lies at the gorge of the Meramec River near Sullivan. On the 7,153 acres of parkland are 20 caves, numerous springs and many trails. You can also explore **Meramec Caverns,** once the site of Jesse James' hideout, at **Stanton.**

Farther east on US 61 is **STE GENEVIEVE,** the oldest settlement in Missouri. See the large red brick church and walled convent which lend credence to its Gallic origins. The **Louis Bolduc House** is a typical Creole dwelling with walls of heavy oak logs, French Canadian furnishings, four-sided gallery, an orchard, and herb garden. An important example of French colonial architecture, **Amoureaux House** is rich in antique furnishings. At the **Church of Ste Genevieve,** built in 1880, are religious paintings dating from 1663. Three French colonial governors are buried here. Pioneer and Indian relics are preserved at the **Fur Trading Post. The Dr Benjamin Shaw (Mammy Shaw) House** is an old cabin, unusual in its furnishings and design. Another Creole tradition is the **Jour de Fête à Ste Genevieve,** featuring tours of historic homes, antique displays, muzzle-loading contests, and a performance of a medieval French song and dance by the townsfolk in mid-August.

Cities To Visit

KANSAS CITY

Kansas City lies in west central Missouri at the confluence of the Missouri and Kansas Rivers. French trappers were the first to arrive in the area and a trading post was established in 1826. Impetus was given to the little community by the gold rush of 1849 and the quickening pace along the Santa Fe and Oregon Trails. In 1850 it received a charter under the name of the Town of Kansas, later changed to the City of Kansas and finally, in 1889, to Kansas City.

The city is a traditional market center for agricultural produce, and in recent years industry has also come to play a prominent role. Across the Missouri River lies the smaller Kansas City, Kansas. The two cities share the same facilities, but are distinct and separate communities. Greater Kansas City is important in the industries of automobile and truck assembly, and its clothing industry is gaining national prestige. The area is noted for winding highways, rolling hills, park areas, and attractive residential neighborhoods. Population of Kansas City, Missouri, 456,907, population of Kansas City, Kansas, 164,250. Population of metropolitan area, including both cities and the suburban area is 1,320,400.

WHAT TO SEE

Worthwhile sites include **Commerce Towers, Federal Building, Civic Center,** and **City Hall;** telescope on City Hall roof available to visitors Monday to Friday 8-4:30. Also visit the **Liberty Memorial,** in the center of 30 landscaped acres, and its museum; **Municipal Market,** outdoor and farmers' market; **Jesse James Bank Museum,** site of famous holdup. **Kansas City Museum of History and Science,** ethnological and archaeological collections; open Monday-Saturday 9-5, Sunday 12-5, free; there are planetarium shows at the museum Saturday and Sunday, from 1pm, adults

$2, students 75¢. See the **Municipal Auditorium, Board of Trade, Missouri Town 1885, 1859 Jail and Museum,** and the **Kansas City Livestock Exchange and Stockyards. Worlds of Fun** is a 140-acre family recreation park; show rides.

Gray Line has sightseeing tours with complimentary pickup available at most downtown, midtown and country club Plaza hotels. Advance reservations are required. Call 816-333-4838.

Convention and Visitors Bureau of Greater Kansas City has outlined a Scenic Tour and Map Guide that includes all the highlights of Kansas City. You can drive it. There are signs marking the prescribed route.

Swope Park, second largest municipal park in the US, is an attractive recreational area with a large playground and zoo; open daily 9-5. There is also a children's zoo. Admission free on holidays except Memorial Day.

Kansas City is world headquarters for the **Church of the Nazarene** and **Unity School of Christianity.**

Kaleidoscope, a creative arts experience for children, kindergarten through 6th grade; open to public June through August, Monday-Saturday. Adm. 75¢. Visit the observation deck City Hall (30th floor); open Mon-Fri, 8:30-4:30, free. Enjoy **Trail Town,** home of Benjamin Stables, re-creation of early western town—horseback, pony rides, picnics, chuckwagon food; open daily at 8:30am. Stroll through **Union Cemetery,** burial place of early pioneers. Visit **Clarke's Point,** lookout site of the Lewis and Clark expedition to the Northwest, a panoramic view of the Missouri and Kansas Rivers and the Kansas City Stock Yards; study **Union Station,** historic landmark, third largest railroad station in the US. For diversion try the **Kansas City Railroad Museum** with its display of passenger and freight cars, steam, and diesel locomotives, open Sat and Sun 1-5, free. At Unity Church Country Club Plaza, **Last Supper Sculpture,** life-size wooden carving of Last Supper by renowned sculptor Domenic Zappia; open Mon-Fri 9:30-3:30, Sat and Sun 2-4pm. **Reorganized Church of Jesus Christ Auditorium,** World Headquarters of the denomination, organ recital daily, guided tours, free.

ACCOMMODATIONS

Alameda Plaza Hotel (756-1800, S$49-65/D$59-75); **Best Western Executive Motor Hotel** (842-8636, S$28-34/D$36-42); **Glenwood Manor Motor Hotel** (649-7000, S$31-45/D$36-47); **Overland Park: Crown Center Hotel** (474-4400, S$65-95/D$80-110); **Continental Hotel** (421-0640, S$28/D$35); **Granada Royal Hometel** (756-1720, S$69/D$79); **Hilton Airport Plaza Inn** (891-8900, S$44-56/D$56-68), International Airport; **Hilton Plaza Inn** (753-7400, S$44-56/D$56-68); **Holiday Inn City Center** (221-8800, S$42-46/D$52-56); **Holiday Inn-Funworld** (455-1060, S$31-35/D$39-43), adjacent to Worlds of Fun Family Amusement Center; **Holiday Inn Sports Complex** (353-5300, S$33 up/D$39 up), across from Truman Sports Complex; **President Hotel** (471-5440, S$19-25/D$23-30); **Radisson Muehleback** (471-1400, S$47-57/D$60-70), downtown; **Ramada Inn Central** (421-1800, S$35-42/D$42-64 up); **Raphael Hotel** (756-3800, S$39-

51/D$49-61) at Country Club Plaza; **Sheraton Downtown** (842-6090, S$29-36/D$33-40); **Sheraton Royal** (737-0200, S$42-52/D$52-62), close to Truman Sports Complex.

In addition, Kansas City's downtown and surrounding area is ringed with a variety of attractive motor hotels for the visitor's selection. Included are a variety of **Best Westerns, Howard Johnsons, Ramada Inns, Interstate Inns,** and **TraveLodges.**

All rates in Kansas City are subject to a 7⅝ percent tax (not included in published rates).

RESTAURANTS
La Bonne Auberge, haute cuisine of the first order; **La Carrousel,** prime rib, boneless trout, flambé items; **Gasteno's,** Italian American; **Hereford House,** steak, chicken, and ribs; **Italian Gardens,** long established Italian specialties; **Savoy Grill,** venerable Kansas City establishment, crab, lobster, steaks; **Top of the Crown,** specialties, extensive wine list; **Alameda Roof,** specialties, scallops veal Francais and rack of spring lamb; **Andreas Swiss Pantry and Candy Shop,** Swiss Pastry and Tea Room; **Annie's Santa Fe,** margaritas by the glass or pitcher; **Harry Starkers Restaurant,** steak, seafood, and specialties; **Houlihan's Old Place,** a variety menu; **Magic Pan Creperia,** crepes; **La Méditerranée,** classic cuisine from France; **Le Carrosel,** French cuisine; The **Raphael,** English inn atmosphere, seafood, shrimp; **Imperial Palace,** Chinese fare; **Jasper's Restaurant,** continental fare-international; **Snead's Bar-b-Q,** casual dining, beef, ham, and pork sandwiches; **Stephenson's** and **Steve Stephenson's Apple Tree Inn,** quality and Southern country style menu; **Sanford and Sons,** extremely varied menu; **Prospect of Westport,** chicken l'orange, decorative salads, and special coffee; **Dolce's High; Farms,** antebellum mansion with chicken, steak, ham and barbeque ribs menu; and **King's Wharf,** steak and seafood menu.

ENTERTAINMENT
Discos: **Dirty Salley's, Scarlet O'Hara's, Plaza Nest,** and **Mother's.** Old Westport for "pub-hopping." Dinner Theaters: **Tiffany's Attic** and **Waldorf Astoria.** Piano Bars: **Signboard, Combo,** and **Quality Bar and Lounge, Alameda Plaza.**

ARTS AND MUSIC
Nelson Gallery and Atkins Museum of Fine Arts, collection of paintings, sculpture, ceramics; open Tuesday to Saturday 10-5, Sunday 2-6; admission adults $1.50, children 75¢, free Sunday. The **Kansas City Philharmonic** offers a varied concert season, often with outstanding guest artists. The **Starlight Theater** in Swope Park has summer musical shows. **Lyric Theatre** opera productions are performed in English. The **Civic Ballet** also offers good programs. There are stage productions at the **UMKC Playhouse** and **Barn Theater** during the summer, and at the **Resident Theater, Music Hall,** and **University Theater** the year round. The **Missouri**

Repertory Theater stages classical and contemporary productions June to September.

SHOPPING

Petticoat Lane, downtown, has a concentration of leading shops. **Hallmark,** famous greeting card company, whose international headquarters is in Kansas City, has a store and shopping mall in **Crown Center Downtown** and another store in the beautiful **Country Club Plaza** retail shopping area. The latter area also has **Seville Square** shopping complex.

SPORTS

Professional baseball is played by the **Kansas City Royals** in the American League; pro football by the **Kansas City Chiefs** in the National Football League; and the **Kansas City Kings** professional basketball team. College sports are played by the **University of Kansas,** Lawrence, Kansas, 32 miles west; particularly notable are the **Big Eight** (Midwest Universities League) football and basketball contests. Boxing and wrestling matches are frequently held. There are many golf, tennis, and swimming facilities, both public and private. The fishing season is throughout the year. The hunting season varies, but is usually in the late fall.

CALENDAR OF EVENTS

Jazz Festival, third Sunday in April; **Rodeo of Champions,** late June to early July; **American Royal Livestock and Horse Show,** November.

WHERE TO GO NEARBY

Arrow Rock Park, about 159 miles from the city, has springs, caves, picnic grounds, historic tavern. **Knob Noster Park,** 100 miles away, has a lake, woods, streams, and fishing. **Lewis and Clark Park,** at Rushville, about 50 miles away, has camping and picnic areas, lake sports, fish hatchery. **Roaring River Park,** at Cassville, less than 200 miles away, has fishing, swimming, boating, hotel, cabins, woods, picnic and camping grounds. There are also caves, horseback riding facilities, and lake sports.

The **Lake of the Ozarks** region offers a wide choice of hotels, motels, cottages and resorts with excellent fishing, boating and water sports. The community of **Lake Ozark** is a convenient starting point for a trip through the region. Other important lake-resort sections are **Lake Wappapello, Taneycomo** (near Table Rock State Park), **Bull Shoals,** and **Norfolk.** Many state parks are ideal for a vacation, having all types of sport, recreational facilities, and accommodation in lodges and cabins. A typical Missouri vacation is a "float trip" on one of the Ozark streams, varying in length from a morning's jaunt to several weeks.

Fort Osage, reconstruction of first US outpost in Louisiana built 1808 by William Clark of Lewis & Clark expedition; open daily 9-5, free; **Heritage Village,** reconstruction of 1821-1860 village, open Sat and Sun free. **Lake Jocomo,** Fleming Park, 1,000-acre lake, 4,000-acre park, picnics, shelter houses, fishing, nature trails, wildlife exhibits. **Line Creek Park,**

235 acres, roaming buffalo, elk, deer, archaeological site of Hopewell Indians. **Loose Park,** 75-acre park, features famous rose garden, lake, promenades.

ST LOUIS

St Louis is in eastern Missouri on the Mississippi River, below the point where it is joined by the Missouri. The first pioneers were a small group of Frenchmen who arrived in 1764; the founder is recognized to be Pierre Laclede Liguest. The new community immediately became prominent as a fur-trading center and began to grow in size. In 1803, after the Louisiana Purchase, the region was ceded to the United States by France. St. Louis was incorporated as a city in 1822, and during the Civil War was a Union supply base.

Often called the "Gateway to the Western United States," St. Louis is an important interchange point for rail, truck and air traffic. It is a progressive city and a center for conventions because of its key location. Population 450,790; greater metropolitan district, about 1,778,959. The city's boundaries have not been extended since 1876.

WHAT TO SEE

Interesting sites include the **Memorial Plaza** and government buildings including the **Old Courthouse** where the Dred Scott case was tried. Scott, a liberated slave, returned to Missouri and sued for liberation on the grounds of his previous independence on free soil. The Southern-dominated court ruled that by voluntarily returning to a slave state, Scott had lost the right to be free. The courthouse is now a museum. **Campbell House,** museum of the fur-trading era; birthplace of Eugene Field, where the poet's "gingham dog and calico cat" are displayed; the fabulous stainless steel **Gateway Arch,** 630 feet high, designed by Eero Saarinen, which has rides to an observation room at the top and museums dedicated to the opening of the West; the **Meeting of the Waters** fountain by Carl Milles; *SS Admiral,* an air-conditioned river steamer with dance floor, which cruises the Mississippi daily, except Monday, from Memorial Day through Labor Day; **Jefferson Memorial** in Forest Park with its famous Lindbergh Collection, open daily 9:30-4:45, free. Also worth seeing are the **Soldiers Memorial Building, City Hall, Powell Hall** (home of the St. Louis Symphony Orchestra), **Old Cathedral** on the riverfront, **St. Louis Cathedral, De Menil House** and **Lemp Mansion** (2 historic restored mansions side by side), **Aloe Plaza,** the **Federal Building** in Memorial Plaza, the 82-acre **St. Louis Zoo,** the **St. Louis Art Museum,** the **Missouri Botanical Gardens** (with its indoor climatron and outdoor Rose gardens and Japanese gardens), the **National Museum of Transport,** the **Museum of Science and Natural History, Grant's Farm** (restored cabin built by Ulysses S. Grant, with a large game preserve and miniature zoo). Also of interest is the restored commercial riverfront district **Laclede's Landing,** and St. Louis' numerous historic residential neighborhoods under restoration, including **Lafayette Square, Soulard,**

The striking Gateway Arch, in St Louis, 630 ft high, is a stainless steel monument, "Gateway to the Western United States."

and **Benton Park.** *Goldenrod Showboat,* authentic turn-of-the-century sternwheeler with performances of old-time melodramas on weekends; and the motored vessels *Huck Finn, Sam Clemens,* and *Tom Sawyer,* which have river trips daily, Memorial Day-Labor Day, weekends in April, May, September and October. The **St Louis Riverfront; Sports Hall of Fame, Busch Memorial Stadium,** museum of St. Louis sports history; **Anheuser-Busch brewery,** with free tours; **St Louis Medical Museum,** open daily.

ACCOMMODATIONS

Downtown: **Bel-Air Hilton Hotel** (621-7900, S$53/D$62); **Holiday Inn Riverfront** (621-8200, S$47/D$55); **Marriott's Pavilion Hotel** (421-1776, S$56-64/D$66-80); **Mayfair Hotel** (231-1500, S$47/D$57); **Radisson Hotel** (421-4000, S$56-65/D$64-76); **Rodeway Inn Downtown** (534-4700, S$35/D$41-44); **St. Louis Gateway Hotel** (231-1400, S$18-21/D$25); **Sheraton St. Louis** (231-1500, S$47/D$57); **Stouffers Riverfront Towers** (241-9500, S$54/D$66). Central West-End and Clayton Area: **Chase-Park Plaza Hotel** (361-2500, S$58-64/D$66-72); **Cheshire Inn & Lodge** (647-7300, S$45/D$57); **Clayton Inn** (726-5400, S$49-59/D$59-69); **Holiday Inn Clayton** (834-0400, S$42-59/D$48-59). West county: **Holiday Inn West Port** (434-0100, S$48-50/D$58-60); **Breckenridge Inn** (993-1100, S$47-65/D$57-75); **Sheraton West Port Inn** (878-1500, S$49/D$55). Near the airport: **Hilton Inn** (S$42-48/D$50-56); **Holiday Inn** (S$40-45/D$49-54); **Marriott Hotel** (S$60-68/D$72-80); **Northwest Airport Inn** (S$35/D$40); **Ramada Inn** (S$42-48/D$48); **Sheraton Airport Inn** (S$40/D$44).

RESTAURANTS

Downtown: **Crest House,** features steaks, moderate to expensive; **Miss Hullings Cafeterias,** good food and moderately priced; **La Sala,** authentic Mexican dishes, moderate; **Top of the Riverfront,** revolving restaurant with spectacular view of Gateway Arch featuring French and American specialties, moderate; **Al's, Tony's** and **Anthony's,** elegant with French, Italian and continental dishes, expensive; **Lantern House,** one of the best Chinese restaurants in the nation; **Trader Vic's,** Oriental and Polynesian dishes, moderate; **Shanghai Inn,** Peking-style Oriental dishes, moderate; **Cafe de France,** French cuisine, moderate to expensive. Riverfront: Several river showboats serve dinner, including the **Belle Angeline,** fresh seafood; the **Robert E. Lee,** good steaks. Laclede's Landing has **Bogart's, Hannegans, Kennedy's, Lucius Boomers,** and **Massuccis,** moderately priced. Near Northside: **Kemoll's Italian Restaurant,** features Gourmet Nights when menus of the world's top restaurants are available, moderately priced. Forest Park area: three English-style dining rooms at **Cheshire Inn,** popular and moderately priced; **Sea Chase,** good seafood; **Tenderloin Room,** good beef and steaks, expensive; **Nantucket Cove,** seafood, expensive; **Musial & Biggie's,** good steaks, moderately priced. On-the-Hill, Italian area: **Ruggeri's** and **Dominic's,** moderate to expensive. **Cunetto's House of Pasta** for fine Italian fare, moderate prices. Near the airport: **The Hanger** in Marriott Hotel features prime rib and Maine lobster, moderately priced; **La Place** in the Hilton, continental cuisine, moderate to expensive. St. Louis has many fine restaurants, including **Rich & Charlie's Del Mar Restaurant**, moderate and **Sunshine Inn**, numerous vegetarian dishes available, also meat. Some, like the **Jefferson Avenue Boarding House**, offer three separate seatings for dinner with one entree each evening, open Tuesday-Saturday, lunch weekdays, brunch Sundays. **Balaban's** in the fashionable central west end has continental cuisine, expensive; **Caleco's, Duff's,** and **Llewellyns Ap Gruffyd's** are moderately priced and informal; **St. Louis Art Museum Cafe, Talayna's Pizza;** west county: **Abernathy's** for moderately priced food, **Boucair's Bistro and Bar,** moderate; **De Bergerac** and **L'Auberge Bretonne** are restaurants with fine French cuisine, expensive.

ENTERTAINMENT

Laclede's Landing has restaurants featuring live musicians playing jazz, ragtime, rock, and blues—places like **First Street Alley, Muddy Waters, Tryst.** Other downtown music spots are **Goldenrod Showboat, Portico's Restaurant and Dinner Theater, BBs Jazz Blues & Soups,** the **Grog Shop.** In addition, the **Banjo Palace, Red Onion, Trap Room,** and **Marty's Ballroom** in the Chase-Park Plaza Hotel. The **Ramada Inn** at Fenton for name entertainment. Near the airport: **Stash's, The Sting** and the **Marriott,** nightclubs.

ARTS AND MUSIC

St Louis Art Museum, regarded as one of the best in the nation; open Tuesday 2:30-9:30, Wednesday through Sunday 10-5; free. **Steinberg Art Gallery,** collection of modern art and traveling exhibits. The **St Louis Symphony Orchestra,** the second oldest in the United States, is one of the country's outstanding orchestras. There is also the **Municipal Opera,** in an outdoor theater in **Forest Park,** light opera and musical comedy; July to Labor Day. Broadway productions are performed throughout the year in St Louis. Summer shows are at the 12,000-seat **Municipal Opera;** also, performances are held at the **Loretto-Hilton Repertory Theater,** the **American Theater** and **Kiel Auditorium.**

SHOPPING

Over twenty-one shopping centers among the St Louis retail group offer a cross-section of what makes the city one of the major retail markets in the nation. Numerous art galleries and boutiques are situated in the **Maryland Plaza** section of midtown St Louis. Many suburban discount department stores have late evening hours daily except Sunday.

SPORTS

Busch Memorial Stadium, so interesting that there are guided tours of it, is home field for the **St. Louis Cardinals,** National League baseball; the **Cardinals,** National League football; and **Stars,** National Soccer League. The **St Louis Blues,** National Hockey League, and **The Streak,** women's basketball team, play in the **Arena.**

Other spectator sports include cricket, rugby, speed skating, polo and horse shows. Canoe racing is held on the **Meramec River** and boat races at **Alton Lake.** There is horse racing at **Fairmount Park** and **Cahokia Downs** in Illinois, just across the Mississippi River, and automobile and motorcycle racing at **Mid-America Raceway** in Wentzville, about 45 minutes from downtown St. Louis. Many kinds of fish are caught in the Mississippi River and in the artificial lakes in the vicinity. Golf, tennis, and swimming are available at public parks and private clubs.

CALENDAR OF EVENTS

St Louis Home Show, St Louis Sports, Travel and Boat Show, Flower Show, March; **Shrine Circus and Parade,** June; **National Ragtime Festival, Strassenfest, Soulard Market Days,** July; **Mississippi River Festival** at Edwardsville, Illinois, July-August; **Veiled Prophet Parade,** September; **Dutchtown Oktoberfest,** October; **Veiled Prophet Ball,** December. There is also recognition of **Founders Day,** 14 February.

WHERE TO GO NEARBY

Six Flags Over Mid America is a 200-acre amusement complex open April through October. One charge for admission and all rides and shows; about 35 minutes drive southwest. **Edmund A. Babler State Park,** across the river from St Louis; peculiar mound formations built by ancient Indians are interesting. **Meramec State Park,** southwest of the city, has cottages, caverns, water sports, and other recreational facilities. Gray Line has sightseeing tours with complimentary pickup at most downtown, midtown hotels. Advance reservations recommended. Call (314) 631-5700.

The Convention and Visitors Bureau of Greater St. Louis provides maps and other materials, and can help you plan any excursions you may want to make.

FURTHER STATE INFORMATION

Missouri Division of Tourism, Box 1055, Jefferson City, MO 65101. Hunting and Fishing: **Missouri Department of Conservation,** Box 180, Jefferson City, MO 65101. The **Convention and Visitors' Bureau of Greater Kansas City,** City Center Square, Kansas City, MO 64105. **Convention and Visitors' Bureau of Greater St Louis,** 500 North Broadway, St. Louis, MO 63102. **St Louis Council on World Affairs** (for foreign visitors), Chase-Park Plaza Hotel, 212 North Kings Highway, St. Louis, MO 63108. **Visitor Information Booth,** St Louis Lambert International Airport.

Consulates in Kansas City: Belgium, Republic of China (Taiwan), Colombia, Costa Rica, Denmark, Finland, Great Britain, Germany, Italy, Japan, Korea, Luxembourg, Mexico, Netherlands, Sierre Leone, Spain, Sweden, Switzerland, Thailand. For other consulates in the Greater Kansas City area, see Kansas.

In St Louis: Belgium, Denmark, Dominican Republic, Italy, Spain, Peru.

USEFUL TELEPHONE NUMBERS IN KANSAS CITY

Area Transportation Authority	221-0660
Police	421-1500
Fire	842-2121
Ambulance (Emergency Only)	471-1111
Highway Patrol	524-9200
Medical Assistance	531-0696
Pan Am Reservations and Information	1-800-621-2909
Research Medical Center	276-4000
University of Kansas Medical Center	588-5000
Visitor Information Phone (VIP)	474-9600
Yellow Cab Co.	471-5000

USEFUL TELEPHONE NUMBERS IN ST. LOUIS

Lambert Airport	426-7777
Emergency	911
City Police	444-5555
County Police	889-2345
City Fire	622-3223
Barnes Hospital	454-2000
County Hospital	727-6300
Visitors Bureau	421-1023
Laclede Cab	652-3456
Yellow Cab	361-2345—991-1200
Pan Am Reservations	800-621-2909

Montana

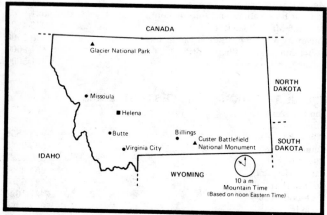

Area	147,138 square miles				**Population**	786,690						
Capital	Helena				**Sales Tax**	None						

Weather	Jan	Feb	Mar	Apr	May	Jun	Jul	Aug	Sep	Oct	Nov	Dec
Av Temp (°C)	−6	−5	−1	6	12	16	21	19	14	9	1	−3
Days Rain/Snow	9	8	9	9	11	13	7	7	7	6	7	7

Montana is a beautiful, big state, good for exploring, especially if you are on a tight budget. Prices in hotels, motels, and dude ranches are among the lowest in the country, and the meals are generally enormous. Montana's wide open spaces are so unpopulated that you'll probably have mile upon mile of spectacular countryside all to yourself. There are no really large cities. In the center of the state the mountains rise sharply against the plains skyline, while in the western area you'll find snow-capped peaks, with sparkling lakes, trout streams, and richly fertile valleys. Since many of the mountains are extensively forested, with fir, pine, spruce amongst others, the timber line becomes a graphic reality. Don't miss the magnificent **Glacier National Park**. Most of the 10 national forests in Montana (covering 20 million acres) have trails for hiking, skiing, or horseback riding through primitive or wilderness areas. Two favorites are the **Bob Marshall Wilderness** near Helena and the **Pintler Wilderness** near Anaconda. Those who prefer driving can still enjoy the wilderness by taking the 65-mile Pintler Scenic Route (US 10-A from Anaconda to Drummond; connects with I-90). In addition, there are seven state forests and 19 wildlife sanctuaries. Boating, fishing, hunting, and winter sports are excellent throughout the year.

The US military expedition led by Lewis and Clark (1805-06) first brought Montana to the attention of white men. One can follow parts of the Lewis-Clark route, starting at Missouri Headwaters State Park near Three Forks, and much of the state must look the same today as when they first set eyes on it. Lewis and Clark were soon followed by fur traders, homesteaders, and miners. The first big gold strike was in 1862 at Bannack, now a state park; there are over 90 ghost towns and worked-out mining camps to explore. Two that vividly recall the rip-roaring past are **Elkhorn**, just off US 91 between **Helena**, the state capital, and **Boulder; Granite**, another unrestored ghost town, is near Philipsburg, to the west on US 10-A.

Buffalo were nearly exterminated in the 1880s, but around 400 still roam the range in a vast refuge near Moiese, off 93 and MT 200. When cattle replaced buffalo, Montana's cowboys became colorful characters in the State's history much like those painted and sculptured by Charles Russell. Russell's paintings and bronzes can be seen in **Helena**, the state capital of Montana, at the State Historical Museum. The free museum is open weekdays 8-5, Saturday and Sunday 12-5. Helena started life as a mining camp known as Last Chance Gulch. While you are in the capital, take the **Last Chancer Tour Train** ride to the site of the 1864 gold discovery. The train departs daily from mid-June through Labor Day. Accommodations include: **Best Western Colonial Inn** (443-2100, S$28-30/D$32-38) and **TraveLodge** (443-2200, S$21-26/D$25-30), both downtown; and at **Coach House Motor Inn** (442-6080, S$20/D$24-28), **Motel 6** (442-1311, S/D$11 up), and **Best Western Jorgenson's Holiday Motel** (442-1770, S$22/D$32-38). Russell's work can also be seen in the Russell Gallery and Studio in Great Falls to the north. Southeast of Helena is **Virginia City**, site of the richest placer gold discovery ever made (1863) and territorial capital during the boom days of 1865-75, and adjacent **Nevada City**, nearby on MT 287, have been brought back to life. Virginia City's restored buildings and museums are free; and 19th-century melodramas are staged nightly mid-June through Labor Day in the Opera House. Hotels have antique furnishings. Reservations are advised well in advance.

Missoula is home of the **University of Montana**, which hosts the Summer Festival of the Performing Arts July-August, and is training headquarters for Forest Service smokejumpers who parachute into primitive areas to fight forest fires; daily tours of the **Aerial Fire Depot 4**, 8-5, June through Labor Day. In Missoula, accommodations are available at: **Red Lion Motel** (728-3300) and **Village Red Lion Motor Inn** (728-3100), averaging S$25-31/D$32-42); **Best Western Executive Motor Inn, Southgate Inn, Westerner Motel**, and **Creekside Inn**, averaging S$24-27/D$29-35; and **Bel-Aire Motel, Trade Winds Motel, TraveLodge**, and **Holiday Inn**, averaging S$16-25/D$29-35. Missoula is also the gateway to **Flathead Lake**, the state's premier recreation area (where lake communities of Polson and Bigfork have summer theaters June-August), and to Glacier National Park.

"The richest hill on earth" was what **Butte** was called in its heyday and still is; you can visit the **Berkeley Open Pit Mine,** where an observation platform is open at all times. Take a tour of the city on "Old No. 1", a replica of an early-day open streetcar; tickets are available at the Butte Chamber of Commerce, 2950 Harrison. Visit the free **World Museum of Mining;** the free mineral display at **Montana College of Mineral Science and Technology;** and the **Copper King Mansion,** the sumptuous home of a 19th-century copper baron, open daily 9-9 in summer and 10-6 in winter, admission $2.50 per person. Butte was one of the country's biggest mining camps. The frontier traditional cheerful, trusting acceptance of strangers continues today and the city prides itself on its hospitality. Accommodations in Butte include: the new **Copper King Inn TraveLodge** (494-6666, S$33/D$37 up); **Best Western War Bonnet Inn** (S$33/D$36-43); **Ramada Inn** (494-3500, S/D$27); and **Mile-Hi Motel** and **Capri Motel,** averaging S$19/D$31. Near Butte is the **Lewis and Clark Cavern State Park,** where you can see some of the most spectacular and colorful stalactite and stalagmite formations; guided tours 1 May to 1 October. Admission is $2 for adults and $1 for children 6-12.

The tragic 1877 flight of the Nez Perce Indians can be recalled at **Big Hole National Battlefield** near Butte, and the **Bear Paws State Monument** near the Canadian border. The military history of the flight comes alive at **Fort Benton** near Great Falls and **Fort Keough** near Miles City. Indian artifacts and cave drawings can be seen at **Medicine Rocks State Park** near Ekalaka and **Pictograph Cave State Monument** west of Billings. Also near Billings is **Custer Battlefield National Monument,** where the Sioux and Cheyenne were victorious over Gen. George Custer is 1876. Billings, today the state's largest city, has a full range of accommodations, including **Best Western Northern Hotel** and **Ponderosa Inn, War Bonnet Inn, Holiday Inns East** and **West,** and **Ramada Inn,** averaging S$25-26/D$33-35; and **Cherry Tree Inn, Dude Rancher Lodge, Esquire Motel, Rimrock Lodge, TraveLodge, Westward Ho Lodge,** and **Friendship Inn,** averaging S$19-25/D$22-30.

Pompey's Pillar, 28 miles east of Billings, is the sandstone rock on which Captain George Clark carved his name on 25 July 1806. **West Yellowstone,** one of three Montana gateways into America's first national park, is the liveliest year-round resort in the state. In West Yellowstone there are the **Best Western Ambassador Motor Inn,** the **Desert Inn Motel,** the **Big Western Pine Motel,** the **Executive Inn,** and the **Lamplighter,** averaging S$22-30/D$25-38; and **Stagecoach Inn** (646-7381, S$16-20/D$20-28). The **Golden Garter Theater** has plays nightly, mid-June through Labor Day. There are snowmobile tours into Yellowstone in winter. **Big Sky of Montana Resort,** the 10,000-acre resort is open year round for a variety of outdoor activities, including skiing, tennis, golf, fishing, and horseback riding. Accommodations at **Big Sky of Montana Resort** (995-4211, S$60-65/D$82-85 up) include lofts, studios, and condominia in addition to comfortable rooms at Huntley Lodge. Less expensive accommodations at motels in the vicinity, averaging S$16-30/D$18-36. Rates at the

Huntley Lodge (995-4500 or toll-free 800 548-4486) S$62/D$72. Hostel accommodations are also available and there are a number of guest ranches in the area. **Big Sky** is located about 40 miles north of West Yellowstone on MT 191.

Glacier National Park

Located in northwest Montana, the park covers 1,583 square miles. It merges with Alberta, Canada, to form the **Waterton-Glacier International Peace Park.** Mountain roads are still lined with snowbanks until early July, while lower elevations are a sea of wild flowers against a background of fir, pine, and spruce. During the winter, US 2, skirting the southern boundary of the park, is the only road open to cars; snowmobiles can be rented in **Kalispell.**

The park has at least 63 mountain peaks averaging 8,624 feet, 60 live glaciers, and 250 trout lakes. The **Going-to-the-Sun Road,** from St. Mary on the east side of the park to West Glacier on the west, is 50 miles of breathtaking views of blue lakes, fern-carpeted forests, plunging waterfalls, and towering peaks. Check opening dates: usually mid-June to mid-October. The road crosses the Continental Divide at **Logan Pass,** elevation 6,664 feet. All-inclusive tours (lodging, meals, and transportation by buses and launches) are the best way to see the park in two-, three-, four-, or five-day trips. More than 700 miles of wilderness trails are laid out for hikers, but carry a noise-maker to scare away roaming animals. Ranger-naturalists conduct free field trips from about 15 June-Labor Day. Saddle horses and guides are available at **Apgar, Lake McDonald, Many Glacier, East Glacier, Waterton,** and several other places. Anglers will find 22 species of fish in the lakes and rivers; the fishing season runs from 15 June through the first weekend in September; no license is required. See over 1,000 types of trees and wild flowers and the showy bear grass which is considered the park flower. The 57 species of park animals include mountain goat, bighorn sheep, bear, elk, deer, and moose. More than 200 bird species include the water ouzel, osprey, bald eagle, the noisy Clark's nutcracker, and pileated woodpecker. Rock formations are in four distinct layers of color and the whole park area, with its glaciers, is of tremendous interest to geologists.

Motels open year round are on the park fringes, but inside the park most hotels are open only from about 15 June through the first weekend in September or 1 October; advance reservations are recommended. Accommodations for Glacier National Park are in and around East and West Glacier, and include **Apgar Village Lodge Inn** (888-5484, S$29/D$32-34; 4 beds $37); **Inwood Motel & Bungalows** (888-5366, S/D$18-22); **Mountain Pine Lodge** (226-4551, S$23-25/D$27-30); **West Glacier Motel** (888-9987, D$18-22); and there are an additional four excellent hotels and three motor inns of Glacier Park, Inc. including **Glacier Park Lodge** (226-4841, a central reservation number; average rates S$29.50-34/D$34-38.50). Cabins within the park with an outhouse cost $10-12, with running water, $21.

FURTHER STATE INFORMATION

Montana Travel Hosts, Division of Montana Chamber of Commerce, Box 1730, Helena, MT 59601. **Travel Promotion Unit,** Montana Department of Highways, Helena, MT 59601. Hunting and Fishing: **Montana Fish and Game Department,** Helena, MT 59601. **USDA Forest Service,** Federal Building, Missoula, MT 59801. National Parks: **Glacier National Park** (Superintendent), West Glacier, MT 59936. Reservations: Glacier Park Inc., East Glacier, MT 59434 (summer); 1735 East Ft Lowell Road, Tucson, AZ 85717 (winter).

USEFUL TELEPHONE NUMBERS IN HELENA

Ambulance	442-1234
Helena Medical Clinic	442-9523
Fire	442-5241
Police	442-3231
Highway Patrol	449-3000
Legal Aid	442-9830
Chamber of Commerce	442-4120
Pan Am Reservations	(800) 227-4840

Nebraska

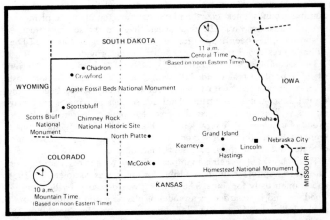

Area	77,227 square miles				**Population**		1,570,000				
Capital	Lincoln				**Sales Tax**		2.5%				

Weather	Jan	Feb	Mar	Apr	May	Jun	Jul	Aug	Sep	Oct	Nov	Dec
Av Temp (°C)	5	3	3	11	17	23	26	25	19	13	4	2
Days Rain/Snow	7	7	9	9	11	11	9	9	8	6	5	6

Once a barren land which bore the tag "Great American Desert," Nebraska is now renowned for its rich farmlands and beef cattle. The state is exceptional for hunting too, and shooting for pheasant, duck, and geese is very good. The Union Pacific railroad, begun in Omaha in 1865, and the Homestead Act of 1862, opened the door for settlers. Under the Homestead Act anyone living on and working land for five years was entitled to buy 160 acres at a special low price. Ranches were quickly set up and by 1890 thousands of acres were under cultivation.

Nebraska ranks among the top five states in total farm receipts, with the largest share coming from livestock. One of the world's largest livestock markets is in **Omaha**, which also is one of the country's largest food-processing centers. Not surprisingly for a state with nearly 20,000,000 acres under cultivation, the largest manufacturing industries are agriculture-related. Oil, discovered in the panhandle region in 1949, is also an important product.

The flat lands of the **Platte River Valley** have been turned to advantage. Because of the high water table, highway builders used dirt from adjacent land to make roads higher. In the process, these "borrow" pits filled with water and, with help from the state government, the manmade lakes became part of more than 50 parks. Most of the lakes are along a 160-mile strip of I-80 from Grand Island to Hershey. Both in the lakes and in the 11,000 miles of streams are trout, pike, bass, catfish, bluegill, crappie, and walleye. The parks are open daily all year; cabins are available mid-May to 15 September. A large national forest provides good hunting grounds; duck, goose, and pheasant are found on the plains and around the waterways. The **Republican River,** in the southwest corner of the state, has been tapped for irrigation projects, and as an offshoot still more reservoirs for water sports have been provided.

The second-largest city in Nebraska, **LINCOLN,** home of the **University of Nebraska,** sits alongside I-80, with Omaha 56 miles to the northeast. After a bit of a feud with Omaha over which city would become the capital, Lincoln emerged triumphant. It also became a major grain market, as well as an insurance and farm equipment center. The city is proud of native sons General John J. ("Blackjack") Pershing and William Jennings Bryan; the latter served the state in Congress and as Secretary of State, and ran in three presidential elections.

The **Nebraska State Fair** is an important event here in early September. The **State Capitol,** a landmark visible for miles, was completed in 1934 and is open daily for tours. The building was designed by Bertram G. Goodhue and is regarded as a model of planning among the country's public buildings. Above the tiled dome stands the bronze statue *The Sower,* symbolizing agriculture. The base of the dome is adorned with the Indian Thunderbird symbol. The **Executive Mansion** (guided tours on Thursdays, April-November) and the **Lincoln Monument,** copied after the original in Springfield, Illinois, are in adjoining grounds. The **University of Nebraska State Museum** (open daily, free) has geology and anthropology exhibits. **Nebraska State Historical Society Museum** has a history of the state depicted in exhibits of Indian history, period rooms, and pioneer relics; reference library, open daily, free. **Pioneers Park** has buffalo, elk, and deer herds, plus an 18-hole golf course. **Antelope, Woods** and **Holmes Parks** also provide natural recreational settings.

The **William Jennings Bryan Home** has the first and second floors restored; open June to September. **Sheldon Memorial Art Gallery** is open Tuesday to Sunday, free, and **Mueller Planetarium** is open daily. **Holiday Inn, Ramada Inn,** and **Villager Motel** are about S$34/D$40. Good accommodations available at the **Hilton** (S$29-39/D$39-49) and the **Clayton House Motel,** S$26/D$33. Good food in Lincoln is available at the **Misty Lounge; Cork and Cleaver; Lee's Restaurant,** fried chicken a speciality; and **Valentino's** and **Tony and Luigi's** for Italian food.

Southeast of Lincoln is the **Arbor Lodge State Historical Park,** at Nebraska City. The 52-room colonial mansion, occupying 65 acres of wooded grounds, was the home of **J. Sterling Morton,** founder of Arbor Day in 1872; open 15 April through October, daily. **John Brown's Cave,** a station on the Underground Railroad which brought blacks to freedom in the north before and during the Civil War, is open all year. **Homestead**

National Monument, near **Beatrice** on NB 4, commemorates the pioneer spirit of the settlers who arrived under provisions of the Homestead Act. The **Visitor Center Museum** exhibits pioneer equipment, household goods, and artifacts. A log cabin, built in 1867, has been restored with period furnishings. The original two-story cabin measured only 14 by 16 feet and housed a family of twelve.

Grand Island, a man made island, has **Stuhr Museum of the Prairie Pioneer,** open all year. The museum, designed by Edward Durell Stone, has outdoor 1900 village, log cabin, farm, and church. Horse racing is held at **Fonner Park** from mid-March through April; pari-mutuel betting. **Holiday Inn** and **Island Inn** are about S$25-29/D$32-45.

Hastings, with a population of 23,019, is the sixth-largest city in Nebraska and is 23 miles south of Grand Island. It has a good museum of local lore in the **House of Yesterday,** and also has the **J.M. McDonald Planetarium.** The **Jacob Fisher Rainbow Fountain,** illuminated nightly in summer, is memorable for its display of colored waters. Comfortable motels make Hastings an ideal touring headquarters; **Midlands Lodge,** the **Rainbow, Redondo,** and **Holiday Inn** average S$18-29/D$22-32. One of America's greatest writers of the pioneer era grew up in **Red Cloud,** 30 miles south of Hastings on US 281. The **Willa Cather Pioneer Memorial and Museum** contains personal memorabilia and the author's letters and first editions; open May through September. Miss Cather's childhood home now has a self-guiding, push-button narration system; open by appointment.

Minden, near Kearney, has the **Harold Warp Pioneer Village,** three city blocks long. There are 23 buildings re-creating the town's early history, including a Pony Express station, sod house, 250 antique autos, tractors, trucks, early locomotives, and thousands of items tracing the pioneer's life; open daily; camping during May through October. **Kearney,** named for the frontier outpost and fort used as a base against the Indians, once had ambitions to be the capital of the United States, due to its central location. **Fort Kearney State Historical Park,** open daily 28 May-1 November, has been restored and displays exhibits of Indian lore. There is also a 40-acre campground. A number of very good motels include **Hammer, Ramada, Holiday Inn, Tel-Star,** and **Western Inn,** all about S$21-41/D$28-42.50.

McCook, near the Kansas border, is the site of the **Red Willow County Fair and Rodeo** in late July or early August, and a fishing derby in mid-May. **Hugh Butler Lake State Recreation Area** is 10 miles north. The **George W. Norris House** is the restored home of the senator who brought the one-house legislature to the state; open Tuesday to Sunday, June to September, free. Pioneer relics and World War II prisoner-of-war paintings are housed in the **Museum of the High Plains;** open daily. Bird shooting is excellent in the rolling plains surrounding the city. **Cedar Motel** and **Chief Motel** average S$19-25/D$24-36.

North Platte, on I-80, features **Nebraskaland Days Celebration,** a series of carnivals, parades, and a four-day rodeo commemorating the world's first rodeo in 1882; late June. The city was the home of Buffalo Bill

Cody. **Buffalo Bill Ranch State Historical Park,** once the winter headquarters for his traveling rodeo, is just outside town. It includes the barn, some out buildings, and 19-room **Buffalo Bill Cody Home** (1886); open daily, free. **Circle C Motels** and **Holiday Inn** are about S$29-39/D$36-44. **Ogallala** seems a perfect setting for a stagecoach; visit the **Cowboy Museum** and the **Crystal Palace;** performances in the summer. A rodeo is held in mid-August.

A landmark of the Oregon Trail, which begins at Independence, Missouri and terminates at the Columbia River in Oregon, is the **Chimney Rock National Historic Site,** located south of Bayard. The sandstone rock begins as a mound, then rises 150 feet in a column above the landscape. For early pioneers going west the site signaled the termination of the dusty prairies. **Scotts Bluff National Monument** is a dramatic bluff, rising 500 feet to confront pioneers on the Oregon Trail. Wagon train relics are displayed in a Visitor Center situated at this historic site. The town of **Scottsbluff** is a center for the large, irrigated North Platte Valley. The **Cavalier Motel, Lamplighter** and **Quality Inn** are about S$18-23/D$22-38. To get to the **Agate Fossil Beds National Monument,** drive nine miles north on US 26 to Mitchell, then 34 miles north on NB 29. Fossil remains of mammals which inhabited the territory 20 million years ago can be seen in the **Visitor Center;** open daily, Memorial Day to Labor Day.

Fort Robinson State Park, where Chief Crazy Horse died in 1877, is outside **Crawford** in the northwestern corner of the state. The fort is partly run by the state historical society and serves as a fishing, camping, and riding center; stagecoach rides are offered in the summer. **Trailside Museum** in the park has exhibits of geologic history and fossil remains; open June-Labor Day. Accommodations are usually available in the lodge or in the former officers' quarters which serve as modern cabins. Reservations obtainable from **Nebraska Game and Parks Commission,** 2200 North 33rd Street, Box 30370, Lincoln NE 68502. The **Museum of the Fur Trade** is located nearby in **Chadron.** The museum, concentrating mainly on the operations of trappers in the 1800s, also has a restored trading post, garden of primitive crops, Indian relics, and a fine gun collection; open daily June to September. Chadron was the starting point of a 1,000-mile horse race to Chicago in 1893. **Little Britches State Rodeo** is held here on two days in mid-July.

City To Visit

OMAHA

Omaha is in eastern Nebraska on the Missouri River. There were some trading posts in the region about 1804, but the earliest permanent settlement dates from 1854. Omaha was the capital of Nebraska from 1855 to 1867. There has been substantial economic and industrial growth, and it now is a major industrial, retail, insurance, and financial center. In the midst of a tremendous area of fertile crop land and countless herds of cattle, Omaha thrives on the agricultural wealth which surrounds it. Although an important city, it has a homey and friendly atmosphere that comes naturally to descendants of pioneers. Population is 314,841.

WHAT TO SEE

Joslyn Art Museum; the **Civic Auditorium; Ak-Sar-Ben Field** and **Coliseum; Union Pacific Museum,** with souvenirs of the railroad's exciting early years, open Monday to Friday 9-5, Saturday 9-2; free. Also the **Mormon Cemetery** and monument, honoring about 600 Mormons who died here in 1847 while on their way to Utah. There are guided tours of the **Strategic Aerospace Museum,** but the huge underground SAC Headquarters is not open to the public. There are, however, guided tours of **Offutt Air Force Base. Boy's Town,** 11 miles west, is a venture in raising homeless boys in a self-governing community; open to visitors daily 8-4, Sunday 9-4:30.

Omaha has almost 120 parks covering well over 7,000 acres. **Henry Doorly Zoo** is open April through October. **Elmwood Park** has a golf course, picnic areas, and springs. **Levi Carter Park** is attractive, with good boating and fishing. Other large parks include **Spring Lake, Hanscom, Miller, Benson, Fontenelle, Hummel,** and the new **N.P. Dodge Park,** located on the Missouri River.

ACCOMMODATIONS

Continental Tower (346-4920, S\$30-65/D\$36-70), near center of town; **Red Lion Inn** (346-7600, S\$34-42/D\$44-52), in midtown with heated pool, parking facilities, shopping arcade; **Imperial 400** (345-9565, S\$22-24/D\$26). There are many motels in and around the city. They include **Holiday Inns, Howard Johnson's, New Tower, Omaha TraveLodge, Ramada Inns, Airport Inn, Granada Royale Homotel;** rates range S\$21-61.80/D\$31-73.80. Hotel Tax: 4½%.

RESTAURANTS

Omaha steaks are the local specialty and almost all restaurants feature them. **Caniglia's World, Gorats, Johnny's Café, The Sparetime, Ross' Steak House, Hilltop House;** all moderate. **Marchio's, Anthony's,** Italian dishes. **The French Café** in the Old Market has a reputation for excellent French cuisine. **Silver Lining,** Eppley Airfield, features many local specialties.

ARTS AND MUSIC

Joslyn Art Museum, notable permanent and special exhibits, special section of Indian art objects, beautiful building; open Tuesday through Saturday 10-5, Thursday to 9, Sunday 1-5; admission \$1. The **Omaha Symphony Orchestra** gives concerts during the winter months and pop concerts during the summer season. The **Community Playhouse** is active during the winter months. Two dinner/theaters also offer entertaining evenings.

SHOPPING

Leading stores are **The Brandeis Store, Younkers-Kilpatrick's, Goldstein-Chapman's, Herzberg's, Nebraska Clothing Co., Sears, Montgomery Ward,** and **J.C. Penney.** An increasingly popular part of town for residents and visitors alike is the **Old Market.** This former warehouse district just south and east of "downtown" is becoming an increasingly pleasant melange of attractive shops and stores, good restaurants, congenial bars, plus a disco—**Cuzz's.**

SPORTS

Collegiate football, basketball, baseball, and other sports events are held throughout the year. The visitor can see the **Omaha Royals,** baseball team. Also of interest are the **College Baseball World Series,** held in June and horse racing at **Ak-Sar-Ben** track, from May through mid-July. Omaha offers good opportunities for golf, tennis, bowling, and other sports; fishing and hunting in the immediate area.

CALENDAR OF EVENTS

Livestock Show at Ak-Sar-Ben, also **World Championship Rodeo,** September.

WHERE TO GO NEARBY

Louisville Recreation Grounds, about 25 miles southwest. **Memphis Lake Recreation Grounds,** 45 miles southwest, has boating, camping, and fishing facilities. **Fremont Recreation Grounds,** 38 miles northwest, features a group of lakes, camping, and picnic areas. **Dead Timber Recreation Grounds,** 62 miles northwest, good fishing facilities. Also nearby are **Two Rivers Recreation Area,** 20 miles west, and **De Soto Bend Recreation Area,** 30 miles north.

FURTHER STATE INFORMATION

Department of Economic Development, Tourism Division, PO Box 94666, Lincoln, NE 68509. Hunting and Fishing: **Nebraska Game and Parks Commission,** 2200 North 33rd Street, Box 30370, Lincoln, NE 68502. **Omaha Chamber of Commerce,** 1620 Dodge Street, Omaha, NE 68102.

Consulates in Omaha: Denmark (344-0500), Norway (342-0982) and Sweden (341-3333).

USEFUL TELEPHONE NUMBERS IN OMAHA

Pan Am Reservations:	(800) 621-7107
St. Joseph's Hospital	449-4590
Archbishop Berhan Mercy Hospital	398-6161
Lutheran Medical Center	536-6600

Nebraska Methodist Hospital	397-3000
Omaha District Dental Society	345-3000
Omaha Chamber of Commerce	341-1234
Legal Aid Society	348-1060
Rotary International	342-0281

Nevada

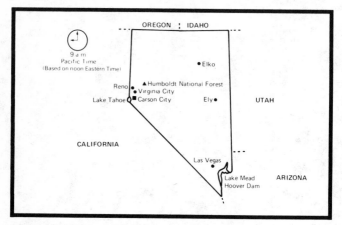

Area	110,540 square miles	Population	800,312
Capital	Carson City	Sales Tax	3%

Weather	Jan	Feb	Mar	Apr	May	Jun	Jul	Aug	Sep	Oct	Nov	Dec
Av Temp (°C)	−1	2	5	9	12	16	20	19	15	10	4	0
Days Rain/Snow	6	5	6	4	5	3	3	2	2	2	5	6

Nevada is a big state with a small permanent population; nearly 50 times as many people visit Nevada every year as live in the state. The name derives from Spanish and means "snow-clad." Almost all of Nevada lies in the **Great Basin,** a vast arid plateau that is mostly 4,000 to 5,000 feet above sea level. The **Sierra Nevada Mountains,** which rise along the western boundary, intercept rain-laden winds from the Pacific with the result that Nevada gets less rainfall than most other states. This is fine for vacationers but a problem for farmers. Piñon and juniper trees grow in the upper mountain slopes, and the valleys produce the desert vegetation valuable for grazing and help to support the state's vast cattle and sheep ranches.

Fur traders and trappers ventured into Nevada in the 1820s and 1830s. Such men as Peter Ogden, Jedediah Smith, Joseph Walker—Los Angeles bound—opened up a new spur to the Santa Fe trail. The first permanent settlement was made by Mormons at **Genoa** in 1849 following the John C. Frémont expeditions, guided by frontier scout Kit Carson in 1843-45. But settlers stayed away in large numbers until, in June of 1859, the Comstock Lode was discovered at Virginia City in the Washoe Mountains. It was one of the greatest strikes of gold and silver of all time. Virginia City's population rocketed almost overnight to 30,000 while Carson City's mushroomed. Today there are still ghostlike, played-out mining towns all over the state, reminders of the big strikes of 1860, '63, '68, and '73. Meanwhile, cattle ranching developed amid frequent skirmishes between the cattle barons and rustlers; the state is still an important producer of livestock. Thanks to modern technology, many of Nevada's mines still produce great quantities of gold, silver, barite, copper, mercury, and lithium. The **Hoover** and **Rye Patch Dams** have provided the needed irrigation for the cultivation of grains, vegetables, and fruit and the pastures for livestock. Gambling was legalized in the state in 1931, with strict controls for honesty. By now, however, **Las Vegas** is probably even more famous for its celebrity-packed night clubs than for its roulette wheels.

At about the time gambling was legalized, a short residency requirement for divorce became law and the state speedily became a national destination for thousands of people seeking legal separation. After six weeks, often spent in a luxurious dude ranch, freedom is almost instantaneous. Other states now also have the six weeks' residency law, but Nevada still gets a lot of the business. Paradoxically it is easier to get married in Nevada than in any other state and the marriage business is booming.

If you head west on Interstate 80 from Salt Lake City, Utah, you enter Nevada at **Wendover** which straddles the state line. The first sizable town is **Elko,** elevation 5,067 feet, which preserves its "Wild West" atmosphere with a horse show the second weekend in June; the **National Basque Festival,** with Basque dancing and typical Basque feasts, is held the first weekend in July; the **Silver State Stampede,** a rodeo, on the first weekend in August; and the **County Fair and Livestock Show** on Labor Day weekend; from the end of August through October, there's the big beef round-up. The **Northeastern Nevada Museum** is a good introduction to the area, its history and natural resources. **Humboldt National Forest** begins south of town, a glorious wilderness of mountains, canyons, abandoned mining towns, and ancient trees; hunting and fishing too. Among numerous good motels: the **Best Western Marquis Motor Inn** (738-7261, S$22-34/D$26-38), **Best Western Thunderbird Motel** (738-7115, S$28-35/D$35-44), and **Holiday Inn** (S$29.75-33.75/D$33.75-38.75) are in downtown Elko. **Esquire Motor Lodge, Ranch-inn Lodge** and **Stockmen's Motor Hotel** are S$21-25/D$25-30 while the **Red Lion Motor Inn** (738-8421, S$29-37/D$37-47). Interesting and delicious Basque-style dishes are served in the **Nevada Dinner House.** The next major stop on the highway is **Winnemucca,** where one of the west's best rodeos is staged along with the **County Fair** on Labor Day weekend. **Lovelock** lies in rich farming land, rare for Nevada, and there are ghost towns to explore nearby as well as some active mines. At Wadsworth, NV 34 veers north to **Pyramid Lake.** See the strange tufa rock formations jutting out of the water. **Anahoe Island** is a sanctuary for thousands of white pelicans. The lake is full of trout; fishing permits are issued by the Paiute Indians who live in the reservation on the lake.

RENO has a quiet, substantial population of 100,943 people who have a rather different routine from the visitors. It proudly calls itself the "Biggest Little City in the World." Long famous for the divorces granted in the **Washoe County Courthouse** and the legend of the wedding rings tossed into the **Truckee River,** Reno glitters with night clubs and gambling casinos open around the clock. Since children are not allowed in gaming rooms, reliable baby sitters are easily acquired through hotels and motels. This is very much a family resort town with lots to see and do besides gambling or unscrambling a marriage. In late June, for example, the **Reno Rodeo** attracts contestants from all over—it's the richest in the West, while in mid-September there's the **Nevada State Fair.** Just east of town is **Harrah's Automobile Collection,** one of the world's biggest displays of vintage automobiles, plus ancient railroad cars, old motorcycles, boats, a Pony Express exhibit, and many more relics related to transportation; open daily. The **University of Nevada** has much for visitors to enjoy including their **Winter Carnival** in February, in which they host twelve top collegiate ski teams. The **Mining Museum** in renowned **Mackay School of Mines,** the **Fleischmann Atmospherium-Planetarium,** the **Nevada State Historical Society Museum,** featuring Indian artifacts and pioneer relics related to the developments of the state, and the theatrical productions in the **J. E. Church Fine Arts Building. The Church Fine Arts Building** also has a permanent collection and features changing exhibitions by nationally recognized local and regional artists. The **Reno Ski Bowl,** south of town, has a string of resorts where you can rent equipment for skiing and ice skating; lessons available. Reno's **Plaza Resort Club Hotel** (786-2200, S$34-44/D$40-50, suites $125 up), being completely remodeled, has superb views of mountains and the city. There are built-in gambling casinos in the handsome **Harrah's** (329-4422, S/D$55-65), where famous entertainers appear in the **Headliner Room.** The **Holiday Hotel, Mapes Hotel, Ponderosa Hotel** average S$22-40/D$24-42, while suites are $60-134.

The **MGM Grand Hotel** (789-2000, or toll free 800-648-5080, S/D$46-62, suites $69-138) boasts the largest casino in the world, the world's largest stage, and over 1,000 accommodation units which range from standard through deluxe. There's a 50-lane bowling center, plus indoor/outdoor tennis courts, men's and women's health spas, two movie theaters, seven restaurants, and over 40 shops and boutiques. There are special cocktail and dinner shows nightly.

South of Reno is **VIRGINIA CITY,** where the Comstock Lode was discovered in 1859. It was one of the most exciting mining camps in the Old West. By the time Nevada became a territory in 1861, three-fourths of its entire population was in Virginia City, either extracting gold from the earth or from those who had found it. By the 1870s, 30,000 people were here, often living in considerable splendor. These days it's better known for its camel races (September), at which visitors are welcome to ride. **The Castle** (1863-68) and the **Mackay Mansion** (1860) are two palatial homes that survived a bad fire in 1875. The figure of Justice on the Courthouse is probably the only one in the country that holds

There's lots of action in the nightclubs and casinos of Reno, Nevada, all day long and through the neon night.

evenly balanced scales but is not blindfolded. Samuel Clemens first started using his Mark Twain *nom de plume* as a reporter on the *Territorial Enterprise;* its office is now restored. Edwin Booth and Sarah Bernhardt played to rapt audiences in the old **Piper's Opera House.** For years a ghost town, Virginia City is now one of Nevada's major attractions. **Sharon House,** with authentic frontier decor, serves very good Chinese food. Accommodation at **Comstock Motel** (847-0233, S/D$18-20).

CARSON CITY, nearby, is one of the nation's smallest state capitals (population 32,114). Named after the frontiersman Kit Carson, the town has a cool, dry, invigorating climate. The federal government established a mint to convert the immense output of silver into coins, and today the **Mint Building** houses the **State Museum** of mining and Indian exhibits; and the Mint Room is a reminder that this was once an important Federal mint. Of special interest is the **Fire Museum** with its collection of Currier & Ives fire-fighting prints. The elegant **Bowers Mansion,** open 15 May to 31 October, shows how at least one millionaire spent his fortune on lavish furnishings. **Lake Tahoe,** 6,228 feet up in the Sierra Nevada mountains, is only 12 miles west of Carson City. The Nevada side of the lake has many gambling casinos and resort hotels. For exciting mountain scenery, genuine Old West atmosphere, and mines, you can follow US 95 down western Nevada from Reno to Las Vegas. The highway passes through **Hawthorne** at the foot of **Walker Lake, Tonopah,** and then skirts the boundary of the **Nellis Air Force Range and Nuclear Test Site.** From US 95 you can cross over into California through **Montgomery Pass,** elevation 7,167 feet, near **Boundary Peak,** 13,140 feet, the highest point in Nevada. Accommodations in Carson City include **Best Western Carson Downtowner Motor Inn** (882-1333, S/D$24-32); **Best Western City Center Motel** (882-5535, S/D$22-38); **Ormsby House** (882-1890, S/D$35 up); **TraveLodge Carson City** (882-3446, S$30-37/D$32-39).

On US 93, which runs south to Las Vegas near the eastern border of the state, you pass through **Ely,** the only sizable town on this route. One of the world's largest open pit copper mines, operated by the Kennecott Corporation, is 6 miles west of town. The **Ward Charcoal Ovens,** 17 miles south of town, are 30-foot high, beehive-shaped remnants of the silver and lead mining boom of the 1870s. **Hamilton,** 42 miles west of Ely, is a ghost town with substantial ruins that recall one of the richest silver cities in the West. The **White Pine Public Museum** in Ely has many relics of these days.

City to Visit

LAS VEGAS

Las Vegas is in the southern tip of Nevada, 290 miles northeast of Los Angeles. The city was the site of a Mormon settlement in 1855-57 but was forgotten until 1903 when the land was purchased by the railroads for a town site and railroad division point. Las Vegas was incorporated as a city in 1911 and today is known primarily as a deluxe resort and convention center.

Metropolitan Las Vegas has grown at a fabulous pace in the last few years. Stringently honest gambling laws, magnificent hotels, elaborate shows, and natural attractions—all at prices kept comparatively moderate by the gambling profits—make the city a unique vacation spot. Population 162,960.

WHAT TO SEE

Every visitor will first want to wander through the luxurious hotels on "The Strip" and downtown, where the biggest names in show business perform year round. The 3½-mile "Strip" still provides the major concentration of resorts, but another casino complex located downtown along Fremont Street (the original main street when the city was founded) is known as "Casino Center," and Las Vegans claim that it's actually brighter at night than Times Square, New York. It is not far from the Civic Center. A "Behind-the-Scenes Tour" in the **Mint Hotel Casino** shows the coin and currency counting room, security measures used for monitoring casino activities, plus a demonstration (and the repair of) one-armed bandits; daily 10-7, over 21 only, free. See the **Convention Center,** one of the world's largest, with seating for some 8,500 persons, and adjacent to the **Las Vegas Country Club.** The **Museum of Natural History** has exhibits of Indian artifacts and early pioneer life, open Monday through Friday, 11-5, Saturday, 10-noon and Sunday, 2-5, free. Visit also the **Desert Research Institute Museum** with an interesting collection of flora and fauna from the surrounding area, including live examples of four regional rattlesnakes, open daily, 9-5. A number of art galleries are to be found within the Strip hotels.

ACCOMMODATIONS

Las Vegas offers an excellent choice of resort, commercial, ranch, or motel accommodations. Leading resort hotels on "The Strip" include the **Aladdin** (736-0111, S/D$45-70), **Caesar's Palace** (734-7110, S/D$45-85), **Desert Inn & Country Club** (733-4444, S/D$45 up), **Desert Inn** (735-7278, S/D$55-75), **Dunes, Flamingo, Frontier, Hacienda, MGM Grand Hotel, Riviera, Sahara, Sands, Stardust, Thunderbird,** and **Tropicana;** all with casinos and pools. Rates range from S/D$30-55 at some hotels to S/D$35-115 at others. The **Landmark** (733-1110, S/D$32 up) and the **Las Vegas Hilton** (732-5111, S/D$51-80) are just off "The Strip" near the Convention Center as are the **Royal Americana Hotel** (734-0711, S/D$30-48), **Best Western Royal Las Vegas** (735-6117, S$28-32/D$32-36), **Convention Center Lodge** (735-1315, S$20-27.50/D$21.50-30), and **Somerset House Motel** (735-4411, S/D$22-36). Downtown hotels include the **El Cortez** (385-5200, S/D$14-23), **Four Queens, Fremont, Mint** and **Showboat;** average rates S$20-35/D$22-50. There are hundreds of motels in the area, some luxurious. Some leading motels on "The Strip" are **Desert Rose, El Morocco, Rodeway Inn, Royal Palms** and **Tam O'Shanter,** averaging S$20-40/D$24.50-45. Downtown there are **Fergusons, Lotus Inn Hyatt Lodge, Orbit Inn, TraveLodge Las Vegas Downtown.** Rates range from S$18-30/D$22-52. Hotel Tax: 6%. Nearby camping facilities are at **Lake Mead, Lake Mohave,** and **Mt Charleston.**

RESTAURANTS

Particularly good meals may be had at the resort hotels, which feature buffet-dining at moderate prices. But Las Vegas offers excess for the sybarite and gourmand, ranging from the seven-course feast at the **Bacchanal Room** at Caesar's Palace, or the nearly understated chic of the surroundings of the **Monte Carlo Room** at the Desert Inn Hotel, or **Top-O-the-Strip** at the Dunes. **Alpine Village Inn,** on Paradise Road, features a Rathskeller, fine German beer, plus choice portions of Swiss and German fare. The **House of Lords** is the Sahara's attempt at a British pub atmosphere, but the food is excellent, including trout salmon and tournedos; **The Lobster Trap,** informal atmosphere, some of the best seafood in town; long-time favorite; **The Golden Steer,** steaks to ravioli, but given 24-hour notice you could dine on quail, suckling pig, pheasant, and so on; **Chin Chin,** for Chinese; **El Burrito** and **Viva Zapata,** Mexican; and **Chateau Vegas,** for romantic evenings with harp, soft music, and fine Italian veal; as well as gourmet dining in the hotel dining rooms, including the **Regency Room** at the Sands, **Top of the Mint** on the 25th floor of the Mint Hotel, **Gourmet** at the Tropicana, **The Sultan's Table** at the Dunes and **Gigi Restaurant** at MGM Grand Hotel. The famous **Golden Nugget,** downtown, 108 South Casino Center Boulevard, featuring steaks and seafood, is open 24 hours a day.

ENTERTAINMENT

Along "The Strip" most hotels feature big-name entertainment nightly, usually in two shows, or present extravaganzas with music and dancing. Hotel guests get first choice of seats, so if there's a show you must see, maybe you'd best check into that hotel. Almost every known gambling game may be found. Most of the hotels have casinos and there are slot machines in every conceivable location. Be sure to see **Binion's Horseshoe** and **Circus Circus,** two of the more unusual casinos. The latter features trapeze stars and highwire artists. Outside the hotels, but still offering entertainment, are **P. J. Bottoms, Dirty Sally's, Silver Dollar Saloon—** live country-western music, and **The Brewery.** Some of the best of American burlesque is to be found at the **Cabaret, Palomino Club,** and **Royal Casino.**

For theatrical productions, check **Repertory Theater** at Judy Bayley Hall (on campus), **Alladin Theater,** and **Meadows Playhouse.** In late June, early July, San Francisco Shakespeare Company plays at **Spring Mountain Ranch.**

SHOPPING

Numerous boutiques and specialty shops, especially along **Fremont Street;** in the **Boulevard Shopping Center,** there are 67 stores in a fully enclosed air-conditioned mall, open weekdays 10-9, Saturday 10-6, Sunday 12-5. There are also gift shops in hotels, open at convenient hours.

SPORTS
Good fishing in **Lake Mead** and **Lake Mohave,** for bass especially, and crappie, trout, and catfish. No closed season; 5-day fishing license for nonresidents, $5.00. These lakes are also ideal for swimming, water-skiing, and sailing. Snow-skiing can be found at **Lee Canyon Ski Area,** 45 miles from Las Vegas, open daily 9-4, December through April, and at **Charleston Mountains,** 35 miles northwest of Las Vegas. Hunting season in the fall for deer, elk, mountain sheep, duck, and goose; nonresident hunting licenses are $50. University of Nevada/Las Vegas with one of the finer collegiate basketball teams plays from November through February at the Las Vegas Convention Center, while the NASL **Quicksilvers** play soccer at home at Las Vegas Stadium from April through August. **Boxing** ranges from major professional heavyweight matches to weekly bouts by talented unknowns at the Silver Slipper hotel, at Caesar's Palace or the Aladdin Hotel. **Jai Alai,** daily at the MGM Grand Hotel arena. Numerous golf courses, admirable tennis facilities include Cambridge Tennis Club on Swenson Avenue.

CALENDAR OF EVENTS
Annual Showboat Invitational Professional Bowlers, January; **Sahara Mid-Winter Trapshooting Tournament,** February; **Las Vegas Symphony Society Concerts** in Las Vegas Convention Center, mid-January, mid-February and mid-March (check for dates); **Mint "400" Del Webb Desert Rally and Parade,** March; **Elk's Helldorado and Rodeo** and **International Gin Rummy Tournament,** May; **Alan King Tennis Tournament,** Caesar's Palace, May; **Del Webb Trapshooting Tournament,** September; **Intermountain Tennis Tournament,** September; **US National Seniors Golf Tournament** and **Sahara International Golf Tournament,** October.

WHERE TO GO NEARBY
A short distance from town is **Hoover Dam,** formerly Boulder Dam, one of the world's great irrigation and power projects. The dam, 726 feet high, impounds **Lake Mead;** at 110 miles long, it is the largest man-made lake. Excursion boats leave **Lake Mead Marina** daily; adults $2, children under 12, $1. The **Desert National Wildlife Range,** 28 miles from Las Vegas, has bighorn sheep on display, open daily 9-5, free. Petrified trees and carvings of ancient peoples are found at the **Valley of Fire State Park** as well as spectacular scenery, about 50 miles out of Las Vegas.

FURTHER STATE INFORMATION
Department of Economic Development, Travel Division, Carson City, NV 89710. Hunting and Fishing; **Nevada Department of Wildlife,** PO Box 10678, Reno, NV 89510. **Greater Las Vegas Chamber of Commerce,** 2301 East Sahara Avenue, Las Vegas, NV 89105. **Las Vegas Convention**

and Visitors' Authority, PO Box 14006, Las Vegas, NV 89114. **Pan Am** office, 2901 Las Vegas Boulevard South, Las Vegas, NV 89109; tel: 637-4904.

Consulates in Las Vegas: Costa Rica, El Salvador, France, Italy.

USEFUL TELEPHONE NUMBERS IN RENO

Fire	785-2345
Police	785-2121
St. Mary's Hospital	323-2041
Reno Medical Plaza	359-0212
Legal Aid Society	786-2695
Chamber of Commerce	786-3030
Tourist Information	847-0177
Pan Am Reservations	(800) 227-4920

New Hampshire

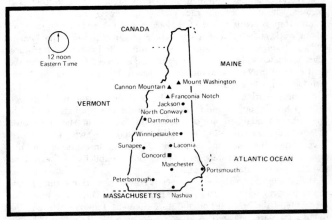

Area	9,304 square miles	Population	920,610
Capital	Concord	Sales Tax	5% state tax on hotels and meals

Weather

	Jan	Feb	Mar	Apr	May	Jun	Jul	Aug	Sep	Oct	Nov	Dec
Av Temp (°C)	−6	−5	0	7	13	18	21	20	15	9	3	−4
Days Rain/Snow	11	10	11	11	12	10	10	10	9	8	12	11

The people of New Hampshire, the "Granite State," may tell you they have a mountain for every visitor. Certainly these mountains are among the most spectacular sights in New England. **Mt Washington** at 6,288 feet is the highest point in northeastern United States and was described by Phineas T. Barnum, the showman, as the "Second greatest show on earth"—his own circus being "the greatest."

The winters are usually long and severe, but the summers are cool and mild. The greatest extremes in temperature occur in the mountain valleys, where it may rise above 27°C in summer and dive to −18°C in winter. The extremes are considerably less along the seacoast. The annual snowfall in the northern section of the state, and in the mountains, is about eight feet, but only about half that amount falls in the southeast.

The oldest ski club in the US was founded near Berlin in 1872; today over 100 ski areas attract winter sports enthusiasts to the famous New Hampshire slopes. The major ski areas: **Mt Washington Valley; Ski 93; Sunapee; Laconia; Monadnock Region;** and **Merrimack Valley;** all offer special package prices on lifts, lessons, and accommodations through local area associations. Century-old inns, luxury resorts, and modern motels provide après-ski comfort and entertainment. Local restaurants supply the added enticement of hearty New England dinners. Winter Carnival time is every February and March, with skiing and ski-jumping events at **Franklin, Gilford, Cannon Mt,** and **Dartmouth College** in Hanover. The World Championship Sled Dog Derby highlights the festivities at **Laconia,** where the 20-mile race ends in the town's main street.

New Hampshire is proud of its local craftsmen and artists, many of whom work at home and market their products through the League of New Hampshire Craftsmen. Fine hand-crafted cabinets, furniture, rugs, needlework, jewelry, and pottery are exhibited and on sale at the craft centers in **Nashua, Manchester, Sharon, Hanover, Concord, Meredith-Laconia,** and **Exeter.**

The people are also noted for their practicality, a trait which proved to be politically opportune in 1916, when the town fathers decided to hold a presidential primary on the second Tuesday in March. Because the monthly town meeting was held that day they would, therefore, have to heat the town hall only once. The tradition continues and this now gives New Hampshire priceless national publicity as the kick-off state for presidential campaigns.

At **Portsmouth,** on the coast in **SOUTHERN** New Hampshire, follow the strawberry signs to "Strawberry Banke" in the **Old South End.** This is the site of the original Portsmouth settlement, founded in 1623. The townspeople are engaged in a project to preserve the original homes on the 10-acre site, and many of the restored houses and buildings, including a blacksmith's shop, are open for inspection, May through October. **Prescott Park,** adjacent to Strawberry Banke, at State and March streets, offers fishing and picnicking. Portsmouth is the state's only harbor. The **US Naval Base** at the Portsmouth-Kittery Naval Shipyard is the principal yard for repairing atomic submarines, and the city's main industry. Excursion boats leave Market Street wharf daily, mid-June through August, for the offshore **Star Island** and the **Isle of Shoals.** The annual **Jubilee Week,** 8 days in late-July, and **Great Bay Day,** featuring an all-class regatta, sailboats, and water-skiing contests on Labor Day weekend, are always crowded. **Holiday Inn** (431-8000, S$28-35/D$32-47) has a heated pool, as does **Howard Johnson's** (436-7600, S$28-43/D$30-43). **Fisherman's Pier,** a very popular local restaurant, has a view of the harbor; **Flagstones** and **Yoken's** "Thar She Blows" are recommended for families, while the **Blue Strawberry** (431-6420, reservations necessary) is for those who want to live it up a little.

Settled by Puritans in 1635, **Durham,** which is west on US 4, is the seat of the **University of New Hampshire. Rochester,** on the Cocheco River, near the Maine border, is the scene of the **Rochester Fair,** which has been held every year in mid-September since 1875. **Colby's Restaurant** has good food at reasonable prices.

Manchester, to the southwest, on the banks of the Merrimack River, is the largest city in the state and is home for over 300 industries. The

Currier Gallery of Art, one of New England's finest small museums, is open daily (except Mondays) year round and there's no admission charge. Manchester also has a large airport, **Grenier,** which has scheduled flights to and from major cities. It is located 3 miles from downtown, and is serviced by public transportation. **Concord,** north of Manchester, the state capital, has the largest legislature of any state, over 400 seats. **Concord Coach Motor Inn** (224-2511, S$28/D$32) has a heated pool and pleasant dining room with colonial decor; **Brick Tower Motel** (244-9565, S$20-25/D$25-32) also has a heated pool. The childhood home of New Hampshire's only US president, Franklin Pierce, is at **Hillsboro. Pat's Peak Ski Area,** at Henniker, is open daily, mid-December through March.

At **Keene,** the chief community in southwest New Hampshire, the old-fashioned Main Street is reminiscent of another era. Swimming is good at **Spofford Lake** and **Otter Brook State Park;** camping at **Wheelock Park** and harness racing and pari-mutuel betting are at **Hinsdale Raceway,** mid-May through late October. The **Cheshire Fair** at Safford Park in early August, includes horse- and ox-pulling contests. Stay at **Valley Green Motel** (352-7350, S/D$20-24); or **Winding Brook Lodge** (352-3111, S/D$20-28), pool. The popular **Black Lantern Restaurant's** specialty is roast beef; Thursday buffet.

Rhododendron State Park, at Fitzwilliam, southeast of Keene, has a 16-acre bed of wild rhododendrons among its 294 acres. The flowers usually bloom in mid-July and there is picnicking, late June through Labor Day. **Fitzwilliam Inn** (585-9000, S$16/D$20), in business since 1796, features a buffet supper, Sundays and Mondays. Nearby, children are encouraged to play with the farm animals at the **Friendly Farm** in **Dublin,** open daily mid-May through October.

Peterborough was the home of composer Edward MacDowell. He attracted authors such as Willa Cather and Thornton Wilder, who came to work at the **MacDowell Colony** and helped to make it famous. Five miles southeast there are ski slopes at **Temple Mountain, Crotched Mountain,** and **Onset.** During the summer relax with a picnic at **Miller State Park;** swimming, fishing and camping at **Greenfield State Park. Brick End Room Restaurant** specializes in New England seafood dishes. Try the **Countryside Lodging** (924-3715, S$26/D$30). **Grandmother's House** is a popular local restaurant serving German and Hungarian dishes. **Old Forge,** in a converted forge, specializes in German dishes.

On the eastern slopes of Mt Monadnock, **Jaffrey** has been a summer resort since the 1840s. **Barrett House,** on Main Street in **New Ipswich,** is an impressive, three-story mansion *circa* 1800 with a ballroom, period furnishings, and spinning and weaving equipment on display in the carriage sheds. Notable summer residents speak at the **Amos Fortune Forum** in the **Old Meeting House,** Friday nights, mid-July through mid-August. There's swimming at the public beach on **Lake Contoocook. Woodbound Inn** (532-8341, S$22/D$47), on the east shore of the lake, has a private beach, fishing, water-skiing, ski tows, lighted ice rink.

Nashua, in the **SOUTH CENTRAL** part of New Hampshire, was originally a fur-trading post and is now the second-largest city in the state.

Benson's Wild Animal Farm, across the river from Nashua, has a well-stocked zoo, rides, wild animal acts, and a picnic area, open mid-April through November. A refreshing summer treat might be a visit to the **Anheuser-Busch Brewery** and sampling room. Swimming at **Silver Lake State Park.** In Nashua try: **Green Ridge Motor Lodge** (888-2500, S$14-20/D$16-20); or the **Suisse Chalet** (889-4151, S$18/D$20). **Green Ridge Turkey Farm Restaurant** is very popular with families. East of Nashua is **Salem,** location of **Mystery Hill,** a 30-acre archeological site with 20 stone structures which are about 3,000 years old. Also in Salem there is thoroughbred racing at **Rockingham Park** from July through October. Horse racing is also at **Hinsdale,** and dog racing at **Seabrook** and **Belmont** tracks. **Fireside Motel** (893-3584, S/D$22-26) is in Salem near the track.

Exeter claims one of the most prominent preparatory schools in the country, **Phillips Exeter Academy,** founded in 1781. The town served as the state capital during the Revolution. The ivy-covered **Exeter Inn** (772-5901, S$16/D$20) is locally famous for its roast beef and steak, while the informal **Loaf and Ladle** is good for light meals.

In **CENTRAL** New Hampshire, **Old Fort Number Four** on NH 11 along the Vermont and New Hampshire state line, at **Charlestown,** was reconstructed from drawings of 1746, depicting pre-Revolutionary frontier life. The project includes the **Great Hall,** stockade, watch-tower, and furnished period houses. **Newport** is the commercial center of the **Lake Sunapee** area with **Mt Sunapee State Park** and ski resort nearby. The **Winter Carnival** here is 4 days in mid-February. To the east, across Lake Sunapee in **New London,** there's skiing at **King Ridge** and, nearby in **Danbury,** at **Ragged Mountain.** The **Dartmouth-Lake Sunapee Region Championship Regatta,** on Little Lake Sunapee, is held the first Sunday in August. In New London the **Barn Playhouse** is open mid-June through Labor Day. In the area stay at **Indian Cave Lodge** (763-2762, S$41-46/D$62-72); **Mount Sunapee Motel** (736-5592, S$16-24/D$18-24), at the entrance to the state park; **Lamplighter Motor Inn** (526-6484, S$25/D$35), near beach; and **New London Inn** (526-2791, S$21-23/D$27-30), established 1792.

Shaker Village in Canterbury, southeast of New London, is one of two remaining Shaker villages in New England. It was once a colony of some 400 farmers and craftsmen, but since the Shakers were celibates, the town is no longer occupied. There are guided tours of the restored buildings, Memorial Day through Labor Day. Daniel Webster's birthplace, a restored frame house, is at **Franklin.** Swimming at **Webster Lake** and **Odell Park** outside of Franklin.

Laconia, one of New England's most popular year-round resort areas, overlooks three lakes—Winnisquam, Opechee, and Winnipesaukee. It is also the headquarters of **White Mountain National Forest,** 737,000 acres of forest, including the **Presidential Range** and a major part of the **White Mountains.** The **National Forest** is described more fully in the section covering Northern New Hampshire. The **Appalachian Trail,** which includes numerous hostels, covers some spectacular peaks; hunting, fishing, camping, picnicking. **Gunstock Recreation Area** has a double chair lift to **Belknap** summit; swimming, picnicking, hiking, late June through Labor Day; also winter skiing. The **Arlberg,** at the foot of Gunstock Mountain Ski Area, specializes in German dishes; **Hickory Stick Farm** is a converted colonial farmhouse with a wonderful view of the mountains; and the **Windmill** is good for families.

Swimming, boating, fishing, sailing, and water-skiing are at **The Weirs,** a series of dams on **Lake Winnipesaukee,** at the south end of Weirs Beach, mid-June through Labor Day. Lake cruises leave Weirs Beach, the main resort section, for a 4-hour cruise around Lake Winnipesaukee, making stops at **Center Harbor, Wolfeboro,** and **Alton Bay,** daily, late June through early September. **Sunfish-Minifish-Hobie Cat Regatta** is on Lake Winnipesaukee in Ellacoya State Park at Gilford, in August; and the 50-mile **Water-ski Marathon** from Weirs Beach on Lake Winnipesaukee is in late August. **Gilford Playhouse** presents Broadway comedies and musicals, late June through early September. Winter events include the **Laconia International Snowmobile Championships,** second weekend in February, and **Winter Carnival,** with the **World Championship Sled Dog Derby,** the last weekend in February. Among the many resorts in the Laconia area: **Flying Cloud** (366-4993, S/D$26-30), in Laconia, overlooking lake, sand beach, heated ice fishing house; **Steele Hill Resort** (524-0500, D$40-50 MAP), all resort facilities plus a high vantage point; **King's Grant Inn and Chalets** (293-4431, S$30-40/D$45-65 MAP), popular winter and summer family resort, complete ski area and ski packages, private beach, ice rink, cottages. Recommended for families: **Driftwood** (366-7393, S/D$27-30), overlooking the lake.

Wolfeboro is the largest town on the 28-mile lake and looks like the old, sedate resort community it is. Governor John Wentworth built the first inland "summer home" in the US here in 1766. **Wentworth State Park,** just north of Wolfeboro, offers swimming, fishing, and picnicking mid-June through mid-September. **Winter Carnival** is the first weekend in February. **Lakeview Inn and Motor Lodge** (569-1335, S$15/D$22-31) in a lovely historical setting on 80 acres; **The Lake Motel** (569-1100, S/D$28-35).

Wakefield, northeast of Wolfeboro, is popular as both a summer and winter resort. The **Moose Mountain Ski Area** is open mid-December through March. Another summer and winter sports region centers around **Ossipee Lake** and the **Ossipee Mountains,** to the north on NH 16. There's skiing at **Mt Whittier Recreation Area;** swimming at Ossipee Lake and **White Lake State Park.** The **Tamworth Inn** is a charming country inn a few miles west.

Meredith is a favorite water sports center between Lakes Winnipesaukee and Waukewan. See the **Meredith-Laconia Arts and Crafts Center. New Hampshire Music Festival,** at Interlakes High School in Center Harbor, has symphony concerts and musical events, mid-July through mid-August. **The Straffordshire Inn** (253-4382, S$39-59/D$54-59), private sandy beach; and **Rob Roy** (476-5571, S$32/D$40), steambath, whirlpool, fully air conditioned with color TV, also good. **Hart's Turkey Farm Restaurant,** with children's plates, is good for families.

Holderness is noted for its fishing, boating, swimming, and water sports at Squam Lake and Little Squam. Twelve miles of waterfront and sandy beaches provide excellent swimming. **Boulders Motel** (968-3600, S$18/D$30), most rooms overlooking Little Squam Lake, private beach; and **Squam Lakes Lodge** (968-3348, S/D$30), on 17 acres, golf, tennis, beach, are excellent. **White Oak Motel** (968-3673, S$17-26/D$22/32) is set on 8 acres, heated pool, private sandy beach. Inland, **Plymouth** has been a popular resort center since the middle of the 19th century. The **State Fair** is held in Plymouth in late August.

To the west, in **Hanover**, 5 miles north of I-89, is **Dartmouth College**. Established in 1769 four years after the first settlers came to Hanover, the college has dominated the town ever since. College Guide Service Tours are available during the summer. **Dartmouth Winter Carnival**, inter-collegiate skiing and winter sports competitions, is held mid-February. **Congregation of the Arts,** Hopkins Center at Dartmouth College Green, presents concerts, films, late June through late August. Stay at the **Hanover Inn** (643-4300, S/D$42-54) or the **Chieftain Motel** (643-2550). **Peter Christian's Tavern** offers hearty and inventive soups, sandwiches, and stews, while **5 Olde Nugget Alley** is a favorite with townspeople and college professors and students alike. Ten miles to the north **Lyme Inn** (795-2222, S$14-25/D$20-30), built in 1809, has fireplaces in some of its guest rooms and an outstanding restaurant; reservations recommended.

Twenty-five miles south, in **Cornish**, is the **Saint-Gaudens National Historic Site,** a former tavern and home of Augustus Saint-Gaudens, the sculptor. His works are on display, and there are concerts and exhibits of important artists, late-May through mid-October.

Many fine resorts are located in the White Mountain National Forest in **NORTHERN** New Hampshire. Crossing the state from west to northeast, the **White Mountains** provide some of the most dramatic vistas in the country, along with the **Appalachian Range.** There is skiing at **Waterville Valley, Mt Tecumseh, Snow's Mountain,** and **Tenney Mountain. Polar Caves,** 5 miles west on NH 25, are glacial caverns; there is also a maple sugar house, cafeteria, open mid-May through mid-October. Waterville Valley summer facilities include tennis, golf, and an Olympic-size pool. The annual **Waterville Valley Ski Touring Derby** in early February and the **Saint Paddy's Day Sprint** in mid-March are family-style competitions. Stay at the **Out Look Inn** (236-8355, S$17-19/D$22-40), **Landmarc Lodge** (236-8355, S$29-46/D$40-59), **Silver Squirrel Inn** (236-8366, S$26/D$36), **Snowy Owl Inn** (236-8383, S$23-36/D$32-46), or **Valley Inn & Tavern** (236-8336, S$24-32/D$32-44).

To the north of Waterville, but still within the National Forest, the 5 ski areas in the **Mount Washington Valley** region, **Black Mountain** at Jackson, **Attitash** at Bartlett, **Cranmore Mountain** in North Conway, **Wildcat** at Pinkham Notch, and **Tyrol,** have special ski plans. For information on Mt Washington Valley's immense trail network, contact the ski touring center at Jackson; tel: 383-9355. **North Conway** is in the heart of the famous Mount Washington Valley region of the White Mountains. Mt

Washington can be seen from Main Street. Mt Cranmore has skiing and summer sightseeing on mile-long tract to the 2,000-foot summit. Good views of White Mountain. **Attitash Ski Area** is in Bartlett, on US 302. Swimming and picnicking at 47-acre **Echo Lake State Park,** within the National Forest area, mid-June through mid-October. Camp-sites are available in **White Mountain National Forest.** Hotels/motels in the Conway area include **Arends Motel** (356-2976, S/D$22-30) in Glen, view of mountains, heated pool in summer; **Cranmore Inn** (356-5502, S$16-20/D$24-32), in North Conway, is informal and popular with skiers; **New England Inn** (356-5541, S$33-38/D$27-38), in Intervale, has spacious grounds, pools, and a good restaurant; **Red Jacket Mountain View Motor Inn** (356-5411, S/D$31-56), in Intervale; **Stonehurst Manor and Motel** (356-2432, S$18-28/D$28), south of Intervale, English-style manor house on 50-acre estate; and **Snowvillage Lodge** (447-2812, S$40-42/D$66-70), in Snowville on a 150-acre estate, has a Swiss kitchen.

At Glen, drive west and then north on US302 to **Crawford Notch,** a spectacular gap in the White Mountains cut by the Saco River, which stretches from Bartlett in the south to Crawford House in the north. **Arethusa Falls,** more than 20 feet high, is one of the highest in New Hampshire. **Crawford Notch State Park** has camping, fishing, picnicking, late-May through mid-October. Just north of Crawford House is the Mount Washington (278-1000, S$50-65/D$90-138 AP), a rambling, thriving relic of the great New England hotels with spacious grounds and a splendid view of Mt Washington; on the grounds is the modern **Bretton Woods Motor Inn** (S$26/D$34), at which you enjoy all the privileges of the hotel.

Returning to Glen and continuing north on US16, children and the young at heart will want to stop at **Storyland;** life-sized exhibits of familiar children's stories, carousel, and train rides, open mid-June through mid-October. **Jackson,** at the southern end of Pinkham Notch, is an all-year resort. **Christmas Farm Inn** (383-4313, S$31-43/D$52-76 MAP), pool; **Covered Bridge Motel** (383-4264, S$24-28/D$26-32), pool; **Dana Place** (383-6822, S$20-32/D$30-44 BB), heated pool, charming restored inn on 300 acres; **Eagle Mountain House** (383-4264, S$35-45/D$50-70 MAP); and **Whitney's** (383-6886, S$36-48/D$76-84 MAP) provide excellent accommodation.

The Mt Washington cog railway was completed in 1869 and is still running. The line offers a scenic 3-hour excursion—a 1-hour ride to the top, 1-hour visit to the observatory museum, US weather station, time out for hot coffee at **Summit House,** and another hour for the return trip. There is also a 45-minute auto route to the top, with the approach along NH 16, going through **Pinkham Notch,** headquarters of the **Appalachian Mountain Club's** hut system. Eight huts are scattered a day's hike apart through the forest preserve. **Wildcat Mountain Recreation Area** is 10 miles north of Jackson on NH 16 in White Mountain National Forest. **Tuckerman Ravine** presents a challenge to the most expert skiers. It has no lifts or tows and is considered the only ski area of Alpine standards in the East. It opens mid-March and closes early July. **Gorham,** 10 miles northeast of Mt Washington at the north end of Pinkham Notch, is a popular winter and summer sports center. Summer recreation facilities at **Moose Brook State Park, Dolly Copp Campground,** and **Libby Memorial Pool and Recreation Area. Town and Country Motor Inn** (466-3381, S$16-22/D$20-24) in Gorham has a pool and restaurant. The **Brabo at Mt Madison** and **Tourist Village** both have heated pools. The **Nansen Ski Jump** at Berlin, north of Gorham, at 181½ feet is the highest steel tower jump in the US. **Winter Carnival** at the ski jump is held the first weekend in March.

To the west **Jefferson** is on the slopes of **Mt Starr King** in the White Mountains. Outside Jefferson, **Santa's Village** and **Gingerbread Forest** have steam train rides, puppet shows, open late June through mid-October; 50 tame deer have a free run. **Lancaster** is the Connecticut Valley farm and shopping center. There are many houses that were built before 1800 on Main Street and superb views of the White Mountains to the east. Nearby **Weeks State Park** with 430 acres, observation tower, forestry museum, covered bridges, dates from the late 19th century. **Lancaster Fair,** Labor Day weekend, has horse show and agricultural exhibits. **Weathervane Theater** at **Whitefield** below Lancaster, performing in a converted barn, features a professional repertory company early July-early September; there is also a children's theater, Friday afternoon. **Mountain View House** (837-2511, S$42-49/D$40-46 AP), on 3,000 acres, is a comfortable resort in a beautiful mountain setting; dine in the restaurant or enjoy a buffet lunch beside the heated pool. **Littleton** is a resort town a few miles northwest of White Mountain National Forest. **Forest Lake State Park** offers swimming, fishing, and picnicking. There is skiing at **Pine Hill Road,** two ski tows right in town in Mt Eustis and Remich Park, free. **Perkins Motel** (444-3971, S$21-27/D$23-29) has a heated pool during the summer.

South of Littleton, **Franconia Notch** is one of the most scenic of the White Mountain notches and has been a top tourist attraction since the mid-19th century. Skiing at **Cannon Mountain** and **Mittersill.** Tram cars also make the 2,000 feet, 8-minute trip, late May through mid-October. **The Great Stone Face,** 1,200 feet above Profile Lake, is best seen from the east shore of the lake. **Echo Lake** has boating, fishing, swimming, and picnicking facilities. **The Flume,** a narrow natural gorge and waterfall at the southern end of the notch, provides an ideal setting for picnicking. Recommended in Franconia: **Best Western Hillwinds Motor Inn** (823-7711, S$20-36/D$26-46); **Lovetts Inn** (823-7761, S/D$40-64), resort on 160 acres, charming restaurant specializing in curried lamb; **The Franconia Inn Resort, Notchway Motel,** and **Raynor's Motor Inn** average S/D$18-34. **Ski 93,** named for the interstate highway that connects the areas, offers a reciprocal ski ticket plan which allows unlimited skiing in any of five major areas: Waterville Valley, Loon Mountain, Cannon Mountain, Mittersill Ski-Town and Tenney Mountain. For information telephone 745-8101.

Due south of Franconia Notch, you enter **North Woodstock** in a spectacular mountain setting, which has many hotels, motels and shops catering to the busy tourist trade. The **Kancamagus Highway,** NH 112, provides a beautiful 42-mile route east to west between Conway and North Woodstock. **Loon Mountain Ski Area's** four-passenger gondola operates daily, late June through mid-October, climbing 7,000 feet up for excellent view of the White Mountains. **Natureland,** on US 3 in Lincoln, has a private zoo with wild and tame animals, rides and picnicking, May through October. **Lost River Reservation** includes 900 acres with garden and picnicking, mid-May through mid-October. In North Woodstock: **Inn at Loon Mountain** (745-8146, S$28-60/D$32-85), hunting and ski package rates; **Parker's** and **Red Doors** in the range of D$30-36; **Jack O'Lantern** (745-8121, S/D$58), tennis, fishing, golf, heated pool on 300 acres; and **Woodward's Motel** (745-8141, S/D$32-48).

FURTHER STATE INFORMATION

Division of Economic Development, PO Box 856, Concord, NH 03301. Hunting and Fishing: **Fish and Game Department,** 34 Bridge Street, Concord, NH 03301. **Mt Washington Valley Association,** North Conway, NH 03860. **White Mountain National Forest,** Laconia, NH 03246. **Chamber of Commerce,** Concord, NH 03301 (tel: 224-2508).

USEFUL TELEPHONE NUMBERS IN MANCHESTER

Medical	669-5300
	883-5521
Police	668-8711
Fire & Ambulance	669-2256
Poison Control	1-643-4000
Pan Am Reservations	800-223-9762

New Jersey

Area	7,495 square miles					**Population** 7,327,000						
Capital	Trenton					**Sales Tax** 5%						
Weather		Jan	Feb	Mar	Apr	May	Jun	Jul	Aug	Sep	Oct	Nov Dec
Av Temp (°C)		2	2	5	11	16	21	24	23	20	14	8 3
Days Rain/Snow		11	10	11	11	10	9	9	9	7	7	9 9

The easiest statistic to accept about New Jersey is that it has more roads, highways, and railroad tracks to the square mile than any other state in America. New Jersey has more people to the square mile than any other state. But two-thirds of the population lives within 30 miles of New York City, leaving nearly one-fourth of the state sparsely populated. On the coast, there are miles of empty beaches where you can have the sea to yourself. The shoreline stretches 127 miles from Atlantic Highlands just south of New York City all the way south to Cape May. And "The Garden State" produces large crops of fruits and vegetables in its non-industrialized areas.

Much of the state's early history is tied to that of New York and Delaware. The area was originally inhabited by tribes of the Algonquin group and it was not until the mid-17th century when the Dutch ceded their interest to the British that New Jersey began to develop its own entity. The British Crown made a grant of the land between the Hudson and Delaware to Lord Berkeley and Sir George Carteret in return for their settling it, under the basic terms of loyalty and dues to the crown.

Quakers had settled what had become known as West Jersey. At the turn of the century until 1738, the Crown—in the person largely of Lewis Morris (and for whom Morristown is named)—and the Colony of New York administered the territory. Morris then became Governor of New Jersey alone.

Because of its geographical location, New Jersey was the site of a number of Revolutionary battles. A high point in the state's evolution was Princeton's service as temporary capital of the Union.

Drive into New Jersey from its northwestern corner, and discover a delightful region of low wooded mountains, countless lakes, and little towns that give no hint of the great industrial region to the southeast. **Stokes State Forest, High Point,** and **Wawayanda State Parks** offer boating, fishing, camping, and hiking opportunities. **Hamburg** has a children's amusement park famous for its **Gingerbread Castle,** witch's cauldron, and miniature railroad. There is skiing at **Great Gorge, Vernon Valley, Hidden Valley** and **Craigmeur. Lake Hopatcong** is one of those beloved summer resorts that families return to year after year. Stanhope is near **Waterloo Village,** a restoration of an 18th-century town with everything in running order from April through December; closed Mondays. **Action Park** in Vernon Valley is a family fun center where you can race speed boats through a lagoon. Alpine slide, water slide, and white water rapid ride are popular features here, and there's outdoor skating on a trail through the woods and a children's play park; daily, 10am to 11pm. The highlight of northeastern New Jersey is the drive down the **Hudson River. Fort Lee,** due west at the approach to the George Washington Bridge, stands on a high bluff where Washington built a fort, hoping to defend West Point from the British. Fort Lee affords a dramatic skyline view of New York City, only 20 minutes away by subway, and the huge suspension bridge. **Holiday Inn** (944-5000, S$40-44/D$45-49), 1 mile west of the George Washington Bridge and just 6 miles from Times Square, has a pool, valet service, and baby-sitter list.

The eastbound highways from Stroudsburg and Bethlehem in Pennsylvania run roughly parallel as they cross New Jersey. On Interstate 78 about 15 miles east of Easton, Pennsylvania, there are two new popular boating, fishing, and picnicking areas. One is **Spruce Run** and the other the **Round Valley Reservoir,** noted for 4-pound trout and sailboating. Both have bathing beaches. There are some charming towns between the two roads. **Madison,** famous for its roses, is the home of **Drew University** where professional repertory productions of Shakespeare and other classic and modern works are staged from late June through Labor Day. The **Florham-Madison Campus** of Fairleigh Dickinson University and the **College of St Elizabeth** also have attractive grounds.

Morristown (population 16,573) was established in 1720 when a large iron ore deposit proved profitable. A supply base for the Continental Army, the troops quartered in **Jockey Hollow,** where their huts and the **Continental Army Hospital** have been reconstructed. The **Wick House,** also in the Hollow, is comfortably and simply furnished in the style of a prosperous 18th-century farmer. **Fort Nonsense** is a focal point for the **Morristown National Historical Park.** Most buildings in the park are open daily except major wintertime holidays. General Washington stayed in the **Ford Mansion** during the winters of 1777-78 and 1779-80. Behind it is the important **Historical Museum and Library** devoted to the Revolution. In town, the **Schuyler-Hamilton House** (1760) was the home of a surgeon whose daughter Alexander Hamilton, the US statesman, wooed and married during the winter of 1779-80. Samuel Morse developed the telegraph at the **Speedwell Ironworks** in Morristown in the 1830s. Near town too is the first school of **Seeing Eye Inc** where blind people come to train with their guide dogs. The **Black Horse Inn** is a popular restaurant. Accommodations are available at: **Governor Morris Inn** (539-7300, S$58-63/D$66-71).

Caldwell is the only New Jersey town that has provided a US President, Grover Cleveland. He was later to lecture at Princeton, write one of the first post-presidential books—*Presidential Problems*—and died in June, 1908. His last words are purported to be "I tried so hard to do what was right." The **Grover Cleveland Museum** displays memorabilia. **Montclair**, northwest of Newark, is outstanding among the many residential suburbs. It stands on the eastern slopes of the **Watchung Mountain**, and on a clear day has a superb view of the New York skyline. The **Montclair Art Museum** is excellent and the city puts on a major antiques fair in May.

The huge complex of industrial cities that face New York City across the Hudson have much of interest. **Paramus** is known for its enormous shopping centers. Interestingly, in 1791 Paterson was the site of the Union's first model factory town. The principals were to create in Britain a similar "model" in the 1840s; it was the first example of a sociological export from the former colonies to the Old Country and was inspired by Alexander Hamilton's *Society for the Establishment of Useful Manufactures*, which might in these times be called a socialist concept in which labor shares responsibility with the providers of capital. Alexander Hamilton chose the advantageous site for **Paterson**, the city made famous in William Carlos Williams' poem. The **Old Gun Mill** (1836) was where Samuel Colt made his first reliable revolvers, and the city's silk weaving business was begun here by his brother Christopher. **Lambert Castle** (1892) shows how one wealthy silk merchant spent his fortune on a splendid decor and art collection. The first modern submarine was invented in 1878 at Paterson; its hull and other exhibits are in the **Paterson Museum.** In **West Orange** were wrought some of the biggest changes to the American way of life. Here are the original laboratory, workshops, and home of Thomas Alva Edison, who lived and worked here from 1886 until his death in 1931. He developed more than 1,000 patented inventions, ranging from the incandescent light bulb to talking motion pictures. Original and replica models are displayed in his laboratory, open daily. **Hackensack** was one of the original Dutch settlements before the British arrived. The **Church on the Green** (1696) and the **Zabriskie-Von Steuben House** are magnificent examples of early Dutch Colonial architecture. **Meadowlands Sports Complex** is located on former swamplands near Hackensack. There are facilities for soccer (Cosmos), football at Giants Stadium, and for horse racing fans, regular trotters meet. Special round-trip bus services are provided for all events from New York Port Authority Building at 8th Avenue and 42nd Street.

Newark, largest city in the state, third oldest in the Union, population 312,412, seems to be all factories and harbor facilities, but its Gutzon Borglum statues may surprise you. He created the **Abraham Lincoln Statue** for Essex County Courthouse, the **Bridge Memorial** just north of Washington Park, and the 42 figures in **Military Park** depicting soldiers in *The Wars of America*. **Elizabeth**, immediately south of Newark, has been an industrial center since before the Revolution, and many old buildings remain from the colonial era. Check with the Chamber of Commerce for visiting hours at the **Bonnell House** (1682), **Belcher-Ogden Mansion** (1700), and **Boxwood Hall** (1750), home of Elias Boudnot, first president of the Continental Congress. A special treat is Newark's Ironbound section, which has been turned into a small Portuguese enclave complete with small shops and restaurants featuring delicious Portuguese seafood dishes. Accommodations in Newark include: the **Hilton-Gateway** (622-5000, S$40-60/D$57-70); **Holiday Inn North-Newark Airport** (589-1000, S$43-62/D$47-67); **Holiday Inn-Jetport** (355-1700, S$55 up/D$60 up); S$49-52/D$53-58); **Howard Johnson's-Newark Airport** (824-4000, S$41-45/D$45-47); **Robert Treat Hotel** (622-1000, S$24/D$29); and **Sheraton Inn-Newark Airport** (527-1600, S$54-63/D$60-70).

The New Jersey Turnpike, maximum $2.70 per car, leads south for 131 miles from the George Washington Bridge to the Delaware Memorial Bridge. Off-ramps lead to some charming communities. **Plainfield**, residential as well as industrial, is just east of **Washington Rock State Park**, a Watchung Mountains vantage point from which Washington kept an eye on British troop movements. He supposedly stayed in the **Nathaniel Drake House** (1746) in the spring of '77. **New Brunswick**, on the Raritan River, is the site of **Rutgers University**, founded in 1766. **The Old Dutch Parsonage** (1751) became the nucleus for Rutgers University. **Somerville** is where General and Mrs Washington stayed in the then-new **Wallace House** while the army bivouacked at **Camp Middlebrook** in the fall of 1778 to June 1779; Washington's oak-lined army trunk, in the hall, was designed to double as his coffin if he died in battle.

Princeton (population 12,423) was a popular luncheon stop for stagecoaches between Philadelphia and New York. The "College of New Jersey" centered around **Nassau Hall** (1756), which changed hands three times during the Battle of Princeton, and was finally won by General Washington in 1777. The Continental Congress met in the hall from June to November 1783, automatically making Princeton the nation's capital. During the late 1890s, a small coterie of wealthy New Yorkers built estates around the little town and it has remained a commuting suburb for New York business people; industrial plants encircle the town without, as yet, affecting its beauty. It's best to make an advance reservation for free guide service for sightseeing on the handsome **Princeton University** campus: call (609) 452-3603 or ask at Stanhope Hall. Major buildings include the **Art Museum, Harvey S. Firestone Library, University Chapel, Nassau Hall, Geological and Natural History Museum, Plasma Physics Laboratory.** During the annual spring visiting day at the university many of the beautiful old homes are open to the public. **Rockingham Historical Site,** open year round, is about 5 miles north of town. Some of the furnishings were in the house when Washington stayed here in 1783 and composed his speech, *Farewell Orders to the Army.* The traditional place to stay in Princeton is the **Nassau Inn.** See the colonial funishings in the **Monmouth County Historical Museum.** Accommodations in Princeton include: **Holiday Inn** (452-9100, S$42-45/D$47-49); **Howard Johnson's Motor Lodge** (896-1100, S$39-41/D$44-46); **Nassau Inn** (921-7500, S$41-46/D$45-55); and **Treadway Inn** (452-2500, S$36-45/D$41-49).

Trenton, the capital of New Jersey (population 94,772), has been a manufacturing town since the first gristmill was built there in 1679. Adjacent to the capitol is the **State Museum,** which focuses on natural and regional history exhibits as well as science and art, Monday through Friday, 9-4:45; weekends, 1-5pm. The museum's **Planetarium** features an unusual space transit program which depicts interplanetary explorations. Telephone 292-6333 for program details and information on special children's programs. The **Old Barracks,** now a museum, were put up in 1758 to house British troops during the French and Indian War, and on 26 December 1776 they were full of sleepy Hessian soldiers who mistakenly thought General Washington was safely in Pennsylvania on the other side of the Delaware River. Markers 8 miles northwest of the city in **Washington Crossing State Park** indicate where Washington and his men crossed the ice-clogged river that night. This 783-acre park offers picnicking, playgrounds, and open-air theater. The **McKonkey Ferry Museum,** now a colonial inn, is also on the park grounds; it is supposed to have sheltered Washington after he reached the New Jersey shore; open Tuesday through Saturday 10-12 and 1-5 pm, Sunday 2-5. The **Battle Monument Historic Site,** on the highest ground in Trenton, is where the Continentals first opened fire on the confused mercenaries. The **William Trent House** (1719) has fine period furnishings and the original fireplaces, stairway, and much of the original flooring. Stay at the **Trenton Inn** (989-7100, S$26-35). **Landwehr's,** an attractive restaurant 2 miles south of Washington's Crossing, specializes in prime ribs and home-style baking and has a view of the Delaware River. The **Glendale Inn** just outside the city provides excellent homestyle Italian fare.

Great Adventure is located in Jackson, 12 miles east of Trenton. It is a $100 million total entertainment complex featuring rides, shows, restaurants, shops, live entertainment, and the largest drive-through safari. Open from Easter through October, daily 10am-midnight, safari 9-5. Combination ticket to safari park and entertainment area: $13.95; amusements only $11.95; safari only $5.25; under 4 free.

Southern New Jersey has large areas of pine barrens, and there is almost no sign of habitation in the middle of the state, but there are interesting little towns along the Delaware River. **Burlington,** for instance, was settled by Quakers in 1677 and is four years older than Philadelphia. It had steamboat service from Philadelphia as early as 1788, 20 years before Robert Fulton's boat began puffing up the Hudson, and a railroad came through in 1824. Interesting old buildings include the **James Fenimore Cooper House**, where the author was born in 1789; the **James Laurence House** (1732), home of the naval hero of the war of 1812; **Friends Meeting House** (1784); **Old St Mary's Church** (1703); and **Thomas Revel House** (1685).

Camden, south Jersey's big industrial city, is where poet Walt Whitman chose to end his days. The **Walt Whitman House** where he lived from 1884 until his death in 1892 contains many of his personal belongings; he designed his own tomb, which is in **Harleigh Cemetery**. **Pomona Hall** (1726) is a museum and library of colonial relics. The suburb of **Cherry Hill** features impressive shopping centers, good restaurants and numerous motels. **Indian King Tavern** (circa 1750) is where the legislature met in 1777 while the British occupied Trenton. When the New Jersey Turnpike ends at the Delaware River Bridge, turn south on route 49 to **Salem,** where dozens of 17th-century houses and buildings are still in use. At nearby **Hancock's Bridge** is the zigzag glazed brick **Hanover House** (1734) where the British massacred a party of patriots in 1778; also see the tiny **Cedar Plank House** (1640) which a Swedish pioneer built of handhewn logs. These and the **Alexander Grant House** (1721) contain rare colonial antiques. **Bridgeton** is another quaint old town that manages to preserve its ancient character amid industries of the sort that have thrived here for centuries.

Cape May is at the southern tip of New Jersey where the broad mouth of Delaware opens into the Atlantic. This is probably the oldest coastal resort in the country, and looks it. Charming old Victorian houses and hotels are the sort that families return to summer after summer, but there are modern ones too. The atmosphere is quiet and redolent of the past. Fine examples of period architecture are carefully preserved. The beaches are famous for bathing, gathering shells, and the smoothed quartz rocks called "Cape May Diamonds." Boats can be chartered for sport fishing. The Cape May County art league has a full schedule of events including an Old House tour in mid-July, a Studio tour in August. In Cape May center, **Atlas Motor Inn** (884-7006, S/D$16-52) is opposite beach with heated pool, sauna, dancing, and entertainment in bar. **Best Western Marquis De Lafayette** (884-3431, S/D$30-44), restaurant with view of the ocean; **Christen Admiral Hotel** (884-8471, S$22/D$44); **Coachman's Motel** (884-8463, S/D$42-44); **Colonial Hotel & Motor Lodge** (884-3483, S$27-31/D$45-49); **Stockholm** (884-5332, S/D$18-43) good for families, golf privileges. **Watson's Merion Inn** (884-8363, a restaurant only, reservations important) specializes in fresh fish and home cooking in a colonial atmosphere. Rates in the area during the late June to Labor Day season range around S/D$15-70. The **Garden State Parkway,** maximum $2.75 toll, runs from Cape May up to the New York State border, 173 miles. But it's more fun to take a leisurely drive up route NJ 585, which follows the shore north to **Atlantic City. Wildwood Crest,**

Wildwood, and **North Wildwood** are neighboring resorts on a little island. Five miles of wide sandy beach and 3 miles of good old-fashioned boardwalk provide ample opportunity here for bicycle riding, promenading, and buying souvenirs and saltwater taffy. The better motels on the beach are **El Coronado** (729-1000, D$40-70), **Nassau Inn** (729-9077, D$17-48), and **Olympic Motor Inn** (522-0206, D$42-48). **Ocean City** sticks to its founders' stipulation that no liquor should be sold, which makes it a popular resort for religious conventions and some family vacations. Situated between **Great Egg Harbor** and the Atlantic, Ocean City offers a choice of protected or open shoreline; a 2½ mile boardwalk, 8½ miles of public beach, and a golf course. The boating, swimming, and fishing, are ideal, and there is a nightly free concert on **Music Pier,** late June through August. Ideal accommodations include: **Flanders Hotel** (399-1000, S$20/D$28-40), at the beach; **Sting Ray Motel** (399-8555, S/D$42-58); and **Port-O-Call Hotel** (399-8812, S/D$48-64). For eating out, try **Watson's,** for seafood or **Simms,** on the Boardwalk.

Only one road, NJ 72, goes out to **Long Beach Island,** a narrow strip of land extending 18 miles north and south along the State's east coast, from the famous **Barnegat Light** down to **Beach Haven Inlet.** Most of the motels are quite small and beaches are blissfully uncrowded; rates from mid-June through Labor Day average S/D$25-39 with a $2 overcharge at some places during the holidays. The **Surflight Summer Theater** at Beach Haven presents a different musical comedy every week that it's open. Farther north, the seaside resorts are packed in a solid line along the ocean front, the most famous being **Asbury Park.** Admission to the immense beach, open 30 May through 15 September, is $2.50 on weekends and holidays, $1.50 on other days, 50¢ for children 6-12, but most motels give their guests free passes. Big name dance bands and well-known entertainers are featured in summer, and there are lots of conventions, exhibitions and all sorts of entertainment. Just south of Asbury Park is **Ocean Grove** which has been the province of the Camp Meeting Association of the United Methodist Church since 1870. The sale of alcoholic beverages, card-playing, and swimming are not allowed on Sundays. Bicycles may not be ridden for 24 hours from Saturday midnight until 12:01 on Monday morning. The people who return regularly every summer probably love Ocean Grove because of its restrictions rather than in spite of them. Restaurant meals are inexpensive and rooms in the older motels are still $10 a night or less.

City To Visit

ATLANTIC CITY

Always an important year-round resort, Atlantic City, resident population 38,239, is changing fast and getting bigger and better every day. In addition to its normal tourist attractions, the *Playground of the World* now has casinos, which are bringing in top-name entertainers nightly.

The "Boardwalk" at Atlantic City.

New and bigger hotels are being built and fine restaurants are springing up. There are convenient buses running daily and frequently from New York and Philadelphia to the casinos. It is built on **Absecon Island,** approximately 1 mile wide and 10 miles in length, which was a sandy, deserted island until 1852, when the Camden and Atlantic Railroad began construction of the roadbed. A local hotelman built the first boardwalk in 1870; Atlantic City immediately became popular and still retains the approval of more than 18 million people who visit it each year. The current boardwalk is the city's fifth. It is built on concrete pilings and is 60 feet wide and more than 5 miles long. More than 25 million people visit the city each year. The success of the casinos already established— **Resort's International** and **Caesar's World** were the first to open—were followed by the openings of the **Golden Nugget, Harrah's, Playboy Club,** and **Balley's Park Place.** For non-gamblers, the ocean side of the boardwalk features sandy beaches and amusement piers, which offer entertainment and exhibits. **The Garden, Steel,** and **Steeplechase Central** all offer family fun. Atlantic City's famous saltwater taffy is available at many stores on the boardwalk.

WHAT TO SEE

Piers on the Boardwalk provide games, exhibits, rides, and displays. **Garden Pier** is the site of exhibitions in summer; free concerts are also staged there in an outdoor amphitheater. **The Steel Pier,** now operated by Resorts International, is open on a limited basis, featuring weekly boxing and wrestling cards during the season. **Absecon Lighthouse State Historic Site,** built in 1853, now fully restored, holds a museum. See performing porpoises, trained sea lions, and exotic fish at **Ocean Wonderworld.**

ACCOMMODATIONS

Since Atlantic City is a convention and new gambling city, reservations should be made in advance. **Bala Midtown Motor Inn** (349-3031, S/D$48-52); **Best Western of Atlantic City** (348-9175, S$42-50/D$46-50); **Lafayette Motor Inn** (345-3251, S$32-56/D$34-58); and on the Boardwalk, **Algiers Hotel** (344-6101, S/D$20-44), **Barclay Motel** (348-1156, S/D$36-50), and many others including **Resorts International, World International,** averaging S/D$42-110, Suites $190-350, **Balley's Park Place** (340-2000, S/D$64-94), **Harrah's Marina Hotel** (800-257-8505, S/D$55-80), **Playboy Hotel** (800-621-8505, S/D$72-97) and the **Boardwalk Regency Casino Hotel** (348-4411), **Golden Nugget Hotel** (800-257-8677) rates upon request, which includes entertainment with your gambling. Hotel tax: 5%.

RESTAURANTS

Seafood is a specialty in Atlantic City, particularly at the famous **Hackney's** and at **Doc's Oyster House.** Good food served in an attractive atmosphere may be obtained at the **Front Porch, Le Palais,** and **Orsatti's** and the **Knife and Fork Inn;** expensive. Less expensive but good value are **Pal's Other Room,** 12 South, **Golden Steer** and **Le Grand Fromage. Smithville Inn** is known for excellent home cooking. Great steak and seafood can be found at **Zaberer's,** which is suitable for family dining. Restaurants at the new casino hotels are excellent and include the **Oyster Bar** at Resort International's complex.

SPORTS
Sport facilities include ocean bathing, surfing, deep-sea fishing, tennis, golf, horseback riding. **Atlantic City Race Course** has thoroughbred horse racing from May through September. An indoor gridiron in **Convention Hall** is the comfortable setting for top collegiate football, played on weekends between Thanksgiving and Christmas, capped in mid-December by the NCAA featured **Boardwalk Bowl.**

CALENDAR OF EVENTS
Annual Art Show, Easter Sunrise Services, Easter Day Parade, April; **Hydrangea Festival,** July; **Wedding of the Sea,** August; **Fishing Tournament, Miss America Pageant,** September.

WHERE TO GO NEARBY
In **Egg Harbor City,** tour the plant and vineyards of L. N. Renault and Sons, producers of American champagne and wines. See also the old **Joseph Wharton Estate.** Restored buildings include the mansion, sawmill, grist mill, and furnace site. Visit the historic town of **Smithville,** 12 miles north of Atlantic City, a well-planned restoration of an 18th-century southern New Jersey community.

FURTHER STATE INFORMATION
New Jersey Office of Tourism and Promotion, Department of Labor and Industry, PO Box 400, Trenton, NJ 08625, 292-2470. Hunting and Fishing: **Division of Fish and Game,** PO Box 1809, Trenton, NJ 08625. **Atlantic City Convention Bureau,** 16 Central Pier, Atlantic City, NJ 08401. **Greater Atlantic City Chamber of Commerce,** 10 Central Pier, Atlantic City, NJ 08401. **Pan Am office,** 146 Haynes Avenue Newark, NJ 07102; tel: 624-1300.

USEFUL TELEPHONE NUMBERS
Newark
Ambulance	733-8724
Fire	733-7400
Police	911
Newark Beth Israel Medical Center	926-7000
Poison Control	733-7620
Legal Aid	622-1513
Chamber of Commerce	624-6888
Pan Am Reservations	624-1300

Trenton
Emergency (Ambulance, Fire, Police)	911
Mercer Medical Center	396-4070

NEW JERSEY

Hamilton Hospital	586-7900
Poison Control	396-1077
Legal Aid Society	695-6249
Chamber of Commerce	393-4143
Pan Am Reservations	800-223-9762

New Mexico

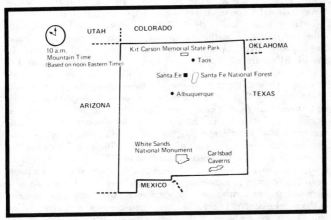

Area	121,666 square miles	Population	1,229,968
Capital	Santa Fe	Sales Tax	4½%

Weather	Jan	Feb	Mar	Apr	May	Jun	Jul	Aug	Sep	Oct	Nov	Dec
Av Temp (°C)	2	4	8	13	18	24	26	25	21	14	6	3
Days Rain/Snow	3	4	4	3	4	4	9	9	6	5	3	4

New Mexico is a land of Spaniards, Indians, and space-age technology, and the former home of the Folsom and Sandia Men, oldest inhabitants of the western world. In 1539, Friar Marcos de Niza first saw this land of mountains over 13,000 feet high and caverns more than 800 feet deep. He returned to Mexico with tales of cities of gold which so impressed the viceroy that in 1540 he dispatched Francisco Vasquez de Coronado with an army of explorers. The soldiers found no gold, but a lot of sagebrush and empty rock formations, and Coronado returned to Mexico 2 years later a broken man. But he had opened the Southwest territory to the white man, and traders following the Santa Fe Trail in the 1800s were luckier. They returned to Missouri with furs, gold, and silver, leading to the establishment of prosperous trade routes which brought territorial status to the region in 1850. The coming of the Santa Fe railroad paved the way for progress and development. Modern machinery was transported along the rails west, and a mining boom began which would become a multi-million-dollar industry. Minerals are the state's richest natural resource, oil and gas are also valuable assets, and the sheep and cattle industries are big, as are the farming belts. But one of the most important industries is the one geared to accommodate the 24 million tourists who visit the state each year. Federal government bureaus, which control 45% of the land in the state, play a large role in New Mexico's life in nuclear and space research and testing at such centers as Los Alamos, White Sands, Holloman and Sandia. The first atomic explosion was set off in July 1945 at a point north of the **White Sands National Monument,** which commemorates the event.

Today vast areas are made fertile by irrigation waters coming from dams and reservoirs on the **Rio Grande, San Juan, Canadian, Gila** and **San Francisco** rivers. Spruce, Ponderosa pine and Douglas fir thrive in the 13,281 square miles of national forests. In the north, the state has semi-desert lands, but most of this area is high mountain country with streams of clear water and snow which often stays on the peaks all year.

The Indians of New Mexico are not a homogeneous people; the Navajos and Apaches are related in origin, yet they are quite distinct in culture. Their 19 pueblos, or "towns," have rather similar societies but the inhabitants speak five very different languages. These differences and their origins are explained in the **Hall of the Modern Indian** in Santa Fe, the museum at **Bandelier National Monument** near Los Alamos located an hour from Santa Fe and at the **Indian Pueblo Cultural Center** located near Old Town in Albuquerque. The Indians are a settled people who farm and work in nearby towns. Their ceremonial dances preserve some of the finest examples of pre-Christian worship on this continent. Indian tribal lands are contained in four major reservations and the pueblos scattered along the Rio Grande from **Isleta** to **Taos** and on the high mesas to the west including **Acoma,** the "sky city" built on top of a 357-foot mesa. Pueblo ruins dating from 1000 AD can be found northeast of **Gallup** in **Chaco Canyon.** Santa Fe is the second oldest city (1609) in the United States. Albuquerque is a beautiful city, New Mexico's largest. From the artists' colonies in Santa Fe and Taos to the White Sands Missile Range, from the ice caves of Bandera Crater to the hot springs at Truth or Consequences, from the coolness of Carlsbad Caverns to the heat of Pecos Valley, New Mexico offers immense and exciting variety.

Eight and a half million acres of scenic playgrounds are found in the national forests—**Carson, Cibola, Coronado, Gila, Lincoln** and **Santa Fe;** and there are 32 state parks. In the mountains are winter sports areas with good skiing from December to April in a variety of scenic surroundings. Mountain streams teem with trout, the reservoirs are full of bass, crappie, bream and catfish. In the wilderness, big game such as deer, bear, Bighorn and Barbary sheep, cougar, turkey and elk are hunted in season. Dove, waterfowl, crane and quail are among the game birds shot in the fields and forests.

In New Mexico's **NORTHEAST CORNER** an inactive volcanic crater is well preserved at the **Capulin Mountain National Monument;** the Visitor Center is open year round. Cars can take a road to the crater rim and two trails provide passage around the rim and into the crater bottom. At the west base is a picnic site. Heading southwest you will find **Fort**

Union National Monument, marking the location of a guardpost for the Santa Fe Trail. Its history (1851-1891) rings with the sound of wagon trains and soldiers battling Kiowas, Comanches, Apaches, and other Indians determined to block the white man's way through their lands. Much of the aura of this frontier fort is captured in the monument's museum; open all year. Camping, fishing, and picnicking are available at nearby **Murphy Lake.** A great trading center for the Plains and Pueblo Indians can be seen at the **Pecos National Monument,** including an old mission erected in 1700 by monks of the Franciscan Order. Some of the original pueblo ruins are mixed among the falling walls of the mission. The multiple-dwelling pueblo was occupied for nearly 600 years until disease and battles with the **Plains Indians,** once friendly traders, forced the Pueblo Indians to move in 1838; open daily, free. A short drive along I-25 brings the visitor to **Santa Fe.** Northwest of Santa Fe in the cliffs of **Frijoles Canyon** are man-made caves, rooms cut from the soft limestone, houses built on slopes, and a large circular community house. Guided walking tours are offered six times daily, June through August, self-guided tours all year. Evening campfire programs, offered at many New Mexico parks and historical sites, are given in the summer. North, in the immediate area, there are four pueblos: **San Ildefonso Pueblo** is the home of Maria Martinez, creator of the renowned black pottery; **San Juan Pueblo** is the site of the first Spanish settlement in New Mexico; **Santa Clara Pueblo** is the site of a two-day ceremony the last weekend in July; and **Pojaaque Pueblo** is the home of the famous Nambe ware. **Puye Cliff Dwellings and Communal House Ruins** run a mile's length along a mesa nearby and stand as samples of the Pajaritan culture, ancient even in these parts. The ruins, a multiple story pueblo, are thought to have once contained 2,000 rooms.

TAOS, at the foothills of the Sangre de Cristo Mountains 70 miles north of Santa Fe, is well known as an art center. Activities include Indian ceremonials, art shows, concerts, summer theater presentations, and five skiing areas within an hour's drive. **Carson National Forest** headquarters is here. **Kachina Lodge** (758-2275, S$34/D$42), **Sagebrush Inn** (758-2254, S$36/D$40), with a great view of the mountains, are good places to stay. **Taos Rodeo** is in late June. There are ceremonial Indian dances at various pueblos; check at your hotel for the schedule. **Kit Carson House and Museum** was occupied by the Indian fighter and explorer from 1843 to 1868. Guns, artifacts, period furniture, and wearing apparel are on display; open daily. Carson is buried in nearby **Kit Carson Memorial State Park.** A hacienda-type house, cultural replicas from the three Taos cultures—Spanish, Indian, and pioneer—are found in the **Millicent A. Rogers Museum;** open Monday to Saturday. The **Stables Gallery** is open daily with exhibits by local artists. The **Mission of St Francis of Assisi** is one of the Southwest's best examples of Spanish church architecture. On display there is the Henri Ault painting *Shadow of the Cross,* which, in a certain light, shows Christ carrying a cross, but at other times the cross is not visible; open in the summer. **Pueblo de Taos,** where 1,700 Indians still make their homes, rises from a mesa outside town to become the tallest such structure in the Southwest. Fiestas are scattered throughout the year; the most notable is the celebration of San Geronimo held 29-30 September. **Taos Ski Valley** and **Sipapu Ski Area** offer novice-to-expert runs. Two other ski centers are at **Red River** and one at **Angel Fire;** moderate prices at all. **Edelweiss** and **St Bernard Inns** offer ski packages including equipment with rooms overlooking the slopes and **La Dona Luz,** with one of the finest wine cellars in the Southwest, and **Casa Cordoba,** outside the town, offer excellent French meals. When not skiing or touring, an entertaining pastime is walking around the town, most of which is clustered around the old Spanish-style plaza. Many shops specialize in handmade turquoise and silver Indian jewelry. About a 2-hour drive from Taos is **Los Alamos,** site of nuclear physics research. Even now, some sections of the town are barred to the general public. A curious statistic distinguishes the city; there are more inhabitants with Ph.D. degrees here than in any city of comparable size in the world. **Bradbury Science Hall** has on display *Fat Man* and *Little Boy,* the first plutonium and uranium bombs; open Monday-Sunday, free.

At the **Aztec Ruins National Monument** in the **NORTHWESTERN CORNER** of New Mexico is one of the country's best-preserved pueblo dwellings. A museum houses weapons, jewelry, and pottery excavated from the ruins. The **Great Kiva,** a mammoth ceremonial building, dominates the surroundings; open all year. South along US 66 is **Gallup,** center for some of the liveliest Indian entertainment in the state. Gallup is best known for its annual Intertribal Indian Ceremonial, usually held during the second weekend in August. The event features a rodeo and Indian performances by dance groups from tribes from all over the country. **Holiday Inn, Royal Inn, Shalimar Inn, TraveLodge,** and **The Inn,** among many others, are S$25-37/D$29-41. At **El Morro National Monument** are petroglyphs hundreds of years old which were carved into the limestone. The earliest readable inscription dates from 1605. **Chaco Canyon National Monument** contains the ruins of 12 large cities which, according to experts, were apparently constructed by highly skilled architects who designed the buildings around the seasons of the year. **Zuni,** 40 miles south of Gallup, is believed to be the first settlement of the "Seven Cities of Cibola," which Coronado searched for in his quest for the gold described by Friar Marcos. The **Zuni Indian Shalako Dance,** a tribal house-blessing ceremony, is held in either late November or early December. East along I-40 is **Grants,** known as a uranium center. At **Ice Caves** and **Bandera Crater,** the crater soars to 500 feet, overlooking the valley below. Inside its walls, where lava trapped water and cooled it to ice despite 38°C temperatures outside, are the ice caves; open year round. **Acoma,** a pueblo which is possibly the oldest continuously habitated Indian homesite in America, is outside Grants as the traveler heads east towards **Albuquerque.** "Sky City," shooting up to 357 feet from the plain, was thriving when, in 1540, the Spaniards rode into the land. The high mesa made the inhabitants secure through 100 years of war with the invaders. It is open 1 hour after sunrise and closed 1 hour before sunset, but is closed 10-13 July and 2 days in October for private

This mission church in New Mexico is part of the Taos Pueblos—founded in 1615.

Indian religious ceremonies. South from Albuquerque, 155 miles on I-25, is **Truth or Consequences,** a name inspired by the old radio program. Hot mineral baths are on the south side of nearby **Elephant Butte Reservoir,** where fishing, boating, and water-skiing provide relaxation for vacationers and natives while supplying water for irrigation. In a remote section of **White Sands Missile Range,** the first man-made atomic explosion was set off in 1945. **Trinity Site,** a sloping crater created by the blast, is a permanent reminder. A tour conducted by the city's chamber of commerce goes to the site the first Sunday in October, the only time it is available for public visit.

Stay at the **Desert Aire** (439-2110, S$25/D$30); **Holiday Inn** (S$30-36/D$36-42); **Satellite Inn** (437-8454, S$20/D$22); or **TraveLodge** (437-1850, S$20/D$25). **Cedar Creek** and **Sierra Blanca** winter sports areas are to the east near the Mescalero Apache Indian Reservation. The ski areas are near **Ruidoso** which is the location of the Ruidoso Downs race track. A $1-million quarterhorse race, the richest in the world, is held at the track every Labor Day weekend. There are many good places to stay in Ruidoso and the **Cloud Country Lodge** in nearby Cloudcroft and the **Inn of the Mountain Gods** on the Apache reservation in Mescalero are also good places to stay. Further to the east is **Roswell,** the home of the **Bitter Lake National Wildlife Refuge** and the host of the **Pecos Valley Horse Show** in mid-June. **The Roswell Museum and Art Center** mixes rocketry in Robert H. Goddard's collection with 20th-century paintings and prints, including those by Peter Hurd and Henriette Wyeth. **El Rancho Palacio** (622-2721, S$24/D$28); **Hilltop House** (623-4021, S$26/D$30); **Roswell Inn** (623-4920, S$28/D$32); **Royal** (622-0110, S$20/D$22); and **TraveLodge** (623-3811, S$20/D$23) are all good places to stay before heading 80 miles south to the exciting **Carlsbad Caverns.**

In **SOUTHWESTERN NEW MEXICO** there is the **Gila National Forest,** Indian ruins, and old mining ghost towns. The area can best be seen from **Silver City,** home of the state's major copper mines. Silver City can be reached by traveling west from I-25 on State Road 90. The Gila Cliff Dwellings and the ghost town at Mogollon are worth a visit. **The Drifter Motel** (538-2916, S$23/D$25) is a good place to stay.

Cities To Visit

ALBUQUERQUE

Albuquerque, on the Rio Grande River, was founded as a Spanish villa in 1706 when Don Francisco Cuervo y Valdes, then governor of New Mexico, moved 30 families from Bernalillo to a spot 15 miles south on the Rio Grande where there was better pasturage. He named the community after the Duke of Albuquerque, then Viceroy of New Spain; the viceroy renamed it San Felipe de Albuquerque in honor of King Philip V of Spain. Old Albuquerque was a way station on the Chihuahua Trail, known as the *Camino Real* (King's Highway). By 1790 the population is reported to have been almost 6,000, a very large city for New Mexico at the time. Except for one brief period, Albuquerque has continued to be the largest city in the state. The present city grew up around the Santa Fe railway station, about 2 miles east of Old Town. It soon became a wool-marketing center and was incorporated in 1890. On a morning in July 1945, the nation's first nuclear device was tested at Trinity Site, 75 miles south; today it is one of the nation's important centers for nuclear and space research. Recently Albuquerque has achieved fame as the hot-air balloon capital of the world by hosting the **International Hot Air Balloon Fiesta** every October.

The city's appeal is universal to physicist and artist, newcomer and native, the young and actively retired. The city has accepted change and contrast with unusual adaptability. In the shadow of its futuristic nuclear laboratories, quaint shops and candlelit restaurants of the **Old Town Plaza** capture the atmosphere of a different era.

WHAT TO SEE

Visit the historic and colorful **Old Town** and the Old Town Plaza ringed with charming restaurants, picturesque shops, patios, art shops, and galleries. Careful shopping may yield good buys if you like Indian jewelry. Also see the **San Felipe de Neri Church,** used as fortress against the Indians. **Sandia Crest,** a 10,678-foot peak easily accessible by car, offers an uninterrupted panorama of more than 11,000 square miles. Spectacular **Sandia Peak Aerial Tramway,** on cables 2.7 miles long, rises about 3,819 feet up the rugged west slope in 10 minutes to the **Summit House;** it also transports skiers to the eastern slope during winter. Other worthwhile things to see are the **Ernie Pyle Memorial Library,** and the **Turquoise Trail** from Albuquerque past **Coronado Monument,** 17 miles north of the city. The **Atomic Museum** at nearby Kirtland AFB displays dozens of awesome nuclear warhead casings. Near the city there are Indian pueblos dating back to 1300 AD; the pueblos of **Sandia, San Felipe, Santo Domingo,** and **Zia** are fascinating, as are **Isleta Pueblo** to the south and **Laguna** and **Acoma Pueblos** to the west.

There are more than 100 public parks in Albuquerque, many of them lush with grass, trees, and shrubbery. **Rio Grande** and **Los Altos** parks have modern swimming pools and tennis courts. Rio Grande has barbecue pits, bicycle riding, and a zoo.

Principal schools: The **University of New Mexico,** founded in 1889, has a 440-acre campus, and is noted for its schools of anthropology, electrical engineering, Romance languages, and medicine. There is also the **University of Albuquerque,** a Roman Catholic coeducational liberal arts institution. For 24-hour visitor information call the Chamber of Commerce (842-0220).

ACCOMMODATIONS

There are over 50 major hotels and motels in and near the city. Those in Albuquerque center include: **American Best Western** (298-7426, S$24.50/D$27); **Capri** (247-1061, S$24/D$30); **Crossroads** (242-2757,

S\$20/D\$22); **DeAnza Motor Lodge** (255-1654, S\$14/D\$16); **Desert Inn** (243-1773, S\$15/D\$20); **Holiday Inn Midtown** (884-2155, S\$34/D\$43); **Hotel Plaza** (243-4421, S\$26/D\$31); **Howard Johnson's Midtown** (243-5693, S\$32/D\$34); and **Ramada Inn** (296-5472, S\$30/D\$40), 1 mile from center. More expensive are the **Hilton Inn** (884-2500, S\$49/D\$59); **The Regent** (247-3344, S\$53/D\$61); **Four Seasons Motor Inn** (265-1221, S/D\$50-64); and the **Sheraton Old Town Inn** (843-6300, S\$54/D\$64); all centrally located. At the airport: **Amfac Hotel** (843-7000, S\$48/D\$60). Near major shopping centers: **The Classic** (881-0000, S\$62/D\$66). Hotel Tax: 4-6%.

RESTAURANTS

La Placita and **La Hacienda Dining Rooms** are good for Mexican dinners; also **El Pinto** for Mexican food and **Montana Mining Co.** for steak; all moderate to expensive. **Summit House,** atop Sandia Peak, overlooks Rio Grande Valley. In Old Town, there is the **High Noon** and **Maria Teresa's,** both of which serve Mexican and American food.

ENTERTAINMENT

Nightclubs are in such motor hotels as the **Hilton Inn, Sundowner, Sheraton Western Skies,** and **Ramada Inn.** Many supper clubs feature stars from the east and west coasts. The *Singles Scene, Albuquerque This Month,* and local papers list the current entertainments.

ARTS AND MUSIC

Many of the state's artists and craftsmen reside in Albuquerque and exhibit regularly at the dozens of galleries and shops throughout the city. The **Galeria del Sol** is a private art gallery in the Patio Market in Old Town, exhibiting traditional paintings; closed Monday. The **New Mexico State Fairgrounds** has a public art gallery featuring the works of outstanding artists of New Mexico; closed Tuesday. An extensive collection of Remington and Russell bronzes and paintings may be seen at the **Lovelace Clinic,** 5200 Gibson Boulevard, SE; Monday through Friday during the year. The **Museum of Albuquerque,** a community museum, has exhibits of history, art, and science; open Tuesday-Sunday. The **University of New Mexico Anthropology Museum** features outstanding exhibits on Indians of the Southwest.

Albuquerque Symphony Orchestra presents nine concerts from November through April and also a Young People's series on Saturday afternoons. The **University of New Mexico Symphony Orchestra** performs four times each season. **Albuquerque Civic Light Opera** presents five musicals each season, at Christmas, Easter, and three times during the summer. All of these performances are in **Popejoy Hall** at the University of New Mexico. The **University of New Mexico Chamber Orchestra** presents four concerts during the academic year at **Recital Hall** on the campus. The university has year-round events of ballet, musicals, and lectures. Broadway shows on tour, and other special programs are held in Popejoy Hall; tel: 277-3121 for the schedule. The **Santa Fe Opera,** an hour's drive from Albuquerque, has an excellent summer season of outdoor opera. The **Albuquerque Little Theater** combines professional and local talent during the winter season. The **Corrales Adobe Theatre,** 12 miles north, in an old Spanish village, has a summer season. The **Barn Dinner Theater,** 20 miles east, in the mountains, gives dinner-theater performances except in winter. The **University of New Mexico Rodey Theater** and the **University of Albuquerque Theater** both present an interesting repertoire of plays during the year.

SHOPPING

Shopping hours are 9 to 5:30 downtown; until 9 Monday-Friday in most shopping centers.

SPORTS

Albuquerque Dukes AAA, owned by the Los Angeles Dodgers, play in **Albuquerque Sports Stadium; Albuquerque Lasers,** a professional volleyball team; University of New Mexico **Lobos** play basketball and football; and there are boxing, wrestling, stock car and go-kart and midget racing. More than 100 miles of irrigation streams adjacent to the city are stocked with fish. Mountain streams and lakes provide an abundance of rainbow trout. There are six public golf courses, one a lighted course for night playing. There are many riding stables and fine horseback riding trails in the foothills of the **Sandia** and **Manzano Mountains** and on the city's **West Mesa.** Mountains throughout the area abound in wild game, elk, deer, antelope, and wild turkey. There are special seasons for bear and other rugged species such as boar, mountain lions, big horn sheep, lynx, ibex, and antelope. A special bow-and-arrow season (which changes every year) is offered in the Sandia Mountains. There is a ski area at **Sandia Peak;** skiing from 15 December through March; chairlift and rentals.

CALENDAR OF EVENTS

New Mexico Arts and Crafts Fair, June; **New Mexico State Fair,** mid-September; **International Hot Air Balloon Fiesta,** October; **Fiesta Encantada,** including **luminaria tours,** December; and Indian ceremonial dances in nearby pueblos year round.

WHERE TO GO NEARBY

One-day jaunts, known as "magic circle" trips, take visitors to ancient missions; pueblo ruins; old mining ghost towns; Spanish mountain villages that are still very much alive but whose culture is geared to another age; mountains; **Carlsbad Caverns,** about 300 miles south; and **Los Alamos Scientific Laboratory.** Within 100 miles are **Bluewater Lake, Hyde Memorial,** and **Santa Fe State Parks.** Camping facilities are available at Bluewater and Hyde; all three have picnic facilities. Bluewater is also good for boating, fishing, and water skiing.

SANTA FE

Santa Fe ("holy faith") is at an altitude of 7,000 feet in the foothills of the Sangre de Cristo mountains in north central New Mexico. The Santa Fe River runs through the town. Originally the site of prehistoric Indian pueblos, Santa Fe was founded in 1609 by Don Pedro de Peralta, who built the **Palace of Governors**, oldest public building in the United States. Now a museum, from 1610 until 1909 the palace was occupied in turn by Spanish, Indian, Spanish again, Mexican and US territorial governors, and the Confederate Army. Diego de Vargas regained Santa Fe from the Indians in 1692. Between 1850 and 1880 pioneers in covered wagons and adventurers in stagecoaches made the long run on the Santa Fe Trail from Independence, Missouri, ending their journeys boisterously in the city's **Plaza**. Santa Fe, relatively unindustrialized, adopted by painters, writers, and skilled craftsmen, is an unusual state capital city.

Modern buildings reproduce the charming and practical architecture developed by the Pueblo Indians, early Spaniards, Mexicans, and the missionaries. Many of the artist residents tend to wear more colorful attire than is seen in most cities, and people who have had Santa Fe "prescribed" for them by their doctors soon adopt the easy-going pattern of life.

WHAT TO SEE

Canyon Road; the museums; the main **Plaza** and **Sena** and **Prince Plazas** with their fascinating shops. The **Miraculous Staircase** in **Our Lady of Light Chapel** has no visible means of support and was built without nails. Visit the **Mission of San Miguel**, oldest church in the nation, begun in 1621; **Cathedral of St Francis of Assisi,** built in 1869 by Bishop Lamy, upon whom Willa Cather based the principal character of her novel *Death Comes for the Archbishop;* **Cristo Rey Church,** largest adobe building in the country, with beautiful stone reredos dating from 1761. Much of the **Scottish Rite Temple** is a replica of the Alhambra in Spain.

Principal schools: **College of Santa Fe,** and **St John's College,** coeducational; **Institute of American Indian Arts.**

ACCOMMODATIONS

Hotel La Fonda (982-5511, S$44/D$52) is a hotel with charming old Spanish atmosphere and decor, the town's social center. Luxurious motels include **Desert Inn** (982-1851, S$37/D$42); **Hilton Inn** (988-2811, S$37-45/D$42-55); **Holiday Inn** (471-8072, S$28/D$32); **La Posada de Santa Fe** (983-6351, S$24/D$29); **The Inn at Loretto** (988-5531, S$56-62/D$66-72). Others include the **Lamplighter Motel, TraveLodge** and **Ramada Inn;** peak rates from May to mid-September. **Tres Lagunas Guest Ranch** (757-6194, S$62-69 AP) has ranch house and log cabins, 12 miles north of Pecos; open all year. Nearest campsite in **Black Canyon,** about 10 miles northeast of town. The **Bishop's Lodge** (983-6378, S$90-152/D$116-165 AP) is a unique resort ranch 3½ miles north on Bishop's Lodge Road; open March-October. Hotel Tax: 4-7%.

RESTAURANTS
Especially attractive patio dining in summer at **El Nido,** near Opera amphitheater; **Palace; Pink Adobe; The Compound; End of the Line; The Shed;** and **Rancho de Chimayo.** Most restaurants display paintings by local artists and have fireplaces for winter coziness. Although there are many very good restaurants featuring Mexican food, Santa Fe is highly cosmopolitan, and a continental cuisine predominates.

ENTERTAINMENT
El Nido and **El Gaucho** feature dining, dancing and Flamenco entertainment; **Casablanca** features disco dancing. Check local newspapers for current schedules.

ARTS AND MUSIC
Canyon Road, a pre-Columbian Indian trail, is about 5 miles of art galleries, artists' studios, homes, and shops selling paintings and handicrafts; the Chamber of Commerce issues an excellent guide map. **Palace of Governors** has art, archaeological, and historical exhibits; **Fine Arts Building** has changing exhibits of New Mexican and Southwestern artists, also Indian craft; **Hall of Ethnology,** Indian sand paintings, jewelry, exhibits of contemporary Indian life; **Museum of International Folk Art,** worldwide collections of folk art; **Museum of Navajo Ceremonial Art,** closed Monday; and, on the grounds of the renowned **Laboratory of Anthropology,** not open to the public is a research center devoted to Indian pottery, textiles, and jewelry. The widely acclaimed **Santa Fe Opera** performs under the stars in the dramatic open-air theater in July and August; 5 miles north visiting musicians participate in the **Community Concert Association.** There are several active community theaters, including the **Greer Garson Theater** which stages productions ranging from classical to experimental.

SHOPPING
Downtown shopping hours are 9-5:30; until 9 on Friday evenings.

SPORTS
Santa Fe has a large municipal swimming pool and a fine 18-hole golf course. The trout-fishing season runs from 11 May to 31 October. Within a few miles of the city, hunters find bear, deer, elk, grouse, and turkey. The **Santa Fe Ski Basin,** 16 miles from town at an elevation of 10,200 feet, offers superb powder snow conditions from November to May; a ½-mile double chair lift has a vertical rise of 1,500 feet. Horse racing is held at **Santa Fe Downs** from mid-May through Labor Day weekend.

CALENDAR OF EVENTS
Rodeo de Santa Fe, with the nation's best cowboys, July; **Santa Fe Horse Show,** mid-August; **Santa Fe Fiesta,** commemorating the reconquest of Santa Fe by De Vargas, brilliant with parades, pageants, Indian dances, authentic early-day costumes, and ceremonies; last Friday in August

through Labor Day. **The Festival of the Arts** is held in early October featuring work by local artists, and there are spring and fall festivals at **El Rancho de las Colondrinas,** a Spanish living folk art museum located 10 miles S.W. of Santa Fe.

WHERE TO GO NEARBY

Within a radius of 70 miles of Santa Fe are 15 Indian villages; pueblos best known for handicrafts are **San Ildefonso,** 22 miles northwest, **Cochiti,** 30 miles southwest, **Santo Domingo,** 31 miles southwest, famous for its elaborate Corn Dance every 4 August, and **San Felipe,** 34 miles south. Visitors are welcome at all pueblos until 6pm. To take pictures, for which a varying fee is charged, permission must be obtained from the pueblo's governor.

Hyde State Park, 9 miles northeast of Santa Fe, is in **Santa Fe National Forest** at an elevation of about 8,000 feet in the Sangre de Cristo mountains; campsites in Black Canyon. The forest, which is in several sections on both sides of the Rio Grande, consists of 1,200,000 acres of deep forests and rangelands. The scenery is stupendous, and so are the hunting and fishing. No roads, resorts, or human habitations destroy the natural beauty of the **San Pedro Parks Wild Area** and the **Pecos Wilderness Area,** which are paradises for sportsmen traveling on foot or by horseback. Dude ranches on the edges of these areas can supply horses. **Bandelier National Monument** has cave dwellings and houses built out from cliffs; self-guiding trails, ranger lectures during the summer, museum, public campground, and trailer sites.

CARLSBAD CAVERNS NATIONAL PARK

Twenty-seven miles southwest of Carlsbad, near the Texas border, is **Carlsbad Caverns National Park.** The caverns and huge underground rooms are estimated to be the oldest in the world. Self-guiding tours will take you nearly 830 feet down for an inspection of 3 miles of chambers. The trip takes 3½ hours and you can buy your lunch underground. The full extent of the caverns is not known but 23 miles have been explored. Your visit will include the **Big Room,** 1,300 feet long, 650 feet wide, and 285 feet high; the **Greenlake Room, King's Palace, Queen's Chamber,** and **Papoose Room.** The stalactites and other crystalline formations glow in yellows, browns, and reds. An elevator takes you from ground level to the main cavern floor. The famous **Bat Flight** occurs during sunset every evening from June through October when the cave bats come out by the hundreds of thousands in search of food. A naturalist lectures on bat habits before the flight begins. Primitive lantern trips into **New Cave,** an undeveloped cave 23 miles from the Visitor Center, are available on a limited basis; advanced reservations necessary.

FURTHER STATE INFORMATION

New Mexico Travel Division, Commerce and Industry Department, Bataan Memorial Building, Santa Fe NM 87503. Tel. Toll-free: 800-545-2041. Hunting and Fishing: **Department of Game and Fish,** State Capitol,

Sante Fe, NM 87503. **Greater Albuquerque Chamber of Commerce,** 401 Second Street, NW, Albuquerque, NM 87101. **Santa Fe Chamber of Commerce,** PO Box 1928, Santa Fe, NM 87501. National Parks: **Carlsbad Caverns National Park** (Superintendent), Box 1598, Carlsbad, NM 88220.

Consulates in Albuquerque: Dominican Republic, France, Mexico, Norway, Spain.

In Santa Fe: West Germany.

USEFUL TELEPHONE NUMBERS

All emergencies	911
Road conditions	1-800-432-4269
Game and fishing	1-800-432-4263
State Police	827-2551
Reservation problems (FBI)	247-1555
Legal problems (attorney general)	982-6000

New York

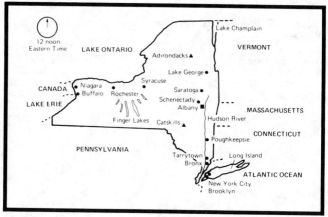

Area	49,576 square miles	**Population**	17,557,288
Capital	Albany	**Sales Tax**	7-8%

Weather

	Jan	Feb	Mar	Apr	May	Jun	Jul	Aug	Sep	Oct	Nov	Dec
Av Temp (°C)	0	1	5	11	17	22	25	24	20	15	8	2
Days Rain/Snow	11	10	12	11	11	10	11	10	8	8	9	10

The state of New York might be divided in a number of ways, but perhaps the greatest division is a psychological one, that which distinguishes New York City from "Upstate" New York.

The areas occupied by the city and by upstate New York were discovered at about the same time. Although the Florentine explorer Verrazano is thought to have been the first to sail into what is now New York Harbor in 1524, he simply had a look around and left, and it was not until 1609 when Henry Hudson, an Englishman in the employ of the Dutch, sailed into the harbor and on up the river which was to bear his name, that the real settlement of New York can be said to have begun. And in the same year, another explorer, Samuel de Champlain, first entered the lake which was to bear his name, and exploration of upstate New York began. The state has played an important part in the development of the United States ever since.

In the American Revolution, New York declared itself a state while still occupied by the British and was the site of some important battles, such as the capture of Ticonderoga by Ethan Allen and his Green Mountain Boys. In the War of 1812, the state witnessed the brilliant naval victory of Thomas MacDonough over the British in Lake Champlain. In 1825 the **Erie Canal** opened, linking the **Great Lakes** with the Atlantic Ocean, via the **Hudson River** and the state began a climb to prosperity which has since rarely faltered. During the Civil War, New York became a great industrial state, with many factories turning out munitions and other war materials, and although the state was far enough north to avoid having any fighting done on its soil, it contributed more to the Union cause in the way of men, money, and supplies than any other state.

It's easy to make a New York vacation a family affair, since many restaurants, hotels, and attractions have special children's programs and prices, and the state has two vast forest preserves—the Adirondacks and the Catskills—abundant outdoor recreational areas, and complete sports and leisure facilities year round. There are more than 120 state parks for boating, camping, hunting, hiking, and swimming. Many historic homes have been designated National Historical Landmarks. New York State has a wide choice of accommodations, ranging from rustic cabins to the finest resort hotels and, at the same location, you can have a choice of a lakeside cottage, a luxury motel, or a campsite.

Begin a tour of the **SOUTHERN REGION** of the state by driving north from New York City alongside the **Hudson River,** where stone memorials mark the Hudson River Valley's role in the American Revolution, or cruise the Hudson to and from New York City. The Hudson River Dayline Cruise Company has daily excursions from May to October as far north as West Point. The **Tarrytown** locale was made internationally famous by **Washington Irving,** with his book *Legend of Sleepy Hollow.* His home **Sunnyside,** in Irvington, has been restored with his library and period furnishings. Irving, Andrew Carnegie, the industrialist, and Samuel Gompers, the labor leader, are buried in the **Sleepy Hollow Cemetery. Lyndhurst,** a castle on the Hudson which was built in 1838 in the Gothic revival style, was once owned by railroad tycoon Jay Gould. See its art gallery and unusual furnishings. An 18th-century water-powered gristmill is still operating at the magnificently restored two-story stone **Philipsburg Manor House** and farm. **Van Cortlandt Manor,** a late 18th-century Dutch-English house, is set on 20 acres of land with a 750-foot landscaped walk and a picnic area. A combination ticket to Washington Irving's home, Philipsburg Manor House, and Van Cortlandt Manor, all along route 9, is available from Sleepy Hollow Restorations, Box 245, Tarrytown 10591 or call (914) 591-7900. Try the **Hilton Inn** (631-5700, S$52-74/D$64-86), at New York State Thruway Exit 9; **Ramada Inn** in Armonk (273-9090, S$54/D$60 up); or **Ramada Inn** in Elmsford (592-3300, S$57/D$63). **Tappan Hill Restaurant** offers a fine view of the Hudson River.

At **Sterling Forest Gardens,** in Tuxedo Park, there's an outstanding 125-acre floral display with rare birds, sculpture, and waterfalls, and a **Farmyard Theater** for children, plus a picnic area, and an observation train; open May through October. The **Sterling Forest Ski Center** is open mid-December through March. **Harriman State Park** includes a picnic area at each developed region, plus pools, boats for rent, fishing, beach and camping sites. **Bear Mountain State Park** has over 5,000 acres, including Bear Mountain, 1,314 feet. The **Bear Mountain Inn** (786-2731, S$25.50/D$35), just south of Bear Mountain Bridge Circle, is open year around. The US Military Academy at **West Point** is five miles north of the park. The Academy was opened in 1802 with a class of 10 on a site originally occupied as a military post during the Revolution. From early September through November and during May, cadet parades are usually scheduled three times a week. Saturday Reviews are held Labor Day through mid-November. For specific information contact the Information Office (914) 938-3507. The **Hotel Thayer** (446-4731, S$26/D$32), on West Point grounds overlooking the Hudson River, is recommended. Rates are higher during Parents' Week, June Week, and Football Week at the Academy.

The oldest harness track in America, built in 1838, and New York's only afternoon trotting track, is just to the west at **Goshen**. The **Hall of Fame of the Trotter** has paintings and original Currier and Ives trotting prints. Annual Race Week is held the first week in July. The **Brotherhood Wine Cellars,** in nearby Washingtonville, has guided tours and wine tastings, February through November, free. George Washington had his headquarters at **Newburgh** in 1782-83 and he announced the end of the Revolution and officially disbanded the army from here. His headquarters, built in 1750, has relics and furniture of the Revolutionary War period. **Howard Johnson's** in Newburgh (565-4100, S$26/D$28 up); **Holiday Inn** in Suffern (357-4800, S$50/D$56); **Sheraton Inn** in Nanuet (623-6000, S$38/D$44 up); and **Howard Johnson's** in Middletown (342-5822, S$31/D$35 up) are recommended. The **Beau Rivage Restaurant** is housed in a charming colonial house overlooking the Hudson River. In Central Valley, **Gasho of Japan** offers authentic Japanese food.

To the northeast, **James Baird State Park** has an 18-hole golf course, a pool and facilities for tennis and picnicking. **Vassar College,** founded in **Poughkeepsie** in 1861, is one of the nation's outstanding coed colleges. Visit **Governor George Clinton's House,** a typical 1765 home that served as his headquarters from 1777 to 1782. In Poughkeepsie, try **Camelot Inn** (462-4600, S$34/D$39) and **Best Western Red Bull Motor Inn** (462-4400, S$32/D$38 up) to the south. **Nick Beni's** offers Italian and American menus, children's plates. **Treasure Chest Inn** has French cuisine in a converted 1741 Dutch colonial home, with candlelit dining on the terrace.

Northeast on US 44 is **Millbrook,** where **Innisfree Garden** is dedicated to the study of Eastern and Western civilization's influence on garden art. West of here is **Hyde Park,** where Franklin D. Roosevelt, the 32nd president, was born in 1882, and he and his wife Eleanor are buried in the rose garden. The Roosevelt house, which was built in 1826 and is now a national historical site, is open to the public; the stables and icehouse are principal attractions. The **Vanderbilt Mansion,** nearby, was completed in 1898 and cost $660,000. Most of the furnishings in the

54 rooms are museum pieces. Visitors may stroll through the 212-acre estate; open daily 9-5, closed only 25 December and 1 January. At the **Ogden and Ruth Livingston Mills Memorial State Park,** the palatial 65-room Mills mansion has been converted into a historical museum, and there are golfing and fishing facilities at the park. The oldest hotel in the United States, the **Beekman Arms,** was built in 1700 at **Rhinebeck.** The **Old Rhinebeck Aerodrome** gives airshows, which include World War I planes, Sundays from mid-May, plus Saturdays from 1 July through October. And the annual **Dutchess County Fair,** complete with harness racing and livestock shows, is held in August.

At the eastern entrance to the **CATSKILL MOUNTAIN** resort area, the **Catskill Game Farm** has amusement rides, 3,000 animals, picnic grounds, and a cafeteria; open mid-April through mid-November, daily 9-6. Every year, in late June, there's an antique auto parade for **Old Catskill Days. Catskill Motor Lodge** (943-5800, S$25/D$30), in the town of Catskill, and **Pleasant View Lodge** (634-2523, S$35/D$50), in Freehold, provide accommodations. The **Friar Tuck Inn** (678-2271, S$35-37/D$70-74), to the west, has heated pools indoors and out, golf, and riding. The **Skyline Restaurant** offers a pleasant view and special seafood dishes.

The 657,600-acre **Catskill Park** has more than 200 miles of marked hiking trails and six public campsites. The forest preserve has three of the best fishing streams in the state; plus facilities for swimming, boating, fishing, and hunting. **Woodstock** is a small, sophisticated artists' colony and a year-round resort in the east-central section of the park. The Art Students' League of New York has a summer school here. Nationally prominent artists exhibit their work at the **Woodstock Artists Association Gallery.** The **Woodstock Playhouse** is open May-September, except Monday for summer stock. In nearby Saugerties, try **Howard Johnson's** (246-9511, S$30/D$32 up) or in Kingston, **Ramada Inn** (339-3900, S$36/D$44 up) or **Howard Johnson's** (338-4200, S$39/D$38 up). **Deanie's Town Tavern** is popular with the local people. You'll like its early American decor, seafood, and prime rib specialties. **Hunter Mountain Ski Bowl,** to the north, offers 32 miles of beginner and expert trails, open December through March. During the summer there are picnic facilities and mile-long chairlift rides, open July-1 September, daily; 24 May-29 June and September-October, weekends only. In Hunter, try **Hunter House** (263-4611, S$45/D$47) or, in Haines Falls to the east, **Villagio Resort** (589-5000, Rates furnished on Request). The area has many hotels, motels, tourist homes, boarding houses, and cottages; write for information to **Catskills Destinations,** Box 91, Malden, NY 12453.

To the south of the Catskill Park area in **Liberty** is **Grossinger's Hotel and Country Club** (292-5000, S$63/D$90 up), set on 1,300 mountain acres with a private lake. It has 600 rooms, an Olympic-size pool, indoor heated pool, sauna and health club, and a day camp. For sports enthusiasts, there's boating, fishing, skating, skiing, tobogganing, and snowmobiling. The night club attracts big name entertainers, and the restaurant features a rich kosher menu; family, weekly, and golf package rates also available. In the **Swan Lake** area, there are 25 hotels, motels, rooming houses, 50 bungalow colonies and a dude ranch, night clubs, and children's day camps.

Monticello is the center of the **SULLIVAN COUNTY** resort area. The **Monticello Raceway** has harness racing daily April through October. **Fort Delaware** depicts the life of the early settlers, with a replica of a 1754 stockade, blockhouses, and cabins; open June through September. **Forestburgh Summer Theater,** open late June through Labor Day, also has weekday matinees for children. **Holiday Mountain Motor Lodge** (796-3000, S$39/D$48 up), at Rock Hill to the east, has a heated pool, playground, golf privileges, and hunting on its 200 acres. Nearby is the **Concord** (794-4000), on **Kiamesha Lake,** one of the most luxurious hotels in the Catskills. It has 1,200 rooms, large pool, heated indoor pool, activities for children and teenagers, three golf courses, putting greens, driving range, turf skiing, riding, tennis, year-round ice rink, skiing, tobogganing, boating, fishing, health clubs and a night club, kosher food; family, weekly and golf package plans. Kosher menus are also provided at **Kutsher's Country Club** (794-6000, S$45-70/D$90-140 AP) and **The Pines** (434-6000, S$36-55/D$72-110 AP).

Ellenville, to the east, is the center of **ULSTER COUNTY'S** resort area where there are lots of hotels, motels, cottages, children's camps, and ranch resorts. **Ice Cave Mountain,** open April through November, features a self-guided tour of the caves with snow and ice, nature trails, and a lookout at the top of the mountain, 2,255 feet above sea level. The **Nevele** (647-6000, S$54/D$108), in Ellenville, has a kosher menu, three pools, golf course, sports, and entertainment. In Kerhonkson to the north, try the **Granite Hotel** (626-3141, S$48/D$90 up) or **Pine Grove Ranch** (626-7345, S$70/D$90 up).

Continuing north along the Hudson River, you enter the **ALBANY-SARATOGA** area, known best for its political history and cultural heritage. The state capital at Albany, on the west bank of the Hudson River, is the oldest city in the United States still operating under its original charter, and because of its proximity to Lake Champlain and Erie canals and the Hudson River, has become an important inland seaport. At the **State Capitol,** the **Legislative Chambers** and **Great Western Staircase** are noted for their architectural beauty. **Schuyler Mansion** was built for General Philip Schuyler in 1762, and his daughter married Alexander Hamilton here; open Wednesday through Sunday. Historic **Cherry Hill** has many original furnishings. It was the home of the Philip Van Rensselaer family in 1768. The annual **Tulip Festival** at Washington Park in May pays tribute to Albany's Dutch heritage. **Rensselaerville,** 30 miles to the southwest in the Helderbergs, is a delightful village founded in 1787, with charming old homes, churches, and inns. Information on guided tours in and around Albany available from Chamber of Commerce (518) 434-1214.

Albany's skyline is dominated by the newly built **Empire State Plaza,** a 98.5 acre tract immediately south of the Capitol that includes massive marble and glass office buildings, an egg-shaped **Performing Arts Center,** reflecting pools used for ice skating in winter, a 3,000 seat **Convention**

Center, a six-block long underground concourse lined with shops, and boutiques and displaying more than 80 works of art commissioned by New York State and created by the nation's outstanding contemporary artists. From the observation level of the 44-story tower building, tallest skyscraper upstate, visitors can see mountains in the distance on all sides: the Berkshires, the Catskills, the Helderbergs, and the Adirondacks. In season, the **Plaza** offers art festivals, ice shows and carnivals, holiday galas, musical and dance events, ethnic fairs, outdoor concerts, and children's theater presentations of the internationally-known **Empire State Youth Theater Institute.** Just south of the Plaza, and entered from it, is the 13-story **Cultural Education Center,** which houses the enlarged **State Museum** and the 4.5-million-volume state Library.

Many motels. Three **Holiday Inns** within 3 to 6 miles of downtown, with heated pools and playgrounds, prices S$28-35/D$37-40. Near Albany County Airport: **Americana Inn** (869-9271, S$41-45/D$55-60); **Sheraton Airport Inn** (458-1000, S$37-42/D$43-48). In midtown near State University: **Thruway House** (459-3100, S$28-33/D$32-37); **Ramada Inn** (459-2981, S$34-40/D$40-45); **Tom Sawyer Motor Inn** (438-3594, S$29-32/D$33-39). The newly built **Albany Hilton Hotel** (462-6611, S$38-48/D$48-58), just downhill from the Capitol, has 392 beds. **Jack's Sea Food & Steak House** has been run by the same family for over 60 years. **L'Auberge des Fougeres** and **L'Epicure** serve French specialties and are chef-owned. Good and attractive are **La Serre,** French, and **Ogden's,** standard. **Veeder's** just west of city offers family dining at reasonable prices.

In downtown **Schenectady,** located on the Mohawk River in the scenic **MOHAWK VALLEY,** the city fathers have retained the **Village-Stockade Area.** Each colonial house is marked with the date of construction and the name of its original owner. A 1½-hour guided tour is available by appointment—call (518) 393-8622—or you can pick up a walking tour folder from the County Historical Society, 32 Washington Avenue; free. The annual **Walkabout** in the Stockade area takes place one Saturday in late September. **Union College,** the oldest planned campus in the US, with its 17-acre **Jackson Botanical Gardens,** is in Schenectady. **Holiday Inn** (393-4141, S$32/D$42), 2 blocks from downtown, is recommended. The **Van Dyck** and the **Ritz** are popular restaurants.

President Grant liked to give parties at the elegant old United States Hotel at **Saratoga Springs.** Though it has gone the way of its era, the horse racing and the mineral springs continue to attract visitors each year. The scenery is still magnificent and the **Saratoga Performing Arts Center** offers enough of a potpourri of entertainment to satisfy the most discerning visitor. The Performing Arts Center amphitheater seats over 5,000 persons under cover and an additional 10,000 in the open air. This is the summer home of the New York City Ballet during July and the Philadelphia Orchestra takes the stage in August. There are also special summer concerts by distinguished guest artists. **Saratoga Spa State Park,** a 2,200-acre recreational and cultural development, is open during the summer. The **Recreation Center** has two golf courses, one 18-hole, one 9-hole, open April to November. Swimming and diving facilities are available, late May through Labor Day, and there's a picnicking area. At the famous mineral spring baths visitors can take treatments throughout the year at the 2,000-acre complex of recreational and health facilities. There's thoroughbred racing in August at the **Saratoga Race Track**, the country's oldest. Off the track, the **National Museum of Thoroughbred Racing** has racing mementos and paintings. Harness racing fans can see the trotters at the **Saratoga Harness Racing Track**, mid-April through mid-November, with weekend racing from January through March. Recommended motels are the **Carriage House** (584-0352, S/D$75); **Holiday Inn** (584-4550, S/D$100); and the **Turf & Spa** (584-2550, S/D$65), with a heated pool. The **Gideon Putnam Hotel** (584-3000, S$63/D$100 AP) is just south of the city on the Saratoga Spa State Park grounds. All rates quoted are for August, and are lower the rest of the year. Caution: motels within a 50-mile radius of Saratoga Springs are usually booked at or near capacity during the August thoroughbred racing season. The **Trade Winds Restaurant** has a glassed-in hearth and elaborate decor and is very popular with the local folk. Also try **Mangino's** on Saratoga Lake and the **Wishing Well. Saratoga County Antiques Center** displays wares of 15 dealers in a home built in 1855. At **Saratoga National Historical Park**, the Visitor Center offers a view of the battlefield which proved to be the turning point of the American Revolution. Exhibits and a 12-minute film explain the battle.

In Glens Falls, farther north, the **Hyde Museum** houses an outstanding collection of paintings in a converted mansion. **Storytown, USA**, offers more than 30 storybook settings, Jungle Land, Ghost Town, and live circus acts from Memorial Day through September. **West Mountain Ski Center** is open mid-December through March. Accommodations in the area include **Howard Johnson's** (793-4173, S$43.50/D$70.50); **Sheraton Glens Falls** (793-7701, S$65/D$70); **Queensbury Hotel and Motor Inn** (792-1121, S$32/D$44), and, 5 miles to the south, **Landmark Motor Lodge** (793-3441, S$45/D$50). Prices quoted are summer rates, and are lower the rest of the year. **Red Coach Grill**, opposite Storytown, has children's plates; the **Gold Room** in the Queensbury Hotel, and the **Blacksmith Shop** at Howard Johnson's steak and salad bar, are all good.

Lake George, 9 miles north of Glens Falls in the foothills of the **ADIRONDACKS**, is a popular winter and summer family resort area. At the base of the lovely **Lake George**, leading artists from American and European opera companies present three operas in English, mid-July through August, at the annual **Lake George Opera Festival**. **Fort William Henry**, of French and Indian War fame, has been rebuilt from original plans, and there are guided tours July through Labor Day. The area abounds in amusement parks. **Gaslight Village** is a replica of a pre-1900 town with continuous Gay 90s rides, silent movies, boardwalk fun houses, and vaudeville entertainment; open late June through early September. **Animal Land**, open May through October, has animal shows, including duck racing and alligator wrestling. **Magic Forest** has Santa and his famous reindeer, Indian ceremonial dances, and a dolphin show, open late June through Labor Day. There are daily sightseeing cruises on Lake George, varying in length from 1 to 4 hours, along the shore-line to **Paradise Bay,** and even a moonlight dance cruise. Try the fishing on Lake George and the swimming at the **Lake George Beach State Park** in the Adirondack Forest Preserve. It's winter carnival time every weekend in February and summer visitors will enjoy **Warren County Sheriff's Mounted Trail Days,** with pleasure and competitive rides, barbecues, and parades; 3 days in late June. **Gore Mountain Ski Center** is at North Creek, 25 miles north; open mid-December through March.

Accommodations for over 25,000 visitors are available in the Lake George area. You have a choice of hotel or motel, tourist home or boarding house, cottages, cabins, and dude ranches. Many of the resorts maintain private beaches and golf courses. Accommodations include **Marine Village Resort Motel** (668-5478, S/D$40 up); **Holiday Inn** (668-5478, S$30-75/D$35-80); **Best Western of Lake George** (668-5781, S$26-83/D$30-83); **Georgian Motel** (668-5401, S/D$48-105). **Roaring Brook Ranch** (668-5767, S$35-53 MAP), 2 miles south, has a children's program summer and winter, plus summer sports activities. Additional motel information available at Chamber of Commerce (668-5755). **Le Chalet Francais** serves fine French food, and the **Montcalm,** with its charming roof garden, is popular with the locals. **Ridge Terrace** and **Mama Riso's** are also recommended.

Schroon Lake is an important summer resort area, extending for 2 miles along the west shore of the lake. Within a 5-mile radius there are some 70 lakes and ponds, numerous beaches and public campsites. At **Frontier Town** recapture the feeling of this area's intriguing history. Take a stagecoach, ride in the cavalry or the wagon train in **Adirondack State Park,** between Lake George and Lake Placid, open Memorial Day to mid-October. **Eagle Point** in Adirondack Forest Preserve has a bathhouse and at **Paradox Lake** there are boat rentals.

The famous **Ticonderoga** resort lies between Lake George and Lake Champlain, with extensive tourist, hunting, and fishing facilities. The great stone **Fort Ticonderoga** fortress has been restored and nearby you can see the well-preserved battle lines. The museum has a collection of uniforms, paintings, and weapons; open mid-May through October. Guided tours and cannon shooting are featured in July and August. For a panoramic view of Lake Champlain, the Champlain Valley, and Green Mountains in Vermont, drive the route the British took in 1777 to the top of **Mt Defiance.** The Fort Ticonderoga Ferry crosses Lake Champlain to Larabees Point, Vermont, in 6 minutes. **Putnam Pond Public Campsite** in Adirondack Forest Preserve has tent sites, and facilities for boating, swimming, fishing, and picnicking.

Blue Mountain Lake is in a central Adirondack location with good fishing and hunting, canoe trips, and lake cruises. There's a 3-mile trail to the 3,800-foot summit, where the observation tower overlooks the Adirondack Forest Preserve, with the highest mountains in the state; facilities for camping, swimming, fishing, and boating. **Adirondacks Lakes Center for the Arts** has concerts, films and art exhibits all year. **Hemlock Hall Inn** (352-7706, S$45-55/D$58-68) is a pleasant, secluded resort hotel in the woods by the lake shore; **The Hedges** (352-7325, S$46/D$56) is also located on the lake.

Lake Placid, the internationally known resort on Mirror Lake and Lake Placid below Whiteface Mountain, is open year round. The most famous winter sports area in the east, Lake Placid hosted the 1980 Winter Olympics Games, with the thrilling gold-medal performance of the US Olympic hockey team. There are two indoor Olympic Arena rinks, an outdoor skating rink, an Olympic bob run for bobsled racing, plus ski centers and over 200 miles of ski trails. **Whiteface Mountain Ski Center** is nearby. Summer sports include riding, swimming at public and private beaches, tennis, and golf. The boat ride from **Holiday Harbor** around Lake Placid is a big favorite with tourists. **Labor Day Figure Skating Operetta** and the **Fourth of July Ski Jump** are annual events. **Sterling-Alaska Fur and Game Farm** has over 1,000 live fur-bearing and game animals from all over the world; llama rides in July and August. Accommodations include: **Art Devlin's Olympic Motor Inn** (523-3700, $D28-60); **Lake Placid Hilton** (523-4411, S/D$50-74); **Whiteface Inn** (523-2551, S$40-50/D$55-65); **Best Western Golden Arrow Motor Inn** (523-3353, S/D$50-63); **Holiday Inn** (523-2556, S$32-72/D$34-74); **Lake Placid Club Resort** (523-3361, S$32/D$50-60); and **Thunderbird Motel** (523-2439, D$30-39). **The Steak & Stinger, Mirror Lake Inn,** and **Frederick's** are recommended restaurants. **The Homestead** is good, too.

Saranac Lake is a major year-round resort center. The **Winter Carnival** is held on Lincoln's Birthday weekend, in February. The **Guideboat Championships, Willard Hanmer Memorial Canoe Races** on Lake Flower and the Saranac River, held on the 4th of July weekend, are annual festivities. **Mt Pisgah Municipal Ski Center** is open mid-December through mid-March. There are facilities for camping at the **Meadowbrook Public Campsite** in Adirondack Forest Preserve and there is swimming on Lake Colby, Prescott Park, and lower Saranac Lake. You may also want to visit **Robert Louis Stevenson Cottage,** open June-September, Tuesdays through Sundays. **Brookside Hotel** has a cheery country inn dining room, with prime ribs the house specialty. The **Tupper Lake Chair Lift** takes you on a 3,000-foot scenic ride to the summit, late June through Labor Day. **Big Tupper Ski Area** is open December through April. During the summer, there's swimming, boating, and camping at **Fish Creek Pond.** The **Tupper Lake Open** golf tournament is the second weekend in August. **Riverside Restaurant** overlooks the lake. Accommodations in Saranac Lake include **Gauthier's Motel** (891-1950, S$20-30/D$30-38), **The Saranac** (891-2200, S$22/D$28), and **Saranac Inn & Country Club** (891-1402, D$50), summer only.

The **Whiteface Mountain Ski Center** at Wilmington is open 8:30-4:30 during the winter season. Off-season, the **Little Whiteface Chair Lift** operates late June through mid-October. There are facilities for camping nearby at **Wilmington Notch Campsite.** Santa Claus is alive and well at Santa's Workshop, off route 86, in **North Pole, NY,** open late May through mid-October.

In the **NORTHWEST CORNER** of the State, **Massena** is the center of the **St Lawrence Seaway** and power installations operated jointly by the US and Canada. Stay at the **Sheraton Inn-Massena** (769-2441, S$21-23/D$25-29). The international boundary is marked by flags at the center of the dam. **Robert Moses State Park, Eisenhower Lock,** and **Snell Lock** provide viewing decks, plus picnicking, camping, and fishing facilities. Take a bus tour of the locks, dams, and boat basin, late June through late September, daily except Sunday. Heading south along the St. Lawrence River, the **Frederic Remington Art Museum** at Ogdensburg has the most complete single collection of the artist's works. He was born and lived in nearby Canton and his oil paintings, bronzes, and sketches of the Old West are housed in an 1809 mansion. The **International Seaway Festival** lasts four days in late July. The **Gran-View Restaurant** of the **Quality Gran-View Motel** (393-4550, S$27-29/D$33-38), overlooking the river 3 miles south of Ogdensburg, will cook your day's catch.

Alexandria, in the **NORTH CENTRAL SECTION** of the State, is the resort center of the area known as Thousand Islands located at the southern end of the St Lawrence River; some of these islands are so small they have only a single tree while others are several miles long. Sightseeing boats leave every hour out of Alexandria Bay and Clayton during July and August. The 2½-hour trip usually stops at the ruins of **Boldt Castle** on Heart Island. A 100-room, $2 million castle, it was intended as a gift from a husband to his wife, but she died and the castle was never completed. While you're in the neighborhood, don't miss the famous Thousand Islands shore dinner; licensed fishing guides specialize in cooking the catch after a day's fishing trip. At **1000 Skydeck**, take the elevator to the observation deck 400 feet above the St Lawrence River, for a magnificent over-all view of the islands; open mid-May through mid-October. Swimming, boating, water sports, and fishing are available at **Scenic View Park. Capt Thomson's Motor Lodge** (482-9961, S/D$29-55), on the St Lawrence Seaway, is a popular motel; **Edgewood** (482-9922, S/D$20-48), and **Pine Tree Point Club** (482-9911, S/D$20-48) are recommended resorts. **Skytown** is a recreational area on **Hill Island.** Storybook characters come to life at **Never Never Land.** Outboard races and special events are held all summer long at **Clayton.** There are facilities for swimming, boating, fishing, and camping at the local state parks and you can take a 3-hour cruise along the St Lawrence through the Thousand Islands, May through early October.

Driving southwest around Lake Ontario to the Canadian border, one finds some of New York's largest cities: Rochester, Niagara, and Buffalo.

Oneida in **CENTRAL NEW YORK STATE,** is probably the best known of the 19th-century Utopian communities. The residents still maintain the silverware factory where they make Community plate and William A. Rogers silver. Harness racing is held at **Vernon Downs,** late April through October. The **Cooperstown** community was founded in 1786 by Judge William Cooper. His son, James Fenimore Cooper, made the area famous when he used the surrounding farmland and meadows for his *Leatherstocking Tales.* As all baseball fans know, the **National Baseball Hall of Fame and Museum** is in Cooperstown. The museum is open daily, May through October, 9-9, and November through April 9-5. You can buy combination tickets to the Baseball Museum and **Farmer's Museum** which depicts farm and rural village life in the early 1800s. There are boat rides and rentals on **Otsego Lake**, the "Glimmerglass" of Cooper's stories, Memorial Day through mid-November. You may prefer a roundtrip ride, July-September, on an old steam locomotive-drawn coach and parlor car with lunch and dinner served on board. There are many motels on Lake Otsego. The **Red Sleigh** is a delightful local restaurant.

Driving west you approach the **Finger Lakes**. This area is called "the champagne district," because of the bubbly local wine produced there. The **Corning Glass Center,** in Corning, has a museum of exhibits showing manmade glass from 1500 BC. You can see the spectacular glassmaking process at the **Steuben** factory, open daily; free. **Corning Summer Theatre,** at the Glass Center is open July and August. The **Best Western Lodge on the Green** (962-2456, S$28/D$31-36) has spacious grounds, a heated pool and a gracious dining room; two miles from Corning Glass Center. High above Cayuga Lake in Ithaca is **Cornell University.** Over 16,000 students attend classes on its beautiful 740-acre campus. The annual **York State Crafts Fair** is held at Ithaca College in early August. The **Station Restaurant,** a converted railroad station, uses ticket punch menus. And the popular **Taughannock Farms Inn** offers family-style dining in an old farm mansion.

Syracuse China in **Syracuse**, northeast of Ithaca, is the oldest and largest china manufacturer in the US. **Syracuse University's** magnificent 640-acre campus serves over 19,000 students. There's a zoo in **Burnet Park,** and **Green Lakes State Park** has swimming, fishing, and picnicking facilities. The **Intercollegiate Rowing Regatta** takes place in mid-May on Onondaga Lake. The **New York State Fair** draws thousands of visitors to Syracuse each year; late August through Labor Day. There are open-air concerts in the city parks; early July through August. **Best Western Dinkler Motor Inn** (472-6961, S$29-39/D$29-44); four **Holiday Inns,** about S$31-36/D$36-41; **Marriott Inn** (432-0200, S$50-56/D$58-64); and **Ramada Inn** (457-8670, S$30/D$32-35) are recommended.

Joseph Smith, the founder of the Mormon Church, had a vision in the frontier town of **Palmyra**, northwest of Syracuse, which eventually led to his founding of the sect. They celebrate the Mormon Pageant at **Hill Cumorah,** seven nights beginning late in July, one of the largest and most colorful religious pageants in the US. Racing fans are drawn to Watkins Glen for the **Watkins Glen Grand Prix Course. Six Hours of Endurance** and **Glen Can-Am** are in mid-July. **Formula 5,000 Trans-American** is in mid-August, and the **US Grand Prix Formula One Championship,** in early October. Write Box 1, Watkins Glen 14891 or call (607) 535-4701. **Watkins Glen State Park** includes a system of stairs and bridges leading through the famous tributary gorge past rapids and waterfalls. The terrain rises 700 feet within 2 miles. Recommended accommodations: **Motel Glen Eden** (535-4800, S$18/D$20-26, higher racing weekends).

Grapevines can be seen rising along the hillside as you enter the center of New York State's grape and wine industry due south of Palmyra. Grapes have been grown in and around **Hammondsport** since 1829. You can sample the fruits of their labor on free tours of the local wineries: **Pleasant Valley Wine Co** (Great Western), call (607) 569-2121; **Taylor Wine Co.** call (607) 569-2111; **Gold Seal Vineyards,** call (607) 868-3232.

Once an oil boom town in the **SOUTHWEST CORNER** of the state, **Olean** has good recreational and picnic areas. The restaurant at the **Castle Inn Motel** (372-1050, S$19-26/D$24-33) has a 16th-century Old English castle atmosphere. Within **Allegheny State Park** are some of the best recreational centers in the country, open year round, with cabins, tents, and trailer sites, tennis courts, skiing on **Bova Slope,** tobogganing, and snowmobiling. Write to Allegheny State Park Commission, Salamanca 14779 for details.

Chautauqua, to the west, is best known as an educational and recreational center. The community began in 1874 as a Sunday School teachers' training camp and developed into a cultural center. Devoted followers return each summer for the full program of art, drama, music, and lectures, non-credit and college study courses. The **Amphitheatre,** with seating for 6,000, features legitimate theater and opera in English. The tour ship **Gadfly** takes visitors on a 1¼-hour sightseeing cruise on Chautauqua Lake. Write to **Chautauqua Institution,** Box 1095, Chautauqua, NY 14722, or phone 357-5635.

Cities To Visit

NEW YORK CITY

New York City is in southeastern New York State at the mouth of the Hudson River, which runs along the west side of Manhattan Island; the East River bounds the east side. The two rivers converge in New York Harbor, one of the great ocean ports of the world. New York City has had a colorful history, starting with its discovery by Henry Hudson at the beginning of the 17th century. According to the story, in 1626, the Dutchman Peter Minuit made one of the most remarkable real estate deals in history when he purchased Manhattan Island from the Indians for a reported $24 worth of trinkets. Sponsored by the Dutch West India Company, the young colony, called New Amsterdam, prospered immediately because of its excellent location as a seaport. In 1664, in support of complicated territorial claims, the English seized the settlement, despite the irascible Dutch governor Peter Stuyvesant, and renamed it New York. War broke out again between Britain and the Dutch Republic and in 1673 a Dutch fleet returned to New York and captured it, renaming it Fort Orange. At the close of the war in 1674, the town was relinquished to Britain, under whose rule it prospered again. During the American Revolution New York remained in British hands until the war was over, but nevertheless, it was here that George Washington was inaugurated as the first president of the United States. The completion of the Erie Canal in 1825, providing a continuous commercial waterway from the Atlantic Ocean to the Great Lakes, gave New York City its great impetus to become a business and financial center. Today the city is perhaps the greatest port in the world and the financial, intellectual, and artistic center of the nation.

New York consists of five boroughs—**Manhattan,** the **Bronx,** on the mainland, **Brooklyn** and **Queens** on Long Island, and **Richmond** on Staten Island. Thousands of commuters live in New Jersey, Westchester County, Long Island, and Connecticut. At least one source of New York's vitality and excitement is the patchwork of national neighborhoods which maintain, with startling accuracy, the mood, the look, even the aromas of the cuisines of their particular nation. To visit Chinatown, the German section uptown in Yorkville, Little Italy, the Syrian section of Atlantic Avenue in Brooklyn, Brooklyn's Bay Ridge, Harlem, and Greenwich Village is to get a real taste of what America is all about.

The population of the Greater New York area is approximately 11,-700,000 including the city's five boroughs and surrounding suburbs in New York State. Manhattan has many different business districts. Starting at the southern tip, you'll find the Wall Street district, where most of the financial, insurance, and stock-exchange activities take place. North of Canal Street there is mixture of light manufacturing and miscellaneous businesses. The garment-manufacturing district is from 34th to 40th streets, centering on Seventh Avenue. The area between 34th and 59th streets is the principal retail shopping district. The Grand Central area, where there has been a considerable amount of new construction, includes the landmark Grand Central Terminal at 42nd Street and Park Avenue. From 60th Street northwards, Manhattan is primarily residential.

WHAT TO SEE

Here are some suggested sights: museums are listed separately under "Arts and Music." **La Guardia** and **Kennedy International** airports both have sightseeing decks and are interesting to visit, as are the **Bronx Zoo; Bronx** and **Brooklyn Botanical Gardens;** Cathedral of St John the Divine; **Central Park** with its many attractions including a zoo, and the **Bethesda Fountain,** is a major meeting ground for young New Yorkers on warm weekends. The City Hall district and the **Foley Square** courthouse area; the **Cloisters** and **Fort Tryon Park; Chinatown; Columbia University;** the view from the top of the Empire State Building; and the view from the observatory and roof of the World Trade Center at the lower end of Manhattan, Grand Central Terminal; Grant's Tomb; Greenwich Village; **Hayden Planetarium; Lincoln Center for the Performing Arts;** Riverside Church; Rockefeller Center; **St Patrick's Cathedral;** shops and stores from 34th Street & Seventh Avenue to Fifth Avenue and up Fifth to 60th Street and avenues east of it; **Statue of Liberty** and **New York Harbor; Times Square** district; United Nations; **Wall Street** district and the **New York Stock Exchange,** 20 Broad Street, open to the public weekdays 10-2, tours free; **Washington Square** and **Washington Arch;** and the **Radio**

City Music Hall, where now only periodically there are movies and elaborate stage shows, including the famous precision dancing of the Rockettes. "The New York Experience," located beneath the McGraw-Hill building, offers a multi-media history of New York City.

There are a variety of ways to view "The City": the Circle Line boats take 3-hour trips around Manhattan Island at least six times a day, leaving from Pier 83 at the foot of 43rd Street, April to mid-November; cost is $7.50 for adults, $3.75 for children under 12. The Statue of Liberty ferry leaves from Battery Park, South Ferry, hourly, 9-4 throughout the year, cost $1.50 for adults, and 50¢ for children under 12. From May to October the Hudson River Day Line has 1-day trips to Bear Mountain, West Point Military Academy, and Poughkeepsie. A typical 2-hour bus tour of the city costs about $8-10 and a 4-hour tour is about $11.50. Gray Line offers city bus tours and helicopter rides over Manhattan, from $8 up to $50. Bus tours are multilingual, in French, German, and Spanish, year round; cost is $10-15. For only 25¢ round trip you can take the picturesque ferry ride from lower Manhattan to Staten Island.

BUILDINGS

Many of the tallest buildings in the world are in New York: **World Trade Center**, 110 floors; **Empire State**, 102; **Chrysler**, 77; **60 Wall Street Tower**, 66; **Bank of Manhattan**, 71; **Radio Corporation of America**, 70; **Chase Manhattan Bank**, 60; **Woolworth**, 60; **Pan Am Building**, 59. Other important buildings: **City Hall** in City Hall Park, built in 1811, is a classic example of the architecture of its period; **Grand Central Terminal**, 42nd Street & Park Avenue, huge railway station; the **New York Public Library** at 42nd Street and Fifth Avenue; the greenery-filled **Ford Foundation Building**, 350 E 43 Street; the impressive **General Motors Building**, 59th Street & Fifth Avenue and the nearby **Citicorp Building** between 53 and 54th on Lexington Avenue. **Park Avenue** is a boulevard of exciting architecture, including such notables as **Lever House, Pepsi-Cola Building, Seagram Building**, and **Union Carbide Building**.

Rockefeller Center, 48th to 52nd streets on Fifth Avenue and Avenue of the Americas, consists of 21 buildings containing exhibits, offices, shops, theaters, and television studios. Escorted tours start every 15 minutes daily 9:30-5:30, but check holiday hours. The **United Nations** is at 42nd to 48th Streets on First Avenue; when in session, the public may attend meetings; tickets available on a first come, first served basis; guided tours; fascinating foreign shops. The Protestant Episcopal **Cathedral of St John the Divine**, 112th Street and Amsterdam Avenue, is the largest church in the United States. **Grant's Tomb**, overlooking the Hudson at 122nd Street & Riverside Drive, is the mausoleum of General Ulysses S. Grant, Commander-in-Chief of the Union Army in the Civil War. **Riverside Church**, 122nd Street & Riverside Drive, is a fine example of French-Gothic architecture. **Trinity Church**, Broadway at Wall Street, dates from the colonial era; and Alexander Hamilton and Robert Fulton are buried in the old churchyard. **Fraunces Tavern**, 54 Pearl Street at Broad Street, was built in 1719 and is still serving meals in the first-floor restaurant;

this was the setting for Washington's farewell to the officers of the Continental Army; museum on the second and third floors.

ACCOMMODATIONS

Although the city is well supplied with hotels, rooms are often scarce. Always write or wire for a reservation and if possible have it confirmed by the hotel. Your Pan Am office or agent will make your reservations prior to your trip to the USA. Checkout time in most hotels is during the afternoon, and, occasionally, a room will not be ready if you arrive early in the day. Budget-priced rooms start at about S$28/D$30; reasonably priced rooms are priced at around S$40/D$46 up; and moderately priced ones are from S$60/D$74 up. In the expensive category, a single room will start at about $95 and a double room at $110. Rooms with twin beds are more expensive than rooms with a double bed. The following is merely a representative list, with minimum prices given. Hotel Tax: 8%

Times Square District

On this west side of town from 42nd Street to 52nd Street hotels are often rather noisy and busy at night, but are convenient to transportation, theaters, restaurants, and nightclubs.

Abbey Victoria (246-9400, S$40/D$46), 151 West 51st Street, all rooms air conditioned; **Algonquin** (840-6800, S$72-76/D$77-82 up), 59 West 44th Street, large, comfortable; **Carter Hotel** (944-6000, S$38/D$40), 250 West 43rd Street, special rates for overseas groups; **Edison** (246-5000, S$40/D$56), 228 West 47th Street, large, busy, some rooms with television and air conditioning, special rates for overseas groups; **Seymour** (840-3480, S$38/D$48), 50 West 45th Street.

Other hotels in the area are the **Diplomat** (921-5666, S$30/D$36), 108 West 43rd Street, good value; **Mansfield** (944-6050, S$40-44/D$42-48), 12 West 44th Street; **President** (246-8800, S$27/D$30), 234 West 48th Street, special rates for groups; and **Royalton**, (730-1344, S$38-80/D$50-95), 44 West 44th Street.

Pennsylvania Station District

Hotels in this central area are conveniently situated near the popular 34th Street shopping region, Madison Square Garden, and the wholesale garment district.

Statler-Hilton (736-5000, S$59-89/D$74-104), 33rd Street and Seventh Avenue, very large, important commercially, a convention center.

West Side

The Sheraton Center (581-1000, S$74-110/D$89-125), 53rd Street and Seventh Avenue, huge modern hotel near theater district; **Barbizon-Plaza** (247-7000, S$77-82/D$81-92), 58th Street and Avenue of the Americas, very large, transient and residential; **Dorset** (247-7300, S$92-125/D$107-140), 30 West 54th Street, moderate-sized, part residential, dignified, on fairly quiet street; **Marriott's Essex House** (247-0300, S$95-140/D$110-

The United Nations Secretariat Building towers over the headquarters complex of the United Nations, centerpiece of the world diplomatic community.

155, special weekend rates), 160 Central Park South, view of Central Park, luxurious; **New York Hilton** (586-7000, S$67-103/D$87-123), at Rockefeller Center, a large, modern hotel; **New York Sheraton** (247-8000, S$75-89/D$90-104), 202 West 56th Street, large, commercial and transient; **St Moritz** (755-5800, S$70-100/D$80-115/Suites $155-285), 50 Central Park South, facing Central Park, a favorite with foreign travelers; **Warwick** (247-2700, S$71-83/D$83-95), 65 West 54th Street, fairly large, part residential.

Chelsea (243-3700, S$35/D$45), 222 West 23rd Street; **Henry Hudson** (265-6100, S$45/D$61), 353 West 57th Street, quiet, self-service laundry, indoor swimming pool and health club, some rooms with air conditioning and television; and **Wellington** (247-3900, S$44/D$54), Seventh Avenue and 55th Street, multilingual staff. The new **Vista International** (938-1990, S$55-115/D$99-135), 3 World Trade Center, is close to the financial district and has a view of the entire city.

Far West Side

Between Broadway and Twelfth Avenue is a concentration of relatively new motels with free indoor parking facilities that are especially convenient for motorists driving into the city from across the Hudson River or down the West Side Highway.

These "skyscraper motels" include the **Best Western Skyline Motor Inn** (586-3400, S$52/D$59), 49th-50th Streets and Twelfth Avenue; **City Squire Motor Inn** (581-3300, S$15 up/D$84-110), Broadway between 51st and 52nd Streets; **Ramada Inn** (581-7000, also toll free, 800-228-2828, S$55-60/D$67-72), Eighth Avenue and 48th Street; **Howard Johnson Motor Lodge** (581-4100, S$50-60/D$62-72), Eighth Avenue and 51st Street; **Holiday Inn Coliseum** (581-8100, S$63/D$72), 57th Street between Ninth and Tenth Avenues; and **TravelInn** (695-7171, S$44/D$48-54), 515 West 42nd Street, near 11th Avenue.

East Side

Moderately priced: **Doral Inn** (755-1200, S$64-82/D$76-94), 49th Street at Lexington Avenue, large, residential and transient; **Beverly** (753-2700, S$69/D$79 up), 50th Street at Lexington Avenue, moderate sized, residential and transient; **Biltmore** (687-7000, S$75-100/D$89-115), 43rd Street and Madison Avenue, very large, partly commercial; **United Nations Plaza Hotel** (355-3400, S$115-135/D$135-155), **The Grand Hyatt New York**, (883-1234, S$115/D$140 up), adjacent to Grand Central Terminal; **Lexington** (755-4400, S$64.50/D$74.50), 48th Street and Lexington Avenue, large, residential and transient; **Roger Smith** (755-1400, S$49-65/D$61-77), 47th Street and Lexington Avenue, small, quiet, features suites; **Roosevelt** (661-9600, S$75-92/D$87-104), 45th Street and Madison Avenue, large, transient, commercial features; **George Washington** (475-1920, S$30-46/D$42.80 up), Lexington Avenue and 23rd Street; **Tudor** (986-8800, S$48-60/D$60 up), 304 East 42nd Street, very near the United Nations; and **Pickwick Arms** (355-0300, S$18-28/D$38/Studios $55 up), 230 East 51st Street.

Since 1886 the Statue of Liberty (by sculptor Frederic Auguste Bartholdi) has welcomed countless visitors and immigrants to the US shores.

Barclay Inter-Continental (755-5900, S$100/D$113), 111 East 48th Street, moderate sized, residential and transient; **Berkshire Palace** (753-5800, S$100-120/D$115-150), 52nd Street and Madison Avenue, moderate sized and luxurious; **Drake** (421-0900, S$85-145/D$100-160), 56th Street and Park Avenue, fairly large, centrally located, distinguished; **Gotham** (247-2200, rates unavailable), 55th Street and Fifth Avenue, convenient, newly renovated, residential and transient; **Park Lane Hotel** (371-4000, S$95-150/D$110-165), 36 Central Park South, luxurious; **Pierre** (838-8000, S$150/D$165 up), 61st Street and Fifth Avenue, smart and exclusive, multilingual staff and special facilities for foreign guests; the **Plaza** (759-3000, S$105-215/D$125-240), 59th Street and Fifth Avenue, famous for its regal Edwardian atmosphere and view of Central Park, pets allowed; **Regency** (759-4100, S$155/D$165), 61st Street and Park Avenue, new and elegant, pets allowed; **St. Regis-Sheraton** (753-4500, S$98-140/D$118-160), Fifth Avenue and 55th Street, large, residential and transient, convenient location; **Sherry Netherland** (355-2800, S/D$115-175), 781 Fifth Avenue, at 59th Street; **Sheraton-Russell** (685-7676, S$90-105/D$105-110), Park Avenue and 37th Street, convenient for shopping; **The Summit of New York** (752-7000, S$65-85/D$77-97), 51st Street and Lexington Avenue, multilingual staff; **Waldorf-Astoria** (355-3000, S$65-140/D$97-172), 50th Street and Park Avenue, world famous, extremely large, all facilities for banquets and balls, shops, pets allowed; **Westbury** (535-2000, S$115-135/D$130-150), 69th Street and Madison Avenue, residential and transient, quiet, dignified, group rates.

For Women Only

Allerton House (753-8841, S$20-30), 130 East 57th Street, transient and permanent; **Martha Washington** (689-1900, S$18 or with minimum stay of two weeks $84 p.w.), 30 East 30th Street, transient and permanent, in business district but quiet at night.

Queens

Howard Johnson Motor Lodge (659-6000, S$57/D$63) and **International Hotel** (995-9000, S$59/D$65), both provide free airport transportation; **Skyway Hotel** (659-6300, S$40/D$46), near Kennedy International Airport provides free airport transportation; **Holiday Inn** (995-5000, S$54/D$61), at 175-15 Rockaway Boulevard, provides free transportation to and from the airport. Other accommodations in Queens, convenient to the airports; **The Laguardia Marriott Hotel** (565-8900, S$75/D$85), 102-05 Ditmars Boulevard, East Elmhurst; **Midway Motor Hotel** (699-4400, S$55/D$63), 108-25 Horace Harding Expressway; **Sheraton Inn** (446-4800, S$77/D$87), at La Guardia, Grand Central Parkway; **Travelers Hotel** (335-1200, S$50/D$58), 9400 Ditmars Boulevard, Elmhurst.

Bronx

Town and Country Motor Lodge (994-9000, S$29/D$39.50), 2244 Tillotson Avenue, off New England Thruway at Exit 5.

Brooklyn

Golden Gate Motor Inn (743-4000, S$37-46/D$46-48), Belt Parkway at Exit number 9.

TRANSPORTATION

As in most big cities, it is very difficult to drive in New York; the streets are overcrowded and parking is hard to find. It is much easier to take the subway, taxis, or buses. Walking is better for sightseeing, particularly in the downtown area. If you are an enthusiastic cyclist, Manhattan is a biker's town.

The island of Manhattan is in the shape of a finger, about 13 miles long from north to south. Fifth Avenue is a dividing line running north-south, and addresses with "East" in them are to the east of it, addresses with "West" in them are west of it. In general, avenues run north to south and streets east to west. Addresses with odd numbers are on the north side of the street; those with even numbers are on the south side. South of 14th Street is the older part of the city; even the numbered streets do not always follow a regular pattern. Usually, even-numbered streets are for eastbound traffic; odd-numbered for westbound.

Buses: Most north-south avenues (uptown-downtown) and all principal east-west streets (crosstown) such as 14th, 23rd, 34th, 42nd, 49th, 50th and 57th Streets, have bus routes. You need exactly 60¢ in coins (no 50¢ pieces) and can purchase an add-a-ride for an additional 25¢, which will allow you to transfer from a crosstown bus to an uptown or downtown one, or vice versa. Special passes for senior citizens, available to New Yorkers, are not available to out-of-towners. Bus maps are available at the informations booths in Grand Central Terminal and Penn Station. The Transit Authority operates two special touring "Bus Loops," $1.75 on Saturdays, Sundays, and holidays. Loop 1, number M41, covers 22 stops at points of interest. Loop 2, number B88, stops at 29 points in Brooklyn and lower Manhattan. After paying your initial fare you can get on and off as often as and wherever you like.

Subways: These are fast, efficient, crowded, and noisy. Subway maps are available at hotels and newsstands and generally at subway token booths at stations. Try to plot your route beforehand. Try to avoid the subways during the rush hours, 7:30-9:30am and 4:40-6:30pm; you will be better off. The **JFK express**, which leaves from mid-town 6am-10pm every 20 minutes on the Avenue of Americas (6th Avenue) express line, connects to a bus that goes to JFK terminals; cost is $4.

Taxis: Fare starts at $1.00 and costs 10¢ for each additional ⅒th mile. The charge chart is displayed on the taxi door. Most taxis accommodate four passengers. Checker cabs will accommodate five. For fares of $5 or more the usual tip is 20%. New York taxicab drivers are famous as conversationalists and can be good sources of miscellaneous information. It is recommended for distance trips to inquire about approximate cost before hiring the taxi.

RESTAURANTS

New York is one of the great restaurant cities of the world, with approximately 10,000 restaurants from which to choose. The cuisines of all nations in all price ranges are well represented. The better known and more expensive restaurants require reservations. New Yorkers tend to eat dinner between 8-10pm, but night owls will find plenty of choices for later dining. Should you be going to the theater, plan to have dinner after the performance and allow ample travel time, because traffic is heavy at theater hours (7:30 and around 11).

In the following list, "reasonable" means $10-15 or less per person for dinner without drinks or tips; "moderate" means from $15-25; "expensive" means $30 per person and up. New York restaurants very quickly open and close, are in vogue and out, and change owners and prices, so this list offers, primarily, just a sampling of the rather awe-inspiring choice available. The yellow pages of the telephone book list many other restaurants by nationality and type of cuisine. Most hotels have inexpensive coffee shops and moderately-priced restaurants.

American Restaurants

Billy's, Coach House, Paul Revere's Tavern & Chop House, Red Coach Grill; moderate to expensive; Mayfair, The Boss, and Steak and Brew restaurants; reasonable. Gage and Tollner, in Brooklyn; reasonable.

Snack Bars

Chock Full 'o Nuts, McDonald's, Burger King, Nedicks, Prexy's, Zum Zum, all at several locations; inexpensive.

Pastry Shops

Cake Masters, Fay & Allen's, Ferrara's, Délices de la Côte Basque, La Bakery, Hungarian Pastry Shop; international pastries and coffee or tea, inexpensive.

Meals with A View

Act I, Rainbow Room, Stouffer's Top-of-the Six's, Top of the Park; moderate to expensive. Windows on the World (World Trade Center); recently refurbished Tavern-on-the-Green, where the view from the Crystal Room is a delight year round; River Café, which, located under Brooklyn Bridge, offers wonderful view of Manhattan's skyline; expensive.

Seafood

Paddy's Clam House, Gloucester House, Grand Central Oyster Bar, Joe's Pier 52, Sea-Fare-of-the-Aegean; moderate to expensive.

Steaks

Beefsteak Charlie's, The Cattleman, Christ Cella, Cristo Steak House, Gallagher's Steak House, Old Homestead, Pen and Pencil, Peter's Backyard, O. Henry's, the Palm, and US Steakhouse; expensive.

Health Food

Brownies, Great American Health Bar, Health Works; reasonable.

Theatrical Atmosphere

Backstage, Downey's, Mildred Pierce, Sardi's, Stage Delicatessen and Restaurant; moderate to expensive.

Elaborate Decor and Menu

The Box Tree (intimate, seats only 23); Four Seasons; Lutèce (one of the best restaurants for *haute cuisine* in the US); La Caravelle (one of Lutèce's closest rivals); The Palace (the most expensive restaurant in the US); Le Périgord and Périgord East, and "21 Club."

RESTAURANTS BY NATIONALITY

Brazilian

Brazilian Coffee Restaurant, Brazilian Pavilion, reasonable to moderate.

British

Bull and Bear, Billymunk, Charlie Brown's, Cheshire Cheese; moderate to expensive.

Chinese

Gold Coin, Mandarin House, Shangri-La, Shun Lee Dynasty, Sun Luck (several locations), Pearl's; moderate. Nom Wah Tea Parlor, Wah Kee, all in Chinatown; reasonable.

Czechoslovakian

Czech Pavilion (winter garden), Ruc (garden-dining in summer), Vasata; moderate.

French

Brittany du Soir, Café Brittany, Larré's, Pierre Au Tunnel, Au Steak Pommes Frites; reasonable. A La Fourchette, Brussels, Café de France, Café Argenteuil, Chez Napoleon, Clos Normand, Du Midi, La Cocotte, Le Cygne, La Mangeoire, La Petite Marmite, Le Chanteclair, Le Moal, Les Pyrénées, Le Veau d'Or; moderate to expensive. La Côte Basque, Le Manoir, Le Périgord; expensive. La Caravelle, La Grenouille, Lutèce, Quo Vadis; very expensive.

German

Heidelberg, Kleine Konditorei, Luchow's, Café Geiger; moderate.

Greek

Pantheon; moderate. Molfetas; reasonable.

Hungarian

Bristol, Paprika, Tik Tak; moderate. Budapest; reasonable.

Indian-Pakistani

Ceylon Indian Inn, Kashmir, Pak-India Curry House, Shalimar, Shezan; reasonable.

Italian

Trattoria da Alfredo, Antica Roma, Gene's, Giambelli, La Scala, Mamma Leone's, Piccolo Mondo, Trattoria, street level of Pan Am Building; moderate. Isle of Capri, La Luna, Eduardo's, Rocco's; reasonable. Barbetta, Giambelli 50th, Giovanni, La Fortuna, Mercurio, Orsini's, Pietro's, Romeo Salta, Vesuvio; expensive.

Japanese

Benihana East, Benihana of Tokyo, Nippon, Saito; moderate. Suehiro; reasonable.

Kosher

Lou G. Siegel (meat), Gross Dairy & Vegetarian, Moishe Peking (kosher Chinese); moderate.

Middle Eastern

Ararat, Balkan, Cedars of Lebanon, Dardanelles, Keneret, Topkapi Palace; moderate.

Philippine

The Philippine Garden; moderate.

Russian

Russian Tea Room; moderate. Russian Bear; expensive.

Scandinavian

Copenhagen; moderate.

Spanish, Latin American and Mexican

Castilian Room, El Faro, El Parador, Victor's; Zapata; moderate.

Swiss

Chalet Suisse, Swiss Center restaurants; moderate.

ENTERTAINMENT

In places which have dancing or entertainment, there is often a "minimum" charge. This is a fixed bill for drinks that must be paid—even if you don't drink. Sometimes there is also a "cover" charge, or an admission fee.

Dinner and Dancing

Carlyle Café, Café at the Pierre Hotel; the Plaza Hotel's **Persian Room; Rainbow Grill,** with a view of the skyline. These rooms often feature well-known entertainers; smart and expensive.

Discothèques

New York New York, Les Mouches, Régine's, Mudd's for the dedicated dancers. **Hippopotamus,** Moroccan setting, ample menu; elegant setting, fine food. **Thursdays,** has dancing to records downstairs; moderately expensive.

Jazz, Rock and Guitar

Half Note, top jazz stars featured; **Hors d'Oeuvrerie** (World Trade Center) jazz every evening; **Jimmy Ryan's,** Dixieland; expensive. **Jimmy Weston's; Lone Star Café** (country and western); **The Cookery, Village Gate, Village Vanguard, West Boondock;** reasonable to moderate.

International Atmosphere: Chateau Madrid, Latin entertainment; **Asti,** continental dining to operatic arias; **La Chansonnette,** French cooking and continental songs; **Mykonos,** Greek dancing; **Adonis,** Aegean scenery, song, dance, and bouzouki.

Restaurant-bars: Along First, Second, and Third Avenues, between 60th and 86th Streets, there are well over a hundred bars. Many serve giant hamburgers and other simple dishes; a few serve more elaborate and expensive meals. Some are "in," with lines of young people waiting to enter. The popularity ratings change constantly; but when a bar becomes unpopular, it doesn't take long to get a new owner, a new decor, and a new name. Many of the names are deliberately droll. **Daly's Dandelion, Maxwell's Plum, Adam's Apple, Friday's, Ma Bell's** and many more.

Other restaurant-bars in nearby neighborhoods, each with a large and interesting clientele, especially late in the evening, include **Elaine's; P. J. Clarke's; Michael's Pub; McSorley's,** in Greenwich Village; **The Ginger Man,** near Lincoln Center, and **Four Seasons Bar.** The **Oak Bar** in the Plaza Hotel, and **Charlie Brown's** in the Pan Am Building, are all popular drinking spots for the business crowd.

Also recommended and serving food and drinks: **Charley O's,** at Rockefeller Center, an attractive place to go at night; **Brasserie,** a popular medium-priced restaurant which never closes, especially popular in the early hours for all kinds of egg dishes; and the lobby of the **Algonquin Hotel,** intimate, popular for decades with writers and publishers, frequented after the theater.

ARTS AND MUSIC

New York is one of the world's major cultural centers. In addition to the museums listed below, there are always exhibits in privately owned galleries, where visitors are welcome, and other events of special interest. These are usually described in the art and music sections of the daily and Sunday newspapers, particularly the *NY Times,* and in such magazines as *Cue-New York* and *The New Yorker*. Consult them, also, for admission fees, if any.

Museums: An enormous collection of plant and animal life is at the **American Museum of Natural History,** 79th Street & Central Park West; open Monday-Saturday 10-4:45, Sundays and holidays 11-5. In the **Hayden Planetarium,** a part of the museum, afternoon lectures and programs are held. **American Numismatic Society,** Broadway & 155 Street; rare and unusual coins and medals; open Tuesday through Saturday 9-4:30. Also see: **Brooklyn Museum,** Washington Avenue & Eastern Parkway, Brooklyn; large general exhibit; open Wednesday to Saturday 10-5, Sunday 11-5, and holidays 1-5. **Cloisters, Fort Tyron Park;** priceless European medieval art in an exquisite setting on the Hudson; open daily except Monday 10-4:45, Sunday 12-4:45, May through September, other months 1-4:45. **Cooper-Hewitt Museum** (Smithsonian Institution's National Museum of Design), 2 East 91st Street; open Tuesday 10-9, Wednesday through Saturday 10-5, Sunday 12-5. **Federal Hall National Memorial,** Wall and Nassau Streets. **Frick Collection,** 70th Street & Fifth Avenue; outstanding art treasures in a beautiful building; chamber music concerts in autumn; open Sunday 1-6, Wednesday to Saturday 10-6; closed holidays; no children under 10 admitted. **Jewish Museum,** 92nd Street & Fifth Avenue, interesting displays of Jewish religious art and antiquities; open Monday to Thursday 12-5, closed Saturdays and Sundays, Jewish and other holidays. **Library-Museum of the Performing Arts,** Lincoln Center, Broadway; open daily 10-4. **Metropolitan Museum of Art,** 82nd Street & Fifth Avenue; one of the great art museums of the world; open Tuesday 10-8:45; Wednesday through Saturday 10-4:45; Sundays and holidays 11-4:45. **Pierpont Morgan Library,** 29 East 36th Street; special exhibits Tuesday-Saturday 10:30-5; Sunday 1-5. **Museum of the American Indian,** 155th Street & Broadway; Indian art of the Western Hemisphere; open Tuesday to Saturday 10-5, Sunday 1-5, closed holidays and during August. **Museum of Modern Art,** 11 West 53rd Street; outstanding collection of modern art in all forms both permanent and special exhibits, beautiful sculpture garden and café, avant garde films, interior designer collection, bookshop featuring the latest museum publications; outdoor jazz concerts in summer; open Monday, Tuesday, Friday, Saturday, and Sunday 11-6, Thursday 11-9, closed Wednesday. **Museum of the City of New York,** 103rd Street & Fifth Avenue; from Indian days to the present in displays and mementos; open Tuesday to Saturday 10-5, Sunday and holidays 1-5. **Museum of Early American Folk Art,** 49 West 53rd Street; changing displays of modern art of all kinds; Tuesday through Sunday 10:30-5:30, Thursday 10:30-8; **New-York Historical Society Museum,** 77th Street & Central Park West; open Tuesday to Friday and Sunday 1-5, Saturday 10-5, closed holidays. **New York Jazz Museum,** 125 W. 55 Street; presents an audio-visual display of jazz history. **Solomon R. Guggenheim Museum,** designed by Frank Lloyd Wright, 88th Street & Fifth Avenue, modern art, permanent and loan exhibitions; open Tuesday 11-8, Wednesday to Sunday 11-5, closed Monday. **South Street Seaport Museum,** 16 Fulton Street; maritime history and seven old sailing

vessels open for inspection. **Spanish Museum, Hispanic Society,** 155th
Street & Broadway; Spanish art; open Tuesday to Saturday 10-4:30, Sunday 2-5. **Studio Museum in Harlem,** 2033 Fifth Avenue (125th Street);
all kinds of African art objects and musical instruments; closed Monday,
open Wednesday 10-9. Tuesday, Thursday and Friday 10-6, Saturday
and Sunday 1-6. **Whitney Museum,** 945 Madison Avenue, contemporary
American art in a futuristic granite building; open Tuesday-Friday 1-8,
Saturday and Sunday 12-6. **International Center of Photography,** Fifth
Avenue at 94th Street, open daily except Monday 11-5.

New York City is also the music center of the United States, and there
are several concerts every day even during the summer. For details
consult the music pages of the *NY Times, Cue-New York,* and *The New
Yorker.* The **New York Philharmonic** is world-renowned and performs
in **Avery Fisher Hall** in Lincoln Center. The **Metropolitan Opera Company** in Lincoln Center presents a full program from September until
Spring. Principal concert halls include the **Brooklyn Academy of Music,
Carnegie Hall, McMillin Theater,** Columbia University, and **Town Hall.**
During the summer there are outdoor concerts in **Central Park** both
on the Mall and on the **Sheep Meadow.** Leading ballet and dance companies perform at different theaters during the winter season. The **New
York State Theater** of Lincoln Center and the **New York City Center**
present opera, ballet, and other musical performances. **The Cathedral
of St John the Divine; St Bartholomews' Fifth Avenue; the Riverside
Church; St Patrick's Cathedral,** and **Temple Emanuel** all offer fine programs of ecclesiastical music.

THEATERS

Getting seats for the hit shows on short notice can be difficult; first try
the box office of the theater. You'll find the shows listed in the newspapers, *The New Yorker,* and *Cue-New York.* "Twofers" are specially priced
pairs of tickets, available at the New York Convention and Visitors
Bureau at 2 Columbus Circle; and at the Visitors Information Bureau
on Times Square discount tickets are sold. In addition you may purchase theater tickets for half price plus a small service charge at Duffy
Square only on the same day of the performance daily between the
hours of 3-8 pm for the evening performance, Wednesday and Saturday between noon and 2 for matinées, and Sunday between noon and
closing time for all performances. If a show is "sold out," try a theater ticker broker; he sells tickets at list prices plus a service charge
for each ticket. If you know what shows you want to see before you
come to New York, write in advance to the theater's box office, offering
at least three choices of dates. Enclose your check or money order and
a self-addressed stamped envelope. Concert tickets for Avery Fisher Hall
are sold at Bloomingdale's at no extra charge. Also Ticketron locations
at the Pan Am Building, Madison Square Garden, World Trade Center, Macy's Department Store, 329 Sixth Avenue in the Village, and 120-
125 Street sell theater, sport, and concert tickets with a nominal service
charge added. The Off-Broadway and Off-Off Broadway theater move-

ments have grown tremendously and offer easy-to-obtain seats at generally low prices. They often have Sunday performances, too.

TELEVISION

Free tickets to shows can be obtained from the broadcasting companies. Write as far in advance as possible. The New York Convention and Visitors Bureau and hotels usually have some TV show tickets on a daily basis only, which they give to guests without charge. The local stations are: Channel 2—WCBS-TV, Columbia Broadcasting System; Channel 4—WNBC-TV, National Broadcasting Company; Channel 5—WNEW-TV, Metromedia Inc; Channel 7—WABC-TV, American Broadcasting Company; Channel 9—WOR-TV, Mutual Broadcasting Company; Channel 11—WPIX, independent; Channel 13—WNET-TV, a Public Broadcasting Service station.

SHOPPING

The principal retail shopping district extends from 34th to 59th Streets in Manhattan. The big department stores, **Macy's** and **Gimbels,** are in the lower west side of this district, and **Bloomingdale's** is in the upper east side. In between run Fifth and Madison Avenues, the shopper and window shopper's heaven. Along Fifth can be found **B. Altman, Lord & Taylor** and **Saks Fifth Avenue.** Discount department stores include **Alexander's** and **Ohrbach's.** Such Fifth Avenue stores as **Bergdorf Goodman, Henri Bendel, Saks Fifth Avenue,** and **Ted Lapidus** specialize in quality apparel for men, women, and children. Stores for young women's fashions include **Paraphernalia** (several locations). Popular-priced men's clothes at **Wallach's, Roger Kent,** and **Mern's. Barney's** has 9 floors and over 60,000 men's suits in all styles and prices. More expensive men's furnishings are to be had at **Tripler's, Brooks Brothers, A. Sulka, Chipp, J. Press,** and **Paul Stuart.** Also expensive but specializing in European imports are **Saint-Germain, Pierre Balmain,** and **De Noyer,** among others. For hip young things **Betsey Bunky & Nini, Courrèges, Honeybee,** and **Laura Ashley. F.A.O. Schwarz** is famous for toys and **Hammacher-Schlemmer** is unique for housewares and unusual gadgets. Fine leather goods can be found at **Mark Cross** and **Gucci.** The largest selections of cameras and photographic equipment is at the **Willoughby Peerless Store.** For records, sheet music, and related equipment, **Sam Goody's, The Record Hunter, G. Schirmer, Liberty Music Shops** are among the outstanding stores. Among the larger bookshops are **Barnes & Noble, B. Dalton's, Brentano's, Schibner's,** and **Doubleday; Rizzoli** specializes in European publications. For business and professional books, try the **McGraw-Hill Book Store.** Among the best stores for jewelry, watches, silver, fine china, and glassware are **Tiffany's, Cartier's, Van Cleef and Arpels, Steuben Glass,** and **H. Stern.**

Imported or specialized merchandise may be obtained in many of the large department stores or at the following shops: **America House,** artistic American handicrafts; **Bazaar Français,** imported kitchen articles; **Conran's,** in the Citicorp Building, European imports; **Sweden House** and **Norsk,** Scandinavian arts and crafts; **The Irish Pavilion,** handkerchiefs, china, and books; **Pan American Shop,** Latin-American decorative objects; **Pottery Barn** for pottery and glassware; **Scottish Products,** Scottish delicacies and woolens; **Azuma,** Japanese items; and **UN Gift Shop,** articles from around the world.

There probably isn't a city in the world where you can buy as many different things, spend as much money, and indulge yourself as much as you can in New York. But sometimes a wealth of choice can be very confusing. There are certain districts that specialize in particular merchandise. **Antiques:** mostly along Second and Third Avenues, from about 47th Street to 57th Street; also in Greenwich Village and the lower east side. **Auctions:** outstanding are **Sotheby Parke Bernet, Christie's,** and **Plaza Art Galleries;** see newspapers for others. **Automobiles:** Broadway in the upper 50s, Park Avenue from 47th Street to 60th Street. **Books:** scattered throughout the city; used books may be found on East 60th Street and on Fourth Avenue from Astor Place to 11th Street. **Brass and Copper:** mostly on the west side of Allen Street. **Women's Clothes:** for expensive shopping, shops on Madison and Fifth Avenues; for less expensive clothes, the West 34th Street district, with popular-priced shopping at **Macy's, Gimbels,** and **Ohrbach's;** for economy shopping, the 14th Street district, and the lower East side, south of Houston Street, closed Saturdays but open Sundays. **Food, Retail:** all over the city; some interesting foreign nationality shops on Ninth Avenue from 38th Street to 42nd Street. **Flower Markets:** concentrated around 28th Street & Sixth Avenue; many of these will sell retail. **Jewelry:** on West 47th Street from Fifth Avenue to Sixth Avenue; if you know values and prices, you can often do well; the **Diamond Center** is here as well as on the lower east side. **Linens:** mostly on Grand Street on the lower east side, if you're looking for bargains; higher-priced merchandise in the department stores, but beware of small linen shops "selling out"! **Machinery:** mostly on Centre Street, north of Canal Street. **Silverware:** two areas, one on Lexington Avenue between 56th Street and 58th Street, the other on Nassau Street.

For further listings and addresses, see the yellow pages of the telephone book and the **New York Convention and Visitors Bureau** at 2 Columbus Circle.

FOREIGN BANKS

Countries maintaining banking facilities in New York City include the following (see also under "Banks" in the Manhattan Yellow Pages): Australia, Belgium, Brazil, Canada, Ecuador, France, Great Britain, Greece, Hong Kong, India, Indonesia, Israel, Italy, Japan, Korea, Mexico, Netherlands, Pakistan, Philippines, Puerto Rico, South Africa, Switzerland, Thailand, Venezuela, and Yugoslavia.

SPORTS

New York has two professional baseball teams: the **New York Mets** of the National League play at **Shea Stadium** near Flushing Meadow Park, and the **New York Yankees** of the American League play their games in **Yankee Stadium.** The season is April through September; games start at 1pm or later, depending on the schedule. Times for both day and night games under artificial lights can be found in local papers the day before. Double-headers, two games for the price of one, are usually scheduled on Sunday; details appear in the newspapers several days in advance. **Columbia University Lions** play collegiate football at **Baker Field;** the nearest other important college football games are played by Yale at New Haven, Connecticut; Princeton University, Princeton, New Jersey and by the University of Pennsylvania in Philadelphia. The **New York Giants** play at **Giants Stadium,** Meadowlands, New Jersey, while the **Jets** play at **Shea Stadium,** Flushing Meadow Park. The **New York Cosmos,** champions of the North American Soccer League, play from mid-April through August at Giants Stadium, Meadowlands, New Jersey. Call the North American Soccer League, 575-0066, for up-to-date soccer information. Both college and professional basketball games may be seen, October through March, particularly at **Madison Square Garden,** which is "home" for the **New York Knicks** of the National Basketball Association. The **New York Nets,** now with the National Basketball Association, play at Rutgers in Piscataway, New Jersey. The **New York Stars,** a women's professional basketball team, have played their games at the Forum in Madison Square Garden. Ice hockey matches are played by the **New York Rangers,** at Madison Square Garden; and by the **New York Islanders,** at Nassau Coliseum, on Long Island, October to April. Horse racing, including trotting racing, is held in New York and vicinity year-round. When **Belmont Park** and the **Aqueduct Track,** which are fairly close to the city, close down, racing is held at **Saratoga** during the month of August and at **Meadowland Race Track,** (trotting January-August and thoroughbred September-January) and **Monmouth** in nearby New Jersey. Trotting races take place at **Roosevelt Raceway** and **Yonkers Raceway** year-round except for 2 weeks at the Christmas season. Pari-mutuel betting is permitted at race tracks and at many locations throughout New York State through off-track betting (OBT). Championship tennis matches are played at the **West Side Tennis Club** in Forest Hills. In the course of the year, it is possible to attend boxing and wrestling contests, track events, and practically every other conceivable sporting event. The sports pages of the newspapers carry all current listings and advertisements.

A wide choice of recreational facilities are available in the New York area. Archery, baseball, swimming, bicycling, boating, cricket, fishing, including deep-sea fishing in **Sheepshead Bay,** football, golf, hockey, horseback riding, ice skating, running, skiing, soccer, and tennis are available, either free or at a moderate cost, through New York's Department of Parks. For a complete list of facilities or additional information, write for a copy of *Recreational Facilities for New Yorkers* to the Department of Parks, Arsenal Building, 64th Street & Fifth Avenue, New York City 10021. There are also numerous private country clubs in and around the city.

WHAT TO DO ON A SUNDAY IN NEW YORK

Being alone in an unfamiliar city on a Sunday can be a dull prospect. But, if you know where to go, that is anything but true in New York City. Late Saturday night, pick up a Sunday newspaper, particularly the *New York Times*, or pick up a magazine during the week, particularly *The New Yorker* or *Cue-New York*, all of which are valuable guides to amusements and special events. Go through the theater sections; many legitimate theaters, especially Off-Broadway, give performances on Sundays, often the easiest days to get tickets.

Sunday, for hard-working New Yorkers, is traditionally the day for "brunch." A clever invention of the late-sleeper, this meal combines breakfast and lunch, and is normally a drawn-out affair, liberally washed down with "Bloody Marys" (an invigorating mixture of tomato juice, vodka and Worcestershire sauce). The **Brasserie, Inn on the Park** (if it's a sunny day), the Plaza's **Palm Court, Thursday's,** and most large hotels take an elegant and expensive approach to brunch; the little restaurant-bars on the upper east and west side are less formal and more convivial. Brunch and later Tea Dancing (beginning 4pm every Sunday) in World Trade Center **Windows on the World Restaurants.**

If you'd like to attend church, look in the Manhattan Yellow Pages telephone directory. Many services are conducted in foreign languages.

Sunday is a good day for a visit to the **Hayden Planetarium,** 81st Street & Central Park West, where you can see an extremely interesting show for $2.75 adults, $1.75 for students and senior citizens, and $1.35 for children 12 and under. Adjacent to the Planetarium and in the same park area is the **American Museum of Natural History,** which has many fine exhibits and lectures, movies, and special shows. There is a little shop in the museum that sells various novelties such as bird's eggs, sea shells, and all sorts of gifts that delight children.

A ride down **Fifth Avenue** on a bus, a ride to **Staten Island** on the ferry, or a walk through the windy corridors of **Wall Street** are specially pleasant on a Sunday, without weekday crowds.

If the weather is good, take a walk down Fifth Avenue or through **Central Park;** just follow the crowds. There will be lots of people, activity, languages, unusual clothes—and dogs of every shape and size. Central park and especially the **Bethesda Fountain** area on a Sunday afternoon are an experience you will not forget. If you prefer not to walk, take any southbound Fifth Avenue bus to 65th Street. New York's **Central Park Zoo** and **Children's Zoo,** a fascinating place to wander through. Ask the attendant about the feeding times of the various animals and join the crowd as it goes from cage to cage. There is a cafeteria where refreshments may be eaten outdoors in good weather. In winter, ice skating in **Rockefeller Center** (rental skates available). Any Sunday in **Central Park,** a ride in horse-drawn carriage through the park.

Famous old films are shown daily (except Wednesday) at the **Museum of Modern Art** on 53rd Street, west of Fifth Avenue. The admission charge of $2.50 for an adult and 75¢ for a child or senior citizen includes the exhibit of modern art and the motion picture.

CALENDAR OF EVENTS

In New York City there probably isn't a day in the year without a dozen or more important and interesting events. The New York Convention and Visitors Bureau, 2 Columbus Circle, issues a quarterly calendar which will be sent to you without charge. The following are typical of the various annual events.

January: Chinese New Year's Festival, Motor Boat Show, opening of thoroughbred racing season.

February: Track Meets, Sportsmen's Show, Westminster Kennel Club Dog Show.

March: St Patrick's Day Parade, Track Meets, Basketball Playoffs.

April: Opening of the professional baseball season, Easter Sunday Fashion Parade, beginning of the circus season.

May: May Day Parades, Outdoor Art Exhibits in Greenwich Village.

June to September: "New York is a Summer Festival Season"; events include outdoor concerts, free Shakespearean performances in Central Park, fireworks displays, outdoor art exhibits, special musical, theatrical, and sports events.

September: Labor Day events, opening of the Metropolitan Opera season.

October: Philharmonic Orchestra season opening.

November: Various flower shows and exhibits, Thanksgiving Day Parade.

December: Christmas celebrations, displays at Rockefeller Center. For details of free programs in parks, museums, libraries, and streets throughout the five boroughs, both indoors and outdoors, call Parks Department information, 472-1003, 10-6 seven days a week.

WHERE TO GO NEARBY

Long Island, stretching 120 miles east by northeast, into the Atlantic Ocean, is known for its fine beaches along its southern shore. **Jones Beach,** nearest the city, **Fire Island,** a ferry-ride off-shore along the barrier beach, and **Montauk,** at the tip end, are among the best. **Southampton** and **East Hampton** are the poshest of the resort towns, as rural in winter as they are sophisticated in summer. Bathing along the nearby **New Jersey** shore is also recommended for a day's fun or a longer vacation. For additional information, consult the travel sections in the Sunday editions of the newspapers.

Coney Island, in Brooklyn, is a large seaside amusement park.

NIAGARA

The westernmost part of the state, the Niagara Frontier features **Niagara Falls,** one of the world's natural wonders, and the historically-significant city of Buffalo. The region has a history which goes back to the time of the pharaohs. Topographically the area ranges from the sandy beaches of two of the Great Lakes to wooded hills rising 2,500 feet. Pottery discovered along the Niagara River Gorge outside Niagara Falls has been traced to Indian burial mounds dating back to about 160 AD. Other evidence points to primitive but thriving Indian cultures in the area dating back more than 4,000 years. The French explorer LaSalle rode down the Niagara River in a canoe in 1628, setting the stage for lucrative fur trading posts run by French trappers. The then Village of Buffalo was raided and burned to the ground by the British during the War of 1812. The area's prosperity was assured when Buffalo became the western terminal of Governor DeWitt Clinton's "Big Ditch"—the famed Erie Canal, in 1825. The first lighthouse on Lake Erie began operating in Buffalo in 1833 and by 1850 the "Queen City of the Great Lakes" was the nation's leading milling center. The Niagara River and the Great Lakes Erie and Ontario separate Canada (Toronto is a 2½-hour ride north from Buffalo) and Western New York, which today is a mixture of industrial communities and vacation spots catering to everything from water sports and fishing to skiing. Via two main cataracts plunging some 194 feet across a 3,500 foot spread over the Niagara River, the falls empties the overflow of Lakes Superior, Huron, Michigan, and Erie into Lake Ontario. The river drops more than 326 feet along its 36 mile course to the falls where the water plunges into the gorge below at a rate of about 748,000 gallons per second, making the falls a significant source of cheap hydroelectric power now utilized by communities across the state via a massive power grid. Were it not for the massive hydroelectric power complex feeding off its flow, the falls would have a flow of about 1,500,000 gallons per second.

WHAT TO SEE

Goat Island, surrounded by the Niagara River and separating the American and Canadian Falls, is easily accessible by foot or vehicular bridges and provides spectacular views from the edges of both falls. Originally called Iris Island, Goat Island was renamed after an early settler named John Stedman put a herd of goats on the island to protect them from wolves and bears. Except for one tough old Billy goat, the Stedman herd died during a severe winter. A third cataract is formed by a water current between Goat Island and the adjoining **Luna Island. The Cave of the Winds tour** on Goat Island follows wooden walkways to within 25 feet of the base of the falls. The Cave Tour (approximately $3.50 for adults and $2.25 for ages 6-11) runs daily 10am to 8pm from late June to Labor Day and from 10am to 5pm 1 May to late June and again from Labor Day to mid-October. Niagara Viewmobile sightseeing trains may be boarded at four locations on Goat Island and at Prospect Point near the Observation Tower for a 30-minute tour of the falls. The 282 foot Observation Tower stands at the base of the American Falls in Prospect Park and rises 100 feet above the cliffs. A superb view of the falls is available from its upper decks and two elevators descend into the gorge where the **Maid-of-the-Mist** boats dock. The boats, which also depart from docks on the Canadian side, ride to the base of the falls. Boats depart every 15 minutes 9am to 8pm 24 June-4 September; Monday-Friday 10-5, Saturday, Sunday and holidays 10-6 mid-May to 23 June and 5 September to 15 October. Waterproof clothing is included in the $3.25 adult fare, $1.75 for children 6-12. Near the falls, popular spots include the **Power Vista** (tel: 285-3211, 4½ miles north of the falls among SR 104) where the observation and information building of the Niagara Power Project offers a free and spectacular view of the river and gorge below. **The Schoellkopf Geological Museum** (tel: 287-1780, ¼ mile north of the Rainbow Bridge off Main Street) tells a fascinating 500-million-year-old story of the region's geology. **The Aquarium of Niagara Falls** (tel: 285-3575, Whirlpool Street at Pine Avenue) was the world's first inland oceanarium. It houses more than 2,000 specimens. **The Winter Gardens,** downtown on Rainbow Boulevard, is an admission-free glass-enclosed garden featuring more than 7,000 tropical and semi-tropical plants and trees. The adventurous and physically fit can walk down a path at **Devil's Hole State Park** 1 mile north of the falls and reach the bottom of the Niagara Gorge. **Whirlpool State Park,** 109 acres on a bluff overlooking the famous whirlpool which results from the Niagara River making a 90-degree turn, offers free picnicking facilities. Fast becoming an internationally-known summer center for the performing arts, **Artpark,** located several minutes from Niagara Falls north in Lewiston, offers a wide range of summer arts and musical entertainment on a 200-acre state park site at the foot of the Niagara Gorge rapids (tel: 694-8191 during the summer and tel: 745-3377 the rest of the year). Artpark offers outdoor programs, fishing and picnic areas and a 2,400-seat auditorium which annually attracts some of the world's top performers in the fields of opera, ballet, theater and popular and classical music each summer. Nearby are **Our Lady of Fatima Shrine** (754-7489) and **Old Fort Niagara** (745-7611) in Youngstown off SR 18F, built by the French in 1726. **The Niagara Falls International Convention Center** (278-8066) offers year-round entertainment. For further information contact the Niagara Falls Convention and Visitors Bureau, Niagara Falls, N.Y. 14303.

ACCOMMODATIONS

Castle Motor Inn (297-3730, D$28-32); **Driftwood Motel** (692-6650, S$12/D$14-28); **Henwood's Motel** (297-2660, D$18-24); **Holiday Inn** (285-2521, S$30-57/D$35-62); **Howard Johnson Motor Lodge** (285-5261, S$25-45/D$30-55); **John's Flaming Hearth Motor Inn** (284-8801, S$24-34/D$30-48); **John's Niagara Hotel** (285-9321, S$24-34/D$30-48); **Niagara Hilton** (285-3361, S$30-60/D$42-77); **Parkway Ramada Inn** (285-2541, S$25-56/D$32-56); **Quality Inn** (297-5050, S$27-29/D$29-41); **Sands Motel** (297-3797, D$14-30); **TraveLodge** (285-7316, D$26-46).

RESTAURANTS

Moderate to expensive: **The Alps, Clarkson House** (a Lewiston landmark), **Como Granato's, John's Flaming Hearth, Red Coach Inn, Speakeasy, Tenderloin, Niagara Hilton** restaurant, **Riverside Inn** (Lewiston).

WHERE TO GO NEARBY

A short drive east from Niagara Falls is the **City of Lockport,** site of the world's first "high school," the **Union School** built in the 1850s. Tours of the old Erie Canal are conducted daily from the heart of the city. A 10-minute drive between Niagara Falls and Buffalo takes vacationers across **Grand Island,** the world's largest freshwater island. **Grand Island Holiday Inn** (773-1111, S$32-53/D$41-58).

In **Buffalo** places to visit include the progressive **Albright-Knox Gallery** of avant-garde modern art, open Tuesday to Saturday 10-5, Sunday 12-6, donations; **Buffalo and Erie County Historical Society,** exhibits covering military exploits and Indian lore, Monday to Friday 10-5, Saturday and Sunday noon to 5, free; **Buffalo Zoological Gardens,** 1,200 animals in barless exhibits, daily, summer 10am-7pm, rest of year to 6; and **Old Fort Erie,** restored star-shaped fort prominent in War of 1812, open mid-May to mid-June 10-6. Sightseeing yachts also offer cruises of Buffalo Harbor and the Niagara River.

ROCHESTER

Rochester is in northwestern New York State, on the **Genesee River,** (which has three falls within the city) and on Lake Ontario. New York City is 363 miles southeast. To the southeast is the **Finger Lakes** region, 9,000 square miles of recreation area, including six major lakes and 18 state parks that provide fishing, boating, and swimming during the summer.

Although there were earlier settlers, credit for the founding of Rochester is usually given to Nathaniel Rochester and two associates who purchased the land in 1803. With the coming of the Erie Canal, Rochester became known as the "Flour City," because the flour milled here was easily shipped to large markets. The name was later changed to "Flower City" because of its many parks.

Rochester is also known as the "photo capital of the world" because of the presence of Xerox, Kodak, and Bausch and Lomb, and is furthermore noted as a precision-industry city and as a graphic arts and a music center. The population is 262,800.

WHAT TO SEE

The **University of Rochester** campus; the handsome **Midtown Plaza,** 7½ acres of business firms under one roof, including a covered shopping mall which is unique for its "Clock of the Nations" puppet and musical show every half hour. The **Lincoln First** highrise office complex with its underground concourse and enclosed walkways to downtown, and **First Federal Plaza,** another highrise complex upon which revolves New York State's only revolving restaurant, the **Changing Scene.** The **Susan B. Anthony House** which contains the furnishings and mementos of the 19th-century feminist; and is open Wednesday-Saturday. The **Rochester Historical Society Museum** has local historical exhibits; and is open Monday to Saturday. The **Rochester Institute of Technology** which has exhibitions of student arts and crafts. Among numerous parks, **Highland** is memorable for the world's largest lilac display, and the **Durand-Eastman** has the country's largest collection of pine tree species. At **Lollypop Farm,** on the Pittsford-Palmyra Road, children can meet friendly animals.

ACCOMMODATIONS

Americana of Rochester (546-3300, S$42-48/D$45-51); **Holiday Inn Downtown** (546-6400, S$35-37/$41-45); **Best Western One Eleven East Avenue** (232-1700, S$29/D$35); and **Rochester TraveLodge** (454-3550, S$26/D$28-37). Near West Henrietta Road, off Exit 46 from New York State Thruway: **Best Western Highlander Motor Inn** (334-1230, S$24-26/D$26-38); and **Howard Johnson Motor Lodge** (475-1661, S$29.50-32.50/D$42.50-44.50) are recommended. Hotel tax: 9%.

RESTAURANTS

Café Avion at the airport, American and French cuisine; **Nathaniel Restaurant,** elegant veal Cordon Bleu, prime ribs; family menu at the **Manhattan Restaurant; Betty's Chop House,** popular, downtown; Alexander Street—known locally as "restaurant row" includes the **Budapest Hungarian** (with traditional violinist), **Hugo's** for continental fare, and **Lloyds; Chez Jean-Pierre** is a local bastion of French cuisine, while **Ebenezer's** at the Marriott Inn includes a number of flambéed items in its menu; **Rio Bamba** and **Don Quixote** are well spoken of, while the **Royal Scot Steak House** also features lobster tails; **Spring House,** homelike colonial atmosphere; dancing nightly except Monday in the elegant **Sword and Sabre** is in the Flagship Rochester; a great view from the 14th floor **Top of the Plaza** in the Midtown Tower Hotel; dancing Friday and Saturday at the **Aloha.**

ARTS AND MUSIC

Rochester Museum & Science Center, natural science, cultural history, American Indian displays; open Monday to Saturday 9-5, Sundays and holidays 1-5; admission $1.00 adults 50¢ children and students. **Strasenburgh Planetarium,** adjoining, has a theater of stars, observation platform and telescope. Admission $2.00. **Memorial Art Gallery,** fine art from predynastic Egypt to the latest moderns; open Tuesday 2-9, Wednesday through Saturday 10-5, Sunday 1-5. The **International Museum of Photography, George Eastman House,** open Tuesday-Sunday 10-4:30, admission $2.50 adults $1.00 children and students. **Eastman School of Music,** operas, recitals, concerts; free. **Sibley Music Library,** one of the world's largest collections of music literature, original scores, and manuscripts; open daily during the academic year, closed Sunday during the summer, free. Frequent recitals are also presented by the **Rochester Oratorio Society,** and there are many concerts at the Eastman School of Music. The **Nazareth Performing Arts Center,** and the **Genesee Valley Arts Foundation Repertory** offer varied dramatic entertainment in Rochester.

SHOPPING

Downtown store hours are generally from 9:45 to 5:45; Tuesday and Thursday evening until 9. There are more than 40 shopping plazas around

Rochester open from about 10 to 9, Monday through Friday, until 5:45 on Saturday.

SPORTS
There are public golf courses at **Churchville, Durand-Eastman** and **Genesee Valley** parks, and tennis courts in most city parks. Thoroughbred horse racing is held at **Finger Lakes Race Track,** 20 miles southeast of the city, and harness racing at **Batavia Downs,** 33 miles west of town. There are some excellent fishing spots south of town, and the **Bristol Mountain** ski area is one of many within an hour's drive.

CALENDAR OF EVENTS
Annual **Lilac Time Festival,** now a 10-day event, variable but usually late May; **All-High Music Festival,** Highland Park, early June; **Hill Cumorah Mormon Pageant,** a colorful seven-day festival, early August; **Highland Park Bowl,** July-August; **Monroe County Fair,** mid-August.

WHERE TO GO NEARBY
Letchworth Park, 40 miles southwest; **Hamlin Beach Park,** 25 miles northwest; and **Braddock Bay Park,** 10 miles west, are state parks with good recreational facilities; usually open Memorial Day to Labor Day. The **Finger Lakes** district, 30 miles southeast, has many hotels and cottages and has long been popular for fishing and water sport vacations.

FURTHER STATE INFORMATION
New York State Department of Commerce, Travel Division, 99 Washington Avenue, Albany, NY 12245. Hunting and Fishing: **Division of Fish and Wildlife,** State Environmental Conservation Department, 50 Wolf Road, Albany, NY 12233. **Rochester Convention and Visitor Bureau,** War Memorial, Rochester, NY 14604. **Buffalo Area Chamber of Commerce,** 107 Delaware Avenue, Buffalo, NY 14202. **Buffalo Convention and Visitors Bureau,** 115 Delaware Avenue, Buffalo, NY 14202. **Pan Am** offices in New York City, Pan Am Building, 45th Street and Vanderbilt Avenue; 100 East 42nd Street; Fifth Avenue & 48th Street; 1 E. 59th Street; One World Trade Center. The telephone number is 973-4000 for reservations.

   New York Convention and Visitors Bureau, 2 Columbus Circle, answers questions for tourists and visitors and supplies maps and folders. **New York Chamber of Commerce and Industry,** 65 Liberty Street.

   Consulates: For representatives in New York City see the listings in the telephone directory.

USEFUL TELEPHONE NUMBERS
New York City
Emergency (Police, Fire, Ambulance)	911
Bellevue Hospital	561-5151
Metropolitan Hospital	360-6262
St Vincent's Hospital	620-1234

Poison Control	340-4494
Dental Emergency	679-3966
Legal Aid	577-3300
Chamber of Commerce	561-2020
Tourist Information	397-8222
Pan Am Reservations	973-4000

Niagara

Police	278-8111
Fire	285-1233
Ambulance	284-4228
Niagara Falls Memorial Hospital	278-4484
Mount St Mary's Hospital	297-4800
Poison Control Center	278-4511
Dental Emergency	278-4000
Legal Aid	284-8831
Chamber of Commerce	285-9141
Pan Am Reservations	(800) 522-7400

Rochester

Emergency (Police, Fire, Ambulance)	911
Genesee Hospital	263-6000
Life Line (for any medical emergency)	275-5151
Legal Aid	473-6550
Chamber of Commerce	454-2220
Pan Am Reservations	232-1934

North Carolina

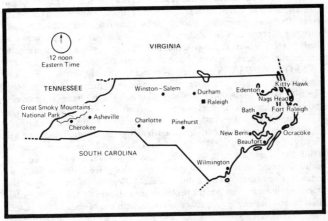

Area	52,712 square miles						**Population**	5,842,110					
Capital	Raleigh						**Sales Tax**	3% with an additional sales tax of 1% added by some counties.					

Weather	Jan	Feb	Mar	Apr	May	Jun	Jul	Aug	Sep	Oct	Nov	Dec
Av Temp (°C)	6	7	10	16	21	25	26	26	23	17	10	6
Days Rain/Snow	10	10	11	9	9	9	12	10	7	7	7	9

Sir Walter Raleigh's colonists founded the first settlement of the colonies on Roanoke Island in 1585. Sir Walter himself *never* came to North Carolina. John White, governor of the colony, journeyed to England and when he returned three years later, the colonists had vanished. The word *Croatoan*, carved on a tree, was the only trace of the group. "The Lost Colony," as it became known, was never found, and the mystery remains unsolved.

In the years that followed there was trouble between the colonists and the owners of the land grants in England, as well as quarrels between Quakers and other groups against the Anglican Church. The Indians were hostile and the swamps and dense forests made it difficult to develop the land. In addition, pirates plagued the coastal settlements until the infamous "Blackbeard," Edward Teach, died in battle off Ocracoke Island. There were border disputes with Virginia and Georgia. Until 1710 North Carolina was part of the territory including what is now South Carolina.

In 1729 North Carolina became a Royal Colony and began to stabilize. From that time, conditions improved until the Revolution. North Carolina experienced very little fighting on her own soil, but sent troops elsewhere to fight for independence. Even when the Revolution was won, the state languished, acquiring the nickname "The Rip Van Winkle State."

After the Civil War and the Reconstruction period, the state began a steady climb to agricultural and industrial prominence which continues today. Its great variety of countryside, about 66% of which is forested, is a special attraction for visitors. Extending for 503 miles from east to west, North Carolina is composed of four distinct regions which are quite different in climate, topography, and activities.

The **OUTER BANKS** are a chain of narrow, sandy, wind-whipped islands that extend for 120 miles and are as far as 30 miles into the Atlantic. The islanders are salty individualists, full of lore about pirates, shipwrecks, and ghostly legends handed down from their ancestors.

Beginning from the north, US 158 crosses from **Point Harbor** to **Kitty Hawk,** from which one can drive south along the Outer Banks. On **Kill Devil Hills** is the soaring **Wright Brothers National Memorial** commemorating the world's first powered airplane flight, which took place here on 17 December 1903. A museum, open daily, free, houses full-scale reproductions of the 1903 flying machine. Replicas of the hangar and workshop used by the Wright brothers are adjacent to the flight center. **Nags Head** is an easy-going old resort town with lots of ocean-front hotels. High season rates average about $30-$65, from about Memorial Day to Labor Day, when the swimming is excellent; fishing and beach-combing go on all year round. You can sand-ski here on dunes over 100 feet high; the tallest dune, **Jockey's Ridge,** is a mecca for hang-gliders. One of America's authentic mystery stories, *The Lost Colony,* is performed nightly except Sundays from about mid-June to late August in the **Waterside Theatre** near Manteo. The **Fort Raleigh National Historic Site** marks the first English settlement in America; the disappearance of these early colonists sometime between 1587 and 1590 remains a mystery to this day. The original fort is reconstructed and a Visitors' Center relates the colony's unfortunate story. **Cape Hatteras National Seashore** stretches some 70 miles from just below Nags Head to **Ocracoke Inlet.** Just a thin strand between the pounding ocean and the shallow **Pamlico Sound,** there is an eerie loneliness to the place, and several remains of shipwrecks are discovered from time to time, a reminder that this is the "Graveyard of the Atlantic." **Cape Hatteras Lighthouse** overlooking **Diamond Shoals** is the nation's tallest; adjacent is a fascinating **Museum of the Sea. The Pea Island National Wildlife Refuge** is the winter home of snow geese, loons, herons, and similar spectacular birds; bird observation platform near **Bodie Island Lighthouse.** The village of **Ocracoke,** legendary headquarters of "Blackbeard" the pirate, is a quaint old fishing village accessible by ferry from Hatteras, Cedar Island or Swan Quarter. There are nice motels here and in **Buxton, Rodanthe,** and **Hatteras;** summer rates average about $25-$60 double occupancy.

The Outer Banks offer some of the nation's finest surf fishing. Fish also like to lurk in the hulls of wrecked ships; at least 2,000 craft have gone down off these treacherous shoals. The new technique of "deep-jigging" brings up great catches of grouper, snapper, king mackerel, cobia, and amberjack from the waters around wrecks. Charter boats are available to rent. Sailing is excellent all summer in the protected waters of the sounds between the Outer Banks and the mainland. Only a few wrecks are buoyed but charter boat captains know the location of the others by compass reading. There is also very good duck and goose hunting during the fall.

The **COASTAL PLAIN** has a subtropical climate of warm-to-hot summers, and mild winters, ideal for growing bright-leaf tobacco, for which North Carolina ranks first in the nation, and a great many other crops. Traveling from north to south along the coast, but inland from the Outer Banks, you first encounter the **Dismal Swamp** on the Virginia border, a dim, shadowy wilderness of great interest to hunters and fishermen. Nearby is **Elizabeth City**, which flourished with West Indies trade in the early 1800s. **Edenton**, 40 miles south of Elizabeth City, held a "Tea Party" when the women of the town gave up tea and other British goods on 25 October 1774 in protest against British excise taxes; a big bronze teapot on Edenton's **Courthouse Green** marks the spot where they held their meeting, and the **Chowan County Courthouse** (1767) has fine paneling and a regal Georgian decor. **St Paul's Church** dates from 1736. Interesting old houses open to the public include the **Barker House** (1782), **Cupola House** (1725), and **Iredell House** (1776). **Bath** was the first incorporated town in North Carolina. Here, **St Thomas Church,** begun in 1734, has altar candelabra that were said to be a gift from King George II of England. The **Visitors' Center** (closed Mondays), located in Bath on NC 92, will provide information on the fine old houses you can visit in this village.

New Bern, another very old town, displays its prosperous past in the stately Georgian town houses and cozy clapboard cottages that line its narrow oak-shaded streets. Among many beautifully restored old homes is **Tryon Palace** (1770), which was built for the royal governor but later became the statehouse of independent North Carolina until the capital was moved to Raleigh. **Beaufort** is an old coastal town full of legends and photogenic old streets; and you can visit many quaint 18th-century houses during the **Old Homes Tour** in June. The **Hampton Mariners Museum** is open year round; there is no admission fee. **Morehead City** is a popular spot for fishermen to show off the big ones caught in the Gulf Stream on Bogue Island. **Fort Macon,** surrounded by a moat, is one of the nation's best preserved forts. **Camp Lejeune** covers 170 square miles and is a famous marine amphibious training center. In the southeastern corner is **Wilmington,** down on the Cape Fear River and 10 miles inland from the Atlantic; this is the state's leading deep-water port city. The old residential section is maintained as an historic area and contains buildings dating from before the Revolutionary War through the Victorian era. The **Burgwin-Wright House** (1772) was a temporary headquarters of General Cornwallis in 1781. The **Azalea Festival,** centering around beautiful **Greenfield Gardens,** is held in mid-April, but camellias and early azaleas are already blooming in March. The *USS North Carolina,* now a memorial to the state's World War II fighting men, is docked on the river; there is a nightly sound and light pageant, viewed from a dockside grandstand, from early June through Labor Day, which depicts the story of this battleship.

The **PIEDMONT PLATEAU** is gently rolling country that makes a nice transition in scenery and climate between the warm low coastal plain and cool western mountains. It's a region of briskly modern cities, old tobacco barns, elegant resorts, and serious-minded universities. **Southern Pines** and **Pinehurst,** in the center of the state, are two of the nation's smartest year-round resorts. Here among the pine-shaded sandhills are beautiful estates, superb golf courses, horse shows, foxhunts, and endless bridle trials. Pinehurst, while owned by a corporation and, therefore, not an official town, is open to the traveler and has excellent recreational facilities. The **Pinehurst Hotel and Country Club** (295-6811, average rate D$75) has six nationally acclaimed golf courses, 20 tennis courts, stables, a gun club, and a variety of other amenities. There is a wide choice of excellent motels in Southern Pines, where the fashionable season is February through May; rates then average D$30 (no meals). **The North Carolina Zoological Park** is open near Asheboro and has a 40-acre interim zoo with trails for hiking.

To the northeast is **Raleigh,** the state capital and a college town. **North Carolina State University** has a **Nuclear Reactor Center** here; open to the public when classes are in session. The **North Carolina Museum of Art** recently relocated to just west of the city limits off Interstate 40. The museum includes the **Kress Collection** and the **Mary Duke Biddle Gallery for the Blind,** a special collection of original sculptures and artifacts that blind and sighted visitors may touch, regardless of their great value. It was the first art collection founded with state funds and the exhibits are now valued at more than $40 million. **Chapel Hill,** northwest of Raleigh, is a charming old town with the nation's oldest state university, chartered in 1789. The nation's astronauts study the stars at **Morehead Planetarium** where informative programs are presented daily to the public. Also here are the **N.C. Botanical Gardens** and the **Ackland Art Museum** containing one of the state's finest collections. **Durham** is the city that the Duke family built with the fortune from the immense American Tobacco Company. Try to attend a tobacco auction if you're there between August and December. **Duke University** has two beautiful campuses, a famous medical center, art museum, and an immense library. The ancestral **Duke Homestead,** six miles north of the city, is open Tuesday through Saturday and Sunday afternoons, year round; free. **Greensboro,** west of Durham, is the home of the **Greater Greensboro Open,** held every year in early April at the **Forest Oaks Country Club.** This tournament has a purse of $300,000. About 27 miles west on I-40 is **Winston-Salem,** a blend of industrial city and religious community. Visit **Reynolds House** on the Reynolds family estate, which contains fine furnishings and valuable art collections; open Tuesday to Sunday, year round. The **Old Salem** district is the restored original town founded in 1766 by devout, industrious Moravians from Pennsylvania. The fine old buildings, ten of which are open to the public, are lovely in their simplicity. See pioneer crafts demonstrated in the **Single Brothers House**, and dine well in the **Salem Tavern** where Washington stayed in 1791. Also visit the delightful **Museum of Early Southern Decorative Arts**, containing 15 period rooms from 1690 to 1820. The largest city in the state, **Charlotte**, is down near the South Carolina border. Here the immense, ultramodern **Coliseum** and **Charlotte Motor Speedway** draw hugh crowds to the city for sports events. **Carowinds** is a theme park emphasizing the heritage of the Carolinas. It's open daily in summer and on weekends in spring and fall.

The **APPALACHIANS**, in the western portion of the state, are thinly populated owing to the rugged nature of the terrain. You'll find old-time crafts still being meticulously practiced in the village of **Penland** and in **Celo**, which specializes in candles. Genuine Indian craftwork is still made on the large **Cherokee Indian Reservation** on the edge of the **Great Smoky Mountains National Park**. Also visit the **Museum of the Cherokee Indian**, the wax museum **Cyclorama** depicting 300 years of Cherokee history, and the **Oconaluftee Indian Village** adjacent to the **Mountainside Theater**, where *Unto These Hills* is presented nightly except Monday, June through Labor Day.

The **Blue Ridge Parkway** is the spectacular scenic highway that connects the national parks of Shenandoah, in Virginia, and the Great Smokies. It is 470 miles long and 649 to 6,053 feet high, with wonderful views all the way. The highway is open all year (the higher sections may be closed in inclement weather) but recreational areas and some campsites are closed from 1 November through April. **Blowing Rock**, high on the Blue Ridge, is where light objects dropped off the cliff are returned to you by the strong wind currents. A scenic, moderately priced summer resort, Blowing Rock is also one of many winter resorts in these mountains where you can ski from December through March; lots of special events in February. Other ski resorts are located at **Beach Mountain, Sugar Mountain, Hound Ears, Seven Devils, Sapphire Valley, Wolf Laurel, Cataloochee, High Meadows, Scaly Mountain,** and **Appalachian Ski Mountain.** If there isn't sufficient snow, it can be sprayed on artificially. Other major mountain towns include **Boone**, where the stirring *Horn in the West* is staged Tuesday through Sunday evenings, late June to late August; **Linville**, at the base of 5,939-foot **Grandfather Mountain**, where the *Singing on the Mountain* is held the fourth Sunday in June, and the **Highland Games** attract Scottish clans from all over the second weekend in July; **Hendersonville**, a popular summer resort; and nearby **Flat Rock**, home of the late poet-biographer Carl Sandburg and the **Flat Rock Playhouse**, performances Tuesday to Saturday, late June through September 4. **Asheville**, in western corner, is the queen of the mountain country and is described at length below.

The entrance to the **Great Smoky Mountain National Park** from the

North Carolina side is at **Oconaluftee**, just north of Cherokee; the **Visitors' Center** is open 8-4:30 1 November through 31 March; 8-6 1 April to mid-June and Labor Day to 31 October; 8-7:30 mid June through Labor Day, closed Christmas Day. You can rent a recorder and self-guiding tour tape at the **Museum of the Cherokee** with an expert description of what to see as you drive across the park. Nearest hotels, before plunging into this splendid, unspoiled wilderness, are at **Cherokee, Bryson City, Maggie,** and **Fontana Dam,** with its resort **Fontana Village** (498-2211, average rates $40-$65), which has an inn, a lodge, and 300 modern housekeeping cottages for 1-10 people. The inn is open year round; lodge opens from 1 April and cottages 1 May through Thanksgiving. A full description of the park is provided in the chapter on Tennessee.

City To Visit

ASHEVILLE

Even before the railroad came through in 1880, Asheville was a resort town that drew visitors who had heard of its ideal climate and beautiful location in the Blue Ridge and Great Smoky Mountains. Today it is a smart-looking modern city with an affinity for preserving skills of the past. The population is 58,000; Buncombe County 155,000.

WHAT TO SEE

Biltmore House, George W. Vanderbilt's huge French Renaissance château, was begun in 1890 and contains priceless art treasures of all kinds. Also on the 12,000-acre estate are superb formal gardens and a dairy farm with one of the nation's finest herds of purebred Jersey cattle. The estate is south of town on US 25. It is open to the public, year-round, 9 am to 6 pm except Thanksgiving, Christmas, and New Year's. The **University Botanical Gardens** is a meticulously controlled wilderness of native wild flowers and plants on the campus of the local branch of the **University of North Carolina.** According to legend the mountains are full of gold and precious stones, and there are exceptional displays in the **Colburn Mineral Museum;** free. The **Folk Art Center of the Southern Highland Handicraft Guild** contains handcarved and handcrafted items of the mountain area. The **Thomas Wolfe Memorial,** on Spruce Street, is the house where the world-famous author grew up; his room is furnished with his few possessions. After he published *Look Homeward, Angel* in 1929, revealing unpleasant truths about Asheville, the book was virtually banned in his hometown. The **Pack Library** now contains a great collection of Wolfe memorabilia. There are sound and light performances at the Wolfe Memorial on 3 October, his birthday, and on an evening of the second week in July. The Memorial is open year round, $1 for adults, 50¢ students. Thomas Wolfe and William Sydney Porter (O. Henry) are buried in **Riverside Cemetery.** About 12 miles northeast of town is the **Vance Pioneer Homestead and Museum,** a typical frontier log house with outbuildings that was the family home of Zebulon B. Vance, the great Civil War governor; open Tuesday to Sunday, free.

ACCOMMODATIONS

Downtown are the **Downtowner Motor Inn** (254-9661, averaging $28), **Smoky Mountains Inn on the Plaza** (252-8211), **Interstate Motel** (254-0945), and **Sheraton Motor Inn** (253-1851, averaging $35). Numerous accommodations elsewhere include: **Holiday Inn Central** (254-4311, averaging $42), **Ramada Inn** (254-7451, averaging $32), **Howard Johnson Motor Lodge** (274-2300), and the **Econo Travel Motor Hotel** (254-9521). Rates vary depending on the season. North of town the **Grove Park Inn and Country Club** (252-2711, averaging $50) is open year round, with lovely mountain views. The **Great Smokies Hotel** (254-3211, S$36-44/ D$44-46), 1 mile west, is also recommended.

RESTAURANTS

Especially good dining in the **Coachlite Restaurant, The Village Square** of the Sheraton, and the **Grove Park Inn. S&W Cafeteria** is very popular. Mixed alcoholic drinks are served within the city limits only, liquor can be purchased in state-owned stores. Carry your own when you go out of the city proper and buy set-ups. Many places are licensed to serve beer and wine, however.

ARTS AND MUSIC

Asheville has a **Community Theater,** an outstanding **Civic Center,** a **Symphony Society, Community Concert Association, Youth Theater,** and ballet. See the **Asheville Art Museum,** whose changing exhibits feature both nationally known and local artists. Art is not a static thing here; many craftsmen turn out items ranging from dulcimers to handwoven table linens, pottery, and jewelry.

SHOPPING

Many stores are an outlet for handmade crafts produced in the mountains. Local goods, which you can see being made, are reasonably priced. **Biltmore Handweavers** turn out beautiful homespuns on their looms. East of town off US 70 on the Blue Ridge Parkway are the shops of the **Southern Highland Handicraft Guild** with a wide variety of unusual things, and the **Stuart Nye Silver Smiths.** South of town on US 25 are the **Biltmore Country Market,** the **Spinning Wheel,** and **Brown's Pottery.** Turn west on NC 280 to reach **Evan's Pottery** and the **Pisgah Forest Potters.** Located downtown is **Allanstand Mountain Craft Shop.** Factory outlet stores are very popular with visitors; they sell fabrics and sportswear at discount prices. Visit **Wall Street** for crafts and boutiques.

SPORTS

Asheville has two public golf courses and two private country clubs; 14 other courses are within easy reach of the city. Most courses are beautifully located. Icy cold mountain rivers and lakes are superb for making big catches of trout, bass, bream, and crappie. **Bee Tree Lake,** east of Asheville, is stocked with 10- to 12-inch rainbow trout. The deer hunting season runs 24 November through 13 December. Bear hunting 13 October through 15 November; 16 December through 1 January. Skiing on natural or man-made snow from late December. Water sports on mountain lakes.

CALENDAR OF EVENTS
Mountain Youth Jamboree, mid-May; **Shindig-on-the-green,** where mountain folk square dance, clog, do buck-and-wing turns, and play folk music, every Saturday night in July and August. **Craftsmen Fair,** handicrafts and folk dances, mid-July and mid-October; **Mountain Dance and Folk Festival** with 5-string banjo, fiddle, and traditional mountain dancing performances Thursday, Friday, and Saturday, the first week in August; **Antique Fair,** mid-August.

WHERE TO GO NEARBY
You will find spectacular views anywhere along the **Blue Ridge Parkway;** wooded mountains rise one after the other in the hazy distance. Among several circle tours mapped by the Asheville Chamber of Commerce is one that takes you north up the Parkway to **Craggy Gardens,** 5,900 feet, and to **Mount Mitchell,** 6,684 feet, the highest mountain in the east. Then on to the **North Carolina Mineral Museum** in the mining town of **Spruce Pine,** dramatic **Linville Gorge, Linville Falls, Grandfather Mountain,** and **Burnsville.** West of Asheville, the Parkway goes through the lofty **Pisgah Mountains** and **Great Balsams** that look to the Great Smokies.

FURTHER STATE INFORMATION
Travel and Tourism Division, Department of Commerce, PO Box 25249, Raleigh, NC 27611. Hunting and Fishing: **North Carolina Wildlife Resources Commission,** Education Division, 325 N. Salisbury Street, Raleigh, NC 27611. **Asheville Area Chamber of Commerce,** PO Box 1011, Asheville, NC 28802.

USEFUL TELEPHONE NUMBERS IN RALEIGH
Emergency Medical Services (Fire, Police, Rescue)	829-1911
Raleigh Community Hospital	872-4800
Wake County Medical Center	755-8000
Chamber of Commerce	833-3005
Travel Council of North Carolina	821-1435
Legal Aid Society	828-4647

North Dakota

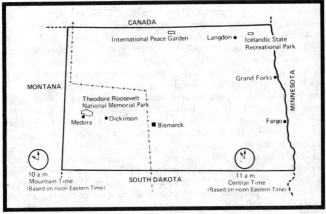

Area	70,665 square miles	**Population**	652,695
Capital	Bismarck	**Sales Tax**	3%

Weather	Jan	Feb	Mar	Apr	May	Jun	Jul	Aug	Sep	Oct	Nov	Dec
Av Temp (°C)	−12	−10	3	6	13	18	22	21	15	8	−2	−8
Days Rain/Snow	8	7	8	8	10	12	9	9	7	5	6	7

North Dakota is characterized by its gigantic wheat fields and vast cattle-and sheep-grazing ranges. Only Kansas produces more wheat in the US. But less publicized is the fact that this state's oil and coal reserves are among the nation's highest, while western North Dakota is the site of the nation's first (1983) plant for turning lignite coal into gas for heating. Food processing has become a major industry, while tourism continues to grow on the excellent opportunities of exciting fishing and hunting. Between 1850 and 1870, as white settlers moved farther into the Dakota Territory, the displaced Dakota Indians fought them every step of the way. Unwilling to shed further blood needlessly, the Indians acceded to the demands of the politicians and removed themselves to an area known as the Badlands, a region of beauty on the Montana Border. The Northern Pacific Railway, which had laid tracks into the capital city of Bismarck in 1873, continued to build westward across the Badlands.

In 1883, while on a hunting trip, Theodore Roosevelt bought the Maltese Cross Ranch near Medora. Although a New Yorker and only 26 years old when he arrived, Roosevelt organized a protective group against cattle thieves, served actively as a deputy sheriff, was the organizer and first president of the Little Missouri Stockman's Association, vigorously ran his newly-acquired and renamed Elkhorn Ranch, and somehow found time to write two biographies.

Today, 70,374 acres of the Badlands have been made into the **THEODORE ROOSEVELT NATIONAL MEMORIAL PARK.** The park has been sculptured by wind and water into curious buttes, and conical hills thrust up in odd formations. The meandering **Little Missouri River** has cut through layers of sediment, exposing multi-colored patterns. Seen at sunrise or sunset, the colors are exquisite. All through the Badlands are open deposits of soft lignite coal, some as deep as 18 feet. Some of the veins, probably ignited by lightning, have burned for years and baked the clay around them into a red "scoria," which is so like brick that it has been used to surface a road near Medora. Remnants of petrified forests remain in the park, and the wind-worn surfaces of rocks are good places to hunt for prehistoric fossils. Study wildlife such as deer, antelope, buffalo, prairie dogs, eagles, falcons and hawks. Within the park are picnic areas, well-marked trails and fine campsites. On summer evenings, rangers give nightly campfire talks.

Park Headquarters, with a museum and information center, is at **Medora,** just off I-94; open 8-8 in summer, 8-4:30 in winter. Just south of Medora is the **Château de Mores,** a mansion filled with French furnishings and the guns, personal belongings and riding gear of the Marquis de Mores, who founded the town in 1883. At the **Gold Seal Amphitheater,** a mile southwest of Medora, a musical variety show reenacts Badlands history; performances nightly in July and August. Accommodations in the Medora area include the historic **Rough Riders Hotel** (623-4433, S$20/D$25), dating from 1885, open May-September, and the **Badlands Motel** (623-4422, S$20/D$25), also open May-September. **Dickinson,** about 35 miles east of Medora, is the shopping center for a large area including parts of Montana and South Dakota. The choice of motels is greater here. Rates at the **Best Western New Oasis** are (225-6703, S$16-25/D$21-27) and **Best Western Prairie Winds Inn** (225-9123, S$16.50-21/D$20-26); **Ramada Inn** (225-6791, S/D$28-30); and **Holiday Inn** (227-1853, S$31-34/D$41-44). Hotel Tax: 4%.

Located on the North Dakota-Manitoba, Canada border is the **INTERNATIONAL PEACE GARDEN.** Dedicated as a monument to the peaceful coexistence the United States and Canada have long enjoyed, the 2,300-acre site has flourished since its official dedication in 1932. A cairn made of native rock, located at the entrance to the garden, states, "To God in His glory, we two nations dedicate this garden and pledge ourselves that as long as men shall live, we will not take up arms against one another." An all-faiths **Peace Chapel** is located in the garden. Engraved in the limestone walls are quotations from men of peace throughout history.

The formal area of the garden lies half in Manitoba and half in North Dakota. **Lake Stormon** in the Canadian section, named after Judge John

A. Stormon, and **Lake Udall** in the American section, named after the late William Udall, of Boissevain, Manitoba, provide excellent scenery for family picnics. Camping facilities are also available.

North of Bismarck is **Garrison Dam,** an immense structure to protect the Missouri River Basin from flood waters. ND 200 goes along the top of the 200-foot dam. There are guided tours of the powerhouse from June-August. **Lake Sakajawea,** formed by the dam, has 1,600 miles of shoreline that has become a year-round center for fishing, boating, camping, hunting, and snowmobiling. Migratory waterfowl, safe from hunters, throng to the **Audubon National Wildlife Refuge** on one side of the lake.

BISMARCK, North Dakota's capital, is bisected by I-94 and the Missouri River. Exuding an aura of prosperity from the surrounding huge farms and oil wells, most vestiges of Bismarck's frontier days are found only in the **State Historical Society Museum** and **Camp Hancock Museum.** There are guided tours of the **State Capitol,** a sleek skyscraper of white limestone. Marcel Breuer, known for his innovations in modern architecture and furniture, designed the buildings for **Mary College,** south of town. **Holiday Inn** (223-9600, S\$28-31/D\$36-39), 1 mile south of I-94 exit 34, and **Town House Motor Inn** (223-8001, S\$34/D\$38), 4 blocks south of I-94 exit 36, offer good accommodations. Also in the neighborhood are **Best Western Fleck House** (255-1450, S\$19-21/D\$22-24); **Best Western Kirkwood Motor Inn** (258-7700, S\$26-30/D\$31-33.50); **Bismarck Motor Hotel** (223-2474, S\$11-15/D\$15-19); **Colonial Motel** (258-9824, S\$14.50/D\$18.50); and **Ramada Inn** (258-7000, S\$23-32/D\$32-34). Hotel Tax: 4%.

Interstate 29 runs north from Fargo in a direct line towards Winnipeg, Canada. En route is **Grand Forks,** site of the **University of North Dakota** where the US Bureau of Mines maintains a **Lignite Research Laboratory.** The huge antiballistic missile installation, which may confound archeologists some day, rises out of the flat landscape near **Langdon,** about 40 miles west of I-29 and about 30 miles south of the Canadian line. It is an incredible sight among the peaceful wheat fields. Another surprise in the northeast corner of the state is the large number of people of recent Icelandic descent, as seen in the little towns of **Cavalier** and **Mountain.** Since **Renwick Dam** has harnessed the treacherous Tongue River, the **Icelandic State Recreational Park** has been created complete with boating and water skiing facilities.

FURTHER STATE INFORMATION
Travel Department, State Capitol Grounds, Bismarck, ND 58505. Hunting and Fishing: **State Game and Fish Department,** Bismarck, ND 58505.

USEFUL TELEPHONE NUMBERS IN BISMARCK
Emergency Assistance (Highway Patrol, Medical)	224-2121
Fire	223-1324
Police	223-1212

NORTH DAKOTA

Bismarck Hospital	223-4700
St. Alexius Hospital	223-5000
Legal Assistance of North Dakota	258-4270
Chamber of Commerce	223-5660
Pan Am Reservations	(800) 621-0595

Ohio

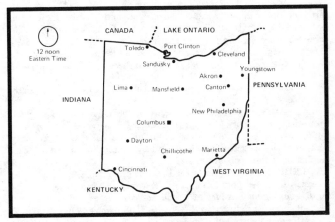

Area	41,222 square miles	Population	10,797,419
Capital	Columbus	Sales Tax	4% State sales tax: 4% (Local sales tax added in some counties and cities).

Weather	Jan	Feb	Mar	Apr	May	Jun	Jul	Aug	Sep	Oct	Nov	Dec
Av Temp (°C)	1	2	6	12	18	23	25	24	21	14	7	2
Days Rain/Snow	12	11	13	12	12	13	10	9	9	9	10	11

It is difficult to imagine now, but Ohio was once as wild and unexplored as any state west of it. In fact, it was regarded by early pioneers as the beginning of the great Northwest. LaSalle, the French explorer, first wandered through the area in 1670, giving the French a claim over which to squabble with England, until the French and Indian wars in the 18th century settled the matter in England's favor—just in time for the American Revolution. After that, a number of the colonies laid various claims to Ohio, until everything was resolved by the Northwest Ordinance in 1787. The following year the first permanent white settlement was established, and Ohio entered the Union in 1803 as the 17th state.

The state developed rapidly and played an important part in events leading up to the Civil War. The abolitionist movement began in Ohio, and the state became a haven for escaped slaves brought north on the

Underground Railway. When the Civil War began, the state made heavy contributions in manpower and material, although little actual fighting took place on her soil.

US Presidents born in Ohio include Ulysses S. Grant, Rutherford B. Hayes, James Garfield, Benjamin Harrison, William McKinley, William Howard Taft, and Warren G. Harding.

The state offers an interesting variety of terrain. Most of the eastern part is occupied by the Appalachian Plateau, and most of the western part by the fertile Till Plains. A narrow strip of the Great Lakes Plain borders **Lake Erie**, and in the south is an extension of the Kentucky Bluegrass Region. Ohio's population has an interesting mixture of "old country" cultures. As you travel around the state you are likely to come across festivals extolling everything from pumpkins to bratwurst. An excellent road system makes travel easy and all areas of the state are easily accessible.

The heaviest traffic crosses the state on the Ohio Turnpike, which helps make short work of the trip between Chicago and Pittsburgh. If you're on vacation, it's nice to follow Lake Erie across Ohio. Entering Ohio from the west from northern Indiana or southwestern Michigan, the first big city is Toledo.

TOLEDO, located on the Great Lakes shipping lanes, has one of the busiest fresh-water port facilities in the world and is a major port for ships to and from Europe, Asia, and South America. Edward Libbey brought the glass industry to the area in 1888; Michael Owens became his partner and invented a machine which formed molten glass into bottles and served as the forerunner of the giant container and flat glass-producing industry of today. The Erie and Kalamazoo Railroad, the first to be constructed west of the Allegheny Mountains, began in Toledo. Today the city has over 1,000 manufacturing plants. The **University of Toledo** is here, which includes a huge arboretum. **Toledo Zoological Gardens,** 3 miles southwest, started with an eagle, two badgers, and a woodchuck and now has more than 2,200 specimens of animals living on 33 acres. A children's zoo, **Wonder Valley,** features a steam train and merry-go-round; admission $2.00 adults, 75¢ children 2-12; open 10-5 daily. The **Toledo Museum of Art,** 1½ miles northwest, open Tuesday to Saturday 9-5, Sunday 1-6 (closed Monday), free, houses a collection of more than 700 paintings and one of the world's finest glass displays. Also here are galleries of 17th-century Dutch, French, and Flemish art, Egyptian mummies, and in the Medieval Cloister ivories, art objects, and tapestries. Seventy-six parks in the Toledo area provide boating, swimming, and playgrounds. The **Toledo Raceway Park** harness races are run from mid-May to mid-September.

Downtown accommodations include: **Holiday Inn-Downtown** and **Hillcrest Hotel** (both S$33/D$39). On the fringes of the city are four more **Holiday Inns,** a **Howard Johnson's, Ramada Inn, Harley Inn,** and **Sheraton-Westgate,** among many other motels. **Sharif's** serves a variety of authentic Lebanese and Syrian foods, with outstanding lamb dishes.

The **Chop House,** on Monroe Street, is good for charcoal-grilled kebabs and lamb chops.

Driving east along Lake Erie from Toledo you come to **Port Clinton** at the neck of Marblehead Peninsula, which juts out between Sandusky Bay and Lake Erie. Camp Perry Military Reservation is on the peninsula where the **National Rifle and Pistol Championship** competitions are held every August. The peninsula is a charming summer resort area with sandy beaches and some excellent fishing. During the summer there is a regularly scheduled ferry service from Port Clinton and from **Catawba,** on the tip of the peninsula, to **Put-in-Bay** on South Bass Island. It was near Put-in-Bay that Commodore Oliver Hazard Perry won his decisive victory during the War of 1812 and it is also near the boundary line between Canada and USA Lake Erie. **The Perry Victory and International Peace Memorial National Monument** commemorates a lasting peace between the United States and Great Britain. Perry's victory over a British naval squadron in the Battle of Lake Erie ended British control of the lake and made possible the invasion of Canada by the Americans. Put-in-Bay is also reached by Island Airlines' famous old Ford tri-motor plane, the "Tin Goose," from Port Clinton. The **Inter-Lake Regatta** is held at Put-in-Bay the first 2 weeks in August.

A diversion south of the Marblehead Peninsula will take you to **Fremont,** where you'll see the last home, library, museum, and tomb of former President Rutherford B. Hayes. Continuing along Lake Erie's shores, **Sandusky** is a major coal-shipping port, but it also has wineries that turn the region's Catawba grapes into a white wine. Stop in Vermilion for the Festival of the Fish, fish dinners, boating events, mid-June; to see the **Neil Armstrong Air and Space Museum,** with exhibits of flights from early balloons to the Gemini 8 space voyage; ship models and other maritime treasures are seen in the **Great Lakes Museum.** Visit the outstanding but expensive **L'Auberge du Port** restaurant, reservation advised (216-967-5333). **Lorain** is a port, ship-building area, and industrial city with such a cosmopolitan population that people of more than 50 nationalities often participate in the big **International Festival** held here the first week in July.

You will next reach Cleveland. (For guide to Cleveland, see page 425). From Cleveland, the lakeshore highway continues northeast throughout **Ashtabula** and **Conneaut** on its way to Erie, Pennsylvania, and on up into New York State. **Conneaut Railroad Museum,** free admission, summer months only. If however you drop down to the Ohio Turnpike south of Cleveland you might drive east to **Warren,** an enthusiastic theater town where famous stars often appear in summer with the Kenley Players in the **W.D. Packard Music Hall;** Stouffer's Avalon Inn (856-1900, S$34-38/D$42-50) is an exceptional resort hotel here. Convenient motels include the **Niles Motor Inn** (S$18-22/D$26-29) and **TraveLodge** (S$27-37/D$31-39).

Just south of Warren is **Youngstown** where steel has been made since 1802. **Mill Creek Park** in the city area is an unusually beautiful natural park of gorges, ravines, and rolling hills extending from the Mahoning River to Lake Newport Dam. An old woolen mill, built in 1821, has been converted into a pavilion for picnics and dancing; the **Fellows Riverside Gardens** are also within the park. **Butler Institute of American Art** has some good antiques, paintings, and etchings by American artists, open Tuesday through Sunday; free.

Directly south, 33 miles from Cleveland, is **AKRON,** rubber capital of the world. The opening of the Ohio Canal in 1827, 2 years after the town of Akron was founded, spurred growth immediately. The Goodrich factory was built in 1870, and soon Akron became synonymous with the new household words of Goodrich, General, Mohawk, Firestone, and Goodyear. Primarily an industrial city, it spreads over rolling hills and is surrounded by scenic areas. **Akron Art Institute** has frequently changing displays; open daily except Monday; Tuesday-Friday 12-5, Saturday 9-5, Sunday 1-5.

Stan Hywet Hall was built in authentic Tudor Revival style between 1911 and 1915 by Frank A. Seiberling, who founded both the Goodyear and Seiberling tire and rubber companies. See antiques and art treasures dating from the 14th to 20th centuries displayed in 33 of the 65 rooms. The magnificent wood paneling, molded plaster ceilings, and leaded windows were created by craftsmen imported from Europe. Guided tours take visitors through the house; a 65-acre garden, featuring May tulips and mid-October chrysanthemums, surrounds the mansion; open Tuesday to Sunday, $3.50 for adults, $1 for children. During the first weekend in October, the **Ohio Mart,** an assembly of the state's artists and craftsmen, holds a 4-day show and crafts demonstrations in the mansion; admission $1.50. Concerts are given by the **Akron Symphony Orchestra,** the **Tuesday Musicals,** and the **University Town and Gown** series.

Blossom Music Center, 8 miles north of Akron, in a beautiful rural area, with an open-air concert hall, features excellent programs by the Cleveland Symphony Orchestra, popular musical groups, and ballet groups in the summer months. The **Goodyear Rubber Exhibits** in Akron are open Monday to Friday, free. The **Goodyear Air Docks,** one of the largest buildings in the world without interior supports, is not open to the public but can be appreciated from a distance. **The Perkins Mansion** and **John Brown Home,** both open daily except Monday. The **Jonathan Hale Homestead & Farm Museum,** a pioneer home and reconstructed 19th-century pioneer village located at Bath near Akron, exhibits the area's Western Reserve colonial heritage and many authentic artifacts, furniture, and implements; open Tues, Thurs, Sat, Sun (adults $3, senior citizens, $2, children $1.50).

Railways of America is 5 miles north of Akron and features a working electric train and models of over 1,000 cars, some over 140 years old. Outside there are displays of railroad cars and engines; open daily; admission: $1.25. The Akron metropolitan park system, with almost 5,000 acres, is four miles from downtown and includes the **Children's Zoo;** admission: 35¢, in conjunction with the **Akron Museum of Natural History;** free. **Portage Lakes State Park,** 12 miles south, offers swimming, boating, and

OHIO

fishing; **Stark Canal,** 25 miles south, has good recreational facilities and **Nelson Ledges State Reserve,** 35 miles northeast, has unusual rock formations and unusual plant life. In the summer, the **Kenley Players** offer outstanding plays and musicals with famous-name stars at the E. J. Thomas Auditorium on University of Akron campus.

Weathervane Playhouse, a little theater group, has productions throughout the year in Akron; its summer shows are given at nearby **Canal Fulton** by the Canal Fulton Summer Stock players. **Coach House Theater** is located at the Women's City Club. The **University of Akron,** a state institution, operates five colleges: **Kent State University** is in the nearby town of Kent. Sporting events bring the attention of the nation's golfers and bowlers to the city annually. The Professional Bowler's Association has its **Firestone Tournament of Champions** in late March or early April, the **American Golf Classic** is played in June and the **World Series of Golf** is held at the Firestone Country Club in early September. The **Summit County Fair** brings farmers and their prize-winning livestock and produce to mix with carnival workers and fun-seekers in September. Industrial tours are available at: **Goodyear Tire and Rubber Co.,** Monday to Friday, 1pm; **Firestone Tire and Rubber Co.,** Monday to Friday 2pm; **General Tire and Rubber,** Monday to Friday, 2pm, and **Goodrich Research Center** in Brecksville, Monday to Friday, 9-2.

Downtown Akron accommodations: **Holiday Inn-Downtown** (253-1181, S$33-37/D$38), **Hilton Inn-West** (867-5000, S$33-45/D$43-55) and the Quaker Square Hilton (253-5970, S$35-60/D$50-75), constructed within the framework of the Quaker Oats' silos; there are five other Holiday Inns on the outskirts of town. In nearby Richfield, **the Taverne of Richfield,** Victorian era hotel, moderate prices. Restaurants; good food at the **Brown Derby; Iacomini's** and **Sanginiti's** for Italian food; **Tangier's West** and **Mark III** for steaks; **Marcel's Embers I, Embers II, Yanko's Seven Seas** at the Yankee Clipper Inn, and **Stouffer's** all have good dinners at moderate to expensive prices.

Canton, 20 miles south of Akron, is where professional football began in America in 1920, and the **Pro Football Hall of Fame** is at 2121 Harrison Street NW. The city is also the last home of President William McKinley and site of the **Canton Art Institute,** open Tue-Sun; free. Continuing south, the **New Philadelphia** area was described as "the edge of paradise" by conservationist-novelist Louis Bromfield. **Atwood Lake Lodge** at Dellroy, on Atwood Lake (735-2211, S$32-35/D$38-41) is a delightful resort hotel some 16 miles southeast of town. Motels in Canton include the **Sheraton-Belden** on a large lake, the **Holiday Inn,** and **L-K,** all about S$25-30/D$35-45. **Schoenbrunn Village,** 4 miles south of New Philadelphia, was established by Moravian missionaries in 1772, and many of the log dwellings have been reconstructed; open April through October. Most of the residents were Indians converted to Christianity who were butchered by over-zealous militiamen from Pennsylvania. The village is now a memorial site and the story is told in a Paul Green drama *Trumpet in the Land,* staged in nearby **Dover** nightly during July and August. Also in Dover is the **Warther Museum** of meticulously hand-

419

carved steam engine models. **Zoar Village State Memorial,** open April to October, was a successful venture in communal living, founded by German Separatists, that thrived from 1817 to 1898; beautiful buildings are furnished with original furniture and implements and a garden laid out as New Jerusalem was described in the Bible; guided tours from May to September; open Wednesday through Saturday, adults $1.50, children 75¢. A good German menu is to be found at the **Zoar Hotel** built in 1833. The **Separatist Festival** in Zoar is held in August. There are also a lot of Swiss descendants here, and a big **Swiss Festival** is held at nearby Sugarcreek in late September.

Marietta, down on the **Muskingum** and **Ohio Rivers** facing West Virginia, was the first permanent settlement in Ohio, founded by General Rufus Putnam in 1788, who gallantly named it in honor of Queen Marie Antoinette. The settlement fared much better than she did, and Putnam's original house is now preserved inside a wing of the **Campus Martius Museum;** admission $1.50 for adults, 75¢ for children, closed Mon-Tues. **Marietta College** is here. Many fascinating relics of Ohio River steamboats are on view in the **Ohio River Museum;** daily; admission: $1.50. The *W.P. Snyder, Jr.* and the *Becky Thatcher* are genuine sternwheeler riverboats, docked in the Muskingum River and fun to explore. Gutzon Borglum was the sculptor of *The Start Westward of the United States* monument that stands in **Muskingum Park.** The *Conus* in **Mound Cemetery** is a 30-foot high prehistoric Indian mound and the burial place of a long-ago chieftain. Revolutionary War officers and pioneers are buried among the Indians here. Farther down the Ohio is **Gallipolis,** founded in 1790 by French Royalists. **Gatewood** was the retirement home of popular newspaper columnist O. O. McIntyre. **Jackson,** northwest of Gallipolis, is in apple orchard country. North of town is the **Leo Petroglyph State Memorial,** with early Indian inscriptions in sandstone.

COLUMBUS, capital of Ohio, is in the center of the state on the Scioto River, and came into existence in 1812 through a vote of the Ohio State Legislature which sought the most central point to be the capital. It was named in honor of Christopher Columbus; the railroad boom of the 1850s changed the city into a busy industrial community. Many people know Columbus is the home of **Ohio State University** and its championship football teams. **Columbus Museum of Art** has general art exhibits; open Tuesday, Thursday, Friday & Sunday. **Ohio State University Art Gallery, Byron's Art Gallery,** and **Schumacher Gallery** at Capital University house contemporary works by Ohio artists. The **Columbus Symphony Orchestra** gives regular concerts during the winter; the "**Floating Bandshell**" and amphitheater on the riverfront is one of Columbus' unique sites for artistic events. The **Ohio Historical Center** is the home of the state's historical society and houses a library, manuscripts, and archives; open daily. Ohio Village, I-71 at 17th Avenue, reconstructed 19th-century Ohio village, Wed-Sun $1.50 after April 1. The **State Capitol,** built of limestone in the Doric architectural style, has exhibits of history and portraits of the state's past governors; rotunda open daily, tours by appointment. Jeffrey Coal Mine No. 1, simulated coal mine tour, and the

The "America," one of the only three lighter-than-air craft operating in the United States today, is named after a famous yacht, as are its two sister blimps, the "Mayflower" and "Enterprise."

Battelle Planetarium are part of the Center of Science and Industry; open daily, except Sunday; admission $3.50 adults, $2.00 students and senior citizens. Points of interest include the Ohio State University campus with its geological museum, medical center, and horticultural gardens; Park of Roses with over 35,000 plants, open daily 30 May to 15 October; the Columbus Municipal Zoo, and the Franklin Park Conservatory where a glass building from the 1893 Chicago World's Fair stands. Downtown is F and R Lazarus Company, Ohio's largest department store. Scioto Downs has harness racing from May through early September. Fishing and boating are permitted at Hoover Dam and at two dams that now control the Scioto River. Columbus Clippers, minor league baseball at Franklin County Stadium, $2-$3.50 seats; Muirfield Memorial (golf) Tournament, PGA tour, in late May. Tickets $50. The Franklin County Fair is in July; the Ohio State Fair attracts big crowds in the last week of August. Summer stock theater is performed during the summer months. An *Oktoberfest* is held over Labor Day weekend in downtown Columbus. The German Village is a delightful restoration of the mid-19th-century homes of German settlers. *Haus und Garten* tours are conducted the last Sunday in June, but handicraft and sausage shops are open throughout the year; also visit the Gothic St Mary's Church, begun in 1866.

In midtown Columbus accommodations include: Sheraton-Columbus Motor Hotel (228-6060, S$49-69/D$59-79), and the Hyatt Regency (463-1234, S$52-83/D$67-98). Christopher Inn, Holiday Inn Downtown, Neil House Motor Hotel, and Southern Hotel range from S$23-43/D$29-49. Near Ohio State University campus: Holiday Inn On The Lane (294-4848, S$38/D$46) and Stouffer's University Inn (267-9291, S$29-36/D$35-43). East of town, off I-70: Marriott Inn (861-7220, S$39-46/D$44-53). Good restaurants in town are the Clarmont Steak House, Jai-Lai (Spanish), Suburban Steak House, Seafood Bay, Kahiki (Polynesian), Presutti's Villa (Italian), 94th Aero Squadron (near the airport), and the Glass Garden in the Hyatt; all moderate to expensive. The Old Mansion, The Inner Circle, L'Armagnac (French), and "A Matter of Taste" are recommended for more elegant fare.

Directly south of Columbus and 4 miles north of Chillicothe is Mound City Group National Monument. The 24 carefully restored burial mounds within an earth wall are monuments to the interesting Hopewell Indian culture, which buried its dead under mounds of earth between 200 BC and 500 AD. The Visitors' Center is open daily; free. In Chillicothe, first capital of Ohio, from 1803-1816, Adena State Memorial is the restored stone mansion of Ohio's Governor Thomas Worthington. Built in 1806-07, it was designed by Benjamin Latrobe and is beautifully furnished; open mid-May to October; fee: $1.50. Holiday Inn and L-K Motel here are about S$29/D$34.

King's Island Amusement Park at King's Mills between Columbus and Cincinnati on I-71, weekends only in winter, daily after 27 May. Admission $10.50; 300-site campground open year-round (513-241-5600).

Mansfield, northeast of Columbus on I-71, is an interesting place to visit. **Malabar Farm,** 12 miles southeast of town, was the home of Louis Bromfield, the famous novelist who was one of the first practicing ecologists; admission: $1.25 adult, 50¢ children. On the west side of Mansfield is the regal **Kingwood Hall** set amid superb formal gardens; in the summer flower shows, art shows, and related programs are conducted here; free. Southwest of Mansfield is **Old Town, USA** (open June to mid-November), a replica of an old-fashioned village. The terrain around Mansfield is good for winter sports and the Ohio ski carnival is held here in mid-February. If you're going northwest of Columbus, you'll pass through **Delaware,** the town where President Rutherford B. Hayes was born in 1822. South of town are the **Olentangy Indian Caves,** where Wyandot Indians hid from their enemies. A re-created pioneer settlement and Indian village (open April to October) add to the atmosphere. **Marion** is the town where Warren Harding started his campaign for the presidency. His home on Mount Vernon Avenue has been preserved very much as it was in his day. **Upper Sandusky,** farther north, was the center of Wyandot Indian Country. The graves of many Indians are in the old **Mission Church Cemetery;** also visit the **Wyandot County Historical Museum** (free) and the **Indian Mill State Memorial** (free). Two other towns of interest in this direction are **Fostoria** and **Tiffin,** famous for table glassware.

Scattered around western Ohio are several historic sites. **Wapakoneta** found a place in history books on 20 July, 1969, when local boy Neil Armstrong became the first man to set foot on the moon. The **Neil Armstrong Museum** has personal memorabilia and samples of moon rocks. The fine old **MacDonell House, Allen County Museum,** and the old-time trains exhibited in **Lincoln Park** make **Lima** worth a stop. Excellent dining here too, at the **Milano Club.** Good motels include **Scot's Inn, Howard Johnson's Motor Lodge, Regency Inn,** and **TraveLodge,** all about S$27-33/D$32-38. **Defiance** was founded as a fort on the Maumee River in 1794 by "Mad Anthony" Wayne, who defied both Indians and British to take it; there are still old earthworks visible around the fort site.

CINCINNATI, on the Ohio River, was founded on the Kentucky border in 1788 and 2 years later combined with two other Ohio River communities. Over $500 million has been spent recently for expressways, public and private buildings and commercial developments. Among them is the **Riverfront Stadium,** home of the **Cincinnati Reds,** National League baseball champions in 1972, 1975, 1976. **The Bengals** play professional football during the fall. The **Cincinnati Art Museum** has a fine collection of old masters and art objects; Tuesday-Sunday, free on Saturday. The **Taft Museum,** built in 1820, has an outstanding display of Duncan Phyff furniture and valuable collections of enamels, jewelry, ceramics, paintings; open Monday to Saturday 10-5, Sunday 2-5; free. Watch for performances by the **Cincinnati Symphony Orchestra.** The **Cincinnati Summer Opera** is held each summer at the Music Hall. The **Zoological Gardens,** possibly the first zoo to exhibit animals in uncaged compounds, is open daily 9-5; fee: $3.25 adults, $1.25 children and senior citizens. A **May Music Festival** is held every year in Cincinnati, and the **Hamilton County**

Fair is in September and the **American Art Exhibit** in October. In addition to the public libraries, there is the **Hebrew Union College Library,** with its world-famous collection of archeological objects and biblical and historical manuscripts. One of the nation's most complete law libraries is in the **Hamilton County Courthouse.** The town's many parks and smaller zoos offer scenic river views; included are **Eden Park** which contains a repertory theater, **Krohn Conservatory** with beautiful floral displays, **Ault Park** and **Mount Airy Forest** and **Arboretum** outside the city; **King's Island Amusement Park** (admission: $10.50 plus $1.50 parking) and **Lion Country Safari** (admission $10.50; $8 for senior citizens) are also of interest. Children large and small often prefer the greater variety (and swimming) at **The Great American Amusement Park** (Americana Amusement Park) at Middletown, about 25-minutes' drive from the city; admission $6.50. **Carew Tower,** 48 stories tall, is a good vantage point to see the city and river front; open daily 9:30-5:30. **Tyler-Davidson Fountain** in Fountain Square Plaza, **Abraham Lincoln Statue, Union Terminal Building,** and the **University of Cincinnati Observatory** are points of interest, along with **Mt Adams,** an unusual art colony and night spot. The **Harriet Beecher Stowe House** is a museum honoring the author of *Uncle Tom's Cabin.* The *Delta Queen* and *Mississippi Queen,* sternwheeler steamboats that make boat trips on the Ohio and Mississippi Rivers, have some tours beginning in Cincinnati. Sightseeing trips of the city are available and average 2 hours. There is an 88-day summer horse-racing meet at **River Downs** track. Hotel and motel accommodations are plentiful. Downtown: **Netherland Hilton** (621-3800, S$34-55/D$44-65); **Terrace Hilton** (381-4000, S$42-75/D$54-87); **Stouffer's Towers** (352-2100, S$39-49/D$50-60) across from the Convention Center. Among numerous motels on the outskirts of the city are **Americana Inn** (371-1776, S$32-46/D$38-52), near the Greater Cincinnati Airport, in Kentucky; **Carrousel Inn** (821-5110, S$32-47/D$38-55); **Holiday Inn; Howard Johnson's** and **Imperial House West,** ranging from S$27-37/D$33-46. Among the city's many good restaurants are **Maisonette,** expensive; **Gourmet Room** at the Terrace Hilton, elegant dining, moderate to expensive; **Grammer's, Mecklenburg Garden, Black Forest,** and **Forest View Gardens,** German old-world dishes; **Nikko Inn,** Japanese specialties; **Adrica's** or **Scotti's,** Italian food; **Pigall's,** French and expensive.

DAYTON, an hour's drive north of Cincinnati on I-75, was founded in 1796. Experiments here by the Wright brothers led to their first successful airplane flight, and the city is still a center of aeronautical research. Dayton combines physical attractiveness with major industrial and military importance. It has an unusual natural setting at the confluence of the **Miami, Mad,** and **Stillwater** Rivers, and is widely recognized as one of the best-governed cities in the country. The **Dayton Art Institute** has an outstanding collection of Oriental art, South and Central American pottery, and special loan exhibits; open daily except Monday, free. There are also many free concerts here throughout the year. There are carillon recitals on summer evenings at **Carillon Park,** where there is a restored

1905 Wright airplane and replica of the Wright brothers' cycle shop; open 1 May to 31 October, daily except Monday, free. There are Philharmonic concerts, opera, summer theater, and the **American Theater League** productions in the summer and fall months. The original **Newcom Tavern,** one of the structures built by the first settlers, now houses collections of pioneer relics. The **Air Force Museum,** 4¾ miles northwest at **Old Wright Field** is the world's largest military aviation museum. The old **Courthouse, Masonic Temple, Orville and Wilbur Wright's Home,** the home of poet Paul Laurence Dunbar, **Wright-Patterson Air Force Base,** and the **Wright Memorial** east of the city are other points of interest. Also see the series of flood control dams and the **Museum of Natural History,** noted for its children's programs, open daily, free on weekdays. Horse-racing at **Lebanon,** 24 miles away, and ice hockey from October to March, as well as collegiate sports at the **University of Dayton** highlight sporting events.

The **Dayton Horse Show** is held in August along with the Amateur Trapshooting Association's world tournament and the **Hydroglobe,** featuring the top outboard, inboard, and hydroplane boat racers. Following in September are the **Montgomery County Fair** and the **Miami Valley Industrial Show.** In the downtown area are many good motels and hotels, including the **Sheraton-Dayton, Dayton Airport Inn, Stouffer's Dayton Plaza, Ramada Inn Downtown, Holiday Inn-Downtown.** All averaging S\$32-57/D\$38-67. Outlying accommodations include **Imperial House, Holiday Inn South, Howard Johnson's, Quality Inn-Red Horse, Ramada Inn-Airport, Red Root Inns, N & S Dayton Airport Inn,** all averaging S\$26-36/D\$29-48. Good places to eat and only moderately expensive include **Anticoli's,** with an American and Italian menu; **Carillon Cafeteria, King Cole Restaurant; Bill Knapp's, Suttmiller's,** with a wide variety of German and American dishes; the **Shrimp Boat, Rike's Dining Room,** and the **Brown Derby.**

City to Visit

CLEVELAND

Cleveland is in northeast Ohio, on the south shore of Lake Erie; it was named after General Moses Cleveland, who in 1796 laid out the main streets of the city. Its growth was slow for about 30 years, but with the completion of the Ohio and Erie Canals, Cleveland began its steady and continuing development to become Ohio's largest city.

The city is well planned and is frequently cited for its progressive slum clearance and other civic projects. Cleveland is primarily an industrial city and an important world seaport; especially since the opening of the Great Lakes-St Lawrence Seaway. The population of the city is 572,532, metropolitan area, 1,893,000. Running through the center of town is the ½-mile wide **Cuyahoga River Valley,** where most of Cleveland's steel mills, heavy industry, and lumber yards are situated. The city stretches for several miles to both the east and west along Lake Erie.

WHAT TO SEE

University Circle, east of the center of the city, is an unusually attractive cultural area. The **Cleveland Museum of Art** is one of the world's major art galleries, with its medieval Guelph Treasure and its collections of Oriental, Renaissance, and modern art. See **Shaker Heights, Cleveland Heights, Gates Mills,** and **Rocky River,** some of the beautiful suburbs of Cleveland. Cleveland's waterfront and shipping areas, and **The Mall,** the city's civic center, are also interesting. **Dunham Tavern,** early Americana museum in an original 1820 stagecoach inn. **Museum of Natural History,** general exhibits; open Monday to Saturday 10-5. Sunday 1-5:30; adults $2.00, children and senior citizens 50¢. **Frederick C. Crawford Auto-Aviation Museum** of Western Reserve Historical Society, an outstanding collection of 140 beautifully restored antique cars and planes; Tuesday to Saturday 10-5, Sundays 12-6, admission $2.00 adults, $1.00 students and senior citizens. See also **Cleveland Health Education Museum,** which has a number of excellent audio-visual exhibits on health, medicine and human anatomy. Boat trips, mid-June through Sept, on "Goodtime II," a 475-passenger ship out on **Lake Erie** or up **Cuyahoga River** take 2-4 hours; fare, $4.75-8.50, children $2.75-4.75.

Cleveland has 12 city parks, and 17,000 acres of metropolitan parks which form an almost continuous half-circle around the city. Important gardens are the **Cultural Gardens** dedicated to 26 nationalities and ethnic in interest; **Fine Arts Garden** and the **Cleveland Garden Center** are located in University Circle area. The **Zoological Gardens** (Zoo) are located in Brookside Park, admission $2.00 adults, $1.00 children, open daily 9:30-5, free Mon-Fri 9-11; **Cleveland Aquarium,** in **Gordon Park,** admission $1.00, children 50¢, is open 10-5 except Monday, noon to 6 on Sunday; free Tuesdays.

Principal colleges: **Case-Western Reserve University,** founded 1826, coeducational, offers complete selection of courses in arts and sciences, engineering, medicine, professions, business. **Cleveland-Marshall Law School; St John's College; Cuyahoga Community College; Baldwin-Wallace College; John Carroll University; Cleveland State University;** and **Notre Dame** and **Ursuline Colleges** for women.

ACCOMMODATIONS

Downtown accommodations include **Bond Court Hotel** (771-7600, S$40-46/D$50-56); attractive **Hollenden House** (621-0700, S$35/D$43-45); **Stouffer's Inn on the Square** (696-5600, S$48-62/D$58-72), conveniently located. Convenient motels and motor inns include **Holiday Inn, Howard Johnson's, Marriott, Ramada, Sheraton, Stouffer's,** and **Turfside.** Rates average: S$34-44/D$39-51. Near the Airport: **Sheraton Hopkins Airport Hotel** (267-9800, S$49-61/D$59-71); **Holiday Inn** (267-1700, S/D$34-42); **Howard Johnson's** (267-2350, S$30-35/D$32-37); **Airport Hilton Inn** (267-

5100, S$49-59/D$59-80); **Marriott Inn** (252-5333, S$47-57/D$54-65); TraveLodge (252-770, S$27-32/D$32-39).

RESTAURANTS
Bond Court and **Hollenden** dining rooms, center of town, moderately expensive; **Theresa's,** for good Italian cuisine, University Circle area, moderate; **Kiefer's Tavern,** German dishes, moderate; **Jim's Steakhouse,** steaks, expensive; **Ho Ho,** for Chinese dishes, expensive; **Red Coach Grill,** steaks, expensive; **Wagon Wheel,** Shaker Heights, 8 miles east of town, excellent French food, expensive; **Fisherman's Wharf, Pier 1, Pier 2,** and **Pier W,** seafood, moderate to expensive; **The Blue Fox** and the **Red Fox Inn** fine continental cooking, 15-20 miles east, moderate; **Stouffer's Top of the Town,** moderate; **Stouffer's Pier W,** expensive. **The Garland,** in the suburb of Westlake, serves excellent French-Italian food at moderate prices.

ENTERTAINMENT

Theatrical Grill; Cleveland Plaza, Cleveland-Sheraton, Hollenden House hotels, orchestras and entertainment; all expensive. **Diamond Jim's** and **Pickle Bill's** in the "Flats" area, moderate. Try the **Cleveland Agora** for disco. All downtown.

ARTS AND MUSIC
Museum of Art, world-famous, large, fine art collection in a beautiful building; open daily except Monday, free; the **Shakespeare and Cultural Gardens,** illustrating the architecture and culture of 22 nations, open daily, free; and the **Hale Homestead Museum,** a reconstructed 19th-century Western Reserve community 25 miles south of Cleveland with original homes, church, stores, and shops moved in to create a village are all well worth seeing. The excellent and famous **Cleveland Symphony** performs regularly at University Circle during the winter season and also gives summer concerts at Blossom Center, 20 miles south of Cleveland from mid-June to early September. The **Cleveland Playhouse, Lakewood Little Theater** and **Karamu** are among the theatrical groups.

SHOPPING
Stores are open Monday to Saturday 10-5. Monday evening until 8. The principal downtown shopping district is to the east along Euclid Avenue from the Public Square to East 14th Street. Suburban shopping malls offer a full range of shops, stores, and services.

SPORTS
Professional baseball is played by the **Cleveland Indians** in the American League, professional football by the **Browns; Cleveland Cavaliers,** professional basketball; **The Force,** soccer at the Coliseum. There is racing at **Thistledown** and **Northfield Park.** College athletic events are also sched-

uled. Professional hockey, basketball, tennis, at **The Coliseum**, Richfield, about 30 miles south of Cleveland.

A wide variety of facilities are available for golf, tennis, and other sports. Some limited good fishing in Lake Erie; the *Northern Ohio Fishing Guide* is complete and useful.

CALENDAR OF EVENTS

Mid-American Boat Show, January; **Sportsmen's Show**, March; **Home and Flower Show**, March; visit of Metropolitan Opera Association, April to May; **Festival of Freedom**, 4 July; **Cuyahoga County Fair**, August; Fountain Arts Festival, June through August.

WHERE TO GO NEARBY

Nelson Ledges State Forest Park, 35 miles east, has interesting, unusual sandstone and rock formations, good picnic areas. There is a good swimming beach and a campsite 20 miles east, at **Mentor Headlands**. **Portage Lakes State Park**, 45 miles south has a series of lakes and reservoirs known for fishing and boating. **Sea World**, in Aurora, features a killer whale, trained dolphins and seals, and complete water shows. Admission $8.95/$7.95, **Geauga Lake Park**, next door, admission $8.95, children under 4 free, is a complete, excellent amusement park.

The **Lake Erie Island** region consists of **Vermilion, Huron, Sandusky, Port Clinton**, and the **Lake Erie Islands**—all favorite spots for vacation, as is **Cedar Point**, a few miles north of Sandusky. The entire region is filled with cottages, camps, and resorts hotels. **Geneva-on-the-Lake**, 45 miles east of Cleveland, and Vermilion to the west are especially popular cottage and hotel districts.

FURTHER STATE INFORMATION

Ohio Office of Travel & Tourism, P.O. Box 1001, Columbus, Ohio 43216; Hunting, Fishing and Parks: **Department of Natural Resources**, Fountain Square, Columbus, OH 43224. **Greater Cleveland Growth Association**, 690 Union Commerce Building, E 9th & Euclid Streets, Cleveland, OH 44115, comprehensive business information; **Cleveland Convention and Visitors' Bureau**, 1301 E 6th Street, Cleveland 44114 (621-4110), travel information and assistance for large groups; **Columbus Convention and Visitors' Bureau**, 50 W Broad Street, Suite 2540, Columbus, OH 43215. **Pan Am**, 323 Hanna Building, 1422 Euclid Ave, Cleveland (621-0120).

Consulates in Cleveland: Austria, Belgium, Canada, Colombia, Denmark, Finland, France, Germany, Great Britain, Italy, Japan, Korea, Norway, Sweden, Switzerland, Yugoslavia.

USEFUL TELEPHONE NUMBERS
Cleveland

Ambulance	771-3355
Forest City Hospital	249-5200
St. Luke's Hospital	368-7000
Poison Control	231-4455

Fire	621-1212
Police	621-1234
Legal Aid Society	861-6242
Chamber of Commerce	621-3300
Tourist Information	721-0726
Pan Am Reservations (all over Ohio)	(800) 621-2909

Columbus

Emergency Information & Referral	462-4545
Mt. Carmel Medical Center	225-5000
Children's Hospital	461-2000
Poison Control Center	228-1323
Fire	221-2345
Police	462-4545
State Highway Police	466-2660
Legal Aid & Defender Society	224-8374
Chamber of Commerce	221-1321

Oklahoma

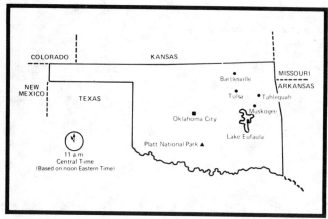

Area	69,919 square miles
Capital	Oklahoma City

Population	3,025,266
Sales Tax	2% (this is a State Tax. Some cities impose an additional amount (1-, 2-, 3%) while others may impose a special hotel tax.)

Weather	Jan	Feb	Mar	Apr	May	Jun	Jul	Aug	Sep	Oct	Nov	Dec
Av Temp (°C)	3	5	9	16	20	26	28	28	23	17	9	5
Days Rain/Snow	5	7	7	8	10	9	7	7	7	6	5	5

When the great package known as the Louisiana Purchase was opened in 1803, Oklahoma looked like the section least likely to succeed. Spanish explorers crossed it in 1541 and a few trappers drifted in some time later. Potential settlers following the Santa Fe Trail saw nothing to tempt them to give up their westward trek. The Indians were able to keep Oklahoma pretty much as it had been for 10,000 years. Elsewhere, however, Indians were occupying lands that white men wanted for themselves.

To solve this problem Congress established the "Indian Territory" in 1830 and into this supposedly worthless area the government forcibly herded Cherokees, Chickasaws, Choctaws, Creeks, and Seminoles. Known as the Five Civilized Tribes, they were removed from their prosperous holdings in Alabama, Arkansas, the Carolinas, Georgia, Mississippi, and Tennessee and given grants of land in Oklahoma. More than 4,000 Cherokees died on the "Trail of Tears," their march to Oklahoma, but those who survived set up a sophisticated system of government and schools, and constructed printing presses for books and newspapers in their own languages.

By the time the Civil War began, some Oklahoma Indians owned slaves and were pro-Confederacy; others were pro-Union, like the whites in neighboring states. In retaliation for siding with the Confederacy, after the war the Five Tribes were forced to share their territory with Indians the government had gathered up from all over the Plains. Between the original Indian Territory and the Oklahoma Territory given to the newly arrived tribes, was a generous section of unassigned land. White settlers had ignored Oklahoma for two centuries but became suddenly anxious to get it. At noon, on 22 April 1889, in the first of five great land rushes, there was a wild scramble as settlers on horseback, bicycles, buggies, and wagons sped over the rough plain in search of good land. Not everyone waited for the signal, however. Some sneaked in sooner to get the best spots, and Oklahoma has been known as the "Sooner State" ever since. Indians and whites since that time have fairly amiably mixed and shared the land. And by now it is a matter of pride if a white can claim at least one Indian ancestor. Will Rogers, the Oklahoman humorist, probably started it when he said: "My forefathers didn't come over on the Mayflower, but they met the boat." Oil was discovered in Oklahoma in 1897, and now there are wells everywhere, even on the grounds of the state capitol in Oklahoma City.

Miami, in **NORTHEASTERN OKLAHOMA,** is at the top of **Lake o'the Cherokees,** a great recreational waterway with 1,300 miles of shoreline. In Miami the **Thunderbird** (542-4435, S$12-15/D$16-18), **Townsman** (542-6631, S$14/D$16), and **Best Western Continental** (542-6681, S$18-20/D$22-24) motels are on Steve Owens Boulevard, 5 miles from downtown. To the south of Miami is the **Shangri-La** resort on Grand Lake o'the Cherokees at Afton (257-4204, S/D$50-67) with some 27 holes of golf, indoor and outdoor tennis, bowling, boating, health spas, swimming, fishing, and its own 4,000-foot airstrip. Will Rogers went to school in **Vinita;** the town puts on an annual **Will Rogers Memorial Rodeo** in August. Southwest of Vinita, in **Claremore,** and on the land where he planned to retire in his old age, is the **Will Rogers Memorial.** The rambling stone ranch house holds his saddles, cowboy trappings, trophies, and personal mementos, and galleries of Indian and pioneer lore. The statue of Rogers is by Jo Davidson. Will and his wife are buried in the garden. The **Will Rogers Celebration** is on 4 November, his birthday, and the **Will Rogers Rodeo** is held here in mid-June. The **Rogers County Fair** is in mid-September. Claremore is also the birthplace of Lynn Riggs, who wrote *Green Grow the Lilacs,* which was converted into the hit musical *Oklahoma.* The original "surrey with the fringe on top" is among other mementos that belonged to the author in **Lynn Riggs Memorial.** Also of considerable interest here is the enormous weapons collection in the **J. M. Davis Gun Museum,** which also contains rare World War I posters, beer steins, and saddles. **Long's Historical Museum** is worth seeing. Just 12 miles north of town, near Oologah, is the two-story white house where Will Rogers was born in 1879; open daily.

Bartlesville is the major city north of **Tulsa.** Among its sleek skyscrapers is **Price Tower,** Frank Lloyd Wright's colorful experiment in combining office and residential space on each floor. A replica of the **Nellie Johnstone Oil Well,** which started Oklahoma on its way to riches, is in Johnstone Park. In the **Phillips Petroleum Building** are comprehensive exhibits related to the oil business. You can dig deeper into this subject with sound-accompanied slides, shown by appointment at the Bureau of Mines' **Energy Research Center** and at the **Frank Phillips Home** (1909), the restored 26-room mansion of the founder of Phillips Petroleum Company. About 14 miles south of Bartlesville is the **Woolaroc Ranch and Museum** where wild animals wander freely. Don't get out of your car until you reach the main building, which displays paintings by Frederic Remington, Charles Russell, and other noted painters and sculptors of Western scenes. Just north of Bartlesville is the little town of **Dewey,** where Tom Mix was US Deputy Marshall until he became one of the highest-paid silent screen stars. The **Tom Mix Museum** is fascinating with his elaborate cowboy gear, including a $15,000 saddle and his famous white sombrero.

The territory known as the **OSAGE NATION** lay west of Bartlesville to the Arkansas River, and **Pawhuska** was its capital. Even before oil was discovered, the Osage were the country's wealthiest tribe, and the decision to divide oil royalties on a per capita basis has made Osage County one of the richest communities in the entire world. The Osage are still loyal to their heritage, and rare and unusual tribal artifacts are proudly displayed in the **Osage Museum** on Agency Hill, where tribal business is transacted. The **Osage County Historical Museum** has Indian and pioneer relics. Special events in town include the **Osage Indian Tribal Dances** in mid-June, the real thing and not just a tourist attraction; the **International Roundup Cavalcade** for 4 days in late July; and the **Ben Johnson Memorial Steer Roping Contest** and **Art Show** in late August. Stop at **Red Corn's Restaurant** for authentic Indian food.

The Muskogee Turnpike runs southeast from Tulsa to **Fort Smith** on the Oklahoma-Arkansas border, but there are some worthwhile digressions along the way. **Tahlequah,** in the foothills of the Ozarks, was the capital of the **CHEROKEE NATION,** founded by the survivors of the "Trail of Tears" in 1839. On the town square are the **County Courthouse** (1867), which was the Cherokee capitol building; and the **Supreme Court Building** (1844), where the Cherokee Supreme Court met until it was converted into the office of the *Cherokee Advocate,* the first Indian newspaper. **Cherokee National Prison** is at the corner of Choctaw and Water streets. **Cherokee Female Seminary** (1851) became the nucleus for today's **Northeastern State University,** where the library contains an outstanding collection of Cherokee manuscripts and publications. The **Murell Home,** south of town, was built in 1844 by a Virginian who had accompanied the Cherokees on their forced march into Oklahoma. Furnished with pieces Murell imported from France, this is one of the finest antebellum houses in the state. **Tsa-La-Gi**, southeast of Tahlequah, is an authentic Indian village where descendants of the area's original Cherokee residents still carry on the traditions and craftsmanship of their ancestors. "The Trail of Tears" pageant is staged in the outdoor amphitheater nightly, except Sunday, from late June through late August, and follows the Cherokees' history from their eviction from Georgia and the Carolinas in 1838 to statehood in 1907. The **Cherokee Arts and Crafts Center** is nearby.

MUSKOGEE, near the junction of the Arkansas, Grand, and Verdigris rivers, was a convenient meeting place for Indians. Today it is an important seaport; barges from New Orleans turn here from the Arkansas River into the Verdigris for the 50-mile trip to the Port of Catoosa at Tulsa. There's the *USS Batfish* submarine, a World War II memorial and more, here. Muskogee may be a completely modern industrial city, but it is still the headquarters for the Five Civilized Tribes. The US Union Agency, formed in 1894, still conducts business with the Indians in the Federal Building. The **Five Civilized Tribes Museum in Honor Heights Park** is a showcase of arts and crafts, documents, costumes, and treaties. In April, more than 25,000 blooms are to be seen during the **Azalea Festival**. Everyday utensils of Indian life are in the fine museum at **Bacone Indian College**. The **Thomas-Foreman Home** (1898) was the home of historians Grant and Carolyn Thomas Foreman, who collaborated on numerous books about the Five Civilized Tribes. Just east of town is **Antiques Inc., Horseless Carriages Unlimited,** a museum with more than 40 antique cars still in mint condition, including a Humber that belonged to Sir Winston Churchill and a 1911 Rolls-Royce once owned by an Indian maharajah. Northeast of town is the reconstruction of **Fort Gibson** (1824), the first army post in the territory. Getting back to the Muskogee Turnpike, at **Sallisaw** turn into the hills to the spot where Sequoyah built his one-room log cabin in 1829. This brilliant Cherokee devised an 84-character alphabet which enabled his people to become literate within a very short time. A stone building now protects his simple cabin, which is maintained as a shrine; open daily except Monday. Sequoia trees were named for this Cherokee.

The **Ouachita Mountains** fill southeastern Oklahoma, a wild and lovely region once known only to hunters and trappers. The **Talimena Skyline Drive**, still completely uncommercialized, twists along ridge crests through a wilderness little changed from the days when it was part of the Choctaw Nation, and extends from the little town of Talihina to Mena in Arkansas; there are campsites along the way.

Okmulgee, about 30 miles south of Tulsa, was the capital of the **CREEK NATION** from 1868 to 1907. In the **Council House**, saved from demolition by Will Rogers, the Creek leaders still meet to discuss tribal business, but it is also an excellent tribal museum of folklore, weapons, and crafts. The sedate sandstone structure is something of an anachronism in the present-day town whose citizens have won affluence from oil wells, glassmaking plants, pecan orchards, and cotton fields. **Henryetta,** where the east-west and north-south highways intersect, is the home of the **Jim Shoulders Rodeo Riding School** (652-7558) where four or five times from May to September intensive 4-day coaching sessions are held to tutor teenagers for rodeo competition. Mr. Shoulders recommends that children—boys and girls—should be in their mid-teens and with good reflexes. Cost of a 4-day course is $200.

McAlester began in 1870 with a tent store put up at the intersection of the Texas Road and California Trail. The store's founder became a Choctaw by marriage, got into tribal trouble over coal mining claims, was sentenced to death, escaped, and lived to become the state's lieutenant governor in 1911. The **Tobusky County Courthouse,** scene of McAlester's trial, was where Choctaw law was carried out from 1870-1907. The town is also the site of the International Headquarters, **Order of Rainbow for Girls, the Oklahoma State Prison Rodeo**—late August, early September, nominal admission. The copper-domed **Scottish Rite Temple** is even more impressive at night when light glows through its multicolored glass inserts. In McAlester, stay at **Best Western McHoma Lodge** (423-1150, S$22-24/D$26-35) or the **Holiday Inn** (423-7766, S$22-69/D$27-69). East of McAlester in Krebs, is **Pete's Place,** highly regarded for its Italian fare and home of the annual Italian festival in late May. Down near the Texas border the highway skirts around **Durant,** a pleasant little city with towering magnolias and stately southern homes. West of town is **Lake Texoma,** formed by damming the Red River. Here Texans and Oklahomans fish, golf, swim, ride horseback, water-ski, cruise around in outboard motor boats, and go hunting in the fall. **Texoma Lodge** (564-2311, S$25-28/D$32-42) is one of Oklahoma's seven state-owned lodges; cottages are also available. On the eastern shore of the lake are the ghostly remains of **Fort Washita,** built by General Zachary Taylor to help protect the Five Civilized Tribes from the more ferocious Plains Indians.

Lake Eufaula, northeast of McAlester, is a huge man-made lake with every facility for water sports. The little town of **Eufaula,** once the home of a boarding school for Indian girls, now provides coed facilities for students attending the local public school. **The Indian Journal,** founded in 1876, still publishes weekly. North of Eufaula is **Fountainhead State Park,** and south of town is **Arrowhead State Park.** Both are excellent recreation areas, and both have palatial state-operated lodges, as well as campsites. **Fountainhead Lodge** and **Arrowhead Lodge** are about S$25-30/D$32-48.

Interstate 35 runs from Salina, Kansas, to Laredo, Texas, neatly bisecting Oklahoma. Up near the Kansas border is **Ponca City,** which sprang up in 1 day, during the 1893 land rush. The **Indian Museum and Pioneer Woman Museum** are worth stopping to see. Turn west off I-35 onto US 64 to get to **Enid** with its enormous grain elevators and flour mills. Visit the **Cherokee Strip Museum** at Fourth and East Market streets. If you want to see the genuine **Homesteader's Sod House,** drive 30 miles west to Cleo Springs and then 6 miles north. It has probably survived because its walls are nearly 3 feet thick and plastered with an alkali and water mixture. It was occupied from 1893 to 1909 and then used as a storehouse until it was rescued and furnished in 1907 decor by the Oklahoma Historical Society. Getting back to I-35, still heading south, turn east on OK 51 to go to **Stillwater,** home of **Oklahoma State University. Pawnee,** 12 miles northeast of Stillwater, is worth a detour to see the **Pawnee Bill Museum.** Pawnee Bill (Major Gordon W. Lillie) was Buffalo Bill's partner in the Wild West Shows, and his large house is packed with mementos. Buffalo and longhorn cattle graze in the adjacent pasture. Regional Indians put on a rousing **Home Coming Pow Wow** in Pawnee during the first weekend in July. **Guthrie,** only about 20 miles north of Oklahoma City, was founded by "spontaneous combustion" during the 1889 land rush, became the capital of Oklahoma Territory in 1890, and was capital of the state from 1907-1910. The town's history is entertainingly revived during the **'89er Celebration** for three days around 22 April. Guthrie's **Scottish Rite Temple** is one of the world's largest Masonic buildings.

Norman, on the southern outskirts of Oklahoma City, is the home of the **University of Oklahoma.** For a tour of its large, interesting campus, pick up a guide from the public relations office in the Memorial Union. Continuing south on I-35 heading for Dallas-Fort Worth, take time to stop at **Platt National Park.** Though the smallest in the national park system, it ranks second highest in visitor attendance. The oil and cattle town of **Ardmore** is conveniently situated between Platt and Arbuckle Mountains to the north, and Lake Texoma to the south and has become a headquarters for vacationers. Accommodations include: **Best Western Inn** (226-1270, S$17-19/D$22-29); **Holiday Inn** (223-7130, S$24-36/D$31-36); **Lake Murray Lodge** (223-6600, S$15-18/D$21-24); and **Ramada Inn** (226-1250, S/D$30-32).

The H. E. Bailey Turnpike in **SOUTHWESTERN OKLAHOMA** is the fast route from Oklahoma City to Wichita Falls, Texas. Go west from the turnpike on OK 9 for about 15 miles, to **Andarko.** This is the headquarters of the **Southern Plains Indian Agency,** and the Federal Building is decorated with handsome murals painted by Kiowa Indians. On the east side of town is an outdoor museum of sculpture, the **Indian Hall of Fame,** where there are busts and statues of America's best known Indians. Nearby is the **Southern Plains Indian Arts and Crafts Museum** with authentic beadwork, carvings, weapons, ceremonial costumes, and paintings. Contemporary articles are for sale. North of town is the **Riverside Indian School,** founded in 1872 and attended by children from 13 different tribes. South of town is **Indian City,** a re-created but true-to-life village that is typical of those once inhabited by Apaches, Caddos, Comanches, Kiowas, Navajos, Pawnees, and Wichitas. Indian guides conduct tours of tepees, mud huts, and tribal lodges, and also perform traditional dances. Try to be in Andarko for the big **American Indian Exposition** held for a week in mid-August. The turnpike crosses **Fort Sill Military Reservation** before it reaches Lawton. Fort Sill was established in 1869 when the Plains Indians were being understandably irritable because white men had slaughtered so many buffalo for their hides. **The Old**

Post, now a national historic landmark, includes the **Fort Sill Museum**, a fascinating treasury of Indian, pioneer, and army lore; the original **Old Post's Chapel;** the original **Guardhouse,** where the notorious Geronimo was among many Indians once detained. Geronimo became a respectable farmer and member of the Dutch Reformed Church, and was buried in 1909 in the Apache cemetery northeast of the fort; **Cannon Walk** displays weapons from all over the world; the **Hall of Flags** has a display of banners; and the history of American artillery is represented in the displays in **McLain Hall** and **Hamilton Hall.**

Lawton, which grew up out of the land lottery of 1901, has plenty of old-timers who can recall the turbulent time of the town's first days. The **Museum of the Great Plains** traces the impact made on the region by successive tides of Indians, fur trappers, buffalo hunters, settlers, and cowboys. Lawton celebrates its birthday for 4 days every year with a big rodeo and general fiesta. **Holiday Inn** (353-1682, S$27-35/D$30-36); **Montego Bay Inn** (353-0200, S$21-23/D$24-26); **Ramada Inn** (355-7155, S$20-23/D$23-27); and **Best Western Sandpiper Inn** (353-0310, S$21-26/D$25-29) are here. West of town is the **Wichita Mountains Wildlife Refuge,** dotted with lakes for fishing and swimming and good places to camp and picnic. On the hills are nearly 1,000 buffalo, carefully nurtured from the 15 that were left when the conservationists arrived in 1907. They are rounded up every year in October and November; many are sold to zoos and to ranchers hoping to start their own herds. Elk, deer, Texas longhorns, and other animals are protected in the refuge. There's a great view of the whole area from the top of **Mt Scott,** 2,464 feet, which has a paved road to the summit. Easter Sunrise Services are held in a natural amphitheater at the foot of **Mt Roosevelt.**

Travelers heading to the **WESTERN SECTION** of the state from Oklahoma City on I-40 come to **El Reno.** Stay at the **Best Western Astro** (262-6490, S$19-22/D$20-24) or **Best Western Cherokee Motor Inn** (884-2931, S$14-24/D$18-28). **Fort Reno,** built in the 1870s as protection against Cheyenne and Arapaho Indians, is now an agricultural and livestock experimental station. **Clinton,** farther west, has an Indian Pow-Wow the third weekend in June, a Rodeo the last weekend in July. Visit the town's **Western Trails Museum,** an unusually good display of what life was like for Oklahoma pioneers. **Elk City,** in the western plains, has oil wells and natural gas. Visit the **Old Town Museum,** a carefully detailed replica of a typical frontier community. The **Sequoyah Intertribal Pow Wow** is held in Elk City in early June. Accommodations include **Best Western Flamingo Motel & Resort** (225-1811, S$16-20/D$20-22); **Quality Inn** (225-1061, S$26-36/D$30-40); and **Ramada Inn** (225-5000, S$20-25/D$28-32).

The **OKLAHOMA PANHANDLE** is 167 miles across and only 34 miles deep. Irrigation produces immense fields of wheat, corn, and alfalfa, and helps to support great herds of beef cattle. The great arid mesas and canyons of numerous rivers once formed a natural barrier to Texans driving their own cattle to railheads in Kansas. **Woodward,** on the southeastern ridge of the Panhandle, is headquarters for the **US Great Plains**

The way of life of the Plains Indians is kept alive at Indian City, near Andarko.

Experimental Station, which tests crops and trees for their ability to survive the region's difficult conditions. The **Pioneer Museum** has exhibits of items that used to help the early settlers to survive. East of town is the **Boiling Springs State Park.** Farther northeast are the **Little Sahara Recreational Area** and **Alabaster Caverns State Park,** two recreation areas built around interesting natural phenomena. Woodward has a good rodeo during the fourth week in July. Motels include the **Best Western Wayfarer Inn** (256-5553, S$19-22/D$22-25); **Holiday Inn** (256-7600, S$24-26/D$30-32); and **Sands Motel** (256-7442, S$14-15/D$17-22). **Guymon,** in almost the precise center of the Panhandle, is on an elevation of 3,119 feet. Try to be in Guymon for **Pioneer Days,** held the first weekend in May; it features a free chuckwagon breakfast, costume parade, and professional rodeo. Accommodations include the **Best Western Townsman Motel** (338-6556, S$18-19/D$20-24) and **Best Western Ambassador Inn** (338-5555, S$22-25/D$28-31). Recalling the days when neither Indians nor white settlers laid much claim to the Panhandle is the **No Man's Land Historical Museum** on the campus of **Panhandle State University** in Goodwell, 10 miles south of Guymon. The **World Championship Cow Chip Throwing Contest** is a unique event held at **Beaver,** also near Guymon, in connection with the **Cimarron Territory Celebration,** the third week in April.

Cities To Visit

OKLAHOMA CITY

Oklahoma City, the capital of Oklahoma, is in the central part of the state. The city had a dramatic beginning in 1889 when the rush for the free prairie land took place. Between noon and sundown of 22 April some 10,000 people arrived by wagon, horseback, and foot to claim land, and by nightfall the settlers had staked their claims on the newly opened territory. The discovery of oil in 1928 gave the city even further impetus.

If the United States is the melting pot of the world, then Oklahoma City is the melting pot of the United States, for people from all over have settled here. Skyscrapers and oil wells dot the flat landscape and the skyline can be seen from miles away. The city has a scrubbed look because natural gas rather than coal is used for industry and private consumption. Population 372,690; metropolitan district 699,100. Oklahoma City is often cited as an example of good industrial city planning.

WHAT TO SEE

The **State Capitol,** surrounded by oil wells; oil is pumped up from a pool directly beneath the building itself. The distinctive modern architecture of **St Luke's Methodist Church** and the **Church of Tomorrow;** the **Civic Center;** the **Stockyards** open to the public from Tuesday through Friday. Also see the **State Historical Building** with one of the largest collections of Indian material in the country; open Monday to Friday

8-9:30pm, Saturday 8-6, Sunday 1:30-4:30, free. **National Cowboy Hall of Fame; Western Heritage Center,** a national shrine, small admission charges. Visit the **Omniplex** (science, industry, arts, planetarium), **Oklahoma Firefighters Museum, Softball Hall of Fame & Museum, zoo,** all in Lincoln Park, small admission charges. Recreational facilities at **Will Rogers Park** and **Springlake Amusement Park.**

ACCOMMODATIONS

Downtown are the **Sheraton-Century Center** (235-2780, S$55-63/D$67-75) and **Skirvin Plaza** (232-4411, S$40-50/D$50-60), both near the Myriad Convention Center; the **Lincoln Plaza Inn** (528-2741, S$36-42/D$42-50) and **Pebbletree Inn** (528-2511, S$30-45/D$36-45) are near the Northeast Expressway. In addition there are about 60 other motels and motor hotels in and near the city. Hotel Tax: 2%.

RESTAURANTS

The White House, the Cellar, Raffles (modeled after the Singapore Hotel), **Juniors, Applewoods, Hungry Peddler, Michael's Plum, Chi Chis** (Mexican), **Steak and Ale. Anna Maude,** very popular cafeteria and restaurant, beer served, moderate. **Sleepy Hollow** is known for its relaxed atmosphere and "down-home" Southern cooking; **Christophers,** located by a swan-filled lake and parkland, serves American dishes; **Jamil's** is known for its Lebanese hors d'oeuvres, steak, and lobster. In Oklahoma City, as in all of the state, the sale of alcoholic beverages is permitted in retail package stores. Cocktails and other drinks, however, are served only in private clubs, which are numerous and easily joined.

ARTS AND MUSIC

Oklahoma Art Center, in State Fair Park, permanent art exhibitions; open daily except Monday 10-5, Sunday 1-5; free. The **Oklahoma City Symphony Orchestra** plays a full concert season. Plays are presented regularly by the **Lyric Theater, Oklahoma Theater Center,** and **Gaslight Dinner Theatre.**

SHOPPING

Stores in the suburbs remain open in the evenings and many on Sunday afternoon. **Shepler's** is the best Western merchandise store in the state; **Tribal Arts Gallery** specializes in Indian paintings, prints, and jewelry; **Creek Nation Crafts, Inc.** specializes in authentic Indian pottery.

SPORTS

College athletic events during the winter season: wrestling, football, car races, and professional hockey. Golf can be played at numerous public and private courses. The local parks have tennis courts, swimming pools, and riding trails. There is good fishing in nearby lakes; hunting is available during the fall.

CALENDAR OF EVENTS
Livestock show, third week in March; **Festival of the Arts,** mid-April; **State Fair,** September; **National Rodeo Finals,** December.

WHERE TO GO NEARBY
Frontier City, northwest of Oklahoma City on US 66, an authentic reproduction of a frontier town complete with daily gun fights; adults $1.56, children (under 12) $1.04. **Roman Nose State Park,** 60 miles northwest; modern cabins, fishing, swimming pool. **Lake Murray State Park,** 110 miles south; lodges and hotel accommodations, camping, water sports. **Platt National Park,** 90 miles south; picnic area, camping grounds, sulphur springs. Fountainhead and Arrowhead Lodges on Lake Eufaula, 120 miles east. Lake Texoma on the Texas border, 125 miles south; excellent camping and fishing.

TULSA

Tulsa is in northeastern Oklahoma, on the Arkansas River. It is the hub of many large lakes in eastern Oklahoma built in recent years under the Arkansas Basin Development program. Each has been well developed as a recreational center with fine resort facilities. The region was settled by a tribal division of Creek Indians who migrated here in 1836. Modern Tulsa's history began with that memorable day in 1882 when the San Francisco Railroad, then called the Atlantic and Pacific, was extended from Vinita, Indian Territory, to the site of the present city. The new town grew rapidly and was incorporated in 1896. The discovery of oil in 1901 also encouraged growth; there was a particularly rapid period of development from 1910 to 1920.

Tulsa, the "Oil Capital of the World," is a clean attractive city. Most oil towns in the country have grown up quickly and Tulsa is no exception; but whereas the others tend to retain their boom town atmosphere, Tulsa has become quite sophisticated and cultured. The boom town of the past is hard to trace in this thriving community. Population about 360,919, metropolitan area 689,628.

WHAT TO SEE
The **Old Council Tree,** traditional gathering place of Creek Indians; **World Museum/Art Center; Gilcrease Institute of American History and Art; Boston Avenue Methodist Church,** startling architecture; **Mohawk Park** and its zoo; **Philbrook Art Center; Oral Roberts University; Fenster Gallery of Jewish Arts,** Sundays 2-4pm, free, other times by appointment; **Tulsa Port of Catoosa,** nation's newest and most inland, year around river port; **Frankoma Pottery** in nearby Sapulpa on US 66, free plant tours, Monday through Saturday; **D-X Sunray Oil Co** and **Texaco Company's** plants, conducted tours on weekdays. **Will Rogers Memorial,** 28 miles northeast. **Tsa-La-Gi,** to the east, is an authentic Cherokee village. **Mohawk Park,** about 7 miles northeast of the city, has a zoo, lake, two

golf courses, and other facilities; open daily. **Tulsa Rose Gardens** are particularly interesting; open daily, free.

ACCOMMODATIONS

Downtowner Motor Inn (583-6251, S$18/D$22-25), 2 blocks from Civic Center; **Williams Plaza** (582-9000, S$55-65/D$75-85); and the **Holiday Inn Civic Center** (587-9441, S$30-46/D$36-52) are located downtown. Also downtown is the city's newest hotel, the **Tulsa Excelsior.** There are many motels on US 66 and I-44, almost all are air-conditioned. Among them are **Camelot Inn,** a 400-room "castle" with a shield-shaped swimming pool, and **Hilton Inn,** averaging S$42-58/D$53-73); and **Howard Johnson's, Ramada Inn, Tradewinds,** and **TraveLodge** averaging S$20-37/D$22-44. Hotel Tax: 3-7%.

RESTAURANTS

Blue Danube, Montaques, the Razor Clam, expensive; **La Louisiann** (seafood a specialty), **The Fountains, Argentina International Steak House, Benihana** (Japanese food), **Chi-Chis (Mexican), Molly Murphy's,** moderate; **Peking Gardens & Tao Tao** (Chinese), inexpensive. **Sleepy Hollow** and **Jamil's** for steak, moderately expensive; **Villa Venice,** good meals, fairly expensive; **Casa Bonita** and **El Chico,** Mexican food; **Italian Inn; Borden's** cafeterias, very reasonable. Among other restaurants are those at the Camelot Inn and Howard Johnson's.

ARTS AND MUSIC

Philbrook Art Center, Indian objects, general art exhibits; open Monday through Saturday, 10-5, Sunday 1-5; $2 adults, $1 senior citizens and college students, free under 18. **Gilcrease Institute of American History and Art,** fine collection of art concerning frontier life and the American Indian; open Monday-Saturday, 9-5, Sunday 1-5, free. **Tulsa Opera** presents operas; concerts are given by the **Tulsa Philharmonic Orchestra;** the **Tulsa Civic Ballet** presents a full season, and the **Theater Tulsa** conducts a year-round program. *Oklahoma* is presented outdoors, June through Aug at **Discoveryland,** 8:15pm, preceded by an optional barbecue dinner; closed Sundays.

SHOPPING

Most store hours are from 10-6 daily except Monday and Thursday, when they are 10-9. Many stores are open on Sundays.

SPORTS

Oral Roberts University basketball and baseball; **Tulsa Roughnecks,** professional soccer; **Tulsa Twisters,** professional team rodeo; **Tulsa Drillers,** baseball; modified and super modified stock cars, 8pm Saturdays—March through October, **Tulsa Speedway;** drag racing, **Tulsa International Raceway,** twice monthly, Sundays, March through October. College football and basketball are played by **Tulsa University;** professional hockey by the **Tulsa Oilers Hockey Club.** There is golf at **La Fortune Park** and at **Mohawk Park's** public course; tennis and swimming at public pools. There is no closed season on fishing; hunting in season.

CALENDAR OF EVENTS

International Finals Rodeo, January; **Northeast Oklahoma Square Dance Festival,** March; **Johnny Lee Wills Rodeo, Horse Show, Music Festival,** May; **Tulsa Pow Wow and Indian Festivities,** August; **Great Raft Race,** Labor Day; **State Fair,** October.

WHERE TO GO NEARBY

Lake Murray, 204 miles southwest, excellent sports facilities, boating, swimming, cabins; **Osage Hills State Park,** 65 miles north, beautiful rugged country, fishing, boating, cabin accommodations; **Sequoyah State Park,** about 50 miles east, many recreational facilities. **Grand Lake,** 75 miles northeast, with cabins for fishing. Fort Gibson, 45 miles east, boating and fishing; **Keystone Lake,** 15 miles west; **Oologah Reservoir,** 35 miles north; **Lake Hudson,** 60 miles east; and Eufaula Lake, 70 miles south of Tulsa are all enjoyable. Lake Texoma, approximately 200 miles south, is a popular resort area.

PLATT NATIONAL PARK— ARBUCKLE RECREATION AREA

The area is adjacent to the city of Sulphur in south central Oklahoma, 30 miles northeast of Ardmore, 30 miles southwest of Ada, and 90 miles south of Oklahoma City. It is open the year round, but is most beautiful during the redbud (an American leguminous tree, sometimes incorrectly called the American Judas Tree) season, the first 2 weeks in April and in October and November.

There are six good campgrounds—three in Platt National Park and three in Arbuckle Recreation Area; 14-day-stay limit in summer and 30-day limit per calendar year. Motels and cottages in the town of Sulphur. Each campground has outdoor lighting, city water, garbage facilities, and washrooms, and each site has a table, a fireplace, and a space for parking.

Platt, a gem of nature, is encircled by the 6-mile **Perimeter Drive** enclosing quiet wooded hills, miniature waterfalls, and **Travertine** and **Rock** creeks. Two large freshwater springs are named **Antelope** and **Buffalo,** after the animals that once watered here, and a small herd of buffalo still lives in the park. The many cold mineral-water, sulphur, and bromide springs were highly regarded by the Choctaw and Chickasaw Indians of long ago. **Travertine Nature Center,** with live exhibits of plants and animals of the area, is open daily all year. During the summer season, visitors may participate in a number of daily programs such as a morning nature walk led by a park naturalist; an afternoon aquatic walk in **Rock Creek,** where interesting features of the creek and its wildlife are discovered; the children's program at 11am for "children" of all ages. Visitors may view a movie, take a mini-walk, paint, or learn more about live animals. Movies are shown at 2, 3, and 4pm. Or enjoy a live evening program in the auditorium on such subjects as the environment, ecology, wildlife, history, insects, and plants of the area.

Arbuckle, about 8 miles southwest of Platt, includes low rolling hills, springs, clear-running streams, rocky bluffs, grassy ridges, and wooded hillsides. Some of the recreational activities in this lovely area include boating, fishing, camping, picnicking, swimming, water-skiing, skin-diving, and hunting.

FURTHER STATE INFORMATION

Oklahoma Department of Tourism and Recreation, 500 Will Rogers Memorial Building, Oklahoma City, OK 73105. **Oklahoma State Chamber of Commerce,** 4020 North Lincoln, Oklahoma City, OK 73105. Hunting and Fishing: **Department of Wildlife Conservation,** 1801 North Lincoln Boulevard, Oklahoma City, OK 73105. **Oklahoma City Chamber of Commerce,** One Santa Fe Plaza, Oklahoma City, OK 73102. **Metropolitan Tulsa Chamber of Commerce,** 616 S. Boston Avenue, Tulsa, OK 74119. National Parks: **Platt National Park—Arbuckle Recreation Area** (Superintendent), PO Box 201, Sulphur, OK 73086.

USEFUL TELEPHONE NUMBERS IN OKLAHOMA CITY

Heart Attack Emergencies	236-0191
Doctors General Hospital	236-3011
Presbyterian Hospital	271-5100
Poison Control Center	271-5454
Fire	235-1313
Police	231-2121
Highway Police	424-4011
Legal Aid Society	272-9461
Chamber of Commerce	634-1436
Tourist Information	942-7088
Pan Am Reservations	235-3631

Oregon

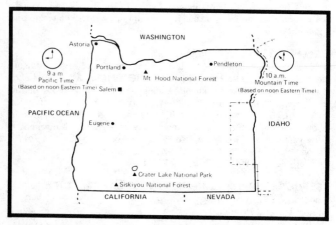

Area	96,981 square miles	Population	2,632,663
Capital	Salem	Sales Tax	None

Weather

	Jan	Feb	Mar	Apr	May	Jun	Jul	Aug	Sep	Oct	Nov	Dec
Av Temp (°C)	4	6	8	11	14	17	20	19	17	12	7	5
Days Rain/Snow	20	16	17	14	12	10	3	5	8	13	18	19

Oregon has one of the finest coastlines in the United States and receives more visitors every year than it has permanent residents. Huge forests, in which the timber stands about as high as the eye can see, lofty mountains, cherry orchards, and hayfields are among the natural delights that help to generate an income of more than $600 million a year from tourism.

The state has several distinct and exciting touring areas, all connected by more than 700 miles of freeways including Interstates 5 and 80 in the north, west, and east. The Pacific shoreline stretches for 400 miles, followed by US 101. Beautiful, sandy, broad beaches from Astoria to Brookings are nearly all public domain. Resort villages, small cities, and campgrounds provide excellent accommodations for those who seek crabbing, fishing, surfing, and sun bathing along the coast.

The **Williamette Valley,** home of **Portland** and the state capital, **Salem,** is a lush region of farms, rivers, forests, and parks bordered by snow-capped mountain peaks, notably **Mt Hood. Crater Lake,** with its sapphire blue water in a former volcano 1,932 feet deep, the deepest lake in the US, is here too. And from **Crown Point State Park** to the spectacular Multnomah Falls, the **Columbia River Gorge** is still remarkably like the vistas which greeted explorers in the last century.

Oregon's 238 state parks and 13 national forests, many of which allow overnight camping, provide excellent opportunities for reeling in a chinook, crappie, sea bass, or rainbow trout. The best hunting is found in the eastern and central sections of the state, where deer, bear, grouse, quail, duck, and elk abound. Seven parks are open year round and most others open their gates in mid-April. Ski areas are located near **Baker, La Grande, Bend, Lakeview, Klamath Falls, Ashland,** and on **Mt Hood.**

One of the prettiest drives in the country, US 101 hugs the **OREGON COAST** from Astoria south to Brookings on the California line. **Astoria,** dating from the days of Lewis and Clark and John Astor, is on the Columbia River 10 miles inland from where it meets the Pacific. **Astoria Column,** 125 feet high, commemorates the first settlement and illustrates it with a sculptured frieze. The view from the top of the column is a spectacular sight of mountains meeting river and river meeting the Pacific; open daily all year. **Fort Clatsop National Monument** marks the spot where the explorers Lewis and Clark wintered in 1805; open daily. The fort now standing is a reconstruction. The **Columbia River Maritime Museum** features memorabilia recalling the drama of the river and the men who worked on its tributaries and the northwest coast; the *Columbia*, a lightship which stood at the river's mouth in the early 1900s, is open in the summer. **Fort Stevens State Park** is about 14 miles west of town and is the only continental US military post that was fired on in World War II; a Japanese submarine fired several shells onto the beach in 1942. Summer evening programs and clamming are fun for campers. In Astoria there is the **Thunderbird Motel** (325-7373, S$27-34/D$35-39), two miles from the airport, and the **Crest Motel** (325-3141, S/D$23-27.50), five miles from the airport, overlooking the Columbia River. **The Astoria Regatta and Fish Festival** is held in late August.

Seaside is the state's oldest resort. A monument marks the spot where Lewis and Clark constructed a salt cairn with which to boil down sea water to obtain needed salt. Deep-sea life and trained seals are entertaining at **Seaside Aquarium;** open year round. **Saddle Mountain State Park** is southeast of Seaside on US 26; hiking, camping, and picnicking. **Haystack Rock,** one of the world's largest monoliths, is at Cannon Beach. Sea lion rookeries are offshore in **Ecola State Park,** which also offers clam digging along six miles of ocean frontage. Enjoy superb scenery around **Tillamook** and its beautiful Loop Drive to **Cape Meares** and **Oceanside** on the Pacific. Watch for **Cape Meares Lighthouse, Three Arch Rocks Federal Sea Lion and Bird Refuge,** and the deformed Sitka spruce known as the "Octopus." **Cape Lookout State Park** has surf bathing and a virgin spruce forest. The **Tillamook County Pioneer Museum** is open Tuesday-Friday 1-5, weekends 10-5, free; it features displays of Indian and pioneer relics and nature lore. Be sure to try the excellent Tillamook cheddar cheese. The **Fleet of Flowers Ceremony** is held the last day of May in Depoe Bay to commemorate drowned sailors. Commercial fishermen ply their way past the rocky inlet to fish the ocean. **Depoe Bay Aquarium** has performing seals and a fish tank; open daily all year.

The Oregon coast can be seen in quiet surroundings from the five state parks in the area. **Lacey's Doll House** in Pixieland features more than 4,000 dolls and an antique collection. The **Cape Foulweather** area is the home of sea lions, birds, and seals, some of which bask in the sun atop **Otter Crest,** a 453-foot high flat rock jutting from the shoreline. When the tide is low, starfish, sea urchins, pools, and sea caves are also visible.

Newport is typical of this entire coastal region, offering everything from four-hour excursion boat rides to far-out metal sculptures and handicrafts at the **Yaquina Art Center. Undersea Gardens** has 3,000 marine creatures and 112 windows through which to view them; open daily. The **Marine Science Center** of Oregon State University conducts research on oceanography and sponsors natural history and marine science lectures and films daily; free. **Devil's Punch Bowl State Park,** where high tide fills a bowl-shaped rock with water in exploding fury, is nearby. **Loyalty Days Festival** is held in Newport on the weekend nearest 1 May. Mineral collecting is a popular sport along the beaches. **7 Seas Motel** (265-2277, S/D$20-32) and the **Jolly Knight Motel** (265-7723, commercial S$18, S$20-24/D$24-28), both at the center of town, along with the **Windjammer Motel** (265-8853, S$30-35/D$35-45), five blocks from downtown, provide good rooms.

Florence is the next sizable town down the coast. **Jessie M. Honeyman State Park** has sand dunes, beaches, and rhododendrons. The state's most powerful beacon is housed at **Heceta Lighthouse.** The **Rhododendron Festival** is held in Florence on the third weekend in May. **Sea Lions Cave** is the home of hundreds of sea lions, which can be seen on daily 30-minute tours the year round. From Florence south to the tip of **North Bend Peninsula** poking into **Coos Bay** is a 50-mile stretch of sand dunes extending one to three miles in from the Pacific. Most of the area is included in the **Oregon Dunes Recreation Area.** With the exception of **Umpqua Lighthouse State Park** at Winchester Bay, where some dunes stand as high as 500 feet, and areas adjacent to **Horsfall Beach Road,** the stretch is open to dune buggy enthusiasts. Three private operators offer rides. From the town of Coos Bay, probably more lumber is shipped than from any other port in the country. Hotels are **Thunderbird Motor Inn** (267-4141, S$29-34/D$39-44), three miles from the airport, and **Royal Dunes Motor Hotel** (269-9371, S$21-23.10/D$25.20-29.40), two miles from the airport. Oregon "jade," gem-quality agates, and fossils reward beachcombers along this stretch of coast. The **Cranberry Festival** is held for three days in mid-September at Brandon, a typical coastal town near **Bullards Beach State Park** which borders on both the Pacific and the Coquille River; good for swimming and boating.

At **Port Orford,** Cape Blanco juts into the Pacific like a chalky facade; **Prehistoric Gardens,** open daily, has life-sized replicas of prehistoric animals displayed in a rain forest; **Sea Crest Motel** (332-3040, S/D$27-34) overlooks the ocean half a mile from town center. South of town, **Humbug**

Mountain State Park, with its 1,750-foot peak, overlooks a beach, trout streams, and a virgin forest. Farther south are **Wedderburn** and **Gold Beach,** center for **Rogue River** excursions. Three companies offer jet boat rides up the river to **Agness** and two offer excursions upstream past Agness in a 104-mile "wildriver" trip. Also on the river, one- to seven-day fishing or hunting trips can be taken. The commercial and sport fishing town of **Brookings** is the last spot on the coastal tour before heading into California. The **Brookings Azalea Festival** is held the last weekend in May in **Azalea State Park,** which grows five varieties of wild azaleas. **Chetco River Road** east of town rises to an elevation of 2,000 feet and gives a terrific view of the Pacific and the Coast Range mountains. Places to stay: **Brookings Thunderbird Motel** (469-2141, S/D$24-39), at city center, and **Best Western Brookings Inn** (469-2173, S$22-28/D$26-36), two miles from city center.

To the east in the **SOUTHWESTERN SECTION** is the **Oregon Caves National Monument,** open all year, on OR 46. A bed of marble has been carved out naturally to create pillars, domes, and passageways reaching 60 feet in height; tours are conducted by park rangers who also give campfire talks. **Grants Pass,** north on OR 199 at I-5, was named by roadbuilders when they heard of Grant's victory at Vicksburg. It is headquarters for the **Siskiyou National Forest.** Lumbering is the chief industry; giant fields of gladioli bloom in late July and early August.

Siskiyou National Forest is popular for its salmon fishing, rare trees and plants, and old goldmines; pack and saddle trips into the rugged backcountry are available. The Oregon Vortex in the **House of Mystery** at nearby Gold Hill is a freakish experience of magnetic forces which cause travelers to bend and weave and seemingly change in height; open daily in summer.

The carefully preserved old gold mining town of **Jacksonville** is the site of **Peter Britt Gardens Music and Arts Festival** for two weeks in mid-August. **Beekman House** and Bank, **Parish House, Methodist Church, Rogue River Valley Railroad Depot** are part of the excellent **Jacksonville Museum** complex, which along with **Pioneer Village,** vividly recalls the Victorian-era gold rush here. **Ashland** is famous for its lithia water mineral springs and **Shakespeare Festival,** conducted from the first week in March to the third week in April in an indoor theater and from mid-June to mid-September on an outside Elizabethan stage.

The closest large town to Crater Lake National Park is **Klamath Falls.** In certain sections of the town, buildings are heated by tapping the strata of hot water underlying the city. Klamath County's 100 lakes and 1,000 streams provide fishing beyond imagination, in addition to varied recreational activities. There is the 40-mile-long **Upper Klamath Lake,** where white pelicans nest; forest-covered mountains surround the lake and its northern end is surrounded by the **Upper Klamath National Wildlife Refuge,** a shelter for waterfoul migrating south from Canada. Numerous good motels in the area are especially popular among hunters and fishermen, including **Cimmarron Motel** (882-4601, S$24/D$26-32) and **Budget Host Inn** (882-4494, S$16-20/D$18.55-23.85), both three miles from the airport; and **Thunderbird Motel** (882-8864, S$27-31/D$32-37). To the east along OR 140 is the town of **Lakeview** with its famous geyser and the **Warner Canyon Winter Sports Area.** In Fremont National Forest, north of the town, are remains of the ice age, such as lava flows and the largest exposed geological fault in North America. **Abert Rim,** on the east side of Lake Abert, is still littered with Indian artifacts. **Old Perpetual Geyser** can be seen just north of Lakeview. It is believed to be the only continuous hot water geyser in the nation.

North from Crater Lake is the town of **Bend,** a good center for trips out into the mountains in **CENTRAL OREGON.** Movie productions are often located here to take advantage of the dramatic western scenery, much of which can be seen from the **Cascade Lakes Highway,** a drive which circles almost 100 miles between the Cascade ridge and the high plateaus. This is a popular resort, as exemplified by two rather palatial lodges. **Sunriver Lodge** (800-452-6874, S/D$40-64), 15 miles from Bend, has golf, tennis, ski bus, and a heated pool; **Inn of the Seventh Mountain** (382-8711, S$34-38/D$34-150), five miles from Bend, features a heated pool, ski bus, tennis, riding, fishing, dancing, and entertainment. Attractive motels include the **Red Lion** (382-8384, S$24-31/D$32-42), seven blocks from downtown; and **Westward Ho** (382-2111, S$18-25/D$23-30), half a mile from downtown.

Mt Bachelor Ski Area is nearby, as well as **Lava Butte** and **Lava River Caves State Park,** formed by ancient lava flows, **Pilot Butte State Park,** containing a cone projecting 500 feet into the sky, and **Newberry Crater.** The **Deschutes River** and the national forest of the same name provide challenging fishing and hunting experiences for the toughest of outdoorsmen. **Petersen's Rock Gardens** in Redmond contains bridges, castles, and rock gardens built from the rock and petrified wood common to the area; open daily, year round. **The Deschutes County Fair and Rodeo** is a big event here during the first week in August. **Prineville,** east of Redmond, is in an area rich in agate, obsidian, petrified wood, and "thundereggs", or chalcedony nodules. The city's chamber of commerce maintains 37 claims where digging is free.

The immense and sparsely populated mountainous **EASTERN REGION** has a number of attractions. The **John Day Fossil Beds National Monument** contains the former **Painted Hills State Park,** at Mitchell on US 26, and the former **Thomas Condon-John Day Fossil Beds State Park,** east on US 26. The Painted Hills section gets its name from the colorful bands of buff, red, yellow, and green hills which also contain fossilized leaves and plants. The 4,600 acres of the Fossil Beds section contain fossils estimated to be 30 million years old. Indian pictographs can be seen at **Picture Gorge,** one of the few areas of the park that is easily accessible. The intersection of US 395 and US 26 is in the **Strawberry Mountains** country where you'll find the town of **Canyon City,** now with a population of 600 but in the gold boom of the 1860s a home for 10,000. The **Herman and Eliza Oliver Museum** maintains the resort cabin of Oregon poet Joaquin Miller; open Tuesday-Saturday 9-5, Sunday 1-5, 1 April to 31 October. **Burns,** a remote trading center and seat of the state's largest county, on US 20 serves a livestock-raising area larger than many states. A four-day fair and rodeo is held here the first weekend of September. **Malheur Cave** has an underground lake at the tunnel. For bird watchers, thousands of ducks and geese migrate over the **Malheur National Wildlife Refuge** from March through May and again in October and November.

The **Wallowa-Whitman National Forest** is headquartered in **Baker,** created as the freight and transportation center for the gold towns of **NORTHEASTERN OREGON.** The forest contains snow-capped peaks, rare wild flowers, meadows, and scenic drives winding to such spots as **Anthony Lake Ski Area** which operates from December to April, and **Hell's Canyon,** through which the Snake River winds along the border with Idaho. The canyon exceeds the Grand Canyon's depth by 1,000 feet. An astonishing campground, in terms of remoteness and scenery, is located at **Hat Point,** overlooking the canyon from the Oregon side. The nearest town, **Joseph,** is as natural as the day it was born except for a handful of resort motels, including the **Indian Lodge Motel** (432-2651, S$18/D$21-23). The state's largest pool filled from warm water springs is at **Haines,** just up I-80 from Baker; open daily 20 April to 20 September. Before moving into the Columbia River Gorge Country, you reach the lively little city of **Pendleton,** where a stop at the **Pendleton Woolen Mills** is a must. Here the famous fine wool shirts worn by hunters the world over are manufactured; plant tours are available. The famous **Pendleton Round-Up,** a rodeo and Old West pageant, has been held annually since 1910 in mid-September. Thousands of working cowboys, visitors, and Indians from the Pacific Northwest gather here for this celebration. Advance reservations are advisable for the round-up, when motels usually increase rates temporarily and have minimum-stay requirements. Try the **Imperial 400** (276-5252, S$22-24/D$26-28), with swimming pool; **Tapadera** (276-3231, S$25-29/D$28-32); or **Pendleton Travel Lodge** (276-6231, S$21-25/D$31.50-37). All are 1½ miles from the airport. **Spout Springs Ski Area** is near Tollgate in the **Umatilla National Forest,** where fishing, horseback riding, and hiking are strictly for the adventurous.

The great **Columbia River** forms most of the **NORTHERN BORDER** with Washington on its majestic route to the Pacific Ocean. Interstate 80 joins the river at **Boardman** and follows it westward to **The Dalles,** once the end of the Oregon Trail. Here the turbulent Columbia was placid enough to allow pioneers to load goods on boats and float westward. The unnavigable rapids east of town, which once caused concern, are now submerged under water backed up from **The Dalles Dam,** which is at the head of a deep-draft boat channel 200 miles from the Pacific. The fish ladder, lock, and dam are open daily. **Fort Dalles Museum** is in the 1856 surgeon's quarters of the original fort; open year round. Petroglyphs, Indian artifacts including Stone Age materials up to 11,000 years old are shown at the **Winquatt Museum.**

Farther to the west is **Bonneville Dam,** built by the US Army Corps of Engineers. Fish ladders on both sides of the river are navigated by fish working their way toward their spawning grounds; open daily, free. **Multnomah Falls,** highest of the many cascades along this section of the Columbia Gorge, thunders down 620 feet 30 miles east of Portland. The highest point in Oregon, the 11,235-foot **Mt Hood,** and its surrounding **Mt Hood National Forest,** are best seen from the scenic **Loop Highway.** Besides various recreational facilities keyed to water sports, camping, hiking, and hunting, the area has six winter sports resorts, the most famous of which is **Timberline Lodge** on the mountain's south slope. At an elevation of 6,000 feet, the skiing facilities include chair lifts, fabulous runs in a variety of settings, a heated swimming pool, and snow tractors which can go to within 1,200 feet of the summit. Ski "packages" are available, as are all other types of ski equipment.

Other centers are **Multorpor Ski Bowl, Cooper Spur, Summit Ski Area,** and **Mt Hood Meadows Ski Area;** the ski season is mid-November to at least late June. The Mt Hood National Forest extends from the foothills outside Portland north to the Columbia River, down along the Cascade Mountains and east to plateaus of the central region. Filling the forest's 1.1 million acres are active glaciers, hot springs, lakes, streams, and tremendous waterfalls. **Lost** and **Timothy Lakes** are excellent campsites. The Loop Highway winds its way through the forest and recreation area passing more than 200 camp and picnic locations and moves through **Bennett Pass,** the Oregon Trail route used by pioneers to cross from The Dalles into the **Willamette Valley. White River** is an excellent example of a glacial river flowing from its source. South of Portland in Oregon City is the **John McLoughlin House National Historic Site.** Built in 1846, now restored, it was the home of the agent for the Hudson's Bay Company who founded the city, which was the capital of the Old Oregon Territory; open daily except Monday. Like "coals to Newcastle," the **McCarver House** (1850) was built of lumber shipped from Maine around the Horn.

As the Willamette River follows I-5 south, the state's capital, **SALEM** comes into view. The **State Capitol** is of modern Greek design topped by a goldleaf statue symbolic of the pioneers who brought settlement to this land. Tours of the capitol include views of Mts Hood and Jefferson; open daily 30 May through Labor Day. The **Oregon State Fair** is held here for 10 days before Labor Day, and an art festival at the **Bush House-Bush Barn Art Center** is held in the third weekend in July. **City Center Motel** (364-0121, S$22/D$24-26), 1½ miles from the airport; **Best Western New Kings Inn** (581-1559, S$26/D$28-31), ten miles from the airport; and the **Tiki Lodge** (581-4441, S$24/D$25-28), five miles from the airport, are a few of the good motels. **Albany's World Champion Timber Carnival,** with contests in axe throwing, log rolling, and tree cutting, takes place on 2-4 July.

Corvallis, in the heart of the **Willamette Valley,** is the home of **Oregon State University; Horner Museum** and **Memorial Union,** on the campus, house art, pioneer, and antique collections. **Junction City** holds a four-day festival in August to honor natives of the Scandinavian countries who have settled in Oregon and helped make it a great state. **Eugene** and **Springfield,** separated by the Willamette River, are set between the

Cascade Range to the east and the Coast Range to the west. The **University of Oregon** is in Eugene. The **Museum of Art** on the university campus houses an extensive collection of Oriental art, including an 18th-century jade pagoda nine feet high and a collection of works by Northwest artists; open Tuesday to Sunday. Forests of Douglas fir support a lumber industry which accounts for 50% of the local payroll. The **Willamette National Forest** is the most heavily timbered national forest in the country with 1.7 million acres. And **Lane County** will make the visitor think he is back in New England with 47 old covered bridges to view. Surrounding state parks and recreation lakes, including **Lookout Lake, Dexter Dam, Fall Creek Reservoir,** and **Armitage Park,** provide boating on the **McKenzie River** and fishing, hunting, and camping in the area. The **Angus Inn** (342-1243, S$21-26/D$22-28), eight miles from the airport; and **Best Western New Oregon Motel** (683-3669, S$26-39/D$32.50-39) and **Willow Tree Motel** (342-4804, S$19-22/D$24-28), both near the University of Oregon campus about 10 miles from the airport, provide excellent accommodations. **Alpine Village Inn** serves hearty German dishes in a Bavarian atmosphere.

Eugene's sister city, Springfield, is the home of the **Broiler Festival** held in Willamette Park during the second week of July. US 126 goes over to the **McKenzie River Recreational Area** east of Springfield. Breathtaking panoramas of the **Three Sisters, Mt Jefferson,** and **Mt Washington** can be had from **Dee Wright Observatory** at the summit of **McKenzie Pass** on OR 242. **Clear Lake,** headwaters for the Upper McKenzie River, lives up to its name by being so transparent that you see to depths of 100 feet. A Douglas fir forest was submerged at the north edge of the lake by a flood resulting from a stray lava flow. The **Bohemia Mining Days Celebration** is held the third weekend in July at Cottage Grove, south of I-5. On summer weekends, you can ride two and a half hours on a steam excursion train deep into the forest and mining districts.

City To Visit

PORTLAND

Portland is in northwestern Oregon on the Willamette River, near its confluence with the Columbia. Although a few cabins were built in the area as early as 1825, there was no permanent settlement until 1844. The city was named after Portland, Maine, and was incorporated in 1851; growth was very rapid after the completion of two transcontinental railroads in 1883-84. Portland's present importance is based upon its key location at the confluence of the two rivers and the abundance of natural resources. An important inland port and industrial area, Portland is becoming increasingly popular as a tourist center. It is known as the "City of Roses" because of its many rose gardens. Portland has snow-covered mountains rising to the north and east, particularly impressive at sunrise and sunset. Population metropolitan area 1,236,000; city area 90 square miles. The downtown hotel and business district is compact and lies to the north of the Willamette River; manufacturing and industrial plants are situated along both banks of the river and in the Industrial Park.

WHAT TO SEE

Sanctuary of Our Sorrowful Mother, a beautifully-landscaped 60-acre religious shrine with grotto carved out of solid rock; continuous organ music. **Auditorium Forecourt Fountain,** an area of waterfalls, pools, streamlets, trees, and grass. **Pittock Mansion,** a beautiful restored French Renaissance mansion set in landscaped gardens. **St John's Bridge,** Gothic spires. **Historical Society,** objects of local historical interest; open Monday to Saturday 10-5, free. **Oregon Museum of Science and Industry,** scientific displays and planetarium; open Monday to Thursday 9-5, Friday 9-9, Saturday and Sunday 9-6; admission $2.50, students and senior citizens $1.50. The city has marked a 69-mile **Scenic Parkway** which passes many local points of scenic beauty. There are numerous conducted sightseeing tours in Portland; a typical three-hour tour of the city costs $7.50.

Principal parks: **Laurelhurst Park,** with a beautiful lake; **Mt Tabor Park,** on the site of an extinct volcano, good view of the city; **Peninsula Park,** known for its sunken rose gardens; **Washington Park,** international rose test gardens; **Hoyt Arboretum,** the country's largest collection of coniferous trees; **Portland Zoological Gardens,** all the latest in animal comfort, and a miniature sightseeing train tours the grounds. **Macleay Park,** about four miles west of the business district, is a large forest area and bird sanctuary; **Council Crest Park** has superb views.

On clear days, from viewpoints high in the city, Mt St Helens (about 45 miles north of Portland), Mt Hood, and Mt Adams can be seen. Since the May 18, 1980, explosive eruption of Mt St Helens, smoke, steam, or ash plumes may occasionally be viewed coming from the mountain. From Portland, the best way to see Mt St Helens is from spots with a clear view to the north.

ACCOMMODATIONS

Portland hotels include **Benson** (228-9611, S$45-77/D$60-92), one of the best; **Corsun Arms** (226-6288, S$23-30/D$27-34), nicely furnished; **Imperial Hotel** (228-7221, S$20-23/D$23-26); **Portland Hilton** (226-1611, S$43-75/D$61-93), very smart, pool, drive-in parking; and **Portland Motor Hotel** (221-1611, S$35-37/D$39-41). All are in the center of the city. **Red Lion Motor Inn** (221-0450, S$48-50/D$54-56) and the **Red Lion Lloyd Center Hotel** (288-6111, S$30-41/D$42-53) are one mile from center city. **Thunderbird Motor Inn Jantzen Beach** (283-2111, S$44-52/D$50-58) is on the banks of the Columbia River, four miles from the airport. Hotel Tax: 5%. Nearest campsite is in **Dabney State Park,** 16 miles east of Portland.

RESTAURANTS

Local food specialties are berries in season, fruit, salmon, crab, clams, and trout. **Couch Street Fish House,** seafood, dinner only; **Dan & Louie's**

Crater Lake in southern Oregon was formed when Mt Mazama erupted and created the crater of approximately 21 square miles.

Oyster Bar and Jake's Famous Crawfish, well known for seafood; 4 and 20 Blackbirds, food excellent, lunches only; Huber's, popular since 1879, unique atmosphere; Nendel's Inn, chicken; Original Pancake House, nothing to do with the chain, authentic and delicious, closed Mondays, Tuesdays; River Queen, a converted paddleboat turned restaurant; Rose's Delicatessen, for blintzes, cakes, sandwiches; Sylvia's Italian Restaurant; Rian's Breadbasket, weekday lunches, good; Rian's Eating Establishment, downtown lunch & cocktail spot, closed Sundays; Rian's Fish & Ale House, seafood, including delicious fish and chips; Thunderbird; Encore; Captain's Corner; and Prime Rib; all excellent. Canlis, with a view from atop the Hilton Hotel; London Grill, very attractive, winner of *Holiday* award. Polynesian food at Trader Vic's in the Benson Hotel and at Kon Tiki in the Sheraton Motor Inn. Authentic Japanese food and atmosphere at Bush Garden; reservation necessary. Japanese cuisine also at Baisen Steak House and Benihana of Tokyo. Jade West, Chinese cooking, has a view overlooking the city. The Rheinlander German Restaurant has strolling musicians. The Woodstove, French provincial decor plus traditional American fare.

ARTS AND MUSIC

Portland Art Museum has permanent and loan art exhibits in a contemporary building; open Friday noon to 10, other days noon to 5; closed Mondays and holidays. The Oregon Symphony Orchestra performs frequently during the fall and winter seasons. During the summer months everything from grand opera to band concerts is presented in Mt Tabor and Washington parks; free. Portland Civic Theater presents a series of excellent plays. Other theaters include Firehouse Theater, Slabtown Stop Theatre, New Theater, the children's Playbox Theatre at the 200, and Lake Oswego Community Theatre.

SHOPPING

Stores are open daily, 9:30-6, Monday and Friday evenings until 9. Lloyd Shopping Center, one of the larger in the US, has parking for 8,000 cars. Open Monday-Friday 10-9:30, Saturday 10-7, Sunday 12-5. For souvenirs and products native to the state, visit the Oregon Products Store in Morgan's Alley.

SPORTS

The Portland Beavers play semi-professional baseball in the Pacific Coast League. The Portland Winter Hawks of the Pacific Western Hockey League play ice hockey, very popular here, in the Memorial Coliseum. The Portland Trial Blazers, NBA basketball team, also meet opponents in the Coliseum. The Portland Timbers of the North American Soccer League play their home matches at the Portland Civic Stadium and indoor soccer at the Coliseum. Weekly wrestling at the Portland Sports Arena. Collegiate football is played during the fall season. There is horse racing at Portland Meadows Wednesday-Sunday, mid-January to late May, and summer dog racing at the Multnomah Kennel Club.

The Portland area has many facilities for golf, tennis, swimming, and other sports. The fishing season runs from April through October. There are also good opportunities for hunting. There is excellent skiing at Mt Hood, one and a half hours from Portland. Timberline Lodge has good skiing December to April with skiing at higher elevations through June. Government Camp, lower on Mt Hood, also has various skiing facilities.

CALENDAR OF EVENTS

All-Indian Rodeo, in Tygh Valley, about a three-hour drive east of Portland, May; **Portland Rose Festival,** June; **World Championship Timber Carnival,** July; **Astoria Regatta,** August; **Pendleton Round-Up,** famous rodeo in Pendleton, a three-and-a-half hour drive east of Portland, August; **Pacific International Livestock Exposition and Rodeo,** November.

WHERE TO GO NEARBY

The state parks facing the Pacific Ocean have good bathing and picnicking facilities—**Short Sand Beach, Cape Meares, Cape Lookout, Boiler Bay, Rocky Creek,** and **Otter Crest State Parks,** all between 65 to 100 miles west and southwest of Portland, and **Rooster Rock State Park,** 30 miles east. To the east of the city are many state parks and recreation areas, particularly on the south shore of the Columbia River. East of Portland through the impressive **Columbia River Gorge** on the beautiful **Columbia River Highway** trips may be taken to **Larch Mountain,** part of the Mt Hood National Forest. A circle tour including Mt Hood and the Columbia River Highway is available as well as boat cruises on the Columbia River; $6.50 for adults, $4 for children, free under 2. **The Mt Hood Recreation Area,** including **Timberline Lodge** (272-3311, S$26/D$38-48), 50 miles from Portland, and **Government Camp,** 56 miles away, is popular summer and winter. **Bonneville Dam,** 42 miles east, is extremely interesting; be sure to see the new visitors' center on **Bradford Island** with displays of fish ladders and hatcheries.

CRATER LAKE NATIONAL PARK

The park, 16 miles north of Klamath Falls and 69 miles northeast of Medford, is in south central Oregon, and covers some 250 square miles. The season is from mid-June through Labor Day. The park averages 50 feet of snowfall a year, but the roads from the south entrance and west entrance to **Rim Village** are kept clear between high falls of snow, and the park in winter is, if possible, even more beautiful than in summer. **Crater Lake Lodge** is open 15 June to 15 September; adjacent cottages available. Campsites are open from about 1 July to 30 September, depending on snow conditions. The cafeteria in Rim Village is open weekends and holidays throughout the winter.

The story of the eruption of **Mt Mazama,** about 6,600 years ago, became an Indian legend very close to geologic facts. When the mountain collapsed after the "war between the gods," the incredibly blue lake, fed by rain and snow, gradually filled the immense caldera. Today Crater Lake is nearly 2,000 feet deep, but only about six miles in diameter, so that you can see the whole panorama in one sweep. Take the bus tour around Rim Drive, a 35-mile road encircling the caldera's edge; the driver provides an interesting commentary and make stops for photographers. Special viewpoints are the **Sinnott Memorial Overlook Building; Cloudcap; the Watchman,** from which you can see **Mt Shasta,** 100 miles away; **Garfield Peak,** overlooking the small volcanic cone known as **Wizard Island;** and **Sun Notch,** overlooking the **Phantom Ship,** a unique rock formation seemingly afloat. Also see the pumice spires called **The Pinnacles** and the **Castle Crest Wildflower Garden.** Take a launch trip on the lake from **Cleetwood Cove,** the only access to the water in the cup of lava cliffs that are 500 to 2,000 feet high. Naturalist programs are held nightly in summer at the Mazama Campground in Rim Village and at Crater Lake Lodge. Animals in the park include ground squirrels, chipmunks, mule, black-tailed deer, and black bears. Bald and golden eagles and the great horned owl can often be seen.

FURTHER STATE INFORMATION

Oregon State Highway Division, Travel Information Section, Salem, OR 97310. **Department of Fish and Wildlife,** Box 3503, Portland, OR 97204. **Portland Chamber of Commerce,** Convention Bureau, 824 SW Fifth Avenue, Portland, OR 97204. National Parks: **Crater Lake National Park** (Superintendent), Crater Lake, OR 97604. **Pan Am** office, 333 SW 5th Avenue, Portland, OR 97204, tel: 249-4975.

  Consulates in Portland: Australia, Austria, Belgium, Canada, Costa Rica, Denmark, El Salvador, Finland, France, Germany, Great Britain, Honduras, Iceland, Italy, Japan, Korea, Lebanon, Mexico, Netherlands, Nicaragua, Norway, Panama, Peru, Philippines, Sweden, Venezuela.

USEFUL TELEPHONE NUMBERS IN PORTLAND

Personal Crisis Intervention	248-5431
Fire	232-2111
Police Emergency	760-6911
Legal Aid	224-6580
Chamber of Commerce	228-9411
Hospitals	
Bess Kaiser Medical Center	285-9321
Good Samaritan	229-7711
St Vincent	297-4411
Emanuel	280-3200
Portland Adventist	239-6155
Providence Medical Center	234-8211
University of Oregon	
Health Sciences Center	225-8311
Emergency Services	225-7551

Pennsylvania

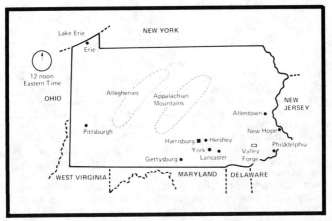

Area	45,333 square miles	**Population**	11,866,728
Capital	Harrisburg	**Sales Tax**	6%

Weather	Jan	Feb	Mar	Apr	May	Jun	Jul	Aug	Sep	Oct	Nov	Dec
Av Temp (°C)	0	1	5	11	17	22	24	23	19	13	7	1
Days Rain/Snow	11	9	11	11	11	10	9	10	8	7	9	10

The keystone of the 13 original colonies, Pennsylvania typifies the kind of America that was a magnet for immigrants. The first settlement was founded in 1643 by Swedish-Finnish colonists on Tinicum Island in the Delaware River, facing what is now Chester. The Dutch appropriated the colony in 1655, and lost it to the English in 1664.

While other Quakers were being persecuted in England for their beliefs, the aristocratic William Penn remained in favor with the court, partly because he had inherited a large claim against the crown. To collect, Penn asked Charles II for a grant of land in the New World where Quakers and other non-conformists could live with complete freedom of religion. Penn arrived in Chester in 1682 and proceeded to establish exactly the sort of colony he had visualized. Land was purchased from the Indians with such fairness that settlers and Indians lived in harmony until 1755, the period of the French and Indian War. Welsh and English Quakers were the first to join Penn, and the established Swedish colony merged with them amicably. The next wave of immigration came from Germany, consisting of members of small religious sects, many of whose descendants to this day maintain the lifestyle of the "Plain People." Happily, this includes skills in folk arts and cooking some of the most delicious food in the country.

While still only a colony Pennsylvania became a formidable commercial center, using ports on the Ohio River, Lake Erie, and the Atlantic to trade with Europe and the colonies. It is worth noting that Pittsburgh itself is a major US port, handling more tonnage per year than presently travels via the Panama Canal. Although an inland port, it is a major gateway to the western US. Huge fortunes were made in this affluent state, and they gave rise to America's first fire insurance company, first life insurance company, and first chartered bank. The first commercial telegraph in the US was used between Philadelphia and Lancaster in 1846, and the first commercial broadcasting station in the world was Pittsburgh's KDKA, which went on the air in 1920.

As the natural hub of the fledging nation, the Commonwealth of Pennsylvania was involved in some of the US's most historic events. Nearly 500 historic sites, state and federal parks, and recreation areas have been set aside for the public in the state.

Pennsylvania is 307 miles wide and 169 miles from north to south. Despite the great industrial centers, rich farm acreage, and mining areas, there are still plenty of forests, lakes, and streams to attract naturalists, hunters, and fishermen. Low mountains slant across nearly the entire state, except for the coastal plains in the southeast and northwest.

Southwest of Philadelphia on US 1 is **Brandywine Battlefield Park**, where Washington and Lafayette's headquarters are open daily except Mondays. Britain's General Howe won that battle of 11 September 1777, and moved on to occupy Philadelphia, living in comfort in Germantown for the rest of the winter while Washington and his troops barely survived after their retreat to Valley Forge. **Chadds Ford** is where illustrator Howard Pyle started a summer art school at the turn of the century. He was joined by N. C. Wyeth, artist father of Andrew Wyeth, America's greatest modern painter. Many original Wyeth works hang in the fine **Brandywine River Museum.** Continuing on US 1, you come to **Longwood Gardens,** one of the country's most magnificent horticultural parks; guided tours in summer, self-guided tours the rest of the year; open daily. The gardens and fountains are illuminated on Tuesday, Thursday, and Saturday evenings, mid-May to mid-October, and there's an outdoor theater for concerts, ballet, and other entertainment.

You can drive northeast from Longwood to **VALLEY FORGE,** via **West Chester** and **Paoli.** If you're there on a cold winter day, try to imagine how 11,000 colonial troops felt as they straggled in to set up camp after their defeat at Germantown. The winter of 1777-78 was bitterly cold, the snow was deep, there was never enough food, and clothing was so inadequate that nearly 3,000 men were without shoes. The **National Memorial Arch** was erected in appreciation of the suffering those troops endured for love of country alone, because even the continental scrip they received for pay was of questionable value. **Washington's Headquarters** is where the General stayed only after quarters had been built to house all his men. Until then, he lived in a field tent which is now in the museum adjoining the impressive **Washington Memorial Chapel.** Among the many relics of that valiant, miserable winter encampment are the **Stable,** the **Bake House,** the **Hospital Hut,** the defensive earthworks, and **General Varnum's Quarters.** The **Grant Parade** is where Baron van Steuben drilled the ragged troops from February to June, turning out a confident, disciplined army eager to confront the British again. Valley Forge is at its loveliest in late April and early May when the dogwood blooms. Air-conditioned bus tours operate daily from 1 April to 31 October; cassette tapes and players can be rented year round for self-guided tours in your own car.

The Liberty Trail is a series of historic tours starting in Philadelphia which suggest routes to points of interest in the five southeastern counties, Bucks, Montgomery, Chester, Delaware, and Philadelphia. You could return to Philadelphia through **Germantown,** the northern suburb which began as a separate settlement in 1763. This was where General Howe settled after his victory at Brandywine, and where the British handed the colonials another defeat which sent them into retreat at Valley Forge. Among many 18th- and 19th-century homes restored and open to visitors is the **Deshler-Morris House** where Washington stayed in 1793-94 when a yellow fever epidemic forced the government out of Philadelphia.

LANCASTER is only 65 miles west of Philadelphia, and was the capital of the country for one day, 27 September 1777, when the Continental Congress held a session here while in flight from the British. The **Old City Hall** on Penn Square dates from 1795. **The Central Market** nearby is open Tuesdays and Fridays, and just about anything that can be produced on a farm is sold here in stalls proudly marked with each owner's name. Others may be offering homemade baked goods, cheeses, pickles and relishes, or sausages and bolognas. The **Southern Market** on South Queen Street is open Saturdays, and Lancaster has two other farmers' markets farther out. James Buchanan, America's only bachelor president, lived at **Wheatland** until his death in 1868. The house is furnished as it was in his day; open 15 March to 1 November. The **Hans Herr House** (1719) is one of the country's oldest examples of Swiss-German architecture, and is the oldest building used by Mennonites as a meetinghouse. Both the Conestoga wagon and the Pennsylvania rifle, which went across the Alleghenies with pioneers in the 18th century, were invented in the Lancaster area. Dutchland Tours run two sightseeing trips daily except Sundays through the surrounding countryside.

Lancaster, York, Dauphin, Lebanon, Berks, and Lehigh counties are the heart of the **PENNSYLVANIA DUTCH COUNTRY,** west and north of Philadelphia. More than any other place in America, this region has remained much as it was in the days of its first settlers. The "Dutch" were actually *Deutsch* of Palatinate Germany, members of small, strict sects who sought sanctuary in the religious freedom guaranteed by William Penn in the late 17th century. The Amish are today the plainest of the "Plain People," and also the most noticeable. The heavily-bearded men wear wide-brimmed black hats, black suits, and suspenders instead of belts. Their wives fasten their homemade ankle-length dresses with pins instead of buttons, and tuck their hair severely back into bonnets or white net caps. Through hard work and ingenuity, they manage to prosper very nicely without electricity or telephones. For safety's sake watch out for their horsedrawn black buggies on country roads. One should respect the wishes of the Amish not to be photographed or drawn into needless conversation. Some Mennonites adhere to the same strictures as the Amish, but others have become modernized in varying degrees. Moravians are among the "Fancy Dutch," which includes German members of Lutheran and Reformed Churches who delight in decorating their barns with those engaging "hex" signs, still used to ward off the "Evil Eye" and offensive spirits. True Pennsylvania Dutch cookery is refreshingly different and delicious. Here a dish is prepared with time, thought, and ingenuity. You can scarcely see the table top for the relishes, well-seasoned meats, homegrown vegetables, salads, homemade breads, puddings, cakes, and cookies, which are all eaten in one course, followed by several different kinds of pie, including shoo-fly pie. You might start eating your way around the Pennsylvania Dutch country in Lancaster County. Chicken-corn soup is probably the most famous dish here, but there are so many good things to eat in this abundant county that it's hard to choose a favorite.

Accommodations in Lancaster are the **Brunswick Motor Inn** (397-4801, S$27/D$38); **Host Town Resort Motel** (299-5700, S/D$30-44); and **TraveLodge** (387-4201, S$30-39/D$43-52). On highways east of Lancaster: **Host Farm Resort** (299-5500, S/D$30-44), a complete summer-winter resort; and **Howard Johnson's** (397-7781, S$26-44/D$28-51). North of Lancaster: **Landis Valley Resort Inn** (569-0477, S$24-28/D$30-36), **Sheraton-Conestoga Village** (656-2101, S$33-56/D$39-62). **Continental Inn** (299-0421, S/D$26-45), **Holiday Inn-East** (299-2551, S$20-40/D$23-43), and **Willow Valley Farms Inn** (463-2711, S$20-40/D$23-43). Prices given are summer rates. Rates are generally lower September-May. The **Plain and Fancy Farm,** nearby in Bird-in-Hand on PA 340, is a famous place for Pennsylvania Dutch cooking, served family-style; closed Sunday. **The Lemon Tree,** west of Lancaster on PA 492, is in a lovely old house, the cuisine is gourmet, continental, and quite elegant; dinner only, closed Sundays and national holidays.

Amish Homestead, 3 miles east of Lancaster on PA 462, is run much as it was when the early settlers arrived in Lancaster County. The **Amish Farm,** on US 30, has lecture tours on how the people live and work. The **Dutch Wonderland** amusement park and **National Wax Museum** of Lancaster County with historic tableaux are 4 miles east of town on US 30. **The Railroad Model Showcase,** a display of handcarved wooden trains, is adjacent to a Dutch Haven Village, 8 miles east of US 30. **Strasburg,** 10 miles south of Lancaster on PA 462, is where you can take an 8-mile ride through lovely farmland on an old-time locomotive the **Strasburg Railroad** has been running since 1832.

Three miles north of Lancaster is the **Pennsylvania Farm Museum of Landis Valley,** just off US 222; see the farm machinery, Conestoga wagons, demonstrations of spinning and weaving, and the exhibitions of everyday items used when Lancaster County was just about as far west as civilization went in colonial days. **Ephrata**, several miles farther north, is where a strictly ascetic colony of German Seventh-Day Adventists lived in retreat from 1732 until as recently as 1934. Ten of the original steep-roofed, typically German-style buildings show how the devout brotherhood lived. The group was known for its music; there is a pageant with religious choral music held here on Saturday evenings from late June through Labor Day. Early every Friday morning, the buggies and carriages of Amish families start arriving at the **Green Dragon** farmers' market, which suddenly blossoms, after being empty all week, into a vast emporium of everything these shy, quiet people are apt to buy. Ephrata also has a big **Street Fair** the last full week of September. **Lititz** was settled by Moravians just 300 years after the first Moravian Church was founded in Lititz, Bohemia, in 1443. Among the 18th-century buildings on **Main Street** is the bakery where the first pretzels were made commercially. Sugar candy, molded into enchanting figures, is another Lititz specialty.

YORK COUNTY is across the Susquehanna River from Lancaster County, and centers around the historic city of **York,** which is 90 miles west of Philadelphia. York was already a thriving town when the Continental Congress fled Philadelphia. After its one-day session in Lancaster, the Congress moved on to York, where the nation's capital was established in **York County Courthouse,** now seen in replica in Farquhar Park, and used from 30 September 1777 to 27 June 1778. During that brief period, a lot happened to move the country towards unity but at the same time there was a group of malcontents agitating to replace General Washington. The ringleader was General Horatio Gates. The **Gates House** (1751) is where Lafayette turned the tide in favor of Washington. Next door is the **Golden Plough Tavern,** the oldest building in town, dating from about 1740, one of the country's last half-timbered buildings in medieval German style. Meetings are still held regularly in the **Friends Meeting House,** built in 1766. The **Bonham House** (1840) is typical of the way prosperous local families lived in the Victorian era. The **Log House** (1812) is furnished in early German colonial style. There's an unusually large collection of nostalgic lithographs in the **Currier and Ives** and **Antiques Gallery,** open Monday to Friday. York has three superb farmers' markets, at least one of which is sure to be bursting with produce if you're in town on a Tuesday, Thursday, Friday, or Saturday. Take home jars of *schnitz* so you can make your own York County dried apple pie.

HERSHEY is in southeastern **Dauphin County.** The aroma of chocolate is everywhere, and there are conducted tours through **Hershey Chocolate World** explaining the production of chocolate; daily, except holidays, free. This tidy little town was founded in 1903 by confectioner Milton S. Hershey, of Mennonite descent. **Hershey Park** has rides and entertainment that appeal to all ages. The park is open from 4 July through Sept. 10:30 to 10, adults $11.50, children under 5 years are free. The **Hershey Museum** features Pennsylvania furnishings and such local crafts as Stiegel glass, old guns and clocks, especially the "Apostolic Clock." Tulips in May and roses all summer in the **Hershey Gardens**, open 15 April to 1 December. Try to be in Hershey for the **Pennsylvania Dutch Days,** a real old-time folk festival for a week in late July. The 4-day rally of the **Antique Automobile Club** is held in early October. Among accommodations are the outstanding **Hershey Motor Lodge** (533-2171, S\$40-42/D\$46-49); the **Hotel Hershey** (Spanish-style architecture) (533-2171, S\$55-72/D\$32-46), a long distinguished resort with all kinds of sport and entertainment; and the **Best Western** (533-5665, S\$30-42/D\$32-46).

BERKS COUNTY has that tidy, substantial Pennsylvania Dutch look and cuisine. **Reading** was laid out on the banks of the Schuylkill River in 1748 by the sons of William Penn. It has been an industrial city ever since it made cannons and served as a supply depot for George Washington's army. It led the nation as an iron and steel center in the mid-19th century and has one of the world's largest hosiery factories today. **Duryea Drive,** named for the speedy automobile made here between 1900 and 1912, winds up to the top of **Mt Penn,** 1,140 feet, topped with a huge **Japanese Pagoda,** from which you get a superb view. Another Reading oddity is **Stokesay Castle,** a replica of a 12th-century English castle that is now an excellent restaurant (375-4588), with an outstanding wine cellar. The city's **Public Museum and Art Gallery** is widely known for its collections of butterflies and insects from the carboniferous age. The **Daniel Boone Homestead,** 9 miles east of town, is where that dauntless frontiersman was born in 1734 and lived until he was 16. The next occupants replaced the Boone cabin with a stone farmhouse, now furnished in 18th-century style, and there is a good museum on the grounds. Tourists come from as far as Canada to shop in the county's numerous factory outlets with items priced below retail.

Hopewell Village, 14 miles southeast of Reading near Birdsboro, is a well-preserved example of an iron-making village, complete with tenant houses, ironmaster's mansion, and many of the buildings where iron stoves and cooking pots were cast even before the Revolution. Surrounding this national historic site is **French Creek State Park** with a variety of campsites and recreation areas. **Shartlesville,** northwest of Reading, is the tiny town where the **Shartlesville Hotel** and **Haag's Hotel** are famous for their belt-bursting, family-style Dutch lunches and dinners. Up the road is **Hamburg.** Turn north here on PA 895 to go to **Hawk Mountain Sanctuary,** a unique gathering place for eagles, hawks and other migratory birds of prey. Surrounding Reading are the **Blue Mountains** where gourmets collect delicious wild mushrooms; **Joe's Restaurant** in Reading is famous for them and so popular because of it that advance reservations are always advisable. **Crystal Cave** and **Onyx Cave** (the latter closed December through February) are southwest of Kutztown, where the **Pennsylvania Dutch Festival** is held for 8 days in late June-July, attracting huge crowds who revel in craftsmanship exhibits and vast quantities of good food. Coil-shaped funnel cakes are a traditional snack.

LEHIGH COUNTY is also Pennsylvania Dutch, but more famous for its largest city, **Allentown.** Allentown, highly industrialized today, began life as a hunting and fishing lodge in the 1750s. **Trout Hall** (1770), the city's first mansion, now houses the county's historical museum. **Zion Reformed Church** is where the Liberty Bell was hidden when it was removed from Philadelphia for safekeeping during the British occupation; a replica of the bell now stands in its place. West of the city is the **Trexler-Lehigh County Game Preserve,** stocked with bison, elk, and deer. **Bethlehem,** one of America's greatest steel-producing cities, began as a Moravian communal-living settlement in 1741, and was named following a Christmas Eve service. **The Central Moravian Church** (1806) is regarded as the leading Moravian church in the country. The **Old Chapel** (1751) is still used, however, on special occasions. Next to it is **Gemein Haus** (1741), oldest building in the city. Other Moravian places of interest are the **Single Brethren's House** (1748), **Piston's House** (1744), **Bell House** (1746), **Moravian Cemetery,** with its uniform flat gravestones and separate sections for men and women, begun in 1742, and the **Moravian College,** founded in 1742. The **Moravian Antique Show** is held on the campus the first week in June. The **Annie S. Kemerer Museum** has an especially fine collection of 18th- and 19th-century American glass, china, furniture, and landscape paintings. One of the nation's most prestigious music events is the **Bach Festival** held in May in Packer Memorial Chapel on the campus of **Lehigh University,** renowned for its engineering school. Mementos of the early days in the steel industry are displayed in the **Charles M. Schwab Memorial Library** in Bethlehem Steel Company's general office building. A notable country inn 17 miles outside of Allentown on route 29 is **Candlewyck,** an old converted farmhouse, featuring delicious homemade specialties; rooms are also available. The new **Hamilton's Mall** in Allentown is a fine shopping center.

GETTYSBURG is near the Maryland border, just west of the Dutch country. The **Gettysburg National Military Park,** which surrounds the little town almost completely, is visited by up to 50,000 people in a day at the height of the summer season. Despite all the monuments, markers, observation towers, roads, and walking paths that have been added to the site, when you see the battlefield where 43,500 men "gave the last full measure of devotion," you cannot fail to be moved. Begin at the Visitors Center, which has a large museum with a lighted map that recounts all the action of that July 1863. Afterwards, you can hire a licensed guide to go in your car with you, or rent a cassette tape that will guide you. Especially notable among monuments erected by states represented in the battle are those given by Pennsylvania, bearing the names of nearly 35,000 men; the Virginia memorial with its statue of General Robert E. Lee on his horse "Traveller"; and the North Carolina monument, designed by Gutzon Borglum. The *Soldiers Monument* in **Gettysburg National Cemetery** stands on the spot where Lincoln stood on 19 November 1863 to deliver the ringing words of the *Gettysburg Address.* **The Hall of Presidents** is a popular historic center. **The Eisenhower National Historic Site,** the farm that President Eisenhower donated to the nation, can be seen from one of the observation towers on the battlefield. The **Dobbin House,** used as a hospital during the battle, is now a restaurant and museum with an excellent diorama of the battlefield. The **Jennie Wade House** was the home of the only civilian who was killed (by a stray bullet) during the battle. The **Wilks House** is where Lincoln completed the writing of his famous speech which marked the end of the Civil War. **Soldier's National Museum of the Civil War** shows dioramas of every major battle during the 4-year conflict; open daily, 9-9. The **National Civil War Wax Museum** is also notable. A good view of the entire battlefield can be seen from the **National Gettysburg Tower** on Baltimore Street. For children, there's **Miniature House Farms,** 3 miles west on Route 30. There are a great many motels in and around Gettysburg, but advance reservations are generally necessary in the summer; **Best Western Stonehenge Lodge** (334-6715, S$26/D$34), **Holiday Inn** (334-6211, S$19-42/D$22-34), **Howard Johnson Motor Lodge** (334-1188, S$18-24/D$24-34), **Quality Inn Gettysburg** (334-1103, S$18-40/D$20-40), and the **Sheraton Inn** (334-8121, S$30-33/D$35-38).

Harrisburg, the capital of Pennsylvania, is dominated by a handsome complex of state office buildings. The 272-foot capitol dome was patterned on St Peter's basilica in Rome. The **John Harris Mansion** (1764-66), built by the city's founder, is furnished with period pieces. The **Fort Hunter Museum** of colonial household items was built in 1789 on the site of a stockaded blockhouse. The **William Penn Memorial Museum** on Capital Hill presents Pennsylvania history in widely diversified exhibits. The **State Farm Show Building** is used for major stock shows from late September to mid-January, and the **Pennsylvania Recreation and Sportsmen's Show** is held there in early February. A $500-million urban redevelopment project—Harristown—is nearing its half-way mark and giving a sparkling new look to center city.

Three Mile Island. This scene of the nation's worst and most fearsome nuclear power plant accident, 28 March 1979, is becoming a major tourist attraction, according to the state Department of Commerce. An observation center on State Route 441, 12 miles southeast of Harrisburg, with telescopes, offers a close-up view of the near-disaster site. The imposing cooling towers that dominate the scene make for good photographs.

BUCKS COUNTY lies along the Delaware River, just northeast of Philadelphia. It is about 40 miles long and 16 miles wide. Around 1900 landscape painter William Lathrop founded the first art colony at **New Hope,** a delightful village on the Delaware surrounded by rich, beautiful, rolling farmland. The residents are still predominantly writers, composers, artists, and actors who have found Bucks County a convenient refuge from New York City. The village, only 33 miles from Philadelphia, is filled with craft shops and art galleries. You can ride a mule-drawn barge through the old **Delaware Canal** near here, built in 1831, and take a 14-mile ride on the **New Hope** and **Ivy Railroad,** a 1911 steam train. You can dine romantically by candlelight in many restaurants. And, with advance reservations, you can see excellent threatrical productions in the famous **Bucks County Playhouse;** shows nightly, except Sundays, and on Wednesday and Saturday afternoons from early May to mid-September. Several miles south of New Hope is **Bowman's Hill**, which Washington used as a lookout, now topped with an observation platform worth climbing for an even more magnificent view of the **Delaware River Valley**. On the other side of the hill is the lovely **Wildflower Preserve**, at its peak of beauty in April through June. Nearby is the **Nature Education Center** with lectures and interesting birdbanding demonstrations on Saturday and Sunday afternoons. A little farther south is **Washington's Crossing State Park.** Just outside the park, the **Thompson-Neely House** (1701), requisitioned by Washington's officers, is where the decision was made to cross the Delaware for the surprise attack on the Hessians at Trenton. The **Memorial Building** contains the familiar Emmanuel Leutze painting *Washington Crossing the Delaware* and steps now lead down from the building to the place where the 2,400 soldiers and Washington made their historic river crossing on Christmas night in 1776. Farther south, below **Morrisville,** home of US Steel's Fairless Works, is **Pennsbury Manor,** closed Mondays, an authentic re-creation of the Georgian-style mansion where William Penn, founder of Pennsylvania and Bucks County, lived in 1700 and 1701. It contains the state's largest collection of 17th-century furnishings; definitely worth a detour. **Doylestown,** 11 miles northwest of New Hope, is the Bucks County seat and a picturesque little town surrounded with impressive estates and superb farms. The **Mercer Museum,** closed in January and February, contains the country's largest collection of American implements and tools, dating back to the earliest pioneers. **Fonthill** (in Doylestown), the home that Dr. Henry Chapman Mercer decorated with an incredible assortment of tiles, is open only by appointment, but the pottery on the grounds, where Moravian tiles are still made, is open at all times.

The **POCONO MOUNTAINS** slant across Pike, Monroe, and Carbon counties in northeastern Pennsylvania. They are only about 1,600 feet high, but high enough to be cool in summer and snowy in winter. This is a popular honeymoon hideaway the year round. It's a very pretty region of wooded hills and deep valleys, small lakes and streams, and picturesque waterfalls. At the latest count, more than 300 facilities offer a choice of just about every vacation amenity, including golf, tennis, lawn games, horseback riding, swimming, fishing, boating, hiking, and mountain climbing in summer; skiing, sledding, skating, and tobogganing in winter. **The Pocono Raceway** hosts the racing car Pocono 500 each June. The larger resorts have dancing and professional entertainment nightly. There are all kinds of special rates for a week or a weekend, for honeymooners, for singles-only, for couples-only, for families, for conventioneers, and what-have-you. A toll-free call to the Pocono Mountain Reservations Service (800-523-4513) can help you select the sort of hotel you'd enjoy most. Some have housekeeping units for an economical prolonged vacation.

The **Buck Hill Inn and Golf Club** (595-7441, S\$60-75/D\$89-95) at **Buck Hill Falls** opened in 1901 as the first resort in the Poconos, and is now one of the largest summer-winter resort estates in the US. **Fernwood** (588-6661, from 37.50 p.p.) is a year-round resort in nearby Bushkill.

Bushkill Falls and **Winona Falls** are major scenic attractions here. The **Delaware Water Gap** is one of the great beauty spots of the east, and is the most popular approach to the Poconos from New Jersey on I-80; especially lovely in mid-April to mid-May, when it is all abloom with azaleas, mountain laurel, dogwood, and wild flowers. Just 3 miles north of the Gap, at Shawnee on the Delaware, is **Shawnee Inn** (421-1500, S$52.50-110/D$62.50-130) open mid-April to mid-October. **Stroudsburg** is the "capital" of the Pocono Mountains. Its wide choice of good motels makes it a convenient, inexpensive base for seeing the scenery. Located downtown: **Holiday Inn** (424-1951, S$25/D$37); **Pocono Hilton** (421-2200, S$20-28/D$30-40); and **Sheraton Pocono Inn** (424-1930, S$41.50-46.75/D$53.50), are all excellent. On the western fringes of the Poconos are the highly industrialized cities of **Scranton** and **Wilkes-Barre**, which were badly devastated during the flood caused by tropical storm Agnes in June 1972.

West of Wilkes-Barre, on the other side of the Appalachian Mountains, is **Williamsport**, on a branch of the Susquehanna River. This was the heart of the US lumber industry in the 1860s. Its prosperity is more diversified these days, and probably every child knows this is where Little League baseball began and is the location of the International Headquarters. The **Little League World Series** is played in Williamsport the last week in August. US 220 curves southwest from Williamsport along the scenic ridges of the **Allegheny Mountains,** passing through **Altoona** where traffic has been heavy ever since Americans first headed west. During the nation's big canal-building spree in the 1830s, the Portage Railroad became a freakish offshoot by hauling canal barges 36 miles from the Juniata River up a series of inclined planes, then easing them down to continue their travels on the Conemaugh River. Part of this remarkable line can still be seen outside Altoona. Most famous, however, is the **Horseshoe Curve** on the Conrail tracks, 5 miles west of town and easily viewed from an observation parking area. Going around the central curve of 220 degrees, each passing train seems to double itself, and for a moment the last cars are almost exactly parallel with the first. Southwest of Altoona is **Johnstown,** western terminus of the Portage Railroad over the Alleghenies. Johnstown's business and industrial districts lie in a deep, narrow river valley, with residential areas on the hillsides. Some of the earliest developments in steel-making were perfected here. By 1873 Johnstown was the country's leading steel center. Then came the Johnstown Flood of 31 May 1889. As the gigantic wall of water crashed through the valley, more than 2,200 people were drowned. A special "Unknown Plot" in **Grandview Cemetery** contains the unmarked headstones of 777 unidentified victims. Other bad floods in 1936 and 1977 temporarily devastated the city. The story of these three floods is in the Johnstown Flood Museum. Ride Johnstown's unique **Inclined Plane Railway** (71 grade), that can carry 50 passengers in a single car up more than 500 feet to attractive residential suburbs high above the valley.

Uniontown, about 40 miles south of Pittsburgh, is a heavily industrial city set in the scenic **Blue Ridge Mountains. Mt Davis,** at 3,213 feet the highest point in the state, is about 35 miles east of town. **Fort Necessity National Battlefield,** 11 miles southeast of Uniontown, is where the young George Washington and a handful of Virginians met superior forces of French and Indians on 3 July 1754 in what proved to be the first battle of the French and Indian War, a conflict that eventually involved most of Europe and India in the Seven Years' War. General Braddock, commander of all the British forces in America, was fatally wounded in the Battle of Monongahela in 1755 and was carried back to Fort Necessity, where a granite monument marks his grave. The fort as it is seen today was reconstructed from a description of the original. Fort Necessity often in the summer has a tour guide dressed in a soldier's uniform to explain his attire and the battle. An enjoyable tourist attraction is the **National Pike Festival** held each Spring along US 40—with displays and fairs held at all the towns from Scenery Hill in Washington, Pa., through Uniontown and east. It's worth seeing. Also well worth-seeing is **Youghiogheny Park** in the same area and its beautiful waterfalls on the Youghiogheny River. Resorts are along the river and guides are available for "white water trips" and camping facilities are also there. Open year-round, good trout fishing. About 10 miles north of here, at **Bear Run** on PA 381, is **Fallingwater,** probably the most stunning of all the houses designed by Frank Lloyd Wright. Natural rock outcroppings, trees, and a plunging stream have been used as integral parts of the design structure for this building, which is cantilevered at various levels over the waterfall. The richly furnished interior may be seen on guided tours daily, except Mondays, from late March to mid-November; reservations tel: 232-0060.

Due north of Pittsburgh is **Meadville,** where the campus of **Allegheny College** is known for **Bentley Hall,** a very good example of the symmetrical Federal architectural style, and the pioneer and Lincoln collections in **Reis Library.** The **Baldwin-Reynolds House** (1843) is an interesting museum of pioneer mementos. Ten miles west of town is **Conneaut Lake,** a resort town on Pennsylvania's largest natural lake, 929 acres. East of Meadville is **Titusville,** where the world's first oil well was drilled by Edwin L. Drake in 1859. An exact replica of Drake's rig is in **Drake Well Memorial Park,** along with a fascinating museum of photographs and relics from the early days of the oil industry. After Drake's success, wildcat drillers swarmed into Crawford County, creating short-lived boom towns. **Pithole City,** southeast of Titusville, is now a ghost town marked with plaques recalling its brief era of glory, which produced the country's first oil-carrying pipeline in 1865. **Allegheny National Forest,** east of here, is a splendid wilderness area teeming with fish, wild game, and birds. Park headquarters are in **Warren,** where recommended accommodations include the **Holiday Inn, Sheraton Inn,** and **Best Western Conley's Motel,** averaging S$22-38/D$25-38.

ERIE is Pennsylvania's great inland port, with one of the best harbors on the Great Lakes. Port facilities are protected by the **Presque Isle Peninsula** that extends 11 miles out into Lake Erie. Presque Isle has excellent beaches and tourist facilities. Within the last 10 years a large amusement park has been built. Coastguards are also based here to protect boaters. Ice fishing is popular in the winter. The **Koeler Brewery** downtown has tours with snacks—a popular attraction. The site was first chosen for a French military fort in 1753. This was later abandoned and appropriated by the British in 1759. They were driven out by Indians in 1763, and Chief Pontiac ordered the fort destroyed. The Americans came along and built another in 1795. The city of Erie was planned by General Andrew Ellicott, the first US surveyor general, at about the same time. Most of Commodore Oliver H. Perry's ships were built at Erie, and he sailed from here to defeat the British on 10 September 1813, securing Lake Erie for the US in the War of 1812. The *USS Niagara,* at the foot of State Street, is a restoration of Perry's flagship. Nearby is the prow of the *USS Wolverine,* the first iron-hulled warship, built in Erie shipyards in 1843. The **Old Customs House** (1839) is in regal Greek revival style. The **Perry Memorial House and Dickson Tavern** (1809) was used as headquarters by Commodore Perry, and is honeycombed with secret passages where runaway slaves were hidden on the pre-Civil War "Underground Railroad." **Presque Isle State Park** is a great recreation area with sandy beaches, fishing, boating, and other summertime fun facilities. The **Land Lighthouse** (1866) on the peninsula is the third that has stood on its site since 1813. **Fort Le Boeuf,** 16 miles south of the city, was the last fort held by the French in the French and Indian War. Midtown motels in Erie include: **Holiday Inn-Downtown** (456-2961, S$31-38/D$38-39); **Quality Inn-Downtowner** (456-6251, S$24-28/D$26-38); and **TraveLodge-Erie** (459-2220, S$30-39/D$38-45). A little farther out are **Holiday Inn-South** (864-4911, S$31-38/D$38-39), 4½ miles south on I-90; **Howard Johnson Motor Lodge** (864-4811, S$28-37/D$36-43), 5 miles south on PA-19; **Ramada Inn** (825-3100, S$34 up/D$40 up), 4 miles south on Wattsburg Road; and **Scott's Quality Inn** (838-1961, S$24-35/D$30-50), overlooking the harbor at the entrance to Presque Isle State Park.

Cities To Visit

PHILADELPHIA

Philadelphia, birthplace of the nation and the fourth largest city in the US, is in southeastern Pennsylvania, on the Delaware and Schuylkill Rivers, 85 miles southwest of New York City. It was founded in 1682 by William Penn, who gave the city its name and laid out its roads. At the time of the American Revolution it was the largest city in the colonies. The First Continental Congress met here, and the city was the focal point of the most stirring events in early American history. The *Declaration of Independence* and the *Constitution of the United States* were adopted and signed in Philadelphia, and the city was the seat of the US Federal Government until 1800. It is the largest freshwater port in the world and the second largest port in the US. The area surrounding the beautiful Independence National Historical Park has been called "America's most historic square mile."

Known as the "City of Brotherly Love" when the American nation was born in 1776, today it is a center of culture, education, science, and religion as well as business and industry with a metropolitan population of 4,696,000.

Philadelphia today has something for everyone. It offers visitors a renaissance of culture, history, and entertainment, including the finest in professional sports—and street peddlers hawking soft pretzels.

Art connoisseurs, history buffs, music lovers, medical scientists, and those who appreciate the culinary arts are finding new interests in a city which has restored much of its historical glamour within walking distance of its bustling business and industry.

WHAT TO SEE

Of great interest are **Independence National Historical Park; Fairmount Park; Philadelphia Zoo; Bartram's Gardens,** a restoration of the great botanist's home; **Morris Arboretum; Franklin Institute and Fels Planetarium,** (both in the same building), **Academy of Natural Sciences, Independence Hall** and the **Liberty Bell; Congress Hall,** which housed Congress from 1790-1800; **Betsy Ross House; Christ Church,** founded 1695, where Washington, Franklin, Morris, and others worshipped; **Franklin Court, Graff House** (where Jefferson wrote the Declaration of Independence), **Afro-American Historical & Cultural Museum,** and the **Visitors Center** run by the National Park Service; **US Mint; Old Custom House; Carpenters' Hall; Elfreth's Alley,** the nation's oldest residential street; colonial and Federal mansions in **Fairmount Park,** open to the public; **Friends Meeting House; City Hall,** with its observation tower; **Edgar Allan Poe House;** *USS Olympia* located at Penn's Landing, Commodore Dewey's flagship during the Spanish-American War. Also, **Old Fort Mifflin,** a well-preserved 18th-century bastion on the banks of the Delaware; **Fire Museum,** memorabilia of the country's first municipal fire department; the **University Museum** and **Philadelphia Museum of Art** are particularly outstanding. **Maritime Museum** with Underwater Hall is interesting. Many antique dealers are located on Pine Street in downtown Philadelphia. There are numerous conducted city tours; a typical trip takes 3 hours. Horse-driven carriages are available in the historical and Society Hill area. **SEPTA** (Southeastern Pennsylvania Transportation Authority) offers the cultural loop bus, which features unlimited rides all day for $1.50 from 3rd & Chestnut streets to the Philadelphia Zoo, and which includes many museums and historical points along the way. Also available is the Fairmount Park trolley-bus to visit mansions in the park. Philadelphia Harbor Cruises run twice daily for two hours.

Colleges and schools in the Philadelphia area include the **University of Pennsylvania,** founded 1740; **Temple University; Drexel University.** Other important institutions are the **Pennsylvania Academy of the Fine**

Arts, the **Philadelphia College of Art**, the **Moore College of Art**, and **La Salle College**. Villanova University, Haverford College, Swarthmore, Ursinus, and Bryn Mawr are nearby.

ACCOMMODATIONS

Located near Independence Hall and the historical area is the **Holiday Inn-Independence Mall** (923-8660, S$49/D$55). Three hotels located in the elegant and stylish Rittenhouse Square area are the **Barclay Hotel** (545-0300, S$65-85/D$80-110), **Warwick Hotel** (735-6000, S$70-90/D$85-105), and **The Latham** (563-7474, S/D$70-85). The newest hotel, located near the Benjamin Franklin Parkway at 17th Street in the business district, is the **Franklin Plaza Hotel** (448-2704, S$64-74/D$76-86). Also located on the Parkway at 18th St is the **Plaza** (963-1800, S$70-90/D$100-125) and near the museums along the Parkway is the **Franklin Motor Inn** (568-8300, S$43/D$46). Other centrally located hotels are: the completely refurbished **Bellevue-Stratford Hotel** (893-7710, S/D$45-65), the **Sheraton Hotel**, (568-3300, S$49-63/D$59-73), the **Holiday Inn-Midtown** (735-9300, S$50/D$55), **Holiday Inn-Penn Center** (561-7500, S$51-57/D$62-74), **Penn Center Inn** (569-3000, S$42-46/D$48-52). The **Hilton** (387-8333, S$46-62/D$56-72) and the **Holiday Inn-University City** (387-8000, S$50/D$56) are located near the University of Pennsylvania campus, near the Civic Center where major conventions are held and near the Amtrak 30th St Station. On the outskirts of the city is the **Marriott Hotel** on City Line Ave. (667-0200, S$58-64/D$68-74). At the airport are the **Holiday Inn-Airport** (521-2400, S$41/D$46) and the **Best Western Airport Inn** (365-7000, S$38/D$45).

RESTAURANTS

Philadelphia has truly become a major restaurant town in recent years, and the city now offers many restaurants worthy of critics' acclaim. Most expensive, and most acclaimed French restaurants are **Le Bec-Fin** and **La Panetière**. Two other fairly expensive French restaurants are **La Truffe** and **La Banana Noire** (Black Banana)—both located in the Society Hill section near the waterfront. Reservations are a must at these French restaurants and at many below. Among the many moderate-to-expensive outstanding restaurants offering a Continental cuisine are the **Frog**; **Copper Penny**; **Garden**; **Bogart's**; **Morgan's**; **Maureen**; **20th Street Café**; and **Friday, Saturday, Sunday & Thursday, Too.** For fast gourmet food in cafeteria style, try the unique **Commissary** or **Eden.** A centrally located Italian restaurant is the **Ristorante da Gaetano**, on Walnut Street. Near Washington Square is **La Buca Ristorante.** For those who like a quiet Italian bistro in the heart of the open Italian market in South Philadelphia try the modestly priced **Villa di Roma** on 9th Street. In Chinatown are many Chinese restaurants which offer modestly priced food; the **Lotus Inn**, the **Imperial Inn**, and **Ho Sai Gai** offer excellent Chinese food. Some of the city's best seafood houses which offer traditional dishes are **Bookbinder's Old Original** (on 2nd Street and not to be confused with the other on 15th Street) and **Kelly's of Mole Street.** One Philadelphia specialty

The Liberty Bell is now enclosed in this glass-fronted pavilion on Independence Square so that visitors can see and study its colorful and dramatic history, at any hour of the day or night.

is snapper soup. For seafood with an expensive Continental flair, try the **Fish Market.** An enjoyable steak dinner is served at **Arthur's Steak House, Mitchell's,** and **Maxwell's Prime** (on South Street where there are many new bistros popular with the under-30 crowd). Also on South Street is **Tang's** for Chinese food. One Philadelphia specialty not to be missed is the soft pretzel with mustard, available from sidewalk vendors. You should also sample **Bassett's** ice cream, cheese-steaks, and hoagie sandwiches (submarines). Near the Echelon Mall in Voorhees, N.J., try **Chez Robert's** in the Coliseum.

ENTERTAINMENT

Many of the hotels, such as the Franklin Plaza in its rooftop **Horizons Room** or the Bellevue-Stratford in the **Versailles Room, Hunt Bar,** or in **O'Brien's,** have dinner music or entertainment. Restaurants featuring entertainment include: **Riverfront Dinner Theater, Middle East,** and **Palumbo's.** Mod entertainment at the **Bijou Café.** For the over-30 crowd, **Ain't Quite Crickett** in the Latham Hotel features piano entertainment and drinks only, the **Middle East** has bellydancers, and **Palumbo's** is a supper club with famous entertainers. The disco crowd has several choices: **Elan** in the Warwick Hotel; on South Street are **Ripley's** and **La Dolce Vita;** another disco on City Line is the **Library,** a popular singles bar, and the **Windjammer Room** of the Marriott.

If you're looking for popular social gathering places, try the **Happy Rooster,** the **Newstand** at Central Square (16th & Market streets), or **Stouffer's** at the Top of Center Square which offers a panoramic view of the city, also **Fran O'Brien's** on City Line Avenue. For the under-30 drinker, there's **PT's** on Front Street (with backgammon tables), **Downey's Saloon,** and **Lickety Split** in the South Street area, **Dr. Watson's Pub** and **McGillin's Old Ale House** for the college crowd.

ARTS AND MUSIC

Academy of Natural Sciences (299-1000), bird, animal, and shell exhibits; open Monday-Saturday 10-4:30, Sunday 1-4:30. **Atwater Kent Museum** (922-3031), folk art; open daily 9:00-5:00. **Civic Center Museum** (686-1776) features "Philadelphia Panorama," the nation's largest exhibit on city planning, also exhibits on commerce and culture of other countries, open Tuesday to Saturday 9-5, Sunday 1-5; free; the restored **Pennsylvania Academy of Fine Arts** (972-7600) featuring American art; **Museum of Art** (736-8100), Western art of 14th through 19th centuries, distinguished collections from the Far East; open daily 9-5. **Philadelphia Art Alliance** (545-4302) features changing exhibitions of contemporary paintings and sculpture. The **Barnes Foundation** (Merion, PA, 664-8880) contains priceless paintings, including works of Degas, Seurat, and Picasso. **Rodin Museum** (763-8100), sculpture collection; open daily 9-5. **University Museum** (386-7400), exceptional archeological collections; open Tuesday through Sunday 10-5.

The excellent **Philadelphia Orchestra** performs regularly at the Academy of Music. In summer there are outdoor concerts at Robin Hood

Dell in **Fairmount Park,** with world-famous conductors and soloists. Members of the **Philadelphia Mummers String Band New Year Association** present 90-minute concerts every Tuesday at 7pm at John F. Kennedy Plaza, and in costume every Friday on Independence Mall at 8pm, June to September. There is a **Mummers Museum** at 2nd & Washington Avenue with displays on the costumes and art of mummery. Other entertainment in summer at **Rittenhouse Square, Independence Hall,** and **John F. Kennedy Plaza.** There is a sound-and-light production in **Independence Hall** at 9pm, daily during the summer.

The **Spectrum** and **Civic Center** present a varied repertoire of music, including big name groups, country music stars, folk singers, and jazz. Philadelphia offers excellent opportunities for theatergoers; many new Broadway shows hold out-of-town premieres here. Leading theaters include the **Shubert, Walnut, Forrest,** and the **Annenberg Center.** The **Playhouse in the Park** is a permanent theater in **Fairmount Park,** open spring-fall. **Bucks County Playhouse,** one of the finest summer stock theaters, is nearby, in New Hope, PA. The city also has a number of dinner theaters, such as the **Riverfront** on the Delaware River, in Central Philadelphia.

SHOPPING

The main shopping area runs from 8th to 18th streets on **Market, Chestnut,** and **Walnut** streets. **The Gallery,** a four-level, modern, enclosed shopping mall located in center city at 9th & Market streets between Gimbels and Strawbridge & Clothier department stores, is the newest place to shop with 125 shops and fast-food restaurants. Open Mon-Sat 10-9, Sun 12-5. Also visit the new market complex of boutiques in the Society Hill area at 2nd & Pine streets; nearby is **Head House Square** with its colonial type shops. Two blocks down is South Street—Philly's **Greenwich Village. Lord & Taylor** and **Saks 5th Av.** have branches on City Line Avenue. The most exclusive shops are on Chestnut & Walnut streets from 17th to 18th streets. **Cherry Hill Mall,** five miles east of Philadelphia on route 38 and Haddonfield Road, is the largest enclosed shopping center east of the Mississippi. Completely covered with glass and air conditioned year round, the Mall has rare tropical plants and birds, and contains nearly every kind of store and service imaginable; open 10-9:30; Monday through Friday, 10-6, Saturday.

SPORTS

Harness and thoroughbred racing at **Liberty Bell Park.** Thoroughbred tracks in neighboring New Jersey, Delaware, and Maryland. **Philadelphia Phillies,** 1980 World Series champs, play baseball in the National League. Professional football is played by the **Eagles.** Both play at the **Veteran's Stadium.** Boxing and wrestling events are scheduled at the **Arena.** The Philadelphia 76ers play basketball and the **Philadelphia Flyers,** hockey at the **Spectrum. Philadelphia Atoms,** of the North American Soccer League, compete at Veteran's Stadium May through August. The **Philadelphia Wings** play Lacrosse, May through September, at the Spectrum.

All college sports, particularly football, are played by Pennsylvania,

Villanova, and Temple universities, and by numerous college teams in the area. There are five public and many private golf courses; numerous tennis courts in the parks. Swimming in nearby lakes, recreation centers, and motor inns.

CALENDAR OF EVENTS

Mummers Parade, New Year's Day; Sports show and "National" Indoor **Tennis Championships,** late January; **Philadelphia Track Classic,** 7 February; **Philadelphia Flower & Garden Show** at Civic Center, mid-March; **Penn Relays,** track competiton, April; **Devon Horse Show,** late May; **IVB Golf Classic,** mid-June; **Freedom Week,** late June; **Philadelphia Fling,** programs June to Labor Day; **Robin Hood Dell Concerts,** late June through July, Festival concerts Tuesday and Thursday nights in August; **Schuylkill Regattas,** July and August; **Hero's Scholarship Thrill Show,** September; **International Horse Show,** October; **Gimbels Toyland Parade,** Thanksgiving Day; **Army-Navy Football Classic,** November.

WHERE TO GO NEARBY

Cherry Hill, 5 miles east; swimming, golf, nearby racetrack, summer theater, and points of historic interest. The **Pocono Mountains** are about 80-95 miles to the north; there are almost 200 vacation resorts in the vicinity of **Stroudsburg.** Other leading resorts, in New Jersey, are **Atlantic City,** now the Las Vegas of the East, 60 miles southeast. Casino gambling is available in Atlantic City, NJ, at **Resorts International, Boardwalk Regency Casino Hotel, Bally, Brighton, Harrah's,** and the **Golden Nugget,** and other casino hotels. Bus excursion packages are available from Philadelphia. Also located in New Jersey are **Ocean City,** 68 miles southeast; **Wildwood,** 90 miles southeast; and **Cape May,** 95 miles southeast. About 35 miles north is **New Hope,** in Bucks County, an artists and writers' colony. The **Pennsylvania Dutch Country** is about 40 miles west. **Valley Forge,** 21 miles northwest of Philadelphia, scene of Washington's winter of 1777, beautiful park area with museum, historic buildings, and observation tower. A trip here takes about 4 hours. **Washington's Crossing State Park,** 30 miles northeast; historic spot where General Washington crossed the Delaware River, old buildings, gristmills, markers. **Ralph Stover State Park,** about 38 miles north, picnic facilities.

PITTSBURGH

Set among the hills of southwestern Pennsylvania at the point where the Allegheny and Monongahela Rivers merge to form the Ohio, Pittsburgh has always played a strategic role in the history and economics of the state and the nation. The peninsula of land between the rivers was a continuous battleground between the French and English as they jockeyed for American colonial supremacy in the 18th century, and was a focal point in the French and Indian War. In 1754 the French ousted the British from the point as they were in the process of building a fort, and built their own called Ft Duquesne. They in turn were routed in 1758 when a British force led by General Forbes captured the fort

Mummer Comics strut up Broad Street in Philadelphia, spreading joy on New Year's morning.

and re-named it "Pitts-Borough," in honor of the English statesman, William Pitt.

Pittsburgh's location, at the junction of three rivers (the only city in the continental US that can boast such a locale) hastened its early growth and earned it the title "Gateway to the West." In the 1800s as immigrants and raw materials, particularly coal, poured into the area, Pittsburgh burgeoned into a rough and rowdy frontier town whose mills supplied armaments to the Union in the Civil War. The huge stores of nearby coal, and the ease of transporting other raw materials by water, have made Pittsburgh one of the most important iron-and-steel producing centers in the world, and the nation's largest inland port.

To supply war materials during World Wars I and II, Pittsburgh's mills went non-stop, blackening the skies and giving the city an almost infernal reputation. In 1945, when the city emerged from the war effort, a smoke-stained, weary urban disaster, Pittsburgh's civic and industrial leaders joined forces to begin a renaissance that continues to this day. Their efforts, which included an active program of smoke control, and rebuilding the most decayed urban areas, have produced a clear-skied metropolis, still heavily industrial, but also boasting the third largest number of corporate headquarters in the nation.

The initial renaissance has been completed and Renaissance Two, as it is now called, has produced a convention center, as well as a portfolio of major building projects that will carry into the late 1980s. More than that, Pittsburgh has emerged as a lively, forward-looking city whose compact business district, girdled by the rivers, throbs with life day and night as people take advantage of restaurants, theaters, entertainment spots, sports arenas, and shopping—nearly all within walking distance of major downtown hotels and motels. Pittsburgh's planners have also managed to retain and renovate some architectural gems from the last century. This, plus the downtown skyscrapers and the rivers against the surrounding hills, with narrow three-story houses clinging precariously to their heights, make Pittsburgh one of the best urban surprises in the country. Population: 423,962; metropolitan area 2,244,620.

WHAT TO SEE

See downtown Pittsburgh's "Golden Triangle" from its best vantage point, **Mt Washington**, especially at night. Take the **Duquesne** or **Monongahela incline**, a vertical cable car, from 5:30am-1:00am (Adults 80¢ roundtrip) from W Carson Street. Walk the promenade and lookout areas along Grandview Avenue atop the mount. You can get a broader view of the city and its environs from the roof of the 64-story **US Steel Building** on Grant St (the tallest building between NY and Chicago) and snack at the **Top of the Triangle Restaurant.** Close by is the **Civic Arena,** crowned by an umbrella-shaped roof taller than a 10-story building. In 2½ minutes this world's largest retractable dome can swing open providing an amphitheater under the stars for sports events, rock concerts, folk events, and festivals of all kinds. Also on Grant Street, heading toward the Monongahela River, is the **Allegheny County Court House,** described as one of America's finest examples of Norman Romanesque architecture. Exhibitions, films, lectures, given in courthouse gallery and foyer. For information 355-5859. Downtown Pittsburgh is dotted with plazas and **Point State Park** is located at the juncture of the rivers. The park's fountain is the focal point of the triangle area and shoots a 200-ft. high column of water into the air. The **Fort Pitt Museum** and **Blockhouse** are located in the heart of Point Park, the former containing 60 exhibits, many with audio aids illustrating the history of the area from early Indian cultures through the 1800s. The Ft Pitt Blockhouse, built in 1764, is all that is left of the original English Fort. Entrance is free. Museum hours Tues-Sat. 10-4:30; Sunday noon-4:30; tel: (471-1764). Admission for adults $1.75, accompanying children—free. On Sunday from mid-June through Labor Day, French and Indian War cannonades are demonstrated by the Royal American Regiment Musketeers. Also in town is **Market Square,** center for nightlife—clubs, singles bars, restaurants, in an atmosphere of cobblestones and gaslights, and the Bank Center, 4th Avenue & Wood Street, a shopping, dining, entertainment bazaar housed in the renovated remains of a number of bank buildings in Pittsburgh's turn-of-the-century financial district. The architectural leftovers alone—ponderous marble staircases, bank vaults with their massive doors permanently opened, stained glass skylights—are enough to make it a memorable stop.

Take the Smithfield Street Bridge and walk across the Monongahela River to **Station Square,** an agora of restaurants, shops, and galleries housed in renovated railway freight houses. The elegant turn-of-the-century stationhouse now contains the **Grand Concourse** restaurant and busy **Gandy Dancer Saloon,** amidst a wealth of railroad memorabilia. Across the Allegheny River on the City's near north side, visitors can see **Three Rivers Stadium Sports Museum** (323-1000); **Buhl Planetarium** which features sky shows (321-4300). Admission for adults $2.50, children through high school $1.25; the **Old Post Office Museum** featuring artifacts and exhibits of Victorian lifestyle around the turn of the century and an outstanding exhibit about stained glass and how it's made; the **Pittsburgh Aviary** (open every day except Christmas, 9-5. 50¢ for adults; 25¢ for children up to 17). **Allegheny Observatory** in Riverview Park features tours, free lectures, movie shows, etc. Weather permitting, visitors can peer through the 13-inch telescope. Tours by appointment April through October (321-2400).

Ten to fifteen minutes east of downtown is **Oakland,** the city's medical and cultural center. Points of interest include **Carnegie Institute,** containing the main branch of the city's public library system; **Museum of Natural History** which houses one of the nation's best dinosaur collections; and the **Carnegie Museum of Art,** including the **Scaife and Heinz Galleries** (622-3131), which feature nationally renowned art exhibitions; closed Mondays. **Schenley Park** has a lake, golf course and the **Phipps Conservatory** open daily with special flower shows in spring and fall (255-2375) free except during shows. The **University of Pittsburgh's** 40-story **Cathedral of Learning** is the nation's only skyscraper university done in neo-Gothic style. The cathedral houses 19 nationality rooms which depict through decor and furnishings the cultural diversity of Pittsburgh's ethnic communities, including Chinese, Syrian, Greek, etc. Tours (624-6000). A few hundred yards away is **Heinz Memorial Chapel,** a non-denominational chapel in 13th-century French Gothic style, outstanding stained-glass windows. **Stephen Foster Memorial,** auditorium and museum adjacent to the Cathedral of Learning, houses memorabilia on the life and career of Pittsburgh-born Stephen Collins Foster, one of America's best-known folk composers. Free tours (621-4100). All of the above-mentioned points of interest are within walking distance of each other, mostly across the street.

Two other not-to-be-missed Pittsburgh attractions (especially if you have children) are the **Pittsburgh Zoo** (441-6262) at **Highland Park** in the East End section of the city; and **Kennywood Amusement Park** (461-0500) in West Mifflin. In addition to the traditional collection of animals, the former includes a children's aqua and twilight zoo which shows the living habits of nocturnal animals in almost natural surroundings. Kennywood features 32 adult rides, a kiddyland, boating lake, miniature golf, games, and daily circus acts. Open daily May through Labor Day. Noon-11pm; closed Mondays July and August.

Because of its rugged terrain, Pittsburgh was not laid out in grids like many other cities. Once outside the downtown area, points of interest are spread out enough that a city map is almost essential. Public transportation is available, and Pittsburgh is one of the few cities left that still uses trolleys. Port Authority Transit (231-5707) can supply commuter information as well as details on their guided bus tours to points of interest in the city and metro areas. The Pittsburgh Council for International Visitors (682-6151) arranges tours and introduces international visitors to other foreigners in the area. Pittsburgh proper has two cab companies—Yellow (665-8100) and People's (681-3131).

Pittsburgh can also be seen from its rivers via the Gateway Clipper Fleet—for children, the good ship lollipop. For adults there are party and dinner cruises as well as narrated tours covering historic sites and points of interest along the river including a ride through a lock (355-7979). For further information on tours, call the Pittsburgh Visitors and Convention Bureau (281-7711).

ACCOMMODATIONS

Downtown hostelries include the **Pittsburgh Hilton** on the Golden Triangle overlooking Point Park (261-5600, S$54-63/D$65-74); **Hyatt House** at Chatham Center near Civic Arena (391-5000, S$60-70/D$72-82); with same occupancy, Hyatt features executive floors with VIP services at $85 and $97; **William Penn** (281-7100, S$42-58/D$52-68), in the heart of downtown overlooking Mellon Square, one of the grand old hotels in process of being renovated, three adequate restaurant facilities within walking distance of everything, cocktail hour in main lobby every day— a meeting place particularly on Fridays. Just across the river is the new **Sheraton** at Station Square. The **Pittsburgh Marriott Inn**—complete resort facility 3 miles from downtown on Parkway West, Greentree exit (922-8400, S$54-70/D$60-75, weekend family rate $40) features swimming, tennis, entertainment, disco, etc.; **Parkway Center Inn** (922-7070, S$38-42), **Parkway West** at Greentree, swimming and sauna; **Holiday Inn at Greentree** (922-8100, S$44/D$50), Parkway West at Greentree.

Oakland: University area—**Crossgates Inn**, (683-3000, S$49/D$58, two- or three-room suites $110-156), fabulous art-deco decor. South Hills: **Sheraton South** across from South Hills Village Shopping Mall (343-7600); **Redwood Motor Hotel**, Banksville Road at Potomac Avenue (343-3000); **Best Western Viking Motor Hotel**, Banksville Road, Greentree (531-8900), averaging S$29-38/D$34-47.

Airport area—**Airport Hotel**, airport terminal building (264-4803); **Allegheny Motor Inn** (264-7790); **Hilton** (262-3800); **Holiday Inn, Ramada Inn, Sheraton, Howard Johnson's**, average S$20.83-57/D$24.04-69.

Monroeville area: **Pittsburgh Marriott** (373-7300, S$48-54/D$56-62), racquet club facilities, Sunday brunch, located in the Monroeville Shopping Mall.

RESTAURANTS

The outstanding **Le Mont** and **Tin Angel** restaurants combine excellent cuisines with panoramic views of Pittsburgh; **Georgetown Inn** offers good food and a view at a more modest price. Best downtown restaurants include **Common Plea, De Foro** (Continental cuisine), **Klein's** (seafood specialities), **Tambellini's Wood Grill** (Wood Street), **Franco Tambellini** (Seventh Street), and **Piccolo Piccolo**, a delightful Italian trattoria. Station Square, within walking distance across the Monongahela River, offers five restaurants including the elegant **Grand Concourse**. To the east are the excellent **La Normande, Park Schenley**, and **Nino's**. In the airport area are **The Colony, Hyehold**, and **Sgrow's**.

ENTERTAINMENT

Les Nuages, Fulton Building, Sixth Avenue, serves food and vies with **The Library**, Bank Center, as the city's poshest disco. The latter serves drinks only. **Happy Landing,** Kossman Bldg, Stanwix Street, serves food. Other discos include the **VIP**, Bridgeville, in the South Hills and another in the North Hills suburbs; **Wonderful Wanda's,** Crossgates Inn, Oakland; and **Johnny Dollar,** near the airport, a Western-style disco. Jazz is the thing at **Encore,** Shadyside's Walnut Street, and the place attracts top musicians. **Walsh's,** Broad Street Mall, East Liberty, is for blue-grass lovers only. **Top of the Triangle,** US Steel Building, Grant Street, offers entertainment, a large bar, and a great view; there are shows Tuesday through Saturday; call ahead for times.

Singles spots: Downtown, **The Rusty Scupper,** Bank Center; **Alexander Graham's Bell** (with telephones on each table to dial prospective dates), Market Square; **Gandy Dancer Saloon,** Grand Concourse, Station Square; **Tramps,** Boulevard of the Allies.

Most of the hotels and motels have entertainment and dancing. The

Marriott's **Trolley Car Lounge** is popular. The only "real" nightclub left is the **Holiday House,** Monroeville. It features big name entertainment, dancing, and a disco on Sunday night. **Ben Gross' Reataurant and Dinner Theater,** route 30, Irwin, Pa., has lively entertainment with good food; reservations 271-6696. In addition to the regular commercial movies, **Pittsburgh's Carnegie Institute** (622-3200), the **Pittsburgh Playhouse** (621-4445), and the **Pittsburgh Film-Makers** (681-5449) offers carefully selected programs of important cinema at inexpensive prices throughout the year.

ARTS AND MUSIC

The **Pittsburgh Center for the Arts** features series of exhibits changed every month, open weekdays 10-5, Sunday 2-5, closed Monday. The **Three Rivers' Art Festival** is held outdoors in the Gateway Center during the end of May or in early June. An **International Folk Festival** is held in the Civic Arena, usually the second week in June. **Carnegie Institute,** art galleries, music hall, library; open weekdays 10-5, Sunday 12-5, closed Monday. **Heinz Hall** for the performing arts is the home of the **Pittsburgh Symphony Orchestra** and the **Pittsburgh Opera and Ballet.** Concerts are held Friday evenings and Sunday afternoons during the winter season. The **Pittsburgh Public Theatre** offers outstanding repertory theater September-June. There is also the **Civic Light Opera** group, which features musical theater at Heinz Hall during the summer. The **American Wind Symphony** entertains from a barge moored in the Allegheny River at Point Park.

SHOPPING

Downtown stores include **Squirrel Hill** (Forbes and Murray Avenues), **Shadyside's** (Walnut Street), and **Sewickly,** particularly for fashion, esthetics. Most downtown stores are open 9:30-5:30. Monday and Thursday nights till 9.

SPORTS

The **Pittsburgh Pirates** play professional baseball and the **Pittsburgh Steelers** play pro football at Three Rivers Stadium, located across the river from the Golden Triangle; ticket information for Pirates (323-1150); Steelers (323-1200). **Pittsburgh Penguins** play hockey at the Civic Arena (765-3939). **Schenley Park** has an ice skating arena open to the public. The city offers bicycling through four of the major parks (255-2350). **University of Pittsburgh, Carnegie-Mellon,** and **Duquesne University** have extensive athletic schedules covering baseball, football, track, tennis, swimming, and wrestling. Harness racing at **The Meadows,** 25 miles away in Washington. Swimming facilities are available. **Schenley Park** has an 18-hole public golf course; there are many other public and private golf clubs. **Bushy Run Battlefield,** about 30 miles east, is the site of an important Revolutionary War battle; it has a museum of Indian relics, also picnic groves. **Kooser Lake Park,** about 55 miles southeast, has cabins to rent by the week during the summer months, as has **Linn Runn,** 50 miles east. **Racoon Creek State Park,** 30 miles west, has a lake and picnic and camping spots.

CALENDAR OF EVENTS

Spring Flower Show, March or April; **Three Rivers Art Festival,** late May or early June; Folk Festival in the Civic Arena, mid-June; Shakespeare Festival, June-August; Three Rivers Regatta, August; **Allegheny County Fair,** late August; **Fall Flower Show,** November.

WHERE TO GO NEARBY

The two outstanding parks nearby are **North Park,** 10 miles north of the city, and **South Park,** 8 miles south, both of which have many recreational facilities.

Conneaut Lake, 90 miles away, has summer cottages, public bathing beach, and other resort facilities. At **Bedford,** in the Alleghenies 98 miles east of Pittsburgh, the attractive **Bedford Springs Hotel** offers mineral springs identical to those of the famed spa in Carlsbad, Czechoslovakia; most sports available; prices moderate. **Jennerstown** is a mountain resort village about 60 miles east, with some magnificent mountain scenery, a small hotel, good restaurants, and a summer theater, the **Mountain Playhouse. Ligonier,** 50 miles away, is a fine old town and the center of a resort area; of special interest are **Linn Run Recreation Area, Rolling Rock Club,** and **Idlewood Park. Oglebay Park,** West Virginia, less than 60 miles, has cabins, golf course, swimming pool, riding horses, and tennis courts. **Cook Forest State Park,** 100 miles northeast, is a natural forest area with hiking trails, picnic grounds, and boating facilities. **Presque Isle State Park** on Lake Erie is well worth a visit.

FURTHER STATE INFORMATION

Pennsylvania Travel Department Bureau, Department of Commerce, 431 South Office Street Building, Harrisburg, PA 17120. **Pennsylvania Dutch Visitors Bureau,** 1800 Hempstead Road, Lancaster, PA 17601. Hunting and Fishing: **State Game Commission,** Box 1567, and **State Fish Commission,** Box 1673, both Harrisburg, PA 17120. **Philadelphia Tourist Center,** 16th Street and John F. Kennedy Boulevard, Philadelphia, PA 19102; tel. 561-1200. **Chamber of Commerce of Greater Pittsburgh,** Chamber of Commerce Building, Pittsburgh, PA 15129. **Pittsburgh Convention and Visitors Bureau Inc.,** Roosevelt Building, Pittsburgh, PA 15222. **Pan Am** offices, 30 North 17th Street, Philadelphia, PA tel: (800)223-9762.

Consulates in Philadelphia: Belgium, Canada, Colombia, Costa Rica, Denmark, Dominican Republic, Ecuador, El Salvador, Finland, France, Germany, Great Britain, Guatemala, Haiti, Honduras, Iceland, Israel, Italy, Lesotho, Liberia, Mexico, Monaco, Netherlands, Nicaragua, Norway, Panama, Portugal, Sweden, Switzerland, Thailand, Uruguay, Venezuela.

In Pittsburgh: France, Great Britain, Italy, Mexico, Netherlands, Switzerland, Yugoslavia.

USEFUL TELEPHONE NUMBERS
Philadelphia

Emergency (Medical, Fire, Police)	911
Children's Hospital of Philadelphia	596-9100
Thomas Jefferson University Hospital	928-6000
Poison Information Control	922-5523
Emergency Dental Service	928-0110
Community Legal Service	893-5300
Chamber of Commerce	568-4040
Independence National Historical Park Information Center	597-8975
Philadelphia Convention & Visitors Bureau	864-1976

Pittsburgh

Children's Hospital	681-7700
Emergency	647-5555
Presbyterian University Hospital	647-2345
Pittsburgh Poison Center	681-6669
Allegheny County Dental Clinic	578-8052
Pittsburgh Help Line	255-1155
Pan Am Reservations	261-5811

Rhode Island

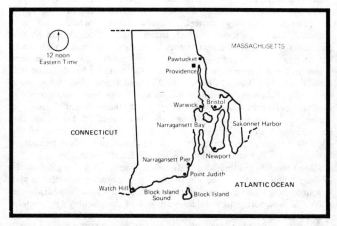

Area	1,214 square miles					**Population**	948,154					
Capital	Providence					**Sales Tax**	6%					
Weather		Jan	Feb	Mar	Apr	May	Jun	Jul	Aug	Sep	Oct	Nov Dec
Av Temp (°C)		−2	−1	3	8	14	19	22	21	17	12	6 0
Days Rain/Snow		11	10	11	11	11	10	9	10	8	8	12 12

If the best things truly come in small packages, then Rhode Island, the smallest of all the states, takes the prize for being the miniature masterpiece. It is quickly gaining ground as one of the most popular vacation spots on the east coast. The state is just 48 miles long and 37 miles across, bounded on the north and east by Massachusetts, on the south by the Atlantic Ocean and on the west by Connecticut.

Giovanni da Verrazano (for whom the famous bridge that spans the entrance to New York harbor is named) is thought to have been the first European to have explored this coast (1524). However, it was not until more than 100 years later (1636) that Roger Williams settled at Providence a community of "persons distressed for conscience" who had quit Puritan-dominated Massachusetts for freer climes. Two years later Williams founded the first Baptist congregation in the US, and the following year Newport was settled. Indeed, Newport was destined to become the northern focal point in the triangular trade that took rum to Africa for slaves, slaves to the Indies for molasses, and molasses back north to make rum. So Rhode Island, which never ranked high as an agricultural state due to small area and poor soil, became dependent on merchants and shipowners for most of its income during the state's early development. Molasses became its chief product before the Revolution. Manufacturing activity grew when Samuel Slater, an English immigrant, established a cotton mill with water-powered machines, marking the beginning of factory textile manufacturing in America. Today, textiles are still one of Rhode Island's most important industries, along with metals and machinery, jewelry, apparel, rubber, and plastic products.

Rhode Island's location on Block Island Sound, Rhode Island Sound, and Narragansett Bay rewards visitors with a variety of vacation pleasures any time of year. One of the great sailing centers of the world, Newport is host to the **America's Cup Classics** and the **Biennial Block Island Regatta Week.** The **Annual Storm Trysail** around Block Island takes place every May. Summertime sailors can escape to the bay's many modern marinas and yacht clubs. Fishermen regard Rhode Island's waters as among the finest in the world and the best salt-water fishing on the east coast can be found here, April through December. Some of the choicest catches of giant tuna between the Bahamas and Newfoundland have been taken between Block Island and Point Judith.

More than 100 public and private beaches, stretching along 400 miles of unmatched coastline, provide swimming and surfing, sunbathing and beachcombing. The first national tennis and golf championships were played at Newport, long established as one of the country's prominent sports centers. There is dog racing at **Lincoln Downs.** Ski buffs take to the slopes at **Yawgoo, Ski Valley, Pinetop,** and **Diamond Hill** ski areas. Local summertime entertainment includes the **Warwick Musical Theater, Theater-by-the-Sea,** at Matunuck, and the **Carriage House Theater** at Little Compton. Proud of its pioneer legacy, Rhode Island has, within its modest boundaries, some of the nation's finest examples of early American architecture. And, of course, the famous great commercial port at Newport is noted for its sumptuous summer "cottages" along Bellevue Avenue.

Seafood is the regional specialty. Don't miss the succulent Block Island swordfish, lobster, crabs, scallops, oysters, and clams. And what outdoor gourmet can resist the unique clambakes and May Day breakfasts; the latter originated in Rhode Island in 1867 and are held in grange halls, homes, and churches throughout the state.

Enter **SOUTHERN** Rhode Island on Interstate 95 from Connecticut and then switch to Rhode Island Routes 3, 1A and US 1, the scenic route along **Little Narragansett Bay** and **Block Island Sound.** At **Watch Hill** in the southwestern corner of the state, the **Ocean House** (348-8161, S$90/D$90-96) offers a private beach and comfortable rooms. There are many summer homes in the area dating from the late 1800s and the **Flying Horse Carousel** at Watch Hill beach is the oldest merry-go-round in America; the original horses are over 100 years old. There are boat charters at Watch Hill, and there is swimming at **Misquamicut State Beach** and the beaches between **Weekapaug** and Watch Hill. **The Weekapaug Inn** (322-0301, S/D$80-90) overlooks the ocean. The **Willows Resort Motel** (364-7727, S/D$72.50-80) in **Charlestown** to the east on

US 1, is set on 300 acres with riding, boating, salt- and fresh-water fishing, swimming; open Memorial Day through Labor Day. Continuing along the coast on US 1, the **Theater-by-the Sea** in **Matunuck** stages professional plays mid-June to Labor Day.

Eastward along the southern route, US 1, is **Narragansett Pier** where **The Towers,** two towers and a bridge, remain as testimony to the beauty of Stanford White's original 19th-century pavilion. Fish off the pier at the waterfront villages of **Galilee** and **Jerusalem** at the southern tip of Narragansett County. **Scarborough State Beach** and **Sand Hill Cove State Beach** nearby offer a variety of facilities for picnicking, swimming, and fishing. The **Dutch Inn** (789-9341, S$50-60/D$60-74), in Narragansett, has a pool, fishing, and boats, is 2 blocks from the ocean. **George's** in Galilee, an unpretentious restaurant, is best known for its clam chowder, fresh seafood platter, and low prices. The **Channel Lounge** has dining on a sundeck overlooking Block Island and Rhode Island Sounds, Sunday breakfast buffet.

Block Island, the State's ocean island resort, is about 10 miles off the Rhode Island coast to the southwest. There are several ways to get there. You can fly from La Guardia or Kennedy Airports in New York to Providence and make a connecting flight to Block Island. Charter flights from La Guardia via Hamptons to Montauk on Montauk-Caribbean Airways can also be arranged. Tel: (516) 537-1010. Or you can drive along the scenic I-95 as far as North Stonington, Connecticut, then switch to US 1 and RI 1A in "South County" and go finally to the village of Galilee where you can catch the ferry. Ferries run between Block Island and Galilee, Providence, Newport, and New London, Connecticut, daily, late June to early September; from Galilee ferries run year round, but less frequently during the rest of the year. Check weekend, holiday, and winter schedules. You can also take a ferry from Montauk to Block Island by making arrangements through Viking Fishing Fleet. Tel. (516) 668-5924. Block Island is usually 10 to 15 degrees cooler than the mainland in the summer, and also milder in winter. The community was once a quiet fishing and farming town with only a few hundred residents, but since the hotels were built, the summer population has swelled to about 5,000, still a relatively small number for one of the East Coast's most popular resort areas. Accommodations in Block Island are few, but include **Narragansett Inn** (466-2626, S$170-190 weekly), **The Old Town Inn** (466-5958, D$50), and **Spring House Hotel** (466-2633, S$33-40/D$52-68).

The fishing off the island is considered among the best in the world. You can surf cast from all the beaches, fish freshwater ponds inland for bass and perch, or charter a deep-sea boat at **New Harbor** and fish for tuna and swordfish. Fall is the hunting season for duck, pheasant, and woodcock. The **Mohegan Bluffs** on the southern shore, are 185-foot clay cliffs with an excellent view of the sea, reminiscent of the English white cliffs of Dover. **Block Island State Beach** has surf bathing, bathhouse, fishing, and picnicking.

Returning to the mainland, west of Narragansett Pier, in **Wakefield** there is patio dining in an 18th-century mansion at the **Larchwood Inn.**

South Kingstown retains its 18th-century charm. **Yawgoo Ski Area** to the northwest in **Exeter** is open December through March. Back along the coast on scenic RI 1A **Silas Casey Farm** operates as a typical 18th-century New England farmhouse with outbuildings. **Gilbert Stuart House** in **North Kingstown,** built in 1751, has been restored. It includes an 18th-century snuff mill which operates by an old wooden water wheel. Stuart was one of America's foremost colonial artists, best known for his portraits of Washington. **Conanicut** is one of the state's three main islands in Narragansett Bay. Bridges connect it to Newport on the east and the mainland on the west near North Kingstown. **Jamestown Village** clusters around the Newport ferry landing. The island's **Mackerel Cove Beach** is popular for swimming, and fishing boats may be rented at **East Ferry Slip.**

North is **Wickford Village,** a completely restored colonial community with beautiful houses on the main and side streets. All were built before 1804 and are still in use. Wickford has one of the largest marinas in New England, and the growing summer art colony is helping it to become a popular resort center in the Narragansett Bay area. Nearby **Smith's Castle** at **Cocumscussoc** was built in 1678, nearly a century before the signing of the Declaration of Independence. It stands on the former site of a trading post owned by Roger Williams, the founder of Rhode Island. Overlooking **Greenwich Bay, Goddard Memorial State Park** covers 472 acres and includes a nine-hole golf course; there is swimming at **Greenwich Cove Beach,** fishing, riding, picnicking, and ice skating in winter. **East Greenwich,** on Narragansett Bay, one of the most attractive old towns in the state, is worth a special visit. The **Kent County Court House,** built in 1750, is still in use. Fishing at the foot of **Duane Street;** swimming at beaches on **Ives Road.**

The cities of **Warwick** and **Cranston,** south of **Providence,** turn out for **Gaspee Days** in early June, celebrating the anniversary of the capture of *Gaspee,* the British revenue ship, by Rhode Island patriots. There's a clam bake, boat races, fireworks, and a parade. **Warwick Musical Theater,** one of the largest theaters-in-the-round in the world, features musical comedies; open late June through early September. Swimming at **Conimicut Point. Great House** serves dinner in an elegant old home and converted caboose with a player-piano in the century-old railroad station bar. **Cathay Terrace** serves excellent Cantonese cuisine; and **Valle's Steak House** is also a place for good food. **General Nathaniel Greene Homestead** at Anthony Village, west of Warwick, built in 1770, has been restored and the 14-room house with period furniture is now a patriotic shrine. Greene was George Washington's second-in-command during the Revolution. The **Carlton House Motor Inn** (739-3000, S$27/ D$31-34) has a pool.

Passing through Providence, **Old Slater Mill Museum,** to the north at **Pawtucket,** was the first successful cotton mill operated by water power in America. Samuel Slater started the American textile industry there in 1793 and the mill has been restored as a museum; hand spinning, hand loom, cotton gin, and weaving demonstrations. It is open 1 June-

5 September, Tuesday-Saturday 10-5, Sunday 1-5; rest of the year open Saturday and Sunday, 1-5. **Slater Memorial Park** has 195 acres, including the **Dagget House,** built in 1685 and furnished with outstanding colonial antiques; it also has one of the best zoos in New England. **Narragansett Race Track,** on the US 1A, has thoroughbred horse racing and pari-mutuel betting; early September through mid-December. **Howard Johnson's Motel** in Pawtucket (723-6700, S$36-38/D$41-43) includes an indoor heated pool. Northwest of Pawtucket, **Lincoln Downs** has flat racing and pari-mutuel betting; January through April. **Lincoln Woods State Park's** 627 acres are sprinkled with freshwater ponds providing facilities for swimming, boating, fishing, riding, picnicking, and skating in winter. Farther north, near **Woonsocket** and the Massachusetts state line, **Diamond Hill** and **Ski Valley** attract winter sports enthusiasts.

South along the east shore of the Narragansett Bay at **Llys-Yr-Rhosyn Rose Gardens** ("Royal Court of the Roses") in Barrington there are 6,500 rose plants of over 1,000 varieties on the private seven-acre estate; open mid-May until the first frost, free. Take the **Colt Drive** along the scenic shoreline to **Colt State Park** nearby. **Fore 'N Aft, The Lobster Pot,** and **Wharf Tavern** all overlook the bay here and feature typical New England menus with seafood specialties. In about 1800, **Bristol** was the fourth-busiest port in the United States and many America's Sailing Cup winners were built there. Today, business is mostly confined to pleasure craft. The historic colonial homes along the elm-shaded avenues are often marked with their date of construction and the name of the original owner. At **Tiverton,** southeast of Bristol, there are actually more farmers than fishermen. South of this popular bay resort is **Adamsville,** where the **Red Hen Monument** commemorates the development of the Rhode Island Red chicken in 1854, now the state bird. **Tiverton** offers swimming at the four local public beaches and salt- and freshwater fishing. **Stone Bridge Inn** (624-6601, S$28/D$30), built in 1794, enjoys a fine view of **Sakonnet Harbor** and has a colonial atmosphere. **Compton Cliffs,** overlooking the Sakonnet River, serves good fresh seafood; **Sunderland's** offers a charming country tavern atmosphere. Across Sakonnet River is **Portsmouth,** site of the landing, at **Founder's Brook,** of Anne Hutchinson and the first settlers from Boston, in 1638. See the **Old School House,** the nation's oldest, *circa* 1716, and the **Green Animals Topiary Gardens** which features 80 trees and shrubs shaped in animal forms, open 10-5 daily, 15 June to end of September. In Portsmouth the **Ramada Inn** (683-3600, S$42/D$53, lower in winter) has golf, swimming, boating, and fishing facilities. Nearby is the **Westport Players Dinner Theater.**

Cities to Visit

NEWPORT

Newport (population 29,266) was a seaport before the Revolution and is still famous for its shipbuilding industry, which began in 1646. Following the Civil War, the famous "Four Hundred," the cream of New York society, built many magnificent summer estates overlooking the spectacular waterfront. Today, Newport is really three towns—the cultural and commercial center of Rhode Island, the US Navy Education and Training Center on Coaster Island, and a distinguished summer colony.

WHAT TO SEE

Cliff Walk, a picturesque 3-mile walk along the Atlantic Ocean shoreline, and the 10-mile **Ocean Drive,** offer unparalleled views of the craggy coastline and fashionable estates. The **National Lawn Tennis Hall of Fame and Museum** is located in the Newport Casino. The **Elms,** on mansionlined Bellevue Avenue, is fashioned after an 18th-century French château, complete with formal sunken gardens and a magnificent collection of unusual trees and shrubs in which each species is labeled. It was built in 1901 for coal magnate Edward J. Berwind and is furnished with elegant antiques and art objects. You can spend "An Evening at the Elms" Thursdays and Saturdays, July through mid-September.

Château-sur-Mer is a fine example of the Victorian style at its most lavish, with an authentic French ballroom and intricate Florentine woodwork. Cornelius Vanderbilt hired Richard Morris Hunt, the great Beaux Arts architect of the 1890s, to design the most elaborate of the Newport summer "cottages," **The Breakers.** This magnificent mansion has 70 rooms including an ornate state dining room with original furnishings. The adjoining **Carriage House and Stable** displays horse-drawn carriages just as they were at the turn of the 19th century. Not to be outdone, Cornelius' brother, William K. Vanderbilt, built **Marble House** in 1892. The central hall is modeled after Versailles and every room is furnished with original pieces. **Rosecliff** is among the most beautiful of Newport's summer residences. Designed by Stanford White, a leading American architect, for California millionaire James Fair's daughter, the 40-room mansion is reminiscent of the Grand Trianon at Versailles. **Belcourt Castle** was the summer home of Oliver Hazard Perry Belmont; members of the present owner's family, in period costumes, guide visitors through the 62-room mansion and serve tea and coffee in the solarium. Combination tickets are available for The Breakers, The Elms, Marble House or Rosecliff and Château-sur-Mer at any one of the houses or from the **Preservation Society of Newport County** at Washington Square; tel: 847-1000. Two- and 3-hour city bus tours are available daily, Memorial Day to early October; and the *Viking Princess* leaves **Goat Island Marina** off Washington Street for a 1-hour sight seeing cruise, daily, May through October; Viking Tours, 4 Bush Street, tel: 847-6921. The elite still meet at **Bailey's Beach,** but there are five public beaches along the waterfront, and amusement rides at **Newport Beach.** Next door to the Newport Historical Society is **Touro Synagogue,** built in 1763 and the oldest synagogue on American soil. Designed in Georgian style by Peter Harrison, its plain exterior gives no hint of the richness within. As was customary in those times, the Sephardim sited the building inconspicuously in a quiet street,

Two 12-meter yachts—Freedom and Enterprise—compete off Newport almost literally head-to-head in preparation for the most prestigious yacht race in the USA, the America's Cup.

so that members at prayer before the Holy Ark face eastwards towards Jerusalem.

Inside, 12 Ionic columns—representing the 12 tribes of ancient Israel—support a gallery. And above these are 12 Corinthian columns supporting a domed ceiling. Above the Ark in Hebrew script is a representation of the 10 Commandments painted by Newport artist Benjamin Howland. Well worth the visit.

ACCOMMODATIONS

Howard Johnson's (849-2000, S/D$48) 1 mile north; **Shamrock Cliff House** (847-7777, S$65/D$75) and **Inn at Castle Hill** (849-3800, D$40-95), both on Ocean Drive; **Newport Harbor Treadway Inn** (847-9000, S/D$79-89), downtown on the harbor, includes private beach facilities and a marina; and **Sheraton Islander Inn** (849-2600, S/D$75-150), on Goat Island with a lovely view of the harbor and bay, indoor pool and tennis court; winter rates lower. Hotel Tax: 5%.

RESTAURANTS

The **Pier Restaurant,** on the pier off Thames Street, is very popular. Also recommended: **Le Bistro, The Chart House** (steaks), **Fricks',** and **La Petite Auberge,** plus **Salas** and **White Horse Tavern. Black Pearl, Clarke-Cooke House, Mack's Clam Shack,** fabulous fried clams, and **Christie's** are on the wharf beside the harbor.

CALENDAR OF EVENTS

Block Island Week Sailing Regatta, held in odd numbered years, late June. Also the **America's Cup Race** held every few years. **Tennis Week** at the Casino, usually late August; the **Outdoor Art Festival,** late July or early August; the **Annual Motor Car Festival,** late June. The famous **Newport Music Festival,** early summer. **Newport Opera Festival,** early August.

PROVIDENCE

Providence, the capital of Rhode Island, is on the Providence River at the head of Narragansett Bay, 43 miles south of Boston. The first settlement was begun in 1636 by Roger Williams, who named the city "in commemoration of God's merciful providence." It was incorporated in 1832 and became well known for its sailing ships. Providence was made the capital of the state in 1900. It is an important industrial city and a busy port, shipping goods to nations all over the world.

WHAT TO SEE

The **State Capitol,** an imposing marble building with its dome the second-largest unsupported structure in the world (second only to St. Peter's Basilica, Rome), contains several important early American paintings including a Gilbert Stuart portrait of George Washington in the baroque anteroom to the governor's office; open Monday through Friday 8:30-4:30, free. Famous old churches in the city include the **First Baptist Church, Beneficent Congregational Church, First Congregational Unitarian Church,** the **Cathedral of Sts. Peter and Paul** at Cathedral Square, and the **Cathedral of St. John's** on North Main Street. Old houses open to the public are **Stephen Hopkins, John Brown, Betsy Williams,** and **Esek Hopkins** houses. See **Brown University's** campus and **University Hall,** which served as a barracks during the revolution. The state's oldest library is at **Providence** Athenaeum, a Greek Revival building, completed in 1838. There is an extremely valuable collection of books, and it was here that Edgar Allen Poe courted Sarah Helen Whitman. **Stephen Hopkins House,** at the next corner on Hopkins Street, was named for its occupant who was state governor no less than 10 times, and a Chief Justice of the Supreme Court. General Washington visited in 1776 following the evacuation of Boston, and in 1781 when he visited the state to meet with General Rochambeau. **Shakespeare's Head,** a frame house (*circa* 1772) which served as post office when Benjamin Franklin was Postmaster General, has a colonial garden.

Other buildings include **Thomas Poynton Ives House,** completed in 1786 and a fine example of Georgian architecture with a splendid collection of furniture from the 18th century. It is presently headquarters of the Rhode Island Historical Society. **Joseph Nightingale House** was built in 1792 and is one of the largest colonial houses still extant. On South Main Street is **Dolphin House,** built by a sailing captain, Joseph Tillinghurst in 1770, while on Planet Street is the site of the **Sabin Tavern,** built in 1763. The building has since gone but is remembered as the place where the American Revolution began.

ACCOMMODATIONS

The **Biltmore Plaza** (421-0700, S$53-65/D$63-75); **Holiday Inn-Downtown** (831-3900, S$45-49/D$50-55); **Marriott Motor Inn** (272-2400, S$50-68/D$55-74); and **Wayland Manor** (751-7700, S$29-36/D$36-44). Hotel Tax: 5-8%.

RESTAURANTS

The great local specialty is the "Rhode Island Shore Dinner" which usually includes steamed clams, corn chowder, fish, and lobster. Public clambakes, made of the same ingredients but cooked together over hot stones under layers of seaweed, are held frequently during the summer, and visitors should make an effort to attend one. Good restaurants include **George Winkler's Steak House,** moderate; and **Camille's Roman Gardens,** Italian-American cuisine; **Rue de L'Espoir,** French cuisine on College Hill. For relaxed and scenic dining, the outskirts and neighboring shore locations offer a large choice of places to eat. Well-known restaurants near Providence include **Eileen Darling's, Wharf Tavern,** and **Fore 'N Aft** in Warren; **The Lobster Pot** in Bristol; **Abraham Manchester's** in Adamsville; **Helm House, Country Inn, Valle's Steak House, Golden Lantern, The Great House,** and **Le Ticoz** in Warwick; **Wickford Marina,**

Wickford; **Larchwood Inn,** Wakefield; **Sweet Meadows,** Narragansett; **Sunderland** and **Stone Bridge Inn** at Tiverton; all moderate to expensive.

ARTS AND MUSIC

Rhode Island School of Design Museum has a general art exhibit and sculpture, excellent collection of 18th-century furnishings and fabrics; open Tuesdays, Wednesdays, Fridays, Saturdays 11-5, Thursdays 1-7, and Sundays and holidays 2-5. **Providence Art Club** shows a fine small art collection. **Roger Williams Museum of Natural History,** planetarium in operation Saturday 2:30 and 3:30 and Sunday 3 and 4; museum open 7am-9pm daily. The **Rhode Island Philharmonic Orchestra** performs during the winter. There are summer theater performances at **Warwick Musical Theater, Newport,** and **Matunuck. Trinity Square Playhouse,** a repertory theater in Providence, is open from September to May. The **Rhode Island Civic Chorale and Orchestra** performs November to May.

SHOPPING

Most stores are open Monday through Saturday and Thursday or Friday evenings.

SPORTS

Professional hockey and college football and collegiate basketball are played in the area. There are many good facilities for golf and tennis in and around the city. Saltwater fishing is a leading sport (no license required) at **Newport, Block Island,** and **Narragansett;** May through October. All water sports including swimming, boating, and sailing are popular. **Narragansett Pier** is the rallying point for surfers in New England.

WHERE TO GO NEARBY

In **Pawtucket,** just north of the city, are two interesting houses, the Daggett House and Old Slater Mill. A pleasant day-trip can be made to the magnificently restored **Newport** which, along with **Narragansett,** 30-35 miles south of Providence, is an important resort area. Three miles south on US 1, **Roger Williams Park** has rose gardens, lakes, a zoo, a natural history museum, and recreational facilities. **Watch Hill, Sakonnet Point,** and **Jamestown** are also places of interest nearby. **Block Island** has good fishing and swimming.

FURTHER STATE INFORMATION

Rhode Island Department of Economic Development, Tourist Promotion Division, One Weybosset Hill, Providence, RI 02903 (tel: 277-2601). Hunting and fishing: **Department of Natural Resources,** 83 Park Street, Providence, RI 02903. **Preservation Society of Newport County,** Washington Square, Newport, RI 02840. **Newport Music Festival,** 25 Bridge Street, Newport, RI 02840. **Greater Providence Chamber of Commerce,** 10 Dorrance Street, Providence, RI 02903 (tel: 521-5000). For information on Ferry to Block Island: **Interstate Navigation,** Box 482, New London, CT 06320. Tel: 442-7891.
Consulate in Providence: Portugal.

USEFUL TELEPHONE NUMBERS
Providence
Police	272-1111
Fire	274-3344
Legal Aid	331-4665

Newport
Police	847-1212
Fire	846-2211
Newport Hospital	846-6400
Rhode Island Hospital	277-4000
Legal Aid	847-1862
Pan Am Reservations	(800) 223-9762

South Carolina

Area	31,055 square miles					Population		3,119,208			
Capital	Columbia					Sales Tax		4%			

Weather	Jan	Feb	Mar	Apr	May	Jun	Jul	Aug	Sep	Oct	Nov	Dec
Av Temp (°C)	8	9	12	18	22	27	28	27	24	18	12	8
Days Rain/Snow	10	10	11	9	8	9	12	11	7	6	7	9

South Carolina has a fascinating, often troubled history, a wealth of natural beauty, and a friendly gracious population. The area was first unsuccessfully settled by the Spanish and French in the 16th century. When the English ultimately gained control, the southern section of the area named for Charles I was settled by Englishmen from the home country and the British Caribbean island of Barbados. The population had been increased in 1740 by the settlement of German-Swiss and Scottish-Irish immigrants, and by Welshmen coming from Delaware.

Although more Revolutionary War battles were fought in South Carolina than in any other state, most skirmishes were far inland, where the wily citizens, renowned for their marksmanship, were victorious in the famous battles of Kings Mountain (1780) and Cowpens (1781), the turning points for ultimate American victory. In 1790 the capital was moved from Charleston to Columbia to accommodate these "up country" fiercely proud farmers.

Slaves were vitally important to the economy of the state, and when

Lincoln was elected president, South Carolina was the first state to secede from the Union. The ensuing Civil War brought much physical destruction, wrought by General Sherman and others, and together with the necessary abolition of slavery after the war the basically agricultural economy was near ruin. The devastation of the boll weevil on the crops of sea-island cotton in the 1920s was widespread, and again affected the economy adversely. Not until after World War II did South Carolina begin on the road to its present relative prosperity. Today it leads the nation in the production of textiles, although more of its land is planted in tobacco than cotton, and is a major producer of wood pulp from the forests that cover a third of the state.

There are superb beaches the full length of the 281-mile coastline, with a choice of Atlantic surf fishing or boating on the protected Intracoastal Waterway. The deep-sea fishing is excellent, but even the less adventurous will probably catch more crabs than they can eat. Inland are big lakes, reservoirs, and rivers where the fishing season lasts throughout the year. The hunting season for most small game is from Thanksgiving through February; the deer season is mid-August through December.

Driving south into the state on US 17, you arrive at **MYRTLE BEACH** and the "Grand Strand," one of the greatest stretches of sand on the eastern seaboard and a wonderful spot for seashell collectors. Choose here from an enormous range of hotels, motels, and efficiency apartments. High-season rates are generally June to August; lower rates from Labor Day through May often include special golf and tennis privileges. In mid-March, Canadians swarm in by the thousands for the **Canadian-American Days Festival.** In addition to the sand beach are thirty-four 18-hole championship golf courses, more than 150 tennis courts, fishing piers, deep-sea party boats, dance pavilions, and five large amusement parks for children. Other annual celebrations include the **Grand Strand Fishing Rodeo,** 1 April-31 October; the **Sun-Fun Festival,** June 6-9; and the **Holiday Fiesta,** 23 November-31 December. The renowned **Brookgreen Gardens,** with magnificent landscaping and an outdoor museum of sculpture, is at Murrells Inlet. Farther south is **Georgetown,** once rich in rice, indigo, and shipping. It now has many original 18th-century buildings which can be seen from the **Historical Train Tour.** Also visit the unusual **Rice Museum,** which traces the development of the crop with the use of maps and has other exhibits.

Beginning near **Charleston** and continuing southward are the Barrier Island resorts, all of which offer luxurious accommodations, excellent dining, and a wide variety of resort activities. The closest and newest of these in the Charleston area is the **Isle of Palms Beach and Racquet Club** (886-6000, S/D$60-170), 12 miles northeast of the downtown Charleston historic district, the club features excellent tennis facilities and the unique oceanside **Wild Dunes Golf Course.** Present accommodations are 1-4 bedroom homes, villas, and condominium units featuring private phones, washer-dryers, fully equipped kitchens, central air/heat, and maid service. Other activities here include Junior Olympic pool, two and one-half miles of private beach, marina with boat rentals and launching ramp, bicycles for rent, a children's vacation program, and both freshwater and saltwater fishing.

Some 20 miles south of Charleston is another Barrier Island resort, **Kiawah Island,** named for a now-extinct Indian tribe. This 10,000-acre island resort has been developed in a series of villages and private residential neighborhoods. Billed as a "walk-to-everything" resort community, it has captured numerous design awards for community planning and is recognized as one of the top tennis and golf resorts in the US. Present guest facilities consist of the **Kiawah Inn** (S/D$80-115) and more than 270 villas with 1-4 bedrooms (768-2121, S/D$115-275). An unusual highlight is the two-and-a-half-hour jeep safari, suitable for all ages. Guests drive individual jeeps on an exploration of back-island forests and old logging trails occasionally encountering deer, raccoon, bobcat, alligators and more than 150 species of birds. An experienced island guide leads the safari and several stops allow time for beachcombing and to see an historic island plantation mansion built around 1772. Fares are $3.75 for children and $7.50 for adults. Reservations are recommended. Other nearby Barrier Island resorts of note are **Seabrook** and **Oristo,** both offering similar fare and accommodations.

South of Charleston is the picturebook old port of **Beaufort** (pronounced *bew-fuht*) with homes of former 18th- and 19th-century cotton magnates. A tour of houses and gardens takes place every spring, but several are open all year under the auspices of the Historic Beaufort Foundation. The **Beaufort Museum** is one of many old structures faced with "tabby," crushed oyster shells mixed with sand and lime to form a cement mixture. On **Parris Island,** five miles south, is the famous US Marine Corps Recruit Depot.

Just north of the Georgia border is **HILTON HEAD ISLAND.** Encountering this spot in 1663 after an arduous voyage on the ship *Adventure* out of Gravesend, England, Captain William Hilton wrote: "Facing on the sea, it is most pines, tall and good. The ayr is clean and sweet, the land passing pleasant . . . the goodliest, best and fruitfullest island ever was seen . . ." A large measure of natural beauty remains just as it was then while other aspects of the island have changed to make it one of the nation's most enjoyable year-round resorts. The area is divided into **plantations,** one of the first being **Sea Pines Plantation** with three championship golf courses, 39 tennis courts, and four and one-half miles of perfect beachfront. The **Hilton Head Inn** (785-5111, S/D$85-100) is one of the outstanding resorts of the US. You may charter boats for fishing and sailing here. See the unique **Harbour Town,** a beautifully designed collection of shops, villas, and apartments that are modern yet quaintly old world in character. The **Harbour Town Marina** is a favorite anchorage for yachtsmen touring the Intracoastal Waterway. Among other places recommended to stay at on Hilton Head are the **Hyatt on Hilton Head** (785-1234, S/D$105-250); **South Beach** (S/D$50-185); **Port Royal Inn & Golf Club** (785-3381, S/D$37 up) which features 11 miles of private beach, complimentary tennis for guests, and villas (1-4 bedrooms, $50-120). Newest among the island's accommodations is the **Marriott-Hilton Head Resort** (842-2400, S/D$80-100), opening July, 1981, featuring 20 tennis courts and the island's only indoor heated pool. Other good bets include the **Holiday Inn on Hilton Head** and the **Sea Crest Motel,** averaging S/D$57-90, **Palmetto Dunes Resort** (S/D$45 up, villas $50 up), and **Sea Cabins** (S$40-75/D$55-95).

COLUMBIA, the capital city, located in the middle of the state, has the **State House,** bearing Civil War scars from General Sherman, the **State Archives Building** with three centuries of records and Confederate relics, and the **University of South Carolina,** where visitors can view old *Movietone* newsreels, now in permanent display. The **South Caroliniana Library,** located on the historic "Horseshoe" portion of the campus, houses a fine genealogical collection and the personal papers of numerous South Carolinians of note. It is the major repository for privately generated historic material in the state and features continuing exhibits of special collections. A short walk next door is the **War Memorial Building,** featuring military relics and artifacts from all periods of the state's history. Military buffs will enjoy a trip to the **Ft. Jackson Museum,** located at the famous Army Basic Training facility east of the city center. Accommodations in town at the **Carolina Inn** (799-8200, S$39.50-41/D$45-48), two blocks from the state capitol; the **Town House** (771-8711, S$33-44/D$38-52), four blocks from the capitol; **The Capitol Inn** (252-3100, S$34/D$40); the **Quality Inn Northeast** (736-1600, S$31/D$41), on Interstate 20; and **Holiday Inn City Center** (799-7800, S$36/D$42). The midland towns of **Aiken** and **Camden** are as "horsey" as many in England and Ireland. Aiken, located southwest of Columbia near the Georgia line, is smartly fashionable where polo is played every Sunday afternoon from February through April. Golf, hunting, shooting, and fishing are popular here. **Camden,** Aiken's counterpart, located northeast of Columbia is known for steeplechases, fox hunts, and horse shows from Thanksgiving through April. The leading event is the **Colonial Cup International Steeplechase** in late November, and the 40-year-old **Carolina Cup** in early spring. Some of the best horses in the United States and from abroad compete on the steeplechase course covering 2 miles, 6½ furlongs, including 18 different jumps. This whole area was once alive with *redcoats,* and 14 Revolutionary War battles were fought within a 30-mile radius of Camden. State parks are open to campers in all seasons.

In the northwest corner of the state is **Spartanburg,** a major textile city, a convenient base for excursions to historic **Kings Mountain National Military Park** and **Cowpens National Battlefield Site.** Cowpens was the scene of the spirited victory of the mountain men over superior British forces, which damaged the British campaign in the South. **Greenville,** the largest city in the South Carolina hills, is the site of the famous **Shriners' Hospital for Crippled Children.** Due east, 13 miles north of Rock Hill on Interstate 77, is **Carowinds,** a family entertainment complex with rides, shows, exhibits, restaurants, and historical attractions.

City to Visit

CHARLESTON

Charleston stands on a peninsula between the estuaries of the Ashley
and Cooper Rivers (named after Anthony Ashley Cooper), facing a bay
which opens into the Atlantic. Originally called Charles Towne by its
British founders, who arrived in 1670, the settlement was moved to its
present site in 1680. Despite its appearance of elegant gentility, Charleston has had a turbulent history stemming from pirates and slave traders,
Indian battles, occupation by British forces, and the first state to separate
from the Union before the Civil War.

WHAT TO SEE

The city has often been referred to as a "living museum" since so many
of the homes, buildings, and points of interest are still used by those
who live there. Entire neighborhoods—such as Ansonborough and Harle-
ston Village—were developed prior to the American Revolution and today restoration is giving vitality to the city. For an overall perspective
of the city, start at the **Visitor Information Center**, 85 Calhoun Street,
where the friendly staff can arrange tours and answer questions regarding
all aspects of the city. Pick up a *Visitors' Guide Map* here to help find
your way. You may also call the Center (722-8338) for information on
a wide range of tours and guide services. A film called **A Kingdom by
the Sea** is shown every half hour in Marion Square Mall (577-2399) as
a unique introduction to the city. The mall is only two and one-half
blocks from the Visitor Information Center. **Carolina Lowcountry Tours,
Inc.,** conducts a 3-hour tour by auto-van of the Old City: tours will leave
from your hotel by reservation. Two firms, **Charleston Carriage Company**
and **Palmetto Carriage Works, Ltd.,** offer horse-drawn carriage tours;
take these either from White Point Gardens on the Battery or from
the **Buggy Whip** at 96 N. Market Street in the historic Market area.
Registered historic guides are available from **Walled City Guides** (722-
8338), **Associated Guides of Historic Charleston** (744-7837), **Charleston
Guide Service** (747-3111), and **Charleston Strolls** (556-5462), which provides walking tours only. Bicycle rentals with free maps, baskets, baby
seats, and locks are available through **Le Grand Tour** at 173 Meeting
Street (722-8168). **Gray Line** provides both yacht tours of the harbor
(722-1112) and bus tours of the city and famous gardens (722-4444). **American International Sightseeing** also provides a number of mini-bus tours
to points of interest in and around the city. **Fort Sumter Tours** (722-
1691) operates the only yacht tour which stops at the island fort. Fort
Sumter was occupied by Federal Forces on 12 April 1861, when Confederate soldiers in Fort Johnson fired the first shot in the Civil War when
the union forces refused to vacate Fort Sumter. The boat tour leaves
from the Municipal Marina daily for the 2-hour cruise and no reservations
are necessary for individuals; check tour times, which vary throughout
the year.

The area between Broad Street and Battery Park is packed with magnificent old mansions, including the **Nathaniel Russell House** (1809), one of the nation's finest examples of Adam architecture and woodwork; the remarkable free-flying staircase curls up to the third floor without touching the walls; open daily 10-5, Sundays 2-5. President Washington was a house guest in 1791 at the **Heyward-Washington House** (1770), open Saturdays and Sundays, 10-5. Close by and worth seeing are the **Edmonston-Alston** house, a Greek revival mansion at 21 E. Battery. See the **Thomas Elf Workshop,** featuring works of this early American furniture maker. Open 10-5, Monday-Friday and 10-1 Saturday. One of the most notable Victorian mansions (1876) is the **Calhoun Mansion** at 16 Meeting Street, still under restoration by a local Charleston lawyer who resides in the Mansion of 54 rooms and 19 baths.

Catfish Row or **Cabbage Row,** 89-91 Church Street, where street vendors once peddled their wares, was also the inspiration for Gershwin's opera, *Porgy and Bess.* **Rainbow Row,** named for the colorful row houses dating from 1740, runs from 83 to 107 East Bay Street.

Among many interesting old buildings between Broad and Wentworth streets, farther north are the **City Hall** (1801), **Old Slave Mart Museum,** and the US' first fireproof building begun in 1822 and designed by the famous architect Robert Mills, who also designed the Washington Monument. The first fire insurance company in the nation was founded in Charleston in 1736.

Visit the **Old Exchange Building** (1767-71) where George Washington was entertained in 1791, **Beth Elohim Synagogue,** whose congregation dates back to 1749-50, and many fine churches. The **French Huguenot Church** (begun in 1844) is the only church in the US that adheres precisely to the original French Protestant liturgy. Farther out, at 350 Meeting Street, is the **Joseph Manigault House** (1802) in the Adam style, beautifully furnished; open daily, 10-5.

Among the smaller museums of specialized interest is the **WCSC Broadcast Museum** (723-8371), in a 175-year-old house at 80 Alexander Street; **The Hunley Museum,** in the basement of one of the oldest bank buildings in the US at 50 Broad Street, features a full-scale replica of the first successful Confederate submarine. **Charles Towne Landing,** on the site of the first settlement, combines beauty, entertainment, and history in one large exhibition park; there's even a seagoing reproduction of the *Adventure,* the 17th-century trading ketch sailed by Captain William Hilton, and a 20-acre animal forest where animals wander unhindered through their native environment. **The Citadel,** distinguished Military College of South Carolina, overlooks the Ashley River on the west side of town. Also of interest on the Citadel campus is the **Military Memorial Museum** (2-5 Monday-Friday, 9-5 Saturday and Sunday) and full-dress parades each Friday afternoon at 3:45 throughout the academic year. See also the **College of Charleston,** the first municipal institution of higher learning in the US, chartered in 1785. The **Older Powder Magazine,** a pre-Revolutionary structure (1712), was used during the Revolutionary

War as a powder storehouse. Open Monday to Friday 9-4, closed September.

Fort Moultrie on Sullivan's Island, now part of the **Fort Sumter National Monument,** added bombardments to the famous battle which began the American Civil War in 1861. Fort Moultrie a palmetto log structure, also handed the British their first major defeat in the Revolutionary War. Edgar Allan Poe, stationed at Moultrie as a sergeant-major, used the island as the setting for his short story, *The Gold Bug.* **Provost Dungeon,** located under the Old Exchange Building, was used by the British as a prison for American patriots (1780). It is closed during December and January. **Patriots Point** houses the *USS Yorktown* aircraft carrier and the **Naval and Maritime Museum.**

ACCOMMODATIONS

The **Mills House Hotel** (577-2400, S/D$80 up), in the center of Charleston, is a tasteful modern version of the distinguished Mills House, built on the same site in 1853. Public rooms are furnished with antiques, bedrooms with reproductions; swimming pool. For historic quaintness, try some of the city's small inns which strive for a personal touch beyond the ordinary. With only a few rooms, reservations are advised at all of these. Situated on the first floor of an 18th-century Charleston home, **The Sword Gate Inn** (723-8518, S$48/D$55) has only four rooms; breakfast is included. The ten units of the **Battery Carriage House** (723-9881, S$48-58/D$58-68) feature 18th-century furnishings with canopied beds and Continental breakfast served in the room. Larger, but still offering a personal touch in the heart of the historical district, is the **Vendue Inn** (577-7970, S$58-63/D$60-72). In the midtown area are the **Francis Marion Hotel** and **Holiday Inn Downtown.** In the historic district—**Golden Eagle Motor Inn,** the **King Charles Inn** and the **Heart of Charleston.** Prices average $35 and up. Hotel Tax: 4%. Overlooking the scenic Ashley River outside of town is the **Sheraton Charleston Hotel** (723-3000, S$56-66/D$68-78). There are also many good motels on highways leading into the city. Camping facilities at the **KOA Kampground,** year round, 15 miles west off I-26 on Highway 78; **Oak Plantation Campground,** 8 miles south on US 17; **Campers Cove** at Folly Beach on US 17; and **Sewee Camp Resort,** 25 miles north on US 17.

RESTAURANTS

With a wide range of traditional and ethnic establishments to choose from, dining out is as much a custom for the native Charlestonian as it is for the visitor. The fine art of *low country* cuisine, preserved and passed down through the generations, is available at a number of the city's restaurants. **Barbadoes Restaurant,** at the Mills House Hotel, offers a fine selection, including the city's famous she-crab soup. For the gourmet, try **Robert's of Charleston,** at 42 N Market Street, which features one seating per evening (Tuesday-Saturday); reservations required. Recommended for seafood are **The Colony House** and its **Wine Cellar** are recommended for good food; **Henry's,** on Market Street; the **Market**

Place Restaurant, which was converted from an old seaman's chapel; the Chart House on Broad Street and Whistler's, in the old market area. For Italian fare, try Frieda's, at 82 Society Street, or Il Giardino-Trattoria Italiana, at 82 Queen Street. For fine French cuisine, Marianne's, at 219 Meeting Street, is hard to top. Mexican lunch and dinner is served at San Miguel's, in the market at 4 Linguard Street; taste the crabmeat enchilada. Perdita's, at 10 Exchange Street, offers good low country cooking, as does Poogan's Porch, at 72 Queen Street, in an old Charleston frame house featuring fireplaces in each of the four dining rooms. Also recommended are East Bay Trading Company and Robert's Other Place. Dining east of the Cooper River, try The Lorelei, and right next door, The Trawler, both on US 17 north in Mount Pleasant. Both are renowned for their seafood. Dining west of the Ashley River, try Adger's Wharf, at 861 Folly Road; The Atlantic House, with its glass porch overlooking the ocean at the end of Highway 17 on Folly Beach. Also recommended are the Cork-n-Cleaver, Le Chateau, and Rast Restaurant. Local specialties throughout the Charleston area include she-crab soup, okra soup, shrimp creole, and roast oysters. Hominy grits for breakfast are as common as toast elsewhere.

ARTS AND MUSIC

Home of the Spoleto Festival U.S.A., Charleston comes vividly to life during the last of May and the first days of June each year with more than a hundred cultural events. In addition to sidewalk art shows, the visitor will find every form of the arts including: grand opera, drama, symphony concerts, chamber music, ballet, films, jazz, traditional country music, plus a wide variety of "mini festivals" in all parts of the city. Gibbes Art Gallery, paintings, sculptures, delightful miniatures, open Tuesday to Saturday 10-5, Sunday 2-5; free. City Hall Portrait Gallery has the original John Trumbull portrait of George Washington, as well as those of other notable visitors to the city in its early days, open Monday to Friday 9-5; free. The Charleston Museum, 360 Meeting Street; open Monday to Saturday 9-5, Sunday and holidays 1-5 is a modern museum of historic and current exhibits. The Charleston Symphony Orchestra gives concerts during the winter months, as does the Charleston Civic Opera Company. Also try to hear performances by the Society for the Preservation of Spirituals, North Charleston Choral Society, and Charleston Jazz Society. The Footlight Players theatrical group performs October to May in the Dock Street Theater, on the site of America's first playhouse.

SHOPPING

King Street, Charleston's oldest commercial district, offers a variety of department stores and is the center for antique shops. Here also are bookstores, art galleries, and clothing stores. Explore Church Street, in the heart of the historic district, for numerous boutiques and specialty shops. The Market Street area has for nearly two hundred years been the market place of the low country. A portion of the old market has been enclosed to house a number of small shops in an authentic setting from the early 1800s, while at the other end, the open market features vendors selling from open stalls. Everything from plants in season to authentic Southern handicrafts in a flea market atmosphere are available here. Low country baskets made and sold in the market are also available at the southwest corner of Meeting and Broad streets where sea-island flower vendors sell bunches of their colorful fresh flowers in season. Popular belief has it that good luck will follow those who purchase the sea-island flowers.

In outlying areas of the city are some 25 modern shopping centers. The newest of these, **Charles Towne Square,** is located off Interstate 26 at the Montague Avenue exit in North Charleston.

SPORTS
Good swimming at nearby beaches. Excellent surf and deep-sea fishing. Freshwater fishing is excellent in nearby lakes **Moultrie** and **Marion.** Golf and tennis facilities available.

CALENDAR OF EVENTS
In Charleston: the exclusive **St. Cecilia's Ball** is held annually in **Hibernian Hall; Founders Festival,** each month; **Festival of Houses,** mid-March to mid-April, when 65 houses are open to the public; **Confederate Memorial Day,** 10 May; **Annual Trident Fishing Tournament,** May through mid-September.

WHERE TO GO NEARBY
Boone Hall, seven miles north on US 17, is probably the most typical and most photographed antebellum-style mansion in the country. Its **Avenue of Oaks** still shades the original slave cabins; open daily except Thanksgiving and Christmas. **Magnolia Gardens,** 10 miles northwest of town on SC 61, are best from mid-February to May, when they are a profusion of camellias, azaleas, magnolias, and other flowers. Three miles farther on is **Middleton Place Gardens, House and Plantation Stableyards;** open year round. Here is America's first formal garden, begun in 1741 under the direction of an English landscape gardener. Some of the original plants still thrive, and in the stableyard are blacksmiths, candlemakers, and others who work as if this were still an 18th-century plantation. Displays of furniture, china, silver, works of art, and historic documents and books are in this plantation house.

Cypress Gardens, just off US 52, 24 miles north of Charleston, was once a great rice plantation. Immense cypress trees, azaleas, camellias, and flowering shrubs reflect in the shallow lake, which can be toured by boat; open 15 February to 30 April. Get off the main highways and follow some back roads through the lovely rural low country. **Cape Romain National Wildlife Refuge** is 15 miles northeast; unusual waterfowl, seabirds, and shorebirds, bright-eyed raccoons, whitetail deer, and the shiny black fox squirrel. The ferry ($5 per adult, $3 for children 6-13, free under 6) leaves from Moore's Landing at 8:30 am and comes back from **Bull Island** at 3:30 pm; take your lunch with you. The **Francis Beidler Forest** in **Four Holes Swamp** contains the largest remaining virgin stand of tupelo and cypress trees in the world. Located north of the city off I-26 at State Route 28, the forest is a National Audubon Society Sanctuary. Native wildlife abounds and visitors can cross a small portion of the swamp on the 6,500-foot boardwalk. Some nine miles northwest of the city on State Route 61 (Ashley River Road) is **Drayton Hall**, a National Historic Landmark plantation house. Built between 1738 and 1742, it is one of the most important examples of early Georgian architecture in the US. The plantation house escaped ruin by Sherman's Civil War troops by posting a small pox hospital sign. The house was held by the Drayton family through seven consecutive generations until 1974, when acquired by the National Trust for Historic Preservation. For picnics and other family-oriented outings, **Palmetto Islands County Park** is ideal. Located off US 17 north on Long Point Road near Boone Hall Plantation, the park offers group and individual picnic facilities, bicycle paths, boardwalks, nature trails, pedal boats, and canoe rentals.

FURTHER STATE INFORMATION
South Carolina Department of Parks, Recreation and Tourism, Box 71, Columbia, SC 29202. Hunting and Fishing: **South Carolina Wildlife and Marine Resources Department**, Box 167, Columbia, SC 29202.

Consulates in Charleston: Denmark, France, and Norway.

USEFUL TELEPHONE NUMBERS IN CHARLESTON
Fire	577-7070
Police	577-7074
Highway Patrol	747-6352
Emergency Medical Service	577-7080
Charleston County Hospital	577-0600
St. Francis Xavier Hospital	577-1000
Legal Assistance Program	722-0107
Chamber of Commerce	577-2510
Visitor Information Center	722-8338
Pan Am Reservations	(800)424-3210

South Dakota

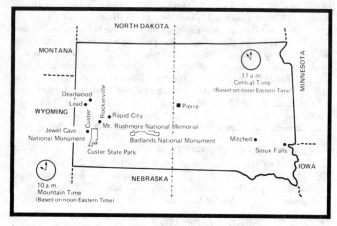

Area	77,047 square miles	Population	690,200
Capital	Pierre	Sales Tax	4%

Weather

	Jan	Feb	Mar	Apr	May	Jun	Jul	Aug	Sep	Oct	Nov	Dec
Av. Temp (°C)	−9	−7	1	8	15	20	24	22	17	10	0	−6
Days Rain/Snow	6	6	8	8	10	12	9	8	8	6	5	6

The first expeditions into the Black Hills and Badlands of South Dakota probably did little to disturb this happy hunting ground of the Sioux Indians. The arrival in 1873 of General George Armstrong Custer and the 7th Regiment of the US Cavalry, however, was a considerably less friendly occasion. And when Custer discovered gold at **French Creek** in August 1874, the days of Sioux supremacy were over forever. There are now, however, more Sioux Indians living on eight reservations than there were in the whole state in pioneer days.

During the great gold rush that followed Custer, some of the most colorful characters on the shadier side of American history arrived and left a trail of violence which has furnished endless plots for books, dramas, and television westerns. In 1862 settlers were offered land under the Homestead Act, but during the next decade fewer than 12,000 people moved in. When settlers did come in force, they were largely of German, Russian, and Scandinavian stock. The Black Hills cover an area about 100 miles long and 40-60 miles from east to west. Strange rock formations, high mountains, caves, and a summer-long program of sports and pageantry make this an ideal vacation area.

South Dakota leads all the other states in the proportion of personal income derived from agriculture. It also leads the nation in the production of gold. Tourism accounts for a considerable income, too; there are 170 state and federal parks, recreation areas, camping and picnicking sites. Fishing is excellent, and the shooting for pheasant, wild duck, geese, deer, and antelope is among the best in the country. Many people go to South Dakota primarily to see the carved faces of **Mt Rushmore**.

RAPID CITY is the "major city to visit" and is in the middle of the Black Hills region and is a good place to stay if you want to explore the area. The city is a center of gold and silver mining. Rapid City attractions include the **Museum of Geology** at the School of Mines, with prehistoric exhibits, rocks and minerals; **Repitle Gardens,** with a large collection of reptiles; and **Marine Life Aquarium,** featuring live porpoise and seal acts. **Storybook Island** brings nursery rhymes to life for the children, free. The **Horseless Carriage Museum,** 10 miles south, displays many old-time objects. Rapid City is host to the **Central States Fair** for five days in August, with lots of Indian pageantry and a Wild West Rodeo. Good moderate to expensive restaurants include the **Ruby House,** the **Gas Light,** and the **Pyrenees II.** Entertainment centers around the **K.J. 79 Club** discothèque and **Sight and Sound LTD.**

In the Rapid City downtown area there are the **Alex Johnson Hotel, Imperial 400, Tip Top Motor Hotel** and **Town House Motel** with rates about S/D$24-39.50. South, on Mt Rushmore Road, are **Jensen's Motor Lodge, Lazy U Motor Lodge, Ramada Inn, Sands Motel of the Black Hills** and **Town 'N Country Motel,** rates averaging S/D$30-41.50. Northeast of town, about two miles away, are **Holiday Inn** and **Howard Johnson's,** about S$37-46/D$42-46. The **Price Motel** is 1½ miles east; rates S/D$22-32. There are many more motels around town; nearly all have lower rates after Labor Day until late May or early June.

Stavekirke Church, a replica of an 800-year-old Norwegian building, is on SD 40 west of Rapid City and is open to the public free of charge. Some of the best views of the Black Hills can be had from Skyline Drive outside Rapid City. **Dinosaur Park,** on the drive, contains life-size concrete reproductions of prehistoric animals. Southwest from Rapid City is **Keystone,** where there are guided tours through **Big Thunder Gold Mine.** The new **Borglum Ranch and Studio** near the entrance to Custer State Park displays memorabilia of the late Gutzon Borglum, Mt Rushmore sculptor. About 9 miles east of Rapid City, **Rockerville,** a ghost town, is very much alive from Memorial Day to mid-September. The **Meller Drammer Theater** in Rockerville takes you back to the Gay '90s with nightly performances, from early June to Labor Day.

MT RUSHMORE NATIONAL MEMORIAL is about 25 miles south of Rapid City. Two million people a year come to see immense granite sculptures of George Washington, Thomas Jefferson, Abraham Lincoln, and Theodore Roosevelt. Each face, an amazing likeness, is from 60 to

70 feet high. The memorial is illuminated 9pm-10:30pm nightly from May through Labor Day. There are horseback and hiking trails to the top of nearby **Harney Peak,** at 7,242 feet the highest point east of the Rockies.

Just southwest of here the **Crazy Horse Memorial** is taking shape. This sculpture by Korczak Ziolkowski, who worked with Gutzon Borglum on Mt Rushmore, will show the Sioux chief on his horse and will be the world's largest statue, 641 feet long, 563 feet high. Still years away from completion, the statue is being carved out of **Thunderhead Mountain,** 6 miles north of Custer. Blasting operations on the statue may be viewed by the public for an admission fee of $5 per automobile. Gold is just one of a number of minerals still mined in Custer. From **Hill City,** a genuine 1880 train puffs its way through magnificent countryside to **Custer,** elevation 5,318 feet, making the 32-mile round trip three times daily, from mid-June to late August. The **Way Park Museum** and the **Custer County Courthouse Museum** (see National Parks Section), both open June to August, are packed with instructive and highly entertaining memorabilia of the area and its colorful personalities. The pageant *Gold Discovery Days,* covering the gold rush, Custer's war with the Sioux, and Indian raids, takes place during late July. Noted beauty spots near Custer include **Sylvan Lake, Needles Highway Scenic Drive,** and **Custer State Park.** West of Custer is the **Jewel Cave National Monument.** There are lovely calcite crystal formations here, but the tour is a bit rough; wear warm, strong clothes. **Wind Cave National Park** is between Hot Springs and Rapid City (see National Parks Section).

Northwest of Rapid City is **Lead** (pronounced *leed*) at an altitude of 5,320 feet. This is the site of the **Homestake Mine,** the greatest gold producer in the Western hemisphere; above ground guided tours are offered, May through October. Nearby **Terry Peak,** 7,071 feet, has superb skiing from mid-November to March, and the chair lift also operates from 1 May to 20 September for summer visitors.

Just northeast of Lead is **Deadwood,** the famous "Living Gold Camp." Main Street lies along the bottom of **Deadwood Gulch,** with the rest of the picturesque town clinging to the steep sides of the canyon. At **Mt Moriah Cemetery,** about 1 mile from town, are the graves of Wild Bill Hickok, Calamity Jane, Potato Creek Johnny, and Preacher Smith, just a few of the characters who gave Deadwood its reputation. A statue of Wild Bill by Korczak Ziolkowski stands in Sherman Street, and *The Trial of Jack McCall for the Murder of Wild Bill Hickok* is dramatized in the old Town Hall nightly except Sunday from June to September. The **Adams Memorial Museum** has one of the finest collections of pioneer mementos in the nation; open daily. **Ghosts of Deadwood Gulch** is a wax museum of local historical events. **Broken Boot Gold Mine,** 1 mile west of town, has underground guided tours daily from mid-May to October. Deadwood's "Days of '76" celebration in early August includes parades and a rodeo. From the top of the **Theodore Roosevelt Monument** on Mt Roosevelt, 4½ miles west of Deadwood, you can see into four states.

Between 1927 and 1941 Gutzon Borglum carved the four presidential faces from Mt Rushmore in South Dakota's Black Hills.

Sturgis, in the heart of the rangeland, has two scenic drives through Boulder Canyon and Vanocker Canyon. Spearfish is the home of the highly praised *Black Hills Passion Play*. The last 7 days in the life of Jesus are re-enacted Sunday, Tuesday, and Thursday evenings in an outdoor amphitheater from early June to late August. Advance reservations are nearly always necessary. Write to the Passion Play Headquarters, Spearfish 57783, or call (605) 642-2646. There are numerous motels for an overnight stay. Other local entertainment includes a night rodeo on Mondays and Wednesdays. One of the West's most famous rodeos is the Black Hills Round Up at Belle Fourche, 3, 4, and 5 July. *Bell foosh*, as the locals call it, is where cattlemen and sheepherders once provided endless plots for range-war movies.

Driving east from Rapid City on I-90, stop at the tiny town of Wall, where the remarkable Wall Drug Store features a mechanical cowboy band, Indian display, animated chuck wagon and lots more old-time recreations. On the fourth Sunday in September, Western history fans swarm into Wall for the annual Vanishing Trails Expedition, to see such pioneer-day reminders as ruts in the prairie that still trace the route of wagons heading for the long-ago Black Hills Gold Rush.

The mighty Missouri River slants down the full length of the center of the state. It is controlled by four immense dams that have created a chain of lakes with a combined shoreline of 2,300 miles. Out here in the middle of the prairie is a superb waterland for fishing and water sports. Pierre, the capital, is in the exact center of the state, and Oahe Dam is the largest rock-and-dirt dam in the world. Pierre, incidentally, is pronounced *peer* by the locals. Chamberlain is where I-90 crosses the Missouri, and is a popular resort town for water sports, hunting, fishing, and exploring the nearby Indian reservations. Mitchell, about midway between the Missouri River and the Minnesota line, is the home of the world's one and only Corn Palace. This large Moorish-style extravaganza is annually redecorated with murals, inside and out, composed entirely of corn kernels in their different natural colors, grasses, and grains. The building is open all year, but designs are freshest for the Corn Palace Festival in the last full week in September. Also visit the city's excellent Museum of Pioneer Life.

SIOUX FALLS, near the juncture of the Minnesota, Iowa, and South Dakota lines, has a population of 81,274 and is by far the largest city in the state. It is the hub of a vast agricultural district, with the accent on meat packing. The Great Plains Zoo includes animals native to the West. Pettigrew Museum contains thousands of Indian relics. The Battleship South Dakota Memorial is the same size as the famous World War II vessel; it contains a museum, open Memorial Day to Labor Day. The nearby EROS Data Center shows the application of space technology to life on earth. From Sioux Falls to the North Dakota border, there are little blue glacial lakes in great profusion and lots of tiny resorts for families and fishermen. Sisseton is near the very well-preserved Fort Sisseton, built during the Sioux Indian troubles in the 1860s. Annual pageants tell the story of how the West was won.

NATIONAL PARKS AND MONUMENTS

The **BLACK HILLS NATIONAL FOREST** comprises an area of 6,000 square miles defined by the Belle Fourche and Cheyenne Rivers. For serious quartz and rock collectors the region has long been known for its variety of samples. The hills rise to altitudes of over 5,000 feet from the great stretches of semi-arid plain below. The species of yellow pine that originally covered this area looked black from a distance; hence the name. The fascinating area includes the beautiful **Custer State Park, Jewel and Wind Cave National Parks,** and **Mt Rushmore Memorial.**

WIND CAVE NATIONAL PARK covers about 44 square miles and includes the interesting Wind Cave, discovered by explorers in 1881, which either sucks air into the cave or explosively expels it. The Visitor Center has information about the strangely decorated passageways that were first explored in 1890. Be dressed for the cave's permanent temperature of 8°C, and wear rubber-soled shoes if you go on one of the daily conducted tours from 1 April-1 November. You'll see limestone caverns netted with honeycomb-like boxwork, bubbly-looking rock, frostwork crystals, lustrous chert, and lacy dendrites. The illuminated trail descends 326 feet, but you can go back up by elevator.

The undulating sea of grass covering the park grounds is the same as it was when the Sioux hunted here and is still inhabited by shaggy bison, graceful pronghorn antelope, elk, mule, deer, badger, coyote, and sociable prairie dogs that live underground. Campfire programs are held here from mid-June through the first weekend in September; there are also spelunking cave tours. To appreciate the interesting merge of Rocky Mountain trees and plants with the contrasting growth of the Great Plains, follow the self-guiding nature trail to the top of Rankin Ridge.

BADLANDS NATIONAL MONUMENT is truly one of the most fantastic of the natural attractions in the midwestern US. East of the Cheyenne River and just south of Wall, the Badlands provide a weird vista of sharp-edged ridges, spires, and pinnacles carved by wind and water erosion and banded with colors. The deeply eroded clay gullies look like a lunar landscape, and there is much of archeological interest in the area. A museum and audio-visual programs about the region are held in **Cedar Pass,** where there are also nature walks and an amphitheater where ranger-naturalists lecture in the summer.

FURTHER STATE INFORMATION

Division of Tourism Development, Pierre, SD 57501. Hunting and Fishing: **Game, Fish and Parks Department,** State Office Building, Pierre, SD 57501. **Wind Cave National Park** (The Superintendent), Hot Springs, SD 57747.

USEFUL TELEPHONE NUMBERS IN RAPID CITY

Rapid City Regional Hospital	394-3000
Chamber of Commerce	343-1744
Pan Am Reservations	(800) 621-0595

Tennessee

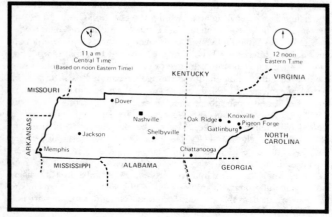

Area	42,224 square miles	Population	4,539,834
Capital	Nashville	Sales Tax	6%

Weather

	Jan	Feb	Mar	Apr	May	Jun	Jul	Aug	Sep	Oct	Nov	Dec
Av Temp (°C)	5	7	11	16	21	26	27	27	23	17	10	6
Days Rain/Snow	10	10	11	10	8	8	9	8	7	5	8	10

Tennessee has earned the title of the "Volunteer State." When the Carolinas were overrun with British redcoats, Tennessee mountain folk hiked down the slopes and helped to win the battle of Kings Mountain in 1780. It was the Tennessee Volunteers with Andrew Jackson ("Old Hickory") who played a key part in the battle of New Orleans in the War of 1812. Jackson later became the seventh President of the United States. Davy Crockett, another Tennessee fighter, left the comparative security of Rutherford Ford to lend a hand to the Texans' struggle against Mexico and died in the Alamo in 1836. James Polk, the eleventh President, was also a native of Tennessee. In 1846, when Polk called upon his home state to furnish a quota of 2,800 men to fight in the Mexican War, 30,000 Tennesseeans volunteered. In World War I, Sergeant Alvin York from "out Jamestown way", put 35 German machine guns out of commission and captured 132 prisoners. In World War II, correspondent Ernie Pyle described the Tennessee "hillbilly" troops as "real gentlemen . . . They are courteous, friendly, and trusting—all by instinct." But the Civil War put the Tennessee fighting men to their greatest test. The western and middle sections of the state were pro-Confederacy and 115,000 men went to fight for the South; 31,000 men from the eastern mountains went to fight for the North. Shiloh Stones River, Chickamauga, Chattanooga, Nashville, and Franklin became Tennessee battlefields printed into the bloodiest pages of American history.

The Tennessee Valley Authority (TVA), bitterly opposed when it was established in the 1930s, proved to be of immeasurable economic benefit to Tennessee. It also turned this landlocked state into one of the nation's great aquatic playgrounds. The system of 34 dams that control the **Tennessee River** have created the 24 "Great Lakes of the South," with a combined shoreline of 10,000 miles. Because of the state's mild climate they can be enjoyed year round for fishing, boating, water skiing, and other sports. Until the TVA brought immense quantities of cheap electricity to the area (hydro, fossil steam plants, and nuclear reactors, in that order), Tennessee was primarily an agricultural state; today, industry and tourism are primarily important. The atomic age might be said to have started here in 1943 when construction of the top secret town of Oak Ridge began. The Nuclear Regulatory Commission is still more active in Tennessee than anywhere else in the nation.

Tennessee is 432 miles wide from the Mississippi River to the North Carolina border, but only a maximum of 112 miles from north to south. Between the Appalachian Mountains and the lowlands of the Mississippi are the rolling hills and valleys of the blue grass country, the home of the Tennessee Walking Horse and prize herds of Jersey, Angus, and Hereford cattle. West Tennessee extends from the Mississippi to the Kentucky Lake-Tennessee River waterway, an area with a Deep South atmosphere; Memphis is the principal city. Middle Tennessee, with the city of Nashville, extends to the edge of the Cumberland Plateau. Chattanooga, the Great Smokies, and Knoxville at the head of the Tennessee-Tombigbee Waterway Project, are the focal points of East Tennessee. Historic landmarks and beautiful recreation parks can be found all across the state.

Cities to Visit

CHATTANOOGA

Lookout Mountain rises to a height of 2,126 feet above the city and justifies Chattanooga's Cherokee Indian name which means "rock rising to a point". Explored by DeSoto in 1540, the city began its life as Ross Landing, a trading post, in 1810 and later became a strategic area during the Civil War when the Union victory at the Battle of Chattanooga marked a turning point in the struggle. There are numerous TVA lakes, rivers, and streams nearby for fishing and water sports, and some fine caves and caverns for exploration. The city population is 165,000, metropolitan area 402,300.

WHAT TO SEE

Orchard Knob, right in town, was General Grant's headquarters during the Battle of Missionary Ridge. There's a road up Lookout Mountain, or you can take the **Incline Railway,** the world's steepest passenger train ride with a 72.7° grade near the top; the "surrey bus" at the top makes hourly tours of the mountaintop. The *Battle Above the Clouds* (1863) is depicted in the **Confederama** at the foot of the mountain. Open 9am-9pm weekdays and 1-9 Sundays in summer and 1-6 in winter. Also explained through electronic automation are the charge up Missionary Ridge, the night attack at Brown's Ferry, and the march on Orchard Knob. Closed Mondays. **Cravens House,** on the mountain, served as a Confederate hospital until it was made a Union headquarters; open March to November. **Point Park,** overlooking Chattanooga and the loop of the river, has a museum and observatory. **Ruby Falls** are in caverns deep inside the mountain underneath the battlefield; view the fascinating and colorful stalagmites, stalactites, and helectites. The falls are 1,120 feet below the mountain's surface and drop 145 feet. This attraction is open daily, 7:30am-9:30pm May through Labor Day, then 8am-8pm until May. Rock City, farther south on the mountain, has **Fairyland Caverns** and **Mother Goose Village** to delight the children, in addition to its magnificent natural rock formations. You can see into seven states from **Lovers' Leap Rock;** open daily year round. **Signal Mountain,** 9 miles north of Chattanooga, was used for smoke signals to Confederate forces. **Nickajack Lake,** which runs through "The Grand Canyon of the Tennessee", is parallel to a scenic highway; the canyon is one of the most beautiful in the nation. Carolenda Tours of Chattanooga offers their services to groups or individuals wishing to explore the city and discover attractions in the surrounding countryside.

ACCOMMODATIONS

In midtown: **Chattanooga Choo-Choo Hilton Inn** (266-6486, S$30-38/D$38-46) in Victorian sleeper cars in restored 1905 train station; **Downtowner Motor Inn** (266-7331, S$19-21/D$22-26); **Sheraton Chattanooga Downtown** (756-5120, S$22-27/D$23-32); **The Read House** (266-4121, S$32-55/D$45-75); **Holiday Inn** (265-8571, S$28-31/D$37-40). One or two miles south are the **Admiral Benbow Inn** (267-9761), S$25-29/D$31-35); **Holiday Inn-Lookout Mountain** (265-0551, S$25-28/D$34); and **Howard Johnson's** (265-3151, S$24-28/D$30-36). The **Holiday Inns, Ramadas,** another **Sheraton,** the **Days Inn, Quality Inns** all offer accommodations on or near major highways leading into and out of the city. There are three public campgrounds on **Lake Chickamauga** and two on **Lookout Mountain.** Hotel Tax: 4-5¼%.

RESTAURANTS

Favored eating places in town include **Fehn's, Green Room,** and **Bethea's.** Enjoy the superb view from the **Rock City Restaurant** on Lookout Mountain. For a unique experience dine at the **Chattanooga Choo-Choo,** in a superbly restored Victorian railway station, within an unusual entertainment complex. Other good restaurants include **The China Garden, The Green Room** at the Read House, **Michael's Cow Palace,** and **Town & Country.**

ARTS AND MUSIC

Hunter Gallery has changing exhibits and a permanent display of 19th-century American artists; open daily, free. **Houston Antique Museum** has a huge collection of jugs and pitchers, pressed glass, and lusterware; closed Sundays and holidays. Chattanooga has a symphony orchestra, an opera association, a civic chorus, community concert association, and conservatory of music. Stage productions at the **Little Theater** and the **Backstage Playhouse.**

SHOPPING

The largest stores are **Millers, Lovemans, J.C. Penney, Picketts,** and **Sears Roebuck.** There are several fine shopping centers in enclosed malls.

SPORTS

Chattanooga has seven public and seven private 18-hole golf courses. **Lake Chickamauga,** 6 miles north of town, is great for fishing, swimming, sailing and power boat races. Hunting in the surrounding hills is usually very good.

CALENDAR OF EVENTS

Chattanooga Allied Arts Festival, usually in April; **Home Show,** May; **Tri-State Fair and Cotton Ball,** September; **Plum Nelly Art Festival,** October; **Annual Fall Foliage Color Cruise,** through Grand Canyon of the Tennessee River, last two weekends of October. **Autumn Leaf Special steam train,** day-long excursions two weekends in October. There are usually special observances of the birthdays of Robert E. Lee, 19 January; Andrew Jackson, 15 March; Jefferson Davis, 3 June, and General Nathan Bedford Forrest, 13 July.

WHERE TO GO NEARBY

The **Chickamauga-Chattanooga National Military Park,** the nation's oldest military park, is south of town and partly in Georgia. Over 2,000 markers, monuments, and tablets describe every action on one of the Civil War's bloodiest battlegrounds. The Visitors' Center, with museum and information for touring the area, is on US 27 9 miles south of Chattanooga. Thirty-five miles from the city are the **Sequoyah Looking Glass Caverns,** which appear to be doubly beautiful because the lakes mirror the rock formations.

KNOXVILLE

The first settlement at Knoxville was secured in 1785 in a peace treaty with the local Cherokees. In 1790, William Blount was appointed Governor of the "Territory of the United States of the Ohio River". Knoxville was Tennessee's first capital in 1796, with Indian fighter John Sevier its first governor. Six of the Great Lakes of the South surround the city. The Tennessee Valley Authority headquartered here. Knoxville population, 181,534 including a University of Tennessee enclave of 40,000; metropolitan population 482,544.

WHAT TO SEE

Blount Mansion, home of William Blount, is recorded as the first weather-boarded house built west of the Alleghenies, open Tues-Sat 9:30-5 and Sun 2-5. **The Craighead-Jackson House** next door and **James White Fort** a block away, furnished with frontier antiques dating from 1818, is also an interesting sidetrip. **Ramsey House,** just east of town, was the home of Colonel Francis Alexander Ramsey. It was the first house in the state with plastered walls and was the "most costly, most admired building" in the state in the 1800s. **Marble Springs** was the farm-home of John Sevier. He is buried on the historic courthouse lawn. **Knoxville Zoological Park** is a prominent zoo, housing exotic animals and reptiles. **Lamar House Bijou Theater,** one of the eight theaters offering live entertainment including Broadway productions, has been restored. **Knoxville Civic Auditorium Coliseum** annual events include **Holiday on Ice, Ringling Brothers-Barnum and Bailey Circus,** and many nationally known entertainers such as Lawrence Welk. **Neyland Stadium** seats 95,000 fans.

ACCOMMODATIONS

Hyatt Regency (637-1234, S$43-53/D$58-68); the new **Hilton Knoxville** (523-2300, S$44-60/D$59-75); **Howard Johnson's Motor Lodge** (688-3141, S$30-34/D$34-38). The **Quality Inn** on Summit Hill Drive and the **Holiday Inn Station '82** were built for the World's Fair.

RESTAURANTS

Specialties of the region are home-cured country ham, hot biscuits, fried chicken, steaks, seafood, and mountain honey. At **Regas**—two locations, including their downtown site with plush lounge-bar-waiting room—steaks and lobsters are specialties; **Cappuccino's** Italian cuisine; **Copper Cellar; Half Shell Restaurant,** seafoods; **Hanna's Restaurant; Steak & Ale; Mr. Steak; the Orangery; Pero's Steak-Spaghetti House; Ye Old Steak House;** an abundance of fast-food places; **S&W, S&S, Morrison's, Weaver's,** and **Ramsey** cafeterias, all at moderate prices.

ARTS AND MUSIC

Dulin Gallery of Art includes famous Thorne Miniature rooms, open noon-4 Tues-Fri, Sat and Sun 1-5. **Confederate Memorial Hall** (1858), antebellum mansion used as headquarters by General James Longstreet during the 1863 Seige of Knoxville, has period furnishings; open daily April-Sept, 2-5, rest of year 1-4. On **University of Tennessee** campus are **Hoskins Library,** with Estes Kefauver Collection in west wing; the **McClung Museum,** a collection of exhibits on anthropology, archeology, fine arts, science, history, and natural history; the **Carousel Theater** (in-the-round) and **Clarence Brown Theater. Civic Auditorium-Coliseum** stages a wide range of entertainment from symphony concerts to ice shows. Knoxville has a **Symphony, Youth Orchestra, Choral Society, Young People's Theatre,** and **Civic Opera. Dogwood Arts Festival** held in April, featuring events including a parade, art festival, many trails of beautiful flowers and white and pink dogwoods.

ENTERTAINMENT
Chantilly's Piano Lounge, Regency Club at Hyatt Regency, **Flanigan's Cabaret, Uncle Sam's, Sam Houston's,** and **The Gathering Place.** The 1982 World's Fair in downtown Knoxville offers a variety of entertainment, from May-Oct. There are 13 different theaters and drive-ins in the city; see newspapers for showings and times.

SHOPPING
There is good shopping on **Market Square Mall,** where amateur and cultural groups sing, dance and, dine in the open. **West Town Mall** has 90 stores, just west of the University campus.

SPORTS
Golf, tennis, bowling, ice and roller skating. Collegiate athletic events at **Knoxville College** and **University of Tennessee. University of Tennessee Volunteer Football**—Basketball has long been "big time".

CALENDAR OF EVENTS
Sportsmen's Show, February; **Dogwood Arts Festival,** 10 days in mid-April; **Home Show,** May; **Redgate Bluegrass Festival,** June; **Parade of Homes,** July; **Holiday on Ice,** August; **Tennessee Valley Agricultural and Industrial Fair,** second week in September; **Ramsey House Country Market and Auction,** last Wed in September; **Artfest,** week-long celebration of the arts, October; **Foothills Craft Guild Sale and Show,** November; **Nativity Pageant,** December.

WHERE TO GO NEARBY
Oak Ridge is 20 miles northwest and worth the trip for the atomic plants and **American Museum of Science and Energy.** The **Great Smoky Mountains National Park,** 1 hour's drive from Knoxville, is within easy reach and you can see quite a bit even on a 1-day trip, including native craft and ceramic wayside demonstrations at **Gatlinburg** and **Pigeon Forge** (US 441). Six immense TVA dams and steam plants and the **Watts Bar Lake Nuclear Plant** are within 30 miles of town and guided tours are available. South of Knoxville in limestone country are some remarkable caves and caverns, such as the **Lost Sea** at Sweetwater, where glass-bottom boats ride you across the largest underground lake in the world, in a cave with rare cave flowers, and where jaguar bones were found in a crevice—they're now in the Smithsonian in Washington DC. **Tuckaleechee Caverns** at **Townsend** were formed by the mountain stream that

rises under **Dry Valley** and **Forbidden Caverns,** near Sevierville, was formed in the same way. **Wonder Cave** is near **Monteagle,** and since cavern temperatures are a year-round 58° F a wrap is sometimes recommended. **Fort Loudoun,** built by the British in 1756 during the French and Indian war, near **Vonore** (US 441), is open to visitors and is mostly restored. The State Park features an interpretive center and historical lectures on the bank of the **Little Tennessee River.** It was a 3-inch long fish from this river—the famed "snail darter"—that stopped the TVA's **Tellico Dam** project before the gates could be closed, thereby endangering this creature. In the end a recreational lake was finally formed by order of Congress.

MEMPHIS

The regal center of a cotton aristocracy, Memphis also once claimed the reputation of being just about the wickedest port city on the entire length of the Mississippi. It is still a big cotton market but soybeans now outvalue cotton as a crop. Memphis is now perhaps the most responsible member of the state, earning national awards for its public environmental standards. A commercially innovative city, it saw the first S. H. Kress & Co store, the first John G. McCrory store, and the first S. S. Kresge store all open here in 1896, making Memphis the dime-store capital of the world at one time. This is also the home of Piggly-Wiggly, the world's first self-service grocery store. That distinctive American song form, the blues, was first set on paper here by W. C. Handy. Memphis was named after the ancient Egyptian capital, whose name meant "place of good abode." The city's population is 907,100.

WHAT TO SEE

Beale Street, made famous by W. C. Handy with his 1909 composition of *Beale Street Blues,* is undergoing extensive redevelopment. The **W. C. Handy Park,** at the corner of Beale and Third streets, is the heartbeat of the area. One of the big recording stars who maintains a home in Memphis is Isaac Hayes. Elvis Presley's **Graceland Mansion** on Elvis Presley Boulevard is now a tourist attraction. The **Mid-South Medical Center** is the largest in the South; it includes 17 hospitals, among which is **St Jude Children's Research Hospital,** founded in 1960 by Danny Thomas. **Mid-America Mall** is the nation's longest Main Street Mall (1 mile).

The **Lorraine Hotel,** where Martin Luther King, Jr. was shot in 1968, and his hotel room, are now kept as a memorial to the Civil Rights martyr. The **Magevney House, Mallory-Neely House,** and the **Fontaine House** on Adams Street are open to the public and are part of **Victorian Village,** 18 landmark buildings in the downtown area. **Mud Island,** opening in July 1982 in downtown Memphis, has an amphitheater, recreational areas, shops, and restaurants. Take a Mississippi River cruise on the *Memphis Queen II* or *III, Showboat,* and *Belle Carol,* which leave from the foot of Monroe Avenue daily, 1 March to 30 November and rest of year, weather permitting; check schedule locally. **The Memphis Zoological**

Garden and Aquarium, in Overton Park, are outstanding. **Overton Square** has a number of specialty shops and night spots. Take a Gray Line sightseeing tour for a comprehensive view of the city or a horse-drawn carriage tour to savor the atmosphere of the Deep South.

ACCOMMODATIONS

Downtown: **Holiday Inn-Downtown** (525-8368, 973-1921, S$25-28/D$35-37). Several blocks east in central-midtown area are **Sheraton Motor Inn; Admiral Benbow; Holiday Inn-Midtown; Holiday Inn—Medical;** and **TraveLodge Downtown;** averaging S$20-31/D$26-35. Two units by the river are **Quality Inn West** and **Best Western Riverbluff Inn,** also in the same rate scale. Also on the river is the **Holiday Inn-Rivermont** (525-0121, S$33-41/D$41-52). **The Sheraton Convention Center Hotel** (525-2511, S$37-42/D$48-53) is 3 blocks from downtown. Near the airport are three moderately priced inns, **Quality Airport Inn** (332-8980, S$28/D$38), **Rodeway Inn Airport** (345-1250, S$32-38/D$38-44), and **Trave-Lodge** (396-9170, S$27.50-29.50/D$35-45). Fancier inns in the airport area: **Hilton** (332-1130, S$32-36/D$39-43) S$34-48/D$44-58) and **Sheraton Airport Inn** (332-2370, S/D$34 up). East of central Memphis is the **Hyatt Regency** (761-1234, S$48-56/D$63-71). **The Peabody Hotel,** long a center of mid-South business and social activity, has undergone a $17-million renovation. Tent and trailer campsites are in **Meeman-Shelby Forest State Park,** about 13 miles north; and in **Lakeland Amusement Park,** about 10 miles east of town. Hotel Tax: 5-10%.

RESTAURANTS

Fine dining with dance music at **Capitan Bilbo's El Matador, El Capitan Supper Club,** the **Vapors Supper Club,** the **River Restaurant** in the Holiday Inn-Rivermont, and the famed **Skyway** at the Peabody. The accent is on familiar American food at **Anderton's Restaurant and Oyster Bar, Café St Clair, The Embers, Knickerbocker, Mark IV, Four Flames, Sawmill, Victoria Station,** the **Loft, Garden Gallery, Wild Mushrooms, Fenwick's,** and the Hyatt Regency. **Rendezvous,** barbeque ribs, beef & pork; **Folks Folly,** Cajun-style vegetables, superb steaks. **Justine's** and the **Four Flames** are French; **Pete and Sam's** and **Grisanti's** are Italian; **Pancho's** is Mexican; **Samovar Restaurant** for Russian food; **Benihand of Tokyo; Jade East, Joy Young, Wah Yens, Wahnam** and **Singaporian** are Chinese; and there's Polynesian food and decor at the **Dobbs House Luau.**

ENTERTAINMENT

TGI Friday's, TJ's, El Morocco, Beale Street, El Chico, Wellington's, The Blues Alley, The Prospector, Trader Dick's, The Cowboy, The Cockpit, Club Caesar, Manhattan Club, The Plantation Roof, and Lafayette's Music Hall are just a few of the livelier Memphis night spots. **Doebler's Dock,** with singing waiters and waitresses, and a piano bar, has a riverfront view and live entertainment in the new **Pier Lounge.** Check with *Key* and *What to Do in Memphis.*

ARTS AND MUSIC

Brooks Memorial Art Gallery, sculptures, paintings, traveling exhibitions; closed Mondays, free. **Memphis Pink Palace Museum,** art, history, natural history and African game trophies; closed Mondays, free. The **Memphis Little Theater** and **West Tennessee Historical Society** are in the same spacious mansion. The **Memphis Academy of Arts** is interesting; open Monday-Friday, free. The Memphis Arts Council co-ordinates the activities of the **Ballet Society, Opera Theater, Orchestral Society, Children's Theater** and similar cultural groups, such as **Memphis Symphony** and **Metropolitan Orchestra.**

SHOPPING

Some downtown stores are open till 9 on Thursdays. Several outstanding shopping malls are open daily till 9. There are some tempting antique shops out in the **Germantown** section, on **Cooper Street,** and throughout the city.

SPORTS

Big sports events in the **Coliseum, Memorial Stadium** and **Memphis Blues Stadium.** The metropolitan area has 10 public and 10 private golf courses with plenty of tennis, bowling, riding, swimming, water-skiing and polo. Freshwater fishing in numerous nearby lakes is good for bass, crappie and blue gill. Duck shooting is great in winter.

CALENDAR OF EVENTS

National Bird Dog Championship, at nearby Grand Junction, February; **Cotton Carnival, Danny Thomas Memphis Golf Classic, Danny Thomas Shower of Stars, New York Metropolitan Opera Company, Heritage House Tours,** and **Memphis in May International Festival,** May; **Annual Memphis Music Awards,** early June; **Germantown Charity Horse Show,** June; **Mid-South Fair,** September; **Liberty Bowl** football game, December.

WHERE TO GO NEARBY

The **Chucalissa Indian Museum,** adjoining T. O. Fuller State Park, about 10 miles from downtown Memphis, is a carefully restored village occupied by the Agnachi tribe between 900 and 1600; open Tuesday through Sunday. The Naval Air Station 19 miles north of Memphis at **Millington** is the world's largest inland naval training center; tours arranged. **Shiloh National Military Park** is 105 miles east. The **Casey Jones Home and Railroad Museum** are at Jackson, 85 miles northeast. **The Land Between the Lakes** is a recreation area in western Kentucky and Tennessee, between Kentucky Lake on the Tennessee River and Lake Barkley on the Cumberland River. **Reelfoot Lake,** 100 miles north, created by a massive earthquake in 1803 and causing the Mississippi to run backwards for 24 hours, has more varieties of fish than any other freshwater body in the US. It is one of the most beautiful lakes in the country, with boat tours daily in summer.

NASHVILLE

Nashville, the state capital, is in middle Tennessee on the Cumberland River amidst tree-covered, gently rolling hills that make it one of the most eye-catching areas in the South. Many lakes are in the area. Nashville is widely known for its music industry which all started with the internationally famed Grand Ole Opry radio broadcast over 50 years ago. Nashville-based entertainers have spread the "Nashville Sound" around the world and the city is the second largest recording center in the nation. It also has 13 colleges and universities, is a major religious center, and was the site of one of the key battles of the Civil War. Population of metropolitan Nashville is 439,599.

WHAT TO SEE

The **Country Music Hall of Fame and Museum** is devoted to the country and western stars whose earthy humor and pure melodies have delighted the nation. On the edges of town are the elaborate mansions of many famous banjo-strummers, fiddlers and guitar players who rose from rags to riches. **Fort Nashborough** is a reconstruction of the first settlement in 1779. The **Upper Room Chapel** houses the great polychrome wood carving of Da Vinci's *Last Supper.* Visit the **Vanderbilt** and **Fisk** university campuses, the **State Capitol** and other government buildings, and the **Tennessee State Museum** in the War Memorial Building.

Ten miles east of midtown, via I-40 and Briley Parkway, is **Opryland, USA,** a vast entertainment complex that depicts the story of American music from jazz and blues through country and western to contemporary. Within the park is the new **Grand Ole Opry House,** which provides the authentic Grand Ole Opry on Friday and Saturday nights. There are a number of excellent shows in the park at Opryland, including *"I Hear America Singing," "On With the Show," "Dixieland,"* and *"Country Music USA."* Opryland is open daily Memorial Day through Labor Day and weekends in April, May, September, and October. Thirteen miles east is **The Hermitage,** home of President Andrew Jackson, furnished as it was when he died there in 1845. "Old Hickory" and his Rachel are buried in a corner of the garden which is still shaded by hickory trees planted from a parcel of hickory nuts sent to Jackson in 1830. Admission fee includes entrance to the **Hermitage Church** and **Tulip Grove** (1836), which Jackson built for his nephew. **Traveller's Rest,** about 6 miles south of town, belonged to Jackson's law partner and was the focal point for visiting celebrities who included Lafayette and Sam Houston. **Belle Meade Mansion,** 7 miles west of town, is a magnificent antebellum mansion with typical outbuildings of the pre-Civil War era.

ACCOMMODATIONS

The highways into Nashville have a total of 10,000 motel rooms within a 20-mile radius. Near the center of town are **Hyatt Regency Nashville** (259-1234, S$42-65/D$57-80); **Best Western Central** (254-1551, S/D$30-

54); and the **Sheraton-Nashville Hotel** (244-0150, S$28-38/D$34-43); **Maxwell House Hotel** (259-4343, S$42-56/D$50-64). Also downtown, the **Downtowner Motor Inn,** (859-2861, S$21-30/D$30-40); **Ramada Inn** (244-6130, S$36 up/D$44 up); **Rodeway Inn** (793-7721, S$26/D$36), and **TraveLodge/Nashville** (244-2630, S$30-36/D$35-41). On the west side of town is a **Holiday Inn** near Vanderbilt University; the **Hilton Airport Inn** and **Music City Rodeway Inn** are convenient for plane passengers. Spanking new is **Opryland Hotel** (889-1000, S$34-75/D$62-75). Hotel Tax: 6% sales tax plus 3% tourism tax.

RESTAURANTS

Regional specialties include Southern-fried chicken, Tennessee country ham, Southern-style barbecue, spiced beef, and rich, sweet chess pie. Good restaurants, moderately priced, include: **Anderson's Cajun Wharf,** seafood; **Barn Dinner Theater, Captain Ray's Sailmaker; Julians,** French cuisine; **Hugo's at Hyatt Regency,** elegant; **Jimmy Kelly's** steak and country ham; **Kobe Steaks,** Japanese; **Mario's, The Squire's Table,** beef and seafood; **TGI Friday's,** and **Vizcaya Spanish Restaurant.**

ENTERTAINMENT

Captain's Table, 4 Guys Harmony House, Boots Randolph's, The Embers-Black Poodle Lounge, The Embers Showcase, The Embers-Western Room, Exit/In, and **Skull's Rainbow Room** are all moderately expensive.

ARTS AND MUSIC

The Parthenon, an exact replica of the original temple in Athens, is especially impressive at night under floodlights. It contains reproductions of the **Elgin Marbles,** now in the British Museum, and the **James M. Cowan** art collection; free. Paintings from the **Kress Collection** and other fine arts exhibits are in the **Peabody Arts Museum;** free. **The Cheekwood Fine Arts Center,** in an impressive Georgian mansion, features *objets d'art* and chamber music recitals in the botanical gardens. There is always a full house at the **Grand Ole Opry House,** where the enduring country music radio program is performed on Friday and Saturday evenings year round and Saturday afternoons, mid-April-October. Reserved seat tickets must be ordered months in advance.

SHOPPING

Leading department stores are **Cain-Sloan, Castner-Knott, Harvey's, J.C. Penney** and **Sears Roebuck.** Many shops sell records and musical instruments.

SPORTS

Seven public and eight private golf courses; numerous tennis courts and swimming pools. Excellent hunting and fishing nearby. The stock-car racing season is from April through October.

TENNESSEE

CALENDAR OF EVENTS
Tennessee Crafts Fair and **Iroquois Steeplechase**, May; **International Country Music Fan Fair**, June; "Down to Earth" Gospel Sing, July; **Tennessee State Fair**, September; **Tennessee Walking Horse Celebration** at Shelbyville, about 60 miles south of Nashville, late August-early September, **Belle Carol Fall Foliage Tours**, September to November.

WHERE TO GO NEARBY
The **Fort Donelson National Military Park** is about 75 miles west of Nashville near Dover; **Stones River National Battlefield** is 30 miles east near Murfreesboro and **Shiloh National Military Park** is 132 miles southwest. Also worth visiting are the **Carter House** and **Carter's Court**, 20 miles south in Franklin.

GREAT SMOKY MOUNTAINS NATIONAL PARK
The Great Smokies, wreathed in their smoke-like haze, reach 6,642 feet at their highest point. The park covers about 800 square miles northwest of Chattanooga and midway between Knoxville and Asheville, North Carolina. **The Appalachian Trail**, winding from Maine to Georgia, follows the spine of the mountains on the states' merged boundary lines for 68 miles, and trailside shelters are spaced about a day's hike apart. **Newfound Gap** overlooks miles of forest seemingly remote from civilization, although there is bumper-to-bumper traffic on the cross-park highway on summer days. On the highest mountain is **Clingmans Dome** observation tower, providing a magnificent view; a ramp-walkway allows easy ascent. **Cades Cove** is a village reminiscent of the early 1900s. The fishing season in the park's 600 miles of rushing streams is 15 April to 15 September, state license required. There are many quiet, remote spots for peaceful trout fishing. Bear, deer, European wild boar, and wild turkey are still found on the Great Smokies. The area is best explored off **Newfound Gap Road** (US 441) following the many nature trails that lead deep into the hills.

Park rangers conduct naturalist walks daily from **Sugarlands Visitors' Center**, near Gatlinburg, from 1 May to 31 October. By late April there's a profusion of wildflowers, and the famous rhododendrons and mountain laurel bloom in June and July. The forest usually becomes a muted tapestry of colors about the last two weeks in October, and from November to March dedicated campers and hikers usually have the vast silent wilderness to themselves. Winter snowfall is unpredictable but the park is beautiful year round.

Try some of the many campsites in the park; 7-day stay limit at developed sites, 14-day limit in other areas from 1 June to Labor Day. **LeConte Lodge**, accessible only by foot or on horseback, is the only hotel-type place to stay in the park, but Asheville and Knoxville are both just an hour's drive away, and Gatlinburg has at least 50 good motels. Handmade pottery, furniture, wood carvings, and handloomed materials by skilled artisans draw big crowds all summer. Try to attend the **Craftsman's Fall**

Exhibition in early October in Gatlinburg and the Craftsman's Fair of the Southern Highlands in the third week in October in Knoxville.

FURTHER STATE INFORMATION

Governor's Staff Division for Tourist Development, Room 1028, Andrew Jackson Building, Nashville, TN 37219. Hunting and Fishing: Tennessee Wildlife Resources Agency, P.O. Box 40747, Nashville, TN 37219. Chatanooga Convention and Visitors Bureau, 1001 Market Street, Chatanooga, TN 37402. Knoxvisit, PO Box 15012, 901 East Vine Avenue, Knoxville, TN 37901. Convention & Visitors Bureau of Memphis, PO Box 3543, 12 South Main, Memphis, TN 38103. Nashville Chamber of Commerce, 161 Fourth Avenue North, Nashville, TN 37219. National Parks: Great Smoky Mountains National Park (Superintendent), Gatlinburg, TN 37738.

Consulates in Memphis: Dominican Republic, Germany, Guatemala, Italy, Mexico, Panama.

In Nashville: Dominican Republic, Mexico.

USEFUL TELEPHONE NUMBERS
Chattanooga

Ambulance	266-2753
Parkridge Hospital	698-6061
East Ridge Community Hospital	894-7870
Poison Control Center	755-6100
Fire	266-2753
Police	698-2525
State Highway Patrol	886-2276
Legal Services	756-4013
Chamber of Commerce	267-2121
Tourist Information	756-2121
Pan Am Reservations	(800) 424-3210

Knoxville

Police	521-1200
Fire	522-7101
University of Tennessee General Hospital	971-3011
St Mary's Medical Center	971-6011
Poison Control Center	971-3261
Chamber of Commerce	637-4550
Knoxvisit	523-7263
Pam Am Reservations	(800) 424-3210

Memphis

Welcome Station	345-5956
Police	528-2222
Fire	458-3311
Ambulance & Medical Service	523-1313
Traveler's Aid	525-5466 & 527-4939

Tennessee Highway Patrol	386-3831
Tourist Information	526-1919
Pan Am Reservations	527-6484

Nashville

Police, Fire, or Ambulance	911
Tennessee Highway Patrol	741-2060
Poison Control Center	322-6435
Drug Abuse Center	244-7444
Tourist Information Center	259-3900 & 242-5606
Vanderbilt Hospital	322-7311
Donelson Hospital	889-5940
St Thomas Hospital	320-2111
Pan Am Reservations	254-6541

Texas

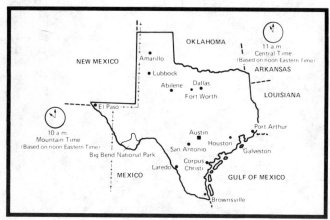

Area	267,339 square miles				**Population**		14,152,339				
Capital	Austin				**Sales Tax**		6%				

Weather	Jan	Feb	Mar	Apr	May	Jun	Jul	Aug	Sep	Oct	Nov	Dec
Av Temp (°C)	8	10	13	18	23	27	29	29	26	20	13	9
Days of Rain	7	8	8	8	9	6	5	5	6	5	6	6

It is hard to believe that this state is really all that the Texans say it is until you see it for yourself. Not every citizen has an oil well in his backyard, but the state leads the nation in the production of petroleum and natural gas. Not all Texans wear Stetson hats and handtooled leather boots and ride "tall in the saddle," but they breed more cattle and sheep than any part of the US and are the source of countless cowboy legends and colorful phraseology. And yet, despite the fact that the span of Texas is greater than the distance between New York and Chicago, 80% of the population clusters in the urban areas, and most Texans earn their livelihoods in business or industry, research or space technology. The name of the state is derived from the Indian word for "friends," and Texans entertain on a gigantic scale.

Texas has 80 state parks, two national parks, a national seashore, four national forests and four state forests for outdoor recreation. It has 90 mountain peaks that are a mile or more high, 624 miles of beachfront on the warm Gulf of Mexico, a total of 6,300 square miles of inland lakes and streams, and 23.4 million acres of woodland. It has some of the nation's most impressive architecture in its modern cities.

From 1519 to 1685 Texas belonged to Spain and from 1685 to 1690 to France; after that the Indians had it pretty much to themselves until the Spanish returned and ruled again from 1719 to 1821. As part of newly independent Mexico, the Mexican flag flew in Texas from 1821 to 1836 and, despite the defeats at Goliad and the Alamo, Texas managed to declare its independence from Mexico in 1836. It was the Republic of Texas until 1845, when it joined the Union as the Lone Star State.

From 1861 to 1865, despite Sam Houston's pleas for national unity, Texas sided with the Confederacy in the Civil War. It existed in a sort of limbo after that debacle and was not formally readmitted to the Union until 1870. The first oil was discovered here in 1894, but only local speculators were interested until 10 January 1901, when the Lucan Well at **Spindletop,** near Beaumont, suddenly flooded the area with "black gold." That was just the beginning. With all the related industries that developed, Texas changed quickly.

Meteorologists have divided Texas into 12 climatic zones. The four major geographical areas are the Coastal Plain, sea level to 800 feet elevation; the Central Lowlands, a richly fertile area rising from 800 to 2,500 feet at the escarpment where the Western Great Plains begin; the L-shaped Great Plains area gradually rising to 4,600 feet over on the New Mexico border, and the Rocky Mountains region, barren but dramatically beautiful, in Western Texas, where **Guadalupe Peak,** 8,751 feet, is the highest point in the state.

In addition to national holidays, Texas observes certain dates in its history: **Confederate Heroes' Day,** 19 January; **Texas Independence Day,** 2 March; **San Jacinto Day,** 21 April; and **Lyndon B. Johnson's birthday,** 27 August.

In a state with more than 700 airports, 13 deep-water seaports, and at least eight major interstate highways entering it from New Mexico, Oklahoma, Arkansas, Louisiana, and Mexico, it is difficult to decide which is the best place to begin a tour. But **AUSTIN,** the state capital, is a convenient starting point. There was nothing here but a fine climate and a lot of natural resources when the city site was chosen in 1839. The **State Capitol,** of pink granite, stands in a complex of unusually handsome state office buildings; included are the **Daughters of the Republic of Texas** and the **Daughters of the Confederacy Museums.** The Colonial Dames, whose ancestry goes back even farther, are responsible for the **Neill-Cochran Museum House** (*circa* 1853), built of hand-hewn native limestone and furnished with elegant Texas colonial antiques. Reception rooms and Sam Houston's bedroom are open to the public in the pillared **Governor's Mansion** (1856), which is being refurbished with antiques. Mementos of "O. Henry" are displayed in the modest cottage where William Sydney Porter lived from 1885 to 1895. France regarded the Republic of Texas as so completely independent that it established a legation in Austin in 1841; the **French Legation,** open daily, contains

TEXAS

ornate doors and furnishings shipped from France. The **Elizabet Ney Museum,** in the sculptress' former home, contains many art treasures. Modern Texas art exhibits are in the **Laguna Gloria Gallery.** Of special interest on the picturesque campus of the **University of Texas** are the **Lyndon Baines Johnson Library,** the **Eugene C. Barker Texas History Center** and the **Art Museum.** Austin was originally founded on the north bank of the Colorado River. Dams have since created the 150-mile chain of **Highland Lakes** and Austin is on **Town Lake,** setting for the 10-day **Austin Aqua Festival** beginning the first weekend in August. There are water shows on the lake all summer at **Fiesta Gardens.** In **Zilker Park,** where plays and concerts are staged under the stars from early June to late August, Scots from all over meet for **Highland Games** in the first week of November. Austin is the only city left that turns on "artificial moonlight" after dark; the streets are bathed in blue-white light from 26 towers each 165 feet tall.

Places to stay in midtown include: **Driskill** (474-5911, S$45-75/D$55-85); **Holiday Inn-Townlake** (472-8211, S$28-32/D$36-40); **Sheraton Crest Inn** (478-9611, S$41-53/D$51-63); **TraveLodge Midtown** (454-6721, S$42-60/D$53-74); **Ramada Inn Capital** (476-7151, S$33-36/D$38-43). On the Inter-regional Highway north of town are **Best Western Chariot Inn** (S$31.75/D$37.75); **Hilton Inn** (451-5757, S$33-60/D$55-72); **Howard Johnson's** (836-8520, S$40/D$42); and **Best Western Villa Capri** (476-6171, ranging from $38-68).

Austin is in **CENTRAL TEXAS,** a richly fertile area where numerous haciendas from the Spanish colonial period and 18th-century German Gothic architecture depict the origins of so many early settlers. This area has more German sausage manufacturers than any other region of Texas. A surprising number of lakes, reservoirs, and rivers all around Austin have made yachting a popular sport and the world's largest fiberglass boat manufacturer is in Austin. **San Marcos** stands beside a mammoth, clear, cold spring in the San Marcos River. A submarine theater features daily mermaid shows in the **Aquarena,** and there are glassbottom boat trips across the remarkably clear lake. The famous **LBJ Ranch** on the Pedernales River is west of Austin near **Johnson City;** this was the "little White House" during President Johnson's tenure, 1963-69. Tourmobiles highlight points of interest in an hour's guided tour of the LBJ Ranch, cemetery, birthplace, and one-room school house.

North of Austin, **Waco** stands near the northern boundary of central Texas in the Brazos River Valley. When the old **Chisholm Trail** came through here in 1866, Waco developed a wild reputation, which is a little hard to visualize when you see some of the magnificent old homes that were built before and during that rambunctious era. A tour of some of the mansions takes place during the **Brazos River Festival and Pilgrimage,** the last weekend in April. **Baylor University,** in Waco, is renowned for its **Armstrong Browning Library,** containing the world's largest collection of the works and memoirs of Robert and Elizabeth Browning.

Near the university are **Best Western Old Main Lodge** (753-0316, S$21/D$21-28), **Holiday Inn I-35** (753-0261, S$26-28/D$32-37), and **La Quinta**

(752-9741, S$15/D$18). On the south side of town are **Ramada Inn** (772-9440, S$32/D$38) and **Best Western Sandman** (756-3781, S$17/D$20).

SOUTHERN TEXAS begins over around **Beaumont,** near the southern Louisiana border, and extends westward to around **Bandera.** In between these two landmarks and the Rio Grande and Gulf of Mexico are some of the most disparate attractions in the whole state. This is the region of mellowed old Spanish missions which contrast with the Lyndon B. Johnson Space Center. Migratory waterfowl in the coastal marshes and white-tailed deer in the brushlands seem in a different world from the gigantic, petrochemical plants; and coastal islands where pirates once hid are now dotted with immense oil tanks. Texas as it is today began in Beaumont where the **Lucas Gusher Monument** in Spindletop Park commemorates the oil well which helped to revolutionize the way of life. **Port Arthur** would be worth seeing just for its immense refineries and oil storage facilities, but it is also an attractive "deep south" city, where everyone seems to find time to take advantage of the superb fishing and hunting in the bayous and salt marshes. From here, you can drive along the edge of the Gulf of Mexico to **Port Bolivar,** where free ferries operate 24 hours a day to **Galveston.** This island city, founded by pirate Jean Lafitte in 1817, lost more than 5,000 citizens in the great flood that accompanied a hurricane in 1900. The 10-mile seawall that now protects the city also provides a scenic drive along its top. Free fishing piers extend out into the gulf. Charter and party boats are available for deep-sea fishermen. A memorable Galveston landmark is the **Bishop's Palace** (1886), open daily except Tuesdays; among its ornate furnishings is a fireplace of satinwood, onyx, and Mexican silver. **Sea-Arama** includes a huge tank stocked with fish native to Texas waters, a collection of exotic fish, and entertaining water shows. For luxurious accommodations in Galveston try the **Flagship Hotel** (762-8681, S$45/D$51), built over the Gulf on a 1,500-foot pier. Overlooking Yacht Basin are the **Holiday Inn** (765-5666, S$32-44/D$40-52) and **Commodore** (763-2375, S$32 up/D$36 up).

From here if you have time and like the water, it is interesting to follow the shoreline south to **Corpus Christi,** where **Padre Island National Seashore** begins. This is a long, thin strip of breeze-swept sand dunes where you can camp, fish, swim, and feel utterly removed from civilization. Corpus Christi is a highly industrialized international seaport, but its climate and location make it also a very popular winter resort. The municipal marina harbors thousands of pleasure boats. Big events here are the **New Year's Day Swim** in Corpus Christi Bay on 1 January; **Buccaneer Days,** a pirate carnival in late April or early May; **All-Jazz Festival** in early July. On Shoreline Blvd. are the **Downtowner Motor Inn** (884-4815, S$17-19/D$21-24); **Holiday Inn-Emerald Beach** (883-5731, S$35/D$48); and **TraveLodge** (882-6181, S$38/D$43). For resortlike accommodations try the **Sheraton Marina Inn** also on Shoreline Blvd. (833-5111, S$27-31/D$29-35). Padre Island accommodations include **Island House,** offering 2- and 3-bedroom apartments. All accommodations have lower winter rates. **Kingsville,** the only sizable city between Corpus Christi and Brownsville, is adjacent to the fabulous **King Ranch,** where Santa Gertrudis cattle were developed as the first new breed of cattle to originate in the western hemisphere.

US 77 goes through the King Ranch, but there is also a 12-mile sightseeing road laid out for visitors. Continue south through cattle ranch country to **Brownsville,** largest city in the Rio Grande Valley, on the Mexican border. It began life in 1846 as Fort Brown, established by General Zachary Taylor, who later became president. The fort was so remote that the Confederates won a brief victory here before they learned that Lee had surrendered over a month before. Although an important seaport, railhead, and commercial center, Brownsville's warm winter climate and proximity to the southern end of Padre Island make it highly popular with vacationers. The Mexican atmosphere predominates in Brownsville's gala **Charro Days,** a 4-day pre-Lenten fiesta which draws huge crowds. Good accommodations can be found at **Best Western Fort Brown** (546-2201, S$25-34/D$30-40); and **Ramada Inn** (541-2201, S$21-27/D$25/33). Local resorts are **Rancho Viejo Resort** (350-4000, S$47/D$56) and **Valley Inn & Country Club** (892-7500, S$28-33.50/D$33-38). Apartments available as well as tennis, swimming, golf, and nightly entertainment. **Matamoros,** an especially colorful Mexican city, is just over the International Bridge and is packed with handicraft shops, nightclubs, and interesting restaurants. Inland is **McAllen,** where the delicious pink Texas grapefruit come from. Its balmy winter climate attracts hosts of Canadians and midwesterners for golfing, swimming, fishing, and hunting for quail and dove. Over the bridge at **Reynosa** is authentic Mexican music and bullfighting. Among the numerous good motels are **Holiday Inn** (686-1741, S/D$19-22); **La Quinta Motor Inn** (687-1101, S$20/D$23); and **Quality Inn** (787-5921, S$13-18/D$17-24). One of the best accommodations to be found in the city is **Best Western La Posada** (686-5411, S$28-39/D$32-42).

Continuing northwest along the Rio Grande you come to **Laredo,** major crossing point for the superhighway down to Monterrey and Mexico City. There may have been "six flags over Texas," but there have been seven over Laredo. Due to some confusion about boundaries after the Texas Revolution, Laredo was the capital of the short-lived "Republic of the Rio Grande" and the white-washed adobe Capitol is now a fascinating museum of pioneer relics, with accent on souvenirs of the Republic (1839-41). **San Agustin Church** was founded in 1767, and **Fort McIntosh,** on the banks of the Rio Grande, was in continuous use from 1848 to 1946. The **Cactus Gardens** display one of the nation's largest collections of these interesting desert plants; also pre-Columbian artifacts, shells, and fossils. Laredo and neighboring Mexico collaborate on an annual 5-day fiesta to celebrate George Washington's birthday. Across the river, **Nuevo Laredo** offers good shopping for Mexican goods. In midtown Laredo are the **New Hamilton** (723-7421, S$14-17.50/D$20-24.50) and **Best Western La Posada** (722-1701, S$32-37/D$40-46), a delightful midtown motel overlooking the river. Farther north are **Holiday Inn** (723-3606, S$25-27/D$27-29); and **Mayan Motor Inn** (722-8181, S$19.95/D$19.95-

24.95); and **Ramada Inn** (722-8133, S$27-30/D$32-34). Reasonably priced accommodations can be found at the **Motel 6** (722-4666, S$11/D$15.95). Higher rates during hunting season in September.

WEST TEXAS has a vast, lonely splendor that daunted pioneers in wagon trains, but it is easily crossed today despite its towering mountain peaks. US 90 heads west from **San Antonio** to **Del Rio** on the Rio Grande. This is sheep country, where Judge Roy Bean was once "the only law west of the Pecos." The dauntless judge held court in his saloon, named the "Jersey Lily" after the much-admired actress Lillie Langtry, and was buried in 1903 in the grounds of what is now the **Whitehead Memorial Museum.** Apart from the mountain scenery and fertile irrigated valleys, the major landmarks in West Texas are **Big Bend National Park** down in the tip of the state and **El Paso** over in the westernmost corner. About 110 miles east of El Paso is **Guadalupe Mountains National Park,** the state's newest national park, established in 1966. The highway presents a superb view of **El Capitan,** which rises 8,078 feet, of which the top 1,000 feet are a dramatic, sheer tower of rock. **Guadalupe Peak,** just north of it, is the highest point in Texas. There is evidence that Indians lived here some 12,000 years ago; their pictographs still decorate rocks and caves and their cooking facilities are still evident.

The **TEXAS PANHANDLE** is almost overpowering in its immensity. Flat plains extend toward the horizon in every direction. Modern breeds of cattle have replaced the tough old Texas Longhorns, but cowboys still ride the vast plains. They are, however, as likely to be in jeeps or helicopters as on horseback. The discovery of a huge underground reservoir of pure water has changed some of the sparse grazing lands into vast fields where cotton, grains, and vegetables grow in enormous quantities. The Panhandle region begins in the southwest at **Odessa** and **Midland** and extends north to the Oklahoma border. The two cities, only a few miles apart, are on a flat prairie that was once an ancient sea. It's called the **Permian Basin** and under the surface is a valuable treasury of oil, natural gas, anhydrite, and potassium salt. Midland was established as a prosperous farming community in the late 1870s and got its name from being midway between Forth Worth and El Paso. The Comanche War Trail went through here first, though, and later this became the Chihuahua Trail for California-bound pioneers. Oil was discovered here in 1923 and today about 700 oil companies and petroleum-related firms have their offices in Midland; actually one fifth of all the office space in Texas is in this city. The new **Permian Basin Petroleum Museum,** at I.H. 20 West and Mission Street, traces the history of petroleum from its formation to modern industrial uses. Open Tuesday-Saturday, 9-5, Sunday 2-5, adults $1.50, under 12—75¢. Midland accommodations: **Best Western of Midland** (684-6611, S$25-28/D$30-34), **Holiday Inn** (694-7774, S$26-35/D$31-40), and **Sheraton Inn Midland** (683-3333, S$24-30/D$31-38).

Odessa struck oil in 1929. Visit the **Permian Playhouse;** in an accurate reproduction of London's Globe Theatre, there is a **Shakespeare Festival** every year from mid-June to mid-August. Odessa motels include **Holiday**

Inn (333-3931, S$32-38/D$37-48), **TraveLodge** (332-0491, S$18-20/D$20-21), and **La Quinta Motor Inn** (S$24/D$28).

Big Spring is host to a spectacular rodeo in mid-June and a Junior Rodeo in early August. Oil refineries and petrochemical plants now stand where herds of buffalo and wild mustangs watered and where Comanche and Shawnee Indians battled for possession of the precious spring.

Lubbock stands in a sun-baked county that had a population of 32,000 in 1940. Shortly thereafter, the underground water supply was discovered and the county's population leaped to 173,979 by the last census taken. Vast cotton fields have made Lubbock the nation's third-largest cotton market and the world's largest processor of cottonseed oil. Crude oil gushes from more than 30,000 wells nearby. **Texas Technological University** claims to have the world's largest university in area. The **Museum of Texas Technological University** concentrates on the region's geological, paleontological, and early pioneer history; an outstanding Peter Hurd mural helps set the scene. The Lubbock **Municipal Auditorium-Coliseum** is the focal point for Panhandle gatherings, ranging from religious revival meetings to basketball games and beauty contests. **Mackenzie State Park** is widely known for its "Prairie Dog Town," where these creatures have found a safe home. Special events in Lubbock are the **ABC Rodeo** and the **South Plains Junior Livestock Show** during the third week in March, the **South Plains Maid of Cotton Pageant** around Easter time, and the **Panhandle South Plains Fair** in late September. Out near Texas Tech are the **Rodeway Inn** (763-8081) and **TraveLodge** (765-8847) averaging S$17-23/D$20-27. South of town is the **Ramada Inn** (747-4346, S$25-35/D$29-38). Midtown accommodations include the **Civic Center Inn** (762-0681, S$18-24/D$24-28).

Amarillo is about 100 miles north of Lubbock, a drive across seemingly endless flat plains. Only 18 miles south of the city, however, is the small town of **Canyon** on the edge of **Palo Duro Canyon State Park,** an almost unbelievable sight in the Panhandle. A branch of the **Red River** started the canyon some 300 million years ago and, aided by wind erosion, produced weird rock formations banded in different colors. Campsites and trailer parks enable you to settle in and explore on foot or on horseback, by miniature train or aerial tramway. A 600-foot canyon wall is the backdrop for Paul Green's musical-historical drama *Texas,* staged nightly except Sunday from mid-June through August. There are water sports and excellent fishing at nearby **Buffalo Lake,** which is in the **Buffalo Lake National Wildlife Refuge.** Canyon is also the home of **West Texas State University,** where some of the most authentic and lively-looking relics of Old West days are preserved in the popular **Panhandle-Plains Historical Museum.** Amarillo's first "buildings" were buffalo hide tents put up by a railroad construction crew in 1887. The only incentives to stay longer on this wind-whipped prairie were the presence of some pleasant lakes and grazing grass for cattle. The discovery of oil and natural gas, back in the 1920s, changed the picture entirely but there is still a lot of cowboy atmosphere in Amarillo. Every week, the year round, cattle are appraised and bought at the **Amarillo Livestock Auction. A Fat Stock**

Show and Rodeo are held in January; **Will Rogers Range Riders Rodeo** on 4 July; **Boys Ranch Rodeo** on Labor Day weekend; the big **Tri-State Fair** in the third week of September. In downtown Amarillo are the **Rodeway Inn** (355-9141, S$19-23/D$22-27) and the **TraveLodge Mid-Town** (373-7433, S$18-22/D$22-26). **Quality Inn** (372-8101, S$28/D$37), and **Howard Johnson's West** (355-9171, S$28-32/D$32-40) also offer good accommodations.

Northwest of the city is **Tascosa,** the ghost of the 1880s "Cowboy Capital of the Plains," complete with its grim **Boot Hill Cemetery.** The abandoned site was taken over in 1939 by **Cal Farley's Boys Ranch** for homeless "maverick" boys from all over the country. The ranch has turned out so many worthwhile citizens, through sports, education, and vocational training that the late J. Edgar Hoover called it a "blueprint for the prevention of crime." About 30 miles north of Amarillo is **Lake Meredith** on the Canadian River; the **Sanford Recreational Area** is great for boating, water-skiing, scuba-diving, hunting, and fishing. **Alibates National Monument,** the place where prehistoric men mined flint for tools and weapons some 12,000 to 15,000 years ago, is still under development by the National Park Service in the southern perimeter of Lake Meredith.

On the western rim of north central Texas is **Abilene** whose wild and woolly past is recreated in the **Old Abilene Town** amusement park; a "Mexican Village," with lots of shops, is in **Burro Alley.** Revenue from oil, livestock, crops, and manufacturing helped to pay for the **Abilene Fine Arts Museum, Philharmonic Orchestra, Community Theater,** two colleges, a university, and numerous spacious, well-equipped parks. Annual events include the **Abilene Fat Livestock Show** in January; **Frontier Arts Festival** and **Hardin-Simmons University Rodeo** in April; and the **West Texas Fair** in September. The **Sheraton** (677-2821, S$24-25/D$27-31) is in midtown, as is the **Windsor Hotel** (672-3261, S$18-22/D$22-24). West of town are **Holiday Inn** (673-5271, S$27-31/D$33-37) and **Sunset Lodge** (677-8546, S$7-9/D$8.50-12.50). East of town is the **Ramada Inn** (677-1461, S$22-26/D$27-31). North of town are the **Best Western American** (677-2463) and the **Colonial Inn Motel** averaging S$19-26/D$22-29.

Wichita Falls has not had a waterfall for years. This is another oil-rich city which has attracted a great many other industries. The city supports its own symphony orchestra and ballet theater, has four nearby lakes for recreation, and is the shopping and entertainment center for personnel of **Sheppard Air Force Base.** The attractive campus of **Midwestern University** is in the south central part of town. **Holiday Inn Downtown** (723-4121, S$28-31/D$33-36) and the **Tradewind** (723-5533, S$17/D$21-23) are convenient in midtown.

EAST TEXAS has a lot more Old South atmosphere than Wild West. Trees are draped with Spanish moss and quiet lakes seem like bayous. Instead of chili and barbecues, the cuisine leans toward southern-fried chicken, catfish, and hush puppies (corn meal deep fried). Antebellum mansions are seen far more often than ranch houses and the lush fertile land produces great crops of rice and peanuts, as well as spectacular

531

roses. All four of the state's national forests are in this region, which extends from just above Beaumont to the Oklahoma border on a line about 120 miles west of Louisiana. At **Bonham**, northeast of Dallas, is the **Sam Rayburn Library**, dedicated in 1957 to the man who served as Speaker of the House of Representatives longer than anyone else in the nation's history. One room duplicates his office in the US Capitol and includes a crystal chandelier that has hung in both the Capitol and the White House. Straddling the Arkansas border, just north of the Louisiana line, is **Texarkana**. The **Red River Army Depot**, 18 miles west of town, occupies an area of 50 square miles. Texarkana's **Four States Fair and Rodeo**, concurrent with a **Quarter Horse and Appaloosa Horse Show**, draws huge crowds in mid-September. Tops among numerous motels are **Coachman's Inn** (794-2504, S$10-11/D$14-15) and **Sheraton Motor Inn** (794-3131, S$26-29/D$32-35). Among the many lakes in northeastern Texas are **Lake Texarkana, Lake O'the Pines,** and **Lake Tawakoni**; all exceptionally good for fishing, boating, and camping.

Longview was doing well with cattle, horses, and hogs when oil was struck in 1931; now it has the greatest concentration of oil derricks on the entire continent. **Tyler** claims to be the Rose Capital of the world and you can easily believe it if you are in town any time from April through October. The most stunning displays, along with parades, floral pageants, and garden tours, can be seen during the **Texas Rose Festival** about the third week in October. Tyler also holds an **Azalea Trails and Spring Flower Show** in late March or early April when azaleas, redbud, dogwood, wisteria, and other plants are in full bloom. The atmosphere is very 1860s, with costumes and displays of Civil War mementos. **Camp Ford,** now recalled only by a tourist marker, held more federal prisoners of the Civil War than any other compound west of the Mississippi River. Tyler motels: **Holiday Inn** (593-7391, S$29-32/D$34-36), **Rodeway Inn** (595-2451, S$20-23/D$24-27), and **Sheraton Inn** (597-1301, S$24-29/D$29-32).

Lufkin, in the "Heart of Piney Woods," lies between **Davy Crockett** and **Angelina National Forests**. The city's industries are diversified but the accent is on lumber and wood products. Meanwhile, the areas which supply the raw materials make great recreation spots for vacationers. The **Sam Rayburn Dam and Reservoir**, about 15 miles east of town, is well equipped for all kinds of water sports. **Huntsville**, on the west side of the **Sam Houston National Forest,** was populated with prominent Texans when it was little more than a trading post. In the **Sam Houston Memorial Park** there is a complex of buildings that were associated with the man who led Texas to victory over Mexico and was twice president of the Republic of Texas. In addition to the **Memorial Museum** are the **Wigwam**, the house Houston built in 1847; the **Steamboat House**, which he built in 1858 and where he died in 1863; the **Carriage House;** and the **Sam Houston Law Office.** While Houston was building his first house, the **Texas State Penitentiary** was also under construction in Huntsville. It has become nationally famous for its unique rodeo, held each Sunday afternoon in October, in which convicts and professional riders compete for top prize money. The proceeds go into a fund for the prisoners' education and rehabilitation. **Best Western Sam Houston Inn** (295-9151, S/D$30-52) and **Holiday Inn** (295-6454, S$28.75/D$35.75) are good accommodations in Huntsville.

Cities To Visit

DALLAS

Dallas is in northeastern Texas, on the Trinity River, about 100 miles south of the Oklahoma border. The city, founded in 1841 by John Neely Bryan and subsequently named after one of his friends, has become an important industrial center. Dallas is known for its diversified economic, civic, and cultural interests. It is still young and vigorous, but with an urban, fashionable look. Population 904,078; metropolitan area, 2,964,342.

WHAT TO SEE

The **First National Bank Building** offers panoramic views; **Hall of State,** considered by many as the most beautiful building in Dallas; **State Fair Grounds; John Neely Bryan's Cabin,** on the County Courthouse lawn; **Memorial Auditorium;** homes and scenery along **Turtle Creek** and around **White Rock Lake;** famous Neiman-Marcus department store; Southern Methodist University campus with its Georgian architecture, and Owen Art Center. The **Health and Science Museum and Planetarium** has permanent exhibits, including *Story of Life,* which traces the story of human development. **Lake Cliff, Reverchon,** and **White Rock Parks** offer good recreational facilities. **Aquarium,** on State Fair Grounds, open weekdays 8-5, Sunday noon to 6, free. **Old City Park,** restored buildings of the 1800s in a park setting that was established as a centennial project 100 years ago, enlarged and refurbished as a Bicentennial project; open Tuesday-Friday 10-4:00; Saturday, Sunday 1:30-4:30; $2.00 adults, 50¢ children, $5.00 family rate.

Principal schools: **Southern Methodist University; Southwestern Medical School,** part of the University of Texas, known for research; **Baylor University School of Dentistry,** good facilities; **Baylor University School of Nursing; University of Texas at Dallas,** advanced courses in research and applied science.

ACCOMMODATIONS

Hotels in the midtown area include the beautiful and popular **Fairmont** (748-5454, S$80-100/D$100-120). Near the airport: **Holiday Inn-Airport North** (255-7147, S$43/D$49) and **Holiday Inn-Airport South** (256-4541, S$42-48/D$49-54). Other good and reasonably priced accommodations include **La Quinta Central** (821-4220, S$28/D$32) and **Rodeway Inn-Central** (827-4310, S$23-27/D$27-29).

RESTAURANTS

Arthur's Beef Barron in the Statler Hilton Hotel, Bavarian Steak House, Cattlemen's Steak House, Copper Cow, and Kirby's Charcoal Steaks, steaks and lobster; Chateaubriand, old New Orleans decor; Ewald's and Mario's for continental cuisine; Ports o'Call, foreign specialties; Old Warsaw, imported game in season; all expensive. Ianni's and Il Sorrento, Italian food; Neiman-Marcus' Zodiac Room, tops for lunch, open for dinner on Thursdays; Southern Kitchen, chicken; Pyramid Room in the Fairmont Hotel; and the Oz, excellent continental cuisine; Vincent's Seafood and Oporto Oyster Bar, for seafood; Little Bit of Sweden, smorgasbord; Sonny Bryan Smokehouse, Love's Wood Pit Barbecue, The Rib, and Roe's Pit Barbecue for barbecues; all are moderate. Two dinner theaters offer appetizing meals with on-stage entertainment: Country Dinner Playhouse (231-9457) Thursday through Sunday; buffet at 6:30, show at 8:00, Sunday matinee lunch 12:00, show at 2:00, $13.50-$17.50, and Granny's Dinner Playhouse (239-0153).

ENTERTAINMENT

Most of the major hotels have lounges which serve drinks and usually have dancing and quite lavish entertainment. For banjo music and sing-along entertainment visit the Levee. For country and western music, Longhorn Ballroom and Western Place. Dancing nightly at Victor's, Purple Orchard, Recovery Room, Travis Street Electric Company, and Wellingtons. Dallas Summer Musicals have a 12-week summer season with Broadway stars and shows. For sleek, sophisticated discoing, there is da Vinci, a semiprivate $200 a year membership club. Temporary 1-night memberships are available at the door for $5.00. The affluent over-40 crowds swarm to Farfallo (12900 Preston Road, 387-0369). Live entertainment Mon-Fri. Reservations are recommended for the restaurant.

ARTS AND MUSIC

Dallas Museum of Fine Arts, one of six permanent museums on State Fair Grounds, is considered among the top five regional art centers in the US; open Tuesday through Saturday 10-5, Sunday 12-6; free. Southern Methodist University's Owen Art Center houses the Bob Hope Theater, the Meadows Museum of Spanish painting, 20th-century sculpture court, and Pollack Art Galleries. The Fall Festival of Art includes many fine art shows. There are performances by the Dallas Symphony, Dallas Civic Opera, and New York Metropolitan Opera Company. There are free concerts at the State Fair Bandshell every Tuesday evening, June through August. Dallas Theater Center is the only public theater designed by Frank Lloyd Wright. Summer musicals in Fair Park draw top talent and pro touring groups.

SHOPPING

Shops are open 9:30-6, until 9 Monday and Thursday nights. Many fine specialty stores include Neiman-Marcus, Sanger-Harris, and Titche-Goettinger. The main shopping areas are the **Quadrangle,** downtown, **North Park Shopping Mall,** and **Town East Mall.**

SPORTS

Professional baseball is played by the **Texas Rangers** in the American League. The **Dallas Black Hawks** play pro ice hockey, the **Dallas Tornadoes** pro soccer. The Southern Methodist University **Mustangs** and the professional **Dallas Cowboys** play football in the new **Texas Stadium.** Southern Methodist teams also participate in basketball, baseball, and track. For horseracing fans **Ross Downs** (481-1071) is open Sundays during racing season.

There are four municipal 18-hole and two 9-hole golf courses, 100 municipal tennis courts, 13 municipal swimming pools, and other sports facilities. Within a 2-hour drive of the city are **Lakes Worth, Eagle Mountain, Bridgeport, Texoma, Garza-Little Elm, Tawakoni,** and others offering swimming, boating, and fishing. The fishing season in Texas is open the year round; there is good hunting in the outlying regions.

CALENDAR OF EVENTS

Garden Tours, Vacation Show, Dallas Open Golf Tournament, April; **Texas State Fair,** the nation's largest state fair, **Neiman-Marcus Fortnight,** October; **Cotton Bowl Festival,** from last week in November through parade and Cotton Bowl football game on 1 January.

WHERE TO GO NEARBY

Lake Texoma, 100 miles from the city; **Bonham State Park,** about 105 miles; **Daingerfield State Park,** 138 miles; **Tyler State Park,** 99 miles; visit also **Possum Kingdom State Park.** All these offer good recreational opportunities. **Six Flags Over Texas** and **Seven Seas** are amusement parks on the Dallas-Forth Worth turnpike, also.

EL PASO

El Paso is in the westernmost tip of Texas, on the Rio Grande—the frontier between the United States and Mexico—and directly across the river from Juarez. The region was first explored by the Rodriguez Expedition in 1581 and in 1598 an unsuccessful settlement was made. In 1659 another Spanish settlement was begun which later became the city of Juarez. In 1827, when still another start was made, the El Paso region was known simply as Ponce de León Ranch. In 1845, the new town, called Franklin, became US territory as a result of the Mexican War, and in 1859 was renamed El Paso, for the nearby pass through the Franklin Mountains, which are part of the Rocky Mountain Highlands, called **El Paso del Norte**—the pass to the *north.* It was incorporated as a city in 1873 and in 1881, with the coming of the railroad, El Paso began to boom. It became a Western town in true Hollywood style, complete with gamblers, "bag men," and frequent shootings. But lawlessness gradually subsided and today El Paso is a respectable business and tourist center. El Paso is an international city and much of the population speaks

Spanish; both Spanish and English newspapers and radio stations are available in the city.

When the Rio Grande changed its course over 100 years ago, 437 acres of Mexican land, known as El Chamizal, became a part of El Paso. This has recently been returned to Mexico, resulting in a building boom to reroute railroads, put up new bridges, and cut a new channel to keep the river from changing the national boundary again. Population 420,000; metropolitan area 450,000.

WHAT TO SEE

Drive out on **Scenic Road** which skirts the edge of Mt Franklin and affords an excellent view of the city and its surroundings. Another must is a visit to Juarez, Mexico, which has a section devoted almost exclusively to the tourist trade with many attractive things to buy; there are also some good restaurants. **Trans Mountain Drive,** the aerial tramway, the *Christ of Peace* statue on Sierra del Cristo Rey, and the replica of the old **Fort Bliss** are worth a visit. Drives can also be taken to the **White Sands National Monument, Ruidoso,** and **Cloudcroft** in New Mexico and to the old missions at **Ysleta, Socorro,** and **San Elizario.** El Paso **Centennial Museum** offers exhibits in astronomy, geology, paleontology, and local archaeology and history, open 10-4:30 Mon-Fri, 1-4:30 Sat and Sun. The **Magoffin Home** is a 20-room territorial-style adobe built in 1875; open 9-4 daily. **Chamizal National Monument,** open daily 10-6, cites the amicable settlement of the border dispute; center contains border memorabilia and exhibits; film in English and Spanish. **Tigua Indian Museum** and arts and crafts center, open Tuesday-Sunday at Ysleta Mission. Conducted tours of El Paso leave from the principal hotels; a typical tour takes about 3½ hours and costs $9.00 adults, $5.00 children. An extensive range of tours is available in El Paso and provided by **Sun Country Tours** (779-6954), **Pan Am Travel Service** (772-8755), and the **Gray Line** (778-4893). For current selection available call companies direct; you can usually be picked up at your hotel. Tourists also enjoy **Exploring El Paso** walking, auto, and bus tours available through the El Paso Visitors' Bureau (544-3650).

Principal parks: **Washington Park,** zoo and swimming pool; **Memorial Park,** garden center; **Grandview Park,** public swimming pool; **McKelligon Canyon Park,** picnicking and location of the **McKelligon Port Amphitheater** where the musical drama *Viva El Paso* is presented from July through August; **Tom Mays Park,** a mile-high desert wilderness in the Franklin Mountains; **Ascarate Park,** lake and amusement park.

Principal school: **University of Texas at El Paso,** coeducational, noted for its courses in mining, engineering, and liberal arts, and its Bhutanese (Tibetan) architectural style.

ACCOMMODATIONS

Sheraton El Paso (533-8241, S$37.50/D$45) and **Holiday Inn** (544-3300, S$29/D$35) are both located in the heart of downtown El Paso. Close to the airport is the **Hilton Inn** (778-4241, S$42/D$51). In and near the city good accommodations can be found at the **Rodeway Inn** (778-6611, S$24/D$37), **Best Western Tom Penny Inn** (779-7700, S$24/D$37), and the **Caballero Motor Inn** (772-4231, S$23/D$25). For accommodations that offer just a little out of the ordinary, there's the **Granada Royal Hometel** (779-6222, S$59.90/D$69.90). Free breakfast in tropical atrium and free cocktails by the fountain.

RESTAURANTS
Although its border location makes El Paso's Mexican cuisine especially appealing, there are restaurants to please any palate. **Billy Crews, Julio's Cafe Corona, Leo's Mexican Restaurant, Casa Juardo, Jersey Lily, Gregory's Penthouse,** the **Stanton Room,** and **Nantucket Lobster Trap** all serve good meals, reasonable to slightly expensive. **Cattlemen's Steakhouse,** on Indian Cliffs just east of the city, offers good meals in an authentic Old West setting, and there are many fine restaurants in Jaurez, Mexico, just a few minutes' drive from El Paso hotels and motels.

ENTERTAINMENT
El Pasoans find nightlife both in El Paso and across the river in Juarez, Mexico. The **Top O'The Inn** in the Holiday Inn-Downtown, the **Mardi Gras Room** at the Sheraton Motor Inn offer fine entertainment. Disco is featured at **Vegas** (592-7860). **Caravan East** (593-7340) is a popular Western entertainment spot. Local business people frequent **Smugglers Inn.** See *El Paso Today* magazine for nightlife information.

ARTS AND MUSIC
El Paso Museum of Art, Indian, Spanish, and Mexican collections, and the Kress collection of 14-17th-century European art; open daily except Monday 10-5; Sunday 1-5; free. **El Paso Symphony Orchestra,** season October to March; outdoor concerts in summer.

SHOPPING
Department stores are open daily 10-5:30. Mexican goods are the best buys, particularly silverware, carved woods, and leather work. At the airport **La Placita,** an international market place, offers wares of three cultures: southwestern American, Indian, and Mexican. Major shopping centers include **Cielo Vista Mall, Morningside Mall, and Basset Mall** all located 10-15 minutes from the heart of town. Juarez, Mexico, offers markets, shops, and malls just minutes from El Paso.

SPORTS
Racing at **Sunland Park,** about 10 minutes from downtown El Paso. Bus service to and from the track in season, which is usually from October through May. The rodeo is a big annual event in February, lasting 5 days. There are collegiate and professional basketball games. Football at the **Sun Bowl Stadium;** annual **Sun Bowl Grid Classic** late December. Golf courses and tennis courts are open all year; swimming pools are open during the summer, some year round.

537

CALENDAR OF EVENTS

Livestock Show and Rodeo, early February; **Tigua Fourth of July Pow Wow**; **Fiesta de las Flores**, Labor Day weekend; and **Mexican Independence Day**, 16 September; **Southwest Sun Carnival**, November to 1 January.

WHERE TO GO NEARBY

All in New Mexico: **White Sands National Monument**, 100 miles north in New Mexico, strange formations of snowy white gypsum; open all year. **Lincoln National Forest**, 90 miles north, open all year round, has tourist accommodations. **Carlsbad Caverns National Park**, 150 miles northwest in New Mexico, noted for its famous stalactite and stalagmite cave formations; good choice of accommodations. Nearer El Paso is **Hueco Tanks State Historical Park**, 32 miles NE, natural water basins with rock and cave formations. Indian pictographs, 10,000 years old, line some of the caves. $2.00/car. **Indian Cliffs Ranch**, 20 miles east of downtown, offers "dude ranch" atmosphere with horseback riding, hay rides, and overnight camping.

FORT WORTH

Fort Worth is in north central Texas, 100 miles south of the Oklahoma border, 32 miles west of Dallas. In 1849, when Major Ripley Arnold and his Second Dragoons established Fort Worth as an army post on the banks of the Trinity River, the country to the west was inhabited by hostile Comanche Indians. Although the post was later abandoned, many private citizens remained behind; the cavalry stables became the first hotel, and stores and homes grew up around it. The coming of the railroad transformed Fort Worth, until then primarily a resting place on the cattle trail, into an important city which is now a major manufacturing center. In the immediate vicinity are six lakes—**Worth, Eagle Mountain, Bridgeport, Grapevine, Arlington,** and **Benbrook**—providing facilities for swimming, fishing, sailing, motorboating, and water-skiing. Fort Worth, "Where the West begins," is a leading livestock and grain-market city. It also has been called, for all its skyscrapers, the most "Texan" of Texas cities—certainly a complete description. Its preoccupations are cattle, oil, business, and very modern diversified industries, but its greatest asset is an alert, progressive and friendly citizenry. Population of Fort Worth is 385,144.

WHAT TO SEE

Will Rogers Memorial Coliseum; Texas Christian University; Tarrant County Convention Center; Noble Planetarium. Trinity Park has a beautiful botanical display and outstanding Japanese garden, also an herbarium, an exhibit of dried plants. **Forest Park** is an attractive area with many facilities, including a zoo, herpetarium, aquarium, miniature railroad, and a unique log cabin village.

Principal schools: **Texas Christian University**, coeducational, schools of fine arts and science, education, and business, graduate and evening schools; **College of Nursing, Southwestern Baptist Theological Seminary,** coeducational; **Texas Wesleyan,** offering primarily courses in business and engineering.

ACCOMMODATIONS
Hotels include the **Fort Worth Hilton** (335-7000, S$42-75/D$54-87) and **Hyatt Regency Fort Worth** (870-1234, S$46-58/D$61-73). There are many convenient motels including **Howard Johnson's** (293-6672, S$36-43/D$41-49), **Best Western Fort Worther** (S$17-19/D$20-22), and **La Quinta** (485-2750, S$25/D$27).

RESTAURANTS
Local specialties include barbecues of all sorts, steaks, seafood, Mexican dishes, and the famous "blackbottom pie" (a layered custard pie with chocolate base and rum-flavored top). Aside from the hotels, which provide excellent meals, there are the **Carriage House, Cattlemen's Steak House, Spanish Galleon,** and **El Fenix;** all prices are moderate.

ARTS AND MUSIC
Fort Worth Art Museum, modern with good displays; open daily except Monday 10-5, Sunday 1-5, free. **Fort Worth Museum of Science and History,** numerous exhibits of interest to children; open weekdays 9-5, Sunday 2-5; free. **Amon Carter Museum of Western Art,** outstanding collection of Remington and Russell paintings and sculptures; open weekdays except Monday 10-5, Sunday 1-5:30; free. The **Fort Worth Opera Association,** the **Fort Worth Symphony,** and the **Texas Boys Choir** present concerts throughout the year. The city is headquarters for the **Van Cliburn International Quadrennial Piano Competition.** The modern **Casa Manana** presents theater-in-the-round throughout the year and Broadway musicals during the summer. **Fort Worth Community Theater** and theater groups at the **Texas Christian University** and **Texas Wesleyan College** have several presentations each year. The modern **William Edrington Scott Theater** is interesting both for its architecture and its dramatic productions.

SHOPPING
Largest department stores are **Stripling's, Monnig's, Cox's, Leonard's,** and **Neiman-Marcus.**

SPORTS
The **Texas Rangers,** the local baseball team, is a member of the American league. Collegiate sports including football, basketball, and track are also played. Golf, tennis, water-skiing, and swimming may be enjoyed here almost the entire year. Fishing and hunting in the vicinity are exceptional; you can fish for bass, crappie, perch, bream, and catfish.

WHERE TO GO NEARBY
Lake Texoma, Bonham State Park, Daingerfield State Park, Tyler State Park, Possum Kingdom State Park, Big Bend National Park. All these

offer good recreational opportunities. **Seven Seas** and **Six Flags Over Texas,** an amusement park, both located on the Dallas-Fort Worth turn-pike, are worthwhile. **Fort Worth Nature Center and Refuge,** 7 miles northwest on Texas 199; 3,300 acres, hiking, riding trails, canoeing, inter-pretive center. Open daily except holidays. **Pate Museum of Transporta-tion,** 14 miles southwest on US 377, has military as well as civilian exhibits including a superb collection of classic foreign and domestic autos. Open Tuesday through Sunday, 9-5, free.

HOUSTON

Houston is in southeastern Texas, 50 miles northwest of the Gulf of Mex-ico. Four of the principal rivers of Texas converge here. A dam on the **San Jacinto River** forms the 14,000-acre **Lake Houston** just north of the city. The **Houston Ship Channel,** a deep-draft canal dredged from Buffalo Bayou, links Houston to Galveston Bay 22 miles to the east. Along it sprawls the enormous petrochemical complex that is the underpinning of the city's economy.

The original settlement, founded in 1836, was the first capital of the Republic of Texas, 1836-45, and named in honor of General Sam Houston, Commander of the Texas Army and first president of the Republic. The important Battle of San Jacinto in 1836, which won Texas its independ-ence from Mexico, was fought 18 miles east of Houston. If the discovery of oil at Spindletop nudged Houston into the petrochemical age, the building of the Lyndon B. Johnson Space Center launched the city into the space age. At JSC, the US trains its astronauts and plans future forays into the universe.

One of the fastest-growing major cities in the country, Houston is bus-tling with life. The social tempo, however, is definitely Southwestern—relaxed and friendly. City population 1,554,992; metropolitan area 2,886,962.

WHAT TO SEE

Downtown: Pennzoil Towers, exciting angular twin office building de-signed by Phillip Johnson; **Tranquility Park,** an oasis of sculpture and plants, created by Charles Tapley; **Allen's Landing Park,** on the site where the city was founded; **Sam Houston Park,** early Houston homes and build-ings restored and relocated by the Harris County Heritage Society; **Cul-len Center Plaza** and fountains; **pedestrian tunnels; No. 1 Shell Plaza,** highest building west of the Mississippi, and the **Old** and **New Houston Public Library,** studies in contrast; the **Civic Center** complex of fortress-like **Alley Theater,** which houses a leading US repertory company; **Jesse H. Jones Hall for Performing Arts,** with its Richard Lippold *Gemini II* sculpture floating overhead; and the **Albert Thomas Convention Center** and **Space Hall of Fame.**

Midtown: Texas Medical Center; Hermann Park with its **Zoo, Rose Garden,** and playground/picnic facilities set among enormous trees; **Mu-seum of Fine Arts; Contemporary Arts Museum;** Rice University; the air-conditioned, covered **Astrodome—**"Eighth Wonder of the World" that's home for the sports of the Astros, Oilers, and University of Houston Cougars (three tours daily, $2.50); **Astroworld,** Houston's answer to DisneyLand (open weekends spring and fall; daily 1 June through Labor Day, noon-midnight, $9.95 1 day/$14.95 2 days).

Other points of interest include the **Galleria** complex of hotels, exclusive department stores, and shops centering on an ice rink, now expanded with **Galleria II; Memorial Park,** with extensive jogging trails and picnic, golf, and tennis facilities; **Aline McAshan Botanical Hall and Arboretum** in Memorial Park, a 260-acre haven for 60 or more native flora and fauna; the posh residential areas of **River Oaks, Shadyside,** and **Memorial.**

Principal schools: **Baylor University College of Medicine; Rice University; Texas Southern University; University of Houston; University of Texas Postgraduate School of Biomedical Sciences, Dental Branch, Division of Continuing Medical Research, M.D. Anderson Hospital and Tumor Institute; Texas Women's University College of Nursing; University of Texas Medical School at Houston.**

ACCOMMODATIONS

All of the following downtown hotels are air conditioned: **Downtown: Hyatt Regency** (654-1234, S$67-70/D$75-85); **Lamar** (658-8511, S$48-62/D$58-72), popular, center of town. Two very modern centrally located hotels, within two to three blocks walking distance from Pan Am office are the **Best Western Savoy** (659-1141, S$38-50/D$44-56) and the **Sheraton Houston** (651-9041, S$57-72/D$72-87). Others include the **Four Seasons-Houston Center** (650-1300, S$90 up/D$100 up), with swimming pool, opening spring 1982; **Harley Hotel** (225-1781, S$40/D$46); **Holiday Inn Downtown** (659-2222, S$46-58/D$56-68); **Meridien** (759-0202, S$72-103/D$87-118); **Memorial Plaza Holiday Inn** (869-8261, S$36-46/D$42-48); and the **Allen Park Inn** (521-9321, S$36-45/D$42-56). All these accommodations have suites, most ranging in price from $150 up.

Medical Center/Midtown Area: Approximately 4½ miles south of the business district are the deluxe **Shamrock Hilton** (668-9211, S$54-80/D$70-96), boasting the world's largest hotel swimming pool, and the luxurious **Warwick** (526-1991, S$65-100/D$80-115), overlooking Hermann Park. Other hotels and motels in the area include the **Astro Village Hotel** (748-3221, S$41-46/D$51-66), with a corporate rate program; **Holiday Inn-Medical Center** (797-1110, S$38/D$43); and **Mariott Hotel** at the Astrodome (932-0808, S$60-70/D$70-80). Special medical rates are available at the **Surrey House Motor Hotel** (667-9261), **Tidelands Motor Inn** (526-4161), and **Towers Hotel—Medical Center** (666-1461); regular rates range S$30-41/D$37-54.

Galleria/Greenway area: Newest hotels in the area are the **INTER-CONTINENTAL HOUSTON** (931-1400, opening late 1982) and the **Inn on the Park-Houston** (871-8181, S$75-95/D$95-115), both with swimming pool and health club, and the former with raquetball and tennis courts. Also in the area are the **Houston Oaks Hotel** (623-4300, S$75-105/D$95-125); the **Greenway Inn** (526-2533, S$26-30/D$30-34), with pool; the **Martinique Motor Lodge** (840-8600, S$39-44/D$44-54), with 3 pools and a nightclub; and the **Galleria Oaks Corporate Inn** (629-7120, 1-bedroom suites $45-65, 2-bedroom $65-85), all with completely equipped kitchens, corporate rates available.

NASA-Clear Lake area: Days Inn-Webster (332-4581, S$24.88/ D$28.88), with pool; Holiday Inn NASA (333-2500, S$38/D$44); and **Space Center Inn** (332-3551, S$22/D$26-28), with kitchenettes.

Intercontinental Airport area: Holiday Inn-Airport (449-2311, S$40-47/ D$44-52); the new **Doubletree Inn** (442-8000, S$58-76/D$72-90), with swimming pool and golf course; **TraveLodge-North** (820-1500, S$33/ D$36); and **Host International Hotel** (443-2310, S$58-62/D$66-70).

RESTAURANTS

Houstonians can count on four basic types of food for consistently good eating: steak, Mexican, barbecue, and seafood. This only scratches the surface, as there is a variety of establishments worth investigating. **Downtown:** Try Brennans and Hubers for Louisiana Creole type cooking; the latter serves a seafood gumbo with jazz. For French cuisine there is **Le Restaurant de France,** in the Hotel Meridien, which serves *nouvelle cuisine* in a posh setting, and Maxim's, Houston's first gourmet French restaurant. **Harry's Kenya Club** is the new spot for continental cuisine, while the **New York Deli** is for homesick New Yorkers. For seafood, try **Massa's,** an old Houston favorite, and for barbecue there is **Otto's,** which serves a mild east Texas variety. **China Garden** serves Mandarin, Szechuan, and Cantonese dishes.

Near town: Ruggles, favorite late-night eatery; **Andres,** Swiss quiche and pastries; **Harrigan's,** continental cuisine; **Birra Poretti's,** a unique combo of Italian restaurant and Irish bar; **Happy Bhudda,** city's oldest Japanese steak house; **Roznovsky's,** old-fashioned burgers; and **Hobbit Hole,** vegetarian.

Medical Center/Midtown area: Che, in the Plaza Hotel, serves continental cuisine; **Warwick** is noted for Sunday champagne brunch; **Le Select,** a small French place, serves deli at lunch; **Museum of Fine Arts Restaurant** has a soup, sandwich, and salad luncheon; **Ouisi's Table** is known for imaginative soups, salads, and entrées; **Alfred's Village** specializes in kosher entrées, sandwiches, and pastries; for seafood try **Kaphan's, Guido's,** or **Pier 21;** steaks are the thing at **Look's SirLoin House** and the **Stables,** while the **Red Lion Inn** serves delicious English prime rib. For barbecue, try the **Cellar Door.**

East/Ship Channel area: Ninfa's is the flagship of a popular new Tex-Mex local chain; **Merida,** opposite Ninfa's, specializes in Yucatecan dishes; a must on a visit to the battleship *Texas* is a stop at the **San Jacinto Inn,** a Houston favorite that serves all the seafood you can eat. Also in the area are **El Mira Sol,** with authentic Tex-Mex dishes, and **Taj Mahal,** exotic Indian food.

Galleria/Post Oak area: Don's Seafood, excellent Louisiana Cajun seafood; **Magic Pan,** crepes of every description; **Tony's,** considered the city's finest and most expensive French restaurant; **Confederate House,** fine Southern cooking; and **Rivoli,** continental cuisine.

Southwest area: **Uncle Tai's Hunan Yuan,** gourmet south China specialties; **La Hacienda de Morales,** exact duplicate of famous Mexico City restaurant and menu by its owners; **Foulards,** gourmet French; **Luther's,** barbecue; **Chili's,** next best thing to Terlingua Chili Cookoff; **Bud Bigelow's,** steaks; **Vargo's,** traditional Southern.

West area: **Brenner's,** best steakhouse in town.

ENTERTAINMENT

Popular spot in town is **Gilley's,** the country-western singer's enormous cabaret in Pasadena, complete with the original mechanical bull. Other country western spots include the **Texas Tumbleweed,** and **San Antone Rose.** The **Athens Bar & Grill** on the Ship Channel is a favorite of Greek sailors and socialites alike. Jazz aficionados will like **Roscoe's, Birdwatchers, Rockefellers, Fitzgeralds, Huber's,** and **Mums.** The **Great Caruso** offers light classical and opera in its ornate Victorian supper club. The **Comedy Workshop** has original revues and budding performers. The **Ritz** and **Elan** are discos. **Steamboat Springs** and **Whiskey River** are showcases for rock groups. The **Bavarian Gardens** offers a beer garden and polkas. **Crystal Forest,** in the Hyatt Regency, hosts big-name entertainers.

ARTS AND MUSIC

The **Houston Symphony Orchestra, Houston Grand Opera Association,** and the **Houston Ballet** perform in **Jones Hall** downtown. In summer, performances by all three are given at **Miller Outdoor Theater,** in Hermann Park. **Theater Under the Stars** (TUT) also appears here. The **Nina Vance Alley Theater,** one of the country's outstanding regional groups, performs year round. Drama is presented by three dinner theaters. Road companies play Houston regularly.

The **Museum of Fine Arts,** with its new wing designed by Mies van der Rohe, boasts the Kress collection of high Italian and Spanish Renaissance art, as well as the Beck collection of impressionist and post-impressionist paintings. MFA's newest branch, **Bayou Bend,** houses an elegant collection of American decorative arts (1650-1850). MFA is open Tuesday-Saturday, 10am-5pm, Sunday, noon-6; Bayou Bend is open second Sundays of the month, 1-5. The **Contemporary Arts Museum** offers paintings, constructions, and sculpture by Buffet, Ernst Calder, Matta, and others plus current shows. Open Tuesday-Saturday, 10-5, Sunday, noon-6. The **Museum of Natural History** and **Burke Baker Planetarium** offer everything from archaeology and geology to a trip through outer space; open Tuesday-Thursday 9-5; Friday-Saturday, 9-5, 7:30-9; Sunday-Monday, noon-5. Other museums include the **Blafter Gallery,** University of Houston; **Rice Museum** and **Sewell Art Gallery,** Rice University; **Rothko Chapel,** adjacent to the University of St Thomas; and the **University of St Thomas Art Gallery.**

SHOPPING

The Galleria/Post Oak area is probably the city's most popular shopping area. Located in adjoining **Galleria I and II** are such well-known department stores as **Neiman-Marcus, Lord & Taylor's,** and **Marshall Field's,** as well as hundreds of specialty shops that face out onto the ice rink at Galleria I or the open-space mall in Galleria II. Nearby are such stores as **Sakowitz, Joske's,** and **Saks Fifth Avenue.** Other shopping centers include **Sharpstown, Memorial City, Town & Country Village, Gulfgate, Almeda Mall, Northline,** and **Greenspoint.** More ambience can be found in the **University Village,** near Rice University/Medical Center, **River Oaks,** and **Westbury Square** shopping centers. Major downtown department stores include **Sakowitz, Foley's,** and **Palais Royal. Jim Mamail & Sons** is the Rolls Royce of gourmet food stores. Downtown stores are open weekdays 9-5:30; some on Monday and Thursday evening until 9.

SPORTS

Houstonians are sports fanatics, especially for the **Houston Oiler** football team and the **Houston Astros** baseball club. Both play in the air-conditioned **Astrodome,** which seats 52,000 for football; 45,000 for baseball. The **Rockets** basketball team, which plays in the **Summit sports arena,** has an avid following. The **Apollos** hockey team plays in the **Coliseum.** Tennis and jogging rank at the top of participant sports, with **Memorial Park** being the best place to run. In the midtown area, joggers prefer to run around the 3-mile perimeter of Rice University. Tennis courts and golf courses are available at city parks. Deep-sea vessels can be chartered out of nearby Galveston for saltwater fishing, or fish from piers and jetties there. Freshwater fishing, particularly for bass and crappie, abounds in the lakes north of Houston. Admission to polo matches in Memorial Park is free.

CALENDAR OF EVENTS

Houston Marathon, January; **Salt Grass Trail Ride, Rodeo Parade, Livestock Show & Rodeo,** late February, early March; **Azalea Trail, Houston Festival,** and **St Patrick's Day Parade,** March; **River Oaks Tennis Tournament,** April; **Houston Open Golf Tournament,** May; **Pine Oaks Horse Show,** Astro Arena, June; outdoor performances by Opera, Symphony, Ballet, and Theater Under the Stars, in Hermann Park, June-September; opening of music, dance, drama season, October; **Foley's Thanksgiving Parade,** November; **Candlelight Tours,** Heritage Park, December; **Bluebonnet Bowl,** New Year's Eve.

WHERE TO GO NEARBY

No trip to Texas would be complete without a visit to the **Roundup Rodeo** at **Simonton,** just west of Houston on FM-1093, Saturday 8pm, $5 adults, $3 children. On the way, stop at **Fulshear** for a fine Texas country meal at **Womack House;** reservations. In the spring a drive through the bluebonnet-blanketed hills to **Brenham** is a favorite event. In **Galveston,** 51 miles south, visit the strand, see the fine Victorian architecture, swim at the beach, and see the shows at **Searama Marine World** or the *Lone Star* epic in the State Park's amphitheater. **Lyndon B. Johnson Space Center,** 25 miles southeast, is open year round except for national holidays. Exhibits of hardware, astronaut training, and moon rocks. Special conducted tours can be prearranged; admission free. In the **Port of Houston,** take a free tour of the *Sam Houston,* reservations necessary; see the facilities of the nation's third-largest port, plus the multibillion-dollar petrochemical complex lining the man-made Ship Channel connecting Houston to the Gulf of Mexico. At the site where Texas won its independence from Mexico, visit the museum in the base of the **San Jacinto Monument,** tour the **Battlefield,** and board the *Texas,* the only remaining battleship of the dreadnought class which saw service in World Wars I and II, and flagship of Eisenhower on D-Day invasion of France; open year round, admission charged. Northeast of Houston is the **Sam Houston National Forest.** Dine there at Cleveland in the lush greenhouse restaurant of **Hilltop Herb Farm;** reservations necessary; open Tuesday-Thursday, lunch; Saturday, dinner; reservations 592-5859. On October weekends drive northwest to **Magnolia** where the **Texas Renaissance Festival** is held on 237 wooded acres; 16th-century European costumes, customs, and food are featured. Continue on to **Washington State Park,** where the Texas Declaration of Independence was signed, and enjoy the picnic facilities. To the northeast of Houston is the **Alabama Coushatta Indian Reservation** in **Livingston.**

SAN ANTONIO

San Antonio is in south central Texas, about 150 miles northeast of the Mexican border. A Spanish outpost as early as 1691, San Antonio was established as a city in 1718 by Philip V of Spain. In 1821 it came under Mexican rule. Its inhabitants, however, were largely American, and in 1835 they attempted to break away from Mexico and the tyranny of its president, Santa Anna. The struggle culminated in the fierce battle in which the **Alamo,** a fortress in the city held by the Texans, was overwhelmed by Mexican troops after the last defender had been killed. This defeat was avenged at the Battle of San Jacinto, when Texas won its independence from Mexico, and San Antonio became part of the new Republic.

Long a vacation spot in the state, San Antonio has become a major convention center. The city's old Spanish missions and Victorian **King William District** offer an interesting study in architectural contrasts. The **Paseo del Rio,** or river walk, is lovely for strolling, dining, or sightseeing. Population 788,049; metropolitan area 1,070,245.

WHAT TO SEE

The leading historical attractions are the **Alamo** and the old Spanish missions—**San Jose, Concepcion, San Juan,** and **Espada; the Spanish Governor's Palace;** and **La Villita,** a reconstructed Spanish village. Downtown, the area along the Paseo del Rio has a variety of quaint shops, exciting nightclubs, and exotic restaurants offering Mexican foods, gondola rides, semitropical scenery, outdoor theater. Especially interesting: **Navarro House; Cos House; Steve's Homestead; Institute of Texan Cultures; Hertzberg Circus Collection; Hemisdair Plaza;** King William District;

TEXAS

Mexican Cultural Institute, exhibits works of contemporary Mexican and South American artists; Southwest Craft Center; and San Fernando Cathedral. Brackenridge Park Zoological Gardens is one of America's best zoos, an early example of barless cages and open pits for animals. Visitors also enjoy the Aquarium and riding the miniature train or skyride. Riding horses are available at the park stables. The San Antonio Botanical Center is a 38-acre tract featuring a miniature version of the diverse Texas landscape. Five military installations—Brooks, Kelly, Lackland, and Randolph Air Force Bases, and Fort Sam Houston—are reminders that the city was founded as a garrison.

Principal schools: Trinity University, coeducational: St Mary's University.

ACCOMMODATIONS

The Hilton Palacia del Rio (222-2481, S$44-58/D$60-74) is across from the city's new Convention Center complex; the dignified Menger (223-4361, S$29-37/D$35-47) has a handsome new wing of balconied rooms and a patio swimming pool, located at Alamo Plaza. The St Anthony INTER·CONTINENTAL HOTEL (227-4392, S$35-52/D$54-62), convenient downtown location, is also very pleasant. Numerous and excellent motor hotels and motels include Pick Motor Inn (344-8331, S$27.50-30/D$33-66); Ramada Inn (344-5418, S$30-32/D$39-40), and several others near the airport; Holiday Inn (732-5141, S$26-31/D$34-40), in northwest business and commercial district. El Montan Motel (826-2349) and Master Hosts Inn (225-5441, S$20-25/D$25-35) are reasonably priced downtown accommodations.

RESTAURANTS

The city is famous for its Mexican dishes, many of which rival the cuisine of Mexico itself. Casa Rio and La Paloma del Rio, both with large patios facing the San Antonio River, and La Fonda, on the outskirts of the business area, serve Mexican food; moderate. Tower of the Americas Restaurant, atop a 622-foot tower, which revolves each hour; Little Rhein Steakhouse, Casey's John Charles, and Old San Francisco for steaks. La Louisiane, a gourmet outpost in the Southwest, is still tops for fine French cuisine. For Chinese food, Hung Fong Restaurant and the Golden Palace, which specializes in Cantonese dishes. Naples and Valerios, Italian fare; Little Bavarian and Schilo's, German; Arthur's and Chez Ardid offer exceptional American food. Viet Nam serves seafood prepared in an Asian style; Night Hawk and Earl Abel's are stalwarts for reasonably priced food.

ENTERTAINMENT

The Esquire, old-fashioned bar near Riverwalk; Number Ten Club and El Pincon, jazz; The Landing, Dixieland; Cotton-Eyed Joe and Doc Holliday, country-western; Skipwilly's and Village Inn, rock; Roaring 20's, speakeasy motif; Big Al's Hill Country and The Shadows, country rock; Jimmy's Party Room, and Mendiola's, a Mexican ballroom, and Durty

Nellie's, a small bistro on Riverwalk, are some of the many nightspots available.

ARTS AND MUSIC

Witte Museum, exhibits of archaeology, modern art, Americana, open weekdays 9-5, weekends 10-6; admission $1.00. **McNay Art Institute,** permanent and special exhibits, changed monthly, open daily except Monday 9-5, Sunday 2-5; free. The **San Antonio Symphony Orchestra** plays November to March and also presents a **Grand Opera Festival.** The **Fiesta Noche del Rio,** Mexican song and dance performances, are presented at the **Arneson River Theater** on Tuesday, Friday, and Sunday nights, June through August. The Arneson Theater is unique in that the audience sits on one side of the San Antonio River and the stage is on the other. At the **Institute of Texas Cultures,** the dome show employs 36 screens on which are projected movies and slides illustrating the diverse cultures in Texas. Plays are performed from fall through spring at the **San Pedro Playhouse;** Trinity University drama department productions are staged at the **Ruth Taylor Theater.**

SHOPPING

Stores are open weekdays 9-5, Thursday evening until 9. Mexican goods, a specialty here, are in the **Mexican Quarter, El Mercado,** near the Governor's Palace, **La Villita,** and at **Paseo del Rio** shops. Also available are imported articles from South America and Western wear, especially fine boots.

SPORTS

The **San Antonio Spurs** professional basketball team is the city's leading athletic organization. With a warm climate and a large number of retired military personnel in residence, San Antonio supports a surprising number of sports facilities, ranging from tennis, golf, and racquetball to swimming, soccer, and polo. Trinity University tennis teams have a wide following. Deer, quail, and wild turkey hunting are good nearby.

WHERE TO GO NEARBY

To the north are **San Marcos-Aquarena Springs** and nearby **Wonder World; Natural Bridge Caverns;** the **LBJ Ranch** and **State Park;** and **New Braunfels,** a delightful German area. To the northwest and west are **Cascade Caverns, Bandera Dude Ranch Country, Alamo Village** at Brackettville, where the John Wayne epic *Alamo* was filmed, and **Castroville,** a French-German town. To the south is **Nuevo Laredo,** Mexico. Good fishing and water sports are available on **McQueeney, Medina, Canyon,** and **Highland Lakes** and the **Guadelupe River.** Nearby is **Inks Lake State Park** (containing **Longhorn,** the world's third-largest cave) and **Kerrville, Gerner,** and **Frio State Parks. Corpus Christi** and **Padre Island** are to the southeast.

BIG BEND NATIONAL PARK

Big Bend National Park is located within the great curve of the Rio Grande in southwestern Texas. This huge park, with 1,103 square miles, is more suggestive of northern Mexico which it borders than the United States. It is an area of dramatic contrasts; mountain ranges abruptly rising above great expanses of desert; winding rivers, defined by flowering desert plants, cutting through steep-walled canyons. The season is year round. Mountain areas are cold in winter and comfortably cool in summer. The desert and Rio Grande Valley can have temperatures around 38°C in summer but they're delightfully comfortable in winter. Humidity is low, and abundant year-round sunshine bathes the cliffs and desert in constantly changing colors.

Chisos Mountains Lodge Motel and cottages at **Chisos Mountain Basin**, elevation 5,400 feet; advance reservations are advisable all year. Good trailer parking at **Rio Grande Village**, elevation 1,800 feet, and **Panther Junction** service stations. Tent camping at the Basin, **Rio Grande Village** and **Cottonwood Campgrounds** is limited to 14 days.

Boquillas Canyon, 34 miles from the Basin on a paved road, is a tremendous gorge, its majestic cliffs turning the color of pure gold in the late afternoon. **Santa Elena Canyon** can also be reached by car and is at its most colorful for an hour or two after sunrise. **Castolon** is a cluster of historic buildings, several of original adobe construction, where Big Bend pioneers lived and where the US Army quartered during the uneasy days of Pancho Villa's raids across the border, 1914-1920; the frontier general store still flourishes. Riding trails lead from the Basin, where horses may be hired to the **South Rim** 7,200 feet high, and **The Window,** a perfect frame for sunset pictures. The **Lost Mine Trail** is only a 5-mile round-trip hike from the Basin. Spectacular flowering plants, such as the huge, creamy-flowered giant dagger yucca, bloom as early as late March. Resident wildlife includes 74 species of mammals and 380 different kinds of birds. Park rangers conduct campfire talks every night except Sunday the year round, on all aspects of the park. Sports are mainly hiking and horseback riding; for fishing in the Rio Grande, no license is required.

FURTHER STATE INFORMATION

Amarillo Board of Convention and Visitor's Activities, 301 South Polk, Suite 112, Amarillo, TX 79101. Hunting and Fishing: **Texas Parks and Wildlife Department,** 4200 Smith School Road, Austin, TX 78744. **Texas State Parks Board,** Austin, TX 78701. **Travel & Information Division,** Texas Department of Highways, PO Box 6054, Austin, TX 78763. **Dallas Chamber of Commerce,** 1507 Pacific Avenue, Dallas, TX 75201. **El Paso Chamber of Commerce,** 5 Civic Center Plaza, El Paso, TX 79901. **Fort Worth Chamber of Commerce,** 700 Throckmorton Street, Fort Worth, TX 76102. **Greater Houston Convention and Visitors' Council,** 1522 Main Street, Houston, TX 77002. **Houston Chamber of Commerce,** Chamber of Commerce Building, Houston, TX 77002. **San Antonio Convention**

and Visitors' **Bureau,** 602 HemisFair Plaza Way, PO Box 2277, San Antonio, TX 78298. Park Information: **Big Bend National Park** (Superintendent), TX 79834. Reservations: **National Park Concessions,** Basin Station, Big Bend National Park, TX 79834. The *Texas Almanac* published by the *Dallas Morning News* is useful. **Pan Am** office, 340 North Belteast, Suite 227, Houston, TX 77002, tel: 447-0088.

Consulates in Dallas: Belgium, Bolivia, Canada, Chile, Costa Rica, Denmark, Dominican Republic, El Salvador, Finland, France, Germany, Guatemala, Honduras, Italy, Korea, Lebanon, Mexico, Monaco, Morocco, Nicaragua, Norway, Panama, Paraguay, Peru, Sweden.

In Houston: Australia, Bahamas, Belgium, Bolivia, Brazil, Canada, Chile, Republic of China, Colombia, Costa Rica, Denmark, Dominican Republic, Ecuador, El Salvador, Finland, France, Germany, Guatemala, Haiti, Honduras, Iceland, India, Ireland, Israel, Italy, Japan, Jordan, Korea, Lebanon, Liberia, Luxembourg, Mexico, Netherlands, Nicaragua, Norway, Panama, Paraguay, Peru, Philippines, Portugal, Saudi Arabia, South Africa, Spain, Sweden, Switzerland, United Kingdom, Venezuela.

In Fort Worth: Costa Rica, Dominican Republic, Guatemala, Mexico, Nicaragua, Peru.

In El Paso: Germany, Mexico, Nicaragua, Panama, Thailand.

In San Antonio: Australia, Costa Rica, El Salvador, Haiti, Honduras, Mexico, South Korea.

USEFUL TELEPHONE NUMBERS
Dallas
County Hospital	638-1800
Legal Aid	742-7650
Legal Clinic	651-9200
	234-4288
Dental Referral	528-6125
Pan Am Reservations	821-3030

Fort Worth
County Hospital	921-3431
Legal Aid/Referral	334-1435
Dental Referral	336-3693
Pan Am Reservations	336-4441

Houston
Ben Taub Triage Treatment	791-7000
Hermann Hospital Life Flight	797-4357 & 797-4014
Ambulance	222-3434
Legal Aid	342-9201
Dental Referral	790-9690
Pan Am Reservations	447-0088

San Antonio
Alamo Doctor's Exchange	349-4411
Ambulance	696-8440

Santa Rosa Medical Center	228-2251
Legal Aid	227-0111
Alama Dental Exchange	349-5411
Pan Am Reservations	227-8196

El Paso

El Paso Medical Exchange	544-7750
Physician/Surgical Exchange	532-2476
Legal Aid	778-6431
Pan Am Reservations	533-1666

Utah

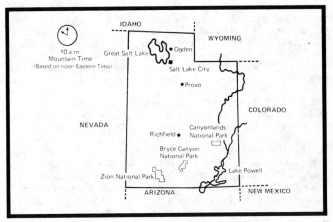

Area	84,916 square miles	Population	1,310,600
Capital	Salt Lake City	Sales Tax	5%

Weather	Jan	Feb	Mar	Apr	May	Jun	Jul	Aug	Sep	Oct	Nov	Dec
Av Temp (°C)	−3	0	5	10	15	20	25	24	18	11	3	−1
Days Rain/Snow	10	9	9	9	8	6	4	6	5	6	7	9

The history of Utah in the last century is inextricably bound up with the progress of the Mormons. Forced out of New York, Missouri, and Illinois, the Mormons trekked west in search of a place where they could settle peacefully and unmolested. They came across a mountain canyon above **Great Salt Lake Valley** where their leader, Brigham Young, declared: "This is the place." The Bible had promised that "the desert shall blossom as the rose," but it was the indomitable courage of the Mormons that transformed Utah's formidably arid land. They plowed, planted, and irrigated, established a theocratic government, and in 1847 called their community the city of the Great Salt Lake. Today, 60% of the state's population is Mormon.

Visitors come from all over the world to see Utah's strange geological formations, and the state has some of the best recreational facilities in the US. Winter sports thrive mid-November until May at high altitudes.

BRIDGERLAND, named for the famous frontiersman Jim Bridger, is in the northeastern corner, bounded by Idaho on the north and Wyoming on the east. **Logan** is the hub city for this area. There are guided tours of the **Mormon Tabernacle** (1878), but only the grounds of the **Temple** (1884) are open to non-Mormons. **Utah State University** maintains an art gallery and the **Man and His Bread Museum,** a display of agricultural equipment from 1750 to the present. Northeast of town are **Cache National Forest** and **Logan Canyon, Sweetwater,** a new resort on Bear Lake, and the **Beaver Mountain Ski Area.** Full facilities for boating, fishing, scuba diving, and water-skiing are available at **Bear Lake State Park.** Glacial lakes offer fishing and water sports; the hunting for deer, elk, and upland game birds has earned much praise. The **Hardware Ranch Elk Preserve** is a winter refuge for elk, from December into early March; winter visitors are allowed to accompany rangers on horse-drawn sleighs as they feed the elk. The **Visitor Center** is open all year 10am - 6pm.

GOLDEN SPIKE EMPIRE is the name of the adjoining area that is bounded on the north by Idaho and on the west by Nevada. The major city here is **Ogden,** only 30 miles north of Salt Lake City. A handsome commercial and industrial city, this was the home of John M. Browning, probably the world's greatest inventor of firearms. See the remarkable collection of weapons in the **John M. Browning Armory,** along with the **Firearms Museum** and the **National Railroad Hall of Fame** at the newly renovated Union Station. Visit also the **Pioneer Relic Hall** and the **Miles Goodyear Cabin,** built in 1846; open 10 June to 10 September, Monday to Friday, free. Ogden stages a good rodeo during **Pioneer Days** held the week of 24 July, and is host to the **Golden Spike National Livestock Show** in November. About 30 miles north of Ogden is **Brigham City,** an exceptionally neat and clean town even for immaculate Utah. The **Box Elder Tabernacle** and the **Intermountain School** for Indians are major attractions; visit the school's **Arts and Crafts Shop.** At Tremonton, north of town, the **Golden Spike Rodeo** is held annually in late August. The **Bear River Migratory Bird Refuge,** the largest migratory bird refuge in North America, is 15 miles from town. And, 30 miles west, is **Promontory,** now the **Golden Spike National Historic Site,** where a monument marks the spot where America's first transcontinental railroad was completed with the driving of a gold spike on 10 May 1869. The historic event is recreated several times a day during the summer months by a group of professional actors. Visitor center and museum open daily 8am-4:30pm (8-6 weekends April through October).

Beyond **Great Salt Lake** is the **Great Salt Lake Desert,** left when the enormous Lake Bonneville dried up. The **Bonneville Salt Flats,** famous as the site of several motor car land-speed records, is just north of I-80, which follows the trail of the ill-fated Donner Party, the pioneers who crossed Utah and Nevada heading for California and were driven to cannibalism before rescue in the Sierra Nevada. Ten miles west of the **Bonneville Salt Flats,** where the world's fastest cars compete during the fourth week in August, is **Wendover,** straddling the Nevada Border. **Best Western Wendover Motel** (665-2211, S/D$28-41) and **Stateline Hotel**

& Casino (668-2221, S/D$23-25) provide accommodations. In the northwestern corner of the state is **Sawtooth National Forest.**

Interstate 15 and US 91 lead south into **PANORAMALAND** towards the Arizona border, skirting mountain and desert country to the west and passing through Fillmore, where the **Territorial Statehouse Museum,** in the building that was Utah's capitol until 1856, has a remarkable display of pioneer relics; open spring to fall. Southeast of Fillmore, **Capitol Reef National Park,** an area of spectacular red-rock sandstone formations, contains huge arches, petrified forests, and the artifacts of pre-Columbian Indians of the Fremont Culture. **Fishlake National Forest,** with deer herds and other wildlife, and rainbow and mackinaw trout in **Fish Lake,** fills in much of the area between I-15/US 91 and the nearly parallel I-70/US 89. **Big Rock Candy Mountain,** of folk song fame, also lies between the two highways.

Cedar City, down in the southwest **COLOR COUNTRY,** is on an elevation of 5,800 feet and is in the middle of one of the most colorful regions on earth. Just east of town is **Brian Head Ski Area,** where there is almost sure to be light, dry powder snow on 10,000-feet-high slopes from December through April. And just beyond is **Cedar Breaks National Monument,** a vividly colored rock amphitheater situated 10,700 feet high in the **Dixie National Forest. St George,** elevation 2,770 feet, down in the hot, dry southwestern corner, has a real southern climate where you can play golf all winter. Between St George and Cedar City is 230-square-mile **Zion National Park,** with some of the deepest and narrowest canyons and strangest rock formations imaginable. **Panguitch,** on US 89, stands at an elevation of 6,666 feet. It is a small town, but there is a good choice of motels because this is the nearest town to **Bryce Canyon National Park. Kanab,** at 4,900 feet, is on the Arizona border but it's almost an annex of Hollywood, on the strength of the many movies that are filmed here. Bryce Canyon, **Zion,** and **Grand Canyon National Parks** are all only 1½ hours away by car. Other nearby attractions include the **Coral Pink Sand Dunes State Park, Old Paria Ghost Town, Vermilion Cliffs,** a petrified forest, and cliff dwellings. Among numerous Kanab motels are **Parry Lodge** (644-2601, S$19.50-24/D$22-30); **Four Seasons Motor Inn** (S$22-26/D$22-30); and **Best Western Red Hills Motel** (644-2675, S$28-30/D$30-34). Some rates are lower offseason.

To drive from Kanab to **CANYONLANDS** country in southeastern Utah, continue on US 89 which detours into Arizona because the Glen Canyon Dam, in Arizona, backs up the Colorado River to form superb **Lake Powell** on the Utah side. There is a vast **Navajo Indian Reservation** here which stretches all across the southeastern corner of Utah. **Rainbow Bridge National Monument** is the world's largest, most perfectly formed natural rock bridge; accessible by horseback from Navajo Mountain Trading Post, or by boat from Lake Powell. **Monument Valley,** which US 163 passes through, is an eerie expanse of free-standing monolithic rocks that are as much as 1,000 feet high. At **Mexican Hat** you can arrange for guided tours to the **Valley of the Gods, Goosenecks State Park,** and other wild regions.

Lake Powell and **Glen Canyon National Recreation Area** can be reached from Mexican Hat and Blanding. **Wahweap** is the most well developed marina on Lake Powell, but there are charter boats at all major marinas, and the area is open year round. The **Hovenweep National Monument** is northeast of town and consists of six groups of Pueblo ruins erected by Anasazi Indians in about 900 to 1276 AD. The little town of **Blanding,** elevation 6,105 feet, has excellent hunting, mainly for deer. It is a convenient take-off point for **Natural Bridges National Monument,** which contains three extraordinary rock bridges and some ancient Indian dwellings.

Monticello, the next town on US 163, is at an elevation of 7,050 feet. Guides, jeeps, and charter planes are all available here to help you see the countryside. **Moab,** elevation 4,000 feet, is the principal town for the Canyonlands area. Places to stay in Moab include the **Apache** (259-5727, S$18/D$23-25), **Best Western Green Well** (259-6151, S$22-32/D$24-32); **Friendship Inn** (259-6147, S$20-30/D$22-32); **Ramada Desert Inn Lodge** (259-7141, S$24-45/D$32-49), and **TraveLodge** (259-6171, S$35-46/D$46-56); most rates are lower in winter. Local gems, minerals, and uranium are displayed in the **Moab Museum.** Just south of town is the **Land of the Magic Lamp,** open May to September, where the exotic Arabian Nights atmosphere seems curiously normal in this setting.

Arches National Park begins only 5 miles northwest of Monticello. It has the world's largest concentrations of natural stone arches, even more stunning when seen snow-covered in winter. Beyond this park, if you have a jeep, a highly detailed map, and some luck, you may come upon the remarkable **Gemini Bridges,** a freak of nature which was discovered by a uranium prospector in 1957. **Dead Horse Point State Park,** on an overlook 2,000 ft above the Colorado River, is also near Moab. Jeep safaris or boat and raft tours down the Colorado River are available in summer (advance reservations are advised) and sightseeing planes can be taken year round. All are available from Moab.

CASTLE COUNTRY, northwest of Moab, is almost overwhelming with its immense sandstone palaces, towers, and citadels rising out of the silent landscape. **Price,** elevation 5,500 feet, is headquarters for this area of coal mines, hunting, fishing, and rock collecting, as well as sightseeing. The **Nine-Mile Canyon,** north of Price, is decorated with petroglyphs, Indian relics, and abandoned log cabins. The **Cleveland-Lloyd Dinosaur Quarry,** south of Price, is the site where dinosaur fossils were unearthed. The **Manti-La Sal National Forest,** southwest of Price, has camping areas, fishing and hunting, Indian cliff dwellings, and strange geological formations, as well as a grove of giant aspen trees. Accommodations in Price include the attractive **Best Western Green Well Motel** (637-3520, S$24-28/D$26-32); rates are lower in winter.

Vernal is the hub of **DINOSAURLAND** in northeastern Utah. It has

Five miles south of Moab, Utah, Arches National Park offers the world's largest concentration of natural stone arches.

a population of about 7,200 and lies at an elevation of 5,248 feet. There's an **Appaloosa Horse Show** and **Race Meet** here in mid-June, **Dinosaurland Art Festival** from mid-June into July, **Dinosaur Roundup Rodeo** in mid-July, and **Pioneer Day Celebration** on 24 July. Northeast of town is **Dinosaur National Monument,** which contains some of the world's most impressive fossils of dinosaurs, crocodiles, turtles, and tropical plants. Raft and canoe trips down the **Green River** are available from early June to early September. **Ashley National Forest,** stretching for miles north of Vernal, is a major recreation area. Here are the **Uinta Mountains,** the only range in the US that runs east-west, a vast primitive area covering 244,000 acres, and the spectacular **Flaming Gorge National Recreation Area.** Excellent motels in Vernal include the **Antlers** and Best Western's **Lamplighter Motel** with summer rates averaging S$18.50-32.50/D$28.50-42.50.

Alta is the most familiar name in the **MOUNTAINLANDS** sector. This famous ski resort is only about a 40-minute drive from Salt Lake City's airport on UT 210. The skiing season begins in mid-November and lasts late into the spring. Every facility is available here—chair lifts, tows, ski school, ski rentals, and handsome lodges. **Alta Ski Lodge** (742-3500, S/D$38-52) is at the head of **Little Cottonwood Canyon; Alta Peruvian Lodge** (742-3000, S$34-38/D$42-54), open 20 November to 30 April, and **Rustler Lodge** (742-2200, S$37-55/D$48-66) are good. Rates given are for peak winter season and do not include a 15% service charge. The dazzling **Snowbird Lodges** (742-2000, S/D$66-75) also have a wide choice of accommodations and "package plans." Their aerial tramway cabins can carry 120 persons at a time to the top of **Hidden Peak,** 11,000 feet, in only 6 minutes.

Park City is a little farther north, and is geared for both winter skiing and summer vacationing; it has an 18-hole golf course and riding stable. The resort-community has a 2½-mile-long ride, nine double chair lifts, and two triple chairs along 65 runs. The gondola operates in summer, too, when you can also ride a real mine train deep into **Treasure Mountain** to see a mining museum. High season rates, about mid-November to mid-April, for Park City accommodations: **Château Après Lodge** (649-9372, S/D$29); **Silver King Lodge** (649-8200, S$25/D$30); **Treasure Mountain Inn** (649-8200, S/D$50-150); **Prospector Square Hotel** (649-7100, S$45-50/D$51-56); and **Park City Racquet Club Village** (642-8200, S$50-80/D$85-165).

Provo is one of the west's largest steel centers. Consult the Provo Chamber of Commerce for industrial tours. The **Pioneer Museum** and the several museums at **Brigham Young University** are worth inspecting. Recreation areas abound nearby at **Utah Lake State Park, Deer Creek Reservoir, Sundance Ski Area, Timpanogos Cave National Monument,** open Memorial Day to Labor Day; and **Bridal Veil Falls,** open mid-May to mid-October. Accommodations in Provo include: **Rodeway Inn** (374-2500, S$25-27/D$29-32); **Village Inn Motel** (375-8600, S$21/D$24.50-26.50), and **The Royal Inn** (373-0800, S$20-25/D$24-37) at Brigham Young University.

City To Visit

SALT LAKE CITY

Salt Lake City, the capital of Utah, is in the north central part of the state, about 15 miles from **Great Salt Lake**, the largest body of water west of the Mississippi: 80 miles long and 35 miles wide.

The city, known at first as Great Salt Lake City, was founded in 1847 by the Mormon leader Brigham Young and his followers and was the capital of the Mormon settlement called the State of Deseret after a Book of Mormon word meaning "honey bee" and understood to by synonymous with industry. The Territory of Utah superseded the State of Deseret in 1851, with Brigham Young as its first governor, and in 1896, when Utah was admitted to the Union, the city became the state capital.

The physical beauty of the city with its attractive trees and gardens is in sharp contrast to the barrenness of the surrounding area. The **Wasatch Mountains**, towering to more than 12,000 feet, form a spectacular background for the city, particularly at their highest point to the southeast. Salt Lake City is laid out in large square blocks with very broad main streets.

WHAT TO SEE

The **State Capitol; Salt Lake Temple** and **Temple Square; Temple grounds** and **Bureau of Information** exhibits, open, with guide service, from 7am to 8pm; the **Tabernacle** and its famous organ; **Lion** and **Beehive Houses; Eagle Gate**. The star programs at the **Hansen Planetarium** are also worth a visit. If time permits, drive through several of the canyons surrounding the city. A trip to the **Great Salt Lake** is particularly worthwhile if made during the warm weather when you can swim. An excursion to **Bingham Canyon** and the world's largest open-pit copper mine is interesting. If you like Western-style scenery, ride out to **Big Cottonwood Canyon**. The Gray Line (bus and limousine) offers several conducted tours of the city and surrounding countryside; a typical 2½-hour tour costs $3.50. Principal parks are **Liberty, Pioneer, Fairmont, Jordan**, with International Peace Gardens, **Riverside, Memory Grove Parks**, and the **Hogle Zoo**.

ACCOMMODATIONS

Good hotels located downtown are **International Dunes Hotel** (521-9500, S$30/D$34-36) and **Hotel Utah** (531-1000, S$23-60/D$38-52). Luxurious motels (all with swimming pools and all either downtown or within 15 blocks of the center) include **Deseret Inn, Holiday Inn Downtown, Howard Johnson's Motor Lodge, Imperial 400, Little America, Ramada Inn, Rodeway Inn, Royal Executive Inn, World Motor Hotel** and **TraveLodge** (four locations); average rates S$24-28/D$30-36). The **Salt Lake Hilton** (532-3344, S$38 up/D$55 up) is also located downtown. The **Holiday Inn Airport** (533-9000, S$35-41/D$42-48) is 2 miles west of downtown. Hotel Tax: 5-6%. Campsites are east of the city in **Mill Creek Canyon**, and in **Big** and **Little Cottonwood Canyons**. Accommodations specializing in skiing (most open only in winter), all within 28 miles southeast of Salt Lake City, include **Mount Majestic Manor** (364-3382, S$21/D$30) at Brighton Bowl, **Silver King Lodge** and **Treasure Mountain Inn** at Park City, and **Alta Ski Lodge** and **Rustler Lodge** at Alta.

RESTAURANTS

Utah's mountain trout are a great delicacy. Most of the local restaurants are moderate in price; these include the **Balsam Embers** and the Hotel Utah **Sky Room.** Other good restaurants are **Andy's Smorgasbord,** the **Print Shop, Royces,** and **Beefeaters** for steak; **Finn's,** Scandinavian dishes; **Tampico,** Mexican food; **Mikado,** Japanese; the **Paprika** for German cooking; and **The Hungarian Restaurant** for Hungarian food. **Ristorante Della Fontana** features Italian food; try the **Athenian** for a Greek meal. Hawaiian specialties are served at the **Polynesian** and **Hawaiian; La Fleur De Lys** is well known for its French cuisine.

ARTS AND MUSIC

State Capitol exhibits, with guide service; **Pioneer Memorial Theatre** and the **Utah Museum of Fine Arts** at the University of Utah; **Salt Lake City Art Center,** frequently changed exhibits of all art forms. Recitals on the famed **Tabernacle Organ** are given daily noon to 12:30 and at 4 on Sundays. Radio broadcasts of the organ and **Tabernacle Choir** are given on Sundays 9:25-10am year round from the Tabernacle, visitors welcome. Tabernacle Choir rehearsals are on Thursday at 7:30pm. The **Utah Symphony Orchestra,** at Symphony Hall, and the **Utah Repertory Dance Theatre** and **Ballet West,** at the Capitol Theatre, are all acclaimed nationally.

SHOPPING

New shopping complexes are **ZCMI Center,** with more than 50 stores on two levels, and **Crossroads Mall. Arrow Press Square,** facing the Salt Palace, is a charming renovation of old structures into a cluster of shops, restaurants, and theater. **Auerbach's** is a principal department store in the downtown area. Some stores are open Monday and Friday, 10am-9pm. Enclosed shopping malls include the **Cottonwood Mall, Fashion Place Mall,** and **Valley Fair. Trolley Square,** an unusual shopping and entertainment center, incorporates vintage trolley barns, antique cast-iron light fixtures, and remnants from local mansions to preserve the local flavor of the community. An indoor farmer's market, boutiques, several theaters, and gourmet restaurants line the newly created brick streets. There are many souvenir and gift shops in the **Temple Square** district featuring objects of local craftsmanship—dolls, shawls, rugs, moccasins, and jewelry. The **Mormon Handicraft Shop** is particularly interesting.

SPORTS

Professional hockey by the **Golden Eagles** is played at the **Salt Palace,** Salt Lake City's **Convention Center** complex. College football and basketball are played at local universities. Automobile speed trials are held on noted **Bonneville Salt Flats** on the western edge of the Great Salt Lake Desert in August and September. Stock and modified auto races Saturday evenings from May through September at the **Bonneville Raceway,** 8 miles west of Salt Lake City. There are many municipal tennis courts and eight municipal golf courses. Many city parks have swimming pools. Great Salt Lake offers boating and swimming facilities. It is now 27% salt, giving swimmers an unsinkable buoyancy; beaches are 15 miles west of town. Some fishing waters are open year round, others open in general season from early June until late fall; hunting seasons vary. The nearby ski areas offer some of the best powder snow skiing in the country.

CALENDAR OF EVENTS
Utah Winter Carnival, February; **Spring Garden Show,** March; **Days of '47,** pioneer celebration, July; **Utah State Fair,** rodeos, stock-judging contests, various amusements, September. In December, the **Salt Lake Oratorio Society** presents the *Messiah,* and the **Utah Symphony** and **Ballet West** stage the *Nutcracker Suite Ballet.*

WHERE TO GO NEARBY
Bear Lake, on the Utah-Idaho state line, has swimming and boating. **Logan Canyon,** east of Logan, has beautiful scenery, camping grounds. **Mirror Lake,** east of Salt Lake City, has opportunities for horseback trips into the **High Uinta Mountains. Provo River** has a large reservoir; there are accommodations in lodges and cottages. **Lake Powell** and **Flaming Gorge Dam** and **Reservoir** offer camping, fishing, and boating; spectacular canyons accessible by boat.

Principal parks: **Dinosaur National Monument,** near Jensen, 190 miles east; fossil relics of prehistoric animals. **Bryce Canyon,** 275 miles south; weird, colorful formations of eroded limestone. **Canyonlands National Park,** one of the newest national parks, features a quarter of a million acres of canyon country; guided tours available. **Zion National Park,** 335 miles southwest, startling canyons, impressive scenery. **Arches National Park,** 232 miles southeast, unusual natural stone arches. Near the Arizona border, due south of Salt Lake City, is **Coral Dunes,** an undeveloped area of constantly shifting sands where you might expect to see a camel caravan.

BRYCE CANYON NATIONAL PARK
Along the 20-mile rim of the **Paunsaugunt Plateau** in this beautiful park are 12 deep amphitheaters, where the elements have shaped what Paiute Indians called "red rocks standing like men in a bowl-shaped canyon." But they are more than red, being every hue from white and pink to lavender, yellow, orange, and brown. And their weird formations also conjure up visions of animals, castles, temples, and a whole wonderland of towering stone sculptures rising from the tough desert vegetation at lower elevations to vivid green pines and firs in the mountains. **Queen's Garden** is an easy trail to follow for a close-up of rocks called Queen

Victoria, Queen's Castle, and Gulliver's Castle. **Navajo Loop,** descending 521 feet, and **Tower Bridge,** 750 feet, are both strenuous on foot; Tower Bridge can be explored on horses accustomed to the steplike switchbacks and shadowy tunnels. Seen from a car traveling along the ridge, the strange rocks seem to glow with light from within, but only tours down into the canyons can truly impart their majesty.

The park is open all year. Bryce is at an elevation of 8,000-9,000 feet, so the weather from November through March is cold and snowy but often sunny. Accommodations include **Bryce Canyon Lodge** (586-7686, S$25-29/D$27-33), in the park, open mid-May through September; two campgrounds, 14-day-stay limit, open about 1 May to 31 October. Good accommodations; **Pink Cliffs** (834-5355, S$17-24/D$19-26), 3 miles outside the park; and at nearby **Panguitch** and **Hatch.**

CANYONLANDS NATIONAL PARK

Grotesquely wild rocks spring out of the desert in myriad forms and colors in this quarter-of-a-million-acre park. This is an eerie primitive area, parts of which are still unexplored. Ordinary cars can reach most points in the **Island in the Sky** district, but it's better to take a conducted tour by jeep. Chesler and Virginia areas are ringed by **The Needles,** fantastic rock spires as much as 30 stories high. Follow capricious **Elephant Canyon** to towering **Druid Arch.** Deeper south is the remarkable **Angel Arch.** West of The Needles are the great parallel valleys of **The Grabens.** In the northern section are such natural oddities as **Upheaval Dome, Monument Basin,** and **Grandview Point.** Boating tours through the rapids are operated in summer, and the **Cataract Canyon** expedition is probably the wildest ride on the continent.

The best season is summer, but the park is open all year. Elevations range from 3,600 feet at **Cataract Canyon** to nearly 7,000 feet at **Cedar Mesa.** Yearly temperatures range from −29°C to 43°C, but summer nights are always cool. Precipitation is mostly limited to late-summer thunderstorms and winter snows. There are elementary trailer and campsites with limited facilities; bring your own water and firewood; stay limited to 14 days. Nearest motels are at **Moab** and **Monticello.**

ZION NATIONAL PARK

Even if you have already visited nearby Bryce Canyon and Grand Canyon, don't miss Zion National Park. Entering from **Mount Carmel** 24 miles east, the highway is an engineering marvel down the mountains to the mile-long **Zion Tunnel,** which has window openings for views of the colorful **East Temple** and the **Great Arch.** In six switchbacks, the road then drops 800 feet in 4 miles to the **Virgin River Bridge.** It has taken at least 200 million years of climatic changes, earth upheavals, and erosion to form these immense rocks that range in color from rust-red at the bottom to white at the top. Go to the **Visitor Center,** open daily the year round, for information about main points of interest, how they were created, and why pioneering Mormons gave them their fanciful names. Schedules are also posted for nightly summer naturalist programs and for horseback trips and conducted hikes.

From the South Entrance, the drive through **Zion Canyon** is 8 miles of magnificent scenery. The road follows the north fork of the Virgin River enclosed by sheer, varicolored cliffs named **Towers of the Virgin, Altar of Sacrifice, Beehives, Sentinel Peak, Three Patriarchs,** and others, to the massive **Great White Throne.** The road ends at the vast natural amphitheater known as **The Temple of Sinawava.**

Leave your car and follow the easy trail to the **Gateway to the Narrows,** tightly squeezed in between cliffs half a mile high. In this cool, moist retreat the **Hanging Gardens of Zion** are luxuriant with flowers, and wildlife take refuge from the hot sun. **Weeping Rock,** also reached by an easy trail, sheds streams of tears that water plants below. The moonflower and evening primrose are two white summer flowers that open in the evening. Daytime species are vivid shades of scarlet, purple, pink, and yellow. Until very recently, the wild canyon-gashed **Kolob Terrace** highlands in the northwestern section of the park have been inaccessible. Now the 5-mile **Taylor Creek Road,** off UT 15, winds through sheer sided, finger-shaped canyons to **Lee Pass.**

The park is always open; May to September is the peak season. May-to-October temperatures may range from 29-43°C during the day, dropping to 18-21°C at night. Winter temperatures vary widely from a low of −9°C to a high of 18°C. **Zion Lodge** is open from late April-November. There's a 14-day limit from 15 May to 15 September at the **Campground South,** which is open all year, and at **Watchman Campground,** open May to September. There are excellent motels just south of the park near **Springdale,** which are open year round.

FURTHER STATE INFORMATION

Utah Travel Council, Council Hall, Capitol Hill, Salt Lake, Salt Lake City, UT 84114. Hunting and Fishing: **Division of Wildlife Resources,** 1596 West North Temple, Salt Lake City, UT 84116. **Salt Lake Valley Convention and Visitor Bureau,** Salt Palace Suite 200, Salt Lake City, UT 84101. **Trolley Square,** 199 Trolley Square, Salt Lake City, UT 84102. National Parks: **Bryce Canyon National Park** (Superintendent), Bryce Canyon, UT 84717; **Canyonlands National Park** (Superintendent), Moab, UT 84552; **Zion National Park** (Superintendent), Springdale, UT 84767. Park Reservations and Information: **Reservations Department,** Parks Division, PO Box 400, Cedar City, UT 84720; Tel: (801) 586-9476.

  Consulates in Salt Lake City: Finland, Peru, Switzerland.

USEFUL TELEPHONE NUMBERS IN SALT LAKE CITY

Emergency (Fire, Police, Rescue)	911
Lakeview Hospital	292-6231
St. Mark's Hospital	268-7074
Holy Cross Hospital	350-4111
Cottonwood Hospital	262-3461

UTAH

LDS Hospital	350-1100
Drug Referral Center	355-7413
Poison Control Center	581-2151
State Highway Assistance	533-5638
Legal Aid Society	328-8849
Chamber of Commerce	364-3631
Tourist Information	521-2822
Pan Am Reservations	328-1672

Vermont

Area	9,609 square miles	Population	511,000
Capital	Montpelier	Sales Tax	3%

Weather

	Jan	Feb	Mar	Apr	May	Jun	Jul	Aug	Sep	Oct	Nov	Dec
Av Temp (°C)	−9	−8	−3	5	12	18	21	19	18	9	2	−6
Days Rain/Snow	13	12	13	12	13	11	12	12	11	11	14	14

In early spring you can head into the Vermont hills for picnics in the snow, better known as old-fashioned "sugarin'-off" parties. The state's sugar maple trees are tapped, and the sap is boiled into a syrup which is poured on the snow to make a maple sugar delicacy. The excellence of the food is one reason why visitors keep returning to Vermont throughout the year. Cob-smoked ham, bacon and sausage, homemade breads and jellies, apple cider, aged cheddar cheese, pickles and relishes, and the state's famed maple products are the highlights of the celebrated Vermont cuisine.

And for winter sports Vermont rates as the leading ski resort in the northeast, offering the largest number of ski areas and skiing facilities. America's first ski lift opened at **Woodstock,** the first organized ski patrol began at **Stowe,** and the first Alpine lift was installed at **Pico Peak** in Rutland.

Vermont got its name, the "Green Mountain State," from the French words *vert mont.* **Green Mountain National Forest** surrounds 34 towns and covers 241,000 acres, north and south, through the state. In the spring when the snow has gone, you can cover miles of farmland or forests, taking in the clean fresh air. Summers are cool and relaxed, perfect for leisurely country strolls and drives, visiting antique shops and craft fairs or resting in old inns that once served as stagecoach stops.

Eastern Vermont is generally colder than the west; the central mountain regions are coolest of all. Snow often arrives in November in the higher altitudes but the heaviest snowfalls usually begin in December, remaining until March. The average annual snowfall is 90 inches, with the heaviest accumulations in the central and eastern sections. Spring comes earliest in the Champlain Valley and southwestern sections, and in lower portions of the Connecticut River Valley.

In 1774, Ethan Allen and his Green Mountain Boys fought to defend the state's independence. Despite external pressure, it continued to function as a free republic for 14 years, 1777 to 1791, with its own postal service and mint; in 1791 Vermont became the 14th state to enter the Union. Vermont was the first state to guarantee universal manhood suffrage, regardless of property or income, the first to forbid slavery, and the first to guarantee public education to all men and women.

BENNINGTON, one of the two oldest counties in the southern region, was incorporated in 1779. **Windham,** the other county, was incorporated in 1781. The city of Bennington was the Revolutionary War headquarters for Ethan Allen's Green Mountain Boys. **Bennington College** (in North Bennington), long one of the nation's most progressive women's colleges, became coeducational in 1969. Also in North Bennington is the **Park/McCullough House. The Victorian Mansion,** open to visitors from 17 June-18 Oct, contains displays of Victorian dresses, fans, eyeglasses, and mirrors. The stable houses a collection of carriages. Old Bennington has beautiful colonial houses and a common; visit the battle monument nearby. Robert Frost, who owned a farm in the area, is buried in the **Old Burying Ground** at the Old First Church. **The Bennington Museum** has displays of Bennington pottery, America's oldest "Stars and Stripes," and a major collection of Grandma Moses paintings—The museum is open 1 March-30 Nov. Bennington Museum also has one of the rarest collections of American blown and pressed glass. The schoolhouse Grandma Moses attended was moved from neighboring New York and serves as a new museum wing. **The Country Store** is the oldest general store still doing business. It sells local produce—homemade bread and Vermont cheese, penny candy, calico goods, and old-time kitchenware and household items. **The Bennington Pottery and Potters Yard** houses local crafts shops, some in authentic New England buildings. **Bennington Battle Day,** on 16 August, is a Vermont holiday. Other annual events are the **Antique and Classic Car Show,** second Saturday in September, and the **Antique Shows** in early October. **Green Mountain Race Track** in Pownal, on US 7, has a glass-enclosed, heated grandstand for greyhound racing. The local country store in Pownal dates back to the early 1800s.

MANCHESTER has been a popular resort area for over a hundred years; **Bromley Mountain, Snow Valley,** and **Stratton Mountain** are nearby. **Southern Vermont Art Center** offers music, dance and art programs, mid-May through October. **Deeley Gallery** in Manchester is a must for art lovers. Also in Manchester is **Orvis,** one of America's oldest manufacturers of fly fishing rods and outdoor clothing. The **American Museum of Fly Fishing** is located at Orvis's. **Bromley Mountain Ski Area,** 8 miles east, is one of the country's oldest winter resorts and in the summer features a ½-mile long Alpine Slide. Accommodations in Manchester include: **Four Winds** (362-1105, S/D$28-50), open Jan-May; **Toll Road Motor Inn** (362-1711, S/D$34-40) and **Weathervane** (362-2444, D$32-42), both with pool and free beverages in room. Manchester has many large old inns. **The 1811 House** (362-1811, S$12-$15/D$18-25). Prices include continental breakfast. Winter rates are higher but haven't yet been established, elegant rooms equipped with fireplaces; **Wilburton Inn,** a Georgian inn with mountain view, has terrace dining; **Worthy Inn** (262-1792, D$18-36 EP, S$18-28 MAP), closed in May; and **The Inn at Manchester** (362-1793, D$23/29 EP summer; S$20-27 MAP winter). Travelers can find both rooms and fine meals at **Colburn House** (D$20 EP). Other dining spots include **Kandahar Lodge;** French cuisine at **Chantecleer Restaurant,** a renovated dairy barn, and at **Pierre's,** formerly of New York City; continental fare at the **Reluctant Panther** and **Toll Gate Lodge. Stratton Mountain Ski Area** is 12 miles to the east. **Mount Equinox,** to the west, at 3,816 feet, is the highest peak in the Taconic Range. **Equinox Sky Line Drive,** on US 7, is a paved road 5.6 miles to the summit, and the scene of sports car races in late June. The **Sky Line Inn and Restaurant** on top of Mt Equinox offers a panoramic view.

The charming village of **Dorset,** above Manchester, is a favorite haunt of artists and writers. Dorset has two colonial inns: **Barrows House** (867-4455, S$45-55 MAP), established 1770; and **Dorset Inn** (867-5500, S$42-52 MAP), since 1796. The **Village Auberge** (867-5715), a completely renovated old country inn, serves a French cuisine and also has rooms; dinner by reservation only. While you are in Dorset, stock up on wooden housewares made by the J. K. Adams Co in its on-premises factory. East of here the **Stratton Mountain Arts Festival** presents the works of Vermont painters, sculptors, photographers, and other artisans, from the end of September to mid-October; on weekends special programs are offered. The **Dorset Playhouse** is one of the oldest summer theaters in the country.

Between Dorset and Bennington is Arlington, where both Norman Rockwell and Dorothy Canfield Fisher lived. **Arlington Inn** (375-6532, D$18-37) w/continental breakfast on lawn. **Grandmother's House** (375-2328, S$37 MAP), in West Arlington, was once the home of Norman Rockwell. **The Candle Mill** in East Arlington still makes candles in original tin molds. Farther south, the giant **Mount Snow** resort complex is open all year and has summer lifts to the summit, swimming, and tennis tournaments. The annual week-long **Winterfest,** in late January, is one of the highlights of the winter ski season. **Wilmington,** at the crossroads of routes 100 and 9, is surrounded by **Mount Olga** in Molly Stark State Forest, Lake Raponda, and the **Mount Snow, Carinthia, Haystack,** and **Hogback Mountain** ski areas. **The 1836 Country Store** on route 9 sells old-fashioned New England wares. **The Coombs Beaver Brook Sugar**

House has sap-boiling demonstrations and the **Deerfield Valley Farmer's Day** is a late summertime treat. The **Hermitage Restaurant** features an excellent continental menu.

The **Marlboro Music Festival** in Marlboro was founded by pianist Rudolph Serkin two decades ago and continues to attract international performers for its chamber music and chamber orchestra concerts, weekends, early July through mid-August. There are more than 500 specimens of wildlife on display at the local **Luman Nelson Museum of New England Wildlife.** Stay at the **Longwood Inn** (257-7272, S/D$40 up). **Silver Skates Inn Reataurant** features a popular French and American menu. At the **Skyline Restaurant,** on the summit of Hogback Mountain, there is a 100-mile view from the dining room; the restaurant is famous for waffles and griddle cakes with pure Vermont maple syrup.

Brattleboro has become famous through the **Brattleboro Chorus and Orchestra's Spring Festival** and **Autumn Bach Festival. Common Ground** is a good natural foods restaurant in Brattleboro, reasonably priced. The **Brattleboro Museum and Art Center** is located in the Old Railroad Station. The first ski jump in Vermont was built here, and the week-long **Winter Carnival** features a parade, ski jumping, and racing events. Accommodations include **Stonybrook Motel** (254-8153, D$16-27).

The **Experiment in International Living** is in **Putney.** Founded in 1932, The Experiment makes arrangements for about 5,000 students each year to live with families of different cultures. During March and April visitors to **Harlow's Sugar House** in Putney can see maple syrup manufactured. An exhibit and movie about sugaring are shown year round. **Santa's Land,** nearby, features baby animals to pet, a replica of his workshop, miniature Alpine railroad, and picnic area; open daily May to Christmas. **Basketville,** on Main Street (Rt. 5), sells Vermont gift items and locally woven baskets. In **Newfane,** on route 30, is a fascinating flea market every Sunday during the summer. **Steamtown USA,** at Bellows Falls, is the world's largest steam engine museum; passenger train ride, weekends May through October, daily July and August; picnic area and restaurant. **Grafton** is a well-restored colonial village whose charming red brick houses and churches and village green seem untouched by the 20th century. The Grafton Historical Society has published a folder with a map describing nine walking tours. Presidents Ulysses S. Grant and William Howard Taft frequented the local stagecoach tavern, the **Old Tavern Inn** (843-2375), established in 1801; it has been renovated and has a pool and café. **The Hayes House** (843-2461, D$27-31 w/fireplace and continental breakfast); **Woodchuck Hill Farm** (843-2398, S$25/D$30 with breakfast), open May-Nov.

To the west **Magic Mountain Ski Area** is 3 miles east of **Londonderry. Stratton Mountain Inn** (297-2500, S$52-62 MAP), closed spring and fall, has a heated pool, sauna, tennis, and golf. **Putney General Store** was originally a grist mill, built in 1790; it reopened as a general store in 1843 and has been in continuous operation since, specializing in local products.

The state's famous marble region is in **RUTLAND COUNTY;** New

Stopping to search for a special "find" in one of the many antique shops in Vermont is a popular pastime whatever the season.

York City's public library and the Supreme Court Building in Washington, DC, are built with Vermont marble. Canoeists can paddle along **Otter Creek,** the state's longest river. To the south, on route 30, are the Revolutionary War **Hubbardton Battlefield** and **Monument** in nearby East Hubbardton. **Colonial Day** in Castleton is a local mid-summer tradition. **Rutland** has been called "Marble City" because of the city's quarrying and finishing industries. There's a marble exhibit in neaby **Proctor,** displaying more than 100 varieties of stone. **Chaffee Art Center** here exhibits works by state artists. **Mid-Vermont Artists Outdoor Show** is held during the **Rutland State Fair;** New England's largest agricultural fair, it runs for a week, the end of August through Labor Day. **Wilson Castle,** a 32-room mansion set on 115 acres in Proctor, has some fine European and Oriental furnishings. Rutland is also the headquarters for the **Green Mountain National Forest. La Cortina Motor Inn** (773-3331, S\$35-37 MAP) has a heated indoor pool; **Mountain Top Inn** (483-2311, S\$30-52MAP), set on 600 acres, on a lake, has a spectacular view of Green Mountain National Forest; the **Summit Lodge** (422-3535, rates on request), a heated pool, restaurant. **Royal's Hearthside Restaurant** (775-0856) serves New England dishes in Early American dining rooms. **Vermont Inn** (D\$22-30 summer, S\$24-34 winter), in an old farm house in Mendon, is known for its lobster and seafood platters. Ten miles east of Rutland, Sherburne is the home of the **Killington** and **Pico Peak** ski areas. Visitors can take Killington's 3½-mile gondola lifts to **Killington Peak,** Vermont's second highest mountain. The observation decks of the new Killington Peak restaurant afford a 200-mile panorama. The **Long Trail** extends some 250 miles, from the Massachusetts line to Canada; for 80 miles this state-long hiking route winds through **Green Mountain National Forest.** A Long Trail guidebook, with maps and distances, available from Green Mountain Club, Box 94, Rutland 05701. **Brandon,** at the western edge of the Green Mountains, is a quiet resort and residential town. Skiing is at **High Mountain;** boating, sailing, and fishing at **Lake Dunmore;** and on the eastern shore of the lake **Branbury State Park** has swimming along a sand beach. **Brandon Inn** (247-5766, D\$43-52 MAP summer, S\$35-45 MAP winter) was built in 1789, and its restaurant is popular with local gourmets.

In the Connecticut River Valley due south, **Orange** and **Windsor Counties** are well known to horse fanciers for their breeding farms, riding stables and trails. **Woodstock,** near the base of the Green Mountains, hosts **Suicide Six** and **Mount Tom** ski areas. Each February there is a citizen ski-touring race. A residential and resort community, Woodstock has earned a reputation as one of New England's most attractive villages. When the steel bridge crossing the **Ottauquechee River** on Union Street wore out in 1968, it was decided to replace it with a covered wooden bridge; all power and telephone lines throughout the city have been kept underground. Classic 18th- and 19th-century townhouses surround the village greens. Four of the local churches have bells cast by Paul Revere. The Historical Society has nine period rooms in **Dana House,** built in 1807. Accommodations are available at the **Woodstock Inn** (457-

1100, S$44-56 MAP); **Cambria House** (457-3077, S/D$12-18); and **Shire Motel** (457-2211, S/D$26-40).

Calvin Coolidge, the 30th US President, was born, raised, and sworn into office in **Plymouth** in 1923. The **Coolidge Homestead**, the century-old Wilder House, is a museum, kept as it was when Coolidge became president; the Wilder Barn is now the **Vermont Agricultural Museum**. **Round Top Mountain Ski Area** is nearby. There are beaches and boat ramps on **Amherst Lake, Lake Echo**, and **Lake Rescue**. Rising in the west, **Okemo Mountain Ski Area** has a paved road to the summit. It's the scene of an **Antiques Fair** in the fall. The century-old **Crowley Cheese Factory** in nearby Wallingford still makes cheese by hand; the best time to visit is between 10:30 and 1 pm. Farther south on route 100, an ancient gristmill, two country stores, and charming old houses surround the small common in **Weston**. **The Inn** at Weston (824-5804, S/D$34-39) and **Friendly Acres Motel** (824-5851, S$20/D$29 up), country breakfast included, are places to stay. Vermont craftsmen, in a restored 1791 mill, have weekend demonstrations and local crafts for sale. The **Farrar Mansur House,** a restored tavern built in 1797 on the north side of the common, was once the political and social center of the town. The authentic 1890 **Vermont Country Store,** south of the village green, is an original Vermont store and sells typical items of that period, from rock candy to calico. The **Weston Playhouse**, on the village green, is open July through Labor Day. Just outside of town on Route 155 the **Weston Priory** is an inspiring place to visit because of its architectural beauty.

Route 11 leads east to **Springfield,** center of the nation's precision tool industry. **Hartness House** (885-2115, S$12-24/D$18-28), a former governor's mansion, is now an attractive inn on 30 garden-covered acres; it has a heated pool, and its restaurent's Saturday buffet is a local treat. The **Paddock Restaurant,** in a converted barn, is also popular. **Penelope's,** an attractive restaurant downtown, is also popular.

To the northeast, **Windsor** was the political center of the Connecticut Valley and is the site of Old Constitution House, the former tavern where the state constitution was signed in 1777. Skiing at **Mount Ascutney;** picnicking at the state parks. The **Joseph Smith Birthplace Memorial** is off VT 14, between Royalton and Sharon; picnicking and camping on the grounds. North of White River Junction, on route 5, is **Norwich,** the original home of Norwich University. The **Norwich Inn** (649-1143, S$27-29/D$37-39) was established in 1797; the restaurant, with year-round terrace dining, specializes in maple sugarcured ham, bacon, and sausage.

Nearby **Fairlee** was the home of Samuel Morey, inventor of the steamboat; the **Vermont State Golf Championships** are held there each June. **Bonnie Oaks** resort (333-4302, S/D$25-55; S$30-50 MAP), on Lake Morey, has heated pool, golf, tennis, riding, fishing, and boating. **Lake Morey Inn & Club** (333-4311, S/D$38; S$44 MAP), a 350-acre estate established in 1900, has heated pool, golf, tennis, riding, fishing, and boating. Special golf and tennis package plans available. **Rutledge Inn & Cottages** (333-9722, S$26-34 AP), on Lake Morey, has a restaurant that specializes in homemade desserts. Farther north, in Bradford, the **Connecticut Valley Fair** is held in midsummer. Westward, the century-old **Tunbridge World's Fair** is held in mid-September, with horse races, pony and ox pulls, craft demonstrations, and auto shows. In Tunbridge, **Whitetail Corners Guest House** (889-5565, adults $18; children 12 and under, $12). The only floating bridge in the east is located near **Brookfield**, between routes 14 and 12. The **Green Trails** riding resort is well known. Enjoy ice fishing, skating, and cross-country skiing near the Country Store.

Beautiful lake and mountain scenery surrounds the four counties of the **CHAMPLAIN VALLEY**. Green Mountain National Forest, 241,000 acres, is in **Addison County** in the northeast. Near **Ripton** is the **Bread Loaf Campus** of Middlebury College, noted for its **School of English** in July, and its famous **Writers Conference** in August, started by Robert Frost in 1921. Frost spent the last years of his life here and Route 125 is the **Robert Frost Memorial Highway**. Visitors can see the four highest peaks in the state from Bread Loaf Mountain—**Mount Mansfield, Mount Ellen, Lincoln Mountain, and Camels Hump. Middlebury College Snow Bowl** sponsors an annual inter-collegiate carnival during the last week in February. Going west on route 125, you'll reach **Middlebury**, a summer and winter resort and the home of the main campus of **Middlebury College**, founded in 1800. The **Sheldon Museum**, regarded as one of the finest small museums in the country, is a restored early 19th-century home with authentic furnishings and tools on exhibit; open 1 June-15 Oct except on Sundays. Visitors are welcome to the **Morgan Horse Farm**, in Weybridge, off route 7. Now a research center of the University of Vermont, the state's famous Morgan horses are still bred here and the cattle and sheep farm is on view. **Mary's Restaurant** in Bristol north of Middlebury is excellent. Menu includes crepes and chocolate cheesecake. **Vermont State Craft Center** at Frog Hollow is in Middlebury. Stay at **The Middlebury Inn & Motel** (388-4961, S$22-40/D$32-50). For dining, try **Mr Up's**, the **Sugarhouse Restaurant, Fire & Ice, Rose Bud Café**, and **Bakery Lane Soup Bowl** (specializes in homemade soups, salads, quiches, breads, and desserts), all in Middlebury. One of the state's oldest inns, the **Waybury Inn** (388-4015, D$19-20), established in 1810 as a stagecoach stop, is in **East Middlebury**; its old colonial restaurant has porch dining during the summer. The **Dog Team Tavern**, on the banks of the New Haven River in the town, features a New England menu on a blackboard and serves Vermont dishes family-style. **Vergennes** is the center of one of the state's dairying areas and claims to be the smallest incorporated city in the country—one square mile. Settled in 1766, it's the third-oldest city in New England. **Button Bay State Park** offers superb views of the **Adirondack Mountains;** camping, fishing, and boating. The luxurious 700-acre **Basin Harbor Club** (475-2311, rates on request) has its own airstrip, golf course, inn, and cottages on Lake Champlain; heated pool, family programs, all sports, and entertainment; the café has a wide porch overlooking the lake. Excellent dining at **Paintur's Tavern** in downtown Vergennes.

Shelburne, in Chittenden County, is best known for the **Shelburne**

Museum, a unique 100-acre outdoor museum depicting early New England life in 35 buildings. The museum is open year round. Many of the structures have been restored to their original state, including six 18th- and 19th-century furnished houses, a railroad depot, covered bridge, country store, blacksmith shop, and the old Lake Champlain steamer S.S. *Ticonderoga.* The **Electra Havemeyer Webb Memorial Building,** and 1830 Greek revival structure with European paintings and furnishings, and the **Webb Gallery of American Art** are also located on the site. You may want to spend a day or two at the museum grounds. A short walk from the museum is the **Shelburne Inn and Motel** (985-3305, S$30.95 MAP); price includes a ticket to the museum, gratuity, and tax; open 15 May-15 Sept. The weekend dining room specialty is lobster. **Harbor Hideaway,** featuring shishkebab, and the **Sirloin Saloon** are also popular. **Café Shelburne,** excellent French cuisine. Try the sailing and iceboating on **Shelburne Bay.** Fischers Landing, in Charlotte, has rental and charter boats and the Champlain Ferry makes a scenic crossing from Charlotte to Essex, New York, in 18 minutes daily, April through late December. **Camel's Hump State Forest,** in Huntington, extends to 12,840 acres, including the famous Camel's Hump, 4,083 feet high. Across the river is the **Vermont Audubon Society Nature Center.**

BURLINGTON, Vermont's largest city, is located on Lake Champlain. **The Scenic Line Ferry** leaves the King Street Dock for 2-hour round trips daily across Lake Champlain to Port Kent, New York, May through early November. The **University of Vermont** was founded here in 1791. Today over 10,000 students attend its campus on the eastern edge of town. North of the city, **Ethan Allen Park,** on part of the original Allen farm, offers picnicking and a marvelous view of the Adirondacks and Lake Champlain to the west and the Green Mountains to the east. **Bolton Valley Ski Area** is nearby. The **Champlain Shakespeare Festival,** in the new **Royal Tyler Theater,** is held every summer. The University of Vermont is also the site of the annual **Vermont Mozart Festival.** The **Champlain Valley Exposition,** at the Fairgrounds in Essex Junction, includes a country fair, the last week in August. And each November the **Vermont Handcrafters Association** holds a 3-day bazaar. Accommodations in the Lake Champlain area include: **Bolton Valley Ski/Summer Resort** (434-2131, S/D$44 summer, S/D$48 winter), set on 8,000 acres, with heated pool, tennis, and skiing. The resort restaurant's specialty is prime ribs. Other area motels are **Colonial, Grand View, Handy's Town House, Holiday Inn, Howard Johnson's, Ramada Inn, Redwood Master Hosts Inn,** and **Sheraton Motor Inn.** The **Black Bear Lodge** (434-2126, S/D$36 summer, S/D$46 winter), rustic, with a heated pool and family rates. The **Crimson Hearth** at the Holiday Inn, and the **Rathskeller,** a converted wool mill with blackboard menu, are favorite local dining spots. In Burlington **Econo Lodge** (800-446-6900, S$20/D$25), **Radisson** (S$35-45/D$45-55), and **Sheraton Burlington Inn** (800-325-3535, S/D$39-47 summer, S/D$30-39 winter). Burlington restaurants include **Ben and Jerry's** (features all-natural ice cream and salads, crepes, soups, and fresh squeezed lemonade and orange juice). **Hunt's,** best spot for music (bluegrass and jazz); good moderately priced, elegant surroundings. **The Ice House** overlooks Lake Champlain, seafood specialty; **Stuft Shirt**, for moderately priced seafood and excellent Sunday brunch; and French cuisine at **Déjà Vu.**

The old stone **South Hero Inn**, in **South Hero**, once frequented by Ethan Allen, is still in business. The **Hyde Log Cabin**, on Route 2, built in 1783 and considered the oldest log cabin in the US, is still standing in its original condition. Camping, swimming, fishing, and boating are available in **Grand Isle State Park**. The **Grand Isle-Cumberland Head Ferry** on the western shore of Grand Isle, makes a 12-minute trip across Lake Champlain to Plattsburgh, New York, year round now. There are many antique shops and country stores worth visiting. Though the mineral springs are no longer popular in **Highgate Springs** in the northwestern corner of the state, tourists still flock to the area for picnicking and hiking, fishing, swimming, and boating. The **Tyler Place** on Lake Champlain (868-3301, S/D$78 up), the largest summer vacation resort in the area, has 27 cottages surrounding the old stagecoach inn; heated pool, children's programs, all sports, entertainment, terrace overlooking the waterfront, and café; open June through Labor Day; lower rates spring and fall.

Montgomery is the center for the **Jay Peak Ski Area,** the state's northernmost all-year resort. There are many motels, inns, lodges, and mountain chalets along route 242 at the foot of **Jay Peak State Forest,** heading toward the ski area. The Jay Peak aerial tramway also operates daily, July through Labor Day. The excellent **On the Rocks Restaurant,** on the Hazens Notch Mountain Pass, offers leisurely dining and splendid views of the mountains; reservations required. **Enosburg Falls,** at the crossroads of routes 108 and 105, is the site of Vermont's big **Dairy Festival** the first weekend in June. Farm exhibits, parades, and contests are all part of the annual festivities.

St Albans is the center of the state's maple syrup and dairy industries, **North Hero House** (372-8237, $20-52), open mid-June to Labor Day, has additional lakeside accommodations, and private tennis court and sauna. The **Vermont Maple Festival** takes place during 3 days in early April. Local maple producers conduct tours and sponsor sugarhouse parties with sugar-on-snow, fresh raised doughnuts, and sour pickles for local and visiting gourmets. There are also Old Time Fiddlers Concerts, country dances, craft and art shows, and country suppers. Passenger ferry service from Burton Island State Park to St Albans State Park. There's a huge mid-October chicken pie dinner given in **Georgia,** west of route 7, to help maintain the local church, which was built in 1800.

Five of Vermont's largest ski areas are located in the center of the state, north and south of the **Winooski River.** The **Smuggler's Notch Resort** lies west of route 108. The **Crown & Anchor Restaurant** between Jeffersonville and Stowe at the foot of the mountain, is known for its year-round sundeck dining and old English country pub atmosphere and mountain view; soups and sandwiches served noon to 6 pm, and singers entertain Friday and Saturday nights during the winter. South on route

100, musical comedies are presented during the summer at **Hyde Park Opera House.** Route 100 continues to **Morrisville,** where Sunday crowds gather at the **Mud City Flea Market** during summer and fall. The Morrisville Historical Society Museum, in a two-story 1820 brick mansion, displays articles of early New England life.

Stowe, in the southernmost corner of **Lamoille County,** along with **Mount Mansfield Ski Area,** is considered by many to be the ski capital of the east. But it has also been a busy summer resort area since the 19th century. Its hiking and mountain trails, riding, golf, theater, crafts, and boutiques make the area an all-round tourist attraction. North of here each August is a composer's conference at the campus of **Johnson State College.** Take the scenic road from route 108, up the Toll Road to the chin of **Mount Mansfield,** 4,393 feet, the state's highest mountain. The panoramic view covers almost the whole length of Lake Champlain. Mount Mansfield's gondola (ski lift) accommodates summer sightseers and fall foliage followers. Restored **Bloody Brook School House** is open year round. While the **Trapp Family Lodge** recently burned down, the annex is still offering cross-country ski touring. The **Viennese Kaffee Haus,** a quarter mile from the former lodge, features Austrian pastries and a light lunch. Other accommodations in Stowe include: **Alpine Motor Lodge** (253-7700, S/D$30-50), heated pool; **Edson Hill Manor** (253-7371, S$40-60 MAP), on 400 woodland acres, with pool, riding, golfing, fishing; **Green Mountain Inn & Motel** (253-7301, rates on request), an 1833 inn and restaurant; the **Lodge at Smuggler's Notch** (253-7311, rates on request), at the base of Mt Mansfield, with a large heated pool, golfing and tennis, restaurant famous for Sunday buffet; **The Inn at the Mountain** (253-7311, D$25-50), overlooking ski slopes, heated pool; **Yodler Motor Inn** (253-4836, D$25-40 summer; S$32-38 MAP winter). **Spruce Pond Inn & Motel** (253-4828, S$30-40 MAP), specializes in brook trout and homemade soups and breads. **Andersen Lodge** (253-7336, S/D$9-17 summer; S$22-33 MAP winter) has an Austrian chef; **Fiddler's Green Inn** (253-8124, S$8.50 summer, S$27-30 MAP winter); **Fox Fire Inn and Restaurant** (253-8459, S$30 MAP), Italian food a specialty, **The Gables Inn** (253-7730, twin, double, bunk room, motel & efficiency accommodations S$9-16); **Hob Knob Inn** (253-8549, S/D$30-50) has fine food and serves breakfast; **Stowehof Inn** (253-8500, S/D$60-105; S$53-75 MAP), sauna, heated pool, cross-country trails & equipment, private tennis and golf, and **TopNotch** (253-8585, S/D$75; S$67.50 MAP), 10 outdoor and 4 indoor tennis courts, riding stable, heated pool, sauna. Expensive but excellent restaurants in Stowe include **La Bicoque, Partridge Inn,** and **TopNotch. The Carpenter Farm** in Moretown (496-3433) is a dairy farm that welcomes clubs, families, and individuals; private rooms and dormitories. Southwest on route 100 is **Waitsfield,** nearest village to **Sugarbush Valley, Mad River Glen,** and **Glen Ellen.** In winter these three adjacent areas combine to provide some of Vermont's most challenging and diverse skiing. In summer and fall Sunday afternoon polo is played in Waitsfield. Accommodations in Waitsfield include **Knoll Farm Country Inn** (496-3939, S$16-27 AP; S$100-170 AP weekly), closed Nov; and

Tucker Hill Lodge (496-3983, S$27-35 MAP), cross-country skiing. Restaurants in the Waitsfield-Warren area are **The Common Man** (583-2800), exceptional European food; and **China Barn** in Waitsfield (496-3579), Mandarin and Szechuan, moderately priced. Also **The Phoenix** in Warren (583-2777). The **Bundy Art Gallery** exhibits contemporary work. Accommodations central to the area include: **Madbush Chalet Motor Inn** (496-3966, S/D$30-40 summer; S$56-72 MAP winter); **Sugarbush Inn** (583-2301, S/D$55-95 EP; S$49-69 MAP), near ski lift, offers soaring instruction, heated pool, golfing, tennis, riding, and homemade pastries. The state fish hatchery in **Roxbury** is open to visitors. **Northfield** is the home of **Norwich University,** the first private military academy in the country. Parades are usually scheduled weekday afternoons during fall and spring. The **Norwich University Ski Area** is open to the public and the annual **Winter Carnival** is a big local event.

MONTPELIER, the capital, on the banks of the Winooski River, hosts the annual **Fall Festival of Vermont Crafts** in October. The **State House,** built in 1859 of Vermont granite, is adjacent to the state **Historical Society Museum,** housed in a replica of an 1800 Greek revival pavilion-style hotel. The **Tavern Motor Inn** (223-5252, rates on request), across the street, has an indoor pool and charming dining room. **Lackey's Tourist Home** (223-7292) is an 1890s Victorian home in Montpelier. Places to eat in Montpelier include the **Brown Derby** and the **Lobster Pot.** Local dining favorites are **Horn of the Moon Café** on Langdon St. (223-2895) for excellent natural foods, daily breakfast and lunch (except Sunday), and dinners Thursday-Saturday, excellent soups, sandwiches, salads, quiches, desserts; and **The Stockyard** (223-7811), steaks and chops, good salad bar, moderately priced. Route 14 passes south to **Barre,** a leading granite center, and north to Calais, location of **Kent Tavern Museum. Rock of Ages Quarries** in Barre has guided tours where visitors can see granite cutting operations from an observation deck. There's also a ½-hour quarry train ride, affording spectacular views, June through September. **Groton State Forest,** with 20,000 acres, is second only to Mount Mansfield for hiking, boating, swimming, fishing, and picnicking. The **Vermont State Farm Show** is held here each January in the Municipal Auditorium and the **National Old Time Fiddler's Contest** is held here in August. The **Hollow Motel** (479-9313, S/D$24-36) has a pool and free breakfast. The **Country House Restaurant** offers homemade Italian soups and New England seafood.

Farther east on route 2 toward Caledonia County **NORTHEASTERN** Vermont has large undeveloped areas covered with dense forest and small farm villages. **St. Johnsbury** is best known for its Fairbanks Scales; Thaddeus Fairbanks, inventor of the platform scale, lived here, and today the town is the scale manufacturing center of the world. Many of the local museums and Victorian mansions are associated with the Fairbanks family. Maple sugar and trucking are also important industries. The **Fairbanks Museum of Natural Science and Planetarium** is open daily throughout the year. The **Maple Grove Maple Museum** on Portland Street gives free samples and tours of the candy factory all year. In nearby lower

Waterford, **Rabbit Hill Motor Inn** (748-5168, S$25/D$30-40/family $34-54) is a converted colonial inn. Traditional game suppers are held every November in **Greensboro Bend,** on route 16. A state fish hatchery is open to visitors in **Newark** and local potters and weavers sell their wares in the village shops. **Victory** and **Granby,** twin villages in the east, just recently installed electricity and telephones with funds from the annual **Holiday in the Hills** fall foliage celebration in late September. The annual **Northeast Kingdom Fall Foliage Festival** is held here in the towns of Walden, Cabot, Plainfield, Peachum, Barnet, and Groton.

Canaan, near the Canadian border, popular for its mineral springs is now famous for Ethan Allen American Traditional furniture made in **Beecher Falls. Newport City,** on Route 5, lies at the southern end of **Lake Memphremagog,** which provides swimming, boating, and camping and is very popular for fishing in summer, ice fishing in winter, and salmon in early spring. **Frank's Steak House** is popular locally. Westward, **Jay Peak,** the state's northernmost ski resort area, has a 60-passenger aerial tramway which operates for sightseers, Memorial Day through Labor Day. Lobster and chicken barbecues are held all summer long. The **County Fair** takes place on the Barton fairgrounds in Orleans in late August.

FURTHER STATE INFORMATION
Vermont Development Agency, 61 Elm Street, Montpelier, VT 05602. Hunting and Fishing: **Fish and Game Department,** Montpelier, VT 05602. **Chamber of Commerce** (Central Vermont), tel: 223-2441, Lake Champlain Regional Chamber of Commerce, tel: 863-3489, Addison County Chamber of Commerce, tel: 388-7579.

USEFUL TELEPHONE NUMBERS IN BURLINGTON
Crisis Clinic	656-3587
Medical Health Care Information, Medical Center Hospital	864-0454
Dental Health Division	862-5701
Burlington Dental Clinic	862-7954
Vermont Legal Aid	863-2871
Pan Am Reservations	(800)223-9762

Virginia

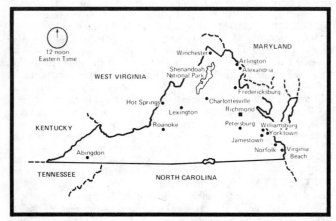

| **Area** | 40,817 square miles | | | | | **Population** | | 5,321,435 | | | |
| **Capital** | Richmond | | | | | **Sales Tax** | | 4% | | | |

Weather	Jan	Feb	Mar	Apr	May	Jun	Jul	Aug	Sep	Oct	Nov	Dec
Av Temp (°C)	1	−1	7	14	18	23	25	27	22	14	11	6
Days Rain/Snow	13	6	12	7	12	12	12	11	4	9	10	9

The colonists who landed at Jamestown in Virginia on 13 May 1607 founded the first permanent English settlement in America. They named their territory Virginia after Queen Elizabeth I (the Virgin Queen). So much has happened since then that there are over 1,500 historical markers along the 35,000 miles of paved roads.

Interested chiefly in gold and exploration, the first colonists could have never survived without Captain John Smith, the tough army man who forced the Jamestown "gentlemen" to dirty their hands with hunting, fishing, and farming. But their enthusiasm improved when John Rolfe arrived in Jamestown in 1610 and developed tobacco growing so successfully that English farmers soon came over by the hundreds to start planting. Once an 8-year truce was signed with Powhatan, father of Pocahontas, the colonists prospered unmolested; Rolfe judiciously married Pocahontas in 1614. In 1619 the first Africans were sold to the planters as slaves, introducing a practice which would first make the colonists wealthy and finally lead to their ruin. In that same year the first legislative assembly in the New World met in Jamestown, and 90 young women arrived seeking husbands and helped found families that are still prominent in Virginia.

Virginians have been deeply involved in creating and molding the nation. Here were the first armed rebellion against His Majesty's Government in 1676 and the inspiring revolutionary debates in Williamsburg and Richmond. Virginians figured prominently in the formation of the US. Yet it was from Virginia that the nation was nearly destroyed, as the state was the mainstay of the Confederacy during the Civil War. Both the Revolution and the Civil War ended on Virginia's soil and since the beginning of the republic, Virginia has given the nation eight Presidents and six First Ladies.

Despite its uneven terrain, Virginia has a rather even climate. The average temperatures at similar elevations are only about 2°C cooler in the west than along the eastern shore, although mountaintop towns are considerably cooler. There's little snow, but artificial ice and snow have made skiing and skating resorts at Hot Springs, Bryce Mountain, and Wintergreen near Charlottesville. Summers are not too hot, even in the Tidewater region, and there's usually good swimming well into October. Spring flowers bloom early and linger on into summer, and the autumn is even nicer; the crisp weather in the mountains turns the leaves to vivid mosaics of color.

If you like freshwater fishing, Virginia has 450 public fishing streams, rivers, lakes, and reservoirs. Many sites are in deep forests, which seem far from civilization. The coastal estuaries are lined with quiet bays and inlets where you can drop a fishing line. There's surf fishing, and big game fish lurk farther out where the Gulf Stream cuts a blue swath through the green Atlantic. Areas open for hunting wild game include the large federal (military) reservations. Virginia contains 22 recreational and seven historical state parks, six natural areas, two national forests, two national parks, a national seashore, and many wildlife areas; camping facilities provided in most state parks and both national parks.

The **Tidewater** region surrounding the Chesapeake Bay, where the first settlements were founded, is a level plain slashed by four great rivers on their way to Chesapeake Bay—the lower Potomac, the Rappahannock, the York, and the James. The fall line, which separates the coastal plain from the rolling countryside of the **Piedmont Plateau,** runs south from Alexandria through Petersburg. The **Blue Ridge Mountains** rise abruptly and scenically from the western rim of the Piedmont. Between the Blue Ridge and **Allegheny Mountains** is a region of great fertile valleys, eerie limestone caverns, strange rock formations, and streams teeming with bass and trout. In the southwestern end of the state is the wall of mountains that thwarted exploration westward until the **Cumberland Gap** was discovered in 1750.

The Virginia suburbs **Arlington** and **Alexandria** are integral parts of metropolitan Washington, DC (the nation's capital). They were originally part of the District of Columbia but returned to Virginia in 1846. Sites to visit in Arlington include the famous **Arlington National Cemetery** with the Tomb of the Unknown Soldier and John F. Kennedy's grave;

Iwo Jima Statue, the Marine Corps Memorial; Curtis-Lee Mansion, once-proud plantation of General Robert E. Lee. During the Civil War Alexandria was quickly occupied by the North to acquire control of the vital Potomac River. A tour of historic places in **Old Town Alexandria** will include the **Stabler-Leadbeater Apothecary Shop** (1792) which served Washington, John Calhoun, Robert E. Lee, and Henry Clay and is now a typical 1800 pharmacy museum. Other Washington, DC, suburbs are **Vienna, Falls Church, Fairfax,** and **Reston. Wolf Trap Farm for the Performing Arts,** in Vienna, attracts thousands with performances as varied as opera and country western.

But to get away from the frenetic pace of this area into an entirely different atmosphere, drive 70 miles westward to **Winchester** in **NORTH-WESTERN VIRGINIA,** which gave its name to the rifle that won the West. Should you be there in mid-May, you'll find the whole area perfumed with apple blossoms; there's the **Shenandoah Apple Blossom Festival** in late April-early May. Sixteen-year-old George Washington came to Winchester in 1748 as an assistant surveyor. He returned in 1755 during the French and Indian War as a colonel under General Braddock; the **Washington Office-Museum** in Winchester is open daily, May to November, admission charged. During the Civil War, Confederate strategists made shrewd use of the Shenandoah Valley (south of Winchester), and "Stonewall" **Jackson's Headquarters,** now a museum, is open daily, admission charged. In a prime strategic location, Winchester changed hands over 70 times during the war; nearly 8,000 soldiers are buried in the Confederate and Union cemeteries.

Heading south from Winchester you come to **Harrisonburg,** where Rockingham County turkeys are processed and frozen. It is in the midst of much beautiful scenery, with the **George Washington National Forest** only 10 miles east and **Shenandoah National Park** 24 miles east. The **Grand Caverns,** a chilly 13°C year round, are where both Union and Confederate troops were quartered during the Civil War; open year round. The castle-like **Natural Chimneys** rock formation, 15 miles southwest of Harrisonburg, is the setting for a medieval **Jousting Tournament** held annually (since 1821) on the third Saturday in August. **Staunton,** south of Harrisonburg, preserves the birthplace of President Woodrow Wilson. The restored farm and workshop of Cyrus Hall McCormick, who invented the mechanical reaper in 1831, is also here.

In the mountains, about 40 miles southwest of Staunton, is **Hot Springs,** where the gentry of Virginia's Tidewater region have gone to escape the summer heat since around 1755. **The Homestead** (839-5500, S$85/D$170 Nov-Sept; S$95-135/D$178-200 Sept-Nov) is unquestionably one of America's most magnificent resort hotels, with just about every facility imaginable for having a good time day or night the year round. It has fine food and superb service, even its own landing field for scheduled flights to and from the hotel. Sports and other facilities of The Homestead are available to guests of the nearby **Cascades Inn** (839-5355, S$49-51/D$90-98). East of Staunton are **Waynesboro** (visit its elaborate **Swannanoa Mansion**) and **Charlottesville,** described below.

Lexington, in the valley south of Staunton, is the lovely little town where you'll find the **Virginia Military Institute (VMI)**. The **George C. Marshall Research Library** is a memorial to the **VMI** graduate who drafted the Marshall Plan. Robert E. Lee was president of **Washington and Lee University,** in Lexington, founded in 1749, from 1865 until his death in 1870. The beloved Confederate general is buried in **Lee Chapel,** with other members of his long-distinguished family, and his office is preserved here. The only house "Stonewall" Jackson ever owned has been restored as **Jackson Museum. Natural Bridge** is the village beside one of the nation's most impressive natural wonders. The stone arch, for which the village is famous, is 215 feet high, 90 feet long, and 50 to 150 feet wide. Local Indians once worshipped it, but Thomas Jefferson bought it and built a guest cottage here so his friends could visit the oddity in comfort. Today visitors can stay in the **Natural Bridge Hotel** (291-2121, S$20-25/D$24-29); and **Natural Bridge Motor Lodge** (291-2131, S$15/D$19). The sound and light *Drama of Creation* is presented under the bridge nightly throughout the year.

Roanoke is the commercial and industrial outlet for **SOUTHWESTERN VIRGINIA,** but it is also beautifully situated in a valley between the **Blue Ridge** and **Allegheny Mountains.** The **Booker T. Washington National Monument** is 24 miles southeast of the city and is on the site of the plantation where he lived as a slave and was freed in 1865. Visitors can stay at the **Hotel Roanoke** (343-6992, S$31-43/D$36-48). **Hotel tax: 5%.** For an elegant dinner with live dinner music, try the **Regency Room** in the hotel.

Southwestern Virginia is a maze of valleys and mountains, most of it within the **Jefferson National Forest.** This is Daniel Boone country and the setting for James Fox's *Trail of the Lonesome Pine.* The book comes alive at the town of **Big Stone Gap** among the pioneer relics and folk art in the **Southwest Virginia State Museum,** and in the musical version of the book performed Thursday-Saturday, July and August.

Abingdon, in the southwest corner of the state near the Tennessee border, reverberates with the chants of auctioneers in the burly tobacco and livestock markets, and is filled with handicraft stores, antique shops, and chinaware dealers. The country's only lusterware factory is located here. So is the nation's oldest professional repertory theater, the **Barter Theater,** which opened in 1933 during the Depression and was glad to accept produce in lieu of cash; the actors wound up as poor as ever, but gained a collective total of 300 pounds of goods during the first season. High-quality productions, from Shakespeare to Agatha Christie mysteries and musicals, are staged here from mid-April to mid-October. The **Virginia Highlands Arts and Crafts Festival** is held the first 2 weeks in August; **Tobacco Festival** for 3 days in mid-October. The **Martha Washington Inn** (628-3161, S$30/D$35) serves good regional food. The **Empire Motel** (628-7131, S$20/D$24-30) is nearby. At Bluefield you can drive your car through the **Pocahontas Exhibition Coal Mine,** and tours are offered daily May to October.

From north to south within **Shenandoah National Park** is the spectacular **Skyline Drive,** which begins at **Front Royal,** just south of Winchester. This is a 105-mile drive, with only two exits between the north and south approaches of this fabulous highway; the speed limit is 35 miles per hour. The drive twists along the crest of the Blue Ridge Mountains and offers one of the finest scenic drives on the nation's eastern coast. Just south of Front Royal on US 340 are the **Skyline Caverns,** with guided tours the year round. The caverns contain probably the world's only "anthodites," calcite formations in the shapes of delicate flowers. The nearby caverns in **Luray** are also spectacular.

About 20 miles east of the juncture of Skyline Drive and the Blue Ridge Parkway is the exquisite little city of **Charlottesville,** home of the **University of Virginia,** which Thomas Jefferson founded and designed. Architect Stanford White called the university "the most beautiful group of collegiate buildings in the world." The boxwood gardens and hedges and the famous serpentine wall, only one brick thick, form a perfect setting for the white-trimmed, classic red brick buildings. The town also has some exceptionally fine statues, such as the superb equestrian ones of Stonewall Jackson on his *Little Sorrel,* and Robert E. Lee on *Traveller,* each in its own square. In Midway Park stands the **Lewis and Clark Monument** to the team that explored the Louisiana Territory; it is a reminder that both Meriweather Lewis and the Clark brothers were born near Charlottesville. The memorial to George Rogers Clark, explorer of the Northwest Territory, is on West Main Street.

Monticello, home of Thomas Jefferson and 3 miles southeast of Charlottesville, was designed by Jefferson in the style of Palladio. From the indoor privies to the dumbwaiter, the house is full of the ingenious devices which Jefferson constructed. He was America's first real gourmet, and the pond in front of the mansion was often stocked with shad, crabs, and other seafood that had been transported live from the shores of eastern Virginia. **Ash Lawn,** 2 miles beyond Monticello, is the house Jefferson designed for James Monroe, another American President and father of the Monroe Doctrine. Both homes are open daily. On the way back to Charlottesville, dine at **Michie Tavern** (pronounced *mic-key*), which has served good Virginia meals for over 200 years and was visited by Monroe, Jefferson, Madison, and Lafayette; open for lunch 11:30-3, colonial museum open 9-5. **The Boar's Head Inn** (296-2181, S$40/D$48) is a picturesque resort located in Charlottesville near the foot hills of the Blue Ridge Mountains and Virginia hunt country. Offers tennis, swimming, squash, health gyms with saunas, club dining room, dancing, and luxurious rooms. South of Charlottesville is **Lynchburg,** a major tobacco market and site of **Randolph-Macon Women's College; Appomattox Courthouse National Park** is 21 miles east of Lynchburg. Here, on the afternoon of 9 April 1865, Lee surrendered to Grant in the parlor of McClean House, thus ending the Civil War. Also south of Charlottesville are **Martinsville,** a textile city, and **Danville,** famous for tobacco auctions and the gigantic Dan River textile mill.

For anyone new to Virginia, southbound I-95, in the eastern portion of the state, seems to cut through some of the most historically exciting

Monticello, designed by Thomas Jefferson, the third President of the US, is set on a mountain top near Charlottesville.

territory in America. After you pass the huge Quantico Marine Reservation, where the **Marine Corps Museum** is open daily, you soon arrive at **Fredericksburg** on the Rappahannock River. Still in mint condition are buildings that were familiar to heroes of both the Revolution and the Civil War. Maps for self-guided tours can be obtained at the **Fredericksburg Visitors Center,** 706 Caroline Street. Good motels include the **Sheraton Motor Inn** (786-8321, S$36/D$46), **Howard Johnson's Motor Lodge,** (898-1800, S$20-24/D$24-32), and **Holiday Inn North** and **South** (S$24-28/D$30-36). **The Rising Sun Tavern** was built by Charles Washington, George's younger brother, in about 1760, and became a hotbed of patriots plotting independence from England. The **Mary Ball Washington House,** with English boxwood gardens, is where George Washington's mother lived from 1772 until her death in 1789. **Kenmore** (1752) nearby is the magnificently restored Georgian home with architect T.S. Adam-inspired plaster decoration where George Washington's sister Betty lived with her husband, Colonel Fielding Lewis. **Hugh Mercer's Apothecary Shop,** still stocked with ancient bottles and ledgers, was where Washington, a frequent visitor, maintained a small library and office. **James Monroe's Law Office and Museum, St George's Church, Stoner's Store,** the **Masonic Lodge,** where Washington was initiated in the Masonic Order, and many more landmarks make Fredericksburg an important stop on your itinerary. Within a 17-mile radius west of town are the great battle-fields of Fredericksburg, **Chancellorsville,** the **Wilderness** and **Spotsylvania Court House,** all encompassed within the **Fredericksburg** and **Spotsylvania National Military Park;** here is the house where Stonewall Jackson died of pneumonia on 10 May 1863. East of Fredericksburg, on the north shore of the peninsula between the Potomac and Rappahannock Rivers, are the birthplaces of George Washington, James Monroe, and Robert E. Lee.

The country south from Fredericksburg is charming. Many of the lovely old homes, which can be seen only from the road most of the year, are open to the public during **Historic Gardens Week** in late April, when all Virginia celebrates the beauty of spring.

Cities To Visit

NORFOLK

The newest cruise port on the Atlantic seaboard is Norfolk, a city already filled with ships and sailors and the lure of the sea. The city was founded in 1682 at the point where the Elizabeth River opens into the magnificent harbor of Hampton Roads. The famous battle between the ironclad *Monitor* and the *Merrimac* took place on 9 March 1862 in full sight of huge crowds on the shores of Hampton Roads. Although Norfolk had to defend itself against the British during the Revolution and the War of 1812, it is the Cunard Line of Britain which launched Norfolk into the profitable and joyous business of sending seagoing vacationers off to foreign ports.

Norfolk also serves as the home base of the US Atlantic Fleet and the Supreme Allied Command of the North Atlantic Treaty Organization (NATO). Other installations include the Naval Air Station at Breezy Point, Amphibious Training Base at Little Creek, Naval Operating Base at Sewell Point, and the Naval Shipyard and Hospital in Portsmouth. Anyone who loves the sea will enjoy Norfolk, the largest city in Virginia.

WHAT TO SEE

Harbor tours (late May through September) with close-up views of ships and submarines; a sightseeing boat leaves from pier at the foot of East Main Street. Cruise ships leave from the terminal at Pier 2. Bus tours of Norfolk Naval Station take visitors on a general tour of the base past nuclear powered aircraft carriers and Polaris submarines, destroyers, support ships, and a variety of aircraft. Selected ships are open free on weekends.

See the **General Douglas MacArthur Memorial** with his tomb and a collection of memorabilia. **St Paul's Church** (1739) was the only major building that survived the great fire of 1776. The building, completed in 1852 was originally Norfolk's former courthouse. The general is buried in the crypt, and lining eight galleries are mementoes, including his famous crushed cap and corncob pipe. A 28-minute documentary film of the life of this American hero is shown, narration by Walter Cronkite. **Gardens-by-the-Sea,** near the airport, is famous for azaleas, camellias, rhododendron, and roses. The **Adam Thoroughgood House,** built in the late 1600s, between Norfolk and Virginia Beach, is probably the oldest brick house in the nation. In **Portsmouth** see the **Naval Shipyard Museum,** open Tuesday to Saturday and Sunday afternoons; **Lightship** and **Coastguard Museum,** same schedule (both free); and the **US Naval Hospital,** founded in 1830 on the site of British headquarters during the Revolution.

The port city of **Newport News** is home of Virginia's largest private employer, the Newport News Shipbuilding and Dry Dock Company. It was from here that the Atlantic Blue Ribbon holder, the 990-foot passenger liner **United States,** and the world's first nuclear powered aircraft carrier, the **US Enterprise,** were launched. Visit the **War Memorial of Virginia,** with military collections ranging from the Revolution through Vietnam wars, open Monday to Saturday and Sunday afternoons; free. **Mariners' Museum,** open Monday to Saturday 9-5; Sunday 12-5, adults $1.50, children 75¢, is a delight of ship models, figureheads, and seafaring equipment. The collection includes walrus skin canoes, and dugouts, a collection of 16 miniature vessels, the work of 28 years by artist August F. Crabtree, which reflects the rise and fall of sailships, and even a two-man submarine. **Army Transportation Museum** at Fort Eustis displays army vehicles of all kinds used from the Revolution to the present day; open Tuesday to Friday and Saturday, Sunday afternoons; free. **The Victory Arch** was built to honor returning servicemen at the end of World War I. The stone arch was replaced in 1962 to honor all local men and women of the Armed Forces.

Visit the Newport News Park for picnics, children's recreation, golf, fishing, canoeing, and camping. Also visit the Peninsula Nature and Science Center/Planetarium. It contains exhibits representing the natural history of Tidewater. In **Hampton** see **Fort Monroe** (1834), with its unusual **Casemate Museum,** offering historical exhibits in its bombproof chambers; open daily, free. **Hampton Institute** has a museum of Indian and African art. Visit the **Kicotan Indian Village** and **Syms Eaton Museum.** The museum traces the history of Hampton. **Langley Air Force Base** and research laboratories of the **National Aeronautics and Space Administration** can be toured by buses leaving from the Hampton Information Center.

ACCOMMODATIONS

In midtown Norfolk: **Omni International Hotel** (622-6664, S$36-50/D$46-60); **Holiday Inn-Midtown** (622-2361, S$26.50-40/D$32-40); **Holiday Inn-Scope** (627-5555, S$30-38.75/D$34-41.75). North of midtown on Ocean Avenue: **Holiday Inn-Ocean View** (587-8761, S$33.50-48.50/D$53-57.50); **Ramada Inn-Ocean View** (583-5211, S$32/D$47). Just southwest of midtown on Military Highway: **Quality Inn-Executive Park** (461-6600, S$32.45/D$38.87). **The Sheraton Inn** (461-9192, S$34-42/D$43-51) is east of midtown near Virginia Beach. Nearest campsites are in **Seashore State Park** between Cape Henry and Virginia Beach. Hotel tax: 9%.

RESTAURANTS

Seafood is a specialty in Virginia but there are also the delicious Smithfield ham and Black Angus beef. The **Nations** has an international gourmet cuisine (dinners only) in Holiday Inn-Scope. **Mason's** is north of midtown on Granby Street; and the **Burroughs Steak House** is on the Military Highway near the Sheraton Inn, where the **Column II** and **The Barn** in the Admiralty Motel are also good. Try **Lockhart's** of Norfolk. **Alexander's** at the Omni International Hotel has steak and seafood, as does **The Judge's Chambers.** Also good are **Le Charlieu,** French cuisine, and **Harvey's** at the Holiday Inn-Scope. Excellent restaurants in Virginia Beach are **The Lighthouse** and **Hurd's** for seafood and **Valle's Steak House** and **Black Angus Restaurant** for steaks.

ENTERTAINMENT

Excellent night spots in Virginia Beach are the **Shipmates, Rogue's Club,** and **Pascal's Discothèque.** In Norfolk, **Alexander's, Fifth National Banque, Jonathan's** and **Stage Door** are all first-rate night spots.

ARTS AND MUSIC

Chrysler Museum open daily; **Hermitage Foundation Museum of Western and Oriental Fine Arts,** also open daily. The **Moses Myers House,** begun in 1791, contains magnificent Adam-style plasterwork, antiques, and family portraits by Gilbert Stuart and Thomas Sully; open daily (10-5, Monday to Saturday April-November; afternoons only, rest of year). The **Norfolk Symphony Orchestra** performs during the fall and winter season. Norfolk also has a civic chorus, **Little Theater,** chamber music group, civic ballet, two dinner playhouses, and the **Virginia Opera Association.** Attend the **Hampton Jazz Festival** which features international and nationally known jazz and blues artists. Performances are held at the Hampton Coliseum during June.

SHOPPING
The leading stores are Rice's, Nachmans, Miller & Rhoads, and Smith & Welton.

SPORTS
Norfolk's professional sports team is the **Tides** (baseball). There are five private and three public golf courses in the vicinity. Year-round freshwater fishing in the **Back Bay** area, **Smith** and **Little Creek.** Saltwater fishing in the **Norfolk-Oceanview-Lynnhaven** district. Sailing regattas and boating of all kinds flourish here.

CALENDAR OF EVENTS
International Azalea Festival, late April; Norfolk **Festival of Arts,** 3 weeks in July; **Old Dominion Kiwanis Classic,** December; **Oyster Bowl Game,** October. **Harborfest,** a weekend in June of water and land festivals centered on the visit of tall masted sailing ships and other vessels.

WHERE TO GO NEARBY
Only 20 miles east of Norfolk is **Virginia Beach,** a 28-mile stretch of really perfect sand for sunning and dabbling, with Atlantic rollers bringing in some of the best surfing waves on the east coast. There are accommodations in all degrees of simplicity or smartness and in a wide range of prices. This is a very popular resort for young families, with sports of all kinds during the day and qualified sitters available. Many hotels are open year round, but the height of the season (and of hotel rates) is June through Labor Day.

South of Norfolk is the **Dismal Swamp,** creepy unless you're a naturalist. Just up the road from Portsmouth is **Smithfield,** the famous town that is pungently redolent of smoking ham. First surveyed in 1728 by Colonel William Byrd II, it was George Washington, who with five other investors, put up the capital required for its reclamation. The swamp, however, proved more than a match for their endeavors. More recently, the Department of the Interior has been turning Old Dismal into a wildlife preserve with facilities for visitors. Do not visit during July and August when insects (of the biting type) abound. The **Chesapeake Bay Bridge-Tunnel** ($8.00 toll per car) is a 17½-mile-long feat of engineering that connects Norfolk with Virginia's Eastern Shore. The bridge-tunnel is 23 miles long, and driving time is approximately 25 minutes. **Sea Gull Fishing Pier and Restaurant** is on the southernmost of the four manmade islands the bridge touches. For the rest of the trip you are above (or below) water, and should make sure you have plenty of gas in your tank. There are public telephones along the bridge to summon help in an emergency.

The **Eastern Shore** is an entirely different world of fishing villages and snug old houses that have stood for 200 to 300 years. **Chincoteague** is famous for its **Wild Pony Roundup** the last week in July. These lovable miniature horses, who live on marsh grass on **Assateague Island,** are auctioned off, usually to become children's pets. The fishing all along the eastern shore is superb.

RICHMOND

Richmond, the capital of Virginia, stands on the fall line of the James River where the Piedmont Plateau meets the Tidewater coastal plain, 100 miles west of Chesapeake Bay. Only 9 days after the first colonists landed at Jamestown, Captain John Smith and a party of explorers followed the James River inland and came upon the river falls and the site where Richmond was eventually established as a town by William Byrd II and William Mayo in 1742.

After the Virginia conventions of 1774 and 1775 were held here with such resounding success, the capital was moved from Williamsburg to Richmond in 1780. Later, as the capital of the Confederacy from 1861, the city was constantly in danger and, in 1865, eventually evacuated. The great fire that followed General Grant's capture of the city on 2 April 1865 miraculously spared the most precious landmarks, including the White House of the Confederacy, Capital Square, and St John's Church where Patrick Henry issued his famed "give me liberty or give me death" speech. At first glance, Richmond is a typically modern city. Yet underneath is the real Old South, with buildings familiar to Thomas Jefferson, Patrick Henry, John Marshall, Robert E. Lee, and a whole roster of other heroes.

WHAT TO SEE

St John's Church (from 1740); antebellum houses around the church are being beautifully restored. **St Paul's Church** is filled with memorials to famous Virginians. The **Old Stone House** (*circa* 1686) has a collection of Edgar Allan Poe memorabilia. Ellen Glasgow, another Richmond author, wrote her regional stories at 1 West Main Street. The homes of other famous people (check visiting hours) are the **John Marshall House,** where the Chief Justice lived for 45 years; the **Robert E. Lee House,** which he briefly occupied after the surrender at Appomattox; the octagonal **Hancock-Wirt-Caskie House;** the **Victorian Lewis Ginter House;** and **Wilton,** a superb mansion built by William Randolph III in 1750-53.

Out in **Windsor Farms,** a suburb northwest of town, is **Virginia House,** constructed mainly of stones from Warwick Priory in England, with fine antique furnishings. Running east of Richmond is a series of colonial mansions where "southern hospitality" was born. They line both sides of the James River, recalling the days when planters had their own private wharves for shipping tobacco, and rowboats were the most convenient mode of transportation for visitors. A complete list of homes is issued by the Garden Club in Richmond, and many are open during **Historic**

Garden Week in April. Several that are open daily are **Shirley Plantation,** home of the Carter family since 1723; **Berkeley Plantation,** birthplace of President William Henry Harrison; **Westover,** built about 1730 by William Byrd II, who founded Richmond, the gardens of which are open to the public; **Brandon Plantation,** 18th-century home of Nathaniel Harrison, which has magnificent grounds, open year round.

East of the city is the **Richmond National Battlefield** where Union forces made repeated attempts to capture the capital until General Grant finally stormed through on 2 April 1865; one week later, General Lee capitulated. Forts and other relics have been preserved. The main **Visitors' Center,** with excellent explanatory exhibits, is in **Chimborazo Park.**

The **State Capitol,** designed by Thomas Jefferson after the Maison Carrée in Nimes, France, is a work of art in itself and contains the only statue for which George Washington posed in person. In its Hall of the House of Delegates, Aaron Burr was tried for treason.

Monument Avenue is lined with statues of Confederate heroes; those facing south survived the war to return home. **Battle Abbey,** with famous Confederacy murals by Charles Hoffbauer, is a treasury of Virginia history; open daily except holidays. **The Museum of the Confederacy,** housed in the White House of Jefferson Davis, contains the world's largest collection of Civil War relics; open daily. **The Valentine Museum,** in three 19th-century mansions, has period furnishings and changing exhibits; open Tuesday to Sunday.

The Philip Morris Tobacco Factory has guided tours Monday to Friday of their $200-million facility, the world's largest cigarette factory.

Two locks have been preserved from the **Kanawha Canal** started during George Washington's time to carry river traffic around the falls of the James River. Open daily 9-5.

ACCOMMODATIONS

There's a wide choice of motels on the highways into Richmond. But if you want to be in the middle of the city, the **Holiday Inn-Downtown** (644-9871, S$31-42/D$31-45) has live entertainment nightly except Sunday; **John Marshall Hotel** (644-4661, S$29-38/D$35-44) has entertainment nightly except Sunday in the **Captain's Grill;** and the **William Byrd Motor Hotel** (358-1571, S$18.02/D$23.32) good dining. In the West End of Richmond, the **Regency Inn of Richmond** (285-9061, S$36-45/D$45-50), and the **Richmond Hyatt House** (285-8666, S$41-55/D$51-59). **Hotel Tax:** 4%.

RESTAURANTS

Spoonbread, Smithfield ham, genuine Southern-fried chicken, home-baked biscuits, and similar regional fare is available at the **William Byrd Hotel, Sherwood, Quality Inn-Intown,** and others. Seafood and steaks are specialties at the **Flying Cloud, Golden Lion, Executive Motel, Top of the Tower, Aberdeen Barn, Hugo's Rotisserie** (Richmond Hyatt), **Omar's, Skilligalee Seafood, Sam Miller's Exchange Café,** and **The To-**

bacco Co. **Jade Isle** has Oriental and American food. **The Capri** is Italian. For elegant French cuisine, try **La Petite France.**

ENTERTAINMENT

Sam Miller's Exchange Café, Poor Richard's, Top of the Tower, Beehive Showroom, Tony's Supper Club, Hyatt House, The Warehouse, and **The Tobacco Co.** are excellent night spots.

ARTS AND MUSIC

Virginia Museum of Fine Arts contains Russian crown jewels by Fabergé among its truly outstanding collections; open Tuesday to Sunday, 50 cents on Saturday and Sunday. In the same building is an exceptionally fine theater of the performing arts, which includes the **Richmond Chamber Music Society. The Richmond Symphony Orchestra** performs from October to May.

SHOPPING

Downtown stores close at 5:30, Tuesday to Saturday and at 9 on Monday evenings. The antique shops are especially interesting. Good shopping malls include **Regency Square, Cloverleaf, Azalea,** and **Chesterfield.**

SPORTS

The biggest sports event of the year is the **Strawberry Hill Races** at the Virginia State Fairgrounds in April. Richmond has professional baseball, and there is a good choice of collegiate sports events. Golf is available at public and private clubs, and most public parks have tennis courts. Just outside the city are several good spots for fishing, swimming, and boating. In late January, the **United Virginia Band Tennis Classic** is one of the tennis Grand Prix tournaments as well as one of the WCT tournaments.

CALENDAR OF EVENTS

Strawberry Hill Races, early April; **Historic Garden Week,** last full week in April; **June Jubilee; Festival of Arts,** mid-June through mid-August; **Virginia State Fair,** late September; **National Tobacco Festival,** late September to early October; **Annual Autumn Pilgrimage,** October.

WHERE TO GO NEARBY

Petersburg, 23 miles south of Richmond, had the distinction of being so vital to the Confederate supply line that it was besieged continuously for the last 10 months of the Civil War. The fighting area is now classified as a National Battlefield; museum in **Visitors' Center,** off VA 36. Visit the city's **Information Center** off I-95 for publications and assistance before taking the newly established self-guided tour of the city. **Kings Dominion** is a family entertainment park located 20 miles north of Richmond on I-95. Open daily from May to September and on Sat and Sun from March to May and September to October. The park includes five worlds of fantasy, 34 thrilling rides, live shows, and Lion Country Safari. Admission is $10.95, which covers rides, shows, and attractions.

WILLIAMSBURG

This little city began life in 1633 as "Middle Plantation," an outpost midway between Jamestown and Yorktown. When malaria and a disastrous fire drove the first settlers out of Jamestown in 1699, they moved inland to this pleasant site, where the **College of William and Mary** had already been founded 6 years before. They changed the name to Williamsburg in honor of William III. It is 27 miles northwest of Newport News and 50 miles southeast of Richmond.

For the first 80 years of the 18th century, Williamsburg was the political, cultural, and social heart of the state, a virtual royal court of the aristocracy in the building nation. But after the capital was moved to Richmond, the spirit went out of Williamsburg and the fine old buildings fell into decay. In 1926, John D. Rockefeller, Jr., sponsored the restoration of the historical areas of the colonial city so that "the future may learn from the past."

Today a visit to Williamsburg is like stepping into the 18th century. More than $96.5 million of patient research, meticulous care, and a devotion to exact accuracy have breathed authenticity into the town you find here now, and it can be a thrilling experience. The historic section of town occupies an area 1 mile long and ½ mile wide.

WHAT TO SEE

Go first to the **Information Center,** Colonial Parkway and VA 132, for a valuable orientation film on the historic area, which will help you enjoy and understand it all better. Admission tickets to the historic area are a bargain at $9-20 for adults and $4.50-10 for children 6-12. The ticket includes 10 exhibition buildings and colonial homes, 15 craft shops, evening lectures and film programs, and use of the historic area bus system; the area is closed only on Christmas Day. Buses circle continuously, and you can get off where you please and reboard by showing your ticket. Streets within the Historic Area are closed to automobile traffic from 8am to 6pm, which greatly helps the illusion of antiquity. By now, nearly 500 buildings have been restored and reconstructed.

The ones you mustn't miss seeing include the completely recreated **Governor's Palace,** an elegant 18th century mansion in a 10-acre garden, which costs $3 for adults and $1.50 for children 6-12, plus the general admission ticket; the **Capitol; Brush-Everard House; Peyton Randolph House; Raleigh Tavern,** frequent meeting place of revolutionary patriots; **Wythe House; Publick Gaol; Wetherburn's Tavern; James Geddy House; Magazine and Guardhouse;** and the **Courthouse of 1770. Duke of Gloucester Street,** where Williamsburg residents wear pre-Revolutionary clothes perfectly naturally, is still the main thoroughfare. At the head of this historic street is the beautiful **College of William and Mary,** founded in 1693. The exquisite building, designed by Sir Christopher Wren, was erected in 1695-99, and is the country's oldest academic building still in use.

Outside the historic area, yet still in Williamsburg, is Busch Gardens, an entertaining journey through the histories of England, France, Germany, and Italy. Admission is $11 for a 1-day ticket.

ACCOMMODATIONS

The most regal and atmospheric place to stay is the **Williamsburg Inn** (229-1000, S/D$63-91 in colonial guest cottages, S/D$54-80 in the main building), the **Williamsburg Lodge** (229-1000, S/D$53-75) is also delightful. The historic area bus serves **Inn, Lodge,** and the **Motor House** (229-1700, S/D$42-47), located opposite the Information Center; advance reservations essential.

Motels within 1 to 2 miles of the historic area are the **Colonial Motel** (229-3621, S/D$18-32), **Commonwealth Inn** (229-6922, S$22-29/D$24-42) closed December to March; **Heritage Inn** (229-6220, S/D$45); **Hilton Inn** (220-2500, S$42-58/D$48-66); **Holiday Inn-East** (229-0200, S/D$36-52); **Howard Johnson Motor Lodge** (229-2781, S$36/D$38); **Quality Inn Colony** (229-1855, S/D$34-38); **Quality Inn Francis Nicholson** (229-6270, S$26-35/D$28-37); **Ramada Inn-West** (229-0260, S/D$34-55); **Rochambeau** (229-2851, S/D$20-30); and **Sheraton Motor Inn** (229-6605, S$36-44/D$40-48). Hotel tax: 4%.

RESTAURANTS

For truly elegant atmosphere, fine service, and lovely food, try the **Dining Room,** at Williamsburg Inn, expensive. Dining at **Williamsburg Lodge** is more moderately priced; entertainment several evenings a week. For lots of atmosphere and Virginia specialties, try **Chowning's Tavern, Christiana Campbell's Tavern,** and **King's Arms Tavern;** all moderately expensive. Also popular are the **Aberdeen Barn, Cascades** in Motor House Motel, which has dancing or entertainment each evening, the **Jefferson Inn,** and the **Lobster House.** Across from the Information Center, the **Cafeteria** offers quick service with a wide choice of high quality foods at reasonable prices.

ARTS AND MUSIC

One of the nation's great collections of folk art is in the **Abby Aldrich Rockefeller Collection,** situated between Williamsburg Inn and the Lodge, open Monday to Saturday and Sunday afternoons; free. The **Williamsburg National Wax Museum,** 3 miles west of town, has life-sized tableaux of important colonial events; open daily 9am-10pm 1 June through Labor Day, 9-5 1 November to 14 March, and 9-9 the rest of the year. From April to mid-October, the **Colonial Williamsburg Fifes and Drums** perform on Saturday mornings and accompany the costumed colonial militia drill in Market Square several times a week.

SHOPPING

The **Craft House** is the sales and exhibition center for authentic reproductions of Williamsburg furniture and decorative accessories; a marvelous place to shop for your home. Many of the handmade crafts in the historic area are also for sale. Souvenir articles and products made for and by

The sounds of fifes and drum fill the air during the Grand Illumination of the City, a tradition in the reconstructed colonial village of Williamsburg.

Colonial Williamsburg craft program may be purchased at **Prentis Store, Tarpley's Store,** and the **Post Office.** The silversmith at the **Geddy House** and the jeweler at the **Golden Ball** also have items, as does the **Raleigh Tavern Bakery.** The modern section of Williamsburg is very well supplied with shops.

SPORTS

Many of the motels have pools; some also have various lawn games. Plenty of golf courses and tennis courts nearby, and there are both fresh-water and saltwater fishing only short drives away.

CALENDAR OF EVENTS

Antique Forum, late January; **Colonial Weekends,** the weekends in February; **Garden Symposium,** late March or early April; **Historic Garden Tours,** late April; **Prelude to Independence,** 15 May to 4 July; **Field Music Day,** the Saturday following Labor Day; and the **Holiday Season,** festive Christmastide celebrations from about 15 December until early January.

WHERE TO GO NEARBY

Carter's Grove Plantation, a great mansion with 400 acres only 6 miles southeast of Williamsburg, was erected in 1750-53 and was once famous for its gala social life; superb wood paneling.

The **Colonial National Historical Parkway,** only 23 miles long, begins in **Jamestown,** the first permanent English settlement, about 6 miles southwest of Williamsburg. Go to the **Visitors' Center** first to get an idea of what was where, because little but foundations remain of buildings put up by the first colonists. The remnants of a church tower, built in 1639, are recognizable, and streets in the "New Towne" that developed about 1620 have house sites clearly defined. Memorials, monuments, and markers recall characters of early American history. A glass factory, established when Jamestown was only a year old, has been reproduced and costumed glass blowers demonstrate their art. **Jamestown Festival Park** is adjacent to the historic site and recreates much of the early colony. The guard is changed with due ceremony at James Fort several times a day (15 June to Labor Day), Chief Powhatan's lodge has been recreated and you go aboard full-scale ship replicas of the *Susan Constant, Godspeed,* and *Discovery* that brought the first 144 settlers to Jamestown. History-tracing exhibits are displayed in the **New World Pavilion** and **Old World Pavilion.**

The Parkway from Jamestown follows the river until it turns inland toward Williamsburg, where it tunnels under the historic area, emerging near the Colonial Williamsburg Information Center. It then heads for the York River and down to little **Yorktown.** There are picnic areas and parking sites along the way.

In 1691, Yorktown was founded as a port to protect Virginia's shipping lanes. Its role had declined as early as 1750, but General Cornwallis regarded Yorktown as a good winter harbor for British warships and fought his way (without any spectacular battles) down the peninsula to the town. Cornwallis expected British ships to arrive any day, but they had been blockaded by the French fleet of Comte de Grasse. Meanwhile, American and French forces under Washington, Lafayette, and Rochambeau surrounded the town and laid siege on 9 October 1781. On the 17th, Cornwallis asked for surrender negotiations to begin, and on the 19th he signed the Articles of Capitulation. From that day the Revolution was over; America was free.

The **Visitors' Center** can provide information on the nine buildings still standing that survived the fighting and the vicissitudes of time. Among them are the **Moore House,** where Cornwallis signed the capitulation papers, and **Grace Episcopal Church,** where the British stored their powder and shot. Some of the old British fortifications were hastily revived by the Confederates during General McClellan's Peninsular Campaign. But, remembering the plight of Cornwallis, they nimbly withdrew on 4 May 1862 and let Union forces hold Yorktown for the rest of the year.

SHENANDOAH NATIONAL PARK

The park, 80 miles west of Washington, DC, covers 331 square miles and extends from Front Royal to Charlottesville. By mid-April the redbud and dogwood are in bloom, followed by pink azaleas and flowering black locust in May and pink and white mountain laurel in June. The trees usually achieve their most flamboyant autumn colors between 10 and 20 October. The park is always open but most active in midsummer, which is blissfully cool in the mountains.

Big Meadows Lodge, open all year, and **Skyland Lodge,** open April to early November, are 19 and 10 miles, respectively, south of the Thornton Gap road down to Luray; for Big Meadows Lodge (999-2221, S/D$22.50-32.50), open May-Oct, and for Skyland Lodge (999-2211, S/D$19-32.50), and advance reservations are advised. Housekeeping cabins are available at **Lewis Mountain,** farther south. There are shops and restaurants within the park.

An ideal wilderness for nature lovers from mid-June until Labor Day, the park has ranger-naturalists conducting hikes and nightly campfire programs. The magnificent **Skyline Drive** follows the full length of the park for a distance of 105 miles, and there are 75 parking overlooks along the way for tremendous views of the soft crests of the **Blue Ridge Mountains,** where the tallest peak, **Hawksbill Mountain,** is a comparatively modest 4,049 feet high.

Dickey Ridge Visitors' Center, near the north entrance, stresses the geological history of this billion-year-old region, and **Byrd Visitors' Center,** midway at Big Meadows, has exhibits on pioneer and Indian history. Hiking enthusiasts will want to follow all or part of the 95 miles of the **Appalachian Trail,** which rambles along the mountain crests. Self-guiding tours also follow the **Swamp Nature Trail,** the 4,010-foot ascent of **Stony Man Mountain** and—more rigorous—the trail to **Dark Hollow Falls.** Trout-fishing is very good from mid-April to mid-October; license required. Some 200 species of birds have been recorded, and there are an estimated 1,200 species of trees and flowering plants. Deer and bear are the largest of 40 varieties of wildlife.

FURTHER STATE INFORMATION

Virginia State Travel Service, 9th St. Office Building, Richmond, VA 23219. Hunting and Fishing: **Game and Inland Fisheries Commission,** 4013 West Broad Street, Richmond, VA 23230. **Norfolk Convention and Visitors' Bureau,** PO Box 238, Norfolk, VA 23501; **Chamber of Commerce—Metropolitan Richmond,** 201 E. Franklin Street, Richmond, VA 23219; the **Colonial Williamsburg Foundation,** PO Drawer C, Williamsburg, VA 23185; Superintendent, **Shenandoah National Park,** Luray, VA 22835.

USEFUL TELEPHONE NUMBERS
Norfolk

Major Hospital and Norfolk General	628-3000
Emergency Dental	627-8534
Legal Aid Society	627-5423
Tourist Information Center	441-5166
Chamber of Commerce	622-2312
Rotary Club	622-7971
Pan Am Reservations	622-1301

Richmond

Medical College of Virginia	786-9000
Legal Aid Society	643-0218
Tourist Information Center	358-5511
Chamber of Commerce	648-1234
Rotary Club	643-4192
Kiwanis	643-1190
Pan Am Reservations	649-9161

Washington

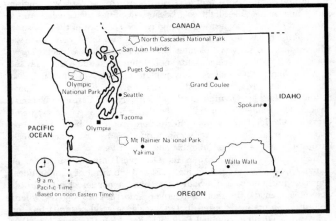

Area	68,192 square miles					**Population**	4,130,000					
Capital	Olympia					**Sales Tax**	5.3%					

Weather	Jan	Feb	Mar	Apr	May	Jun	Jul	Aug	Sep	Oct	Nov	Dec
Av Temp (°C)	4	5	7	10	13	15	18	18	16	11	7	5
Days Rain/Snow	20	16	18	14	10	10	5	7	9	15	18	21

In the autumn of 1805 a US military expedition led by Lewis and Clark crossed the Continental Divide to the headwaters of the Clearwater River in Idaho. Here they made canoes and let the river carry them into the Snake, which flowed into the Columbia River. It was not the Northwest Passage they'd hoped to find but it must have been an overwhelmingly beautiful trip; it still is, especially through the 60-mile-long gorge that the river has carved through the Cascades.

Sculptured by volcanic action and glaciers, Washington is edged with miles of uncrowded Pacific beaches, but the coastal lowland gives way to the **Olympic Mountains,** which run south from the **Strait of Juan de Fuca.** This is a region of shadowed rain forests where huge Douglas fir trees tower up to 300 feet and have diameters of 15 feet. Moisture-laden winds off the Pacific keep the area cool in summer and warm in winter, but they pour upon it as much as 140 inches of rain per year. It is the wettest region in the nation and, understandably, still one of its least explored areas. Once past the Olympic Mountains, the Pacific air currents around the **Puget Sound** bring only moderate rainfall and a mild climate; the **Cascade Range** divides the state nearly equally. Up to 108 inches of rain may fall on the western slopes of the Cascades, but leave a semi-desert parched for rain on the eastern side of the mountains. Farther east, around Spokane, rainfall is normal again and the Rocky Mountains in the state of Montana usually intercept frigid northeasterly winds that can blow across from the northern Great Plains. Spring and summer are pretty reliably warm in most of Washington state, but you'll want a light coat because evenings turn cool. Autumn and winter are the rainiest seasons and can be cold east of the Cascades.

Washington has more than 100 state parks and eight heritage areas where museums preserve pioneer and other historical artifacts. There are about 275 special regions for sport fishing and some 20 areas set aside for hunting, as well as many wildlife refuges. Washington is also an ideal winter resort with just the right terrain, weather, and snow conditions. Besides **Olympic National Park, North Cascades National Park,** and **Mt Rainier National Park,** the National Park Service also administers the **Coulee Dam National Recreation Area,** and there are superb recreation areas along the reservoirs formed by the great dams which harness the power of the Columbia and other rivers.

An intricate shoreline borders the Olympic Peninsula on the Puget Sound. However, along the Pacific Coast and the Strait of Juan de Fuca, which lies north between the State's coast and Vancouver Island in British Columbia, Canada, the shore is relatively smooth. **Port Angeles,** where English explorers first docked in 1787, makes a good headquarters for visits to the Olympic National Park. The **Red Lion Bayshore Inn** (452-9215, S$28-38/D$35-46), nestled on the waterfront, has a great view of the harbor. **Aggie's Motel** (457-0471, S$22/D$28) has an excellent restaurant with dancing six nights a week. The **Aircrest, Hill Haus, Royal Victorian** and **Uptown** motels are about S$21-27/D$25-42. Most rates are lower from October to May.

US 101 continues westward from the park, then south towards the large **Quinault Indian Reservation** and down to the adjoining cities of **Aberdeen** and **Hoquiam** on Grays Harbor, 12 miles inland. These are great centers for lumbermen and fishermen. WA 109 leads to a string of little resort towns right on the Pacific coast. Inland, on the southwestern side of Puget Sound, is **Olympia,** capital of the state, with one of the nation's handsomest collection of administrative buildings. Visit the **State Capitol Museum.** Tiny, plump Olympia oysters are the local delicacy and they taste even better with the view you get at the **Jacaranda** or **Olympic Oyster House** restaurants.

SOUTHWESTERN WASHINGTON is a great place for sportsmen. **Long Beach** has a hard-packed sand beach, firm enough for driving on, stretching for 28 miles. Residents on the little peninsula that separates **Willapa Bay** from the Pacific are busy year round oystering, logging, fishing, and growing cranberries, while vacationers revel in free clambakes, duck hunting, boating, and swimming. King salmon run from April to October at **Fort Canby** and you can charter a boat at **Ilwaco** or **Westport. Longview,** another place with fine fishing for salmon and steelhead, lies inland on the Columbia River. It has other industries but is most famous for the world's largest wood-products plant, operated by the Weyerhaeuser Company. Guided tours, using your own car, begin at the Guest House, Monday to Friday at 9:30 and 1:30 from 17 June-30 August, off-season tours by arrangement. Nearby **Kelso** has the fascinating **Cowlitz County Museum** that recalls pioneer conditions in the lumber country. A branch road north of Kelso leads to the deep blue **Spirit Lake** and offers on clear days views of the still-steaming active **Mt St Helens**, the volcano which in 1980 blew off 1,200 feet of its former 9,677-foot peak. This is a popular non-commercialized winter sports area. **Vancouver**, south of Kelso, was founded as a Hudson's Bay Company fort and trading post in 1824. Visit the **Fort Vancouver National Historic Site, Clark County Historical Museum**, and the **Ulysses S. Grant Museum** in "Officers Row," where Grant was stationed in 1852-53.

The **Puget Sound** area is said to be one of the prettiest places in the world and one of the most satisfying to live in. The metropolitan district of **Seattle-Tacoma-Everett** has fine stores, smart restaurants, all kinds of cultural activities, and handsome residential suburbs. Bridges and ferries provide glorious waterway views, as well as transportation to the islands. Yet within easy drive from all this sophisticated bustle are seashore and mountain resorts, trout-filled lakes, and forests. **Mt Rainier National Park** is southwest of this metropolitan area.

NORTHWESTERN WASHINGTON is a vast region of snowy mountains, great forests, and an island-dotted shoreline. **Anacortes** is an industrial city on Fidalgo Island. Enjoy the beaches, lakes, and parks or take a ferryboat which puts out several times a day for a sail through the **San Juan Islands**. This historic archipelago was probably where the first white men came ashore in Washington. Accommodations range from modest fishing camps to the luxurious **Rosario Resort Hotel** (376-2222, S$33-45/D$45-125) on Orcas Island; prices are 20% lower in the winter off-season. The **San Juan Island National Historical Park** commemorates America's final boundary dispute with the British, which ended in 1872. The park consists of two units: American Camp at the southern end, and English Camp at the northern end of the island. **Bellingham** stands on high bluffs overlooking Puget Sound and the distant Olympic Mountains to the west, while the snowy Cascades rise regally on the eastern skyline. Try not to miss the view from **Chuckanut Drive**, carved out on mountainside cliffs high above the Sound. Interesting regional exhibits are in the **Whatcom Museum of History and Art**. North of Bellingham, near Blaine, is the **Peace Arch** commemorating friendship with Canada. The US-Canadian customs post is at Blaine. East of Bellingham is **Mt Baker National Forest**, a rugged wilderness of forests and mountains that are a refuge for hunters and fishermen. Great skiing on **Mt Baker** from November until early July. **North Cascades National Park** is adjacent to **Mt Baker**.

NORTH CENTRAL WASHINGTON presents more superb scenery, both natural and man-made. The world's largest concrete gravity dam is **Grand Coulee Dam**, begun in 1933 and completed in 1942. There are conducted sightseeing tours. A "coulee" is a deep valley gouged out by glacial waters, and **Grand Coulee** is grandest of all. It is about 50 miles long and its walls are from 500 to 1,000 feet high. **Dry Falls Lake** is a quiet spot for trout fishermen. Just beyond is **Sun Lakes State Park** with golf, horseback riding, fishing, and water sports. Along the eastern edge of the Cascades is **Wenatchee,** the apple capital of the nation. Wenatchee plays host to the **Washington State Apple Blossom Festival,** held in May. **Rocky Reach Dam,** north of town, has an unusually good local museum. Just west of town are Cashmere with the **Willis Carey Pioneer Village Museum,** and **Leavenworth,** a little town rebuilt to look like a Bavarian village. The **Washington State Autumn Leaf Festival** is held here at the height of the fall foliage season, in late September and early October. There is good cross-country and downhill skiing here from December to March. About 30 miles northwest is the famous **Stevens Pass Ski Area.** Some 30 miles southeast is the large **Mission Ridge** ski area, while farther north is **Lake Chelan,** 55 miles long and only ¼ to 2 miles wide; daily boat trips from **Chelan** to **Stehekin** from 15 May through September, reduced schedule the rest of the year. Chelan has a rodeo in mid-July and a sailboat regatta the last weekend in September. Campsites, motels, and cottages make this a popular resort for outdoor recreation. **Omak** is a lumber and cattle town where the exciting **Stampede and Suicide Race** involving cattle is held the second weekend in August. From Omak, east to **Franklin D. Roosevelt Lake** and south to Grand Coulee Dam, is the **Colville Indian Reservation.** The information center is in the **Colville Tribal Office** just south of Nespelem on WA 155.

NORTHEAST WASHINGTON is the sparsely settled region bounded on the west by the Columbia River and the Franklin D. Roosevelt Lake— 150 miles long and a superb recreation area. North of Spokane are abandoned goldmining towns: **Gardner Caves,** near the Canadian border; and **Sherman Pass,** which crosses the mountains at an elevation of 5,675 feet.

Yakima in **SOUTH CENTRAL WASHINGTON** claims 300 days of sunshine a year. Here you will find the world's largest facilities for storing and processing fruits. Horses are regarded nearly as highly as fruit, and the **Washington State Open Horse Show** is held every Memorial Day weekend. There are thoroughbred and quarter horse races at **Yakima Meadows** from mid-April to mid-May and in October and November. Using Yakima as a base you can easily visit the Wild West town of **Ellensburg** for the big rodeo on Labor Day weekend; wander through **Fort Simcoe State Park,** near Toppenish, where the original buildings are much as they were during the Indian troubles of the last century. See the **Ginkgo Petrified Forest;** visit the **Wanapum Dam** with its excellent museum of Indian and pioneer lore; and go to **Maryhill,** near Goldendale, where there is a remarkable art museum and, surprisingly, a replica of England's Stonehenge. East of Yakima is the **Hanford Works US Energy Research and Development Administration's Reservation,** which covers 620 square miles. The **Hanford Science Center,** with exhibits that make atomic energy understandable, is in **Richland,** a bright new industrial city. Clustered with it, where the Snake River joins the Columbia, are **Pasco** and **Kennewick.**

The **Snake River** forms the boundary between Washington and Idaho for about 30 miles in **SOUTHEAST WASHINGTON** and here it has carved the deepest gorge on the North American continent. It is more than 40 miles long and as much as 7,000 feet deep. The **Grand Ronde Canyon** in the same area is also spectacular. **Palouse Falls,** due north of Walla Walla, is another remarkable sight. Although primarily a wheat-growing region, this part of the state has great opportunities for sportsmen. Apart from the fishing available in the rivers, the reservoirs formed by dams provide all kinds of water sports. The **Blue Mountains** have fine hunting for deer and elk, and the valleys teem with wild duck, geese, and other game birds. There is also skiing in the **Blue Ridge** area. The key city is **Walla Walla,** just north of the Oregon line. The **Whitman Mission Historical Site,** seven miles west of Walla Walla, is a museum and a memorial to the medical missionary, Dr Marcus Whitman.

Cities To Visit

SEATTLE

Seattle was first settled in 1851 at **Alki Point.** It was then called New York, but later renamed in honor of a friendly Indian, Chief Sealth. The city was incorporated in 1869 and saw considerable growth as a lumber town and later as a departure point for gold prospectors. A disastrous fire leveled much of the city in 1889. Like most seaports, Seattle is cosmopolitan with many diversified interests. The city has a blend of many races, creeds, and cultures which helps to make life here sophisticated and exciting. The population of the metropolitan area is 1,600,000.

WHAT TO SEE
University of Washington campus; **Lake Washington Ship Canal; Floating Bridges** spanning Lake Washington; **Chinatown; Rose Gardens; Ye Old Curiosity Shop,** an interesting place with gifts from the Pacific Northwest and Alaska; the statue honoring Chief Sealth, the Indian for whom the city is named, is located at 5th Ave. and Denning. **The Hansen Baking Co.** for dining and shops; the **Rainer Brewery**—free tours daily 1-6, Monday through Friday; or tour underground Seattle, where you'll see remains of the original city, adults $2.50, $1.25 children. **Museum of History and Industry,** illustrating the story of the city's first 100 years; Tuesday to Friday 11-5. Saturday from 10, Sunday from noon. **Smith Tower Observatory** and **Chinese Temple; Public Market; Seattle Center** with its magnificent **Pacific Science Center** and the 607-foot **Space Needle.** An interesting tour on both land and water is offered by Gray Line for $14 adults, $9 children; tours leave several times daily during the summer months. To see the city properly, you should take a boat trip; most of

these cost about $8. Trips to the **Cascade Mountains, Chinook Pass,** and **Mt Rainier** cost $18. A tour of the **Mt St Helens** volcanic area costs $17.50. This includes a stop at the **Forest Service Visitors' Center,** with a videotape viewing of the eruption and a seismograph monitoring the volcano's current activity.

There are about 44 city parks and playgrounds. **Alki Beach, Carkeek Park,** and **Golden Gardens** have ocean beaches and picnic facilities; **Lincoln Park** has a salt-water swimming pool. **Volunteer Park** is known for its formal gardens, flowers, and conservatory. **Woodland Park** has rose gardens, a fine zoo, including a new children's zoo, and recreational area. The University of Washington's 97-acre **Arboretum** features an authentic Japanese tea garden. **The Seattle Marine Aquarium,** Pier 56, has a variety of marine life from the Puget Sound area. **The Freeway Park** with its numerous flowers and a waterfall is built atop 8 lanes of downtown freeway.

ACCOMMODATIONS

Downtown hotels include: **Camlin** (682-0100, S$35-40/D$40-50); **Park Hilton Downtown** (682-1750, S$68/D$82). The 40-story circular **Washington Plaza Hotel** (624-7400, S$60-80/D$85-95) is the finest in the city; luxury accommodation with huge view windows and a 375-car garage. Other hotels include **Edgewater Inn, Vance, Sixth Avenue Motor Hotel, Towne Motor Hotel,** and **Tropics,** averaging S$25-38/D$31-42. Those located near the airport include **Holiday Inn Airport, Hyatt House, Jet Inn, Red Lion, Seattle Airport Hilton, Seattle Marriott Sea-Tac,** and **TraveLodge at Sea-Tac.** Average rates are S$37-70/D$42-73. All are comfortable and provide complimentary shuttle service between the hotel and airport. Hotel Tax: 5%

RESTAURANTS

Canlis' for steaks and continental cuisine, marvelous salads, served in an exotic atmosphere, expensive; **Rosellini's Other Place,** considered the best for French cuisine, expensive; **Mirabeau,** atop the Sea-First Bank Building, expensive; **Cloud Room,** Camlin Hotel, dining with a view, moderate to expensive. **Trader Vic's** in the Washington Plaza Hotel, expensive; **Space Needle** restaurant, revolving, moderate to expensive; **Ivar's Acres of Clams** and **Ivar's Indian Salmon House,** both with waterfront views and marine atmosphere, picturesque, excellent seafood, moderate prices; and **Hidden Harbor** on Lake Union, marine views, moderate to expensive. The **Quins** at Shilshole Marina, overlooking one of the world's largest and most modern yacht harbors, fine food, marvelous views of the Puget Sound country, moderate to expensive; **Gasperetti's Roma Café,** fine Italian food; **Thirteen Coins,** in the Northwest Furniture Mart, Italian theme, excellent food and delightful atmosphere, moderate to expensive; **Brasserie Pittsbourg,** oldest restaurant in continuous operation in Seattle, excellent French menu, moderate to expensive. Across from the Kingdome is **F.X. McRory's,** an Irish oyster house, moderate; the **Smuggler** in Pier 70 features a wide variety of fresh seafood as you

The Science Pavilion and the 607-ft Space Needle are just two of the futuristic attractions offered at the 74-acre Seattle Center in Washington.

watch the ferries ply to and fro, moderate; **Henry's Off Braodway,** a luxurious "in" restaurant and oyster bar, moderate; **Hiram's,** with a view of the locks and Salmon Bay, moderate to expensive; **Horatio's,** with its turn-of-the-century nautical theme, moderate; also at Shilshole Marina is **Stuart's,** with a view of the sun setting behind the Olympic mountains, moderate to expensive.

ENTERTAINMENT

Fine dining and entertainment are found in the **Washington Plaza Hotel, Olympic Hotel, University Tower, Hyatt House, Doubletree Inn,** and **The Goose.** Other excellent nightspots include **Jack McGovern's Music Hall,** a dinner theater with Las Vegas-type reviews, the **Wharf Restaurant** and the **Quins,** the **Space Needle, Pier 70 Restaurant & Chowder House,** all moderate to expensive. Off-beat modern jazz establishments, such as **Parnell's,** abound in the "Old Seattle" Pioneer Square area. For nightclub tours, call "Seattle by Night," tel: 762-3727.

ARTS AND MUSIC

Seattle's major new arts center, the **5th Avenue Theatre,** houses first-run Broadway productions, especially musicals. It has a year-round schedule replete with big names and national touring companies of current Broadway hits. The **Seattle Repertory Theater** plays a full season of fine professional productions at **Seattle Center.** The "Rep" is augmented by a lively schedule of contemporary works and road shows. There is a full seasonal program of works by the **Seattle Symphony Orchestra** and by the **University of Washington School of Music** and by **The Pacific Northwest Ballet,** a resident professional company. There are frequent free concerts at the Seattle Center. Legitimate stage productions are presented by the **Repertory Theater, Black Arts West, ACT, Cirque Dinner Theater,** and **Bathhouse Theater.** Road shows appear at the **Seattle Opera House,** Seattle Center. There also are many fine amateur or semi-professional groups. The **Seattle Art Museum,** collection of oriental and occidental art; Tuesday to Saturday 10-5, Sunday 12-5. **Free Public Art Museum,** general displays of art; Monday to Saturday 10-5, Sunday and holidays 12-6. **Washington State Museum,** art of the Pacific, Asia, and Alaska; **Henry Art Gallery,** examples of modern art; **Pacific Science Center,** Laserium light concert, open daily; **Seligman Gallery,** local works and loaned collections.

SHOPPING

Downtown Seattle has everything from major department stores to high fashion shops and specialty stores. There are also shopping malls in the suburbs. Many stores remain open on various evenings until 9. Visit **Pike Place Market,** a fascinating market featuring unusual bazaars, country produce, flowers, and seafood. **Pier 70** has more than 40 distinctive shops and restaurants on the waterfront. Don't miss the elegant **Rainier Square Mall** which stretches several blocks underground, fanning out from beneath Rainier Bank's unique pedestal skyscraper.

SPORTS

The **University of Washington, Seattle Pacific College,** and **Seattle University** offer all major collegiate sports. American League Seattle Mariners play in the Seattle Kingdome during baseball season. There is summer horse racing at **Longacres** and the winter season offers professional ice hockey and basketball. Golf may be played on 10 public and six private courses; tennis, in schools, parks, and private clubs. There are innumerable spots for fresh- and saltwater swimming and other water sports. Boating is particularly important in Seattle with many people owning all sorts of small craft. Hunting seasons vary; non-resident license is $60. Trout fishing is good; the open season, with some limitations, is from April through October; non-resident seven-day license is $7.50. Saltwater fishing has no closed season, requires no license. Many ski resorts in the area are only an hour's drive from the city. The largest ski area with accommodations is at **Crystal Mountain,** a beautiful alpine setting where rooms average $30. For mountain climbers, guided trips to the summit of Mt Rainier, as well as instructions in mountain climbing techniques, are available.

CALENDAR OF EVENTS

Seattle Seafair marks the height of the summer season with parades, boating and yachting events, hydroplane racing. Numerous small county and regional fairs; most of these special events are held between June and October.

WHERE TO GO NEARBY

Olympic National Park is west of Seattle and the **North Cascades National Park** is about 125 miles northeast of the city. Washington also has 144 state parks and historical sites; near Seattle are **Lake Sammamish, Saltwater, Twanoh, Fay Bainbridge, Kitsap Memorial, Illahee,** and **Belfair** state parks. Other places of interest are the **San Juan Islands, Olympic Peninsula** area, **Mt Baker, Spirit Lake** at **Mt St Helens,** and **Deception Pass.** If time permits, take a boat trip to **Vancouver** or **Victoria** in Canada.

SPOKANE

Spokane is in east central Washington, on the Spokane River. A fur-trading post was established in 1810 and a mission in 1838 at nearby Tshimakin, but the earliest permanent settlement dates only from 1871. The largest city in a huge and distinct geographical region, Spokane refers to itself as the "Capital of the Inland Empire." The surrounding area is rich in timber, water power, farmland, and minerals, and other natural resources.

WHAT TO SEE

Spokane Falls, 70 feet high, in the central business district; **Duncan Gardens** in the lovely **Manito Park; Cathedral of St John; Cheney Cowles**

and **Grace Campbell** memorial museums, Indian and pioneer artifacts, open Tuesday to Saturday 10-5, Sunday 2-5, free. Visit the **Crosby Library** and see the collection of Bing Crosby's records, Oscars, and trophies; Spokane was the singer's boyhood home. Spokane has 60 public parks with good recreational facilities. **Manito Park** has beautiful sunken gardens; **Cliff Park** offers a fine view of the city; **Riverside State Park** has interesting geological formations. **Riverview Park** is fifty-five acres in the downtown area along the Spokane River where the **Ice Palace,** the Northwest's largest outdoor ice rink, open daily from October 13 through April 13 is located and where the site for Expo '74, the Mini International Fair was held. Within a 50 mile radius of downtowm Spokane, there are more than 75 lakes. A pleasant automobile trip may be made on **Downriver Drive** to **Indian Canyon** and **Rimrock.**

ACCOMMODATIONS

Davenport Hotel (624-2121, S$30/D$46-140), heated rooftop swimming pool, famous cuisine in Matador Room; **Sheraton-Spokane** (226-7700, S$46/D$55), on Expo '74 grounds; **Holiday Inn-Downtown** (838-6101, S$30-D$36), **Ridpath Hotel and Motor Inn** (838-2711, S$30-39/D$38-105), rooftop dining and dancing. All are in downtown Spokane. **Spokane House Motor Hotel** (838-1471, S$25-29/D$31-47) is on I-90 at Garden Spring exit, and **The Trade Winds Motel** (838-1571, S$25-29/D$31-55) is downtown. **The Ramada Inn** (838-5211, S$30/D$36) is located at the Spokane International Airport. Camping near the city at **Smoky Trail Campsite** and also at **Riverside State Park,** 5 miles northwest of Spokane. Camping is also available at the **KOA Campground, Trailer Inns R.V. Park,** and **Sunset Campgrounds,** all some 5 miles to the west of Spokane. Hotel Tax: 5%

RESTAURANTS

Be sure to try Washington's famous fruits in season. A local treat is smoked bluetacks, a silver salmon about 10 inches long which makes a good appetizer. **King Cole Room** and the **Desert Sahara** both have good American cuisine. **Stockyards Inn, Black Angus Steakhouse,** and **Beef 'n Brew** are all known for their steaks. Italian food at **Luigi's** and **Pupo's;** Davenport Hotel's **Matador,** Spanish decor; **Madge's Hedgehouse,** good American dinners. **Smitty's Pancake House** has great pancakes and Southern-fried chicken. Ridpath Hotel's **Legend Room** serves good beef amid murals of Spokane history. All of these are moderate in price.

ARTS AND MUSIC

Cheney Cowles Memorial Museum and **Eastern Washington State Historical Society** have collections of Indian arts and crafts, pioneer relics, geology displays, and changing art exhibits; there is also the **Pacific Northwest Indian Center,** 5-story teepee-shaped museum and Indian language research library, one of the finest in the country. **Spokane Symphony Orchestra** performs in season. Dramas and musicals at the **Spokane Civic Theater.**

SHOPPING
Downtown stores remain open until 9 on Monday and Friday. Several interesting shopping centers include **Second City, Old Port Spokane,** and the **Flour Mill.**

SPORTS
There is horse racing at **Playfair** during the fall season. Pro-hockey by the **Jets,** college basketball and football by **Washington State University, Whitworth College, Spokane Falls Community College,** and **Gonzaga University.** Golf can be played at three municipal, two public, two county, and two private 18-hole courses. There are good facilities for tennis, swimming and other sports. Hunting and fishing in the area are often good.

CALENDAR OF EVENTS
Boat Show, February; annual **Spokane Diamond Spur Rodeo,** April; **Lilac Festival,** May; **Spokane Interstate Fair,** September; **Home Show,** October; **Auto Show,** November.

WHERE TO GO NEARBY
Mt Spokane State Park, 30 miles northeast, has a road to the summit of Mt Spokane which offers a superlative view of the surrounding area. **Steptoe Butte State Park and Battlefield** are 47 miles south. **Riverside State Park,** 5 miles northwest on the Spokane River, has picnic and camping facilities, wood area, and interesting lava outcroppings. **Grand Coulee Dam** is 89 miles west and is a worthwhile trip. There is a network of 75 lakes in the immediate neighborhood, offering a wide selection of recreational facilities. Within a day's drive are 13 national or state parks, many with camping facilities.

TACOMA

The Hudson's Bay Company built a fort 18 miles south of the present site of Tacoma in 1833 and 31 years later Job Carr filed a land claim on what is now Old Tacoma. General McCarver, seeking a location for the terminus of the Northern Pacific Railroad, bought some of Carr's land in 1868 and when the railroad was completed the community was called **New Tacoma.** The town grew with amazing rapidity during the decade that followed. Tacoma is an important world port and shipping center and its citizens are particularly interested in sailing and boating, with a high per capita ownership of pleasure craft.

WHAT TO SEE
Kla-ho-ya Trail, a marked 2-hour tour of the city, may be covered by following special street markers. Taxi tours around the trail may be arranged through the **Oliver Taxi Company.** Highlights of a visit should include the **Tacoma Narrows Suspension Bridge,** 5,450 feet long, successor to the ill-fated "Galloping Gertie," which collapsed in 1940; **Stadium High School,** housed in an astonishing French Renaissance-style castle; **Point Defiance Park,** containing a restoration of a Hudson's Bay Company

fort; **Washington State Museum; Job Carr House; Old Fort Nisqually; Camp Six,** a reconstructed lumber camp. Near the city are **Fort Lewis** and **McChord Air Force Base,** large US military installations. Tacoma is a good starting point for a trip to **Mt Rainier National Park.** Charter boats are available at **Tacoma Boat Mart,** 2315 Ruston Way.

Tacoma has 44 parks, **Point Defiance** being the outstanding one, with an aquarium, boat house, zoo, rose gardens, bathing beach, and picnic areas; the park is mostly of natural evergreen, full of beautiful trails. **Wapato Park** has picnic grounds and a lake; **Wright Park** is known for its conservatory and trees. Near **Eatonville,** about 25 miles southeast of Tacoma, is the new **Northwest Trek,** a 600-acre animal preserve. A narrated 50-minute tram trip gives the visitor a close-up view of elk, bison, caribou, bighorn mountain sheep, and many others.

ACCOMMODATIONS
Doris Tacoma Motor Hotel (572-9572, S$22/D$26), downtown, overlooking the bay; **Holiday Inn** (922-0550, S$30/D$36), at Port of Tacoma exit of I-5, 3 miles from downtown; **Olympus Hotel** (572-8533, S$15/D$20), downtown; **Rodeway Inn** (475-5900, S$27/D$35-39), 5 miles south of downtown; **Sherwood Inn** (475-4400, S$25/D$27-29), adjoining Freeway, 5 miles south of business district; **TraveLodge** (383-3557, S$25-29/D$27-30), downtown; and **Lakewood Motor Inn** (584-2212, S$27-29/D$30-35), 12 miles from the business district. Hotel Tax: 5%

RESTAURANTS
Seafood is the specialty of the Puget Sound area; particularly recommended are salmon, crab, clams, and shrimp. Raspberries and other fruits are excellent during the late summer season. **Johnny's Dock, Cliff House, Ceccanti's,** and **Harbor Lights, Clinkerdagger, Bickerstaff & Petts** for steaks and seafood; all are moderately expensive. The **Bavarian** serves German food, moderate; **Steve's Gay 90's,** smorgasbord; **Lakewood Terrace,** moderately expensive, 7 miles south of town.

ENTERTAINMENT
Ceccanti's, New Yorker, Top of the Ocean, and **Steve's Gay 90's;** moderately expensive.

ARTS AND MUSIC
State Historical Museum, noted for its illuminated photo murals and exhibits of pioneer, Indian, and Alaskan materials; open Tuesday through Saturday 9-4 except holidays, free. **Allied Arts Center** and **Tacoma Art Museum;** open Monday to Saturday 10-4, Sunday 12-5, free. Tacoma has an active **Little Theater** which presents a different show each month. **Lakewood Players** also present stage shows as announced.

SHOPPING
The downtown shopping area is the **Broadway Plaza,** with pedestrian traffic only and fountains and play areas for children. Stores remain open

Monday and Friday evenings until 9. Also downtown is the recently renovated **Old City Hall,** now a beautiful landmark and filled with a variety of shops and boutiques. The **Tacoma Mall,** a regional shopping center on an 85-acre complex with two department stores, numerous specialty shops, and service establishments, theater, and office buildings, is about a mile south from downtown, in Lakewood.

SPORTS

There is horse racing at **Longacres,** 25 miles northeast, near Renton, from May through September. The **Tacoma Twins** are members of the Pacific Coast AAA Baseball League. College basketball, baseball and football are played in season.

Boating is the favorite local sport. The boathouse in Point Defiance Park is one of the largest in the country; rowboats rent for only $15 a day, outboard boats and motors $19 up. Golf is available at several public and private courses; tennis at various public parks; saltwater swimming at Point Defiance and freshwater swimming at public pools and lakes. No license is required for saltwater fishing of salmon, sea bass and salmon trout.

CALENDAR OF EVENTS

Puyallup Valley Daffodil Festival, April; **Rose and Rhododendron Shows,** May; **Western Washington Fair,** at Puyallup, September.

WHERE TO GO NEARBY

Saltwater State Park, 15 miles north, a fine bathing beach, fishing, camping, and picnicking areas facing Puget Sound. **Belfair State Park,** 37 miles northwest, facilities for swimming and camping. **Twanoh State Park,** 43 miles west, on the Hood Canal, fishing, swimming, and picnic facilities. **Federation Forest,** 42 miles east, natural wooded area with good fishing. **Mt Rainier National Park** is 56 miles southeast. The **North Cascades National Park** is northeast of Tacoma and **Olympic National Park,** northwest. The **Olympic Peninsula** is the outstanding local vacation district. Washington State Ferries and Canadian Pacific operate ferry service from Port Angeles and Seattle to Victoria, British Columbia, June to September.

MT RAINIER NATIONAL PARK

This park occupies 378 square miles in central Washington, about 60 miles southeast of Tacoma or 1½ hours from Seattle. The season is principally mid-June to mid-September, with July and August the most free of clouds and fog. The **Road to Paradise,** from the **Nisqually Entrance** in the southwestern corner, is open all year. **Mather Memorial Highway,** which crosses the park from north to south on the east side of the mountain, is kept open most of the year. The normal climbing season is from Memorial Day to Labor Day. The winter-sports season is from early December to early May. Lake fishing is usually 4 July to 31 October.

National Park Inn (475-6260, S/D$16-37) at Longmire, elevation 2,761 feet, is open from early May until October. The famous **Paradise Inn** (475-6260, S/D$17-43) at 5,400 feet is open from mid-June until Labor Day. There are four well-developed campgrounds and three primitive sites.

Mt Rainier, a dormant volcano of the Cascade Mountains, appears to be a perfectly shaped white cone from the northwest. But it consists of three peaks: **Liberty Cap,** 14,112 feet; **Point Success,** 14,150 feet; and **Columbia Crest,** 14,410 feet. The 20 or more living glaciers on Rainier include 15 that originate at the summit icecap or in glacier-carved hollows at elevations of between 10,000 and 12,000 feet. The **Emmons** and **Nisqually** glaciers are easily visited; the Nisqually is estimated to move from 50 to more than 400 feet a year at the 6,000 foot level. The small **Paradise** and **Stevens** glaciers, only 3 miles from **Paradise Visitor Center,** are easy to explore and, within a relatively small area, display all the geological oddities typical of valley glaciers. The snowy grandeur of the mountain is seen against stately forests of firs and hemlock. Wildflowers carpet the valleys and slopes from early May through the summer; little fawn lilies even shoot up through the snow. Wilderness trails are the best places to view the park's bears, elk, mule deer, mountain goats, and the stout, furry marmots who live in the higher rocks. More than 130 species of birds have been seen in the park. There are daily "Round-the-Mountain" sightseeing bus tours from Seattle and Tacoma in summer. **Rainier Mountaineering,** an organization managed by Lou Whittaker, twin brother of Everest-conqueror Jim Whittaker, features instruction in the latest ice and snow climbing technique or will escort you on a 2-day climb to the summit of Mt Rainier (14,410 feet).

NORTH CASCADES NATIONAL PARK

The park covers 1,053 square miles about 125 miles northeast of Seattle. The season is from mid-June to mid-September for mountain climbers; early April to mid-October for hikers at lower elevations. The western side of the mountains is rainier and cooler in summer than the eastern side. Winters can be bitter and formidable.

The park, created in 1968, presents a panorama of jagged mountain peaks and deep-plunging valleys. There are more than 300 active glaciers and valleys are filled with wildflowers. About 350 miles of trails have been laid out; some of them are for the casual hiker, others can tax the most determined climber. You may catch a glimpse of black bears, mountain goats, and deer but such animals as grizzly bears, cougars, and moose are rarely seen. The park is in two sections. The northern part, reaching to the Canadian border, is the most mountainous. The southern section is gentler, encompassing the **Eldorado High Country** and **Stehekin River Valley.** The two parts are separated by WA 20, the village of Newhalem and Lakes Ross and Diablo, formed by damming the Skagit River; lake tours available at **Newhalem.** This was, until a few years ago, the end of the line. For 80 years, off and on, attempts were made to blast the highway through the mountains; the road is finally open to form the only east-west route in northern Washington. The park can also be seen from lake-landing seaplanes chartered in **Ana-cortes, Bellingham,** and **Chelan.**

Camping is the only way you can spend the night inside the park. The nearest motels, at present, are in **Sedro Woolley** and **Concrete,** the nearest towns on WA 20 which goes through **Ross Lake National Recreation Area.** This park has three camping grounds and a small resort on Ross Lake. The campground at **Colonial Creek** is especially good; open 15 April to 1 November. The **Lake Chelan National Recreation Area,** south of the park, has campsites at **Stehekin,** where the village store has been outfitting hunters and prospectors since pioneer days. Travel into Stehekin is by *The Lady of the Lake* that sails up from Chelan, and chartered aircraft.

OLYMPIC NATIONAL PARK

The park occupies 1,400 square miles of the Olympic Peninsula, west of Seattle and Tacoma, and bounded by the Pacific Ocean, Juan de Fuca Strait, and Puget Sound. It is never out of season. Summers are mostly cool and sunny; September and October are sometimes delightfully warm. The luxuriant rain forests on the west side of the peninsula thrive under 140 to 200 inches of precipitation annually. Most of the rain falls in the winter but it's wise to have rainwear handy at any time of year.

Pioneer Memorial Museum at the northern entrance is open daily year round. **Hurricane Ridge Road** climbs to an elevation of 5,200 feet, affording tremendous views of all the Olympic Mountains and meadows that are a glorious profusion of wildflowers from June through September; this road also leads to ski slopes in winter. **Obstruction Point Lookout,** elevation 6,450 feet, is the end of the road and the beginning of **Deer Park Trail.** Altogether, 15 roads lead into the park from all sides, quickly terminating to become hiking trails with conveniently placed overnight shelters. Tallest of the park's peaks, **Mt Olympus,** rising to 7,965 feet, is laced with glaciers and requires considerable mountaineering skill. West and south of Olympus are the gigantic rain forests in the valleys of the **Hoh, Quinault,** and **Queets** rivers. Here Douglas fir and western red cedar stand nearly 300 feet tall, and Sitka spruce, western hemlock, and other species rise to shade the forest with green light. Nearly 6,000 elk live in the park, as well as black-tailed deer, black bear, marmot, and many other species. No license is required to fish for trout in the cold mountain streams and lakes, or to dig for clams along the Hood Canal and the Pacific beaches where seals cavort on offshore rocks. Naturalist programs are held nightly at major campgrounds in summer. Winters along the beaches are cold and not at all suitable for picnicking; but some people enjoy beachcombing and looking for Japanese glass fishing net floats.

There are 16 well-equipped campgrounds in the park, seven of them accessible even to large trailers. There are also numerous primitive campsites. More sophisticated quarters are available in five different clusters of lodges and housekeeping cabins, three of these units being open year round. Excellent motels are found in Port Angeles, just north of the main park entrance.

FURTHER STATE INFORMATION

Tourist Development Division, Department of Commerce and Economic Development, General Administration Building, Olympia, WA 98501. Hunting and Fishing: **Department of Game,** 600 North Capital Way, Olympia, WA 98504. State Parks: Booklet, *Washington State Parks,* published by the **State Parks and Recreation Commission,** Olympia, WA 98504. **Seattle/King County Convention and Visitors' Bureau,** 1815 Seventh Avenue, Seattle, WA 98101. **Spokane Chamber of Commerce,** Convention and Visitors' Bureau, 1020 West Riverside Avenue, Spokane, WA 99201. **Tacoma Area Chamber of Commerce,** 752 Broadway, PO Box 1933, Tacoma, WA 98401. National Parks: **Mt Rainier National Park** (Superintendent) Longmire, WA 98397; **Rainier National Park Company,** Box 1136, Tacoma, WA 98401 (reservations, rates and bus tours). **North Cascades National Park** (Superintendent), Sedro-Wooley, WA 98284. **Olympic National Park** (Superintendent), 600 E Park Avenue, Port Angeles, WA 98362. **Olympic Peninsula Resort and Hotel Association,** Colman Ferry Terminal, Seattle, WA 98104 for accommodations. **Pan Am** offices, 1301 4th Avenue, Seattle WA 98101 tel: 624-2121, or call 800-227-4920 or 800-227-4840; Passenger Terminal, Seattle/Tacoma International Airport, Seattle, WA 98158, tel: 433-4545.

Consulates in Seattle: Austria, Belgium, Canada, Chile, Republic of China, Denmark, Ecuador, El Salvador, Finland, France, Germany, Great Britain, Guatemala, Iceland, Italy, Japan, Mexico, Netherlands, Nicaragua, Norway, Peru, Sweden, Switzerland.

In Spokane: Germany.

USEFUL TELEPHONE NUMBERS
Seattle

Emergency (Police, Fire, Ambulance)	911
Georgetown Dental Clinic	762-4070
Harborview Hospital	223-3000
Providence Hospital	326-5555
Evergreen Legal Services	464-5911
Seattle Visitors Bureau	477-7273

Spokane

Pan Am	800-227-4920
Beaconess Hospital	624-0171
Legal Aid Society	838-3671
Tourism Info Assistance	(509) 624-1341
Riverfront 24-hour FunFone (for entertainment)	456-5518

West Virginia

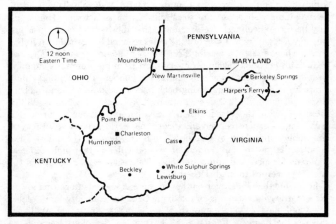

Area	24,181 square miles	Population	1,949,644
Capital	Charleston	Sales Tax	5%

Weather

	Jan	Feb	Mar	Apr	May	Jun	Jul	Aug	Sep	Oct	Nov	Dec
Av Temp (°C)	3	3	7	13	18	22	24	23	20	14	7	3
Days Rain/Snow	15	14	15	14	13	11	13	10	9	9	11	13

West Virginia's most compelling attraction is that it is still largely unspoiled. Although known for its coal and other industries, the state has vast areas of undeveloped territory just waiting to be discovered. Over one million acres are open for public recreation; there are 34 state parks, 9 state forests, and 27 public hunting and fishing areas.

The most mountainous state in the east, West Virginia has the **Appalachian Mountains** slanting down the eastern third of its territory; the **Allegheny Plateau** covers the rest of it. As if the earth had been pleated, the great hills are separated by valleys and canyons that have been worn deep by rushing rivers. Since it was such a difficult terrain to cross in early times, even the Indians stayed mostly in the gentler regions of the Ohio and Kanawha river valleys. The first permanent settlement in the western part of the state was not established until 1730, well over a century after the eastern side had been colonized.

Many battles of the French and Indian War (1754-63) were fought on West Virginia soil. The last battle of the Revolutionary War was fought here, and the first battle in the Civil War. In colonial days the populated area extended from the Ohio River to the Atlantic Ocean, but the tough mountaineers had little in common with the elegant Virginians to the east. When Virginia joined the Confederacy in the Civil War, the inevitable split came, and West Virginia was proclaimed a separate state in 1863.

The northwestern panhandle of the state is squeezed between the Ohio River and the western boundary of Pennsylvania. This is an intensely industrialized area of steel mills and glass factories. The largest city here is **Wheeling,** once so remote that the Revolutionary War had been over for 11 months before the news reached the British and Indian forces who were still attacking Fort Henry in September 1782. **Oglebay Park,** with facilities for almost every sport from midsummer swimming to midwinter tobogganing and skiing, also contains the **Mansion House Museum** with furnishings dating back to colonial days and an excellent display of local glass. Out on Bethany Pike near Wheeling is **Willow Glen** (1914-20), the vast mansion a coal baron built for his bride. His collection of expensive souvenirs from the world over is on display to the public; open May to October. South of Wheeling (12 miles) is the country's largest Indian mound, at **Moundsville,** 69 feet high, 927 feet in circumference, and approximately 2,000 years old. A museum on the site is open April through December.

Following the Ohio River south, you come to several interesting towns. **New Martinsville** is famous for its Viking Glass; the company offers guided tours and glass-blowing demonstrations by master craftsmen. **Williamstown** is the home of Fenton Art Glass, which also offers tours of the factories year round. **Point Pleasant,** so-named by George Washington when he was a young surveyor, was the scene of a furious battle between frontiersmen and British-incited Shawnees in 1774. **The Mansion House** (1796), built of hewn logs, has colonial furnishings and relics of the battle. Over at **Cedar Lakes** in Ripley, a few miles east of Pt Pleasant, the **Mountain State Art and Craft Fair** is held in late June to early July. It is an important showcase for the mountaineers to display their wares. **Huntington,** protected by floodwalls from the capricious Ohio River, is highly industrialized and the Huntington division of the Viking Glass company has tours Monday through Friday. **Huntington Art Galleries** are also worth a visit; admission by donation. See **Heritage Village,** a collection of boutiques housed in late 1700 and early 1800 buildings moved to the site, and eat at **Heritage Station,** a restaurant located in the old railway terminal. Only 14 miles east is **Milton,** where the Blenko glassblowers produce most of America's stained-glass windows, using age-old techniques. There's a special observation deck for watching the ingenious process and a museum in Visitors Center; open daily.

Continuing east is **Charleston,** capital of West Virginia, with an exceptionally handsome capitol building lavishly decorated with marble, carved bronze doors, and a huge crystal chandelier. The newest addition to the capital complex is the Science and Culture Center, a showcase of West Virginia history and art. The building—the size of three football fields—contains the archives, a library, museum, theater, and craft shop. **Sunrise** (1905), a great estate overlooking the **Kanawha River,** has a children's museum, art gallery, lovely gardens, and live animal fair; all free. There is also a planetarium; small fee.

The mountains south and southeast of Charleston may be coal mining country, but the scenery is so glorious that the state's three major resorts—Pipestem, The Greenbrier, and Glade Springs—and about 20 special recreation parks are in this region. **Mingo County** along the Kentucky border is the scene of the famous 40-year feud between the Hatfields and the McCoys; it was also a focus for violent strikes that finally brought about greatly improved working conditions and higher wages for the coal miners. **In Williamson,** (Mingo County), the **Chamber of Commerce** building has walls built entirely of local coal.

Continuing south from Williamson to the bottom of the state, take the Ridge Runner narrow-gauge railroad out of **Bluefield** for some breathtaking mountain scenery; it runs April through December. Heading north, between Bluefield and the tidy little riverside town of **Hinton,** is the resort of **Pipestem** (tel: 466-1922), a remarkable community that is bringing prosperity to this forgotten niche of Appalachia. Try the **Pipestem Resort State Park Lodge** (466-1800, S$29/D$35). **Bluestone Gorge Lodge,** built into the cliffside, and **Mountain Creek Lodge,** at the foot of the gorge, are connected by aerial tramway. Delightful housekeeping cottages, with two to four bedrooms, are priced from $175 to $192 per week, depending upon the number of people. Activities include two championship golf courses, indoor and outdoor swimming, horseback riding, tennis, woodland nature trails, and great fishing. Join an excursion to the hills and see the country women stitching patchwork quilts that sell for hundreds of dollars in metropolitan stores. The Big Bend railroad tunnel at nearby **Talcott** is the place where the legendary John Henry drove steel with his hammer and "made fourteen feet, while the stream drill, it made only nine." Twenty-four miles northwest of Hinton is **Beckley.** Here the **Exhibition Mine** offers an underground visit to an actual coal mine; open May through September. The **Cliffside Amphitheater** repertory company stages *The Hatfields and McCoys* and *Honey in the Rock,* both historical musical dramas, on alternative evenings, June through Labor Day. Twenty-three miles to the north is **Thurmond** where **Wildwater Expeditions Unlimited** offers 1- or 2-day thrilling rafting adventures on the white water of the **New River Canyon,** known as the "Grand Canyon of the East." The trip covers 30 miles of turbulent waters through a majestic area in the foothills of the Appalachian Mountains.

Northeast of Hinton is **Lewisburg,** once a center of pioneer and colonial activity and now host to the **West Virginia State Fair** the last full week in August. Five miles away is **Ronceverte,** starting point of the **Greenbrier Valley Scenic Railroad,** which operates on fall weekends.

Tucked away near the southern border of the state, at **White Sulphur Springs,** is the world-famous **Greenbrier Hotel** (536-1110, S$95 up/D$150-

195 MAP). The springs were discovered in 1798 and have been the site of a fashionable spa ever since. The majestic hotel overlooks miles of beautiful mountain scenery. Diversions include dancing nightly, creative arts colony, three golf courses, tennis, skeet- and trapshooting, horseback riding, carriage rides, swimming pools, and special festivities over the Christmas holidays. A large indoor tennis complex is the latest attraction.

Heading north from this luxurious haven, you will encounter the **Monongahela National Forest,** deep in the Allegheny Mountains. One of the many activities offered by this area is the **Cass Scenic Railroad** whose steam locomotives chug deep into the rugged wilderness to discover the primitive majesty of the mountains. Still within the forest but farther north is the **Snowshoe** area with miles of ski slopes. A variety of lodgings is now available at the resort where extensive recreational facilities have been opened. Two lodges, condominiums, chalets, villas, and cabins provide accommodations for this recreational facility which includes 10 base slopes (with an average 700 foot vertical drop), a chairlift, plus the well known Cup Run with its 1500 vertical drop. There accommodations are at **Spruce** and **Timberline Lodges** (tel: 799-6600). Snow information by calling 1-800-642-8507. At the northern tip of the forest are the state-run ski resort **Canaan Valley State Park,** where the **Canaan Valley Lodge** (tel: 866-4121) provides the focal point for some 5 slopes and 7 ski trails, and **Elkins,** home of the **Mountain State Forest Festival,** which annually attracts thousands of visitors during the height of the foliage season in October.

In the eastern panhandle is an even older resort, originally named Bath but now known as **Berkeley Springs,** often visited by George Washington. Nearby **Charles Town** was named after George's younger brother Charles, who laid out the town in 1786; a number of fine old homes built by various relatives of Washington still stand. **Jefferson County Courthouse** was the place where John Brown was convicted of treason after his raid on the **Harpers Ferry** arsenal. Harpers Ferry, just east of Charles Town and only 54 miles from Washington, DC, was built at the confluence of the Potomac and Shenandoah rivers in 1796. John Brown, a fanatical abolitionist who planned to arm black slaves, captured the arsenal with a small group of men on 16 October 1859. He and his followers were soon captured, but John Brown's "martyrdom" became a rally point for Union soldiers. The execution was heavily guarded and some of the troops, including John Wilkes Booth who later assassinated Abraham Lincoln, were commended for maintaining order at the execution by young Major Jackson (later known as "Stonewall" Jackson). A street marker identifies the spot where the gallows stood. **The Harpers Ferry National Historical Park** commemorates John Brown's raid and Civil War battles fought in the vicinity. The Visitors Center provides information and pertinent exhibits. Buildings of interest include the old **Harper House** (1772-82) and the **Gerald B. Wagner Building,** which houses the John Brown Museum.

FURTHER STATE INFORMATION
Travel Development Division, Governor's Office of Economic and Community Development, State Capitol, Charleston, W. Va. 25305. **West Virginia Department of Commerce,** State Capitol, Charleston, WV 25305.

USEFUL TELEPHONE NUMBERS IN CHARLESTON
Ambulance	345-2558
Fire	348-8111
Police	348-8111
State Police	348-6370
St Francis Hospital	348-8500
Charleston Area Medical Center	348-5432
Legal Aid Society	343-4481
Chamber of Commerce	345-0770
Pan Am Reservations	800-424-3210

Wisconsin

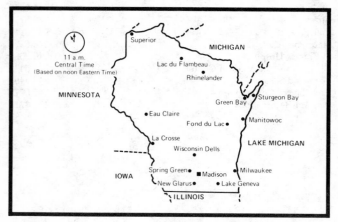

Area	56,154 miles	Population	4,705,335
Capital	Madison	Sales Tax	4%

Weather	Jan	Feb	Mar	Apr	May	Jun	Jul	Aug	Sep	Oct	Nov	Dec
Av Temp (°C)	−6	−5	−1	6	12	17	20	20	16	10	2	−4
Days Rain/Snow	11	9	11	12	12	11	9	8	9	8	10	10

If you need to be reminded that the United States is one of the richest, prettiest, best-fed, and most comfortable countries on earth, you should drive through Wisconsin. Much of the scenery is rich, rolling farmland, studded with sleek silos and well-painted barns. One can imagine the comfortable farmhouses as traditional family gathering places at Christmas. Wisconsin exudes an aura of affluent security. A long-ago slogan read: "It's harder to get lost in Wisconsin than it is to find your way in most other states." Those words apply to more than just the highly efficient way the state's roads are signposted.

Wisconsin's strongly ethnic/farming origins still dominate all demographic aspects of the state (Milwaukee notwithstanding). Wisconsin was settled primarily in the late 18th century by Swedes, Norwegians, Finns, Poles, and Germans. Each ethnic group settled in a specific area of the state in a predominantly agricultural motif. Each imported its own unique approach to agriculture, animal husbandry, and the architecture of their homes and farm buildings. Those ethnic distinctions remain today, and in driving through rural Wisconsin you often have the illusion of traveling through pastoral Europe—from Poland to Sweden to Germany to Finland to Norway.

As "America's Dairyland," Wisconsin formerly produced more milk and cheese than any other state. It is now third. This industry began long ago with the early Swiss, German, and Danish settlers. Lead and zinc mining is not as important as it was in the early 19th century, though massive zinc deposits have recently been discovered in south central Wisconsin. At one time the entire northern half of the state was covered by trees. This attracted many Scandinavians, who helped build up the lumber industry. Today nearly 14 million acres of ground are still forested and wood pulp products are still a major business. Wisconsin is happily situated with the Mississippi River down its western border, Lake Superior across the north and Lake Michigan down the east side. Inexpensive waterway transportation and abundant water power has helped make this state an industrial giant, ranking among the top 11 states. Wisconsin's excellent highways roll through one pretty location after another, and there are plenty of places to have a splendid vacation.

Wisconsin is the most interesting place in the world from the standpoint of glacial geology. Wisconsin is the most recently glaciated area in the world—having been glaciated by the "Wisconsinin" glacier late in the Pleistocene Age. Wisconsin abounds with the "youngest" and hence the most spectacular glacial landforms in the world: drumlins, eskers, kames, ground moraine, end moraine, terminal moraine, glacial lake bed, outwash plain, etc. However, glacial landforms are very subtle and it is advised that the Wisconsin visitor study glacial landforms before visiting so they know what to look for and can fully appreciate it.

Wisconsin has more than 50 state parks, 9 state forests, and 2 national forests, all devoted to recreation. When the ice age glaciers went through they left nearly 15,000 lakes, many of which are unnamed. Now northern Wisconsin has more lakes for its land area than any place else in the world. There are hundreds of little forest-rimmed lakes with only deer, beaver, otter, muskrat, bear, and other wild animals to enjoy them. There are also about 150 species of fish. Pheasant, grouse, and other game birds are abundant. For the hunter and fisherman Wisconsin is hard to beat. On the larger developed lakes, there are charming resort towns with fine boating and water skiing. Good swimming, too, in midsummer.

The third major point of interest in Wisconsin—and by far the most beautiful part of the state and that most well worth visiting—is Lake Superior's South Shore. It is without doubt the most pristine, beautiful wilderness area in the nation; and the Lake Superior beaches and water far surpass any of the America's seacoasts in quality and untouched natural beauty. The entire north boundary of Wisconsin is one giant, broad sand/gravel beach along the cleanest water in the world. Lake Superior water along the Wisconsin border is literally so clean that you can drink it; in fact, water-quality studies have found it to be far cleaner than the municipal household water of most cities; and the few towns that border Lake Superior have no need for drinking water treatment plants—they pump it right from the lake into the homes. The most amazing thing about Lake Superior's South Shore is that it is virtually deserted at all times of the year—even in the hottest summer months. Thus anyone who wants to can simply drive along US 3 or 13, and pick a gravel road leading to the lake at random and have miles of untouched sandy beach to themselves for as long as they want. The vast majority of the lakeshore is owned by the government, so that there are only a smattering of cottages on it—primarily around Ashland, Superior, and Bayfield. Twenty-five percent of the lakeshore is on Indian Reservation land.

In many respects Lake Superior off the Wisconsin coast is remarkably like the Mediterranean. The most notable feature is the Apostle Islands— virtual gems of the pristine wilderness scattered throughout Chequamo- gan Bay and on out into the open lake like a string of pearls. The largest— Madeline Island—is accessible ten times a day by ferry from Bayfield Wharf; and is well worth the visit. It is somewhat of an anomaly among the Apostle Islands in that it is half pristine, and half luxury. A $500,- 000,000 real-estate development covers 20% of the island—complete with luxury hotels; a beautiful marina boasting some of the most beautiful pleasure sailing vessels in the Great Lakes for rent or hire; one of the most beautiful 18-hole golf courses in the nation; dozens of tennis courts and swimming pools. The rest of the island is a "gold-mine" of Indian lore (including a many-centuries old Indian burial ground) and artifacts from the 17th-century French explorers and fur traders (for which Made- line Island was a major meeting place); and a beautiful, quaint French Mission built in 1832, which is well worth visiting.

Wisconsin summers are sunny and warm, the winters usually long and cold but great for skiing, ice skating, sledding, snowmobiling, and tobog- ganing. **Lake Geneva** is a little resort town. It is best visited out of season. There are numerous water sports here in summer, as well as skiing, both downhill and cross-country, and snowmobiling in winter. Many fa- mous entertainers perform at the **Playboy Resort** at Lake Geneva (248- 8811, S$63-68/D$68-73). Farther west is **Monroe,** the Swiss cheese capital of the country. The town's interesting little shops contain many unusual items as well as a glorious assortment of cheeses. Traveling north you come to **New Glarus,** settled by the Swiss in 1844. Here you'll see the **Swiss Historical Village** and the **Chalet of the Golden Fleece,** both remi- niscent of the area's Swiss heritage. Other places of interest include the lace, embroidery, and cheese factories. Stop at the **Wilhelm Tell Supper Club** for superb food. Major events here are the **Heidi Festival** in late June; **Swiss Volksfest,** including yodeling, the first Sunday in August; and the big **Wilhelm Tell Pageant and Festival** on Labor Day weekend.

MADISON is the handsome state capital, beautifully situated on Lakes **Mendota, Monona,** and **Wingra,** with little **Waubesa** and **Kegonsa** to the southeast, all of which provide boating. Some capitol watchers say that Wisconsin's is one of the most beautifully constructed capitol buildings in the nation. Tours are available every day of the year. Time and time again Madison has been cited by national magazines as one of the top ten most beautiful cities in the nation. **The State Capitol Building** is widely acknowledged to be one of the top five most beautiful in the nation, and is well worth visiting for its spectacular artwork, architecture, and myriad of intricate pseudo-Greek sculptures. **The State Historical Library & Museum,** located on the UW Campus across from the **Memorial Library** off the State Street Mall is also well worth a visit for its fascinating exhibits on Wisconsin pioneer and Indian lore. The **University of Wisconsin,** with an enrollment of about 38,000, stands on wooded hills overlooking Lake Mendota; tour maps available from the information booth at Memorial Union. The **Elvehjem Art Center,** on the campus, has a remarkably sophisticated collection of Russian icons, 16th- and 17th-century Dutch and Italian works, as well as East Indian miniatures and modern masterpieces. There are guided tours of the highly advanced **US Forest Products Laboratory,** Monday-Friday, 2pm. Frank Lloyd Wright, Wisconsin's most famous citizen, designed the unusual **First Unitarian Church** at 900 University Bay Drive. Convenient motels and hotels include the **Concourse** (257-6000, S$40/D$48), one block north of Capitol Square; the **Edgewater** (256-9071, S$40-60/D$40-65), on Lake Mendota, four blocks northwest of Capitol Square; **Howard Johnson's Downtown Motor Lodge** (251-5511, S$31/D$39), adjacent to the University of Wisconsin campus, six blocks southwest of Capitol Square; **Madison Inn** (257-4391, S$23-33/D$28-38), amid sororities and fraternities on Langdon Street, four blocks from Capitol Square; **Inn on the Park** (257-8811, S$31-33/D$38-40), on Capitol Square; **Town-Campus Motel** (257-4881, S$29-33/D$36-40), convenient to campus and capitol. Other good motels ranging from three to five miles of the downtown area include **Holiday Inn, Quality Inn, Ramada Inn, Midway Motor Lodge,** and **TraveLodge.** Madison makes a good headquarters for excursions through southwestern Wisconsin. There are lots of good tips on places to go in the free *Madison Area Guide* and *This Week in Madison.*

Cave of the Mounds, known for its colorful stalactite formations, and **Little Norway,** a restored Norwegian homestead and Norse museum, are west of Madison on US 18 and 151. **Spring Green,** on US 14, is where Frank Lloyd Wright began his famous building complex, *Taliesin* in 1911, where he founded his first architectural school. The **Spring Green Restaurant** is the only restaurant building designed by Wright. **The House on the Rock,** by Alexander Jordan, is another unusual architectural wonder six miles south of town. The house is poised 450 feet above the lovely Wisconsin River valley. It contains numerous music and antique collections, as well as "Streets of Yesterday" on the grounds; open April–mid-November. **Baraboo** is where the Ringling Brothers got their start, and the **Circus World Museum,** where posters, equipment, and musical instruments used in the circus are on display, is a big attraction here; open mid-May to mid-September. West of town is the **Mid-Continent Railway Museum** with oldtime coaches and a ride on a real steam train; open Memorial Day to Labor Day. **Devil's Lake State Park,** south of Baraboo, is exceptionally pretty and a good place to camp. A scenic route from Madison to Baraboo and Devil's Lake State Park is via Highway 113 north to the free **Merrimac Ferry** across the Wisconsin River. The ferry runs from March through November, depending on ice conditions. The

Wisconsin Dells, just north of Baraboo, are one of the nation's geological beauty spots. There are sightseeing boat trips between the dramatically shaped rock formations from April through October. Winnebago Indians put on a rousing show of tribal dances and ceremonials nightly from late June through Labor Day. The **Bartlett Water Show** is a dazzling performance on nearby Lake Delton, mid-June to mid-September. Other attractions here are the **Biblical Gardens, Fort Dells, Lost Canyon, Storybook Gardens,** a four-mile railroad ride through wooded canyons on a renovated 19th-century train—complete with an original 100-year-old steam locomotive, $2.50 round trip. The original railroad station—built in the late 19th century—has also been renovated and has many interesting displays from early railroad days. Free. **Wisconsin Deer Park,** and boat rides on the *Wisconsin Ducks* and *Good Ship Lollipop* are available.

Also easily accessible from Madison is the old town of **Prairie du Chien,** pronounced *sheen,* at the confluence of the Wisconsin and Mississippi Rivers. First a trading post in 1763 and then fortified during the War of 1812, the town was chosen by fur trader Hercules Dousman as the site for his *Villa Louis.* The house was begun in 1842 and rebuilt in 1872. As Wisconsin's first millionaire, Dousman collected some fabulous furnishings which remain in the house. He also devised an ingenious "air conditioning" system from blocks of ice gathered in the winter from the Mississippi. There are conducted tours of the house and pioneer museum from May-October. To travel north from Prairie du Chien, take WI 35. This drive, called the **Great River Road,** is filled with fantastic scenery and wildlife. In **La Crosse** the Black and La Crosse Rivers join the Mississippi. This area is characterized by towering bluffs with varicolored rock pinnacles and outcroppings; dense forests interlaced with rivers, streams, and lakes. It is not at all "developed" and has very few vacation homes, a great place to camp in seclusion. There are old-time paddlewheeler cruises from mid-June to Labor Day. You can get a good view of the river, the city, and its surrounding bluffs from **Grandad Bluff,** 1,172 feet high. La Crosse stages an exuberant *Oktoberfest* for five days in early October, when autumn foliage should be at its best.

If you continue north from here, the last sizable city is the pretty **Eau Claire.** See the **Paul Bunyan Logging Camp,** open May-September. Between here and Lake Superior, the map is thickly dotted with hundreds of little lakes and rivers where the fishing is great. In **Hayward** you can visit **Historyland** where there are tours through a Chippewa Indian Village and through a replica logging camp. The **Lumberjack World Championships** are held here in late July. The **Mt Telemark Ski Area** provides year-round resort facilities near the little town of **Cable.** You really feel up north by the time you get to **Superior** which, with Duluth, Minnesota, is the western terminus of the **Great Lakes-St Lawrence Seaway.** By ship, Superior is 2,342 miles from Quebec City, where the Seaway begins. Superior's enormous docks are among the largest in the country and ship out millions of tons of ore and grain. The docks are really exciting to see, and there are harbor boat excursions from June–mid-September. The rugged, primitive and beautiful **Apostle Is-**

lands National Lakeshore may be seen on cruises from Bayfield, mid-June to September. There is also a ferry service April to December to Madeline Island where the village of La Pointe has a very good museum of Indian and pioneer life. Ashland, on the scenic Chequamegon Bay, is a well known headquarters for hunters and fishermen.

Lac du Flambeau is a village in the middle of the big Chippewa Indian Reservation. There are powwows twice weekly in summer in the lakeshore Indian Bowl Amphitheater. Dillman's Sand Lake Lodge (588-3143, S\$30.75/D\$47.25) is geared for all summer and winter sports, and will even clean and freeze the fish you catch; lower rates are available in winter. Hundreds of little lakes are dropped like jewels all over this part of northern Wisconsin. Some are completely uninhabited, while others are the retreats of tycoons who maintain secluded palatial hideaways. The little towns of Minocqua, Tomahawk, and Eagle River are especially popular and have some beautiful summer homes. Sugar Camp, on WI 17, is worth a detour for a meal at Louis Widule's White Stag Inn. Sayner, another small town, has the excellent Heritage Room at Froelich's Sayner Lodge. In nearby Rhinelander there's more extremely good food in the Cavalier Dining Room of the excellent Claridge Motor Inn (362-7100, S\$28.50-30.50/D\$34.50-39.50). Rhinelander, the site of one of the country's largest paper mills and formerly a logging town, has a "hogdag" as mascot. You can see a replica of the strange creature in the Logging Museum; there's a Hogdag Snowmobile Marathon in January. Tourists love the town for the fishing, hunting, and water sports in its surrounding lakes, streams, and deep forests.

GREEN BAY is the home of the famous Green Bay Packers football team, and there's a Packer Hall of Fame Museum that thrills the team's many fans. Home games and practice sessions are played at Lambeau Field. Part of an area discovered by Jean Nicolet in 1634, Green Bay is Wisconsin's oldest town. The Roi-Porlier-Tank Cottage was begun in 1776 by a French trader and enlarged by subsequent owners; open Tuesday to Sunday, May to October. Hazelwood (1837) is where the state's constitution was written; open Tuesday to Sunday, May-October, weekends in April. The Cotton House (1840s) and Baird Law Office (1830s) are on the same grounds. The house is probably the finest example of Greek revival architecture in the midwest. The law office was the first in the state; both open Tuesday to Sunday, May to October. There are some fascinating regional antiquities in the Fort Howard Hospital Museum (1816); open Tuesday to Sunday, May to October. The National Railroad Museum has old coaches dating back to 1880 and steam locomotives from 1910; open mid-May to Labor Day. Downtown accommodations include the fine Beaumont Ramada Inn (435-4484, S\$25-29/D\$34-37) and the Imperial 400 (437-0525, S\$18/D\$22-26). North of Green Bay is fruit country, and it is impossible to drive past all those roadside stands without stopping for apples, grapes, cherries, or whatever is in season.

DOOR COUNTY, on the breezy peninsula between Green Bay and Lake Michigan, is the Midwest's version of Cape Cod. Once just a refuge for hayfever sufferers, it has been taken over by artists and vacationers reveling in vast sand beaches and gorgeous scenery. The best time to visit it is in October or early spring (April/May). Otherwise it's standing-room only. **Sturgeon Bay** is the county's largest town and located on the shipping canal. The area is, in summer, swamped with cherries. The orchards bloom in late May, and the fruit is ripe for picking in July. Ice fishing, skiing, and snowmobiling thrive in winter. Throughout Door County are modest inns, familiar motels, and quite luxurious resorts.

The **Fox River** connects Green Bay with **Lake Winnebago**, which has some well-known cities along its shores. **Appleton**, home of esteemed **Lawrence University** and the interesting **Institute of Paper Chemistry**, was the world's first city to have water-powered electricity in 1882. There is an interesting replica here of the first hydroelectric power station. **Fond du Lac**, literally at the base of the lake, is another very pretty industrial city. Visit the **Galloway House and Museum** (1868), open Memorial Day to September, and **St Paul's Episcopal Cathedral**, which contains German wood carvings and imported stained glass windows. The geologically interesting **Kettle Moraine State Forest** begins southeast of town. The unusual terrain of strange holes and ridges was created by glaciers during the Ice Age. Over on the shore of Lake Michigan are more busy industrial-and-resort towns. **Manitowoc** has an especially interesting **Maritime Museum,** and there are tours through *USS Cobia*, a World War II submarine. Car ferries depart day and night for Ludington, on the other side of Lake Michigan.

Brule River, which empties into Lake Superior, has been rated in the top ten trout streams in the nation, and the top for steelhead fishing. The steelhead run in late September/early October. They are actually rainbow trout going to spawn and are among the largest of all trout in the world.

City To Visit

MILWAUKEE

Milwaukee is in southeastern Wisconsin, on the west shore of Lake Michigan, 90 miles north of Chicago. The **Milwaukee, Menomonee,** and **Kinnickinnic Rivers** have all played an important part in Milwaukee's growth. The first explorer to visit the region was the French missionary Father Marquette. In 1673 he arrived at the site of modern Milwaukee, then the Indian village of Mahnawaukee-Seepe, the "meeting place of great councils." A fur-trading post was established there in 1795 by Jacques Vieau and it became a stopping place on the trail between Chicago and Green Bay. The city was incorporated in 1846.

Although it is the 16th largest city in the nation, Milwaukee has much of the congenial atmosphere of a small town. It is often cited as a well-run community with a low crime rate. There is much interest in art and education and a considerable amount of civic pride. Population

632,989; metropolitan area 1,390,000. Manufacturing and industrial areas are located along the banks of the three rivers flowing through the city. Milwaukee is where Oktoberfest is enjoyed—thousands of people fill the streets day and night with revelry having, among other things, marathon beer drinking contests, often lasting for days.

WHAT TO SEE

Milwaukee Public Museum, outstanding anthropology, history, and natural science exhibits; open daily 9-5; non-residents, $1.50 adults, 75¢ children. **State Fair Park; Milwaukee Harbor; War Memorial; Art Museum; New YWCA; Annunciation Greek Orthodox Church,** last building designed by Frank Lloyd Wright; **Joan of Arc Chapel** at Marquette University; and the **Experimental Aircraft Museum,** large collection of antique and experimental aircraft. The three-and-a-half mile lakefront drive is one of the most beautiful in the country. A typical conducted tour, summer only, costs $3.25 adults; $2.50 for ages 13 to 17; and $1.75 below 13.

Milwaukee County has 92 parks offering golf, tennis, and water sports. **Lake Park,** overlooking Lake Michigan, and the excellent **Milwaukee County Zoological Park,** which is considered one of the top zoos in the nation, with animals all in their recreated environment, are particularly attractive. **Mitchell Park** has lovely enclosed gardens. **Whitnall Park** has flower shows, displays, and the **Boerner Botanical Gardens. Estabrook Park** has restorations of old houses.

There are 163 inland lakes within an hour's drive of the city; these afford numerous opportunities for fishing, swimming, and boating. Several ferries and pleasure cruises leave for trips across Lake Michigan.

ACCOMMODATIONS

The **Marc Plaza** (271-7250, S$41-60/D$53-72) is conveniently located downtown; **Pfister** (273-8222, S$46-60/D$60-74), with its deluxe Tower addition, is the leading downtown hotel; the recently opened **Hyatt Regency** (276-1234, S$49-57/D$64-72) is next to the convention center and a short walk to the beautiful Performing Arts Center. **Holiday Inn-West** is near the State Fair Park and the zoo. In a quiet residential area near Lake Michigan: **Astor** (271-4220, S$23.50-30/D$27.50-35) and **Park East Hotel** (276-8800, S$35-40/D$43-48). At the airport: **Holiday Inn-South** (764-1500, S$36/D$41-43), **Ramada Inn** (764-5300, S$42/D$46), and **Red Carpet Inn** (481-8000, S$45-48/D$55-58). There are many other tourist courts and motels. Hotel Tax: 4-7%.

RESTAURANTS

A meal at a German restaurant should not be missed. **Mader's, Karl Ratzsch, John Ernst,** and **Pandl's,** all moderate, are recommended for German food and beer. **Toy's** is a beautiful Chinese restaurant. Other good places: **Alioto's, Jakes, Nino's,** and **Black Steer** for steak or beef, moderate to expensive; **Grenadier's** and **Jean Paul** for continental food, moderately expensive. **J. J. Garlic** and **Jacques,** moderate. **Someplace**

Else for beer and bratwurst, inexpensive. **Kosta's,** Greek food, moderate; **Old Town,** and the **Brothers** for Serbian Food, moderate; **Pieces of Eight,** Polynesian, moderate; **Smith Bros, Port Washington,** sea food.

ENTERTAINMENT
Live entertainment at the Pfister's **Crown Room, Frenchy's, Gatsby's,** "The Attic," Someplace Else, **Marc Plaza,** and many other night spots. **Marriott, Ramada Inn** at the airport, and **Red Carpet Inn** have dancing and entertainment nightly. **The New Park Avenue** is the city's poshest disco, open nightly. **The Jazz Riverboat** and the **Bull Ring** offer jazz. And the **Blue River Cafe** has folk music. Discos include **The Baron, Oliver's Cabaret,** and **Teddy's.**

ARTS AND MUSIC
Milwaukee Art Center, housed in the War Memorial Building, features a variety of exhibits; open Tuesday through Sunday 10-5, closed Monday; free. Ceramics are predominant at the **Charles Allis Art Library.** The **Milwaukee Symphony Orchestra** has a 40-week concert schedule. The **Performing Arts Center** presents concerts and the excellent **Milwaukee Repertory Theater Company** produces plays the year round. During the summer there is **Music Under the Stars** at Washington Park. The **Melody Top Theater** stages Broadway musicals, June through September.

SHOPPING
Shops downtown remain open Monday, Wednesday, and Thursday evenings until 9. Wisconsin, a dairy state, produces enormous quantities of cheese and also sausage; local varieties are a good buy.

SPORTS
Milwaukee schedules top attractions in boxing, wrestling, polo, auto racing, and soccer, plus various college events. Sport fishing, especially for coho and trout, is good. The **Green Bay Packers** play several games each year at the **County Stadium,** which is also the home of the **Milwaukee Brewers** American League baseball team. The **Milwaukee Bucks** of the National Basketball Association play at the **Arena.**

CALENDAR OF EVENTS
Home Show, Sports Show, March; **Old Milwaukee Days,** July; **Summer Fest,** July; **Musical Festival, Wisconsin State Fair,** August; **Folk Fair,** November.

WHERE TO GO NEARBY
Old World Wisconsin, well worth seeing, about 30 miles southwest, is open from May through October. This is an outdoor museum built by the Wisconsin State Historical Society, which moved dozens of original buildings built 100-300 years ago from all over the state to the site. The "museum" covers over 3 square miles and contains numerous completely reconstructed households and farms—exactly as they were one

A proud symbol of Milwaukee's Old World charm, the City Hall *features a 393-foot tower built in 1895 in Flemish Renaissance style.*

to three centuries ago. Each "display" represents the heritage of a different Wisconsin ethnic group. Northwest of the city are **Lake Winnebago,** the largest inland lake in the state, and **Fond du Lac,** with many vacation facilities in the immediate region. About 125 miles northwest are the **Wisconsin Dells,** 13 miles north of Baraboo, with beautiful scenery, boat trips, and Indian dances during the summer. **Vilas** and **Oneida** counties are just below the Wisconsin-Michigan state line. If time permits, drive to **Devil's Lake State Park** 120 miles northwest, three miles south of Baraboo. It is always open and has interesting Indian mound formations. **Devil's Lake** is enclosed by cliffs on three sides.

FURTHER STATE INFORMATION

Division of Tourism, Department of Business Development, Box 177, Madison, WI 53701. **Greater Madison Convention and Visitors' Bureau, Inc,** PO Box 3353, Madison, WI 53704. **Milwaukee Convention and Visitors' Bureau,** 828 North Broadway, Milwaukee, WI 53202; *Milwaukee Journal,* 333 W. State Street, Milwaukee, WI 53203. **Door County Chamber of Commerce,** Green Bay Road, Sturgeon Bay, WI 54235. **Pan Am** office, 111 E. Wisconsin Avenue, Milwaukee, WI 53202, tel: 621-2909.

Consulates in Milwaukee: Costa Rica, Dominican Republic, Mexico, Nicaragua, Norway, Pakistan, Sweden.

USEFUL TELEPHONE NUMBERS FOR MILWAUKEE

Police	765-2323
Rescue Squad/Fire	347-2323
Mount Sinai Medical Center	289-8200
St. Mary's Hospital	289-7000
Legal Aid Society	765-0600
Chamber of Commerce	273-3000
Tourist Information	747-4808

Wyoming

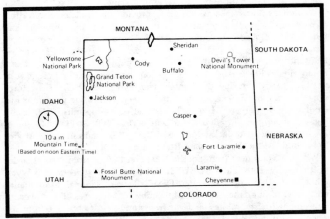

Area	97,914 square miles	Population	470,000
Capital	Cheyenne	Sales Tax	3%

Weather	Jan	Feb	Mar	Apr	May	Jun	Jul	Aug	Sep	Oct	Nov	Dec
Av Temp (°C)	−4	−3	0	6	12	17	21	20	15	9	1	−1
Days Rain/Snow	6	7	10	10	12	11	11	9	7	5	5	5

Wyoming is the land of historic trails, rushing rivers, jagged mountains, plains, and flowering meadows that have been woven so vividly in the art and music of the Old West. Wyoming's firsts are many. They include the first state to grant women the right to vote; the first national park; the first national monument; and the first timberland to be reserved under the national forest system. In addition there are the spectacular mountains, two national recreational areas, 10 national forests, and eight state parks. Wyoming is also the main source for the three greatest rivers of the West—the Colorado, Columbia, and Missouri. The primary mountain ranges are the Big Horn, the Absaroka, Teton, Gros Ventre, and Wind River, which cut across the northwestern corner, and the Medicine Bow Range and Laramie Mountains in the southeast.

The flags of Spain, Britain, Mexico, France, the Republic of Texas, and the United States have all flown here. The Oregon Trail and the Mormon Trail crossed Wyoming, but settlement began in earnest only when the Union Pacific Railroad pushed its way through in 1867-68. News of valuable grazing land lured Texas cattlemen in the early 1870s and the discovery of gold and coal brought further settlers. Finally organized as a territory in 1868, Wyoming was admitted to the Union 22 years later. The determined women of the state, who were granted the right to vote in 1869, were not content with just political participation. They pushed through an excellent county library system, first-class schools, and the financing of the University of Wyoming from the proceeds of the state's three million acres of oil land.

Wyoming's clear streams and lakes provide unparalleled fishing for all varieties of trout; most of the state is open for year-round fishing but check the Wyoming Game and Fish Commission in Cheyenne for local exceptions. A 5-day nonresident license costs $10. Pronghorn antelope and mule deer are the most widely hunted game. An elk herd numbering 8,000 to 10,000 is located on the **Federal Elk Refuge** just north of Jackson during the winter. The high country of the western slopes offers moose, bear, and mountain sheep. Nonresident permits for antelope and deer are $100 each; elk and moose permits, $250 each; bighorn sheep permit, $300; black bear permit, $60. At Pinedale, some 70 miles southeast of Jackson, some of the better steaks in the west are to be found at the **Fort William Restaurant**.

Whether you enter from South Dakota on I-90 or from Nebraska on I-80 along the **EASTERN BORDER** of the state, the attractions of Wyoming are immediately evident. **Devil's Tower National Monument,** northwest of Sundance via US 14, occupies 1,346 acres. The tower, a huge monolith resembling a stone tree stump, rises 865 feet from its wooded base and 1,280 feet above the flowing Belle Fourche River. Geologists say the formation was once molten rock born of volcanic activity millions of years ago. In a certain light the many subdued shades produce an effect so fascinating that there is temptation to believe in the supernatural powers attributed to the tower by Indians. A visitor center contains geological specimens, artifacts, and exhibits; open daily May-September.

Newcastle, 50 miles southeast on US 16, is a community of farms and ranches belying its history as a center of large-scale coal mining activity. East of the junction of US 16 and 85 is the only known hand-dug oil well in the United States. A viewing room at the bottom provides an opportunity to see how oil is produced and refined. Drilling and pumping equipment from the early 1900s are on display; open year round. **Best Western Fountain Motor Inn,** on the outskirts of New Castle on US 16 (746-4426, S$24-26/D$26-28) has landscaped grounds. Continuing south through the **Thunder Basin National Grassland** is **Fort Laramie National Historic Site,** 3 miles southwest of the town of Fort Laramie. This national site covers 564 acres near the meeting of Laramie and North Platte Rivers. It offers the preserved remains of old Fort Laramie, a fur trading center and military post on the Oregon Trail. The fort was built in 1834, and associated with it are pioneer characters like Kit Carson, Buffalo Bill Cody, and John C. Frémont. From mid-June through Labor Day the grounds are open daily 7-7, rest of the year 8-4:30.

In the **SOUTHEAST** corner of Wyoming are **Cheyenne,** the state capital, and **Laramie,** home of the **University of Wyoming,** the state's only

4-year institution of higher learning. The **Western Historical Collection and University Archives** are open Monday to Friday, free. Thirty miles west in **Medicine Bow National Forest** is the **Snowy Range,** one of the west's most beautiful recreation areas. Winter sports areas are **Happy Jack,** 9 miles east of Laramie; **Medicine Bow Ski Area,** 40 miles northwest; and **Ryan Park Ski Area,** 25 miles east of Saratoga. North toward Casper is the **Alcova Dam,** stretching 700 feet in length and rising 800 feet from the canyon riverbed. The **Alcova Reservoir** offers swimming, boating, and horseback riding, with tent and trailer camping available in **Alcova County Park.**

About 150 miles north of Laramie is **Casper,** the state's leading industrial city, fed on a rich diet of oil and uranium. **Salt Creek Oilfield** is 45 miles to the north and is one of the world's largest light oil fields, covering 20,000 acres. The **Central Wyoming State Fair and Night Rodeo** is held in early August. **Casper Mountain State Park** offers panoramic views of the area, including **Hell's Half Acre,** a depression with highly colored and grotesque rock formations, and **Independence Rock,** a 193-foot "Great Record of the Desert," a name acquired from the thousands of names inscribed by pioneers who traveled the Oregon Trail. **Best Western Galley** and **Showboat Motels,** S$22-32/D$24-34, and **Holiday** and **Ramada Inns,** S$36-44.40/D$41-49.50, provide good rooms. **Benham's Supper Club** is very popular and has a varied menu.

Heading **NORTH** you will find **Buffalo,** at the junction of I-25 and I-90, in an area where many Indian battles were fought including the **Dull Knife Battle,** the last major skirmish in the Indian campaign. The **Johnson County Cattle War** in 1892 was fought on the **TA Ranch.** Southwest of the town is a section of prairie accessible only through a narrow, concealed defile, termed the "hole-in-the-wall" by rustlers who used it to conceal stolen cattle. Many dude ranches are nearby, and 13 miles east stands a petrified forest of ancient sequoias. **Best Western Cross Roads Inn** (684-2256, S$24-30/D$26-36) has a heated pool. **Sheridan,** 36 miles to the north, is the largest city in northern Wyoming, but the frontier spirit is still manifested in the **All-American Indian Days,** held in late July or early August, a colorful, 3-day celebration featuring exhibits from over 40 tribes of Plains Indians. The **Sheridan Rodeo** is held in July. **Bradford Brinton Memorial Ranch** recreates the atmosphere of western ranch life. The history of the ranch, established in 1893, is extensively displayed in a reception gallery, the 20-room main house, and other ranch buildings; open daily 15 May to 15 September, free. **Best Western Sheridan Center Motor Inn** and **Trail's End Motel** average S$26/D$26-38. A good selection of well-prepared food is served in the dining room of the **Sheridan Inn,** a National Historic Landmark that serves as a restaurant, convention center, and small museum. **Bighorn National Forest,** to the north of Buffalo on US 14, encompasses over a million acres. Facilities in the forest include roads and trails which afford access to numerous streams and lakes. Saddle and pack trips may be taken into the **Cloud Peak Primitive Area.** Skiing is available at **Antelope Butte Ski Area** and at **Meadow Lark Lake. Medicine Wheel,** constructed of stones laid side by side, is 70 feet in diameter and has 28 spokes. It is believed to have been a complex used by Indians for religious purposes. A narrow forest road, open only in summer, leads from US 14A to the site.

Southwest of the forest on WY 789 passing through Worland is **Thermopolis**, a health center famous for the hot springs of the Bighorn River. **Hot Springs State Park** covers 957 acres and contains four large and hundreds of smaller springs. **Bighorn Hot Springs**, flowing with 18.6 million gallons daily, is the largest mineral hot springs in the world. An Indian pageant, **Gift of the Waters**, is held annually in early August. **Holiday Inn of the Waters** (864-3131, S$28-30/D$30-35), adjacent to the hot mineral springs, offers mineral baths, sauna, and therapy rooms. Good dinners are served at the **Legion Town and Country Club** at the airport. Farther south, just below the Wind River Indian Reservation, is the town of **Lander**, a convenient port of call for exploration. Accommodations at **Best Western Holiday Lodge** (332-2511, S$21-26/D$26-30). **The Hitching Rack Restaurant** serves fine food, and provides entertainment weekends. The **Atlantic City Mercantile**, some 20 miles south in Atlantic City, serves the best steaks in the state.

Cody, named after "Buffalo Bill," is in the **NORTHWEST REGION** of the state on US 14. In the immediate area are some of the state's most scenic spots, **Buffalo Bill Dam** and **Shoshone Canyon**, where a river has cut a deep gorge separating two mountains. The town is the scene of the **Cody Stampede** held 3-4 July. The **Pioneer Playhouse**, in Buffalo Bill Village, presents nightly rodeos and entertainment during the summer months. **Buffalo Bill Historical Center**, open May through September, features museums of the famous hunter and the Northern Plains Indians. The **Whitney Gallery of Western Art**, part of the center, displays a famous and comprehensive collection of documentary art of the Old West, featuring such artists as Frederic Remington, Charles M. Russell, and Albert Bierstadt. **Colonial Inn, Holiday Inn** and **Best Western Sunset Motor Inn** range from S$18-35/D$20-39; good food served at the **Irma Hotel**, the **Bronze Boot** and **Cassie's Supper Club**. **Sleeping Giant Winter Sport Area** is west of here, near the eastern entrance to Yellowstone. **Yellowstone** and **Grand Teton National Parks** consume the northwestern section of the state's border with Idaho and Montana. (See park section for details.)

South along US 89 is **Jackson**, at the southern entrance to Grand Teton National Park. The **Jackson Hole Aerial Tram**, a 2½-mile tramway, carries passengers to the 10,446-foot **Rendezvous Peak**, which affords a spectacular view of the **Grand Teton Range** and the entire **Jackson Hole Valley**. The **Jackson Hole Ski Area** is open all year, with skiing from mid-December to mid-April. In addition to the tramway, there are four chairlifts and 100 miles of trails. **Snow King Mountain Chair Lift** is 4,000 feet long. The **All-American Cutter Racing Association** originated here. Rope tows and ski schools are maintained; open 30 May to Labor Day and 15 December to 1 April. Float and fishing trips are available on guided tours of the **Snake River**. The **Laubin Ancient Indian Dances** are faithful recreations dating from before the arrival of the white man; performances are held every Friday from the end of June through mid-September. **Best Western Alpenhof Lodge** (733-3462, S/D$65-105), one of six lodges in the **Teton Village** resort area at the base of **Rendezvous Peak**, has a heated pool, sundeck, and sauna. Others include **Crystal Springs Inn** (S/D$36-46), **The Inn at Jackson Hole** (S/D$65-105), and **Soujourner Inn** (S/D$60-75), with heated swimming pools. Accommodations are also available in Jackson, at the **Snow King Ramada Inn** (733-5200, S$30-50/D$40-60) and at the **Antler** (S$26/D$32) and **Virginian** (S$28-30/D$34-36) motels. The **Open Range** and the **Cowboy Steakhouse** are favorite local eating spots.

City To Visit

CHEYENNE

The site of Cheyenne was first surveyed by General Grenville M. Dodge, chief surveyor for the Union Pacific Railroad, in July 1867. Four months later, when the tracks of the Union Pacific arrived, Cheyenne had become a town of 4,000 people, with its own government and two newspapers. The city, incorporated under special charter on 24 December 1867, was named after a tribe of Algonquian Indians, originally called "Shey-an-nah." Cheyenne became the state capital in 1869. It combines the robust glamour of the Wild West with sedate Victorian structures and all the cosmopolitan aspects of a modern, growing industrial and retail community.

WHAT TO SEE
State Capitol Building; **State Museum**, with cowboy and Indian mementos and a mineralogical display. The museum also houses the **Wyoming State Art Gallery**; open daily. A 2-city-block area in downtown Cheyenne has been remodeled into a "Frontier Town" with a mall, visitor information center, and an old cavalry fort for children to play in. **Holiday Park** contains a steam locomotive, donated by the Union Pacific Railroad, one of the last of the giants which used to haul passengers and freight over the Rocky Mountains. **Lions Park** is open all year, free, and **Francis E. Warren Air Force ICBM Base,** on the western city limits, was originally a pioneer military outpost. **Frontier Days,** featuring the world's oldest and biggest rodeo, has been held since 1897 and provides a thrilling 9 days at the end of July, when the best riders and ropers in the nation compete for the highest purses on the rodeo circuit. Four western parades, square dancing, Indian dancing, chuckwagon races, nightly shows, and free chuckwagon breakfasts make up the rest of the Frontier Days celebration.

ACCOMMODATIONS
Accommodations include **Best Western Hitching Post Inn** (638-3301, S$36/D$56); **Downtowner Motor Inn** (634-1351, S$28-36/D$53-43); Fire-

bird Motel (632-5505, S$20-34/D$26-36); **Ramada Inn** (634-2171, S$27.50/D$31.50); **Sands Motel** (634-7771, S$8-11/D$9-17) and **Trave-Lodge** (634-2137, S$27-31/D$33-37).

RESTAURANTS

All restaurants are moderately priced, and among the better ones are at the **Best Western Hitching Post, Ramada Inn, Holiday Inn, Mayflower, Cal's Restaurant,** and **Little America.** Also try **Petersen's Buffet** and the **Chefs Inn.** About 7 miles north of Cheyenne on I-25 is **Little Bear Inn,** recommended for steaks and lobster.

ARTS AND MUSIC

The **Cheyenne Art Center** in **Holliday Park** is open Tuesday to Saturday 10:30-4:30, Sunday 2:30-4:30; free. During the season, plays are produced by the **Cheyenne Little Theater Group,** which sponsors the "Meller-drama" all summer at the **Atlas Theatre.** Musical concerts are presented by the **Community Concert Association** and **Symphony and Choral Society.**

SPORTS

Swimming, tennis, golf, baseball, horseshoe pitching, and bowling are popular. Some skiing, boating, and water-skiing.

WHERE TO GO NEARBY

Few places are "nearby" in this vast, thinly populated state. **Wyoming Hereford Ranch,** 10 miles east on US 30, was founded in the 1880s with purebred cattle imported from England and is one of the world's largest Hereford ranches; visitors welcome. Snow skiing at **Happy Jack Ski Area** in **Medicine Bow National Forest,** 38 miles west of Cheyenne; open daily, November through April, rental equipment available.

GRAND TETON NATIONAL PARK

The park covers 484 square miles south of Yellowstone National Park near the Idaho-Wyoming border. **Jackson Hole,** a forested valley of pine, fir, spruce, and cottonwood is about 50 miles long and 6 to 12 miles wide. The lively **Snake River** divides the basin. To the east the park blends into the **Bridger-Teton National Forest.** To the west the majestic range of the **Grand Tetons** continues for nearly 40 miles of jagged peaks, glaciated canyons, and dazzling snowfields. Eleven of these mountains range in height from 11,412 to 13,770 feet. Rising steeply 7,000 feet above the almost-level basin of sagebrush flats, the most scenic part of the Teton Range was a landmark for hunters and Indians. The **Grand, Middle,** and **South Tetons** were called "Les Trois Tetons" by French trappers and explorers of the early 19th century. The larger lakes of the park, **Jackson, Leigh, Jenny, Bradley, Taggart,** and **Phelps,** are all nestled close to the range.

The park is a sanctuary for wildlife. It is the home of the biggest elk herd in America and pronghorn, bighorn, mule deer, and moose. The

Upper Yellowstone Falls, WY, continues with a constant cascade of clear waters in one of the world's most scenic parks.

bald eagle, the rare trumpeter swan, and white pelican are among the more than 200 species of birds recorded in the park.

The park is open year round, with 200 miles of well-marked hiking trails which penetrate into deep canyons and eventually lead to high alpine meadows of flowers. The climbing season is about 15 June to 15 September; guide services and a mountaineering school are available. Floating the Snake River is an exhilarating experience; a number of concessionaires offer such trips. Boating, swimming, and fishing for cutthroat, mackinaw, and German brown trout are offered at the numerous lakes. A fishing license is needed as well as a boating permit. Horseback riding is available at most inns. With modern snow vehicles, it is now possible to visit many sections of the park to enjoy the spectacular winter scenery. Skiing, snowplaning, and ice fishing are also available.

From early June to Labor Day, naturalist talks are presented each evening at five campgrounds in the park. **Colter Bay Center** has an **Indian Arts Museum** which is designated to give an appreciation and understanding of the American Indian. The **Fur Trade Museum** at **Moose Station**, park headquarters, explains the trappers' role in the exploration of the Teton area, while a small museum at **Jenny Lake** provides information about the park's geology, flora, and fauna.

Most facilities and accommodations are available only from early June through September. There are five campgrounds. House trailers are permitted at all campgrounds except Jenny Lake; 10-day limit at Jenny Lake, 14 days at other sites. Overnight accommodations available in the park in the form of rustic log cabins at **Jenny Lake Lodge** (733-4647, open early June-early Sept, S$135-215/D$150-215 MAP); motor lodge or main lodge rooms at **Jackson Lake Lodge** (543-2855, open early June-mid Sept, S/D$46 up), or cabins at **Colter Bay Village** (543-2855, open late May-late Sept, S$24-41/D$41-52), also at Jackson Lake. Excellent year-round services are available in nearby Teton Village and Jackson.

YELLOWSTONE NATIONAL PARK

The park covers 3,471 square miles or over two million acres of northwestern Wyoming, lapping over into Idaho on the west and Montana on the north. The nation's oldest, largest national park is also the world's greatest center of geyser activity. It is famous for its wildlife, scenery, and magnificent trout fishing. Deer, moose, American elk, bison, pronghorn, coyote, bighorn sheep, American black bears, and grizzly bears roam freely in the park. Also 200 species of birds, including the bald eagle, the nation's symbol, and the almost extinct trumpeter swan, inhabit the park.

The main points of interest can be seen in a day, following the 140-mile **Grand Loop Road** connected by five approach roads. It is worthwhile, however, spending at least a week in Yellowstone. There are six major areas with nightly campfire programs, stores, restaurants, church services, and ranger-conducted nature walks. Saddle horses are for hire at two areas. Plan to spend at least a day in each area. **"Old Faithful"** reliably shoots its immense cloud of steam into the air at an average interval of every 65 minutes, and the display lasts from 2 to 5 minutes. Follow **Firehole River** to **Lower, Midway,** and **Upper Geyser Basins** where most of the park's 10,000 thermal features are concentrated. Bear, deer, and elk are abundant north and east of Old Faithful during the spring and fall months; and farther north is **Norris Geyser Basin** where "**Steamboat**" has flung steam as high as 300 feet. **West Thumb** juts off from **Yellowstone Lake,** 7,731 feet, the highest large mass of water in North America; it features the **Fishing Cone,** a hot spring mound surrounded by cold lake waters; excellent fishing for cutthroat (a non-fee fishing permit is required); and boats for rent. There are scenic cruiser lake trips, which rouse wild waterfowl and elk and moose in coves, a museum, and a campground. **Lake Fishing Bridge Area** has boating and fishing, a campground and trailer park, naturalist programs, wildlife museum, and midsummer all-day hikes to the top of the **Absaroka Range. Roosevelt Lodge Area** has a dude-ranch lodge, campground, Concord stagecoach rides, and bus trips to the summit of **Mt Washburn** (10,243 feet) every ½ hour, 8-4 from 1 July to 2 September. See beautiful **Tower Fall,** spilling 132 feet; watch for antelope, bear, buffalo, deer, elk, and moose. **Mammoth Hot Springs Area,** the only section of the park accessible by road year round, has a campground; well-marked trails to hot springs bubbling down terraced rock formations; a museum of geology, natural science, and human history; and fishing in **Gardiner** and **Yellowstone River.** The **Canyon Area** has motel-type cottages, campground entertainment, a museum, and an overwhelming view from **Inspiration Point** down into the sheer-sided **Grand Canyon** of the **Yellowstone River,** with its myriad yellows, oranges, and reds. See the much-photographed **Upper** and **Lower Falls,** thundering and foaming 417 feet into the gorge; take the all-day hike to the petrified forests on **Specimen Ridge.** Winter tours of Yellowstone are available from late December to mid-March. Snowcoaches carry 10 or 12 passengers across snow in warm comfort. Daytime tours originate at Gardiner, Montana, and West Yellowstone and Jackson, Wyoming. Tour prices range from \$20-40 for adults and \$10-20 for children. Week-long tours are also available.

Other focal areas in the park are **Madison Junction,** campground, nature talks; **Grant Village,** campground, nature talks, museum; and **Norris Geyser Basin,** campground, museum, conducted walks. Three hotels, motel units, numerous housekeeping cabins, including 200 recently added luxury cabins, seven modern campgrounds, a trailer park, and wilderness campsites are located here. Campgrounds are open from about 1 June to 15 September and are usually filled to capacity by noon every day July and August; 14-day stay limit 1 July to Labor Day; reservations advisable for cabins and hotel rooms in summer; most are open from June to September. **Lake Yellowstone Hotel** (344-7311, open mid-May-mid-Sept, S/D\$20.28-40.56) has an unparalleled view of America's largest alpine lake, dining facilities in the **Anchorage Dining Room,** cocktails and entertainment at the **Drydock. Old Faithful Inn** (344-7311, open May-mid-Oct, S/D\$20.28-42.12), and **Mammoth Hot Springs Hotel & Cabins** (344-7311, open June-mid-Sept, S/D\$25.45-37.08) both have dining facilities and cocktail lounges. **Old Faithful Cabins & Lodge,** open late May-late Sept, offers cabins S/D$9.36. Cabins also offered at **Canyon Village, Fishing Bridge Campers Village,** and **Lake Lodge.**

FURTHER STATE INFORMATION

Wyoming Travel Commission, Cheyenne, WY 82002. Hunting and Fishing: **Wyoming Game and Fish Commission,** Cheyenne, WY 82002. National Parks: **Grand Teton National Park** (Superintendent), Moose, WY 83012. Accommodations: **Grand Teton Lodge Company,** Moran, WY 83013. **Yellowstone National Park** (Superintendent), WY 82190. Accommodations: **Yellowstone Park Company,** Yellowstone National Park, WY 82190. **State Travel Information Centers:** I-25 at Etchepare Circle, Cheyenne, WY 82002, Tel: 777-7777; I-90 at 5th Street, Sheridan, WY 82801, Tel: 672-5665; 532 North Cache Street, Jackson, WY 83001, Tel: 733-6677.

USEFUL TELEPHONE NUMBERS IN CHEYENNE

Emergency (Fire, Police)	911
Memorial Hospital of Laramie County	634-3341
Poison Control	1-800-442-2704
State Patrol	777-7244
Legal Services for Laramie County	634-1566
Pan Am Reservations	(800)525-6006

Washington DC

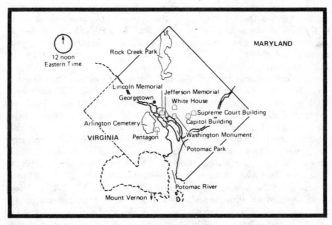

Area	69 square miles					**Population**				637,651				
Sales Tax	6%					**Metropolitan Area**				3,045,399				

Weather	Jan	Feb	Mar	Apr	May	Jun	Jul	Aug	Sep	Oct	Nov	Dec
Av Temp (°C)	3	3	7	13	19	23	26	25	21	15	9	3
Days Rain/Snow	11	9	11	10	11	9	10	9	8	7	8	9

After the Revolution, the North and South competed for the privilege of providing a suitable location for the new nation's capital. As a result of a compromise in 1790, a site was selected on the Potomac River and Maryland donated 69 square miles of its land for the new city. With experience in the baroque style of Paris, a Frenchman, Major Pierre L'Enfant, planned the city on grand scale with bold avenues and inspirational vistas appropriate to the spirit of a vigorous young nation. The city has led a peaceful existence with the notable exception of the British assault during the War of 1812. On 14 August 1814, the capital was set ablaze and the First Lady, Dolley Madison, was able to rescue Gilbert Stuart's famous portrait of Washington from the White House with only minutes to spare. When the executive mansion was rebuilt, the walls were covered with a thick coat of white paint, thus giving the home its familiar name, "White House." Today Washington is a vibrant, cosmopolitan city as well as an impressive, dignified national capital. Its principal function is to serve as headquarters for the federal government which is composed of the Presidency, the Congress, the Supreme Court and all major federal departments.

WHAT TO SEE

Capitol district includes the **Capitol** building, galleries open to the public 9-4:30 when Congress is in session; US citizens must obtain a pass to the galleries from their Congressman or Senator; foreign visitors may apply to either the Doorkeeper of the House or the Sergeant at Arms of the Senate. **House** and **Senate Office Buildings; Supreme Court Building;** the Supreme Court announces opinions three Mondays per month, open to the public. Guided tours conducted when court is not sitting. For reservations call (202) 252-3499 or write: Curator's Office, US Supreme Court, Washington DC 20543. **Library of Congress. State Department** tours, reservations needed two weeks ahead, call (202) 632-3241. Highly recommended: **Marine Corps Barracks Friday Evening parade,** 7:30 pm. Call 3 weeks in advance (202) 433-4073 or write Marine Corps Barracks, Public Affairs, 8th & Eye Streets, S.E., Washington, DC 20390. Walking tours of **Lafayette Square, Pennsylvania Ave,** or **Georgetown** conducted by **Architour,** a nonprofit organization that promotes the history and architecture of a city. Call 626-7546 for reservations. The **White House** on Pennsylvania Avenue has been the official home of the Presidents since John Adams. US Government exhibitions; VIP White House tours—less crowded, includes several more rooms than general public tour—request tickets well in advance through your Congressman's office; non US citizens contact a Congressman's office for information. Some past Presidents' homes: **Decatur House,** 748 Jackson Pl., N.W., home of Martin Van Buren when he was Secretary of State; **Woodrow Wilson House,** 2340 S. St., NW. **National Archives** displays the *Declaration of Independence,* the *Constitution,* the *Bill of Rights;* **Bureau of Engraving and Printing** gives a tour showing how stamps and money are made; **Voice of America** headquarters in the Department of Health, Education and Welfare; **FBI** in the new J. Edgar Hoover FBI Building. The **Smithsonian Institution** has been called the US government's "attic" because it's filled with a vast miscellany of objects in its many buildings: **Museum of Natural History; Museum of History and Technology; Arts and Industries Building; Smithsonian Building; Air and Space Building; National Portrait Gallery; National Gallery of American Art** housed in the refurbished Old Patent Office Building where President Lincoln held one of his inaugural balls; **National Gallery of Art** and new East Wing; **Renwick Gallery; Hirshhorn Museum & Sculpture Garden; Museum of African Art.** Worthwhile visits: National Geographic Society's **Explorers Hall; National Historical Wax Museum.** Children will be particularly interested in the **Explore Gallery,** a room of different textures, shapes and colors; **The National Air and Space Museum,** a "must," don't miss the movie *To Fly.* Also shown: *Living Planet,* an earth voyage; *Worlds of Tomorrow,* a space voyage. At the Natural History Museum, children will delight in the Discovery Room where exhibits can be touched and handled, and the **Insect Zoo.** For a recording giving information on Smithsonian events, call Dial a Museum, 357-2020. **The Textile Museum,** 2320 S. St., N.W. an outstanding collection of textiles, tapestries, and rugs. **The Freer Gallery** for Oriental Art. **Dumbarton Oaks** Byzantine and **Pre-Columbian Collection** and gardens (closed July-August). The Children's Attic in the **DAR Museum,** 1776 D. St., N.W., has an extensive doll collection. **Department of Interior,** C. St., between 18 & 19 Sts., has various exhibits on wildlife preservation, national parks, and Indian affairs. **National Aquarium,** Department of Commerce, 14th St. between Constitution Ave. and E. St., N.W. **Folger Shakespeare Library,** fine collection of Elizabethan books and materials; **Octagon House,** temporary residence of President and Mrs. Madison after the British burned the original executive mansion in 1814. **Ford's Theater,** where Lincoln was shot, is completely restored; contains museum and library. **Petersen House,** in which Lincoln died. Washington honors the men who have molded and served the nation with the **Washington Monument,** the **Lincoln Memorial,** the **Jefferson Memorial, Tomb of the Unknown Soldier,** and **Kennedy** memorials in **Arlington Cemetery.** A typical half-day tour of places of interest costs $11-15; a full day tour (usually with more time for visiting buildings) $18-30. Children under 12 half price. On a Tourmobile you can stop over as long as you like at 12 historic sites for $5.50. Children $3.25. Various attractions along the river offer a leisurely change of pace with the lovely **Potomac Park** barge trip along canal, April to October; **Georgetown,** fine homes of Washington's elite in colonial setting; boat trip along the Potomac to **Mount Vernon,** George Washington's home. There are 780 park areas and over 39,000 acres of park lands in the District of Columbia and its environs in Maryland and Virginia. **US Botanic Garden Conservatory** has tropical plants; **National Zoological Park** in wooded **Rock Creek Park.** There are also many important schools in the area including **George Washington University,** founded 1821; **Georgetown University,** founded 1789; **American University; Howard University; University of Maryland; Catholic University.** Theaters: **Kennedy Center,** a complex of five theaters: **Eisenhower,** for drama, Opera House, Concert Hall, Terrace, and American Film Institute. In addition, other Washington theaters include the **National Theater,** for drama and stage productions, **Arena Stage,** theater in the round, **Folger Theater** located in the Elizabethan Folger Shakespeare Library, for Shakespeare plays as well as new plays and playwrights. **Ford's Theater,** restored historical playhouse, presents touring productions—chairs are uncomfortable, but productions do not run overly long. Summer theater attractions: **Post Pavilion, Wolf Trap Farm Park for Performing Arts,** in nearby Virginia, and the **Olney summer theater** in Olney, Md.

ACCOMMODATIONS

Downtown area: **Hyatt Regency** (737-1234, S$85-105/D$105-125), striking 5-floor lobby with a waterfall, **Georgetown Inn** (333-8900, S$92-96/D$107-111), **Four Seasons Hotel** (342-0444, S$96-119/D$116-139), **Park Central** (393-4700, S$42-46/D$50-60), on Capitol Hill; **Hay-Adams Hotel** (638-2260, S$79-125/D$109-145), across from the White House; **Loews**

L'Enfant Plaza (484-1000, S$100-135/D$115-150), at the new Cosmopolitan center; **Mid-Town Motor Inn** (783-3040, S$40/D$46); **Sheraton Carlton** (638-2626, S$65-115/D$85-135), two blocks from the White House; **Capitol Hilton** (393-1000, S$60-90/D$80-110), popular, terminal for limousine buses to Baltimore-Washington and Dulles airports; **Hotel Washington** (638-5900, S$55-66/D$66-76) across from White House, fine food; **Watergate** (965-2300, S$92-128/D$112-148), overlooking the Potomac; and the **Mayflower** (347-3000, S$60-95/D$87-115).

Just north of the downtown area are the **Madison** (862-1600, S$96-115/D$116-135), elegant; **Dupont Plaza** (484-600, S$75-105/D$85-125); and the **Washington Hilton** (483-300, S$60-100/D$78-118).

Northwest in the fashionable Rock Creek Park area: **Sheraton Washington** (328-2000, S$70-85/D$85-100), pool and ice rink; **Shoreham** (234-0700, S$65-90/D$77-102).

Two large Marriott motor hotels are the **Marriott Key Bridge,** Arlington, Virginia (524-6400, S$70-90/D$85-105) and the **Marriott Twin Bridges** on US1 and I-95 (628-4200, S$61-79/D$71-89). Many others line the highways into Washington. Hotel Tax: 6%. Virginia Hotel Tax: 9%.

RESTAURANTS

The **Jockey Club; Paul Young's; Rive Gauche; La Fonda; Sans Souci; Tiberios,** Italian; **The Palm,** steak; **Cantina D'Italia,** Italian; **Harvey's,** seafood; **Le Lion D'Or, Dominique, Le Provencal,** French; **Le Bagatelle** and **Jean Pierre** are all expensive. **O'Donnell's Sea Grill** and **Hogates,** seafood; **Blackie's House of Beef; Gusti's,** Italian; **Anna Maria's** for pizza; all are moderately priced. Sidewalk cafes are **Afterwards, Arboughs, Garvin's, Napoleon's** and **The Buck Stops Here.** Excellent cafeterias in National Gallery of Art, Museum of American Art, and Smithsonian History and Technology. These are only a few of the many fine restaurants in Washington.

ENTERTAINMENT

Dinner and dancing at the Shoreham's **Marquee Lounge.** Entertainment at **Childe Harold, Blues Alley,** progressive jazz; **Cellar Door.** M Street clubs catering to the younger set are **Clyde's** and the **Crazy Horse.** Discothèques are **The Apple of Eve, The Plum, Deja Vu, Samantha's, Tramps,** and **The Tombs.** Reservations are recommended at nightclubs.

ARTS AND MUSIC

The **Kennedy Center** incorporates an opera house, concert hall, movie theater, **Eisenhower Theater** and **The Terrace Theater** for drama. **Corcoran Gallery of Art** has 18th-20th century American art; the **National Gallery of Art** and the new East Wing, one of the country's outstanding museum buildings, houses a fine art collection; **Museum of African Art, Phillips Gallery,** mostly modern art. **Smithsonian Institution** includes the National Gallery of American Art, National Portrait Gallery, Freer Gallery, Renwick Gallery and the Hirshhorn Museum and Sculpture Garden. **Dumbarton Oaks Museum** has a good art collection. Regular Broadway

The tallest building in Washington, DC at 555 ft (and the tallest masonry structure in the world), the Washington Monument pays fitting tribute to the first President of the USA.

productions are given at the **National Theater** and the **Arena Stage,** national repertory productions in **Ford's Theater.** There is a **Shakespeare Festival** at the **Sylvan Theater** in summer. The **National Symphony Orchestra** gives regular concerts during the winter season. There are numerous recitals and concerts by smaller groups during the winter as well as outdoor summer concerts, and there are band concerts at the East Front of the Capitol. Consult the local newspapers for details.

SHOPPING

For all types of boutiques, antiques, wander streets of the Georgetown, Wisconsin Ave and M. St., N.W., delightful gift store: **Little Caledonia Shop** on Wisconsin Ave. In the **Watergate Complex** (across from Kennedy Center) the **Les Champs** arcade offers many boutiques: **Pierre Cardin, Yves St. Laurent,** craft and specialty shops. For unusual gifts don't miss the many museum shops (no tax). **The Pan American Union** has Indian jewelry and the Department of Interior has an **Indian Craft Shop.** Government shops at Treasury Department for souvenir coin sets. Library of Congress for reproductions of posters, cards, pamphlets. National Archives sells facsimiles of American documents. Department of Commerce bookstore offers wide selection of books and pamphlets. Army Map Service, Bethesda, Md. for relief maps. Downtown shopping area (F St. between 14th & 9th): **Woodward and Lothrop** and **Hecht's** are the two department stores, with **Garfinckel's** the nicest specialty store. For a wider selection of specialty stores, Connecticut Ave. K St. to Dupont Circle, N.W., offers **Raleigh's, Rizik's,** and **Lewis,** and **Thos. Saltz.** The larger chains, **Neiman Marcus, Saks Fifth Ave., Lord & Taylor** are located on upper Wisconsin Ave., N.W., north of the downtown area. Stores are open until 6 except on Mondays & Thursdays, when they are open until 9.

SPORTS

The **Redskins** is the professional football team; pro-basketball is played by the **Bullets.** The **Capitals** is the professional hockey team. Washington has a good selection of golf courses and tennis courts, both public and private. There are fishing and hunting for small game birds in the Chesapeake Bay area.

CALENDAR OF EVENTS

Presidential Inauguration, 20 January (every four years); **Cherry Blossom Time,** early April; **President's Cup Regatta,** early summer; **Festival of American Folklife,** June to Labor Day; **Lighting of National Community Christmas Tree,** mid-December; **Pageant of Peace,** December. The famous Washington DC international horse race is run at Laurel, Maryland, in mid-November.

FURTHER INFORMATION

Washington Area Convention and Visitors' Assoc., 1575 I Street, NW, Washington DC 20005 (202-789-7000), **National Visitor Center,** Union

Station, 50 Massachusetts Avenue, NE, Washington, DC 20002 (202-523-5300), **International Visitors' Information Service,** 801 19th Street, NW, Washington, DC 20006 (202-872-8747), offers all kinds of information, as well as language assistance for visitors from abroad. **Pan Am** offices, World Center Building, 16th and K Streets, NW, Washington, DC 20006 (tel: 833-1000), and at Baltimore-Washington International and Dulles Airports.

   Embassies and Legations: Practically every country in the world is represented in Washington. The local telephone directory will supply the addresses and telephone numbers.

For daily listing of government & congressional activities, see *Washington Post* newspaper.

For all cultural and recreational activities, see *Washington Post* Weekend Section of the Friday *Post.*

USEFUL TELEPHONE NUMBERS

Police Ambulance Fire	911
Police Information	727-1000
Medical Bureau (doctor referral)	223-2200
Peoples Drug Store, 14th St. & Thomas Circle, N.W., 24-hr. service	628-0720
Travelers Aid	347-0101
International Visitors Information Services	872-8747
Pan Am Reservations	833-1000

Guam

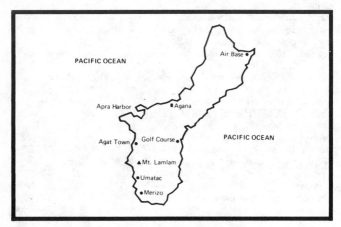

Area	212 square miles					**Population**	109,900					

Capital Agana   **Sales Tax** None

Weather	Jan	Feb	Mar	Apr	May	Jun	Jul	Aug	Sep	Oct	Nov	Dec
Av Temp (°C)	25	25	25	26	26	27	27	26	26	26	26	26
Days of Rain	12	10	7	10	6	10	12	12	13	13	8	15

Time Zone No named zone. When it is 12 noon Monday in New York City it is 3am Tuesday in Guam.

The largest of the volcanic Mariana Islands in the Western Pacific between the Philippines and Hawaii, Guam combines the beauty of the tropics with the modern conveniences of the Western world. It has a healthy and pleasant climate, beautiful sunsets, fragrant flowers, white beaches, and a crystal-clear sea. Guam's strange formations of rock and coral are the result of the immense volcanic upheavals that formed the Marianas and the surrounding Pacific deeps. Man-made history ranges from early cave drawings and the mysterious latte stones which signposted the Malaysian migration across the Pacific, to Magellan's arrival in 1521, and more recent reminders of Spanish occupation, and later of World War II.

The island is now an unincorporated territory of the United States and is populated by 60% indigenous Chamorros and 20% mainland Americans, with a heavy sprinkling of Hawaiians, Filipinos, Chinese, Japanese, Koreans, and Micronesians. Its people are US citizens and, although they do not vote in national elections, they are represented in Congress. The island elects its own governor and there is an elected, one-house legislature. The US Department of the Interior supervises the government of the island.

All Guamanians are fluent in **English,** although "Chamorro" is widely spoken. The predominant **religion** is Roman Catholic; however, Protestant denominations are represented. Several major American **banks** have offices on the island; US currency is used. There is a daily air mail service and overseas **phone** calls can be made through the overseas operator. **Electrical** outlets are 120 volts, 60 cycles AC.

WHAT TO SEE

Guam Museum in Agana gives a digest of over 5,000 years of history; also visit the **Micronesian Area Research Center** in the **University of Guam Library.** See the Spanish buildings, forts and bridges around the charming Chamorro villages of **Merizo, Umatac,** and **Inarajan;** the mysterious coral columns called *latte*. Take a coral-watching trip in a glass-bottom boat. Visit the **Plaza de Espana** in Agana or Lovers' Point at **Puntan dos Amantes,** which also boasts one of the world's finest sunsets nightly. Several companies offer bus tours of the island for six hours, $30 per person with lunch, or four-hour tours of the central area, $22, including lunch. Private cars with guides are available through major hotels at $100 per half day. **Lanchon Antigo** or "Old Village" is a living museum in Inarajan Village—oldest community in Guam. It provides an authentic re-creation of Chamorro village life with demonstrations of traditional craft working, food preparation and the performing arts.

HOW TO GET THERE

Flying time to Guam International Airport from San Francisco is 12 hours; from Honolulu, 7 hours; from Manila, 3½ hours. The airport is 2 miles from Agana, the main village; resort hotels of Tumon Bay are less than 15 minutes from the airport. Taxi fare into Agana is about $5. In addition, hotel buses meet planes, cost about $3.80 to hotel row; hotel call phones are available in the airport customs area. Rental cars are handy everywhere.

ACCOMMODATIONS

A wide range of modern hotels is available overlooking picturesque Tumon Bay. Among the higher priced are the **Hilton** (646-1841), **Okura** (646-6811), and **Reef** (646-6881), averaging from about S/D$57. A new resort is the **Pacific Islands Club** (646-7865, S/D$75), part of a beach complex. Medium priced hotels include the **Dai-Ichi, Fujita Guam Tumon Beach, Guam Horizon, Terraza Tumon Villa, Joinus:** average, S/D$34. Economy priced hotels in the Agana area include the **Magellan,** about S/D$25. Hotel room tax: 10%; most hotels have an additional 10% service charge.

RESTAURANTS

Restaurants reflect the cultural heritage of the island; there is American, Japanese, Spanish, Filipino, Mexican, Chinese, and Chamorro as well as continental cuisine. Chamorro dishes are primarily made of coconuts, rice and taro with roast pig, barbecued spare ribs, and chicken all spiced with finadeni sauce. True Chamorro food is almost impossible to get except at the Public Market stands in downtown Agana, and at the frequent village or private fiestas, but restaurants for other foods abound. Elegant American and continental dining can be had at the **Galleon Grill** in the Hilton, the **Flamboyan** at the Okura, **La Fuente** at the Kakuei, the **Salzburg Chalet, Don Pedro's Castle;** all are in the Tumon resort hotel area. Japanese food excels at the **Kuramaya** at the Dai-Ichi, **Genji** at the Hilton, the **Top of the Reef.** The **Sakura, Yakitori II, Furosata,** and others are slightly less expensive. Go to **Nina's Papagayo** or **Joe and Flo's** for Mexican food; to the **Toh Kah Lin** in the Okura, **China House** at the Dai-Ichi, plus a half dozen others around town for Chinese food; **Chuck's** or **Suehiro's** for steaks, both in the Tumon area. And the **Hale Kai** on San Vitores Road for fresh seafood. There are **McDonald's, Colonel Sanders, Shakey's,** and other pizza and hamburger havens, too.

SHOPPING

The superb duty-free shops are full of low-priced luxury items. Look for Oriental goods; gems, art objects, jewelry, silks, brocades, batiks, pearls.

Other good buys include photographic and stereo equipment, European and Japanese china and crystal, perfume and Swiss watches. Wood carvings and needlework from the Philippines can be purchased as well as shell products, ceramics and wood carvings.

Americans can purchase up to $600 (instead of $300) of non-US-made goods and be exempt from duty on returning home.

SPORTS

First-class water sports of every conceivable kind are available; scuba-diving is outstanding. Equipment may be rented from the **Coral Reef Marine Center** or the **Marianas Divers** in Agana. Guam's offshore waters are a fisherman's paradise; trawling for marlin, tuna, dolphin, barracuda, bonito, and sailfish can be done in chartered boats from **Coral Reef Marine Center, Agana,** or **Merizo Boaters Association, Merizo.** There are several 18-hole golf courses; **Country Club of the Pacific** and the **Windwards Hills Golf Course** have clubhouses and swimming pools. Horseback riding is available at **Talofofo Bay;** bowling, tennis, greyhound racing, and cock-fighting are also offered.

FURTHER GUAM INFORMATION

Guam Chamber of Commerce, PO Box 283, Guam 96910. **Guam Visitors' Bureau,** PO Box 3520, Agana, 96910; tel: 646-5278/9.

USEFUL TELEPHONE NUMBERS

Police	472-8911
Fire	2-2222
Ambulance	646-8801
Guam Memorial Hospital	646-5801
Air/Sea Rescue	344-7100
F.B.I.	477-7896
Guam Visitors Bureau	472-6014

Micronesia

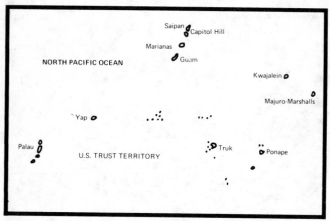

Area 700 square miles	**Population** 135,660
Capital —	**Sales Tax** None

Weather

	Jan	Feb	Mar	Apr	May	Jun	Jul	Aug	Sep	Oct	Nov	Dec
Av Temp (°C)	25	28	28	28	30	30	30	30	28	28	28	25
Days Rain	8	9	12	16	9	23	22	22	19	17	14	12

Time Zone No named zone. When it is 12 noon Monday in New York City, it is 3 am Tuesday in Guam.

Micronesia is many separate places: 2,141 variations on the tropical theme, with the usual liberal lacings of sand, sea, surf. The name itself means, literally, "tiny islands"; there are in fact seven districts—Yap, Truk, Ponape, Kosrae, Palau, the Marshalls, and the Marianas. The whole territory is equal in size to the continental United States, while its actual land mass is about half the size of Rhode Island. Culturally and ethnically Micronesia has a chequered past. The original natives came from Southeast Asia, but from the 18th century onwards the islands have been occupied in turn by the Spanish, Germans, Japanese, and Americans; all left their marks. The Mariana Islands are on their way to attaining Commonwealth status with the US, while the other six districts currently are deliberating their future political status. The US trusteeship which provides the binding link of these distant territories comes to an end in the near future. Already residents of the islands of Koror, Babelthuap, Peleliu, Angaur, Kayangel, Sonsorol, Tobi and Pulo Anna have voted to join together as the Republic of Belau. (Belau appears at left on the map as Palau, and the new Republic will have an area of 190.6 sq miles with a population of 14,800.)

Meanwhile, in the northwest Trust Territory, Saipan and residents of adjacent isles have already proclaimed the Commonwealth of the Northern Marianas. Area, 184.5 sq miles with a population of 15,790. The bulk of the population lives on Saipan, the remaining 3,000 divided between Agrihan, Alamagan, Pagan, Rota and Tinian.

The islands of the central Trust Territory, including Ponape, Truk, Kosrae, Yap, and the numerous atolls around, will be part of the Federated States of Micronesia. Kolonia on Panape is to become the seat of the new federal government. Land area is some 280 sq miles with a population of around 65,000.

At the eastern edge of the Trust Territory are the Marshall Islands (and atolls), who have voted for independence. Majuro will become the seat of government for the 29,670 islanders. Total area of this new territory is about 70 sq miles. All new mini-nations are expected to maintain alliances with the US in matters of foreign affairs and defense, which will result in the continuation of funding for government/economic and related activities.

The islands are, by and large, unspoiled and undeveloped, and visiting many of this is likely to be an adventure in the truest sense of the word. There *are* facilities for tourists—currently a great number of comfortable new hotels are opening on most of the islands—but life is still primitive. However, the sea is blue and inviting, the beaches are white and empty, and the lush backdrop of island scenery is as widely varied as the tropical climate.

Tropical Climate—rainy season in southern districts mid-May to late November, but the rain is rarely heavy.

Government—US Trust Territory with appointed Resident Commissioner for the Marianas and High Commissioner for the other six districts.

Language—English, Japanese, Micronesian dialects.

Religion—About 50% Catholic.

Currency—US dollar.

Public Holidays are the same as USA.

REQUIREMENTS FOR ENTRY AND CUSTOMS REGULATIONS

Passport, United States visa, and round-trip ticket are required for periods of 30 days or less. US citizens, visiting for the same amount of time, only need proof of identity for entry. Smallpox and cholera inoculations are required only if entering from an infected area. Tetanus, typhoid, and paratyphoid injections are strongly recommended. Change currency other than US dollars before arrival, as facilities are limited.

AIRPORT INFORMATION

Continental/Air Micronesia has regular services from Guam to Saipan, the Majuro-Marshall Islands, Ponape, Truk, Palau, and Yap. Airports have no hotel reservations counters. Hotel representatives meet flights in all districts and provide transportation. Taxis are generally available.

ACCOMMODATIONS

Accommodations are extremely varied—from good to practical—and are within minutes of airports. Due to the scarcity of rooms in some districts, single guests may be asked to share twin-bedded rooms with other single guests. (See district sections for specific hotels.)

USEFUL INFORMATION

Banks are open Mon-Fri. Currency can be changed only at a bank, although hotels and some shops take travelers' checks. Each district has a branch of a major bank (e.g. Bank of America or Bank of Hawaii), whose opening hours vary.

Only post offices sell stamps, and letters can be mailed only at district post offices or through hotel facilities. P.O. Hours: 7:30am-4:30pm; Sat. 9am-noon.

Phone systems are found in hotels, restaurants, and other public facilities. Saipan has the only pay phones (25¢ local calls). To operate the interisland service, dial direct. Radio-telephone communications are in operation for other districts.

English-language newspapers and magazines are available. The former include the *Guam Pacific Daily News, Marianas Variety*, and *Micronesian Independent*.

Tipping is neither customary nor expected, and there are no service charges.

Electricity—110 volts 60 cycles AC in areas that have electricity.

Laundry service is adequate in most hotels, but dry-cleaning is available only in the Marianas.

Very few hairdressers, except at hotels on Saipan; shampoo and set from US$10, man's haircut from US$3.

Photographic equipment is available in hotels and shopping areas. Processing, however, is not available.

Rotary Club in Saipan only. Kiwanis in Commonwealth of the Northern Marianas.

Babysitting facilities can be found in hotels.

Rest rooms can be found in hotels, restaurants, and stores. No charge.

Doctors and dentists speak English. Imported pharmaceuticals are available in government clinics in each district.

TRANSPORTATION

There are no buses on the islands other than tourist services and taxis are the best and most reliable form of transportation. Alternatively, one can rent a car; prices are from US$15-20 a day, and chauffeur-driven cars cost more. Roads can be rough. The internal airlines are Air Micronesia and Air Pacific International, both of which link up most of the islands. Government field trip ships travel to outer islands; a boat with outboard motor can be hired for US$40 and up per day, guide/operator included.

FOOD AND RESTAURANTS

Fish, of course, is available in vast quantities—clams, eels, *langusta*, octopus—plus coconut crabs, mangrove clams, fruit bats, and yams. Try *kelaguin* (a chewy mixture of diced chicken and shredded coconut) in the Marianas and breadfruit in Truk. The Japanese *sashimi* (slices of raw fish dipped in a peppery sauce) make a tasty snack with beer throughout the islands. The **Chamorro Village** is a new restaurant offering local food specialties and entertainment. Prices are reasonable. The food served in hotels is basically American, and adventurous eating will depend on your willingness to look for something more exciting. If you let people know that you want more than ordinary tourist food, you may be quite agreeably surprised. Hotel staff members can usually arrange for you to eat "out" somewhere—if you're in luck, it may be at the wedding feast of a member of their own family, where the eating is likely to be notably different. Otherwise, look for small native restaurants near the various town centers.

DRINKING TIPS

When on Ponape, drink *sakau,* which is obtained from the root of the sakau plant. Otherwise, imported wines, liquor, and beers are available. Alcoholic-beverage drinking permits, varying in cost from US$1-3, are required in the Marshalls, Ponape, and Yap districts. The best bars are in hotels, most of which have food and are near the ocean. Truk recently became "dry" but that legislation may be repealed.

ENTERTAINMENT

Amateur theater groups, old films, local bands in nightclubs, and some native dance performances brighten the island evenings. Nightclubs with music include the following: Saipan—major hotels, **Oleai Room, Marianas Inn, Big K, Puppy Club, Tapa Bar;** Palau—**Peleliu Club, Factory Club;** Ponape—**Nan Madol Hotel;** the Marshalls—**Kitco Downtown Club;** Truk—**Christopher Inn, Maramar Hotel;** Yap—**Rai View Inn, O'Keefe's Community Club.**

SHOPPING

Handicraft shops can be found on all the islands, and Ponape black pepper and wood carvings are two of the best buys at handicraft cooperatives and stores. **Majuro** has *kili* bags woven by former Bikini islanders, stick charts, seashells, and coconut-fiber flowers. **Palau** and **Ponape** are known for their carvers, who make wooden story-boards depicting island legends, model outrigger canoes, carved wooden houses, and tortoiseshell jewelry. The **Yapese** make miniature stone money, lavalavas, and grass skirts. On **Saipan** buy lacquered turtles, stuffed coconut crabs, and all kinds of seashell goods. On **Truk** look for love sticks and war clubs. The **Marianas** offer wishing dolls, coconut masks, and wood carvings.

SPORTS

Scuba-diving, snorkeling, deep-sea fishing, and swimming are enjoyed in all districts. There is outstanding scuba-diving among the coral reefs and drop-offs of Palau and the 60 or so sunken Japanese warships in the Truk Lagoon. Tennis and hiking are available in all districts, golf in Saipan only. Hunting and yachting are limited.

WHAT TO SEE

Yap: On Yap, life in the small, thriving District Center of **Colonia** provides an interesting mixture of loincloths and jukeboxes, grass skirts and motorcycles. In the villages see the huge slabs of stone money, some of them 14 feet across, lying about near roadsides and houses. Visit the **Yap Museum** in Colonia, or see the stone money bank in Rull. Hotels are the **Rai View Inn, Colonia** (tel:485, from US$22 double), and the **ESA Hotel** (from US$25 double).

Northern Marianas: Saipan is the center of the Marianas, background for some of the fiercest battles of World War II. The best beaches of the Marianas are on Saipan, most of them decorated with rusty remnants of the war. Hotels here are **Hafadai Beach Hotel** (S$23/D$26) and at the beach; **Mariana Hotel** (S/D$25) on the hillside overlooking the village of Garapan; **Royal Taga Hotel,** on the beach at Susupe (from US$30 double); and the **Saipan Continental,** Micro Beach (from US$67 double). There is also the new **SAIPAN BEACH INTER-CONTINENTAL INN,** Micro Beach (from US$45 double, and **Saipan Grand** (from US$50 double).

Tinian: Fleming Hotel (S$15/D$25).

Palau: Two hundred islands make up the district of Palau, the central town of which is **Koror.** Take a boat through the **Rock Islands** and see the atoll of **Kayangel.** Hotels are **Palau Continental,** Koror (from US$53 double); the **New Koror Hotel,** Koror (from US$20 double); the **Barsakesau Hotel,** Koror (US$30 double).

Truk: One of the world's largest lagoons, this circle of coral has the largest population of all the six districts. More war mementoes are here, scattered about the island. See the **Japanese Lighthouse** and the **Truk Trading Company,** called "a general store to end all general stores—part tropical outpost, part American frontier." Hotels are the **Bayview,** Moen (from US$14 double), the **Christopher Inn** (from US$20 double), in Moen near the airport. There is also **Truk Continental Hotel,** Moen (S$53-58/D$58-65).

Ponape: Perhaps the most beautiful and most "typical" of all South Sea islands, Ponape has few beaches but numerous freshwater streams, waterfalls, and lagoons where you can picnic and swim.

Kolonia is the district center of Ponape—a wonderful shanty of a town. Forty minutes away from Kolonia by boat is **Nan Madol**—ruined walls, pathways, canals, and the temple of **Nan Dowas.** Hotels in Kolonia: **Cliff Rainbow Hotel** (S$15-22/D$18-25) just 15 minutes from the airport, near Kapinga Village; **South Park Hotel,** (S$25-40/D$28-45) overlooking Sokehs Bay; **Hotel Nan Madol,** also at Sokehs (S$16-19/D$24-26); **Hotel Pohnpei** (US$20 double); and **The Village** (S$35-45/D$40-50).

Majuro-Marshalls: Thirty-four island groups, 870 reefs, and the sea available in more than a dozen shades of blue—those are the attractions of the Majuro-Marshalls. The sea predominates here and provides all the entertainment you'll want. Hotels are the **Eastern Gateway Hotel,** Majuro (US$30 a/c, US$21 non-a/c double), and the **Hotel Majuro,** Majuro (from US$18 double).

SOURCES OF FURTHER INFORMATION

Pan Am: Skinner Plaza, Agana, Guam, and any Pan Am office around the world; **Micronesia Regional Tourism Council,** PO Box 682, Agona, Guam 96910 (tel: 649-1250); **Northern Marianas Visitors Bureau,** PO Box 861, Saipan, Marianas Islands 96950; **Pacific Area Travel Association,** 228 Grant Avenue, San Francisco, CA 94108.

Puerto Rico

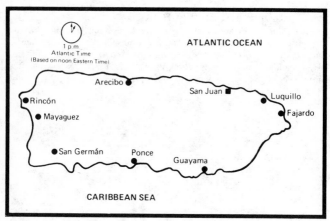

| **Area** | 3,435 square miles | | | | **Population** | 3,334,000 | | | | | | |
| **Capital** | San Juan | | | | **Sales Tax** | None | | | | | | |

Weather	Jan	Feb	Mar	Apr	May	Jun	Jul	Aug	Sep	Oct	Nov	Dec
Av Temp (°C)	24	24	25	26	27	27	27	27	27	27	26	25
Days of Rain	17	13	11	14	19	18	21	19	18	17	18	19

Time Zone Atlantic

Puerto Rico, a hilly and tropical island 100 miles long and 35 miles wide lying between the Atlantic and the Caribbean, gives you the assurance of year-round sunshine. The food has a definite Spanish flavor and the leading hotels are among the most luxurious anywhere in the Caribbean. The island became a possession of the United States after the Spanish-American War of 1898. In 1948 the Honorable Luis Muñoz Marin became the first elected governor. Puerto Rico became a commonwealth in July 1952, with a constitution giving the island limited autonomy. A resident commissioner in Washington has a voice but no floor vote in Congress (he may vote in committee).

Driving round the island is an enjoyable way of sightseeing. Roads have improved immensely during the past few years and apart from Route 52, as the expressway which joins Ponce and San Juan is officially called, even some of the smallest of byways have been actually improved. For the driver, there are now some 4,000 miles of good roads. Traveling along the coast on route 3 you approach **Luquillo Beach** (30 miles east on San Juan), a beautiful crescent-shaped area lined with coconut groves. The parador **Martorell** is an excellent place to stay overnight here, and provides a classic example of what the Puerto Rican parador system is about. The concept is an old Spanish one, dating back to the 16th century and reborn in 20th-century Spain to develop tourism. The concept is to provide comfortable, basic, ethnic accommodation at a reasonable price. The early paradors were what we would term inns or hostelries and were situated at convenient way points where travelers would want to change horses, catch a nap, have a meal. For latest rates contact Tourism Company, since these can fluctuate with the season. Figure around S$23-43/D$30-53 in the low season. Above Luquillo Beach stands **El Yunque,** the only tropical rainforest in the US National Forest system, with over 200 species of trees and a bird sanctuary. **Fajardo,** on the northeast corner of the island, overlooks the village of **La Croabas** and the sea from a height of 280 feet. From the village take a ferry to the offshore islands of **Culebra** and **Vieques.**

Continuing on route 3 you pass through **Humacao, Guayama,** and other small towns before reaching **PONCE,** second largest city in Puerto Rico, on the southern coast. A visit to Ponce used to be considered worthwhile if only to see its famous fire station, the Parque de Bombas: these days it's better known for the $5-million **Ponce Museum of Art** designed by Edward Durell Stone; closed Tuesdays; admission $1 adults, 50¢ children. The museum houses an impressive collection of Spanish, Puertorriquenian, and European art of the last five centuries. By all means visit the fire station, too, with its red-and-black striped building splashed with yellow and green designs. It has an *opéra bouffe* quality that is almost unbelievable. Behind the firehouse is the stately **Cathedral of Our Lady of Guadalupe.** The Melia Hotel (843-8181, S$36-40/D$40-45) is a good downtown hotel with an excellent restaurant. The **Holiday Inn** (844-1200, S$65-70/D$70-75) is across from **El Tuque Public Beach,** 4 miles west of the city. The beach has become popular and more facilities seem to be added each year. About 35 miles from Ponce, near the southwest corner of the island, is the historic town of **San Germán** where **Porta Coeli Church,** built in the 17th century, houses a religious art museum that is closed for restoration at the present time. **Inter-American University** is also here. Interestingly, San Germán was one of the earlier communities to be founded on the island, in 1573. Indeed, it was once rival to the present capital of San Juan. (It was here that Ponce de León himself searched for the Elixir of Life, it should be remembered.) San Germán's present claim to fame is that it provides the center for the **Inter-American University.** Follow a winding road down to the coastal village of **Parguera,** from where it is a short boat ride to **Phosphorescent Bay** which looks like liquid diamonds on a moonless night. **Villa Parguera** (892-9588, S$25-42/D$42) provides deep-sea fishing facilities and an unforgettable trip by motor launch over the glittering bay. The hotel restaurant is recommended.

On the west coast you pass through sugarcane fields along the sea to **Mayagüez,** once known for its exquisite handmade embroidery and lace, today regarded for its tuna fishing fleet which works in the Pacific Ocean off the coasts of Ecuador and Peru; visit the exotic garden at the US Department of Agriculture Experimental Station. Well-known restaurants here are La Palma and Bolo's. Driving inland you pass through coffee country en route to Maricao State Forest, where you can visit the government fish hatchery which stocks Puerto Rico's lakes and rivers. Returning to the coast, you pass through the towns of Aguada, near where Columbus landed when he discovered the island in 1493, and Aguadilla.

In Arecibo along the Atlantic coast stop for a tour of the Ronrico Rum Distillery and a free drink. A 35-minute drive inland in the *karst* country is the Arecibo Ionospheric Observatory, the largest radar-radio telescope in the world; grounds open to the public 2-4:30, Sundays only. The *karst* country is named for a similar area in Yugoslavia with a similar broken terrain of deep conical sinkholes and small abrupt hills called haystacks, or *mogotes,* locally. You will get good views of these weird geological formations as you approach the 5,800-acre Rio Abajo State Forest, with a recreation and picnic area. Nearby on Dos Bocas Lake, take a free 2-hour launch ride at 7, 10, 2, or 5. West of Utuado on route 111 are the ruins of an ancient Taino Indian ceremonial park constructed 700 years ago. It is believed to have been used by the Indians for religious ceremonies. The museum diaplays artifacts excavated at the site.

Returning to route 2 along the Atlantic coast, you pass through pineapple country to Dorado just 20 miles outside San Juan. There are two luxury hotels with championship golf courses here, as well as magnificent palm-sheltered beaches. The Cerromar Beach Hotel (796-1010, S/D$135 MAP), complete convention facilities, two 18-hole golf courses, olympic-size swimming pool; the Dorado Beach Hotel (796-1600, S$165/D$185 MAP), a beautifully landscaped 1700-acre resort directly on the beach with two 18-hole championship golf courses; and villas are obtainable at the Villa Dorado Condominium Resort (796-1600, rates on request). Prices quoted are for the winter season; rates are lower in the summer.

City To Visit

SAN JUAN

San Juan, the capital and principal city of Puerto Rico, is an important port and is connected to the mainland by a series of bridges. Curiously enough, it was originally the island that was known as San Juan and its capital city as Rich Port, or Puerto Rico. No one knows how the switch occurred. Ponce de León himself named the bay, while searching for the Elixir of Life, and the second most important city in the island bears his name.

Founded about 1521, San Juan has an old city—subject to much painstaking restoration—in addition to the vast sprawl of its modern area. There are numerous small shops and houses in the older part of town,

*The assurance of year-round warm weather and the many miles of beauti-
ful beaches makes Puerto Rico a tropical island paradise.*

set along many charming narrow streets, or *calles*, as they are called. There are also some impressive historic buildings. Population is 522,700.

The national language is Spanish; however, English is widely spoken. Eighty percent of the population is Catholic.

WHAT TO SEE

Old San Juan itself is an islet, connected to the modern **Condado** section by bridge. In old San Juan visit **El Morro** (1539), one of the most interesting forts in the western hemisphere, begun in the 16th century to block invasion from the sea; open daily 8-5. Also see the old fortress of **San Jeronimo,** now housing the fascinating **Museum of Military History; La Fortaleza** (1540), home of the island's governors, is the oldest executive mansion in continuous use in the hemisphere; and **San Juan Cathedral,** where Juan Ponce de León, Puerto Rico's first governor, is buried. The mansion of the Ponce de León family, a 16th-century structure called **Casa Blanca,** has been impressively restored. **San Cristobal Fort** guards the landside entrance to the walled city of Old San Juan. At 2:30 and 4:30 on Sunday and holiday afternoons, there are ferry cruises around San Juan Bay with panoramic views of the city's most historic landmarks; adults $1.50, children under 12, $1.00. The **Institute of Puerto Rican Culture,** in the beautifully restored 16th-century **Dominican Convent,** is the commonwealth's workshop for the study and preservation of island culture. **La Casa del Libro** houses a notable collection of rare books in a restored 18th-century building and **La Casa del Callejon,** another restored building, contains the **Museum of Colonial Architecture** and the **Museum of the Puerto Rican Family.**

The **Botanical Garden** of the University of Puerto Rico contains a profusion of tropical flowers and trees, open 9-5 daily. In the **Bacardi** plant near Cataño, across San Juan Bay, guided tours explaining the distilling of rum and a free rum drink are given, open Monday through Saturday.

ACCOMMODATIONS

San Juan offers a wide range of accommodations from luxurious beachfront hotels to attractive, modestly priced guest houses. Prices listed are for winter season; most rates lower for the summer.

Condado section: the 706-room **Caribe Hilton** (725-0303, S$89-137/ D$99-147) offers a balcony and ocean view with every room; **La Concha Hotel** (723-6090, S$73-109/D$80-116) and **Hotel Condado** (723-6090, S$55-71/D$59-75) with the Exhibition Hall that joins them to form the **Condado Convention Center;** the colorful **Da Vinci** (725-2323, S$85-125/ D$90-130); **Condado Holiday Inn** is joined by a walkway over Avenida Ashford to the former Flamboyan Hotel, to form a resort and casino complex (724-4000, S$55-75/D$60-80); and the **Dupont Plaza San Juan** (724-6161, S$80-110). Long popular with business visitors is **Best Western's Hotel Pierre** (724-1200, S$49-55/D$55-61), in nearby Santurce, with the famous Swiss Chalet restaurant next door.

Isla Verde section: the **Hotel Palace** (791-2020, S$85-130/D$90-135); **El San Juan** (790-1100, S$85-130/D$90-135); **Holiday Inn** (791-2300,

S\$70-95/D\$75-100); the **Carib Inn** (791-3535, S\$59-74/D\$64-79); these hotels are all air-conditioned, have bars, restaurants, their own beaches (except the Carib Inn) and pools, evening entertainment during the season, and sports facilities.

In Old San Juan, the beautiful **Hotel El Convento** (723-4370, S\$60/D\$70), an exquisitely restored 17th-century Carmelite convent, with wood panelling, wall tapestries, and furnished with antiques.

In Miramar: **Hotel Gran Bahia** (725-1212, S\$42-62/D\$48-68) and the tallest hotel in the Caribbean; **Hotel Excelsior** (725-7400, S\$50-54/D\$55-58); and used by business visitors to the city, **Hotel Olimpo Court** (724-0600, S\$26/D\$32).

RESTAURANTS

Puerto Rico food is definitely Creole-Spanish. Famous are *arroz con pollo,* chicken with rice; *asopao,* a soupy dish of rice cooked with seafood or chicken; *pasteles,* a meat filling with grated plantain wrapped in plantain leaves and boiled; *lechon asado,* a barbecued pig; *jueyes,* fresh land crabs, shelled and boiled; and *pastelillos,* thin dough filled with meat or cheese and deep-fat fried. Good American, French, Chinese, Arabian, Jewish, and Italian food, too.

Most famous and oldest of the island's restaurants is **La Mallorquina** in Old San Juan, where the a la carte menu features Puerto Rican and Spanish dishes, with a balance between seafood and meat. The *plats du jour* are worth noting, while house specialties include Caribbean sea turtle steak, *asapao,* and black bean soup. In Old San Juan, local atmosphere and food can be found at **La Fonda de la Capilla** and **La Danza; La Zaragozana,** and **Barrachina** are other favorites in this area. **El Meson Vasco,** old established Basque restaurant, in a lofty building with tall windows, reaching to a beamed ceiling, offers traditional Basque and island fare including gazpacho (an ice-cold vegetable soup), piperade, seafood, and tortillas. Recommended is a fish dish—hake in a green sauce made from parsley, stock and white wine. For French cuisine, visit **La Chaumière.** The Condado area offers the **El Cid, Novel Castilla Fabiana,** and **La Reina** in Puerto de Tierra for Spanish food. For seafood specialties, visit **El Cabildo. Rotisserie Castillo** at the Caribe Hilton and the **Segovia** offer international cuisine. **El Consulado** offers both enclosed and outdoor dining with international and Italian cuisine, while **Cookies** features Argentinean specialties. The **Scotch and Sirloin** in the La Rada Building and the **Beef and Wine Room,** Hotel Da Vinci, specialize in steaks. The **Swiss Chalet** is known for its continental cuisine; **El Zipperle** features Spanish and German food. In Isla Verde, **Cecilia's Place** specializes in Puerto Rican dishes and seafood. The **Four Winds and Seven Seas** in El San Juan Hotel is well known for its charcoal steaks. **The Metropol** features Cuban and Puerto Rican cooking.

ENTERTAINMENT

You can find almost any sort of night life you want in and around San Juan, from the lavish clubs and restaurants of the luxury hotels to the native cabarets. **El Club Caribe,** in the Caribe Hilton, attracts "big name" entertainers; several hotels feature glittering revues. Gambling is legal in Puerto Rico; hotels with casinos are the Hotel Palace, Caribe Hilton, Condado Holiday Inn, El San Juan, Dupont Plaza San Juan, Dorado Hilton, and Dorado Beach. Popular night spots outside the hotels are **Café Tetuan 20, La Tea, Monologo, Los Balcones, The Place,** all in Old San Juan. In the Condado area, **Horizons** attracts the young crowd. Disclothèques include **Isadora's, The Flying Saucer, Juliana's,** and **Pier One.** Visitors can usually obtain complimentary admission from their local hotel managers.

ARTS AND MUSIC

In Rio Piedras, the **University of Puerto Rico** has a good museum located off the main quadrangle. The **Ponce de León Museum,** with exhibits relating to the early history of the island, is open daily except Sunday 9-5. Be sure to visit the **Puerto Rico Museum of Art.** The museums of **Fort El Morro** and **Fort San Jeronimo** are also worth a visit. Puerto Rican music is distinctive and ear-catching. It is usually heard at religious festivals, home gatherings, private parties, and sometimes at night clubs. Records are easily obtainable. One of the most important musical events is the **Casals Festival** usually held in June. Ballets and plays in Spanish at the **Tapia Theater** in Old San Juna. The **Civic Theater of Puerto Rico** puts on frequent productions.

SHOPPING

In addition to **Plaza las Americas** shopping center and shops in leading hotels, there are over 400 shops lining the streets of Old San Juan. **The Folk Arts Center** (Centro de Artes Populares) in the Dominican Convent and **El Centro de Productos de Puerto Rico** are good places to buy local handicrafts. **Crazy Alice** and **Casa Cavanaugh** have a variety of island-made sports clothes. **Timi's** specializes in tortoise shell, horn, and amber jewelry. **Fernando Pena** in the Condado section carries haute couture fashions. Handrolled cigars are found at **Antillas Cigars** or **Caribe Cigars.**

SPORTS

In the San Juan area, enjoy a wide choice of spectator sports. Cockfights are held in Isla Verde at the **Coliseo Gallistico,** open Friday, Saturday, and Sunday, and in every little village; the **Gallera Canta Gallo** in Santurce is easily reached from the city, as is **Tres Palmas Gallera** on the Bayamon Road. Horse racing on holidays, Wednesdays, Friday, and Sunday afternoons at **El Comandante;** baseball at the **Estadio Municipal Hiram Bithorn** is also very popular and during the US Leagues' training season, major league teams play exhibition games. Boxing, wrestling, and basketball at **Roberto Clemente Coliseum.**

Outside of San Juan, there are nine-hole courses at **Aguirre Sugar Central** and at the **Ponce Country Club.** Tuesday through Friday, the 18-hole golf course at the **Berwind Country Club,** Rio Grande, is open to the public. At Aguadilla, **Punta Borinquen,** an 18-hole public golf course, is open daily. The big hotels have their own tennis courts, and guest privileges are accorded at some of the private beaches.

Swimming, of course, is superb. There are pools and beaches at the hotels. **Isla Verde,** next to the San Juan airport, has a beach with showers and lockers for the public. **Luquillo Beach,** one hour's drive from San Juan, is magnificent. Skeet and trap shooting is available at the **Club Metropolitano de Tiro.** Horses can be hired at some hotels located outside San Juan.

Fishing, as you might expect, is excellent. In San Juan, charter boats are available through **Captain Mike Benitez** (tel: 723-2292) and the **San Juan Marina** (tel: 725-1039). Big game fishing with Captain Benitez costs $400 full day, $240 half day, or $65 one person; the Marina charges $325 full day, $190 half day, or $65 one person half day. All baits, rods, lines, tackle, and refreshments provided. Sailboats can be rented at the **Dorado Beach, El Conquistador,** and **Villa Parguera** hotels; at Fajardo, **Captain Jack Becker** (tel: 836-1905) offers a day's sail on his 40-foot catamaran to **Icacos Island** for $25 per person. All major resorts have facilities for snorkeling, skin diving, and water skiing.

CALENDAR OF EVENTS

In addition to the same US national holidays that are observed on the mainland, the following are celebrated: Epiphany, 6 January; Hostos' Birthday, 13 January; Abolition of Slavery, 22 March; Good Friday; De Diego's Birthday, 6 April; Muñoz Rivera's Birthday, 16 July; Constitution Day, 23 July; Barbosa's Birthday, 27 July; Discovery of America, 12 October.

WHERE TO GO NEARBY

West of San Juan on route 2, visit **Vega Baja,** one of Puerto Rico's finest 19th-century churches. Inland, passing through **Ciales,** the road is bordered by coffee groves. You then enter the **Toro Negro Forest** with a recreation area and observation tower where you have a magnificent view of the countryside. At **Barranquitas,** 35 miles from San Juan, visit the house where Puerto Rico's statesman Luis Muñoz Rivera was born, now a museum and library. Near the town is the 230-acre mountain resort, the **Barranquitas Hotel** (857-2400, S$20-24/D$26-30). Twenty-five miles east of San Juan is **El Yunque,** a tropical rainforest of 28,000 acres with an elevation of 3,493 feet; **Luquillo Beach** has bathing facilities and picnic areas. All are easy day trips by car.

FURTHER PUERTO RICO INFORMATION

Puerto Rico Tourism Company, Calle San Justo, corner Recinto Sur, Old San Juan, PR (tel: 809-721-2400); 1290 Avenue of the Americas, New York, NY 10019 (tel: 212-541-6630). Tourism Company also operates several tourism information offices which include International Airport, 791-1014; San Juan Marina, Miramar, 725-0139; City Hall, Old San Juan, 724-7171. For tourism complaints, call 721-2400. And for information about the Parador Inn system—a government sponsored program of rural inns—call 754-9265. **Pan Am** offices, Pan Am Building, 255 Ponce de León Avenue, Hato Rey, Puerto Rico 00917, tel: 754-7470 or 757-7470.

Consulates in San Juan: Argentina, Austria, Belgium, Bolivia, Canada, Colombia, Costa Rica, Denmark, Dominican Republic, Ecuador, El Salvador, Finland, France, Germany, Great Britain, Guatemala, Haiti, Honduras, Italy, Japan, Lebanon, Mexico, Monaco, Netherlands, Nicaragua, Norway, Panama, Paraguay, Philippines, Portugal, Spain, Sweden, Switzerland, Uruguay, Venezuela.

USEFUL TELEPHONE NUMBERS

Police	343-2020
Fire	343-2330
Medical	769-3838
Ambulance (government)	343-2550
Ambulance (private)	764-0685 & 726-5116
Weather (information in English & Spanish)	791-0320
Traveler's Aid	791-1054
Tourism Information	791-1014 & 791-3443
Postal Information	753-4951
Chamber of Commerce	723-1300
All night towing services:	
Beaucham Towing Service	785-2344 & 785-0444
Metropolitan Tow Service	727-4132 & 727-0573
Borinquen Tours	725-7133
Turismo Internacional	724-1297
United Tour Guides	723-5578
Pan Am Reservations	(800) 327-1320

Samoa & Cook Islands

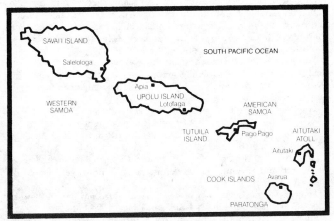

Area	1,173 square miles	Population	155,000
Capital	Pago Pago, American Samoa; Apia, Western Samoa	Sales Tax	none

Weather

	Jan	Feb	Mar	Apr	May	Jun	Jul	Aug	Sep	Oct	Nov	Dec
Av Temp (°C)	25	28	28	28	30	30	30	30	28	28	28	25
Days Rain	8	9	12	16	9	23	22	22	19	17	14	12

Time Zone At the International Date Line—12GMT, it will be midnight in Samoa

Samoa is two countries, Western Samoa and American Samoa, united by a single description—lush green mountainous Pacific islands halfway between Hawaii and Australia. It's inspiring, too. Robert Louis Stevenson, Margaret Mead, and Somerset Maugham, with his legendary Sadie Thompson, found in its easy and peaceful ways much refreshment.

Despite the arrival of missionaries in the early 1800s and then the big jets 150 years later, Samoa is still one of the few places left whose culture and tradition have survived untouched, though in harmony with the modern world. Far away from the white sands, blue sea, and bustle of legendary Pago Pago, capital of American Samoa and gateway to both Samoas, the small villages in the sweep of the perfumed forests live on in timeless and almost tribal tradition. It is a tradition and a mood you will find very embracing. The two Samoas are ethnically identical though dissimilar sociologically and in their level of development. Western Samoa is an independent country (actually a constitutional monarchy), less developed but more picturesque than American Samoa, which is an unincorporated territory of the US, administered by the Dept. of the Interior.

On January 1st, 1962, Western Samoa became the first fully independent Polynesian State. Until then the group had been under foreign control or rule since their apportionment in 1899 when Germany and the United States undertook their protection. New Zealand became the protector of Western Samoa during World War I.

The most crucial problem facing the two nations is the struggle to hold on to the extended family groupings—or aigas—while enriching the people through a move away from the traditional agricultural economy towards tourism.

Tropical Climate: The rainy season is December through April, and most visitors prefer to visit between May and November.

The official language is Samoan, although English is spoken by about 85% of the population.

Christian Congregational Church; Roman Catholic; Mormon; Methodist Church and Seventh Day Adventists are the principal religions on the islands.

American Samoa's currency is the US dollar. Currency unit in Western Samoa is the tala; 100 sene = 1 tala and 1 tala = US$1.40.

Public holidays are the same as US in American Samoa, with the addition of Flag Day, 17 April; White Sunday, 2nd Sunday in October; and the Swarm of the Palolo in late October or early November. Public holidays in Western Samoa are as follows:

Good Friday
Easter Monday
Anzac Day, 25 Apr
Whit Monday

Independence Celebration, 1 June
Christmas Day, 25 Dec
Boxing Day, 26 Dec

Sunday is the regular weekly holiday and is strictly observed.

REQUIREMENTS FOR ENTRY AND CUSTOMS REGULATIONS

For entry into American Samoa, US citizens require proof of citizenship and round-trip ticket; other nationals require passport, round-trip ticket, and all require a permit for stays of more than 30 days. For Western Samoa, requirements are valid passport, round-trip ticket, and a visa obtainable from New Zealand or British Consulates, for stays of more than 30 days. Proof of adequate funds is also required. A smallpox vaccination certificate or yellow fever and cholera shots are not required for either territory for passengers from the United States, provided they do not arrive via an infected area. Duty-free allowance: 200 cigarettes or 50 cigars or 1½ pounds of tobacco in Western Samoa; 2 fifths of liquor, 1 fifth for Western Samoa. US citizens returning home may leave American Samoa with US$600 worth of duty-free merchandise.

AIRPORT INFORMATION

Tafuna International Airport is 7 miles from Pago Pago. Bus fare into town is about US$1.50—luggage is charged by the piece. Taxis will do the trip for about US$5. No airport tax. Airport has a duty-free shop. Airport for Western Samoa is Faleolo, 23 miles from Apia. Bus transfer US$2; taxi US$10. Departure tax in Western Samoa about US$3.00.

ACCOMMODATIONS

Mostly up-to-date hotels, some with pools. There is an accommodation bureau at the **Office of Tourism**, PO Box 1147, Pago Pago, American Samoa 96799, tel: 633-5187. In Western Samoa, visitor information is available from the Department of Economic Development, PO Box 862, Apia, tel: 731-630. Hotels in Samoa:

Rates are in US$ for a double/twin room with bath or shower

Aggie Grey's Hotel, PO Box 67, Apia, Western Samoa, S$29/D$61, near beachfront.

Pago Pago Rainmaker, Pago Pago Bay, American Samoa, S$30/D$36.

Samoan Hideaway, PO Box 1195, Apia, Western Samoa; located at Mulivai Beach, 16 miles from Apia, from S$19/D$24.

Tiafau Hotel, PO Box 34, Apia, Western Samoa, S$34/D$40, located at town center overlooking beach.

Hotel Tusitala, PO Box 101, Apia, Western Samoa, S$50/D$57, heart of downtown, at waterfront.

USEFUL INFORMATION

When visiting a Samoan home or *fale* that has no chairs, it is traditional etiquette to sit in a cross-legged position while addressing your hosts. If you want to stretch out your legs, they should be covered. One should not eat while walking through a village. If you are offered a cup of *kava* in a *kava* ceremony, it is customary to first tip a bit out of the cup onto the ground before drinking. If there is any *kava* left in the cup when you have finished, this should also be poured on the ground.

Banks are open 9-3 Mon-Fri; outside windows open till 4 Mon-Thurs and till 5 Friday. No banks outside the principal cities. Hotels and a few shops will change currency.

Local calls cost 10¢.

English-language newspapers are available in addition to the *Samoan News* and *News Bulletin,* in American Samoa, and the *Samoa Times Observer, Samoa Weekly,* and *Savali* in Western Samoa.

There is no tipping in Samoa.

Electricity—110 volts (occasionally 230) 60 cycles AC. Hotels do have converters.

There is a good selection of photographic equipment available throughout the country. Processing takes about a week.

The Rotary Club meets at the Pago Pago Rainmaker Hotel, American Samoa, and at the Apian Way Inn, Western Samoa.

Public facilities are available in restaurants, hotels, bars, and around public places. There is no charge. Women, *Tamai'ta'i;* men, *Tane* (in Samoan).

Health: Most doctors and dentists speak English, and inexpensive pharmaceuticals are available at drugstores.

TRANSPORTATION

Buses or taxis. Polynesian Airlines and South Pacific Island Airways provide daily services between American and Western Samoa. Taxis are readily available for short journeys or sightseeing trips and can be identified by the "T" on their license plates. It is possible to rent a car from US$10.50 per day.

FOOD AND RESTAURANTS

National dishes in Samoa include *palusami* (coconut juice, banana, and taro leaves), roast pig, taro, breadfruit, bananas, fish, and *poi* (mashed ripe bananas and coconut milk.) Meal times are similar to US and European hours. The **Rainmaker Restaurant** in Pago Pago (in the Pago Pago Rainmaker Hotel—tel: 633-4241) serves international cuisine and is noted for its *fia fia,* traditional Samoan entertainment. **The Golden Dragon** (Pago Pago Village—tel: 32545) serves Chinese food exclusively. **Soli's Restaurant** in Pago Pago serves good food and is a lively night spot. Western Samoa: **Aggie Grey's Hotel,** famous for Polynesian cuisine and its weekly (usually Thursday) staging of *fia fia;* **Hotel Tusitala** for European food, and the **Tiafau Hotel.**

DRINKING TIPS

In American Samoa bars are open from 8am-5pm daily and 8am-12 noon on Saturday. All bars are closed on Sunday. Local drinks are *kava,* which comes from the root of the ava tree and is used as a ceremonial drink, and coconut milk. Other liquor, wines, and beers are imported and cost about US75¢ for a whiskey and soda, US$1.70 plus for a bottle of ordinary wine. Bars worth visiting are the **Bamboo Room** in Pago Pago, the **Pago Bar,** which caters very much to the locals, the **Tumua Palace, Soli's,** and the **Tikki Club.** In Apia there are the **Tanoa-o-Alii, Surfside, Aggie's Bar, Hotel Tusitala, Tiafau Hotel, Tui Savalalo, Mt Vaea,** and **Polyeurasian Club.**

SHOPPING

There is an excellent assortment of local crafts—handwoven *tapa* cloth, *lava-lavas* and *puletasi* (traditional men's and women's costumes), shells, *laufala* mats, and carvings. US citizens may take home US$600 worth of goods dutyfree. Western Samoa has fine handwoven fabrics, baskets, bags, superb teak bowls, and shell and coconut jewelry. In Apia, **Burns Philp, Morris Hedstrom's, I.H. Carruthers, S.V. Mackenzie's, Bartley & Sons,** plus several Chinese stores such as **Ah Chong's** have almost everything you could want. Or for the really local souvenirs investigate the **New Market.** The best handicrafts are in the well-stocked **Government**

Western Samoans are still subsistence farmers, gathering and making most of the things they use, growing crops such as taro and ta' amu (pictured), which are starchy roots that form the staples of Samoans' diets, and fishing in the ocean.

Handicrafts Corporation store, next to the tourist office in downtown Apia.

SPORTS

Golf, tennis, swimming, surfing, yachting, climbing, or fishing are available year round. The beaches are magnificent—long and sandy and clean—and there are swimming holes on **Upolu,** Western Samoa.

WHAT TO SEE

Samoa is its own best attraction, and **Blunt's Point, Breaker's Point, Virgin Falls,** and **Solo Hill**—all within a short distance of Pago Pago—provide a visitor with a wide selection of Samoan scenery. From **Solo Hill** you can swing across Pago Pago Bay and up 1,600 feet to the top of **Mount Alva** on the Aerial Tramway.

On **Upolu,** Western Samoa, see the "scenic route," a 40-mile coastal stretch that takes in the **Falefa Falls,** the **Mafa Pass,** and the **Fuipisia Falls.** The atmosphere of Upolu is perhaps more quintessentially Polynesian than that of any of the other islands. It was on Upolu, at **Vailima,** that Robert Louis Stevenson made his home, and today you can see the restored house where he lived and his grave on **Mount Vaea.** In October or early November, Samoans celebrate the **Swarm of the Palolo.** At this time the *palolo,* or coral worms, swarm in the reef waters to lay their eggs, and the Samoans, who call the palolo the "caviar of the South Pacific," wade out with nets and cheesecloths to gather the eggs. The atmosphere is festival-like, and everyone is invited to go Samoan and join in the fun.

Where To Go Nearby

COOK ISLANDS

An independent nation only since 1965, the 15 Cook Islands spread their 93 square miles of land area over 850,000 square miles of the Pacific Ocean, flanked to the west by Tonga and Samoa and to the east by French Polynesia. Formerly a New Zealand dependency, the islands are now self-governed, although outside affairs are still handled by New Zealand. Population of the Cook Islands is 18,128. The island of Rarotonga is the largest and most developed of the Cooks and is capital of the group.

Rarotonga has excellent tourist accommodations and a newly expanded International Airport close to Avarua, where approximately half of Rarotonga's 9,811 people live. Flying time to the Cook Islands from Western Samoa is about 4 hours. Most of the islands were discovered by Captain Cook (hence their name), although Aitutaki, 140 miles north and the only other island offering tourist facilities, was discovered by Captain Bligh shortly before the mutiny on the *Bounty.*

The climate of all the Cook Islands is pleasantly warm and mostly sunny year round. December to March is warmest and wettest and known as hurricane season, although such storms are a rarity. On Rarotonga, where the weather is perennially ideal, annual rainfall totals 80 inches.

There is a growing number of restaurants in Rarotonga. The **Arorangi Lodge** (from $20) 4 miles from town, stages three cabarets a week, including an excellent island-style buffet dinner. Bicycles and Honda scooters are available to rent at low rates. Luxury goods are duty-free in all shops. Accommodations on Rarotonga are also available at the **Raratonga Hotel** (S$39/D$44, suite $65), and **Lagoon Lodges** (S$20/D$25) at the beach. On the island of Aitutaki is the **Rapae Motel** (S$18.10/D$21.30). For reservations contact the Cook Island Tourist Authority.

REQUIREMENTS FOR ENTRY AND CUSTOMS REGULATIONS

Bona fide visitors do not require an entry permit provided they possess a valid passport, have onward passage, and do not intend staying more than 31 days. A valid smallpox certificate is required of all visitors except citizens of Australia, Canada, New Zealand, the Pacific islands, and the United States, who are exempted provided they have not traveled outside those countries during the 14 days prior to entering the Cook Islands. Baggage is fumigated on arrival and delivered to the hotel about two hours after guests check in.

Visitors may bring 200 cigarettes, 1-fifth of wine and 1-fifth of spirits, 2 still cameras with 10 rolls of film, 1 pair binoculars, 1 portable radio, 1 record player (and 10 records), 1 typewriter, one portable musical instrument, all without duty. The importation of firearms, cartridges, and fireworks is expressly prohibited.

SOURCES OF FURTHER INFORMATION

Any **Pan Am** office around the world; **Department of Tourism,** Government of American Samoa, PO Box 1147, Pago Pago. **Office of Territories,** US Department of the Interior, Washington DC. **Department of Economic Development,** PO Box 862, Apia, Western Samoa; **Cook Island Tourist Authority,** P.O. Box 14, Rarotonga, Cook Islands.

USEFUL TELEPHONE NUMBERS IN PAGO PAGO

Police	633-4441
Fire	633-5858
Airport Information	688-9145
Directory Inquiries and Operator	0
Weather	688-9130
Time	633-4949
Tourist Offices	633-5187

The Virgin Islands

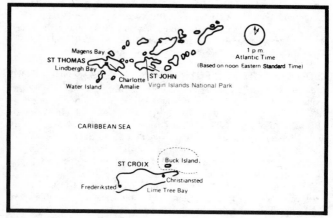

Area	133 square miles				Population	97,000					
Capital	Charlotte Amalie				**Sales Tax**	None					

Weather	Jan	Feb	Mar	Apr	May	Jun	Jul	Aug	Sep	Oct	Nov	Dec
Av Temp (°C)	24	25	26	26	27	28	28	28	28	28	26	25
Days of Rain	19	13	13	13	16	15	19	18	17	17	18	18

Time Zone Atlantic standard (no daylight saving time)

The Virgin Islands of the United States consist of the islands of **St Thomas, St Croix, St John,** and about 50 nearby islets in the Caribbean. The islands were first sighted by Christopher Columbus during his second voyage and named by him "Las Virgenes" in honor of St Ursula and martyred virgins. When he anchored for fresh water he named one of the islands Santa Cruz, now St Croix. Peace was broken in 1555 when Charles V of Spain's expeditions defeated the Carib Indians and claimed the territory. During the 17th century ownership was fought over by France and Britain as well as Holland and Denmark who colonized St Thomas in 1672. St John was purchased by Denmark in 1716 and St Croix was purchased from the French during the Napoleonic wars. In 1917 the Danes sold the Danish West Indies to the US government for 25 million dollars. These delightful islands offer excellent vacation facilities and a salubrious climate. Since they are practically duty free, it is possible to purchase many imports from all over the world at a considerable reduction of their costs elsewhere. The islands are governed by a legislative assembly made up of 15 locally elected senators and an elected governor. For a typical tropical vacation, the Virgin Islands are popular with Americans visiting the Caribbean for the first time. Everyone speaks English and the local currency is the US dollar.

ST JOHN, 22 square miles in area, with a population of just over 2,000, is the smallest and most beautiful of the Virgin Islands. Two-thirds of this mountainous island is the **Virgin Islands National Park.** The island is accessible only by boat, seaplane, or ferry. A daily ferry service from Red Hook on St Thomas docks at Cruz Bay, about 15 minutes away, every hour on the hour until 7 pm; fare is $2 each way. Jeep taxis meet all boats or you can rent a self-drive car. Day package tours for $25 are available from St Thomas to the Virgin Islands National Park, Trunk Bay, an outstanding beach, and to Caneel Bay. Accommodations range from the luxurious **Caneel Bay Plantation** to tents at **Cinnamon Bay,** one of St John's campsites. **Caneel Bay Plantation** (776-6111, S$165-225/D$180-240, with breakfast and dinner, winter rates; S/D$115-130 in summer) is an exclusive resort on a secluded bay on the northwest tip of St John. Resort cottages are available elsewhere on St John from $250 to $1,000 per week. Campsites at **Cinnamon Bay** should be reserved up to a year in advance. Call 776-6330, tents $24 a day, cottages $32 a day; baresites are $3 a day. **Maho Bay** is a private campground resort ($40 a day) (776-6226 or 776-6240). Most rates are lower from 1 May to 15 December.

ST CROIX

The largest of the islands, **St Croix** is 84 square miles. The terrain varies from flowering cactus and spiny scrub on the east end to the rain forest of mahogany, mango, and palm trees in the west end. Columbus discovered the island in 1493 and named it Santa Cruz. Later in 1625 the Dutch set up a small colony near what is now Christiansted, the English near the Frederiksted area. The French and Spanish made alternate attempts to govern the island. Eventually in 1733, France sold the island to the Danish West India and Guinea Co. Danish settlers were promptly recruited. The new owners experienced initial difficulties in collecting taxes and duty from the freebooters who had filled the vacuum while the island government had been changing. In 1755 all the islands were declared a Crown Colony, and in 1764 a free port for all. Prosperity almost doubled overnight, and the islands became an important Caribbean trade center, including running of arms to be used in the Revolutionary War. Alexander Hamilton, one of America's founding fathers, spent a number of years here before moving to the mainland. The island reflects the heritage of its early colonists: Danish, French, Dutch, English, the Knights of Malta, and Spanish. Population is about 50,000.

WHAT TO SEE

Despite modern developments, many old buildings remain and several worthwhile restorations have been undertaken. In Christiansted, the **National Historic Site** includes **Fort Christiansvaern,** originally constructed in 1744 primarily for harbor defense and gradually added to over the years; Steeple Building, housing the **St Croix Museum** of Amerindian artifacts and the exhibits of the **East India and Guinea Company Warehouse; Lutheran Church,** ostensibly built prior to 1740; **Government House,** the former residence of the Danish Governors, with its impressive Reception Hall (with facsimile reproductions of the original Danish government furnishings), and the West Wing—dating back to 1747—with its magnificent second-story ballroom; currently undergoing restoration is the former Danish **Customs House,** an original one-story structure completed in 1751 but added to until 1830. You'll also enjoy the interesting archways and architecture; the **Christiansted Wharf** with trading schooners and downtown business area; and **Rachael Lavien Monument** at Grange. At the east end windmills dot the island; see the ruins of sugar estates; visit the ancient estate that was the headquarters of the Knights of Malta in the 17th century; **Salt River,** where Columbus first landed in the Virgin Islands. Also, go to **Buck Island,** with its beautiful beaches, one and a half miles off the northeast coast of St Croix. Buck Island is the only US National Park that is underwater and has two fantastic underwater snorkeling trails through the crystal sea and coral reefs, with marine growth clearly labeled on sunken blocks. Some of the best skin-diving and snorkeling in the Caribbean is found in the Virgin Islands.

At the other side of the island is the town of Frederiksted which was almost totally wiped out by a fire in 1879. The enterprising townfolk decided the quickest way of solving their problem would be to reconstruct by using wood above the stone foundations. The result is surprisingly pleasing. **Fort Frederik** (1671) has been restored and looks very much as it did in its heyday. A number of late 18th-century buildings include **Apothecary Hall** (Queen Street), the **Customs House,** and **Holy Trinity Lutheran Church** (1791). **St. Paul's Anglican Church** (Prince Street) was originally founded in 1772, but the new structure was completed around 1815.

One of the great showplaces in the island is an estate some two miles east of Frederiksted. Formerly known as John's Rest, it is now called the **Whim Greathouse,** and has been painstakingly restored to its former glory. The main building is of neoclassic design, consisting of three large rooms, a small wing to the rear, and a gallery. It was built around 1794 by one Christopher MacEvoy, Jr. (a Dane despite his Scottish name—his father had become a naturalized Danish citizen). MacEvoy Junior became extemely wealthy from his inheritance and his apparent business skills, and in 1811 decided to move to England. He would later buy a sugar refinery and castle in Denmark, and resettle there to become Chamberlain to King Frederik VI. A tale is still told of how he appeared one day—following his court appointment—on the streets of Copenhagen in a magnificent coach drawn by four white horses. The problem was that only Danish nobility were entitled to use white horses and the court was outraged. MacEvoy was severely rebuked, and in a huff decided to resign his post and return to St Croix. His fortunes continued to prosper and he became even more wealthy, but the island must have seemed exceedingly provincial after the bright court scene. So it appears that having refilled his coffers, he made his way back to Copenhagen this time to appear in an even more magnificent coach drawn by eight white mules. No rules were transgressed, the Danish nobility could appreciate that the joke was on them, and MacEvoy was reappointed Royal Chamberlain to the king.

ACCOMMODATIONS

Most rates are lower from 1 May to 15 December.

Christiansted: The **Caravelle** (773-0687, S$40-54/D$48-62) and **Club Comanche** (773-0210, S$32-38/D$53-60) are good places to stay. Others in town are **Holger Danske,** the **King Christian Hotel, King's Alley Hotel,** and **The Lodge.** The enchanting **Hotel on the Cay** (773-2035, S$98-100/ D$125-135) is on its own tiny island in the harbor. Two miles east of town is the popular **Buccaneer Hotel** (773-2100, S$90-155/D$100-165). The **Turquoise Bay Cottages** (773-0244, Apts $475, Cottages $575 per week) just two miles from town is excellent. North shore, west of Christiansted, **St Croix by the Sea** (773-0385, S$95/D$110); on the south shore, east of town, there is the **Grapetree Beach Hotel** (773-3300, S$85-120/ D$90-150) with complete water sports facilities, cocktail lounge, and nightly entertainment.

Frederiksted area: **Cottages by the Sea** (772-0495, S$30/D$36-42) offers good accommodations as does **Sunset Beach Cottages** (772-0199, S$30-45/D$45-75) directly on beach, with full maid service, and **Sprat Hall Hotel. Arawak Cottages,** only a mile from Frederiksted, is in the oldest plantation greathouse on the island (772-0305, S/D$90) and offers horseback riding, deep-sea fishing, snorkeling, and scuba, in addition to tennis. **Cane Bay Plantation** (778-0410, S$70-95/D$85-115) is on the north shore.

RESTAURANTS

Christiansted: **Club Comanche** and **Frank's** are good. For Danish specialties try the **Top Hat,** and for Sunday buffet, **St Croix by the Sea.** Island dishes are featured at **Villa Morales** and **Sprat Hall.** Outside of Christiansted the **Buccaneer Hotel** and **Cane Bay Plantation** offer fine cuisine.

Frederiksted: **Smithfield Inn** and the **Swashbuckler** are recommended.

ENTERTAINMENT

In or near Christiansted are the **Buccaneer, Grapetree Beach Club, St Croix by the Sea, Club Comanche,** the **Limin' Inn,** and **Guthrie's. The Island Center** also features occasional live plays and other imported performers.

SHOPPING

In Christiansted see the shops in the **Caravelle Arcade** and **King's Alley.** There are still more in the **Pan Am Pavilion** and all over town. In Frederiksted visit **Royal Frederik Shop.**

SPORTS

Water sports, deep-sea fishing, spear fishing, lobster and conch diving, sailing in yawls, sloops and schooners, and motor cruises are available. Swimming at **Cramer's Park, Fort Louise Augusta, Sandy Point,** and **Davis Bay Beach.** The island also offers baseball, cricket, basketball, horse racing. **Sprat Hall Hotel** has the only riding stables on the island. There is the spectacular **Fountain Valley Golf Course** designed by Robert Trent Jones. **Buccaneer Hotel** also has an 18-hole golf course and eight tennis courts. **Hotel on the Cay, St Croix by the Sea,** and the **Gentle Winds Condominium** also have tennis courts. There are 12 championship courts at the **Caribbean Tennis Club.** The **Reef Hotel** offers both tennis and golf.

ST THOMAS

St Thomas, 80 miles east of San Juan, Puerto Rico, is the liveliest of the three islands and offers alluring duty-free shopping. Population is about 49,000 in an area of 32 square miles.

WHAT TO SEE

Charlotte Amalie, the capital, is a lively town of narrow streets and steps with villas perched where, supposedly, Sir Francis Drake sat while he was charting the channels and passages of the islands. Some three-fifths of the buildings in downtown St Thomas are more than 100 years old. The local Masonic Lodge, which maintains its affiliation with the Grand Lodge of England to this day, was founded in 1818. Here too is the second-oldest Jewish synagogue and Jewish cemetery on American soil. Rebuilt after a disastrous fire is the 17th-century **Nisky Moravian Mission** building, while the **Dutch Reformed Church** is also one of the first to have been built in the hemisphere. Take a hike up the **99 Steps** on Government Hill, just up from **Government House,** the official residence of the Governor; don't miss the collection of paintings, including two by Pissarro, a native of St Thomas. There is also an ancient Danish cemetery. The oldest building on the island is **Fort Christian,** built in 1671, which houses a museum. See **Sts Peter and Paul Church,** and **All Saints Anglican Church.** In **Emancipation Park,** the proclamation was issued freeing the island slaves in 1848. There are many legends about **Bluebeard's Hill and Castle.** The biggest attraction on St Thomas is the **Coral World** underwater observatory at Coki Point beach (it is the only one of its kind in the Western Hemisphere). Admission is $5 for adults and $2.50 for children under 12. **Coral World** also has a restaurant, bar, and duty-free shops.

ACCOMMODATIONS

Most rates are lower from 1 May to 15 December.

Charlotte Amalie: Designated as a national historic site, the **Hotel 1829** (774-1829, S$40-80/D$50-125) is notable; **Midtown Guesthouse** (774-6677, S$25.10/D$28.25-33.50) is also located in the midtown area. The **Windward Passage Hotel** (774-5200, S$65-85/D$70-90) is good. On an island, seven minutes out by launch, is the delightful **Sugar Bird Beach Hotel** (774-1213, S$83-103/D$85-105).

In the hills surrounding the shopping streets: **Bluebeard's Castle** (774-1600, S$95-119/D$98-122), **Island View Guest House** (774-4270, S$22-31/D$28-49), and **Mafolie** (774-2790, S$36-42/D$48-52) are very nice. There are many guest houses in the hills near town, such as **Estate Thomas, Maison Greaux, Miller Manor Guest House, Villa Fairview, Villa Santana,** and **West Indian Manor,** rates averaging S$20-45/D$30-45. High on a hill is the **Shibui Resort** (774-1001, S$75/D$95), a colony of Japanese-style cottages. Recently re-opened is the **Virgin Isle Hotel** (774-1500, S$78-108/D$83-113); it sits high on a hill, and has shuttle bus service to its beach.

West of town, near the airport, are the **Carib Beach Hotel** (774-2525, S$65-105/D$68-108) and **Island Beachcomber** (774-5250, S$55-65/D$60-70).

East of town, on the sea, are the huge, Miami Beach-like **Frenchman's Reef Holiday Inn** (774-8500, S$118-148/D$120-150); the secluded **Morningstar Beach Resort** (774-2650, S$50-60/D$60-71); the attractive **Lime Tree Beach Hotel** (774-4770, S$84-96/D$94-106); and the **Bolongo Bay Beach Hotel** (775-1800, S$110/D$120). Farther east is the **Secret Harbour House Resort Hotel** (775-1010, S/D$85-140).

On the north shore: **Pavilions and Pools Hotel** (775-1110, S/D$114-124), **Pelican Beach Club** (775-0855, closed for the summer; winter rates S/D$95-135), **Pineapple Beach Club** (775-1510, S$84-108/D$96-120), and **Sapphire Bay Beach Apartments** (775-2660, S/D$81-92). Newly opened is the 120-room **Mahogany Run Golf and Tennis Resort** (774-8418, S/D$108-198).

RESTAURANTS

Hotels and resorts offer good food, often terrace dining and entertainment. Most hotels, guest houses, and beach resorts offer good dining with special dishes, and barbecues on certain nights. Danish, French, Italian, Oriental, American, as well as local dishes are represented. Local dishes include *fungi* (spiced cornmeal boiled with okra), *gundi* (cold salad of seafood and vegetables), *kallaloo* (seasoned meat and seafood stew with kallaloo greens and okra), *souse* (spicey pig's feet soup), fish soups, and soursop (local fruit) ice cream. Downtown, **The Kalabash** and **Doris King's Kitchens** serve native dishes. Sebastian's, on the waterfront, is extremely popular.

Au Bon Vivant and the two **L'Escargot** restaurants are excellent. Chinese food is inexpensive and good at **Kum Wah.** For steaks try **Mafolie. Harbor View** and the **Fish Market Restaurant,** outside town, have excellent cuisine. For country dining, try **Daddy's Restaurant,** 20 minutes from town, and the **Lime Tree;** the **Mountain Top** is good for lunch, and for its specialty, banana daiquiris. Also popular is **Bartolino's** in Frenchtown.

ENTERTAINMENT

Leading hotels feature entertainment and dancing. Among the better known are **Frenchman's Reef**, and the **Virgin Isle Hotel** and **Bluebeard Castle.** Nightclubs stay open until the small hours; some of the best are the **Safari Club, Cheetah,** and the **Greenhouse.** **Reichhold Center** for the performing arts at the College of the Virgin Islands features live concerts and other entertainments, such as Marcel Marceau. The **Virgin Isle Hotel** has recently opened a new and popular disco, called **Studio 54.**

SHOPPING

All luxury goods are at almost duty-free prices. Good buys are cigarettes, watches, perfume, liquor, crystal, and jewelry. There are over 100 enticing shops in Charlotte Amalie along **Main Street** and its quaint little side streets, especially **Drake's Passage, International Plaza, Palm Passage,** and **Back Street Mall.** Island scents can be purchased at **Tropicana Perfume Shoppes;** the **Mahogany Center of the Virgin Isles** displays carving and lovely tortoiseshell jewelry. **H. Stern** is world known for jewelry. Stores open 8-5, 8:45-5, closed Sunday except when a great many cruise ships are in port, when shops may or may not be open. Under new federal law, US residents are now allowed to bring back $600 in duty-free merchandise from the US Virgin Islands. This amount includes the cost of 1 gallon of liquor and 5 cartons of cigarettes when purchased in the Virgin Islands. All other visitors are to be guided by their local customs regulations.

SPORTS

Cricket, basketball, horse racing, tennis, and golf are available on the island. An 18-hole golf course is now under construction at Mahogany Run on the north coast. Deep-sea fishing, charter sailboats and cruisers with crews available, and swimming and snorkeling mostly excellent. Several beaches that offer water sports activities include **Morningstar** and **Lindberg Beaches** on the Caribbean, and **Sapphire Bay Resort** and **Pineapple Beach Resort** on the Atlantic.

VIRGIN ISLANDS NATIONAL PARK

The park, which covers 9,485 acres or nearly two-thirds of St John Island, has vast white coral sand beaches, crescent-shaped bays and peaceful coves of clear warm water, wooded mountains, ruins of old sugar plantations, and complete quiet and serenity that make an idyllic paradise.

Stop at the park **Visitor Center** in Cruz Bay for information; there are orientation talks offered for a general introduction to the island. Guided snorkel trips as well as history and nature walks are conducted weekly.

Trunk Bay has the fascinating **Underwater Trail,** which anyone who can swim can follow. You'll glide through a wonderland of lacy sea fans, strange brain coral, and all sorts of odd underwater formations, neatly identified by sunken plaques. **Centerline Road** winds across the middle of the island, reaching its apex at **Bordeaux Mountain,** 1,277 feet high. Trails from the road lead down to **Petroglyph Falls,** where rocks are decorated with drawings believed to have been made long ago by Arawak and Carib Indians; and to the ruins of an 18th-century sugar mill. There is a profusion of tropical fruit trees and vividly colored tropical flowers. There are sail and motorboat cruises, and big game fish are caught off St John. Package jeep tours and scenic boat charters are available from St Thomas. Also taxi tours through the park with a guide are for hire from Cruz Bay costing about $4 per hour for up to four persons plus $1 per person for each additional person.

A 15-minute ferry leaves every hour from Red Hook on St Thomas and docks at Cruz Bay. You can rent jeeps at $30 per day or by the week. Many roads are roller-coasterish, some requiring a four-wheel-drive car.

Cinnamon Bay Campground has cottage units, completely equipped tents, and tent sites with picnic tables and charcoal grills. Advance reservations must be made.

FURTHER VIRGIN ISLAND INFORMATION

Virgin Island Government Tourist Office, PO Box 1692, Charlotte Amalie, St Thomas, VI 00801. National Parks: **Virgin Islands National Park** (Superintendent), Box 806, St Thomas, VI 00801; Concessioner, **Cinnamon Bay Campground,** Box 120, St John, US Virgin Islands 00830.

Free trip-planning literature also available from the **Virgin Island Government Tourist Office,** 307 N Michigan Avenue, Chicago, IL 60611; 100 N Biscayne Boulevard, Miama FL 33132; 1270 Avenue of the Americas, New York 10020; 1300 Ashford Avenue, Condado, San Juan PR 00907; 1050 17th Street NW, Washington, DC 20036.

Consulates in St Thomas: Belgian, British, Danish, Swedish

USEFUL TELEPHONE NUMBERS

Telephone calls can now be made from the US mainland to the US Virgin Islands toll free on "800" numbers and WATS-line services.

Police	915		
Fire	921		
Ambulance	922		
	St Thomas	**St John**	**St Croix**
Hospital (Emergency)	774-1212	776-6222	773-1212
Red Cross	774-0375	774-0375	773-1104
Legal Aid Serv.	774-6720	774-6720	773-2626
Chamber of Commerce	774-0463	774-0463	773-1435
Tourist Information	774-2566	776-6450	773-0495

Index